The **Rough Guide** to

Kenya

written and researched by

Richard Trillo

with additional research by

Matt Brown, Robert Gordon and Alex Trillo

and a contribution on music by

Doug Paterson

ROUGH GUIDES

www.roughguides.com

Contents

Crafts and shopping
colour section
following p.124

Traditional dress
colour section
following p.444

3

Introduction to

Kenya

Lapped by the Indian Ocean, straddling the equator, and with Mount Kenya rising from its magnificent natural environment, Kenya is a rewarding place to travel. The country's dramatic geography has resulted in a great range of natural habitats, harbouring a huge variety of wildlife, while its complex history of migration and conquest has brought about a fascinating social panorama, which includes the Swahili city-states of the coast and the Maasai of the Rift Valley.

The country's world-famous national parks, tribal peoples and superb beaches lend Kenya an exotic image with magnetic appeal. But treating the country as a succession of tourist sights isn't the most stimulating way to experience it. If you get off the beaten track, you can enter the world inhabited by most Kenyans: a ceaselessly active scene of farm and field, corrugated-iron shacks, tea shops and lodging houses, crammed buses and streets wandered by goats and toddlers. Both on and off the tourist routes, you'll find warmth and openness, and an abundance of superb scenery – rolling savanna dotted with Maasai herds and wild animals, high Kikuyu moorlands grazed by cattle and sheep, and dense forests full of monkeys and bird song. But Kenya is not all postcard-perfect: start a conversation with any Kenyan and you'll soon find out about the country's deep economic and social tensions.

Where to go

The **coast** and major **game parks** are the most obvious targets. If you come to Kenya on an inclusive tour, you're likely to have your time divided between these two attractions. Despite the impact of human population pressures, Kenya's **wildlife spectacle** remains a compelling experience. Its million-odd annual visitors are easily absorbed in such a large country, and there's nothing to prevent you escaping the predictable tourist bottlenecks. Even on an organized tour, you should not feel constrained to follow the prescribed plan.

The major **national parks and reserves**, watered by seasonal streams, are mostly located in savanna on the fringes of the Highlands that take up much of the **southwest** quarter of the country. The vast majority of Kenyans live in these rugged hills, where the ridges are a mix of *shamba* smallholdings and plantations. Through the heart of the Highlands sprawls the **Great Rift Valley**, an archetypal East African scene of dry, thorn-tree savanna, splashed with lakes and studded by volcanoes. It's great walking country, as are the high forests and moors of the **Central Highlands** and **Mount Kenya** itself – a major target and a feasible climb for most people. **Nairobi**, the capital, on the highlands' southern edge, is generally used only as a gateway, but has plenty of diversions to occupy your time while arranging your travels.

In the far west, towards **Lake Victoria**, lies gentler countryside, where you can travel for days without seeing another foreign visitor and where you will get perhaps the best immersion in Kenyan life and culture. Beyond the rolling tea plantations of Kericho and the hot plains around the port of Kisumu lies the steep volcanic massif of **Mount Elgon**, astride the Ugandan border. The little-known **Kakamega Forest** rainforest reserve, with its unique wildlife, is nearby, and more than enough reason to strike out west.

In the north, the land is **desert** or semi-desert, broken only by the highlight of gigantic **Lake Turkana** in the northwest, almost unnaturally blue in the brown wilderness. **Northeast Kenya**, towards the Somalian border, is currently unsafe for travellers, but the routes to Turkana are open and offer access to one of the most spectacular and memorable of all African regions.

▲ Hippo, Tsavo West National Park

6

▼ Kogelo: "Obama's Village"

Fact file

• With an **area** of 580,400 square kilometres (224,100 square miles), Kenya is about two and a half times the size of Britain and nearly one and a half times the size of California. The **population**, which for many years had a growth rate higher than that of any other country, has now started to stabilize at around 32 million.

• Kenya regained **independence** in 1963 after nearly eighty years of British occupation and colonial rule. The republic is a multiparty democracy, ruled by a "Grand Coalition" of parties, headed by **President Mwai Kibaki** and **Prime Minister Raila Odinga**.

• Kenya has a huge **debt burden**, currently (2010) running at nearly $7 billion, or roughly $220 for every man, woman and child. Every month, Kenya spends as much on servicing this debt as it does on health care for the whole year.

• With little oil or natural gas and few mineral resources, most of the foreign currency Kenya needs for vital imports is earned from coffee and tea exports, and tourism. Most Kenyans scrape a living by subsistence **agriculture**.

• Kenyan society consists of a huge, impoverished under-class, a small but growing middle class and a tiny, rich elite whose success often owes much to nepotism and graft. **Corruption** percolates every corner of the country and affects every aspect of the economy.

Kenya's "upcountry" interior is separated from the **Indian Ocean** by the arid plains around Tsavo East National Park. Historically, these have formed a barrier that accounts in part for the distinctive culture around **Mombasa and the coastal region**. Here, the historical record, preserved in mosques, tombs and the ruins of ancient towns cut from the jungle, marks out the area's **Swahili civilization**. Along the length of the coast, beyond the white-sand beaches – invariably shaded by coconut palms or casuarina trees – runs an almost continuous **coral reef**, protecting a shallow, safe lagoon from the Indian Ocean.

When to go

Kenya has a complicated and rather unpredictable **climate** – even more so with the impact of climate change striking hard. Broadly, the seasons are: hot and dry from January to March; hot and wet from April to June (the "long rains"); warm and dry from July to October; and warm and wet from

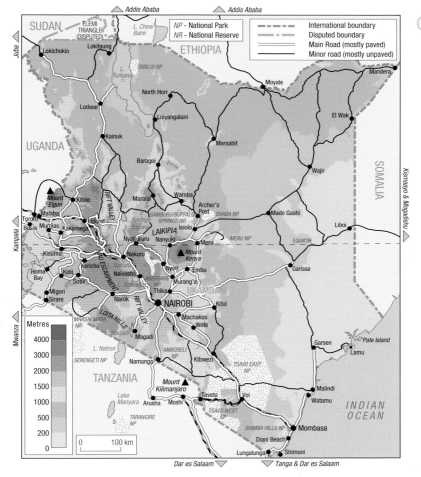

Map legend:

NP – National Park
NR – National Reserve

- - - - International boundary
- · - · - Disputed boundary
——— Main Road (mostly paved)
——— Minor road (mostly unpaved)

Metres
4000
3000
2000
1500
1000
500
200
0

0   100 km

November to December (the "short rains"). At high altitudes, it may rain at almost any time. Western Kenya has a scattered rainfall pattern influenced by Lake Victoria, while the eastern half of the country, and especially the coast itself, are largely controlled by the Indian Ocean's monsoon winds –

"Kenya" or "Keenya"?

Although you'll hear "Kenya" most of the time, the second pronunciation is still used, and not exclusively by the old settler set. The colonial pronunciation was closer to the original name of Mount Kenya, "Kirinyaga". This was abbreviated to "Ki-nya", spelt Kenya, which came to be pronounced with a short "e". When Jomo Kenyatta became president after Independence, the pure coincidence of his surname was exploited.

Kenya's peoples

Certain language groups remain easily identifiable through dress and lifestyle, although urban growth and intermarriage are blurring distinctions. The brilliantly beaded and closely related Maasai and Samburu peoples are associated with the parks named after them, but they herd their animals across vast reaches of savanna and, when access to water demands it, even into the big towns. Many Turkana and members of some of the other remote northern groups also retain their traditional garb and rather tooled-up appearance, with spears much in evidence.

Some of Kenya's biggest ethnic groups have had a largely Westernized orientation for three or four generations – notably the Kikuyu in the central highlands, the Kamba east of Nairobi, and the Luo in the west – and their economic and political influence is notable. There's more on language and tribes on p.548; for more on traditional dress, see the *Traditional dress* colour section.

▼ Riyadha Mosque, Lamu

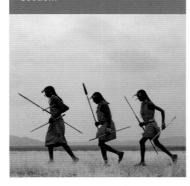

8

the dry northeast monsoon (*kaskazi*) blowing from November to March or April and the moist southeast monsoon (*kusi*) from April or May to October. The *kusi* normally brings the heaviest rain to the coast in May.

Temperatures are determined largely by altitude: you can reckon on a drop of 6°C (or 11°F) for every 1000m you climb from sea level. Nairobi, for example (1660m or 5450ft), has a moderate climate, and can drop to 5°C (41°F) at night. Swimming pools are rarely heated, and are only guaranteed to be warm on the coast.

The main **tourist seasons** tie in with the rainfall patterns: the biggest influxes are in December and January and, to a lesser extent, July and August. **Dry-season** travel has a number of advantages, not least of which is the greater visibility of wildlife as animals are concentrated along the diminishing

watercourses. July and August are probably the best months, overall, for **game-viewing**, with August almost certain to coincide with the annual wildebeest migration in the Maasai Mara. October, November and March are the months with the clearest seas for **snorkelling** and **diving**. In the long rains, the mountain parks are occasionally closed, as the muddy tracks are undriveable. But the **rainy seasons** shouldn't deter travel unduly: the rains usually come only in short afternoon or evening cloudbursts, and the landscape is strikingly green and fresh even if the skies may be cloudy. There are bonuses, too: in the absence of other tourists, hotel and other prices are reduced and people generally have more time for you.

Kenya's climate

	Jan	Feb	Mar	Apr	May	Jun	Jul	Aug	Sep	Oct	Nov	Dec
Nairobi (Alt 1660m/5450ft)												
Av day temp (°C)	25	26	25	24	22	21	21	21	24	24	23	23
Av night temp (°C)	12	13	14	14	13	12	11	11	11	13	13	13
Rainfall (mm)	38	64	125	211	158	46	15	23	31	53	109	86
Days with rainfall	5	6	11	16	17	9	6	7	6	8	15	11
Mombasa (sea level)												
Av day temp (°C)	31	31	31	30	28	28	27	27	28	29	29	30
Av night temp (°C)	24	24	25	24	24	23	22	22	22	23	24	24
Rainfall (mm)	25	18	64	196	320	119	89	66	63	86	97	61
Days with rainfall	6	3	7	15	20	15	14	16	14	10	10	9
Kisumu (Alt 1135m/3724ft)												
Av day temp (°C)	29	29	28	28	27	27	27	27	28	29	29	29
Av night temp (°C)	18	19	19	18	18	17	17	17	17	18	18	18
Rainfall (mm)	48	81	140	191	155	84	58	76	64	56	86	102
Days with rainfall	6	8	12	14	14	9	8	10	8	7	9	8

12

things not to miss

It's not possible to see everything Kenya has to offer in one trip – and we don't suggest you try. Here's a taste of the country's highlights, arranged in five colour-coded categories, to help you find the very best things to experience.

01 Maasai Mara wildebeest migration Page **374** • Observing the cacophonous herds from the banks of the flood-swollen Mara River – especially at one of the deadly, crocodile-infested crossing points – is one of nature's most awe-inspiring experiences.

02 **Turkana overland safaris** Page **506** • Remote Turkana can be visited on a camping safari from Nairobi, involving several days of bumping through arid wilderness. This is Nabuiyatom or Teleki's volcano, at the southern end of the lake.

03 **Climbing Mount Kenya** Page **156** • Africa's second highest peak, glacier-topped Mount Kenya is an extinct volcano straddling the equator. You can hike the lower slopes at will, but if you attempt the 5200-metre summit you need to go slowly enough to acclimatize to the altitude.

04 **Nyama choma** Page **52** • Kenya's most popular big meal out is *nyama choma* or roast meat – goat, mutton or beef – and lots of beer. Nyama choma bars are to be found throughout the country.

06 Dhow trips Page **486** • Play Sinbad for a day on a tranquil dhow cruise around Lamu.

05 Kakamega Forest Page **308** • An isolated patch of the equatorial forest that once girdled the breadth of Africa, Kakamega is a haven for hundreds of species that exist nowhere else in Kenya.

07 Diving and snorkelling Pages **384**, **436** & **441** • Kenya's coral reef has superb underwater opportunities, with diving schools in all the main centres, and snorkelling equipment widely available to rent for a couple of hours. Wasini, Watamu and Kiwaiyu are outstanding sites.

08 Tiwi Beach Page **429** • Simply one of the nicest beaches in Kenya, easily accessed from Mombasa, and less crowded than Diani Beach, further south.

09 Gedi ruins

Page **456** • Eerily atmospheric ruins of a Swahili town abandoned in the seventeenth century – take time to wander the jungle-shaded lanes away from the main site.

10 Crafts

See *Crafts and shopping colour section* • Wooden carvings are the stock-in-trade of Kenya's curio sellers, but there's a huge range of other crafts to be tempted by, from gorgeous cloth wrap garments to musical instruments.

12 Birdwatching

Page **577** • Kenya's diversity of habitats explains its extraordinary 1070 species of birds, including this superb starling. Even the uninitiated are soon converted, so take a pair of binoculars.

11 Eco lodges

Page **179** • Kenya boasts some superb, if pricey, accommodation in pristine parks and reserves, such as at Il Ngwesi, north of Lewa Wildlife Conservancy.

The mammals of Kenya

This field guide provides a quick reference to help you identify the larger mammals likely to be encountered in Kenya, together with their Swahili names. Straightforward photos show easily identified markings and features. The notes give you clear pointers about the kinds of habitat in which you are most likely to see each mammal; its daily rhythm (usually either nocturnal or diurnal); the kind of social groups it usually forms; and general tips about sighting it on safari, its rarity and its relations with humans. For further details and background, see p.567.

Yellow Baboon
Papio cynocephalus (Nyani)

 open country with trees and cliffs; adaptable, but always near water

● diurnal

♥ troops led by a dominant male

✓ common throughout East Africa; two species, *P. cynocephalus* (illustrated) and *P. anubis* (Olive); both species adapt quickly to humans, are frequently a nuisance and occasionally dangerous

Black-and-White Colobus Monkey
Colobus guereza (Mbega)

open forest, both in highlands and along watercourses in otherwise arid savanna; almost entirely arboreal

● diurnal

♥ small troops

✓ two species of black-and-whites, *C. angolensis* on the Indian Ocean coast, and the much larger *C. guereza*, in upcountry Kenya; troops maintain a limited home territory, so easily located, but can be hard to see at a great height

🐾 HABITAT ● DAILY RHYTHM ♥ SOCIAL LIFE ✓ SIGHTING TIPS

Patas Monkey
Erythrocebus patas (Ngedere)

🐾 savanna and forest margins; tolerates some aridity; terrestrial except for sleeping and lookouts

🌓 diurnal

🛡 small troops

✓ endangered and infrequently seen; can run at high speed and stand on hind feet supported by tail

Vervet Monkey
Cercopithecus aethiops or C. pygerythrus (Tumbili)

🐾 most habitats except rainforest and arid lands; arboreal and terrestrial

🌓 diurnal

🛡 troops

✓ widespread and common; occasionally a nuisance where used to humans (will steal food and anything else to hand)

Blue or Sykes' Monkey
Cercopithecus mitis (Nyabu)

🐾 forests; arboreal and occasionally terrestrial

🌓 diurnal

🛡 families or small troops

✓ widespread; shyer and less easily habituated to humans than the Vervet; can be a pest to farmers

Lesser Bushbaby or Galago
Galago senegalensis (Komba)

🐾 woodland; arboreal

🌓 nocturnal

🛡 solitary or in small family groups

✓ unfazed by humans, these small foragers often frequent lodge restaurants; call is a distinctive wail like a baby's; huge eyes, inquisitive fingers, fondness for bananas

Aardvark
Orycteropus afer (Mhanga)

🌼 open or wooded termite country; softer soil preferred

🌓 nocturnal

🛡 solitary

✓ rarely seen animal, the size of a small pig; old burrows are common and often used by warthogs

Pangolin or Scaly Anteater
Manis temminckii (Kakakuona)

🌼 termite savanna and woodland; terrestrial

🌓 nocturnal

🛡 solitary or in pairs; baby carried on mother's back

✓ armoured ant and termite eater resembling an armadillo; when frightened, they secrete a smelly liquid from anal glands and roll into a ball with their scales erect (*pangolin* is Malay for "rolling over")

Crested Porcupine
Hystrix cristata (Nungu or Nungunungu)

🌼 adaptable to a wide range of habitats, often in caves

🌓 nocturnal and sometimes active at dusk

🛡 family groups

✓ large rodent (up to 90cm in length), rarely seen, but common away from croplands, where it's hunted as a pest, or for its quills

Bat-eared Fox or Cape Fox
Otocyon megalotis (Mbweha masikio)

🌼 open country

🌓 mainly nocturnal; diurnal activity increases in cooler months

🛡 monogamous pairs

✓ distribution coincides with termites, their favoured diet; they spend many hours foraging using sensitive hearing to pinpoint their underground prey

🌼 HABITAT   🌓 DAILY RHYTHM   🛡 SOCIAL LIFE   ✓ SIGHTING TIPS

Black-backed Jackal

Canis mesomeles (Bweha)

❀ broad range from moist mountain regions to desert, but drier areas preferred

◖ normally nocturnal, but diurnal in the safety of game reserves

▽ mostly monogamous pairs; sometimes family groups

✓ a common, bold scavenger the size of a mid-sized dog that steals even from lions; three species in East Africa: black-backed with a "saddle" (illustrated); the shy side-striped (*C. adustus*); and golden (*C. aureus*) – restricted in Kenya to the Rift Valley and Laikipia

African Hunting Dog or Wild Dog

Lycaon pictus (Mbwa mwitu)

❀ open savanna in the vicinity of grazing herds

◖ diurnal

▽ nomadic packs

✓ extremely rare and rarely seen, but widely noted when in the area; the size of a large dog, with distinctively rounded ears and blotchy orange and brown fur

Honey Badger or Ratel

Mellivora capensis (Nyegere)

❀ very broad range of habitats

◖ mainly nocturnal

▽ usually solitary, but also found in pairs

✓ widespread, omnivorous, badger-sized animal; nowhere common; extremely aggressive

African Civet

Civettictis civetta (Fungo)

❀ prefers woodland and dense vegetation

◖ mainly nocturnal

▽ solitary

✓ omnivorous, medium-dog-sized, short-legged prowler; not to be confused with the smaller genet

❀ HABITAT   ◖ DAILY RHYTHM   ▽ SOCIAL LIFE   ✓ SIGHTING TIPS

Genet
Genetta genetta (Kanu)

✿ light bush country, even arid areas; partly arboreal

◐ nocturnal, but becomes active at dusk

☒ solitary

✓ quite common, slender, cat-sized omnivore, often seen at game lodges, where it easily becomes habituated to humans

Banded Mongoose
Mungos mungo (Nguchiro)

✿ thick bush and dry forest

◐ diurnal

☒ lives in burrow colonies of up to thirty animals

✓ widespread and quite common, the size of a small cat; often seen in a group, hurriedly foraging through the undergrowth. The main East African species are the banded (illustrated); dwarf (*Helogale parvula*); and black-tipped or slender (*Galerella sanguinea*)

Spotted Hyena
Crocuta crocuta (Fisi madoa)

✿ tolerates a wide variety of habitat, with the exception of dense forest

◐ nocturnal but also active at dusk; also diurnal in many parks

☒ highly social, usually living in extended family groups

✓ the size of a large dog with a distinctive loping gait, quite common in parks, especially early in the morning; carnivorous scavenger and cooperative hunter; dangerous; not to be confused with the shy, solitary and rarely seen striped hyena (*Hyaena hyaena*; Fisi miraba)

Caracal
Caracal caracal (Simba mangu)

✿ open bush and plains; occasionally arboreal

◐ mostly nocturnal

☒ solitary

✓ lynx-like wild cat; rather uncommon and rarely seen

✿ HABITAT ◐ DAILY RHYTHM ☒ SOCIAL LIFE ✓ SIGHTING TIPS

Cheetah
Acinonyx jubatus (Duma)

savanna, in the vicinity of plains grazers

diurnal

solitary or temporary nuclear family groups

✓ widespread but low population;
much slighter build than the leopard, and distinguished from it by a small head, square snout and dark "tear mark" running from eye to jowl

Leopard
Panthera pardus (Chui)

highly adaptable; frequently arboreal

nocturnal; also cooler daylight hours

solitary

✓ the size of a very large dog; not uncommon, but shy and infrequently seen; rests in thick undergrowth or up trees; very dangerous

Lion
Panthera leo (Simba)

all habitats except desert and thick forest

nocturnal and diurnal

prides of three to forty; more usually six to twelve

✓ commonly seen resting in shade; dangerous

Serval
Felis serval (Mondo)

reed beds or tall grassland near water

normally nocturnal but more diurnal than most cats

usually solitary

✓ some resemblance to the cheetah but far smaller; most likely to be seen on roadsides or at water margins at dawn or dusk

HABITAT   DAILY RHYTHM   SOCIAL LIFE   ✓ SIGHTING TIPS

Rock Hyrax
Procavia capensis (Pimbi or Wibari)

🌸 rocky areas, from mountains to isolated outcrops

🌓 diurnal

🔖 colonies consisting of a territorial male with as many as thirty related females

✓ rabbit-sized; very common; often seen sunning themselves in the early morning on rocks

African Elephant
Loxodonta africana (Tembo or Ndovu)

🌸 wide range of habitats, wherever there are trees and water

🌓 nocturnal and diurnal; sleeps as little as four hours a day

🔖 almost human in its complexity; cows and offspring in herds headed by a matriarch; bulls solitary or in bachelor herds

✓ look out for fresh dung (football-sized) and recently damaged trees; frequently seen at waterholes from late afternoon; dangerous

Black Rhinoceros
Diceros bicornis (Faru/Kifaru)

🌸 usually thick bush, altitudes up to 3500m

🌓 active day and night, resting between periods of activity

🔖 solitary

✓ extremely rare and in danger of extinction; largely confined to parks and heavily protected wildlife reserves; distinctive hooked lip for browsing; bad eyesight; very dangerous

White Rhinoceros
Ceratotherium simum (Faru/Kifaru)

🌸 savanna

🌓 active day and night, resting between periods of activity

🔖 males solitary, otherwise small same-sex herd or nursery group

✓ A reintroduced species, confined to protected reserves; distinctive wide mouth (hence "white" from Afrikaans *wijd*) for grazing; docile

🌸 HABITAT   🌓 DAILY RHYTHM   🔖 SOCIAL LIFE   ✓ SIGHTING TIPS

Burchell's Zebra

Equus burchelli (Punda milia)

✿ savanna, with or without trees, up to 4500m

◐ active day and night, resting intermittently

💭 harems of several mares and foals led by a dominant stallion are usually grouped together, in herds of up to several thousand

✓ widespread and common inside and outside the parks

Grevy's Zebra

Equus grevyi (Punda milia)

✿ arid regions

◐ largely diurnal

💭 mares with foals and stallions generally keep to separate troops; stallions sometimes solitary and territorial

✓ easily distinguished from smaller Burchell's Zebra by narrow stripes and very large ears; rare and localized but easily seen

Bush Pig

Potamochoerus larvatus (Nguruwe mwitu)

✿ forest and dense thickets close to water

◐ nocturnal

💭 groups (sounders) of up to twenty animals

✓ resembles a long-haired domestic pig with tasselled hair on its ears and white-crested back

Warthog

Phacochoerus aethiopicus (Ngiri or Gwasi)

✿ savanna, up to an altitude of over 2000m

◐ diurnal

💭 family groups, usually of a female and her litter

✓ common; boars are distinguishable from sows by their prominent facial "warts"

✿ HABITAT　　◐ DAILY RHYTHM　　💭 SOCIAL LIFE　　✓ SIGHTING TIPS

Hippopotamus
Hippopotamus amphibius (Kiboko)

🌸 slow-flowing rivers, dams and lakes

◑ principally nocturnal, leaving the water to graze

🔖 bulls are solitary, but other animals live in family groups headed by a matriarch

✓ usually seen by day in water, with top of head and ears breaking the surface; frequently aggressive and very dangerous when threatened or when retreat to water is blocked

Giraffe
Giraffa camelopardalis (Twiga)

🌸 wooded savanna and thorn country

◑ diurnal

🔖 loose, non-territorial, leaderless herds

✓ common; many subspecies, of which Maasai (*G. c. tippelskirchi*, left), Reticulated (*G. c. reticulata*, bottom l.) and Rothschild's (*G. c. rothschildi*, below) are East African

African or Cape Buffalo
Syncerus caffer (Nyati or Mbogo)

🌸 wide range of habitats, always near water, up to altitudes of 4000m

◑ nocturnal and diurnal, but inactive during the heat of the day

🔖 gregarious, with cows and calves in huge herds; young bulls often form small bachelor herds; old bulls are usually solitary

✓ very common; scent much more acute than other senses; dangerous, old bulls especially so

🌸 HABITAT   ◑ DAILY RHYTHM   🔖 SOCIAL LIFE   ✓ SIGHTING TIPS

Red Hartebeest
Alcelaphus buselaphus (Kongoni)

🌼 wide range of grassy habitats

◑ diurnal

🔲 females and calves in small, wandering herds; territorial males solitary

✓ hard to confuse with any other antelope except the topi; many varieties, distinguishable by horn shape; most common is the Red or Cape (illustrated); others include Coke's (*A. cokei*), Lichtenstein's (*A. lichtensteinii*), and Jackson's (*A. jacksoni*)

Topi or Sassaby
Damaliscus lunatus (Nyamera)

🌼 grasslands, showing a marked preference for moist savanna, near water

◑ diurnal

🔲 females and young form herds with an old male

✓ widespread, very fast runners; male often stands sentry on an abandoned termite hill, actually marking the territory against rivals, rather than defending against predators

Blue Wildebeest or Brindled Gnu
Connochaetes taurinus (Nyumbu)

🌼 grasslands

◑ diurnal, occasionally also nocturnal

🔲 intensely gregarious; wide variety of associations within mega-herds which may number over one million animals

✓ unmistakeable, nomadic grazer; long tail, mane and beard

Gerenuk
Litocranius walleri (Swala twiga)

🌼 arid thorn country and semi-desert

◑ diurnal

🔲 solitary or in small, territorial harems

✓ not uncommon; unmistakeable, its name is Somali for "giraffe-necked"; often browses standing upright on hind legs; the female is hornless

🌼 HABITAT   ◑ DAILY RHYTHM   🔲 SOCIAL LIFE   ✓ SIGHTING TIPS

23

Grant's Gazelle
Gazella granti (Swala granti)

 wide grassy plains with good visibility, sometimes far from water

◐ diurnal

🔾 small, territorial harems

✓ larger than the similar Thomson's Gazelle, distinguished from it by the white rump patch which extends onto the back; the female has smaller horns than the male

Thomson's Gazelle
Gazella thomsoni (Swala tomi)

 flat, short-grass savanna, near water

◐ diurnal

🔾 gregarious, in a wide variety of social structures, often massing in the hundreds with other grazing species

✓ smaller than the similar Grant's Gazelle, distinguished from it by the black band on flank; the female has tiny horns

Impala
Aepyceros melampus (Swala pala)

❀ open savanna near light woodland cover

◐ diurnal

🔾 large herds of females overlap with several male territories; males highly territorial during the rut when they separate out breeding harems of up to twenty females

✓ common, medium-sized, no close relatives; distinctive high leaps when fleeing; the only antelope with a black tuft above the hooves; males have long, lyre-shaped horns

Common (or Southern) Reedbuck
Redunca arundinum (Tohe)

❀ reedbeds and tall grass near water

◐ nocturnal and diurnal

🔾 monogamous pairs or family groups in territory defended by the male

✓ medium-sized antelope, with a plant diet unpalatable to other herbivores; only males have horns

❀ HABITAT   ◐ DAILY RHYTHM   🔾 SOCIAL LIFE   ✓ SIGHTING TIPS

Common Waterbuck
Kobus ellipsiprymnus (Kuro)

🐾 open woodland and savanna, near water

🌗 nocturnal and diurnal

🛡 territorial herds of females and young, led by dominant male, or territorial males visited by wandering female herds

✓ common, rather tame, large antelope; plant diet unpalatable to other herbivores; shaggy coat; only males have horns

Kirk's Dik-dik
Madoqua kirkii (Digidigi or Dika)

🐾 scrub and thornbush, often far from water

🌗 nocturnal and diurnal, most active morning and evening

🛡 monogamous pairs for life, often accompanied by current and previous young

✓ tiny, hare-sized antelope, named after its alarm cry; males are horned; females slightly larger; found in bushes, and almost always in pairs; territory marked by piles of droppings and black secretions deposited on grass stems

Common Duiker
Sylvicapra grimmia (Nysa)

🐾 adaptable; prefers dense scrub and woodland, some subspecies prefer mountainous forests

🌗 nocturnal and diurnal

🛡 most commonly solitary; sometimes in pairs; occasionally monogamous

✓ widespread and common small antelope with a rounded back; seen close to cover; males have short straight horns.

Suni *Neotragus moschatus* (Suni)

🐾 forest, or dense, dry bush

🌗 nocturnal and crepuscular; hide in shade by day

🛡 monogamous pairs, sometimes with additional non-breeding females

✓ even smaller than dik-diks, no higher than 32cm; extremely isolated populations scattered throughout Kenya, particularly in forested coastal hills; freeze when threatened before darting into undergrowth

🐾 HABITAT   🌗 DAILY RHYTHM   🛡 SOCIAL LIFE   ✓ SIGHTING TIPS

Sitatunga
Tragelaphus spekei (Nzohe)

🏵 swamps

🌓 nocturnal and sometimes diurnal

🛡 territorial and mostly solitary or in pairs

✓ very localized and not likely to be mistaken for anything else; usually seen half submerged; females have no horns

Bushbuck
Tragelaphus scriptus (Kulungu or Mbawala)

🏵 thick bush and woodland close to water

🌓 principally nocturnal, but also active during the day when cool

🛡 solitary, but casually sociable; sometimes grazes in small groups

✓ medium-sized antelope with white stripes and spots; often seen in thickets, or heard crashing through them; the male has shortish straight, spiralled horns

Eland
Taurotragus oryx (Mpofu or Mbungu)

🏵 highly adaptable; semi-desert to mountains, but prefers scrubby plains

🌓 nocturnal and diurnal

🛡 non-territorial herds of up to sixty with temporary gatherings of as many as a thousand

✓ common but shy; the largest and most powerful African antelope; both sexes have straight horns with a slight spiral

Greater Kudu
Tragelaphus strepsiceros (Tandala mkubwa)

🏵 semi-arid, hilly or undulating bush country; tolerant of drought

🌓 diurnal when secure; otherwise nocturnal

🛡 territorial; males usually solitary; females in small troops with young

✓ impressively big antelope (up to 1.5m at shoulder) with very long, spiral horns in the male; very localized; shy of humans and not often seen

🏵 HABITAT　🌓 DAILY RHYTHM　🛡 SOCIAL LIFE　✓ SIGHTING TIPS

Lesser Kudu
Tragelaphus imberbis (Tandala mdogo)

🌸 semi-arid, hilly or undulating bush country; tolerant of drought

🌓 diurnal when secure; otherwise nocturnal

🔲 territorial; males usually solitary; females in small troops with young

✔️ smaller than the Greater Kudu; only the male has horns; extremely shy and usually seen only as it disappears

Fringe-eared Oryx
Oryx gazella callotis (Choroa)

🌸 open grasslands; also waterless wastelands; tolerant of prolonged drought

🌓 nocturnal and diurnal

🔲 highly hierarchical mixed herds of up to fifteen, led by a dominant bull

✔️ the *callotis* subspecies is one of two found in East Africa, the other, in northeastern Kenya, being the Beisa Oryx (*Oryx g. beisa*)

Sable Antelope
Hippotragus niger (Palahala)

🌸 open woodland with medium to tall grassland near water

🌓 nocturnal and diurnal

🔲 territorial; bulls divide into sub-territories, through which cows and young roam; herds of immature males; sometimes pairs in season

✔️ large antelope; upper body dark brown to black; mask-like markings on the face; both sexes have huge curved horns

Roan Antelope
Hippotragus equinus (Kirongo)

🌸 tall grassland near water

🌓 nocturnal and diurnal; peak afternoon feeding

🔲 small herds led by a dominant bull; herds of immature males; sometimes pairs in season

✔️ large antelope, distinguished from the Sable by lighter, greyish colour, shorter horns (both sexes) and narrow, tufted ears

🌸 HABITAT   🌓 DAILY RHYTHM   🔲 SOCIAL LIFE   ✔️ SIGHTING TIPS

Steenbok
Raphicerus campestris (Dondoo or Dondoro)

❀ dry savanna

◑ nocturnal and diurnal

♡ solitary or (less often) in pairs

✓ widespread small antelope, surprisingly aggressive towards attackers but shy with humans; males have horns

Grysbok
Raphicerus melanotis sharpei (Dondoo or Dondoro)

❀ thicket adjacent to open grassland

◑ nocturnal

♡ males territorial; loose pairings

✓ small, rarely seen antelope; the East African subspecies is Sharpe's (illustrated); distinguished from the more slender Steinbok by light underparts; males have short horns

Oribi
Ourebia ourebia (Kasia)

❀ open grassland

◑ diurnal

♡ territorial harems consisting of male and one to four females

✓ localized small antelope, but not hard to see where common; only males have horns; the Oribi is distinguished from the smaller Grysbok and Steinbok by a black tail and dark skin patch below the eye

Klipspringer
Oreotragus oreotragus (Mbuzi mawe)

❀ rocky country; cliffs and *kopjes*

◑ diurnal

♡ territorial male with mate or small family group; often restricted to small long-term territories

✓ small antelope; horns normally only on male; extremely agile on rocky terrain; unusually high hooves, giving the impression of walking on tiptoe

❀ HABITAT　　◑ DAILY RHYTHM　　♡ SOCIAL LIFE　　✓ SIGHTING TIPS

Basics

Basics

Getting there

Flying is the only straightforward way of getting to Kenya, apart from taking overland routes which are currently only really feasible from southern Africa. Flights to Kenya are generally most expensive from late June to mid-August, and from mid-December to mid-January.

Return tickets on scheduled flights are generally of three types: short excursions of up to a month; three-month excursions; and one-year tickets. Cheaper tickets generally have fixed dates that you won't be able to change without paying an extra fee. Some airlines offer various **restricted eligibility fares** for students and under-26s which may be cheaper and more flexible than ordinary adult fares.

Charter flights, available from Britain and Europe, are often cheaper than scheduled flights, but there's usually a maximum stay in Kenya of two to four weeks.

Make **reservations** as far in advance as possible, especially if you want to travel in high season, as flights frequently fill up. Prices can fluctuate, however, on a particular flight as the date of departure approaches.

An inclusive **package holiday** can make a lot of sense. Some packages, based around mid-range coast hotels, are relatively inexpensive and, if you choose carefully, you shouldn't feel too packaged. Based on your flight, plus two weeks' of half-board accommodation (dinner, bed and breakfast) they can cost from as little as £700 from the UK, or $2400 from the US. Beach hotels vary greatly in price, atmosphere and amenities, so choose carefully, though note that you aren't obliged to stay at your hotel all the time, so you could use it as a base to make independent trips around the country.

Adding some **safari** travel to a package holiday will increase the price by at least £200 ($300) per day of safari. If you have more time and flexibility, book a safari in Kenya; see p.65, as well as the end of the Nairobi chapter or the end of the Mombasa city section for recommended companies.

From Britain and Ireland

London Heathrow is the only British airport with **direct flights to Nairobi**, operated by Kenya Airways, British Airways and Virgin Atlantic, and taking around eight-and-a-half to nine hours. Kenya Airways and Ethiopian Airlines fly to Mombasa (connecting in Nairobi and Addis Ababa). **Fares** for flights on fixed dates start at around £450 return in low season and rise to around £800 in high season. It may well be cheaper to take an **indirect flight**, changing planes in the airline's hub city in Europe, Africa or the Middle East.

There are also several **charter operators** with whom you can get seats to Mombasa, out of London and some regional airports, from around £500. These tend to change from year to year and normally offer seats with accommodation included (which at the budget end doesn't affect the price much), but you can also get "seat-only" deals. Any online or high-street travel agent can give you a quote. Last-minute high-street window deals can also be very good value.

Flying from Ireland, your easiest bet is to fly to Heathrow, connecting there for a BA, Virgin Atlantic or Kenya Airways flight. Flights should cost between €650 and €900, depending on the season.

Airlines from Britain and Ireland

British Airways UK ☎ 0844/493 0787, ⓦ www .ba.com. London Heathrow direct to Nairobi, with connecting flights from most UK airports, and connecting Aer Lingus flights from Ireland.
Egyptair UK ☎ 020/7734 2343, ⓦ www.egyptair .com.eg. London Heathrow to Nairobi via Cairo.
Emirates UK ☎ 0844/800 2777, ⓦ www.emirates .com. London and UK regional airports to Nairobi via Dubai.

Ethiopian Airlines UK ☎ 020/8987 7000, ⓦ www
.ethiopianairlines.com. London to Nairobi via Addis
Ababa.

Kenya Airways UK ☎ 020/8283 1800,
ⓦ www.kenya-airways.com. London Heathrow
direct to Nairobi.

KLM UK ☎ 0871 222 7474, Ireland ☎ 1850/747
400; ⓦ www.klm.com. London, Dublin and UK
regional airports to Nairobi, via Amsterdam.

Lufthansa UK ☎ 0871 945 9747, Ireland ☎ 01/844
5544; ⓦ www.lufthansa.com. London, Dublin and UK
regional airports to Nairobi, via Frankfurt.

Qatar Airways UK ☎ 0870/389 8090,
ⓦ www.qatarairways.com. London and Manchester
to Nairobi via Doha.

Saudia UK ☎ 020/7798 9898, ⓦ www
.saudiairlines.com. London and Manchester to
Nairobi via Jeddah.

SN Brussels Airlines UK ☎ 0905 60 95 609,
ⓦ www.brusselsairlines.com. London and UK
regional airports to Nairobi, via Brussels.

Swiss UK ☎ 0845/601 0956, Ireland ☎ 01/890
200 515; ⓦ www.swiss.com. London, Dublin and UK
regional airports to Nairobi, via Zürich.

Virgin Atlantic UK ☎ 0870/380 2007, ⓦ www
.virgin-atlantic.com. London Heathrow direct to
Nairobi.

UK discount flight agents

Africa Travel Centre UK ☎ 0845/450 1520,
ⓦ www.africatravel.co.uk. Helpful and resourceful.

Flight Centre UK ☎ 0870/499 0040, ⓦ www
.flightcentre.co.uk. Flights and safari packages.

North South Travel UK ☎ 01245/608291,
ⓦ www.northsouthtravel.co.uk. Excellent personal
service and discounted fares, with all profits going to
grassroots development charities.

STA Travel UK ☎ 0871/230 0040, ⓦ www.statravel
.co.uk. Specialists in flights and tours for students and
under-26s, though others are catered for.

Trailfinders UK ☎ 0845/058 5858, ⓦ www
.trailfinders.com; Ireland ☎ 01/677 7888, ⓦ www
.trailfinders.ie. Long-established, reputable agent,
with good-value flights and a small range of Kenya
accommodation.

Travel Bag UK ☎ 0871/703 4700, ⓦ www
.travelbag.co.uk. Discount flight deals.

USIT Ireland ☎ 01/602 1906, Northern Ireland
☎ 028/9032 7111; ⓦ www.usit.ie. Student and
youth specialists.

World Express Travel UK ☎ 020/7434 1654,
ⓦ worldexpresstravel.co.uk. Consolidators for Kenya
Airways, Brussels Airlines and Ethiopian.

World Travel Centre Ireland ☎ 01/416 7007,
ⓦ www.worldtravel.ie. Cheap flight deals.

UK Kenya and Africa specialists

See also the specialists in the US and
Canada listings on p.36, who often have
UK offices and agents listed on their
websites.

Aardvark Safaris ☎ 01980/849160, ⓦ www
.aardvarksafaris.co.uk. Committed and enthusiastic
tailor-made Africa specialists who spend a lot of time
getting to know the high-end camps and lodges they
work with – more than 60 in Kenya.

Africa Archipelago ☎ 020/7471 8780, ⓦ www
.kenyaodyssey.com. Packages and tailor-made tours
featuring safaris, beach holidays, and small lodges off
the beaten track.

Africa Select ☎ 01670/787646, ⓦ www
.africaselect.com. Like it says on the tin, a select
little outfit, offering tailor-made safaris, with some
interesting suggestions – such as a fitness holiday
in Watamu.

African Travel Resource ☎ 01306/880 770,
ⓦ www.africatravelresource.com. Intelligent and
quirky travel company with a website offering more
than 300 liberally illustrated lodges and camps in
Kenya, all visited by them, for the purpose of tailor-
making your safari.

Africa Sky ☎ 0845/543 2194, ⓦ www. africasky
.co.uk. Very well-established and knowledgeable
agent-operator with a helpfully clear website and a
host of offerings in Kenya, most of them responsible
and mid-priced.

Camp Kenya ☎ 0844/800 1127, ⓦ www
.campsinternational.com. Expertly run,
community-facing, gap-year, school-team and
career-break programmes for people of all ages,
doing genuinely useful work.

Cazenove & Loyd UK ☎ 020/7384 2332, ⓦ www
. cazenoveandloyd.com. Intelligently designed, entirely
tailor-made, private safaris from around £3000, relying
on clients who know what they're looking for.

Exodus ☎ 0845/863 9600, ⓦ www.exodus.co.uk.
Long-established overland and adventure company,
with an interesting selection of Kenya tours, including
a photographic trip to the Mara, a Mount Kenya
climb on the Sirimon route and a Kenya/Rwanda
combination.

Extreme-Safari ☎ 020/7450 1223, ⓦ www
.extreme-safari.com. London- and Diani-based
adventure and adrenaline sports company specializing
exclusively in Kenya.

Footloose Adventure Travel ☎ 01943/604030,
ⓦ www.footlooseadventure.co.uk. Enthusiastic
independent outfit based in West Yorkshire, offering
a selection of treks and safaris; they'll tailor-make a
safari to fit your budget and interests, offer advice and
track down flights.

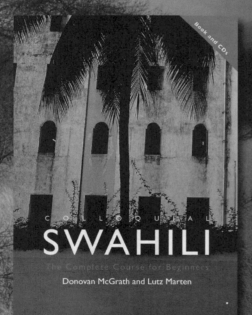

Gane & Marshall ☎01822/600600, ⊕www
.ganeandmarshall.co.uk. Africa specialists, with
responsible travel credentials and a good Kenya
programme, including Mount Kenya and Laikipia.
Gecko's Grassroots Adventures ☎0844/736
0175, ⊕www.geckosadventures.com. Budget brand
of Australian company Peregrine, with some down-to-
earth Kenya and overland tours.
GSE-Ecotours ☎0870/766 9891, ⊕www
.gse-ecotours.com. Village homestay holidays in half
a dozen Kenyan locations, aiming to give a lift to the
local economy while supporting conservation and
sustainability. From £364 for seven nights including
all meals, accommodation and local transport.
Intrepid Guerba ☎020/3147 7777, ⊕www
.intrepidtravel.com. Guerba, the acknowledged
African truck-travel experts, now part of Intrepid
Travel, run a string of Kenya trips including "Roots of
Obama" and "Walking with the Maasai".
IntoAfrica ☎0114/255 5610, ⊕www.intoafrica
.co.uk. Small, good, eco-minded tour operator, whose
trips (five in Kenya, five in Tanzania) give a genuine
insight into the country while having minimum
negative impact on people and environment.
Kumuka ☎0800/991 503, ⊕www.kumuka.com.
Overland truck tours and lodge-and-camp-based
safaris with a youthful edge, from a long-established
company with an excellent reputation and a very
impressive website.

Natural High Safaris ☎01747/898104, ⊕www
.naturalhighsafaris.com. Very cool consultancy,
safari-planner and booking agent, with highly
experienced staff.
On The Go Tours UK ☎020/7371 1113, ⊕www
.onthegotours.com. Lively and competitively priced
range of Kenya tours from a no-frills "Kenyan Capers"
camping trip to a "Gorilla and Game Trek" that
includes Uganda.
Responsible Travel ☎01273/600030, ⊕www
.responsibletravel.com. Online travel agent,
marketing more than 100 pre-screened holidays in
Kenya from dozens of socially and environmentally
responsible companies.
Safari Consultants ☎01787/888590, ⊕www
.safari-consultants.co.uk. Long established and very
personal Africa specialists who rely on direct contact
with clients.
Steppes Travel ☎01285/650011, ⊕www
.steppestravel.co.uk. Innovative travel stylists with a
personal approach, specializing in tailor-made trips,
based in luxury lodges.
To Escape To ☎020/7060 6747, ⊕www
.toescapeto.com. Property rental and accommodation
agent, offering more then 60 hotels, lodges and
camps in Kenya, including mid-priced options.
Theobald Barber ☎020/7723 5858, ⊕www
.theobaldbarber.com. Bespoke safari planners,
offering a very personalized service.

Tim Best Travel ☎ 020/7591 0300, ⓦ www
.timbesttravel.com. Eco-luxurious holiday company
with a great reputation for delivering off-the-beaten-
track arrangements.

Tribes Travel ☎ 01728/685971, ⓦ www
.tribes.co.uk. Highly recommended small
company in the vanguard of responsibly operated
and traded tourism, including more
than 90 places to stay in Kenya, all individually
reviewed and rated.

Wildlife Worldwide ☎ 0845/630 6982, ⓦ www
.wildlifeworldwide.com. Tailor-made trips for wildlife
enthusiasts and packages including a "Migration
Special".

From the US and Canada

There are no direct flights from the USA or
Canada to East Africa, although the 2008
signing of an "open skies" agreement
between Kenya and the US may mean the
start of direct services soon. The fastest
routes to Nairobi are usually via **London**,
either on British Airways or a combination of
Virgin Atlantic and Kenya Airways.

Fares start from around $1300 for a
two-week return out of New York in low
season, $1850 in high season, or, out of
Los Angeles, from $1400 or $2250
respectively.

Airlines from the US and Canada

British Airways ☎ 1-800/AIRWAYS, ⓦ www
.ba.com. From several US and Canadian airports to
Nairobi via London.

Brussels Airlines US ☎ 516/740 5200, Canada
☎ 1-866/308 2230; ⓦ www. brusselsairlines.
com. Chicago and Toronto to Nairobi via Brussels.

Egyptair US ☎ 212/581 5600, Canada ☎ 416/960
2441; ⓦ www.egyptair.com.eg. New York to Nairobi
via Cairo.

Emirates ☎ 1-800/777 3999, ⓦ www.emirates
.com. New York, San Francisco, Los Angeles and
Houston to Nairobi via Dubai.

Ethiopian Airlines ☎ 1-800/445 2733, ⓦ www
.flyethiopian.com. Washington DC to Nairobi via
Addis Ababa.

KLM/Northwest ☎ 1-800/225 2525, ⓦ www.klm
.com. From several US and Canadian cities to Nairobi
via Amsterdam.

Saudia ☎ 1-800/472 8342, ⓦ www.saudiairlines
.com. New York and Washington DC to Nairobi via
Jeddah.

Swiss ☎ 1-877/359 7947, ⓦ www.swiss.com.
Boston, Chicago, Los Angeles, Miami, Montreal and
New York to Nairobi, via Zürich.

Virgin Atlantic ☎ 1-800/821 5438, ⓦ www
.virgin-atlantic.com. Tickets from several US cities to
Nairobi via London.

US & Canadian discount flight agents

Air Brokers International US ☎ 1-800/883 3273,
ⓦ www.airbrokers.com. Consolidator and round-the-
world specialist.

Airtech US ☎ 212/219 7000, ⓦ www.airtech.com.
Standby-seat broker, and also deals in consolidator fares.

Airtreks US ☎ 1-877/AIR-TREKS, ⓦ www.airtreks
.com. Specialist in round-the-world and multi-sector
tickets.

Educational Travel Center US ☎ 1-800/747
5551 or 608/256 5551, ⓦ www.edtrav.com.
Student/youth discount agent.

Flight Centre US ☎ 1-866/967 5351, ⓦ www
.flightcentre.us; Canada ☎ 1-877/967 5302,
ⓦ www.flightcentre.ca. Low airfares to Kenya.

STA Travel US ☎ 1-800/781 4040, ⓦ www
.statravel.com. Independent travel specialists, geared
up to students and under-26s, though not exclusively.

Travel Cuts US ☎ 1-800/592-CUTS, Canada
☎ 1-888/246 9762; ⓦ www.travelcuts.com.
Popular, long-established student travel organization.

Travelosophy US ☎ 1-800/332 2687, ⓦ www
.itravelosophy.com. Discount and student fares.

US & Canadian Kenya and Africa specialists

See also the specialists in the UK listings on
p.32, who often have North American offices
and agents listed on their websites.

Abercrombie & Kent US ☎ 1-800/554 7016,
ⓦ www.abercrombiekent.com. Upscale operator
with more than thirty years of experience organizing
African safaris, and a wide knowledge of Kenya,
where the company originated.

Adventure Center Canada ☎ 1-800/228 8747
or 403/439 9118, ⓦ www.adventure-center.com.
Hiking and soft-adventure specialists, agents for a very
wide range of tours focusing or touching on Kenya.

African Horizons US ☎ 877/256 1074, ⓦ www
.africanhorizons.com. Decent range of well-priced
Kenya safaris with flexible departures.

Africa Tours US ☎ 1-800/235 3692, ⓦ www
.africasafaris.com. A choice of eight off-the-shelf
Kenya safaris and three combined with Tanzania.

African Adventure Company US ☎ 1-800/882
9453 or 954/491 8877, ⓦ www.africa-adventure
.com. One of the best agencies in the business,
offering nine safari options in Kenya, including a
"voluntourism" trip to Rukinga Ranch.

Born Free Safaris US ☎ 1-800/4-SAFARI or
720/524 9683, ⓦ www.bornfreesafaris.com.

Plain-speaking safari operator established in the 1970s, with a what-you-see-is-what-you-get approach and good value safaris on offer.

GAP Adventures Canada ☎1-800/708 7761, ⓦwww.gapadventures.com. Long list of Kenya tours from super-luxurious short breaks to basic camping trips.

Geographic Expeditions US ☎1-800/777 8183, ⓦwww.geoex.com. Fifteen-day off-the-shelf Kenya safaris, private deluxe safaris, and combination Kenya/Tanzania safaris.

Good Earth Tours US ☎888/776 7173, goodearthtours.com. Very good value safaris, starting at $210/day for minibus camping trips, excluding air travel.

Journeys International US ☎1-800/255 8735 or 734/665 4407, ⓦwww.journeys-intl.com. Award-winning ecotourism operator with two Kenya trips: a mainstream 9-day safari and an unusual culture-and-wildlife 14-day safari that ventures off the beaten track into Ukambani.

Ker & Downey US ☎1-800/423 4236 or 281/371 2500, ⓦwww.kerdowney.com. Renowned and much-commended upmarket travel company, working closely with top Kenya property groups Cheli & Peacock and Bush & Beyond.

Micato Safaris US ☎1-800/MICATO-1 or 212/545 7111, ⓦwww.micato.com. Multi-award-winning Kenyan-American tour operator with a variety of Kenya offerings.

Mountain Madness US ☎1-800/328 5925 or 206/937 8389, ⓦwww.mountainmadness.com. Seattle-based adventure travel firm, offering really good-value, well-planned, well-paced Mount Kenya climbs, though only once a year.

Mountain Travel Sobek US ☎1-888/831 7526 or 510/594 6000, ⓦwww.mtsobek .com. Wonderful foot safaris through Tsavo East, Maasailand and the northern deserts in the footsteps of Teleki, in association with Tropical Ice Safaris of Nairobi.

Nature Expeditions International US ☎1-800/869 0639 or 954/693 8852, ⓦwww.naturexp .com. Good value, flexible educational tours – one just in Kenya, one including Tanzania – with optional lectures on wildlife, natural history and culture. Good for older kids and teens.

Safari Consultants US ☎1-866/SEE-GAME, ⓦwww.safariconsultants.com. Wide range of clearly presented and well-priced options from budget to top-end.

Six steps to a better kind of travel

At Rough Guides we are passionately committed to travel. We feel strongly that only through travelling do we truly come to understand the world we live in and the people we share it with – plus tourism has brought a great deal of **benefit** to developing economies around the world over the last few decades. But the extraordinary growth in tourism has also damaged some places irreparably, and of course **climate change** is exacerbated by most forms of transport, especially flying. This means that now more than ever it's important to **travel thoughtfully** and **responsibly**, with respect for the cultures you're visiting – not only to derive the most benefit from your trip but also to preserve the best bits of the planet for everyone to enjoy. At Rough Guides we feel there are six main areas in which you can make a difference:

- Consider what you're contributing to the **local economy**, and how much the services you use do the same, whether it's through employing local workers and guides or sourcing locally grown produce and local services.
- Consider the **environment** on holiday as well as at home. Water is scarce in many developing destinations, and the biodiversity of local flora and fauna can be adversely affected by tourism. Try to patronize businesses that take account of this.
- Travel with a purpose, not just to tick off experiences. Consider **spending longer** in a place, and getting to know it and its people.
- Give thought to how often you **fly**. Try to avoid short hops by air and more harmful night flights.
- Consider **alternatives to flying**, travelling instead by bus, train, boat and even by bike or on foot where possible.
- Make your trips "**climate neutral**" via a reputable carbon offset scheme. All Rough Guide flights are offset, and every year we donate money to a variety of charities devoted to combating the effects of climate change.

From Australia and NZ

There are no direct flights to Kenya from Australia or New Zealand. From **Australia**, South African Airways (SAA) has some good connections to Nairobi via Johannesburg, while Emirates also offer good connections and fares. From **New Zealand**, Emirates via Dubai is your most obvious bet, but Air New Zealand and Qantas can get you to Kenya in combination with other airlines, such as SAA from Johannesburg.

Except for the Christmas period, when you will have to pay more, **fares** to Kenya from Australia and New Zealand are generally not seasonal. The lowest-priced return tickets bought from a discount agent or direct from the airline cost around Aus\$2100–3000 from Australia or NZ\$2800–4000 from New Zealand.

Airlines from Australia and New Zealand

Air Mauritius Australia ℡02/9264 7771, ⓦwww .airmauritius.com. Nairobi via Mauritius.

Air New Zealand New Zealand ℡0800/737 000, ⓦwww.airnewzealand.co.nz. To Nairobi from Auckland and regional airports in conjunction with another carrier.

Emirates Australia ℡1300/303 777, New Zealand ℡0508/364 728; ⓦwww.emirates.com. Sydney, Melbourne, Perth and Auckland to Nairobi via Dubai.

Qantas Australia ℡13/1313, New Zealand ℡0800/808 767 or 09/357 8900; ⓦwww.qantas .com. To Nairobi from most Australian and New Zealand airports in conjunction with another carrier.

South African Airways Australia ℡1300/435 972, New Zealand ℡09/977 2237; ⓦwww.2flysaa .com. From Sydney, Melbourne and Perth with Qantas to Johannesburg, connecting with SAA to Nairobi.

Australia and New Zealand Travel agents

Airfares Flights Australia ⓦwww.airfaresflights .com.au. Fare-comparison site.

Best Flights Australia ℡1300/767 757, ⓦbestflights.com.au. Well-priced and user-friendly agent.

Flight Centre Australia ℡133 133, ⓦwww .flightcentre.com.au; New Zealand ℡0800/243 544 ⓦwww.flightcentre.co.nz. Some of the best Nairobi fare deals.

STA Travel Australia ℡134/STA, ⓦwww.statravel .com.au; New Zealand ℡0800/474 400,

ⓦwww.statravel.co.nz. Specialists in flights and holiday deals for students and under-26s.

Trailfinders Australia ℡1300/780 212, ⓦwww .trailfinders.com.au. One of the best-informed agents for independent travellers.

Australia and New Zealand Kenya and Africa specialists

See also the specialists in the UK and North America listings on pp.32–36, who often have Australian and New Zealand offices and agents listed on their websites.

Abercrombie & Kent Australia ℡1300/851 800, New Zealand ℡0800/441 638; ⓦwww .abercrombiekent.com.au. Classy operator with a strong reputation, offering a limited number of well-constructed lodge-, camp- and mobile-camp-based trips in Kenya and Tanzania.

Adventure World Australia ℡1300/363 055, ⓦwww.adventureworld.com.au; New Zealand ℡0800/238 368, ⓦwww.adventureworld.co.nz. Agents for mostly overland operators who include Kenya, such as Acacia Africa, Dragoman, Explore!, G.A.P and Drifters.

African Travel Specialists Australia ℡03//9576 1980, ⓦwww.africantravel.com.au. Well-established agent, part of the Four Corners Travel Group, with an excellent reputation and a team of highly experienced staff, many of whom know Kenya well.

African Wildlife Safaris Australia ℡1300/363 302 or 03/9249 3777, ⓦwww.africanwildlifesafaris .com.au. Slick and confident upmarket lodge- and camp-based safaris, many run by renowned Nairobi-based operator, Origins Safaris.

Classic Safari Company Australia ℡1300/130 218 or 02/9327 0666, ⓦwww .classicsafaricompany.com.au. Tailor-made safaris ranging from comfortable to luxurious including mobile camping, riding and walking options.

Peregrine Australia ℡03/8601 4444, ⓦwww .peregrine.net.au. A number of safari options in Kenya alone, or in combination with Uganda and/or Tanzania.

Wildlife Safari Australia ℡1-800/998 558, ⓦwww.wildlife-safari.com.au. Kenya specialist operator run by a Kenyan Australian using 4WDs and mid-priced lodges or internal flights and more luxurious bases.

From South Africa

There are daily **direct flights** to Nairobi from Johannesburg on South African Airways (℡0861/808 808, ⓦwww.2flysaa.com) and

Kenya Airways (☎082/234 5786, ⓦwww
.kenya-airways.com). Return fares start at
around R5000.

South African operators and agents

See also the specialists in the UK and North
America listings on pp.32–36, who
sometimes have South African agents listed
on their websites.

African Routes ☎031/563 5080, ⓦwww
.africanroutes.co.za. Durban-based overland operator
and agent for northbound trips.
Drifters Adventure Tours ☎011/888 1160,
ⓦwww.safarishop.co.za. A range of options.
Free Spirit Adventures ☎082/558 8959, ⓦwww
.freespiritadventures.co.za. Exclusive package tours.
STA Travel ☎0861/781 781, ⓦwww.statravel
.co.za. Good youth and student fares.
Wild Frontiers ☎011/702 2035, ⓦwww
.wildfrontiers.com. An excellent range of mid-priced
tours to Maasai Mara, Mombasa, Lamu and other
popular Kenyan destinations.

Overlanding to Kenya

With unlimited time and a sense of
adventure, **travelling overland** can be an
exciting and rewarding way of getting to
Kenya. Central African conflicts have effectively closed routes from West Africa for the
time being, and while it is possible to get to
Kenya from Egypt, by taking a boat from
Aswan to Wadi Halfa in Sudan, crossing into
Ethiopia at Humera or Metema, and entering
Kenya at Moyale, this route is not an easy
one, although adventurous **self-drive**
overlanders are using it. With the settlement
in southern Sudan, it is also now possible to
travel via Juba, entering Kenya at Lokichokio.

Currently the only advisable route is from
southern Africa. You can take the train up
through Zambia and Tanzania, go overland
by local transport, or hook up with any
number of overland operators from Cape
Town to Nairobi. Scrutinizing their websites
gives an indication of their preparedness
and know-how; if the blurb looks cheap or
hasty, you should probably give them a
wide berth. A useful resource is ⓦwww
.overlandingcommunity.com: they have
news and forum comment about many
companies.

Most of the following **recommended
operators** (see also p.32) offer five- to
ten-week Nairobi–Cape Town trips, which
are usually possible in the other direction
too. Prices vary widely: for a six-to-ten-
week Cape Town–Nairobi trip, taking in
Namibia, Victoria Falls, Uganda and other
highlights, you're looking at anything from
$250–600 per week, including the local
kitty. As usual, you tend to get what you
pay for.

UK-based overland operators

Absolute Africa UK ☎020/8742 0226, ⓦwww
.absoluteafrica.com. Budget.
Acacia Africa Adventures UK ☎020/7706
4700, ⓦwww.acacia-africa.com. Expensive, but
good value.
African Trails UK ☎01580/761 171, ⓦwww
.africantrails.co.uk. Budget.
Dragoman UK ☎01728/861 133, ⓦwww
.dragoman.com. Expensive but worth it.
Kumuka Expeditions UK ☎0800/991
503, ⓦwww.kumuka.com. Expensive, and
recommended.

Ivory

Although you will rarely be offered it, it's worth knowing that possession of **ivory** is
strictly illegal in Kenya, and most countries have banned all trade. If it's found by
customs you are likely to be heavily fined or imprisioned

Getting around

As well as domestic flights, travelling as part of a safari tour, or renting a vehicle for self-drive or with a driver, Kenya has a wide range of public transport. Alongside the flashy air-conditioned coaches, you'll find smaller companies operating a single battered minibus. And in towns of any size, crowds of Nissan minibuses and pick-ups (both operating as shared taxis and referred to as matatus) hustle for business constantly. A quick round-up of regional public transport information is given at the end of each chapter.

Car rental and driving

All the parks and reserves are open to private vehicles, and there's a lot to be said for the freedom of choice that **renting a car** gives you. Unless there are more than two of you, though, it won't save you money over one of the cheaper camping safaris. If you're going to be in Kenya for some time, or you're planning to travel more widely, buying a **secondhand** vehicle in Nairobi is a realistic possibility, though prices are high for what you can get, relative to Europe or North America. Check the poster boards at any big mall or shopping centre such as Village Market or the Sarit Centre.

Before renting, shop around for the best deals and try to negotiate as you might with any purchase, bearing in mind how long you need and the season. July, August and Christmas are busy, so you might want to book ahead. **Rates** vary greatly: some are quoted in Kenyan shillings and some in dollars or euros; some include unlimited mileage while others don't. The minimum age to rent a car is usually 23, sometimes 25.

You can often rent with a **driver or driver-guide** supplied by the rental company, which can be more relaxing and a great introduction to the country. This should add around Ksh500–1000 per day to your bill for the driver's salary, and up to another Ksh1000 per day for his daily living expenses. Be clear precisely what the arrangements are before you set off: it's always best to have things in writing.

Check the insurance details and always pay the daily **collision damage waiver (CDW)** premium, sometimes included in the price; even a small bump could be very costly otherwise. **Theft protection waiver (TPW)** should also be taken. Even with these, however, you'll still be liable for an **excess**, usually $500–1000, for which you are liable if there is any claim. You're also required to leave a hefty deposit, roughly equivalent to the anticipated bill, normally on a credit card.

If stopped at a police checkpoint, you may be asked to produce evidence that the rental car has a **PSV** (passenger service vehicle) **licence**. You should have a windscreen sticker for this as well as the letters "PSV" written somewhere on the body; if in doubt, check this out with the rental company before you leave. All PSV vehicles are, in theory, fitted with 80kph speed governors, physically limiting your top speed to about 50mph. In practice, few companies leave them operational, but your speed limit is still 80.

Being **stopped by the police** is a common occurrence. Checkpoints are generally marked by low strips of spikes across the road, with just enough room to slalom round. Always stop, greet the officer and wait to be waved through. If they accuse you of breaking any law, then politely accept what you are told, including the possibility of a court appearance (highly unlikely). Being set up for a bribe used to be fairly common, but the police have cleaned up their act and will normally wave tourists on their way with a warning.

If you have a **breakdown**, before seeking assistance, you should pile bundles of sticks or foliage 50m or so behind and in front of the car. These are the universally recognized "red warning triangles" of Africa, and their placing is always scrupulously observed, as is the wedging of a stone behind at least one wheel to stop it rolling away.

You might consider joining **AA Kenya** (🌐www.aakenya.co.ke) which offers termporary membership for up to six months for Ksh1500, which includes the usual breakdown and rescue services, where available.

Choosing and running a vehicle

Four-wheel drive (4WD) is always useful, but except in mountainous areas and on some dirt roads during rain, it is rarely essential. **High clearance**, however, is, thanks to the dire state of many roads. Few, if any, agencies will rent out non-4WD vehicles for use in the parks, and most park rangers will turn away such cars at the gate. Maasai Mara and the mountain parks (Mount Elgon, Mount Kenya and the Aberdare range) are the most safety-minded.

Four-wheel drive **Suzuki jeeps** are the most widely available vehicles, but ensure you get a long wheelbase model with rear seats, room for four people (or five at a pinch) and luggage space at the back. These are more stable than the stumpy short-wheelbase versions. Beware of the notorious tendency of Suzukis to topple over on bends or on the dangerously sloping gravel hard shoulders that line so many roads. Warnings aside, Suzukis are light and dependable, capable of great feats in negotiating rough terrain, and can nearly always be fixed by a local repair shop.

Don't assume, however, that the vehicle is roadworthy before you set off. Have a good look at the engine and tyres, and don't set off without checking the spare (preferably two) and making sure that you have a few vital tools. Ideally, always carry a tow rope, spare water and fuel in a jerrican (it's quite common for petrol stations to have no supplies, even in large towns). You might also take a spare fan belt, brake pads, and brake fluid. You are responsible for any **repair** and **maintenance work** that needs doing while you're renting the vehicle, but the better firms will expect you to call them if you have a breakdown, and will even come out to help you. They should always reimburse you for any running repairs, against receipts.

When you get a **flat tyre**, as you will, get it mended straight away: it costs very little (Ksh50–100) and can be done almost anywhere. Local mechanics are usually very good and can apply ingenuity to the most disastrous situations. But spare parts, tools and proper equipment are rare off the main routes. Always settle on a price before work begins.

At the time of writing, the **price of petrol** (gasoline, always unleaded) ranges from roughly Ksh70–100 per litre (£0.63–90 per litre or $3.60–5.10 per US gallon) depending on the retailer, the remoteness of the town and Kenya's latest oil imports. There is occasionally a choice of regular or premium, but the latter is the norm. **Diesel** is around five to ten percent more expensive. When filling, which is always done by an attendant, check the pump is set to zero. In city petrol stations you can sometimes pay by credit card, but don't count on it as their card reader may be out of action.

Driving on the roads

You can drive in Kenya with either a valid **driving licence** from your home country, or an international one. Although there is still very little satellite mapping of Kenya, a **GPS** SatNav device is very useful as there are very few road signs and no detailed, accurate road maps. A basic GPS that draws your route as you go enables you to retrace your route back to where you came from meaning you'll never lose your bearings.

Be cautious of abrupt changes in **road surface**. On busy, tarmac roads, "tramlines" often develop. Caused by heavy trucks ploughing over hot blacktop, these can be deep and treacherous, making steering difficult. Slow down.

Beware of animals, people, rocks, branches, ditches and potholes – any combination of which may appear at any time. It is accepted practice to honk your horn stridently to warn pedestrians and cyclists. **Other vehicles** are probably the biggest menace, especially in busy areas close to towns where matatus are constantly pulling over to drop and pick up passengers. It's common practice to flash oncoming vehicles, especially if they're leaving you little room to pass. Try to **avoid driving at night**, and be extra careful when passing heavy vehicles – the diesel fumes can cut off your visibility without warning.

In theory Kenya **drives on the left**, though in reality vehicles keep to the best part of the road until they have to pass each other. You should recognize the supplementary meanings of **left and right signals** particularly common among truck drivers. A right signal by the driver ahead of you means "Don't try to pass me", while the left signal which usually follows means "Feel free to pass me now". Do not, however, automatically assume the driver can really see that it is safe for you to pass. In fact, never assume anything about other drivers.

Beware of **speed bumps**, found wherever a busy road has been built through a village, and on the roads in and out of nearly every town. Try to look out for small bollards or painted rocks at the roadside, but usually the first you'll know of speed bumps is when your head hits the roof.

Driving in town, you may need to adopt a more robust approach than you would use at home, or risk waiting permanently at the first busy junction you come to. There is no concept of yielding or giving way in Kenya: most drivers occupy the road forcefully and only concede when physically blocked by another vehicle or someone in uniform with a weapon. Although it sounds highly confrontational, incidents of "road rage" seem few and far between.

Finding somewhere to **park** is rarely a problem, even in Nairobi or Mombasa. There are council traffic wardens in most large towns from Monday to Saturday, from whom you can buy a ticket for 24 hours for Ksh40–100. If you don't, your car may be clamped or towed away. Be careful not to inadvertently park on yellow lines, which are often faded to near-invisibility.

Off-road driving

Although there are few parts of Kenya where 4WD vehicles are mandatory (some of the private ranches and game reserves do insist on them), you would be well advised not to go far off tarmac in a two-wheel-drive vehicle, if only because a short cloudburst can transform an otherwise good dirt road

into a quagmire. Take local advice if attempting unsurfaced roads in the rainy season, when mud pits with a smooth and apparently firm surface can disguise deep traps. A covering of vegetation usually means a relatively solid surface.

If you have to go through a large muddy puddle, first kick off your shoes and wade the entire length to check it out (better to get muddy than bogged down). If it's less than 30cm (a foot) deep, and the base is relatively firm (ie your feet don't sink far), you should be able to drive through. Engage 4WD, slip into first gear, and drive slowly straight across, or, if there's a sufficiently firm area to one side, drive across at speed with one wheel in the water and one out (beware of toppling over in a Suzuki). For smaller puddles, gathering up speed on the approach and then charging across in second gear usually works.

Approaching **deep mud** is harder to advise upon. Drive as fast as you dare, never over-steer when skidding, and pray.

On a mushy surface of "**black cotton soil**" especially during or after rain, you'll need all your wits about you, as even the sturdiest 4WDs have little or no grip on this and some – Land Cruisers for example – are notoriously useless. It's best to keep your speed down and stay in second gear as much as possible. Try to keep at least one wheel on vegetation-covered ground or in a well-defined rut.

If you do **get stuck**, stop immediately, as spinning the wheels will only make it worse. Try reversing, just once, by revving the engine as far as you can before engaging reverse gear. If it doesn't work, you'll just have to wait for another vehicle to pull you out.

Buses, matatus, taxis

Matatus, and to a lesser extent buses, have a bad **safety record**. The most dangerous matatus are those billed as "express" (they mean it). Don't hesitate to ask to get out of the vehicle if you feel unsafe, and to demand a partial refund, which will usually be forthcoming. On all public transport, it's worth considering your general **direction** through the trip and which side of the vehicle will be shadier. This is especially important on dirt roads when the combination of dust, a slow, bumpy ride, and fierce sun through closed windows can be unbearable. Note that in more remote areas, where a service has no clear schedule, if a driver tells you he's going somewhere "today", it doesn't necessarily mean he expects to arrive today.

Inter-city bus and matatu **fares** are typically around Ksh1.50–3 per kilometre (or if the vehicle is "deluxe" in some way, up to Ksh4.50). Even the longest journey by matatu, the 300km, six-hour journey from Nairobi to Kisumu, should cost no more than Ksh900 (or Ksh1300 by "deluxe" vehicle). Rarely does anyone attempt to charge more than the approved rate. Baggage charges should not normally be levied unless you're transporting a huge load. If you think you're being overcharged, check with other passengers.

Buses

Buses cover almost the whole country. Some, on the main runs between Nairobi and Mombasa, and to a lesser extent the centre and west, are fast, comfortable and keep to schedules; you generally need to **reserve** seats in advance. The large companies, in particular Akamba (ⓦwww.akambabus.com), have ticket offices near the bus stations in most towns, where they list their routes and prices. Their parking bays are rarely marked, however, and there are no published timetables. The easiest procedure is to mention your destination to a few people at the bus park, and then check out the torrent of offers. Keep asking – it's virtually impossible to get on the wrong bus. Once you've acquired a seat, the wait can be almost a pleasure if you're in no hurry, as you watch the throng outside and field a continuous stream of vendors proffering wares through the window.

Matatus and other vehicles

Along most routes the matatus these days are Nissan **minibuses**, while occasionally in rural areas old-style **pick-up trucks** still ply their trade, fitted with wooden benches and a canvas roof. The Nissans can be fast and are the more dangerous: try to sit at the back, to avoid too graphic a view of blind overtaking.

After new **regulations** were introduced by the Kibaki government in 2003, all seats are supposed to be fitted with seat belts (which are often broken), loud music is banned (it is often still played: it's actually the one saving grace for some passengers) and electronic speed governors are supposed to prevent speeds above 80kph (but are often broken or deliberately disabled). Passenger numbers are, in theory, strictly limited, but on many routes, especially off the main roads, the old maxim of "room for one more" still applies. *Kitu kidogo*, a "little something" for police officers at road blocks, ensures blind eyes are turned towards many infringements.

Nonetheless, matatus can on occasions be an enjoyable way of getting about, giving you close contact, literally, with local people, and some hilarious encounters. They are also often the most convenient and sometimes the only means of transport to smaller places off the main roads.

Always choose a matatu that's close to full or you'll have to wait inside until they're ready to go, sometimes for hours. Beware of being used as bait by the driver to encourage passengers to choose his vehicle, and equally of a driver filling his car with young touts pretending to be passengers (spot them by the newspapers and lack of luggage). Competition is intense and people will tell brazen lies to persuade you the vehicle is going "just now". Try not to hand over any money before you've left town. This isn't a question of being ripped off, but too often the first departure is just a soft launch, cruising around town rounding up more passengers and buying petrol, and then going back to square one.

If your destination isn't on a main matatu route, or if you don't want to wait for a vehicle to fill up (or, indeed, if you just want to travel in style), drivers will happily negotiate a price for the charter or rental of the whole car. The sum will normally be equivalent to the amount they would receive from all the passengers in a full vehicle over the same distance.

The following terms are worth knowing: a **stage or stand** is the matatu yard; a **manamba or turn boy** is the tout who takes the fares and hangs on dramatically; and

dropping is what you do when you disembark, as in "I'm dropping here".

Transport in towns often comes down to **private taxis**. You'll need to discuss the fare in advance: most drivers will want to be earning something like Ksh400 per hour, so Ksh100–200 should cover most journeys. In some towns, there's also the option of using a **tuk-tuk** (three-wheeled vehicles imported from Asia, on which fares are around half the price of an ordinary taxi). Alternatively, many areas have the two-wheel taxis consisting of a motorcycle which can carry one or two people without luggage (known as a **piki-piki**) or a bicycle with a padded passenger seat for one (known as a **boda-boda**). As you'd expect, you get what you pay for.

Trains

The overnight **Nairobi–Mombasa** train leaves three times a week in each direction, taking around 14–17 hours to complete the journey. There's also a thrice-weekly **Nairobi–Kisumu** service, which takes a similar time. On both routes, the train can pull in anything up to four hours late. Frustrating though the almost routine delays are, they at least mean you are likely to have a few hours of morning light to watch the passing scene: approaching Nairobi from Mombasa, the animals on the Athi Plains; approaching the capital from Kisumu, the

Rift Valley; approaching Mombasa, the sultry crawl down to the ocean. If you want to book tickets before you arrive in Kenya, the agents Let's Go Travel (ⓦwww .lets-go-travel.net) do a reliable job, but you pay a little extra. You can always book at the local station, ideally the day before.

Trains have three **seat classes**, but only first and second offer any kind of comfort. In first class, you get a private, two-berth compartment; second class has four-berth compartments, which are usually single-sex, though this may be disregarded, for example if all four people are travelling as a party; third class has hard seats only and is packed with local passengers.

The carriages and compartments aren't luxurious, and the toilets are not all European-style, but the train usually starts its journey clean, and in a reasonably good state of repair. **Meals and bedding**, available in first and second class only, cost a little extra, and must be paid for when you buy your ticket, though it's normally assumed you will take them. The linen (Ksh320) is always clean, washing water usually flows from the compartment basins, and meals are freshly prepared and service is good. On the Mombasa train, dinner is served in two sittings (7.15pm & 8.45pm; Ksh700). You should go for the first sitting for the best food and service, and the second if you'd rather take your time. Breakfast, served from 6am, is Ksh470. Singles and couples will usually have to share their tables with other diners. On the Kisumu train, dinner costs Ksh350 and breakfast Ksh250.

There are **disused railway tracks** in many parts of Kenya and occasionally sections are refurbished. At the time of writing, a weekly, Saturday daytime service was running between Nairobi and **Nanyuki** (see p.167). In addition, a weekly local service still runs from Kisumu to **Butere** (see p.305).

Boats and ferries

There is no passenger **shipping** along the Kenya coast apart from the small vessels connecting the islands of the Lamu archipelago. Informally, you can hitch lifts with dhow captains, though there are few working dhows left. On Lake Victoria, the network of steamer routes was suspended

---

Nairobi–Mombasa timetable

Dep. Nairobi Mon, Wed, Fri 7pm
Arr. Mombasa Tues, Thurs, Sat 8.25am
Dep. Mombasa Tues, Thurs, Sun 7pm
Arr. Nairobi Wed, Fri, Mon 9am
Fares, without meals, but including bedding: 1st class Ksh2490, 2nd class Ksh1470.

Nairobi–Kisumu timetable

Dep. Nairobi Mon, Wed, Fri 6.30pm
Arr. Kisumu Tues, Thurs, Sat 7.45am
Dep. Kisumu Tues, Thurs, Sun 7pm
Arr. Nairobi Wed, Fri, Mon 8am
Fares, without meals, but including bedding: 1st class Ksh1950, 2nd class Ksh1150.

when the lake became clogged up with water hyacinth, and although there are occasional services, there's nothing regular that you can really on.

Hitchhiking

Hitching is how the majority of rural people get around, in the sense that they wait by the roadside for whatever comes, and will pay for a ride in a passing lorry or a private vehicle, the cost being close to what it would be in a matatu. Private vehicles with spare seats are comparatively rare, but Kenyans are happy enough to give lifts, if often bemused by the idea of a tourist without a vehicle. Hitching rides with other tourists at the gates of national parks and reserves is also sometimes possible, but only if you have lots of time on your hands. Highway hitching **techniques** need to be fairly exuberant: beckon the driver to stop with a palm-down action, then quickly establish how much the ride will cost. And be sure to choose a safe spot with room to pull over. Alternatively, use a busy petrol station and ask every driver. You'll soon get a ride. In terms of **safety**, it's highly unlikely you would run into any unsavoury characters, but don't get in if you think the vehicle is unroadworthy, or the driver unfit to drive.

Bicycles

Kenya's climate and varied terrain make it challenging and thrilling **cycling** country, and you can rent bikes or go on organized tours in a number of places, or sign up for one of the charity-fundraising rides that regularly take place.

With a bike, given time and average determination, you can get to parts of the country that would be hard to visit except perhaps on foot. Cycling is also one way you will get to see wildlife outside the confines of the game parks, while several of the smaller game parks allow bikes, including Hell's Gate at Naivasha and Kakamega Forest. You need to consider the **seasons**, however, as you won't make much progress on dirt roads during the rains. On **main roads**, a mirror is essential and, if the road surface is broken at the edge, give yourself plenty of space and be ready to leave the road if necessary.

You can take a bike with you, or buy one locally. Most towns have bicycle shops selling basic mountain bikes and trusty Indian three-speed roadsters, starting from around Ksh5000. We've mentioned some outlets in the Mombasa and Nairobi "Listings" sections. Whatever you take, and a mountain bike is certainly best, it will need low gears and strongly built wheels, and you should have some essential spare parts.

If you're taking a bike with you, then you'll probably want to carry your gear in **panniers**. These are inconvenient, however, when not on the bike, and you might instead consider strapping your luggage onto the rear carrier. You can adapt your carrier locally with furniture cane and lashings of inner tube strips (any market will fix you up for pennies), thus creating your own highly un-aerodynamic touring carrier, with room for a box of food and a gallon of water underneath.

If you're taking a bike from home, take a battery **lighting system**: it's surprising how often you'll need it. The front light will double as a torch, and getting the large-sized U2 batteries is no problem. Also take a **U-bolt cycle lock**. In situations where you have to lock the bike, you'll always find something to lock it to (out in the bush, locking is less important). Local bikes can be locked with a padlock and chain passed through a length of hosepipe, which you can buy and fix up in any market.

Buses and matatus with **roof racks** will always carry bicycles for about half-fare, even if flagged down at the roadside, and trucks will often give you a lift. The trains take bikes, too, at a low fixed fare.

Planes

The main operators for **internal flights** are Safarilink (ⓦ www.safarilink-kenya.com), Kenya Airways (ⓦ www.kenya-airways.com), Airkenya (ⓦ www.airkenya.com), Mombasa Air Safari (ⓦ www.mombasaairsafari.com), 540 Aviation (ⓦ www.fly540.com) and Jetlink (ⓦ www.jetlink.co.ke). The destinations served include the main towns and cities (**Nairobi, Mombasa, Kisumu, Eldoret, Kitale, Nanyuki**), coastal resorts (**Diani Beach, Malindi, Lamu, Kiwayu**), the Sudan aid centre at **Lokichokio** and airfields serving safari clients in the main parks and reserves of

Amboseli, **Maasai Mara**, **Meru**, **Tsavo West** and **Samburu-Shaba**, and at **Lewa** and **Loisaba** north of Mount Kenya. Most services are daily, sometimes more, but even if you can afford it, don't expect to flit effortlessly from one corner of the country to another as there are not that many same-day connections. Bear in mind that ordinary **connecting times** shouldn't be relied on if you're flying to catch an international departure.

For some ballpark return **fares**, reckon on Nairobi–Maasai Mara costing $240, Nairobi–Lamu $320 and Nairobi Mombasa $210. **Baggage allowances** on some internal flights are less than 20kg. Fortunately, the excess baggage charges are nominal.

Chartering a small plane for trips to safari parks and remote airstrips is an option worth considering if money is less important to you than time. Costs for a two-seater are typically around $2 per kilometre, or $5 for a 5-seater. Remember the plane has to make a round trip, even if you don't. Two of the best charter companies are Tropic Air (Ⓦwww.tropicairkenya.com), based at Nanyuki airfield and Boskovic Air Charters (Ⓦwww.boskovicaircharters.com) based at Wilson Airport in Nairobi.

Accommodation

There's a fine diversity of accommodation in Kenya, ranging from campsites and local lodging houses for a few hundred shillings a night to luxury lodges and boutique tented camps.

If you're planning a trip to Kenya using moderate or expensive accommodation, it's useful to know that a lot of money can be saved by not going in the **high season**. Most resort hotels and safari lodges and tented camps have separate high-, mid- and low-season (sometimes called "green-season") rates. There's sometimes a peak-season too, just covering the Christmas and New Year break from December 21 to January 2. Low-season rates can be anything from a third to a half of the high-season tariff.

Many of the smaller camps and lodges close for a couple of months between mid-April and June, and some places also close for the month of November. Closures are not just due to lack of demand or less-than-ideal weather conditions, but to allow for maintenance and refurbishment.

Hotels, lodges and tented camps

The term **hotel** covers a very broad spectrum in Kenya (the word *hoteli* means a cheap café-restaurant, not a place to sleep). At the top end are the big tourist establishments, many in one of the country's handful of small chains. In the game parks, they're known as lodges. Some establishments are very good value, but others are shabby and overpriced, so check carefully before splurging. Try to reserve the more popular places in advance, especially for the busiest season in December and January.

At the mid-price level, some hotels are old settlers' haunts that were once slightly grand and no longer quite fit in modern Kenya, while others are newer and cater for the Kenyan

Seasons (approximate)
High: Dec 21 to Jan 2, July 1 to Sept 30
Mid: Jan 3 to April 14, Oct 1 to Dec 20
Low/Green/Closed: April 15 to May 31

middle class. A few are fine – charmingly decrepit or fairly smart and semi-efficient – but a fair few are just boozy and uninteresting.

As a rule, expect to pay anything from Ksh3000–10,000 for a decent double or twin room in a town hotel, with bathroom en suite, known in Kenya as "self-contained" or sometimes just "self" (and abbreviated throughout this book to s/c). Breakfast is usually included, but if you want to have breakfast elsewhere, the price will be deducted. Features such as TVs, room safes, fans and air-conditioning will all put the price up, and are sometimes optional, allowing you to make significant savings at cheaper hotels.

Older **safari lodges** may show their age with rather unimaginative design and boring little rooms, but those which date back to the 1960s were built when just having a hotel in the bush was considered an achievement. Today, the best of the big lodges have public areas offering spectacular panoramas and game-viewing decks, while the rooms are often comfortable chalets or *bandas*. The vogue in the most expensive, boutique lodges tends to be Tarzan-like, incorporating deadwood branches and bare rock, and eschewing straight lines wherever possible. Some places have just half a dozen "rooms", constructed entirely of local materials, ingeniously open-fronted yet secure, with stunning views, and invigorating open-air showers.

If you want something that reminds you of what you're missing by not camping, then opt for a **tented camp**, consisting of large, custom-made tents permanently erected over hard floors. The walls flap in the breeze but the toilet and bathroom at the back are plumbed in and all the usual lodge amenities, including electricity and big, comfy beds, are installed. At night, the tents zip up tight to keep the insects out. In the centre of the camp, the usual public areas will include a dining room and bar, or in smaller camps a luxurious "mess tent" with sofas and waiters proffering drinks, where you'll eat together with your hosts and the other guests and share the day's experiences in an atmosphere that always has a little "Out of Africa" in it.

Because tented camps are relatively easy to construct and re-configure, they're at the vanguard of Kenya's **environmentally responsible tourism** movement. The most innovative camps limit their use of electricity to what can be generated by solar panels, provide safari showers to order rather than permanent hot water, and take care to limit their environmental footprint in other ways, for example by composting all their organic waste and trucking out non-biodegradable trash rather than burning it. Scavenging **marabou storks** at camps and lodges are a sure sign of poor waste management, and a bad advert if you were thinking of staying. For more on Kenya's environment and responsible travel, see p.584.

Some lodges and camps are surrounded by a discreet, or not so discreet, **electric fence**. This gives you the freedom to wander at will, but detracts from the sense of being in the wild. Those places which don't have such security may ask you to sign a disclaimer to limit their liability in the event that a large mammalian intruder should abruptly terminate your holiday. In practice, although elephants, buffaloes and other big animals are always wandering into camps, serious incidents are exceptionally rare and you have nothing to worry about. After dark, unfenced camps employ traditionally dressed, spear-carrying *askaris* (see box, p.49) to see you safely to your room.

Meals in the lodges and camps are prepared in fully equipped kitchens and served by waiters who are often surprisingly knowledgeable about local wildlife and customs. Although the food can occasionally be dull and repetitive, the best places have their own organic vegetable and herb gardens and prepare gourmet dinners in the middle of nowhere.

Where hotels and camps have **swimming pools**, they are free to guests, and generally open to casual visitors for a small fee per person, indicated in our listings.

All the more expensive hotels, lodges and tented camps quote their **rates** in US dollars or sometimes euros. You can always settle your bill in Kenya shillings, but the exchange rate is often poor. Prices can be high, with $400 or more for two, on a full-board basis, not unusual, and some properties hitting $1000 or more, usually on a "package" basis, which essentially covers all meals, drinks and most activities.

It's always worth trying to negotiate a **discount**. Many cheap hotels will bend over backwards to remind you that their rates can be discussed. And in the more expensive places with a two-tier tariff for residents and non-residents, it's a perfectly acceptable negotiating tactic to claim to be a resident, though you may have to eat humble pie if they demand to see proof. If you need a **single room**, expect a single-occupancy rate around two-thirds of the double or twin rate.

Boarding & Lodgings

In any town you'll find basic guesthouses called **Boarding & Lodgings** (for which we've coined the abbreviation "B&Ls"). These can vary from a mud shack with water from the well, to a multi-storey building of self-contained rooms, complete with a bar and restaurant, and usually built around a lock-in courtyard-cum-parking area. Most B&L bathrooms include rather alarmingly wired "instant showers", giving a meagre spray of hot water 24 hours a day.

Toilets

Town public toilets (*wanawake* for women; *wanaume* for men) are invariably disgusting, as are those in cheaper B&Ls. You can buy toilet paper everywhere, but some cheap B&Ls don't provide it. Public buildings and hotels are unlikely to turn you away if you ask to use their facilities.

While in any town you can always find a room for under Ksh1000, and sometimes much less, **room prices** are not a good indication of the standard. If the bathrooms don't have instant showers, then check the water supply and find out when the boiler will be on. The very cheapest places (Ksh200–500) will not usually have self-contained rooms, so you should check the state of the shared showers and toilets. You won't cause offence by saying no thanks.

The better B&Ls are clean and comfortable, but they tend to be airless and often double

Accommodation price codes

Accommodation rates in this guide have been price-coded according to the price bands below. The prices indicated are the non-resident "rack rates", the regular walk-in rates for a standard **twin** room (if you book through an agent you may get a cheaper deal, or it may be more expensive). For dorm beds and campsites charging per person, the exact price at the time of writing has been given, as it has for cottages and houses where the whole unit is rented. Where there are seasonal differences, the price code refers to the high-season price: occasionally the peak price over Christmas and New Year is very much higher and the range from ordinary high season to peak is shown. All Nairobi hotels, most up-country hotels and most places in the cheapest five price bands have non-seasonal tariffs. Coast hotels and safari camps and lodges are highly seasonal. Prices for luxury hotels, lodges and tented camps above $400 are given in full throughout the guide

Cheap hotels quote their rates in Kenyan shillings, while hotels in band ❻ and above tend to quote their rates in dollars or euros. Special rates for Kenya residents (typically around 30–40 percent discount) are offered at many establishments in band ❹ and above.

❶ Ksh1000 and under: basic B&L usually with s/c rooms, rarely including breakfast.

❷ Ksh1001–2000: B&L or cheap hotel with elementary comforts; BB.

❸ Ksh2001–3000: adequate hotel with s/c rooms.

❹ Ksh3001–5000: mid-range local hotel or modest tourist-class hotel.

❺ Ksh5001–10,000: tourist-class hotel.

❻ $120–200: tourist-class hotel or cheap lodge.

❼ $201–300: standard tourist hotels and lodges.

❽ $301–400: hotels and lodges with good facilities.

as informal brothels, especially if they have a bar. If the place seems noisy in the afternoon, it will become cacophonous during the night, so you may want to ask for a room away from the source of the din. Moreover, if it relies on its bar for income, security becomes an important deciding factor. Well-run B&Ls, even noisy, sleazy ones, always have uniformed security staff and gated access to the room floors. You can leave valuables with the manager in reception (usually a small cell protected by metal grills), though you'll need to use your judgement. Leaving valuables like cameras in your room is usually safe enough if they're packed away in your bags. It's money and small items left lying around that tend to disappear.

The terms twin, double and single aren't much in use in B&Ls: what matters is how many beds will be used, not the number of people sleeping in them. A couple sharing a double bed will nearly always pay the same price as a single guest, though they'll have to pay for an extra breakfast. If you want a double bed, just ask for a room with "one big bed". If you ask for a double room you may get two beds.

Cottages and homestays

Increasingly, it's possible to book **self-catering apartments**, **villas** or **cottages**. Home from Home (☎020/890699, Ⓦwww.kenyasafarihomes.com), are agents for a wide range of holiday homes especially on the coast. Also on the increase are **homestays**. GSE-Ecotours (Ⓦwww.gse-ecotours.com; see p.35) offers village homestays, giving a deep insight into local life while integrating development and conservation. At the other end of the economic spectrum, a limited range of all-inclusive accommodation in a usually Anglo-Kenyan household in the countryside, with optional excursions and safaris, can be booked by Let's Go Travel (Ⓦwww.lets-go-travel.net). Kenya Beach

---

Accommodation terms

A/c Air-conditioned

AI All-inclusive

askari Guard, nightwatchman

banda Thatched cottage or chalet, usually rented out on a self-catering basis, but sometimes referring to chalet-style rooms at lodges

BB Bed and breakfast

B&L Boarding and Lodging, a cheap guesthouse

FB Full board, ie lunch, dinner, bed and breakfast

fly camp Mobile camp used on private safaris

HB Half board, ie dinner, bed and breakfast

hoteli Cheap restaurant or café, not a hotel

lodge Safari hotel in the bush

long-drop Non-flushing toilet

mabati Corrugated iron roof

package Usual obligatory arrangement in high-end safari camps and lodges, in which all meals, drinks and activities are included

rondavel Small, round hut, containing beds but no bathroom

safari shower Refillable reservoir of hot water above the shower area, in eco-friendly tented camps

s/c Self-contained room, with en-suite bathroom

star-bed 4-poster bed mounted on vehicle wheels, pulled onto a deck at night and guarded by *askaris*

tented camp Lodge in the bush, or in a game park, using large tents with a solid bathroom at the back

tree-hotel Animal-viewing hotel on stilts, after the style of *Treetops* (see p.187).

Rentals (ⓦwww.kenya-beachrentals.com) specializes in coastal properties.

Youth hostels

Only two Kenyan **youth hostels**, Nairobi and Naro Moru, are affiliated to Hostelling International (ⓦwww.hihostels.com). Both are fairly basic, but good places to hook up with other budget travellers. Non-members pay Ksh120 per night in addition to the normal rate (Ksh600 in dorms). The hostels can be booked through HI or the local association (ⓦwww.yhak.org). There are also **YMCAs**, **YWCAs** and **church-run hostels** in a number of towns. The better ones are mentioned in accommodation listings.

Camping

If you're on a budget and have a flexible itinerary, there are enough **campsites** in Kenya to make it worthwhile carrying a tent, and camping wild is sometimes a viable option, too. Bring the lightest tent you can afford and remember its main purpose is to keep insects out. You might consider making your own simple ridge tent: nylon netting with a sewn-in groundsheet is the basic tent. A rip-stop nylon flysheet adds privacy. Poles, back and front, are tensioned using guy lines, tied to trees where possible.

Campsites in the parks are usually very basic, though a handful of privately owned sites have more in the way of facilities. **Kenya Wildlife Service** (KWS) manages all the campsites in national parks, for which the current per person rate ranges from $15–25 per day. For that hefty price, you often get little more than a place to pitch your tent and park your vehicle: showers and toilets are often rudimentary and the

other normal features of a campsite, such as a shop or café, non-existent.

The so-called **special campsites**, found in a number of parks, are in reality simply campsites which have to be reserved on an exclusive basis for private use. Some of them are especially attractive and they can cost up to $40 per person per night, depending on the park, but unlike standard campsites they have no facilities whatsoever: you need to be entirely self-sufficient to use them. To reserve a special campsite, which costs a flat fee of Ksh7500 per week, plus the daily per-person rates, contact ⓦreservations@kws.go.ke or visit KWS headquarters in Nairobi.

Camping wild depends on whether you can find a suitable, safe site. In the more heavily populated and farmed highland districts, you should always ask someone before pitching in an empty spot, and never leave your tent unattended. Far out in the wilds, hard or thorny ground is likely to be the only obstacle. During the dry seasons, you'll rarely have trouble finding dead wood for a fire, so a stove is optional, but don't burn more fuel than you need. Camping gas cartridges and packaged, dried food is available in variety in Nairobi, but the easiest and cheapest camping food is *ugali* (see p.619), flavoured with curry powder or sauce mixes if you like.

Camping near roads, in dry river beds, or on trails used by animals going to water, are all highly inadvisable (for more on safety and wildlife, see p.77). On the coast, almost anywhere between Malindi and the Tanzanian border, sleeping out or camping on the **beaches** should be counted as an invitation to robbery.

Eating and drinking

Kenya has no great national dishes, and eating out is not a Kenyan tradition. The living standards of the majority of people don't allow for frills so food is generally plain and filling. For culinary culture, it's only the coast, with its long association with Indian Ocean trade, that has produced distinctive regional cuisine, where rice and fish, flavoured with coconut, tamarind and exotic spices, are the dominant ingredients. For food terms and help translating Swahili menus, see pp.618–619.

In the most basic local restaurant, decent meals can be had for less than Ksh200. Fancier meals in touristy places rarely cost more than Ksh1500 a head, though there are a number of classy establishments where you could happily spend Ksh4000 or more.

Home-style fare and nyama choma

If meals are unlikely to be a lasting memory, at least you'll never go hungry. In any **hoteli** (small restaurant) there is always a list of predictable dishes intended to fill customers' stomachs. Potatoes, rice and especially **ugali** (a stiff, cornmeal porridge) are the national staples, eaten with chicken, goat, beef, or vegetable stew, various kinds of spinach, beans and sometimes fish. Portions are usually gigantic; half-portions (ask for *nusu*) aren't much smaller. But even in small towns, more and more cafés are appearing where most of the menu is fried – eggs, sausages, chips, fish, chicken and burgers.

The standard blow-out feast for most Kenyans is a huge pile of **nyama choma** (roast meat). *Nyama choma* is usually eaten at a purpose-built *nyama choma* bar, with beer and music the standard accompaniments, and *ugali* and greens optional. You go to the kitchen and order by weight (half a kilo is plenty), direct from the butcher's hook or out of the fridge. There's usually a choice of *nyama*, either goat, beef or mutton. After roasting, the meat is brought to your table on a wooden platter and chopped to bite-size with a sharp knife.

Snacks and breakfast

Snacks, which can easily become meals, include samosas, chapatis, miniature kebabs,

roasted corncobs, *mandaazi* (sweet, puffy, deep-fried dough cakes) and "egg-bread". *Mandaazi* are made before breakfast and served until evening time, when they've become cold and solid. Egg-bread (misleadingly translated from the Swahili *mkate mayai*) is a light wheat-flour "pancake" wrapped around fried eggs and minced meat, usually cooked on a huge griddle. While you won't find it everywhere, it's a delicious Kenyan response to the creeping burger menace (McDonald's, happily, is still not here). Snacks sold on the street include cassava chips and, if you're very lucky, in country areas, roasted termites (which go well as a bar snack with beer).

Breakfast varies widely. Standard fare in a *hoteli* consists of a cup of sweet tea and a chapati or a doorstep of white bread thickly spread with margarine. Modest hotels offer a "full breakfast" of cereal, eggs and sausage, bread and jam, and a banana, with instant coffee or tea. If you're staying in an upmarket hotel or lodge, breakfast is usually a lavish acreage of hot and cold buffets that you can't possibly do justice to.

Restaurant meals

Kenya's seafood, beef and lamb are renowned, and they are the basis of most serious meals. **Game meat** used to be something of a Kenyan speciality, most of it farmed on ranches. Giraffe, zebra, impala, and warthog all regularly appeared at various restaurants. These days, only captive-farmed ostrich and crocodile are legal.

Indian restaurants in the larger towns, notably Nairobi and Mombasa, are generally excellent (locally, there's often a strong Indian influence in *hoteli* food as well), with dhal lunches a good standby and much fancier regional dishes widely available too. When you splurge, apart from eating Indian, it will usually be in **hotel restaurants**, with food often very similar to what you might be served in a restaurant at home. The **lodges** usually have buffet lunches at about Ksh800–1000, which can be great value, with table-loads of salads and cold meat. Among Kenya's exotic cuisines, you'll find Italian restaurants and pizzerias, various Chinese options, and French, Japanese, Thai, and even Korean food.

Phone numbers are given in the Guide for those restaurants where it's advisable to make reservations.

Fruit

Fruit is a major delight. Bananas, avocados, pawpaws and pineapples are in the markets all year, mangoes and citrus fruits more seasonally. Look out for passion fruit (the familiar shrivelled brown variety, and the sweeter and less acidic smooth yellow ones), cape gooseberries (*Physalis*), custard apples and guavas – all highly distinctive and delicious. On the coast, roasted **cashew nuts** are widely available, but not cheap (never buy any with dark marks on them). **Coconuts**, widely seen at roadside stalls in their freshly cut, green-husked condition, are filling and nutritious. At this stage, when the nuts are young, they're full of coconut water and the flesh is like soft-boiled egg white. If left to ripen on the tree until the husk goes brown, the liquid reduces, and the flesh becomes firm.

Drinking

The national beverage is **chai** – tea. Universally drunk at breakfast and as a pick-me-up at any time, it's a weird variant on the classic British brew: milk, water, lots of sugar and tea leaves, brought to the boil in a kettle and served scalding hot. It must eventually do diabolical dental damage, but it's addictive and very reviving. The main tea-producing region is around Kericho in the west, but the best tea is made on the coast. These days, it's all too often a tea bag in a cup of vaguely warm water or milk. Instant **coffee** – fresh is rare – is normally available in *hotelis* as well. Only in upmarket places will you find real coffee, often served in a *cafetière*.

Soft drinks (sodas) are usually very cheap, and crates of Coke, Fanta and Sprite find their way to the wildest corners of the country. Krest, a bitter lemon, is not bad, and Krest also makes a ginger ale, but it's watery and insipid; instead go for Stoney ginger beer, which has more of a punch. Sometimes you can get plain soda water. A newer drink is Alvaro, a malty, pineapple-flavoured non-alcoholic alternative to beer, which is very popular but too sweet for some tastes.

Fresh fruit **juices** are available in the towns, especially on the coast (Lamu is fruit juice heaven). Passion fruit, the cheapest, is excellent, though nowadays it's likely to be watered-down concentrate. Some places serve a variety: you'll sometimes find carrot juice and even tiger milk, made from a small tuber (the tiger nut or Spanish *chufa*). Bottled Picana mango juice is also available at some shops that sell sodas.

Special diets

If you're a **vegetarian** staying in tourist-class hotels, you should have no problems, as there's usually a meat-free pasta dish, or various egg-based dishes. If you're on a strict budget you'll gravitate to Indian vegetarian restaurants where you can often eat remarkably well very cheaply. Otherwise, it can be tricky, because meat is the conventional focus of any meal not eaten at home, and *hotelis* rarely have much else to accompany the starch; even vegetable stews are normally cooked in meat gravy.

If you're a vegan, you'll find there are nearly always good vegetables and lots of fruit at lodges and camps and the more expensive hotels. Once again, where you'll struggle is if you're on a strict budget and eating local restaurant food. Many restaurants on the coast serve **halal fare**, while in most areas, you'll usually be able to find a Somali-run *hoteli* that has halal meat.

Plastic-bottled **spring water** is relatively expensive but widely available in 300ml, 500ml and one litre bottles. Mains water used to be very drinkable, and in some places still is, but it's safer to stick with bottled (see p.70 for more information).

Beer

If you like **lager**, you'll find Kenyan brands generally good. The main lagers are Tusker and White Cap (both 4.2 percent) and Pilsner (4.72 percent), sold in half-litre bottles, with the better-flavoured Tusker Malt (52 percent) in 300ml bottles. They all cost from Ksh90 in local bars up to about Ksh350 in the most expensive establishments. All brewed by East African Breweries, they are fairly inconsistent in flavour: try a blind taste test. You can also get a head-thumping 6.52 percent-alcohol version of Guinness, and the cheaper Senator beer, devised to move drinkers of illicit brews to something safer by drawing on the mass appeal of Senator Barack Obama (briefly rebranded after his election win as President beer. Recent competition for East African Breweries includes Summit and Senior, but the jury is still out on whether they're distinctive enough to survive.

In **cheap bars**, the counter is usually protected by a metal grill, putting the staff in a kind of cage. In this kind of place, you'll need to specify whether you want your beer cold or warm. Warm is the usual, local preference. A point of drinking **etiquette** worth remembering is that you should never take your bottle away. As bottles carry deposits, this is considered theft and surprisingly ugly misunderstandings can ensue.

Other alcoholic drinks

Most of the usually familiar **wines** sold in Kenya come from South Africa and Italy, with California, Chile, France and Spain also featuring. Locally made wines struggle a little, but Richard Leakey's Pinot Noir vineyard is finally breaking through with Zabibu (Ⓦ www.zabibu.org).

You won't often find **cocktails** except in expensive hotels and restaurants. **Kenya Cane** (white rum) and **Kenya Gold** (a gooey, coffee-flavoured liqueur) deserve a try perhaps, but they're nothing special. One popular and highly addictive Kenyan mix to try is a **dawa** ("medicine"), which is simply vodka, white rum, honey and lime juice.

There's a battery of laws against **home brewing** and distilling, perhaps because of the loss of tax revenue on legal booze, but these are central aspects of Kenyan culture and they go on. You can sample *pombe* (bush brews) of different sorts all over the country. It's as varied in taste, colour and consistency as its ingredients: basically fermented sugar and millet or banana, with herbs and roots for flavouring. The results are frothy and deceptively strong.

On the coast, where coconuts grow most plentifully, merely lopping off the growing shoot produces a naturally fermented **palm wine** (*mnazi*), which is indisputably Kenya's finest contribution to the art of self-intoxication. There's another variety of palm wine, tapped from the doum palm, called *mukoma*. Though there's usually a furtive discretion about *pombe* or *tembo* sessions, consumers rarely get busted.

Not so with spirits: think twice before accepting a mug of **chang'aa**. It's treacherous firewater, and is also frequently contaminated, regularly killing drinking parties en masse. Sentences for distilling and possessing *chang'aa* are harsh, and police or vigilante raids common.

The media

The press in Kenya is lively and provides reasonable coverage of international news, while the BBC, CNN and European sports stations are available on satellite TV.

Radio and TV

Kenya Broadcasting Corporation has three main **radio** services, broadcasting in English, Swahili and local languages, as well as a 24-hour Nairobi reggae station, Metro FM (101.9FM), competing with the independent Capital FM (98.4Mhz). Better for music is another independent station, Kiss 100 (100.3FM). The *Nation* newspaper runs a news station, Nation Radio (96.4FM). The BBC World Service can be picked up on FM in Nairobi (93.9MHz), Mombasa (93.9MHz) and Kisumu (88.1MHz). Capital and a number of FM stations are also available on the **internet**.

Kenyan **television**, much of it imported, carries a mix of English and Swahili programmes. There are three main channels: the stuffy and hesitant state-run KBC, which carries BBC World for much of the day; the upbeat, mainly urban KTN, which carries CNN during the night and much of the morning; and the *Nation* newspaper's channel, NTV. In addition to these, KBC operates a pay channel, KBC2, which is run in conjunction with South Africa's M-NET. An increasing number of homes, bars and hotels have **satellite dishes**, giving access to Britain's Sky TV, Eurosport and other foreign channels. Kenya's SuperSport 3 pay-channel shows a lot of English premiership football.

The press

Kenya is a nation absorbed in its press, which is often quite outspoken. At one time, the mainstream press was joined by a gaggle of scandal sheets, which were even more outspoken, but the government banned all of them in 2004, since when a number of them have registered as newspapers and returned to the streets.

The leading mainstream **newspaper** is the *Nation* (ⓦ www.nationmedia.com), part-owned by the Aga Khan, which has meaty news coverage, including international news and European football results, a forthright editorial line, and a letters page full of insights into Kenyan life. Its main competitor, *The Standard* (ⓦ www.eastandard.net) is somewhat lightweight in comparison. The Nation Group's *Business Daily* (ⓦ www .bdafrica.com) is always a solid read, as is their excellent weekly *The East African* (Mondays; ⓦ www.theeastafrican.co.ke), a conservatively styled round-up of the week's regional news, shot through with an admirable measure of cynicism. *Weekly Review* magazine is always worth picking up, but it tends to toe whatever government line it discerns.

Less reliable are: *The People*, whose logo "Fair, Frank and Fearless" is about right, and which verges on the scurrilous; the stodgy government-owned *Kenya Times* (ⓦ www .kenyatimes.com); and the *Nairobi Star*, which is read more for gossip than news. *Taifa Leo* is the most important Swahili daily.

Of the **foreign press**, weekly editions of the UK's *Daily Telegraph* and other papers reach areas with substantial white populations, and you can find a fair number of foreign papers in busy areas on the coast in high season. *Time* and *Newsweek* are hawked widely and, together with old *National Geographic*s and copies of *The Economist*, filter through many hands before reaching the secondhand booksellers.

Public holidays and festivals

The main Christian religious holidays and the Muslim festival of Id al-Fitr are observed, as well as secular national holidays. Other Muslim festivals are not public holidays but are observed in Muslim areas. Local seasonal and cyclical events, peculiar to particular ethnic groups, are less well advertised.

On the coast, throughout the northeast, and in Muslim communities everywhere, the lunar **Islamic calendar** is used for religious purposes. The Muslim year has 354 days, so dates recede against the Western calendar by an average of eleven days each year. Only the month of fasting called **Ramadan**, and the festival of **Id-al-Fitr** – the feast at the end of it, which begins on the first sighting of the new moon – will have much effect on your travels. In smaller towns in Islamic districts during Ramadan, most stores and *hotelis* are closed through the daylight hours, while all businesses will close in time for sunset, to break the daily fast. Public transport and most government offices continue as usual. **Maulidi**, the celebration of the prophet's birthday, is worth catching if you're on the coast at the right time, especially if you'll be in Lamu.

Agricultural shows

The Agricultural Society of Kenya (ASK; ⓦ www.ask.co.ke) puts on a series of annual **agricultural shows**, featuring livestock and produce competitions, beer and snack tents, as well as some less expected booths, such as family planning and herbalism. These can be lively, revealing events, borrowing a lot from the British farming-show tradition, but infused with Kenyan style.

Public holidays and Muslim festivals

Note that if a public holiday falls on a Sunday, the following Monday is usually declared a public holiday.

Jan 1	New Year's Day	**Oct 20**	Kenyatta Day
March/April	Good Friday	**Shawwal 1**	Id al-Fitr
March/April	Easter Monday	**Dec 12**	Jamhuri Day
May 1	Labour Day	**Dec 25**	Christmas Day
June 1	Madaraka Day	**Dec 26**	Boxing Day
Oct 10	Moi Day		

Islamic festivals: approximate dates

	2010	2011	2012	2013
Maulidi/Mouloud (12th Rabia I)	26 Feb	16 Feb	5 Feb	24 Jan
Beginning of Ramadan (1st Ramadan)	11 Aug	1 Aug	20 Jul	9 July
Id al-Fitr/Id al-Saghir (1st Shawwal)	10 Sept	31 Aug	19 Aug	8 Aug
Tabaski/Id al-Kabir (10th Dhu'l Hijja)	17 Nov	7 Nov	26 Oct	15 Oct
Muslim New Year (1st Moharem)	8 Dec	27 Nov	15 Nov	5 Nov
Ashoura (10th Moharem)	17 Dec	6 Dec	24 Nov	14 Nov

Entertainment and sport

Kenya's espousal of Western values has belittled much traditional culture, so only in remote areas are you likely to come across traditional dancing and drumming which doesn't somehow involve you as a paying audience. If you're patient and a little adventurous, you're likely to witness something more authentic sooner or later, especially if you stay somewhere long enough to make friends. On a short visit, popular music and spectator sports are more accessible.

Dance

The hypnotic swaying and displays of effortless leaping found in **Maasai and Samburu dancing** are the best-known forms of Kenyan dance. Similar dance forms occur widely among other non-agricultural peoples. **Mijikenda dance troupes** (notably from the Giriama people) perform up and down the coast at tourist venues, while all-round dance troupes perform for tourists a range of "tribal dances" in hotels all over the country. It's best to ignore any purist misgivings you might have about the authenticity of such performances and enjoy them as distinctive and exuberant entertainments in their own right.

Music

Your ears will pick up a fair amount of current music on the streets or on buses and matatus, but the live spectacle of **popular music** is mostly limited to Nairobi, a few coastal entertainment spots, and a scattering of upcountry **discos** and "**country clubs**". The indigenous music scene is somewhat overshadowed by American soul and hip hop, Jamaican reggae (especially in the sacred image of Bob Marley) and a vigorous Congolese contribution from Congo. See p.586 for a history of music in Kenya and a discography.

Theatre and film

Theatrical performances are effectively limited to one or two semi-professional clubs in Nairobi and Mombasa and a handful of upcountry amateur dramatic groups. African actors and scripts tend to be rare, but things are improving, at least in Nairobi, where there are a several groups performing in English.

Cinema in Kenya revolves almost entirely around imports. The big towns have a few cinemas and drive-ins, but DVDs are how most people get their movies, with US and Bollywood box-office hits the staple diet. Homegrown Kenyan cinema has barely got off the ground, though the new Kenya Film Commission (Ⓦ www.kenyafilmcommission .com) may stimulate an industry that up to now has mostly been about servicing foreign productions, from *Out of Africa* to *The Constant Gardener*.

Sport

Kenya's ongoing **Olympic success story** is internationally recognized, with a regular clutch of gold and silver in the **track events**. Kenya's athletes are among the continent's leaders and the country's long-distance runners are some of the best in the world. It has even been suggested that certain Kalenjin communities may have a genetic make-up which makes them more likely to be strong athletes, but Kalenjins as much as anyone else have played down this idea. What is indisputable is that Kenya has possibly the most successful athletics training school in the world in St Patrick's High School at Iten, up at an altitude of 2400m in the Rift Valley (see p.241).

Football is wildly popular, with English Premiership teams having thousands of devoted fans. Any small bar with a satellite TV has a blackboard showing the next fixtures. You'll even see matatus decorated with the colours of Arsenal or Liverpool. Kenya's national team, known as the Harambee Stars, has won the East and

Central African CECAFA Cup several times, most recently in 2002, and hosted it at the end of 2009. But it has never qualified for the World Cup finals, nor done especially well in the African Nations Cup. In the Premier League, Nairobi's AFC Leopards and Gor Mahia rank with the best clubs on the continent, alongside another Nairobi club, Tusker FC, and Nakuru's Ulinzi Stars. Crowds are pretty well behaved, perhaps because forking out for the modest gate fee precludes getting drunk as well.

Kenyan **cricket** received a boost when Kenya beat the West Indies at the World Cup in 1996 and came third overall in 2003. Most matches are played in the Nairobi area. Check out CricInfoKenya Ⓦtinyurl .com/qlkr5t.

Other spectator sports include: **racing** at the racecourse in Nairobi (see p.132), which dates from early colonial times; and **camel-racing**, spotlighted annually at the international camel derby in Maralal (see p.514) and now co-promoted with some serious international **mountain-bike racing** at the same event.

Car rallies

Once considered "the world's toughest rally", but dropped by the World Rally Championship in 2003, the **KCB Safari Rally** blazes a smaller trail across Kenya than it used to, doing a couple of "clover leaf" routes, out from Nairobi and back. The rally is usually at Easter and uses public roads. Depending on weather conditions, drivers spin through acres of mud or chase each other blind in enormous clouds of dust.

Another annual motor event is the **Rhino Charge** motor race, which attracts adventurers from across the globe (though these days is largely restricted to those who can raise the most funds). The funds raised go to the Rhino Ark Charitable Trust, which has already fenced Aberdare National Park to project its rhinos (Ⓦwww.rhinoark.org). The challenge is to reach ten control posts in remote locations, whose whereabouts are revealed to the entrants only the night before the event. Speed is not the objective, the winner being the team that completes the course with the least distance recorded, "charging" through and over the obstacles.

Outdoor activities

Kenya is a country with huge untapped potential for outdoor activities. The following notes suggest the possibilities for walking, climbing, caving, riding, fishing, diving and snorkeling, wind- and kite- surfing, rafting and golf.

It's worth seeking advice from the Mountain Club of Kenya (see opposite), not just on climbing but on outdoor pursuits in general. For detailed descriptions of various climbing, hiking and caving locations in Kenya, see the "East Africa Mountain Guide" section of Ⓦwww.kilimanjaro.cc.

Walking and running

If you have plenty of time, **walking** is highly recommended and gives you unparalleled contact with local people. In isolated parts, it's often preferable to waiting for a lift, while

in the Aberdares, Mau and Cherangani ranges, and on mounts Kenya and Elgon, it's the only practical way of moving away from the main tracks. You will sometimes come across animals out in the bush, but buffaloes and elephants (the most likely dangers), unless solitary or with young, usually move off. Don't ignore the dangers, however, and stay alert. You'll need to carry several litres of water much of the time, especially in lower, drier regions. You might prefer to go on an organized **walking safari**, at least as a starter. Such trips are offered by a number of companies in Nairobi (see p.128) and by most of the smaller lodges and camps in the private game sanctuaries, especially in Laikipia (see p.175).

Jogging and **running** are popular in Kenya, which produces some of the world's top long-distance runners. If you're a **marathon** runner, there are several events to tie your trip in with, which usually offer fun runs and half-marathons too. The Safaricom marathon is the best known, on account of its location, in the prestigious Lewa conservancy north of Mount Kenya, and altitude (an average of more than 1600m), both of which make for a tough and exciting race. Marshalls ensure your safety in the wildlife areas, but you'll be running on dirt tracks through the bush. It usually takes place in June (🌐tinyurl.com/mxcwua). The Nairobi marathon takes place in October (🌐www .nairobimarathon.com), running on roads.

Climbing

Apart from Mount Kenya, there are **climbing** opportunities of all grades in the Aberdare, Cherangani and Mathews ranges, in Hell's Gate National Park and on the Rift Valley volcanoes, including Longonot and Suswa. The Mountain Club of Kenya (🌐www.mck .or.ke; clubhouse at Wilson Airport; $30 joining fee, plus $30 annual membership) is a good source of advice and contacts. If you intend to do any serious climbing in the country, you should make early contact. Don't expect them to answer detailed route questions, however; leave that until you arrive. Safari companies in Nairobi offer everything from a simple hike to technical ascents of Mount Kenya.

Caving

Kenya's big attractions for cavers are its unusual **lava tube caves**, created when molten lava flowing downhill solidified on the surface while still flowing beneath. Holes in the surface layer allowed air to enter behind the lava flow, forming the caves. Lava tubes in Kenya include the Suswa caves near Narok, and Leviathan cave in the Chyulu Hills, one of the world's biggest lava tube systems, with more than 11km of underground passages. Caving should, of course, not be undertaken without the right

equipment, training and safety precautions. For more information, contact one of the lodges in the Chyulu area (see p.345).

Riding

There are good opportunities for **horse riding** in the Central Highlands and Laikipia and there's an active equestrian community in Nairobi and scattered throughout the country. Safaris Unlimited (see p.130) offers riding safaris near the Maasai Mara National Reserve. **Camel safaris** are popular too, though the best operators to contact tend to change from year to year. Contact any of the addresses under "Camel Safaris in the North" on p.518.

Fishing

Some of the highlands' streams are still stocked with **trout**, which were imported early in the twentieth century by British settlers. A few local fishing associations are still active. The Fisheries Department, next to the National Museum in Nairobi (☎020/3742320) can supply more details and permits. For **lake fishing**, it's possible to rent rods and boats at lakes Baringo, Naivasha and Turkana, and there are luxury fishing lodges on Rusinga, Mfangano and Takawiri islands on Lake Victoria.

Kenya's superb stretch of offshore coral reef, with its deep-water drop-offs and predictable northerly currents, is ideal for **near-shore angling**. For **ocean fishing**, Watamu and Malindi are the most popular centres.

Diving and snorkelling

Kenya's coastal waters are warm all year round so it's possible to **dive** without a wetsuit and have a rewarding dip under the waves almost anywhere, though the best period is October to April with October, November and March ideal. Most of the diving bases are located at Malindi, Watamu or on the coast north or south of Mombasa, and will provide training from a beginner's dive to PADI leader level. For underwater photographers, in particular, the immense coral reef is a major draw. The undersea landscape is spectacularly varied, with shallow coral gardens and blue-water drop-offs sinking as deep as 200m, and as there are few rivers to bring down sediment, visibility is generally excellent. Useful books are mentioned on p.600. If you plan to do a fair bit of **snorkelling**, it makes sense to bring your own mask and snorkel, though they can always be rented.

Wind- and kite- surfing

Windsurfing has been a feature of the Kenya coast since the 1970s. **Kitesurfing**, however, is a fast-growing new sport and Diani Beach (see p.435) and *Che Shale* north of Malindi are increasingly popular among enthusiasts. Kite-surfers use a large inflatable kite to harness the wind, and ride on a board not dissimilar to a wakeboard or snowboard. The coast has excellent kitesurfing conditions from December to February, with the northeast monsoon tending to get up in the afternoon, blowing between 16 and 22 knots (Force 4 to 5 Beaufort), which is ideal for both beginners and experienced riders. While the southeast monsoon, blowing from June through to September, isn't as reliable as the northeast-erly, it can offer some exceptional conditions.

Rafting

Both the Tana and Athi rivers have sections that can be **rafted** when they're in spate. Approximate dates are early November to mid-March, and mid-April to the end of August. Savage Wilderness Safaris is the main operator (see p.152), and offers trips from one to several days.

Golf

Kenya has almost forty **golf clubs**, mostly patronized by the European and Asian communities, notably around the old colonial centres of Nairobi, Naivasha, Thika, Nanyuki and Nyeri in the central highlands, and Kisumu and Kitale in western Kenya. There are also several courses on the coast, and – incontestably the most bizarre – on the scorched moonscape shore of Lake Magadi (see p.201). Green fees vary widely, usually from about $30 per person per day. Details for all of these can be had from the Kenya Golf Union (Ⓦ www.kgu.or.ke). For organized upmarket **golfing safaris**, contact Tobs Golf Safaris Ltd (Ⓦ www.kenya-golf-safaris.com).

National parks and reserves

Kenya's national parks are administered by the Kenya Wildlife Service (KWS) as total sanctuaries where human habitation, apart from the tourist lodges, is prohibited. National reserves, run by local councils, tend to be less strict on the question of human encroachment.

Most parks and reserves are not fenced in (Lake Nakuru, Aberdare and the north side of Nairobi National Park being exceptions). The wildlife is free to come and go, though animals do tend to stay within the boundaries, especially in the dry season when cattle outside compete for water.

Nearly all the parks and reserves are open to **private visits** (though foreign-registered commercial overland vehicles are not allowed in). A few parks have been heavily developed for tourism with graded tracks, signposts and lodges, but none has any

kind of transport at the gate for people without their own transport. You may be able to hitch a lift at the park gate with visitors in a private vehicle, but in general, without your own transport, you'll have to go on an organized safari. The largest and most frequently visited parks are covered in depth in Chapter 5, with others covered in regional chapters. An introduction to the main game parks, giving you some idea of what to expect from them is given in the table on pp.62–63.

Smartcard Points of Issue and Points of Sale

	POI	POS
Nairobi NP main gate (KWS HQ)	✓	✓
KWS offices Mombasa town centre	✓	✓
Lake Nakuru NP main gate (south of town)	✓	✓
Tsavo East NP main gate (Voi)	✓	✓
Tsavo West NP main gate (Mtito Andei)	✗	✓
Amboseli NP Meshanani gate	✗	✓
KWS mountain parks HQ, Mweiga	✗	✓
Malindi Marine NP (south of town)	✗	✓

It's important to bear in mind some simple facts to ensure that you leave the park and the animals as you found them. **Harassment** of animals disturbs feeding, breeding and reproductive cycles, and too many vehicles surrounding wildlife is not only unpleasant for you, but also distresses the animals. Take only photos and leave nothing behind. If you're camping, collecting **firewood** is strictly prohibited, as is picking any flora. If you **smoke** always use an ashtray. Cigarette butts start numerous bush fires every year.

Entry fees

Park and reserve entry fees, payable in UK pounds, US dollars, euros or Kenya shillings, are charged per person per 24-hour visit. Your ticket will indicate your time of arrival. For most parks and reserves, you pay at the gate where you enter, in cash only. However, entry to the six most popular national parks – Aberdare, Amboseli, Lake Nakuru, Nairobi, Tsavo East and Tsavo West – is by a cash-loaded **smartcard**. You can obtain smartcards only at **Points of Issue (POI)** with proof of identity. You need to be over 18 (under-18s' fees go on adult cards). Once you've got your smartcard, you load it with credit at a **Point of Sale (POS)**, the precise sum determined by which park or parks you're visiting and for how long. If you have sufficient credit, your smartcard is good for entry by any entrance to any smartcard park. Unused credit is non-refundable, and the card is retained as soon as credit runs out – meaning you have to go to a POI to get a new one if you want to make further visits to smartcard parks.

If you're visiting the relevant parks in a tour group, all this is handled and paid for on your behalf. But if you're travelling independently, it does require some planning and makes last-minute changes of itinerary problematic – in theory. Happily, there seems to be plenty of **flexibility** in the system, which allows for most gates to process independent visitors who turn up hoping to pay in cash. If your itinerary has gone awry, or you're entering through a minor gate, you can also usually persuade KWS rangers to allow you to travel through the park to a gate where you can rectify your status. Likewise, if you stay another day, you can always pay the balance owing on departure.

Note that if you **overstay** by more than an hour or so you will very likely have to pay the full 24-hour fee. If you can foresee this possibility at the time you enter, it's a good plan to alert the rangers and ask them to radio ahead, as the gate you exit through is more likely to waive the excess fee if they have been notified about your late departure. Don't, however, expect to use this plan to do an extra game drive or stay for lunch: they do watch the clock.

Non-residents' fees range from $15 to $60. Residents' rates range from Ksh300 to Ksh1000. Children's rates apply to anyone over 3 but under 18, while students under 23 can apply for student discounts in advance direct to KWS (Ⓦ www.kws.go.ke). Students need to be studying or researching in Kenya to get the reductions: leisure trips don't count.

KWS park fees were hiked in 2009 to great opposition from tour operators and agents, but it is likely they will increase again during the lifetime of this edition.

In the **national reserves** (the main ones are Maasai Mara, Samburu, Buffalo Springs and Shaba), revenue is not controlled by

National Park/ National Reserve	Description	Main attractions	Accommodation
*(Non-resident entry fee; * indicates payment by Smartcard)*			
Aberdare NP * $50/$25 See p.185	Forest and montane grassland, access by 4WD only	Hiking; elephant, buffalo, black rhino, giant forest hog, rare bongo antelope	*Treetops* and *The Ark*, KWS cottage, camping
Amboseli NP * $60/$30 See p.338	Small and busy, dominated by Kilimanjaro	Kilimanjaro; elephant, hyena, buffalo, zebra, hippo, giraffe, cheetah, lion	Lodges, KWS cottages, camping
Arabuko-Sokoke NP $20/$10 See p.451	Coastal forest, home to pioneering community conservation projects	Walking; Aders' duiker, elephant shrew, birds and butterflies	Camping in the park, hotels in Watamu
Buffalo Springs NR $40/$20 See p.375	Smallish reserve adjacent to Samburu	Ewaso Nyiro River; lion, elephant, reticulated giraffe, Somali ostrich, gerenuk, crocodile	Lodges, camping
Chyulu Hills NP $50/$25 See p.345	Rarely visited volcanic hills near Tsavo West	Hiking, riding, cloud forest; black rhino, elephant, buffalo, eland	One lodge and one tented camp outside the park, camping
Hell's Gate NP $25/$10 See p.212	Small, scenic park next to Lake Naivasha	Walking, cycling, rock-climbing; zebra, giraffe, buffalo, Thomson's gazelle	Camping
Kakamega Forest NR $20/$10 See p.308	Last stand of lowland tropical forest in western Kenya	Walking, birdwatching; great blue turaco, monkeys, chameleons	KWS *bandas*, camping, small lodges nearby
Lake Bogoria NR $25/$10 See p.231	Rift Valley soda lake with limited facilities	Hot springs; flamingos, greater kudu	Hotel outside reserve, camping
Lake Nakuru NP * $60/$30 See p.223	Soda lake, accessible by taxia	Lakeshore circuit; flamingoes, pelicans, lion leopard, buffalo, white and black rhino	Lodges, KWS cottage, camping
Maasai Mara NR $60/$30 See p.355	Best park for game-watching, but often very busy	Wildebeest migration (Aug–Sept); huge variety of savanna wildlife	Dozens of lodges and tented camps, some budget accommodation and camping outside the gates
Meru NP $40/$25 See p.380	Beautiful landscapes, few tourists, wildlife hard to spot	Lion, elephant, buffalo, reticulated giraffe, Grevy's zebra, white rhino	Lodges and a tented camp, *bandas*, camping

B

National Park/ National Reserve	Description	Main attractions	Accommodation
(Non-resident entry fee; * indicates payment by Smartcard)			
Mount Elgon NP $25/$10 See p.297	Kenyan slopes of an extinct volcano on the Ugandan border	Hiking; salt-lick caves, hot springs, scenery, elephants	KWS cottage and *bandas*, camping, rudimentary lodge
Mount Kenya NP $55/$20 See p.155	Kenya's highest mountain, an extinct volcano	Hiking and climbing; high-altitude afro-alpine flora; buffalo, elephant	Hiking huts, hotels at the base
Nairobi NP * $40/$20 See p.136	Close to downtown Nairobi	Full variety of plains game, including giraffe, lion, cheetah, black rhino (no elephants)	None; hotels in Nairobi
Saiwa Swamp NP $20/$10 See p.295	Smallest park in Kenya, access on foot only	Walking on boardwalks; birdlife, sitatunga antelope	Small treehouse, plus, *Sirikwa Safaris* 11km away
Samburu NR $40/$20 See p.375	Peaceful and beautiful park in the arid lowlands north of Mt Kenya	Ewaso Nyiro River; leopard, elephant, reticulated giraffe, Grevy's zebra, Somali ostrich, gerenuk, cheetah, Beisa oryx, crocodile	Lodges and tented camps
Shaba NR $40/$20 See p.378	Close to Samburu, but better watered and less visited	Ewaso Nyiro River; elephant, jackal, lion, Grevy's zebra, reticulated giraffe	One lodge, one tented camp
Shimba Hills NR $20/$10 See p.425	Hilly terrain near Diani Beach, with grassland and scattered jungle	Views; elephant, sable antelope, leopard, bushbabies	Tree-hotel, KWS *bandas*, camping
Tsavo East NP * $50/$25 See p.351	Biggest park in Kenya, popular for short safaris from the coast	Mudanda Rock, Lugard's Falls; elephant, black rhino, lion, zebra	Lodges and tented camps, camping
Tsavo West NP * $50/$25 See p.346	Busy and popular core area, surrounded by wilderness	Mzima Springs (underwater hippo-watching), lava flows; elephant, zebra, giraffe, lion, buffalo, lesser kudu, black rhino	Lodges and tented camps, KWS *bandas*, camping

www.roughguides.com

KWS but by rangers employed by the local county councils. Fees are comparable to national park fees, and strictly for periods of 24 hours, but transactions usually take place only at the gates. In 2009, Narok County Council began an experiment with pre-payments in Nairobi, using the tour operator Somak as their agent. At the time of writing rangers at the gates and airstrips were still happy to accept fees in cash.

Seasons

Most of the parks get two **rainy seasons** – brief rains in November or December, more earnest in April and May – but these can vary widely. As a general rule, you'll see more animals during the dry season when they are concentrated near water and the grasses are low. After the rains break and fill the seasonal watering places, the game tends to disperse deep into the bush. Moreover, if your visit coincides with the rains, you may have to put up with some frustrating game drives, and with mud and stranded vehicles. The effects of climate change have led to several temporary closures over recent years, and park conditions are often unpredictable. By way of compensation, if your plans include upmarket accommodation, you'll save a fortune at lodges and tented camps in the low season. Most places reduce their tariffs by anything from a third to a half between April and June.

Driving in the parks

If you're driving during the rains, remember that none of the park roads are paved and unless you're content to keep to the main graded tracks, you will need a 4WD vehicle to venture down the smaller ones. A night spent stuck in the mud in Maasai Mara isn't recommended, nor is trying to reverse down a boulder-strewn slope in Tsavo West. In any case, a normal saloon will be shaken to bits on the average park road, and most car-rental companies will insist you have 4WD. For more on driving in wet conditions, see p.42.

Be sensitive to the great damage that can be done to delicate ecosystems by **driving off marked roads**. Even apparently innocent diversions can scour fragile, root-connected grasslands for years, spreading dust, destroying the integrity of the lowest levels of vegetation and hindering the life cycles and movements of insects and smaller animals, with consequent disruption to the lives of their predators. The effects of this are especially visible in Amboseli and Maasai Mara, both of which are now ecologically at risk. Use only the obvious dirt roads and tracks (admittedly, it can sometimes be hard to judge whether you're following a permitted route, or simply the tyre marks of others who broke the rule), and if you have a driver, ask him to do the same. If this means being denied the opportunity to see one of the "Big Five", then so be it. Consider the fact that cheetahs, for example, which hunt by day, are very sensitive to noise and interference by vehicles. When surrounded by minibuses, they may offer great photo opportunities, but are unable to hunt.

Stick to the official maximum **speed limit** posted at the gates, usually 30kph. **Night driving** (usually between 7pm and 6am) is illegal in all Kenyan parks and reserves without permission from the warden.

For more on Kenya's environment and responsible travel, see p.584.

Park accommodation

If you're visiting the parks independently it may well be worth bringing a **tent** (consider renting or buying one in Nairobi, see p.131). If you don't have one, you will find the budget options fairly limited, and in some parks and reserves a campsite may be the only affordable place to stay, as well as significantly adding to the adventure. If you're visiting the parks with deeper pockets and staying in **lodges or tented camps**, it would be wise to make advance reservations as there is often heavy pressure on beds, especially during the peak seasons. Note that if you book through an agent, you may get discounts on the establishment's normal, walk-in "rack rates".

Besides their campsites, KWS have a limited range of self-catering cottages, houses and *bandas* in most of the parks. See ⓦwww.kws.org for reservations or take a chance at the gate.

Game-viewing

Many lodges and camps have their own 4WD vehicles and offer regular **game drives**. These can be very worthwhile because the drivers usually know the animals and the area. Expect to pay around $50 per person for scheduled departures and around $200 for exclusive use of the vehicle for two to three hours. The usual pattern is two (or sometimes three) game drives a day: at dawn, mid-morning and late afternoon, though if you keep this up for more than a day or two you'll be exhausted. In the middle of the day, the parks are usually left to the animals. While the overhead sunlight makes it a poor time to take photos, the animals are around, if sleepy. If you can put up with the heat while most people are resting back at the lodge, it can be a tranquil and satisfying time.

Rangers can usually be hired for the day: the official KWS rates are Ksh3000 for a full 24-hour period, or Ksh1500 for six hours. If you have room in your vehicle, someone with intimate local knowledge and a trained eye is a good companion.

There are a number of fairly obvious **rules** to adhere to when watching animals. If you're stopping, switch off your engine and be as quiet as possible, speaking in low murmurs rather than whispering. Obviously, never get out of the vehicle except at the occasional (often rather vaguely designated) parking areas and viewpoints. Never feed wildlife, as it upsets their diet and leads to dependence on humans (habituated baboons and vervet monkeys can become violent if refused handouts). Remember that animals have the right of way, and shouldn't be disturbed, even if they're sitting on the road in front of you. This means keeping a minimum distance of twenty metres away, having no more than five vehicles viewing an animal at any one time (wait your turn if necessary), and not following your subjects if they start to move away.

To see as much game as possible, stop frequently to scan with binoculars, watch what the herds of antelope and other grazers are doing (a predator will usually be watched intently by them all), and pause to talk to any drivers you pass along the way. Most enthusiastic wildlife-watchers agree the best time of day is just before sunrise, when nocturnal animals are often still out and about, and you might see that weird dictionary leader, the aardvark.

Safaris

Before anything else, bear in mind that the professionalism and experience of your safari guide can transform any visit to the parks. Then think about whether you want comfort or a grittier experience, and whether you want the convenience of having it pre-booked as part of a package holiday, or the independence of picking and choosing online, or once you're in Kenya. Remember that the parks can be visited privately, allowing you to arrange your own itinerary. If you have the time, this is a good alternative to an organized trip.

Types of safari

Air safaris, using internal flights to get around, will add significantly to the cost and comfort of your trip and give you spectacular views, but a much less intimate contact with Kenya. A week-long air safari will work out in the range of $500–800 per day per person, assuming four scheduled flights and three different camps or lodges, but will depend on the quality of your accommodation (though less on the size of your party).

On a **road safari**, on the other hand, long bumpy drives to meet the demands of the itinerary can be exhausting, while hours of your time are eaten away in a cloud of dust. Moreover, opportunities to see much of the landscape or communities through which you're passing can be somewhat limited, though this will depend on the route you take, the quality of your vehicle and the level of engagement of your guide, and thus the cost of the trip. Most road safaris take you, using **minibuses** with pop-top roofs for photography, from one lodge or camp to another, staying two or three nights at each lodge, in two or three parks. Samburu–Nakuru–Maasai Mara would be a typical route. Make sure you have a window seat and ask about the number of passengers and whether the vehicle is shared by several operators or is for your group only. A week's safari by road, staying at lodges or tented camps, will cost in the range of $300–700 per day per person, assuming at least five or six clients.

The alternative to a standard lodge safari is a **camping safari**, again usually in a minibus, where the crew (or you, if it's a budget trip) pitch your tents each day. With this kind of trip you have to be prepared for a degree of discomfort along with the self-sufficiency: insects can occasionally be a menace; you may not get a shower every night; the food won't be so lavish; and the beer not so cold. The price should be in the range of $150–250 per day per person, depending on the itinerary.

It's common on camping safaris to spend the hot **middle of the day** at the campsite. Some of these are shady and pleasant, but that's not always the case and, where there are nearby lodges with swimming pools, cold beer and other amenities, it's worth spending a few hours in comfort. Similarly, if you want to go on an early game drive, or spend the whole morning out, don't be afraid to suggest to the tour leader that you skip breakfast, or take sandwiches. Too often, the itinerary is a product of what tour operators think customers want (passed from management to drivers and cooks) constrained by the driver's fuel allowance.

The fact that so many safaris are run using 2WD minibuses in conditions that are really only suited to 4WD vehicles speaks volumes about the nature of tourism in Kenya. On better camping safaris, you travel in a more **rugged vehicle** that's higher off the ground – a 4WD Land Rover or Land Cruiser or even an open-sided lorry – giving more flexibility about where you go and how long you stay.

The most **expensive camping safaris** come very expensive indeed: you can easily expect to pay $600–1000 per day per person. But you'll be guided by expert guides (you want a silver guide, see opposite) and usually looked after superbly, with top-quality tents ready for your arrival at your fly-camp every evening, good meals, cold drinks and informed conversation.

When on your trip, it's important not to take a passive attitude. Although some of the **itinerary** may be fixed, it's not all cast in stone, and daily routines may be altered to suit the clients easily enough if you ask, though going over-budget on fuel is likely to be an issue.

Increasingly, **horse-riding**, **camel-assisted**, **walking** and **cycling** safaris are also being offered: they are generally comparable in price with mid-range or expensive conventional safaris. Note that the "balloon safaris" you see advertised are short balloon flights, not complete tours. They take place at dawn and last a couple of hours. They can be done in a number of parks, most popularly in the Maasai Mara, and the bill is a big one, around $400 per person.

Booking safaris direct

If you want the flexibility of booking your own safari, rather than having a travel agent or operator at home organize the whole trip for you, then you will be dealing with agents or operators either in Nairobi or Mombasa. It's worth noting that the **minibus safaris** that are included in inexpensive Mombasa-based charter packages venture no further afield than the three national parks easily accessible from the coast, Tsavo East, Tsavo West and Amboseli. Trips north to Samburu or west to the Maasai Mara are cheaper if arranged from Nairobi.

Choosing a **safari company** independently can feel fairly hit-or-miss. Unless you have the luxury of a long stay, your choice will probably be limited by what is available during your visit. If you're booking at the last minute, many companies are willing to offer a discount in order to fill unsold seats and some outfits will also give student discounts if you ask. In fact, you should use any angle you can employ to get a good deal. This is not to recommend the very cheapest outfits.

Responsible tourism

Kenya's diverse and fragile environments, its traditional lifestyles and its reliance on tourism make it especially vulnerable to irresponsible exploitation by insensitive visitors and the local tourist industry. For an account of wildlife, the environment and responsible tourism, see p.567. As a first port of call, check out Kenya's main responsible tourism body, Ecotourism Kenya ⓦ www.ecotourismkenya.org), which awards bronze, silver and gold eco-ratings to hotels and operators.

Some camping operators, not all of them licensed, sell safaris at the very bottom of the market in a price war that completely undercuts the legitimate firms. Any safari which is offered at less than $100 per day is going to be cutting corners one way or another. The easiest way for disreputable operators to cut costs is to avoid paying park entry fees. Some companies also make a habit of failing to deliver on their promises, knowing that a combination of their clients' goodwill and inadequate legal recourse will allow them to get away with it.

Some **recommended operators** are listed in the Nairobi section on p.128, but it's difficult to find a company that's absolutely consistent, and this is particularly the case among the budget operators. The Nairobi grapevine is probably your best guide. Membership of **KATO** (Kenya Association of Tour Operators (ⓦ www .katokenya.org) is a good sign, but don't take it as a guarantee.

Unpredictable factors such as weather, illness and visibility of animals all contribute to the degree of success of the trip and group relations among the passengers can assume surprising significance in a very short time. More controllable factors like breakdowns, food, equipment and competence of the drivers, guides and tour leaders, really determine reputations. If anything goes wrong, reputable companies will do their best to compensate on the spot (a partial refund, an extra day if you broke down, a night in a lodge if you didn't make it to a campsite). If your grievance is unresolved, you might want to contact KATO, who can intercede with its members.

Guides and tips

Leaving aside your choice of itinerary, transport, and standard of accommodation,

the one aspect of your safari that is right out of your hands once you've booked is the calibre of your **guide**. Since the late 1990s, the Kenya Professional Safari Guides Association (ⓦ www.safariguides.org) has taken the lead in setting benchmarks for professional guides in Kenya. They hold monthly exams and there are now more than seven hundred accredited KPSGA bronze guides in the country. Of these, more than eighty have now passed their silver exam and just three have reached gold.

It's highly rewarding to go out **game-watching with a silver guide**. They can offer memorable insights into animal behaviour and can be astonishingly adept at tracking animals and interpreting their observations: a good guide will know, for example, why two male lions are being chased by a lioness, and what you might expect to find if you discreetly follow the lioness later. And all silver guides have a wealth of knowledge about natural history in general, not just big game. Bronze guides can be very good, too: they have to wait three years before they can take their silver exam, and many bronze guides will spend hours every day reading the literature. You can check the association's bronze, silver and gold members at the KPSGA website, and it's perfectly fair to ask your company if they have any accredited guides and if so whether they will be guiding your safari.

Good guides are far more than animal-spotters: they are often gifted linguists, highly practical in every way, and excellent bush companions. Many visitors become close friends of their guides and are drawn back to the same company repeatedly to renew the friendship.

Guides earn reasonable salaries by Kenyan standards, but clients' tips still make up a large proportion of their income, accounting sometimes for more than half their earnings.

Tipping, of guides, drivers and other staff, can often cause misunderstandings between clients, who are usually expected to organize themselves to give collective gratuities on the last day. Good companies make suggestions in their briefing packs. You should budget for Ksh500, or around $5–10 per member of staff per day from each client, slightly more for a small group of two or three, and less for a very large group, or one that includes children (who are not expected to tip). If you're a couple, in a group being looked after by a driver and a guide-leader, then you might give $200 in tips at the end of a week's safari. If this sounds like a lot in Kenyan terms, bear in mind that they may spend many weeks each year not working.

Health

Although disease is an ever-present threat to most Kenyans, health should not be a big issue for visitors. Malaria is endemic and HIV infection rates are high, but so long as you take sensible precautions – remember your malaria pills, clean any cuts or scrapes, and avoid food that has been left out after cooking – you should have no problems beyond the chance of minor tummy trouble.

One of the biggest hazards is the fierce **UV radiation** of the equatorial sun. Brightness rather than heat is the damaging element, so wear a hat and use high-factor **sunblock**, especially in your first two weeks. If you're going to be on the road for a long time, it may be worth considering taking some **vitamin** tablets with you, though they are no substitute for a balanced diet with plenty of fresh fruit and vegetables. If you're going to Kenya for longer than a short holiday, get a thorough **dental checkup** before leaving home. A freshly cut "toothbrush twig" (*msuake*) is a useful supplement, and some varieties contain a plaque-destroying enzyme. You can buy them at markets.

Sexually transmitted diseases, including **HIV**, are rife in Kenya. Four out of five deaths among 25- to 35-year-olds are AIDS-related. Using a condom will help to protect you from this and other STDs, including **hepatitis B**, which is quite widespread and can lead to chronic liver disease.

Medical resources

Your family doctor is your best first source of advice and probable supplier of jabs and prescriptions. Depending on your doctor and your health provider, you may get your requirements free of charge, or have to pay.

International and emergency

IAMAT Ⓦ www.iamat.org. A free-membership non-profit organization, providing travel health info and lists of approved participating hospitals and clinics in Kenya.
International SOS Assistance Ⓦ www.intsos .com. Emergency evacuation and assistance to members.
MEDJET Assistance Ⓦ www.medjetassistance .com. Medical evacuation specialists.

UK

MASTA Ⓦ www.masta-travel-health.com. Clinic locations throughout the UK, but expensive.
NHS Choices Travel Health Ⓦ tinyurl.com /pvrsmb. Detailed, free advice.
NHS Scotland Fit for Travel Ⓦ www.fitfortravel .scot.nhs.uk. Scottish NHS website on travellers' health.
Nomad Pharmacy Ⓦ www.nomadtravel.co.uk. Three locations in London, plus Bristol, Southampton and Manchester.

Ireland

Tropical Medical Bureau Ⓦ www.tmb.ie. More than a dozen clinics throughout Ireland.

USA and Canada

Centers for Disease Control and Prevention Ⓦ www.cdc.gov/travel. US government official site for travel health.

Public Health Agency of Canada ⓦtinyurl.com
/db3vnc. Complete listing of all travel health clinics
across Canada.
Travel Health Online
ⓦ www.tripprep.com. Well-updated, US, private-
sector health and safety site with substantial Kenya
information.

Australia, NZ, South Africa

The Travel Doctor TMVC ⓦ www.tmvc
.com.au. 19 clinics in Australia, 7 in New Zealand and
1 in South Africa.

Inoculations

For arrivals **by air** from Europe, Australia, New
Zealand and North America, Kenya has no
required inoculations. Entering **overland**,
though, you may well be required to show an
International Vaccination Certificate for **yellow
fever**, and it is just possible that you may be
asked for a **cholera** certificate too (vaccination
centres will usually provide a "cholera vaccination not required" stamp in your certificate for
just such an eventuality). If you intend to enter
Kenya by land or to break your journey to
Kenya elsewhere in Africa, plan ahead and
start organizing your jabs at least six weeks
before departure. A yellow fever certificate
only becomes valid ten days after you've had
the jab, but is then valid for ten years.

You should ensure that you are up to date
with your childhood **tetanus** and **polio**
protection: boosters are necessary every ten
years (your doctor will check your records)
and it's as well to check before travelling.

Although not necessary for an ordinary
safari-and-beach holiday, if you're going to
be exposed to unhygienic conditions,
doctors recommend jabs for **typhoid**,
hepatitis A and **hepatitis B** (or a combined
vaccination course). Effective protection
takes some time to develop after the vaccination, so if you're going to be working
locally or travelling extensively, talk to your
doctor as far ahead as you can.

Malaria

Malaria is endemic in tropical Africa and has
a variable **incubation period** of a few days
to several weeks, meaning you can get it
long after being bitten. It's caused by a
parasite called *Plasmodium*, carried in the
saliva of the female *Anopheles* mosquito.

Anopheles prefers to **bite** in the evening,
and can be distinguished by the eager,
head-down position as she settles to bite.
Anopheles is rarely found above 1500m,
which means Nairobi and much of central
Kenya is naturally malaria-free, but mosquitoes can travel in luggage and public
transport so you should assume the whole
country is risky.

Though not infectious, the disease can be
very dangerous and sometimes fatal if not
treated quickly. The destruction of red blood
cells by the *Plasmodium falciparum* type of
malaria parasite can lead to **cerebral
malaria** (blocking of the brain capillaries) and
is the cause of a nasty complication called
blackwater fever in which the urine is
stained by excreted blood cells.

Wherever you travel, mosquito bites are
almost a certainty and protection against
malaria is essential. The best and most
obvious method is to reduce your risk of
being bitten. Keep your arms, legs and feet
covered as much as possible after dusk
(long, light-coloured sleeves and trousers are
best), and cover exposed skin with a strong
repellent. **Deet-based repellants** ("deet" is
the insecticide diethyltoluamide) are best;
citronella oil is considered much less
effective, and has the disadvantage that
elephants are attracted to the smell, and
have been known to break into cars and
tents to get at it. Sleep under a **mosquito
net** (if you're using your own, you might
want to impregnate it with Deet) and burn
mosquito coils, or mosquito-repellant
tablets on a plug-in electric burner, both
readily available in Kenya. Electronic buzzers
have been shown not to work.

However much you can avoid being bitten,
most medical professionals consider it
essential to take **anti-malaria tablets**. The
commonly recommended preventatives are
the weekly mefloquine (sold as **Lariam**), which
has a poor record for side effects, the
antibiotic **doxycycline**, taken daily, and
atovaquone-with-proguanil, taken daily (sold
as **Malarone**), which, while expensive, has
few, if any, side effects and can be started just
two days before you leave. Your doctor may
be able to advise further on which of these
pills is the best one for you, and what the
various side effects can be. It's important

to maintain a careful routine and cover the period **before and after** your trip with doses.

If you do get a **dose of malaria**, you'll soon know about it: the fever, shivering and headaches are something like severe flu and come in unpleasant waves, making you pour with sweat for half an hour and then shiver uncontrollably. If you suspect anything, go to a hospital or clinic immediately. You will be rapidly tested and sold the appropriate treatment. If you can't get to a doctor, seeing a pharmacist is a good plan B.

Note that if you're visiting Kenya for an extended period, it makes sense to buy the bulk of your anti-malarial tablets in Kenya. You can buy all of them over the counter and they can be much cheaper than at home – a box of one hundred doxycycline for example, costs only Ksh1000.

Waterborne diseases

Serious stomach upsets don't afflict a large proportion of travellers. That said, Kenya's once fairly safe **tap water** is increasingly unfit to drink and the supply can be particularly suspect during periods of drought or heavy flooding. Where there is no mains supply, be very cautious of rain- or well-water. To purify water intended for drinking, use purifying tablets or, better, iodine (six drops per litre of water, then wait for half an hour), or boil it (if at high altitude, for thirty minutes).

If your stay in Kenya is short, you might as well stick to **bottled water**, which is widely available. For longer stays, think of **re-educating your stomach**; it's virtually impossible to travel around the country without exposing yourself to strange bugs from time to time. Take it easy at first, don't overdo the fruit (and wash it in clean water), don't keep food too long, and be wary of salads. It is also wise to eat food that is freshly cooked and piping hot.

Should you go down with **diarrhoea**, it will probably sort itself out without treatment within 48 hours. In the meantime, and especially with children, for whom it may be more serious, it's essential to replace the fluids and salts lost, so drink lots of water with oral rehydration salts (if you can't get them from pharmacies, use half a teaspoon of salt and eight teaspoons of sugar in a litre of water). It's a good idea to avoid greasy food, heavy spices, caffeine and most fruit and dairy products. Plain rice or *ugali* with boiled vegetables is the best diet. Drugs like Lomotil and Imodium simply plug you up, undermining the body's efforts to rid itself of infection, though they can be useful if you have to travel.

Avoid jumping for antibiotics at the first sign of trouble: they annihilate what's nicely known as your "gut flora" and will not work on viruses. But if your diarrhoea continues for more than five days, seek medical help. Be aware of the fact that diarrhoea reduces the efficacy of malaria and contraceptive pills as they may pass straight through your system without being absorbed.

Bilharzia (medical name schistosomiasis) is a dangerous disease. It comes from tiny worm-like flukes, the schistosomes, that live in freshwater snails and which burrow into animal or human skin to multiply in the bloodstream. The snails only favour stagnant water and the chances of picking up bilharzia are small. The usual recommendation is never to swim in, wash with, or even touch, lake water that can't be vouched for. The stagnant and weed-infested parts of Kenyan lakes and rivers often harbour bilharzia, but the danger of crocodile attack means you're unlikely to want any close contact with inland waters. If you suffer serious fatigue and pass blood, which are the first symptoms of bilharzia, see a doctor: it's curable.

Heat and altitude

It's important not to underestimate the power of the **equatorial sun**: a hat and sunglasses are strongly recommended to protect you from the bright light. The sun can quickly burn, or even cause **sunstroke**, so a high-factor sunblock is vital on exposed skin, especially when you first arrive. Be aware that overheating can cause **heatstroke**, which is potentially fatal. Signs are a very high body temperature, without a feeling of fever but accompanied by headaches and disorientation. Lowering the body temperature (by taking a tepid shower for example) and resting in a cool place, are the first steps in treatment.

The sun's radiation is stronger at higher altitudes, but the biggest risk if you climb to over 2500m above sea level is **altitude**

Medicine bag

Various items worth taking on a trip include:

- **Alcohol swabs** Invaluable for cleaning minor wounds or insect bites.
- **Antihistamine cream** Apply immediately after insect bites to reduce itchiness.
- **Anti-malaria tablets** Essential.
- **Antibiotics** If you are likely to be far from medical help for any length of time, your doctor should be able to prescribe you suitable antibiotics in case you need to treat a serious lower bowel crisis or dysentery.
- **Antiseptic cream**
- **Aspirin or paracetamol**
- **Iodine tincture, with dropper, or water purifying tablets** If you can't get clean water, these will do the trick.
- **Lip-salve/chap stick**
- **Tampons** Available in town chemists but expensive, so bring your own supplies.
- **Thermometer** Get a plastic one that sticks on your forehead.
- **Zinc oxide powder** Useful anti-fungal powder for sweaty crevices.

sickness, which may affect climbers on Mount Kenya, and even walkers in the Cherangani Hills. For further advice see p.159 of the Mount Kenya section.

On the coast, many people get occasional **heat rashes**, especially at first. A warm shower to open the pores, and loose cotton clothes, should help, as can zinc oxide powder. **Dehydration** is another possible problem, so make sure you are drinking enough fluids (but not alcohol or caffeine), especially when you're hot or tired. The main danger sign is irregular urination, and dark urine definitely means you're not drinking enough water.

Cuts and bites

Take more care than usual over minor **cuts and scrapes**. In the tropics, the most trivial scratch can quickly become a throbbing infection if you ignore it. Take a small tube of antiseptic with you, or apply alcohol or iodine.

As for animal bites, **dogs** are usually sad and skulking, and pose little threat, but rabies does exist in Kenya, and can be transmitted by a bite or even a lick, so it's best to avoid playing with pets unless you know the owner and are sure they are safe. On the smaller scale, **scorpions and spiders** abound, but are hardly ever seen unless you deliberately turn over rocks or logs. Scorpion stings are painful but rarely dangerous, while spiders are mostly quite harmless, even the really big ones. **Snakes** are common but, again, the vast majority are harmless. To see one at all, you need to search stealthily. If you walk heavily they obligingly disappear. For more on other potentially dangerous animals, see p.77.

Medical treatment

For serious treatment Kenya has too few well-equipped hospitals, and in most you're expected to pay for all treatment and drugs. The Consolata Sisters' Nazareth Hospital on Riara Ridge, northwest of Nairobi (☏020/2017401), and in Nyeri (☏061/2031010), are well run and modestly priced, as is Kijabe Hospital on the east side of the Rift Valley near Naivasha (☏020/3246500). The best local hospitals are mentioned throughout the text in the "Listings" sections.

Kenya's **flying doctors** air ambulance service (☏020/6993000, ⊛www.amref.org) offers free evacuation by air, which is very reassuring if you'll be spending time out in the wilds. Tourist membership costs $15 per person for two weeks, or $25 for two months for cover up to a radius of 500km from Nairobi, or $30/$50 for up to 1000km. The income goes back into their outreach programme and the African Medical Research Foundation (AMREF) behind it. They have an office at Wilson Airport, from where most of their rescue missions take off.

Culture and etiquette

Although it's not essential on a short visit, understanding something of the subtle rituals and traditions that underpin everyday life will make a big difference to your appreciation of Kenyan culture. And if you're staying for an extended period, you'll need to make some adjustments yourself. There's more detailed information about Kenya's tribes and cultural traditions throughout the guide. Language coverage starts on p.611.

Greetings

Every contact between people in Kenya starts with a greeting. Even when entering a shop, you shake hands and make polite small talk with the shopkeeper. **Shaking hands** upon meeting and departure is normal between all the men present. Women shake hands with each other, but with men only in more sophisticated contexts. Soul-brother handshakes and other, finger-clicking variations are popular among young men, while a common, very respectful handshake involves clutching your right arm with your left hand as you shake or, in Muslim areas, touching your left hand to your chest when shaking hands.

Traditionally, **greeting exchanges** last a minute or two, and you'll often hear them performed in a formal manner between two men, especially in rural areas. Long greetings help subsequent negotiations. In English or Swahili you can exchange something like "How are you?" "Fine, how's the day?" "Fine, how's business?" "Fine, how's the family?", "Fine, thank God". It's usually considered polite, while someone is speaking to you at length, to grunt in the affirmative, or say thank you at short intervals. Breaks in conversation are filled with more greetings.

Hissing ("Tsss!") is an ordinary way to attract a stranger's attention, though less common in more sophisticated urban situations. You may get a fair bit of it yourself, and it's quite in order to hiss at the waiter in a restaurant: it won't cause any offence.

If you're **asking questions**, avoid yes/no ones, as answering anything in the negative is often considered impolite. And when making enquiries, try not to phrase your query in the negative ("Isn't the bus leaving?") because the answer will often be "Yes" (it isn't leaving).

If you'll be staying in Kenya for some time and really want to prepare, print a batch of **photos** of you and your family with your contact details on the back. Personalized "business cards" like this are greatly appreciated.

Body language, gestures and dress

You are likely to notice a widespread and unselfconscious ease with close **physical contact**, especially on the coast. Male visitors may need to get used to holding hands with strangers as they're shown around the guesthouse, or guided down the street, and, on public transport, to strangers' hands and limbs draped naturally wherever is most comfortable, which can include your legs or shoulders.

It's good to be aware of the **left hand rule**: traditionally the left hand is reserved for unhygienic acts and the right for eating and touching, or passing things to others. Like many "rules" it's very often broken, at which times you have to avoid thinking about it.

Unless you're looking for a confrontation, never **point** with your finger, which is equivalent to an obscene gesture. For similar reasons, **beckoning** is done with the palm down, not up, which if you're not familiar with the action can inadvertently convey a dismissive gesture.

Don't be put off by apparent shiftiness in **eye contact**, especially if you're talking to someone much younger than you. It's normal for those deferring to others to avoid a direct gaze.

In coastal towns, wearing **shorts and T-shirts** (which are considered fine on the beach), won't get you into trouble, as people are far too polite to admonish strangers, but it's better to dress in loose-fitting long sleeves and skirts or trousers. Lamu calls more for *kikoi* and *kanga* wraps for both sexes and, because it's so small, more consideration for local feelings. For more on suitable dress for women, see p.76. You'll also need to be suitably attired to enter **mosques**. Few are very grand, however, and you rarely miss much by staying outside.

Beggars

In central Nairobi and Mombasa **beggars** are fairly common. Most are visibly destitute, and many are disabled, or homeless mothers with children. While some have regular pitches, others keep on the move, and all are harassed by the police. Kenyans often give to the same beggar on a regular basis: to the many Kenyans who are Muslim, alms-giving is a religious requirement. This kind of charity is also an important safety net for the destitute in a country with no social security system.

Sexual attitudes

Although there is a certain amount of ethnic and religious variation in attitudes, **sexual mores** in Kenya are generally hedonistic and uncluttered. Expressive sexuality is a very obvious part of the social fabric in most communities, and in Muslim areas Islamic moral strictures tend to be generously interpreted. The age of consent for heterosexual relations is 16.

Female **prostitution** flourishes almost everywhere, with a remarkable number of cheaper hotels doubling as informal brothels. There are no signs of any organized sex trade and such prostitution appears to merge seamlessly into casual promiscuity. If you're a man, you're likely to find flirtatious pestering a constant part of the scene, especially if you visit bars and clubs. With HIV infection rates extremely high, even protected sex is extremely inadvisable. On the coast there's increasing evidence of child prostitution and, apart from the odd poster, little effort by the authorities to control it.

Sex between men is illegal in Kenya, and **homosexuality** is still largely a taboo subject; lesbianism doubly so, although no law specifically outlaws it. Many Kenyans take the attitude that gay sex is a foreign, un-African practice. While there is no gay scene as such, male homosexuality is an accepted undercurrent on the coast, where it finds most room for expression in Lamu and Malindi (*msenge* is the Swahili for a gay man), and to a small extent in Nairobi. The Lake Victoria region has a fairly relaxed attitude, too. You'll find a small amount of information on the male gay scene in Kenya in the *Spartacus Gay Guide*. **Acceptance & Visibility** (ⓦwww.gaykenya .com) is a Kenyan website offering "a safe space for LGBTI Kenyans" and the South African portal **Behind the Mask** (ⓦwww .mask.org.za) has a good page of Kenya info and links. Blogs include ⓦkenyangay .blogspot.com and ⓦthegaykenyan.blogspot .com. Two gay-friendly travel companies are Novta Tours in Malindi (☎042/21067 or 0720/693053, ⓦwww.kenya-travel.com) and Magical Africa in Nairobi (☎020/6314442, ⓦwww.magicalafrica.net).

Rules of bargaining

Don't begin if you're in a hurry; don't show interest if you're not thinking of buying; and never offer a price you are not prepared to pay.

Crime and safety

Though things have improved since the change of government in 2002, there's no denying that petty crime is a problem in Kenya, and you have a higher chance of being a victim in touristy areas, where pickings are richer. It's important to bear in mind, however, that most of the large number of tourists who visit the country each year experience no difficulties. For advice on wildlife safety, see p.77.

For official government warnings, check the travel advisories on the websites of the UK Foreign Office (ⓦwww.fco.gov.uk/travel or ⓦtinyurl.com/qnb2zw), the US State Department (ⓦtravel.state.gov or tinyurl .com/bc44cp) or the travel advisory service of your own country. But bear in mind that travel advisories have an inherent tendency to be somewhat cautious and nannying, and are only as good as the information fed into them on the ground. You may also find the security section of KATO's website (ⓦtinyurl .com/qua6hn) useful. They run a **24-hour tourist helpline** on ☏020/604767 and also advertise two mobile numbers of staff in their Safety and Communication Centre: ☏0722/745645 and ☏0733/617499.

Avoiding trouble

After **arriving** in Kenya, a fair few people get robbed on their first day or two in Nairobi, before they've had chance to get used to the place. Try to be acutely conscious of your belongings: never leave anything unguarded even for five seconds; never take out cameras or other valuables unless absolutely necessary; and be careful of where you walk, at least until you've dropped off your luggage and settled in somewhere.

It's hard not to look like a tourist, but try to **dress like a local**, in a short-sleeved shirt, slacks or skirt and sunglasses, and try not to wear anything brand-new. Wearing **sunglasses** lessens your vulnerability, as your inexperience is harder to read.

In Nairobi, the rush hour at dusk is probably the worst time for pickpockets, but it's a good idea to be alert when getting off a night bus early in the morning, too. When you're out and about, avoid carrying a **bag**, particularly not a day-pack over your shoulder which will instantly identify you as a tourist. And don't wear fancy earrings or any kind of chain or necklace. There's usually less risk in leaving your valuables, tucked in your luggage in a locked hotel room, than in taking them with you.

The only substantial **risks** outside Nairobi are down at the coast, where valuables often disappear from the beach or occasionally get grabbed, and in a few tourist-traffic towns such as Naivasha, Nakuru and Nanyuki.

If you're **driving**, it's never a good idea to leave your vehicle unguarded, even if it's locked, if it has anything of value in it. In towns, there's usually someone who will volunteer to guard it for you for a tip (Ksh100 is plenty).

When you have to carry **cash and other valuables**, try to put them in several places. A money belt or pouch tucked into your trousers or skirt is invisible and the most secure, while pouches hanging around your neck are easy targets for grab-and-run robberies and ordinary wallets in the back pocket are an invitation to pickpockets. Similarly, the voluminous "bum bags", worn back to front by many tourists over their clothing, invite a slash-and-grab mugging. You'll be carrying around large quantities of coins and paper money, so make sure you have a reasonably safe but accessible purse or zip pocket to stuff all the small denominations in.

All of this isn't meant to induce paranoia, but if you flaunt the trappings of wealth where there's poverty and a degree of desperation, somebody will try to remove them. If you clearly have nothing on you, and look like you know what you're doing, you're unlikely to feel, or be, threatened.

Cons and scams

On public transport, **doping scams** have occasionally been a problem, with individuals managing to drug tourists and relieve them of their belongings. It's best not to accept gifts of food or drink on public transport, even at the risk of causing offence.

Approaches in the street from "schoolboys" with **sponsorship** forms (only primary education is free, and even then, books, uniforms, even furniture have to be bought) and from "refugees" with long stories are not uncommon and probably best shrugged off, even though some, unfortunately, may be genuine. Also beware of people offering to **change money** on the street, especially in Nairobi, which is usually a trick to get you down an alley where you can be relieved of your cash.

One scam, now almost a tradition, and surprisingly successful to judge by the number of tourists who fall for it, relies entirely on people's belief in the paranoid republic. It involves an approach by a "student" who then requests a small sum of money, or sometimes just someone who engages you for a chat and claims to be a Sudanese or Somali refugee. Shortly after you part company, a group of heavies surround you and claim to be undercover police, interested in the discussion you've been having with that "terrorist", or "criminal", and a large fine is demanded, or they may tell you you're under arrest. You can ask to see their IDs, or just tell them to go to hell. If you're being intimidated, make a big scene and they will vanish.

A particularly unpleasant new scam on the **coast** involves a male tourist being approached by children who start a brief conversation, which is then followed up by an adult minder accusing the tourist of soliciting for sex. He then demands a payment or threatens a visit from the police. As with the "terrorist" scams, never agree anything or pay any money.

Police and thieves

If you get mugged, **don't resist**, as knives and guns are occasionally carried. It will be over in an instant and you're unlikely to be hurt. But the hassles, and worse, that gather when you try to do anything about it make it imperative not to let it happen in the first place. Thieves caught red-handed are usually mobbed, and often killed, so avoid the usual Kenyan response of shouting "Thief!" ("*Mwizi!*" in Swahili), unless you're ready to intercede instantly once you've retrieved your belongings.

Usually you'll have no chance of catching the thief, and if you've lost something valuable, the first reaction is to go to the **police**. Unless you've lost irreplaceable property, however, think twice about doing this. Firstly, they rarely do something for nothing, and even stamping an **insurance form** will probably cost you (though you will need it to claim) and secondly, you should consider the ramifications of trying to catch the culprits, with you in the back of a police car expected to point out the thief in the crowds. Never agree to act as a decoy in the hope that the same thing will happen again in front of a police ambush. Police shootings take place all the time and you may prefer not to be involved in a cold-blooded murder.

If you have **official business** with the police, which is only likely at police roadblocks when

---

Would-be helpers

It's very easy to fall prey to **misunderstandings** in your dealings with people (usually boys and young men) who offer their services as guides, helpers or "facilitators" of any kind. You should absolutely never assume anything is being done out of simple kindness. It may well be, but if it isn't you must expect to pay something. If you have any suspicion, it's best to deal with the matter head-on at an early stage and either apologize for the offence caused, or agree a price. What you must never do, as when bargaining, is enter into an unspoken contract and then break it by refusing to pay for the service. If you're being bugged by someone whose help you don't need, just let them know you can't pay anything for their trouble. It may not make you a friend, but it always works and it's better than a row and recriminations.

you are the driver, then politeness, smiles and handshakes always help to limit the damage. If they claim you have committed a misdemeanour, whether or not you really have (exceeding the speed limit, committing a driving error, talking on your mobile while at the wheel, or having something wrong with your vehicle) and you think you are being solicited for a bribe (*chai*, meaning "tea", or *kitu kidogo*, "something small"), to be allowed to go on your way ("Are you in a hurry?"), *and* if you're prepared to get into that, then haggle over the sum as you would any payment. Calling their bluff usually works just as well, however: agree that this is all unfortunate but you need to be sure it's being dealt with in the proper way, and if they would just explain the procedure to you, you will be happy to oblige. Of course, court appearances and official fines are rarely on their radar. And if you, and they, know you've done nothing wrong and you're not in any rush, then politely refusing to play their game will only cost a short delay until they give up on you and try another potential source of income.

In **unofficial dealings**, the police, especially in remote outposts, can go out of their way to help you with food, transport or accommodation. Try to reciprocate. Police salaries are low and they rely on unofficial income to get by. Only a completely new police force and realistic salaries could alter a situation that is now entrenched.

Drug and other offences

Though **illegal**, marijuana (*bhang* or *bangi*) is widely cultivated and smoked, and is remarkably cheap. However, with the authorities making efforts to control it and penalties of up to ten years for possession (or life and a million-shilling fine for trafficking), its use is not advisable. Official busts result in a heavy fine and deportation at the very least, and quite often a prison sentence, with little or no sympathy from your embassy. Heroin is becoming a major problem on the coast, and possession of that, or of anything harder than marijuana, will get you in a lot worse trouble if you're caught. *Miraa* (or *qat*; see p.172), a herbal stimulant, is legal and widely available, especially in Meru, Nairobi, Mombasa and in the north, but local police chiefs sometimes

order crackdowns on its transport, claiming it is associated with criminality.

Be warned that failure to observe the following points of **behaviour** can get you arrested. Always stand on occasions when the **national anthem** is playing. Stand still when the **national flag** is being raised or lowered in your field of view. Don't take photos of the flag or the **president**, who is quite often seen on state occasions, especially in Nairobi. And if the presidential **motorcade** appears, pull off the road to let it pass. **Smoking** in a public place is prohibited (it's usually okay to smoke outdoors, though not advisable to do so on the street, but check before lighting up). It's also a criminal offence to tear or deface a **banknote** of any denomination, and, officially, to **urinate** in a public place.

Sexual harassment

Women travellers will be glad to find that machismo, in its fully-fledged Latin varieties, is rare in Kenya and male egos are usually softened by reserves of humour. Whether travelling alone or together, women may come across occasional **persistent hasslers**, but seldom much worse. **Drinking** in bars unaccompanied by men, you can expect a lot of male attention, as you can in many other situations. Universal rules apply: if you suspect ulterior motives, turn down all offers and stonily refuse to converse, though you needn't fear expressing your anger if that's how you feel. You will, eventually, be left alone. Really obnoxious individuals are usually alone, fortunately. These tactics are hardly necessary except on the coast, and then particularly in Lamu.

Travelling on your own, you'll usually be welcomed with generous hospitality. On **public transport** a single woman traveller causes quite a stir and fellow passengers don't want to see you treated badly. Women get offers of **accommodation** in people's homes more often than male travellers. And, if you're staying in less reputable hotels, there'll often be female company – employees, family, residents – to look after you.

The way you look and behave get noticed by everyone, and they're more important if you don't appear to have a male escort. Your **head** and everything from **waist to** ankles are the sensitive zones, particularly in Islamic regions. Long, loose hair is seen as extraordinarily provocative, and doubly so if blonde. Pay attention to these areas by keeping your hair fairly short or tied up (or by wearing a scarf) and wearing long skirts or, at a pinch, very baggy long pants.

Wildlife dangers

Although **wild animals** are found all over Kenya, not just inside the parks, dangerous predators like **lions** and **hyenas** are occasionally curious of campfires, but no more than that, and they rarely attack unprovoked. More dangerous are **elephants** and **buffaloes**, and you should stay well clear of both, especially of solitary bulls. In the vicinity of lakes and slow-moving rivers you should watch out for **hippos**, which will attack if you're blocking their route back to water, and **crocodiles**, which can be found in most inland waters and do occasionally attack swimmers. Never swim in inland lakes or rivers. A persistent and growing problem is the continued, unstoppable damage done by those loutish hooligans, **baboons**. A locked vehicle might be safe; an unwatched tent or an open-fronted lodge room certainly isn't.

Travel essentials

Bargaining and receipts

Bargaining is an important skill to acquire, and you'll need to get into it quickly; once you do, you'll rarely end up paying more than the going rate for food, transport or accommodation. If you do pay an unreasonable price for goods or services, you contribute to local inflation, so be cautious over your purchases until you've established the value of things.

It's surprising how little is sold at a fixed price: even hotel rooms are often negotiable and it's always worth making an offer. You're expected to knock down most negotiable prices by anything from ten percent to a half. **Souvenirs** are sometimes offered at first prices ten times what the vendor is actually prepared to accept. You can avoid the silly asking prices by having a chat and establishing your streetwise credentials. The bluffing on both sides is part of the fun; don't be shy of making a big scene. Where prices are marked, they are generally fixed, which you'll quickly discover if you walk away and aren't called back.

Petty bureaucracy is deeply engrained in Kenya and you will often be given a **handwritten receipt** after making the most elementary payment. If you doubt whether the sum you're being asked to pay is officially sanctioned, however – for example, an obscure entrance fee, a fee for a guide, or on occasions when police try to impose an on-the-spot fine – just asking for a receipt before you pay will often clarify matters.

Costs for low budgets

Kenya can be expensive for **budget travellers** if you want to rent a car or go on organized safaris, especially in high season. By staying in B&Ls, eating in local places and using public transport, you can get by okay on $20–30 a day, though $50 would be more comfortable. It's always cheaper per person if you're travelling with others. Getting around by bus and matatu is inexpensive, but the main disadvantage is that you can't use public transport to visit the game parks. Renting a vehicle, and paying for fuel, will add at least $100 a day to your costs. If you're in a group of three or more, it starts to become more reasonable. Don't be tempted, however, to use the very cheap camping safari companies touted on the street (see p.128).

Customs and duty-free

Duty-free allowances on entering Kenya are one bottle of spirits or wine and one carton of two hundred cigarettes (or 50 cigars or 225g of tobacco). If you're stopped at customs, you may be asked if you have any cameras, camcorders or the like. Unless you're a professional with mountains of specialist gear, there should not be any question of paying duty on personal equipment, though some officials like to note it down in your passport to ensure it is re-exported. If you are taking presents for friends in Kenya, however, you are likely to have to pay duty if you declare the items.

Electricity

Kenya's **electricity supply** (220–240V) is inconsistent and unreliable, and all but the most basic establishments have backup generators and/or solar panels. Most hotels have electric-shaver sockets in the bathrooms. Wall sockets are the square, three-pin variety used in Britain. Appliances using other plug fittings will need an adaptor to fit Kenyan sockets (available in major supermarkets), while North American appliances that work only on 110V (most work on 110–240V) will also need a transformer.

Emergencies

For police, fire and ambulance dial ☎999. They often take ages to arrive. There's also a national disaster line ☎911.

Entry requirements

Most nationals, including British, Irish, US, Canadian, Australian, New Zealand, South African and EU passport-holders, need visas to visit Kenya, either obtained in advance or at the immigration counter on arrival. A number of Commonwealth nationals are exempt, while citizens of certain African and Middle Eastern nations must apply in advance. Under-16s don't require visas. It's a good idea, however, to check with a Kenyan embassy website to confirm the current situation. Also ensure that your passport will remain valid for at least six months beyond the end of your projected stay.

Visas and visitor's passes

Visas can be obtained in advance from Kenyan embassies, consulates or high commissions. Applications take up to three weeks to process, and require two passport-size photos. Since 2009, a single-entry tourist visa costs $25 or equivalent, multiple-entry visas $50 and transit visas, if you're simply changing planes, $10. Remember that Kenyan diplomatic missions are closed on Kenyan public holidays (see p.56 for a list of holidays). Visas are variously valid for entry to Kenya within three months or six months of the date of issue, depending on which embassy you use.

You can also get your visa **on arrival**. If you're doing this, it's a good idea to download the application form from an embassy website, and have it filled in and ready on arrival, in order to reduce your waiting time.

The **price of visas** was cut by fifty percent in 2009 to stimulate tourism (a single-entry visa was formerly $50), but this information seems to have taken some time to reach all of Kenya's embassies and ports of entry. One thing is certain: if you're planning to get your visa on arrival in Kenya, the only guaranteed acceptable payment is US dollars, cash.

Once you have your visa, your passport will be stamped with a **visitor's pass**. Various factors may influence the length of time actually granted, including your appearance, how much money you have and, fortunately, how long a stay you ask for. The maximum length of a visitor's pass is three months.

A valid visitor's pass issued on a single-entry visa allows **re-entry** to Kenya after a visit to Uganda or Tanzania. For other trips outside Kenya, unless you have a multiple-entry visa, you'll need another visa to get back in.

If you intend to stay beyond the visitor's pass date stamped in your passport, you should renew it before it expires, assuming your visa is still valid. Confusion over expiry dates can arise if, for example, you can't decipher KVP5W/H ("Kenya Visitor's Pass 5-Week Holiday") – if you're in any doubt, ask. If your visa is also about to expire, you'll need to get a new one. You can stay in Kenya for a maximum of six months as a tourist, after which time you'll have to leave East Africa. Visitor's pass and **visa renewals** can be done at the immigration offices in Nairobi, Mombasa, Lamu, Malindi and Kisumu. Addresses for these are given in the relevant "Listings" sections in the Guide.

Kenyan embassies

The Kenyan diplomatic missions that readers are likely to find most useful are listed here. See the "Missions" section of ⓦwww.statehousekenya.go.ke for a full list.

Australia 33–35 Ainslie Ave, Canberra ☏02/6247 4788, ⓦwww.kenya.asn.au
Canada 415 Laurier Ave E, Ottawa, K1N 6R4 ☏613/563 1773, ⓦwww.kenyahighcommission.ca
Ethiopia Fikremariam St, W16 K01, Addis Ababa ☏011/661 0033, ⓔkengad@telecom.net.et
Ireland 11 Elgin Rd, Ballsbridge, Dublin 4 ☏01/613 6380, ⓦwww.kenyaembassyireland.net
New Zealand Closest representation: Australia
South Africa 302 Brooks St, Menlo Park, Pretoria 0081 ☏012/362 2249, ⓦwww.kenya.org.za
Sudan Block 1 No 516, West Giraif, Street 60, Khartoum ☏0155/772 801, ⓦwww.kenembsud.org; Juba Consulate, Hai-Neem, Juba ☏0811/823 664
Tanzania 127 Mafinga St, Kinondoni, Dar-es-Salaam ☏022/266 8285, ⓦwww.kenyahighcomtz.org
Uganda Plot 41, Nakasero Rd, Kampala ☏041/258 2325
UK 45 Portland Place, London W1B 4AS ☏020/7636 2371, ⓦwww.kenyahighcommission.net
USA 2249 R St NW, Washington DC 20008 ☏202/387 6101, ⓦwww.kenyaembassy.com; Los Angeles consulate, Park Mile Plaza, 4801 Wilshire Boulevard, CA 90010 ☏0323/939 2408

Insurance

You'd do well to take out a **travel insurance policy** prior to travelling to cover against theft, loss, illness and injury. It's worth checking, however, that you won't duplicate the coverage of any existing plans you may have. For example, many private medical schemes include cover when abroad.

A typical travel insurance policy usually provides cover for the loss of baggage, tickets and cash or cheques up to a certain limit, as well as cancellation or curtailment of your journey. Most of them exclude so-called dangerous sports unless an extra premium is paid: in Kenya these could mean scuba-diving, windsurfing and climbing, though not safaris. If you take medical coverage, check there's a 24-hour medical emergency number. When securing baggage cover, make sure that the per-article limit, which is typically less than $1000, will cover your most valuable possessions, like a camera. If you need to make a claim, you should keep receipts for medicines and medical treatment, and in the event you have anything stolen, you must obtain an official statement from the police.

Internet access

Internet cafés are increasingly widespread in Kenya, but they can still be thin on the ground in rural areas and connections can be painfully slow. Mornings are the best time to get a fast connection. If you can't find a cybercafé, many post offices have internet facilities where you buy credit on a prepaid card. The **browsing charge** in most cyber cafés is Ksh1 per minute, though you'll pay much more (up to Ksh25 per min) in hotel "business centres". **Wi-fi** hot spots have yet to take off in a big way, but again some hotels offer them, either as an extra, or more rarely as one of the benefits of staying with them – like electricity.

Rough Guides travel insurance

Rough Guides has teamed up with WorldNomads.com to offer great **travel insurance** deals. Policies are available to residents of more than 150 countries, with cover for a wide range of **adventure sports**, 24hr emergency assistance, high levels of medical and evacuation cover and a stream of **travel safety information**. Roughguides.com-users can take advantage of their policies online 24/7, from anywhere in the world – even if you're already travelling. And since plans often change when you're on the road, you can extend your policy and even claim online. Roughguides.com-users who buy travel insurance with WorldNomads.com can also leave a positive footprint and donate to a community development project. For more information go to ⓦ**www.roughguides.com/shop**.

With a **3G mobile phone**, you can get online either roaming with your home service provider or using a local SIM card (see p.82). Alternatively, if you have your **laptop** with you, you can buy a local ISP's modem and SIM card to give you mobile broadband access. The set-up cost, currently around $50, is coming down all the time. On top of that, some pre-paid plans (for example Ksh1000 for 300Mb, valid for a month, with Safaricom) allow remaining usage to be rolled into the next month. Connectivity and speeds are improving, but be prepared for some frustration if you're aiming to do more than email and browse. Whatever you select, ensure everything is working before you leave the shop.

Laundry

There are virtually no launderettes in Kenya, but all hotels, lodges and tented camps run a **laundry service** for guests. Female underwear is normally excluded (soap powder is provided for guests to do their own). In cheap hotels, you'll easily find people offering the same service (*dobi* in Swahili), but again they often won't accept female, and sometimes male, underwear. If you're camping, you'll find small packets of Omo widely available, and clothes dry fast in the sun. Beware of **tumbu flies**, however, which lay their eggs on wet clothes where the larvae subsequently hatch and burrow into your skin. A good, hot iron should kill the eggs.

Mail

There are main **post offices** in all the towns and, except in the far north, sub-post offices throughout the rural areas. Post offices are usually open Mon–Fri 8am–5pm, Sat 9am–noon. Letters and airmailed parcels take a few days to reach Europe and around ten days to North America, Australia and New Zealand. If you want speedy delivery, pay a little extra for express. Times from these places to Kenya are slightly longer, and things go missing fairly frequently. The internal service, like the international one, is not entirely reliable.

There is no mail delivery service in Kenya: all **postal addresses** comprise a post office box number and the name of a town or city and recipients have to collect their mail.

Some post offices now have five-number postal codes (the Nairobi GPO is 00100).

If you want to receive a letter, the **Poste Restante** (general delivery) service is free, and fairly reliable in Nairobi, Mombasa, Malindi and Lamu. Have your family name marked clearly, followed by "Poste Restante, GPO" and the name of the town. You'll need to show your passport. Packages can be received, too, but many go missing, and expect to haggle over import duty when they're opened in your presence. Ask the sender to mark the package "Contents To Be Re-exported From Kenya". For large or valuable items, always use a courier. FedEx, DHL and UPS have branches or agents in all large towns.

Maps

The best **map** available of the country is the Rough Guide Map: Kenya & Northern Tanzania (1:950,000) printed on rip-proof, waterproof plastic paper, which is designed to work alongside this guide.

You can get a limited range of more detailed **regional maps** of Kenya from the Survey of Kenya's Public Map Office in Nairobi (see p.133). A local company (ⓦwww.touristmapskenya.com) has also licensed some of the Survey of Kenya material and published a number of **maps of parks and reserves**, which are available in bookshops and at park gates. Nairobi and Mombasa **A-Z street atlases** are available in bookshops, but will gradually be superseded by the all-enveloping **Google Maps**, which has already started on Nairobi, and a number of other Kenyan towns.

Money

Kenya's currency, the Kenyan shilling (Ksh), is a colonial legacy based on the old British currency (as in pre-decimal Britain, Kenyans occasionally refer to shillings as "bob"). There are notes of Ksh1000, 500, 200, 100 and 50, and coins of Ksh20, 10, 5, 1 and 50 cents (half a shilling). Some foreign banks stock shillings should you wish to buy some before you leave, but you'll get rates about ten percent less than what you might find in Kenya. You can import or export up to Ksh100,000 (you need the exchange receipts if exporting).

Because the Kenya shilling is a weak currency, prices for anything connected to the tourist industry tend to be quoted in **US dollars**. Cash dollars, together with British pounds and euros, are invariably acceptable, and often preferred, as payment. People often have calculators and know the latest exchange rates. At the time of writing, the **rates of exchange** were approximately Ksh120 to £1, Ksh80 to $1 and Ksh100 to €1. If you take **$100 bills** to Kenya be sure they are less than five years old as they won't be exchangeable in many places otherwise.

While most **prices** in this book are given in Kenyan shillings, the various currencies we have used reflect the prices advertised by hotels, tour operators and other service providers.

Exchanging money

You can **exchange** hard currency in cash at banks and foreign exchange ("forex") bureaux all over the country, and also at most large hotels, though for a substantially poorer rate. US dollars, British pounds and euros are always the most easily changed. Always check the commission and any charges, as they may vary mysteriously, even within branches of the same bank.

Cash invariably attracts better rates than **traveller's cheques** which, in the age of the ATM, are becoming increasingly unpopular and cumbersome, especially as you need to have the original receipts as well as your passport and the patience of a saint when waiting in the bank to cash them.

Banks are usually open Mon–Fri 9am–3pm, Sat 9–11am (some branches are not open every Sat). In out-of-the-way places, you may have to wait until the rates arrive from Nairobi.

Street moneychangers in Nairobi, Mombasa and Malindi may offer slightly better than official rates, but this **black market** is illegal, and many of them are chancers aiming to rip you off or even muggers looking to lure you into an alley. An exception is when entering Kenya by land from Uganda or Tanzania, where moneychangers in the border towns will give Kenyan shillings for Ugandan or Tanzanian shillings for cash US dollars. Local authorities turn a blind eye, but always count the shillings very carefully before handing over your hard currency.

Credit and debit cards, and ATMs

The best way to carry your money is in the form of **plastic**. This is not so much because you can use credit or debit cards to buy things (though increasingly you can), but because they're more secure than cash, and you can use them at **ATMs**. Some bank branches have ATMs inside a secure booth or guards on the street outside. There's almost always a line of local people waiting to withdraw cash, though you rarely have to wait long.

Most branches of Barclays Ⓦtinyurl.com /yeno468), Standard Chartered (Ⓦtinyurl .com/yj59opt) and Kenya Commercial (Ⓦtinyurl.com/yahmmjl) banks have 24-hour ATMs. The machines variously accept cards with Visa, Visa Electron, MasterCard, Plus or Cirrus symbols. Most branches of Barclays and Standard Chartered also give **cash advances** in Kenya shillings, US dollars or pounds sterling on Visa and MasterCard credit cards. The maximum amount you can withdraw per day is usually Ksh40,000 from an ATM, or Ksh50,000 over the counter.

Visa and American Express **credit cards** are widely accepted for tourist services such as upmarket hotels and restaurants, flights, safaris, and car rental; MasterCard and others are more limited. There's usually a two- to five-percent mark-up on top of the price for the cost of the transaction to the company. Chip-and-pin transactions have not yet arrived in Kenya, and **credit card fraud** is not uncommon. If you're paying a sum in shillings, make sure you've filled in the leading digits with zeros and the voucher specifies the currency before you sign. If it doesn't, it's all too easy for the vendor to fill in a $, € or £ sign in front of the total after you've left.

Wiring money

Having **money wired** from home is not cheap, but it is relatively easy. You can have it sent with Western Union (Ⓦwww .westernunion.com) to branches of PostBank and KCB, or with MoneyGram (Ⓦwww .moneygram.com) to branches of the Co-op Bank and some forex bureaux. The transfer is instantaneous, and fees depend on the amount being transferred. Wiring $1000, for example, will cost around $65.

At the time of writing, **M-Pesa**, the much more affordable mobile-to-mobile money transfer system that has transformed Kenya's rural economy, was planning to go international. Operated by Safaricom, M-Pesa could allow Kenyans to make payments overseas and, potentially, enable overseas mobile-phone users to make payments to people with mobiles in Kenya.

Museums and historical monuments

Kenya's **museums** are always worth visiting if you're in the neighbourhood, although perhaps only the National Museum in Nairobi, Fort Jesus in Mombasa and Lamu Museum deserve a special visit. They're run by the National Museums of Kenya (Ⓦwww .museums.or.ke), which also coordinates archeological digs and looks after various sites and monuments – several of which, such as the ruins of **Gedi** on the coast, and **Thimlich Ohinga** near Lake Victoria, are impressive and highly recommended. If you're visiting Nairobi, it's worth getting the special-rate pass that entitles you to free entry to all the sites and museums for a month (see p.111).

Opening hours

Opening hours tend to follow familiar patterns. In larger towns, the major stores and tourist services are open Mon–Sat 8am–5pm or 9am–6pm, often with a break for lunch. Large supermarkets are increasingly open late in the evenings and big towns often have at least one 24-hour Nakumatt hypermarket. Banks are usually open Mon–Fri 9am–3pm, and Sat 9–11am. Museums are usually open seven days a week. Post offices are usually open Mon–Fri 8am–5pm, Sat 9am–noon. Other offices may be open Saturday mornings but are usually closed all weekend. In rural areas, small shops can be open at almost any hour. Some petrol stations stay open late, but very few are open all night.

Phones and mobiles

Kenya's conventional **landline telephone system**, run by Telkom (operator ☏900),

appears to be in terminal decline. Where it works, people use it because it's the cheapest way to make a call, but in many towns, the local phones, including the call boxes, are all but defunct. If you borrow someone's phone, or you can find a working payphone (some large post offices have working boxes), then you should be able to call internationally as well as in Kenya (see box opposite for country codes). The easiest way is with a Telkom Kenya scratch card, available in various values and durations. You scratch off a panel on the back, revealing the card's password number, which you key in every time you make a call. The cards can be used for local and international calls from any landline phone with tone dialling, including call boxes. The rate for calls in Kenya to landlines ranges from Ksh3.30 per minute to Ksh14 per minute, a flat Ksh31 per minute to mobiles and from Ksh35 per minute to Ksh46 per minute to Uganda or Tanzania. For all other international calls the rate is $1 per minute Mon–Fri 8am–10pm or $0.70 per minute at other times.

Kenya's **area codes** are all three figures, comprising 0 plus two digits. The subscriber numbers are five, six or seven digits, with all numbers moving (in theory) to seven digits.

Kenya also has CDMA **wireless lines**, which are vastly more reliable than land lines. Like Nairobi land lines, wireless lines always have the code 020, plus a 7-digit number.

Cell phones

Mobile (cell) phones outnumber landlines in Kenya, and most of the country has coverage. The main exception is the far north, but reception can also be patchy in thinly populated rural areas.

Mobile phone services are provided by **Safaricom** (the biggest, on GSM 900 and 1800), **Zain** (the former Celtel, on GSM 900), **Orange/Telkom** (GSM 900) and one or two smaller operators. All Zain and Safaricom numbers begin with a 4-digit code starting 07, followed by a 6-digit number.

Unless your mobile is very old, it is almost certain to work in Kenya, but very high charges make using it on **roaming** unattractive for anything but emergencies.

Instead, you might find it worthwhile to buy a Kenyan **pay-as-you-go SIM card** (around

Ksh200) to temporarily replace your ordinary SIM card. Check with your service provider that your phone is not locked to their network (unlocking, if necessary, can be done anywhere).

Once you have your Kenyan SIM (any phone shop, from the airport onwards, will sell you one and put it in your phone), you can buy **airtime** cards literally anywhere, rubbing a scratch number, which you use to key in the top-up. Most Kenyans top up with Ksh20 or Ksh50, a deeply resented pricing structure that gives them poor rates per minute. Ksh1000 will give you very low-price calls (as low as Ksh3 per minute and Ksh2 per text on the same network) and should last you for a short holiday.

For most short-term visitors to Kenya, it's fairly immaterial whether you choose a Zain, Orange or Safaricom SIM card. They continually outbid each other for value and flexibility. If, however, you're travelling more widely in **East Africa**, you'll find Zain's One Network service handy. It allows you to use the same SIM card throughout Kenya, Tanzania, Uganda and several other countries, while topping up in the local currency.

International calls

To **call Kenya from abroad**, dial your country's international access code followed by 254 for Kenya, then the Kenyan area code or mobile-phone code (omitting the initial 0), and then the number itself.

Kenya, Uganda and Tanzania have a special telephone code agreement, used just between them, which replaces their international access and country codes

with a single 3-digit code, ⊤005 for Kenya, ⊤006 for Uganda and ⊤007 for Tanzania. So, if you're calling Kenya from Uganda or Tanzania, you dial ⊤005, then the Kenya area code (omitting the initial zero), then the number. Note, however, that on mobiles, no matter where you're dialling from, the codes for Kenya, Tanzania and Uganda are the usual, international +254, +255 and +256.

To **call out of Kenya**, the international access code is 000, followed by the country code (see below) followed by the number, omitting any initial 0 (this includes calls to foreign-registered mobiles).

Photography

Kenya is immensely photogenic, and with any kind of camera you'll get beautiful pictures. But if you want good wildlife shots, you'll need a **camera** with an optical magnification of at least 10x on a point-and-shoot camera or 400mm-equivalent on an SLR. Such telephoto capabilities are essential if you want pictures of animals rather than savanna. **Wildlife photography** is largely about timing and patience. While shooting, keep both eyes open. And, in a vehicle, always turn off the engine.

Keep your camera in a dust-proof bag. If it uses a rechargeable **battery**, take a spare – you will always run out of power at the critical moment if you don't. If you intend to email digital pictures home or store them online, note that cybercafés don't always have computers with USB ports, and that uploading can take a very long time. The lack of USB also means you may have difficulty archiving your photos to CD (at least you can buy CDs and DVDs widely), so it pays to take plenty of memory cards with you or a separate storage device.

When **photographing local people** you need to be sensitive and always ask permission first. If you don't accept that some kind of interaction and exchange are warranted, you won't get many pictures. Though most people are tolerant of cameras, the superstition that photos capture part of the soul is still prevalent in some areas, and there can be a special objection to photography of children or animals, whose souls may be considered

---

Australia ⊤000+61

Canada ⊤000+1

Ireland ⊤000+353

Netherlands ⊤000+31

New Zealand ⊤000+64

South Africa ⊤000+27

Tanzania ⊤000+255 (⊤007 from East African landlines)

Uganda ⊤000+256 (⊤006 from East Africa landlines)

UK ⊤000+44

USA ⊤000+1

especially vulnerable. The idea that your photos may show Kenya in a poor light is also common. The Maasai and Samburu, Kenya's most colourful and photographed people, are usually prepared to do a deal (bargain, as you would for any payment), and in some places you'll even find professional posers making a living at the roadside. Other people may be happy to let you take their picture for free, but will certainly appreciate it if you take their name and address, and send a print when you get home.

Note that it's always a bad idea to take pictures of anything that could be construed as strategic, including any military or police building, prisons, airports, harbours, bridges and the president or his entourage.

Place names

Place names in Kenya can be remarkably confusing to outsiders. In some parts, every town or village seems to have a name starting with the same syllable. In the Kenya highlands, you'll find Kiambu, Kikuyu, Kiganjo, Kinangop and so on. Further west you confront Kaptagat, Kapsabet, Kapenguria and Kapsowar. If you find his problematic, just get into the habit of "de-stressing" the first syllable and remembering the second.

A more practical problem all over rural Kenya is the vague use of names to denote a whole district and, at the same time, its nucleus, be it a small town, a village, or just a cluster of corrugated-iron shops and bars. Sometimes there'll be two such focuses. They often move in a matter of a few years, so what looks like a junction town on the map turns out to be away from the road, or in a different place altogether. Ask for the "shopping centre" and you'll usually find the local hive of activity and the place with the name you were looking for. Note that **Makutano**, a very common name, just means "junction".

Time

Kenya's **time zone** is three hours ahead of Greenwich Mean Time (UTC) all year round. It's eight hours ahead of North American Eastern Standard Time, and eleven hours ahead of Pacific Standard Time. Take off an hour from these during summer daylight saving time. Kenya is seven hours behind Sydney and nine behind New Zealand; add an hour to these during summer daylight saving time.

With slight variations across the country and through the year, **sunrise** comes between 6am and 6.40am and **sunset** between 6.10pm and 6.50pm. If you're learning Swahili, remember that "Swahili time" runs from dawn to dusk to dawn rather than midnight to midday to midnight: 7am and 7pm are both called *saa moja* (one o'clock) while midnight and midday are *saa sita* (six o'clock). It's not as confusing as it first sounds – just add or subtract six hours to work out Swahili time (or read the opposite side of your watch).

Tipping and gifts

If you're staying in tourist-class establishments, **tipping** is expected, though ironically, in the cheapest establishments, where employees are likely to be on very low wages, it is not the custom. In expensive hotels, Ksh100 wouldn't be out of place for seeing you to your room with your bags (and £1, $1 or €1 would also be very acceptable). It isn't necessary to tip waiting staff constantly while staying in a hotel. Fortunately, many hotels have a gratuities box in reception, where you can leave a single tip for all the staff – including room staff and backroom staff – when you leave, in which case Ksh500 or Ksh1000 per room per day is about right. In tourist-class restaurants, tips aren't essential, but leaving a tip equivalent to 10 percent of the bill for your waiter would be generous. Note that on safaris, tips are considered very much part of the pay and you're expected to shell out at the end of the trip (see p.67).

As for **gifts**, ballpoint pens and pencils are always worth taking and will be appreciated by children as well as adults. Many visitors take more clothes with them than they intend to return with, leaving T-shirts and other items with hotel staff and others along the way: there's even a website devoted to this concept where your philanthropic instincts can be more precisely honed (ⓦ www.stuffyourrucksack.com). Bear in mind, however, that all this largesse deprives local shops and businesses of your surplus wealth. Assuming you can spare a little, it's always better to make a positive gift of cash to a recognized institution which can go into the local economy while providing local needs in a school, clinic or other organization.

Tourist information

The **Kenya Tourist Board** (KTB Ⓦwww .magicalkenya.com) no longer runs walk-in offices abroad, but has franchised its operations to local PR companies, who are often very helpful. In addition to the addresses below, there are KTB representative offices in Amsterdam, Dusseldorf, Hong Kong, Madrid, Paris, Rome and Stockholm (addresses at Ⓦwww.magicalkenya.com). For further reading and online advice, see p.606.

UK Kenya Tourist Board
c/o Hills Balfour, Colechurch House
1, London Bridge Walk, London SEI 2SX
☎020/7367 0900, ✉kenya@hillsbalfoursynergy .com

US & Canada Kenya Tourist Board
c/o Carlson Destination Marketing Services,
6442 City West Parkway, Minneapolis, MN 55344
☎1-866/44-KENYA, ✉infousa@magicalkenya.com

Travelling with children

Wherever you go, local people will be welcoming to your **children**, and only in exceptional cases are under-7s barred from certain lodges (the tree-hotels, for example). Babies, if they're easy-going, can be relatively straightforward, but taking young children to Kenya can be quite a hassle. If they're not old enough to be enchanted by the wildlife and environment, you may find the overall adventure isn't enough reward for journeys that can be long and tiring.

Health issues figure most prominently in most people's minds but you can largely discount fears about your children getting a tropical disease in Kenya (remember how many healthy expatriate children have been brought up there: the biggest health problem for Kenyan children is poverty). It can, however, be very difficult to persuade small children to take **malaria pills**. Be sure to cover them carefully with a Deet-based mosquito repellent early each evening and ensure they sleep under secure nets. Every

morning, thoroughly smother them in factor 40 sunscreen, insist they wear hats, and make sure they get plenty of fluids. For more on malaria and other health issues, see p.69.

In terms of what to bring, while disposable **nappies/diapers** are available, they're quite expensive, so bring your own supply. **Baby foods** are also available, but hotel kitchens usually have a good variety of fresh food and, given some warning, staff will happily prepare it to infants' tastes. If you have a light, easily collapsible **buggy**, bring it. Many hotels and lodges have long paths from the central public areas to the rooms or cottages. A **child-carrier** backpack is another very useful accessory. Unless you're exclusively staying on the coast, bring some **warm clothing** for upcountry mornings and evenings, when temperatures can drop quite low. If the children are old enough to enjoy spotting animals, make sure they have their own **binoculars**.

For a young family, going on a group **safari** with other travellers (whether organized from home as part of a package or booked in Kenya) is probably inadvisable. Renting a vehicle and driving yourself, or taking a driver, is quite feasible, however, and gives you the flexibility and privacy you need for toilet stops and other interruptions. For babies and young children you'll need a car seat, which, if you have the right model, also works as an all-purpose carrier, poolside recliner and picnic throne.

Some **parks** are more child-friendly than others. At Nairobi and Lake Nakuru distances are small and the animals close, and Amboseli is usually a hit, too, for its manageable size and large numbers of elephants.

Most tourist hotels and lodges can organize a **babysitter**, given a few hours' notice, which should cost around Ksh500 for an evening. In safari camps and lodges, you can speak to the restaurant manager and arrange for an *askari* (night watchman) to sit outside while you're having dinner.

Travellers with disabilities

Although by no means easy, Kenya does not pose insurmountable problems for **people with disabilities**. While there is little

Things to take

- **Binoculars** for each member of your party
- **Cotton clothes** (loose and few), plus a warm, light, jacket or fleece
- **GPS** (basic handheld version), immensely useful in the bush
- **Multipurpose penknife** (be sure to put it in your checked luggage)
- **Sheet sleeping bag**, essential in the very cheapest accommodation.
- **Torch** (flashlight), ideally a wind-up one.
- **Water shoes** (easy to swim in) to protect your feet.

government support for improving access, travel industry staff and passers-by are usually prepared to help whenever necessary. For wheelchair-users and those who find stairs hard to manage, many hotels have ground-floor rooms, a number on the coast have ramped access, walks and larger hotels in Nairobi have elevators. While the vast majority of hotels, lodges and tented camps have at least some rooms that are ramped or with only or two steps, most only one have showers. The majority of safari vehicles, too, are not ideal for people with impaired mobility. **Off-road trips** can be very arduous and you should take a pressure cushion for game drives.

If you're flying from the UK, you can avoid a change of plane by going with BA, Virgin Atlantic or Kenya Airways direct from London to Nairobi. All charter flights are direct (if not always non-stop, at least you won't need to change) but they only go to Mombasa.

If you're looking for a **tour**, contact the disabled and special needs travel specialists Go Africa in Diani Beach (Ⓦwww.go-africa-safaris.com) and the highly recommended Mombasa-based Southern Cross (see p.406; Ⓦwww.southerncrosssafaris.com) who are one of the few mainstream companies to offer special safaris for people with mobility impairments.

Work and volunteering

Unless you have lined up a job or voluntary work before arriving in Kenya, you have little chance of getting **employment**. Wages are extremely low – for school teachers, for example, they start at the equivalent of less than $200 per month, while hotel staff wages can be less than half that – and

there is serious unemployment in the towns. Particular skills are sometimes in demand but the employer will need to arrange the necessary papers. It's illegal to obtain income in Kenya while staying on a visitor's pass.

An international **work camp** is no holiday, and conditions are usually primitive, but it can be a lot of fun, too, and is undoubtedly worthwhile. One group to contact is the Kenya Voluntary Development Association (Ⓦwww.geocities.com /kvdaonline), a locally inspired organization bringing Kenyans and foreigners together in a number of locations across the country, digging irrigation trenches, making roads, building schools, or just producing as many mud bricks as possible. The minimum age is 18 and there's no formal upper age limit, but volunteers older than 25 are unusual. The groups are very mixed in terms of nationality. The programmes, which include basic accommodation, meals and transport in Kenya, start at €250 for two weeks, and go up to €450 for six weeks.

Other groups employing volunteers in community projects are Volunteer Kenya (Ⓦwww.volunteerkenya.org), whose main focus is on AIDS awareness, education and women's income generation, and Kenya Voluntary Community Development Project (Ⓦwww.kvcdp.org), which works in a variety of fields. Both organizations have quite local bases in western Kenya and the fees for a month range from approximately $600–1200.

An alternative would be to compromise and take a **working holiday** with a commercial organization. One of the better companies is Camp Kenya (see p.32).

Guide

Guide

www.roughguides.com

Nairobi and around

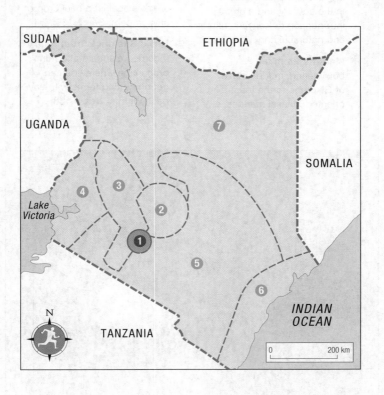

CHAPTER 1 # Highlights

* **Kibera** Take away some added awareness and leave a little extra cash behind on a tour of Kenya's biggest slum district – a sobering but not a depressing experience. See p.109

* **National Museum** By far the biggest and best museum in the country and a great introduction to Kenyan culture and natural history. See p.112

* **Markets** From the bewildering, muddy maze of Gikomba to the tourist oriented Maasai markets, these are excellent places to sample a slice of Nairobi life, eat street food or pick up souvenirs. See p.126

* **Nairobi National Park** On Nairobi's doorstep, the park is home to most of Kenya's big mammals, and is the location for classic photos of plains animals against a backdrop of skyscrapers. See p.136

* **David Sheldrick Trust** Highly regarded elephant and rhino orphanage where you can get on petting terms with tiny pachyderms. See p.138

▲ David Sheldrick Trust

Nairobi and around

Easily the largest city in East Africa, NAIROBI is also the youngest, the most modern, the fastest growing, the largest and, at 1700m, the highest. The superlatives could go on forever. "Green City in the Sun", runs one tour-brochure sobriquet, "City of Flowers" another. Less enchanted visitors growl "Nairobbery". The city catches your attention, at least: this is no tropical backwater. Most roads, particularly paved ones, lead to Nairobi and, like it or not, you're almost bound to spend some time here. And yet, strolling around the malls in Westlands or negotiating Kenyatta Avenue at rush hour, it's perhaps easy to forget how quickly you can leave the city and be in the bush.

Apart from being the safari capital of the world, Nairobi is an excellent base for Kenyan travel in general. To the coast, it's as little as six hours by road or an overnight train journey. It takes about the same time to get to the far west and barely two hours to get to the great trough of the Rift Valley or the slopes of Mount Kenya. An excellent day-trip, literally on the city's doorstep, is Nairobi National Park, a wild attraction where you'd expect to find suburbs.

Nairobi

NAIROBI is one of Africa's major cities: the UN's fourth "World Centre", East Africa's commercial, media and NGO hub, and a significant capital in its own right, with a population of between a million and a half and three million, depending on how big an area you include. As a traveller, your first impressions are likely to depend on how – and where – you arrive. If you've come here overland, some time resting up in comfort can seem an appealing proposition. Newly arrived by air from Europe, though, you may wonder – amid the rash of roadside ads persuading you to upgrade your mobile-phone package or catch the latest TV offering – just how far you've travelled. Nairobi, little more than a century old, has real claims to Western-style sophistication but, as you'll soon find, it lacks a convincing heart. Apart from some lively musical attractions – some of East Africa's busiest clubs and best bands – there's little here of magnetic appeal, and most travellers stay long enough only to take stock, make some travel arrangements and maybe visit the National Museum, before moving on.

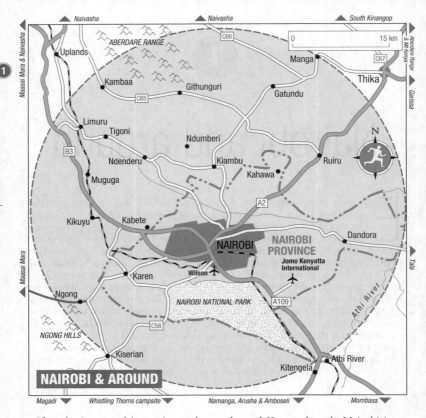

If you're interested in getting to know the real Kenya, though, Nairobi is as compelling a place as any and displays enormous vitality and buzz. The controlling ethos is commerce rather than community, and there's an almost wilful superficiality in the free-for-all of commuters, shoppers, police, hustlers and tourists. It's hard to imagine a city with a more fascinating variety of people, mostly immigrants from the rural areas, drawn to the presence of wealth. On the surface the city accepts everyone with tolerance, and, in any downtown street, you can see a complete cross section of Kenyans, every variety of tourist, and migrants and refugees from many African countries.

Nairobi's rapid growth, however, inevitably has a downside. Read any newspaper or talk to a resident and you'll hear jaw-dropping stories of crime and police shootings. Although the city has become safer in recent years, you should certainly be aware of its reputation for **bag-snatching and robbery**, frequently directed at new tourist arrivals (see the box on security on p.94). If you plan to stay in Nairobi for any length of time, you'll soon get the hang of balancing reasonable caution with a fairly relaxed attitude: thousands of visitors do it every year. If you're only here for a few days, you're likely to find it a stimulating city.

Some history

Nairobi came into being in May 1899, an artificial settlement created by Europeans at Mile 327 of the East African railway line, then being systematically forged from Mombasa on the coast to Kampala, now the capital of Uganda. It was initially a supply depot, switching yard and campsite for the thousands of Indian labourers employed by the British. The bleak, swampy site was simply the spot where operations came to a halt while the engineers figured out their next move – getting the line up the steep slopes that lay ahead. The name came from the local Maasai word for the area, *enkare nyarobi*, "the place of cold water", though the spot itself was originally called *Nakusontelon*, "Beginning of all Beauty".

Surprisingly, the unplanned settlement took root. A few years later it was totally rebuilt after an outbreak of plague and the burning of the original town compound. By 1907, it was so firmly established that the colonists took it as the capital of the newly formed "British East Africa" (BEA). Europeans, encouraged by the authorities, settled in large numbers, while Africans were forced into employment by tax demands (without representation) or onto specially created **reserves** – the Maasai to the Southern Reserve and the Kikuyu to their own reserve in the highlands.

The capital, lacking development from any established community, was somewhat characterless – and remains so. The **original centre** retains an Asian influence in its older buildings, but today it's shot through with glassy, high-rise blocks. Surrounding the core of the old **Central Business District** is a vast area of suburbs: wealthiest in the west and north, increasingly poor to the south and east.

The names of these **suburbs** – Karen, Parklands, Eastleigh, Spring Valley, Kibera, among many others – reflect the jumble of African, Asian and European elements in Nairobi's original population, none of whom was local. The term "Nairobian" is a new one that still applies mostly to the younger generation. Although it has a predominance of Kikuyu, the city is not the preserve of a single ethnic group, standing as it does at the meeting point of Maasai, Kikuyu and Kamba territories. Its choice as capital, accidental though it may have been (the Kikuyu town of Limuru and the Kamba capital, Machakos, were also considered), was a fortunate one for the future of the country.

Since the 1990s, the Central Business District has seen the steady flight of businesses into the suburbs, particularly to **Upper Hill** and the surrounding districts to the west of the CBD, to the booming satellite city of **Westlands**, just a couple of kilometres to the northwest, and out along the **Mombasa road** to the south.

Orientation and arrival

Nairobi has widespread suburbs but the **Central Business District** is relatively small: a triangle of stores, offices and public buildings, with the railway station on the southern flank and the main bus stations to the east. The triangle of central Nairobi divides into three principal districts bisected by the main thoroughfares of **Kenyatta Avenue** and **Moi Avenue**. The grandest and most formal part of the CBD is the area around **City Square**, in the southwest. This square kilometre is Nairobi's heart: government buildings, banks and offices merge to the north and east with upmarket shopping streets and major hotels. The area's big landmarks are the **Kenyatta International Conference Centre**, with its huge cylindrical tower and artichoke-shaped conference centre, the blue-glass skyscraper of **Lonrho House**, and the bizarre zebra-striped "legs" of the **Nation Centre**, all visible from miles outside the city. To the south of this area, towards the train station, stands the **Memorial Park** on the site of the bombed US Embassy.

Security

Nairobi isn't nearly as bad as its **"Nairobbery"** reputation would suggest. The city has cleaned up considerably over the past few years: the city centre is less chaotic, there are fewer street children, beggars and touts, and a dedicated tourist police force patrols the streets. That said, it pays to take some precautions against crime. It helps to memorize any route you're walking, as lost-looking tourists are easiest targets. Keep your hands out of reach and be – rationally – suspicious of everyone until you've caught your breath. It doesn't take long to get a little street-wise. Every rural Kenyan coming to the city for the first time goes through exactly the same process, and many are considerably greener than you, having never been in a city before.

Most areas of the city are fine in daylight, but be extra vigilant if you're walking at night within the city centre and don't wander outside the CBD unless you're really clued-in. Be especially wary in the following parts of the city, where tourist pickings are fairly rich. The **River Road district**, which in practical terms means anything east of Moi Avenue, and indeed sometimes including the avenue, has become something of a **no-go area for tourists** at night. Even locals avoid walking there and taxi drivers are quite often reluctant to venture into certain parts of the district. **Uhuru Highway** plus **Uhuru** and **Central parks** are fine during the day but prime muggers' territory at night, with occasional shootings. At night, the stretch of Valley Road between the *Serena Hotel* and *Nairobi Youth Hostel* is unsafe, and the area near the **Museum** and **Casino** is considered to be downright dangerous – again, at night.

All the main **bus** and **matatu stations** are somewhat chaotic and ideal for pickpockets and snatch-and-run robberies; it's best not to accept food, drinks, sweets or cigarettes from strangers, as doping goes through phases as a popular tactic. If you're **driving**, keeping your windows rolled up is a good idea, especially at traffic lights.

North of Kenyatta Avenue, there's a shift to smaller scale and lesser finance. The **City Market** is here, surrounded by a denser district of shops, restaurants and hotels. The modest-sized **Jeevanjee Gardens** are a welcome patch of greenery, and a little further north is the university district and Nairobi's oldest establishment, the Norfolk Hotel, contemporary with the original rebuilding of the city.

East of Moi Avenue, the character changes more radically. Here, and down towards the reeking Nairobi River, is the relatively poor, inner-city district identified with **River Road**, its main thoroughfare. The River Road quarter is where most long-distance buses and matatus start and terminate, and where you'll find the capital's cheapest restaurants and hotels, as well as the highest concentration of African-owned businesses. It's also a somewhat notorious area, with a traditional concentration of sharks and pickpockets (see the "Security" box above). You can meet European residents who work five minutes' walk away and in all their years in Nairobi have never been to this part of town.

Getting around Nairobi has been a headache for decades: the lack of transport planning and the absence of any light rail transport means **traffic jams** for four or five hours on weekday mornings and evenings, and serious delays in getting from one suburb to another, except late at night and before dawn.

International arrivals & departures: JKI Airport (NBO)

International flights and domestic **Kenya Airways** services use Jomo Kenyatta International Airport (☎020/822111 or 020/822206 or 020/661200, ⓦwww.kenyaairports.co.ke) – commonly abbreviated to JKA or JKIA – 15km southeast of the CBD, off the Mombasa highway.

JKIA **arrivals** are normally straightforward. There's normally a cursory customs check, where you may be asked what you're bringing into the country, but obvious tourists are usually waved through. If at any stage someone asks you for a **bribe**, or "a little something", refuse politely.

In the arrivals hall, there are branches of Barclay's and Standard Chartered **banks** (open to meet most planes, if not 24/7) with ATMs, and one or two other bank exchange desks and forex bureaux. Count the notes carefully if you're exchanging money. The airport has **mobile phone shops** and an office of the **Flying Doctors** organization (see p.71). There's little choice in terms of food and drink: the always busy branch of *Java House* coffee shop near Gate 14 is most people's retreat.

If your plane arrives **late at night**, and you're not booked into a hotel, it's best to wait until morning to go into the city. If you have a long layover you may want to use either the air-conditioned **First/Business Class lounge** near Gate 10, which gives you a comfy sofa to curl up on, papers and TV, and unlimited snacks and drinks ($20) or investigate the basic but clean **sleep–and–shower** facility down the steps at the end of the same corridor ($40 per person for up to eight hours). If you need to store bags, the domestic terminal has a left luggage store (Ksh300 per bag).

Airport taxis
Once you're out of the arrivals hall, a horde of **private taxi** touts invariably assails new arrivals. Ignore them and walk straight to the waiting cabs lined up outside, or else to the Kenatco office. If you'd prefer to be met, contact a travel agent like Let's Go Travel (p.129) who will organize a cab. There's an official fixed price to the city centre, currently around Ksh1500, depending on which hotel you want to go to. Taxis don't have meters, so always agree the exact price before getting in.

Airport buses
There is no public airport shuttle, but some hotels will pick you up if you make prior arrangements. The local Citi Hoppa **bus #34** leaves from outside the arrivals hall roughly every twenty minutes (daily 6am–9pm; Ksh50), entering the city through the eastern suburbs (rather than running straight up Uhuru Highway) and stopping in Accra Road/*Ambassadeur Hotel*. People have been robbed on this bus, so be on your guard.

Domestic arrivals & departures: Wilson Airport (WIL)
If you fly into Nairobi on a domestic flight, you'll probably arrive at **Wilson Airport** (☎020/501941), 5km from the city centre between the CBD and the National Park. It's a small facility, right by Langata Road, and there are always taxis awaiting passengers. You can also get into town by bus. Getting out to Wilson for a flight, taxis from the CBD cost around Ksh800–1000, or use a bus or matatu #15, #24, #31, #34, #125 or #126, alighting at the petrol station on your left.

Arrivals and departures by train
The **railway station** is virtually in the city centre, with one of Nairobi's biggest matatu stages right in front. Arriving on the train, you can just walk straight out through the station concourse and follow Moi Avenue into town. Watch out for taxi drivers and porters who will more or less kidnap your luggage if you don't prevent them. Otherwise, the main attention you'll attract is from **safari touts**, who are persistent, but friendly enough, and

useful if you need an escort to one of the cheaper River Road addresses. A small tip agreed between you (say Ksh100) would be appreciated. There is a **left luggage** facility at the station (Ksh80 per bag).

If you're planning to take the train from Nairobi, it's important to make **reservations**, especially if you want a first-class compartment. While you may get away with leaving this until a couple of hours before departure, it's always advisable to reserve well in advance, especially during busy travel periods like Christmas and New Year. It's best, and cheapest, to buy tickets in person at the station (T020/221211 or 0728/787301), but agents will also obtain tickets for you (see p.128).

Arrivals and departures by bus and matatu

Most **bus companies** have their booking offices or parking areas in the River Road district, and many of the matatu stages are here, too. On the way into town, you can ask to be dropped off anywhere along the route. Suburban matatu services using Thika Road all arrive at and depart from the Globe roundabout.

All the bus terminals are marked on the "Central Business District and River Road Area" map on p.100. The smaller companies operate out of the **Country Bus Station** (aka "Machakos Airport"), 1.5km east of the city centre just past Wakulima market, between Pumwani Road and Landhies Road (buses #4, #18 or #28 from the *Ambassadeur*). Always try to reserve tickets in advance. As the most useful services often leave at night, take a taxi to the bus station or hire an *askari* from your hotel rather than walk unaccompanied with your luggage. Bus company contact details are given in "Listings", p.131.

Information and city transport

Nairobi has no official **tourist information** service, but the *Standard* and *Nation* newspapers are useful sources of current information and special offers, and the free and widely circulated monthly *Go Places* (from most hotels; W www.goplaceskenya.com) is always worth a glance. If you need a detailed **map** of the city, buy the Nairobi *A–Z*, available from bookshops. The city has now been comprehensively Google-mapped, so if you're prepared to put up with roaming charges or you've got a Safaricom SIM card (you'll need to get their internet settings), your **GPS-enabled 3G mobile phone** will be able to guide you around. Beware of displaying expensive gadgets on street corners.

Getting around the CBD is so straightforward you won't need much assistance. By day, you'll probably want to walk; by night, you'll want to take a taxi. If you're on any kind of budget, though, it's certainly worth getting to know what passes for the city's public transport system: and look out for the new **bus and matatu map** published by Kenya Buzz (W www.kenyabuzz .com).

Taxis

By Kenyan standards, Nairobi's **taxis** – the registered ones all bear a yellow stripe – are expensive. Grey, **London-style** taxi cabs, operated by the Kenya

Driving in Nairobi

Avoid **driving** in or through the city if you can. The congestion has to be seen to be believed, and your average speed can be as little as 3kph. Commuting has become nightmarish and many city workers spend four hours a day behind the wheel. The driving itself can be a nerve-wracking experience, too, though you do get used to it. Watch out for matatus, which lurch into the fray as suddenly as they stop to pick up fares. And beware of roundabouts (traffic circles). These labour under "priority traffic" regulations, which in theory means cars already on the roundabout have priority, but in practice means chaos as nobody is prepared to give way. Try to stay in lane.

If you're **hiring a car**, if possible, pick it up at the airport, or have it delivered there, which gives you time to get used to the vehicle and the traffic before joining the city-centre madness. For general driving advice, see p.41.

Parking in the CBD can be difficult during business hours, though there's usually space at the Loita Street Car Park, next to Barclays Plaza (Ksh150 per day) or at the Kenyatta International Conference Centre (entrance off City Hall Way). If you park on the street, assuming you can find a legal space, you'll need to buy a daily parking ticket from one of the city's many, uniformed parking wardens (Ksh150 for 24hr; 8am–8pm).

Driving out of Nairobi, allow plenty of time to get clear of the city traffic. Nairobi has no ring road or bypass – all vehicles, including trans-continental trucks, go through the city centre. If you make an early start from Westlands or Karen, for example, bound for the coast or Mount Kenya, you are likely to be bumper to bumper for more than an hour before you really get going.

Taxi Cabs Association (℡0722/464675), crowd around key spots in the city and have fixed prices, with the current bottom-line fare for any trip in the city centre well known by all (the cheapest ride is currently around Ksh300, with Ngong Road to the CBD costing Ksh500). Another reliable company is Kenatco, who have a 24-hour office at Uchumi House on Aga Khan Walk (℡020/2225123 or 020/316611), and a branch at the airport (℡020/827283). If you're prepared to chance a ride with one of the private (sometimes astonishingly battered) cabs, you'll find them angling for business in a number of spots around town, including along Mama Ngina Street, on Kimathi Street outside the *Oakwood Hotel*, and at the junction of Standard and Muindi Mbingu streets, by the *680 Hotel*. Motorized rickshaws, or tuk-tuks, imported from Asia, are also available. They cost a little less than regular taxis, though you should bargain hard.

Buses and matatus

Buses and matatus save you money on getting around, certainly for longer trips out of the city centre, but take some figuring out. The green Citi Hoppa buses which roar around Nairobi all day are cheap (Ksh10–40; pay the conductor) and very unpredictable. The buses are numbered, but bus stops aren't and routes change frequently. Nairobi's **matatus** – which, like the city's taxis, must bear a yellow stripe – tend to take the same routes as buses and often display the same route numbers. They're generally faster, more dangerous and even more packed, though serious accidents rarely happen in the city. Matatu parks (also known as stages or stands) are scattered throughout the River Road district.

Accommodation

Finding **accommodation** in Nairobi isn't difficult. The main question is which area fits your needs. Travellers end up congregating at a number of different spots and many visitors never even set foot in the Central Business District. If you're arriving in town very early, be aware that most places won't allow you to take a room before 10am.

If you're travelling by rented car and concerned about safe parking, don't panic – the city council and most hotels employ *askaris* (security guards), who can be persuaded to add to their workload for a modest tip. Most top-of-the-range places have guarded or enclosed parking anyway. Naturally, leave nothing of value in, or attached to, the vehicle.

Near Jomo Kenyatta International Airport

The pickings **close to the airport** are a bit thin, and there's nowhere at the budget level, but the following hotels are very convenient if you're travelling early or late as they are clear of the city centre traffic. Depending on your needs, you might want to stay for a few hours in the basic rooms at the airport itself (see p.95).

Panari Panari Sky Center, Mombasa Rd ☎020/3946000 or 0725/694600, ⊛www .panarihotels.com. Beyond the gaudy exterior, the pricey rooms here, less than 10km (and 10min) from JKIA, are modern and surprisingly well appointed. The bottom three floors include a shopping mall, skating rink (the only one in East Africa) and a gym with an indoor pool. The upper floors offer great views of Nairobi National Park across the road. ❽

Redcourt Kenya Red Cross Complex, Red Cross Rd, off Mombasa Rd, Belle Vue ☎020/604528 or 0728/606476, ⊛www.redcourt.co.ke. A new hotel 12km from the airport, wholly owned by the Kenya Red Cross. The standard rooms are on the small side, but stylish enough, and include nternet access and DSTV. There's a gym with a sauna, and a garden at the front with a fish pond. BB ❼

River Road area

The very cheapest lodgings are around **River Road**, the main drag through the city centre's poorest quarter – although in recent years, a number of more expensive hotels have been built here. Despite the constant worry about safety, River Road is the city's most stimulating and animated area, and offers a plunge into a world which would pass you by if you stayed in the CBD or out in the suburbs.

The cheapest places often have rowdy bars and clubs attached to them; their rooms aren't terribly clean or secure and they're not recommended for solo females. If you want a modicum of hygiene and self-contained facilities, you're looking at Ksh1500-plus for a double room. All the establishments below are shown on the "Central Business District and River Road Area" map, p.100.

Inexpensive

Abbey Gaberone Rd ☎020/2243256 or 020/241562. A noisy, boozy place, rather pricey for what it offers, but the rooms have nets, TVs and are mostly clean and fresh, with tiled bathrooms and hot showers. Unlovely but adequate. ❷

Africana Dubois Rd; ☎020/2220654. Lino-floored s/c rooms with hot water. The single beds are tiny.

Only really recommended if you want to be near the Latema Rd area. ❶

Destiny Duruma Rd ☎020/2228450. This four-storey block offers good value and is conscientiously run, with airy, s/c rooms and hot showers. There's a payphone in the corridor and a laundry service, but only single rooms are available. ❶

Eureka Highrise Tom Mboya St ☎020/2247459. Three floors up, with large s/c rooms, each with a desk and hot shower. Security is good, and there's a pub/restaurant. **②**

Evamay Lodge River Rd at the junction with Duruma Rd ☎020/2216218. Very good value for the price, the s/c rooms have phones, TVs and mosquito nets, and the whole place has good security. **②**

🏃 **Mercury** Tom Mboya St ☎020/2212504. Comfortable, carpeted rooms with perks like small dining tables and chairs and free mineral water. Doubles have bathtubs. There's also quite a nice courtyard restaurant with a bizarre miniature rockery in the corner, and a *nyama choma* bar. A cut above others in its class. **②**

Mid-View Central Latema Rd ☎020/2223351. One of the newer and better options in the River Road district, this large hotel has spotless, spacious s/c rooms. Room only **②**

Nawas Nawas Building, corner of Latema Rd & River Rd ☎020/243148. Small rooms with hot water, and a good, friendly restaurant on the first floor. **②**

New Kenya Lodge River Rd at the top of Latema Rd ☎020/2222202 or 020/2248225, ⓦwww.nksafari.com. A long-established backpackers' haunt, with a popular communal area and a book exchange. There's a second branch a stone's throw away. They organize reasonable camping safaris from around $100 per day. Dorms Ksh450. **①**

New Swanga Lodge corner of Duruma Rd and Accra Rd ☎020/213777 or 020/213827. The rooms here, though not large, are comfortable, s/c, have telephones and nets, and are securely bolted away behind spectacular, time-consuming, triple locks. Good-value, though hardly quiet. **①**

Princess Tom Mboya St ☎020/2214640. Very busy establishment, with a restaurant and bar. The rooms are rather cramped but have good showers. Basic but adequate, and it fills up quickly so they must be getting it mostly right. **②**

Samagat Park House, Taveta Rd ☎020/2220604. A former apartment block, this has spacious s/c rooms, the upper ones with views of the CBD's high-rises. There's a ninth-floor dining room and TV lounge. **②**

Sirikwa Lodge Munyu Rd, on the corner of Accra Rd ☎020/2226687. Reasonable s/c rooms above a *miraa* shop, with 24-hour hot water, ideally located for enjoying the chaos of the Accra Road matatu stands. **①**

Moderate

Arkland Palace Interfina House, corner of Ronald Ngala and Tom Mboya sts ☎020/2142600, ⓦwww.arklandpalace.com. Above a shopping centre, this large hotel has s/c rooms with TVs. None of the rooms have a/c, however, which you might expect at this price, and a big drawback is the excruciating noise, into the early hours, from the bar below. BB **③**

Marble Arch Lagos Rd ☎020/2240940 or 020/2245656, ⓦwww.marblearchhotel @kenyaweb.com. While the polished fake marble, brass fixtures and tacky fountains of the public areas are encouragingly not in keeping with the area's generally slummy accommodation, the rooms turn out to be a disappointment at this price, with grubby tiled floors and seriously uncomfortable beds. They have large bathtubs however, and there's secure parking. BB **⑤**

Meridian Court Murang'a Rd ☎0733/502747 or 020/313991, ⓦwww.meridian@bidii.com. Grimly hemmed in by traffic on all sides, the rooms here have baths, safes, DSTV and in most cases separate living rooms. These facilities don't compensate for the generally shabby state of the hotel, though amenities do include a rooftop pool, bar, sauna, 24hour room service, and a pretty good Indian restaurant, the *Khyber* (see p.117). Underground parking. BB **⑤**

Sandton Palace Taveta Rd ☎020/342104, ⓦwww.sandtonhotels.co.ke. One of the best-appointed hotels in the district, although rather overpriced. All 106 rooms have TV (with in-house video), direct-dial phone and, fortunately, ceiling fans (no a/c), which help to dispel some of the aromas wafting up from the *Little India* restaurant on the ground floor. Similarly appointed and priced sister hotel *Sandton City* is on Duruma Road. BB **⑤**

Central Business District and further west

The following listings cover the more moneyed parts of the city centre, roughly north as far as the museum and west as far as Central and Uhuru parks. There are also several inexpensive places on the west side of Moi Avenue up near Jeevanjee Gardens and City Market. Most of the places reviewed appear on the "Central Business District and River Road Area" map, though some are shown on the "West Nairobi" (p.104) or "Greater Nairobi" maps (p.134).

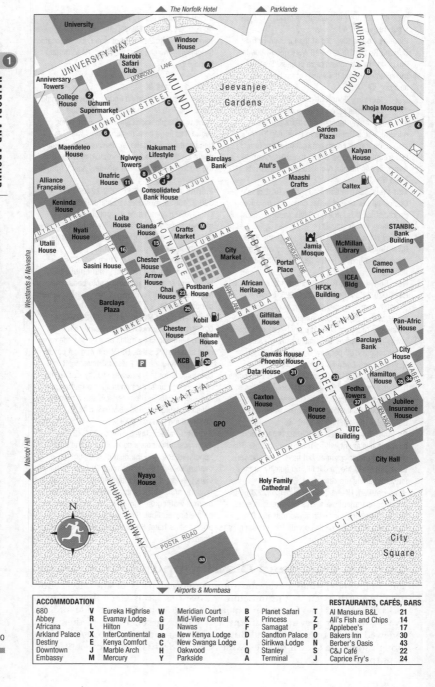

The Norfolk Hotel ▲   ▲ Parklands

University

MURANG'A ROAD

Windsor House

UNIVERSITY WAY

Nairobi Safari Club

MONROVIA

LANE

Anniversary Towers

College House

MUINDI

Ⓐ

Jeevanjee Gardens

RIVER

Uchumi Supermarket ❷

MONROVIA STREET

Ⓒ

STREET

Khoja Mosque

Ⓑ

❻

❸

DADDAH

Garden Plaza

Maendeleo House

Nakumatt Lifestyle

❼

LANE

Kalyan House

KIMATHI

Ngiwyo Towers

MOKTAR

Barclays Bank

Atul's

BIASHARA STREET

Unafric House

❽ ❾

Maashi Crafts

Alliance Française

❶❶

Consolidated Bank House

NJUGU

ROAD

Caltex

Keninda House

KIGALI ROAD

STANBIC Bank Building

UTALII STREET

Loita House

Cianda House

KOINANGE

TUBMAN

Crafts Market

Ⓜ

Jamia Mosque

McMillan Library

Cameo Cinema

Nyati House

❶❻

❶❺

City Market

MBINGU

Utalii House

Chester House

Portal Place

ICEA Bldg

Sasini House

Arrow House

STREET

African Heritage

HFCK Building

Chai House ❷❸

Postbank House

MARKET LANE

Barclays Plaza

MARKET

STREET

❷❺

Kobil

BANDA

Gilfillan House

AVENUE

Pan-Afric House

Chester House

Rehani House

Barclays Bank

City House

KCB

BP

❸❶

Canvas House/Phoenix House

STREET

Hamilton House

❸❺ ❸❹

P

Data House

Ⓥ

❸❸

STANDARD

Fedha Towers ❸❼

Jubilee Insurance House

KENYATTA

Caxton House

Bruce House

KAUNDA

UTC Building

GPO

KAUNDA STREET

Nyayo House

Holy Family Cathedral

City Hall

UHURU HIGHWAY

POSTA ROAD

N

CITY

HALL

City Square

aa

Westlands & Naivasha ▲

Nairobi Hill ▲

Airports & Mombasa ▼

ACCOMMODATION								RESTAURANTS, CAFÉS, BARS	
680	V	Eureka Highrise	W	Meridian Court	B	Planet Safari	T	Al Mansura B&L	21
Abbey	R	Evamay Lodge	G	Mid-View Central	K	Princess	Z	Ali's Fish and Chips	14
Africana	L	Hilton	U	Nawas	F	Samagat	P	Applebee's	17
Arkland Palace	X	InterContinental	aa	New Kenya Lodge	D	Sandton Palace	O	Bakers Inn	30
Destiny	E	Kenya Comfort	C	New Swanga Lodge	I	Sirikwa Lodge	N	Berber's Oasis	43
Downtown	J	Marble Arch	H	Oakwood	Y	Stanley	S	C&J Café	22
Embassy	M	Mercury	Y	Parkside	A	Terminal	J	Caprice Fry's	24

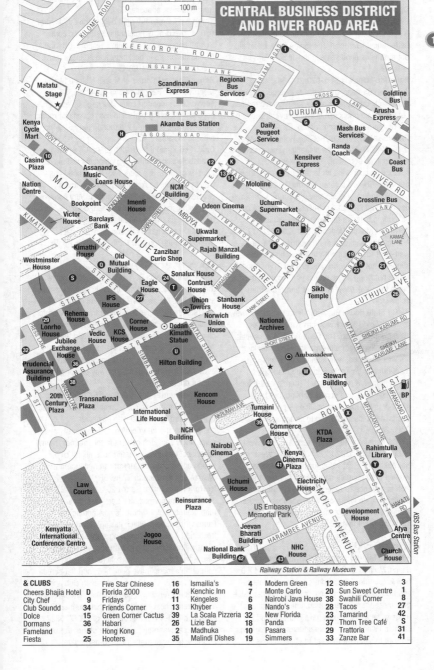

CENTRAL BUSINESS DISTRICT AND RIVER ROAD AREA

Matatu Stage

Kenya Cycle Mart

Casino Plaza

Nation Centre

Assanand's Music
Loans House

Bookpoint

Victor House

Barclays Bank

Imenti House

NCM Building

Scandinavian Express

Regional Bus Services

Goldline Bus

Arusha Express

Mash Bus Services

Randa Coach

Coast Bus

Crossline Bus

Akamba Bus Station

Daily Peugeot Service

Kensilver Express

Mololine

Odeon Cinema

Uchumi Supermarket

Caltex

Ukwala Supermarket

Rajab Manzal Building

Westminster House

Kimathi House

Old Mutual Building

Zanzibar Curio Shop

Sonalux House

Eagle House

Contrust House

Union Towers

Stanbank House

Sikh Temple

Crossline Bus

IPS House

Rehema House

Lonrho House

Jubilee Exchange House

Vedic House

KCS House

Corner House

Dedan Kimathi Statue

Norwich Union House

National Archives

Ambassadeur

Prudencial Assurance Building

20th Century Plaza

Transnational Plaza

Hilton Building

Stewart Building

International Life House

Kencom House

Tumaini House

Commerce House

KTDA Plaza

Rahimtulla Library

NCH Building

Nairobi Cinema

Kenya Cinema Plaza

Electricity House

Law Courts

Uchumi House

Reinsurance Plaza

US Embassy Memorial Park

Development House

Afya Centre

Kenyatta International Conference Centre

Jogoo House

Jeevan Bharati Building

National Bank Building

NHC House

Church House

Railway Station & Railway Museum

KBS Bus Station

BP

& CLUBS							
Cheers Bhajia Hotel	D	Five Star Chinese	16	Ismailia's	4	Modern Green	12	Steers	3
City Chef	9	Florida 2000	40	Kenchic Inn	7	Monte Carlo	20	Sun Sweet Centre	1
Club Soundd	34	Fridays	11	Kengeles	6	Nairobi Java House	38	Swahili Corner	8
Dolce	15	Friends Corner	13	Khyber	B	Nando's	28	Tacos	27
Dormans	36	Green Corner Cactus	39	La Scala Pizzeria	32	New Florida	23	Tamarind	42
Fameland	5	Habari	26	Lizie Bar	18	Panda	2	Thorn Tree Café	S
Fiesta	25	Hong Kong	2	Madhuka	10	Pasara	29	Trattoria	31
		Hooters	35	Malindi Dishes	19	Simmers	33	Zanze Bar	41

Inexpensive

Downtown Moktar Daddah St ☏0721/417832 or 0738/787787, ✉downtownhotel2000@yahoo.com. A clean and quiet alternative to its neighbour, the better-known *Terminal*. The rooms are a bit small, but it remains good value in the Jeevanjee Gardens area. ❷

Parkside Monrovia St ☏020/214154. Facing Jeevanjee Gardens, the *Parkside* is large, secure, reasonably quiet and has airy, pleasant s/c rooms, hot water and phones. It is slightly overpriced and the restaurant is nothing special. ❷

Planet Safari 9th floor, Sonalux House, Moi Ave ☏020/2229799, ⓦwww.planetkenyasafaris.com. Very popular, dorm-only, backpacker place, reached by taking the lift to the eighth floor, then the stairs. There's a safari booking office for its captive market (you can stay free for up to three days if you do a trip). Security is fine, despite some off-putting hangers-on. Dorm beds Ksh500.

Terminal Moktar Daddah St ☏020/2228817. A long-time backpackers' favourite, with large, well-kept rooms, all with nets, telephone and sporadic hot water. No guests after 7pm. Good value, but bring some earplugs to counter the noise from the *Dove Cage* bar and restaurant below. ❷

YMCA State House Rd, 300m from Uhuru Highway ☏020/2724116, ⓦwww.kenyaymca.org. See "West Nairobi" map. The Central YMCA is popular with travellers not quite on a shoestring budget; it's well equipped, with a choice of dorms (Ksh900) and s/c rooms, and isn't markedly different from a modest hotel. There's well-priced if average food, and secure parking, but the clincher is the excellent facilities – pool, tennis courts, aerobics studio and massage services. Open 24hr. ❷

YWCA Mamlaka Rd, off Nyerere Ave, just west of Central Park ☏020/2724789. See "West Nairobi" map. Best value for men as well as women (and couples can share). Contact them well in advance to reserve. Monthly rates are available: a double room with washbasin costs around $150 per month. Dorm beds Ksh1500 including breakfast. ❷

Moderate

680 (Six-Eighty) Corner of Kenyatta Ave and Muindi Mbingu St ☏020/315680 or 020/344000, ⓦwww.sentrim-hotels.com. Somewhat soulless and becoming run-down but still much better value than most of the other central hotels with a full range of facilities. Rooms have bathtubs and satellite TV and there's safe underground parking. Be sure to ask for a room at the back unless you

want to be kept awake by the nightly live music from *Simmers*, opposite. BB ❺

Embassy Tubman Rd, right behind the City Market; ☏020/2224087, ✉hotelembassy@yahoo.com. Scruffy but quite decent, with a reliable restaurant. Discounts for group bookings, and an inexpensive breakfast is included. BB ❸

Kenya Comfort Corner of Muindi Mbingu St and Monrovia St ☏020/317606 or 020/2365577, ⓦwww.kenyacomfort.com. This large hotel is popular with tour groups and has reasonable rooms with nets and satellite TV, a rooftop terrace, 24hr bar and restaurant. ❹

Oakwood Kimathi St ☏020/2220592, ⓦwww.madahotels.com. An endearing oddity lost amid the skyscrapers, this older two-storey hotel has wood panelling, basic phones and TVs, and a wonderful antique lift. The location is very convenient, with good rooms and excellent clean bathrooms (hot water and tubs), and there's good security. It also has a relaxing first-floor bar overlooking the touristy *Thorn Tree Café*. BB ❺

Expensive

Hilton Mama Ngina St ☏020/2790000, ⓦwww.hilton.com. The cylindrical tower is unmistakeable, and the lobby impressive, but the impersonal *Hilton* caters more for expense-account travellers than for leisure visitors. Rooms get better the higher you climb, but they all need refurbishing, and the "rooftop pool" is rather overshadowed at second-floor level. Health club, spa, sauna and steam room, as well as four restaurants, but way overpriced for what it offers. BB ❻

InterContinental City Hall Way ☏020/3200000, ⓦwww.ichotelsgroup.com. Some 30 years old and working hard to keep up with its newer competitors, the *InterContinental* has some surprisingly secluded corners in the grounds, many amenities (including a heated pool, health club, casino and a good Mediterranean restaurant, *Le Mistral*) and disabled facilities. BB

Norfolk Harry Thuku Rd ☏020/2265000, ⓦwww.fairmont.com/norfolkhotel. See "West Nairobi" map. Nairobi's oldest hotel is now getting the Fairmont treatment, which has lightened and freshened it all over, improving standards while slightly diminishing the reason you want to stay here – the Edwardian atmosphere. The very comfortable rooms have good beds and flat-screen TVs and facilities include a pool, health club and sauna, and it remains a good, central rendezvous and Nairobi's best celebrity-watching venue. BB ❽

Panafric Valley Rd, Nairobi Hill ☏020/720822, ⓦwww.sarovahotels.com. Not a standout luxury address, but well managed and perfectly

▲ Norfolk Hotel

comfortable for a night or two in the city, with all the room amenities you would expect, and walking distance to Kenyatta Ave (by day – don't walk it at night). Get a room at the back, overlooking the gardens and pool, however, as the front rooms can be very noisy. The pleasant terrace restaurant does good breakfast buffets. BB ❻

Serena Nyerere Rd, off Kenyatta Ave, near Central Park ☏020/2822000 ⓦwww.serenahotels.com. See "West Nairobi" map. Impeccably decked out in a Pan-African style, replete with sculptures and wall hangings, the rooms are very comfortable and feature intricately carved wooden furniture, marble bathrooms, African art and internet access. Amenities include a health club, pool and shops. Altogether it's a very safe bet, though don't venture out of the grounds on foot after dark. BB ❽

Stanley Corner of Kimathi St and Kenyatta Ave ☏020/2228830 ⓦwww.sarovahotels.com. Complete with its famous *Thorn Tree Café* rendezvous, this is as central as you can get, and a popular base for tourists and business travellers alike. The rooms are equipped with DSTV, minibar and noise-excluding double glazing, and some are designed for disabled guests. Facilities include a modern gym and sauna and a heated rooftop pool and bar. $470

Away from the centre

Many of Nairobi's better-value mid-range and upmarket hotels – often independently owned establishments – are located out of the city centre, in the relatively affluent **suburbs** of Westlands and Parklands (also the main focus for more sophisticated nightlife), and along the main roads radiating out of the city. Buses/matatus #22, #23, #29, #30 and #119 go to Westlands; for Parklands, catch a matatu on Latema Road. Both areas are relatively safe for walking around with luggage during the day. Unless otherwise noted, the places listed below appear on the "West Nairobi" map overleaf, or, in the case of Westlands and Parklands hotels, on the "Westlands Centre" map, p.118.

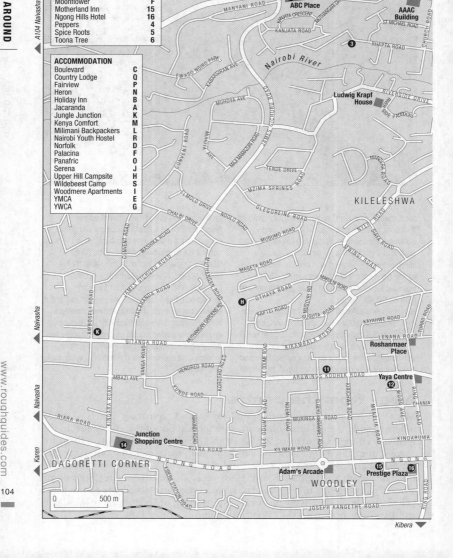

RESTAURANTS, CAFÉS, BARS & CLUBS

Alan Bobbe's Bistro	3
Annie Oakley's	7
Azalea	12
Blue Nile	13
Casablanca	8
Cedars	9
Club Afrique	6
Furusato	1
Habesha	11
Lord Delamere Terrace Bar	E
Mediterraneo	14
Mercury Lounge ABC Place	2
Misono	10
Moonflower	F
Motherland Inn	15
Ngong Hills Hotel	16
Peppers	4
Spice Roots	5
Toona Tree	6

ACCOMMODATION

Boulevard	C
Country Lodge	Q
Fairview	P
Heron	N
Holiday Inn	B
Jacaranda	A
Jungle Junction	K
Kenya Comfort	M
Milimani Backpackers	L
Nairobi Youth Hostel	R
Norfolk	D
Palacina	F
Panafric	O
Serena	J
Upper Hill Campsite	H
Wildebeest Camp	S
Woodmere Apartments	I
YMCA	E
YWCA	G

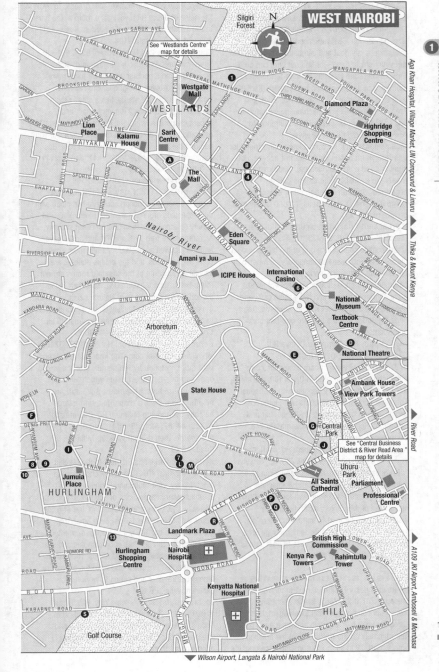

WEST NAIROBI

N

Silgiri Forest

Aga Khan Hospital, Village Market, UN Compound & Limuru ▶

Thika & Mount Kenya ▶

See "Westlands Centre" map for details

DONYO SABUK AVE

GENERAL MATHENGE DRIVE

LOWER KABETE ROAD

BROOKSIDE DRIVE

GARDEN

MUGUGA GREEN

MATUNDU LANE

SCHOOL LANE

LANE

GENERAL MATHENGE DRIVE

HIGH RIDGE

Westgate Mall

❶

NGAO ROAD

WANGAPALA ROAD

FOURTH PARKLANDS ROAD

SUSWA ROAD

THIRD PARKLANDS AVE

MUTATI RD.

WESTLANDS

BEGONIA LANE

RING ROAD PARKLANDS

Diamond Plaza

MPAKA ROAD

SECOND PARKLANDS AVE

Highridge Shopping Centre

Lion Place

Kalamu House

WAIYAKI WAY

Sarit Centre

A

FIRST PARKLANDS AVE

PARKLANDS ROAD

WAMBUGU ROAD

WESTLANDS AVE

The Mall

B

❹

HARIF ROAD

MASARI ROAD

❺

PARKLANDS ROAD

SPORTS RD.

RHAPTA ROAD

MNYItHI ROAD

MUTHITHI ROAD

CRESCENT

NG'E

MUGOYA ROAD

GATUDU ROAD

CHIROMO LANE ROAD

FURESI ROAD

MNYItH

CHIROMO ROAD

Nairobi River

RIVERSIDE LANE

RIVERSIDE DRIVE

Eden Square

Amani ya Juu

WESTLANDS ROAD

KOLDBOT ROAD

NGAMIA ROAD

GALANA

ICIPE House

International Casino

❻

NGARA ROAD

TSAVERO ROAD

LAIKIPIA ROAD

RING ROAD

MANDERA ROAD

KANDARA ROAD

GICHUGU ROAD

KANGUNDO RD.

LEBERE LN.

NGOBICHA ROAD

GITHUNGURI ROAD

Arboretum

C

UHURU HIGHWAY

National Museum

KIPANDE ROAD

TUMBERS ROAD

Textbook Centre

KIJABE ST

MAMAKA ROAD

D

National Theatre

E

UHURU THURI

UHURU HIGHWAY

UNIVERSITY WY.

Ambank House

View Park Towers

River Road ▶

State House

STATE HOUSE ROAD

DOROBO ROAD

MAZIWA ROAD

G

Central Park

J

KENYATTA AVE

See "Central Business District & River Road Area" map for details

WITHN LN.

F

DENIS PRITT ROAD

ROSE AVE

WANG'OMBE AVE

STATE HOUSE AVE

STATE HOUSE ROAD

I

THETA LANE

❽ ❾

❿

LENANA ROAD

Jumuia Place

HURLINGHAM

JABAVU ROAD

❼

L M

MILIMANI ROAD

N

VALLEY ROAD

O

All Saints Cathedral

Uhuru Park

Parliament

Professional Centre

P

FIRST NGONG AVE

SECOND NGONG AVE

THIRD NGONG AVE

MARCUS GARVEY ROAD

PADMORE RD

AMBANK LANE

ROAD

❸

Hurlingham Shopping Centre

Landmark Plaza

R

DR PHILIP ROAD

Nairobi Hospital ✚

NGONG ROAD

British High Commission

Kenya Re Towers

Rahimtulla Tower

LOWER HILL ROAD

UPPER HILL ROAD

A109 JKI Airport, Amboseli & Mombasa ▶

KABARNET ROAD

S

MUGATI DRIVE

MBAGATHI WAY

Kenyatta National Hospital ✚

HOSPITAL ROAD

MARA ROAD

KILIMANJARO RD

HILL

ELGON ROAD

MATUMBATO ROAD

MATUMBATO CLOSE

▼ *Wilson Airport, Langata & Nairobi National Park*

www.roughguides.com

105

Camping and hostels

Jungle Junction Amboseli Rd, Lavington, near Dagoretti Corner, ℡0722/7452865 ℮c_handschuh_68@yahoo.com. Legendary overlanders' hangout and campsite, where you can get your vehicle fixed – or find out who can do it for you. There are facilities for long-term vehicle storage, and a large garden for camping (Ksh600), with clean, communal toilets, showers, kitchen area, wi-fi and washing machine, plus rooms. ❸

Milimani Backpackers Milimani Rd ℡020/2343920, ⓦwww .milimanibackpackers.com. Cleaner and friendlier than the youth hostel, with internet access, hot showers and a self-service bar. Good evening meals are available, and safaris can be organized. Good for meeting other travellers. Camping Ksh450, dorm beds Ksh600 and some private rooms. ❷

Nairobi Youth Hostel Ralph Bunche Rd, near Nairobi Hospital ℡020/2723012, ℮kyha @africaonline.co.ke. Once one of the better budget places in Nairobi (Ksh120 temporary membership), but now the dorms are rundown and the bathrooms are often dirty or lack hot water. Still, there's internet access and a passable café, and it's a good place to meet Kenyan students. Dorm beds Ksh600 or there's two, s/c one-bedroom apartments. ❷

Upper Hill Campsite Othaya Rd, Kileleshwa ℡020/6750202 or 0721/517869, ⓦwww.upperhillcampsite.com. Although no longer located in Upper Hill, this small, relaxed campsite is very popular with overlanders. There are dorms, double rooms and eight nice cabins all with hot showers, a kitchen, bar and restaurant. Security is good. Take matatu #48. Dorm beds Ksh500. ❷

Wildebeest Camp Kibera Rd, off Ngong Rd ℡020/2103505 or 0734/770733, ⓦwww .wildebeesttravels.com. A quiet, family-run place catering across the range, from backpackers to upmarket guests. Pitch your own tent (Ksh500) or stay in one of their luxury safari tents with electricity and plumbed-in bathroom. There's a good restaurant and an outside bar/lounge area, and the helpful staff can organize budget safaris. Dorm beds Ksh800. BB ❹

Hotels and apartments

Boulevard Harry Thuku Rd, next to the National Museum ℡020/2227567, ⓦwww.sentrim-hotels .com. Functional rather than extravagant, this well-cared-for hotel has a garden setting, a good pool (unfortunately on the traffic side of the building), tennis court, TV in all rooms and ample parking. It's always lively with mid-market tour groups. To avoid the noise of Uhuru Highway, get a room at the back in the middle, overlooking the garden. Buses #21, #23 and #119, matatu #104. BB ❻

Country Lodge 2nd Ngong Ave ℡020/2881600, ⓦwww.countrylodge.co.ke. Stylish and affordable new hotel, and a popular alternative to its more expensive, co-owned neighbour the *Fairview*. Rooms can feel a bit sterile, like a small private hospital, but accordingly it's very clean, and security is positively airtight. A pleasant garden, gym and free wi-fi complete the amenities and you can use the *Fairview's* restaurants and pool. Bus/matatu #1, #2, #3, #4, #7, #24, #41, #46 or #111 to 3rd Ngong Ave. BB ❺

Fairview Bishops Rd, Nairobi Hill ℡020/2711321, ⓦwww.fairviewkenya .com. A peaceful, rambling country-style place with quite spacious grounds (great for birding), a wide variety of accommodation and excellent security. All rooms have free wi-fi and TV, and some have bathtubs as well as showers. Family rooms have bunk beds for kids, and the deluxe doubles are excellent, but some of the standard rooms are not much better than a decent B&L. Meals are good though, as they have one of Nairobi's best chefs in the celebrated Eamon Mullen, and it's popular with families, so reserve ahead. Same bus/matatu as *Country Lodge*, then a 3min walk. BB ❻

Heron Milimani Rd, Nairobi Hill ℡02/2720740, ⓦwww.heronhotel.com. The impressive exterior isn't quite matched by the standard of the studio, one- and two-bed apartments which, while adequate, are hardly luxurious. Still, staff are helpful, and there's a restaurant with a large balcony overlooking Milimani Rd. Bus/matatu #1, #2, #3, #4, #7, #24, #34, #41, #46 or #111 to *Panafric*, then a 5min walk up Milimani Road. BB ❺

Holiday Inn Parklands Rd, next to the Mayfair casino ℡020/3740920, ⓦwww.ichotelsgroup .com. Classy, well-maintained, modern establishment in a pastiche of Edwardian and Art Nouveau styles (the original building, the *Mayfair Court*, was built in the 1930s), with small tropical gardens and a bar. It's rather business-oriented, but efficiently run and has good disabled access, with some specially designed rooms. They do an excellent buffet breakfast and have the obligatory fitness centre, pool and sauna to work it off. Excellent value. BB ❼

Jacaranda Hotel Off Waiyaki Way, Westlands ℡020/4448713, ⓦwww.jacarandahotels.com. Rooms here are a bit small, but have fans and satellite TV. Service varies from excellent to middling, but there's a pool and a nice pizza garden with live music every night. Be careful when walking in the vicinity after dark. BB **7**

Palacina Hotel and Suites Kitale Lane, off Denis Pritt Rd ⊕020/2715517, ⊛www .palacina.com. A wonderful boutique hotel tucked

away in the suburbs, offering suites and long-stay apartments that manage to be both luxuriously stylish and homely. The service is efficient and very friendly and there's a top-class restaurant attached. Highly recommended. BB **8**

The outskirts

The places reviewed below appear on the "Greater Nairobi" map on p.134. Where public transport isn't suggested, take a taxi.

Giraffe Manor Koitobos Rd, adjacent to the AFEW Giraffe Centre, Langata ⊕020/891078, ⊛www .giraffemanor.com. Neck and shoulders above Nairobi's other places to stay is this wonderfully eccentric Scottish-style manor house in the grounds of the AFEW Giraffe Centre, to which profits go, and whose inhabitants like to share your breakfast through the windows. All meals are taken with the genial hosts who encourage breakfast in dressing gown and bare feet – a real home-from-home. HB $580.

House of Waine Corner of Masai Lane and Bogani Rd, Karen ⊕020/891920 or 020/891553, ⊛www .houseofwaine.co.ke. Eleven luxurious, individually themed rooms set in peaceful gardens in the suburbs of Karen. BB **6**

Karen Blixen Coffee Gardens 336 Karen Rd, ⊕020/882138 or 0733/616206, ⊛www .blixencoffeegarden.co.ke. Accommodation is in quaint cottages ranged through the gardens, all of which have satellite TVs, Internet connections and pleasant verandas for enjoying the ground (good bird-watching). There's a pool, gym and spa. BB $465.

Karen Camp Marula Lane, Karen ⊕020/8833475 or 0723/314053 ⊛www.karencamp.com. A bed-and-breakfast-cum-overlander's camp with pleasant s/c rooms, permanent tents, dorms and a big lawn for camping as well as good food and a bar. Quiet and peaceful, but a long way from town. Rate excludes breakfast. Dorms $5, camping $3. **2**

Kentmere Club Limuru Rd, 20km northwest of Nairobi ⊕020/3585511 or 0722/276357, ⊛www.kentmereclub.com. Situated amid the tea and coffee plantations of the Tigoni highlands, this small, friendly country inn – all beams and wood-tile roofs – has 16 self-contained rooms in cosy cottages with fireplaces, surrounded by beautiful gardens. It's a restful place to be based for a few days, and you meet some interesting Anglo-Kenyan and Kikuyu locals who pop in for a drink, or to eat at the restaurant, which serves traditional English meals, including a good Sunday roast. BB **5**

Nairobi Campsite Magadi Rd, 1.5km south of Langata Rd ⊕020/890661 or

0728/333476, ⊛www.nairobicampsite.com. One of the best-equipped campsites in Nairobi, popular with overlanders, with single and double rooms and some dorm beds. The site is secure, and the bar is a good place to talk to staff from a number of safari operators. Food is available and there's a cybercafé, laundry facilities and DSTV. Matatu #125 or bus #126. Camping Ksh300, dorm beds Ksh500. **2**

Safari Park Thika Rd, 14km from town ⊕02/3633000, ⊛www.safaripark-hotel.com. A huge, purpose-built "inland resort" offering a wholly sanitized version of "Real Africa". Nonetheless it's an attractive base for an upmarket stay, with faultless service, landscaped gardens, a massive pool, health club, tennis courts, stables, four-poster beds in all rooms, seven excellent and surprisingly affordable restaurants, and – should you have any money left over – a casino. There's a regular shuttle into town, or you could use bus/matatu #45, #137, #145, #160 or #237. BB **7**

Silole Sanctuary South side of Nairobi National Park, between the Kiserian & Empakasi gorges ⊕0721/646588, ⊛www.silolesanctuary.com. Private game sanctuary with excellent wildlife and affordable accommodation in the shape of *Maasai Lodge* – once on the package tour circuit, now refurbished (BB **5**) – and *Silole Cottage* (Ksh5000 self-catering).

Tribe Next to Village Market, Gigiri ⊕020/7200000, ⊛www l.africanpridehotels.com/tribe. The chicest establishment in Nairobi, this boutique hotel is popular with diplomats and business travellers for its proximity to the UN building and many embassies. The natural-stone facade and expansive, African art-draped lounge are winners, though the rooms are on the small side, compensating with orthopaedic mattresses, flat-screen TVs and wi-fi. The *Epic* restaurant serves good meals by the heated pool and waterfall, and the gym and spa are all you'd expect. For Nairobi, great value. BB **8**

Windsor Golf & Country Club Off Kigwa Rd, Ridgeways, 15km north of the city ⊕020/8562300, ⊛www.windsorgolfresort.com. Situated on an old coffee plantation, this golfing resort has been styled in a mix of faux-Victorian and Georgian, complete with landscaped gardens, clock tower, gazebos, and even designer creaking floorboards. Slightly absurd but superbly run, it has services and amenities second to none, including an outdoor heated pool, health club, tennis and squash courts, croquet, fishing, riding, and birdwatching with the resident ornithologist. Accommodation ranges from rooms and suites to some lovely twin cottages. BB ❼

Long stays

Cheap **apartments**, **rooms** and **studios** are advertised in the classified columns of the *Nation* and the *Standard*. Otherwise, contact an apartment agency (Westlands is probably the most promising area), or check out the notice boards outside most large supermarkets. For stays of a month or two, the *YWCA* is your best bet (see p.102). Note that if the place you're considering has no *askari*, the danger of burglary is very real and you should certainly hire somebody. The places below are on the "West Nairobi" map, p.104.

Fairview Bishops Rd (details on p.106). Three-room apartments available for a minimum stay of three-months from Ksh115,000 per month.
Kenya Comfort Hotel Suites corner of Milimani Rd and Ralph Bunche Rd ☎ 020/2719060, ⓦ www .kenyacomfort.com. The building is all ugly concrete but the apartments, from studios to three-bedroom affairs, are nice enough and there's a pool, daily maid service and 24hr reception and parking. Studios from $850 per month.

Woodmere Apartments Rose Ave, off Lenana Rd, three blocks from the Yaya Centre ☎ 020/2712511, ⓦ www.woodmerenairobi.com. Well-guarded premises with a small pool, sauna, garden and space for kids. Accommodation ranges from fully-furnished, serviced studios with tiny kitchen and loft sleeping area to spacious, tasteful apartments. Budget studios from $1300 per month, four-bed apartments from $3800 per month.

Central Nairobi

Kenyatta Avenue is the obvious place to start looking around Central Nairobi. A good initial overview of the CBD can be had from the vertigo-inducing, glass elevators in the **ICEA building**, on the northwest corner of Wabera Street. The guards at the bottom may want to escort you onto the roof (a tip might be helpful).

The avenue was originally designed to allow a twelve-oxen team to make a full turn, though livestock is nowadays no longer permitted within the city limits. Broad, multi-laned and planted with flowering trees and shrubs, it remains (along with the Kenyatta Conference Centre) the capital's favourite tourist image. The avenue is smartest – and most touristy – on its south side, with would-be moneychangers, itinerant souvenir hawkers and safari touts assailing you from every direction.

The focus of the avenue's eastern end is the *Stanley Hotel*'s **Thorn Tree Café**, diagonally opposite Nakumatt supermarket on the corner of Kimathi Street. Nairobi's one proper pavement café, the *Thorn Tree* is an enduring meeting place despite its prices and largely *wazungu* (white people) and rich businessman clientele. The thorn tree in question (the notice boards fixed to its trunk were once Nairobi's main information exchange) was cut down in 1997 and replaced with a new sapling and a smaller message board – though mobiles and the internet have largely usurped its role.

Still on Kenyatta Avenue, close to Uhuru Highway, is the skyscraper of the **General Post Office** (GPO) and, just before it, **Koinange Street**, named after the Kikuyu Senior Chief Koinange of the colonial era. The peculiar, caged **Galton–Fenzi Memorial**, just here on the left, is a monument to the

Kibera

Said to be the largest shanty town in sub-Saharan Africa, **Kibera** is a sprawling mass of shacks, just a few kilometres west of Nairobi's city centre. Although it's perhaps best not to just wander down there, it is safe to visit if you're accompanied by local residents or NGO workers, and is now an option as a morning excursion, offered by a number of local operators. The slums were a flashpoint during the post-election violence in January 2008. Protestors torched buildings and uprooted the Nairobi-Nakuru railway line that runs right through the slum. Few Kibera residents buy newspapers or own TVs: the Kibera community radio station **Pamoja FM** (99.9 FM; @tinyurl.com/ydrf3z3), the community radio station, provides a vital "glue" that helped prevent Kibera from ripping apart.

Kibera started at the end of World War I as a village housing Sudanese Nubian soldiers of the demobilized armies of British East Africa. Subsequently, as rural-to-urban migration increased, people moved into the area and began putting up mud-and-wattle structures. Today, Kibera is home to more than one million Nairobi residents – over a quarter of the city's population, most of whom live in makeshift huts. The typical home in Kibera measures three metres by three metres, with an average of five people per dwelling. Access to electricity, running water and sanitation ranges from zero to very minimal – the occasional makeshift pit latrines are shared between anything from ten to one hundred homes, though foreign donors have constructed some new toilet blocks. The streets are a mass of seemingly endless trenches, alleyways and open gutters clogged with waste and sewage. In addition to lacking even the most basic services, Kibera has an HIV infection rate of more than twenty percent and the number of orphans rises daily. However, the slum somehow works and is full of small **businesses**, from video cinemas to bakeries.

Several tour operators now run escorted visits to Kibera. Make sure before you sign up that you know exactly where your money is going: some businesses are not above running "pro-poor" tourism as part of their activities while pocketing much of the cash supposed to be supporting slum projects. As you visit various premises and community projects, you should find the experience deeply affecting, if not enjoyable, and not without its lighter moments. Contact: Kibera Tours (@www.kiberatours.com); or Victoria Safaris (@www.victoriasafaris.com/kenyatours/kiberaslumtours.htm).

man who founded, of all things, the Nairobi branch of the Automobile Association. In 1926, Galton-Fenzi was also the first motorist to drive from Nairobi to Mombasa.

City Square and Parliament

Heading south down Koinange Street and on to Kaunda Street, passing the *InterContinental* on your right and Holy Family Cathedral on your left, you cross City Hall Way and enter **City Square**. Jomo Kenyatta's statue sits benevolently, mace in hand, on the far side of the wide, flagstoned court; his mausoleum, with flickering eternal flames, is on the right as you approach the Parliament building further on. When the flags are out for a conference it all looks very bright and confident.

The legend over the main doors of Kenya's **Parliament** reads: "For a Just Society and the Fair Government of Men". The motto seems finally to be losing its edge of irony, the government having been forced by both national and international pressures to allow greater democracy and accountability in its business. A host of contentious motions are openly debated here, concerning corruption and ethnic violence, and there's even the occasional vote of no confidence in the government.

▲ *Mabati* (corrugated iron roofs) in Kibera

To sit in the **public gallery** you first have to register for a visitor's permit at the gatehouse on the corner of Parliament Road and Harambee Avenue, leaving all your belongings with the attendant outside. The gallery tends to be full of schoolchildren who are very well behaved – which of course is more than can be said of the members of parliament. Try to get hold of a copy of the Orders of the Day – there may be a juicy question or two worth anticipating. The guards at the gate can tell you when the next parliamentary session is taking place (usually Wed & Thurs at 2.30pm from mid-Oct to mid-July) or, when it's not in session, how to get a tour of the building. If you are assigned a guide, make sure both parties are clear about how much you'll pay.

The Kenyatta International Conference Centre

From Parliament, walking down Harambee Avenue along the shady pavement, you come to Nairobi's pride and joy – the 105-metre-high **Kenyatta International Conference Centre** or KICC. This, for a long time the tallest building in Kenya, is capped by a revolving restaurant, now closed. It's still worth going to the top (Ksh400 for a visit, accompanied by the *askari*), as the view of Nairobi is without equal and a firm reminder of the vastness of Africa. Just 4km to the south, the Mombasa road can be seen trailing through the suburbs and across the yellow plains; northwards, hills of coffee – and, at higher altitudes, tea – roll into the distance. On a clear day, as you'll be told, you really can see Mount Kenya in one direction and Kilimanjaro in the other. Immediately below you, the traffic swarms, and **Jogoo House**, containing government offices, is suddenly seen to be built remarkably like a Roman villa. In 2000, the KICC was overtaken by the nearby **Times Tower**, the tallest building in East Africa at 140m, but occupied by Kenya's tax authority and inaccessible to tourists.

National Archives

Straight down Harambee Avenue, if you cut across Moi Avenue and walk 300m north, you reach the **National Archives** (Mon–Fri 8.15am–4.15pm, Sat 8.15am–1pm; ⓦwww.kenyarchives.go.ke; free). Housed in the striking old

Bank of India building on the bend of Moi Avenue across from the *Hilton*, the "archives" amount to a museum and art gallery in the heart of the city that few visitors to Nairobi know about.

The ground floor is a public gallery with a range of paintings from Kenya and throughout the African continent; an enormous display of Maasai, Luo, Turkana, Luhya and Ethiopian weaponry; and a wall of tribal photographs. In the centre of the floor there's also a delightfully jumbled collection of African ethnographia – musical instruments, masks, weapon and domestic artefacts.

Past the first floor and its photograph library, the second floor houses a photographic exhibition of the struggle for **independence** – compelling not just for its content but because this is one of the few public places in the country where Kenyans can be reminded of the period in their history euphemistically called "The Emergency". If you want to see the archives themselves (mainly books, papers, correspondence and some recordings) you can pay a token fee for a year's access.

Dedan Kimathi Memorial

Just opposite the *Hilton Hotel* on the corner of Kimathi Street and Mama Ngina Street, stands a statue honouring **Dedan Kimathi**, the Mau Mau freedom fighter who was executed by the British in 1957. The statue – an imposing two-metre bronze sculpture atop a three-metre base – is hard to miss. Kimathi, sporting the dreadlocks typical of Mau Mau fighters, holds a gun in one hand and his *rungu* (club) in the other. The statue was erected in February 2007 on the fiftieth anniversary of his death.

The Jamia Mosque

The **Jamia Mosque** stands near the City Market, north of Kenyatta Avenue. The ornate green-and-white exterior contrasts strikingly with the simple interior, and the large central dome appears far larger from beneath than it does from the courtyard outside. Although most Kenyan towns now have at least one mosque, often financed by Saudi patrons, few are as large or as beautiful as Nairobi's Jamia. It's unlikely that non-Muslims will be allowed in, although polite requests, a genuine interest in Islam and the usual modesty of attire may help. For a bird's-eye view of the mosque, the top of the ICEA building is a good vantage point.

The Railway Museum

Nairobi's privately run **Railway Museum** (daily 8.15am–5pm; Ksh400; free guides) is a natural draw for rail fans and of more than passing interest for anyone else. It's a signposted, 1km west of the railway station (be careful if you walk, as there was a rash of grab-and-run robberies down here a few years back).

Museums in Kenya

To keep up with developments in Kenya's museums, contact the Kenya Museum Society (℡020/3743808, ⓦwww.kenyamuseumsociety.org), based off Kipande Road, behind the National Museum. As well as publishing the excellent annual journal *Kenya Past and Present*, they organize a one-week "Know Kenya" course (Ksh5000) in October or November every year, featuring behind-the-scenes access to museums, visits to places of historical or environmental interest and lectures by well-known Kenyan writers and academics. You can take out **one-month temporary membership** of KMS for Ksh500, which entitles you to free entry in all NMK museums and sites around the country – a very good deal.

The main hall contains a mass of memorabilia, including photos of early stations, of the "Lunatic Express" East African Railway from Mombasa to Kampala being built, pictures of the engineering feats involved in getting the carriages up and down the escarpment, and of strange pieces of hardware, such as the game-viewing seat mounted at the front of the train. Passengers who risked this perch were reminded that "The High Commissioner will not be liable for personal injury (fatal or otherwise)". In the museum annexe, the motorized bicycle inspection trolley is quite a sight but, as the write-up explains, the experiment in the 1950s "was not really successful", as the wheels kept slipping off the rail.

Outside, exposed to the elements, is the museum's collection of old **locomotives**, most of them built in Britain. You can clamber inside any of the cabs to play with the massive levers and switches. The restriction on forward visibility in some of the engines seems incredible; the driver of the *Karamoja Express* couldn't have had any idea what was in front of him while steaming down a straight line. If it all fills you with nostalgic delight, you should also note that Nairobi and Mombasa stations both have locomotive graveyards, which, with persistence, you should be able to look around.

Lions figure prominently in the early history of the railway. Look in the shed for first-class coach no. 12 to learn the story of Superintendent C. H. Ryall. During the hunt for the "Man-eaters of Tsavo" in 1898, Ryall had readied his gun one evening, settled down in the carriage and offered himself as bait. Unfortunately, he nodded off and was dragged from this carriage and devoured while colleagues sat frozen in horror. The coach, together with the repainted loco no. 301, took part in the filming of *Out of Africa* at Kajiado.

The National Museum

In 2008, the **Nairobi National Museum** (daily 9.30am–6pm; Ksh800) re-opened its doors after a three-year, Ksh800 million facelift. The refurbished result is a sparkling, showpiece attraction and the best prelude to any tour around the country. The museum is easy to reach from the centre of town (a 30-minute walk from Kenyatta Avenue or a few minutes by bus – #21, #23 or #119) and provides a good overview of Kenya's culture, history and wildlife. Note that the **Snake Park**, a reptile exhibit in the museum grounds, was still closed at the time of writing.

Hall of Kenya

This expansive entry hall into the museum is sparsely appointed with some of Kenya's most impressive and unusual artefacts and artworks. In one display case is a Swahili **siwa** from the 1680s. The *siwa*, a ceremonial horn intricately carved from an elephant tusk, was traditionally blown on celebratory occasions as a symbol of unity and was considered to possess magical powers. There is also a **sambu**, a Kalenjin elder's cloak made from the skins of Sykes' monkeys. Beautiful photos of some of Kenya's animals adorn the wall of this hall, and prepare you for the next gallery.

The Great Hall of Mammals

Dedicated to Africa's charismatic, endangered **megafauna**, and the plains animals that are still found in some abundance in Kenya, this hall features some impressive dioramas. In the centre of the room are examples of a giraffe, an elephant, a buffalo, a zebra and an okapi, the strange forest-dwelling relative of the giraffe found only in the jungles of eastern DR Congo. Along the walls are displays of most of Kenya's mammals, including the big cats, primates and

Birdwatching in Nairobi

Birdwatching need not be exclusively a bush pursuit. For any visitor staying in central Nairobi, an impressive sight during the early morning and late evening is groups of **black kites** circling as they move between feeding and roosting sites and among these are readily identified black-and-white **pied crows**. **Marabou storks**, **sacred ibises** and **silvery-cheeked hornbills** can sometimes be seen flying over the city (dramatically large marabous may also be seen in the thorn trees on Uhuru Highway, near Nyayo Stadium), while flocks of **superb starlings** call noisily from office buildings. The leafier areas of the city are likely to produce even more birds.

The gardens adjacent to the National Museum are an interesting and relatively safe area to start birding. Here, keen bird-watchers may encounter the **cinnamon-chested bee-eater**, while the plants and flowering shrubs outside the front steps of the museum provide excellent opportunities to observe **sunbirds** (variable and Hunter's sunbirds can be seen here). Another bird of the gardens is the **African paradise monarch**, a species of flycatcher. In breeding plumage, the rufous males have long tail streamers, which trail behind them like ribbons as they flit from tree to tree.

Nature Kenya organizes bird walks from the National Museum every Wednesday morning at 8.45am for Ksh100. They usually proceed to another part of Nairobi. Longer trips are also held at least once a month. For more information, contact Nature Kenya at the museum (☏020/3749957, ⊛www.naturekenya.org).

antelopes, with explanations of their habitats, diets and life cycles. Also displayed in this gallery is the skeleton of **Ahmed**, the most famous of the giant-tusked bull elephants of Marsabit, in the north of the country. In the 1970s, when poaching was rampant in northern Kenya, conservationists feared that Ahmed would be targeted because of his enormous tusks. Kenya's first president, Jomo Kenyatta, assigned two rangers to track Ahmed day and night until he died of natural causes at the age of 55. His tusks weighed in at 68 kilos (150lb) each.

Just off this gallery is a room devoted to **ornithology**, featuring 1600 specimens in glass cases. Kenya's birdlife usually makes a strong impression, even on non-bird-watchers. Look out for the various species of hornbill, turaco and roller, and for the extraordinary standard-wing nightjar, which is frequently seen fluttering low over a swimming pool at dusk, hunting for insects.

The Cradle of Human Kind

The unique interest of the Nairobi museum lies in the **human origins** exhibit, where palaeontology displays are housed. Along the walls, skeletons and skull casts of ancient hominids trace primate diversity and the evolution of the human species back millions of years. Of particular importance is the almost complete skeleton of "Turkana Boy", the 1.6 million-year-old remains of an immature male hominid found near Lake Turkana. Hardcore palaeontology fans will want to pay the extra fee to enter the **Hominid Skull Room**, which contains the skulls of some of our ancient ancestors and non-ancestral cousins, such as *Homo erectus*. Our understanding of human evolution is itself a rapidly evolving field, with new theories about human origins and ancestry appearing almost yearly, but East Africa is invariably its field-research location.

Cycles of Life

Upstairs, next to the temporary galleries of local art, the Cycles of Life exhibit covers Kenya's tribes and cultures, in neatly laid-out displays of artefacts telling the story of each ethnic group from childhood through adulthood to ancestor status. If you're planning on travelling through any of the areas inhabited by pastoral peoples (especially Pokot, Samburu, Maasai or Turkana), then seeing some old and authentic handicrafts beforehand is a good idea.

The room begins with a display of traditional birthing methods and child-rearing techniques, including a traditional Pokot child carrier made from monkey skin and children's toys made from discarded scraps of metal. The exhibit moves on to explain initiation and circumcision rituals. On display here is a Maasai warrior outfit, complete with spear and shield. The adulthood display contains various clothing and beauty products including beaded necklaces and earplugs used by some of the semi-nomadic tribes to stretch the earlobes. A display of grave markers and artefacts used to send someone into the afterlife marks the end of the exhibit.

Parks and gardens

Closer to the city centre, the **Arboretum**, northwest of Uhuru Park on Arboretum Drive (matatu #48), is a lovely place to wander or picnic and, of course, a must if you're botanically inclined. Somewhat overgrown, almost jungly in parts, it contains more than two hundred varieties of tree, and even the odd monkey. There are security notices everywhere, so don't take any valuables, and note that the gates close at dusk. On the last Monday of each month there is usually a guided walk; be at the gate by 9.30am if you're interested.

Otherwise, the biggest and best park is **City Park** in the north, a half-hour stroll from the National Museum down Forest Road and Limuru Road, or by matatu #11. City Park has a wealth of tropical trees and birdlife, several troops of vervet monkeys, a small stream with wooden bridges, gravel paths, shady lawns and, on weekends, families everywhere. During the week it's delightful, though not for women alone.

Uhuru and **Central** parks, on the western side of Uhuru Highway, are unfenced and never closed, but they have the city's worst reputation for muggings, particularly after dark. There are rowing boats for rent in the small murky lake in Uhuru Park, which are very popular at weekends and holidays. A poignant **memorial** to the many lives lost in political violence over the past decade can be seen at the roadside verge of **Uhuru Park** at Kenyatta Avenue, also known as "Freedom Corner", where the Green Belt Movement (see p.585) have planted "Trees of Peace", each bearing a simple wooden cross with the name of a victim and the words "Saba-Saba", meaning "Seven-Seven", after the crackdown on pro-democracy demonstrators on July 7, 1990.

In a more reputable part of the city – though even here a night walk would be foolish – try **Jeevanjee Gardens**, especially during a weekday lunchtime when you can picnic on a bench and chat with the office workers not thronging the nearby restaurants. You can listen, too, to the preachers who have made Jeevanjee their church and the bemused picnickers their congregation. The park contains a curiously small statue, just about recognizable, of Queen Victoria, presented to Nairobi by the nineteenth-century business tycoon A.M. Jeevanjee, who founded the *Standard* newspaper.

The **August 7th Memorial Park**, on the corner of Haile Selassie and Moi Avenue, occupies the site of the former American embassy, which was bombed by al-Qaeda in 1998 (see p.562). The park is a peaceful refuge from the free-for-all of downtown Nairobi, with grassy lawns and statues built from the rubble. It is also a chilling reminder of the horror perpetrated here. In the centre of the park, near the fountain, a wall commemorates each of the 218 victims of the blast. The park is open daily from 7am–6pm (entry Ksh20) and there's a memorial centre (daily 9am–6pm; Ksh100), with artefacts from the bombing and a video about the atrocity.

Eating

Nairobi has no shortage of **eating places**. Their diversity is one of the city's best points, and eating out is an evening pastime that never dulls. Admittedly, African food is generally not highlighted in the more expensive restaurants, which concentrate on offering a range of Asian and European cuisines, and spectacular quantities of meat. **Westlands** in particular is a culinary growth area (reachable on bus or matatu #22, #23, #29, #30 or #119), where every street and shopping mall has a handful of restaurants.

Downtown, most of the *hotelis* around River Road serve up stacks of well-prepared eggs, sausages, beans and toast. The big hotels do lavish breakfast **buffets**, of which the *Panafric's* is one of the best. For something simpler, all the cafés and snack bars listed below cater for early birds, as do *Pasara* and *Berber's Oasis*.

To avoid cluttering up the "Central Business District and River Road Area" map on p.100, we've omitted marking some places located in buildings that are already marked on the map. Restaurants located out of the centre on other maps are noted accordingly. For further eating-out listings, check the bars and nightlife section (see p.120) which includes a number of venues that double as very good restaurants.

Specialist food shops

Gourmet Meat Products, in the Yaya Centre, Hurlingham, are first-class **butchers**. You can get good **wines** at Wines of the World in Mandera Road (west of the Arboretum). The Cocoa Bean at Village Market sells excellent handmade **chocolates**. There are a several excellent **delicatessens** in Lenana Forest Centre on Ngong Road, and in various malls in Westlands (see "Shopping malls" on p.127). A very good, downtown **bakery**, with daily supplies of fresh rye and wholemeal bread, is Oscarsson's in 20th Century Plaza on Mama Ngina Street (they have a second branch at Rank Xerox House in Westlands); *Vasili & Sons*, on Mpaka Road in Westlands, is also very good. For **health foods**, try Healthy U, which has branches in most shopping malls.

City-wide café and restaurant chains

Some of Nairobi's best-known eating and drinking venues have multiple venues in the city. This isn't to say that each branch maintains consistent standards, but they're generally fairly predictable.

Nairobi's drinking water

Nairobi's tap water, once fine, is now either unfit to drink or too unpredictable to be worth the risk. Most people, even those on very low incomes, boil their water, and the more affluent drink only bottled water. If in any doubt, or if eating in cheap places where bottled water is not offered, stick to sodas.

Bakers Inn The best and cleanest branch is on Kenyatta Ave, between Koinange and Loita streets. They make excellent spicy meat pies.

Dormans Jubilee Exchange House, Mama Ngina St ☏0724/238976. Among the best of Nairobi's many coffee shops, *Dormans* is always full of cool young Nairobians and business people. Serving an excellent range of flavoured coffees and home-made cakes, it also has branches in the Sarit Centre, Village Market, Dagoretti Corner and Yaya Centre, Hurlingham.

Nairobi Java House Transnational Plaza, Mama Ngina St ☏020/4452273. This hugely popular coffee shop has some of the best breakfasts in Nairobi, good-value lunches, and a great variety of coffees. Branches at ABC Place in Westlands, Nakumatt Junction and JKIA airport.

Kengeles Koinange St. Fast-food joints serving cheap burgers, steaks, toasted sandwiches and Kenyan dishes to a non-stop loud music accompaniment. There's a pleasant balcony at the Koinange St branch. Other branches include Lavington and Yaya Centre.

Steers Muindi Mbingu St, opposite Jeevanjee Gardens. The South African fast-food chain's venture into Kenya offers the usual fast food, plus toasted sandwiches, salads, shakes, juices and great toffee ice cream. Other branches include Wabera St, the Mall in Westlands and Village Market, Gigiri.

Hotelis and street food around River Road

The **River Road area** has one *hoteli* after another on most streets, generally dishing up standard meals of chips or *ugali* with fish or fried chicken. Most of the places reviewed below are in this area (see the "Central Business District and River Road Area" map, p.100; for Westlands places, see the map on p.118). If you're feeling adventurous, then try **Kariokor Market**, which has an enclosure containing dozens of *chai*, *ugali* and *nyama choma* joints vying for business. The meat and fish is very fresh and sizzles on charcoal grills as reggae music blares out. Steaks, brains or sweetbreads, it's all there, and, for the thirsty, several dodgy bars oblige. Other very cheap places to eat include the shacks near the **Country Bus Station**, where you can fill up on *chai* and *mandaazi* for next to nothing, and itinerant stands selling sausages, *mandaazi*, fruit and roasted corncobs – which are so tough and take so long to eat you'll feel you've had a whole meal.

Al Mansura B&L Munyu Rd (open from 6am). Good for a breakfast of *mandaazi na chai*.

Ali's Fish and Chips Tsavo Rd. Cheap, greasy and satisfying.

Cheers Bhajia Hotel Under the *New Kenya Lodge*. Popular, inexpensive south Indian vegetarian.

C&J Cafe Gaberone Rd. Cheerful and well-run café-diner serving good fish curries and meat stews with a choice of rice, *ugali* or chapatti.

Fameland Duruma Rd. Good solid meals (notably *nyama choma* with *ugali*) with excellent music, sometimes live, in this unusually good "day and night club".

Ismailia's River Rd. Very inexpensive, welcoming and comfortable, with a good vegetarian selection.

Malindi Dishes Gaberone Rd (daily 7.30am–10pm). Self-service cafeteria with good cheap Swahili dishes.

Cafés, snacks and fast food in the CBD

You'll find most cafés and snack bars as well as lots of international-style fast-food joints situated in the relatively upmarket business district **north of City Hall Square**. Most are closed all day Sunday, some open Sunday morning.

Caprice Fry's Moi Ave. Busy fast-food joint, popular with the local office crowd for fried chicken and fish and chips.

City Chef Moktar Daddah St. Fresh passion-fruit juice and good-quality cakes, with especially good doughnuts.

Creamy Inn Union Towers, corner of Moi Ave and Mama Ngina St. Serves great ice cream, including a spectacular honey crunch waffle sundae.

Fridays Unafric House, corner of Koinange and Moktar Daddah streets. A lively place, popular with the lunch and post-work crowd, serving cheap burgers, cocktails and grills.

Hooters Hamilton House, Kaunda St. American-style sports bar and fast-food joint (milkshakes, burgers, pizzas), with music videos on the screens. Prices are affordable, and the service is good.

Kenchic Inn Corner of Moktar Daddah and Muindi Mbingu streets. No-frills halal fish and chicken bar, busier than most and therefore fresher.

La Scala Pizzeria Phoenix House Arcade, Standard St/Kenyatta Ave (daily until midnight). Inexpensive place, serving a mix of Italian and Kenyan food. The pizzas and pastas are under Ksh500, service is good and the lunchtime specials are a bargain.

Nando's Union Towers, corner of Mama Ngina St and Moi Ave. Three fast-food emporia in one at this branch of the Portuguese-themed, South African chain, serving pizzas, Portuguese snacks and fried chicken, with a large and spotless dining room upstairs overlooking the busy junction. Same prices as its European counterparts, but always busy.

Pasara 2nd mezzanine floor, Lonrho House, Standard St. At the front is the coffee shop, decorated with old black-and-white movie posters; at the back are the restaurant and bar, with a vaulted ceiling. Excellent cooked breakfasts and cakes.

Thorn Tree Café *Stanley Hotel*, Kimathi St. Hard to avoid as it's in the thick of the worst zone for tourist hustling, so a welcome refuge, and a handy meeting place, but in truth nothing special. The snacks are average and way overpriced. There's usually a cheesy band in the evenings. Closes around 11pm.

Restaurants

The following listings are mostly for more **upmarket** eating houses, where it's often a good idea to reserve a table. Most are closed between 3pm and 6pm and many close once a week, often Tuesday or Sunday. The city has famously good beef and lamb so, if you enjoy meat, indulge while you're here, as the rest of the country is much less well. Prices, without drinks, normally work out between Ksh800 and Ksh2000 a head, though you can certainly eat more cheaply at several of the curry houses. In the more international league, prices are a little higher, and you can pay up to Ksh3000–4000 for a good dinner, without wine.

Central Business District

Berber's Oasis Mezzanine Floor, NHC Building, Aga Khan Walk 0722/679076. Good, filling African food – *kisamvu na karanga* (cassava leaves with groundnuts) and *githeri* – served in a quirky dining room with rather overbearing palm tree wallpaper. The attached terrace bar is not bad, so long as you don't mind country music.

Fiesta 3rd floor, Chester House, Koinange St ☎020/240326. Despite the name and the hacienda-gone-wrong interior, this is a reliable standby for pasta, fish and grilled meat, often used by journalists based in the same building.

Five Star Chinese Restaurant 1st floor, Loita House, Loita St ☎020/2244286. Friendly place, serving very tasty food and cheaper than most other Chinese restaurants in the vicinity.

Hong Kong Ground floor, Kenya House, Koinange St ☎020/2228612 (closed Mon). Very good Cantonese. Try the tasty "steam boat", a communal fondue in which you cook meat and seafood slices in bubbling stock at the table.

Khyber At the *Meridian Court Hotel*. Excellent and very reasonably priced Mughlai cuisine, with a good-value lunchtime set menu (around Ksh800).

Panda 1st floor, Fedha Towers, Kaunda St ☎020/2213018. One of the best Chinese restaurants in the city, with an elegant dining room, wood-lattice screens, flowers and Chinese pottery. Staff are extremely efficient and friendly.

Simmers Corner of Muindi Mbingu St and Standard St ☎0722/593185 (daily 7am–midnight). Large and laid-back, the CBD's only *nyama choma*-style joint, and thus very popular (especially with office workers deferring the misery of commuting home). There are live bands nearly every night of the week.

Swahili Corner Nginyo Towers, Koinange St ☎020/316854. Superb Kenyan restaurant serving Swahili delights, such as coconut chicken curry, kingfish marinated in coriander and chilli, and freshly squeezed juices. Ksh350–400 per head for a main course including salad, rice and assorted condiments.

Sun Sweet Centre Ngariama Rd (open till late). Vegetarian Indian place, large, sparse and slightly lacking in atmosphere, but with excellent vegetarian food and tempting sweets.

Tamarind National Bank Building, Harambee Ave ☎020/2217990 ⊕www.tamarind.co.ke. Nairobi's largest, most expensive – and fortunately best – seafood restaurant.

Highly rated, reservations essential. Daily lunch & dinner.

Trattoria corner of Wabera and Kaunda sts ☎020/340855. This still gets enthusiastic notices from budget travellers having a splurge. The pasta dishes and pizzas are the real thing and the cakes and ice cream magnificent.

Westlands and Parklands

Addis Ababa Woodvale Place, Woodvale Grove, Westlands ☎020/447321. Upmarket Ethiopian, with beautiful decor, attentive service, fantastic food, and regular live music and dancing, in which patrons are encouraged to participate.

RESTAURANTS, CAFÉS, BARS & CLUBS

Addis Ababa	9	Open House	6
Art Café	1	Pavement	12
Gipsy Bar/Tropicana	7	Phoenician	2
Haandi	11	Siam Thai	5
Havana	10	Tamambo	11
Hidden Agenda	3	Three Bells	4
Hutch	13	Wheels	11
Kebab King	8		

Central Business District & Mombasa ▼

Alan Bobbe's Bistro Andrews Apartments, Rhapta Road (west), Westlands ☎020/4252000. Opened in 1962, the oldest restaurant in the city is still devoutly French and devotedly patronized. The manicured poodle logo is a touch of absurd humour, and any impression of camp pretentiousness is belied by the genuine interest in good food. Around Ksh3500. Mon–Fri lunch & dinner, Sat dinner only.

Artcaffé Westgate Mall, Westlands. ☎020/3741197. A great place to have a coffee and a pastry and check your email on the free wi-fi. Also serves good pasta dishes, soups and sandwiches.

Furusato Ring Rd, off General Mathenge Dr, Westlands ☎020/4442508. Japanese food, rather expensive, though the restaurant has the benefit of a fantastically elegant dining room and large garden terrace.

Haandi The Mall, Westlands ☎020/4448295. Nairobi's best north Indian restaurant, specializing in tandoori cooking. It's a little expensive (Ksh1200 per head), but you could miss breakfast to make room.

Hidden Agenda 2nd Floor, Sarit Centre, Westlands ☎020/3743872 or 0722/522552. Upmarket café and bar, popular with Westlands teenagers, with smart leather decor and outdoor tables. Serves great breakfast pancakes.

Kebab King Waiyaki Way, Westlands. Permanent kebab stand, serving fantastic shawarmas and shish kebabs. A great place to soak up one too many at the nearby *Gipsy* bar.

Open House Centro House, opposite The Mall, Westlands ☎020/4445902. Delicious Indian dishes such as ginger chicken and curry prawns. Not at all touristy, the place is usually packed with local Indian families.

Peppers Parklands Rd, opposite *Holiday Inn*, Parklands ☎020/3755267 or 0722/201880. Great steaks, grilled chicken and fish as well as a nice line in cocktails served with style by knowledge-able bar staff. It's popular with families for its huge garden and indoor and outdoor kids' play areas.

Phoenician Karuna Rd, Westlands ☎020/3744279. A surprising mix of Lebanese and Japanese food, including some of the best sushi in town from the full sushi bar.

Siam Thai 1st floor, Unga House, Muthithi Rd, Westlands ☎020/3751727 (open daily). Run by an Indian family in love with Thai food, this is probably the best Thai in town, despite the uninspired decor. Try the tangy *tom yam goong* soup, spare ribs, or *larb gai* – spiced chicken mince with onions, mint and lemon grass. Dinner around Ksh1000, with cheaper lunchtime set menus, often under Ksh700.

Spice Roots Masari Rd at Parklands Rd, Parklands ☎020/3754860 or 0733/601802. Very good Indian, half the price of the more prestigiously located *Haandi*.

Tamambo 2nd floor, The Mall, Westlands ☎020/4448064, ⊛www.tamarind.co.ke. Modern African brasserie serving delicious African and European food (try the crab cigars or the Kachos – Kenyan nachos made with cassava). The dining room is appealingly understated, decked out with plants and African artefacts. The attached bar serves excellent frozen *dawas*, and there's live jazz Fri eve and Sun lunch, and a Sat night disco.

Three Bells Reliance Centre, Woodvale Grove, Westlands ☎020/4443735. Long-established and good value Indian restaurant, formerly in the city centre.

Toona Tree International Casino, Westlands Rd, off Museum Hill ☎020/3740820. Very nice, open-air place, set among the boughs of the eponymous tree, and majoring on seafood, though the food tends to be fairly ordinary. There's a playground for kids and *Blue Times*, next door, is a club with DJ music and an occasional live band (Wed karaoke). Buses #21, #23 or #119. Open daily.

Wheels 2nd floor, The Mall, Westlands ☎020/4458799. Primarily an inexpensive *nyama choma* joint (you can order other local dishes too) with a pleasant veranda overlooking Chiromo Rd, and a local business clientele on weekday lunchtimes.

Nairobi Hill, Kilimani, Hurlingham and Ngong Road

Blue Nile Argwings Kodhek Rd, Hurlingham ☎020/2728709. Very laid-back, enjoyable place (unless you're averse to chilli), with a great value "mix dish" where you can try a bit of everything. Wash it down with *tej*, a mead-like Ethiopian honey beer. Buses #41 or #46/46B.

Cedars Lenana Rd, Kilimani ☎020/2710399. Excellent Lebanese food, if a little pricey. The dining room is charming, with understated Middle Eastern decor and a roaring fire for chilly July evenings.

Habesha Argwings Kodhek Rd, Hurlingham ☎020/3867035. Arguably the best, yet least expensive Ethiopian food in town, and popular with expats. Huge portions served on spongy *injera* flat bread. The best tables are outside in the garden next to the fire pits.

Mediterraneo Junction Mall, Ngong Rd ☎020/3878608. Elegant Italian cuisine in a cosily romantic setting. The menu is huge, almost overwhelming, and they serve everything from pasta to seafood and meat dishes, as well as excellent desserts. They also have a location at Pamstech House, Woodvale Grove, in Westlands (020/4447494 or 0733/576630).

Misono Lenana Rd, next to the South African High Commission, Kilimani ☎020/3868959. Japanese venue, popular at lunchtime with nearby office workers. Good set menus, lunchtime specials and bento boxes served in a large and lovely tree-filled garden.

Moonflower Restaurant at the *Palacina Hotel*, Kitale Lane, off Denis Pritt Rd, Kilimani ☎020/2715517. Stylish and expensive restaurant where grills, lobster and Asian dishes are the main focuses. The outdoor, tented setting is fun, and there's live jazz at weekends.

Karen, Langata, Gigiri and Kasarani

Carnivore Langata Rd, towards the National Park entrance ☎020/602786, ⊛www.tamarind.co.ke Nairobi's most famous restaurant no longer serves game meat, but a meal here is still part of every package itinerary, and very few people seem to dislike it. The all-you-can-eat menu (lunch Ksh1700, dinner Ksh1900) includes camel, ostrich and crocodile, but the very good lamb and beef, carved, Brazilian-style, off the roasting sword, are what you should fast for – don't be tempted by early-evening distractions of burgers and sausages. There's a good vegetarian selection, too. Buses/matatus #15, #24, #31, #125, #126 all pass the entrance road, from where it's a 1km walk. Go by taxi. Daily, lunch and dinner; Sat afternoons kids can disappear to their Funland, with a fairground, donkey and camel rides, magic shows and face-painting; Wed–Sun discos and live music in the adjoining *Simba Saloon*.

The Lord Erroll Ruaka Rd, Runda Estate, behind Village Market, Gigiri ☎020/7122433, ⊛www.lord-erroll.com. A colonial-style house containing an old-fashioned, mahogany-panelled bar, the *Highlander*, and three dining rooms. The best of these is the *Claremont*: its food and service are excellent, and there are good imported wines to accompany the classic French menu. Allow Ksh4000 a head, without wine.

Nyama Choma Ranch at the *Safari Park Hotel*, Thika Rd, Kasarani ☎020/3633000. At once classy and tacky, with perfectly grilled food served by an assortment of dancers, and wildlife videos to keep you entertained. Better value than *Carnivore*, but quite far from the city centre.

Talisman 320 Ngong Rd, Karen ☎020/883213. Pleasant gardens, sofas and some tables outdoors – all in funky-colonial style– serving a diverse variety of international dishes. Allow about Ksh2000 a head. Daily, noon to late, closed Mon.

Nightlife

Drinking and dancing are what a night out in Nairobi is usually about. Earthy, local discos have free entry or very cheap **entrance fees**, while in the glitzier places, men usually pay more than women; around Ksh200 to 400 as against Ksh100 to 200. Drinks prices are much the same as you'll pay in similar establishments around the country and clubs are open nightly, and often on weekend afternoons too. Be warned, however, that, male or female, if you're not accompanied by a partner of the opposite sex, you soon will be.

Bars, clubs and local dives

If you just want a **drink**, the CBD is mostly a bit of a dead loss after about 9pm, when the last commuters finally set off home to avoid the traffic: most people gravitate towards Westlands for its sleeker, more upmarket bars, or else pack into a number of sweaty discos.

There's a scattering of international-style **nightclubs** complete with flashy interiors and the latest African and foreign dance hits. If this appeals, try one of the established places below, or *Simba Saloon* at the *Carnivore* (see p.119). All the big nightclubs put on floor shows for those who stay late enough – gyrating trios, limbo-dancing and explicit contortions.

Meanwhile, people are doing contortions just to get into the most famous of the **"day and night clubs"** (24hr bars) in downtown Nairobi's grittiest quarter – the *Modern Green Day and Night Club*, on Latema Road, just east of the CBD. Opened in 1968 and never voluntarily closed, this might appear – with the usual drunken arguments and hustle going on in the doorway – as a place to avoid. But squeeze inside, drink a beer or two, and soak up the elevated and extremely relaxed atmosphere. People make friends quickly here, though having a conversation over the racket is exhausting. Entrance is free, the floor show is you and the rest of the customers, and cold beer is not the fashion, though it's available, from the barman in his security cage.

If you're suitably stripped down, to just the clothes you're wearing and a little cash, there's nothing to stop you from checking out dozens of similar places in nearby streets. **Munyu Road**, for example, has more bars and clubs per hundred metres than any other place in Kenya: try *Lizie Bar* on the corner of Munyu Road and Gaberone Lane, *Fameland* on Duruma Road (great music and food), *Habari*, on Luthuli Avenue, or tiny *Madhuka*, in Casino Plaza on Moi Avenue.

The CBD and River Road area

Applebee's Gaberone Rd, corner of Luthuli Ave. Cheap beer, friendly staff, slightly kitsch decor, and a lively soundtrack of mostly Lingala music. Can be a congenial spot for a drink, though it has evolved into something of a strip joint and lap-dancing venue in recent years, so beware you don't stray into the wrong room.

Club Sound 2nd floor, Hamilton House, Kaunda St ☎0722/571382. Upmarket place featuring live bands and poetry readings. On Sundays there are salsa lessons in the afternoon, followed by a salsa club night.

Dolce Club Cianda House, Koinange St ☎020/2218275 (daily). Slick, smooth *soukous* soul for a glitzy crowd; deafening sound system.

Florida 2000 1st floor, Commerce House, Moi Ave, near the Kenya Cinema ☎020/2229036, ⓦwww.floridaclubskenya.com. The *New Florida*'s sister, often just called *F2*, attracts similar clients and offering equally unambiguous entertainment, pumped up with what they call "most exotic floor shows". For the local ladies, this means grabbing drunken *wazungu* and persuading them to part with their money. But the Sunday afternoon disco is *the* place to keep on swinging if sleep has somehow eluded you.

Lord Delamere Terrace Bar At the *Norfolk Hotel* ☎020/2265000 ext. 2056. See "West Nairobi" map. Sooner or later a people-watching drink or a snack here is a must, though at times it can feel a bit stuffy. It does, however, offer the full range of Tusker beers, and the snacks aren't as expensive as you might expect.

Monte Carlo Club Accra Rd ☎020/2223181. A cavernous place with a good atmosphere and music. "No weapons or *miraa*", say the signs – a necessary notice, judging from a few unsavoury types lurking within. Daily till dawn; reggae disco Wed from 8pm, Sat from 4pm, Sun from 2pm.

New Florida Club Chai House, Koinange St ☎020/2215014, ⓦwww.floridaclubskenya.com (floor shows 1am). Popularly known as *F1* or *Mad House*, and irresistible for its tackiness, this big red-and-white mushroom of a building above the Total filling station is always full of prostitutes and rather desperate-looking business types, but the atmosphere is merely steamy, not heavy.

Tacos Eagle House, Kimathi St ☎0723/785879. An exuberant, young crowd packs this bar, one of several at this end of Kimathi St, and spills out onto the balcony. There's an infectious mix of Kenyan and international hip hop and pop, and as the night wears on, tables and chairs are pushed aside and the venue becomes an impromptu dance floor.

Zanze Bar 5th floor, Kenya Cinema Plaza, Moi Ave ☎020/222568. A good place to down beers or cocktails in the afternoons or evenings, before it gets disco-feverish.

Kilimani, Westlands and Karen

Annie Oakley's Milimani Rd, behind *Nairobi Backpackers*, Kilimani ☎0712/138234. Very friendly bar with a mixed crowd of locals, expats, backpackers and the usual working women. It has several pool tables, a big-screen TV for sporting events, and good, cheap food. Open daily.

Azalea Bar & Restaurant Komo Lane, off Wood Ave, Hurlingham ☎0710/700539 or 0713/222555. Famous for its array of single malts and creative cocktails. There's a charming garden for hanging out and they also serve good fried bar snacks.

Casablanca Lenana Rd, Kilimani, attached to the highly recommended *Osteria Del Chianti* restaurant ☎020/2723173. Stylish Moroccan-themed bar with a wonderful oasis-style garden, complete with sand, baby palms, outdoor fireplaces and bright blue deckchairs. The cocktails are expensive, but delicious and very potent.

Gipsy Bar/Tropicana Woodvale Grove, Westlands ☎020/4440836. Near the *Jacaranda Hotel*, this is a popular upmarket choice, with a gay-friendly reputation. It serves tapas, remains open to the early hours and has daily drinks specials.

Havana Opposite Bandari Plaza, Woodvale Grove, Westlands ☎020/4450653, ⓦwww.havana.co.ke. Dark and smoky Latin restaurant and bar, with a chic young crowd attracted by good Cuban snacks and cheap cocktail pitchers.

Hutch Bar Grill and Carwash Chiromo Rd, Westlands. Large, boisterous, loud and very local open-air bar, playing Kenyan and Kenyan pop. There's a good *nyama choma* bar, and cheap beer.

Mercury Lounge ABC Place, off Waiyaki Way, Westlands ☎020/4451875. Cool designer watering hole with a curved wooden bar and dark green and purple leather furniture. In keeping with the retro feel, the DJ tends to spin Seventies funk and soul.

Black Cotton At the Jolly Roger, Langata Rd, Karen (first Fri of every month) ☎0727/938739. Large and very popular open-air disco attracting clubbers from far and wide, but the traditional rendezvous of Anglo-Kenyan youngsters.

Pavement Westview Centre, Ring Rd, Westlands ☎020/4441711. In-place for the young and funky, but a sizeable crowd of the not-so-youthful and less-than-trendy hang on with a vengeance.

The live music scene

Although there are a few downtown **live music venues**, much of Nairobi's live music performances take place on the perimeter of the city, and most places are permanent *nyama choma* gardens. Promoting bands in Nairobi is as precarious a business as anywhere and, given the volatile nature of the music business, venues and bands change at a moment's notice. Check out ⓦnairobinow.wordpress.com and look at the *Nation* newspaper on a Friday and Saturday for one-off gigs.

Many clubs have Sunday afternoon "**jam sessions**" that can be just as lively as the evening shows, and often include acrobats, jugglers, magicians or comedians as well – excellent for families and convenient if you don't want to be taking taxis around the city late at night. And every September the **Alliance Française** puts on an event called "Spotlight on Kenyan Music", which can be a good opportunity to see the newest talents on the scene (see "Cultural Centres", p.131).

▲ Afro-jazz singer Achieng Abura

Starting times vary considerably for all the clubs: on weekdays, 7.30pm or 8pm wouldn't be too early to turn up, while at weekends even the warm-ups don't usually begin before 9 or 10pm, and some shows may not get rolling until midnight.

Music venues

Calabash Bezique Thika Rd at Kahawa Sukari, opposite Kenyatta University ☎020/811084. A large 24hr *nyama choma* place with studenty discos Thurs–Sat and occasional live bands – call in advance for details. Bus/matatu #137 or #237.

Club Afrique International Casino, Westlands Rd ☎020/375579. A popular place with young Kenyans, *Club Afrique* has great live music and a good dance scene. Eric Wainaina, Kenya's star benga singer, performs every Thurs and some weekend nights. Afrodizzia, a Lingala band, plays the last Fri of each month.

Fameland Club Duruma Rd, off River Rd ☎020/2248000. Live bands and good DJs at the weekend in this dingy and weathered joint. Thursday is African disco night, with plenty of hip-gyrating rhythms to grind to.

Green Corner Cactus Club Tumaini House, corner of Nkrumah Ave and Moi Ave ☎020/335864 or 020/335342. The first-floor veranda has live music, which can be anything – Congolese, Kikuyu, Luo – on Fri & Sat nights. Very danceable, very local, and entrance is free.

Hillock Inn Enterprise Rd, Industrial Area ☎020/544819 or 020/545668. Long-established venue, with several bars, tacky fountains, inexpensive s/c rooms and resident band on Wed, Fri & Sat (6pm to late), and Sun afternoons. Get there by matatu for "Industrial Area/Hillock" from outside the Afya Centre, junction of Tom Mboya St and Hakati Rd.

Motherland Inn Ngong Rd, opposite Menelik Rd, near Adams Arcade. Slightly more subdued than central venues, this bar serves good Ethiopian food and has regular live music. Buses/matatus #1, #2, #3, #4, #102, #103 and #111.

🏃 **Ngong Hills Hotel** Prestige Plaza, Ngong Rd at Mugo Kibiru Rd ☎02/3860894 ⓦwww.ngonghillshotel.com. One of the best venues, not at all intimidating and with uniformly excellent acts on Fri & Sat nights (8pm–3am). On Sun afternoons they host a very laid-back jam session, complete with dancers, and other entertainers. Bus/matatu #1, #2, #3, #4, #102, #103 or #111.

Roasters Inn Garden Estate Rd, opposite Kenya Breweries, Ruaraka ☎020/8561000. Usually has classic Kenyan pop, and cabaret. Wed, Fri & Sat are the main nights. Bus/matatu #45, #137, #145, #160 or #237.

Simba Saloon At the *Carnivore* ☎020/602764 ⓦwww.tamarind.co.ke (see p.119). A successful melding of live music and disco in a pleasant outdoor environment. There's frequent live music, both Kenyan and international: big names such as Manu Dibango and Youssou N'dour have played here. The adjacent *Carnivore Gardens* concert venue holds up to 15,000.

Simmers Corner of Muindi Mbingu St and Standard St ☎0722/593185. Locals and tourists gather here to listen to live Kenyan and Congolese music nightly.

Theatre and cinema

After years of stagnation, the Nairobi **arts scene** seems to be finally finding a rhythm of its own, independent of the tourist market, which had previously driven much of it. Although still modest by international standards, it is well worth discovering. Besides checking out the theatres and arts centres listed below, your first base should be the excellent arts-scene blog Ⓦnairobinow.wordpress.com, which posts news of up-and-coming performers, shows and events. Also worth having a look at are the theatre pages in the Thursday edition of the *Standard* and the *Nation* on Friday and Saturday. The French **Alliance Française**, the German **Goethe–Institut**, the **Italian Cultural Institute** and the **British Council** all host events (see "Cultural Centres", p.131), though funding comes and goes over the years. One arts organization that has been active for many years is the **Kuona Trust**, in Hurlingham (Likoni Close, off Likoni Lane, off Dennis Pritt Road Ⓦwww.kuonatrust.org) which brings together Kenyan and international artists and performers for residencies, workshops and events.

The major malls – the Sarit Centre, Village Market, Prestige Plaza, Westgate and Nakumatt Junction – all have modern **multiplex movie theatres**, most of them part of the Silverbird (Nu-Metro) chain, showing recent mainstream movies. In the CBD, the 20th Century on Mama Ngina Street (☎020/2210606) and the Kenya Cinema on Moi Avenue (☎020/2226982) show fairly recent mainstream releases – usually blockbusters or award winners. Seats cost up to Ksh200 in the mainstream cinemas, and around Ksh100 in the cheaper places. Daily programmes can be found in the *Nation* and the *Standard* newspapers.

Theatres and arts centres

GoDown Arts Centre Dunga Rd, Industrial Area ☎020/555770 or 0726/992200, Ⓦwww .thegodownartscentre.com. A not-for-profit entity featuring an art gallery, dance studio and performance space, a painters' studio and state-of-the-art recording studio.

Kenya National Theatre Opposite the *Norfolk Hotel*, Harry Thuku Rd ☎020/2086748 or 0712/6008677. Kenya's national stage gives special emphasis to African theatre and Kenyan drama in particular. Built in 1952, the National Theatre was refurbished in the early 2000s by a combination of government funds and the private sector and has now been restored in all its Art Deco glory.

Professional Centre/Phoenix Players Parliament Rd ☎020/2225506, Ⓦwww.phoenixplayers.net. This small theatre has assumed the mantle of Nairobi's leading playhouse, and is highly recommended. Its energetic repertory company, the Phoenix Players, formed in 1948, stages contemporary works by Kenyan or foreign playwrights and classics adapted for Kenya. Their productions are always worth catching and sometimes outstanding.

Sarakasi Dome Ngara Crescent, east of the Nairobi River from River Rd ☎020/3742990 or 020/ 3742994, Ⓦwww.sarakasi.org. A recently renovated performance space for the very active Sarakasi Trust and their Sarakasi Players, promoting contemporary African art, music and dance.

Shopping

It doesn't take long to realize that commerce is Nairobi's *raison d'être*. Disappointingly perhaps, the form which trade takes here is not always very exotic. But Nairobi is the best place in East Africa to buy **handicrafts**, with the widest, if not the cheapest, selection. The city also has some lavish **produce markets**, enjoyable even if you only want to browse. The upper part of Moi Avenue is Nairobi's busiest ordinary shopping street, all colonnaded shop-fronts and antiquated name-boards, and fun to wander past.

Bargaining is expected at all Nairobi's markets and most shops – with the exception of supermarkets and stores selling imported goods. Be aware, however, that the "last price" tends to vary seasonally and can skyrocket when a major conference hits town.

Produce markets and food

Though it doesn't offer the city's lowest prices, for a colourful and high-quality range of fruit and vegetables, the **City Market** (Mon–Fri 7.30am–6.30pm, Sat 7.30am–3pm, Sun 8.30am–noon) is the obvious target, but beware of bag-snatching in the area. The other large produce markets are the **Wakulima** (or Farmers) market, also known simply as Marikiti, a cavernous, dank hall at the bottom of River Road, and the excellent, if totally chaotic, open-air **Kariokor market** at the north end of Racecourse Road at the junction with General Waruingi Street. Also good for fruit and vegetables is the **Forest Road open-air market** on Limuru Road in Parklands, opposite the Aga Khan Primary School (daily 6am–6pm). **Specialist food shops** are rounded up on p.115.

Crafts

For the exhausting business of buying **crafts and curios**, it's advisable to decide what you want before stepping into a shop or looking at a stall. There are dozens of **curio shops** and you might get a good deal at almost any of them, though you should never accept their first price, and always bargain hard. The upmarket places are increasingly relocating to the city's suburban malls. In the CBD they're clustered on Standard, Kaunda and Mama Ngina streets.

At some of the fancier places you can browse for ages undisturbed, but at the cheaper outlets dilly-dallying is not encouraged and the pressure may be on to part with your money. To browse and to establish comparative values, pay a visit to the excellent **Zanzibar Curio Shop** on Moi Avenue, which has a huge range of stuff at fixed and realistic prices. Unless you're after certain antique sculptures, masks and xylophones, you'd be hard-pressed to match its prices by bargaining anywhere else.

Curio shops and hawkers

If you are in no hurry and after something unique, but not necessarily Kenyan, Kashmir Crafts on Biashara Street is worth a visit. They have a great selection of carvings, masks and jewellery from across the continent at very reasonable prices, as do Batik Heritage on Muindi Mbingu Street and Shah's on Moktar Daddah Street, west of Muindi Mbingu. African Heritage, in Libra House on the Mombasa road, on the way to JKI Airport, has some beautiful items including great musical instruments such as thumb pianos and lyres. It also has a branch at *Carnivore* (see p.119).

You'll find lots more curio shops in the streets around the **City Market**, mostly overpriced and unresponsive to substantial bargaining. Usually cheaper are places where they don't have to pay a shop rent – **street stands** and **market booths** – though these are an almost-extinct species, constantly being harassed and demolished by the city council. The more permanent booths in the enclosure at the back of the City Market off Koinange Street are an obvious choice, especially for soapstone, batiks and basketwork, but the whole area is something of a tourist trap and, while you'll probably find what you're looking for, you're unlikely to knock it down to a good price.

For **traditional fabrics and clothes** such as *kikois* and *kangas*, there are around a dozen shops to browse through along **Biashara Street**. Of these, Haria's Stamp

Crafts and shopping

Kenya is a good place to buy carvings and textiles in
particular, the former usually made specifically for the
tourist market. Beadwork and traditional utensils made
from gourds are also popular, but Kenya's most important
artisanal traditions are ironwork and metal jewellery, and
basketware, both of which go back centuries in some
communities. What you take home will depend, to some
extent, on what you can carry. It's easy, when bargaining
on the beach or at the roadside, to get carried away: some
wooden and soapstone carvings are heavy as well as fragile,
and can be hard to cart home. Bigger shops and large
cooperatives will ship items for you.

Crafts market ▲

Basket-making ▼

Carvings

Kenya is one of the world's biggest manufacturers of **wooden carvings**. From the ubiquitous animals of doubtful appearance to finely chiselled bowls and plates, carvings are created here in the millions, mostly by Kamba carvers (see p.321). The most striking carvings are in the dramatic and delicate **makonde style** (after the Makonde people of Mozambique and Tanzania, a group of whom live west of the Taita Hills). Makonde carvings are ostensibly done in **ebony**, but most are blackened rosewood or something similar, a fact which shouldn't deter you from buying – this conserves ebony forest stocks and the result looks just as wonderful in your living room. The other very popular carving material is **soapstone** or steatite – a soft, lustrous stone mined from one locality, Tabaka (see p.279), near Kisii. Apart from having a tendency to snap when carved too thin (which makes soapstone hippos more popular than giraffes), soapstone is one of the most versatile materials, and the industry has sprouted in the last few decades to encompass a wide variety of plates, bowls, boxes and utensils, as well as decorative items such as chess sets and candlesticks.

Baskets

The Kamba are also big basket-makers (see p.319): the familiar **sisal baskets** (*chondo*, or *vyondo* in the plural) come in a huge variety of patterns and can be made from nylon string as well as sisal and, much more rarely, baobab bark twine, with beads woven in. The baskets are all light and functional and, since becoming fashion accessories in the West, are much more expensive than they were: buying direct from weavers, especially when leather

Try to buy from **cooperatives** and development organizations. Places such as Kazuri in Nairobi (see p.125), Makindu Handicrafts Cooperative (see p.320), Kamba Woodcarvers Village (see p.405) and Bombolulu (see p.413) provide their employees with above-average rewards.

straps and other decorations have still to be added, can be an excellent deal for all.

Beads and tribal items

Beadwork (*ushanga, mkufu*) and **tribal regalia** – weapons such as spears and clubs, shields, drums (*ngoma*), carved stools and headrests, traditional utensils made from gourds (sometimes beaded), cowhorn keepsafes and metal jewellery – are fairly common, but much more expensive when they're the genuine article rather than made for the tourist industry. The best region in which to buy metal goods is the north: Turkana-land can yield some fairly spectacular examples of lethal weaponry, crafted indiscriminately for murderous assault or apartment wall. The bracelet-like wrist knives, or *aberait*, used to slash an enemy, are particularly impressive.

Toys

Look out for beautifully fashioned, push-along buses, cars and lorries made entirely of **wire**. These used to have tall rods, fitted with steering wheels, and would be given to lucky boys in rural areas by older brothers and uncles. Today, they're vastly outnumbered by mass-produced (though still handmade) wire vehicle toys, manufactured as tourist souvenirs. Also widely available are amusing, push-along birds, monkeys and cyclists, that flap, bob or crank as they're rolled.

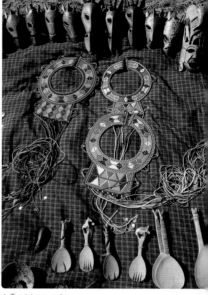

▲ Tourist souvenirs

▼ Wire toys

Local footwear ▲

Playing the *siwa* ▼

Textiles and footwear

Textiles, although always imported, bear a certain stamp of authenticity in that they are worn locally and make good-value, and practical, souvenirs. The printed women's wraps – **kanga** – in cotton, and the heavier-weave men's sarongs – **kikoi** – are really good buys on the coast, and older ones represent collectable items worth seeking out. Kangas are always sold in pairs and are printed with intriguing Swahili proverbs. Local tailors will make them into garments for you at very reasonable prices.

Footwear can also be really good value. The widespread Bata chain has great deals, but you can get much more interesting sandals from tourist stalls, including pretty, beaded leather sandals, and the much tougher and more local sandals made from discarded vehicle tyres – "five-thousand-mile shoes".

Music and musical instruments

Other good buys include **music CDs** (though try to listen before buying), and **musical instruments** – for example the *nyatiti*, a Luo lyre – although it's very hard to get quality instruments rather than souvenir facsimiles. Drums can be bulky and some people even buy them to use as tables, but check the skins have been properly cured. Those designed to be held under one arm, more common on the coast, are the most practical as souvenirs. Lamu has its own wind instrument called a *siwa*, a huge side-blown thing traditionally made from an elephant tusk, but these days fashioned from hardwood.

Shop has an excellent and very reasonably priced range, including single pieces of fabric or *kikois* at Ksh 300–2000 per *kanga*. The **traditional masks** you'll see everywhere are imported – only a handful of Kenyan tribes make masks, the Kikuyu being the best known, and these are exceedingly rare.

Community craft centres

Nairobi has a number of craft shops with charitable status, or associated with development or self-help projects. Although sometimes a little expensive – and bargaining isn't possible – they often have unusual and well-made stock, some of which finds its way into the Christmas charity catalogues overseas. A few are a little way out of town, but well worth making special journeys to visit, and they're good tonics if you're suffering from curio shop fatigue.

Amani ya Juu Riverside Drive ☎020/4449071, ⓦwww.amaniafrica.org. The project employs fifty women who have been marginalized by poverty and war. It's great for gifts – the boutique sells colourful handmade clothes and bags. Matatu #48. Mon–Fri 9am–5pm.

Bega Kwa Bega Korogocho Projects ☎0720/234228, ⓦwww.begakwabega.com. Federation of small handicrafts producers from the Korogocho slums of eastern Nairobi, offering sisal bags, necklaces, batiks, furniture and cloth puppets. Take a taxi.

Craft banda Sarit centre, Westlands. Hassle-free browsing and fair prices. Buses #25, #29, #30 and many others.

Kamili Designs Langata Rd, Karen ☎020/883640. This textile workshop sells locally designed, hand-printed fabrics. The designs are typically bold and colourful, available both by the metre and as cushions, bedspreads and the like. Buses/matatus #24, #111 or #126. Mon–Fri 9am–5pm.

Kazuri Beads & Pottery Centre Mbagathi Ridge, Karen ☎020/883500, ⓦwww.kazuri .com. Kazuri, which means "small and beautiful", employs nearly a hundred formerly destitute women, who make an extraordinary variety of handmade, mostly ceramic, jewellery and beads. You can watch the whole process from shaping and colouring to firing, and there's also a pottery showroom. It's expensive, but the stuff is lovely. They also have retail outlets at Village Market in Gigiri and the Junction Shopping Centre, Ngong Rd. Buses/matatus #24, #111 or #126. Workshops Mon–Fri 8am–4.30pm, Sat 8am–1pm; shop Mon–Sat 8am–5pm, Sun 9am–5pm.

Kitengela Glass Off the Magadi road, south of Nairobi National Park ☎020/6750602 or 0734/287887, ⓦwww.kitengela-glass.com. Inspiring community of glass-blowers and crafts-people in a photogenic creative village. Visitors are welcome and you can observe, browse and buy unhassled. You'll need your own transport to get here: it makes for a good extra visit if you're at the

Giraffe Centre or visiting Daphne Sheldrick's elephant orphans (see p.139 & p.138).

Maridadi Fabrics City Stadium roundabout, Landhies/Jogoo Rd, 2km east of the train station ☎020/554250. Church-based Maridadi was created in 1966 as an income-generating community project for women in one of Nairobi's oldest slum areas – Pumwani and Shauri Moyo. The main workshop is a delight if you're into making your own clothes. A large screen-printing workshop (on view from the visitors' gallery) produces the wide range of prints for sale in the shop. Especially appealing are the bark cloth prints – a natural weave used for clothing by many East African peoples until the end of the nineteenth century. Buses #34 or #36. Mon–Fri 8am–5pm.

Mikono Craft Shop Opposite Ratna Fitness Studio, Gitanga Rd, Kawangware, just north of Dagoretti Corner ☎020/3877498. The outlet of the Jesuit Refugee Service, with well-made work (especially beautiful patchwork textiles) from refugees, and superb Mozambican carvings. Bus #46 or #46B.

Spinner's Web 2nd floor, Viking House, Waiyaki Way, Westlands ☎020/4440882, ⓦwww .spinnerswebkenya.com. A large shop selling a lot of good stuff – crafts, textiles, woollen goods and jewellery, much of it made by self-help groups and individuals, including Meru's Makena Textile Workshop. Bus/matatu – any to Westlands.

Undugu Upstairs at The Mall, Westlands ☎020/4443525, ⓦwww.undugukenya.org. With its roots in the church, Undugu ("fraternity") is the most vigorous society of its kind in the country and organizes regular guided visits to their slum projects. The shop sells a good selection of well-priced, high-quality crafts with some more unusual items, such as Ethiopian jewellery, basketwork, and crafts from DRC, Tanzania and Uganda. You may be able to have a look around the workshops. Bus/matatu – any to Westlands. Mon–Fri 9am–6pm, Sat 9am–5.30pm.

Utamaduni Crafts Centre Bogoni East Rd, Langata ☎020/891798. Eighteen individual craft shops in one large house, opened by Richard Leakey in 1991 (a portion of the profits go to the Kenya Wildlife Service). It has everything you might want, much of it made on site or from street-kid projects; quality and prices are high. The attached *Verandah* restaurant is excellent. Bus/matatu #24. Daily 9.30am–6pm.

Woodley Weavers Chaka Rd, Hurlingham ☎0733/612028 ⓦwww.woodleyweavers.com. Known to many as the "rug gallery", this place has a variety of rugs made by local women, often single mothers from the Kibera slum, using local wool, cotton and plant dyes. Any bus or matatu to Ngong Rd.

Maasai and crafts markets

If you're after Maasai crafts (whether traditional beaded jewellery or items made up for the tourist industry), or carvings and crafts in general, the various "**Maasai Markets**" are recommended, though they are no longer the cheap, hot tip they once were. Initiated downtown opposite the post office in the mid-1990s, the group of Maasai and other women from rural areas, as well as a number of men, were moved several times by city council *askaris* and now convene to display their wares at various places throughout the week: on Friday at the rooftop car park at Village Market, Gigiri; on Tuesday at Westgate Mall in Westlands; on Saturday and Sunday at the Law Courts car park off City Hall Way; and on Sunday at the Yaya Centre in Hurlingham. They usually start around 9am and finish mid-afternoon. You'll sometimes find prices well below those in the tourist markets, with good deals on the simpler designs of beaded jewellery, baskets and gourds. But more usually you'll have to bargain hard to get what seems like an acceptable price. The Saturday Law Courts market is probably the most promising of the three for a bargain.

The **Embakasi Village Crafts Market**, located on the Mombasa road on the way to the airport (second turning on the left just after *City Cabanas Restaurant*; bus #34 and #34B), is perhaps one of the most organized in Kenya, and most items are much cheaper than in other Nairobi markets. There is an area where you can watch the carvers in progress, and commission individual carvers.

Kariokor Market

Between Racecourse Road and Ring Road, **Kariokor Market** (named after the despised wartime "Carrier Corps"; bus/matatu #4, #6, #14, #15, #30, #31, #32, #40, #42, or #46/46B) is closer to an oriental bazaar than most markets in Kenya, with permanent booths for the traders. Inside, there's as much manufacturing and finishing going on as selling – you'll find sisal weavers, leather workers, makers of tyre-rubber sandals ("5000-mile shoes", about Ksh200 a pair and surprisingly comfortable), carpenters, toy-makers, tailors, hairdressers, and a row of good, very cheap, amazingly clean eating places, popular at lunchtime with local workers. Note that you may sometimes be mobbed by kids and touts here.

Kariokor is the best place in Nairobi to buy **baskets** (*vyondo*), made with sisal, coloured with natural or artificial dyes; with garish plastic; or with cord manufactured from the bark of the baobab tree. The cord baskets can be truly exquisite, with tiny beads included in the tight weave. A number of booths sell vaguely pharmaceutical oddities – snuff, remedies, charms, amulets and so on – where you can also pick up anything from feathers to snakeskin. Outside you'll find the odd African literary gem on the secondhand bookstalls.

Clothes, shoes, toys and music

The largest general market in Nairobi is **Gikomba Market**, off Landhies Road, past the Country Bus Station (to get there by public transport, take any bus or matatu for Jogoo Road and get off at Gikomba). This is a spot that few tourists ever see, a labyrinth of muddy alleyways, courtyards, and open sewers. It's also a place to experience an exhilarating slice of Nairobi life, and just about anything can be found on sale, from school uniforms and electronic equipment to industrial-size ovens. There are also tailors, shoe repair shops, hairdressers and numerous little bars and food stalls. Come with someone who knows the place, though; it's very easy to get lost and Gikomba can be unsafe.

For everyday **general merchandise stores**, back in the CBD, the eastern part of the City Market district is the most worthwhile area. **Biashara Street** (*biashara* means commerce) is the street for fabrics and the best place to buy tents and mosquito nets (see "Listings" on p.131). For cheap and not-so-cheap imports, the hangar-like Freemark Pavilion in south **Uhuru Park** has hundreds of stalls.

You'll find **clothes** shops all over, with fashion outlets on Standard and Kaunda streets, and more down-to-earth gear on Kenyatta Avenue, Moi Avenue and Kimathi Street. Good-value **footwear** is available from the African Boot Co, on Moi Avenue opposite Bookpoint, and Bata, which has numerous branches around the city. Even cheaper footwear can be found at Miniprice Footwear Supermarket on River Road.

If you wish to buy **toys**, you'll find the best items are locally made wire-and-fabric contraptions – cars, bicycles, flapping birds – which are sometimes beautiful works of art. You'll find them in the markets, but the best ones are usually made at home for sons and nephews and not for sale. The best general toyshop in the CBD is Hobby Centre in Jubilee Insurance House on Kaunda Street, but Village Market also has a good toyshop, Toy World.

The huge volume of **music** on CD – whether legitimate, murky, or illegal – makes Nairobi a great place for music fans, especially if you have a taste for Kenya's stunning variety of ethnic musical strands, not to mention the plethora of recordings from elsewhere in east and central Africa, especially Congo. Try Assanand's and Musikland on Moi Avenue, Melodica on Tom Mboya Street or, better still, any of the host of shops and stalls on and around River Road and Accra Road.

Shopping malls

Nairobi now has the dubious distinction of having more **shopping malls** – more than twenty and counting – than any other African city outside South Africa, providing a hassle-free environment for getting on with ordinary shopping and business. You'll find most of them stuffed into the western and northern suburbs where they cater to the expat and wealthy Kenyan markets. They all include banks, travel agents, specialist food suppliers and an assortment of cafés and restaurants.

Junction Dagoretti Corner, Ngong Rd. Also known as Nakumatt Junction, it encompasses a large Nakumatt supermarket, cinema, bookstore, greengrocer, restaurants, a good boutique selling leather products, the Kitengela glass shop and fashion stores.

The Mall Westlands. Shops and offices including a branch of Let's Go Travel, a sports shop, a French bakery, ice-cream parlour, a 711-style convenience store and numerous fashion and clothing stores. Buses #25, #29, #30 and many others.

Prestige Plaza Ngong Rd. Features a large supermarket, coffee shop and brand new cinema showing the latest Hollywood blockbusters.

Sarit Centre Westlands ⓦ www.saritcentre.com. A big, established complex, with more than sixty shops and offices, including a dry-cleaner, a health-food shop, a watch repairer, a post office, a multiplex cinema, an Uchumi Hypermarket, the Arena Health Club, a large branch of the Textbook Centre and an Apple computer store. There are some good sports and hobbies retailers on the lower ground floor. Buses as for The Mall.

Village Market Limuru Rd, Gigiri ⓦ www
.villagemarket-kenya.com. Upmarket shopping centre that's more California than Nairobi, complete with miniature waterfall. More than 100

shops compete for your custom as well as a four-screen cinema, a Nakumatt hypermarket, a bowling alley and an excellent food court with great German, Thai and African outlets. Bus/matatu #106 and #108.

Westgate Westlands. The newest and one of the most impressive malls in Nairobi – a vast Singapore-style space, housing a huge Nakumatt supermarket, a good Safaricom service centre,

high-end clothing boutiques, a cinema and a good bookstore.

Yaya Centre Argwings Kodhek Rd, Hurlingham Ⓦ www.yaya-centre.co.ke. There's a good deli here, a useful newsagent with a wide selection of mainly British magazines, a bookshop, super-market, health-food shop, French bakery, post office, chemist, camping supply store and a good toyshop. Bus/matatu #41, #46 or 46B.

Safari transport and operators

Nairobi is the travel hub of Africa, with a mass of opportunities for **safaris** around Kenya and literally hundreds of safari operators, car-rental outlets and travel agents to provide you with everything you need for your trip. See the "Safaris" section in Basics (p.65) for general information about **safaris and guides**. If you're organizing your own self-drive safari in Kenya (with or without a driver), see the list of **car rental** companies on p.131.

One possibility not often considered is **cycling**: Hell's Gate at Naivasha, Kakamega Forest and a number of other small parks allow bikes, and there's a lot of wonderful cycling country besides these areas. For listings of bike shops, see p.131; for bicycle rental, contact Bike Treks (Ksh2000 per day; see opposite), though note that they prefer you to cycle out of town as there's a risk of theft in Nairobi.

At the other end of the budget spectrum, the opportunities for photography and seeing the country are without equal if you **charter a plane**. A few small operators, mostly based at Wilson Airport, will oblige; see "Air charter companies", p.130, for details.

Safari operators

You can pick up plenty of leaflets about safaris from most **travel agents**, the best of whom are honest and reputable. It's always a good idea, however, to meet staff from the operator you are travelling with in advance of departure. Check whether the advertised safari is actually run by the company in question, as the practice of one company sub-contracting a safari to another is common, especially in low season when advertised departures tend to get consolidated. The practice gives you less redress if things go wrong. This is especially important for safaris going into **Tanzania** and **Uganda**, on which you should ensure your company has at least an office in the relevant country. **Safari touts** who hang around on the street, or at various hotels and lodgings, are keen to take you to operators' offices, but should be avoided – no reputable company uses them.

The **Kenya Association of Tour Operators**, Longonot Rd, off Kilimanjaro Ave, Upper Hill (KATO, ☏020/2713348 or 0722/434845 or 0735/917589, Ⓦ www.katokenya.org), publishes full lists of its members, and can offer advice if you have problems with any of them. KATO membership is not a guarantee of a good operator, but it's a good start. The KATO website runs a quotation service, which forwards your needs and interests to their members who then contact you directly by email. If you choose a cheaper company that is not a member of KATO, you should ensure they are registered with the Ministry of Tourism, though this does not mean much on the ground. Take your time, ask to see their vehicles, demand everything in writing, signed and stamped, and including a breakdown of the costs, and don't be pressured into making any decisions until you are ready.

Every other business in Nairobi seems to be a safari outfit and it's obviously impossible to mention more than a few. In the challenging environment of Kenya, spotless reputations are hard to maintain, but the following businesses rarely come in for criticism. The pricing categories are a rough guide only: most companies will be able to offer safaris for more – or sometimes less.

Budget: up to $200 per day

Best Camping 2nd floor, Amee Arcade/Rank Xerox House, corner of Muthithi Rd and Parklands Rd, Westlands ☎0733/630053 or 0733/603090, Ⓦwww.bestcampingkenya.com. Long-established operator whose budget camping trips are generally recommended.

Bike Treks Westlands ☎020/2141757 or 0722/727257 Ⓦwww.biketreks.co.ke. One of Kenya's few bike tour operators, they have a basic camp, *Olperr Elongo*, in the wooded Sekenani valley, just outside the Maasai Mara National Reserve.

Dallago Corner of Nyeri and Olegoreine roads, Kileleshwa ☎020/3877361, Ⓦwww.dallagotours.com. One of the few budget companies to have a bronze-certified guide, Dallago offers a very good value 9-day camping safari to Maasai Mara, Lake Nakuru, Samburu and Amboseli, from $150 per day all-in, based on six clients.

Gametrackers 5th floor, Nginyo Towers, corner of Koinange and Moktar Daddah streets ☎020/2222703, Ⓦwww.gametrackersafaris.com. Popular and consistently good operator with strong northern Kenya credentials (8-day "Turkana truck" $800 plus local payments) and some unusual offerings, including a 7-day "Obama Kogelo" to western Kenya $760.

Green Belt Safaris Kilimani Lane, off Elgeo Marakwet Road ☎020/2211842, Ⓦwww.greenbeltmovement.org. Community homestays, where the guests participate in rural activities (seed collection, nursery preparation, tree planting, harvesting and meal preparation) for up to a week.

Ice Rock Mountain Treks and Safaris 4th floor, NCM Building, Tom Mboya St ☎020/2244608, Ⓦwww.icerockclimbing.com. A small professional set-up with knowledgeable guides, mainly dealing with safaris to Mount Kenya, Kilimanjaro and Hell's Gate. The owner, who used to be a member of the Mount Kenya rescue team, organizes and leads most trips.

Kenia Tours and Safaris 4th floor, Jubilee Insurance House, Kaunda/Wabera sts ☎020/2223699, Ⓦwww.keniatours.com. Keenly priced, budget camping safaris specialist.

Let's Go Travel ABC Place, Waiyaki Way, Westlands ☎020/4447151, Ⓦwww.letsgosafari.com. Branches in the CBD at Caxton House, Standard St (☎020/340331) and Crossroads, Karen (☎020/882505). First and best port of call for independent travellers in Kenya, Let's Go is agent for a large number of homestays and independent lodges throughout Kenya and also runs its own well-organized budget camping and other safaris. One of the few companies to have offices in both Tanzania and Uganda and to run trips to both of Kenya's neighbours.

Savage Wilderness Safaris Sarit Centre, Westlands ☎0733/735508, Ⓦwww.whitewaterkenya.com. Excellent programme of technical climbing and walking trips on Mount Kenya, white-water rafting, and walking safaris.

Savuka Tours & Safaris 4th floor, Panafric House, Kenyatta Ave ☎02/225108, Ⓕ215016, Ⓦwww.savuka-travels.com. Good-value camping safaris that get favourable recommendations from budget travellers for their good food and driver/guides, though accommodation is basic.

Spirit of Africa Safaris 7th floor, Sonalux House, Moi Ave ☎020/211596 or 0722/842819, Ⓦwww.spiritofafricatours.com. Good budget safaris aimed at the backpacker market. As well as the usual camping safaris, they feature more unusual offerings, such as a visit to a witch doctor in eastern Kenya.

Mid-priced: $200–500 per day

Africa Expeditions Ngong Racecourse, Ngong Rd ☎020/3002711, Ⓦwww.africaexpeditions.com. Photographic safaris specialists, offering largely tailor-made trips, with their own camps in the Mara and (unusually) the Loita Hills, and a good record and highly professional approach.

Gamewatchers UN Crescent, behind Village Market ☎020/7123129 or 0722/509200, Ⓦwww.porini.com. Innovative, eco-conscious operators with a strong list of bronze and silver guides among their staff. As well as running excellent safaris, they also own and manage the outstanding *Porini* eco-camps in the Mara, Amboseli area and Ol Pejeta. Highly recommended.

Magical Africa Caxton House, Standard St ☎020/251303 or 0722/608169. General operator, in business since 2003, billing itself as Kenya's only gay-friendly safari operator.

Naturetrek Adventure Safaris 1st floor, Imenti House, Moi Ave ☎020/341188 www.naturetreksafaris.com. Specialists in walking safaris, from 3 to 10 days, plus a range of more conventional options.

Nguruman Safaris Vanga Road, off Gitanga Rd, Lavington ☏ 020/3874434 or 0733/2722818, Ⓦ www.ngurumansafaris.com. Specializes in camping safaris in Land Cruisers and overland trucks. Trips include the usual safaris, as well as trips to the Chalbi desert. They offer good meals, knowledgeable guides and well-maintained vehicles.

Southern Cross Symbion House, Karen Rd ☏ 020/2434600, Ⓦ www.southerncross safaris.com. Considering they have a number of silver

as well as bronze guides, their lodge and tented camp safaris offer extremely good value for money.

Sunworld Riverside Lane, off Riverside Drive, Westlands ☏ 020/4445669 or 0722/525400, Ⓦ www.sunworld-safari.com. Extremely proficient 4WD specialists with a good fleet of vehicles, excellent bronze and silver driver-guides and a well-organized, walk-in bookings operation.

Tour Africa Safaris Palacina Court, Denis Pritt Rd ☏ 020/2729333, Ⓦ www.tourafrica-safaris.com. Long-established and well-run travel agency with its own tailor-made lodge safaris (camping safaris are arranged through other companies).

Luxury: more than $500 per day

Expensive safari outfits are mostly operated to very high standards. The following firms will give good return for your money if you are in the $500–1000-plus per day league, per person, and want something special. At this level, what you do is largely up to you. Transport is usually by comfortable 4WD, accommodation is in boutique lodges or tented camps, or private mobile camps, and the safari guides are some of the best in the world.

Cheli & Peacock Langata, Wilson Airport ☏ 020/603090, Ⓦ www.chelipeacock.com. As owners and marketing agents for some of Kenya's very best small lodges and tented camps, C&P have a savvy and personal approach that keeps them at the forefront of safari operation and lodge design: you tend to see it here first. Highly recommended for their lodges, and they also have a good number of bronze and sliver guides among their staff.

Ker & Downey Safaris Langata Link, off Langata South Rd, Karen ☏ 020/890725, Ⓦ www .kerdowneysafaris.com. The archetypal old-style safari outfitter (Kenya's oldest, dating from 1946), Ker & Downey are the people to choose if you want a no-expense-spared, tailor-made safari, either fully mobile, or using lodges and camps. Many silver and bronze guides work for them.

Origins Safaris 5th floor, Landmark Plaza, Argwings Kodhek Rd ☏ 020/2042695, Ⓦ www.originsafaris.info. Excellent bird-watching trips and a huge range of other safaris, for all interests, with more than twenty bronze and silver guides and one of only four gold guides in the

country. Not cheap, but very highly recommended if you have specific interests, with accommodation at well-selected lodges and tented camps.

Safaris Unlimited 328 Langata Rd, near Hillcrest Schools, 3km west of Bomas turning ☏ 020/890435, Ⓦ www.safarisunlimited.com. Riding safari specialists, for confident riders only, covering the Mara, Chyulu Hills and other wilderness areas, and including stays at their own Longonot Ranch House at Naivasha.

Tropical Ice 98 Marula Lane, Karen ☏ 020/884652, Ⓦ www.tropical-ice.com. High-end adventure safaris like they used to be, combining 4WD vehicles with hiking, led by expert safari guides, operating their own, traditional-style, mobile camps.

Micato Safaris 3rd floor, View Park Towers, Utalii Lane, off Uhuru Highway ☏ 020 2226944, Ⓦ www .micato.com. Much lauded Kenyan-American tour operator with off-the-peg and tailor-made trips run by crews who include more bronze and silver safari guides than any other operator in the country – all trips are run by a driver-guide with at least a bronze certificate.

Listings

Air charter companies Blue Bird Aviation, Wilson Airport ☏ 020/602338 or 0720/251000, Ⓦ www .bluebirdaviation.com; Boskovic Air Charters Ltd, Wilson Airport ☏ 020/606364 or 0733/600208, Ⓦ www.boskovicaircharters.com; East African

Charters, Wilson Airport ☏ 020/603860, Ⓦ www .eaaircharters.co.ke; Mission Aviation Fellowship, Wilson Airport ☏ 020/607051, Ⓦ www.maf.or.ke (flights to northern Kenya); Safarilink (contact details below; from $2.70 per mile – 2-seater Cessna 182).

Airlines, Domestic AirKenya Express, Wilson Airport ☎ 020/605745, 🖳 www.airkenya.com; ALS, Wilson Airport ☎ 020/60986 or 0727/666222, 🖳 www.als.co.ke; East African Safari Air Express, Wilson Airport ☎ 020/6654321, 🖳 www .bookeastafrican.com; Fly540, ABC Place, Waiyaki Way, Westlands ☎ 020/4453252 or 0722/540540, 🖳 www.fly540.com; Jetlink, JKI Airport ☎ 020/8021444 or 0737/222444, 🖳 www.jetlink .co.ke; ✈ Safarilink, Wilson Airport ☎ 020/600777 or 0734/338888, 🖳 www.safarilink-kenya.com.

Airlines, International Air India, 1st floor, Jeevan Bharati Building, Harambee Ave ☎ 020/313300; Air Madagascar, 1st floor, Hilton Building, City Hall Way ☎ 020/225286; Air Malawi, International Life House, Mama Ngina St ☎ 020/317113; Air Mauritius, 2nd flood Sasini House, Loita St ☎ 020/2240024; Air Tanzania, Mezzanine floor, International Life House, Mama Ngina St ☎ 020/2227486; British Airways, International Life House, Mama Ngina St ☎ 020/3277000; Egyptair, Hilton Building, City Hall Way ☎ 020/2226821; El Al, 9th floor, KCS House, Mama Ngina St ☎ 020/2228123; Emirates, 20th floor, View Park Towers, Utalii Lane ☎ 020/3290000; Ethiopian Airlines, Bruce House, Muindi Mbingu St ☎ 020/2217558; Gulf Air, 8th floor, International Life House, Mama Ngina St ☎ 020/2214441; Kenya Airways, 5th floor, Barclays Plaza, Loita St ☎ 020/3274100; KLM, Barclays Plaza, Loita St ☎ 020/3274210; Saudi Arabian Airlines, 15th floor, Ambank House, University Way ☎ 020/2230337; South African Airways, Mezzanine floor, International Life House ☎ 020/2229663; Swiss Airlines, 1st floor, Caltex Plaza, Limuru Rd ☎ 020/3744045.

Airport Information JKI Airport ☎ 020/6612000.

American Express Middle East Bank building, Upper Hill ☎ 020/2734971.

Art galleries Gallery Watatu, Lonrho House, Standard St, promotes contemporary African art (☎ 020/2228737, 🖳 www.gallerywatatu.com), as does the Rahimtulla Museum of Modern Art, aka RaMoMa, Rahimtulla Tower, Upper Hill ☎ 020/2729181.

Banks and exchange There are branches of Barclays and Standard Chartered everywhere, most with ATMs. All banks are closed on Sun except those at the airport, but ATMs operate.

Bike shops Kenya Cycle Mart, the best parts, repair and sales shop, is in Butere Road, Industrial Area. Also try Cycleland, lower ground floor, Sarit Centre, Westlands.

Books Good bookshops include: Textbook Centre, Kijabe St; Nation Bookshop, Kenyatta Ave at the *Stanley Hotel*; Bookpoint, Loans House, Moi Ave; the Textbook Centre, at the Sarit Centre, Westlands; and Books First at Village Market, Gigiri.

Bus companies Akamba Bus, Lagos Rd, and booking office in Wabera St ☎ 020/2222027 or 020/2225488, 🖳 www.akambabus.com; Coastline, Accra Rd/Duruma Rd ☎ 0722/206448; Davanu Shuttle, 4th floor, Windsor House, University Way ☎ 0722/852788; East Africa Shuttles (agent for buses to Tanzania), Portal Place, Muindi Mbingu St ☎ 020/2248453, 🖳 www.eastafricashuttles.com; Easy Coach, Kalamu House, Waiyaki Way, Westlands ☎ 020/3003290 and from Haile Selassie Ave ☎ 0738/200301; Grand Bus Services, top of Accra Rd/Cross Rd ☎ 020/3535786; Impala Shuttle (for Tanzania; pick up from city centre hotels) *Silver Springs Hotel*, Hurlingham ☎ 020/2730953, 🖳 www.impalashuttle.com; Kalita Busline, Cross Rd ☎ 020/2248255; Kensilver Express, Dubois Rd ☎ 0722/509918; Modern Coast, Cross Rd/River Rd ☎ 0733/715553; Riverside Shuttle (for Tanzania; pick up from city centre hotels), Monrovia St, opposite Jeevanjee Gardens ☎ 0725/999121 or 020/2229618, 🖳 www.riverside-shuttle.com. In addition, the following are also in operation: Easy Coach, from Haile Selassie Ave ☎ 0738/200301; Falcon Coach (ex-Tawfiq), from Shell station, Kirinyaga Rd and Voi Rd ☎ 0710/319641; Jolly Coach, from Sheikh Karume Rd, off Munyu Rd ☎ 0720/610088; and MASH from the corner of Accra Rd and Duruma Rd ☎ 0733/929626.

Camping equipment Try Atul's, Biashara St ☎ 020/2225935; Kenya Canvas, Canvas House, Muindi Mbingu St ☎ 020/343262; or Xtreme Outdoors, Yaya Centre, Hurlingham ☎ 020/722224, 🖳 www.xtremeoutdoors.co.ke.

Car rental Avis, College House, University Way ☎ 020/336074, 🖳 bit.ly/2C1Gr; Budget, Muindi Mbingu St ☎ 020/223581, 🖳 www.budget-kenya .com; Central Rent-A-Car, *680 Hotel*, Muindi Mbingu St ☎ 020/2222888, 🖳 www.carhirekenya.com; ✈ Concorde Car Hire, Shell Petrol Station, Lower Kabete Rd, Westlands ☎ 020/4448953, 🖳 www .concorde.co.ke; Cruising Cruisers, ground floor, Motherland Centre, corner of Ngong Rd and Karen Rd ☎ 0736/219639, 🖳 www.cruisingcruisers.com; ✈ Sunworld, Riverside Lane, off Riverside Drive, Westlands ☎ 020/4445669 or 0722/525400, 🖳 www.sunworld-safari.com.

Car repairs Stantech Motors, Shimo la Tewa Rd, off Lusaka Rd, Industrial Area (☎ 020/530662, 🖳 www.stantechmotors.co.ke), is reliable and recommended.

Cultural Centres Alliance Française, Utalii Lane, off Uhuru Highway ☎ 020/340054, 🖳 www .alliancefrnairobi.org; British Council, Upper Hill Rd

☎020/2836000, ⊕www.britishcouncil.org; Goethe-Institut, Maendeleo House, corner of Loita St and Monrovia St ☎020/2224640, ⊕www .goethe.de/ins/ke/nai; Italian Cultural Institute, 5th floor, Grenadier Tower, Woodvale Grove, Westlands ☎020/4451266, ⊕www.iicnairobi.esteri.it; Japan Africa Culture Interchange Institute (Jacii), Kamburu Dr, off Ngong Rd ☎020/3866262, ⊕www.jacii.net.

Dentists Peter Griffiths & Associates, Kolloh Rd, off James Gichuru Rd, Lavington ☎020/4348211 or 0722 736439; Hurlingham Dental Care, Argwings Kodhek Rd, Hurlingham ☎020/2720331, ⊕www .kalaiya.eastafrica247.com.

Doctors See "Hospitals" opposite, or ask your embassy for a list of recommended practitioners.

Embassies, high commissions and consulates Australia, ICIPE House, Riverside Drive, off Chiromo Rd ☎020/4445034; Burundi, 14th floor, Development House, Moi Ave, ☎020/575249; Canada, Limuru Rd, Gigiri ☎020/3663000; DR Congo, 12th floor, Electricity House, Harambee Ave ☎020/3754253; Egypt, 24 Othaya Rd (south), off Gitanga Rd, Kileleshwa B☎020/3870298; Eritrea, 2nd floor, New Rehema House, Rhapta Rd ☎020/4443163; Ethiopia, State House Ave, Nairobi Hill ☎020/2732050; France, 9th floor, Barclays Plaza, Loita St ☎020/2778000; Germany, Ludwig Krapf House, 113 Riverside Drive ☎020/4262100 ,⊕www.nairobi.diplo.de; India, 2nd floor, Jeevan Bharati Building, Harambee Ave ☎020/2222566; Ireland, Dante Diesel Workshop Building, Masai Rd, Karen ☎020/556647; Italy, 9th floor, International Life House, Mama Ngina St ☎020/2247750; Japan, Mara Rd, Upper Hill ☎020/2898000; Madagascar, AACC Building, Westlands ☎020/4452410; Malawi, Mvuli Rd/Church Rd, off Waiyaki Way, Westlands ☎020/4440569; Mozambique, 3rd floor, Bruce House, Standard St ☎020/2214191; Netherlands, Riverside Lane, off Riverside Drive ☎020/4288000; New Zealand, Wajiiri House, Argwings Kodhek Rd ☎020/2712466; Nigeria, Lenana Rd (west), Hurlingham ☎020/570226; Poland, Kabarnet Rd, off Ngong Rd, Woodley ☎020/566288; Rwanda, 12th floor, International Life House, Mama Ngina St ☎020/317400; Seychelles, 114 James Gichuru Rd ☎020/577628; Somalia, 5th floor, International Life House, Mama Ngina St ☎020/580165; South Africa, 3rd floor, Roshanmaer Place, Lenana Rd ☎020/2827100; Spain, 3rd floor, International Life House, Mama Ngina St ☎020/2226568; Sudan, Kabarnet Rd, off Ngong Rd, Woodley ☎020/3875118; Tanzania, 9th floor, Reinsurance Plaza, Taifa Rd ☎020/311948; Uganda, Riverside Paddocks, off Riverside Drive ☎020/4445420; UK, Upper Hill Rd, off Haile Selassie Ave

☎020/2844000; US, United Nations Ave, Gigiri ☎020/3636000; Zambia, Nyerere Rd ☎020/2724796; Zimbabwe, 2 Westlands Close, Westlands Rd ☎020/3744052.

Football (soccer) Nyayo Stadium, at the junction of Uhuru Highway and Langata Rd (☎020/501825). Seats start from Ksh100.

Golf Courses in Nairobi include Windsor Golf & Country Club, Kigwa Rd, 5km north of the city ☎020/8562300; Nairobi Golf Club, Mucai Drive, off Ngong Rd ☎020/725769; Muthaiga Golf Club, Muthaiga Rd ☎020/3761280; and Karen Golf & Country Club, Karen Rd ☎020/884089. Tobs Golf Safaris Ltd, (☎020/2710825, ⊕www .kenya-golf-safaris.com), organizes golfing excursions around the country.

Horse racing The Kenya Jockey Club's racecourse is on Ngong Road, bus #24 or matatu #111. Races are every Sun, with viewing free – or grandstand entry Ksh200.

Hospitals Aga Khan Hospital, Third Parklands Ave ☎020/3662020; Kenyatta National Hospital, Hospital Rd ☎020/2726300 (buses #7C, #34, #56, #61B); Nairobi Hospital, Argwings Kodhek Rd ☎020/2722160, bus #46 (reputedly the best in East Africa, and accordingly priced); and Nazareth Hospital, Riara Ridge, outside Nairobi off the Limuru road ☎020/2017401.

Internet access There are internet cafés all over the city. In the CBD, try the many places round the junction of Loita St and Monrovia St. Wi-fi spots include several in Westlands – the cybercafé on the top floor of the Sarit Centre, the Art Café in Westgate mall and Ukay Nakumatt across from Westgate – plus the Yaya Centre in Hurlingham.

Left luggage Bags can be left safely at the luggage store at the railway station (Ksh80 per day). There is also a left-luggage store at JKI airport (Ksh300 per day).

Libraries British Council Library, Upper Hill Rd (Tues–Fri 10am–5pm, Sat 9am–noon ☎020/2836000); McMillan Memorial Library, Banda St (Mon–Fri 9am–5pm, Sat 9.30am–1pm ☎020/2224281 ext 2253); British Institute in Eastern Africa, Laikipia Rd, off Arboretum Drive, Kileleshwa (☎020/4343190, ⊕www.biea.ac.uk).

Opticians Eye Modes Ltd, Kenya Cinema Plaza, Moi Ave ☎020/2222601 (Mon–Fri 7.30am–6pm, Sat 9am–2pm); Family Eye Care Centre, Princely House, Moi Ave ☎020/312426 (Mon–Sat 8.30am–5pm, Sun 9am–noon.

Pharmacies AAA Pharmaceuticals, Sarit Centre, Westlands ☎020/4451091; Acacia Pharmacy, ICEA Building, Kenyatta Ave ☎020/2212175 and Ralph Bunche Rd ☎020/2711611.

Photography For camera repairs, try Camera Clinic, Kamae Lane, off Luthuli Ave ☎020/2222492. Spectrum Colour Lab, ABC Place, Westlands ☎020/4448352, are also helpful.

Post The GPO on Kenyatta Ave (Mon–Fri 8am–6pm, Sat 9am–noon) has *poste restante* and the usual services.

Public Map Office Survey of Kenya HQ, Thika road (see map overleaf) ☎020/8562902. Turn to left (north) immediately after the footbridge.

Riding Karen Riding School ☎0712/292630, ✉garycattermole@yahoo.com (Tues–Sun 8am–6pm).

Sports Bowling: Cosmic Bowling & Pool Centre in Sound Plaza, Woodvale Grove, Westlands ☎020/4444742; Diving: Nairobi Sailing and Sub-Aqua Club ☎0733/608810, ✉asdearing @gmail.com (BSAC training and trips to coastal and lake diving sites); Jogging: the jogging trails through the golf course at the *Windsor* (see p.107) are useful, but you can jog in many parks and suburban streets, and you'll often have the company of others; Karting: GP-Karting, next to *Carnivore*, with a 500m circuit (Tues–Sun 10am–7pm, closed Mon ☎020/608444 or 0733/66633; from Ksh1000); Skating: Panari Sky Centre, near JKI Airport (daily, 11am–10pm, Ksh800 per hr, including skates).

Swimming pools Nayo Stadium (see "Football") has a 50-metre pool. Other pools open to the public include those at the *Boulevard* and *Panafric* hotels and the *YMCA*. For water-babies, the slides and fountains at the *Splash!* water park next to *Carnivore* (see p.119) are a must (☎020/603777; Wed–Sun 10am–5.30pm, closed Mon & Tues).

Supermarkets Supermarkets and grocery stores can be found all over the city. Nakumatt, the biggest and cleanest, has branches in most big malls (all open daily, some open 24/7) and a downtown branch on the corner of Moktar Daddah and Monrovia streets. Branches of Uchumi (Aga Khan Walk and Monrovia St) are open Mon–Sat 8.30am–8.30pm & Sun 10am–7pm. Both chains are also good for camping supplies and sleeping bags.

Travel agents for airline bookings Most travel agents can book you international airline seats, but the following should be able to offer discounted seats: Akarim Agencies, ground floor, Kenyatta International Conference Centre ☎020/2218880, ⓦwww.akarim.net; Bunson Travel, Pan Africa House, Standard St ☎020/2221992, ⓦwww .bunsonkenya.com; Jet Travel 7th floor, Rehani House, corner of Kenyatta Ave and Koinange St ☎020/310360, ⓦwww.jettravelkenya.com; Kambo Travel 1st floor, Mpaka House, Mpaka Road, Westlands ☎020/4448505.

Vaccinations Cholera, yellow fever, typhoid and hepatitis jabs can be obtained from the Inoculation centre, City Hall, City Hall Way, ☎020/224281 ext. 2526 (Mon–Fri 8.30am–12.30pm & 2–4.30pm).

Visitor's passes/visas Visitor's pass extensions can be obtained at Nyayo House, Posta Rd, behind the GPO ☎020/2222022 (Mon–Fri 8.30am–12.30pm & 2–3.30pm).

Nairobi Province

NAIROBI PROVINCE stretches way beyond the city suburbs, taking in an area of some 690 square kilometres (270 square miles) and ranging from agricultural and ranching land to savanna and mountain forest. For visitors, most of the interest lies to the **southwest**, in the predominantly Maasai land that begins with **Nairobi National Park**, and includes the watershed ridge of the **Ngong Hills**. It's a striking landscape, vividly described in Karen Blixen's *Out of Africa* (see "Books", p.603). **North** of the city, the land is also distinctive, with narrow valleys twisting up into the Kinangop plateau, some still filled with jungle and, it's said, leopards. In spite of that, the steep slopes here are high-value real estate, still being developed as exclusive suburbs, planted with shady gardens and festooned with security signs. To the **west** lies largely Kikuyu farmland, densely cultivated with corn, bananas and the cash crop insecticide plant, pyrethrum. **Southeast**, beyond the shanty suburb of Dandora, are the wide Athi plains, which are traditionally mostly ranching country but nowadays increasingly invaded by the spread of Nairobi's industrial satellites.

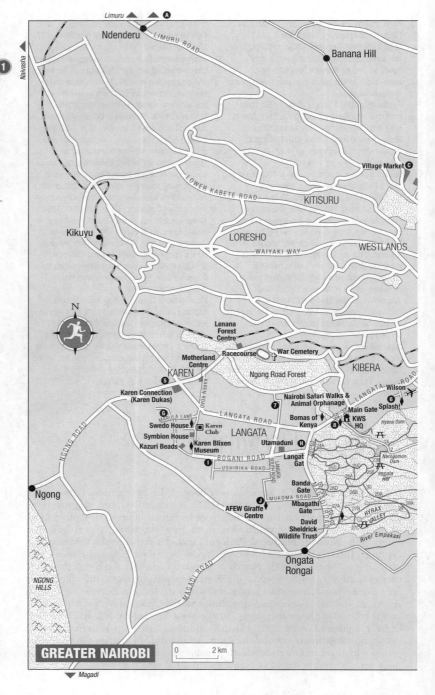

Limuru ▲ ▲ ▲ Ⓐ

Naivasha ◀

Ndenderu

LIMURU ROAD

Banana Hill

Village Market Ⓒ

LOWER KABETE ROAD

KITISURU

Kikuyu

LORESHO

WESTLANDS

WAIYAKI WAY

N

Lenana Forest Centre

Racecourse

War Cemetery

KIBERA

Motherland Centre

KAREN

Ngong Road Forest

Ⓖ

Ⓢ

KAREN ROAD

Karen Connection (Karen Dukas)

Nairobi Safari Walks & Animal Orphanage

Langata– Wilson

LANGATA ROAD

Ⓖ
MARULA LANE
Swedo House

Symbion House

Kazuri Beads

Karen Club

LANGATA ROAD

Ⓖ

Bomas of Kenya

Main Gate Ⓖ

Splash

KWS HQ

Ⓖ

Hyena Dam

NGONG ROAD

Karen Blixen Museum

Ⓘ

LANGATA

Utamaduni Ⓗ

BOGANI ROAD

Langat Gat

LANGATA SOUTH ROAD

24A

Narogomon Dam

USHIRIKA ROAD

25D

26A

25B

26C

Impala Hill

AFEW Giraffe Centre

Ⓙ

MUKOMA ROAD

Banda Gate

26D

26B

30

27A

HYRAX VALLEY

27B

Ngong

Mbagathi Gate

27C

David Sheldrick Wildlife Trust

River Empakasi

NGONG HILLS

MAGADI ROAD

Ongata Rongai

▼ Magadi

GREATER NAIROBI

0   2 km

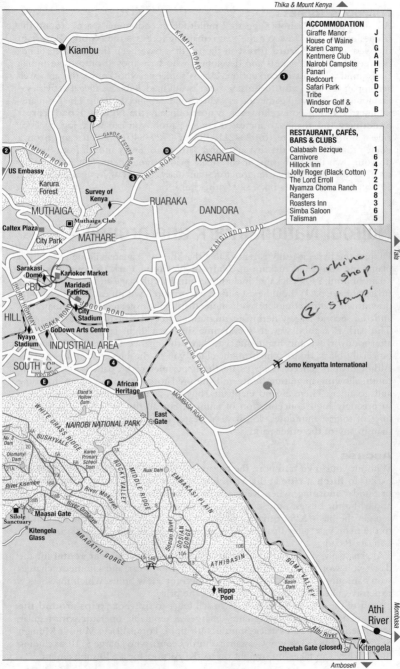

Thika & Mount Kenya

ACCOMMODATION

Giraffe Manor	J
House of Waine	I
Karen Camp	G
Kentmere Club	A
Nairobi Campsite	H
Panari	F
Redcourt	E
Safari Park	D
Tribe	C
Windsor Golf & Country Club	B

RESTAURANT, CAFÉS, BARS & CLUBS

Calabash Bezique	1
Carnivore	6
Hillock Inn	4
Jolly Roger (Black Cotton)	7
The Lord Erroll	2
Nyamza Choma Ranch	C
Rangers	8
Roasters Inn	3
Simba Saloon	6
Talisman	5

① rhino shop
② stamp!

Kiambu

KAMITI ROAD

US Embassy

Karura Forest

Survey of Kenya

LIMURU ROAD

GARDEN ESTATE ROAD

THIKA ROAD

KASARANI

RUARAKA

DANDORA

MUTHAIGA

Muthaiga Club

Caltex Plaza

City Park

MATHARE

KANGUNDO ROAD

Tala

Sarakasi Dome

Kariokor Market

Maridadi Fabrics

CBD

City Stadium

JOGOO ROAD

HILL

UHURU HIGHWAY

LUSAKA ROAD

GoDown Arts Centre

Nyayo Stadium

INDUSTRIAL AREA

OUTER RING ROAD

SOUTH "C"

POPO ROAD

Jomo Kenyatta International

African Heritage

East Gate

MOMBASA ROAD

Eland's Hollow Dam

NAIROBI NATIONAL PARK

WHITE GRASS RIDGE

BUSHYVALE

No 3 Dam

Otomanyi Dam

Karen Primary School Dam

Ruai Dam

ROCKY VALLEY

MIDDLE RIDGE

EMBAKASI PLAIN

River Kisembe

River Mokoyeti

River Ombaye

Silole Sanctuary

Maasai Gate

Kitengela Glass

MBAGATHI GORGE

SOSIAN GORGE

Sosian River

ATHI BASIN

BOMA VALLEY

Athi Basin Dam

Hippo Pool

Athi River

Athi River

Mombasa

Cheetah Gate (closed)

Kitengela

Amboseli

NAIROBI AND AROUND

www.roughguides.com

135

Nairobi's forests

A colour map of Nairobi suggests a multitude of cool green spaces around the fringes of the city. However, the two remaining forests – the **Ngong Forest** in the west and the **Karura forest** in the north – have been fierce battlegrounds between environmentalists and developers who have moved onto these public lands amid a morass of corruption. Unless someone who knows the area well accompanies you, a visit to Karura forest is still inadvisable, as illegal activities – including hunting and gathering as well as building – persist there. The 6-square-kilometre Ngong Forest, however, is now officially the **Ngong Road Forest Sanctuary** and, thanks to increased ranger patrols, you can walk, jog, cycle or ride a horse safely here (☎020/2113358 or 0729/840715). You can go on a guided forest walk on the first and third Saturday of every month from 9am, or do your own thing any time if you make prior arrangements (☎0729/840715 or 0720/360307, ✉office@ngongforestsanctuary.com, ⓦwww.ngongforest.org; $10 on foot, $15 with a bike, $20 with a horse).

Nairobi National Park and around

Despite the hype, it really is remarkable that the 117-square-kilometre patch of plains and woodland making up **Nairobi National Park** (ⓦwww.kws.go.ke /nairobi.html; $40, "package" including Animal Orphanage and Safari Walk $65; smartcard, see p.61) should exist almost uncorrupted within earshot of Nairobi's downtown traffic, complete with more than eighty species of large mammals and the second-largest herbivore migration after that of the Mara/Serengeti. The park is a good way to spend time during a flight layover, or before an afternoon or evening flight, and you have the chance to see certain species, especially black rhino, which might elude you in the bigger Kenyan reserves. Although it is fenced along its northern perimeter, the park is open to the south, allowing migrating herds, and the predators that follow them, to come and go freely. There are no elephants, but this is a small deficiency among a surprisingly high concentration of animals. For all the low-flying planes and lines of tourist minibuses, you have a greater chance of witnessing a kill here than in any of the other parks.

Access

Without your own transport, the cheapest and most adventurous way into the park is to **hitch a ride** at the Main Gate. This is probably easiest on a Saturday or Sunday morning, when Kenyans are most likely to visit. The weekends are also by far the busiest time; during the week you'll find it very quiet. Early birds can get the bus #125 or matatu #126 (at around 5.40am) from the bus station to the main gate; after that time you can use any bus or matatu that goes down Langata Road.

Alternatively, you should be able to swing a good deal on **car rental** for the day – you won't need anything more than a saloon car, and kilometre charges won't amount to much. If you charter a **taxi** for a few hours, which may be less expensive, check that fuel is included in the price.

Most of the safari operators in town sell four- to five-hour **trips around the park** for $90–120, including entry charges. A reputable operator with regular, scheduled trips is East Africa Shuttles, 4th floor, Portal Place, Muindi Mbingu St (☎020/2248453, ⓦwww.eastafricashuttles.com), who charge $110, excluding lunch. They can take you straight on to JKI Airport for a $20 supplement.

The park

The first few hours of the day are always best for **game-watching**. Ask any ranger on arrival and you'll get the day's results: "Number 13 for a cheetah; two rhinos at 6; lions at number 4 . . .", the numbers referring to the road junctions, marked on every map of the park. Alternatively, just follow your nose. If you're driving around independently, go to the western end, near the main entrance, where most of the woodland is concentrated. This is where you are most likely to see giraffe and, just after dawn, if you're very lucky, a leopard – back perhaps from a nocturnal foray into Langata, hunting for guard dogs (apparently quite a problem). The highest point here, known as **Impala Hill**, is also a **picnic site** (with toilets) and a good spot from which to scan the park with binoculars. **Lions**, usually found in more open country, are best located by checking with the rangers at the gate. There are a few families of **cheetahs** in the park, though seasonal long grass can make seeing them very difficult. It's less tricky, however, to see some of the park's fifty-odd **black rhinos**, which are most often found in the forest glades in the west. The park has one of the largest populations anywhere in Kenya, attesting in part to the perseverance of the David Sheldrick Trust (see p.overleaf).

The Mbagathi or Athi River forms the **southern boundary** of the park and is its only permanent river. It's fringed with the yellow acacias that early explorers and settlers dubbed "fever trees" because they seemed to grow in the areas where malaria was most common. Several of the park's seasonal streams are dammed to regulate the water supply; in the dry season, these **dams** – all located on the northern side of the park where the streams come down off the Embakasi plain – draw the heaviest concentrations of animals. Many of the herds cross the Mbagathi every year and disperse across the Athi plains as the rains improve the pasture, returning to the park during the drought. Before 1946, when the park was opened, only the physical barrier of Nairobi itself diverted the northward migration. The erection of fences along the park's northern perimeter has changed that, but lions occasionally still sneak out of the park through gaps in the fence to terrorize early-morning drivers in Langata.

Birdlife in Nairobi National Park is staggering – a count of more than four hundred species. Enthusiasts won't need priming, and will see rarities from European latitudes as well as the exotics. Even if you're fresh off the plane and ornithologically illiterate, the first glimpses of ostrich, secretary bird, crowned crane and the outlandishly hideous marabou stork never fail to impress.

If you're looking for a spot to **picnic**, go a couple of kilometres in from the main gate, to the first fork. There's a shady site on the left, beside a raised mound of elephant-tusk ash, publicly burned in 1989 by President Moi to mark the start of a major (and remarkably successful) offensive on ivory poaching and smuggling, led by the then-director of the Kenya Wildlife Service, Dr Richard Leakey.

There is a gate out to the Mombasa road to the east, East Gate, so you don't have to retrace your route from the park's western end. Cheetah Gate, in the far southeast of the park, is permanently closed, but it's worth driving down here, to the lovely **Mokoyeti picnic site** at junction 14B, near the "Leopard Cliffs" where the Mokoyeti stream flows into the Mbagathi, just below Mbagathi gorge. This route gives you a chance to drive through the open savanna country favoured by **zebra** and **antelope**. There are large herds of **buffalo**, which you can see out here and almost anywhere in the park. **Hippos** can usually be viewed at a pretty pool at the confluence of the Mbagathi and Athi rivers (junction 12), beyond the Leopard Cliffs, which has the added attraction of a **nature trail** and **picnic site** where you can leave your vehicle and disappear into the thickets for closer communion with nature (there's usually an armed ranger on guard). As you're wandering, look out for crocodiles in the river, which look little different from submerged logs to an untrained eye, and monkeys in the bushes.

Nairobi Education Centre and Animal Orphanage

Mainly intended for children, the **Animal Orphanage** (daily 8am–6.30pm; Ⓦwww.kws.go.ke/nbi-edu.html; $15, children $5) by the park's Main Gate is moderately interesting if you're fed up with seeing animals only from a distance. Here, a motley and shifting collection of waifs and strays, protected from nature, have for some years been allowed to regain strength before being released. That, anyway, was the idea, though many of the inmates seem to be established residents and it appears doubtful whether "this orphanage is not a zoo", as the sign claims. At least it's a zoo with a difference; there are as many wild monkeys outside the cages as in them.

Nairobi Safari Walk

More inspiring than the orphanage is the **Nairobi Safari Walk** (daily 8am–6.30pm; $20; Ⓦwww.kws.go.ke/nsw.html), to the right of the Main Gate before entering the park. Showcasing Kenya's great ecological diversity, the walk simulates the country's wetlands, savanna and forest in a captivating, semi-natural environment. This is the closest you can come to seeing captive animals behaving as they would in their natural habitats. The boardwalks to the open-air pens, observation points and platforms are clearly signposted and full of useful information about the animals. Also accessible from the walk is the *New Rangers Restaurant* (Ⓣ020/2357470 or 0723/457480, Ⓦwww.rangersnairobi.com; 7am–10.30pm), which has a pretty extensive menu of reliable African, continental and vegetarian dishes, and is an enjoyable venue after dark, when its comfortable veranda, part of which is inside the national park, overlooks a floodlit water hole.

The David Sheldrick Wildlife Trust

Off the Magadi road, the **David Sheldrick Wildlife Trust** elephant and rhino orphanage (daily 11am–noon; Ⓣ020/891996, Ⓦwww.sheldrickwildlifetrust.org; Ksh300), inside the western end of the park, offers a chance to see baby elephants, and sometimes baby rhino, which have been orphaned by poachers, lost or abandoned for natural reasons, being cared for. Its run by Daphne Sheldrick in memory of her husband, the founding warden of Tsavo National Park, and, during the hour-long open house, the elephant keepers bring their juvenile charges up to an informal rope barrier where you can easily touch them and take photos.

After many years of trial and error, Sheldrick and her staff have become the world's experts on hand-rearing baby African elephants, sometimes from birth, using a special milk formula for the youngest infants and assigning keepers to individual 24-hour guardianship of their charges, a responsibility that includes sleeping in their stables. Without the love of a surrogate family and plenty of stimulation, orphaned baby elephants fail to thrive: they can succumb to fatal infections when teething, and, even if they survive, can grow up disturbed and unhappy and badly prepared for reintroduction to the wild.

Rehabilitation is one of the Sheldrick Trust's major preoccupations. For rhinos, which mature at twice the speed of elephants, this involves a year or more of walks with their keeper, introducing the orphan's scent, via habitual dung middens and "urinal" bushes, to the wild population. Many of Nairobi National Park's rhinos grew up in the Sheldrick nursery; the last surviving member of Amboseli's famous long-horned rhino herd was rescued by the Trust in 1987 and is now a successful breeding female, having been released in Tsavo East. In the case of elephants, which mature at about the same rate as humans, the process of reintroduction is more attuned to the individual: outgoing animals are encouraged while young to meet wild friends and potential adoptive mothers, again through walks with their keepers, most often in Tsavo National Park. More traumatized elephants take longer to find their feet. Matriarchs who were Sheldrick orphans themselves, such as Eleanor at Tsavo East, have been responsible for adopting many returnees.

To get here, head south out of town on the Magadi road, and you'll pass the Nairobi National Park's Banda gate on the left; the next gate on the left, some 4.5km from the start of the Magadi road, is the entrance to the Kenya Wildlife Service central workshop. Once through this gate, follow signs for "Sheldrick" to reach the orphanage.

The Bomas of Kenya

The **Bomas of Kenya** (ⓦwww.bomasofkenya.co.ke, ☎020/891391; shows Mon–Fri 2.30–4pm, Sat, Sun & holidays 3.30–5.15pm; Ksh600; bus/matatu from CBD – #15, #125 or #126), Forest Edge Road, 1km past the National Park Main Gate at the junction with the Langata and Magadi roads, were originally an attempt to create a living museum of Kenyan culture, with a display of eleven traditional homesteads (*bomas*) and an emphasis on regional dances. Unfortunately, the place has always had a touristy feel, not helped by the huge indoor amphitheatre where the dances are performed. In fact the vitality of the Bomas is channelled mainly into souvenir-selling and conferences, most famously the constitutional conference of 2003 leading to the so-called Bomas draft constitution calling for decentralized government. The ethnic homesteads recreating Kenya's vernacular architecture, a guided tour of which is included in the price, are for the most part sadly unkempt. Even so, if you're looking to fill an afternoon, they can be enjoyable enough, particularly on weekends, when they're busier, and when an evening disco sometimes follows the dance show.

Surprisingly, perhaps, the dances are not performed by the appropriate Kenyan tribes; instead, the **Harambee Dancers** do fast costume changes between acts and present the nation's traditional repertoire as professional performers rather than participants. If the acoustics were better and the whole place less of an amphitheatre, the impression would undoubtedly be stronger. As it is, you at least get a very comprehensive taste of Kenyan dance styles, from the mesmeric jumps and sinuous movements of the Maa-speaking peoples, to the wild acrobatics of some of the Mijikenda dances.

AFEW Giraffe Centre

Although promoted as a children's outing, the **AFEW Giraffe Centre** (daily 9am–5.30pm; ⓦgiraffecenter.org, ☎020/891658; Ksh700) on Koitobos Road, 3km off Langata Road (signposted), has serious intentions. Run by the African Fund for Endangered Wildlife, it has successfully boosted the population of the rare **Rothschild's giraffe** from an original nucleus of animals that came from a wild herd near Soy (see p.290). Its other main mission is to educate children about conservation. You'll get some great mug shots from the giraffe-level observation tower, where the giraffes push their huge heads through to be fed the pellets you're given to offer them. There are various other animals around, including a number of tame warthogs, and a fine "Safari Walk" boardwalk, along which you can see what Nairobi looked like before the city existed – a great

▲ Close encounters of the giraffe kind

bird-watching opportunity. If you really like it here, and have deep pockets, stay overnight at the wonderful, Scottish-style **Giraffe Manor** (p.107).

Karen

Always associated with its famous resident, the author **Karen Blixen** (pen name Isak Dinesen) the suburb of **KAREN** was actually named after her cousin, Karen Melchior, whose father was the chairman of the Karen Coffee Company – the estate that was sold for residential development and named Karen – though most people, including Blixen herself, were not aware of the coincidence.

While the number of African residents is rising steadily, until recently, Karen was the quintessential white suburb – five-acre plots spaciously set on eucalyptus-lined avenues amid fields grazed by horses. Still separated from Nairobi by a dwindling patch of dense, bird-filled woodland, the Ngong Road Forest (see p.136), Karen is a reminder of how completely the settlers visualized and created little Europes for themselves. In Karen, you could almost be in the English shires – or, for that matter, northern California.

If you're driving the most direct route to Karen from the city centre, along Ngong Road, you pass **Jamhuri Park** (the Agricultural Society of Kenya showground, see p.56), the **racecourse** (see p.132), and the **Nairobi War Cemetery**. The World War II cemetery is a peaceful and dignified place, set far back from the busy road among shady trees, with pink stonework and carefully tended lawns. Buses to Karen include the fast #111 from the bus station and the interminably slow bus or matatu #24.

Karen's central **shopping centre**, at the crossroads of the Langata and Ngong roads, officially now called Karen Connection, but usually referred to as Karen *dukas*, includes a growing cluster of safari businesses and other services, including branches of Barclays and Standard Chartered banks, both with ATMs.

Karen Blixen Museum

Bus #24 can drop you on Karen Road at the **Karen Blixen Museum** (daily 9.30am–6pm; ☎020/882779, ⓦwww.museums.or.ke; Ksh800), the house where much of the action of Karen Blixen's *Out of Africa* took place (see p.603). If you're on a budget, note that temporary membership of the museum society only costs Ksh500 and allows free entry (see p.111). An organized tour from town, which may also include the AFEW Giraffe Centre, costs anything from $70 to $100.

The epitome of colonial Africa, the **house** was presented to Kenya by the Danish government as an Uhuru gift at the time of Independence, along with the agricultural college built in the grounds. It's a beautiful, well-proportioned home with square, wood-panelled rooms. The restoration of its original appearance and furnishings has evidently been very thorough and the **gardens**, laid out as in former times, are delightful. A guided tour is included in the price but can be somewhat rushed, especially at weekends, and there's no guarantee that they'll let you wander around on your own. On weekends, too, you may be suffocated by Mozart, as well as by tour groups complaining about how little Denys Finch Hatton resembles Robert Redford. The fake-1920s Nairobi that was built nearby for the shooting of *Out of Africa* would have been a magnetic attraction, but the dictates of licensing agreements ensured its demolition once the film crews left.

Swedo House (Karen Blixen Coffee Garden)

Just up the road towards Karen shopping centre, at 336 Karen Road, is **Swedo House**, an old Swedish coffee plantation manager's residence, built in 1912. It's stuffed with archetypal colonial memorabilia and fittings, but the house itself is not always fully open. Still, the grounds are delightful, and there's a bar and restaurant, the *Karen Blixen Coffee Garden*, with tables in the gardens under the trees (℡020/882138 or 0733/616206, Ⓦwww.blixencoffeegarden.co.ke; 9.30am–11pm). The food is variable, but the Ksh1000 Sunday lunch is always popular and the pricey accommodation in cottages around the grounds is very comfortable (see p.107). There's also a craft shop here, although much better local handicrafts can be bought at the nearby **Kazuri Bead Centre**, behind Hillcrest School (see p.125 for more details).

The Ngong Hills

The town of **NGONG**, the jumping-off point for the **Ngong Hills**, is 8km past Karen shopping centre (bus #111 or #126); turn right after the police station in Ngong. If you have the chance, stop on the way at **Bulbul** and take a look at the pretty mosque of this largely Muslim village. As often happened in Kenya, Islam spread here through the settlement of discharged troops from other British-ruled territories, in this case from Nubia in Sudan. Ngong itself is basically just a small junction town with limited shops and services and the rough D523 road trailing out to the west towards the Maasai Mara.

The hills are revered by the Maasai, who have several traditional explanations of how they were formed. The best known says that a giant, stumbling north with his head in the clouds, tripped on Kilimanjaro. Thundering to the ground, his hand squeezed the earth into the Ngongs' familiar, knuckled outline. An even more momentous story explains the Ngongs as the bits of earth left under God's fingernails after he'd finished creating.

The walk along the sharp spine of the Ngong Hills was once a popular weekend hike and picnic outing, easily feasible in a day. The views, of Nairobi on one side and the Rift Valley on the other, are magnificent, and the forested slopes are still inhabited by buffalo and antelope. Unfortunately, the slopes acquired a reputation for muggings in the 1980s, curtailing independent expeditions, and KWS rangers usually provide an escort (negotiable, from

Ksh500 per ranger for 3hr). With a car, and it has to be 4WD if it's been raining, you can get to the summit, **Point Lamwia** (2459m), which offers a 360-degree view. If you want to walk, and are reasonably fit, then allow a minimum of three hours to get to the summit and back to your car. Or you could organize transport to meet you west of Kiserian, on the C58 Magadi road, and spend four to five hours traversing the length of the peaks. On the ridges below the summit, on privately owned land, almost due east of the highest point, is the **Finch Memorial**, Karen Blixen's tribute to the man who took her flying.

Travel details

Trains

Nairobi to/from: Kisumu (3 weekly; 13hr); Mombasa (3 weekly; 14hr); Nakuru (3 weekly; 5hr) Voi (3 weekly; 9hr).

Buses

Most of the services below operate from the Country Bus Station – or "Machakos Airport". For bus company booking offices, see "Listings", p.131.
Nairobi to/from: Arusha (6 daily; 4hr); Chogoria (6 daily; 4hr); Eldoret (hourly; 6hr 30min); Embu (6 daily; 2hr 30min); Isiolo (2 daily; 6hr); Kakamega (10 daily; 8hr); Kampala (Uganda; 2 daily; 12hr); Kericho (frequent; 5hr); Kisumu (frequent; 8hr); Kitale (several services daily and overnight; 8hr); Kitui (several daily; 3hr); Machakos (frequent; 1hr 30min); Maralal (2 daily; 8hr); Meru (6 daily; 5hr); Mombasa (frequent, especially around 7am and 7pm; 7–9hr); Moshi (6 daily; 5hr 30min); Naivasha (several daily; 1hr 30min); Nakuru (20 daily; 2hr 30min); Namanga (2 daily; 3hr); Nanyuki (3 daily; 3hr 30min); Narok (4 daily; 5hr); Nyeri (4 daily; 2hr 30min); Thika (frequent; 1hr).

Matatus and shared taxis

Note that there are no direct matatus to the coast.
Nairobi (Accra Rd between River Rd and Duruma Rd) to/from: Embu (frequent; 2hr 30min); Isiolo (2–3 daily; 5hr).
Nairobi (Accra Rd between River Rd and Tsavo Rd) to/from: Meru (frequent; 4hr 30min); Nanyuki (6 daily; 3hr).
Nairobi (Accra Rd/Dubois Rd to/from: Busia (hourly; 9hr); Kakamega (4 daily; 7hr); Kericho (hourly; 6hr); Kisii (hourly; 6hr); Kisumu (frequent; 7hr).
Nairobi (Accra Rd/River Rd) to/from: Archers Post (daily; 6hr); Nyeri (6 daily; 2hr 30min).
Nairobi (car park just to the north of Country bus station) to/from: Machakos (frequent; 1hr 30min).

Nairobi (Globe roundabout) to/from: Thika (frequent; 1hr).
Nairobi (Latema Rd) to/from: Nyahururu (2 daily; 3hr).
Nairobi (*Nyamakima Bar*, Duruma Rd) to/from: Eldoret (frequent; 5hr 30min); Gilgil (hourly; 2hr); Kitale (hourly; 7hr); Maralal (2 daily; 7hr); Naivasha (frequent; 1hr 30min); Nakuru (frequent 2hr 30min); Narok (4 daily; 4hr).
Nairobi (railway station stage) to/from: Magadi (2 daily; 2hr).
Nairobi (Ronald Ngala St) to/from: Kajiado (6 daily; 1hr 30min); Namanga (4 daily; 3hr).

Flights

JKI Airport (domestic and regional flights on Kenya Airways, Jetlink and Fly540) to/from: Eldoret (3 daily; 45min–1hr 45min, depending on route); Entebbe, Uganda (2 daily; 1hr 20min); Juba, South Sudan (2 daily; 1hr 45min); Kilimanjaro (daily; 45min); Kisumu (6–7 daily; 50min); Kitale (daily; 50min); Lamu (daily; 2hr); Malindi (1 or more daily; 1hr–1hr 15min); Mombasa (at least 12 daily, more in season; 1hr–1hr 10min); Zanzibar (2–3 daily; 2hr 20min).
Wilson Airport (domestic flights on AirKenya Express and Safarilink) to/from: Amboseli NP lodges (2 daily; roughly 45min); Diani Beach (2 daily; 1hr 30min); Kilimanjaro (2 daily; 1hr 10min); Kiwayu (Safarilink; 1 daily; 2hr); Lamu (2 daily; 1hr 10min–1hr 45min); Lewa Downs (2–3 daily; 1hr); Loisaba (daily; 1hr 45min, depending on route); Maasai Mara NR lodges (4-plus daily; 1hr, depending on lodge); Malindi (3 daily; 2hr); Meru NP (1 daily; 50 min); Mombasa (2 daily; 1hr 5min); Naivasha (1 daily; 15min); Nanyuki (3 daily; 40min); Samburu NR (3 daily; 1hr 10min, depending on route); Shaba NR (2 daily; 1hr 10min, depending on route); Tsavo West NP lodges (1 daily; 50min, depending on route). Domestic flights are also available on ALS to/from Kisumu (daily; 1hr) and Lokichokio (4 weekly; 1hr 45min).

The Central Highlands

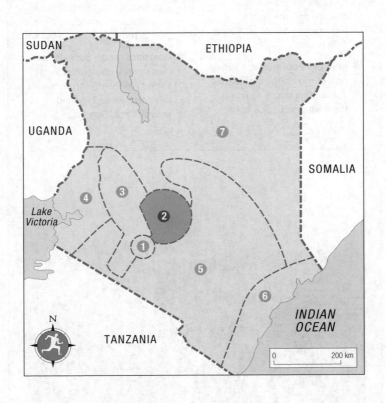

CHAPTER 2   # Highlights

* **Climbing Mount Kenya**
Africa's second-highest
mountain is a highly
recommended trekking area,
with various routes and
diverse flora and fauna.
See p.155

* **Nanyuki** Good hotels and
restaurants, a beautiful
climate and the best
information centre in Kenya.
See p.166

* **Laikipia eco-lodges** Visiting
one of the game sanctuaries
in this high plains region is
the best way to see some

of Kenya's surviving black
rhinos. See p.175

* **Walking with baboons**
Pay a visit to a habituated
baboon troop accompanied
by an informative primate
researcher. See p.182

* **Track wild dogs** Participate
in conservation research on a
working conservancy.
See p.183

* **Aberdare range** Sensational
views and a good chance of
seeing elephants and buffaloes
in a compelling, highland
environment. See p.185

▲ Mount Kenya at dawn

The Central Highlands

A s the political and economic heartland of the country, the **Central Highlands** stand at the focal point of Kenyan history. Mount Kenya, Africa's second-highest peak, gave the colonial nation its name, and the majority of British and European settlers carved their farms from the countryside around it. Later, and as a direct consequence, it was this region which saw the development of organized anti-colonial resistance culminating in Mau Mau.

Until independence, the fertile highland soils ("A more charming region is not to be found in all Africa," thought Joseph Thomson, exploring in the 1880s) were reserved largely for Europeans and considered, in Governor Eliot's breathtaking phrase, "White Man's Country". The **Kikuyu peoples** were skilled farmers and herders who had held the land for several centuries before the Europeans arrived. They were at first mystified to find themselves "squatters" on land whose ownership, in the sense of exclusive right, had never been an issue in traditional society. They were certainly not alone in losing land but, by supplying most of the fighters for the Land and Freedom Army (see "Contexts", p.553), they were placed squarely in the political limelight. In return, they received a large proportion of what used to be known as the "Fruits of Independence". Today, most of the land is in African hands again, and it supports the country's largest rural population. There's intensive farming on almost all the lower slopes, and rising to much of the higher ground as well, beneath the national parks of Mount Kenya and the Aberdare.

There are some great rewards in travel through the Highlands. Above all, if you're into hiking, there's the ascent of **Mount Kenya**. And, while hikes lower down and in the **Aberdare range** are easier, they are still dramatic, with the added bonus that you might see some **wildlife**.

Another great draw is the **Laikipia plateau**, spanning eight thousand square kilometres of wild savanna northwest of Mount Kenya. Second in wildlife density only to the Maasai Mara, it boasts more endangered species than anywhere else in the country (including the country's biggest population of black rhino), a variety of interesting experiments in mixed ranching and conservation and some extremely upmarket boutique lodges and camps.

Travel itself is never dull in the Highlands, where the range of scenery is a spectacular draw in its own right: primary-coloured **jungle** and **shambas**,

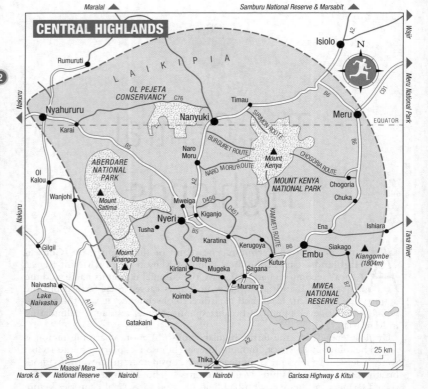

pale, windswept **moors** and dense **conifer plantations**, all with a mountain backdrop. People everywhere are friendly and quick to strike up a conversation, the towns are animated and the markets colourfully chaotic. Most roads are in good shape and bus and matatu journeys invariably packed with interest and amusement.

Mount Kenya and around

After the main game-viewing areas and the coast, the circuit provided by the **Mount Kenya ring road** is one of the most travelled in Kenya, and there are always a few tourist vehicles to be seen. Apart from the high forests, moors and peaks, little of this remains wild country, with *shambas* steadily encroaching the ridges. The Kikuyu, Meru and Embu peoples have created an extraordinary spectacle of cultivation on the steep slopes, gashed by the road to reveal brilliant red earth.

As you travel, the mountain is a constant, looming presence, even if you can't often see much of it. With a base 80km across, Mount Kenya is one of the largest free-standing volcanic cones in the world. The twin peaks, always distant when visible from the road, are normally obscured by clouds, but early in the morning and just before sunset the shroud can vanish suddenly, leaving them magically exposed for a few minutes. To the east and south, the mountain drops steeply away to the broad expanse of Ukambani (Kamba-land) and the Tana River basin. Westwards, and to the north, it slopes away more gently to the rolling uplands of Laikipia.

The Kikuyu

The ancestors of the **Kikuyu** migrated to the Central Highlands between the sixteenth and eighteenth centuries, from northeast of Mount Kenya. Stories describe how they found various hunter-gatherer peoples already in the region (the **Gumba** on the plains and the **Athi** in the forests), and a great deal of intermarriage, trade and adoption took place. The newcomers cleared the forests and planted crops, giving the hunters gifts of livestock, honey or wives in return for using the land.

Likewise, there was trade and intermarriage between the Kikuyu and the **Maasai**, both peoples placing high value on cattle ownership, with the Maasai depending entirely on livestock. During bad droughts, Maasai would raid Kikuyu herds, with retaliation at a later date being almost inevitable. But such **intertribal warfare** often had long-term benefits, as ancient debts were forever being renegotiated and paid off by both sides, thus sustaining the relationship. Married Kikuyu women enjoyed a special immunity that enabled them to organize trading expeditions deep into Maasai-land, often with the help of a *hinga*, a middleman, to oil the wheels.

Like the Maasai, the Kikuyu advanced in status as they grew older, through named age-sets and rituals still important today. For Kikuyu boys, **circumcision** marks the important transition into adulthood, (female circumcision, or clitoridectomy, is illegal and rarely performed today). In the past, boys would grow their hair and dye it with ochre in the style of Maasai warriors (in fact, the Maasai got their ochre from the Kikuyu, so it may really have been the other way around). They also wore glass beads around their necks, metal rings on their legs and arms, and pulled their ear lobes out with ear plugs. Women wore a similar collection of ornaments and, between initiation and marriage, a headband of beads and discs, still worn today by most Maasai women.

Traditionally, the Kikuyu had no centralized **authority**. The elders of a district would meet as a council and disputes or important decisions would be dealt with in public, with a party to follow. After their deaths, elders – now known as ancestors – continued to be respected and consulted. Christianity has altered beliefs in the last few decades, though many church-goers still believe strongly in an **ancestor world** where the dead have powers over their living descendants. The Kikuyu traditionally believed that the most likely abode of God (Ngai), or at least his frequent resting place, was Mount Kenya, which they called **Kirinyaga** (Place of Brightness). Accordingly, they used to build their houses with the door always looking out towards the mountain, hence the title of Jomo Kenyatta's book, *Facing Mount Kenya*.

Today, the Kikuyu are at the forefront of Kenyan **development** and, despite entrenched nepotism, are accorded grudging respect as successful business people, skilled media operators and formidable politicians. There is considerable political rivalry between the Kiambu Kikuyu of the tea- and coffee-growing district north of Nairobi and the Nyeri Kikuyu (one of whose number is President Mwai Kibaki, who rely on a more mixed economy. Alarmingly, the emergence in recent years of the secret and violent **Mungiki** cult, somewhat modelled after the colonial era's Mau Mau independence movement but based around extortion and gangster operations, has brought terror to slum districts in parts of Central Kenya.

Getting to the Mount Kenya area is an easy trip from Nairobi up a busy highway. If you're not driving, you could buy a bus ticket from Nairobi direct to any of the towns in this section, or make **Thika** or **Murang'a** a first destination before heading around the mountain. **Naro Moru**, a popular base for climbing the mountain, lies on its west side, while **Nanyuki**, 25km further north, offers a good alternative hiking base. On the eastern slopes, **Chogoria**, between **Meru** and **Embu**, offers arguably the finest route up the mountain. Or you could head up to the southern slopes, where **Castle Forest Lodge** is an excellent, low-key staging post.

Thika and around

THIKA, a bustling Nairobi satellite just off the main road to Mount Kenya, is not redeemed by the profusion of flame trees you might expect from its famous literary connection, Elspeth Huxley's *The Flame Trees of Thika*, recording her family's move there in 1913. It's a surprisingly laid-back, friendly sort of place, with a bit of light manufacturing, but best known for its pineapples. The fruit was introduced in 1905 and thousands of acres flourish here, mostly owned by Del Monte and easily confused with the sisal also grown in the area.

There are no major attractions in town, but if you're passing through it's worth visiting the **Blue Posts hotel**, where the grounds include a small **zoo** (Ksh200), the best viewpoints for the **Chania and Thika Falls**, a clutch of well-stocked, competitively priced **curio shops** and a small children's playground and boating pond.

In practical terms, the town centre is compact and straightforward, with Barclays and Standard Chartered **ATMs**, the Mbambu **Cyber Café** (Mon–Sat 7.30am–7.30pm; Sun 11am–4pm), a Mathai **supermarket** (daily 8am–7.30pm), a good **pharmacy**, The Chemists (Mon–Sat 8am–6pm, Sun 9am–4pm), and a **market** east of the town centre, past the street stalls at the stadium roundabout.

Accommodation

Thika doesn't offer a wide variety of choice for an overnight stay. The B&Ls are basic and don't have instant showers, while the only "upmarket" option is out of town and somewhat overpriced.

Blue Posts Just to the east of the Nairobi–Murang'a road (no signpost), 1.3km north of the turning to downtown Thika ☎020/2080606 or 0721/578245, ℮blueposthotel@africaonline .co.ke. Coming from Nairobi, take the slip road signposted "Thika Coffee Mills 3km" and traverse the A2 on the flyover to reach the hotel. Dating from 1908, older than Thika, this has modest, tourist-class rooms, with good nets, small TVs and garden views from the Chania Wing. The relatively primitive bathrooms do have instant showers but no tubs, and don't expect hot water in your basin. ❹

December Commercial St ☎067/24296 or 0712/726716. Worn, but good-sized, mostly light, airy, fairly clean rooms with outside windows. Not all rooms have nets and hot water is available mornings only. ❶

New Fulilia Uhuru St ☎067/31286. Reasonably clean lodgings, though only one of the fifty-odd rooms has two beds. Frenetic bar, plus *nyama choma* and a decent *hoteli*. ❶

New Fulilia 1987 Kwame Nkrumah St ☎067/21840. Like its sister establishment, a friendly, if noisy, courtyard-style B&L with plenty of small, dark singles, only a couple of rooms with two beds, and no guarantee of hot water. Busy, ground-floor *hoteli* and second-floor bar. ❶

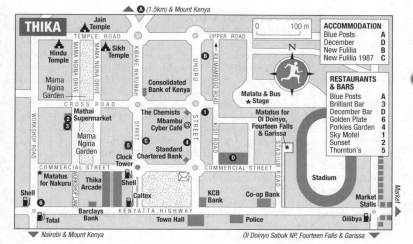

Eating and drinking

Blue Posts Nairobi–Murang'a road. Popular local venue, especially at weekends, with its tables on the lawns, and sweeping views of the Chania Falls. The restaurant offers good lunchtime buffets (Ksh700) and various dinner dishes for around Ksh500.

Brilliant Bar Mama Ngina Drive. Less than sparkling, but a good place to meet inebriated locals.

Cascades at the *Blue Posts Hotel*. This big disco turns up its sound system at weekends, but don't expect a crowd to form much before midnight.

December Bar/Kenchic Inn Beneath the *December Hotel*, Commercial St. Popular place for cakes and sodas, sharing premises with a branch of the reliable fried chicken franchise.

Golden Plate Kenyatta Highway, across from Total. Busy, friendly and well-run *hoteli* with plenty on the menu, much of it available.

Porkies Garden Uhuru St. Bar and limited restaurant in a covered courtyard, offering live English football and a pool table.

Sky Motel Day & Night Club corner of Uhuru St and Cross Rd. Place for heavy drinkers to fade away.

Sunset Bar & Restaurant Mama Ngina Drive. Includes a busy *hoteli* as well as the beer cage.

Thornton's Sports Pub 1st Floor, MTC Building, Uhuru St. TV-festooned watering hole, with decent snacks.

Fourteen Falls and Ol Donyo Sabuk National Park

The trip to **Fourteen Falls** on the Athi River and the nearby **Ol Donyo Sabuk National Park** is popular with locals. To get to either location, head for the village of Kilima Mbogo, 18km east of Thika, along the Garissa road. Some matatus stop at Kilima Mbogo, while others go on to the village of **DONYO**, 4km off to the south, down a dirt track that passes 900m from the entrance to Fourteen Falls. Donyo, on the south side of the river, is a busy centre, with dozens of *dukas* and *hotelis*.

Fourteen Falls (daily 9am–5pm; $4, children $2, vehicles $5, cameras $5, camcorders $10) is a broad cascade, plunging 30m over a precipice with many lips, hence the name. The falls are modestly spectacular after rain, when they flood into a single, thundering red cataract, but perhaps not worth the entrance fees otherwise. You can **camp**, or stay in spartan but dirt-cheap *bandas*, at the council-run *Fourteen Falls Campsite* by the river.

Ol Donyo Sabuk National Park

Seen from a distance, **Ol Donyo Sabuk** ("Big Mountain" in Maa Ⓦwww
.kws.go.ke/oldonyo.html; $20), also known as Kilima Mbogo ("Buffalo
Mountain" in Kikuyu), is not especially inspiring, and nor is it high in Kenyan
terms, rising to 2146m. The attractions of the national park only become
apparent when you approach the gate, as the flat, dry scrubland gives way to red
soil, cool air and fine views. The national park encloses the entirety of the
mountain, and protects diverse birdlife and indigenous forest, though the
mammals – buffaloes, Sykes' and colobus monkeys, and porcupines – make
themselves scarce in the thick vegetation.

For the **national park gate** you take a signposted right turn, at the end of
Kilima Mbogo village. The gate is 2km further on. **Accommodation** in the
park is limited to *Turacco campsite* by the gate (shady lawns, free firewood,
rudimentary showers and toilets; $15), *Lookout campsite* 7km up the hill (no
facilities, wonderful views; $15) and the very large and nicely situated *Sabuk
House*, formerly the warden's residence, 1km south of the gate (self-service
accommodation for up to eight; $250 per night for the whole house;
Ⓣ020/600800, Ⓔreservations@kws.go.ke).

Walking the 9km track to the summit requires being accompanied by an
armed ranger (Ksh1500), but if you drive in, you're allowed to leave your
vehicle for short walks at your own discretion. Beyond signboard #8, at the
7km mark, on the left, you come to the grave of Sir William Northrup
MacMillan, the fattest of famous settlers, whose intended burial place on the
summit had to be abandoned when the modified tractor-hearse's clutch
burned out. He rests here with his wife, maid and dog. Between the
MacMillans' graves and just below the summit, the track winds steeply up
through dense forest. The occasional clearings offer good views, including a
huge oxbow in the Athi River and, when the air is clear enough (usually Dec
& Jan), Mount Kenya and Kilimanjaro. The vegetation at the summit is more
open, with shrubs and grassland, spoiled by a humming grove of communications towers.

Murang'a and southwest Mount Kenya

Established as the administrative outpost of **Fort Hall** in 1900, **MURANG'A**
has since come to be thought of as the "Kikuyu Homeland" because of its
proximity to Mukuruwe wa Nyagathanga, a sort of Kikuyu Garden of Eden.
Here, in Kikuyu mythology, God made husbands for the nine daughters of
Gikuyu and Mumbi, spiritual ancestors of all the Kikuyu people. The husbands,
who became the ancestors of the nine Kikuyu clans, were found by Gikuyu
under a large fig tree. Although the original *mukuruwe* (fig tree) disappeared
long ago, you can take a matatu to nearby **Mugeka** and walk from there to
Gakuyu village if you'd like to see the site.

At the beginning of the twentieth century, Fort Hall consisted of "two grass
huts within a stone wall and a ditch". Although a British military base, it was
never a settlers' town: Fort Hall district was outside the zone earmarked for
white settlement and most of it comprised the "Kikuyu reserve". Colonel
Richard Meinertzhagen, an officer in the King's African Rifles, posted here in
1902, found time, when not shooting animals (or people) to write, "If white
settlement really takes hold in this country it is bound to do so at the expense
of the Kikuyu who own the best land, and I foresee much trouble." That said,

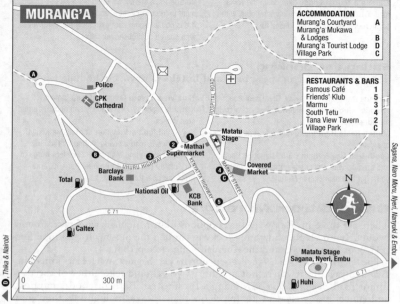

Meinertzhagen helped put down some of this trouble, launching "punitive expeditions" from Fort Hall with his African troops (see "Books", p.604).

Present-day Murang'a, perched above the busy Mount Kenya road, remains a small commercial centre, bustling energetically, and outwardly a happy enough place, despite its recent notoriety as an area of Mungiki gang violence (see p.565). But this won't impact in any way on your visit, and there's no reason not to call in. There's even a bit of sightseeing in the **CPK Cathedral** (formerly the Church of St James and All Martyrs), where an unusual mural sequence depicts the life story of an African Christ in an African landscape. The murals were painted by the Tanzanian artist Rekiya Elimoo Njau in 1955 – the year the church was founded by the Archbishop of Canterbury – as a memorial to the thousands of Kikuyu victims of Mau Mau attacks.

Practicalities

Barclays and KCB both have **ATMs** and there's **internet access** at the Post Office, off Kenyatta Highway. There's a Mathai **supermarket** at the western end of Market Street.

Accommodation

Murang'a has several recommended **lodgings** providing bed and breakfast at knock-down prices; however there is nowhere upmarket.

Murang'a Courtyard Kangema Rd ☏ 060/30736 or 0721/166878. Six cramped rooms, each with a small double bed, over a popular bar-restaurant. Very affordable, but you get what you pay for. ❶

Murang'a Mukawa & Lodges Ltd Uhuru Highway ☏ 020/2085407 or 0723/701409. A cut above the other lodgings, with a nice terrace bar with views across the hills. ❷

Murang'a Tourist Lodge 2km down the Thika road ☏ 0726/495060. Clean and agreeable, with bright rooms and good breakfasts. ❶

Village Park Market St. Good bet for a dirt-cheap night in the town centre, and relatively peaceful as it has no bar. Rooms are extremely basic, however, with shared bucket showers. ❶

Eating and drinking

There's no shortage of cheap **bars and hotelis** in town, but nothing fancy.

Famous Café Uhuru Highway. Great samosas.
Friends' Klub Kenyatta Highway. Spicy *chai* by the matatu stage.
Marmu Restaurant Uhuru Highway. A good range of snacks.
South Tetu Day & Night Club Market St. Boozy and friendly, with a pool table, this is the closest you'll get to a nightclub in Murang'a.

Tana View Tavern Corner of Uhuru Highway/ Kenyatta Highway. Fine balcony and decent curried goat dishes.
Village Park Market St. Reliable Kikuyu *hoteli*, with a vivid painting by Richard Njoroge celebrating Mau Mau. Excellent range of very cheap dishes, all for under Ksh100, and first-rate *chai* for Ksh10.

Onward from Murang'a

There are three main onward travel options from Murang'a: clockwise around Mount Kenya via Karatina; anti-clockwise around the mountain via Embu (see p.173); or up to Nyeri and the Aberdare range (see p.188).

The main route to Nyeri goes north via Sagana where it joins the A2 highway. But if you're not in a hurry, you should take either of the two minor roads leading out of Murang'a to the west. Both in good condition, and much more pleasant to travel on than the main highway, they join at Kiriani. Here, the route dips north through fertile *shambas* via Othaya – the home area and parliamentary constituency of President Mwai Kibaki – to Nyeri.

Sagana and around

SAGANA has little to recommend it, though the thatched *Roots Motel* on the Nairobi road 500m before the junction, is a pleasant enough spot for a meal, and its bar and tables under the trees get busy at weekends. If you need accommodation, try *Hotel Chakaka* at the Murang'a end of town, though the just-about-s/c rooms are basic and not very appealing (❶). Next door, decent food and internet connections can be had at the *Savannah Cafeteria*.

If you have transport, you might prefer to **camp** at ⚔ *Sagana Camp Site*, the adventure activities base run by *Savage Wilderness Safaris* (☏020/7121590 or 0733/835963, ⓦ www.whitewaterkenya.com; see p.129), 7km south of Sagana on the Nairobi road (signposted to the west). It's on the east bank of the Sagana river and specializes in **whitewater rafting**. They also have a sixty-metre **bungee jump** over the river. The shaded, grassy site (Ksh350 basic overnight fee per person), is entirely powered by a home-made hydro-electric system. Options include two 2-person tents (Ksh2500), a simple 4-bed cottage (Ksh2000), several small 2-person dome tents (Ksh300) and bunkhouse beds with mattresses (Ksh300). The site also has plenty of space to pitch your own tent.

The market at **KAGIO** (Tues & Fri), 7km northeast of Sagana on the way towards Kutus and Embu, is recommended for animated scenes and wonderful fruit and vegetables. South of here, the land levels out into a series of intricately irrigated **rice paddies**, part of the Mwea rice scheme, originally a resettlement area for landless farmers supported by Japanese NGOs.

Karatina and Wajee Nature Park

If you pass through the feverish commercial centre of **KARATINA** on a Saturday, or from Tuesday to Thursday, stop to have a look around the market; it's one of East Africa's biggest cattle and produce sales. There are several **lodgings** in town, including the reasonable *Karatina Tourist Lodge*, which has safe parking (℡061/533968; ❸), the *Three-In-One* (℡061/72710; ❷) and the *Ibis* (℡061/72777; ❷). There's good, filling **food** at the *Express Café*, with a shaded terrace and smooth service. The town's main **nightspot** is the *Galaxy*.

If you want to camp near Karatina, you could stay at the **campsite** at Wajee Nature Park (℡061/60359 or 0723/830516, Ⓦwww.wajeenaturepark.com; Ksh500), which also offers a cottage with four self-contained triple rooms, hot water and a kitchen with gas and firewood (Ksh700 per person). To get here, turn southwest onto the Gakonya road (off the main A2 road from Karatina to Nyeri, 3km northwest of Karatina at Tumu Tumu) then go south about 17km via Mukurweini and Mihuti. **Wajee Nature Park**, also called the Mount Kenya Avian Conservation Education Centre, is a 10-hectare sanctuary managed by the Wildlife Clubs of Kenya. It's a magnet for ornithologists, who can spot more than one hundred bird species here, including the Hinde's Babbler, a very localized endemic.

Mountain Lodge and Thego Fishing Camp

Heading clockwise around the A2, up on the southwest slopes of Mount Kenya, *Mountain Lodge* is the best of Kenya's three highland tree-hotels. It's a forty-minute drive from the main road; either take the right (east) turning at **TUMU TUMU**, 3km northwest of Karatina, then follow directions for 31km, or take the right (east) turning at the market centre of **CHAKA**, 4km north of Kiganjo, and drive 27km to the lodge. Both routes are paved and in good shape and join at Sagana State Lodge, a well-guarded presidential retreat 14km short of *Mountain Lodge*.

Along the Chaka route, 7km from the highway, you pass *Thego Fishing Camp*, a pretty spot by the Thego stream with camping allowed and rudimentary *bandas*, but no electricity (℡0716/465831; Ksh100). If you don't already have a fishing licence, you can get one here for Ksh500, giving you a year's worth of fishing, and allowing you up to six fish per day (if you're lucky).

🏃 *Serena Mountain Lodge* (℡061/2030785 or 0733/203078, Ⓦwww .serenahotels.com; ❼), set at an altitude of 2200m, offers consistently good game-viewing. Reminiscent of an old-style ski lodge in its cosy, dark wood design, it has public balconies facing the forest-encircled, floodlit waterhole, en-suite rooms and excellent food. The lodge is inside the Mount Kenya National Reserve and you pass through the Kihari gate where you pay KWS's normal national park fees for your stay (see p.157), but the experience is well worth it. Remember to visit the underground bunker for close-up waterhole views.

Southern Mount Kenya and Castle Forest Lodge

A private home built for British royalty before World War I, 🏃 *Castle Forest Lodge* (℡0721/422908 or 0722/314918, Ⓦwww.castleforestlodge.com; ❺), camping $8) nestles in a fragrantly piney forest clearing at 2100m on the southern slopes of the mountain. Remotely sited and personally managed by its Dutch leaseholder, it is far from the main road and overlooks a waterhole regularly visited by most of the usual suspects. Even if you're simply passing by, there are few nicer ways to spend an afternoon than sitting on the veranda with tea and home-made cakes.

The old house has several modest, comfortable rooms with camphor-wood floors. In the grounds there are three bungalows, each sleeping four, an arc of stylish, individually decorated double and twin cottages with fireplaces, and also the option of DIY camping. They use solar panels for electricity, but most lighting is by kerosene lamp. Good-value meals are available to order and there's a well-stocked bar. In between sleeping and eating, you can walk in the woods, sit by the waterfalls of the Karute stream (a short walk from the house through beautiful thick forest), fish the stream for trout or take a horse out for a ride.

If you're keen to try an unusual approach to the summit of Mount Kenya, consider the seldom-used **Kamweti route** which begins at the road-head, a steep 8km north of *Castle Forest*. This southern part of the mountain shelters the last remaining wild **bongos** on Mount Kenya, as researchers' night-surveillance cameras proved in 2008. The lodge can arrange a hiking trip for you for $120 a day all-inclusive, regardless of the size of the party, via *Mackinder's Camp* and Point Lenana, terminating either in Naro Moru (4–6 days) or Chogoria (6–9 days).

Castle Forest Lodge is 40km from Sagana via Kagio. Take the C73, direction Embu. After 18km, reaching Kutus, continue east on the C73 for 400m, then turn left on the tarmac D458 signposted "Castle Forest Lodge 22km". After 2km, turn left onto an excellent road which eventually becomes a forest track in reasonable condition. En route, 5km before the lodge, you pass the moribund *Thiba Fishing Camp*.

Naro Moru and north to Nanyuki

Heading north up the A2 towards Naro Moru from Kiganjo, you emerge from the folded landscape of Kikuyu cultivation onto a high, windswept plain. Here, you're crossing one of Kenya's great animal migration routes, severed by human population pressure. Until 1948, when the two mountain parks were created, every few years used to see a mass migration of **elephants** from one side to the other. When the parks were opened, it was decided to keep the elephants away from the crowded farmlands in between, so an eight-kilometre-long ditch was dug across their route.

The road climbs gently and steadily to nondescript **NARO MORU**, which stands on the watershed between the Tana and the Ewaso Nyiro river basins. Built around its now disused train station, Naro Moru is the most straightforward base for climbing Mount Kenya, either independently or on an organized trek. The town has a post office and KCB bank with ATM, but no Barclays. There's not a lot in the **food** department; the centre's offerings are strictly in the *karanga* and *chapati* line. If you want to eat in more style, head to *Naro Moru River Lodge*, which does good buffets (signposted 1.5km northwest of the town centre, see below), or the *Trout Tree Restaurant* (☏062/62053; daily 11am–4pm), about 9km north of Naro Moru just past *Bantu Mountain Lodge* (see opposite). Built on wooden platforms among giant fig trees, overlooking former trout ponds, the restaurant serves very good fish in a variety of styles.

If you want a **guided trek** up Mount Kenya, as well as the two big lodges (see opposite), a recommended outfit in Naro Moru is Mount Kenya Guides and Porters Safari Club (☏020/3524393 or 0723/112483, ⓦwww.mtkenyaguides .com), whose office is 6km along the Naro Moru trail, about 3km before the youth hostel.

Accommodation

The area around Naro Moru and the route north to Nanyuki offers a good variety of **accommodation**. If you're camping, the rather exposed campsite at *Naro Moru River Lodge* ($10) is the obvious destination.

Bantu Mountain Lodge (aka *Mountain Rock Lodge*) 8km north of Naro Moru ☏0728/559364, ⓦwww.mountainrockkenya.com. A decent mid-range trekking base, rated for its grounds full of indigenous trees and for its organized treks using its own mountain bunkhouses. The standard rooms at the lodge are nothing to write home about and you might want to upgrade to "superior" (Ksh1320 extra) for the quaintly preferable furnishings, with a fireplace and TV. All their prices are highly negotiable. You can also camp in the grounds (Ksh500) and there's horseriding (Ksh1000 per hr) and escorted walks on offer, as well as the trekking. BB ❹

Colobus Cottages Signposted, 1km north of *Bantu Mountain Lodge*, then 2km west of the A2☏020/2327776 or 0722/840195, ⓦwww.colobuscottages.com. Three delightful new self-service cottages on the banks of the Burguret stream, built and managed by a former jeweller and restaurateur. Funkily designed with natty decor and fireplaces, they perch by the stream, overlooking colobus-laden trees (2-bedroom cottage Ksh8000, 3-bedroom Ksh12,000).

Naro Moru River Lodge Naro Moru ☏062/62023, ⓦwww.alliancehotels.com. The town's upmarket base, this is also the area's main climbing rendezvous, with a pricey but decently stocked kit-rental shop. It has a welcoming atmosphere, pretty gardens along the Naro Moru stream, and superb bird-watching, as well as a sauna, squash, tennis, a pool and riding. Although some rooms need refurbishment, most have fireplaces and balconies and are reasonable value for money, as are the 12 self-service cottages (most sleep 6 or 7 at around $40 per person). Hearty breakfasts and lunches are $10, dinner $15. BB ❻

Naro Moru Timberland Lodging Naro Moru, no phone. Clean, fresh rooms (though no external windows) with instant showers and squat toilets. ❶

Youth hostel 9km up the well-signposted track to Mount Kenya National Park's Naro Moru gate ☏062/62412, ⓦwww.hihostels.com. This excellent hostel has comfortable if basic dorms (Ksh700 per bed) and camping (Ksh500), with hot showers and a well-equipped kitchen. A good place to team up with others for climbing the mountain independently.

Mount Kenya National Park

An extinct volcano some 3.5 million years old, **Mount Kenya** (ⓦwww.kws.go.ke/mt-kenya.html; $55) is Africa's second-highest mountain, with two jagged peaks. Formed from the remains of a gigantic volcanic plug – it rose more than 7000m above sea level until a million years ago – most of its erupted lava and ash have been eroded by glacial action to create the distinctive, craggy silhouette. The peaks are permanently iced with snow and glaciers, the latter under retreat due to climate change. On the upper slopes, altitude and the equatorial location combine to nurture forms of **vegetation**, seemingly designed by some 1950s science-fiction writer, that exist only here and at one or two other lofty points in East Africa. When you first see them, it's hard to believe the "water-holding cabbage", "ostrich plume plant" or "giant groundsel".

Europeans first heard about the mountain when the German missionary **Johann Ludwig Krapf** saw it in 1849, but his stories of snow on the equator were not taken seriously. But in 1883 the young Scottish traveller, Joseph Thomson, confirmed its existence to the outside world. The Kikuyu, Maasai and other peoples living in the region had venerated the mountain for centuries, and park rangers still occasionally report finding elderly Kikuyu high up on the moorlands, drawn by the presence of God – Ngai – whose dwelling place this is. It is not known, however, whether anyone had scaled the peaks before Sir Halford Mackinder reached the higher of the two, **Batian**, in 1899. Another thirty years passed before **Nelion**, a tougher summit, was conquered. Both were named by Mackinder's expedition after nineteenth-century Maasai *laibon*, or ritual leaders.

The **KWS-managed national park** encloses all parts of the mountain above 3200m plus salients down the Naro Moru and Sirimon streams, and, inside this area fees have to be paid, and strict rules control your activities. Outside this zone, surrounding the national park, lies the Mount Kenya National Reserve, in which your movements are normally only limited by your inclinations and equipment (though on some access roads, such as the one for *Mountain Lodge*, fees are payable even in the reserve). For suggested specialist **guidebooks and maps**, see "Books", p.600.

Climbing Mount Kenya

There are **four main routes** up Mount Kenya. From the west, the **Naro Moru trail** provides the shortest and steepest way to the top. The **Burguret** and **Sirimon trails** from the northwest are less well trodden; Sirimon has a reputation for lots of wildlife, while Burguret passes through a long stretch of

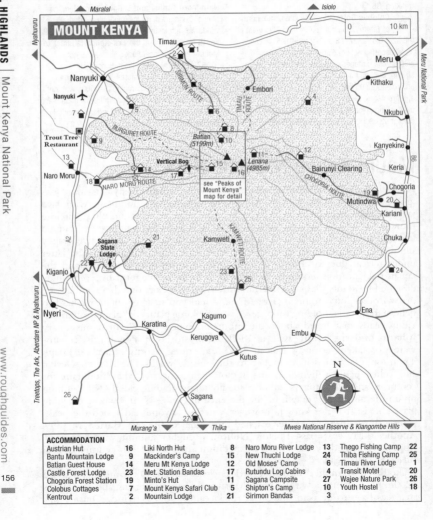

ACCOMMODATION							
Austrian Hut	16	Liki North Hut	8	Naro Moru River Lodge	13	Thego Fishing Camp	22
Bantu Mountain Lodge	9	Mackinder's Camp	15	New Thuchi Lodge	24	Thiba Fishing Camp	25
Batian Guest House	14	Meru Mt Kenya Lodge	12	Old Moses' Camp	6	Timau River Lodge	1
Castle Forest Lodge	23	Met. Station Bandas	17	Rutundu Log Cabins	4	Transit Motel	20
Chogoria Forest Station	19	Minto's Hut	11	Sagana Campsite	27	Wajee Nature Park	26
Colobus Cottages	7	Mount Kenya Safari Club	10	Shipton's Camp	10	Youth Hostel	18
Kentrout	2	Mountain Lodge	21	Sirimon Bandas	3		

Keeping Mount Kenya clean

The Kikuyu and other tribes venerated Mount Kenya as the dwelling place of God. It was believed that if you went up to the peaks you would find him, and medicine men and diviners routinely trekked up the mountain to seek miraculous cures or spiritual inspiration. Nowadays, it's mainly tourists, some 15,000 each year, who tread in their steps. Few of them, it seems, particularly respect, never mind venerate, the old mountain deity, and many tonnes of rubbish are left behind every year. You should take all your trash back down with you.

dense forest. The fourth trail, **Chogoria**, is a beautiful, much longer ascent up the eastern flank of the mountain, on which you have to carry tents. In practice, Naro Moru, Sirimon and Chogoria account for nearly all hikes; if you want to use any other route, you have to inform the warden in advance (this can be done by radio by the rangers at any park gate).

The technical peaks of **Batian** (5199m) and **Nelion** (5189m) are accessible only to experienced, fully-equipped mountaineers, and the easiest route is Grade IV, making them a lot more testing, for example, than most of the routes up the Matterhorn. If you want to climb these peaks, you should join the Mountain Club of Kenya (Ⓦwww.mck.or.ke, see p.59) who will put you in touch with the right people, and can give reductions on hut fees and other accommodation charges.

Anyone who is reasonably fit can have a crack at the third highest peak, **Point Lenana** (4985m). This climb, however, has somehow acquired a reputation for being fairly easy, and lots of people set off quite unprepared for high-altitude living. Indeed, a quarter of attempts fail for this reason. Above about 4000m the mountain is often foggy or windy and freezing cold, wickedly so after dark. The air is thin, and it rains or snows, at least briefly, almost every day, though most precipitation comes at night.

Mount Kenya's **weather** is notoriously unpredictable. There are days when it's fairly clear even during the rainy seasons, but driving up the muddy roads to the park gates may be nearly impossible. If it's really bad, you probably won't be allowed in anyway. The most **reliable months** are February and August, although January and most of July can be fine, too.

National Park rules

KWS operates a sign-in/sign-out system and you register your details and plans at your gate of entry. This is where you pay **fees** for your anticipated stay ($55 per 24-hour period, or a special $150 "mountaineering" fee for your first three days; no refunds). You can change your plans once on the mountain, or extend your stay and pay the balance on departure, but you must leave by one of the three main gates – Naro Moru, Sirimon or Chogoria – and formally sign out. It's a bad idea to use any alternative exit: KWS will look for you and eventually organize an air search if you don't show up. Stories circulate of people being pursued to Nairobi and beyond for non-payment of huge rescue service bills.

Costs, guides and porters

Climbing Mount Kenya is a fairly expensive business, though still significantly cheaper than Kilimanjaro. Doing the trek independently from Naro Moru, the cheapest possible four-day trip (three up, one down) for two people, including park fees, overnight accommodation, transport to the road-head and a basic self-catering food budget of $10 per day, but excluding any equipment rental,

157

▲ Peaks of Mount Kenya

would cost around $330 per person. Organized trips start from around $100 per person per day.

Note that the $150 three-day "mountaineering" fee for national park entry includes three nights of camping fees, which would otherwise cost $15 per night. Note, also, that the smallest party allowed to hike on the mountain is two people, which in practice means solo independent travellers have to team up with others or hire a **guide/porter**.

If you take a guide and/or porter, expect to pay around $10–20 per day per porter, plus Ksh50 for his special-discount park fees. Every guide needs to have an official **KWS guiding permit**. Ask to see it, and don't be fobbed off with local guiding association cards. It's best to agree terms in writing in advance and to pay half or two-thirds of the wages up front and the balance on safe delivery back to base. You can hire **guides** and **porters** in Naro Moru at *Naro Moru River Lodge*, *Bantu Mountain Lodge* or the Mount Kenya Guides and Porters Safari Club (see p.154), in Nanyuki at the *Jambo House Hotel* and in Chogoria at the *Joywood Hotel* (see p.163).

What to bring

Above all, it's essential to have a really **warm sleeping bag**, ideally with an additional liner and/or a Gore-Tex bivouac bag, capable of keeping you warm below freezing point. One **thick sweater**, or better still, several thinner ones, and either a **windproof jacket** or a down- or fibre-filled one are also essential, as is a **change of footwear**, as you're bound to have wet feet by the end of each day. **Gloves** and a **balaclava** or **woolly hat** are also handy. A light cagoule or anorak is good to have, as is a set or two of thermal underwear for the often shivering nights. A **torch**, ideally a wind-up one, is always handy, and essential if you're trekking without a guide. An **emergency foil blanket** is advisable, weighs next to nothing and packs down very small. Another prerequisite is a **stove**, as you'll be miserable without regular hot drinks. Firewood is not available and cannot be collected once you enter the park (no burning is allowed). For **food**, dehydrated soup and chocolate are perhaps the most useful.

The *Naro Moru River Lodge* (see p.155) has a **rental** shop where you can get just about anything, though at prices that may make you wish you'd simply bought it in Nairobi (see "Camping equipment", p.131).

Altitude and health

The various ascents themselves are mostly just steep hikes, if rough underfoot in parts. It's the **altitude** rather than the climb that may stop you reaching the top. Much more relevant than the training programmes that some people embark on is giving yourself enough time to acclimatize, so that your body has a chance to produce extra oxygen-carrying red blood cells.

Above 3000–4000m, you will be well outside your normal comfort zone and are likely to notice the effects of altitude. You may want to take Diamox (acetazolamide) to speed up your acclimatization and keep painkillers handy for headaches, which are fairly normal at first, especially at night. Keeping your **fluid intake** as high as possible will also help – three to five litres a day is recommended. Most water sources on the mountain are reckoned to be safe (one or two exceptions are noted). It's best to avoid alcohol while climbing The effects of altitude can be largely avoided if you **take your time** over the trek, as minor symptoms gradually disappear. Going up the Naro Moru route, you shouldn't attempt to climb from the base of the mountain (that is, from Naro Moru town at 2000m) to Point Lenana (just under 5000m) in less than 72 hours. Five or six days is much better, especially if you've just arrived in Kenya and are used to living at sea level. Assuming you allow a day to get down again, giving yourself a week for the whole trip is a good idea. Always aim to climb for an hour or two higher than the altitude you are going to sleep at; alternatively, spend two nights at the same altitude.

The symptoms of **altitude sickness**, also known as acute mountain sickness, vary between individuals, and appear unrelated to how fit you are – indeed, fit young males often suffer the most acute symptoms. If you climb too fast, extreme breathlessness, nausea, disorientation and even slurred speech are all possible. If someone in your group shows signs of being seriously tired and weak, you should descend a few hundred metres. If the symptoms develop into unsteadiness on the feet and drowsiness, **descend rapidly** until the symptoms improve. The effects of altitude, especially on bodies tuned only to sea level, are remarkable, and they can quickly become very dangerous and even fatal if high-altitude pulmonary or cerebral oedema (water in the lungs or brain cavity) develop.

Accommodation

With a tent, you can camp anywhere in the park, the only practical advantage of the campsites at the *Met Station Bandas*, *Mackinder's* and various other designated campsites on the mountain being water pipes and long-drop toilets. Accommodation on the mountain includes some basic lodges with limited facilities and a number of rudimentary mountain huts which provide little more than shelter and bare bunks.

On the Naro Moru route, the KWS-run, self-service *Batian Guest House* at 2400m near the park gate needs to be booked in advance (Ⓦ www.kws.go.ke; 6 beds in 4 bedrooms, $180 for the whole house) while the *Met Station Bandas* at 3050m ($12 per person) and *Mackinder's Camp* at 4200m ($15 per person) are owned by *Naro Moru River Lodge* and can be booked and paid for in advance, or on arrival if they have space.

On the Sirimon route, the KWS-run *Sirimon Bandas* at 2650m (two 4-bed *bandas* at $80 each) are just outside the gate, together with a campsite ($15), while *Old Moses Camp* at 3400m (formerly *Judmeier's Camp*; $12 per person) and

Shipton's Camp at 4230m ($10 per person) are owned by *Bantu Mountain Lodge* (Ⓦwww.mountainrockkenya.com) and offer basic accommodation. Book in advance or pay on site.

Just before the departure point for the camping-only Chogoria route, there is *banda* accommodation at ⚑ *Meru Mount Kenya Lodge* at 3015m (from Ksh1050 per person, reservations at Ⓦwww.lets-go-travel.net).

Austrian Hut (4785m) and *Liki North Hut* (3990m) are owned by KWS and you should reserve in advance at Ⓦwww.kws.go.ke or pay at the gate (Ksh1000 per person). *Austrian* is usually staffed by KWS rangers. A number of other huts, in various states of repair, are owned by the MCK and reserved for their members.

The Naro Moru route

The earth road between Naro Moru town and the road-head at the Meteorological Station is a 26-kilometre haul. There are no regular matatus; private transport with a driver, booked with *Naro Moru River Lodge*, will set you back $80. If you walk, you may get a paying lift some of the way, but the very light traffic thins out as you head east and if you don't get transport past the youth hostel after 9km, you should allow five hours to walk the rest of the way. Another 9km beyond the youth hostel, you come to the **park gate** and usually a few buffalo chewing the cud on the lawn.

From the park gate to the Meteorological Station

From the park gate, you leave the conifer plantations and occasional *shambas* behind as the road twists and climbs through shaggy forest into a zone of colossal **bamboo**. Look out for elephant and particularly **buffalo** if you walk this stretch, though you'll more often see just their droppings and footprints. If you find buffalo on the path, you're supposed to lob stones at them, and they're supposed to move out of the way. Much safer is the tried and trusted retreat-steadily-without-taking-your-eyes-off-them approach.

The final ascent to the Met Station is a three-kilometre series of steep hairpins usually driveable only in a 4WD (and often not at all when wet). You start to get some magnificent views out over the plains from up here, while right under your nose you may find a three-horned **chameleon**, stalking cautiously through the foliage like a miniature dinosaur. The high forest is their favourite habitat. **Lions** and **black panthers** – the melanistic form of the leopard found at high altitudes – can occasionally be seen in this area.

With an early start, it's physically perfectly possible to reach *Mackinder's Camp* in one day, but unless you're already well acclimatized, you'll probably feel very below par by the time you get there. It's far better to take it easy and get used to the Met Station's 3050-metre altitude, or, if you have a tent, climb an hour or so up to the tree line and camp there. The mountain's weather is another good reason to stop at the Met Station. After midday, it often gets foul, and the infamous **vertical bog** (not far beyond the Met Station) is no fun at all in heavy drizzle and twenty-metre visibility.

The Teleki Valley and Point Lenana

An early start from the Met Station should see you to *Mackinder's* by lunchtime, before the clouds start to thicken up. In fair weather the vertical bog en route is not as daunting as it sounds: you keep to the left of the red-and-white marker posts where it isn't as wet. In wet conditions, however, it can be ghastly, as the rosette plants hold just enough icy water to reach certain parts in a bracing

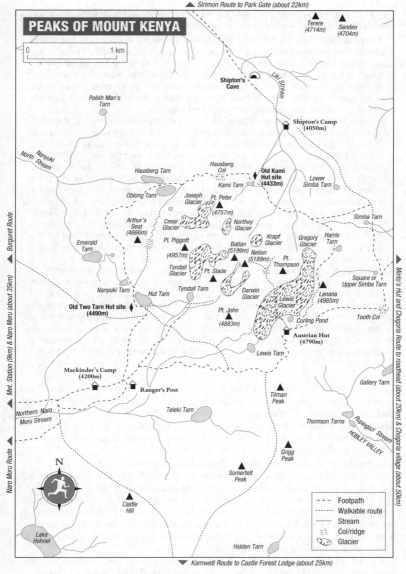

PEAKS OF MOUNT KENYA

0   1 km

▲ Sirimon Route to Park Gate (about 22km)

Terere (4714m)
Sendeo (4704m)

Liki Stream

Shipton's Cave

Shipton's Camp (4050m)

Polish Man's Tarn

Nanyuki North Stream

Hausberg Tarn

Hausberg Col

Old Kami Hut site (4433m)

Lower Simba Tarn

Kami Tarn

Oblong Tarn

Joseph Glacier

Pt. Peter (4757m)

Burguret Route

Arthur's Seat (4666m)

Cesar Glacier

Northey Glacier

Simba Tarn

Emerald Tarn

Pt. Piggott (4957m)

Batian (5199m)

Krapf Glacier

Gregory Glacier

Harris Tarn

Nelion (5189m)

Pt. Thompson

Tyndall Glacier

Pt. Slade

Square or Upper Simba Tarn

Nanyuki Tarn

Hut Tarn

Tyndall Tarn

Darwin Glacier

Lewis Glacier

Lenana (4985m)

Old Two Tarn Hut site (4490m)

Pt. John (4883m)

Curling Pond

Tooth Col

Austrian Hut (4790m)

Lewis Tarn

Mackinder's Camp (4200m)

Gallery Tarn

Ranger's Post

Tilman Peak

Teleki Tarn

Thomson Tarns

Rupingazi Stream

HOBLEY VALLEY

Northern Naro Moru Stream

Grigg Peak

Naro Moru Route

N

Somerfelt Peak

Castle Hill

Lake Hohnel

Hidden Tarn

▼ Kamweti Route to Castle Forest Lodge (about 25km)

Met. Station (9km) & Naro Moru (about 35km)

Minto's Hut and Chogoria Route to roadhead (about 20km) & Chogoria village (about 50km)

Mount Kenya National Park

www.roughguides.com

- - - Footpath
········· Walkable route
——— Stream
Col/ridge
Glacier

manner whenever you slip. As you reach the bog, you enter another vegetation zone, that of **giant heather**. Beyond and above the bog, the path follows a ridge high above the **Teleki Valley** with the peaks straight ahead, rising brilliantly over a landscape that seems to have nothing in common with the hazy plains below.

For *Mackinder's*, you follow the contours across the valley side and jump, or cross by stepping stones, over the snowmelt Northern Naro Moru stream. The

Mount Kenya's high-altitude flora and fauna

The mountain's vegetation is zoned by **altitude**. Above about 2000m, *shambas* and coniferous plantations cease and the original, dense cloud forest takes over, with the best areas on the mountain's southern and eastern, rain-facing slopes. At 2400m, forest gives way to giant bamboo, with clumps up to 20m high. The bamboo, a member of the grass family, appears impenetrable, but dark-walled passages are kept open by elephants and buffalo. Again, it's the south that has the best bamboo areas; on the dry, northern slopes, there's very little of it.

Above the bamboo at about 2800m you come into more open country of scattered, twisted *Hagena* and St John's Wort trees (*Hypericum*), then the tree line (3000m) and the start of peculiar, Afro-Alpine moorlands. Above about 3300m, you reach the land of the giants; giant heather, giant groundsel, giant lobelia. Identities are confusing: the cabbages on stumps and the larger candelabra-like "trees" are the same species, giant groundsel or tree senecio, an intermediate stage of which has a sheaf of yellow flowers. They are slow growers and, for such weedy-looking vegetables, they may be extraordinarily old, up to 200 years. The tall, fluffy, less abundant plants are a species of giant lobelia discovered by the explorer Teleki and found only on Mount Kenya. The name plaque below one of these (there's a little nature trail along the ridge above the Naro Moru stream) calls it an "ostrich plume plant" (*Lobelia telekii*), and it's the only plant that could fairly be described as cuddly. The furriness, which gives it such an animal quality, acts as insulation for the delicate flowers.

Any nights you spend up in the mountain huts will normally be shared with large numbers of persistent **rodents**, which you won't see until it's too late. Remember to isolate your food from them by suspending it from the roof. The familiar diurnal scavengers that you'll see are **rock hyraxes**, which are especially tame at *Mackinder's Camp*; the welfare service provided to them by tourists preserves elderly specimens long past their natural life span. Hyraxes are not rodents; the anatomy of their feet indicates they share a distant ancestry with elephants. You're likely to come across other animals at quite high altitudes, too, notably **duiker antelope** on the moorlands.

camp, at 4200m, virtually at the head of Teleki Valley, is a long stone and concrete bunkhouse. Certainly no hotel, it does at least provide some warmth and the company of other climbers, Kikuyu guides and porters. The peaks of **Batian** and **Nelion** tower magnificently over the valley, with a third pinnacle, **Point John**, even closer. There's usually a fresh icing of snow every morning, but early sunlight melts most of it by midday.

If you want to climb straight to **Point Lenana**, you're likely to find at least one group leaving with a guide from around 2am the following morning. Leaving this early, with a three-to-five-hour hike ahead of you, allows you to get to the summit by dawn for a fabulous view, in the right conditions, from northern Kenya on one side to Kilimanjaro on the other. If you're planning to go without a guide, it's probably safest to scramble straight up the ridge to Point Lenana from *Austrian Hut* rather than cross the unpredictable vestiges of the Lewis glacier without proper equipment.

It's not advisable to rush into doing this final ascent. For most people, day three is better spent getting acclimatized in the Teleki Valley, and not making the climb to Point Lenana until the morning of the fourth day. Note that spending your third night on the mountain at *Austrian Hut*, just below Point Lenana, is not a good idea if you're not used to the altitude. Sleeping unacclimatized here can be, literally, a nightmare.

The **descent** doesn't take long. After summiting, you can get all the way down to Naro Moru in one day, assuming you have transport arranged at the Met

Station or manage to find a lift there. If you're not ready to go straight back down, you might want to do the circular **hike around the peaks** (see p.165).

The Chogoria route

The **Chogoria trail** is scenically superior to the others, but it's also the longest route. You should allow a *minimum* of five days from Chogoria village up to Point Lenana and down the west side to Naro Moru, or six days if you're returning to Chogoria. Note that the Chogoria route is a camping-only trek: you have to show you have tents for your party when passing through the park gate.

Chogoria village

The muddy, Land Rover-choked village of **CHOGORIA** off the B6 highway is your first target. Public transport sometimes drops passengers on the highway (a 1km walk into Chogoria village) and sometimes drives into the small centre. There's a KCB bank with **ATM**, but no Barclay's. There are several **porter/guide** associations in Chogoria, most of whose members are extremely pushy. The most reliable is the Mount Kenya Chogoria Guides Association based at the *Joywood Hotel* (☎064/22266 or 0733/262448). Expect to negotiate a wage of around Ksh500–1000 per day per porter. By far the best of several **lodgings**, with reasonable self-contained rooms, is the *Transit Motel*, 1.5km off the main road south of Chogoria at Karaa Market (☎064/22096; ②). To get here, alight from your bus or matatu at Kiriani stage, 3km south of the Chogoria turn-off.

Up to the park entrance

The road from Karaa/Kiriani meets the one from Chogoria 5km kilometres west of the highway at a rural junction hamlet called **Mutindwa**. From here, it's about 26km to the park gate. En route, some 2km from Mutindwa at Chogoria Forest Station, there's a decent **campsite** (Ksh220, firewood available), dominated by a fine, huge-leaved *Anthocleista zambesiaca* tree.

If you're driving, 4WD is vital on this steep track, but even with it, getting up to the park gate in wet weather can't be guaranteed. If you haven't got your own vehicle, you can charter transport at the *Transit Motel* or elsewhere in Chogoria. Expect to pay around Ksh1000 for a ride on the back of a motorbike or around Ksh8000 to charter a Land Rover for your group. It's a good idea not to pay in full until you get up to the gate. You may prefer to walk up in any case, as it helps you acclimatize. There's exciting, dense rainforest along much of the road, and you're likely to see colobus monkeys, hyena, buffalo and lots of elephant dung. The next available campsite is the only clearing in the forest, at a place called **Bairunyi Clearing**, 15km further up the track, with no water. The national park's **Chogoria Gate** is 9km further up the increasingly steep and rough track, flanked by giant, creaking bamboo forest.

Meru Mount Kenya Lodge and the road-head

The very good and beautifully located *bandas* of 🏕 *Meru Mount Kenya Lodge* (see booking details and prices on p.160) are just before the gate. Firewood is available for the fireplaces in each *banda*, and there's a basic shop that usually has beer. The lodge is often visited by buffaloes, and you can sometimes see elephants at the nearby waterholes.

If you're not staying in the *bandas*, but it's time to stop for the day, you camp by the gate; alternatively follow the main track up from the park gate and you'll come to a **special campsite** with running water and toilet. This is a beautiful place to camp (reservable through KWS; ☎020/600800, ⓦwww.kws.go.ke; $15).

Both the main track and the side branch, via the site of the old *Urumandi* hut, eventually meet up at the **road-head**, 7km further on. The side branch is the more interesting walk, but tougher on vehicles. The road-head, with a small parking area, is on the north side of the Nithi stream and there's another very pleasant **campsite** here, with good stream water.

There are good walks round about, useful for acclimatizing to the 3000-metre-plus altitude. Short scrambles from the road-head take you to the four sets of waterfalls at **Nithi Falls**, while longer walks (3–6hr round trip) take you north to **Mugi Hill**, **Lake Ellis** and the flat-topped peak known as the **Giant's Billiard Table** or Mount Kilingo.

Minto's to Point Lenana

From the road-head (a three-hour trek from *Meru Mount Kenya Lodge*), all wheels are abandoned as you slog on foot up towards *Minto's Hut*, a six-hour stint away in the high moorlands. The route tracks along the axis of an ascending ridge, then flattens onto the rim of the spectacular **Gorges Valley**, carved deep by glaciation. There are unobstructed and encouraging views up to the peaks as you hug the contours of the valley wall.

Minto's Hut, at 4300m is, like *Mackinder's* on the west side of the mountain, a three-to-five-hour hike from Point Lenana. Situated by the four small **Hall Tarns**, it's perched above the larger Lake Michaelson at the head of the valley below – a very beautiful place, inspiringly set off by giant groundsel, lobelia plants and weird volcanic formations inhabited by rock hyraxes. The hut is only for porters. Beware of the tarn water, which is not pure; boiling it at this altitude (water boils at 85–90°C) will kill fewer bugs than usual, so you should use purifying tablets or iodine.

On the morning of day three you have two options. The first is to head up to the ridge west of *Minto's* and follow it, through pretty scenery, to **Simba Tarn**, below Simba Col. From there, head due south around the peaks and past little **Square Tarn** before turning right to follow the contours for a tough kilometre to the so-called **Curling Pond** (matches have been held on the ice here) and *Austrian Hut*. If you're thinking of a short cut straight up to Square Tarn, note that it's very steep. Alternatively, from *Minto's* make for the base of the ridge extending east from Point Lenana, then tackle the cruel scree slope to the south for a ninety-minute scramble up to a saddle, followed by a straight drop to the head of the **Hobley Valley** with its two tarns. From here, it's just an hour across to the base of Lenana Ridge, behind which, again, is *Austrian Hut*. Mercifully, whichever route you choose, this day's hike is a short one and at this altitude (over 4000m), you'll be glad to spend the rest of the day at one of the huts, recuperating for the final ascent. Considering the altitude, a safer and probably more comfortable option would be to spend a second night, acclimatizing at the base of Simba Tarn, followed by a pre-dawn assault on Point Lenana on day four.

After the climb to Lenana, you have a ninety-minute **descent** from *Austrian Hut*, tracking back and forth over miserable scree, to the Teleki Tarn at the head of the Naro Moru stream. *Mackinder's*, and the scent of civilization, is just an hour away down the valley. But if you can resist that lure, and it is still early in the day, *and* if you have enough food and water, you can continue around the west side of the peaks to Hut Tarn, then up and down over the ridges to the site of the former *Kami Hut,* at the head of the Sirimon route on the north side. If you want to do it, and you feel acclimatized, there's no problem making it from *Minto's* to Point Lenana and on down to the Met Station in one day.

The Sirimon route

The **Sirimon route** leads up from the A2 highway from a point some 14km east of Nanyuki. The route climbs over the northern moorlands, giving superb views of the main peaks as well as the twin lesser peaks of Terere (4714m) and Sendeyo (4704m), which have small glaciers of their own. Accommodation consists of the *Sirimon Bandas* and campsite at the gate, *Old Moses Camp* at the road-head (3400m up and accessible only by 4WD), the porters' *Liki North Hut* at 3990m (with camping nearby) and *Shipton's Camp* bunkhouses at 4200m (see p.160).

There are certain advantages in using this route: it's the driest route, the scenery is more open, and it's renowned for wildlife. *Bantu Mountain Lodge* (see p.155) offers all-inclusive **guided tours** up to Point Lenana using this route, as do other Naro Moru and Nanyuki operators. Independent trekking is fine if you're in a small group, but if you're looking to team up with others, you're much less likely to find company here than on the Chogoria or Naro Moru routes as, apart from the huddle of *dukas* on the highway, 9km below the park gate, there isn't any real base to start from.

Treks around the peaks

Though most people head straight up to Point Lenana, trekking round the peaks is an even more exhilarating experience, with the bonus of exploring some of the tarns and glacial valleys on the north side. It is reckoned to be easier to do this anticlockwise in two or three days. If you want to do it in one day, however, set off clockwise from *Mackinder's* via the site of the former *Two Tarn Hut* next to **Hut Tarn**, set in a glorious and eerily silent col beneath the glaciers and scree. The walk from here round to Point Lenana is very much a switchback affair but, as long as the mists stay away, the scenery is fairy-tale. If you're fairly fit and acclimatized, it should take eight to ten hours. Both the *Two Tarn Hut* and *Kami Hut*, on the north side of the peaks, have been demolished, but you can still camp at both sites.

Other routes: Burguret and Kamweti

The trails described above represent only the most obvious and well-trodden of the mountain's hiking possibilities. With time and the right gear, you could hike the moorland and peaks area for as long as you liked. Note, however, that you must be fully self-sufficient, you must inform the rangers at the park gate where you buy your tickets of the route you intend to take and you must exit and sign out via one of three approved gates, paying any fees owed.

Bantu Mountain Lodge's preferred route used to follow the **Burguret River** up from the lodge through thick bamboo forest and moorland, but this is now mostly overgrown and hard to follow without a guide. The lower trail passes a clutch of caves described as a "Mau Mau conference centre" (the lodge offers half-day hikes or mountain-bike trips on this trail).

The southern flanks of the mountain seem to have largely escaped the notice of hikers, but there are several forest stations in the vicinity of Embu and plenty of scope for exploration. Most of the southern slopes were a designated "Kikuyu reserve" during the colonial period, so few European climbers created routes up here, but the **Kamweti route** from *Castle Forest Lodge* is one that is becoming more popular (see p.153).

Nanyuki and on to Meru

North of Naro Moru, the A2 runs across the yellow-and-grey downs, scattered with stands of tall blue gums, roamed by cattle and overflown by brilliant roller birds, before dropping to **Nanyuki**. You might be forgiven for expecting something momentous to take place at the **equator**, just south of town. There's a sprouting of curio shops and signs ("This sign is on the Equator") and even an "Equator Professor" who claims to demonstrate the Coriolis effect of the earth's rotation using a bucket of water and a matchstick (aided by sleight of hand). In the northern hemisphere a large body of still water in a perfectly formed vessel would gurgle through a plug hole anticlockwise, whereas in the southern hemisphere it would flow clockwise – though in practice the direction of flow is controlled by the operator because the Coriolis effect is too tiny to have an impact, especially anywhere near the equator itself where the effect is zero. The demonstration is free; the "certificate" comes for a fee.

NANYUKI

Prison

Sikh Temple

Covered Market

Cloth & Hardware Market

Matatu Stage

PARK ROAD

Modern Sanitary Stores

United Stores

Standard Chartered   KCB   Caltex

Max Global   Barclays

Mitimayo   Juttsons

Market

Nanyuki River

Railway Station

Airstrip, Ol Pejeta & Nairobi

Meru & Isiolo

Cathedral, Meru & Isiolo

Nyahururu and Nanyuki Spinners & Weavers

Nyahururu

LUMUMBA STREET

KIMATHI ROAD

A2

Show-ground

War Cemetery

RESTAURANTS, CAFÉS & BARS

Barney's	6
Boulangerie	3
Cape Chestnut	7
Kongoni Camp	F
Marina	5
Mother's Choice	4
Old House	E
Pilau Centre	1
Sportsman's Arms	G
Stage View Pub	2

ACCOMMODATION

Equator Chalet	C
Jambo House	A
Joskaki	B
Kongoni Camp	F
Lions Court Lodge	D
Mount Kenya Safari Club	H
Old House	E
Sportsman's Arms	G

0   200 m

Arrival

Nanyuki's **airfield** is 9km south of the town centre on the way to Naro Moru and has several scheduled flights a day to and from Nairobi. It's also the home of local charter company Tropic Air (℡020/2033032 or 0722/207300, Ⓦwww.tropicairkenya.com) and has a very pleasant bar-restaurant and the excellent **Laikipia Wildlife Forum info centre** and Laikipia Outpost shop, where you can pick up gifts and essential leaflets on regional attractions and accommodation (Mon–Fri 8am–5pm). As well as plenty of matatu transport, Nanyuki once again has a **rail link to Nairobi**, with one service every weekend (departure: Nairobi Sat 7am, arrival: Nanyuki 5.30pm; departure: Nanyuki Sun 7am, arrival: Nairobi 5.30pm; 3rd class only, Ksh230).

There are **ATMs** at KCB, Barclays and Standard Chartered, all in the town centre. For the **internet**, try Max Global (Mon–Sat 8am–8pm, Sun 11am–8pm), next to the *Marina Grill* or the cybercafé at the Equatorial Supermarket. If you're looking for **guides/porters** for the Sirimon route up Mount Kenya, try Montana Treks in the *Jambo House Hotel* building (℡062/32731), but be sure to insist on card-carrying KWS-approved personnel.

Wandering around Nanyuki's small **shops** is quite fun. Juttsons Ltd (Mon–Sat 8am–5pm) is the main bookseller and stationer, and they have good local knowledge, while Mitimayo Craft Shop, next to Barclays, has superior bric-a-brac, crafts and souvenirs.

Accommodation

You can **camp** at *Kongoni Camp* and usually at the *Sportsman's Arms*. Also bear in mind that Naro Moru (see p.154), is only a twenty-minute drive away, and there are some good places to stay and eat between the two town centres.

Equator Chalet north end of the town centre ℡062/314801 or 0729/749158. About as nice a cheap hotel as you could hope to find anywhere in Kenya: airy, spacious rooms with satellite TV, instant showers and nets, grouped around a pleasant courtyard (safe parking) with a balcony overlooking the street. To maintain its reputation, it claims, the bar sells wine but not beer. BB ❸

Jambo House Lumumba St, opposite the park ℡062/31894. You get what you pay for here, an unembellished place to sleep, and most rooms are dark and airless, albeit with hot water. ❶

Joskaki Lumumba St ℡062/31403. Vast, corridor-riddled warren that can be indescribably noisy when the bar is open all night or there's a disco. Smallish rooms, no nets and uncertain hot water, but the food can be excellent and there are rooftop views of the town and occasionally Mount Kenya. Worth paying extra for a bigger (and, if possible, quieter) room. ❶

Kongoni Camp 1km north of the town centre on the way out to Meru, then 200m off the highway south ℡0720/542159. Campsite, restaurant and bar, deservedly popular as a curry-and-beer celebration spot for returning Mount Kenya trekkers. The *bandas* aren't huge, but

they're clean and cosy, with instant showers, and the overall setting and mood of the place are spot on. BB ❹

Lions Court Lodge 1km south of the town centre, 200m along the road to Ol Pejeta Conservancy ℡062/31639, Ⓔlionscourtlodge@yahoo.com. Out-of-town hotel, with views of Mount Kenya. The *bandas* are rather dark and gloomy, but the newer cottages are good value, with satellite TV and small terraces looking onto the gardens. Can get busy at weekends when the whole of Nanyuki shows up for the disco and DJs. BB ❸

Mount Kenya Safari Club 8km southeast of the town centre ℡020/2216940, Ⓦwww.fairmont .com/kenyasafariclub. Founded by Hollywood star William Holden, and recently entirely renovated, this lavish resort hotel offers extraordinary levels of comfort but seems to relate little to its local environment. Plenty of activities and facilities in and around the hotel, including tennis, riding, bird walks, golf, swimming and visiting the animal orphanage and stylish art gallery. Good value online advance purchase deals available. BB ❻–❾

Old House Haile Selassie Rd, 1km south of the town centre ℡0722/697868. A clutch of cool, clean, modern cottages, overlooking the

gardens and the little Nanyuki river, each divided into two comfortable rooms with TVs (but no nets, fans or a/c), with a well established bar-restaurant. BB ❹
Sportsman's Arms north side of town ☎062/32348 or 0734/944077. An old establishment, with various parts renovated, improved or neglected.

The old cottages ooze atmosphere but main-block rooms and newer cottages are better equipped, though not with nets or a/c. Decent-sized outdoor pool (Ksh200 for non-residents), hot tub and sauna (residents only). Weekend discos can be testing if you're a light sleeper. BB ❹

The Town

NANYUKI has the dual distinction of being Kenya's air-force town as well as playing host to the British Army's training and operations centre. And although it has taken in thousands of refugees in recent decades, escaping from rural poverty and ethnic violence, it nevertheless remains very much a country town in atmosphere, and an oddly charming one. A wide, tree-lined main street and the mild climate lent by its two-thousand-metre altitude bestow an unfamiliar, cool spaciousness that seems to reinforce its colonial character: shops lining the main road include the Modern Sanitary Stores (aka Modsan; they sell camping gas) and the Settlers Store ("1938").

The first party of settlers arrived in the district in 1907 to find "several old Maasai *manyattas*, a great deal of game and nothing else". Nanyuki is still something of a settlers' town and European locals are always around. The animals, sadly, are not. Although you may see a few grazers on the plains, the vast herds of zebra that once roamed the banks of the Ngare Nanyuki (Maasai for Red River) were decimated by hunters seeking hides, by others seeking meat (particularly during World War II, when eighty thousand Italian prisoners of war were fed a pound of meat each day), but most of all by ranchers protecting their pastures.

As the zebra herds dwindled, so lions became a greater threat to livestock and the predators retreated, under fire, to the mountain forests and moors. These days, the non-profit **Animal Orphanage and Wildlife Conservancy** (Ksh1000) at *Mount Kenya Safari Club* is doing good work with waifs and strays and has an active **bongo breeding programme** which is now working on reintroductions.

A recommended local visit is to the 🏃 **Nanyuki Spinners and Weavers** workshop (☎0720/220899, ⓦwww.spinnersandweavers.org), located about 1km down the Nyahururu road, on the left. This women's group employs more than 130 local women and sells their rugs and blankets, woven on hand looms, at decent prices (Ksh500–10,000). They appreciate visitors.

Eating and drinking

One of Nanyuki's best restaurants is down at the airfield, but there are several good places competing with it, plus the usual snack bars and drinking dens.

🏃 **Barney's Bar & Restaurant** Nanyuki airfield, 9km south of the town centre ☎0723/310064, ⓦwww.barneysnanyuki.com. The people here have created an effortlessly cool ambiance on a veranda overlooking lawns next to the runway. Drop in for a big English breakfast or call ahead for a list of the day's specials. It's a little pricey (Ksh300 for chips and salad, Ksh800 for steak frites) but everything is fresh, tasty and really well prepared and they have the nicest loos in Nanyuki – pity it's not open in the evening. Daily 8am–5pm.

Boulangerie Coffee Shop In the town centre. Tempting, expensive coffee, pastries and light dishes.
Cape Chestnut South of the town centre, take a left (300m before the road to *Mount Kenya Safari Club*) for 700m ☎062/32526. A popular local rendezvous for English-style home cooking and curries, with wine and beer available. Dishes around Ksh500. Mon–Fri 9am–6pm, Sat 9am–2pm, closed Sun.

Kongoni Camp 1km north of town on the south side of the Meru road ☎0720/542159. A rising star in Nanyuki, this popular bar-restaurant specializes in "curries, steaks and everything". It's quite a big place with room for 60, and you can eat in the welcoming high-ceilinged timber and *mabati* bar-dining room, or at thatched-roof garden tables. Daily from morning to midnight or later.

Marina Grill & Restaurant Main St, opposite the post office. For a lively drink, and perhaps a meal, try this popular hangout of tourists and soldiers. Something from the snacks and fast-food menu will set you back around Ksh150, with mains taking a lot longer and costing around Ksh300–400.

Mother's Choice Café Main St, next to Marina Grill. Cheap snacks and cakes.

Old House Off Haile Selassie Rd, 1km south of the town centre ☎0722/697868. Pub and restaurant, formerly the popular *Horse's Mouth*, which still does good food, with curries from Ksh250, *nyama choma* at Ksh250 a half kilo and snacks in the Ksh50–200 range. A great spot for a pint with the locals.

Pilau Centre Restaurant On the Nyahururu road. Good snacks and great curries.

Sportsman's Arms North side of town. Time appears to have stood still for 70 years in the downstairs pub at this old hotel, while their big, upstairs deck bar conforms more to twenty-first century norms, with table football, pool and occasional discos.

Timau and east to Meru

Leaving Nanyuki eastwards, the ring road skirts closer to the mountain than at any other point in its circumference. The land here, extremely fertile, is for the most part covered by rolling wheatfields and commercial estates; many people work on the acreages of poly-covered flower and vegetable fields.

After 19km you come to the high-altitude village of **TIMAU**, unremarkable but for two outstanding stopover possibilities with accommodation. Rates at both are per person, so offer very good value if you're on your own. *Kentrout trout farm*, 3km to the south up a rough, signposted track from the village (4WD in rainy weather; ☎0722/775881 or reservations at ⓦwww.lets-go-travel.net; B&B Ksh2000 per person), is a delightful retreat, the gardens, river and indigenous forest teeming with birdlife and colobus monkeys. They have delicious al fresco lunch buffets (Ksh1000), the ingredients for which are grown or bred on the farm. There are three rooms in a rambling old ranch house and a number of self-contained *bandas*, plus two self-service stone cottages for rent.

The other great draw is *Timau River Lodge*, 2km east from Timau and 1km off to the south (☎062/41230; B&B Ksh2000 per person). The dream of a charming Afghan couple, the lodge (a diverse collection of log, mud and underground houses) was built to run on ecological principles. Every *banda* has its own small kitchen (there's also a communal cooking area with ancient Scottish cast-iron ovens) and children will adore the loft bedrooms in the largest *bandas*. You can **camp** anywhere you like (Ksh500 including hot showers). Trout-fishing, mountain-climbing, camel- and horseriding are on offer, and there are secluded waterfalls and river pools for bathing in, and a huge expanse of forest to explore.

After Timau, the scenery acquires a real grandeur as you pass along the southern fringes of the Lewa Wildlife Conservancy (see p.178). The 70km from Timau to Meru couldn't illustrate better the amazing variety of climate and landscape in Kenya. The road climbs steeply to almost 3000m, passing alternative routes to the peaks and giving unparalleled views of them in the early morning. A spectacle you might not have guessed at, however, is the panorama that spreads out to the north as the road drops once again. On a really clear day, after rain has settled the dust, this is devastatingly beautiful. Even on an average day, you can see as far as the dramatic mesa of **Ol Olokwe**, nearly 100km north in the desert. Isiolo (p.530) lies out there, too, first stop on the way to the northern wilderness. Beyond the Isiolo and Lewa turn-off, the road to Meru suddenly plunges through verdant jungle, with glimpses through the trees of the Nyambeni Hills and volcanic pimples dotting the plain.

About 20km east of Timau you reach the North Imenti petrol station, and 300m beyond that, the hour-and-a-half, 4WD-only track to a rustic retreat on the rarely visited northeast side of Mount Kenya, *Rutundu Log Cabins* (Ⓦ www .rutundu.com; self-catering fishing *bandas*, sleeping 4–8; $300). On the moorland shore of little **Lake Rutundu** at 3000m, beneath the dramatically flat-topped Rutundu hill, it's the perfect place for getting away from it all, and even better if you want to have large trout for dinner every night.

Meru

The moist, jungly atmosphere around **MERU**, with wood smoke curling up against a background of dark forest, is very reminiscent of parts of West Africa, and a change of mood after the dryish grasslands on the northwest side of the mountain. **Meru oak** is the commercial prize of this forested eastern side of the mountain, though judging by the number of active sawmills at the upper end of the town, supplies won't last much longer. The forest still comes almost to the town's edge, however, with tall forest giants still looming high, and paths lead off to cleared *shambas* where, for a year or two, just about anything will grow.

Arrival

Meru is a hub for transport south, west and east. Numerous **bus and matatu** companies have their offices between the mosque and *miraa* trading area and most major destinations are served from the main stage, with the exception of Embu, vehicles for which leave from the western end of Moi Avenue. All three main **banks** have ATMs here, and you can use the **internet** at the cybercafés outside Nakumatt (Mon–Sat 8am–10pm, Sun 10am–10pm) and under the *Meru Safari Hotel* (Mon–Sat 8.30am–9.30pm, closed Sun), among other places.

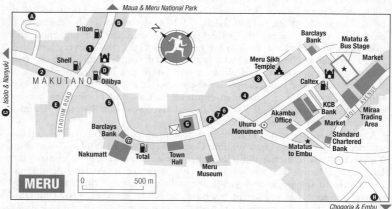

ACCOMMODATION				RESTAURANTS, BARS & CLUBS			
Blue Towers	D	Rocky Hill Inn	C	Afrikana	3	Terah's	2
Meru County	G	Three Steers	A	Ivory Springs Café	4	Three Steers	A
Meru Safari	F	White Star	B	Millie 2000	7	Zulu Roasters	
New Milimani	E			Nana's	6	Cabanas	1
Pig and Whistle	H			Simba Wells	5		

Accommodation

In keeping with its market-town functions, Meru has no shortage of **accommodation**, but there's nowhere much above adequate.

Blue Towers At the junction in Makutano ☎064/30309 or 0720/283666. Decorated with paintings and posters, this offers excellent value with TVs, nets and safes in every room. Deluxe rooms, with enormous bathrooms, cost a few hundred shillings more. BB ❸

Meru County Near the town centre ☎020/8007994 or 0724/278579. Resting on its laurels and now rather tired and overpriced, but most rooms have balconies, and all have nets and satellite TVs. Hot water, however, is only available mornings and evenings. BB ❸

Meru Safari Tom Mboya St ☎064/31500 or 0725/259852. Large hotel, with a rather institutional feel and smallish rooms with instant showers, but clean and pleasant enough, with a nice terrace bar-restaurant and, overall, better value than its *County* neighbour. BB ❷

Pig and Whistle On the lower side of town on the way out towards Embu ☎064/31411. An old colonial-era pub, surprisingly still open. The new rooms attached to the old building are slightly better, but tend to be noisy, while the garden rooms have TVs, nets and big windows but older style shower-baths. BB ❷

Rocky Hill Inn 8km northwest of Meru on the Nanyuki road ☎0714/190424. An ornate creation with chalets almost hidden among the landscaping and overgrown gardens, this has an unreliable water supply and is perhaps more a weekend *nyama choma* venue than a hotel, but is endearingly weird and worth a visit. The quaint little rooms are non-s/c. ❶

Three Steers 2km along the Nanyuki road, past Makutano ☎0728/588005 or 0725/683724. This large motel-type complex has good rooms with nets and TVs, though conventional rather than instant showers, a *nyama choma* joint, two bars and a cheap Indian-influenced restaurant. Safe parking. BB ❷

White Star Moi Stadium Rd; PO Box 259 ☎064/32989. Sister hotel of the *Blue Towers* at the junction, and similarly decorated with garish artworks and equally high standards and facilities. Standard rooms are large and airy and include TVs, safes and nets ("Hippo" is the best), while deluxe rooms have four-poster beds with a separate shower and tub. The restaurant doesn't serve alcohol. BB ❸

The Town

Meru town stretches for several kilometres down the mountain slopes, with great views from the upper (**Makutano**) half of town over the densely settled lower areas. The municipal **market** is large, and it's the obvious place to sample the excellent agricultural produce of the district: they grow the best **custard apples** in Kenya here, and you won't find cheaper, bigger or better bunches of *miraa* anywhere (see box overleaf).

The tiny but fascinating **Meru Museum** (Ⓦtinyurl.com/cletop; daily 9am–6pm; Ksh500) is a treat. It occupies the oldest stone building in town, a former District Commissioner's office, where you're likely to be the only visitor, except at weekends when they also do special film shows for local children. The emphasis is on the traditional culture of the Meru people: small ethnographic exhibits, pick-up-and-feel blocks of fossilized wood, stone tools from a prehistoric site at Lewa Downs and some woeful stuffed animals. There's a particularly good **herbal pharmacopoeia** – a collection of traditional medicinal plants growing in the garden, where you can see what a *miraa* bush looks like – and the museum's **Meru homestead** is well presented.

If you're interested in the Meru tribe, ask at the museum about the **Njuri-Ncheke traditional courthouse**, approximately 9km north of Meru on the road to Maua. The Njuri-Ncheke is a semi-secret society of elders sworn to preserve and uphold traditional cultural structures and religion.

Miraa

Throughout Kenya, and especially in the Central Highlands and on the coast, you'll often see people selling and chewing what looks like a bunch of twigs wrapped in a banana leaf. This is, in fact, **miraa**, more commonly known abroad by its Somali name **qat**, a natural stimulant that is particularly popular among Somalians, Somali Kenyans and Yemenis. The shrub (*Catha edulis*) grows in the hills around Meru (the world centre for its production), and the red-green young bark from the shrub's new shoots is washed, stripped with the teeth and chewed, with the bitter result being something of an acquired taste (it's usually taken with bubble gum to sweeten it). *Miraa* contains an alkaloid called cathinone, a distant relative of amphetamine, with similar **effects**, though you have to chew it for some time before you'll feel them. When they do kick in, they include a feeling of alertness, ease of conversation and loss of appetite. Long-term daily use can lead to addiction. It's not always looked upon favourably, with signs prohibiting the chewing of it in many hotels and bars.

Miraa comes in bundles of a hundred sticks called "kilos" (not a reference to their weight) and various **qualities**, from long, twiggy *kangeta*, which is the ordinary, bog-standard version, to short, fat *gisa kolombo*, which is the strongest. As it loses its potency within 48 hours of picking, it's wrapped in banana leaves and transported at speed. Street stalls selling it often display the banana leaves to show that they have it, and the best place to buy *miraa* in many towns is where the express matatus arrive from Meru. The use of *miraa* by bus, truck and matatu drivers goes a long way towards explaining why they have so many accidents. There are no **legal restrictions** on the use of *miraa* in Kenya, although imams have issued a *fatwa* (legal judgement) condemning it as an intoxicant, like alcohol, which means that it is forbidden to true believers. In fact, in most countries (but not the UK), *miraa* is a controlled narcotic, the possession of which is a criminal offence.

Eating and drinking

For **eating**, Meru doesn't have any outstanding stars, but everywhere is reasonably cheap. The most upmarket place is the clean and appetizing restaurant at the *Three Steers Hotel*, whose Indian dishes include plenty of vegetarian options (Ksh200–300). A popular new address is the *Afrikana Restaurant* on Moi Avenue, for excellent, solid meals in a fresh environment (most dishes Ksh150–200, *chai* Ksh15) and you can't go far wrong with the fast food and drinks at *Zulu Roasters Cabanas*, an outdoor courtyard opposite the mosque, where you can stuff yourself for about Ksh100. *Millie 2000* also does good snacks, as does *Nana's* next door, while *Ivory Springs Café* is a friendly place, and its samosas are satisfyingly tasty.

If you're self-catering, there's a huge new Nakumatt at the upper, Makutano, end of town. Makutano district is also the centre for **nightlife**. Try *Terah's*, a huge beer hall and *nyama choma* garden with weekend discos, or *Simba Wells*. Also at the weekend, you might want to venture out to *Rocky Hill Inn* (see p.171) for their *nyama choma*. They even do a bring-your-own deal: you supply the animal, they do the rest (goat roast Ksh2500, chicken Ksh200).

Embu and around

The fast road from Meru to Embu swoops around the eastern slopes of Mount Kenya through vibrant scenery. Five kilometres south of Meru, you cross the **equator**, and it's indicative of the lack of tourism round here that there's not a single curio stand, let alone a "Professor Coriolis" (see p.166). Hundreds of streams, the run-off from luxuriant rainfall blown in by the southeast monsoon, cut deeply into the volcanic soil of this eastern flank of the mountain. As a result, this side has a much broader covering of jungle, which extends, *shambas* permitting, down to the level of the road and beyond. Driving along, you plunge from one green and tan gorge to the next – early in the morning (the safest time to travel) you can sit back and admire the scenery. Sit on the right side of the vehicle for glimpses of snow-capped peaks, normally visible at this time of day.

Most public transport between Meru and Embu stops at **Chogoria**, a base for the eastern Mount Kenya ascent (see p.163), although if you're staying overnight you might consider continuing to the livelier market town of **CHUKA**. Chuka has a bank with exchange facilities and accommodation at the *Kimwa Farmer's Hotel* (T064/630570; ❸), with *nyama choma*, a busy disco and sometimes live music at weekends.

A more upmarket local haunt is the back-in-business *New Thuchi Lodge* (T020/2074559 or 0734/465625, E karueinvestco@yahoo.com; BB ❸), with beautifully tended tropical gardens, a large pool (Ksh150 for non-residents), well-kept rooms with nets and TVs and very spacious two-bedroom cottages ($70). To get here, turn off the main B6 road 8km south of Chuka at Kathegeri, and take the easterly direction on the E652 signposted "Kigumo 7km". The lodge is 3km down this decent earth road.

Embu town

There's very little to get excited about at **Embu**, and it's not obvious why it was chosen as the capital of Eastern Province. Certainly, without the apparatus of a provincial headquarters, the town wouldn't amount to much.

Embu has a number of decent **hotelis** doing reliable food: *Morning Glory Hotel,* opposite the Exhibition Centre, for chicken and chips and other inexpensive fare; the Somali-run *Zamzam*, which serves sweetly spiced pilau and *mataha* (rice, maize, beans, vegetables and potatoes all mashed together and eaten with beef); and *Rehana's Café*, a little way up the hill near the post office, which has been busily serving up excellent spicy samosas for more than 25 years.

If you need **accommodation**, by far the best place is the ⚔ *Izaak Walton Inn* (T068/31128 or 0712/781810, E manager@izaakwaltoninn.co.ke; BB ❹), a colonial-era former farmhouse, now an assemblage of green-*mabati*-roofed and newer buildings, with pleasant gardens, welcoming staff and an enthusiastic local clientele. It's at the top end of town, on the way out northwards, towards Meru. Rooms are clean and comfortable, with nets and TVs, and mix colonial fixtures and fittings with refurbishments. There's quite a range to choose from, so check several rooms before deciding. It's also a decent place for a drink or meal. For something closer to rock-bottom, try *Prime Lodge* (T068/30692; ❷) on the way out towards Nairobi, or the small, comfortable rooms at the *Kubu Kubu*, along the Kitui road, above the Mugo Shopping Centre (T068/20191; ❷).

Moving on, most **public transport** from Embu along the Kangonde route goes to Thika, with only a few matatus bound for Kitui. The two-hour trip to Nairobi via Sagana is covered by dozens of buses and matatus. If you want to climb **Mount Kenya** from Embu, the closest route is via the idyllic *Castle Forest Lodge* (see p.153).

The Kiangombe Hills and Mwea Reserve

The relatively modest altitudes of the **Kiangombe Hills** (Kiangombe peak is 1804m) aren't enough to lure climbers, but the unspoilt district, upstaged by Mount Kenya and ignored by tourists and travellers, is worth a visit if you have an interest in mysterious folklore. The hills are the home of the **Mbere**, who are related to the Kikuyu, Embu and Meru, and have a reputation in Kenya as possessors of magical powers. Some villages have elderly sages, **Arogi**, credited with terrifying abilities, though others – the **Ago** – have more beneficent gifts like the ability to foretell the future or find missing goats. The identity of these "witches" is at best a hazy and mysterious one which people aren't in any hurry to talk about and is further confused by the supposed existence in the hills of a race of "**little red men**" whose diminutive size (estimated at 1.2m) and fleeting appearances in the bush have led more imaginative scientists to suppose that they might be *australopithecines*, or ape-men, hanging on into the twenty-first century. They and the Ago-Arogi may be just part of the "old people" mytho-history of central Kenya, which is at least partially based on the real, ancient and probably Cushitic-speaking peoples of two thousand or more years ago. Such, anyway, are the stories that might draw you from the main highway.

Siakago

The main centre of the Kiangombe Hills, **SIAKAGO**, can be reached from Embu by matatu five or six times a day. Driving, you take the B7 road from Embu, turning off at Musonoke. Siakago isn't a ki-Mbere word and its derivation is uncertain. It may well have derived from "Chicago", after a group of American anthropologists based themselves here in the 1930s and started the ape-men stories. Siakago is a pleasant and relaxed one-street town, all deep-red earth, green vegetation and colourfully painted shop fronts. There's a scattering of *hotelis* (usually combined with butcheries), a petrol station, two B&Ls, a noisy little market (main days Tues & Fri), which mostly sells livestock at extortionate prices, and several mission churches set amid the huts and *shambas* on the outskirts.

The Kiangombe Hills

The Kiangombes rise behind Siakago and look deceptively easy to **climb**. In fact, it's a stiff hike to the top, better as a two-day trip with an overnight camp in the hills. You start with a 10km hike to **KUNE**, northeast of Siakago, followed by a 2km hike to a **forest station**, where you'll find the start of the main approach to the summit area. You should pick up a **guide** at the forest station (expect to pay around Ksh1000), which may have to be coordinated in Siakago or Kune the day before. From the forest station, ignore the disused vehicle track winding into the hills; it soon becomes difficult to follow. Instead, use the **footpath** leading straight up from behind the huts, which takes you in about four hours' hike to the peaks area. Much of your way is likely to be impeded by thick vegetation and, if you're alert to every photographic possibility, you'll find following the overgrown trail can be tiresome, so ensure someone in your party has a *panga* to trail-blaze it with. As you climb, human population quickly thins out; this is "red-people" territory and traditionally feared by the Mbere.

Mwea National Reserve

The **Mwea National Reserve** (Ⓦ www.kws.go.ke/mwea.html; $20) is well worth the effort if you're looking for solitude and want to avoid the touristy atmosphere of some other parks and reserves. It's a beautiful area with a wealth of ornithological interest and wildlife including giraffes, buffaloes, antelopes and elephants, though the big beasts can be hard to see. With your own tent you can camp either by the main gate or on the sloping site near the shore of the reservoir, though swimming is highly inadvisable – the crocs have a mean reputation.

The easiest way to get to the reserve is via the tarmac B7 Embu–Kangonde road. Some 15km south of Embu, the signposted *murram* road off the B7 to the reserve is passable all year round. Further along the B7, on the south side of the hydro-electric Kamburu dam, another signposted road heads in via Masinga Dam from just before the village of **Kaewa**: the first 11km are tarmac, the remaining 12km *murram*, liable to be impassable in wet weather. One kilometre to the left, at the end of the tarmac, is the hilltop *Masinga Resort Club* (bookings through KWS ☎020/600800, ⓦ www.kws.go.ke; ④), overlooking the reservoir, which has a pool and a choice of rooms – either prefab or stone-and-tile ones with better views.

Laikipia

Northwest of Mount Kenya, **Laikipia District** is a vast plateau of two million acres (8000 square kilometres, about the size of Wales) encompassing much of the transitional land between the well-watered central highlands to the south and the semi-desert grazing steppe of the Samburu in the north. On the face of it, Laikipia is not an obvious destination and the few roads that cross it are mostly poor and sometimes impassable in the rains. It straddles the increasingly blurred divisions between Samburu and Kalenjin pastoralists and Kikuyu agriculturalists, which has led periodically to **ethnic violence**. It also remains the focus of a century-old land dispute between the Laikipiak Maasai and white ranchers. At the same time, while competition with wildlife has increased, there is now widespread cooperation between local people and ranchers, resulting in some of Kenya's most encouraging conservation success stories, where community land is managed in ways that respect traditional lifestyles while meeting the needs of wildlife and producing revenues from tourism. As tourist numbers grow, indigenously owned group ranches are also beginning to work independently to achieve the same ends.

In terms of land use and community, Laikipia is complicated and fascinating. There are no national parks or reserves here – all the conservation initiatives are undertaken privately or in the voluntary sector – and it is one of the best regions in Kenya to see **wildlife**. Indeed, increasingly it is recognized as one of the jewels in Kenya's safari crown. The district contains a wealth of endangered species, including **black rhinos**, whose world population is between three thousand and four thousand, nearly six hundred of them in Kenya. Of those, half are in Laikipia. As browsers rather than grazers, black rhinos don't interfere with cattle pasture, and do well in the same environment so long as the bush isn't cleared. Apart from the rhinos, more than two thousand **elephants** still undertake a seasonal migration during the long rains from Laikipia northwards into the Samburu rangelands. The district also supports an estimated 25 percent of the world's remaining population of **Grevy's zebra**, a

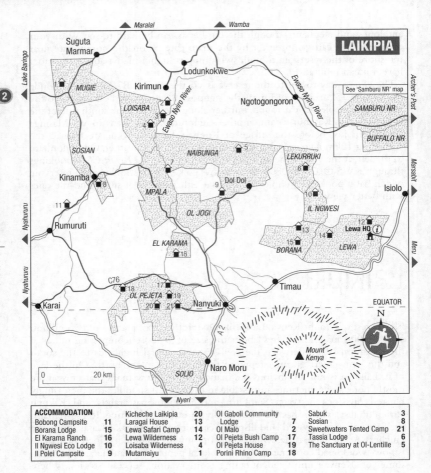

LAIKIPIA

See 'Samburu NR' map

ACCOMMODATION							
Bobong Campsite	11	Kicheche Laikipia	20	Ol Gaboli Community		Sabuk	3
Borana Lodge	15	Laragai House	13	Lodge	7	Sosian	8
El Karama Ranch	16	Lewa Safari Camp	14	Ol Malo	2	Sweetwaters Tented Camp	21
Il Ngwesi Eco Lodge	10	Lewa Wilderness	12	Ol Pejeta Bush Camp	17	Tassia Lodge	6
Il Polei Campsite	9	Loisaba Wilderness	4	Ol Pejeta House	19	The Sanctuary at Ol-Lentille	5
		Mutamaiyu	1	Porini Rhino Camp	18		

species fast disappearing in its other habitats in Ethiopia. There are also several, extremely elusive packs of **African wild dogs**.

In Laikipia, wildlife tends to be more closely managed than in the national parks. Rhinos are individually monitored by assigned rangers, while predators are often radio-collared to enable them to be tracked. Recently, some conservancies have experimented with SIM-card-tagging problem elephants so that rangers receive a text on their mobiles when they stray into farmlands. The solutions may seem unnatural, but they seem to work, and visitors are often encouraged to participate, in radio-tracking wild dogs for example. For further information, check out the excellent website of the Laikipia Wildlife Forum (Ⓦwww.laikipia.org), the body that coordinates the region's various interest groups and visitor facilities.

Many **game ranches** in Laikipia have opened their doors to guests, and combine a warm, quasi-colonial welcome and atmosphere with an all-inclusive package that includes all meals and drinks, game drives and night game drives, and walks. With few exceptions, **accommodation** is for the well-heeled – there's very little public transport up here and most people fly in. You can use Safarilink and Airkenya's scheduled daily services to Nanyuki and Lewa, or Safarilink's daily service to Loisaba (from where you'll be met by a transfer vehicle), or the charter company Tropic Air (☎020/2033032 or 0722/207300, Ⓦwww.tropicairkenya. com) who will fly you to the airstrip of your chosen lodge from anywhere in the country. All the visitable ranches charge a conservancy fee, ranging from $20–90 per person per day on top of accommodation-package rates which frequently reach $800 per day for two people.

Ol Pejeta Conservancy

For immersion in the Laikipia eco-system, **Ol Pejeta Conservancy** (daily 7am–7pm; $47; Ⓦwww.olpejetaconservancy.org), just a few kilometres west of Nanyuki, is a good place to start. Formerly a Lonrho cattle ranch, it is now owned by Fauna and Flora International (Ⓦwww.fauna-flora.org) and run as a not-for-profit business. Consisting mostly of rolling grasslands and acacia thicket, with boreholes providing ample water, it contains some of Laikipia's greatest concentrations of mammals, including all the big plains game.

The ranch covers some 365 square kilometres and combines wildlife management with running the world's largest herd of **Boran cattle** – the breed considered to be the best beef producer for Africa. The cattle are kept in mobile *bomas* at night to protect them from predators, and the cattle-wildlife combination is judged to be a model of integrated ranching and conservation, as cattle-grazing stimulates new pasture for the wildlife, while the surrounding communities benefit from slaughtering facilities and stock improvement for their own herds.

The Eastern sector of Ol Pejeta is the oldest part of the reserve, formerly the Sweetwaters Rhino Sanctuary (now seamlessly incorporated into the rest of Ol Pejeta), one inhabitant of which, a black rhino bull called **Morani**, was tame enough to be fed by visitors and became an icon for Ol Pejeta's conservation work. Morani died in 2008 and, at the time of writing, a successor, a blind black rhino called **Baraka**, is being introduced to close encounters with tourists in Morani's special square-kilometre paddock. Apart from Baraka, it's hard to see **black rhinos**, of which there are between seventy and eighty roaming through Ol Pejeta, as they stay well away from the tracks, seeking out good browsing in the thickets. But you may spot the conservancy's less timid and even larger **white rhinos** as they tank their way through the bush in search of pasture.

Ol Pejeta also contains a **chimpanzee sanctuary** (9–10.30am & 3–4.30pm; free), with chimps from the Jane Goodall Institute in Burundi, and confiscated pets and bushmeat-trade orphans from other parts of Africa. The one-square-kilometre haven, unique in Kenya – a country that has had no wild chimps in historical times – protects 43 of the great apes in two troops; a younger troop on the west side of the Ewaso Nyiro river, and an older troop, that visitors can view, on the east side. This is strictly an animal refuge, supported by a number of charities and individuals at a cost of more than $4000 a year per chimp. The chimps, all of which have suffered varying degrees of psychological trauma, are sterilized to prevent breeding, and fed on a daily supply of fruit and vegetables supplied by the rangers. As the crazier of the chimps smash sticks against the electric fence to the amusement of visitors, it all feels sadly institutionalized, despite the relative space and freedom, and may leave you wondering what connection it has, if any, with the long-term conservation of this highly endangered species.

If you're **driving to Ol Pejeta**, just south of the "Equator" signs south of Nanyuki, turn left (west) signposted "Ol Pejeta House 20km – Sweetwaters

15km". It's a 13-kilometre drive through the dusty Nanyuki hinterland to the Conservancy's **Rongai gate** where you pay your fees if you're a day visitor.

Accommodation

Serena Hotels run *Sweetwaters* and *Ol Pejeta House* – the oldest places to stay, where you pay for game drives and all extras – while smaller operators have opened three camps further to the west, in which everything is included in the package and guests and hosts dine together in a "mess tent". Note that the daily fee of $47, plus $17 "bed night fee", is paid for by the smaller camps and added to your total bill. If you're staying in an Ol Pejeta-owned property you don't pay the bed night fee.

Kicheche Laikipia Nairobi reservations ℡020/890358, ⓦwww.kicheche.com. Opened in 2009 in a remote stretch of bush, on a gentle slope above a broad, seasonal lake, this is the first *Kicheche* camp outside the Mara. Six very comfortable and extremely spacious tents, with stylish extra touches – plants, rugs, wooden bathroom furniture, excellent food and wine – and warm, enthusiastic and highly experienced hosts. Lion-tracking drives available, submitting data to predator researchers. Closed April–May; package $770.
Ol Pejeta Bush Camp ℡0734/445283, ⓦwww.insidersafrica.com; Nairobi reservations ⓦwww.chelipeacock.com. Six comfortable tents on the banks of the Ewaso Nyiro, including one big family tent, with solar lighting, local community guides and lots of game walks. Excellent for photographers. Salt scattered on the opposite bank often brings rhinos at night. Closed May; package $780.
Ol Pejeta House Owned by Ol Pejeta Conservancy ℡062/31970, ⓦwww.serenahotels.com. Bursting with design novelties, original art and flawed magnificence, this is arms tycoon Adnan Khashoggi's former holiday retreat, comprising the flamboyant and monster-bedded "Mr Khashoggi's

Room" and "Mrs Khashoggi's Room", plus two upper guest rooms (1 dbl, 1 twin), and a cottage with two large suites. Giraffe stalk the gardens and there are two pools. FB $500.
Porini Rhino Camp Nairobi reservations ℡020/7123129 or 0722/509200, ⓦwww.porini.com. A low-impact bush camp, consisting of six very spacious tents erected along a *lugga*. Deliberately, nothing here is strictly permanent, but the entire set-up is superbly comfortable and run on entirely sustainable principles, with safari showers, solar-power throughout and all non-biodegradable waste returned to Nairobi. Excellent staff and guides. Closed May; package $1000.
Sweetwaters Tented Camp Owned by Ol Pejeta Conservancy ℡062/31970 or 0734/699852, ⓦwww.serenahotels.com. The most affordable camp, with a small pool and decent and varied food on a rather unexciting site (flat, but very wheelchair-accessible). The tents, mostly facing the electric-fence-protected waterholes, are unimaginative by current standards, and the bland public areas and night lights from Nanyuki's flower farms are drawbacks. Most tents face Mt Kenya (be up by 6.45am for photos). FB ⑧

Eastern Laikipia

In the far southeast of Laikipia lies **Lewa Downs**, a former cattle ranch that was one of the earliest to convert to wildlife conservation. A little to the north and in much wilder country are the locally owned group ranches of **Il Ngwesi** and **Lekurruki**, while bordering Lewa to the west is an exemplary game-and-cattle ranch, **Borana**.

Lewa Wildlife Conservancy

The Matunda gate on the west side of the Timau–Isiolo road, 4km from the Meru junction, takes you 8km along an earth road to the headquarters of the world-famous **Lewa Wildlife Conservancy** (ⓦwww.lewa.org; $80). Entry is by 4WD only. Lewa, fenced all around and carefully managed, is conservation as a business: as well as the high daily fees, the revenue from the café and gift shop (closed Sun) and expensive accommodation all help to support the **Northern Rangelands Trust**, partnering Lewa with local communities.

The 250 square kilometres of Lewa incorporate the former Ngare Sergoi Rhino Sanctuary set up by the owners in 1983; the entire Lewa area is now home to more than 65 black and 45 white rhinos. This grassland environment, a mixture of open plains, scrub bush and woodland in the valleys, is one area in Kenya where sightings of black rhinos are the norm rather than a special event. In addition, there are some 350 Grevy's zebra, accounting for more than a tenth of the world's remaining wild population and, unusually, a population of rare semi-aquatic sitatunga antelope in Lewa swamp.

The annual **Lewa Marathon**, in June, has been run on the conservancy since 1999 to raise funds for conservation and development in Kenya, and now attracts close to one thousand entrants. It's a well-organized international event – see p.59 for further details.

Accommodation

There are various **accommodation** options across Lewa (all on an all-inclusive "package" basis), including the colonial-style *Lewa House*, the newer *Kifaru House* and the very upmarket *Sirikoi Camp* (formerly *Willie's Camp*). Together with the two bases below, *Lewa* and *Kifaru* houses can be contacted via ☎062/31405, ⓦwww.lewa.org and reservations made in Nairobi with Cheli & Peacock on ☎020/604054 or ⓦwww.chelipeacock.com, while *Sirikoi* can be booked through Safari & Conservation on ☎0722/ 464413 or ⓦwww.scckenya.com.

Lewa Safari Camp Formerly called *Lerai Tented Camp*, this is the most affordable, relatively speaking, of the Lewa options – twelve well-spaced, homely and very comfortably furnished tents, some with fine views. The main lodge building is thatched cedar, with a lounge overlooking a floodlit waterhole where rhino and elephant come to drink. Service is usually excellent and there's a pool. Package $980.

Lewa Wilderness Formerly called *Wilderness Trails*, the former home of the Craig family who came to Lewa in the 1920s. Eight cottages and a pre-war English-country-house atmosphere – plus an infinity pool. Congenial hosts and staff and superior cooking (often using ingredients from the organic garden) and slightly more polished service than *Lewa Safari Camp*. Riding is also available at the large stables. Closed Nov; package $1220.

Il Ngwesi and Lekurruki Group Ranches

While Lewa is surrounded by a fence, the group ranches northwest of Lewa Downs are traditional, unfenced community land, incorporating fixed and transient communities, grazing herds and substantial wildlife. Foremost among them is the six thousand-strong Laikipiak Maasai community of **Il Ngwesi Group Ranch**, a 145-square-kilometre slab of wilderness, adjoining Lewa and bounded by the Ngare Ndare and Tinga rivers to the east and north, and by the dramatic hills of the **Mukogodo Forest** to the west. Inclusive options include night drives, bush walks, riverside breakfasts, hikes in the Mukogodo forest and visits to *Il Ngwesi's* rhino sanctuary, where the first transplant from Lewa, a black rhino male called Omni, is tame enough for very close encounters through the wire.

The 240-square kilometre **Lekurruki Group Ranch**, adjoining Il Ngwesi's north side, is even further afield: it takes at least two hours to drive to *Tassia Lodge* from Lewa HQ. The community here own the lodge but don't manage it. Like Il Ngwesi, but even wilder and hillier, this is superb wildlife territory, but more about chance encounters and close-up discoveries than vistas of mammals on every horizon. In both areas, you'll get the most out of the experience if you get out into the bush **on foot**, with armed guides. At Lekurruki, the Tusk Trust has trained two dozen rangers to patrol

▲ Star-bed at Il Ngwesi Lodge

the no-grazing areas of the ranch where the wildlife has pre-eminence (unlike Ol Pejeta, this less controlled environment isn't amenable to the mixed herding-wildlife conservation model).

Most people fly in, either to the Lewa HQ airfield, or to the airstrips at *Il Ngwesi* or *Tassia*. If you drive up, ensure you leave a clear ninety minutes to two hours to get from Lewa HQ to *Il Ngwesi* and at least two hours to reach *Tassia*. From Nanyuki, it can be quicker to drive via Borana Ranch (see below, and check with them). Tracks are rough in parts and hard to follow and a GPS, or better still a guide, is very useful.

Il Ngwesi Eco Lodge Il Ngwesi Group Ranch, Laipha House, Nanyuki ☎020/2033122, ⓦwww.ilngwesi.com; Nairobi reservations ⓦwww.lets-go-travel.net. A much lauded eco-lodge, owned and managed by the local Maasai community, perched along a ridge facing a game-rich valley. Uniquely, *all* the proceeds go to the local community. The six, spacious, raised, open-fronted *bandas* incorporate twisting branches and wonderful views, while *bandas* 1 and 5 have star-beds which can be pulled out onto their decks. There's a small infinity pool. Guaranteed wildlife, including elephants, seen daily at the waterhole. FB $550.

Tassia Lodge ☎0725/972923 or 0727/049489, ⓦwww.tassiasafaris.com. Owned by the Lekurruki Community Conservation Ranch, this beautifully sited lodge, with just six rooms emerging seemingly organically from the landscape, overlooks a scenic valley where you have a good chance of spotting elephants. There's a naturally formed swimming pool nestled in the rocks and exceptionally good and varied food, including plenty of salads and vegetarian options. Package $800.

Borana Ranch

The 32,000 acre, 130 square-kilometre **Borana Ranch** (ⓦwww.borana.com; $80) is a settler farm that has evolved into a model of twenty-first century holistic land management. Unlike Ol Pejeta, Borana hasn't had a succession of owners, but in much the same way it has successfully integrated farming with conservation by allowing intensive short-term livestock grazing of managed areas, followed by long periods of recovery and game grazing. The ranch mixes **beef production** from a two thousand-strong herd of Boran cattle with **wool production** and textile and leather manufacture (Hide and Sheep Ltd, employing disabled members of the local community), along with **rare species conservation** and **high-end tourism** for a maximum of 32 visitors at any one time.

Working closely with Lewa Conservancy, the plan is to open the fence-line between the two areas to enable the Lewa rhinos to wander even more freely. Borana currently has around three hundred **elephants** (twelve matriarchs with collars so that tabs can be kept on where they are) and four prides of **lions** (again, with a radio-collared lioness in each pride). They also monitor **wild dogs**, **hyenas** and **cheetahs** and have stable populations of all three.

For visitors, apart from the chance to participate in game and wildlife management, the big activity at Borana is **riding**, allowing you to get very close to wildlife that would move away from vehicles or visitors on foot. Most of the thoroughbreds here are not really for beginners but perfect for experienced equestrians – although, on the eastern side of the ranch, they have a stable of children's and novice mounts too. As well as **walking**, another hugely enjoyable option here is **mountain biking**. Most activities are included in the packages.

Practicalities

To get here, drive through Timau towards Meru and turn left after 500m. It's 20km up to *Borana Lodge*, via the small centre of **ETHI**. There are two **places to stay** at Borana. Both can be contacted via Ⓦwww.borana.com and reservations made in Nairobi with Safari & Conservation on ☎0722/ 464413 or Ⓦwww.scckenya.com.

Borana Lodge A *Responsible Tourism Award* winner in 2007, built in 1992 in a hilly area with dramatic views in every direction and eight immaculate, privately spaced cottages of cedar, thatch and stone, with fireplaces (at 2000m, you'll often need a fire). The lodge overlooks a waterhole-dam where elephants sometimes swim, and close-up views from the hide are possible. The infinity pool is sited high, with awe-inspiring views. Closed Nov; package $1220.

Laragai House Extraordinarily sited, *Laragai* is perched on the edge of an escarpment looking north. A house of almost palatial proportions, it has a large, heated pool, a waterhole-dam 400m down the hillside and extraordinary views all around. There's a superb sound system in the lounge, and you get the sort of meals and service you would expect. It's perfect for a luxury house party, which is just as well as you have to take the whole house (minimum six people). Closed Nov; package $1220.

Central Laikipia

A great chunk of land in central Laikipia, on the east side of the Ewaso Nyiro, is now managed as the **Naibunga Conservancy**, comprising swathes of conservation land ceded by seven community-owned group ranches in the area: **Il Motiok**, **Il Polei**, **Kijabe**, **Kuri-Kuri**, **Morupusi**, **Nkiloriti** and **Tiemamut**. Naibunga Conservancy covers more than 170 square kilometres. There are, as yet, a limited range of places to stay, though several of the group ranches are encouraging wild camping, with guides (further details at Ⓦwww.laikipia.org)

Privately owned ranches northwest of Nanyuki include El Karama, Ol Jogi and Mpala. **El Karama**, a settler ranch since the early 1960s, covers nearly sixty square kilometres and is home to Grevy's zebra and (fleetingly glimpsed) wild dogs, among other species. **Mpala Ranch and Conservancy**, owned by the American Mpala Wildlife Foundation, ranges across two hundred square kilometres and incorporates a state-of-the-art wildlife and environmental research centre. **Ol Jogi** is a 270-square kilometre ranch owned by the art-dealing and horse-racing Wildenstein family, where KWS staff and US government vets are engaged in a long-term project to extract **gerenuk** semen for captive breeding, sponsored by the Howard Gilman foundation.

An interesting new community activity at Il Polei Group Ranch is **Walking with Baboons** (call Jonathan Rana on ☎0724/943948, ⊛www.baboonsrus.com), a chance for visitors to overturn some of the popular myths and prejudices that our species holds for this less cultured, but no less social, primate. In the early morning or at dusk you go out with a guide trained by the Uaso Ngiro Baboon Project to observe a habituated troop at close quarters on their rocky sleeping ledges. You'll learn about the importance of avoiding eye contact, and the subtlety of baboon family and social life. It's a fascinating and highly recommended experience. The cost, for up to about two hours, is normally Ksh3000 per person in a group of up to four people. The money goes to support local community projects.

Practicalities

The **main road** through central Laikipia goes northwest from Nanyuki, passing the turning off left to Rumuruti after 9km, then continues, still paved, via the small centres of **Jua Kali** and **Naibor** and turns into dirt road after 25km, where the track to **Dol-Dol** and Il Polei heads off to the right. Having passed the turning for Ol Jogi Ranch (right, 39km), it crosses the big metal bridge over the Ewaso Nyiro after 47km, immediately passing the turning for Mpala Ranch and, after 77km, reaches Sosian Ranch (see "Northwestern Laikipia", below).

El Karama Ranch 42km northwest of Nanyuki (fork right 9km from Nanyuki, continue for 23km, then turn left at the signboard "Ol Jogi – No Shooting" for 10km) ☎0727 532091, ⊛www.horsebackinkenya.com. An exceptionally nice and affordable set-up on the banks of the Ewaso Nyiro River, with four rustic cottages. Excellent opportunities for experienced riders (English saddle) at Ksh4000 per ride. Self-catering Ksh4350 per person. FB ❻

Il Polei Campsite Northern slopes of the Lolldaiga Hills on Il Polei Group Ranch, a 1.5hr drive from Nanyuki along the Dol-Dol road ☎062/31650, ✉info@oljogiltd.com. This campsite can only be rented out as a whole and can cater for up to three families. It's a good place to hook up for the "Walking with Baboons" experience (see above). Ksh3000 for exclusive use.

Ol Gaboli Community Lodge On the banks of the Ewaso Nyiro, on Il Motiok group ranch; Nanyuki reservations ⊛www.riftvalleyadventures.com. Named after the huge fig tree that towers above the lodge, *Ol Gaboli* is run by the women of the Il Motiok Group Ranch, and is Kenya's first all-women-pastoralist lodge. There are five stone *bandas* with thatched roofs and a main lounge and dining area. There's also a larger family house. It's self-catering, so you'll need to come fully provisioned. ❹

The Sanctuary at Ol-Lentille Kijabe Group Ranch ⊛www.ol-lentille.com. Spectacular all round, this Maasai-owned lodge (with strong local community links) is Laikipia's most expensive address: four houses, each sleeping two to six and with its own staff, guide and Land Rover. Most activities, including riding, quad-bikes and game drives (relatively limited wildlife but occasional wild dogs), are included, but simply relaxing and soaking up the peaceful environment – there's a good pool and spa – is a large part of the appeal. Package from $1060 (14-day standby deals offer 50% reductions).

Northwestern Laikipia

The ranches to the **west of the Ewaso Nyiro** are the most remote of the Laikipia range lands. See p.513 for route coverage from Nyahururu via Rumuruti to Maralal, from which these ranches and lodges are most easily accessed if you're coming by road. Some are tough to reach by road, however, especially those down towards the Ewaso Nyiro river, such as Loisaba, Sabuk and Ol Malo, for which most visitors use Safarilink (see p.131) to the Loisaba airstrip.

The 250-square-kilometre **Loisaba** (⊛www.loisaba.com) is a private ranch-cum-game sanctuary with a 2500 herd of Boran cattle, stretching from the bush-covered slopes and valleys near the river to high, flat grasslands in the west, bordering Mugie Ranch. If you're driving, it's 120km from Nanyuki and

110km from Nyahururu. Their array of activities includes camel rides, mountain-biking, quad-biking (from which all revenue goes to a local education trust), hot-air-balloon trips, helicopter flights and river-rafting.

Mugie Ranch, based around the junction of the Rumuruti–Maralal road with the road to Lake Baringo, covers two hundred square kilometres, of which Mugie Rhino Sanctuary accounts for half. As in most of the lodges in north-western Laikipia, the wildlife is not just out in the bush, but encountered on the paths, in your outdoor shower or on the way to dinner: warriors always accompany guests when anything dangerous is nearby. As well as stays at *Mutamaiyu* lodge, they offer day visitors guided, self-drive tours of the rhino sanctuary for $30 per person per day (T0722/903179, Wwww.mugie.org).

At the northern-most ranch in this area, **Ol Malo**, elephants and leopards are seen right below the lodge almost every day and a tame kudu wanders the grounds. The 24,000 acre **Sosian Ranch** (100 sq km) has superb wildlife, with all the large mammals you would expect (bar rhinos), including a resident, breeding pack of wild dogs, and does active work in predator research.

Accommodation

All the lodge stays below are based on a full-board and drinks package. All have pools and most activities are included, including game drives. At **Sabuk**, if you give notice, you can also opt to convert part of your stay to a camel-assisted walking safari, lasting from a morning to a fortnight, staying in comfortable fly camps. If you're on any kind of budget, *Bobong* at **Ol Maisor Ranch** is a good – in fact your only – choice.

Bobong Campsite Ol Maisor Ranch, 18km north of Rumuruti, on a bluff just to the west of the road T062/32718, 0735/243075 or 0722/936177 (SMS only), Eolmaisor@africaonline.co.ke. Boasting fantastic views over the Laikipia plains, a small pool, a jungle gym and a range of activities from bird walks along the Ewaso Narok river and Turkana cultural village visits to camel rides and longer camel safaris (Ksh2000 per day), *Bobong* is deliberately low-key and child-friendly. Animal orphans are always around and the daily life of the family farm is part of the appeal. Camping Ksh500, fully equipped self-catering *bandas* Ksh4000.

Loisaba Wilderness T062/31072, Wwww .loisaba.com; Nairobi reservations Wwww .chelipeacock.com. Energetic and enthusiastic, the multi-award-winning *Loisaba* is as much about getting the adrenalin flowing as it is about watching kudu or tracking wild dogs, with a vast range of activities on offer. The set-up includes a seven-room hotel-style lodge set in manicured gardens with staggering views towards Mount Kenya, two fully staffed houses and two star-bed sites: *Loisaba Starbeds* above a dam and the even better community-run *Koija Starbeds* on the east bank of the river (both fun but relatively basic). Package $1190.

Mutamaiyu Mugie conservancy T062/31235 or 0722/903179, Wwww.mugie.org. Expansive and gracious American-owned country house,

decorated with tribal art, surrounded by African olives (*mutamaiyu*) and beautifully tended gardens, with a heated pool, in a relatively gentle, hilly landscape. Four cottages are also available. Wi-fi throughout. Closed Jan & June; package $980.

Ol Malo T062/32715 or 0721/630686, Wwww .olmalo.com; Nairobi reservations T020/605108, Wwww.bush-and-beyond.com. A *Responsible Tourism Award*-winning family-owned lodge commanding a vantage point high above the valley of the Ewaso Nyiro. Guest rooms, annexed off the main building, feature window glass (most Laikipia rooms are open-fronted) and are big on polished stone and wood. The new *Ol Malo House* (sleeps 12) is similar, but with a kitsch, animal theme in the coloured-cement decor. Closed April, May & Nov; package $1220.

Sabuk Wwww.sabuklodge.com; Nairobi reservations Wwww.chelipeacock.com. Intimate and compellingly sited lodge, bursting with character, built on the edge of a remote gorge through which the Ewaso Nyiro permanently rushes and where elephants frequently cross. The six rooms are spacious cottages, including one with its own plunge pool. Warmly and intelligently hosted by a highly experienced safari guide, it's great for children and serves superb food. Closed May; package $1190.

Sosian Near Kinamba T062/31081, Wwww .sosian.com. Built in 1920, abandoned in the 1990s and completely restored as a riding and ecotourism base in 2002, this is peaceful, roomy and supremely relaxing, with huge bathrooms, well-designed furniture in the seven rooms, charming hosts and excellent guides and cuisine.

Driving here, 28km north of Rumuruti, at Kinamba village, bear right under the open boom gate; after 5.5km you reach a sign on a stone and the house is 1.5km further. Package $800.

The Aberdare range

The **Aberdare range**, which peaks at 4001m, is less well known than Mount Kenya. The lower, eastern slopes have long been farmed by the Kikuyu (more recently by European tea and coffee planters), and the dense mountain forests covering the middle reaches are the habitat of leopard, buffalo, some six thousand elephants and a few small herds of critically endangered bongo antelope. Above about 3500m, lions and other open-country animals roam the cloudy moorlands. Melanistic forms, especially of leopard, but also of serval cat and even bushbuck, are also present.

The Kikuyu called these mountains Nyandarua ("drying hide", for their silhouette) long before Thomson, in 1884, named them after Lord Aberdare, president of the Royal Geographical Society. In their bamboo thickets and tangled forests, Kikuyu **Mau Mau guerrillas** hid out for years during the 1950s, living off the jungle and surviving thanks to techniques learned under British officers during the Burma campaign in World War II, in which many of them had fought. Despite the manhunts through the forests and the bombing of hideouts, little damage was done to the natural habitat, and Aberdare National Park remains one of Kenya's most pristine forest reserves.

On the western side, the range drops away steeply to the Rift Valley. It was here, in the high Wanjohi Valley, that a concentration of settlers in the 1920s and 1930s created the myth of **Happy Valley** out of their obsessive, and unsettled, lives. There's not much to see (or hear) these days. The old wheat and pyrethrum farms were subdivided after independence and the valley's new settlers are more concerned with making their market gardens pay. The memories live on only among veteran *wazungu*.

The Kinangop plateau (p.215) was settled by Europeans, too, but in 1950 the high forest and moorland here was declared **Aberdare National Park**. The park stretches 60km along the length of the peaks, with the Salient on the lower slopes reaching out east. Like Mount Kenya National Park, it includes the worst of the weather: rainfall up here is high, often closing the park to vehicles in the wet season, although in the Salient the "tree-hotel" **game lodges** – The Ark and Treetops – stay open all year. The park is nevertheless close enough to Nairobi to be well worth the effort of getting to **Naivasha** or **Nyeri**, the usual bases. **Driving** in the park is beautiful, with waterfalls and sensational views more than compensating for comparatively scarce **wildlife**. You'll find less **transport** in the lower parts of the range than around Mount Kenya, but it's still relatively easy to get around, with regular bus and matatu services between the villages. To head over the mountains and through the park, however, you need your own 4WD vehicle unless you're prepared to wait for a lift for days (you could try the *Outspan Hotel* in Nyeri). Few organized tours venture up there.

Nyahururu, the other important town in the region, has **Thomson's Falls** as a postcard attraction, and is also the setting-off point for a wild cross-country journey to Lake Bogoria, 1500m below, in the Rift Valley (see p.233). From here, too, begins the main route to Maralal and Loiyangalani on the eastern shore of Lake Turkana (see p.513).

Aberdare National Park

Aberdare National Park (ⓦwww.kws.go.ke/aberdare.html; $50; smartcard; see p.62) splits into two different environments: the **high moorland and peaks** which form its bulk, and the lower **Salient** to the east where the vegetation is dense rainforest and there is considerably more wildlife. The Salient slopes (location of *Treetops* and the *Ark*) are closed to casual visitors; all the earth access roads have locked barriers.

In order to protect the park's **wildlife,** in particular its fifty-odd black rhino (one of the largest populations in Kenya), but mainly to arrest the conflict between wildlife and humans, which most visibly manifested itself in the trashing of crops and homes fringing the park by "rogue" or "rampaging" elephants, the KWS has built a 388-kilometre electric fence to encircle the national park and the forests of the Aberdare Conservation Area, with the support of **Rhino Ark** (ⓦwww.rhinoark.org) and the annual Rhino Charge **motor race** (see p.58).

The high park

The high moorlands have some exceptional **walking** and include **three peaks**, Lesatima (the highest at 4001m) in the north, Il Kinangop (3906m) in the south, and Kipipiri (3349m), an isolated cone outside the park above the Wanjohi Valley in the west. They can be climbed relatively easily, given good weather conditions. It takes about three hours to climb Lesatima and two hours back down again. *Sandai* (see p.191) organize climbs, or ask the Mountain Club of Kenya in Nairobi for details (see p.59). *El Paraiso* (see overleaf) can also arrange guiding. Hiking in the park is allowed only with the approval of the warden, so apply in good time. You may be required to take a guide (whom you'll have to pay).

Unless you're planning several days of walking, fishing or camping, the most straightforward visit to the moorlands is to spend a day driving through from one side to the other between the **main gates**, Matubio and Ruhuruini. There are two other eastern gates further from Nyeri (Wandere and Kiandongoro) and two at the remote north end of the park (Shamata, accessible from Nyahururu, and Rhino Gate, from the B5 Nyeri–Nyahururu road), but there's no reliable route through the park between north and south, and the small circuit of tracks in the north is very rough. Driving via the park from Naivasha to Nyeri (or vice versa) is easy enough in good weather with 4WD. If conditions are less than ideal, however, and you get stuck, you could be in for a long day, or a miserable night. You need to check **road conditions** with the rangers at the park gates. Surfaces are mostly red *murram*, though there are also a few, very steep, rocky sections. It's usually permissible to wander a short distance from your car, though the lion situation changes from time to time.

Naivasha to Matubio Gate

From Naivasha, follow the signs for the national park via the Uplands road as if going to Nairobi, as far as the junction for Kinangop on the east side of town. From here, you climb about 14km, on reasonably intact tarmac past

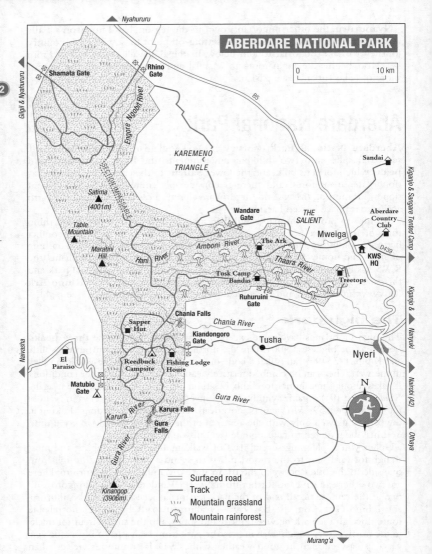

ABERDARE NATIONAL PARK

0   10 km

▲ Nyahururu

◄ Gilgil & Nyahururu

✠ Shamata Gate

✠ Rhino Gate

Engore Ngoort River

SECTION IMPASSABLE

KAREMENO TRIANGLE

B5

Sandai ⌂

Satima (4001m) ▲

Table Mountain ▲

Wandare Gate

THE SALIENT

Aberdare Country Club

Mweiga ●

Kiganjo & Sangare Tented Camp ►

Maratini Hill ▲

Amboni River

The Ark

Thaara River

KWS HQ

D439

Hani River

Tusk Camp Bandas

Treetops

Ruhuruini Gate

◄ Naivasha

Sapper Hut

Chania Falls

Chania River

Kiandongoro Gate

Tusha ●

Nyeri

Kiganjo & ► Nanyuki

El Paraiso ▲

Reedbuck Campsite

Fishing Lodge House

Matubio Gate

Karura River

Karura Falls

Gura River

Nairobi (A2) ►

Gura River

Gura Falls

Othaya ►

N

Kinangop (3906m) ▲

═══ Surfaced road
──── Track
⌂ Mountain grassland
🌳 Mountain rainforest

Murang'a ▼

the National Youth Service camp to Karima, where you turn left onto a good dirt road. After another 5km or so, you reach Kipipiri junction, where you keep right.

At **Ndunyu Njeru** centre, you pass the last chance of fuel and the final stop of matatus up from Naivasha. About 9km north of here, a pleasantly rustic adventure centre, *El Paraiso/Outdoor Africa* (☏050/50246 or 0722/715853, Ⓦwww.kipipiri.com), offers **camping** (Ksh500), meals (Ksh300–600), guided walks and safaris. Back on the route to the gate, the road finally runs out of reasons to continue except to the national park itself, becoming a narrow, quite acceptable, tarmac switchback, and climbs through the vegetation zones, with increasing evidence of elephants (dung everywhere), to pitch out finally through the highest extent of the forest at Matubio Gate, on the threshold of the moorland. Along the last 7km there are some excellent views back down to Lake Naivasha. Allow two to three hours to get this far.

Matubio Gate to Ruhuruini Gate

Allowing four hours from Matubio Gate to Ruhuruini Gate gives time enough, in good weather, for visits to Chania Falls and Karura Giant Falls. Proper access to the top of the **Karura Falls** (there's no way down to the bottom) was built only in 1992, by the British Army's Royal Engineers. They've created two superb, dizzy, timber viewpoints, one on each side, from which you can look across through dripping, Afro-Alpine vegetation to the babbling, four-metre-wide Karura stream as it plunges over the abyss, dropping nearly 300m in three stages. To the south, the distant veil of the **Gura Falls**, a kilometre or two across the yawning canyon, seems to make for a surfeit of dramatic beauty.

The much lower, sheer drop of the **Chania Falls** has rickety access walks and platforms (be careful) and you can gaze from the top, or the bottom, and even contemplate a swim in the pool. It was near here, in 1984, that an American tourist was badly mauled by a lion, an incident that so unnerved the park's authorities that for many years there were tough rules on unaccompanied walking. In 2000, this was followed by a cull of more than one hundred lions, many of which had been relocated from Solio Ranch. The cull was intended to rebuild the safe reputation of the park and give various herbivores, such as the giant forest hog and bongo, a chance to increase their endangered populations. In the case of the giant forest hogs, that has been rather *too* successful, but the bongos are still recovering only slowly.

The 15km east to **Ruhuruini Gate** descends in a breathtaking helter-skelter through the cloud forest, with stunning views across jungle-cloaked valleys. The road down to Nyeri from the gate is in good condition and you soon reach tarmac.

Accommodation

There are several accommodation options in the **high park**, including **camping** at the basic *Reedbuck Campsite* near *Fishing Lodge House*. All are reservable in advance through KWS (☎020/600800, ⊛www.kws.go.ke).

Fishing Lodge House Some 2km inside the Kiandongoro Gate, located on open moors above the Magura River. Two stone-built, *mabati*-roofed cottages, each with three bedrooms and seven beds. Central, open-fire cooking and eating area. You need to take food, warm sleeping bags and firewood; wood-fired boiler tanks outside produce hot water. $180 per night for each cottage.

Sapper Hut Some 10km west of the *Fishing Lodge*, on a little tributary of the Chania river, at an altitude of around 3000m. A wooden *banda* with living room, double bedroom, fireplace, veranda, wood-fired boiler and chilly outside bathroom. Paraffin lamps (bring paraffin), bed sheets, firewood and basic cooking facilities are provided, but take bedding, towels, food and drinking water. Collect the key from the *Fishing Lodge*. $50 for the hut.

Tusk Camp Bandas About 2km inside the park from Ruhuruini Gate, at 2300m. Tucked into a glade surrounded by forest, there are two wooden *bandas* here (1 with 2 double beds, 1 with 4 single beds), an ill-equipped kitchen (bring pots, pans and cutlery), a pit latrine with one of Kenya's most regal views, and a caretaker to help you out. Visits from here to the Salient should be possible if you enquire first with the rangers at the gate. $120 per night for the whole place.

The tree-hotels

Kenya's most famous hotel, **Treetops**, was hosting Princess Elizabeth in February 1952 when she became Queen Elizabeth II on the death of her father George VI. The original tree house she stayed in was burned down in 1955 by Mau Mau freedom fighters; the present, much larger construction is an ugly box, built on stilts, with a few trees growing through it. The main Nyeri road passes by just 3km away, and *shambas* and villages are easily visible: this is no jungle hideaway.

Both tree-hotels (*Treetops* and *The Ark*) are located in the controlled area called **The Salient**, a lower-altitude extension of the Aberdare National Park, where no independent access is allowed. Depending on the season, mist and low temperatures can affect both lodges: take warm clothes.

The problem at *Treetops* is clear when you survey the scene from the open-air "top deck". It is a victim of its own success. The laying of **salt** by the waterhole guarantees the nightly arrival of heavyweight camera fodder, but has brought about the destruction of all the nearby forest by elephants. The current scene – tree-planting areas enclosed by electric fences and acres of mud – is neither popular with visitors nor good for wildlife. That shy forest antelope, the bongo, hasn't put in an appearance since 1988. Despite the lack of cover, black rhino are seen roughly every other night, and leopard two or three times a month. But efforts to encourage hardwood forest regeneration behind the electric wires seem doomed to fail – they've been trying for thirty years.

The Ark Reservations through ⓦ www.fairmont .com. The normally good game-viewing here is helped by the wide variety of viewing points. Accommodation is a little more spacious than at *Treetops* (see below), though don't expect luxury; while all the rooms have their own bathrooms, they are small, basic and in need of refurbishment. Dinner is usually excellent, and you eat breakfast up here before returning to the *Aberdare Country Club*. Children under 7 not accepted. FB ❼
Treetops Reservations through ⓦ www .aberdaresafarihotels.com. The tall, thin lodge, only

six metres from front to back, has something of the creaking atmosphere of a wooden ship, and the corridors and standard rooms are very cramped. Use the few shared showers and toilets early in the evening if you want them to be in a reasonable state (the two, small "suites", the best of which is Suite A, are self-contained). Ensure your batteries are charged: there are no plug sockets in standard rooms. Dinner is notoriously variable, excellent and copious one night, like a school dinner the next. Children under 5 not accepted; unsuitable for wheelchair-users. One-night stays only FB ❽

Nyeri and around

Self-styled capital of Kikuyu-land – a title the Kikuyu of Kiambu might dispute – **NYERI** is the administrative headquarters of Central Province and a lively, chaotic and friendly highland town, whose name derives from the Maa word *nyiro*, meaning reddish brown, after its earth. An attractive trading centre, it nestles in the green hills where the broad vale between Mount Kenya and the Aberdare range drops towards Nairobi. Tumultuous markets, scores of *dukas*, even a few street entertainers, lend it an air of irrepressible commercialism.

Another former British military camp, Nyeri emerged as a market town for European coffee growers in the hills and for settlers on the ranching and wheat farms further north. Nyeri was also the last home of Robert **Lord Baden-Powell**, founder of the worldwide scouting movement, whose cryptically named Paxtu cottage, now a small museum ($5), stands in the grounds of the *Outspan Hotel* and whose grave and memorial are to be found on the north side of town in the cemetery. The **Baden-Powell Scouts Information Centre** (optional donation) plans a small museum and guesthouse here, and it's interesting, as ever, to have a look at the old graves in the cemetery.

The extraordinary density of **cultivation** in the tightly spaced *shambas* around Nyeri (crops include maize, cassava, sugar cane, millet, squash and citrus fruits, as well as tea, coffee and macadamia nuts) is partly a hangover from white settlerdom, when a rapidly growing population was deprived of huge tracts of land and forced to cultivate intensively. Partly, too, it's the result of land consolidation – the "rationalization" of fragmented land holdings into unitary *shambas* that took place in the 1950s, turning people who had held traditional verbal rights into deed-holding property owners. It's also the simple consequence of an excellent climate and soil, plus a birth rate reckoned to be one of the highest in the world.

There's no doubt that the changes which have taken place in Nyeri District have been some of the most profound and rapid anywhere in the country. Even the villages of Kikuyu-land are nearly all innovations of the last sixty years, the irreversible effects of the Emergency. Until then, the Kikuyu had mostly lived in scattered homesteads among their crops and herds. British security forces, unable to contain open revolt in the countryside, began the systematic internment of the whole Kikuyu population into fenced and guarded villages, forcing the guerrillas into the high forests, and the villages of today have mostly grown from such places.

Practicalities

The bus stage and main matatu stage are on Kimathi Way. Nyeri has branches of all the **banks**, including Barclays, KCB, and Standard Chartered, all with ATMs. **Internet** access is widely available, especially along Market Street.

Accommodation

Nyeri's role as a rural business centre and major transport crossroads means there are plenty of cheap places to stay in town, as well as the historic *Outspan* and, out of town, the atmospheric *Aberdare Country Club*.

Aberdare Country Club 11km out on the Nyahururu road near Mweiga, then signposted 3km along the D439 *murram* road ☎061/55224 or 0722/564317, ⓦwww.fairmont.com. Parts of this former farmhouse date from 1930 and much of it, such as the dining room in the old house, is still attractive. The 49 rooms are in 25 cottages, built in the 1960s and still furnished comfortably, if not stylishly, while the old "Nursery Wing" has spacious family rooms with older fittings. The whole property sits on the 1300-acre ACC game sanctuary, with warthogs, bushbucks, suni and even the odd leopard, together with 170 species of birds. Activities include an unheated pool, tennis and game walks. FB ❼

Batian Grand Market St ☎061/2030743 or 0722/265863. Ageing but acceptable block of small rooms around a central courtyard, with nets and TVs in every room. Conscientiously run but overpriced. BB ❸

Central Kanisa Rd ☎061/2030296 or 0722/667437. Secure s/c rooms, all with nets and instant showers, some with balconies and TVs. The newer rooms are good value and breakfast is included. It's the best place in Nyeri for *kienyeji* and there's occasional live music at weekends. ❷

Green Hills Bishop Gatimu Rd, 1km south of town ☎061/2030604, ⓦwww.greenhills.co.ke. A decently run, busy hotel but not as slick as its prices, which

for non-residents are nearly twice the residents' rates (ask about their more basic rondavels). Rooms are fine, with nets. This is mostly a conference base, with a big gym and aerobics suite, a pool and extensive gardens and lawns. BB ❺

Maru B Court Off Kimathi Way ☎0720/850303. Reasonable, and probably better than the *Batian* for its good security and busy bar-restaurant below the rooms – as long as you don't rule out a place where the rooms have nets but no toilet seats or instant showers. BB ❷

Outspan Off the Kiandongoro Gate road (2km west of the clock tower on Kanisa Rd) ☎061/2032424 or 0722/207762; reservations through ⓦwww.aberdaresafarihotels.com. Built in 1927 and set in splendid grounds, the stately *Outspan* (base for visits to *Treetops*) is comfortable enough, but has the irritating flaws of its era which won't endear it to visitors expecting international standards: there are, for example no fans, nets, a/c or room safes. The showers can be iffy, and some rooms are on the small side. The new (Chania) wing rooms are larger, with better showers, tubs and fireplaces, while the rooms in the old building have the most character (especially those downstairs, with balconies) and lovely garden views. Activities include a chilly pool, guided bird walks, the neighbouring 9-hole golf course and various excursions. FB ❼

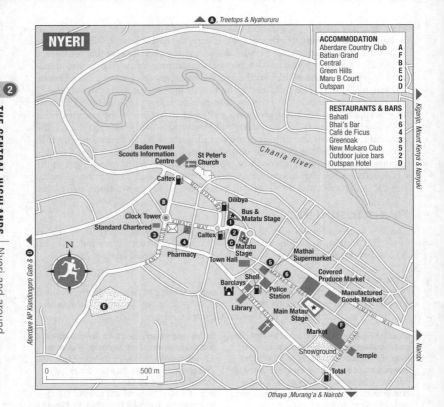

NYERI

▲ **A**, Treetops & Nyahururu

ACCOMMODATION
Aberdare Country Club	A
Batian Grand	F
Central	B
Green Hills	E
Maru B Court	C
Outspan	D

RESTAURANTS & BARS
Bahati	1
Bhai's Bar	6
Café de Ficus	4
Greenoak	3
New Mukaro Club	5
Outdoor juice bars	2
Outspan Hotel	D

Chania River

Baden Powell
Scouts Information
Centre

St Peter's
Church

Caltex

Oilibya

Clock Tower

Bus &
Matatu Stage

Standard Chartered

Caltex

Matatu
Stage

Mathai
Supermarket

Pharmacy

Town Hall

Shell

Police
Station

Covered
Produce Market

Barclays

Library

Main Matatu
Stage

Manufactured
Goods Market

Market

Showground

Temple

Total

N

Kiganjo, Mount Kenya & Nanyuki

Aberdare NP Kiandongoro Gate & ⓓ

Nairobi

Othaya, Murang'a & Nairobi ▼

0 — 500 m

Eating and drinking

Nyeri has a number of interesting **restaurants** and **bars**, a **cheese** factory (from which lots of produce is available locally) and a clutch of **juice bars** near the Standard Chartered bank, which do very nice, tall glasses of avocado, beetroot and regular fruit juices for around Ksh20.

Bahati Kimathi Way. Renowned for its chicken cooked any way you want. At around Ksh200 for chicken, chips and chapati, this is a very popular local restaurant, and it also has a cheap bar.
Café de Ficus Kenyatta Rd. A bar with *nyama choma* and prominent booths where local couples meet.
Greenoak Very good value, serving up top-quality *nyama choma* at Ksh280 per kilo or stews and curries and fried dishes for Ksh150–200. If the weather's okay, the first-floor terrace-bar, overlooking the commotion below, is fun too.

Bhai's Bar Market St. Lively little place serving good samosas and *mandaazi*, as well as beer.
Outspan Hotel This atmospheric pile welcomes day-visitors for its excellent buffet lunches (Ksh1400), or for tea on the lawn and a swim in the pool (Ksh500). The hotel's *Kirinyaga Bar* is pleasant enough for a beer in the evening in civilized surroundings.
New Mukaro Club Opposite the Mathai supermarket. A pleasant boozer with a balcony.

From Nyeri to Nyahururu

A signposted route leads **west**, past the *Outspan*, up into the Aberdare range and the park's Kiandongoro gate in the high moorland. In the other direction, the road splits out of town, forking **south** to Murang'a via Othaya, Kiriani and

Koimbi (a good road all the way), or continuing **east** to the A2 highway and the quickest return route to Nairobi via Sagana.

A fourth route takes you in a northwest direction out of town, splitting in two after 2km. Take the right fork if you want the A2 highway for Naro Moru and Nanyuki, via Kiganjo. Fork left to take the B5, which sweeps past, in succession, the road for Aberdare Park's **Ruhuruini Gate**, the track for *Treetops*, the turning to the right (east, on the D439) for the *Aberdare Country Club*, the hilltop centre of **Mweiga** (8km from Nyeri), and, finally, the track up to *The Ark*. A kilometre or so south of Mweiga, on the east side of the road, is the national park's **KWS headquarters**, the only point of sale for smartcards in the highlands.

If you're looking for a relaxing rural **homestay**, exactly 4.2km north of Mweiga's small town centre, note the white tyre in the earth on the east side of the road, marked "Sandai 7km" (beneath a sign announcing "St Joseph Mahiga Secondary School"). After 5.3km, turn left and after a further 600m right, then follow the white tyres to the charming, German-family-run farmhouse. *Sandai* (☎0733/734619, ⓦwww.africanfootprints.de; FB ❼) has comfortable and very attractive rooms and specializes in horseriding (€55 per day), painting and yoga.

Near *Sandai*, you'll also find the **Sangare Conservancy** (turn east north of Mweiga on the D439 and drive 5km past the *Aberdare Country Club*) with the low-key and affordable *Sangare Tented Camp* (☎020/3594639, ⓦwww .sangaretentedcamp.com; conservancy fee $17; FB ❽) offering twelve large, permanent tents with well-constructed bathrooms and generator-powered plugs, plus two cottages, all ranged along the shores of Sangare Lake. The **birdlife** is the main draw here, with migratory pelicans, glimpses of crowned eagles and black-headed herons squawking loudly in the trees over the tents. There are usually some elephants and buffalo in the vicinity, as well as zebra, gazelle, hyena, Sykes' and colobus monkeys, and the occasional leopard, while darkness brings a fantastic chorus of frogs and toads. If you're driving yourself, the camp is accessible from the Kiganjo side, off the *murram* D439 road, which branches off the A2 3.5km north of Kiganjo and 20km south of Naro Moru.

Further north along the B5 from Mweiga, **Solio Game Ranch** (☎020/249177 or 061/55271; Ksh2000) lies a few kilometres further, off to the right. Privately run, Solio more or less single-handedly saved the Kenyan black rhino population from extinction, breeding them here for subsequent translocation into the national parks and other Kenyan reserves. From an original population of 23 black rhino, there are now 70, and of the original 16 white rhino, imported from South Africa, the population now stands at more than 140. Without your own 4WD, you can visit the ranch by joining a trip from *Sandai* or the *Aberdare Country Club*.

Nyahururu (Thomson's Falls)

Like Nanyuki, **NYAHURURU** is almost on the equator, and it shares much of Nanyuki's character. It's high up (at 2360m, Kenya's highest town), cool and set on open savanna lands with patches of indigenous forest and plenty of coniferous plantation. Since the B5 road to Nyeri was completed, Nyahururu has been less cut off, but it's still something of a frontier town for routes north to Lake Turkana and the desert. A tarmac road goes out as far as Rumuruti and then the fun begins (see p.513).

Joseph Thomson gave the town its original name when he named the nearby waterfall after his father in 1883. Many still call it "T. Falls", and not just the old settlers you might expect. Thomson's Falls was one of the last settler towns to be established. The first sign of urbanization was a hut built by the

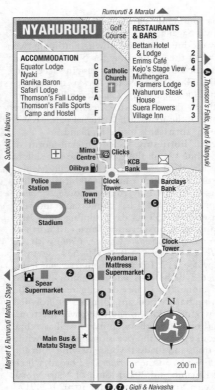

Narok Angling Club in the early 1920s to allow its members to fish for the newly introduced trout in the Ewaso Narok, Pesi and Equator rivers. In 1929, when the railway branch line arrived, the town began to take shape. The line has closed now, but the hotel built in 1931, *Thomson's Falls Lodge*, is still going strong, and Nyahururu remains an important market town, and not really a tourist centre. The **market** is well worth a browse, especially on Saturdays. It sprawls out over most of the district west of the stadium, an indication of the town's rapid growth over the last couple of decades.

The falls

On the northeast outskirts of town, **Thomson's Falls** are pretty rather than spectacular, though they can be dramatic when the Ewaso Narok is in flood after heavy rain. The falls are a popular stop-off for tourists travelling between Samburu and Maasai Mara game reserves, and the hotel lawns above the falls get crowded with picnickers from town at weekends. Uniformed council officials have taken to extracting an "entrance fee" at the turning from unwary tourists: only pay if they can give you an official ticket or receipt, otherwise tell them you have business at the hotel. The path leading down to the bottom of the 75-metre falls is somewhat dangerous, especially when wet, and you should ensure there have been no recent incidents of robbery. Don't attempt to climb up again by any other route, because the cliffs are extremely unstable.

Excursions around Nyahururu

With a couple of hours to spare, you can search for a longer walk down into the forested valley, following the **Ewaso Narok River**. If you want to try this, cross the road bridge first, then look for a way downstream. The spray-laden trees are shaken periodically by troops of colobus monkeys and chameleons are always around. The area is also fruitful for ornithologists. A much shorter stroll also takes you over the bridge and then past the electricity substation, beyond which the first trail you come to leads to the top of a hill with a communications tower and a skeletal lookout post. Excellent views from here stretch south towards Ol Kalou and the marshy trough of Lake Ol' Bolossat.

A longer excursion takes you in quest of the highest **hippos** in Kenya. A kilometre from the turning off to *Thomson's Falls Lodge* on the Nyeri road, you come to a small cluster of *dukas* on the right. Walk down towards the houses closest to town and, about 300m from the road, you emerge by a swampy area

▲ Thomson's Fallls

fed by Lake Ol Bolossat. The area immediately by the access path is thick with reeds, but walk round the lake to the clump of trees and you can shin up one of these and select a natural observation platform. Sit and watch and you may see as many as half a dozen or so hippos. If you don't find them here, then they're likely to be in Lake Ol Bolossat itself, which has its north shore some 15km south of Nyahururu on the road to Aberdare National Park's Shamata gate.

Practicalities

Nyahururu is busy but fairly compact. The town has branches of KCB and Barclays, both with **ATMs**, and there's **internet** access at *Clicks Cybercafé* (Mon–Sat 8am–6pm) in the Mima Centre, among quite a few other places.

For **meals**, *Kejo's Stage View Restaurant* has a lively atmosphere and good, filling dishes and snacks; *Muthengera Farmers Lodge* is recommended for chicken; *Emms Café* below *Cyrus Lodging*, opposite the market, is a good standby; and the balcony at the *Bettan Hotel & Lodge* is always full of people drinking *chai* above the bustling commerce below. *Nyahururu Steak House* (daily 7am–11pm) is a cut above the others – a restaurant, coffee house and bar doing decent steaks (Ksh200–350) and good samosas. Lastly, if you're driving south to Gilgil, there's *Suera Flowers*, a slightly upmarket restaurant and *nyama choma* joint, 5km south of the town centre by the Caltex station, where you can eat well for Ksh250.

For T. Falls' idea of **nightlife**, check out the *Village Inn*, where the soundtrack is reggae and soukous; it has, seen better days, though.

Accommodation

For accommodation, most people head out to *Thomson's Falls Lodge*, which is also the place to **camp**.

Equator Lodge Sharpe Rd ☎0710/205809. Basic, small, dark rooms, with TVs and nets. It also has a very good-value restaurant and bar, and safe parking in the courtyard. ❶

Nyaki North side of town, across from *Nyahururu Steak House* ☎065/22313. The reasonable rooms are on the top floor, with nets, TVs and instant showers, but are perhaps a little pricey as they don't include breakfast. There's a restaurant on the first floor and a bar on the second. ❷

Ranika Baron in the town centre ☎065/22883. Decent value, as it includes a good breakfast, but the handy location makes it noisy. ❶

Safari Lodge ☎065/22334 or 0722/305735. Relatively spacious, clean rooms, some with balcony and all with TV and instant shower, but no nets. There's an alcohol ban here, and safe parking. Probably the best of the cheapies. BB ❷

Thomson's Fall Lodge ☎065/22006 or 065/32170. Abidingly pleasant, friendly old

hotel, with a highlands-farmhouse atmosphere and log fires in the rooms, which include nets, lots of polished floors and old-style bathtub-showers. The camping price (Ksh500) includes hot showers and ample firewood. BB ❹

Thomson's Falls Sports Camp and Hostel 6km south of town on the Gilgil road, then east 1.5km ☎0711/626017. If you have transport, this is a reasonable place to camp, but it's run-down. As well as weary s/c rooms, there's a large campsite (Ksh200), plus dorm accommodation in an old London bus (Ksh250). Hot water mornings only. ❶

Moving on

When you're ready to move on, there are several options: regular matatus run down the fairly fast **B5 road** to Nyeri through forested valleys and over immense plains of swaying grass; the mostly unsurfaced **C76 road** to Ol Pejeta Conservancy and Nanyuki begins at **KARAI**, 15km east of Nyahururu; the **B5 road** westwards out of Nyahururu descends the **escarpment** to Nakuru, via the Subukia valley, following the route to Lake Bogoria described in chapter 3; and lastly, the reasonably quiet **C77 road** to Gilgil and the Rift Valley heads south out of town, crossing the Equator, with the usual smattering of souvenir stalls and eager demonstrators of the "Coriolis effect" (see p.166).

Travel details

Trains

Nanyuki to Nairobi (1 weekly, Sat; 4hr).

Buses

Chogoria to/from: Embu (several daily; 1hr 30min); Meru (several daily; 1hr); Nairobi (several daily; 4hr).

Embu to/from: Meru (several daily; 2hr); Nairobi (several daily; 2hr 30min); Sagana (several daily; 1hr); Thika (several daily; 2hr).

Meru to/from: Embu (several daily; 2hr); Maua (3 daily; 1hr); Mombasa (4 weekly; 12hr); Nairobi (several daily; 5hr); Nanyuki (2–3 daily; 2hr); Thika (several daily; 4hr).

Nanyuki to/from: Nairobi (2–3 daily; 3hr 30min); Nakuru (1 daily; 5hr); Naro Moru (2–3 daily; 30min); Nyahururu (1 daily; 3hr); Nyeri (2–3 daily; 1hr 30min).

Nyahururu to/from: Nairobi (1 daily; 3–4hr); Nakuru (1 daily; 2hr); Nyeri (1 daily; 1hr 30min).

Nyeri to/from: Eldoret (1 daily; 5hr); Nairobi (2–3 daily; 2hr 30min); Sagana (2–3 daily; 1hr).

Matatus

Frequent service unless stated otherwise.
Embu to/from: Isiolo (3hr 30min);

Meru (2hr 30min); Nairobi (2hr 30min); Sagana (1hr); Siakago (several daily; 1hr).

Meru to/from: Isiolo (1hr); Maua (several daily; 1hr); Nairobi (6hr); Nanyuki (2hr).

Nanyuki to/from: Isiolo (several daily; 2hr); Nakuru (several daily; 5hr); Nairobi (several daily; 3hr 30min); Nyeri (1hr 30min); Nyahururu (3hr).

Nyahururu to/from: Maralal (several daily; 4hr); Naivasha (several daily; 1hr 30min); Nakuru (several daily; 2hr); Nyeri (1hr 30min).

Nyeri to/from: Eldoret (4 daily; 5hr); Kisumu (7hr); Nairobi (3hr); Nakuru (3hr 30min).

Flights

Lewa to/from: Maasai Mara (1 daily; 1hr 45min); Nairobi (1 daily; 1hr 15min).

Loisaba to/from: Kiwayu & Lamu (1 daily, connect in Nairobi); Maasai Mara (1 daily; 1hr 45min) Nairobi (1 daily; 1hr). NB, no Loisaba service 1 April–15 June & 1 Nov–15 Dec.

Nanyuki to/from: Maasai Mara (2 daily; 1hr 15min); Nairobi (2 daily; 40min).

The Rift Valley

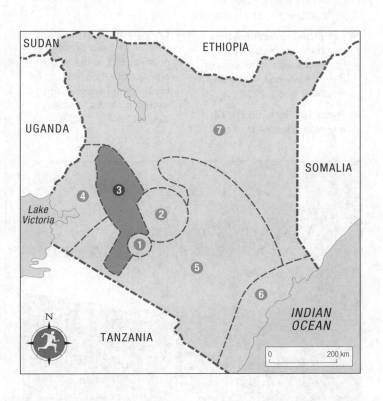

SUDAN   ETHIOPIA

UGANDA

7

SOMALIA

4   3

Lake
Victoria

2

1

5

6

INDIAN
OCEAN

N

TANZANIA

0   200 km

CHAPTER 3 # Highlights

✳ **Olorgesailie prehistoric site**
Stark site in the southern Rift
Valley, with huge numbers
of early hominid stone tools
preserved *in situ*. See p.199

✳ **Lake Naivasha & Hell's Gate
National Park** Hauntingly
atmospheric freshwater lake
near Hell's Gate's sheer, red
cliffs and ravine. See p.203

✳ **Lake Nakuru National Park**
Woods, grasslands and
lakeshore, with the chance of
seeing flamingos, rhinos and
leopards. See p.223

✳ **Hyrax Hill** If you don't visit
any other stone-age site in

Kenya, try to take an hour
out for a wander around
Hyrax Hill, just outside
Nakuru. See p.227

✳ **Lake Bogoria** Steaming
hot springs, greater kudu
antelope and remote
campsites make this a
highly recommended visit.
See p.231

✳ **Lake Baringo** A beautiful
freshwater oasis in the dry
northern Rift, with hippos,
crocs, more than four
hundred bird species and
excellent places to stay.
See p.236

▲ Hell's Gate

3

The Rift Valley

K enya's **Rift Valley** is only part of a continental fault system that runs 6000km across Africa from Jordan to Mozambique. Perhaps Kenya's most important topographical feature, it is certainly one of the country's great distinguishing marks, acting as a human and natural divide. With its spectacular scenery of lakes and savanna, it has come to be seen as a monumental valley of teeming game and Maasai herders, a trough of grasslands older than humanity. Although the iconic image is not entirely borne out by reality, the valley certainly is magnificent, a literal rift across the country, with all the stunning panoramas and gaunt escarpment backdrops you could wish for, and the plains animals are still abundant in places. Nevertheless, much of the game has been dispersed by human population pressure onto the higher plateaus to the southwest, and today most of the Maasai live further south.

At least the Rift Valley's **historical influence** cannot be diluted. People have trekked down it, generation after generation, over perhaps the last two or three thousand years, from the wetlands of southern Sudan and the Ethiopian highlands. Some of the more recent immigrants were the ancestors of the **Maasai**, who dominated much of the valley and its surroundings for several centuries before the Europeans arrived. Until the beginning of the twentieth century, they lived on both sides of the valley, and the northern **Ilaikipiak** group were a constant threat to trading caravans coming up from the coast. With European settlement, the Maasai were forced from their former grazing grounds in the valley's turbulent bottleneck and confined to the "Southern Reserve" for much of the colonial era. Although many have now returned to the valley, and many towns retain their ancient Maa names, the Maasai are at their most conservative and traditional in southern Kenya (see p.372).

In practical terms, the parts of the Rift Valley covered in this chapter offer several exceptional **lakes**, lots of rocky, twisting roads, and some of central Kenya's wildest areas. If you're at all interested in wildlife, especially **birds**, you'll find this area a source of endless fascination, with wonderful nature reserves at **Lake Nakuru** and **Lake Bogoria**, freshwater ecosystems at **Lake Naivasha** and **Lake Baringo**, and a weird soda lake at **Magadi**. In addition, there are several interesting **prehistoric sites** with a refreshing rawness about them.

Apart from **Naivasha**, **Nakuru** and the string of towns up the western escarpment (**Njoro**, **Elburgon** and **Molo**), the area covered in this chapter contains few places larger than a village. Though there is usually somewhere to lay your head, this is a region where, if you're on a budget, a **tent** will be worth its extra weight, and good walking shoes are a definite advantage. **Transport** around Naivasha is generally fine, but down towards Magadi, or northwards off the main Nakuru–Baringo–Kabarnet axis, you can expect

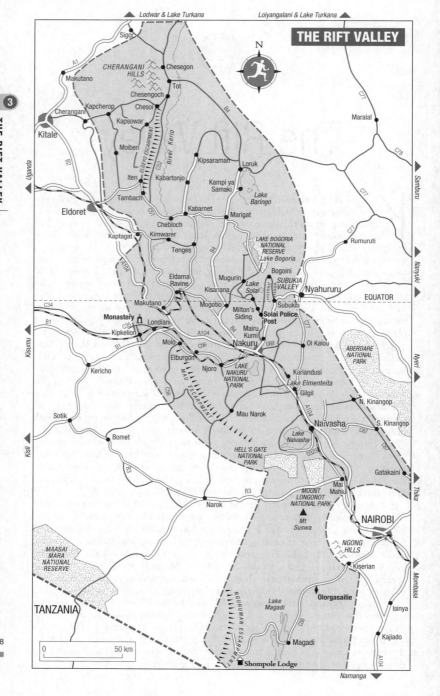

THE RIFT VALLEY

N

Lodwar & Lake Turkana   Loiyangalani & Lake Turkana

Sigor

Makutano

A1

CHERANGANI HILLS

Chesegon

Tot

Chesengoch

Cherangani

Kapcherop

Chesol

Kitale

Kapsowar

B2

Moiben

Uganda

Iten

Kabartonjo

ELGEYO ESCARPMENT

C52

River Kerio

Kipsaraman

B4

Loruk

Maralal

C77

C78

Tambach

Eldoret

Kampi ya Samaki

Lake Baringo

Kaptagat

Chebloch

Kabarnet

Marigat

A104

Kimwarer

Tenges

B4

LAKE BOGORIA NATIONAL RESERVE
Lake Bogoria

Rumuruti

C77

Samburu

Nanyuki

C34

Eldama Ravine

Mugurin

Kisanana

Lake Solai

Bogoini

SUBUKIA VALLEY

Nyahururu

EQUATOR

B1

Kisumu

Makutano

Mogotio

Milton's Siding

Subukia

Kipkelion

Monastery

Londiani

C51

A104

Mairu Kumi

B4

Solai Police Post

C77

Molo

C56

Nakuru

C69

Ol Kalou

ABERDARE NATIONAL PARK

Kericho

Elburgon

Njoro

LAKE NAKURU NATIONAL PARK

Kariandusi
Lake Elmenteita

Nyeri

Sotik

MAU ESCARPMENT

C56

Gilgil

N. Kinangop

Mau Narok

Lake Naivasha

A104

Naivasha

C67

S. Kinangop

Bomet

B3

HELL'S GATE NATIONAL PARK

C61

Gatakaini

Thika

MAASAI MARA NATIONAL RESERVE

Narok

B3

MOUNT LONGONOT NATIONAL PARK

Mt Suswa

Mai Mahiu

D922

NAIROBI

NGONG HILLS

Mombasa

TANZANIA

NGURUMAN ESCARPMENT

Lake Magadi

Olorgasailie

Kiserian

Isinya

C58

Magadi

Kajiado

A104

0   50 km

Shompole Lodge

Namanga

long waits, next-to-no buses and infrequent matatus. Watch out for the climate too: the northern Rift is lower, and consequently hotter, than most upcountry regions, so be prepared for some very high temperatures and don't underestimate your **water** requirements.

The southern Rift Valley

The journey south from Nairobi down into the hot, sparsely inhabited southern districts of the Rift Valley takes you first to the prehistoric site at **Olorgesailie**, then on to the dramatic salt lake of **Magadi**, and finally to the **Nguruman Escarpment** and the remote nature conservancy at **Shompole**. The scenery opens out dramatically as you skirt the southern flank of the Ngong Hills and descend steeply down the escarpment; if you're travelling by public transport, try to get a front seat as giraffe and other animals are often seen.

KISERIAN, 15km from Nairobi National Park's main gate, is your chance to buy last-minute provisions, as there's almost no food available further south. There are several basic B&Ls and bang in the centre of town, the *Eureka Hotel* (☏020/522346; ❸) has a lively restaurant and bar with occasional live music, as well as decent s/c rooms.

A different kind of place altogether is *Whistling Thorns*, 13km east of Kiserian on the road to Isinya (☏020/3540720 or 0722/721933, Ⓦwww .whistlingthorns.com; ❸). Overlooking the Ngong Hills and the plains south of Nairobi National Park, this offers en-suite tents, one and two-bedroomed cottages, and a campsite (Ksh400). There's a swimming pool, good food – including excellent pizzas, grills and vegetarian options (lunch Ksh950, dinner Ksh1250) – and opportunities for walks, cycling and horseriding.

Some 12km southwest of Kiserian, there's a pleasant picnic site at *Olepolos Country Club*. In **Olepolos** itself, there are a number of *nyama choma* joints, a good bar with chairs on the roadside under some trees, and entirely Maasai clientele.

Olorgesailie

Olorgesailie Prehistoric Site (1500m from the main road; daily dawn–dusk; Ksh500) is signposted 3km south of **Oltepesi**. The site is endowed with numerous pathways, boardwalks and informative signs, and is a peaceful place to stay, while the **guided tour** around the excavations (included in the entrance charge) is not to be missed.

The accommodation and **museum** are just above the excavations on a ridge overlooking what was once a wide, shallow lake. Between 400,000 and 500,000 years ago, the lakeshore was inhabited by a species of hominid, probably *Homo erectus* of the **Acheulian culture** (after St Acheul in France, where it was first discovered). They made a range of identifiable stone tools: cleavers for skinning animals; round balls for crushing bones, perhaps for hurling or possibly tied to vines to be used, like gauchos, as *bolas*; and heavy hand axes, for which the culture is best known, but for which, as Richard Leakey writes, "embarrassingly, no one can think of a good use". The guides tell you they were used for chopping meat and digging. This seems reasonable, but some are very large, while hundreds of others (particularly at the so-called "factory site") seem far too small, the theory being that they were made by youngsters, practising their toolmaking.

Mary and Louis Leakey's team did most of the unearthing here in the 1940s. Thousands of the stone tools they found have been left undisturbed, *in situ*, under protective roofs. Perhaps the most impressive find, however, is the fossilized leg bone of a gigantic, extinct elephant, dwarfing a similar bone from a modern elephant placed next to it. It was long hoped that human remains would also be uncovered at Olorgesailie, but despite extensive digging none have been found – more scope for speculation.

Practicalities

It only takes a couple of hours to look around the site, and most visitors choose not to spend the night. If you don't have your own transport, make sure you find out exactly when the next matatu will be passing by, as they are few and far between.

There are eight basic **bandas** on site, which can be booked through the public relations office at the National Museum in Nairobi (⌕020/3741424; Ksh500 or Ksh800), though it's rarely necessary, or you can **camp** (Ksh250). Do-it-yourself showers and free firewood are available, but you'll need to bring food and bedding. Sitting with a pair of binoculars and looking out over what used to be the lake can yield some rewarding animal-watching, especially in the brief dusk. Go for a walk out past the excavations towards the gorge and you may see baboons, duiker, giraffe, eland and even gerenuk if you're lucky (Olorgesailie is about the western-most extent of their range in southern Kenya).

Contacts with Maasai are good at Olorgesailie and there's usually some jewellery for sale. You can cultivate further friendships – and collect some scant **provisions** – at the cluster of desolate *dukas* at Oltepesi, 3km back along the Nairobi road, where they also have warm beer and soft drinks.

Lake Magadi

Lying in a Rift Valley depression, 1000m below Nairobi, **Lake Magadi** is a vast shallow pool of soda (sodium carbonate), a sludge of alkaline water and crystal trona deposits, and one of the hottest places in the country. Magadi is also the second largest source of soda in the world, after the Salton Sea in the USA.

The Magadi Soda Company, formerly an ICI business, now owned by the Indian company Tata, has built the very model of a company town, on a barren spit of land jutting out across the multicoloured soda. The company's investment here is guaranteed – hot springs gush out of the earth's crust to provide an inexhaustible supply of briney water for evaporation. Everything you see, apart from the homes of a few Maasai on the shore and a few *dukas* and places to eat in town, is owned and run by the corporation. You pass a company police barrier where you sign in and enter over a causeway, past surreal pink salt ponds. On company territory, a sign advises visitors that "it is dangerous to walk across the lake surface", just in case you were wondering. Note that some of the company police are touchy about you taking photos of the factory installations. Despite this, the atmosphere here, somewhat surprisingly because of the nature of the work and harshness of the environment, is relaxed and welcoming. By comparison with the rest of Kenya, the company pays high wages; people tend to get drunk a lot, and staff accommodation and many services are free.

Many visitors come to Magadi specifically for its **birdlife**. There's a wealth of avifauna here including, usually, large numbers of flamingos at the southern end of the lake. At this end, there are also freshwater swamps, which attract many species.

The lake

Lake Magadi is fascinating to walk across (on the causeways: in practice only the inlet between Magadi and the eastern shore). On the eastern side, where you first arrive, you can watch the sweepers in rubber boots shovelling the by-product, sodium chloride or common salt, into ridges on the technicolour "fields". Common salt crystallizes on top of the sodium carbonate, and is then loaded onto tractor-drawn trailers and taken away to be purified for human and animal consumption. Magadi soda, used principally for glass-making, is Kenya's most valuable mineral resource. The dried soda is exported, first by rail to Mombasa via Kajiado and Konza, thence, much of it, to Japan. But, despite the "high" wages, you wonder how anyone can be persuaded to work in this lurid inferno: the first rains here are usually so-called phantom rain, the ground so hot that the raindrops evaporate before hitting the surface. It's important to wear sunglasses and a hat while out in the sun, and bring plenty of water.

Practicalities

Behind the police station, which stands on the highest point of the peninsula, is the lake. If you look the other way (to the west), the road to the left leads to the "European" end of town, where a dozen or so managers live and where there's a strange, barren golf course; to the right, the town slopes gently down to a crusty shore where most of the Kenyan employees live. There's a Co-operative Bank in the building behind the Total station, but there's no ATM in town. However, the company has built not only blocks of apartments, a church, mosque, and schools but also, with a touch of inspiration, a glittering **swimming pool** which is "for residents only", although you can use the poolside bar and *nyama choma* kiosk. For a drink and cheap **meals**, try the *Flamingo* staff club, which accepts guests. Also good is the unnamed **bar** opposite the petrol station off Duka Hill Road, which is full of friendly Maasai. Across from the town, on the western shore, the same crowd will sell you *pombe* (bush brew) made from a base of roots and herbs, and fermented with honey. It's a lot cheaper than beer, and stronger, too.

Magadi has a thriving daily market and two **places to stay**, with good doubles and hot showers: the *Lower Guesthouse*, opposite the hospital (T0720/755457; ❷) and the slightly more upmarket *Sportsclub Hotel* (T020/6999265; ❸). Alternatively, you could pitch a tent almost anywhere south of the town, but it's baking hot during the day and a favourite haunt for baboons, so hardly ideal camping territory. You're likely to be invited home by employees, anyway.

The matatu **to Nairobi** leaves at 5am, or you could ask about hitching a ride on the soda **train** to Kajiado (on the main Kenya–Tanzania highway) or to Konza and Mombasa if you're headed that way.

The Nguruman Escarpment

With your own vehicle you can drive on from Magadi, across the lake to the **hot springs** on the western side. You're very likely to find a local in town who'll offer to guide you there. From the hot springs, you can drive to the Ewaso Ngiro River at the foot of the Ol Choroi plateau, also known as the **Nguruman Escarpment**. By the river is the Olkiramatian **campsite** run by the Maasai Olkiramatian Group Ranch. Forget about trying to take a 4WD up the rough track beyond the river, over the escarpment and on to the Mara. People have done that in the past, but the whole area is privately owned Maasai land and, for the moment at least, not accessible.

Further south, along the escarpment, is the 142-square-kilometre **Shompole Conservancy**, an ecotourism venture involving the Maasai Shompole Group Ranch. Access is usually by chartered plane, to the private **airstrip**. The only **accommodation** is at *Shompole Lodge* (Ⓦwww .shompole.com; package $1050 plus conservation fee $45 per day), a beautiful community eco-lodge constructed from natural materials and featuring the area's abundant natural water supply around the lodge in the form of streams and pools. There are eight tented rooms in the main lodge, each with a plunge pool, sitting area and stunning views. Away from the main lodge are two luxury suites, known as "Little Shompole", sharing a lounge and dining area, with their own staff and guide. Although Shompole's forte is the whole experience of being here, rather than a base for game drives, you are likely to see buffalo, elephant, zebra and wildebeest in the area, and, occasionally, a pride of lions.

The central Rift Valley

Many travellers' first proper view of the Rift Valley is from the souvenir-draped **B3 Escarpment Road**, originally built by Italian prisoners-of-war during World War II. This flirts with the precipice before dropping steeply down to the Rift through candelabra euphorbia and spikey agave. The little **chapel** at the bottom, also Italian-built, and often used as a picnic site, seems fitting in this Mediterranean scene.

The alternative route, the **A104 Uplands Road**, goes slightly further north and joins the B3 at Naivasha. Out of northwest Nairobi, it crosses a broad, bleak plateau, where roadside traders sell rhubarb, plums, carrots and potatoes and where, in the wet season, you can find yourself driving over a thick carpet of hailstones between gloomy conifer plantations. All this contrasts dramatically with the dusty plains of the Rift Valley. When you start descending, get out your binoculars and you can pick out herds of gazelle, Maasai with their cattle and, bizarrely, a satellite-tracking station.

For years the Uplands Road was the better of the two routes, but they're currently both in reasonable shape, though if you're climbing the steep and winding B3 back towards Nairobi on a busy day, it can be slow-going in the fumes and traffic. On the escarpment section, roadside souvenir stands sell crafts and small sheepskins (the latter often excellent value, but check they have been properly cured). The big woven grass baskets are also good value.

Lake Naivasha and around

Naivasha, like so many Kenyan place names, is a corruption of a local Maasai name, this time meaning heaving waters, *E-na-iposha*, a pronunciation still used by Maa-speakers in the area. The grassy shores of the lake were traditional Maasai grazing land for two centuries or more, prior to its "discovery" by Joseph Thomson in 1884. Before the nineteenth century was out, however, the "glimmering many-isled expanse" had seen the arrival, with the railway, of the first European settlers. Soon after, the *laibon* Ole Gilisho, whom the British had appointed chief of the Naivasha Maasai, was persuaded to sign an agreement ceding his people's grazing rights all around the lake – and the country houses and ranches went up. Today the Maasai are back, though very much as outsiders, either disputing grazing rights with the many European landowners still left here, working their herds around the boundary fences, or as workers on the vast horticultural farms around the lake.

The **lake**, slightly forbidding but picturesque with its purple mountain backdrop and floating islands of papyrus and water hyacinth, has some curious characteristics. It is fresh water – Lake Baringo is the only other example in the Rift – and the water level has always been prone to mysterious fluctuations. It dropped massively in the 1980s (partly the unmysterious result of farmers to the north taking off some of the Thurusha River's inflow), though the shore did not recede enough to regain the areas that were cultivated in the 1950s, when the lake was half its present size. Even though the lake level rose in 1998 following the El Niño floods, the shoreline the settlers knew is still marked by the outer edge of the fringing band of papyrus, and you can still see fence posts sticking up.

Perhaps of more immediate and visible interest is the lake's **wildlife**, especially its protected **hippo** population. Despite their bulk, hippos are remarkably sensitive creatures, with good night vision, for never is a camper's guy-line twanged. By day you can, occasionally, still see **giraffes**, floating blithely through the trees, taking barbed wire and gates in their stride. Naivasha has extraordinary **birdlife** of all kinds, from grotesque, garbage-scavenging marabou storks to pet-shop lovebirds, doves cooing in the woods, and splendid fish eagles, whose mournful cries fill the air like seagulls. Southwest of the lake, **Hell's Gate National Park** boasts the best expedition in the area – the hike through the Njorowa gorge. Not far away, **Mount Longonot**, also a national park, is worth climbing for the fabulous views in every direction as you circle the rim. All these attractions, and the area's climate, with a light breeze always drifting through the acacias, make Naivasha hard to beat as a first stop out from Nairobi.

Naivasha town

NAIVASHA town has little to offer as a place to stay. Unless you arrive late in the day, you may as well head straight down to the lake. If you plan to spend any time in the area, however, you may want to go into town to stock up on essentials first. For **food supplies**, try the Happy Valley Supermarket at the upper end of Biashara Road, or *La Belle Inn*, which has good picnic food (if you've got your own transport, you could also stop for fresh milk and yoghurts

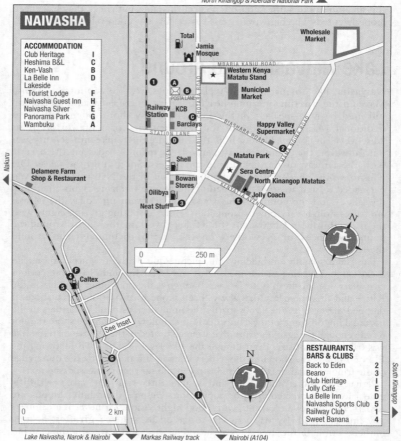

NAIVASHA

ACCOMMODATION
Club Heritage	I
Heshima B&L	C
Ken-Vash	B
La Belle Inn	D
Lakeside Tourist Lodge	F
Naivasha Guest Inn	H
Naivasha Silver	E
Panorama Park	G
Wambuku	A

RESTAURANTS, BARS & CLUBS
Back to Eden	2
Beano	3
Club Heritage	I
Jolly Café	E
La Belle Inn	D
Naivasha Sports Club	5
Railway Club	1
Sweet Banana	4

Lake Naivasha, Narok & Nairobi ▼ ▼ *Markas Railway track* ▼ *Nairobi (A104)*

at *Delamere Farm Shop & Restaurant*, 3km north of town on the Nakuru road). Shopping in Naivasha is a bit limited, with no large supermarkets, but Bowani Stores (Mon–Sat 8.15am–6pm) is well stocked, and you can get fruit – and crafts – in the *dukas* opposite Shell and *La Belle Inn*.

There's always a cluster of **artists** and art salesmen in Naivasha, offering various works, some quite good, but if you get tired of their pestering, dive into the little shop called Neat Stuff, at the south end of town (Mon–Sat 9am–6pm), which sells bric-a-brac, souvenirs, crafts and secondhand books.

There's a **post office** on Moi Avenue and a full showing of banks with **ATMs** (Barclays and KCB are both on Moi Ave). The Sera Centre on Kenyatta Avenue is the best place to look for an **internet** café, but they come and go in Naivasha faster than usual, so you may have to look around.

Naivasha has excellent **transport** connections, with most matatus crowding in a mass up Kenyatta Avenue. Nearby, the cheap and useful Jolly Coach offers a continuous service to Nairobi (Ksh100). Matatus going up to North Kinangop go from the alley alongside the Sera Centre.

Accommodation

You'll find many of the rooms in town surprisingly pricey. Nowhere has fans or air-conditioning. There's not much to choose between the many B&Ls, but those below are all at least adequate.

Club Heritage Top end of town, on the A104 highway ☎050/2030101 or 020/2090371. Attached to this big nightclub are 17 fairly small s/c rooms with instant showers, nets and TV. It's clean and well looked after and decent value for Naivasha, but inclined to be noisy at weekends. ❸

Heshima B&L Kariuki Chotara Rd ☎050/2020631. The rough facade isn't indicative of this extremely cheap B&L with non-s/c rooms (with nets, but no other frills). The shared toilets are all squatters, however, and you shouldn't expect much hot water in the showers. Safe parking. ❶

Ken-Vash Posta Lane ☎050/2021503 or 050/2030049, ✉ken-vash@kenyaweb.com. Though lacking in atmosphere and – strangely – carpeted throughout, this is reasonably comfortable and very clean, with good nets and TVs in all rooms. Still, it's overpriced and, as in most Naivasha hotels, the instant electric shower has yet to make an appearance. Good service and safe parking. ❸

🏃 **La Belle Inn** Moi Ave ☎020/3510404, ✉labelleinn@kenyaweb.com. Popular and atmospheric old staging post on the main street through town, with a variety of good-value, homely, English-B&B-style s/c rooms, with nets and TV, set around a garden courtyard. Rooms are mostly spacious and well furnished and the whole place is well looked after, though the bathrooms are tatty, verging on decrepit, with old plumbing and hot water mornings and evenings. Safe parking. BB ❹

Lakeside Tourist Lodge Moi Ave ☎050/2020856 or 0722/524565, ✉lakesidetlodge@yahoo.com. Large, pleasant place on the north side of the town centre, with good, clean, mostly bright, s/c rooms with nets and TV (some on the 1st floor with verandas) and efficient service. Go for a window room, as inside rooms are small and dark – and negotiate on the price, which is a bit steep. BB ❹

Naivasha Guest Inn Kenyatta Ave ☎050/2021227. Two kilometres from the town centre, this is handy if you've just been dropped at the junction, but is basically a dressed-up B&L. The cosily furnished, s/c rooms with nets and instant showers (and TV in two of them) are reasonable, and there's a busy *hoteli* and bar behind. Secure parking. Negotiable rates, which is good as the price is far too high. ❸

Naivasha Silver Kenyatta Ave ☎0726/045451. Not much of a step up from an ordinary B&L, but perfectly okay on a budget, with clean rooms (with nets, but no instant showers). Very busy *hoteli* at the front and safe parking. ❶

Panorama Park On the cliff-edge, off Koinange Rd on the south side of town ☎050/2030128 or 0712/091777. A new place with great views across the lake and a good, "resort" atmosphere, this has neat little rooms with nets, TV and instant showers, each occupying half a rondavel, and some larger chalets with boiler-heated showers. They have a campsite ($12) down the cliff on the plain. Rates are somewhat confusing and highly negotiable. BB ❹

Wambuku Moi Ave next to the post office ☎050/2030287. Big and impersonal, the *Wambuku* has stuffy, rather cramped s/c rooms with nets and TV, but old-style showers, ranged around a trough-like courtyard. ❷

Eating, drinking and nightlife

There's a clutch of cheap, local **places to eat** on Moi Avenue north of the Caltex gas station, among the better of which is *Sweet Banana*, which serves great *nyama choma* and features one-man guitar shows at the weekend.

🏃 **Back to Eden** Corner of Mama Ngina Rd and Biashara Rd. Wonderful little juice bar with freshly squeezed juices and fruit salads to take away.

Beano Bar & Pool Hall Kariuki Chotara Rd. For a game of pool and a few beers with the locals, you could do worse than this spot at the south end of town.

🏃 **La Belle Inn** Moi Ave. The terrace bar-restaurant here serves great, fried breakfasts and is a good place to while away a few hours. For lunch and dinner the fish – including barbecued tilapia, spiced crayfish, Naivasha bisque and the like – is particularly recommended and there's usually a vegetarian choice. They also have a good pastry chef and always have fresh bread and croissants in the shop.

Club Heritage Top end of town, on the A104 highway. One of Naivasha's busiest nightspots, with discos and, sometimes, live music Fri–Sun.

Entry, if you're not staying here, is around Ksh200–300, depending on who is playing.

Jolly Café At the front of the *Naivasha Silver Hotel*, on the ground floor, this lively *hoteli* has lots of reliable staples (main dishes around Ksh200–300) and *chai* for Ksh20.

Naivasha Sports Club Across the railway tracks, on the way down towards the lakeshore, this old institution usually waives its "members only" rule for out-of-towners with a bit of cash to spend propping up the bar.

Railway Club Near the tracks, west of the post office. With free entry, bands most nights except Mon & Tues, and beers at Ksh100, this is an amiable-to-riotous local dive. Note the list of "breakage charges" posted on the wall: "glass Ksh60, window pane Ksh300 ...".

Lake Naivasha

The fast lakeside road has brought tens of thousands of migrant workers to the **farming estates**, where they grow beans, mangetout and flowers, mostly in giant, polythene greenhouses, for export by air to European supermarkets. Since the late 1980s, great stretches of acacia scrub have been cleared for the expansion of the farms, and ugly lines of squalid field-hand housing have sprouted in the dust between the plantations. Impoverished **Karagita**, the largest lakeshore community, saw some of the worst violence after the December 2007 elections. Thankfully, peace quickly returned to the area, which, despite the ever-growing encroachment of farms and job-seekers, still retains some patches of fairly unspoiled savanna and woodland, and plenty of local wildlife. Even today, you can still see the odd giraffe, taking the fences in its stride, as it lopes down to Crescent Island.

Travel practicalities

Besides Naivasha's good transport connections from Nairobi, Nakuru, western Kenya and the central highlands, there's a daily Safarilink **flight** from Nairobi's Wilson Airport to **Loldia airstrip** on the west side of the lake (however it continues to Maasai Mara and then directly back to Nairobi). It's also possible to charter small planes to the short **Airspray airstrip** on the southeast shore.

To get to the lake from Naivasha town, there's a regular shuttle of matatus and you can hitchhike down there fairly easily. Circumnavigating the lake in a vehicle, you soon reach the 30km mark on the **Moi South Lake Road** and hit the dust and potholes of **Moi North Lake Road**, which represented the condition of the whole lake road until a few years back; there's 35km of this (between an hour and two hours' worth) before you return to the A104 Naivasha–Nakuru highway at a point 9km north of Naivasha. If you're hitching or using public transport, you'll find very few vehicles have reason to go beyond Kongoni village, and it's not really worth trying to go the whole way.

Lake dangers

Beware, out on Lake Naivasha. The possibility that underground springs may feed the lake, its location on the floor of the Rift Valley, and its shallowness all combine to produce notoriously fast changes of mood and weather: grey and placid one minute, suddenly green and choppy with whitecaps the next. Boating mishaps are all too common. Watch out, too, for hippos, which can overturn a small boat easily enough if frightened or harassed. Although there's no bilharzia in Naivasha, the hippos, the dense weeds, and the occasional sightings of crocodiles combine to offset any enthusiasm you might have had for a swim.

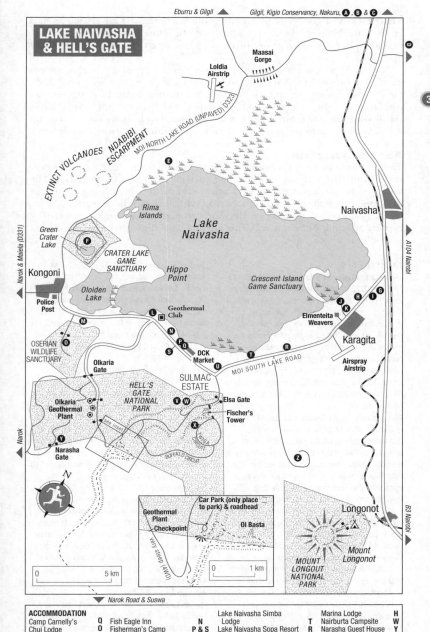

LAKE NAIVASHA & HELL'S GATE

Eburru & Gilgil ▲   Gilgil, Kigio Conservancy, Nakuru, **A**, **B** & **C** ▲

D

Maasai Gorge

Loldia Airstrip

MOI NORTH LAKE ROAD (UNPAVED) D323

E

Rima Islands

Lake Naivasha

Naivasha

EXTINCT VOLCANOES

NDABIBI ESCARPMENT

Green Crater Lake

F

CRATER LAKE GAME SANCTUARY

Hippo Point

Crescent Island Game Sanctuary

J **H** **I** **G**

Kongoni

Oloiden Lake

Geothermal Club

L

N **P** **O**

S **Q**

DCK Market

U

T

R

MOI SOUTH LAKE ROAD

Elmenteita Weavers

K

Karagita

Airspray Airstrip

Police Post

M

O

OSERIAN WILDLIFE SANCTUARY

Olkaria Gate

SULMAC ESTATE

HELL'S GATE NATIONAL PARK

Olkaria Geothermal Plant

see inset

V **W**

X

Elsa Gate

Fischer's Tower

IMPALA CIRCUIT

BUFFALO CIRCUIT

Z

Y

Narasha Gate

N

Narok & Maiela (D331)

Kongoni

Narok

A104 Nairobi

B3 Nairobi

Geothermal Plant Checkpoint

Car Park (only place to park) & roadhead

Ol Basta

very steep (4WD)

0   1 km

0   5 km

Longonot

Mount Longonot

MOUNT LONGONOT NATIONAL PARK

Narok Road & Suswa ▼

Narok Road & Suswa

ACCOMMODATION					
Camp Carnelly's	**Q**	Fish Eagle Inn	**O**	Lake Naivasha Simba	
Chui Lodge	**O**	Fisherman's Camp	**P & S**	Lodge	**T**	Marina Lodge	**H**
Crater Lake Camp	**F**	Kiangazi House	**M**	Lake Naivasha Sopa Resort	**R**	Nairburta Campsite	**W**
Elsamere	**L**	Kigio Wildlife Camp	**C**	Longonot Ranch House	**Z**	Narasha Guest House	**Y**
Endachata Campsite	**V**	Lake Naivasha Country Club	**J**	Malewa Wildlife Lodge	**A**	Ol Dubai Campsite	**X**
Fischers Tower Hotel	**I**	Lake Naivasha Holiday Inn	**K**	Malewa Ranch House	**B**	Olerai House	**E**
				Malu	**D**	Yelo Green Hotel	**G**
						YMCA	**U**

Bicycles are a good way of exploring the lakeshore, and for getting around Hell's Gate National Park, and several of the more independent-traveller-oriented places to stay rent out bikes, as do one or two independent roadside operators.

It's possible to go out in a **boat** at many of the lakeshore establishments, usually for around Ksh3000 per hr with room for up to eight passengers. Check the life vests before you embark. An hour in a reasonably fast boat will see you over to the main concentration of hippos and back to the south shore. **Exploring on foot** can also be very pleasant. From *Fisherman's Camp*, it's worth walking up to the superb viewpoint, and visiting *Elsamere* (see opposite).

Accommodation

There's a wide variety of accommodation along Moi South Lake Road – everything from frugal *bandas* and camping to stately hotels and homestays. The distances mentioned in the reviews below refer to the distance from the lake road junction with the main Nairobi road (which is 3km from Naivasha town itself). Note that a number of lakeshore properties are regularly visited by **hippos** at night. Although accidents are rare, you should take great care and follow local advice.

Budget

Camp Carnelly's 17.9km ☎0722/260749 or 0722/329465, ⓦwww.campcarnelleys .com. Funky offshoot of Fisherman's Camp, with 4-person, s/c *bandas* (Ksh5000), twin rooms (Ksh1600), dorm bunks (Ksh600) and camping (Ksh400). The welcoming and convivial ambiance here, with a relaxing bar-dining area decked in cushions, is serious competition for *Fisherman's* (see below) among the independent and overland crowd. The bar-restaurant does slightly unusual things like smoothies, Camembert samosas and beef wraps. ❷

Fisherman's Camp (Bottom Camp) 18.2km ☎050/2030276 or 0726/870590, ⓦwww .fishermanscamp.com. This long-established budget hideaway has one of the best locations by the lake, right by the water's edge and set in a magnificent grove of fever trees that creates open shade without making the area dark. Besides camping (Ksh400; optional tent rental Ksh500 per two-person tent), there's a choice of s/c, if rather dingy three to four-person *bandas* (Ksh4000 per night at weekends, otherwise negotiable for smaller groups) and the 6-person Kasuku Cottage (Ksh8000 per night at weekends, otherwise equally negotiable for smaller groups).

Fisherman's Camp (Top Camp) Location and contact details as above, plus manager ☎0720/550409. Up on the cliffs above the lakeshore on the other side of the road, *Top Camp* offers several basic-to-rudimentary *bandas* and cottages, more or less s/c and with bedding and kitchenettes, but lacking mosquito nets. ❷

Fischer's Tower 1km ☎050/2020062. Two hundred metre past the *Yelo Green Hotel*, right by the main road and a fair walk from the lake. Although it has a pleasant garden setting with a large bar and a *nyama choma* joint, and there's more chance of live music here than at the *Yelo Green*, the rooms are not as nice. Friendly, and mainly frequented by Kenyans. BB ❸

Fish Eagle Inn 18.2km ☎050/2030306 or 0725/157370, ⓦwww.fisheagleinn.co.ke. Big, reasonably well-run, middle-of-the-road, resort establishment with a variety of accommodation options, including dull, but well-equipped "standard rooms" (with nets, hot water and spotless toilets). Most campers head for nearby *Fisherman's* or *Carnelly's*, but the pool, gym, sauna and steam room may appeal (Ksh200 per visit). Internet Ksh10 per min. Bikes Ksh500 per day. Meals Ksh500–750. Camping Ksh500. BB ❹

Lake Naivasha Holiday Inn 3.6km ☎020/2350149, ⓦwww.lakenaivashaholidayinn .com. No connection with the chain, this is a new place with a slightly Mediterranean feel and pretty, well-maintained grounds. The rooms, in a variety of styles and buildings, are well furnished, with big rustic beds and a nod to African style, while deluxe rooms have huge bathrooms and outside showers. Very good value. BB ❹

Marina Lodge 1.9 (plus 1km down to the site) ☎0722/728054 or 0725/003225. Lovely grassy campsite under acacias with washrooms and hot water and some decent, large rooms with clean bathrooms. This is a good place to hang out with a cool, Kenyan vibe. Go elsewhere for boat trips, however, as they've been known to cut corners. Camping Ksh300. ②

Yelo Green 0.8km ☎050/2030269. Far from the lake itself, and a little tatty, but with acceptable chalet-style *bandas* a cut above those at neighbouring *Fischer's Tower* (all s/c with hot water), set in rambling, bougainvillea-filled gardens. The owners are charming and helpful, and there's a restaurant and bar, popular with locals at weekends. BB ④

YMCA 15.1km ☎050/2030396. Still one of the lake's cheapest (and friendliest) places to stay, a ten-minute walk from the shore itself – and certainly the easiest base if you're planning an early-morning hike into Hell's Gate National Park, as the Elsa Gate is just up the road. You can camp in the acacia grove (showers and toilets are very basic), stay in the dorm (Ksh400; you need bedding), or rent one of the spartan *bandas* (s/c 2000; non-s/c 1000). Firewood, eggs, lake fish and milk are sporadically available. There's hot water, and food can be cooked to order. Camping Ksh250.

Mid-range to expensive

Crater Lake Tented Camp Green Crater Lake (see p.211) ☎050/2020613, ⓦwww.mericagrouphotels .com. Tucked at the base of an old crater on the shore of a hidden satellite-lake of Lake Naivasha, this once fairly luxurious establishment is in an idyllically peaceful spot. Unfortunately, the twin and double tents and family *bandas* are getting tatty. Still, the birding is superb, with birdbaths everywhere, so your subjects effectively come to you (and don't miss the silent electric boat trip). BB ⑥

Elsamere 20.7km ☎020/2050964 or 0722/648123, ⓦwww.elsamere.com. Joy Adamson's former home, open to the public as a conservation centre (see overleaf), offers comfortable, English-holiday-home-style rooms in cottages, each with a veranda facing the lake. There's no bar, but no ban on bringing your own alcohol. Reservations are advisable. FB ⑥

🏃 **Kiangazi House** 25.5km ☎050/2020792 or 0722/200596, ⓦwww.oserianwildlife .com. Stylish and personable, family-run guesthouse with a strong flavour of the Med, and a broad veranda overlooking the southwest corner of the lake. Three artificial pools (two for buffalo, zebra and antelope, the other for you to swim in) provide entertainment, while day and night game drives into the extraordinarily well-stocked Oserian Game Sanctuary are included in the price. Superb meals are accompanied by excellent wines. FB ⑦

🏃 **Lake Naivasha Country Club** 3.8km ☎020/2370368 or 020/2367300, ⓦwww .kenyahotelsltd.com. Once the only – and later the best – hotel on the lake, with sweeping lawns and a colonial-style lounge, the *Lake Hotel*, as it's still usually known, has seen better days. Like a 1930s English Lake District hotel, it's a little too old-fashioned (especially in its bathrooms) for some visitors, but a good place for families, with a small adventure playground, a big pool, and huge gardens to roam, and its all-ground-floor rooms make it suitable for visitors with mobility problems. Day visits Ksh100. FB ⑦

Lake Naivasha Simba Lodge 12.2km ☎050/50305 or 050/50042, ⓦwww.marasimba .com. One of Naivasha's newest lodges, with villas built of ugly, grey concrete blocks, housing seventy rooms, each with a double and a single bed, this has good service and features some nice little touches such as bush dinners in the gardens with traditional music. The pool (unusually, heated) is large and inviting, and there's a tennis court, gym and sauna, and proper apparatus in the children's playground. Day guests Ksh200 (though entering is like getting into Fort Knox) and additional facilities charges. FB ⑦

Lake Naivasha Sopa Resort 8.6km ☎050/50398, ⓦwww.sopalodges.com. With its ostentatious public areas sprawling from an impressive euphorbia grove, this total makeover of the 1970s *Safariland Lodge* has 21 cottages, each with four exceptionally spacious rooms with TV and safe; two rooms upstairs with a big bed, shower and balcony; and two downstairs with two big beds, a terrace, shower and bath. Like the nearby *Simba Lodge* it has a pool, sauna and gym, but as a place to stay it easily outclasses its neighbour. FB ⑧

🏃 **Longonot Ranch House** 10.5km, then left (south) 10.2km up a farm track ☎0722/712026 or 0722/818128, ⓦwww .samawati.co.ke. Charmingly hosted, colonial-style homestay built by journo-aviatrix Martha Gellhorn on a hill between Mt Longonot and the lake, within the 32,000 hectare Kedong Ranch (some 10,000 head of plains game graze all around). The three twin/double rooms in two cottages near the main house are delightfully comfortable and you're on a working farm with a small dairy herd and stables (riding $30 per hr). Reservations essential. Package $470 ⑨

Olerai House 19km along Moi North Lake Road (turning off A104 9km north of Naivasha) ☎020/891112, ⓦwww.olerai.com. The former home of Iain and Oria Douglas-Hamilton, who were involved in the struggle to ban the ivory trade (they still live on the estate), this has six double rooms, full of cool touches and idiosyncratic design ideas, in guesthouses surrounding the main, flower-covered house. FB $600.

Elsamere

Elsamere (see p.209; Ksh650) is the former home of naturalist and painter Joy Adamson and now a field studies centre and the focus for Lake Naivasha's environmental issues. For visitors, there's a video about Adamson, a visit to the small museum and a copious and civilized afternoon tea on the lawn. Book ahead if you want to have lunch as well as the afternoon tea (Ksh950 during the week or Ksh1400 at weekends) or dinner (Ksh1400). It's unlicensed, but you can bring your own wine or beer. While the house and museum are somewhat shrine-like, the garden is a fine place to while away a couple of hours with a pair of binoculars: a troop of colobus monkeys can be seen in the acacias around the grounds.

The thorns of the rose

Cynics in the environmentalist community were unimpressed when the Lake Naivasha Riparian Association (LNRA) and Earthwatch succeeded in getting Naivasha listed as a Ramsar site in 1995. The designation of Naivasha as a wetland of global ecological importance obliges both government and local inhabitants to preserve the lake. The ecological consequences of Naivasha's multimillion-dollar **horticultural industry** were the cause for concern among the sceptics, who worried about the continuing use of **pesticides** on the lakeshore's huge flower and vegetable farms and the huge volumes of water used by them in irrigation.

In 1999, the LNRA won the Ramsar Wetland Award and was commended as an inspiring example of community leadership, demonstrating that conservation and the wise use of wetlands could be achieved in Kenya. However, it's become increasingly apparent that the survival of the lake and its wildlife depends on a multitude of other factors ultimately linked to the country's growing **population**. Since 1977 the number of people living near the lake has risen at least fivefold, and human waste has become a major problem because of inadequate sewage treatment facilities, with the result that some partially treated effluent is finding its way into the lake. Recently, the Malewa and Gilgil rivers (which flow into Lake Naivasha from the north) have been dammed, rendering the lake even more vulnerable.

Consequently, the lake's wildlife is seriously threatened. Until the exceptional 1997 rains raised the lake levels, thereby diluting the pollutants, the **fish eagle** had been especially badly affected, though its numbers now appear to be stable. The birds were not getting enough to eat and **Louisiana crayfish**, introduced in the 1970s for commercial fishing, were largely to blame. By eating their way through the lake's flora (which as well as acting as a soak for excess nutrients and a sediment trap, is food and cover for some fish species and birds), the crayfish caused the water to become murkier, making hunting harder for the eagles. Torrential rains in 2000 washed huge amounts of agrochemicals into the lake, killing fish and other aquatic life, prompting the government to impose a ban on fishing. The ban has since been lifted but fishermen complain that tilapia and black bass have sharply declined and much of the area's 350 species of birds, as well as the hippos and other wildlife, are still in danger: already the lily-trotter, the great crested grebe and the crested helmet shrike have all but disappeared.

Some **companies** finally appear to be waking up to their responsibilities. Oserian, the huge Dutch-owned flower exporter, has developed a new way of fighting fungal diseases without resorting to chemicals, by using geothermal steam in the greenhouse to purge diseases. Other companies have adopted computerized drip-irrigation to optimize their water efficiency. Unfortunately, the severe drought of 2009 caused the shore to recede by at least 500m, and the lake depth to drop to its lowest-ever level. Flower and vegetable growers laid off employees and put their operations into low gear.

Crescent Island Game Sanctuary

A very popular short trip is a visit to **Crescent Island Game Sanctuary** ($20; ⓔgaymer@kenyaweb.com; ⓣ0733/579935 or 0726/878767). The "crescent" is the outer rim of a volcanic crater, which forms a deep bay, the deepest part of the lake. The island, barely two square kilometres in size, is attached to the shore by a narrow causeway on the private land of Sanctuary Farm, about 2km from Moi South Lake Road. You pay cash on arrival and you can stay on the island, having a picnic and pottering about, until 6pm. Free guides are available – ask the ticket-seller. Alternatively, take a boat trip from a recognized operator (*Lake Naivasha Country Club*, whose jetty is inside the bay, are reliable: Ksh3000) and arrange to be picked up later in the day.

At first you may think there's nothing much on the island, but you'll soon come across a wealth of wildlife, including hundreds of species of birds, as many as four hundred wildebeest and two hundred impala, more than one hundred zebra, a variable-sized herd of giraffe, as well as hippos, waterbuck, Grant's and Thomson's gazelles and some startlingly large, though harmless, pythons. If you'd like to visit on horseback, note that **riding** is available at Sanctuary Farm (ⓣ050/2021324; around Ksh1500 per hr).

Oserian Wildlife Sanctuary

Although it's not on the tourist minibus circuit, and the entry fee doesn't encourage independent visits, **Oserian Wildlife Sanctuary** (ⓦwww .oserianwildlife.com; $80) is an accessible and very worthwhile conservation area, in a former ranch away from the lakeshore and the road. You might not guess, from the polythene horticulture so prevalent in the area, that the same Dutch family behind the biggest flower farm in Kenya – the Zwagers – have set aside this forty-square-kilometre sanctuary. There are rarely more than one or two other vehicles visiting the reserve, and although the proximity of the lake and its burgeoning population can't be set aside, it is an extensive wild area with a good array of big mammals, excellent birdlife (birders won't need reminding about the rare **grey-crested helmet shrike** that can be seen here) and a notable conservation success story in its white rhinos.

Most visitors come on day or night game drives included in a stay at Oserian's *Kiangazi House* (see p.209), but you could also stay in its sister establishment, the very comfortable and well located *Chui Lodge* (ⓣ050/2020792 or 0722/200596, ⓦwww.oserianwildlife.com; package $850), set by a waterhole inside the sanctuary. Every guide will be able to find you some of Oserian's impressively long-horned **white rhinos**, which are now into their second generation here and number at least fifteen. Look out, too, for species translocated from northern Kenya – **greater kudu**, **Grevy's zebra** and **Beisa oryx** – and for **wildebeest** and **topi** from the Mara. One species they are going to have to do something about is the **warthog** – the sanctuary swarms with them, and there are not enough **leopards**, **cheetahs** and **hyenas** to keep the numbers down.

Green Crater Lake

The teardrop-shaped **Green Crater Lake** (Ksh700) is a straightforward target for a short trip, but preferably with your own vehicle, as it's 17km past *Fisherman's Camp* and 6km beyond the end of the tarmac and regular transport. A **game sanctuary** has been set up all round the crater, with various tracks you can take, though the one to the crater rim is only for hikers or 4WD vehicles. The birdlife is exceptional and there's a host of wildlife in the vicinity, including colobus monkeys and bushbuck and excellent guides to accompany you from *Crater Lake Tented Camp* (see p.209). The brilliant, jade lake is quite breathtaking: the Maasai consider its deep alkaline waters good for sick cattle, but it's also a favourite sacred place. From the main viewpoint on the west rim, it's possible to scramble up for ten minutes to the highest point. There are not many places where you can get down to the crater floor – the easiest trails are on the southwest side near the tented camp.

Eating and drinking

You can drop in for meals and drinks at all the camps and lodges around the lake, and it's probably worth calling ahead to see what specials they're offering. Some charge casual visitors an entry fee, usually recoupable from whatever you spend. *Lake Naivasha County Club* remains a favourite spot for lunch, and even though the flying-boat era (passengers from London landed just offshore between 1937 and 1950) is long past, the buffet meals are reliable, although always best when the hotel is fairly full. Children love the grounds, but note that the tangled undergrowth at the bottom of the garden is still trampled by big beasts, including waterbuck and, at night, hippo. Apart from the other establishments listed under "Accommodation", you might also check out the *Geothermal Club* (19.6km from the junction). It's a pretty spot, with great views, but, at last check, the swimming pool was empty and little was available on the long menu of dishes. It's basically a bar, where you should be able to get a bite to eat. There's the possibility of wakeboard or waterskiing here for Ksh5000 per hr. *Drifters*, the enjoyable floating restaurant about 1km from the junction, is closed, currently high and dry because of the low water level.

Shopping

There are one or two places to shop around the lake. For general souvenirs, the best hotel gift shops are at the *Simba* and *Sopa* lodges. As in the accommodation reviews, the number of kilometres noted below refers to the distance along Moi South Lake Road from the junction with the main Nairobi road. There are Barclay's **ATMs** at Karagita (3.5km from the junction; limited hours) and DCK Market (between the *YMCA* and *Carnelly's*).

DCK Market (aka *Sulmac dukas*) 17.6km, just before *Carnelly's*. Sulmac is one of the biggest flower plantations in the area. Near the main entrance is a small shopping centre where you can eat for next to nothing. Newspapers are on sale every morning and you'll usually find a gathering of ladies selling produce from their *shambas*.

Elmenteita Weavers 4.3km, and 800m along the signposted track ☎ 050/2030115. A very friendly weaving shop, with looms behind the showroom. Carpets and rugs, sweaters (some superb), *kangas* and *kikois* compete with various other crafts from Fired Earth and Eastleigh Women's Group. Credit cards accepted. Mon–Sat 9am–5.30pm, Sun 9am–5pm.

Hell's Gate National Park

Hell's Gate (Ⓦ www.kws.go.ke/hells-gate.html; $25) was the outlet for the prehistoric freshwater lake that stretched from here to Nakuru and which, it's believed, would have supported early human communities on its shores. Today it's a spectacular and exciting area, the Njorowa gorge's red cliffs and undulating expanse of grassland providing one of the few remaining places in Kenya where you can walk among herds of **plains game** without having to go a long way off the beaten track. Buffalo, zebra, eland, hartebeest, Thomson's gazelle and baboons are all usually seen, lions and leopards hardly ever, but you might just see a cheetah, and you'll certainly come across their footprints if you scan the trail. There are also servals – one of the most elegant cats – and, high on the cliffs, small numbers of klipspringer ("cliffjumper") antelope. The gorge can, however, occasionally be rather empty of wildlife, as numbers vary seasonally.

The main entrance road to Hell's Gate is just south of the *YMCA*, with the Elsa Gate a further 1500m along this track. If you're driving a small vehicle, be aware of the need for high clearance on some of the tracks. If you want to **cycle** through Hell's Gate, you're better off entering by Olkaria Gate, which makes for an easier downhill ride to Elsa Gate. The tarmac road to Olkaria Gate is 28km from the lake road junction (5km south of Moi South Lake Road) followed by a steep descent to the gorge. The third entrance to the park is the more remote Narasha Gate, in the southwest corner, the dirt-track, motorable link with the C12 Narok–Mai Mahiu road.

From Elsa Gate, it's about 25km to the road-head and back and, if you need a lift, note that while a fair number of vehicles visit at weekends, there are far fewer during the week. The best time to arrive is dawn, when most animals are about, and you should try to avoid the midday hours, as the heat away from the lake can be intense. You'll need to carry plenty of water and some food (the only place to buy anything in the park is a simple staff kiosk in the Olkaria Geothermal Area).

As far as **accommodation** goes, there are several **campsites** in the park, with picnic benches, shower stands, taps and pit latrines. The nicest place to camp is the shady and superbly sited *Ol Dubai* campsite ($15) on the clifftop south of Fischer's Tower. *Naiburta* and *Endachata* campsites (also $15) are across the gorge on the northern cliffs. In addition, the KWS-run *Narasha Guest House* is an undistinguished **self-catering bungalow** near Narasha Gate, with two double rooms and a single for $150 per night (reservations ☏020/600800, ⓦwww.kws.go.ke).

The upper gorge

From Elsa Gate, first take a look at the rock known as **Fischer's Tower**, after the German explorer who arrived at Lake Naivasha via Hell's Gate. The rock is a volcanic plug, the hard lava remaining from an ancient volcano after the cone itself has been eroded. It's now the home of a colony of very astute rock hyraxes, which look like large, shaggy guinea pigs and expect to be fed.

Through the gorge along the main track, you'll find more and more animals visible on the slopes leading up to the sheer cliffs. Secretary birds are nearly always seen, mincing carefully through the grass at a safe distance. At least one pair of rare **lammergeier eagles** used to nest on the cliffs, but they are rarely seen – report any sightings to a ranger.

If you're driving or on a bike, rather than heading straight down to the gorge, you can take the longer Twiga or Buffalo circuits. Twiga climbs up to the left from just inside Elsa Gate before you reach Fischer's Tower. Branching off Twiga is Buffalo Circuit, which ploughs through thick bush. Don't go anywhere near the buffaloes, as they can be unpredictable and dangerous. Both tracks are insanely dusty, but when the dust clears, the views out over Hell's Gate and across to the Aberdare range are magnificent.

The lower gorge

Towards the southern end of the gorge (12km from Elsa Gate), a second rock tower – **Ol Basta** – marks its transition into a deep, tangled ravine. There's a car park here but nowhere to park on the narrow, rocky track that follows the gorge to the south for a short distance. The nearby "Interpretation Centre" is now a **viewpoint**, a good place to picnic and take shelter from the sun. The best move you can make from this road-head is to cross the gorge and follow the "Nature

Trail" round the north side of Ol Basta. There's really nothing nature-trail about it, but it's easy enough to follow as far as the rock tower, where most people turn back.

Hiking in the ravine itself is tough but exhilarating. Note that the trail from Ol Basta – the only realistic route – becomes more indistinct as you go, and it's quite easy to lose your way until you turn down into the head of the ravine itself. Beware of suggestions that there's a path around the south side of Ol Basta, directly above the eastern branch of the ravine: there isn't, and trying to prove otherwise is dangerous. Equally dodgy is the very steep way down into the ravine just south of the gorge crossing, near the car park. You need tough walking shoes for this and shouldn't attempt it alone. Once down on the **ravine floor**, it's about a one-hour walk southwards to the point where you can climb up to the road on its west side. Watch out for unexpected slippery surfaces and seek advice if it's been raining, as flash floods sometimes rip through the ravine.

If you've come equipped for a night out, you can press on, to emerge after a further (and difficult) 12km at the end of the canyon – still 15km short of the Narok road. For orientation, aim for **Mount Suswa** – itself an area of great exploring interest, only properly documented in the last couple of decades. Otherwise, either turn back and retrace your path to Elsa Gate, or else climb up towards the noise and steam of **Olkaria geothermal station**, which is inside the national park. On the clifftop you can look out over the gorge and a Maasai village below, with your back to the first productive geothermal installation in Africa. The underground temperature of the super-heated, pressurized water is up to 304°C, one of the hottest sources in the world, and the station is eventually expected to supply half of Kenya's energy requirements. Although the whole complex is working at full tilt, the impact on the local environment appears to be small, and it certainly doesn't spoil the landscape.

Heading for the main buildings through the scrub, and the maze of pipes and hissing steam jets, you meet a perfect **tarmac road**. From here, you shouldn't have any problem getting a ride with employees the 5km down to the lake road at a point 2km west of *Elsamere*. If you hike it (and there are fine views of Oloiden and Green Crater lakes), allow about three hours after leaving the ravine to complete this section.

Mount Longonot National Park

The prominent cone of the dormant volcano **Mount Longonot** (2777m) looms high above Lake Naivasha, flanked by thorny savanna slopes and visible for miles around. It's a relatively easy ascent, and since it became a national park (Ⓦwww.kws.org/mt-longonot.html; $20) it's safe to do, even on your own.

Don't try to make the ascent from the lake road or Hell's Gate – it's further and steeper than it looks, and the north slopes are covered in dense bush, frequented by buffalo. Instead, head for **Longonot** village on the old Nairobi road. About 500m south of the village, just beyond the railway bridge, a 4km dirt road leads to the national park gate at the base of the mountain and a further 3km to the crater rim. You can leave your car safely at the gate and get a drink (remember to take ample water with you), and you can also camp here (simple facilities; Ksh500). Longonot village itself has a couple of basic B&Ls (❶).

Up the mountain

There's only one straightforward route up to the crater rim, which takes about an hour. At the top you can collapse (the last section is rather steep) and look back over the Rift Valley on one side and the enormous, silent crater on the other. Joseph Thomson, the first *mzungu* up here in 1884, was overcome:

> The scene was of such an astounding character that I was completely fascinated, and felt under an almost irresistible impulse madly to plunge into the fearful chasm. So overpowering was this feeling that I had to withdraw myself from the side of the pit.

Avoiding the same urge, it's now possible to scramble down **into the crater**, where exciting encounters with buffalo aren't uncommon: a 1937 guidebook observes "any attempt to descend into the crater is accompanied by hazard". You should preferably be accompanied by a guide if you want to go down to the crater floor.

Most climbers do the walk around the **crater rim**. The anticlockwise route is easier because the climb to the summit on the western side is quicker and steep sections more negotiable. It doesn't look far, but allow two to three hours to circumnavigate the 2km-diameter bowl. Longonot's name comes from the Maasai *oloonong'ot*, "mountain of many spurs" or "steep ridges", and you soon find out why. The cone is composed of very soft volcanic deposits that have eroded into deep gulches and narrow ridges: much of the path is over crumbly volcanic tufa worn into a channel so deep and narrow that it's difficult to put one foot in front of the other.

Until recently, Longonot's crater was famous for its steam jets; the volcano is classed as "senile", rather than extinct. Although their vents, like pockmarks, are still visible in several places around the rim and on the crater walls, emissions of steam have decreased since the Olkaria geothermal plant went on line, though the hot-air currents are said to be still sufficient to deflect light aircraft.

For **overnight stays** on the mountain, you need a tent (there are no official campsites) and you should get formal permission in advance from the rangers.

Naivasha to Thika via the Kinangop

If you're serious about hiking, biking, or fairly adventurous expeditionary driving, a route to take to **Thika** (see p.148) is the dramatic one from **North Kinangop**. It cuts up from the Rift Valley and right over the southern flank of the Nyandarua (Aberdare) range – still, in large part, virgin mountain rainforest. The approach **from Naivasha** is quite straightforward, as frequent matatus make the journey up to North Kinangop. Routine though it may be, this part of the journey is still spectacular. The road climbs constantly towards the **Kinangop Plateau**, with the Rift Valley and Lake Naivasha way below. The land hereabouts is Kikuyu farming country, once widely settled by Europeans, who were lured by the wide open moors, rocky outcrops and gushing streams. Sheep and cattle graze everywhere.

NORTH KINANGOP is nowadays a rather isolated rural community, a village of gumboots and raggy sweaters (it can freeze here at night), whose road becomes nearly impassable during the long rains. Transport onwards is usually little problem outside the rainy season – at least as far as South Kinangop. Tractors will pick you up and there are a few old lorries, trundling around, too. **SOUTH KINANGOP** (also known as **Njabini**) is livelier than its northern counterpart, a small trading centre with regular matatus from Naivasha.

South Kinangop to Gatura is approximately 36km, a good eight hours on foot, or a great, half-day mountain-bike trip. The dirt road (the C67) has very little traffic, even to begin with, as it switchbacks in descent, across a series of streams flowing south from the Aberdare range to the Chania River. The road follows the river, with tremendous scenic variation, though almost always through forest – sometimes indigenous, sometimes conifer plantation. After the turn-off (left) for **South Kinangop forest station**, the occasional *shambas* and all signs of human habitation stop completely. From here down, the forest is untouched mountain jungle – trees with huge leaves, bamboo thickets, birds shrieking in alarm, the crashing of colobus monkeys, chameleons wobbling across the road and tell-tale elephant dung. After rain, the "road" can become a complete quagmire, really just fit for tractors. If you try this route by 4WD, you'd better have a winch, and a good saw, if not a chain saw, as elephants push a lot of trees across the route, and for months if not years on end it can be all but impassable to motor vehicles (as was the case in 2009). When the foresters can't drive in, the road soon becomes overgrown. On foot or mountain bike, or possibly a good, light, trial motorbike, there's no danger of getting stuck, though you should ensure you have food and water, and ideally a GPS.

You finally reach human habitation again at the **Kimakia Forest Station**, where there's normally a barrier across the road. If you've arrived by 4WD, someone will unlock it for you. If you're on foot, or two wheels, you can go round. Now on a proper road, you meet some tarmac a few kilometres later outside the Ngere tea factory, but the tarmac road doesn't start properly until you reach the outskirts of **Gatura** (B&Ls, petrol, shops, matatus), the first of a chain of small towns and villages along the scenic road down to Thika. Gatura is 31km from Thika.

Gilgil, Lake Elmenteita and around

Often overlooked by people rushing from Lake Naivasha to Lake Nakuru, the area around **Lake Elmenteita** and up into the lower foothills of the Aberdare range offers some enticing overnight or short-stay options and off-the-beaten-track attractions such as **Kariandusi** prehistoric site.

Ranch stays

Malu Farm, tucked away about half an hour's drive north of the highway, just a little west of Naivasha, offers great accommodation and a diverse range of activities. Even more active is **Malewa Bush Ventures**, a community-focused team-building and activities centre on the banks of the Malewa river near Gilgil where you can try the high-ropes challenge course, do rock-climbing and abseiling, shoot on a zip line across the swirling river, and go on more mainstream bird walks and game viewing excursions. The activities centre manages and supports the Malewa Trust, which drives resources into the local community.

Between these two establishments lies **Kigio Wildlife Conservancy** a 14-square-kilometre former cattle ranch rolling from the scrubby plains near the highway and railway line down through lightly wooded hills to the lush valley of the **Malewa River**. Established in 1997, Kigio has a good conservation record, with the herd of **Rothschild's giraffe** relocated here in 2002 now breeding. The conservancy is entirely fenced except along its riverbank side, and rarely contains any large predators, which means that you can walk or cycle here safely. The large mammal count is very healthy, and includes hippo, buffalo, impala, Thomson's gazelle, eland, waterbuck, zebra, warthog and more than 250 species of birds, including ostriches. The reserve is a great place to visit for a few hours or as an alternative to being based at Naivasha. As well as wildlife-viewing (by car, on foot or with mountain bikes) and riverside birding, Kigio offers hikes up the densely wooded Kasuki gorge, and river swims and rock-jumping just 1500m downstream from the *Malewa Wildlife Lodge*.

Accommodation

Kigio Wildlife Camp Kigio Wildlife Conservancy ☏020/3748369, ⊛www.kigio.com. New tented camp in the conservancy, above the Malewa River, with nature walks, fishing and bike hire included. FB $500 ❾

Malewa Ranch House Part of Malewa Bush Ventures, near Gilgil ☏020/3535878 or 020/3510720, ⊛www.malewa.co.ke. Originally built in the 1920s, this old farmstead has been renovated to a high standard with five bedrooms and three bathrooms, taken on an exclusive basis, with all meals included. $700 for the whole house with four adults staying. At the adjoining Malewa Bush School, comfortable safari tents ($50 per person) or basic dome tents ($20 per person) are also available, with the option of meals in the central building.

Malewa Wildlife Lodge Kigio Wildlife Conservancy ☏020/3748369, ⊛www.kigio.com. This riverside bush lodge, formerly *Malewa River Lodge*, now considerably expanded and upgraded, offers delightfully eccentric accommodation, based around reclaimed timber, mud walls and thatched roofs. The main lodge has a public lounge with an open fireplace and dining terrace, and there are five private cottages and four river suites on stilts in the grounds. It's all designed to be an eco-lodge, using a combination of solar panels and deadwood-fired *kuni-boilers*. FB $500 ❾

Malu 15km north of Naivasha (3.7km from the A104 junction, after Kobil, turn right, then drive 11km) ☏050/2030181 or 0720/899530, ⊛www.malu-kenya.com. Located in a 7-square-kilometre indigenous forest reserve of cedar and olive, with breathtaking views of Lake Naivasha and Longonot, Malu has a variety of great-value accommodation in cottages, family villas and a superb "treehouse". The Italian-based food from the farm is excellent. Activities include fishing in the Malewa River, visiting the landscaped warm-spring plunge pool, horseriding and mountain biking. ❼

Gilgil

GILGIL is as dull a town as you could expect to find anywhere, with fragile-looking *dukas* and dusty streets scavenged by goats. On the outskirts lie the serried, pastel-coloured ranks of housing for the local Gilgil Telecoms Industries workers. The town has a Gilgil Mattresses supermarket, a Barclays with **ATM**, a post office and several filling stations and car repair yards, but not much else.

If you need to stay or stop for a bite to eat, the best place is the *Hotel Freci* (☏050/4002060 or 0711/713813, ⊛www.hotelfreci.com; ❷), an outwardly unremarkable motel-style place on the south of town. Inside, the pastel-coloured rooms are well insulated against the heat, and comfortable, though without any frills apart from nets. There's a busy bar-restaurant, with main meals around Ksh300 and plenty of snacks and side dishes for Ksh30–80. Come here at the end of the week and you could find a crowd with live music in the "club room".

Gilgil War Cemetery

If you have a half an hour to spare, have a look on the north side of town at the **Gilgil Commonwealth War Cemetery**. Of more than forty cemeteries in Kenya tended by the Commonwealth War Graves Commission, this is one of the most meticulously kept, and a good place to stop for a picnic and some moments of contemplation. There are about two hundred graves here from the East African campaign of World War II and from the war for independence – "the Emergency" – in the 1950s. Whether by accident (which doesn't seem likely) or design, the African graves are all at the bottom of the slope, and record no personal details apart from name, age and rank. The graves of British soldiers are higher up, the stones inscribed with family messages. As well as graves from World War II, there are also poignant reminders of lives lost between 1959 and 1962, after the British government's futile attempt to prevent the inevitable.

Lake Elmenteita

Beyond the turn for Gilgil, the fast A104 road sweeps the eastern wall of the Rift Valley and pushes up high above **Lake Elmenteita**. This shallow soda lake, which has been known to shrivel to a huge white salt pond, is a good site for flamingos when Lake Nakuru is out of favour, and always good for pelicans; there are an estimated three hundred bird species in all. Like Lake Nakuru, Elmenteita has no outflow, and its accumulated alkaline salts make it uninhabitable for all but one species of fish, the indomitable *Tilapia grahami*.

Elmenteita's setting is spectacular and primeval, framed by the broken caldera walls of several extinct volcanoes, which resemble a reclining human figure. The Maasai know these peaks as Elngiragata Olmorani (Sleeping Warrior) – a name that is ironically fitting, since the lake and its lands were expropriated from the Maasai at the start of the colonial period by Lord Delamere (the caldera is now also known as "Delamere's Nose"). You can get a good view from the big "parking lane" viewpoint – if you survive the occasionally desperate assaults by the curio sellers.

Nearly all the land around the lake is part of the private and fenced **Soysambu Wildlife Sanctuary**. In practice, the eastern shoreline is accessible if you're staying at one of the small camps or lodges in the area, such as the very good value *Sleeping Warrior Camp* (T0733/385156 or 0735/408698, Wwww.sleepingwarriorcamp.com; FB ⑥), or the spectacularly sited cottages at *Sunbird Lodge* (T0715/555777 or 733/555777, Wwww.sunbirdkenya.com; ⑦). Go Ballooning Kenya (T0727/741883, 020/2717373 or 0723/702181, Wwww.goballooningkenya.com), based at the sanctuary, runs one-hour **balloon flights** over the lake for $365 per person. The price includes a champagne breakfast and transfers to and from wherever you're staying in the area.

Down on terra firma, a number of prehistoric sites are scattered around the lake's once-lush shores, of which **Gambles Cave**, 10km southwest of Elmenteita village at Eburru, is the most famous. It can be visited by making arrangements ahead of time – ask at the National Museum in Nairobi.

Kariandusi

For an easier shot of prehistory, try a visit to **Kariandusi** (daily 8am–6pm; Ksh500, under 16s Ksh250), signposted off the A104 highway, 1km south of *Lake Elmenteita Lodge* and 1.5km to the east of the highway. This is an **Acheulian site** characterized, like Olorgesailie (see p.199), by heavy hand-axes and cleavers. The site is very small, consisting of just two excavated areas cleared by Louis Leakey in 1928–31 and 1947, each displaying a scattered assortment of stone tools, many of them made of the black glassy volcanic rock, obsidian. The small **museum** explains the formation of the Rift Valley, and has comparative skull specimens of various distant human ancestors. Neither Kariandusi nor Olorgesailie have any signs of permanent habitation, and it's been suggested that they were simply places where the kill was habitually butchered and consumed, the tools being made on the spot and left for the next occasion. Nothing much is known about the toolmakers themselves, apart from the fact that they obviously had a formidable grip. The most likely candidate is a primitive form of *Homo erectus*, an early hominid whose remains have been found at Olduvai Gorge in Tanzania alongside Acheulian artefacts.

Nakuru

As you approach **Nakuru** along the main highway from Nairobi, the *shamba*- and conifer-cloaked mound directly ahead is the southern flank of the vast **Menengai crater**, while to the left are the scrub-covered eastern heights of the justly celebrated **Lake Nakuru National Park**. It also boasts the important but largely ignored prehistoric settlement site at **Hyrax Hill**. A noisy, dusty and hustly town, Nakuru is a major transport focus and the departure point for trips to lakes **Bogoria and Baringo** and the **northern Rift Valley**.

Nakuru came into existence on the thrust of the Uganda railway and owed its early growth, at least in part, to **Lord Delamere**, the Kenya Colony's most famous figure. In 1903 he acquired four hundred square kilometres of land on the lower slopes of the Mau escarpment, followed by two hundred more at Soysambu, on the other side of the lake. Eager to share the empty vistas with compatriots – though preferably with other Cheshire or Lancashire men – he promoted in England the mile-square plots being offered free by the Foreign Office. Eventually, some two hundred new settler families arrived and Nakuru – a name that as usual could mean various things, including "Place of the Waterbuck" (Swahili) and "Swirling Dust" or "Little Soda Lake" (Maasai) – became their country capital. It lies on the unprepossessing steppe between the lake and the flanks of Menengai crater. This desolate shelf has a nickname: "the place where the cows won't eat grass" (the pasture was found to be iron-deficient). Farmers near the town turned to pyrethrum, the plant used to make insecticide, as a cash crop.

Arrival

The **train and matatu stations** are packed together at the east end of the town centre, with **cheap lodgings** all around. Better places to stay are all within easy walking distance. The national park gate and campsite (5km) is a bit of a slog without transport – take a taxi, *tuk-tuk*, *piki-piki* or *boda-boda*.

Accommodation

You're spoilt for choice for **cheap rooms**, though few of them stand out. A number of **mid-range hotels** are dotted about the western avenues, and are amazingly good value if you've just come from Nairobi. However, the sewers there can turn even the hardiest stomachs, and the throbbing of discos from Wednesday to Sunday can also be a nuisance. If you're **camping**, go to the national park: you may have to pay entry fees (see p.223) to use the site inside the gate, but it's worth a try.

> ### Roadside rip-offs
>
> If you're driving, beware of any likely-looking individuals around Nakuru telling you there's anything wrong with your car – this is the **con-mechanic capital of Kenya**. Tricksters hang around along the roadside either between the eastern suburb of Lanet and Nakuru town centre or between the town centre and the national park main gate, and have also been seen along the road to Eldoret. They work in teams, pointing one after another at your wheels as you drive past or, if you stop anywhere, "discovering" oil dripping from your engine – anything to get you into their garage for a bogus repair job.

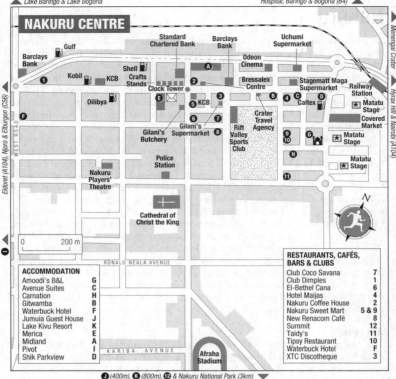

NAKURU CENTRE

Eldoret (A104), Njoro & Elburgon (C56)

THE RIFT VALLEY | Nakuru

0 — 200 m

RONALD NEALA AVENUE

KARIBA AVENUE

ACCOMMODATION

Amoodi's B&L	G
Avenue Suites	C
Carnation	H
Gitwamba	B
Waterbuck Hotel	F
Jumuia Guest House	J
Lake Kivu Resort	K
Merica	E
Midland	A
Pivot	I
Shik Parkview	D

RESTAURANTS, CAFÉS, BARS & CLUBS

Club Coco Savana	7
Club Dimples	1
El-Bethel Cana	6
Hotel Maijas	4
Nakuru Coffee House	2
Nakuru Sweet Mart	5 & 9
New Renacom Café	8
Summit	12
Taidy's	11
Tipsy's Restaurant	10
Waterbuck Hotel	F
XTC Discotheque	3

J (400m), **K** (800m), **12** & Nakuru National Park (3km) ▼

www.roughguides.com

220

Amoodi's B&L Nehru Rd ☎051/41939 or 0721/681596. A no-frills B&L with excellent security, plenty of hot water, clean toilets and the cheapest twin beds in town, in shoebox rooms. Cramped but okay, with towels and nets. **1**

Avenue Suites Kenyatta Ave ☎051/2210607, @avenuesuiteshotel@yahoo.co.uk. Opened in 2007, this has more than sixty rooms, all with nets, TVs and reasonable bathrooms, and most with balconies and views down over Nakuru's main street, and accessed by fast lifts. Good value. BB **3**

Carnation Mosque Rd, 1st floor ☎051/2215360. Although music is piped to every room, you can turn it off and this is a well-run and attentive establishment with a good restaurant, though the showers are old-style. Beware, however, of the travel companies and would-be operators who hang out here. BB **2**

Gitwamba Gusii Rd ☎020/2439270. One of the best joints in this quarter of town, with light and spacious s/c rooms with nets and TV, good cheap breakfasts and a matatu stage opposite. Very good

value, but can be raucous on disco nights – Wed and weekends. **1**

Jumuia Guest House 900m down Stadium Rd towards the park, on the right ☎051/2213477, @www.resortjumuia.com. This National Christian Council of Kenya hotel isn't bad – clean, dull and secure – though overpriced. BB **4**

Lake Kivu Resort 1.5km from main park gate ☎0726/026894, @www.kivuretreat.com. Secure, fairly close to the park, good-value and negotiable. BB **2**

Merica Corner of Court Rd and Kenyatta Ave ☎051/2216013, @www.mericagrouphotels.com. Nearly one hundred large, bright rooms with nets, in a busy, town hotel built on the central-courtyard model, with a good restaurant, large pool and live music at the weekends. Internet Ksh2/min. Rates highly negotiable. BB **5**

Midland GK Kamau Highway ☎051/2212125, @midlandhotel11977@yahoo.com. Terminally dull, 50s-style-institutional Nakuru landmark, but adequate for a comfortable night. The attached bar-restaurant is lively enough, but the food isn't great. Rooms with nets and TV (though the tubs prove more reliable than the showers), at very negotiable rates. BB **⑤**

Nakuru Backpackers' Hostel Mburu Gichua Rd ⓣ0716/705149 or 0721/543406, ⓦwww .nakurubackpackershostel.webs.com. Centrally located, clean, new hostel that seems determined to succeed. Dorm beds with nets Ksh800.

Pivot Lower Factory Rd ⓣ051/2217088, ⓔpivothotel@gmail.com. Despite an uncanny resemblance to a military hospital, this is recommended: the seventy rooms are clean and they all have nets, though no instant showers. Choosing one of rooms #1–15 will lessen the deafening disco din on some weekend nights. BB **②**

Shik Parkview Kenyatta Ave ⓣ051/2212345 or 2212346. Straightforward B&L, with reasonably airy s/c and non s/c rooms, on the small side, and without nets, but very clean. Hot water comes from a wood boiler on the roof terrace, from where you get great views of downtown Nakuru. There's good security and a very busy restaurant. **①**

Waterbuck West Rd ⓣ051/2215672, ⓔwaterbuck @waterbuck.co.ke. The *Waterbuck* is a bit of an oddity, its garish reception area with Maasai maiden statues trumpeting rooms that turn out to be plain, well-kept and clean, with nets, TVs and decent bathrooms (if uncertain hot water). Lively swimming pool and friendly bar area, often full of Kenyan families at weekends. Safe parking. BB **④**

The Town

Nakuru is Kenya's fourth largest city (though it projects a noticeably busier and more energetic image than Kisumu, the third), and capital of the enormous, sprawling Rift Valley Province that stretches from the Sudanese border to the slopes of Kilimanjaro. Still largely a workaday farmers' town, with unadorned old seed shops and veterinary paraphernalia much in evidence on the main street, Nakuru is a little Nairobi without the flashy veneer, its streets frequently undergoing ear-shattering repairs. The town can appear intimidating at first, and most visitors on their way to the national park stay in one of the lodges there. Still, Nakuru has some positive aspects: the **market** is animated and a pleasure to look around (though it, too, has its fair share of hassle), and there's a glimmer of charm remaining in the colonnaded old streets and jacaranda-lined avenues at the edge of town.

Eating and drinking

Finding good **meals** isn't that easy in Nakuru. As a guide, the older, more down-at-heel establishments are bunched towards the east end of town near the train station, while the west end, especially along Kenyatta Avenue, tends to be more upmarket. For a **drink**, especially on Saturday nights, the bar at the *Waterbuck* is a lively place to be.

El-Bethel Cana Meeting Place Moi Rd. Good standby for rice, stews and cold sodas. Pleasant, outside seating area.

Hotel Maijas Gusii Rd, next to *Ribbons* (6am–8pm). Very popular breakfast and lunch spot, with lots of fish and chicken dishes, and pilau rice only Ksh100. Chips and salad Ksh50.

Nakuru Coffee House Moi Rd. Good venue for real coffee and tasty pastries.

Nakuru Sweet Mart Gusii Rd. Long-established Indian for massive vegetarian *dhals*, great *bhajias, masala tea* and a good range of breads. Very cheap, and highly caloric. A sister *Sweet Mart*, in Moi Rd, opposite Gilani's butchery is more of a café, with pastries and coffee.

New Renacom Café Government Rd. Laid-back and friendly bar/café with outdoor seating, serving good curries, steaks and grilled fish.

Ribbons Cafe Gusii Rd. Good first-floor terrace snack bar, with a stripey pink and white exterior, overlooking the commotion below.

Summit Resort Near the national park main gate, Lake Rd. A few minutes' drive from town, this is a large, friendly, mostly open-air complex, with a dance floor and large swimming pool. Several different dining areas serve excellent *nyama choma* and grills.

Tipsy Restaurant Gusii Rd. A cheaper option than *Nakuru Sweet Mart*, but with smaller portions.

Waterbuck West Rd. A good all-day snack menu – samosas, burgers and soups.

Taidy's Corner of Oginga Odinga Ave and Gusii Rd. Popular open-air terrace bar and grill, overlooking a busy corner.

Moving on from Nakuru

Apart from the three-times-weekly **trains** to **Kisumu** (Tues, Thurs, Sat; around 1am) and **Nairobi** (Wed, Fri, Mon; around 5am; see p.44), the **bus** lines all run regular and frequent services to **Naivasha** and **Nairobi**, as well as **Eldoret**, **Kisumu**, **Kitale**, **Kisii** and other points west (Akamba is the best; ☎051/2213775 or 020/3500982). Alternatively, you can take the quieter road west, through the highland towns of **Njoro**, **Elburgon** and **Molo**, a route covered on p.228. Southwards, you can get to **Narok** (for the **Maasai Mara**) by **matatu** up the fantastic Mau escarpment (allow a day to arrive). A string of matatus run daily to **Marigat** at **Lake Baringo**, and matatus also make the run to **Kabarnet** in the hills to the west.

Lastly, there's also a lavishly scenic route to **Nyahururu** through the **Subukia Valley**, an ascent of the Rift that, for sheer grandeur, comes close to the Naivasha escarpment (daily matatu runs). If you're driving this, note that the turn-off 2.5km along the Nairobi road is not signposted – turn left at the Shell petrol station by *Kunste Hotel*.

Nightlife and entertainment

Surprisingly, Nakuru is jumping when it comes to **nightlife**. Try *Club Dimples* or *Club Coco Savana* on Club Road. One of the best places is the *Summit* (see p.221), packed out at the weekends with patrons of all ages getting down to Western and Kenyan pop and golden oldies. Also worth investigating is the glitzy *XTC Disco*. If you're in town for more than a day, you may get the chance to see the Nakuru Players in action at their dour-looking **theatre** (☎051/40805) on Kipchoge Avenue.

Listings

Banks Scattered all over Nakuru, most of them with ATMs.

Clinic Nakuru Medical Clinics, by Barclays on Kenyatta Ave (☎051/214655) has a range of specialists.

Internet access There are two internet cafes in the Bressalex Centre on Kenyatta Ave (both closed Sun). Telephone and fax facilities available also.

Market The main produce market, near the transport parks and railway station, has the full display of fruit and vegetables, but watch out for pickpockets and petty thieves.

Pharmacy Medika Chemists, 1st floor, Equator House, Kenyatta Lane (☎051/214847), next to Uchumi.

Supermarkets The best supermarkets in town are the main Uchumi on Kenyatta Lane, just off GK Kamau Highway (Mon–Sat 9.30am–8pm, Sun 9.30am–2pm) and Stagematt Mega on Kenyatta Avenue (same hours). A smaller grocery is Gilani's on Club Road, while Gilani's Butchery on Moi Road has a good cheese counter.

Travel agents Crater Travel, Inder Singh Building, just off Kenyatta Ave (☎051/2215019 or 051/2214896), offers a full service for air ticketing, plus the usual range of tour and safari deals.

Around Nakuru

Though not large, **Lake Nakuru** is a beautiful park, the terra firma mostly under light acacia forest, well provided with tracks to a variety of hides and lookouts. It's also one of the easiest parks to visit, with or without a vehicle, and the contrast and apparent dislocation between the shallow soda lake, with its primeval birds, and the animated woodlands all about give it a very distinctive appeal. The easy-to-follow topography means you really can't get lost and it's a pleasure to drive around, which takes about three hours.

Rising directly behind Nakuru town is the extinct volcanic giant **Menengai**, its sloping mass somehow not especially noticeable from the town. Another easy target is **Hyrax Hill**, a human settlement site for at least three thousand years, with finds dating from the Neolithic period immediately before the modern era.

Lake Nakuru National Park

With more than 300,000 visitors each year, **Lake Nakuru National Park** (ⓦ www.kws.org/nakuru.html; $60; smartcard, see p.61) is one of the Kenya Wildlife Service's two "premier parks", the other being Amboseli. The park has three gates: Main Gate, Lanet and Nderit. **Main Gate**, the point of issue for smartcards, is on the southern edge of Nakuru town, and is the location of the park headquarters, together with a large shop and the main campsite. Entering through **Lanet Gate**, on the northeast side of the park, gives the most direct access from Naivasha or Nairobi to the park's two **lodges**, and allows you to avoid the congestion of Nakuru town. The 1500-metre dirt road to Lanet Gate starts opposite the *Stem Hotel*: if you're coming from Naivasha heading towards Nakuru and you cross the railway bridge, you've overshot. **Nderit Gate**, in the southeast corner, would be useful only if you were driving cross-country from Lake Naivasha or over the Mau escarpment from Narok.

If you don't have a vehicle, the most straightforward way to see the park is **by taxi**, especially as some of the taxi drivers around Nakuru town know the park well. The *Midland Hotel* (see p.220) is as good a place as any to track one down. Reckon on some hard bargaining, then three hours at about $15 an hour, with park fees on top. An alternative – though not always a very practical one – is to **hitchhike** for a lift at the Main Gate, about an hour's walk from the town centre. The rangers are usually sympathetic, but you should expect to spend the night in the park once you get a ride, so be prepared for that.

Accommodation

The main campsite, known as **Njoro** or **Backpackers'** ($25 per person) is on a grassy site under fine old yellow acacias just inside the Main Gate. The meagre facilities – cold showers, unpleasant squat toilets and communal tap – are a let-down, yet the rates are so high because Lake Nakuru is one of KWS's top-league parks. If you can persuade the rangers you're a Kenya resident, the price is a modest Ksh300. Beware the audacious vervet monkeys and

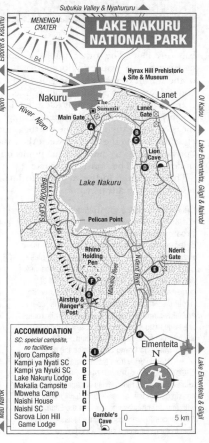

www.roughguides.com

223

▲ Flamingos and pelicans at Lake Nakuru

baboons here. The other public campsite is the somewhat elusive **Makalia campsite**, in a wonderful location at the southern tip of the park, on either side of the stream of the same name and close to a waterfall. Very few organized tours come down this way, but should you feel isolated, you may be reassured to know there's a ranger station fairly close by. There are also several "special campsites", notably **Kampi ya Nyati** (Buffalo Camp) and **Kampi ya Nyuki** (Bee Camp, the nicer of the two), both in the northeast part of the park. They're both located in clearings among the trees between the road and the open shore, and have splendid "private" access to quiet vantage points on the shore through driveable tunnels of undergrowth. The non-resident rate for these is $40 per person per night.

There's limited **lodge accommodation** in the park, and it's a good idea to reserve well in advance.

Lake Nakuru Lodge ⓣ051/850228 or 051/850518, ⓦwww.lakenakurulodge.com. On a wooded rise in the southeast corner of the park, based around an old Delamere Estate house in shady gardens, *Lake Nakuru Lodge's* main plus point is a good, large pool and uninterrupted views across the savanna with a distant glimpse of a corner of the lake. On the downside, most of the rather discordantly decorated *banda*-style rooms are fairly small and dark, though the family rooms are large, with big bathrooms. Casual pool visits $5. Internet access Ksh25 per min. FB ⑧

Mbweha Camp Just outside the park, a 15-min drive from Nderit Gate ⓣ020/4450035 or 0722/677449, ⓦwww.atua-enkop.com. Nine private cottages tucked among euphorbias, all made from local materials and with private verandas and views of the Eburru and Mau ranges. There's also a sunken lounge and bar area looking out onto a small waterhole, and a fantastic restaurant. A range of activities is on offer including bike rides, game drives, bush dinners and sundowners. Camping is available (Ksh500), with hot showers and bush toilets. FB ⑧

Naishi House Southwest part of the park; bookings through KWS ⓣ020/600800 ⓦwww.kws.go.ke. A popular and peaceful little country house surrounded by savanna, with a fully equipped kitchen and four bedrooms to suit a self-catering group of up to six (2 doubles in the main house, each with a large bed, and two singles in a separate annexe). A cleaner is on hand, firewood is provided and the generator is fired up from 6.30–10.30am. There's a good front terrace, and spotlights shine on a small water point at night. Expect to see zebras all the time, plus the local black rhino and the occasional lion. Ranger-guided game drives can be organized. Reservations advised. $200 for the whole house.

Sarova Lion Hill Game Lodge On the park's eastern slopes, high above the lake ⓣ051/850235 or

051/850212, ⓦ www.sarovahotels.com. Typically high Sarova standards, but the rooms, ranged along the hillside through the trees, while comfortable, are undistinguished, making this one of their less exciting lodges. The pairs of rooms, in grey block cottages, can be joined together for families. Each room has a large double plus a single bed, and good nets, but few other embellishments. Meals are excellent and slightly cheaper than at *Lake Nakuru Lodge*. Pool and sauna (small fee for casual visitors). FB $480.

Around the park

The **northern shores** of the lake are the most opened-up, with a busy route between the Main Gate and *Sarova Lion Hill Lodge*; the southern parts are usually empty. The vegetation in the north is mostly lightly wooded acacia forest and this area, close to Nakuru town, is the least interesting for wildlife.

Taken clockwise, the main park road runs through the woods, past *Lion Hill* and into an exotic-looking forest of candelabra **euphorbia** – great cactus-like trees up to 15m high. At the southern end of this zone you come into a spell of more open country, past the turning (left) up to *Lake Nakuru Lodge*, and one or two side tracks down to the mud and the lakeshore (right); then the road turns west into the southern park's dense acacia jungle. This is where you may see a **leopard** and – if they overcome their shyness – one of the park's forty-odd **black rhino**. Several kilometres further, the road opens again onto wider horizons with plenty of buffalo, waterbuck, impala and eland all around. You're likely to see one of the park's fifty **white rhino** here, looking for good grazing, and this is also the most likely area for seeing the park's introduced **Rothschild's giraffe** herd.

The **west shore**, especially "pelican point", has the best opportunities for seeing the **flamingos**, if they've returned (see box below). In places, the road

The mystery of the vanishing flamingos

Lake Nakuru has always been viewed as a flamingo lake par excellence. At one time, it was believed that up to two million **lesser flamingos** (maybe a third of the world's population) were massing in the warm alkaline water to feed on the abundant blue-green algae cultivated by their own droppings. In addition, the lake was also home to a small population of the much rarer **greater flamingo**, a species which tips its head upside down to use its beak to sift for small crustaceans and plankton.

Like Lake Elmenteita, Lake Nakuru has no outlet, meaning that its level fluctuates wildly. In 1962, it dried up almost completely, while in the late 1970s, increased rainfall lowered the lake's salinity and raised the water level. The flamingos began to disperse, some to lakes Elmenteita, Magadi and Natron (the latter in Tanzania), some up to Turkana, and the majority to Lake Bogoria. Since then, flamingos have been sporadically seen again in the surreal pink flocks that have become a photographic cliché. There are always hundreds, probably thousands, but the presence of mass flocks is unpredictable.

Over the last twenty years, large areas of forest in the lake's catchment area have been converted to small farms, and Nakuru town has industrialized and grown massively. Sewage and industrial pollution is believed to be a major factor behind the flamingos' decline, as are water diversion, soil erosion leading to siltation and even sand-harvesting along the Njoro River. The introduction in the 1960s of a hardy species of fish, *Tilapia grahami* – partly to control mosquitoes – has encouraged large flocks of **white pelicans** and it's likely that their presence is another disruptive element (a breeding colony of greater flamingos at Lake Elmenteita was forced off by the pelicans). The Nakuru Wildlife Trust has been studying the ecology of Rift Valley lakes since 1971 in an effort to find some of the answers, and the WWF now organizes educational trips to the park for local children, as well as running a scheme to monitor pollution from individual industries.

Lake Nakuru's wildlife

Fortunately, in view of the flamingos' here-today-gone-tomorrow caprice, there's a lot more to the lake's spectacle than the pink flocks. Its shores and surrounding woodlands are home to some four hundred other species of **birds** including, during the northern winter, many migratory European species. Towards the end of the dry season in March, the lake is often much smaller than the maps suggest and, consequently, water birds are a greater distance from the park roads.

There's a good number of **mammals** here as well. The lake isn't too briny for **hippos** – a herd of a dozen or more snort and splash by day and graze by night at the northern end. Nakuru has also become a popular venue for introduced species: there are **Rothschild's giraffe** from the wild herd near Kitale, and **lions** and secretive **leopards** from wherever they're causing a nuisance.

In the early 1990s, a number of **black rhinos** were relocated from Solio Game Ranch (see p.191), and ten **white rhinos** were donated by South Africa in 1994; the park now has one of the highest concentrations of rhino in the country. Electric fencing has been installed around the entire perimeter of the park – the only park in the country to be so enclosed – with the intention of maintaining a viable number of rhinos in a zone secure from poachers.

Nakuru is possibly Swahili for "place of the waterbuck", and the park is **waterbuck** heaven. With only a handful of lions and small numbers of leopards to check their population, the large, shaggy beasts number several thousand, and the herds (either bachelor groups or a buck and his harem) are large and exceptionally tame. **Impala**, too, are very numerous, though their lack of fear means you rarely witness the graceful flight of a herd vaulting through the bush.

The two other most often seen mammals are **buffalo** – which you'll repeatedly mistake for rhinos until you get a look through binoculars – and **warthog**, scuttling nervously in singles and family parties everywhere you look. Elephants are absent, but you're likely to see **zebra**, **dik-dik**, **ostrich** and **jackals** and, in the southern part of the park, **eland** and **Thomson's and Grant's gazelles**. More rarely you can encounter the odd **striped hyena** loping along the road in the eastern euphorbia forest at dawn, **reedbuck** down by the shore and **bushbuck** dashing briskly through the herbage. Along the eastern road, near *Lake Nakuru Lodge*, are several over-tame **baboon troops** to be wary of. The park is also renowned for its very large **pythons** – the patches of dense **woodland** in the southwest, between the lakeshore and the steep cliffs, are a favourite habitat.

Lastly, if you tire of the living spectacle, go looking for the **Lion Cave**, beneath Lion Hill ridge in the northeast; it's an excavated prehistoric rock shelter and rarely contains lions.

runs on what is virtually a causeway, past the lake's edge, with high cliffs rearing up behind. Finally, the main route leaves the shore and ploughs north, through thick forest with many tall trees and dense undergrowth, back to the Main Gate.

Good **vantage points** around the lake include the northern **mud flats** (follow established tracks across the dry surface); the dead tree **watchtower** (northeast); *Kampi ya Nyuki* and *Kampi ya Nyati* campsites; *Lake Nakuru Lodge*, for a general view across unobstructed savanna; and the high "**baboon cliffs**" in the west.

Menengai crater

Containing an enormous caldera, **Menengai crater** is 12km across and nearly 500m deep in places. From Nakuru town centre, it's an eight-kilometre hike to the crater rim. Allow three hours if you're walking. At weekends, you might be lucky and get a lift, but there's no public transport other than taxis.

If you walk, you're best advised to go up in a group as muggings are a possibility. To reach the crater, head up Menengai Drive and take the fourth left turn (Crater Climb) through the modestly affluent suburbs above the town. Some 4.5km up the hill is a telecommunications tower; head for this, then turn right, following the path through a fragrant forest of gum trees for twenty minutes, to a fire lookout tower on the bare cliff. From the top of this, the massive crater spreads out beneath you, a spectacular sea of bush-covered lava, its black waves frozen solid.

The crater was the site of a battle around 1854 in which the Ilpurko Maasai defeated the Ilaikipiak Maasai, whom they considered upstarts disrespectful to Batian, the *laibon* (paramount chief) of the time, after whom the highest peak of Mount Kenya was named. At intervals throughout the nineteenth century, these **Maasai civil wars** flared up over the issue of true Maasai identity. In this case, it was not simply a matter of honour but also of grazing rights in the Rift Valley, especially around Lake Naivasha and on the scarp slopes. The Ilpurko were herders, while the Ilaikipiak from the north grew crops as well. Both had been preparing for battle for some time and it is said that hundreds of Ilaikipiak *morani* were hurled over the crater rim to their deaths. The place retains a sinister reputation – even the normally fearless Maasai traditionally have it as the dwelling place of devils and evil spirits – and local people prefer not to go near the edge.

A century later, at the highest point of this windy crest, the Rotary Club erected a signpost. Apart from informing you that Nairobi is 140km away and Rome 2997km in the opposite direction, it also points out that the crater wall is 2272m above sea level and its area covers some 90 square kilometres – the whole dramatic extent of which you can see. You'll get fantastic views over Lake Nakuru if you walk down the dirt road along the south side of the gum-tree plantation.

Hyrax Hill

Named for the hyraxes that once scampered over this ancient tongue of lava, **Hyrax Hill** (daily 8am–6pm; Ksh500) is an easy target, 3.5km from the town centre, just off the Nairobi road on the north side. Matatus bound for Lanet and Gilgil will drop you at the turn, then it's a 600-metre walk to the small museum where you pay the fee.

The settlement site here was discovered by Louis Leakey in 1926 and excavated by Mary Leakey ten years later and by others between 1965 and 1987. An excellent guide published in 1983 is on sale in the museum. You can normally **camp** here, free or for a small fee (staff facilities only).

The Northeast Village

The path leading out to the right of the museum winds its way around the north side of the hill to an excavated pit dwelling or "sunken enclosure", with baulks left in place to show the depth of material that was removed during the digging. There are thirteen similar depressions in this "**Northeast Village**", but it's uncertain exactly how they were used. They have yielded a tremendous quantity of pottery shards, tools made from flakes of obsidian and animal-bone fragments. The absence of postholes normally needed to support a roof suggests they may have been shelters for livestock, but just as plausibly, a roof might have been added whenever needed, leaving no trace, and animals and people may have shared the shelters.

It's believed the inhabitants would have been semi-nomadic Sirikwa- or Nandi-speaking (Kalenjin) herders. Today, the Kalenjin mostly live further west, but they're associated with so-called pit-dwellings elsewhere (see p.245) and, in the case of Hyrax Hill, they may have been forced to flee by an expanding Maasai population from the north.

The fort and burial sites

Following the path towards the top of the hill, you come to an exposed "**fort**" facing out towards Nakuru, which consists of a circle of hefty boulders enclosing a flattened area. It may have been an Iron Age lookout post, but there's no way of being certain, or of knowing how old it might be, since no artefacts have been found. From here, you can scramble over the volcanic boulders to the summit, where you get a good view of the southern part of the site and the lake. Now several kilometres away, Lake Nakuru once extended, probably as fresh water, right to the base of the hill and across much of the Rift Valley, turning Hyrax Hill into a peninsula or even an island.

A hundred metres down the hillside in a fenced-in shelter, the massive stone slab which sealed a **Neolithic burial mound** has been removed to display part of a skull and some limb bones. The remains of a further nineteen Neolithic skeletons were discovered north of this, beneath a more recent Iron Age occupation area marked by the two stone circles (which were hut foundations). Nineteen Iron Age skeletons were also discovered, overlying the Neolithic graves, mostly of young men, possibly slain warriors, apparently buried unceremoniously or in a hurry, their skulls and limbs in tangled heaps. The coincidence of nineteen skeletons at each level may be just that – coincidence. Or perhaps the Iron Age survivors who buried their young men knew about the ancient Neolithic graves beneath.

Neolithic recreation

For a less dramatic, but more accessible, impression of life at Hyrax Hill, the **game of bau**, cut into the rock just before you get back to the museum, is a delightfully fresh record. *Bau* is the Bantu name for a game of skill and – depending on the rules used – amazing complexity that has been played all over Africa for a very long time. Two people play, moving pieces (cowries, seeds or pebbles) from one hole to another to win. There are a number of these "boards" around the hill; the one near the museum is a particularly good example.

West of Nakuru: out of the Rift Valley

West of Nakuru, the **A104** is a busy, often dangerous highway along which lorries, buses and matatus thunder at top speed over a surface which varies, unpredictably, from perfect to perfectly awful and which has been the subject of a massive re-surfacing and road-building operation in recent years. It's hair-raising if you're driving yourself or with a driver, and even more wearing on the nerves if you're travelling by public transport.

To head into Western Kenya, the **C56** is a scenic and much quieter alternative to the main highway. It climbs gently up to Njoro, Elburgon and Molo – in ascending order of altitude and size – before rejoining the Kisumu-bound fork of the main A104. If you're heading towards **Lake Baringo** in your own vehicle, you can avoid doubling back to Nakuru by heading north to the A104 from Molo and turning west towards Eldoret. After 5km, when you reach Makutano, take the surfaced road to the right, which goes through some wonderful mountain scenery via Eldama Ravine and Tenges, up to the C51 where you can turn right and join the B4 to the lake.

The Kalenjin peoples

The **Kalenjin** form the majority of the population in the central part of the Rift Valley. Their name, actually a recent adoption by a number of peoples speaking dialects of Nandi, means "I tell you". The principal Kalenjin are the Nandi, Terik, Tugen, Elgeyo, Elkony, Sabaot, Marakwet and Kipsigis, and, more contentiously, the Pokot. They were some of the earliest inhabitants of Kenya and probably absorbed the early bushmen or pygmy peoples who had already been here for 200–300,000 years.

Primarily **farmers**, the Kalenjin have often adapted their economies to local circumstances. The first Kalenjin were probably herdsmen whose lifestyle has changed over the centuries. The pastoral **Pokot** group, who still spurn all kinds of cultivation and despise peoples who rely on anything but livestock, call the **Marakwet**, living against the western Rift escarpment, *Cheblong* ("The Poor"), for their lack of cattle.

The **Okiek** are another interesting clue to the past. Hunter-gatherers, they live in scattered groups in the forests of the high slopes flanking the Rift, but unlike most hunter-gatherers, they do very little gathering. Meat and honey are the traditional staples. They consider wild fruits and vegetables barely palatable, though cornmeal and gardening have been introduced, and they now keep some domestic animals too. They may be the descendants of Kalenjin forebears who lost (or ate) their herds. There are other groups in Kenya who live mostly by hunting – Ndorobo or Wanderoo – for whom such a background is very likely, and who are all gradually abandoning their old lifestyles and dislikes in the inexorable advance of "civilization".

Many Kalenjin played key roles in the founding of the Kenya African Democratic Union (KADU – now disbanded), but the most famous of their number in recent years was Kenya's second president, Daniel Arap Moi, a **Tugen** from Baringo District. As he was from a small ethnic group, his presidency for years avoided the accusations of tribalism levelled so bitterly against Kenyatta. But Moi's firm grip on the reins of power was increasingly exercised through the Kalenjin-dominated civil service, rather than the more ethnically mixed cabinet. In 1992, when democratic elections first took place, there were **tribal clashes**, often coordinated from behind the scenes, with the "ethnic cleansing" of non-Kalenjin (usually Kikuyu incomers) from the Rift Valley by groups of surprisingly well-organized young men. The same story was repeated at election time in 1997, 2002 and 2007. For more background and detail see "History", p.564.

Njoro

The turn-off to the south to Njoro and the Mau escarpment is 5km west of Nakuru, and usually marked by a police roadblock. **NJORO** is the hometown of **Egerton University** (main campus 5km out of town on the main road to Narok), which has several other campuses scattered through the highlands. The jacaranda-fringed main road runs straight past the "centre" of town – a great acreage of mud (or, at best, dust), backed by a humble row of *dukas* and *hotelis*. Beyond the Narok junction, there's another and more soulful Njoro of wooden-colonnaded, tin-roofed, one-storey *dukas*. Here you'll also find a KCB bank and the Njoro Farmer's Petrol Station, a Shell garage. On the other side of town, past timber yards, is flat cereal country, with herds of dairy cattle and racehorses between the lines of gum trees and copses of acacia.

Further along the C56 to Elburgon, 18km from the A104/C56 junction west of Nakuru, is the excellent ≮ *Kembu Campsite and Cottages* (☎0722/361102, ⓦ www.kembu.com). The site is well signposted, 1.2km from the main road. Run by the Nightingale family, *Kembu* offers a variety of relaxing cottages, a delightful "Tree House" and an old wooden caravan, "Cobb's Carriage". Prices range from Ksh2000 for Cobb's (you have to use campsite ablutions) to Ksh8000 for a fully s/c cottage sleeping four, or you can camp (Ksh300). Three excellent meals a day will add Ksh1900 to your bill. Popular with overland groups, and with mountain bikes to rent, farm produce for sale and a convivial bar-restaurant and pizza oven ensuring regular company, this is a spot many people are happy to hang out at for days at a time. Kembu, incidentally, is Kikuyu for **chameleon**, and you can find little Van Hoehnell's chameleons all around the site.

An equally wonderful place to stay in this area, though more luxurious, and comfortable in every way, is the exquisitely chilled and magnificent ⌖ *Deloraine House* (☎051/343122 or 0722/870161, ⓦwww.offbeatsafaris.com; package including riding $600) a stately colonial pile built in 1920 on a vast estate beneath the **Mount Londiani forest**, just a few kilometres northwest of, but a million miles from, the straggling truck-stop of **Salgaa** (Rongai). *Deloraine's* long, shady terrace looks east across luxuriant borders and lawns and there's a large swimming pool, lovingly maintained stables with eighty horses, and a gentle Happy Valley atmosphere. The rooms are baronial and the meals delicious, copious and garden-fresh. It particularly appeals to **riders**, who often stay here as part of a safari with Offbeat; see p.365.

Elburgon, Molo and the Mau Forest

ELBURGON is a good deal bigger than Njoro, and higher up. You're into seriously muddy, conifer country up here, and the buildings, characteristically chalet-style, are built of dark, weathered planks. It's timber money that gives Elburgon a degree of commercial prosperity and can be the only reason for the massive investment in the *Hotel Eel* (☎020/2052195; ❷), the centre of gravity for local entertainments, on the east side of town. On offer here are reasonable s/c rooms without nets, secure parking, and a disco at weekends.

West of Elburgon, the road winds and dips through patches of Mau forest for several kilometres, with glimpses of railway viaducts across the valleys, until it emerges, still higher up, among the cereals and pyrethrum fields at **MOLO**. Molo straggles for several kilometres down into a broad valley across the rail tracks and up the other side on to Mau Summit Road, where you find a post office, banks and several petrol stations. Just over 3km west of the last fuel stop, the *Highlands Hotel* (☎0722/501267; ❷) is extremely quiet, the gardens well looked after and very pretty, but the huge, wood-floored rooms with fireplaces (s/c, no nets) are long overdue for a major refit. There's a bar and dining room, where lamb with baked potatoes is the speciality (Ksh500, but give them plenty of notice).

South of Molo, up into the **Mau forest**, a graded road runs to **Keringet**, where the huge old estate, once owned by Italians, is gradually crumbling, and on to **Olenguerone**. From here, the road tunnels eerily through a forest of huge gum trees, to Bomet (see p.360). There are several daily matatu runs along this route from Molo. The Kenya Wildlife Service has been trying for years to open up the mountain forest, like the Aberdare National Park, but there is stubborn resistance, not least from the forest's indigenous Okiek (Dorobo) hunter-gatherers, as well as from the loggers. There's more background on this area, on p.566.

Kipkelion Monastery

The **Our Lady of Victoria Abbey** is a Cistercian monastery between **Londiani** and **Kipkelion**, in an area formerly known by the Maasai as "Lumbwa", though Kipkelion ("Kif-*kel*-ion") is the original and much-preferred Kipsigis name. Founded in 1956, this is the only Cistercian monastery in Kenya and, deep in this rural hill country, the tall cement-block church is a remarkable sight. The monks make a living from their dairy herd and chickens, and run the only hospital in the area and an important school.

Our Lady of Victoria began as a Trappist monastery, with the silence the reformist order stipulates, but later reverted to the rather less stringent code of the older Cistercian order. The brothers still talk only when necessary, but they are happy to receive visitors. If you like the idea of silence and contemplation in a harmonious rural setting, write to let them know you're coming (PO Box 40 Kipkelion). You should obviously leave an appropriate donation.

The monastery is 11km up a rough track – signposted "Monastery Hospital" – from the small centre of **Baisheli** on the C35 (15km west of Londiani), and the track is rough, narrow and steep in parts, winding through intensively cultivated Kipsigis *shambas*. Only one or two matatus service this route. If you're approaching from the west, the easiest route to the monastery is via **Kipkelion railway station**, signposted off the main B1 highway, 25km east of Kericho. From the station, you have a rocky, three-kilometre climb; then, turning right onto the C35, a further 6km takes you to the track, left, up to the abbey.

The northern Rift Valley

North of Nakuru, the Rift Valley drops away gently and, as the road descends, so temperatures rise, the landscape dries and human population becomes sparser. Not far from Nakuru or Nairobi, and not necessarily a difficult journey, this region has a bright, harsh beauty, quite different from the central Rift. Its **lakes**, Bogoria and Baringo, both make alluring targets. This region also offers three possible routes up to Lake Turkana (see p.504), two of them joining with the Kitale–Lodwar road west of the lake, and the third curving up to Maralal for the east side. Although public transport is virtually nonexistent and the roads pretty rough, the **Kerio Valley** route (see p.241) deserves a special recommendation if you're visiting the west side of Turkana.

Lake Bogoria National Reserve

One of the least-visited lakes in the Rift Valley, despite being a globally recognized Ramsar wetlands site since 2002, **Lake Bogoria** (Chief warden's mobile ☏0720/317760; Ksh2000) is a sliver of saline water – unbelievably foul-tasting – entrenched beneath towering hills, 60km north of Nakuru. With the increasing pollution of Lake Nakuru, Lake Bogoria has become the adopted feeding ground of tens (at times hundreds) of thousands of **lesser flamingos**. The lakeshore is one of the few places where **greater kudu** antelope can easily be seen. The chief warden William Kimosop is a local authority on birds and, with prior arrangement, may be able to accompany you into the reserve. But the reserve is worth visiting as much for its physical spectacle as for the wildlife. It's largely a barren, baking wilderness of scrub and rocks, from which a series of furious **hot springs** erupts on the western shore, and the bleak walls of the Siracho range rise from the east.

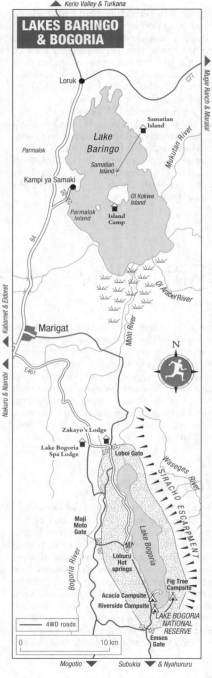

LAKES BARINGO & BOGORIA

Kerio Valley & Turkana

Loruk

Lake Baringo

Parmalok

Samatian Island

Samatian Island

Mukutan River

Kampi ya Samaki

Ol Kokwe Island

Parmalok Island

Island Camp

Ol Arabel River

Molo River

Marigat

N

Zakayo's Lodge

Lake Bogoria Spa Lodge

Loboi Gate

Waseges River

SIRACHO ESCARPMENT

Maji Moto Gate

Lake Bogoria

Loburu Hot springs

Fig Tree Campsite

Bogoria River

Acacia Campsite

Riverside Campsite

LAKE BOGORIA NATIONAL RESERVE

Emsos Gate

4WD roads

0   10 km

Mogotio   Subukia   & Nyahururu

Mugie Ranch & Maralai

C77

Kabarnet & Eldoret

Nakuru & Nairobi

B4

E461

Fortunately, the rigour of the landscape is relieved by three superb, shady **campsites** at the southern end of the lake (Ksh500), though they're difficult to get to unless you have 4WD. There are also a few **accommodation** options just outside the reserve's main Loboi Gate in the north. While you are allowed into the reserve on foot or by bicycle, in theory this is only permitted from Loboi as far as the Loburu hot springs, but exceptions may be made (and perhaps a ranger provided, for a fee) if you're heading for one of the three campsites.

Routes to the lake

The **B4** road north from Nakuru skirts to the west of Lake Bogoria by a margin of 20km and carries little traffic; tortoises in the road present the greatest hazard to motorists. The reserve is signposted to the right, 36km from Nakuru at **Mogotio** (fill up on petrol here), from where a good *murram* road, easily motorable in the dry season, cuts across to the lake. Some 23km from this junction, shortly after **Mugurin** (see p.235), you fork left for the western **Maji Moto Gate** (an incredibly rough 17km further, bringing you to the hot springs and tarmac lakeshore road), or right/straight ahead for the southern **Emsos Gate** (an equally rough 13km), which brings you to the wooded part of the reserve from where a further rough track leads to the springs. You'll need 4WD beyond Mugurin; there's no public transport.

It's easier and quicker, to continue northwards up the B4 to the signposted junction a few kilometres before **Marigat** (see p.236). From here, a fast tarmac road, the E461, takes you straight to the **Loboi Gate**, (20km further). There are infrequent matatus from Marigat to Loboi Gate, but if you're staying at Lake Baringo you might try to arrange a lift from there as most vehicles visiting Bogoria come from Lake Baringo.

The case of the Endorois

The **Endorois** are a small tribe of Kalenjin pastoralists, closely related to the **Tugen**. They used to range over a large area around Lake Bogoria, but were evicted from the narrow shores of the lake when the **reserve** was created in 1974 (ⓦtinyurl.com/ybezkjt). Although they lost little of their traditional grazing lands within the reserve's narrow confines, what they did lose was precious and fertile, along the wooded southern shore, where several streams provided valuable **fresh water**, and at Loboi in the north, where the ill-conceived spa-hotel owned by the family of former president Daniel Arap Moi expropriated the warm springs. They also lost valuable **honey** and sources of **herbal medicine**. Like every one of Kenya's indigenous groups, they have valid claims, and their four percent share of the gate receipts is pitifully low – especially since Bogoria rarely figures on safari itineraries. Inspired community leadership has seen them pursue restitution of their lands and compensation as far as the African Union's Commission on Human and Peoples' Rights. The case is ongoing.

For **accommodation** in the area there's, *Lake Bogoria Spa Resort* (ⓣ051/2216687 or 0710/445627, ⓦwww.lbogoriasparesort.com; BB ❺), 3km before Loboi Gate. Tasteless and not quite functional enough (a/c, nets but no proper showers in the main-block rooms), with the slightly better appointed and larger cottage rooms the same price, this is an ordinary town hotel stranded in the bush. If you have a tent, you can camp near the swimming pool for a negotiable Ksh1000, using the pool facilities. The best feature could be the naturally replenished **thermal spring pool**, always a steady 37°C; but it's not quite clean enough, and the whole facility is too poorly maintained, to be tempting.

Of one or two basic alternatives, *Zakayo's Lodge* (ⓣ0724/081876; ❷) in Loboi village, about 500m from the gate, is a barely adequate fallback if you have no choice, with safe parking, electric sockets (but no guarantee of power) and doubtful hot water. Alternatively, you could camp at Loboi Gate, next to the Environmental Education Centre, just outside the reserve. There's usually water here but you'll need your own stove or firewood and supplies.

The cross-country route to Lake Bogoria

If you have a 4WD vehicle or are into hiking or mountain biking, you might like to approach the Emsos Gate from the southeast, initially using the B5 tarmac route between Nakuru and Nyahururu. Along the way there are several turnings northwest towards the lake. If you don't have your own transport, the tarmac portions of this trip can be made by bus or matatu (there are several daily runs between Nyahururu and Nakuru via **Subukia**), but you'll have to **hike** the rest of the way down to Bogoria – a good two days. Aside from the pleasure of tackling roads used by very few tourists, this route gives you a special feel for the Rift Valley's striking topography as it drops from one monumental block of land to another, with dramatic changes of climate and scenery. When you reach the plain at the bottom, you get an indelible impression of the way the earth has split apart and sunk to form the Rift over the last twenty million years.

Coming from Nakuru, it's a 14km trip past Menengai crater to **Mairu Kumi** ("Ten Miles"), where the road divides. The left fork (unsignposted) leads, after 14km of rough *murram*, to the **police post** at Solai (see overleaf), while the right fork continues on tarmac to Subukia and Nyahururu. Beyond the fork, you enter a steep, hilly landscape of Kikuyu *shambas*, increasingly interspersed with plots of tea bushes and pyrethrum.

Coming from Nyahururu, the target is also the Solai police post. The early part of the route is stunning. It falls in a series of breathtaking steps over the fault lines until it reaches a high scarp above Subukia, where it hairpins its way steeply down to the valley. Descending from the cool highlands around Nyahururu, you start to feel the heat building up. Fields of sugar cane and bananas seem to grow before your eyes in the hothouse atmosphere and the earth takes on a rich, redolent smell.

The police post at **Solai** is served rather infrequently by direct matatus from Nakuru, but a better bet for getting there from Nakuru (or from Nyahururu or Subukia) is to take a matatu to Mairu Kumi and another one from there.

The Subukia Valley and Lake Solai

The **Subukia Valley** was the Maasai's "Beautiful Place" (Ol Momoi Sidai) and its lush pastures were their insurance against the failure of the grass up on the Laikipia plateau. But they were evicted in 1911 to the "Maasai Reserve" and the way was clear for the **settler families**. It's easy to see why the Europeans chose this high valley because, despite its isolation, it has a soft, arcadian beauty far removed from the windy plateaus above or the austere furnace of the Rift Valley floor below.

The village of **SUBUKIA**, just 4km north of the equator, has a scattering of *hotelis* and *dukas*, and a filling station. Simple lodgings are available at the friendly *Malindi Hotel* at the southern end of the village (☎0734/980423; ●), and beer and *nyama choma* at *Uncle's Pub* next door. Buses and matatus stop near the T-junction where the Subukia Valley road meets the B5, and there's regular transport to Nakuru and Nyahururu.

If you have your own transport and two or three hours to spare, or a couple of days to walk it, you can take a major **diversion** up the Subukia Valley to **Bogoini**, then turn west and cut back south again, past Lake Solai (about 45km in total). From the grubby junction at Subukia village where the main road passes, head north about 700m to an old T-junction, with roads to Nakuru (left) and Lower Subukia (right), then take the latter. The track, consisting of rough dirt and rocks, is easy to follow, but sources of food along the way are negligible, so you must be self-sufficient, and transport is sparse, with only four matatus daily between Subukia and Bogoini. Matatus between Bogoini and Mairu Kumi via Solai are slightly more frequent, but you may still have to wait hours. Travel between Subukia and Bogoini is also possible by *boda-boda*.

Little **Lake Solai** is a curiously isolated soda lake with a reedy shoreline grazed by cattle and a scattering of sisal plots. For many years it was a seasonal lake, but it has been a permanent feature of the landscape since the early 1980s. South of Lake Solai, the road climbs through scattered euphorbia and acacias to the junction (hard right) at **Solai police post**. Lines of jacaranda streak the scenery at intervals all over this district, bordering old driveways – evidence of the erstwhile community of white settlers.

Down to the Emsos Gate and Bogoria

The most **direct route** from Subukia village to Lake Bogoria begins by climbing 4km out of the valley on the tarmac to Nakuru. An unsignposted right turn (or left if you've just come from Nakuru) goes over the hill past the curious **St Peter's** church – a quaint Anglican church that looks as if it just flew in from England – and then 15km down to the Solai police post. From here, the 50-kilometre route to Bogoria is rough in many places, though normally negotiable in a 4WD, for which you should allow at least three hours. Matatus are sparse, though they do run. If you're on foot or bicycle and still want to do it, check your emergency water and food supplies, tighten your bootlaces – or check your brakes – and set off west.

The road descends steeply to the Solai Valley with its disused railway line, which you cross at a place called **Milton's Siding**. When you reach the tracks, follow the road, parallel to the tracks, to the right, for a kilometre, and then turn sharp left to cross them. The road descends in a series of steps to a broad, flat valley with a sharp, right-hand bend up the hill on the far side, which it crosses to reach **Kisanana** – life-saving *chai* and a place to stop for the night if necessary, though there's no formal accommodation.

From Kisanana, you turn left at the old signpost and follow decent *murram* tracks for some 5km to a fork around some buildings. Here you head left and are soon pitching up a diabolical slope – rarely used by motor vehicles and by all appearances dynamited out of solid bedrock – which winds up and over a scrub-covered **hog's back ridge** for some 7km, eventually twisting north and dropping to better red *murram*, interspersed with white, rocky stretches. You come to a crossroads (turn left), then after a few hundred metres a T-junction at a place of a few huts called **Mugurin** (turn right), where you may find a solitary *hoteli* open. From here, you're within the compass of the lake, with Emsos Gate some 25km away. The road descends steadily now as you travel north – there's only the odd signpost but no danger of taking a wrong turn. If in doubt, head right.

The reserve

Hidden in its deep bowl, **Lake Bogoria** – when approached from Mugurin – is only visible when you're almost on top of it. The final stretch of the track leading down to Emsos Gate is steep and rocky as well as being savagely beautiful, the landscape transformed into a strident dazzle of red and blue and splashes of green. The lake itself, a glistening pool of soapy blue and white, usually has a mirage of pink flamingos tinting its shores.

While the Bogoria Reserve **paved road** between the Loboi Gate and the Loburu hot springs is in good condition, the **east shore road** has been quite impassable for years, owing to a huge rock fall coupled with higher water levels, so there is no circuit round the lake. If you're driving northwest from Emsos Gate, there's a river bed to negotiate before you reach the tarmac, for which 4WD is essential. It may be best to take a ranger who knows the road: ask at the gate.

The three public campsites at the southern end of the lake, *Acacia*, *Riverside* and *Fig Tree* (all Ksh500), are accessible only by 4WD or, if you get permission, on foot. The furthest, **Fig Tree Campsite** (a 40min walk from Emsos Gate), is an absolute delight, unless your visit coincides with a fresh covering of vegetation after the rains, when squadrons of determined tsetse flies can ruin what is otherwise a verdant and picturesque scene. Enquire with the rangers about heading down further to the thickly wooded shore at the south end (they might provide an escort, for a fee), and also check with them about **food**; a few basics are usually available just outside Emsos Gate to eke out your rations. **Water** is not a problem – a permanent, miniature brook, clear and sweet, runs right through *Fig Tree campsite* and provides a natural spa. Less delightfully, the magnificent glade of giant fig trees that shades the site is a favourite haunt of baboons who gorge themselves day and night. In the fruiting season (Dec–Feb), be wary of camping directly beneath any concentrations of figs. Buffalo also graze near here and are not to be trifled with.

Fig Tree is something of a dead end and, if you're down here and don't have your own vehicle, you may be in for a long wait before someone turns up to give you a lift out. Your only option is to walk the 15km around to the hot springs on the western shore, passing *Riverside* and *Acacia Tree* campsites. *Riverside* is the most basic of the three campsites, without even a water source.

Wildlife, with the exception of the flamingos at the hot springs, makes itself scarce, most animals – including buffalo, hyena, klipspringer, impala, dik-dik, zebra, warthog and Grant's gazelle – preferring the remote and inaccessible eastern shore, though you may see **greater kudu** anywhere. The **flamingos**, for some curious reason – possibly chemical – tend to flock in their greatest numbers to the shallows opposite where the hot springs flow into the lake (they appear immune to the heat). The Bogoria **fish eagles** have made a gruesome adjustment to their fierce, fishless environment: they prey on flamingos. Other birds to look out for include avocets, transitory pelicans and migratory steppe eagles.

The Loburu hot springs

However you enter the reserve, you're bound to want to see the **hot springs**, a series of boiling water spouts on the shore. Although they hardly touch Yellowstone or Rotorua standards, "hot springs" is a tame appellation for this very impressive, terrifying, and photogenic, phenomenon. Depending on the lake level one or more of the springs may break the surface of the lake (while the others show their presence by the agitated green water above them, some steam and a strong smell), or they all may all be visible on the shore.

With normal water levels, the springs burst up from huge natural cauldrons of super-heated water not far below the ground and drain into steaming rivulets that cut through the crusty earth, continuously collapsing and reforming their courses down to the lake. Even at midday, when the sun glares like a furnace, clouds of steam drift across this infernal scene. Near the lakeshore, the macabre bleached skeletons of flamingos lie strewn in the sand and, in the background, the dull thundering of the springs fills the air. It's like some water garden in Hell.

There's a **drinks kiosk** at the springs, but no food. Picnickers sometimes think it's fun to boil eggs and heat tins of food in the pools, but the consequences of a fall can be messy and even fatal: over the years a number of people have slipped and died as a result. An *askari* has now been posted to watch out for visitors, but if you scald yourself, help might still be a long time coming.

Lake Baringo

At one time a barely accessible retreat favoured by just a few weekenders, **Lake Baringo**, an internationally recognized Ramsar wetlands site since 2002, is well connected from Nakuru and Eldoret, and has more than a handful of places to stay. The lake remains a peaceful oasis in the dry-thorn country, rich in **birdlife** and with a captivating character entirely its own. The waters are heavily silted with the red topsoil of the region, and they run through a whole range of colours every day from yellow to coral to purple, according to the sun's position and the state of the sky. On the lakeshore are villages inhabited by the **Il Chamus** (Njemps) people, who live by an unusual mixture of fishing and livestock-herding, breaking the taboo on the eating of fish, which is the norm among pastoralists. Speaking a dialect of Maa – the Maasai language – these fishermen paddle out in half-submerged dinghies made from the spongy and buoyant saplings of the fibrous *ambatch* tree that grows in profusion around the lake.

Practicalities

Most matatus from Nakuru come up only as far as the small district town of **Marigat**. This ought to be the hub of the Baringo–Bogoria tourist circuit, but it's a bland, dust-blown little place. There's a KCB with **ATM** (but no Barclay's) and, among the tin shacks, an impressive bright green and white **mosque** funded by a wealthy Saudi, with two tiers of large windows and a capacity that obviously exceeds

Moving on from Baringo

If you're travelling **via Marigat**, get up early for the matatu into town, from where there are plenty of onward vehicles to Nakuru or Kabarnet. A matatu direct to Nakuru leaves Kampi ya Samaki around 6am.

Travelling **north of Baringo** is a hit-or-miss affair without your own wheels: there's no public transport either to Maralal or to Tot or Lodwar from here, so try to arrange something with mobile tourists. If you're **driving**, note that there is **fuel** at Marigat and sometimes at Kampi Ya Samaki, but none after that until Maralal or Archer's Post. The highly recommended and not too rough road from Lake Baringo to **Maralal** (one day) or the rougher continuation to **Samburu National Reserve** (best done over two days) are only really viable with your own vehicle – there's effectively no public transport on these routes. The Maralal route starts by swinging north from the shore of Lake Baringo, leaving tarmac and tourism behind, and taking you up into the rugged country of the Lerochi plateau, dotted with Tugen and Pokot settlements. When the air is clear, there are stunning views back over Baringo. After two to three hours, you join the Rumuruti–Maralal *murram* road at Mugie Ranch (see p.183), then go north as far as Kisima, where you choose between a short journey onwards to Maralal or some inspiring but wheel-shattering driving along the C78/79 east to Archer's Post and Samburu (see p.513).

the area's Muslim population. There are a couple of B&Ls on the main street, close to the junction with the highway, of are which *Dadina* (☎0735/359351; ❶) is reasonably well kept, with self-contained singles or non-self-contained doubles.

Just a few matatus come all the way to the lakeside village, and de facto capital of Lake Baringo, **KAMPI YA SAMAKI** ("Fish Camp"). Kampi ya Samaki is 2km from the main road, past the council-run roadblock where you pay your curious daily **admission fee** (all above-board and receipted; Ksh200, children Ksh50, vehicles Ksh100). There are very few facilities in the scruffy little village itself; a small post office, but no bank and little in the way of shops. There's not a whole lot to do here, either, but it does have a small **reptile park** (daily 8am–6pm; Ksh200), signposted, near the *Island Camp* boat stage, where you can see some of the local snakes, lizards and tortoises at close range.

There's nowhere in the village that stands out for food and drink: the one real focus in the area is the Roberts' *Thirsty Goat Pub and Restaurant*. There's always a buzz here, with pizzas or goat curry around Ksh450 and beer and wine Ksh120.

Accommodation

All the following are in Kampi ya Samaki except *Samatian Island* and *Island Camp*.

Bahari Lodge Next to the post office ☎0726/857947. By far the best of the village B&Ls, warm and welcoming, with good food and decent, non-s/c rooms with electric sockets (upstairs ones are best, though the doubles are tiny and the shared toilets are squatters). This is the local drivers' favourite and there's a bar and *hoteli* as well. ❶

Island Camp On the southern tip of Ol Kokwe Island ☎0728/478638 or 0735/919878, ⓦ www .islandcamp.co.ke. Although not as luxurious as some tented camps, this has real atmosphere and loyal guests who return year after year. The location is superb, dense with birdlife, as well as numerous species of lizard. The 23, small, comfortable tents

have expansive views directly over the lake, which lulls you to sleep with its lapping just metres away. Boat trips, waterskiing, guided island walks and a good-sized if chilly pool are on offer, and the price includes boat transfer from their jetty at Kampi ya Samaki. ❽

Lake Baringo Club South of Kampi ya Samaki ☎053/51401, ⓦ www.kenyahotelsltd.com. Struggling to keep going, this former oasis dating from the 1960s is still pleasant and worth a visit, and occasionally hosts birding groups, but either of the island-based camps is infinitely better to stay at. The 48 plain, high-ceilinged, well-insulated rooms with ceiling fans and nets tend to be occupied by conference delegates rather than tourists. Hippos graze the lawns at night, under the watchful eyes of the club *askaris*. Pool Ksh200 (Ksh100 under-12s). FB ⑥

Roberts' Camp South of Kampi ya Samaki ☎0733/3207775, ⓦwww.robertscamp .com. Lovely campsite in a large, acacia-shaded garden dipping into the lake, with lots of space, good facilities and great birding. Most visitors camp (Ksh350), but there are four, very nice, non-s/c twin *bandas* with towels, soap, electricity, shared kitchen and bathrooms with hot water (Ksh1500 per person; Ksh500 5–12s), and four self-catering cottages which range from Ksh6500–9500 for four guests, depending on size and season, with extra guests Ksh1000 each. At the heart of the camp is the *Thirsty Goat* pub (see p.237). Book ahead.

Samatian Island ☎0722/207772, ⓦwww .samatianislandlodge.com. The lodge and the minuscule, private island are one and the same, with room for no more than about a dozen guests. Managed with casual efficiency by the young family who also look after *Roberts' Camp*, this is one of Kenya's very best and most relaxing lodges. Birds hop and flit everywhere, and in every direction you get fantastic, ever-changing lake views. Rooms (individual *bandas*) are very spacious and fully open-plan, with baths and showers set close to the lake and no windows or walls to block out the idyllic natural environment. The food is first-rate and there's an infinity pool. Homely yet cool, and effortlessly unfussy, it's hard to think of a better place to unwind – or honeymoon. Most activities included. Package $720.

Soi Safari Lodge Kampi ya Samaki ☎053/51242 or 0720/223853, ⓦwww. soisafarilodge-lkbaringo .com. The newest big place by the lake is one hotel too many for Baringo. The fifty rooms with a/c, nets and TV (but hot water evenings only) are airy but plain. There's no direct lakeshore access and the large pool is surrounded by about an acre of crazy paving. "Suswa Wing" rooms are nicer, with more of a lake view, but still it's hard to see why you would choose to stay. Pool Ksh200. FB ⑥

View Point Lodge On the way into the village on the left ☎0724/472785. Very basic and run-down B&L with slummy non-s/c single rooms at rock-bottom prices and bucket showers (warm water on request). Food can be ordered. A fallback. ❶

Weavers Lodge On the left, behind *Bahari* ☎0727/966362. Quite large s/c rooms with nets, but not as homely as the *Bahari* (and, equally, no instant showers) so overpriced at this level. TV bar in same compound. ❶

Around the lake

Lake Baringo is fresh water (Naivasha being the only other non-saline Rift Valley lake), so its fish support a wide variety of **birds** and there are also sizeable populations of crocodiles and hippos. Though you rarely see much more than ears and snout by day, **hippos** come ashore after dark to graze, and on a moonlit night

▲ Transport on Lake Baringo

Baringo's 458 species of **birds** are one of its biggest draws, and even if you don't know a superb starling from an ordinary one, the enthusiasm of others tends to be infectious. Former Baringo ornithologist Terry Stevenson holds the world record "bird-watch" for 24 hours – 342 species. Baringo's bird population rises and falls with the seasons (the dry season is the leanest time for birders), but the lakeshore resounds with birdsong (and frogs) at most times of year. It's surprisingly easy to get within close range of the birds – some species, such as the starlings and the white-bellied go-away bird, are positively brazen – so you'll find rapt amateur photographers lurking behind practically every bush. There are some interesting areas just south of *Lake Baringo Club*, where you should see some unusual species such as the white phase of the paradise flycatcher, grey-headed bush shrike, violet wood hoopoe and various kingfishers. Hippos commonly graze here, too, even in daylight hours. Wherever you're staying, an early-morning, birding boat trip along the lake's reedy shore is likely to be on offer, possibly in combination with a visit to the **Goliath Heronry** and one or two **hippo** and **croc** haunts. Afternoons can profitably be taken up on a trip out near the main road under some striking red cliffs, an utterly different habitat where, apart from hyraxes and baboons, you can see several species of hornbill, sometimes the massive nest of a hammerkop (wonderful-looking birds in flight, resembling miniature pterodactyls with their strange crests) and, with luck, the rare Verreaux's Eagle.

their presence can be unnervingly obvious, and even in pitch darkness they're too noisy to be ignored. Although it used to be commonly understood that Baringo **crocodiles** were too small to pose a danger to swimmers, what constitutes a dangerous size in a Nile crocodile is perhaps a reckless debate. A regular local swimmer was badly mauled in 2008 so swimming is certainly highly inadvisable.

Activities tend to centre around the more upmarket places to stay and include boat trips around the shores (Ksh5000/hr for up to seven people) and water-skiing (Ksh5000 per hr). Motorboats to Ol Kokwe Island (Ksh1000) leave on request from *Island Camp*'s jetty on the north side of Kampi ya Samaki. A small landing fee is normally payable unless you're staying or eating at *Island Camp*. The trips are always enjoyable, and many operators know their birds and most are old hands at luring fish eagles by tossing them fresh fish. Take your camera for spectacular close-ups as the eagles swoop down for the bait.

Community Boats and Excursions (☎0720/523874) opposite *Roberts' Camp*, offer similar prices, but if you charter one of their boats, make sure that life jackets are provided, and that no more than seven passengers are carried – should those conditions not be met, it's best not to take the excursion. Marina Boats (☎0728/724344), next to *View Point Lodge*, is an independent offshoot of Community Boats, and the same caveats apply. Baringo can get rough and the boats are rarely what you'd call seaworthy: in 2004, a number of people drowned when their boat capsized on the lake.

On dry land, **cultural visits** to a traditional Il Chamus compound (where you may feel obliged to buy decorated gourds and other crafts but at least your presence is not resented) and **bird walks** (see box above) are also available. In addition, most people hire a bike, and just do some gentle pottering: *Roberts' Camp* does **bike rental** for Ksh200 per hour or Ksh800 per day. *Roberts'* also do **Island Camp buffet lunch and pool trips** (Ksh1500 per person, for a minimum of two), which is a wonderful way to splurge a little if you're on a budget.

The new **Ruko Wildlife Conservancy** on the northern shore is still in its infancy, but with support from the Northern Rangelands Trust, *Samatian* and other local businesses, it is likely to consolidate in the next few years. At present based out of *Samatian* and using a small motorboat, you can do some basic exploratory bush walks in the area, in the company of Pokot and Il Chamus game scouts. You're likely to see warthog, ostrich, common (Grant's) zebra, waterbuck, impala, and possibly serval, and the numbers and variety of species will increase with planned KWS trans-locations in the next few years.

Kabarnet and the Kerio Valley

The journey between Lake Baringo and Kabarnet mirrors the exciting trip to Lake Bogoria down the eastern side of the Rift, covered on p.233. Frequent matatus from Marigat climb the first stage to **Kabarnet**, the road soaring and plunging through at times almost alpine scenery. From Kabarnet, matatus run to **Eldoret** across the hot and fascinating **Kerio Valley**. If you're using public transport, set off early.

KABARNET has a superb setting on the **Kamasia massif** – the slab also known as the Tugen Hills, which remained upstanding on the brink of the Kerio Valley when the rest of the area sank – and the road up the escarpment offers breathtaking views over the Rift Valley floor to Lake Baringo. But the town of Kabarnet itself is fairly featureless and dull. From a small nucleus of administration buildings and *dukas* on the hillside in colonial times, it has expanded in every direction since becoming capital of Baringo District, undoubtedly related to its status as former president Daniel Arap Moi's home town (he was born in Sacho, 30km away). But apart from its **post office**, banks with **ATMs** and a few **supermarkets**, Kabarnet's only point of interest is a small **museum** (daily 9.30am–6pm; Ksh500) featuring exhibits on human evolution, headdresses from around the country, and artefacts and homesteads of the Tugen, Pokot and Il Chamus peoples who inhabit the region, plus a small snake farm.

Standing above the town, the *Kabarnet Hotel* (℡053/22094; ❹) is quiet and a bit tatty, but is worth a visit for its pool, mountain views and above-average food. *New Hotel Sinkoro*, by the matatu stage (℡0733/785745; ❷), has safe parking, a bar and a passable restaurant, but it's not cheap for what you get.

Moving on from Kabarnet, you'll find buses to Nakuru and Eldoret, but none after 9am. Matatus serve Nakuru and Eldoret, and also Iten, Marigat, Tenges and occasionally even Loruk.

The Kerio Valley

The quickest and easiest route across the valley is the paved **C51**. The excitement of this route builds only after you leave Kabarnet and plunge into the **Kerio Valley**, a drop of 1000m in not much more than the same distance. There are magnificent views as the road rolls through **Chebloch**, with its old bridge over the Kerio River. The road then turns sharply up the **Tambach escarpment** on the western side of the Kerio Valley. A turn right just before the hamlet of **Biretwo** is the start of the lonely trans-valley route north to Tot (see p.241). Also before Biretwo, look out for the **Torok Falls**, looming high above and to your left at the top of the Tambach escarpment. They're worth a visit if you like waterfalls; count on a good half-day if you're hiking up.

Iten

After a few more hairpins and a spectacular viewpoint (with obligatory curio and drinks stall), the road finally levels out at **ITEN**, a busy little grass-verged market town on the rim of the escarpment. Iten is the main centre on this west side of the Kerio Valley, with fuel, a KCB bank with **ATM** and a small market (recognized for leather goods). Iten is also home to the remarkable **St Patrick's High School**, which must be the world's top school for runners, having produced middle-distance stars such as Peter Rono, Wilson Kipketer and Ibrahim Hussein, while its associated athletics camps have produced female runners such as Lydia Cheromei, Susan Chepkemei and Lornah Kiplagat. The phenomenon is one that sports scientists have yet to explain fully, but has a lot to do with climate, altitude and physiological factors, and seems particularly to involve the Nandi. The school is just after the main shops of Iten, on the road north to Kapsowar.

In terms of **accommodation in Iten**, the huge building on the south side of the main road, at the eastern end of town, houses, among many other businesses, the *Jumbo Hotel* (T053/42265; ❶), which has chaotic plumbing and dodgy electrics, but is basically okay and has a good **bar and restaurant**. You may even meet foreign athletes here: the *Jumbo* in Iten is an affordable place to base yourself for a few weeks of high-altitude training. If you're really more of an athlete than a tourist, you'll already know about Lornah Kiplagat's **High Altitude Training Camp** (HATC; T053/42278, Wwww.lornah.com; ❸) but if you'd simply like to stay in Iten and do some running and training, or just relax, it's open to all-comers. It's next to the district police headquarters. Another option lies 6km out on the Kabarnet road, signposted off the main road, just south of **Kessup** – the *Lelin Overland Campsite* (T0722/349859; camping Ksh600, *bandas* ❷), a friendly overlanders' place with magnificent views and the choice of camping or non-self-contained *bandas* with wood-fired hot showers. **Food** is available, though the menu isn't large and you need to pre-order. The fourth, and possibly best, accommodation option in the area is *Kerio View* (T020/2039559 or 0722/781916; ❺), a very cool bar-restaurant with cottages, with nets, and stunning views from the panoramic all-glass frontage of the main building. It's about 2.5km south of Iten, turning off the Eldoret road after 1.5km.

To Iten via Tenges and Kimwarer

An **alternative** trans-valley route to the C51 is the turn-off from the C51 east of Kabarnet, taking you south to **Tenges** on a surfaced road that twists spectacularly along the spine of the Tugen Hills, with lovely views across the valley. You'll find some public transport to Tenges from Kabarnet, but very little when you turn right, west, for Kimwarer down in the valley. Kimwarer is more easily reached via a better road that meets the C51 just west of Chebloch.

KIMWARER is a company town for the **fluorspar mine** at the head of the Kerio River (fluorspar – calcium fluoride – is used in the manufacture of steel, aluminium and cement). With nothing but bush, Kalenjin herders and the occasional party of honey-hunters round about, Kimwarer's tidy managerial villas and staff quarters come as a surprise. The nearest **accommodation** is on the west side of the Kerio River, at the very good value *Sego Safari Lodge* (go 2km west of the Kerio bridge, then turn left, south; T053/21399 or 0722/407470, Wwww .segosafarilodge.co.ke; ❸), which has self-contained cottages, a pool, restaurant and views of the escarpment. You can camp here, too (Ksh300).

North up the Kerio Valley

There's a dearth of public transport through the **Kerio Valley** off the main Kabarnet–Iten C51 road. The route north from Chebloch along the east side of **Lake Kamnarok National Reserve** is passable only by 4WD (forget it when it rains). The road from **Biretwo to Chesongoch** on the west side of the reserve has a good *murram* surface passable in an ordinary car; north of Chesongoch, it's very rough as far as Tot, but improves after that.

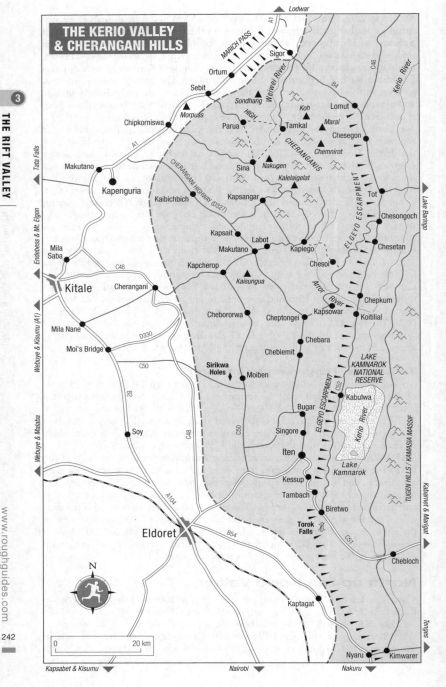

THE KERIO VALLEY & CHERANGANI HILLS

Lodwar

MARICH PASS

Sigor

Ortum

Sebit

Chipkorniswa

Morpuss

Sondhang

HIGH

Parua

Tamkal

Koh

Maral

Lomut

Chesegon

Chemnirot

CHERANGANIS

Sina

Nakugen

Kalelaigelat

Tot

Kaibichbich

Kapsangar

Chesongoch

Kapsait

Labot

Chesetan

Makutano

Kapiego

Kapcherop

Chesoi

Kaisungua

Chepkum

Koitilial

Chebororwa

Cheptongei

Kapsowar

Chebara

Chebiemit

LAKE KAMNAROK NATIONAL RESERVE

Sirikwa Holes

Moiben

Kabulwa

Bugar

Kerio River

Singore

Iten

Lake Kamnarok

Kessup

Tambach

Biretwo

Torok Falls

Chebloch

Eldoret

Kaptagat

Nyaru

Kimwarer

Makutano

Kapenguria

Mila Saba

Kitale

Cherangani

Mila Nane

Moi's Bridge

Soy

N

0   20 km

Kapsabet & Kisumu   Nairobi   Nakuru   Tenges

It's possible to **hitchhike** along this road north to Tot, Lomut and Marich, especially in mango season (Nov–Jan), when lorries come down as far as Tot and Chesongoch for the fruit. Otherwise, transport is sparse until you reach Lomut, where there are regular matatus to Sigor, Marich and Kapenguria, especially on Lomut's market day (Sat). Between Biretwo and Tot, you may well end up "footing" or waiting by the side of the road. No matter, as long as you have several days, for this road, following one of Kenya's most beautiful valleys, is worth a few blisters. Note, however, that the villages along the way have no facilities for travellers, and only limited supplies. For most of the year the valley, wooded and not much cultivated, resonates with dry heat and the rattle of cicadas and crickets. Climatic conditions are best in the few months of vivid greenery after the long rains, in theory from April to June – and fiercest in February and March, just before they break. The section from Tot to the Marich Pass is covered below.

The Elgeyo Escarpment and Cherangani Hills

You can head **north from Iten** along a good *murram* road to Kapsowar, passing the villages of Singore and Bugar; frequent matatus do the run from Eldoret. Some 4km after Bugar, the road branches right to continue north via Chebiemit, Chebara and Cheptongei. Bearing right at Cheptongei will bring you to Kapsowar. The road from Kapsowar to **Chesengoch** and thence to **Tot** along the **Elgeyo Escarpment** is usually in pretty bad shape. Most easily approached on the return leg of a trip to Turkana (make sure you have enough petrol as there's no fuel along the way), the road is diabolical, too rocky for any kind of ordinary car and too steep for any but the most steel-nerved of drivers. It's a thrilling, gut-wrenching trip in a Land Rover – someone else's preferably – but think twice before driving up this road yourself: it is *very* steep.

Lomut

North of Tot, the B4 road continues through the villages of **Chesegon**, **Lomut** and **Sigor** to meet the A1 at the Marich Pass (see p.297). Between Tot and Sigor, there are very occasional matatus – one or two a day if you're lucky – but transport opportunities improve if you can coincide with weekly markets at Chesegon (Wed), Lomut (Sat) and Sigor (Thurs). The market at **Lomut** is particularly worth a visit. Matatus operate between Lomut and Makutano, near Kapenguria on the A1 (see p.296). **Accommodation** is available in Lomut at *Pokot Village Lomut* or *PoViLo* (☏0733/847883, ✉rgloor@icipe.org; ❹), a compound in the style of a Pokot homestead, run by the Lomut Traditional Dancers group, with nine *bandas*. *PoViLo* is part of Project Cabesi (Camels, Bees, Silk) under the steerage of the International Centre of Insect Physiology and Ecology (ICIPE) which works here on sustainable bee-keeping and silk-production and also helps with camel husbandry. It's a great place to meet Pokot people in an environment far removed from the safari industry.

The Marakwet canals and Chesoi

CHESOI is only 8km away from Kapsowar as the crow flies, but 20km by road – a hike around the highland spurs which is much more easily accomplished in the other direction, a fine and easy, mostly downhill, walk. The land here buckles like a patchwork quilt, with the Cherangani Hills stretching west. The area up near Chesoi is the best place to see the area's remarkable **irrigation system** (see box below), which is impressive in scope, if not particularly in appearance when you see the canals close-up. From Chesoi, you can walk or hitch (but don't count on seeing a vehicle, much less on its having space) the 25 breathtaking kilometres down to **Tot**, turning left at **Chesengoch** in the valley.

The rocky, almost perpendicular slopes around Chesoi are dotted with **Marakwet** homesteads, the huts unusual in being built of stone (there's a limitless supply up here), which gives them an ancient-looking permanence rarely seen in Kenyan rural architecture. A thousand metres below, spreading like a grey-green carpet into the haze, are the scrubby, bush-covered plains of Pokot and south Turkana. Dozens of tiny wisps of smoke from charcoal burners combine to smudge out the distant peaks of Mount Kenya to the southeast. The places where the trees grow thicker mark the passage of seasonal streams, which flood and dry up with the rains; Pokot gold-panners still find enough gold in them to trade with anyone passing through.

To add to this distinctive sense of place, the escarpment itself is the location of an ancient **irrigation system**, stretching north-to-south for over 40km, diverting water from the gushing streams of the Cherangani Hills into a branching layout of furrows and aqueducts. Complex, unwritten laws ensure that each Marakwet sub-clan is fairly provided for by the system, which is without parallel anywhere else in the country; the results, as you'll see along the base of the scarp, are spectacular. Indeed, for a considerable distance up the Kerio Valley, there's a band of intensive, luxuriant gardening: tiny *shambas* slotted back-to-back between the spurs and down towards the main river. Magnificent, richly flavoured bananas are on sale everywhere. Many of the irrigation channels now pass under the road, but a few still flow over it and a great deal of ongoing repair work is needed to keep the streams flowing in the right direction.

Chesoi canal is a major water supply a couple of kilometres behind Chesoi centre, a metre-wide channel clinging to the hillside which any local will show you. In other places, the irrigation system has become almost a piped water supply, with hollow logs used as aqueducts, but the Chesoi channel has been built with cement. Unfortunately, the water round about, diverted from the Arror River, tastes disgusting even when boiled (it's a problem you encounter often in the Cheranganis).

The Marakwet irrigation system

The Marakwet – part of the broadly related Kalenjin group of peoples – may have arrived on these slopes as long as a thousand years ago. They say the **irrigation** channels were there long before their own forefathers arrived, and it is possible the original irrigators were a mysterious group called the **Sirikwa**. These people have disappeared, or more likely been absorbed, and the only reminders of them are their name and a lot of curious **holes**, earthworks and cairns, noticed by archeologists around the Kerio Valley and in other parts of western Kenya (see opposite).

Marakwet elders still remember stories of a small people called the **Terngeng**, who may have lived in pits in the ground something like those at Hyrax Hill and Moiben. Other stories refer to tall, longhaired, bearded men who roamed the Rift Valley. Either or both of these groups might have been responsible for the building of the irrigation system, but perhaps the Marakwet's claim to have inherited the system, but not built it, is just a way of saying how old it really is.

The Sirikwa holes

Near **Moiben**, the **Sirikwa holes** are a collection of depressions, some circular, about 10m across and a few metres deep, others a longer oval shape, all ringed by large stones. Matatus run daily from Eldoret or Iten to Moiben; you might have to change at the junction where the *murram* road to Moiben leaves the paved C51.

The holes are some 6km west of Moiben. From the crossroads by the upper primary school and chief's office, follow the dirt track past another school on the left and out into farmland. You may need to ask directions, first for Rany Moi Farm and then for the holes themselves – known locally as "Maasai holes" or "Maasai homes". Some holes are isolated examples; others are joined by passages dug a metre or so into the ground. They are thought to have been cattle pens rather than dwellings, but would each have had a small hut by the entrance. The Moiben site is relatively undisturbed, but as the pressure from local farms increases, it seems likely that these enigmatic remains will–eventually be demolished and ploughed over. You'll find more, though less well-preserved, holes at the *Naiberi River Campsite* near Kaptagat (see p.290), and there are others scattered around the district.

Walking in the Cheranganis

If you have the time and inclination, **walking in the Cheranganis** is exhilarating. The thickly forested hills are wild, hardly explored, and still home to a few bongo antelope. Higher up (Kamelogon peak on Mount Chemnirot is 3581m), they merge into mountain moorland and giant Afro-alpine vegetation, superb hiking country where you're very unlikely to meet any others doing the same. A couple of days of hiking will see you over the southern ridges to **Kapcherop**, where you'll have no difficulty picking up transport west to Kitale or Eldoret.

For this route, you first climb through Chesoi village and past the mission for about ninety minutes through *shambas*; then there's an hour's walk through forest, mostly flat; ninety minutes of climbing through bamboo forest; and a further two hours though hilly pasturelands and woods before you reach **Kapiego**. If you're driving, note that the Chesoi–Kapiego part of this route is non-motorable and that you can only drive to Kapiego from the south or west. Kapiego is a crossroads centre, a suitable stop for the night with a few *hotelis* and at least a daily matatu run to Eldoret.

From Kapiego, routes lead northwest to Kalelaigelat summit (motorable to the base in a couple of hours, but with no matatus and no water); north to the main Cherangani peaks (again, motorable in 2–3hr or a day's walk); and west on a little-used road to **Labot** and – 5km further – **Makutano**. One or two matatus pass through Makutano most days on their way between Kapcherop and Kapsait, and there's one to Kapiego. There's usually one matatu a day between Labot (leaving around 7am) and the other Makutano near Kapenguria (leaving there at lunchtime). South of the Makutano near Kapsait, a quiet road leads down through grassland, then forest to **Kapcherop** (home of Kenya's former international athletics champion Moses Kiptanui) – about a three-hour walk. From there you'll find matatus to Cherangani, and thence to Eldoret and Kitale.

If your hiking plans are more ambitious, try to get hold of the relevant Survey of Kenya 1:50m-scale maps and set off, suitably equipped, over the high central districts of the massif. There are several, relatively easily scaled peaks up here. The best base for exploring this area is *Sirikwa Guesthouse* (see p.292), with *Marich Field Studies Centre* (see p.297) a lower-budget alternative. You can hire local guides at both.

The Cherangani Highway circuit

The scenic D327 road from Makutano through **Kapsait** and **Kaibichbich** is known as the "Cherangani Highway", and the northern stretch forms part of a popular driving circuit. The road does, however, suffer landfalls, and you should check on the current state of it before setting out (*Sirikwa Guesthouse*, see p.292, should be able to advise).

If you start at the junction on the A1 near Kapenguria, you can drive down through Kaibichbich to a junction north of Kapsait, where you take a left, passing through Kapsangar towards the peak of Kalelaigelat. Another left turn takes you northwest through **Sina** and back to meet the A1 at **Chipkorniswa**. The hills between Sina and the villages of **Parua** and **Tamkal** to its north are popular for hiking, with footpaths connecting the three villages, although you'll need a guide to follow them. All three villages are connected to the A1 by *murram* roads. If you are going to Tamkal, it's worth trying to coincide with market day, which is Tuesday.

Travel details

Trains

Nakuru to: Kisumu (3 weekly; 8hr); Nairobi (3 weekly; 5hr); Naivasha (3 weekly; 2hr).

Buses

Kabarnet to/from: Eldoret (2 daily; 1hr 30min); Nakuru (3 daily; 3hr).
Naivasha to/from: Nairobi (several daily; 1hr 30min); Nakuru (several daily; 1hr).
Nakuru to/from: Eldoret (3 daily; 4hr); Kericho (2 daily; 3hr); Kisii (2 daily; 5hr); Kisumu (7 daily; 4hr 30min); Kitale (3 daily; 5hr); Marigat (1 daily; 1hr 30min); Nairobi (20 daily; 2hr 30min); Nanyuki (1 daily; 5hr); Nyahururu (1 daily; 2hr).

Matatus

Kabarnet to/from: Eldoret (several daily; 1hr 30min); Iten (frequent; 1hr); Kabartonjo (2 daily; 30min); Marigat (frequent; 1hr); Naivasha (several daily; 2hr); Nakuru (daily; 3hr); Tenges (occasional; 1hr).
Magadi to/from: Nairobi (2 daily; 2hr); Olorgesailie (2 daily; 1hr).
Marigat to/from Kabarnet (frequent; 1hr); Kampi ya Samaki (frequent; 30min); Nakuru (several daily; 1hr 30min).
Naivasha to/from: Eldoret (several daily; 4hr); Kabarnet (several daily; 2hr); Kericho (several daily; 2hr).
Nakuru to/from: Eldoret (several daily; 3hr); Kabarnet (several daily; 2hr 30min); Kericho (several daily; 2hr 30min); Kisumu (several daily; 4hr); Kitale (several daily; 4hr 30min); Marigat (frequent; 1hr 30min); Nairobi (frequent; 2hr 30min); Narok (1 daily; 5hr); Nyahururu (several daily; 1hr 30min); Subukia (frequent; 1hr).

Flights

Naivasha to: Maasai Mara (1 daily; 40min)

Western Kenya

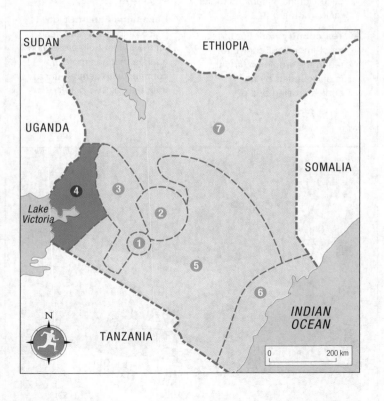

SUDAN

ETHIOPIA

UGANDA

⑦

SOMALIA

④

③

Lake Victoria

②

①

⑤

⑥

INDIAN OCEAN

N

TANZANIA

0   200 km

CHAPTER 4 Highlights

✳ **Kisumu Museum**
Action-packed taxidermy and cultural illumination, at one of Kenya' best regional collections. **See p.257**

✳ **Mfangano Island** Vehicle-less, remote and rarely visited, Mfangano Island, in Lake Victoria, is famous for its rock art. **See p.272**

✳ **Tea country** Kericho, the most important centre for tea in the whole of Africa, is surrounded by an endless rolling sea of brilliant green plantations. **See p.280**

✳ **Saiwa Swamp National Park** Home to the unusual sitatunga antelope, monkeys and a huge variety of birds, with the chance to explore on foot – no vehicles are allowed. **See p.295**

✳ **Kakamega Forest** Unique patch of lowland rainforest off the tourist trail, preserving a fauna that has more in common with central Africa than Kenya. **See p.308**

▲ Fishing boats at Dunga, near Kisumu

Western Kenya

L ike the tiers of a great amphitheatre, **western Kenya** slopes away from Nairobi, the major game parks and the coast, down to the stage of Lake Victoria. Cut off by the high Rift wall of the **Mau and Elgeyo escarpments**, this western region of dense agriculture, rolling green valleys and pockets of thick jungle is one of the parts of the country least known to travellers. Although more accessible than the far north, or even some of the major parks, it has been neglected by the safari operators – and that's all to the good. You can travel for days through lush landscapes from one busy market town to the next and rarely, if ever, meet other tourists.

It's not easy to see why it has been so ignored. Granted, Uganda's disastrous first two decades after independence discouraged the through traffic that might otherwise have thrived. But there's a great deal more of intrinsic interest than the tourist literature's sparse coverage would suggest. While the west undeniably lacks teeming herds of game stalked by lions and narcissistic warriors in full regalia, what it offers is a series of delightfully low-key, easily visited attractions. For a start there are **national parks**: at **Kakamega Forest**, a magnificent tract of equatorial rainforest bursting with species found nowhere else in Kenya; at **Saiwa Swamp**, where you have to visit on foot; at **Ruma**, where a lush valley harbours giraffe and roan antelope; and at **Mount Elgon**, a volcano to rival Mount Kenya in everything but crowds. Then there is the draw of **Lake Victoria**, with the region's major town, **Kisumu**, on its shores, dotted with out-of-the-way islands and populated by exceptionally friendly people. And there's the offbeat, if admittedly very minor, new attraction of **Kogelo**, the home village of the father of US president Barack Obama.

Travel is generally easy. The region has a high population and plenty of roads (though these days they're often in poor condition), so you'll rarely have long to wait for transport. Although the west has only a handful of luxury or inter-national-class hotels, there is no lack of good, modest **lodgings**. If you like to plan ahead, one obvious circuit begins in Kisumu and runs through **Kisii** (of soapstone fame), **Kericho**, **Eldoret**, **Kitale** and **Kakamega**. You could also head southwest from Kisumu to **Rusinga Island**, then further south along a spectacular, hilly stretch of the lakeshore, through **Ruma National Park** and back up to Kisii, or even east to the Maasai Mara. If you don't plan your travels, it's not necessarily a problem: it can be equally rewarding to let events dictate your next move. This is an area that will repay your interest repeatedly if you take time to look around. Much of it, even the areas of intensive farming, is ravishingly beautiful: densely animated jungle near Kakamega and Kitale, regimented landscapes of tea bushes around Kericho, and many areas of swamp and grassland alive with birds.

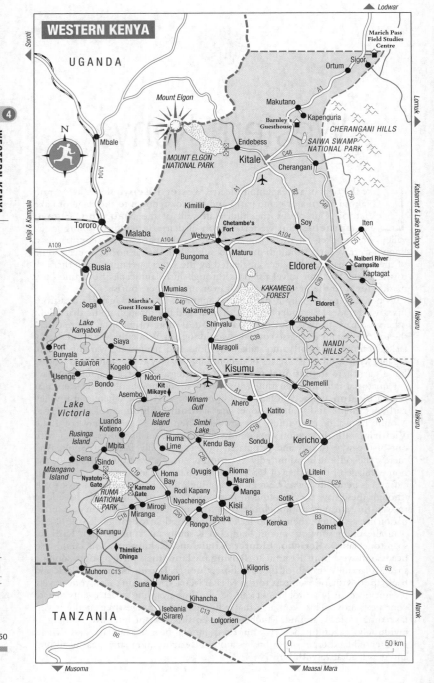

WESTERN KENYA

Lodwar

Soroti

UGANDA

Mount Elgon

Mbale

N

MOUNT ELGON
NATIONAL PARK

Marich Pass
Field Studies
Centre

Sigor

Ortum

A1

Makutano

Barnley's
Guesthouse

Kapenguria

CHERANGANI HILLS

Endebess

Kitale

SAIWA SWAMP
NATIONAL PARK

C46

Cherangani

B2

Kimilili

Chetambe's
Fort

Webuye

Soy

C49

C50

Iten

C51

Tororo

Malaba

A104

Bungoma

Maturu

A104

Eldoret

Naiberi River
Campsite

Kaptagat

A109

C43

A1

Busia

Mumias

C38

Sega

C40

Kakamega

KAKAMEGA
FOREST

Eldoret

A104

Martha's
Guest House

Butere

Shinyalu

Kapsabet

Lake
Kanyaboli

B1

Siaya

Maragoli

C39

NANDI
HILLS

Port
Bunyala

EQUATOR

Kogelo

Ndori

Kisumu

Chemelil

Usenge

Bondo

Kit
Mikaye

Winam
Gulf

Ahero

A1

Katito

B1

Asembo

Ndere
Island

Simbi
Lake

C19

Sondu

Lake
Victoria

Luanda
Kotieno

Huma
Lime

Kendu Bay

Kericho

Rusinga
Island

Mbita

C26

Oyugis

Rioma

Litein

C23

Sena

Sindo

Homa
Bay

Marani

Sotik

C24

Mfangano
Island

Nyatoto
Gate

RUMA
NATIONAL PARK

Kamato
Gate

Rodi Kapany

Nyachenge

Manga

Kisii

Keroka

B3

Bomet

Mirogi

Miranga

C18

C20

Rongo

Tabaka

Keroka

B3

Karungu

A1

Thimlich
Ohinga

Muhoro

C13

Migori

Suna

Kilgoris

B3

Narok

Isebania
(Sirare)

Kihancha

Lolgorien

TANZANIA

C13

0   50 km

Musoma

Maasai Mara

Jinja & Kampala

Kabarnet & Lake Baringo

Nakuru

Lomuk

Ethnically, the region is dominated by the **Luo** on the lakeshore, but there are Bantu-speaking **Luhya** in the sugar lands, north of Kisumu, and **Gusii** in the formidably fertile Kisii Hills. Other important groups speak one or other of the Kalenjin languages, principally the **Nandi**, around Eldoret, and the **Kipsigis** in the district around Kericho.

Lake Victoria and Luoland

Lake Victoria is the obvious place to make for in the west, but frustratingly few main roads get really close to its shores – the best drive is the scenic route from **Mbita** to **Sindo**. Most travellers arrive in Kisumu, which used to have ferries linking it with several Kenyan ports, as well as ports in Tanzania and Uganda. Unfortunately, all services – apart from a ferry across the mouth of the Winam Gulf between Luanda Kotieno and Mbita – are suspended, because low water levels, and stretches clogged by water hyacinth, make navigation unsafe. Currently, the only transport from Kisumu to other lakeshore towns is by road. If you want to get out on the lake, the best place to head for is **Mbita**, which has regular matatu-boats to Mfangano Island, one of the least-visited corners of Kenya, with the added attraction of some wonderful prehistoric **rock art**.

Kisumu

In the sultry atmosphere of **KISUMU**, a distinctive smell from the lake – fish, mud and rotting vegetation – drifts in on a vague breeze from central Africa. Distinctively different from any other big town, Kisumu's position might lead you to expect a bustling waterfront and a lake-facing atmosphere. It was founded as a railway town and lake port, and as its fortunes rose with the growth of trade in colonial East Africa and the newly independent nations, it became Kenya's third largest town. It suffered badly following the East African Community's break-up, however, and, throughout the 1980s and early 1990s, the port was mostly dormant, with signs of dereliction – empty warehouses, broken windows – everywhere. Although some commercial shipping has resumed, and the port sporadically buzzes with loading or unloading (and people looking for a lift to Uganda or Tanzania), low water levels and water hyacinth have held back progress. Today, the layout of the town turns its back on the lake, focusing instead on the commercial centre and land links to the rest of Kenya.

Even if the time-warped atmosphere of a place that's been treading water for three decades may not be much comfort to its inhabitants, Kisumu is one of the few upcountry towns with real **character**. It's a tranquil, easy-going town, where the *manambas* at the bus station are unusually laid-back. Any anticipation of claustrophobia is quickly soothed by the spacious, shady layout. The contrast with Nakuru, if you've just come from there, is striking.

The Luo

The **Luo** are the second largest ethnic group and one of the most cohesive "tribes" in Kenya. Their language, Dholuo, is distinctive and closely resembles the Nuer and Dinka languages of southern Sudan, from where their ancestors migrated south at the end of the fifteenth century. They found the shore and hinterland of Lake Victoria only sparsely populated by hunter-gatherers, scattered with occasional clearings where Bantu-speaking farmers had settled over the previous few centuries. Otherwise, the region was wild: untouched grassland and tropical forest, dense with heavy concentrations of wildlife.

The Luo were swift invaders, driving their herds before them, from water point to water point, always on the move, restless and acquisitive. They raided other groups' cattle incessantly and, within a few decades, had forced the Bantu-speakers away from the lakeshore. Despite the conflict, **intermarriage** (essentially the buying of wives) was common and the pastoral nomads were greatly influenced by their Bantu-speaking in-laws and neighbours, ancestors of the present-day Luhya and Gusii.

The Luo today are best known as fishermen, a lifestyle that had sustained them while migrating along the rivers. But they also cultivate widely and still keep livestock. Culturally, they have remained surprisingly independent, and are one of the few Kenyan peoples who don't perform circumcision. Traditionally, children had six teeth knocked out from the lower jaw to mark their initiation into adulthood, but the operation is hardly ever carried out these days. **Christianity** has made spectacular inroads among the Luo, with an estimated ninety percent being believers, but it does not seem to have destroyed their traditional culture quite as thoroughly as it has elsewhere. Despite the ubiquity of Gospel singing, **traditional music**, especially the playing of the *nyatiti* lyre, is still very much alive and well worth listening out for.

Some history

The **railway line** from Mombasa had reached the lake by 1901, reassuring the British public who were having serious doubts that the "Lunatic Line", as it was dubbed, would ever reach completion, but the first train only chugged into the station at **Port Florence**, as Kisumu was originally known, in 1903 when the Mau Escarpment viaducts were completed. By then, European transport had already arrived at the lake in the form of a steamship brought up from Mombasa piece by portered piece, having steamed out from Scotland in 1895. Many of the ship's parts were seized en route from the coast and recycled into Nandi ornamentation and weaponry, and it was five years before a complete vessel could be assembled and launched on its maiden voyage across the lake to Port Bell in Uganda.

By all accounts Kisumu was a pretty disagreeable place in the early years. Apart from the endemic sleeping sickness, bilharzia and malaria, the climate was sweltering and municipal hygiene primitive. But it quickly grew into an important administrative and military base and, with the consolidation of the colonies in the 1930s and 1940s, became a leading East African entrepôt and transport hub, attracting Asian investment on top of the businesses that had been set up at the railway terminus when the Indian labourers were laid off. Kisumu's rise seemed unstoppable until 1977, when the sudden **collapse of the East African Community**, more or less overnight, robbed the town of its *raison d'être*. The partial reformation of the community in 1996 brightened prospects, and by 1999 the port was relatively busy, thanks largely to UN World Food Programme transit goods destined for war-torn Rwanda and Congo.

Since then, however, Kisumu has again seen a downturn in its fortunes, due to the decline of the local **sugar** industry, sugar cane being the surrounding

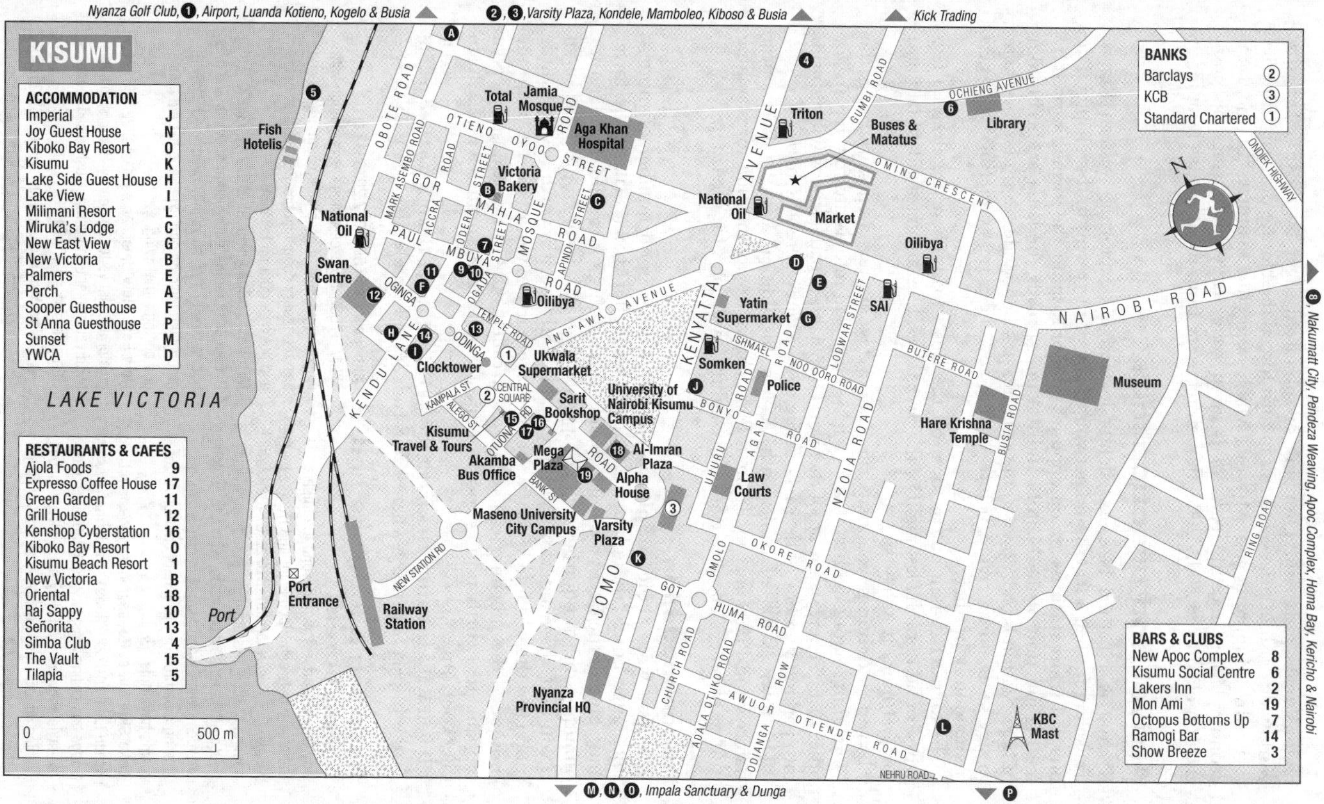

KISUMU

ACCOMMODATION
Imperial	J
Joy Guest House	N
Kiboko Bay Resort	O
Kisumu	K
Lake Side Guest House	H
Lake View	I
Milimani Resort	L
Miruka's Lodge	C
New East View	G
New Victoria	B
Palmers	E
Perch	A
Sooper Guesthouse	F
St Anna Guesthouse	P
Sunset	M
YWCA	D

BANKS
Barclays	②
KCB	③
Standard Chartered	①

BARS & CLUBS
New Apoc Complex	8
Kisumu Social Centre	6
Lakers Inn	2
Mon Ami	19
Octopus Bottoms Up	7
Ramogi Bar	14
Show Breeze	3

RESTAURANTS & CAFÉS
Ajola Foods	9
Expresso Coffee House	17
Green Garden	11
Grill House	12
Kenshop Cyberstation	16
Kiboko Bay Resort	0
Kisumu Beach Resort	1
New Victoria	B
Oriental	18
Raj Sappy	10
Señorita	13
Simba Club	4
The Vault	15
Tilapia	5

LAKE VICTORIA

Port

WESTERN KENYA

4

www.roughguides.com

253

region's main cash crop. Dumping of subsidized sugar by the EU led to a worldwide crash in prices, and this in turn forced the closure of sugar refineries at nearby Muhoroni and Miwani, which were the mainstays of the local economy. More recently, parts of Kisumu were badly hit during the post-election **clashes** in 2007/2008, though recovery from them has been rapid.

Arrival and practicalities

Kisumu is a natural base, excellently located for exploring western Kenya. Travelling for half a day should get you to any of the towns in this chapter. The **bus** and **train stations** are on opposite sides of Kisumu, the former located by the big junction of the Nairobi and Kakamega roads, the latter at the bottom of New Station Road, down in the port area. It's a good idea to find somewhere to stay soon after arriving, before starting any energetic wanderings, as it gets tremendously hot here.

The **airport** is 4km out of town off the Busia road. There are always a few cabs around until the last flight of the day arrives. The current standard fare into town (10min) is Ksh400.

If you're **driving**, you may run into a few wasters in town trying the "something wrong with your car" trick to lure you into a yard for "repairs" or other scams. There's a group of them on Gor Mahia Road. Drivers will also run into parking wardens – the 24-hour fee to park anywhere is Ksh40.

The town is full of banks with **ATMs**. In addition, Victoria Forex near Barclays and PEL Forex in al-Imran Plaza charge no commission for changing cash or traveller's cheques, with only slightly lower rates for the latter.

Accommodation

There's a wide choice of **places to stay**, with a good number of modest, mid-range hotels, though prices tend to be higher than usual. At the lower end, some of the B&Ls are pretty basic, even verging on squalid. Temperature, humidity and mosquitoes will conspire to give you an uncomfortable night if you don't have a net or a fan (preferably both), so it's worth paying a little more for them. Unless you want to leave early, try not to stay near the mosque – the morning call to prayer is called out on the loudspeakers at 5.30am. It's worth noting too that most hotels in Kisumu have a 9.30am checkout time.

If you want to **camp**, check out the *YWCA*, *Kisumu Beach Resort* (see p.258) or the Impala Sanctuary where KWS runs several simple sites (see p.257).

Boarding & lodgings and cheap hotels

Joy Guest House 1.4km beyond the Impala Sanctuary between Hippo Point and Dunga, by the *Kiboko Bay Resort* turning ☎0725/074837. While nothing special, this ordinary, European-style house offers reasonable value, with a large double s/c room with TV and two, twin non-s/c rooms sharing a bathroom with instant shower. All the rooms have nets. ❶

Lake Side Guest House (formerly *Western Lodge*) Kendu Lane ☎0722/725591. The former *Western Lodge* has ceiling fans, lock-up cupboards and old-style showers – an okay place all round, but nothing special. It's right above a pizzeria (daily 11am–midnight). ❶

Lake View Alego St ☎057/2020982 or 0721/117038. No exceptional views, though with its corner position, it does offer some breeze and also has a very congenial bar. Rooms have nets and hot water but no fans. BB ❷

Miruka's Lodge Apindi St ☎0727/233887. Decent, light rooms, with instant showers and nets but no fans or TVs, so slightly overpriced. They're gradually rebuilding and extending the old house and adding a new wing. ❷

New East View Omolo Agar Rd ☎0722/556721. A quieter alternative to the nearby *Palmers*, this has twenty, well-kept and scrupulously clean rooms, with safe parking. BB ❷

New Victoria Gor Mahia Rd ☎057/2021067 or 0722/555443. This well-maintained and efficiently run hotel is perennially popular with travellers and bright and cheerful inside and out. Most rooms have balconies and rooms 206–209 have good lake views. The very good breakfasts alone are worth the visit. BB ❷

Palmers Omolo Agar Rd ☏057/2024867 or 0722/999691. Handy for the bus and matatu stand, and with safe parking, this friendly place has a relaxed bar and breezy *nyama choma* joint at the side. BB ❸

Perch Corner of Mark Asembo Rd and Obote Rd ☏0722/974607. A cavernous block behind the port area, with too much wood panelling and carpeting to be attractive, this is reasonably comfortable, and the s/c rooms (some with lake views) have nets, TV and instant showers, but no fans. There's a busy bar-restaurant, safe, basement parking and rates that are just about okay. BB ❷

🏃 **Sooper Guesthouse** Oginga Odinga Rd ☏0725/281733 or 0723/292781, ⓦsooperguesthse.com The best cheap lodging in Kisumu, still living up to its name, with light, clean s/c rooms, instant showers, nets, TV, lock-up cupboards and electric sockets. Best rooms are the two at the front that share the balcony overlooking the street. Cold drinks, snacks and breakfast are available and there's a kind of roof terrace. ❷

🏃 **St Anna Guesthouse** Signposted left, 450m south down Tom Mboya Drive next to Care Kenya (near the KBC tower, off Ring Road), Milimani Estate ☏057/2024792 or 0734/600119, ⓦwww.stannaguesthouse.com. Although tricky to find, *St Anna* is worth the effort. Nets and instant showers equip the 35 well-kept, value-for-money rooms. Although managed by Franciscan sisters, it's open to all and has no guest requirements beyond refraining from alcohol. The top-value restaurant serves filling staples. Safe parking. BB ❸

YWCA Off Ang'awa Ave ☏057/2024788 or 0733/992982. Friendly, cheap but rather bland, with a canteen, camping facilities (Ksh200 using dorm shared showers and loos) and four double rooms. Ksh350 per person in 3- or 4-bed dorms. ❶

Mid-range hotels

Imperial Jomo Kenyatta Ave ☏057/2020002 or 0721/240515, ⓦwww.imperialkisumu.com. With lifts to its eighty rooms, which have big, hanging mosquito nets, DSTV, a/c and proper showers, this is a clear notch above the *Kisumu* and *Sunset*, its only rivals, and the usual choice of business-account travellers. The modest-sized courtyard pool (10am–12.30pm & 2.30–7pm; Ksh120) is the cleanest in Kisumu. BB ❺

Kiboko Bay Resort 1.5km south of the Impala Sanctuary, between Hippo Point and Dunga ☏0733/532709 or 0722/960860. On the site of the former *Dunga Refreshments*, this very pleasant tented camp on the lakeshore has nine well-equipped tents with mains electricity, generator backup, nets, fridges, full solid bathrooms and floor fans. A popular alternative to staying in town, and popular for lunch at weekends, too. Pool (Ksh150) and terrace by the lake. BB ❻

Kisumu Jomo Kenyatta Ave ☏057/2024157, ⓦwww.maseno.ac.ke/hotelkisumu. Once Kisumu's top hotel (when it was the *Royale*), the eighty, carpeted, average-sized rooms here have TV, full nets, a/c and old-style baths and showers. There are three bars and a moderately priced restaurant and the good-sized pool (11am–6pm, Ksh200) is nicely situated on a shaded terrace, though rather green. BB ❺

Milimani Resort Off Got Huma Rd ☏057/2023245 or 0725/141666, ⓔinfo @milimaniresort.com. Fifty, mostly quite attractive, tile-floored rooms in a quiet, residential street, with nets, a/c, DSTV, good views (from the upper floors) and old-fashioned tubs and showers. The staff are friendly and gracious, and facilities include a restaurant and lounge, though no bar. Large pool (Ksh150). BB ❹

Sunset Aput Lane, 2.5km south of the town centre ☏057/2020464, ⓔhotelsunset1977 @yahoo.co.uk. Above and behind the Impala Sanctuary, this five-storey complex dating from the 1960s is fraying around the edges, but offers great lake views and beautiful sunsets from rooms on the second, third and fourth floors, most of which have small balconies as well as nets, TV, floor fans, a/c and instant showers. The business centre has decent internet, but don't count on swimming in the very green pool (10am–6pm; Ksh120). BB ❹

The Town

Kisumu's **market**, by the bus station, is the biggest and best in western Kenya, and an absorbing place to wander, crammed with fruit and vegetables (including some oddities like breadfruit) and all the usual household paraphernalia – pots and plates, reed brushes, wickerwork and wooden spoons. The market is such a success that it has mushroomed out into the adjacent municipal park, much to the consternation of the local authorities.

4

Lake Victoria's discovery and exploration

The westward view from Kisumu gives you little sense of the vastness of **Victoria Nyanza** (**Lake Victoria**). From the shores of the narrow Winam Gulf it's difficult to grasp the fact that there's another 300km of water between the horizon and the opposite shore in Uganda, and an even greater distance south to Mwanza, the main Tanzanian port. Victoria, the second largest freshwater lake in the world after Lake Superior, covers a total area of nearly 70,000 square kilometres – almost the size of Scotland or Nebraska – of which only a fraction is in Kenya.

It was barely five centuries ago that the **Luo** first settled beside the vast equatorial lake they called **Ukerewe**, and the lake remained uncharted and virtually unknown outside Africa until well into the second half of the nineteenth century. Then, in the midst of the race to pinpoint the **source of the Nile**, the lake suddenly became a focus of attention. When English adventurer **John Hanning Speke** first saw Ukerewe in 1858, he was convinced that the long search was over, and promptly renamed the lake after his Queen. In 1862, he became the first person to follow the Nile downstream from Lake Victoria to Cairo, and triumphantly cabled the Royal Geographical Society in London with the words "The Nile is settled". Sceptics, however, doubted the issue was settled, countering that Lake Tanganyika was the true source, and it took a daring circumnavigation of Lake Victoria, led by the American journalist **Henry Morton Stanley**, in 1875, to prove Speke right. Sadly, Speke did not live to enjoy the vindication – he was killed in a shooting accident in 1874.

For **crafts and souvenirs**, there used to be a row of craft stalls opposite the *Kisumu Hotel* that was one of the region's best hunting grounds. The sellers have decamped to various spots around the town, but the best place to find them is at the tourist market by the **museum** (see opposite). The things to buy here, if you have space, are the heavy, three-legged Luo stools, the best of which are intricately inlaid with beads, and dark brown from repeated oiling. Also on offer are bangles, wooden carvings and rows of soapstone knick-knacks. A very worthwhile crafts set-up in is the Fairtrade small enterprise umbrella group **Kick Trading** (℡0722/432208 or 710/663990, ⓦwww.kicktrading.org) in the northeast part of town on Ramogi Rise Rd, opposite the SDA Central Church, where local artisans fashion a wealth of jewellery, toys, stationery, clothes and hyacinth-based products. The **Hope** souvenir shop, at the airport (℡0710/663990), where the UN-award-winning owner sells crafts made from water hyacinth, has further information about Kick. Another worthwhile visit for crafts, just out of town, is **Pendeza Weaving** (℡0735/229904, ⓦwww.globalcrafts.org/partner/pendeza.htm), about 3km along the Nairobi road, past the chief's camp and indicated by a small white sign on the right. The prayer calls from Kisumu's pastel green-and-white **Jamia mosque**, on Otieno Oyoo Street, sound odd in this town, but Islam is well established here and is an important regional influence dating from well back into the nineteenth century. This orthodox Shafi'ite mosque was built in 1919, though the women's section on the right was only finished in 1984. The beautiful long mats inside are from Saudi Arabia.

If you're interested in **visiting the port**, it's easy enough to go down there, buy a Ksh20 "port visitor" ticket at the port gates and wander along the dock. There is, in truth, practically nothing to see, although if a ship or two are in port, the scene can be quite animated. Your visit may be improved, however, by having a local guide to stroll with you, especially if you want to take photos. Paul Waswa (℡0720/406954; around Ksh200 per 30min) is helpful and can tell you all about water hyacinth and shipping movements.

Kisumu Museum

Foremost among the town's sights is the engaging and ambitious **Kisumu Museum** (daily 9.30am–6pm; Ksh500), just a short walk east from the market. Set in a large garden with carefully labelled trees, the main gallery happily mingles **zoological** exhibits with ethnographic displays. Apart from the rows of trophy-style game heads around the walls, the stuffed animals and preserved insects and crustaceans are displayed with considerable flair and imagination. Particularly good use has been made of old exhibits from Nairobi's National Museum. A free-swinging vulture, for example, spins like a model aircraft overhead while, centre stage, a lion is caught in full, savage pounce, leaping onto the back of a hysterical wildebeest in the most action-packed piece of taxidermy you're ever likely to see.

The **ethnographic** exhibits are illuminating, too. The Maasai aren't the only people who take blood from their cattle for food: Kalenjin peoples like the Nandi and the Kipsigis once did the same, and even the Luo lived mostly on cow's blood mixed with milk before they arrived at Lake Victoria and began to cultivate and fish.

In separate halls from the main gallery are a small, but worthwhile **aquarium**, illustrating the problem of fish depletion in the lake (see what your tilapia looked like before it became a curry), and a **snake house** with a fairly comprehensive collection of Kenyan species. Outside, the tortoise pen and croc pond seem rather pointless extras. The crocodiles, getting extremely large, are fed on Monday afternoons.

Kisumu Impala Sanctuary

For a fine walk out of town, follow any road southwest and you pass the entrance to the small **Impala Sanctuary** (ⓦwww.kws.go.ke/impala.html; $15). Here, more than twenty tame impala (said to be the remnants of wild herds from early railway days) run free, with vervet monkeys and plenty of birdlife in the dense woodland. A single main footpath (no cars allowed) runs through the sanctuary from end to end, taking you between the lakeshore and a few cramped pens and cages that contain a pair of bored **leopards**, an **ostrich**, and a **hyena** that looks as if it might well escape from its insecure confinement. More of a city park than a nature reserve, the sanctuary is worth a visit for the chance to stretch your legs in the shade and stroll near the lakeshore. And, cages aside, it's a pleasant place for an hour or too and a good escape from the heat. Railway buffs will be pleased to find a bit of old **railway line** along the lakeshore at the far end. **Camping** ($10), recently not possible while they've been "renovating" should now once again be a pleasure. But watch out for that hyena.

Hippo Point and Dunga

Beyond the Impala Sanctuary, most people make for the Luo fishing village of **Dunga**. Some 800m south of the sanctuary, passing the largely out-of-action yacht club, you come to **Hippo Point**, where you can watch riotously hued sunsets from the rock-strewn shore. There's a strong, warm breeze at dusk, and it's a curious sensation to experience this giant body of water without the characteristic smell of the ocean in the air. Hippos are still seen here, and the small crowd of friendly local boatmen will offer to take you out to view them (around Ksh2500). They use "long shaft" outboard motors for manoeuvrability in the shallows and, as well as hippos, can often show you spotted-necked otters in the area – but, they say, not crocodiles. As a contribution to local environmental restoration, they've planted a patch of what they call "freshwater mangrove", or ambatch, as in Lake Baringo.

The village of **Dunga** is some 2km further, on the headland, a picturesque settlement with Dunga Fishermen's Co-operative Society and the Dunga Environmental and Eco-Tourism Team (DECTT) the main focuses on the shore. The DECTT people have taken a new approach to the problem of earning a sustainable living that doesn't count just on increasingly uncertain fishing. They have a small office and cold sodas and will gladly assist you with any lake activities you might want to pursue, from night fishing to birdwatching.

Although going out on the lake is fun, it unfortunately is, a disease-ridden body of water. Although there aren't always clouds of mosquitoes, the malaria risk is quite high. Moreover, snails carrying **bilharzia** flourish in the reeds around the fringes of the lake, and although the Luo wash and swim in it and sail their vividly painted, dhow-like, mahogany canoes on it, the danger of bilharzia is all too real. It's very rare to get the disease after brief contact with infected water, but you should avoid getting wet, as far as possible, if you're fishing or boating, and don't even think about swimming.

Eating and drinking

Kisumu has lots of good **places to eat**, but it's worth starting early as many places close shortly after dusk. In addition to the listings below, some of the hotels are worth checking out: the *New Victoria* for a good breakfast, the *Kiboko Bay Resort* for lunch at the weekend, and the top-flight *Kisumu* for more expensive meals at any time.

At the budget end, **nyama choma** can be had in shack-type kiosks at the top of Omolo Agar Road, by the market. The best deal in town, however, is **fresh fried tilapia** in a series of *hotelis* down by the lakeside at the far northern end of Oginga Odinga Road. They're served with either *ugali* or chapatis. The best of them is really a full-fledged restaurant, *Tilapia*, right at the end of the dirt track that goes beyond the group of *hotelis*; it even has parking.

If you're self-catering, you'll find several good **supermarkets** including the 24-hour Nakumatt Nyanza at Mega Plaza. Of several good **bakeries** in town, Victoria (Mon–Sat 7am–6.30pm, Sun 8am–2pm) by the *New Victoria Hotel* in Gor Mahia Road, has probably the best selection of cakes and pastries in western Kenya.

The best **coffee shop** in town is probably upstairs at Tusky's Mall. They also have wi-fi.

Ajola Foods Paul Mbuya Rd. The former *Hunter's Café* is great value for Kenyan dishes at around Ksh80–200 for a meal, and chips for Ksh60. Mon–Sat 7am–6.30pm.

Expresso Coffee House Otuona Rd. A long menu of fry-ups, but the coffee is instant, despite the name, and the "juice" isn't fresh-pressed either. Not bad for breakfast or lunch nonetheless. Mon–Sat 7am–6pm.

Green Garden Odera St ☎ 0727/738000 or 0725/082465. Very popular NGO and traveller haunt on an unpromising side street, serving a long menu of dishes in the courtyard dining area – pizzas, vegetarian, grills – accompanied by a wonderful range of African music. Daily 11am–11pm.

Grill House Swan Centre, Accra Rd ☎ 0735/554036 or 0727/257584. First-rate

location with pavement tables. Locals will tell you it's not what it was, and it's true service can be *very* slow, but it remains an expat favourite and a good spot for breakfasts, snacks and moderately priced meals, with steaks, chicken and lamb dishes, a selection of vegetarian options and their speciality, mixed grills. They have a bar, too.

Kenshop Cyberstation Oginga Odinga Rd. An excellent base for breakfast or tea, with real espresso coffee, fresh juices (the cane juice with ginger is superb), plus pies, sandwiches, burgers and snacks. Tasty and spotless and right next to Kenshop Supermarket's really good bakery with nice fresh loaves. Mon–Sat 8am–6pm, Sun 10am–6pm.

Kisumu Beach Resort 1.6km past the airport ☎ 0733/749327. Sprawling, formerly busy fishing and lunch spot, with public areas near the hyacinth-clogged shore. Worth checking out at the weekend if you have transport.

Mavis The best place for a drink or a bite to eat at the airport, across the yard from the main terminal building. They do good tilapia and chips and it's a friendly place to while away an airport wait out of the heat. Daily 7am–last flight.

Oriental Upstairs at al-Imran Plaza, Oginga Odinga Rd ☎057/2025462 or 0722/289185. All the usual Chinese favourites, including soya chicken and squid in white sauce, plus some Thai starters; good but quite pricey with most dishes Ksh500–900. Expect to spend Ksh2000 for two, without drinks. All cards accepted. Daily 11am–11pm.

🏃 **Raj Sappy** Paul Mbuya Rd. The only vegetarian restaurant in Kisumu, with spicy south, east and north Indian food. Their excellent poppadums are sold in Nakumatt. Daily 7am–7pm.

Señorita Oginga Odinga Rd ☎0733/744588. A long and varied menu of Indian and African dishes,

and good for steaks and stews, but nothing Latin American or Spanish, despite the name. Mon–Sat 8am–7pm.

🏃 **Simba Club** Jomo Kenyatta Ave. The Sikh Union's restaurant here is open to non-members (11am–3pm for lunch, 7pm–midnight for dinner), with an excellent menu of tandoori dishes and curries. Specialities include Amritsari fish (in a tandoori-style marinade, but fried rather than baked) and fish à la Simba (marinated in coriander and green chilli). Friday evening is the best time to go, when it's full of families relaxing into the weekend.

The Vault Corner of Oginga Odinga and New Station roads. Pizzas, pizzas and more pizzas (pricey at around Ksh800), alongside a few other Italian dishes, an Indian menu with lots of vegetarian and non-vegetarian options, mostly around Ksh400, and an "African" menu. You can eat inside, or at the screened-off pavement tables. There's a bar and, upstairs, the *Rivera Casino* (4–11pm or later). Daily 6.30am–11pm.

Bars and clubs

Kisumu has good **nightlife**, with opportunities for catching **live bands**, and sometimes even big-name stars. More run-of-the-mill **discos** are plentiful, too. The regional music speciality is *ohangala*, based on Luo folk music, which is just as danceable as the alternatives of Congolese Lingala, or *benga*, which is also largely a Luo creation (see p.590).

Apoc Complex Nyamasaria district, 4km from town on the Nairobi road, reached by matatu or *boda-boda* from the main stage. Live bands, mainly Lingala, in what is essentially a lively beer hall and *nyama choma* joint. Wed–Sun 6pm–midnight.

Kisumu Social Centre Off Gumbi Rd, by the library. Live bands – this is a hub of *ohangala* – with a bar. Usually free entry, sometimes up to Ksh200. Daily, 6pm–midnight.

Lakers Inn On the Kiboso road, 5km from Kisumu market (head first for Kakamega, then fork right at Kondele district ☎057/2024897. Big-name Congolese bands and others, with Sunday a family day. Also has food and accommodation.

Mon Ami Ground floor, Mega Plaza, Oginga Odinga Rd. Cold beer, pub-like atmosphere, and CNN or English Premiership football on the TV, plus English

and Indian food, and dancing in the evenings. A favourite of expats and more affluent Kenyans. Sun–Thurs until midnight, Fri & Sat until 5am.

Octopus Bottoms Up Ogada St. A pick-up joint of the first order, so not for the easily shocked, but relaxed enough if you just want to mingle over a beer or two. The restaurant is often empty, but the disco is always lively, and the roof terrace (with BBQ and dartboard) is a popular, breezy rendez-vous, albeit with dire service. Open 24/7.

Ramogi Bar Kendu Lane. A satisfyingly seedy and friendly little bar, with the remains of a vintage jukebox. Mon–Sat 7am–6pm.

Show Breeze Mamboleo district, 5km from Kisumu market (past Kondele district along the Kakamega road). Live *ohangala* and *benga*, in fierce competition with *Lakers Inn* for the big stars.

Listings

Airlines East African Safari Air Express, upper ground floor, block B, Mega Plaza ☎057/2025707; Fly540, second floor, Al-Imran Plaza ☎057/2025331 or 0724/563009; Jetlink, second floor, Jubilee Insurance House, corner of

Oginga Odinga St and Ang'awa Ave ☎0714/333377 or 0737/999956; Kenya Airways, Alpha House, Oginga Odinga Rd ☎057/2056000 or 0734/106000; For airport details and numbers, see overleaf.

Birdwatching Lake Victoria Sunset Birders is the local birding group (w lvsb.50megs.com, ☎057/2024162 or 0734/994938). You can join up for Ksh500 and participate in their internationally recognized monitoring work or simply go on one of their regular bird walks – the area along the golf club shore and the 50 hectares of Dunga swamp are very productive areas.

Books Try Sarit Bookshop, Oginga Odinga Rd on the corner of New Station Road, which has a few novels and guides, or FK Shah, Oginga Odinga Rd by *Señorita* restaurant.

Car rental and travel agents Rav4s and similar small 4WDs are available from around Ksh5000/day. Try Piepercaps, Swan Centre, Accra St ☎057/2024249 or 0722/344148, w www.piepercaps.org; Kisumu Travel & Tours, Central Square ☎057/2020785 or 0722/206020; or Helpys Tours & Travels, Varsity Plaza, Kenyatta Highway, opposite the Kisumu Hotel ☎0733/537500 or 0721/804300.

Golf Nyanza Golf Club is on the lakeshore, the first left down the airport road, about 4km from the town centre.

Hospitals The main treatment centre is Nyanza Provincial General Hospital ☎057/2020801. The best private hospital is Aga Khan Hospital ☎057/2020005.

Immigration The Immigration Department, first floor, Reinsurance Plaza, behind Alpha House on Oginga Odinga Rd (☎057/2024935), is generally helpful, usually stamping visitor's pass extensions on the spot without objection.

Internet access There are numerous places around town. Kenshop Cyberstation is good (see "Eating & Drinking"), or try Arcade Cyber Zone, in Stationery Arcade in Mega Plaza (Mon–Sat 8am–7pm, Sun 9am–2pm).

Kisumu Show The annual Agricultural Society of Kenya show is held in the first week of August, 6km north of town on the Miwani road (off to the east of the Kakamega road).

Library Off Gumbi Rd, behind the bus and matatu station (Mon–Thurs 8am–6.30pm, Fri & Sat 8am–4pm).

Mobiles Safaricom Service Centre, Mezzanine floor, Mega Plaza.

Pharmacies Several are open late and on Sundays, including Dosefield, Mega Plaza, Oginga Odinga St ☎057/2023500 (daily 9am–9pm) and Winam, Ang'awa Ave, 100m from the clock tower (daily 7am–7.30pm).

Police Omolo Agar Rd ☎057/2024719.

Swimming Forget the lake – bilharzia, hippos and crocs are all unfriendly – and instead swim at the *Sunset*, the *Milimani*, the *Kisumu* or the *Imperial*. The small fee is usually waived if you're having a meal.

Moving on from Kisumu

Kisumu is very well connected to the rest of the country by **bus** and **matatu**. The bus and matatu stage is on Gumbi Road, at the intersection of Kenyatta Avenue and Otieno Oyoo Street. They run to more or less everywhere in western Kenya, and further afield to Nakuru, Nairobi and Mombasa.

Akamba has its office on Alego St (☎057/2023554 or 020/3500981 or 0720/891114), with four buses daily to Nairobi (9am, 11am, 1pm & 9pm), and one for Kampala (1pm). **Coast Bus** (☎057/2024141) has an overnight run to Mombasa at 6pm, taking fifteen hours, and a service to Nairobi at 9.30pm, arriving inconveniently at 3 or 4am. Departures, along with those of cheaper firms, are from the main stand, though tickets can be bought at Coast's Alego St office.

The **train to Nairobi** departs, in theory, on Tuesday, Thursday & Sunday at 6.30pm (13hr; 1st class bunks Ksh1415; dinner Ksh350). The local train to **Butere** leaves on Tues, Thurs & Sun at 8.45am after the Nairobi service has arrived (3hr; 3rd class only; Ksh115). Book in person at the station.

Ferry services, formerly run by Kenya Railways from Kisumu to Kendu Bay, Kowuor, Homa Bay, Mbita and Asembo, are currently suspended due to low water levels.

From 2009, **Kisumu airport** (☎020/6611000 or 020/6612000) is undergoing renovations and runway expansion. There are numerous daily flights to Nairobi on Fly540 (☎057/2025363, w www.flyt540.com; $69) East African Safari Air Express (☎020/3530428 or 0733/766326), Jetlink (☎0714/111888) and Kenya Airways (☎057/2056000), plus onwards flights to Mombasa (Fly540; $138) and short hops to Eldoret (Fly540; $25). The airport has a KCB **ATM**, though it's not always working.

Kogelo and the road to Uganda

Heading northwest out of Kisumu, down a broad avenue of flame trees, you pass first the Sunni Muslim, Ismailia and Hindu cemeteries, then Nyanza Golf Club and emerge into the rolling plains of Nyanza province's **Siaya District**. There's a constant stream of transport to the town of **Busia**, on the Ugandan boarder. If you're driving to **Kogelo**, you take the left turn at **Kisian**, 10km past the Kisumu airport, where the roads to Usenge (C27) and Busia (B1) split. The C27 to Bondo and Usenge is a very pretty road, in good shape and well worth the trip, even without the minor justification of Kogelo along the way.

Just 14km after the Kisian junction there's a locally famous landmark and minor pilgrimage site at a place called **Kit Mikaye**. Meaning Place (*kit*) of the First Wife (*mikaye*), it's the largest balancing act in a landscape of giant boulders. This scenic, rocky place is where the first wife of the Luo is supposed to have rested on the tribe's journey south from Sudan, and local women often go there for cures and meditation. It's signposted, and about 1km off the highway to the south. You don't have to go so far, however, if you just want to stop and stretch your legs: there's a huge example of a boulder-pile directly by the road on the north side, and on the south side of the highway the mobile-phone operator Zain has taken the trouble to brand a big clump of the giant boulders in their subtle pink and yellow paint.

The easy route to Mbita (see p.270) ends with a short boat ride from **Luanda Kotieno**, reached by turning left off the C27 at **Ndori**. The small car ferry leaves the port at Luanda Kotieno at 8am, 11am, 3pm and 6pm, taking 45 minutes.

Kogelo

To reach Kogelo, you turn right (north) at Ndori, just 200m west of the turning for Asembo and Luanda Kotieno (if you're travelling by matatu, you may have to wait an hour or two in Ndori). After around 8km heading north on this *murram* road, you cross the Yala River bridge, then wind gently up the hill for a couple of kilometres to reach a small junction with a few *dukas* and some shady trees. You're exactly one kilometre south of the equator, and this is **KOGELO**. Despite the fact that there are still no outward signs of its place in the background of the most powerful man on earth (apart from the Senator Obama Secondary School) – and equally no signs of the development and investment that the media speculated would transform it after the 2008 US elections – nevertheless some of the roots of President Barack Obama's family story are embedded here. More precisely, they're in the compound of the third wife of Obama's paternal grandfather, a kilometre of so out of the "centre" of Kogelo, to the northwest, where her stepson, the US president's father (who died in a car crash in 1982), is buried. You can take a look from the outside, and possibly even pay a visit. The Mama Obama homestead is now a gated and *askari*-guarded plot, with several tents for the security detail in the front garden and Mama Sarah Onyango Obama herself the host of frequent local delegations. Plans to build an **Obama Museum** here have been put on hold while the competing claim of the village of Kanyadhiang near Kendu Bay – where Obama Senior was born, according to some family members – are considered (see p.265).

Tiny Kogelo isn't a place you can "tour" on your own: the only point to being here is to have a local to show you around. You may find a guide on the spot, but the best people for the job are the couple who run Erokamano Destinations at *Village Camp*, in Siaya (see below). They can organize various local excursions based around Obama Senior's background and the local environment, and may be able to secure you an audience with Mama Obama if she is available. Erokomano are also proficient birders and are knowledgeable about the natural history and ecology of this corner of Kenya. If you want to stay the night in Kogelo (there are no hotels), they'll organize a village homestay on BB (②) or a more comfortable residence on FB (⑤).

If you want to continue north from Kogelo to reach the B1 Busia road, you can take one of the occasional matatus from Kogelo to Siaya and points north. If you're driving, the C28 road from Ndori continues north, across the equator, to meet the C30 road that goes west to Siaya (it's 7km from Kogelo to the C30).

Siaya and Usenge

The district capital, **SIAYA**, locally known as Tat Yien ("Roof of Herbs"), has a large community of traditional **herbalists** and is a well-known healing (and bewitching) town. More prosaically, there's a KCB with **ATM**, and the useful Siaya Self Service supermarket in the same street as Akamba Bus. There are plenty of **cybercafés** (all a bit pricier than usual), but the only speedy connection is at DBSC in the Kenya Industrial Estate on the western outskirts of town. If you're staying overnight, you'll probably end up at the noisy *Mwisho Mwisho Tourist Hotel* (☏057/321026; ❸), which offers good-value rooms with breakfast, and the occasional live band, but rather slow meal service; there's a snappier, more customer-facing approach at *The Place*, next to the law courts. For camping, the *Village Camp* (☏020/2443806/7 or 0725/179500, ⓦwww.**erokamano**.com; ❺) at **Tingwangi** market, on the road out to Bondo, has tent pitches or homestay arrangements on full board. They can organize bicycle hire, birdwatching (Lake Kanyaboli and Yala Swamp are superb birding sites) and village excursions, especially on market days, and will help you visit Kogelo (see p000).

USENGE (or Usengi), at the end of the C27 road from Kisumu, is something of a diversion if you're en route to Uganda, but a good target if you're planning an exploration of the district. It's also a town of pre-colonial historical significance

Gem of an idea

In the early **colonial period**, the Luo benefited from some inspired, if dictatorial, leadership. They had inherited the institution of the *ruoth* (king or chief) from the original immigrants from Sudan. The *ruoth* of Gem, a location just east of Siaya, was Odera Akang'o, an ambitious and perceptive young man with an almost puritanical attitude to his duties. He had a private police force to inspect farms and report any idleness to him, and he regularly had his subjects beaten or fined for "unprogressive" behaviour. He introduced new crops and, under British protection, made himself quite a sizeable fortune. He was widely feared.

In 1915, the colonial government sent him, with two other chiefs, to Kampala. He returned full of admiration for the European education and health standards there, and ashamed of Gem and Luoland in general. Fired with enthusiasm, he applied his style of schooling and hygiene, bullying his subjects into sending their children to classes and keeping their shirts clean, while the British turned a blind eye. The results were rapid educational advances in Gem, which is still considered a progressive district today. Odera, unfortunately for him, was employed by the British to use his methods on the Teso people in Uganda, where they singularly failed. He was accused of corruption and sent into internal exile, where he died.

in its own right. The nearby hill, Got Ramogi, is by tradition the site where the first Luo arrived at the lake from further north. It's not a hard climb to the top for a satisfying view over Yala Swamp, Lake Sare and the land that the Luo fought for and eventually won from the Bantu-speakers at the end of the fifteenth century. Usenge itself is a pretty town and lodgings there are cheap, but there are no banks and few services. There's a small stone house available to rent, with a lake view from the lookout tower, living room, double bed and mosquito net (contact Grace Akinge Headrick; ☎0734/213882).

Busia

The **road to Busia** is beautifully smooth and broad and lined with the colourful evidence of everyday rural life, including women carrying huge head-loads of bananas, sugar cane and baskets, often in brilliantly pleated, floral-print dresses.

BUSIA, on the Uganda border, is a surprisingly bearable and increasingly big town and a better place to cross the border than Malaba, the frontier post on the railway line further north. If you're staying the night, the *Emmanuel Hotel*, on the north side of the main drag, 300m from the border post (☎0724/958158; ❶), is the best budget option, though try for room #1, which has better windows and is less stuffy. Better, and popular with NGOs, are the *Blue York*, south of the main drag on Bulanda Road (☎055/22081; ❷), and *Farm View* on Hospital Road, a kilometre south of the main drag (☎055/23036; ❷), with good self-contained rooms with nets, a kids' play area, and traditional dancers and discos at weekends.

There are several daily **buses** from Busia to Nairobi (8hr) via Kisumu (2hr 30min). Most companies run one morning and one evening service; Akamba (☎020/2365821) has departures at 10am and 8pm. **Matatus** serve Kisumu, Malaba and Bungoma, with morning departures to Kitale and Nairobi. On the Ugandan side, there are matatus to Jinja and Kampala. **Moneychangers** on both sides of the border will change Ugandan and Kenyan shillings, or give either for dollars, euros or pounds but check the rates in advance. There is also a Barclays with an **ATM**.

South Nyanza

The territory south of Kisumu is interesting to explore and easy enough to get around, if you're willing to go by matatu. This section covers the agreeable little town of **Kendu Bay**, the main town of **Homa Bay**, the unjustly overlooked **Ruma National Park**, the intriguing ruins of **Thimlich Ohinga**, the islands of **Rusinga and Mfangano** and, down near the Tanzanian border, the one-street town of **Migori**. The **lakeshore** west of Migori is remote and, in parts, beautiful, with **Karungu Bay** and the scenic route via **Sindo** to **Mbita** a rewarding side trip. East of Migori is a feasible backcountry route to Maasai Mara National Reserve, via **Kihancha**.

Kendu Bay and Simbi Lake

The best route from Kisumu to **KENDU BAY** is straight along the lakeshore from Katito, south of Ahero. Although Kendu Bay has a good deal of intrinsic charm, there's little to offer the casual visitor in the town itself. The old part, 500m off the Kisumu–Homa Bay main road, has one notable building in the

▲ Tawakal mosque, Kendu Bay

gorgeous **Tawakal mosque**. You can look around it, though there's not much to see, and climb on the roof. The smaller **Jamia mosque** is less ornate, but older, built in 1902.

Kendu Bay's local fame comes from the curiosity of **Simbi Lake**, about 4km or a 45-minute walk, west of the centre. If you don't have transport, you could also take a *boda-boda*. Head out on the Homa Bay road and pass the left turn to Oyugis and Kisii. Some 2km beyond, over the river bridge before you reach Kanyadhiang, turn right down the path and walk for another fifteen minutes along the left bank of the river before scaling the gentle rise to the lake's rim.

Lake Simbi and the nearby Ondago Swamp have been adopted as June and July feeding grounds by a couple of thousand **lesser flamingos**, refugees from Lake Nakuru (see p.225). Although some locals and officials would like to exploit the attraction, it remains a tranquil beauty spot, with a footpath around the rim, where the only commerce is the odd local resident selling sugar cane. Even without the flamingos, this is unquestionably a weird body of water: around 25 hectares of bright green, alkaline water, sunk twenty to thirty metres below the surrounding land and less than 2km from Lake Victoria itself. It has no apparent source and its origins are somewhat mysterious: it looks like a huge meteorite crater. It's only a couple of kilometres around the perimeter path – an easy half-hour walk.

The **story** goes that an elderly woman, travelling alone, was refused hospitality one rainy night at the village that once occupied the site of the lake. A big beer party was going on and she was ignored. Only one woman would allow her to warm herself and the old woman insisted she and her family leave the village with her. The young woman tried in vain to persuade her husband to come with them, fearing the old lady's revenge for her ill-treatment. So the two women left alone. Later that night there was a tremendous cloudburst and the rain came down so hard that the village was swamped to become Simbi Lake. Further variations on the story (there are many) improve on the theme of drunkenness and debauchery to give a Sodom and Gomorrah ring to the tale. Other lakes in Kenya have similar tales of origin.

The little lake's shores are almost devoid of vegetation. It's of volcanic origin and is apparently extraordinarily deep. According to one local belief, visitors should throw money in to avoid bad luck. Whatever the natural explanation, it seems plausible that the area was inhabited when the lake was formed, and that a natural disaster accounts for the legends.

An interesting new twist on the fame of Simbi is the claim by locals from the hamlet of **Kanyadhiang** (just south of the bridge on the C19 road) that their village is the true birthplace of Barack Obama Senior, rather than Kogelo, and hence the rightful location of any western Kenya Obama museum (see p.261). This dispute is likely to run a lot longer than the president's time in office.

If you're heading on to Homa Bay, you might like to see the **Oriang Pottery Centre** in the village of the same name, 2km past the Simbi Lake turning. It's a UNDEP-funded programme, relying on clay from the local riverbed.

Practicalities

The Total petrol station is on the main road by the junction with the road to Oyugis, and the post office is about 100m west of the junction. There are no banks. The ferry **dock** (a pier partly made of concrete-filled barges) is about a kilometre from the old town, with no boat services at the time of writing due to low water levels in the lake.

There's one **B&L** in the old town, *Milimani Bar & Restaurant* (℡0735/861614; ❶), which has eight basic non-self-contained singles, bucket showers and solar-powered electric lights. Handier for transport, the *Hotel Big Five* at the Total station (℡0724/157955; ❷) is decorated with Disney-esque concrete trees and animals, with rooms set apart from its **restaurant**, which serves excellent fish, and its **nightclub**, which plays music every night, but is only really lively on Saturdays. A few doors east, the *New Wedewo*, a shacky-like *hoteli* that's not much to look at, serves unbeatable *mandaazi*, and pretty good meals too.

Leaving Kendu Bay, you'll have no difficulty getting a matatu up to Oyugis or west to Homa Bay. The obvious alternative escape route is the **lakeshore road** from Kendu Bay to Katito, where it meets the A1 between Kisii and Kisumu. There's a wealth of interest in the surrounding Luo countryside, most of it until recently a rural backwater, with scenes of fishing boats and compounds of square, mud-brick-built, thatched houses (a fairly recent change; traditionally they were round).

Homa Bay

At first glance a scruffy and unremarkable place, the small port town of **Homa Bay**, the region's main centre and also a good base for visits to Ruma National Park, Rusinga Island and Simbi Lake, is one of the friendliest towns in Kenya. The town, admittedly, has nothing much of interest, just a few potholed streets and the unusual straw-hat-shaped **St Paul's Catholic Cathedral**, atop a low hill behind town, with its central altar-in-the-round and great views from the back of the pews. However, if you're into **traditional Luo music**, Homa Bay is the place to track down tapes of *nyatiti* (lyre), *orutu* (single-stringed bow fiddle) and *onand* (accordion) music, as well as the ubiquitous gospel pop.

Homa Bay used to have a busy port, but in 1997 this, and much of the shoreline, became hemmed in by more than a kilometre of **water hyacinth**. The weed infestation happened quickly, trapping some boats. Ferries were

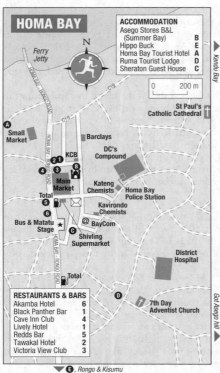

suspended, and people sold off their boats. The hyacinth was eventually cleared mechanically, and fishermen keep the remainder at bay by hand, but the port is a shadow of its former self.

A **hike** up **Got Asego**, the impressive conical hill on the east side of town, is recommended. The hill is the highest of dozens of volcanic plugs (cores of old volcanoes) across the plain; from its table-sized summit, you'll have a 360-degree panorama of lakeshore and surrounding plains. It is remarkable how little of the land is not used. Luo thatched huts are interspersed with tin-roofed homesteads, a patchwork of small plots and agave hedges. Take binoculars and you can see more: clumps of papyrus drifting across the lake, and traffic along the road where it snakes east to Kendu Bay. It takes about an hour to reach the top from the centre of town (actual ascent 30–45min), an easy climb but best tackled late in the afternoon (early morning ascents, though cooler, can be treacherous thanks to dew on the rocks). Head up the Rongo road, turn left 500m south of the Total petrol station and turn right up the *murram* road after Homa Bay School. The hill itself is best approached up the northwest ridge, where there's a well-defined footpath.

Practicalities

Most of the town is strung out along the main street, which starts at the jetty and runs uphill. The little town centre fills a small grid of dusty streets between this main road and the higher, residential area to the east. There are Barclays and KCB **ATMs** but the shopping chains haven't yet reached Homa Bay: Shivling Supermarket (daily 7am–7pm) has most of what you might need. BayCom has Ksh1.50 per minute **internet** access (Mon–Sat 8am–6pm, Sun 2–6pm) and pharmaceutical needs are well served by Kateng (℡0725/483964) and Kavirondo (℡0733/431141).

Matatus leave Homa Bay from the stage on the main road, serving Kendu Bay, Kisii, Kisumu, Mbita and Migori. If you don't find a direct vehicle to Kisii, then take a Migori matatu, which drops you at Rongo on the A1 highway, where you can soon find a Kisii-bound vehicle coming up from the south. **Bus** companies operating to Nairobi include Akamba (℡0329/22578), which has an office 100m down from the matatu stage, opposite the Total petrol station, and runs a day service at 7am and a night service at 7.30pm (8–10hr; Ksh850).

Accommodation

Asego Stores (Summer Bay) Next to the mosque, opposite KCB bank. Nice, bright lodgings, basic but clean, with large beds, squat loos and bucket showers, all set around a courtyard-style dining area. Great-value, especially as it includes breakfast. The best room here is the large triple – worth the little extra. BB ❶

Hippo Buck 2km up the Rongo road, south of the town centre ☎059/22032 or 0733/262000. Competing with *Homa Bay* (below), the standard rooms are functional and clean, and the dining area, food and staff all improve the stay. The deep canal that gushes through the courtyard after heavy rain is a nice feature, and on some weekends there's live *orutu* and *onand* music. ❹

Homa Bay Tourist Hotel Down near the old port, just west of the road ☎059/22788 or 0727/112615, ⓦwww.homabaytouristhotel.com. With 23 renovated rooms in this formerly state-run hotel (including TVs, nets, floor fans, and instant showers) and six safari tents planned, the owners clearly see a future for tourism here. It's a nice spot, with tree-dotted lawns shelving to the lake. Superior rooms are lake-facing and have bigger beds for a Ksh1000 supplement. ❹

Ruma Tourist Lodge South end of town backing onto Total ☎0735/701869. Small, but clean and pleasant, s/c rooms in cottages, set apart from a very congenial outdoor bar-restaurant, with safe parking and even an indoor badminton court. The "executive rooms" are certainly worth the Ksh200 extra. ❷

Sheraton Guest House Up behind the matatu stage ☎0712/128476. Don't be seduced by the fancy facade of the main house – the non-s/c rooms are ranged around a small courtyard at the back, and are small and stuffy, but very clean, with nets and electric sockets, and cheap as chips. Separate showers and (clean) squat loos. ❶

Eating and drinking

For **food**, there are inexpensive *hotelis* everywhere. One of the best is *Akamba*, opposite Total and next to *Redds Bar*. *Lively Hotel* has good, cheap basics and is spot-on for a *chai na mandaazi* breakfast (Ksh50) and *Tawakal Hotel* is worth checking out for its "coastal-style" dishes.

Homa Bay is not especially hot on **nightlife**, but it does have a few bars worth checking out in the evening. Most notably, there's the *Cave Inn Club* on the main road, which has a disco playing *benga* and other local sounds – a nice spot with a shady terrace for a sundowner. Then there's *Redds* near the Akamba office, the most sophisticated drinking spot in town, with a little terrace; the airy *Black Panther Bar*, above *Lively Hotel* on the KCB bank road; and the *Victoria View Club*, opposite, which sometimes has live music at weekends.

Ruma National Park

The Lambwe valley's two hundred-odd square kilometres of tsetse-fly-ridden bush, protected as **Ruma National Park** (ⓦwww.kws.go.ke/ruma.html; $15), is one of the few places in Kenya where you can see **Jackson's hartebeest** and two extremes of the antelope family: the miniature **oribi** and the enormous, horse-like **roan**, which is found only here. The roan is extremely rare, and the best place to see them is in the park's western grasslands, which are often hit by community fires that spread into the park from the west – they like the fresh grazing on the burnt ground. Ruma also has about seventy beautiful **Rothschild's giraffe** and they're not hard to see above the tall grass. You'll have more difficulty spotting **leopard**, the only large predator.

The park is tricky to reach by public transport – the busiest matatu route, Homa Bay to Mbita, skirts it by 11km – but if you're driving, and self-sufficient, it's worth the effort, as you're virtually guaranteed the park to yourself. There are two main gates, Kamato, in the east, with the park HQ and the *Oribi Guest House* (signposted, 21km from Homa Bay) and the more remote Nyatoto in the northwest, on the road between Mbita and Karungu (24km from Mbita; the road crosses the park). If you're coming along the A1 from Migori or Kisii, a signposted *murram* road leads straight to Kamato gate. There are two campsites in the park, *Kamato* and *Nyati*, both close to Kamato gate and the Park HQ (bring all your own equipment, food and water; $15) and one self-catering house, the *Oribi Guest House* ($100 for the whole house; ☎020/600800, ✆reservations@kws.go.ke), just outside the gate, with two double rooms and a triple, plus shared bathroom and kitchen. Although Ruma isn't really practical without your own vehicle, if you have time and would like to visit, you might try making contact with the park warden in Homa Bay (in the DC's compound ☎059/22544).

Thimlich Ohinga

Thimlich Ohinga (daily; no formal hours or entry price; tips welcome) is an archeological site of potentially huge significance: "the greatest stone enclosures in East Africa", according to the Kisumu Museum (see p.257). For sheer visual impact, you won't find a more impressive or atmospheric ancient site anywhere in Kenya, aside from the coast.

Covering an area of 52 acres (21 hectares), the site is the most striking example of an architecture whose remnants are scattered across South Nyanza. Similar to the dry stone enclosures of southern Africa (of which Great Zimbabwe is the classic example), the biggest structure is a compound about 150m in diameter, inside which are five smaller enclosures, probably used as cattle pens, and at least six house pits, the sites of former dwellings. The walls, which range in height from 1m to 4.2m, are built from a combination of natural boulders and dressed stone, the latter used particularly in the construction of the low doorways through the walls. A combination of gradual excavation, and continued restoration work means it's a little hard to get a clear grasp of the whole layout of the site (and there's no map or guidebook), but there are at least four large walled enclosures, each with smaller enclosures inside them.

The precise meaning of "thimlich ohinga" in archaic Luo is open to interpretation, but it is generally held to mean "scary, walled enclosures", though some say the "scary" is a reference to the wild bush country from which the occupants of the site were protected. It's estimated the compounds were built around the fifteenth century by a people whose history has been forgotten, but were almost certainly Bantu-speaking predecessors of the Luo. It probably came to be occupied by Luos displaced in inter-clan fighting in the early eighteenth century, within a few decades of their arrival here. Elsewhere in the district, successive generations of various communities have used stone enclosures and, in some places, modern Luo families have their homesteads inside the remnants of such walls.

Practicalities

You really need your own transport to get to Thimlich Ohinga. From Kisii (105km) or Homa Bay (60km), head for Rodi Kopany on the C20 between Homa Bay and Rongo, where you take the C18 southwest, through **Mirogi** and **Ndhiwa** to **Miranga**. Just beyond Miranga's shops, a signpost shows the direction of Thimlich Ohinga down a rough *murram* track that can take an ordinary car when dry, but requires 4WD in the wet. The site is about 30km south of here. If you're very determined and intrepid, it is just about possible to do this **by public transport**, but there's nowhere to stay, barely anywhere to eat, and you'll need a tent and supplies in case you can't get there and back in a day.

It's easier to approach Thimlich Ohinga from **Migori**. Take the Tanzania road and after 4km, in **Soma**, turn off right (west) onto *murram*, at the junction for Muhoro Bay, where there is a National Cereals and Produce Board depot. A couple of kilometres from the depot you reach another junction where you take a right and drive straight on via **Suna** and **Macalder**. Exactly 4.8km after you cross the big bridge over the Migori River, you cross the Gucha on a smaller bridge. Eight hundred metres west of the Gucha you reach a place called **Ayego** (or Ombo) and turn right (north). A basic farm/bush track, in fair condition and a bit stony in dry weather but liable to be tricky in wet, goes north 12.3km, following the ridge to the west of the Gucha river valley, as far as another junction at another small location, Masara. Turn right here onto a broad stretch of *murram*, following a fence, and 200m further you'll find the entrance to the site (55km from the Cereals Board Depot). You can also reach Thimlich Ohinga, using the last part of these directions, by driving east from Karungu (the junction at Ayego is 21.2km east of Karungu). Like the Miranga route, it's possible to get most of the way to the site using the occasional matatus that ply between Migori and Karungu, getting out at Ayego. But you might have to walk that last twelve kilometres.

Lake Victoria's ecology and economy

Lake Victoria fills a shallow depression (no deeper than eighty metres in depth) between the Western and Eastern Rift valleys, yet it is not part of the Rift system. Until the 1960s, it was home to around five hundred different species of brilliantly coloured tropical **fish**, known as haplochromines or **cichlids,** all of them endemic – unique to the lake. Scientists, puzzling over how such a dazzling variety of species came to evolve in this largely uniform environment in the space of no more than a million years, have suggested that, at some stage in its history, the lake must have dried into a series of small lakes in which the fish evolved separately. Lake Victoria's cichlids are popular aquarium fish, and one of the commonest larger species, the tilapia, is a regional speciality, grilled or fried and served whole.

In the early 1960s, a voracious carnivore, the **Nile Perch**, was introduced to the lake, and proceeded to eat its way through the cichlid population, driving some species close to extinction, though many have held on in parts of the lake which were too shallow for perch, or in smaller lakes around the main one. For local people, the introduction of the perch, which can reach a weight of 250kg, has been a bit of a Trojan horse: while they're consumed locally and sold for export (good news for the lakeshore economy), traditional fishing and processing have been hit hard by the arrival of modern vessels and factories joining in the feast and taking their profits elsewhere.

The lake has other problems, however. **Algae** has proliferated, due to industrial and sewage pollution, depriving the lake of oxygen. More than three million litres of human waste drain into the lake every day, and the Swedish development agency, SIDA, estimates that Kenya, with the smallest share of the lake's shoreline, is its main polluter. As well as suffering a dramatic fall in oxygen levels, the lake is becoming so murky that the remaining cichlids are unable to identify mates, so that hybridization is occurring. Meanwhile, the building of the causeway between Mbita and Rusinga Island has turned the Winam Gulf into even more of a pond, with only one outlet, inhibiting currents and making its water even less healthy.

Another threat comes from the **water hyacinth**, originally native to Brazil. This floating weed grows quickly around the lakeshore and spreads like a carpet across the surface, blocking out the light, choking the lake to death and snaring up vessels. Since the mid-1990s, Homa Bay, Kendu Bay and Kisumu have all at times been strangled by mile-wide cordons of the weed, inhibiting passage to all but the smallest canoes, with disastrous results for the local economy. Solutions have included the promotion of products (furniture, paper, even building materials) made from harvested hyacinth. In 2001, mechanical clearance enabled passenger ferries to start functioning again, only for falling water levels to cause their suspension once more.

Rusinga Island

Much easier than Ruma National Park or Thimlich Ohinga is a trip to **Rusinga Island**. The narrow channel between Mbita and the island was bridged by a **causeway** in 1984, so driving around Rusinga is quite feasible. A steady stream of matatus plies the Homa Bay–Mbita route throughout the day, but they're often packed, and the road is rough *murram* the whole way, and very difficult when wet. You do get some good lakeshore views, and access if you're driving and want a break, for a couple of kilometres south of **LUANDA** (29km from Homa Bay's Mbita junction). From Kisumu, it can be quicker to get a matatu to **Luanda Kotieno** (see p.261), from where there are ferries over to Mbita at 8am, 11am, 3pm and 6pm, taking 45 minutes (matatus leave Kisumu three to four hours earlier to connect).

Mbita, straddled on either side of the causeway, is very unprepossessing indeed, but things improve once you get on to the island. The building of the causeway – partly over two dumper trucks that fell into the lake during the operation and couldn't be recovered – has had some unwanted side effects. Vervet monkeys now move onto the island to raid crops, and fish have become scarce on the Kisumu side of Rusinga because the causeway blocks the current, turning the water there into a stagnant pond. A bridge to replace the old chain ferry would have been the best solution to the island's access problem. As it is, the single bit of civil engineering represented by the causeway has ended Rusinga's slight isolation at what many local people feel is an unacceptable cost.

Mbita

Apart from the odd matatu that runs around Rusinga Island, and the occasional ones that venture down to **Sindo**, the locally important town of **MBITA** is as far as you can go by public road transport. The last matatu returns to Homa Bay around 3pm. There are, however, some wooden "**engine boats**" connecting Mbita daily (until around 2pm) with various ports on Mfangano Island, Takawiri Island, and the **car ferry** to Luanda Kotieno.

Accommodation in the village itself is basic but decent. *Elk Lodge*, across the square from the matatu stand (℡0720/716665, ⓦwww.safarikenya.net/elk.htm; ❷), has clean rooms around a patio garden with flowers and pawpaw trees, but no hot water, though they may provide some in a bucket if you ask. The same landlady also runs the cheaper *Viking Rest House*, just 20m away (℡0720/716665, ⓦwww.safarikenya.net/Viking.htm; ❶), with smaller, non-self-contained rooms, but reasonable enough for the price. *Patroba Ogweno Lodge*, behind the *Elk* (℡0733/731638; ❷), is also very good value. The hot water is on tap and the downstairs rooms are nice and cool.

Some 2km further down the road, ⚓ *Lake Victoria Safari Village* (℡0721/912120, ⓦwww.safarikenya.net; BB ❺), run by the Norwegian husband of the *Elk*'s landlady, is an excellent place to stay, with delightfully restful, high-vaulted *bandas*, divided to create good, spacious twin or double rooms, with clean, well-appointed bathrooms and little terraces out front, overlooking a lakeside beach, and a rather magnificent honeymoon suite in a mock-lighthouse. If you're pining for the Indian Ocean, this almost recaptures that feeling. At night, *omena* fishermen "make more light than Nairobi" as one waiter put it. These tiny fish, which, when dried and pounded, form such an important part of the local diet, are attracted to the hurricane lamps taken out by the fishermen. You can watch all this from the very nice terrace dining room of the "Village", where the food, when it comes, is always good (most dishes around Ksh400, beer Ksh120).

Leaving Mbita, you can take the **car ferry** across the Winam Gulf the ten short kilometres to Luanda Kotieno. The ferry goes four times a day, currently leaving

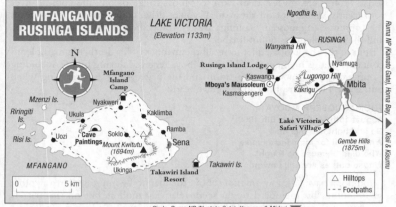

MFANGANO & RUSINGA ISLANDS

LAKE VICTORIA
(Elevation 1133m)

N

Ngodha Is.

RUSINGA

Wanyama Hill

Ruma NP (Kamato Gate), Homa Bay,

Kisii & Kisumu

Mfangano
Island
Camp

Mzenzi Is.

Nyakweri

Rusinga Island Lodge

Kaswanga
Mboya's Mausoleum
Kasmasengere

Nyamuga

Lugongo Hill
Kakrigu

Mbita

Riringiti
Is.

Ukula

Kaklimba

Risi Is.

Uozi

Cave
Paintings
Mount Kwitutu
(1694m)

Soklo

Ramba

Sena

Lake Victoria
Safari Village

Gembe Hills
(1875m)

MFANGANO

Ukinga

Takawiri Island
Resort

Takawiri Is.

0   5 km

△ Hilltops
--- Footpaths

Sindo, Ruma NP (Nyatoto Gate), Karungu & Midori ▼

Mbita at 7am, 10am, 2pm and 5pm, returning an hour later (passengers Ksh60, cars Ksh500). Matatus complete the journey to Kisumu via Asembo and Ndori, and this is usually a faster way of reaching Kisumu than going via Homa Bay.

The island

RUSINGA is small and austerely pretty, with high crags dominating the desolate, goat-grazed centre, and a single dirt road running around the circumference. Life here is difficult, with drought commonplace, and high winds a frequent torment. The occasional heavy rain either washes away the soil or sinks into the porous rock, emerging lower down where it creates swamps. Ecologically, the island is in very dire straits: almost all its trees have been cut down for cooking fuel or to be converted into lucrative charcoal. These conditions make harvests highly unpredictable and most people fish to make ends meet, either selling the catch on to refrigerated lorries or bartering directly for produce with traders from Kisii, and the causeway has forced them to make longer fishing trips. Yet the islanders, in common with their mainland cousins, remain an unfailingly friendly and cheerful bunch, who are more than happy to make contact with wayward travellers.

The island is rich in **fossils**, and was the site of Mary Leakey's discovery of a skull of *Proconsul africanus* (a primitive anthropoid ape), which can be seen in the National Museum (see p.257). It was also the birthplace of **Tom Mboya** (see p.555), the civil rights champion, trade unionist and charismatic young Luo politician who was assassinated in Nairobi in 1969, sparking off a crisis that led to more than forty deaths in widespread rioting and demonstrations, and was a turning point for the worse in Kenya's post-Independence history.

Tom Mboya's mausoleum lies on family land at **Kasawanga** on the north side of the island, about 7km by the dirt road from Mbita, or roughly 5km directly across the island. The odd matatu will pick you up, as will the lorries that travel round the island collecting fish from local communities, but otherwise you'll need to walk the whole way there and back if necessary (allow four hours and take some water). Local residents will show you the way, but Rusinga is so small you're unlikely to get lost. Aim for the crags in the centre, skirt them to the right and then walk down to rejoin the road on the other side of the Tom Mboya Memorial Health Centre. There's a little *hoteli* here with cold sodas. From here, it's less than 2km to Mboya's mausoleum, the conical silver roof clearly visible just off the road. If you're driving, turn right 11.7km from the causeway (signposted "Kolunga Beach"), and then right again after 150m, and the mausoleum is 600m further.

Built in the shape of a bullet to recall the manner of his death, the mausoleum contains various mementoes and gifts Mboya received during his life, including a cup won in a dancing competition and the briefcase he was carrying when murdered. The inscription on the grave reads:

THOMAS JOSEPH MBOYA
August 15th 1930 – July 5th 1969
Go and fight like this man
Who fought for mankind's cause
Who died because he fought
Whose battles are still unwon!

You don't have to know anything about the man to be impressed. In any other surroundings his memorial might seem relatively modest, but on this barren, windswept shore, it stands out like a beacon. Members of Mboya's family live nearby, and are usually on hand to open the gates. They are happy to see foreign visitors, and they maintain the mausoleum themselves, so they always appreciate donations, though these are not obligatory. If you're interested, take a look at the rather good folder of press cuttings about Mboya. The nearby **Rusinga Island Museum** (donations welcome), just across the lawn, has various artefacts and crafts connected to Tom Mboya and Luo life. It's maintained by an enthusiastic and informative young curator, who will open up when you arrive.

Fifty metres past the Tom Mboya Secondary School, the path to the right takes you through *shambas* of millet and corn to a seasonally grassy lakeside called Hippo Bay. Here you can watch nesting fish eagles as well as, usually, hippos. If you're lucky, you may see the pretty and little-known spotted-necked otters that live around Lake Victoria and nowhere else in Kenya.

Also on the north side of the island, 10.5km from the causeway around the north side, or 9.5km around the south side, is *Rusinga Island Lodge* (T0716/055924 or 0734/402932, W www.rusinga.com; package $880, flights extra), a rustic-luxury retreat, most of whose clients fly in from the Maasai Mara to the lodge's airstrip. Part-fishing lodge, part-spa retreat, part-water sports club, part-birders' paradise (369 species have been recorded), this is a sumptuous and relaxing escape with comfortable, safari-style cottages and large bathrooms. Much of the produce for the sixteen guests is grown on their own two acres. There's also the chance to do a **fossil walk** to the site where Mary Leakey discovered *Proconsul africanus*.

Mfangano Island

Said to have been inhabited for centuries, enigmatic **Mfangano Island** is out of range of the smallest fishing boats, and entirely without vehicles. The island is populated by a curious mixture of immigrants from all over Kenya, administered by a chief and three sub-chiefs with help from a trio of policemen. Monitor lizards swarm on the sandy shores and **hippos** are much in evidence out in the water.

Larger and more populous than Rusinga, with a similarly rugged landscape but better vegetation cover, Mfangano's greatest economic resource is still the lake itself. As on Rusinga, the local **fishing techniques** are unusual: the islanders fish with floating kerosene lamps hauled shorewards, or towards a boat, to draw in the schools to be netted. Local residents rely on a network of temporary **footpaths** that are constantly changing course. If you arrive at Sena by boat, you can walk all over the island, though it's always easier if you have a guide – Ksh500 per day is considered a fair fee.

The island's **rock paintings** are certainly worth the trip alone. Thought to be at least a thousand and possibly four thousand years old, they are believed to have been painted by the island's original hunter-gatherer inhabitants who were displaced in around the sixteenth century by Luo incomers, who were themselves displaced a couple of centuries ago by a Bantu people called the Abasuba.

The rock paintings

The Peace Museum can arrange trips to three sites featuring prehistoric **rock paintings** in the form of reddish spirals and whorls, some with rays, up to 50cm across, that could come from any Von Daniken paperback. The main sites (at Kwitone and Mawanga) are close to Ukula on the north coast. You pay a Ksh500 guiding fee to be taken to them from Sena, and a Ksh200 entry fee at each site. The paintings were probably used for rainmaking ceremonies, and all kinds of rituals and taboos are still supposed to apply to people visiting them – a period of sexual abstinence, for example, and not telling anybody that you are coming to the site before you actually do so.

The painting at the Odengere Hills, also on Mfangano, are unique among these at Lake Victoria's prehistoric sites in that they have depictions of insects, some of them so fine that even the species can be identified. Experts are at a loss as to their significance. Site-by-site descriptions of Lake Victoria's rock art can be found in the academic journal *Azania* (1994: vol.9; ⊚ www.biea.ac.uk). The Peace Museum also publishes a pamphlet explaining local rock art.

Practicalities

Unless you fly in, the only means of access to Mfangano is on the large wooden boats with outboard motors ("matatu" or "engine" boats) that shuttle local people and their produce between Mbita and the surrounding islands and peninsulas. Most stop at Takawiri then head around Mfangano in an anti-clockwise direction, calling at Sena, Nyakweri and Ukula, though others go around clockwise. The first boat leaves Mbita around 8.30am (the last around 3pm), with the last boat back from Sena at around 2.30pm, so a day-trip isn't really a practical proposition unless you have enough money (around Ksh4000) to hire a boat and skipper for the day.

It's a ninety-minute crossing to **SENA,** the chief's camp and also the capital of Mfangano. Sena has a couple of small *dukas* and *hotelis* and a post office, and is home to the **Abasuba Community Peace Museum** (Mon–Sat 9am–5pm; Ksh500), which displays cultural artefacts such as traditional cooking pots and farming implements, and is also of interest because you can camp in its grounds (Ksh500), or stay in a traditional Abasuba hut; with drinking and washing water, but no showers (Ksh500). The museum can organize guided excursions to the island's main sights, and can even arrange transport from Mbita. For further information, contact the museum director, Jack Obonyo (☎0723/898406). There is no other accommodation as such in Sena, though local people may be prepared to put you up at B&L-type rates. Don't forget in such cases that Mfangano is desperately poor, without mains electricity or piped water, and you should bring anything you think you might need.

The alternative accommodation, at the other end of the spectrum, is the exclusive and expensive **Mfangano Island Camp** (☎0733/268888, ⊚ www.governorscamp.com; closed April & May; $890 package; flights extra), a fishing lodge similar to Rusinga's (see p.271). Most of the camp's visitors fly in from the Maasai Mara on a day-trip (fishing and birding in the morning, lunching and lounging in the afternoon), but some stay on to enjoy the beautiful setting, gourmet food and attentive service. The price includes all meals and a boat with driver at your disposal. The camp, a huddle of clay-and-thatch buildings laid out in the shape of a Luo homestead, but fitted out in deluxe style, overlooks a private bay and sleeps twelve.

Mbita to Sindo and Karungu

Going beyond Mbita to the south, to **Sindo and Karungu**, is slow going by matatu. The road can be very difficult during the rains and, at the best of times, there's only a limited demand, so one daily departure is the norm. Karungu is better linked with Migori: the stretch between Sindo and Karungu, while remote and beautiful in parts, is best done in your own 4WD.

Some of the most scenic landscapes in western Kenya are to be found around the **Gembe Hills**, south of Mbita. As you approach **Sindo** from the north, the little lakeside town, with the impressive towering backdrop of the **Gwasi Hills**, soaring nearly 1000m above the level of the lake, makes for some memorable views, which seem to have more in common with the Greek islands than with equatorial Africa. The road then turns inland, between the Gembe and Gwasi hills, and runs down to **Kwoyo** and the northwestern Nyatoto Gate entrance to Ruma National Park (see p.267). The narrow public road, mostly of treacherous black cotton soil, follows the eastern border of the park, just inside the fence line. If you can take your eyes off the road, you're likely to get some excellent free game-viewing and can expect to see Rothschild's giraffe and various antelope out on the grassy plain to the east. After you leave the park zone, the road improves to a wider, stonier surface, and you should be able to keep up a decent speed to Karungu. Seventy kilometres from Mbita, **Karungu** is a small town on the lakeshore, greatly occupied with *omena* catching and drying, with one or two basic lodgings and *hotelis*. All the streets in the town seem to have been surfaced, but the road out to the east, to Suna and Migori is *murram*.

Migori

MIGORI is a border town spread out along 4km of the A1 highway. More of a western highlands town than you might imagine, conifer-covered hills rise up to the east. There's a Barclays with **ATM** and one or two small supermarkets. There are **buses to Nairobi** via Kisii, Kericho and Nakuru leaving early morning or evening, and there are also morning buses to Eldoret, and matatus to Kisumu, Kisii and Homa Bay. Heading down **to Tanzania**, there are direct buses to Mwanza mornings and evenings, but otherwise you'll have to take a matatu to the border post at Isebania (also called Sirare, and served by direct matatus from Kisumu), or at Kianja, cross on foot and take an onward vehicle from the other side.

Market days are interesting for the variety of peoples and for traditional activities untainted by tourism. There are one or two decent, modest **hotels**, but water supplies are sporadic, and even cold water may not be available on tap. *Girango*, at the south end of town (☎059/20014; BB ❸), is friendly and peaceful, with rooms in pleasant gardens and guarded parking. If you need something cheaper, try one of the B&Ls around the matatu stand and north of the bridge. For **food**, the *Exile Chis Palace* is the best of the *hotelis* just north of the post office, serving good, wholesome Kenyan staples.

Kuria moves

Kihancha is the capital of the **Kuria** people, who live in scattered, rural communities. The Kuria have an interesting, quasi-matriarchal system found in various parts of Africa, which essentially allows women of means to "marry" younger women in order to have children without the need to live with a man. In practice, it's often a married woman who can't have children who invites a younger woman into her home. The young "bride", in turn, chooses a male partner, often in secret, to father her children, who are brought up by the two women without the involvement of the father or the older woman's husband. The older woman is sometimes a widow, sometimes simply a single woman. In any case, she lives like a male elder – attending to light business affairs but essentially waited upon hand and foot from dawn to dusk. It's a system with much to recommend it, especially when it takes care of unmarried mothers (who are barred from marrying men), who come into the family as "wives" – surrogate mothers – and whose children are automatically adopted. Ironically, despite these apparently female-controlled arrangements, it's male children that women-families want, and men who inherit land.

Migori to Maasai Mara National Reserve

Much of the C13 road east to **Maasai Mara** (p.360) is in a pretty dreadful state, and if you're driving should only be attempted in a 4WD. Some matatus do parts of this route, and one or two services go right through to Narok and back, which, if you're on a low budget, is one way of visiting the Maasai Mara (or at least saying you've been there) without paying for the privilege. You won't enter the reserve itself, but you will see some wildlife en route, especially in the great conservancy areas north of the reserve, though it's a long and often miserably uncomfortable journey.

The Maasai Mara junction is at **Suna**, Migori's little brother, 4km south of Migori down the A1, where the *murram* road to Karungu also meets the highway. From here, it's 22km to the **Kihancha** turning (keep on straight: the small town is to the right) and you cross the Migori River 2km later. Halfway between Kihancha and Lolgorien, the road improves to fair-to-good *murram*, with the odd rough patch. You reach **Lolgorien**, 46km from Suna, and another 20km sees you at the top of the escarpment above the Oloololo Gate, with the plains of the Mara spread out to the east. Allow at least two hours to get here.

The Western Highlands

The Western Highlands rise all around Lake Victoria in a great bowl. There's superb walking country throughout, in the **Nandi Hills**, for example, or in the little-known **Mau Massif**, east of Kericho. But the undoubted highlights are the tiny **Saiwa Swamp National Park** and **Kakamega Forest National Park**, both areas where visiting on foot is essential to appreciate the forest environment. For well-equipped hikers, **Mount Elgon** is also a major temptation, sharing much of Mount Kenya's flora and fauna, but with very few visitors. There's more wonderful walking country in the high hills of the **Cheranganis**, though you need to build in some extra time for accessing them. On the whole, the highland **towns** are not particularly arresting. **Kisii** is unjustly dismissed by most travellers but has a couple of good excursions; **Kericho**, the tea capital of Kenya, is certainly worth an overnight stay; and **Kitale** has some museums; but **Eldoret** and **Kakamega** are essentially route-hubs and supply towns with little for visitors to do.

Kisii and around

Headquarters of the **Gusii** people, and district town of a region vying with Nyeri in having the fastest-growing population in the country, **KISII** is a prosperous, hard-working trading centre in the hills. Notoriously muddy and rubbish-strewn, with a minor reputation for hassle which really only reflects the friendliness of the locals, the town is undergoing something of a makeover, with its sloping streets gradually being resurfaced with paving blocks. Kisii is most famous for its fine **soapstone**, though there's little to be seen in the town itself (*Hotel Kawanji's* usually has some for sale, see p.279). The best locality for

Gusii history and culture

The Bantu-speaking **Gusii** (after whom the town is named) were only awakened to the brutal realities of British conquest in 1905, when they rebelled, pitching themselves with spears against a machine gun. It was "not so much a battle as a massacre", one of the participants recalled, leaving "several hundred dead and wounded spearsmen heaped up outside the square of bayonets". In 1908, after the District Commissioner was speared in a personal attack, the same thing happened again, only this time the Gusii were trying to escape, not attacking. Crops were burned and whole villages razed to the ground. **Winston Churchill**, at the time the Under-Secretary of State for the Colonies, telegraphed from the Colonial Office: "Surely it cannot be necessary to go on killing these defenceless people on such an enormous scale."

The Gusii were totally demoralized. In a few brief years, the fabric of their communities had been torn apart, hut taxes imposed, and cattle confiscated to be returned only in exchange for labour. And then came World War I. Kisii was the site of the first Anglo-German engagements in East Africa, and thousands of men were press-ganged into the hated Carrier Corps.

It seems extraordinary that the exceptionally friendly people of Kisii are the grandchildren of the conscripts. The powerful, millennial religious movements that burst among them during the colonial period under the name Mumboism may partly account for the very strong ties of community they've maintained against all odds. Prophets and medicine men have always been important here, and even in today's superficially Christianized society, the Gusii have solidly kept their cultural identity. The practice of **trepanning**, for example, which involves tapping a small hole in the skull to relieve headache or mental illness, seems to be as old as the Gusii themselves. "Brain operations" are still performed, clandestinely, but apparently quite successfully.

Witchcraft and **sorcery** also continue to play important roles in the life of the town and its district, and often make headlines. The growing influence of Christianity has led to spates of **lynchings** of suspected witches. Residents are often reticent to come forward as witnesses, which can lead to an interesting collision of worldviews in the media. On one occasion the local police chief was quoted saying: "We hope we can get them [the witches] and if possible charge them in court. This way we shall save their lives."

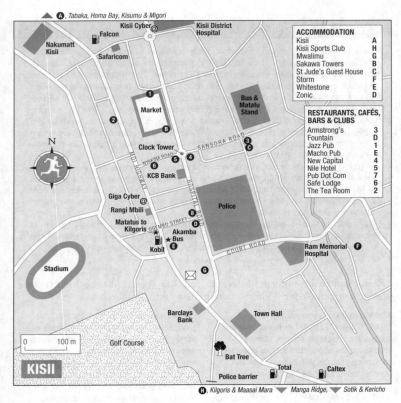

Kisii Cyber @
Falcon
Kisii District Hospital
Nakumatt Kisii
Safaricom

ACCOMMODATION
Kisii	A
Kisii Sports Club	H
Mwalimu	G
Sakawa Towers	B
St Jude's Guest House	C
Storm	F
Whitestone	E
Zonic	D

Ⓐ
Market
Ⓑ
Ⓑ

Bus & Matatu Stand

RESTAURANTS, CAFÉS, BARS & CLUBS
Armstrong's	3
Fountain	D
Jazz Pub	1
Macho Pub	E
New Capital	4
Nile Hotel	5
Pub Dot Com	7
Safe Lodge	6
The Tea Room	2

Clock Tower
SANSORA ROAD
NYAKINA ROAD
Ⓐ Ⓐ Ⓐ
KCB Bank
MOI HIGHWAY

Giga Cyber @
Rangi Mbili
Matatus to Kilgoris
OSEMBO STREET
Akamba Bus ★
Ⓑ
Kobil
Ⓐ
Ⓐ

Police
HOSPITAL ROAD

COURT ROAD

Ram Memorial Hospital Ⓕ

✉ Ⓖ

Stadium

N

Barclays Bank

Town Hall

0   100 m

Golf Course

Bat Tree

Total Caltex

Police barrier

KISII

Ⓗ, Kilgoris & Maasai Mara ▼ Manga Ridge, ▼ Sotik & Kericho

watching the carvers and making on-the-spot purchases is **Tabaka**, some way south (see overleaf). One thing you may notice if you stay overnight in Kisii is the occasional **earth tremor** – the town lies on a fault line and minor earthquakes are not uncommon, only a slight worry if you're asleep at the top of the *Zonic* hotel at the time. Wildlife enthusiasts will want to check out the tree full of **giant bats** in the government compound between Moi Highway and Kisii Sports Club at the southern end of town.

Practicalities

Getting around tends to be on foot or by taxi, as Kisii is too hilly for *boda-bodas*. There are SCB and Barclay's banks with **ATMs**, and **internet** access at Giga Cyber (daily 7am–8pm) at the back on an unlikely-looking courtyard off Moi Avenue. The main **hospital** is Kisii District, but the private option (Ksh400 to see a doctor) is Ram Memorial Hospital on Court Road. If you're driving and need advice or assistance, try Rangi Mbili, a very helpful **parts store and workshop**; they're always happy to meet travellers.

Accommodation

You'll find plenty of **places to stay**, although some are pretty awful, and most are noisy, especially on Wednesdays and weekends when bars and discos are at their loudest, and women travelling alone will want to avoid cheaper places.

Moving on from Kisii

Kisii is something of a route focus, with both regional and national bus and matatu services passing through. There are plenty of **matatus** leaving throughout the day. Most leave from the main stage in front of the market. The exceptions are matatus for Nyachenge and Tabaka, which leave from opposite the Falcon station at the north end of town; and for Kericho and Kilgoris, which go from the bus park beside Rangi Mbili. There are also useful early-morning departures for Narok via the B3, passing the junctions for the C12 and C13 Maasai Mara access roads. **Bus services** are numerous. Akamba, with its office by the *Whitestone Hotel*, departs for Nairobi (9am & 9pm; Ksh800), Homa Bay (4pm; Ksh200), and Migori (4am, using the Nairobi–Mwanza service; Ksh200).

If you're driving and are planning to take the minor but increasingly popular route to the **Maasai Mara** via Kilgoris and Lolgorien, note that beyond Kilgoris, the road to the Mara is difficult, even with 4WD, and the section down the Oloololo Escarpment can be impossible after rain. Heading for the north or east of the reserve, the fastest route is via Sotik and Bomet.

Tanzania is accessible by services to the **border crossing**, variously known as Isebania or Nyabikaye on the Kenyan side, and Serira, Sirare or Siria on the Tanzanian, as well as by a daily Akamba bus service to Mwanza (4am).

Water supplies are notoriously erratic and you should also be prepared for power fluctuations during heavy rain, so have some candles handy.

Kisii Moi Highway, on the road out to Kisumu ☎058/30134 or 0721/493749. Ramshackle but quiet, with an agreeable, creaking colonial atmosphere and helpful staff, the *Kisii Hotel* belies outward appearances with its twelve spacious, clean s/c rooms with nets, TVs, and instant showers. There's guarded parking and a huge and beautiful bird-filled garden, perfect for relaxing with a cold beer or three, though the food in the restaurant isn't great. BB ❶

Kisii Sports Club ☎020/2415537 or 0725/964164. The club is now open to all, and has good-sized, clean, well-furnished standard rooms, with nets, TVs and instant showers (executive rooms have fridges and even more space). But it's a very mixed bag of impressions, with the pool empty and most public areas appearing as if halfway through a very slow refurbishment: the bar functions, the kitchen apparently doesn't, and the peaceful grounds are perfect for kids, with lots of space to run around on the lawns. ❸

Mwalimu Moi Highway ☎058/30357. This 1979 concrete block at the southern end of town was once a teachers' hostel and is still run by the teachers' union, with parking facilities and a bar. The decent s/c rooms are comfortable and carpeted, though some are rather cramped, with nets and hot water, and some with nice views, but they tend to feel like offices converted into bedrooms. ❷

Sakawa Towers Hospital Rd ☎058/30477 or 020/2336977. Named after a Gusii medicine man and prophet, this six-storey block, with great town views from the roof and upper floors, offers good value, though they're still bringing water (even hot water) in buckets "because the showers get destroyed". All the rooms are s/c with nets and balconies, but some are small and cramped, so be choosy. BB ❶

St Jude's Guest House ☎0722/797365 or 0714/231007. Very decent B&L, with s/c rooms with instant showers, nets and TVs throughout, and many with balconies. Rooms 11–19 have good views over the town and countryside, but the best room, "executive room" #10, has magnificent views from a 270° balcony and a bit of a honeymoon theme going on, complete with plastic flowers and slightly more mirrors than necessary. Also has a nice, well-lit upper-floor *hoteli*. ❷

Storm Court Rd ☎058/30649 or 0727/630021. The quietest hotel in Kisii offers a choice of adequate rooms, all s/c with nets, TV and instant showers, plus some more expensive suites, and an outside bar and *nyama choma* joint. Good value and well managed. ❷

Whitestone Moi Highway ☎058/300014 or 0720/020330. Excellent-value cheapie, secure and clean with s/c doubles, and s/c or non-s/c singles, hot water, a cramped little bar called the *Macho Pub*, that lives up to its name, and a good cheap restaurant. An extremely good deal if you're counting the pennies. ❶

Zonic ☎ 058/30298. Supposedly Kisii's top hotel, eight storeys high with balconies for most rooms (a real plus point), with instant showers and short bath tubs, TV and nets on request. It's all a bit fading and frayed but basically sound. Safe, underground parking. ❷

Eating and drinking

Despite the noxious drain smells, the overflowing **market** is the first base for hungry travellers. Kisii is also blessed with a big supermarket, Nakumatt Kisii (Mon–Sat 8.30am–8.30pm, Sun 10am–8am).

The lodgings mostly have **dining rooms** or **restaurants** of their own, of which the *Fountain*, underneath the *Zonic* hotel, is the best, though its main role is as a giant bar with African sounds and widescreen TV. Reliable places for a shot of cholesterol include the *Tea Room* on Moi Highway, which, true to its name, does a gorgeous cup of Indian-style *chai*, and *Hotel Kawanji's*, with its pleasant atmosphere and wooden tables, offers the usual choice of stewed or fried meat with *ugali*, chips or rice. Somewhere better all round is the ⚜ *Nile Hotel*, a very popular first-floor terrace restaurant, offering huge portions of all the usual staples, plus a few more unusual items, and it has a good corner position for hanging out and people-watching.

Kisii has some excellent **drinking** spots. Perennially popular is the ⚜ *Jazz Pub* on Hospital Road, a relaxed venue open until midnight, with waiter service and an eclectic mix of sounds. *Armstrong's*, on the ground floor of *St Jude's Guest House*, is a long bar with a congenial atmosphere, plus several screens of sport (usually English football), and good music, but it closes at 10pm. Another place, with its own rough and ready charm, is *Safe Lodge*, open round the clock on Nyakina Road, which has three pool tables (called Arsenal, Chelsea and Manchester United), and pounding reggae accompaniment.

Tabaka

TABAKA is one of the most important centres in the world for **soapstone** (steatite) production. Most of the carvings are bought up by buyers from the curio shops in Nairobi and elsewhere, but shops selling the carvings now line the road through the little town, and are happy to sell direct to visitors.

The turn-off for Tabaka is at **Nyachenge**, 18km west of Kisii on the A1 Migori road. A sign to the left, if coming from Kisii, points to the St Amillus Tabaka Mission Hospital and Kisii Soapstone Carvers Co-operative Society. From here it's 5km into the village (6km to the Co-operative Society) on a rough dirt road that's treacherous in wet weather, though an ordinary car can make it when it's dry. Coming by matatu from Kisii, it's best to get one that goes direct to Tabaka, even if that means waiting. The alternative is hanging around just as long at the halfway point, or a long walk from Nyachenge. The last matatus from Tabaka back to Kisii leave around 5pm.

Beyond Tabaka centre are the four **quarries**, with two main ones, the first on the left, and the other further down on the right. There must, however, be vast reserves of stone under the ground all over the district. The stone emerges in a variety of colours and densities: white is easiest to work, shades of orange and pink harder, and rosy-red the hardest and heaviest. A number of families have become full-time carvers, but for most people it's simply a spare-time occupation after agriculture, a way of making a few shillings. You'll even see children walking home from school carving little animals from chips of stone. The professional carvers often specialize in a variety of designs from chess sets and traditional animals, to vases, cups and human figures. The stone is dampened to bring up the colour and make it easier to work, and then waxed to retain the lustre.

Manga Ridge

The lavishly fertile district around Kisii gets rain all year, in remarkable contrast to the semi-arid lowlands of the lakeshore just a few kilometres away. A walk to the dramatic escarpment **cliff** of Manga Ridge is a good way of getting into the countryside. It's a two-to-three hour walk north of the town, wonderful either in the early morning, or, if you can arrange a lift back, the late afternoon.

Leaving Kisii on the Kericho road, turn left into Manga Road at the bottom of the hill, 500m after Barclays, and follow the road as it sweeps you towards and then alongside the ridge. After about 5km you can cut down one of the tracks across the lush valley to your left and continue straight up the escarpment (several hundred metres high). Beware of snakes lurking among the rocks and grass on the upward scramble. Alternatively, you can continue along the road for a further 5km to come up behind the ridge. From here it's a ten-minute hike up to the edge, where a path follows the cliff for a kilometre or two. Magnificent views out over Kisii and down to Lake Victoria are your reward. It's possible to get a matatu to the village of **Manga** from Kisii town (in front of *St Jude's Guest House*), but make it clear you want to get off at the ridge.

Kisii to Sotik and Kericho

The road to Sotik is all roadworks, bumps and dust, and **Sotik** when you reach it, is nothing more than a couple of petrol stations (the no-name *makutano* town at the Bomet junction 4km east of Sotik is probably bigger). But **Keroka**, halfway between Kisii and Sotik, has become a sizeable town and has a huge **Sunday market** drawing people from miles around.

From Sotik to Kericho, the new road is now finished and smooth. It's worth stopping at **Kapkatet**, 12km east of Sotik, to take a look around the little **Museum of History, Art and Science of the Kipsigis People** (Mon–Fri 9am–5.30pm, Sat & Sun 9am–6.30pm; ☎0721/274453 or 0724/249705, ✉tumpaul45@yahoo.com; Ksh200), just 150m off the north side of the road. Through the turnstile awaits a diverse little collection of traditional garments, tools, weapons, containers and musical instruments, all of it well-lit and well captioned, with pronunciation guides, putting many of the country's official national-museum collections to shame. Look out for the young girls' FGM cloaks and for the *chepchingilit* – bells that would have been worn by sheep or goats (and by girls, after their operations and only removed after marriage). Finally, there's a fascinating and pretty successful attempt to recreate a cross-section of a traditional Kipsigis home, with wooden sliding door ("with a peephole for anticipating attacks").

Kericho and the tea country

KERICHO, named after the early English tea planter John Kerich, is Kenya's **tea capital**, a fact that – with much hype from the tourism machine embellished by the presence of the *Tea Hotel* – is not likely to escape you. Its equable climate and famously reliable, year-round afternoon rain showers make it the most important tea-growing area in Africa. While many of the European estates have been divided and reallocated to small farmers since independence, the area is still dominated by giant tea plantations.

Compact Kericho seems as neat as the serried rows of bushes that surround it. The central square has shady trees and flowering shrubs – a bandstand would

▲ Picking tea

make it complete – and even the matatu park has lawns around it. It's a gentle, hassle-free place to wander, the people mild-mannered. In many ways, it's an oddity. Clipped, clean and functional, there's little of the shambolic appearance of most upcountry towns. With so many people earning some sort of salary on the tea plantations or in connection with them, and so few acres under food or market crops, the patterns of small-town life are changed here. Most workers live out on the estates, their families often left behind in the home villages. Kericho is above all an administrative and shopping centre, and a relay point for the needs of the estates. The produce market is small and trading limited. Most places seem to close early.

In town, there's a substantial Asian population: note the vast Sikh temple. Many of the streets have a vaguely Oriental feel, with single-storey *dukas* fronted by colonnaded walkways where the plantation "memsahibs" of fifty years ago presumably did their shopping. This curious, composite picture is completed by the grey stone **Holy Trinity Church**, with its small assembly of deceased planters in a miniature cemetery. Straight out of the English shires, it tries so hard to be Norman that it's a pity to point out that it was only built in 1952. Unfortunately (at least from an aesthetic point of view) it is now overshadowed by the modernist **AIC Kericho Town Church**, with its welcoming perimeter of razor wire. At the other extreme, aesthetically, is the stunning **Sikh Gujwara**: it's not clear if outsiders are really permitted to enter and wander around, but it is quite an awe-inspiring temple and has superb gardens.

Practicalities

Kericho is fairly compact, fortunately, for if you don't have your own vehicle, **getting around town** can be a bit of a problem unless you walk, as there are very few town taxis, and no *boda-bodas*. All three main **banks** have **ATMs** and are on Moi Highway at the Kisumu end of town. For **internet** access try the Blistaz Digital Centre on Moi Road. **Medical** facilities are good here, with the

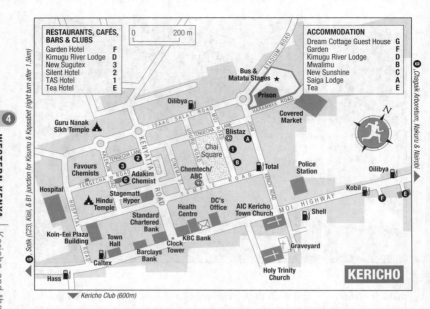

superior Central Hospital 1km past the *Tea Hotel*, on the Unilever tea estate. There are no night or late **pharmacists**, but Adkaim Chemists are on the ball (daily 8am–7pm; ☎052/21013 or 0726/290103) and Favours Chemists (☎0724/729860) are open on Sunday.

Accommodation

Dream Cottage Guest House Moi Highway, 700m west of Caltex on the south side of the road ☎020/3527838 or 0722/647240, ℮thedream cottage@gmail.com. Rather British-style bed and breakfast place with attentive management, offering ten rooms with big nets, instant showers and DSTV. A safe choice, and all very cosy, but strictly no alcohol served or allowed to be consumed. ②

Garden Moi Highway ☎052/8000244. Out-of-town B&L with bar-*hoteli* and twenty rooms, which are clean enough, with instant showers and nets, but have no fans (could be a problem as the asbestos roofing makes it rather stuffy). Some rooms have views out to the garden and car park. The popular beer garden can make it a little rowdy at times and the public areas are grubby and unappetizing. Still, if you're counting every penny, this is cheap and bearable. ①

Kimugu River Lodge Off Moi Highway, opposite the BP station, 700m northeast of the town centre ☎0720/861079, ℮kimuguriverlodge@yahoo.com. Take the signposted turning and follow this track for 600m to this rather downmarket-looking, peaceful alpine chalet-like place, with a great

location above a weir in the Kimugu River. The rooms in brick and wood chalets, some with instant showers, one with a log fire, are simple but comfortable (best are B and D) and there's also a decent bar and quite a good restaurant. ②

Mwalimu Moi Rd ☎0720/899341 or 0723/019212. Well-run cheapie in a bustling mini-mall of businesses. 36 rooms, mostly a bit bigger and brighter than its miserable neighbour the *TAS*, but still without nets or any added comforts. Don't expect hot water except in the evenings. ②

New Sunshine Tengecha Rd ☎052/30037 or 0724/146601. Small, neat, extremely clean rooms with TV, nets and instant showers, in a very well-run lodging that's easily the best in the town centre and worth the small premium in price. Busy *hoteli* downstairs. Good, courtyard parking. ②

Saiga Lodge John Kerich Rd ☎0721/868661. A surprisingly large establishment hidden away behind the shops, with a selection of very cheap s/c and non-s/c rooms, hot water, and parking in the yard. Most of the rooms, which have nets and electric sockets, but no fans, have inward-facing windows, so they're a bit dark; not bad value for the low price. ①

Tea Moi Highway ⓣ020/2050790, ⓔteahotel @africaonline.co.ke. Built in 1952 by the Brooke Bond tea company, and at one time the best place in town, the *Tea Hotel* has been in slow decline ever since, though it retains a faded charm. Standard rooms are large and comfortable enough, with instant showers and nets but no fans or a/c, and quite overpriced if you weren't also getting the beautiful gardens and a large, if predictably green, swimming pool. Choose your room carefully as the main house can be noisy. You can also camp (Ksh500) using room showers or pool-changing facilities. Pool Ksh100. BB ❺

Eating and drinking

If you're buying food, you'll find Kericho's **market** is best at weekends, when there's more variety of fruit and vegetables, and snacks and spices, at good prices. The town's best **supermarket** is Stagematt Hyper (Mon–Sat 8am–7.30pm, Sun 8.30am–7.30pm).

Kericho has its fair share of cheap and fairly un-gastronomic **hotelis**, heavy on the chips and *ugali*. The best is *Silent Hotel* on Kenyatta Road, but the best-value and busiest is *TAS Hotel*, which is packed with workers at lunchtime. Of the upmarket hotels, the *Tea Hotel*'s snack menu isn't particularly expensive, and they rarely go far wrong with club sandwiches and chips, though if you're dining here as a guest, be warned: the meals can be inedible. **Tea for two** here costs Ksh160; if you'd rather have good strong, boiled-in-the-pot, African tea, ask for *chai majani*.

The best food in town (and not expensive) is at ⚑ *Kimugu River Lodge*, which has an extensive menu of mainly Indian food, including chicken *methi*, *malai kofta* and, not always available, a wonderful crayfish *masala*. Dishes are around Ksh300. You'll have to wait, but it's worth it.

If you want a **drink** you might try the *New Sugutex* on Tengecha Road, a typically rowdy tavern, mainly for men. A similar clientele hangs out at the *Garden Hotel*'s bar and beer garden. The bar at the *Kimugu River Lodge* is quiet and civilized.

Around Kericho

This is **tea country**: Kenya is the world's third largest producer after India and Sri Lanka, and the biggest exporter to Britain. As you gaze across the dark green hills, you might pause to consider that the land, now covered in vast regimented swathes of tea bushes, was, until not much more than a century ago, virgin rainforest, only a tiny part of which, the Kakamega Forest, survives. The estates were first set up after World War I with tea bushes imported from India and China. Big business as it is, you can't help feeling that local people

---

Moving on from Kericho

Kericho has hassle-free travel options in every direction: southwest to **Kisii** and **Migori**, east over the Mau Escarpment to **Nakuru via Molo** (see p.359), or northwest to **Kisumu** and **Kapsabet**. Heading south to the **Maasai Mara**, the first part of the route, to Bomet, follows a good road through splendid farming country and then links with the highway to Narok (see p.230). If you're going east, Nairobi and Nakuru buses and matatus generally originate in Kisumu and Kisii and pass through Kericho throughout the day and night. **Matatus** leave for most destinations from the main stage. The Akamba office (ⓣ052/32092 or 020/2365816) is on the Caltex forecourt, and that is the place to board all Nairobi-bound buses. Akamba has departures for Nairobi (Ksh700), Kisii (Ksh300), Kisumu (Ksh300), Busia (Ksh600), Homa Bay (Ksh500), Kampala (Ksh1400) and Mombasa (Ksh1500).

might be better off if this fertile land were given over instead to intensive cultivation of food.

It is possible to **visit the tea estates** on a guided tour (enquire at the *Tea Hotel*'s lobby). The factories operate every day except Monday, the day after the pickers' day off. If you want to visit a tea factory and see the whole process, you should aim to book two weeks in advance (2hr; Ksh200 per person, minimum two people, plus Ksh500 for transport if required). If you can't give the required notice, you may be able to tag along with a group that has already booked. Alternatively, you can just take a tour of the tea fields combined with a nature walk (Ksh200 per person).

The *Tea Hotel*'s guide can also be hired for **birding** excursions in the neighbourhood, at Chagaik Arboretum, and to **Lelartet Cliff**, which is also home to a large number of red colobus and black and white colobus monkeys.

Kimugu Valley and Chagaik Dam

Down in the **Kimugu Valley**, behind the *Tea Hotel* and *Kimugu River Lodge*, you can get some idea of what the land was like before the settlers arrived. The valley is a deep, tangled channel of sprawling trees and undergrowth, with shafts of sunlight picking out clouds of butterflies. The cold brown waters of the Kimugu flow down from Chagaik Dam and allegedly harbour **trout**.

Tea

Tea (*Camellia sinensis*) is a psychoactive shrub originally native to China. Its effects are said to have been discovered by the legendary third millennium BC Chinese emperor Shen Nung, who was apparently taking a cup of hot water in the shade of a shrub when one of the buds fell into it, making him an invigorating drink. For centuries the Chinese had a monopoly on tea, but with its rise in popularity at home, the British were keen for an independent source of supply, and eventually managed to smuggle some cuttings to India. In Kenya, tea was first grown in 1903, though it was nearly twenty years before commercial production got under way. Kenyan teas are known for their strength and full flavour, and are a major component of most commercial blends sold in the UK and Ireland. Kenya's other main customers are Egypt, Pakistan and Afghanistan.

Tea production, though not complicated, is very labour-intensive. Picking continues throughout the year, and you'll see the pickers moving through the bushes in their brilliant yellow-and-green (KETEPA) plastic smocks, nipping off the top two leaves and bud of each bush (nothing more is taken) and tossing them into baskets. Working fast, a picker can collect up to seventy kilos in a day, though half that is a more typical figure; the piece-rate is set at less than eight shillings per kilo picked. After withering, mashing, a couple of hours' fermentation and a final drying in hot air, the tea leaves are ready for packing and export. The whole process can take as little as 24 hours.

Tea can be harvested three years after planting, and in the first year of production it must be picked every eight days, then every fourteen days in the second year and every seventeen in the fourth, after which the bush must be pruned to keep it at the right height for picking, which can begin again after three months. Weeding is not necessary as the foliage is sufficiently dense to prevent other plants from growing under it.

The stimulating **effects** of tea are due to the presence of caffeine, and a cup of strong tea can contain as much caffeine as a cup of medium-strength coffee. The effect feels different because it is moderated by other alkaloids such as thebaine, which is a relaxant. Because the human body requires fluid to process caffeine and thebaine, tea depletes the body of water, even though it appears to quench your thirst. Like beer, therefore, strong tea should not be taken as a fluid against dehydration.

The Nandi and the Nandi bear

At the end of the nineteenth century, the **Nandi** (dialects of whose language is spoken by all the Kalenjin peoples) were probably in the strongest position in their history. Their warriors had drummed up a reputation for such ferocity and daring that much of western Kenya lived in fear of them. Even the Maasai, at a low point in their own fortunes, suffered repeated losses of livestock to Nandi spearsmen, whose prestige accumulated with every herd of cattle driven back to their stockades. The Nandi even crossed the Rift Valley to raid Subukia and the Laikipia plateau. They were intensely protective of their own territory, relentlessly xenophobic and fearful of any adulteration of their way of life. Foreigners of any kind were welcome only with express permission.

With the killing of a British traveller, Peter West, who tried to cross their country in 1895, the Nandi opened a decade of guerrilla warfare against the British. Above all, they repeatedly frustrated attempts to lay the railway line and keep communications open with Uganda. They dismantled the "iron snake", transformed the copper telegraph wires into jewellery, and took whatever livestock and provisions they could find. Despite increased security, the establishment of forts, and some efforts to reach agreements with Nandi elders, the raiding went on, often costing the lives of African soldiers and policemen under the British. In retaliation, a series of **punitive expeditions** shot more than a thousand Nandi warriors (about one young man in ten), captured tens of thousands of head of livestock, and torched scores of villages. The war was ended by the killing of Koitalel Arap Samoiei, the *Orkoiyot* or spiritual head of the Nandi who, having agreed to a temporary truce, was then murdered at a meeting with a delegation led by the British officer Richard Meinertzhagen, who shot him in cold blood (see p.604). As expected, resistance collapsed. His people had believed Koitalel to be unassailable and the Nandi were subsequently hounded into a reserve and their lands opened to settlers.

Traditionally keepers of livestock, the Nandi have turned to agriculture with little enthusiasm and focus instead on their district's milk production, the highest in Kenya. *Shambas*, however, are widespread enough to make your chances of seeing a **Nandi bear**, the source of scores of Yeti-type rumours, remote. Variously said to resemble a bear, a big wild dog or a very large ape, the Nandi bear is believed to have been exterminated in most areas. But in the less accessible regions, on the way up to Kapsabet, many locals believe it still exists – they call it *chemoset*. Exactly what it is is another matter, but it doesn't seem to inspire quite the terror you might expect; the occasional savagely mutilated sheep and cattle reported in the press are probably attributable to leopards. A giant anthropoid ape, perhaps a gorilla, seems the most likely candidate for the original *chemoset*, and the proximity of the Kakamega Forest may account for the stories. This is a surviving tract of the rainforest that once stretched in a continuous belt across equatorial Africa and is still home to many western and central African species of wildlife (though not giant apes). The *chemoset* possibly survived up until the early twentieth century in isolated valleys, even if it is now extinct. Whatever the truth, if you camp out in the Nandi Hills, you won't need reminding to zip your fly-sheet.

To get to **Chagaik Dam** and the graceful **arboretum** nearby, you'll need to drive, or get a lift, in the Nairobi direction, past the KETEPA buildings to the right turn marked "Chagaik", 6.5km from *Kimugu River Lodge*. From here, it's a five-minute walk to the arboretum "Founded by Tom Grumbley, Tea Planter 1946–75". Acres of beautiful trees from all over the tropical and subtropical world lead steeply down through well-tended lawns to a lily-covered lake. There are magnificent stands of bamboo on the banks. Entry to this haven of landscaped tranquillity is unrestricted and you can picnic or rest up as long as you like, though there are gardeners around who won't let you camp. It gets quite popular at weekends and holidays when families come out here to enjoy the space and air. Across the lake, thick **jungle** drops to the water's edge. Mysterious splashes and rustles, prolific bird and insect life, and at least one troop of colobus monkeys are a surprising testament to the tenacity of wildlife in an environment hemmed in on all sides by the alien ranks of the tea bushes.

④ Eldoret and around

The direct journey from Kericho to Eldoret through the **Nandi Hills** is one of the most varied and spectacular in the west, through countryside that is often far wilder than you'd expect, including bleak mountainous scrublands and jungle-packed ravines. Midway, you cross the Kano Plains and you may have to change transport at **Chemelil**, a major crossroads in the Nyando valley, down in the flat sugar lands. Beyond, the road zigzags northwards into high tea country again, the homeland of the **Nandi**, the fiercest early opponents of the British, and the haunt of a crypto-zoological mystery known as the **Nandi bear** (see box, p.285). The only town of any size before Eldoret is **Kapsabet**, which has a couple of banks, a market, and a trio of reasonable lodgings, but nothing to warrant a stopover unless, again, you need to change matatus. If you're driving, you might pause at the **Kingwal swamp**, north of Kapsabet (the road passes right through it), where more than sixty **sitatunga** antelope (see p.295) hang on in an unprotected wetland area.

Although more bustling than Kericho, and somewhat healthier and pleasanter than Nakuru, **ELDORET** really has hardly anything to differentiate if from dozens of other highland centres, though as Kenya's fifth largest town, it's a good deal bigger. The **Uasin Gishu Plateau** all around is reliably fertile cereal, vegetable and stock-raising country; wattle plantations provide the tannin for the town's leather industry; the Raymond, Rivatex, Raiply and Ken-Knit **textile factories** provide employment; and **Moi University**, has proved a shot in the arm for local schools. Eldoret's prosperity is shown clearly enough by the windows of Eldoret Jewellers on the main road.

Though there are no sights as such to keep you here for very long, you may well find Eldoret a useful stopover, and it's refreshingly unthreatening and friendly despite its size. The town's affluence is reflected in a wide variety of places to stay, eat and drink, and enough nightlife to see you through an evening or two.

If you need **health treatment** or advice, go to Eldoret Hospital (℡053/2062000) on Mark Asembo Road which has a good reputation. There are several pharmacies on Kenyatta and Oginga Odinga streets; out of normal hours, try Asisco Pharmacy (℡053/2062496; daily 8am–midnight), Bandaptai House, off Nandi Road, one block east of Nyala Road.

Some history

Eldoret was initially a backwoods post office on Farm 64, later chosen in 1912 as an administrative centre because the farm's soil was poor and the deeds were never taken up by the owner. The name started as Eldare (a river), was then Nandi-ized to Eldaret, and finally misprinted in the *Official Gazette* as Eldoret.

Before the town existed, the area was settled by **Afrikaners**. They gave it much of the dour worthiness that seems to have characterized its first half-century and which is perceptible even today – though most of the Boers

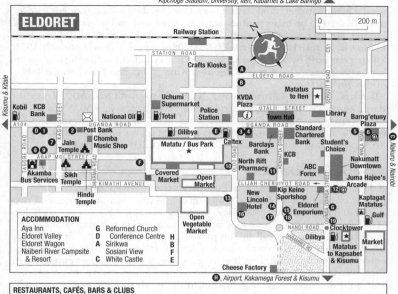

Kipchoge Stadium, University, Iten, Kabarnet & Lake Baringo ▲

ELDORET

0   200 m

Railway Station

STATION ROAD

Crafts Kiosks

ELGEYO ROAD

Kisumu & Kitale ◄

A104

Kobil KCB Bank

Uchumi Supermarket

Total

KVDA Plaza

Police Station

Matatus to Iten ★

UTALII STREET

Library

Barng'etuny Plaza

National Oil

UGANDA ROAD

Post Bank

Chomba Music Shop

Jain Temple

Oilibya

Matatu / Bus Park ★

Town Hall

UGANDA ROAD

Caltex

Barclays Bank

Standard Chartered Bank

KCB

Student's Choice

Nakumatt Downtown

► Nakuru & Nairobi

ARAP MOI STREET

North Rift Pharmacy

ABC Forex

Akamba Bus Services

Sikh Temple

Covered Market

Open Market

ELIJAH CHERUIYOT ROAD

Juma Hajee's Arcade

KIMATHI AVENUE

Hindu Temple

New Lincoln Hotel

Kip Keino Sportshop

Eldoret Emporium

Kaptagat Matatus

Gulf

Open Vegetable Market

NANDI ROAD

Clocktower

Oilibya

Matatus to Kapsabet & Kisumu

Market

Cheese Factory

H, Airport, Kakamega Forest & Kisumu ▼

ACCOMMODATION

Aya Inn	G	Reformed Church	
Eldoret Valley	D	Conference Centre	H
Eldoret Wagon	A	Sirikwa	B
Naiberi River Campsite		Sosiani View	F
& Resort	C	White Castle	E

RESTAURANTS, CAFÉS, BARS & CLUBS					
Baker's Yard	12	Eldoret Garden Square	6	Otto Café	4	Siam	5
Biharlal Catering	7	Kutana Club	16	Places	1	Sizzlers Café	18
Bismilahi Lengut Hotel	10	New Tawfiq Hotel	9	Prime Chic Inn	15	Smiles	2
Caesar's Palace	14	Opera House		Sam's	8	Will's Pub	3
Café Delicious	19	(Club Santa Cruz)	13	Sunjeel Palace	17	Wood House	11

trekked on after Kenya's Independence. In the era of **President Moi**, whose roots were in nearby Kabarnet, Eldoret was a special focus for investment and development: this is when its university was founded and its "international" airport opened. Although most modern inhabitants are Kalenjin-language-speakers from the Elgeyo and Nandi tribes, there are also Somali-speakers, the remnants of the European settler community, and a long-established and respected Asian community (Juma Hajee's supermarket, now a shopping arcade, is the oldest business in the town). In addition, there are enough immigrants from the rest of Kenya for Eldoret to have been a brutal flashpoint in the post-election violence of 2007/8. This culminated in the massacre of more than forty Kikuyu people, including many children, in an arson attack on the Assemblies of God church in the suburb of Kiambaa, where they had taken refuge.. Outwardly, Eldoret has already recovered from the trauma of the clashes: most Kikuyu fled the area, as did members of many other non-Rift Valley and non-Western tribes, some of whom seem resigned to staying in internally displaced person (IDP) camps in the district for years. But the anger released did nothing to resolve the tensions that remain.

Arrival and information

Eldoret sprawls widely and inelegantly in all directions. If you're **driving through**, it can be a real bottleneck, with the streets choked with traffic, and it can easily take half an hour to get through town from one end to the other, as it stretches some 10km along the highway. In order to park here, you'll need a parking ticket, valid 24 hours and sold by the parking wardens all over town (Ksh50). The main **matatu** stage is at the east end of Arap Moi Street. Eldoret **airport** is 16km south of town on the Kapsabet road. Unusually, Eldoret has a **tourist office** (℡053/2032086) on the second floor of KVDA Plaza; it has little by way of handouts, but is very helpful with information on local attractions. A local **travel agent** is Kim's Tours and Travel, in the lobby of the *Sirikwa Hotel*.

Barclays, Standard Chartered and KCB all have **ATMs**. ABC Forex in Barng'etuny Plaza on Uganda Street and Safari Forex in KVDA Plaza give similar rates for cash (but don't take small bills), and slightly lower rates for traveller's cheques. There are numerous **internet** offices include Ndimo (Mon–Sat 8am–8pm) in Juma Hajee's Arcade on Elijah Cheruiyot Road.

Accommodation

Eldoret has no shortage of **accommodation**. Cheap places tend to be grubby or clearly intended for "short-term guests". There are also one or two quaint old haunts from way back, in particular the *New Lincoln* on Oloo Road, but this old pile is now of curiosity value only, with zero facilities and no security. It's fun to call in and maybe get a drink from the fusty old bar off the courtyard, but you really wouldn't want to stay here, even if they could offer you a room. The Reformed Church Centre allows **camping** in the front-yard field. Alternatively, if there's time left in the day to do another half-hour journey, consider going out to the lovely *Naiberi River Campsite & Resort* (see p.290).

Aya Inn Oginga Odinga St ℡053/2062259. A friendly place with large, clean rooms (those on the so-called ground floor are best), with nets and instant showers, good security and safe parking. There are two rowdy but good-natured bars and a quiet and popular *hoteli*. ❷

🏃 **Eldoret Valley** Uganda Rd ℡053/2032314 or 0722/816108. Small but scrupulously clean rooms in an orderly B&L established for more than thirty years. Water comes in a large bucket, however, and the nearby *Places* disco makes rooms at the back noisy, so while it's very good value it won't suit everyone. The restaurant serves decent Kenyan fare and good tea. ❶

🏃 **Eldoret Wagon** Elgeyo Rd ℡053/2062270, ✉wagonhotel@africaonline.co.ke. Helpful, friendly, charmingly old-fashioned but profession-ally managed, the *Wagon* has 92 light, airy rooms, with nets, TV and instant showers, and a *nyama choma* bar. The Eldoret Jambo Casino is by the front gate and the whole place gets quite lively at weekends. Unusually, they take most credit cards. Very good value. ❸

Reformed Church of East Africa Conference and Training Centre 2km out of town on the Kapsabet road (if coming by taxi or *boda-boda*, ask for "Conference") ℡0721/822018 or 0722/456019, ✉rceaguesthouse@africaonline .com. Rambling and rudimentary accommodation

for those on very low budgets. Campers and overland vehicles are welcome, but they're vague about security and rates (around Ksh200 per person). There's a simple cafeteria. ❶

Sirikwa Elgeyo Rd ℡053/2063614 or 0728/680000, ✉hotelsirikwa@gmail.com. The town's "premier" hotel, this is a monolithic and faintly pompous pile, fairly bright and clean, but very tired and overpriced. The 105 rooms, all with TVs and nets, have showers, bathtubs and, in theory, 24-hour hot water. Discounting the pool, which is in good shape (Ksh200), the more low-key and much cheaper *Eldoret Wagon*, opposite, is a better bet any day. BB ❺

Sosiani View Arap Moi St ℡053/2033215. Situated by the transport terminus, this five-storey block has good views – the best are from the fifth floor, which is also the quietest – and nice large rooms with nets, but primitive plumbing. The first-floor bar is a good place to down a beer or two. ❶

White Castle Uganda Rd ℡053/2062773 or 053/2061362, ✉whitecastle@deepafrica.com. Although first impressions are very unpromising – a bland modern building on the noisy main road through town – the rooms turn out to be better than average, spacious and comfy, though with old-fashioned showers and questionable hot water. There's a lift, and even a sauna and health club. ❸

Eating and drinking

Eldoret has plenty of good places to grab a bite, with a clutch of established snack bars, several options for dinner, and one or two evening haunts. For your own supplies, head for the markets west of Oloo Road, or a supermarket such as Eldo at Juma Hajee's Arcade, or Naivasha opposite the market on Nandi Road. Also worth a visit is the **Doinyo Lessos Creamery and Cheese Factory** (daily 8am–6pm) at the end of the track south of Kenyatta Street, where you can buy various European-style cheeses (minimum purchase 250g, all around Ksh500 per kg), plus yoghurt and ice cream.

Restaurants

Baker's Yard Juma Hajee's Arcade, Elijah Cheruiyot Rd. Excellent place that draws you in with a warm bread aroma, offering biscuits, pies, cakes and pastries as well as bread, and also good for filter coffee. Mon–Sat 9am–6pm, closed Sun.

Biharlal Catering Kago St. Charming snacks and sweetmeats shop, an excellent place for vegetarian Indian meals, and good for lunch. Daily 8am–6.30pm.

Eldoret Garden Square Barng'etuny Plaza. Courtyard snack bar and restaurant with the usual variety of fry-ups, stews, chicken and *hoteli* fare, but more ambience than most. Full breakfast Ksh200. Daily 6am–11pm.

Prime Chic Inn Kenyatta St. New place with high standards and keen prices, offering chicken, burgers, fry-ups and chips every which way, beneath a widescreen TV. There's also an "African" menu, with stews, fish and vegetables from around Ksh100. Open 24/7.

Siam Nyala Rd, corner of Uganda Rd. The Chinese dishes, with the accent on chilli, aren't bad, but the "Thai" dishes aren't even a vague approximation. What makes it worthwhile are the great-value Ksh200–300 lunchtime specials. Daily 11am–3pm, 6pm–late.

Sizzlers Café Kenyatta St. Popular American-style joint, offering speedy, high-quality burgers, excellent samosas, plus ice cream and other desserts. Mon–Sat 8.30am–6pm.

Sunjeel Palace Kenyatta St ☏ 053/2030568 or 0720/554747. Operating very much in British-style Indian-restaurant mode, this is where Eldoret's Asian community often come for a good meal out, usually ordering ahead (allow at least 30min). Fine curries (veg and non-veg), plus good *naan*, and a selection of European and African dishes at moderate prices.

Expect to pay Ksh500–600 per head, without drinks. Daily, noon–midnight.

Will's Pub Uganda Rd. Mostly patronized by local businessmen, this is a good place for a beer, but also for solid Kenyan food and snacks, including tasty meat samosas. Full breakfasts Ksh250, pizzas Ksh450. Mon–Thurs 8.30am–11pm, Fri & Sat 8.30am–midnight, Sun 10am–10.30pm.

Bars and clubs

Most of these places charge a small entry fee at weekends but, with the exception of *Caesar's Palace*, are free midweek.

Caesar's Palace Kenyatta St. A revamped disco, loud and enjoyable, with ladies' night on Wed, generally packed at weekends when they play soul, ragga and hip hop, with live English and European football on screen. Evenings only.

Kutana Club Oloo Rd, tucked away, next to the decrepit *Eldoret New Lincoln Hotel*. Rustic African atmosphere and beery bonhomie, with a live visiting band at weekends. Music is mostly African, especially Congolese.

Opera House (Club Santa Cruz) Oloo Rd. Very firmly established nightspot, playing mainly reggae on Fri & Sat until dawn. The rest of the week it's basically just a bar. It is pronounced "O-pair-a", not "Oprah".

Places Uganda Rd. Sophisticated decor, a sunken dance floor, and a fairly well-mannered clientele, with snacks available and good DJs. Music is mainly Western disco.

Wood House Kenyatta St. An ordinary bar midweek, but a lively nightspot on Fri, Sat & Sun afternoon (jam till dawn) with a mix of soul and reggae. Beer Ksh90, jam sessions Ksh50, other eves free.

Shopping

The obvious focus for **shopping** needs is the big, 24-hour Nakumatt Downtown in Oginga Odinga Street. For **souvenirs**, check out the row of crafts traders on Oloo Road, near the station. If you like **music**, you'll love

Chomba Sounds Music Store, in Dharma Road (☎0722/747675; Mon–Sat 8am–7pm), which has lots of local sounds. You might also want to visit the **Kip Keino Sports Shop** on Kenyatta Street, set up by athlete and Christian philanthropist Kepchugi Keino. Keino's double gold at the 1964 Olympics blazed a trail that has since been followed by other Kenyan runners, mainly from around Eldoret. For **books**, Eldoret Emporium on the corner of Elijah Cheruiyot and Oginga Odinga streets has a good selection of Kenyan books, as does Student's Choice on Oginga Odinga St, which is easier to browse and also carries foreign titles plus magazines such as *Time* and *Newsweek*.

Around Eldoret

If you arrived in Eldoret early enough in the day, there's a very worthwhile base outside town, ⚑ **Naiberi River Campsite & Resort** (☎053/2062916 or 0722/686512, ⓦ www.naiberi.com; BB ❹), a very popular stop for independent overlanders and tour trucks heading for Uganda. This has a fine scenic location above the small Naiberi River, with comfortable, s/c cabin-style rooms, as well as dorm accommodation (Ksh1000 or Ksh1500 with good, shared showers and toilets) and camping (Ksh400). The centrepiece is a sprawling and enjoyable **pub-restaurant** built into the hillside, incorporating streams and waterfalls, a central fireplace and the remains of what are said to be Sirikwa holes (see p.245). The Nepali chef cooks up excellent, sizzling, hot-plate dishes and a variety of other meals, and there's a congenial bar with DSTV. It's a delightfully relaxing place to hang out for a day or two, the hilly grounds leading down to the river, and a sparkling (if chilly) **swimming pool** making it hard to tear yourself away. Facilities include **internet** access (Ksh10 per min). If you drive here, take the turning (east, on the B54 towards Kaptagat), at the Petro gas station 3km southeast of Eldoret town centre on the Nairobi road. From the Petro junction, drive 15.3km and *Naiberi* is on your left. Lifts are available from town if you call ahead.

More sedate, and at one time also rather special, the **Kaptagat Hotel** (☎0722/778654; ❷), 1km off the main road 5km east of *Naiberi*, is a colonial anachronism, set in extensive and beautiful grounds, with excellent birdwatching from the terraces of the cottages. These have wooden floors, open fires, and the dodgy bathroom plumbing you'd expect. There's a bar and TV lounge and meals can be rustled up (assuming you have plenty of time). All told, there's a good atmosphere here, or there would be if there were anyone else staying.

Beyond the small centre of **Kaptagat**, the unpaved route down to the fluorspar mine at Kimwarer – which, believe it or not, used to be the main way across the Kerio Valley – no longer sees much traffic, though you can usually hitch a ride with a lorry travelling to or from the mine. It's an incredible hairpin descent that seems to go on forever. Route details for the Kerio Valley continue on p.241.

In the other direction (northwest) out of Eldoret, the old tarmac on the way to Kitale is in very poor condition. The only real town along this route is **SOY**, 9km past the B2/A104 junction, formerly a tiny community but now a sizeable centre. The once rather pukka **Soy Club** is now the *Soy Safari Resort* (☎0723/803683 or 0720/745089; BB ❶), a *nyama choma* bar and watering hole, and the once sparkling swimming pool is green and murky. Still, at the prices on offer for two or three people (most rooms are triples) it's pretty good value, with nets, clean sheets and towels, and despite the wheezing pipes you should get hot water mornings and evenings.

Moving on from Eldoret

Matatus from the main stage run to Kakamega, Kisumu, Kitale and Kaptagat. **Buses** also service most of these towns. Matatus for Iten and Kabarnet (with connections to Lake Baringo and Lake Bogoria) leave from the stage on the corner of Oginga Odinga and Utalii streets using the spectacular Tambach Escarpment route. The Akamba office (☎053/2061047, 020/2365827 or 0727/660251) is on Arap Moi Street, opposite *New Tawfiq Hotel*, with departures for Nairobi (9.30am & 9.30pm; 6hr; Ksh800) among other destinations. Heading directly to **Uganda**, there's little to delay your progress to Malaba on the border, two or three hours away, via Webuye and Bungoma. The busy **A104** road from Eldoret southeast to **Nakuru**, rolls uphill and then down again, with the sombre scenery dotted with moors and conifers. For the **Kakamega Forest**, take a bus or matatu going to Kisumu via Kapsabet, and get off at the D267 turning about 20km west of Kapsabet (signposted "Kisieni 12km"), from where you should get another lift (if necessary, it's a walk of about three hours to the *Forest Rest House*, see p.311).

There are freight **trains** from Eldoret station, but no passenger services. From the airport (☎053/2063377), there are twice daily **flights** on Fly540 to Nairobi ($69).

Beyond Soy, the bumpy, narrow road continues through **Matunda**, formerly the railway station of Springfield Halt (18km past Soy and 25km short of Kitale), and the small trading centre of **Moi's Bridge**, 21km short of Kitale, where its condition improves.

Kitale

KITALE is smaller than Eldoret, and not much more exciting, but it has more going for it from a traveller's point of view, primarily as the base for visits to **Mount Elgon**, Kenya's second giant volcanic cone, and the superb, very underrated, hiking country in the area. It's also an obvious springboard for the **Cherangani Hills**, and a straightforward departure point for trips to the west side of **Lake Turkana**. There's a **national park** nearby – the little-known but easily accessible **Saiwa Swamp**, which can only be explored on foot. In addition, the town also has two **museums** and a couple of other sites to visit.

Originally Quitale, a relay station on the old slave route between Uganda and Bagamoyo in Tanzania, the modern town was only founded in 1920, as the capital of Trans-Nzoia District. When the first white settlers arrived after World War I, this vale of rich grasslands between Mount Elgon and the Cherangani Hills was supposedly almost uninhabited. But just a few years earlier it had been a Maasai grazing area, and a group of people who consider themselves Maasai still live on the eastern slopes of Elgon. With the arrival of the railway in 1925, the town and the region around it began to flourish, with a fantastic array of fruit, cereals, vegetables and livestock, and all the attendant settler paraphernalia of agricultural and flower shows, church fetes and gymkhanas. This heady era lasted barely forty years, but the region's **agriculture** is still famous; almost anything, including such exotic fruit as apples and pears, can be grown here. The Kitale Show happens each year in late October or early November.

The town's present population is a mix of tribes, including Nandi, Pokot, Marakwet, Sabaot and Sengwer, as well as a few Luhya, Kisii and Kikuyu and an influential Asian community. Like most towns in Rift Valley and Western

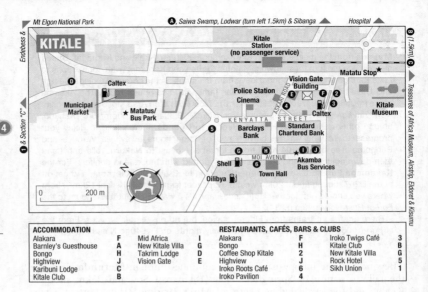

ACCOMMODATION		RESTAURANTS, CAFÉS, BARS & CLUBS	
Alakara	F	Alakara	F
Barnley's Guesthouse	A	Bongo	H
Bongo	H	Coffee Shop Kitale	2
Highview	J	Highview	J
Karibuni Lodge	C	Iroko Roots Café	6
Kitale Club	B	Iroko Pavilion	4
Mid Africa	F	Iroko Twigs Café	3
New Kitale Villa	G	Kitale Club	B
Takrim Lodge	D	New Kitale Villa	G
Vision Gate	E	Rock Hotel	5
		Sikh Union	1

provinces, it was seriously affected by the post-election clashes of 2007/8, but seems to have made a swift recovery.

Arrival and information

Barclays and SCB both have **ATMs**. Soy **supermarket** in Kenyatta Street sells weekly editions of some UK newspapers, but for provisions, there's a wider choice at Transmatt across the street. **Internet** access is available at Multitech on the first floor of the Vision Gate Building at the eastern end of Askari Road and at the Silver Springs Centre next door.

Accommodation

In town, there are quite a few **cheap lodgings**, the very cheapest of which are at the grubby north end of town, past the market. For **mid-range hotels**, you're spoilt for choice, but there's nothing top-end. You can camp at *Karibuni Lodge*.

If you have your own transport, or you're heading north anyway, and it's not too late in the day, the best place to stay around Kitale is 🌂 **Barnley's Guesthouse** (☎0737/133170 or 0733/793524, ✉sirikwabarnley@gmail.com; BB ⑤), also known as *Sirikwa Safaris*. Signposted off to the right precisely 23.1km north of Kitale on the A1, this old farmhouse is situated on a tree-covered hill, with superb gardens to camp in (Ksh450 per person including firewood and use of bathroom facilities and electric sockets), three furnished tents with electricity (❷ tent only) and the Barnley family's fine old house with full-on highlands atmosphere and shared facilities. Excellent meals are provided to order, eaten with the charmingly hospitable and informative hosts (Ksh600–900). Another great draw here are the guides (Ksh700 per day for a field guide, Ksh1900 per day for the ornithologist) who are the perfect companions for Saiwa Swamp, or for a trip to the Cherangani Hills for anything from a day to a week. Given notice, the Barnleys will organize just about anything and, for sheer, robust great company, there are few homestays their equal anywhere in the country.

Alakara Kenyatta St ☏054/20395 or 0728/234865. A large, bright place with surprisingly good beds, alongside nets, TVs and instant showers. The busy bar-restaurant is good, too, and there's safe parking nearby. ❷

Bongo Moi Ave ☏0325/20593. Decent, properly furnished s/c rooms with good breakfasts and (barring the odd hiccup in the supply) hot showers. Slightly cheaper than the *Highview* and *Alakara*, but not quite as good. ❷

Highview Moi Ave ☏0325/31570. A friendly high-rise with good, breezy and relatively clean s/c rooms with nets; the luxury rooms, which cost slightly more than the ordinary ones, are much bigger, with a sitting area, and there's also one cheaper room, actually a suite of sorts, with a box-like bedroom and separate sitting room. ❷

Karibuni Lodge Milimani district, 2km from the town centre (heading for Eldoret, turn left at Total) ☏0735/573798, ⓦwww.karibunikitale.com. Very nice place catering to NGOs and backpackers, with camping (Ksh400), dorm beds (Ksh750) or s/c rooms with nets and hot water, and a good line in locally sourced home cooking, including vegetarian options. Guests also have use of the kitchen. ❷

Kitale Club 1.5km out on the road towards Eldoret ☏0726/610241 or 0733/330924, ⓔktlclub @rocketmail.com. On the site of the former slave headquarters, this institution has old cottages with cement floors, a new block with larger rooms and wooden floors, and new cottages with wooden floors, TVs and fireplaces. The price includes temporary membership and access to club facilities including the golf course (Ksh800) and pool (Ksh300). If you can wade through the slightly stuffy atmosphere of club rules, it's not a bad place to stay. ❹

Mid Africa Moi Ave ☏020/2017825 or 0727/277077, ⓦwww.midafricahotel.com. Downtown Kitale's slickest place to stay, relatively speaking, with a restaurant and rooftop *nyama choma* bar. The decent s/c rooms (some with balconies) have DSTV, and there are cheaper non-s/c rooms available too. ❸

Takrim Lodge On the main road at the northern end of town ☏0725/496394. Basic but neat and clean, Somali-run and by a mosque, with quite a Middle Eastern feel. The basic, s/c rooms have cold showers, but hot water is provided in a bucket on request. ❶

The Town

Given its location, the town's most famous site, **Kitale Museum** (daily 9.30am–6pm; Ksh500) is remarkably successful. Originally the "Stoneham Museum", a collection opened to the public by a lieutenant colonel on his Cherangani farm in 1927, it was transferred here in 1972. For the most part, Stoneham's curious collections are just that: collected curiosities in striking contrast to the recent, more educationally motivated, Kenyan additions.

In the main hall, the **ethnographic displays** on Pokot, Elkony (Elgon), Luhya, Maasai, Turkana and Luo are interesting, though perhaps more so if you've seen examples in real life and now have a chance to return and see it again. Among the artefacts are Kamba carvings, including skin-covered animals and smooth polished abstracts; a Pokot goat bell made from a tortoise shell; and intricate Turkana belts and beadwork. In the small room to the right of the entrance in the main building is an old piano and accordion and a collection of traditional musical instruments, which really are becoming museum pieces as younger generations embrace more cosmopolitan musical genres (though you can buy cassettes of traditional Luhya music in town). Outside, the recreations of Nandi and Luhya homesteads make an interesting point of comparison with the realities of present-day villages.

Next to the Kitale Museum, though its entrance is 300m further east, the Swedish Co-operative Centre's **Agroforestry Project** (daily; free; ⓦwww .sccportal.org) was set up to educate cultivators in Trans-Nzoia and West Pokot about the basics of tree planting. This accomplished, it now deals with soil erosion and over-grazing, and offers practical advice to farmers on the selection of species best suited to local conditions. There's a small gallery and demonstration *shamba*, showcasing sound techniques for increasing crop yield.

The quirkiest of Kitale's sites is the **Treasures of Africa Museum** (Mon–Sat 9am–noon & 2–5.30pm; Ksh250; ☏054/30867, ⓔtoam@multitechweb.com), northeast of the main road, out past the Kitale Club. Run by John Wilson, a retired

Moving on from Kitale

Matatus spill out from the stage near the municipal market onto the adjoining main road, and there's a smaller gathering of Nissans bound for Eldoret, Kakamega and Kisumu opposite Kitale Museum on the corner of the Lodwar road.

Heading west, if you plan to explore **Mount Elgon** (see p.297), matatus leave daily around 3–5pm for *Mount Elgon Lodge* near the national park's Chorlim Gate. Otherwise, the next closest destination is **Endebess**, reached quickly enough by regular matatus. Southwards, Kakamega and Kisumu are no more than two or three hours away down the busy and bumpy A1. As ever, Akamba **buses** (☎054/31732 or 020/2365828) are the best bet for long hauls back to Nakuru and Nairobi, though with only two buses daily (9am & 9pm), you may find Eldoret Express's frequent departures more useful: they leave when full, roughly every hour.

The road to **Lodwar** for Lake Turkana (see p.506) is in such an appalling condition beyond Marich that it may as well not be paved at all. There are several buses a day, best caught early, from around 8am. Remember to take water, and also to stock up on provisions, as you'll only find more basic stuff on sale further north (fresh fruit and vegetables are expensive and poor quality in Lodwar). If you're driving yourself, note that there is nowhere to get fuel between Ortum and Lodwar.

From the airport, 6km southwest of town, off the A1 road to Webuye, there are twice daily **flights** on Fly540 to Nairobi ($79).

---

former colonial administrator in Uganda, the museum displays cultural artefacts, mainly from the Karamojong pastoralists of northern Uganda. The exhibits are arranged in robustly un-scientific fashion to illustrate the proprietor's case, based on supposed linguisitic parallels between Karamojong and other languages, such as Gaelic, that a single worldwide farming culture existed tens of thousands of years before is normally believed to be the case. The curator-proprietor is usually on hand to explain his theory in person, but if you want to be sure of a guided tour – and the visit is fascinating – it's best to call or email in advance of your visit.

Lastly, the **Kitale Nature Conservancy** (daily 8am–6pm; Ksh700), about 5km north of Kitale en route to Saiwa Swamp and Kapenguria, is a small zoo combined with a bizarre collection of natural freaks and oddities – five-legged cows and the like – that would normally be slaughtered at birth. It's grotesque, but morbidly fascinating.

Eating, drinking and nightlife

Kitale has several quite good **places to eat**, including the lively, local *Iroko* franchise. Some of the best food in Kitale is to be found at the *Alakara* and *Highview* hotels, and the *Kitale Club* – if you don't mind paying for temporary membership (Ksh500) on top of the price of a set meal (Ksh350) to eat at the Kitale.

After dark, a number of places provide drink and lively conversation. The **bars** at the *Bongo*, *Alakara* and *Highview* are quiet but congenial. Of the more energetic **nightclubs**, the best is *New Kitale Villa* on Moi Avenue, a cheerful and friendly dive with upbeat music 24/7, and a live band nearly every evening. The *Rock Hotel* disco, at the north end of Kenyatta Street, is also fun, but more rough and ready.

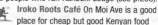

Coffee Shop Kitale Opposite the *Alakara Hotel*. A good spot to start the day – and a useful, central rendezvous – is this very nice establishment, combining a café-bistro with a library, tourist information and crafts sales. It's owned by the people who run *Karibuni Lodge* (see p.293).

Iroko Roots Café On Moi Ave is a good place for cheap but good Kenyan food including stews, curries and pilau. More upscale is the *Iroko Pavilion*, on Askari Road.

Iroko Twigs Café Kenyatta St. Sister establishment to *Iroko Roots* and equally nice; always busy and good value, with most dishes around Ksh100.

Sikh Union dining room Section C district, north side of Kitale. For something a little more adventurous, try this excellent community dining hall, which does superb curries.

Saiwa Swamp National Park

Created specifically for the protection of the **sitatunga**, a rare and vulnerable semi-aquatic antelope, **Saiwa Swamp National Park** (Ⓦ www.kws.go.ke/saiwa .html; $20) is the country's smallest park. Despite its accessibility – 11km from *Barnley's Guesthouse* (see p.292), and easily reached by matatu from there or from Kitale – it is rarely visited, which is a pity. The requirement that you walk (rather than drive) around the 1.9 square kilometres of jungle and swamp, plus the chance of seeing the antelope as well as various monkeys and birds, make it an exciting and interesting goal for a day. If you're staying at *Barnley's*, think about hiring a guide there for the trip, which is not at all expensive, and really worthwhile.

Wildlife-watching

The **sitatunga** is an unusual antelope with strangely splayed and elongated hooves. Although you're almost bound to see the sitatunga, you probably won't see its feet, because the animal lives most of its life partly submerged in water and weed. It is indeed a little hard to see how much help its feet really are as the hooves are only moderately elongated: the theory makes sense, but evolution has a little more work to do here, and the antelope pick their way gingerly through the swamp to avoid sinking. Similar in size and general appearance to the bushbuck, the sitatunga is reddish-brown with a slightly shaggy coat and very large ears, and the males have spiral horns. Due to poaching, numbers in the park are down from more than seventy in the 1980s to fewer than twenty at the last count.

Sitatunga can be found in scattered locations throughout western and central Africa, but in Kenya they are restricted to Saiwa Swamp, the Kingwal swamp south of Eldoret (see p.245), a few spots around Lake Victoria, and Lewa Downs, which has a trans-located group (see p.179). Only at Saiwa Swamp, however, have they grown really used to humans. They can be watched from the **observation platforms**, which have been built in the trees at the side of the swamp – two on the east side, two on the west. The best times are early morning and, to a lesser extent, late afternoon, and the furthest platform is less than a kilometre from the campsites. These lookouts are somewhat precarious, Tarzan-esque structures that enable you to spy down on the life in the reeds. One of them – *Treetop House* – has been converted into a snug overnight stay for two (see overleaf).

The drier parts of the park also shelter **bushbuck**, easily distinguished from the sitatunga by their terrified, crashing escape through the undergrowth as you approach. As well as the antelopes, Saiwa Swamp is a magnet for ornithologists, with a number of unusual **bird species**, including several turacos, many kingfishers, and the splendid black-and-white casqued hornbill. Most conspicuous of all are the **crowned cranes** – elegance personified when not airborne, but whose lurching flight is almost as risible as their ghastly honking call.

A delightful, easily followed, **early-morning walk** takes you across the rickety duckboards over the swamp and along a jungle path on the eastern shore. Here you're almost bound to see the park's four species of **monkey**: colobus, vervet, blue, and the distinctively white-bearded de Brazza monkey.

Practicalities

The park lies to the east of the main Kitale–Lodwar road, near the village of **Kipsain**. Matatus call at the village, which is 17.5km from Kitale. From here, it's Ksh100 each way by *boda-boda*, or a poorly signposted 4.8km walk to the park gates. You can pitch a tent in the park campsite ($15), which has basic facilities, or stay in the *Treetop House* (☎020/600800, ✉reservations@kws.go.k; $50), which is great for overnight atmosphere and dawn birdwatching and animal-spotting from the deck. Otherwise, the best base is *Barnley's Guesthouse*, just up the road (see p.292), where the Barnleys are a mine of information about the park and have some extremely knowledgeable guides. If you're heading straight to the park from Kitale, you can also turn right 11.5km north of Kitale (signposted "Sibanga") for Saiwa Swamp's main gate (7km).

Kapenguria, Ortum and the Marich Pass

KAPENGURIA, off the highway north of Saiwa Swamp, is surprisingly small given its status as the capital of West Pokot District, and is notable only for its role of minor notoriety in colonial history. The excellent **Kapenguria Museum** (daily 9.30am–6pm; Ksh500), occupies the prison where Jomo Kenyatta and his colleagues were detained during their parody of a trial. Their individually named cells have been restored, and contain copies of contemporary press reports, photos, depositions and the charges laid against each of the "Kapenguria Six" (some almost laughably nebulous). All six defendants were found guilty of belonging to Mau Mau and sentenced to seven years in jail with hard labour. More visually interesting are the **ethnographic displays** of local cultures, including well-described photographs of traditional circumcision dances and initiation groups, musical instruments, and a telling series on the changes wrought by modern life. Look out for the chisel for removing teeth, and the small horn "for sucking after making incisions on both sides of the head if one has a headache". In the museum grounds are some traditional Pokot family compounds, which the museum caretaker will explain to you.

Matatus from Kitale will drop you on the main A1 road at **Makutano**, the main town of the western Cherangani Hills, which has more services than Kapenguria itself (the turning for Kapenguria is a couple of kilometres further north). If you're heading towards the Kerio Valley (p.241) on the other side of the Cheranganis, you'll find plenty of matatus between Makutano and Lomut, especially on market day in **Sigor** (Thurs) or **Lomut** (Sat), with fewer onwards to **Tot**, unless you coincide with the weekly market at **Chesegon** (Wed).

Makutano has a KCB **ATM**, opposite Caltex (the local Barclays, also with an ATM, is in Kapenguria, opposite the *posta*). There are more accommodation choices in Makutano than Kapenguria: the s/c rooms at the *Sebit Hotel*, west of the main road, north of Caltex (☎0734/406521; ❶), are clean and well kept, and *Perkau Princess Lodge* (☎054/62405; ❶), next to Caltex, and owned by the Olympic marathon runner Tegla Loroupe, offers decent rooms. In Kapenguria itself, the *White House Resort Club*, on the right 400m before the museum (❶), is a bar and nightspot with s/c double rooms.

North of Makutano, the road enters the truly spectacular countryside of West Pokot proper, winding up the western ridge of Lenan forest, then plunging steeply to the Marun (or Moruny) river. After some 45km you reach **ORTUM**, beautifully positioned beneath the heights of the Cheranganis, close to the **Marich Pass**, and a good locale to start hiking in the hills. If you're heading north by car, Ortum has the last petrol before Lodwar, though it's better to fill up at Makutano to be on the safe side. There are several cheap B&Ls in the village (try *Sondany* or *Simotwo*, both ➊) and no shortage of *hotelis*.

An excellent base to make for in this district is the 🏕 **Marich Pass Field Studies Centre** (☏0722/139151, ⓦwww.gg.rhul.ac.uk/MarichPass; BB ➋), beautifully sited on the banks of the Marun River, 1km north of the small shopping centre of **Marich**, which is at the junction of the A1 Lodwar and B4 road to Sigor, Tot and the Kerio Valley. It's signposted, 1km down a track south of the Lodwar road. The centre has a lovely shaded **campsite** (Ksh360), some good **cottages** with mosquito nets, including two s/c cottages adapted for wheelchair use, and **dorm beds** (Ksh420). Firewood, stoves and lamps are available for a small charge. The **food** is basic but wholesome and plentiful (order well in advance; Ksh120–480) and drinking water comes pure from the well. Even if you're not staying, it's well worth dropping in for a picnic (admission Ksh120), as the centre is surrounded by dense bush, quivering with bird and animal life, and there are guides to help you on excursions around the hills, to Pokot homesteads and to the local markets if you've got the energy (Ksh550 for 5hr, Ksh750 for 10hr).

Mount Sekerr (or Mount Mtelo, 3354m) is the peak that looms to the northwest – it's a three-day hike to the top and back down. It's possible to stay overnight at the stunning 🏕 *Mount Mtelo View Campsite*, either camping (Ksh400) or staying in traditional, round, thatched huts (☏0737/941400, ⓦwww.freewebs.com/mbara1; ➊). Nearer Marich, 3206-metre **Mount Koh** to the southeast is a one-day hike if you've got 4WD to get halfway up; two full days otherwise.

Mount Elgon National Park

Straddling the Kenya-Uganda border, **Mount Elgon** (ⓦwww.kws.go.ke/mt-elgon.html; $25) is hidden in clouds most of the time, its precise outline hard to discern. The name comes from the Maasai **Ol Doinyo Ilgoon**, meaning "Breast Mountain", and, like Mount Kenya, it's an extinct volcano, around whose jagged and much-eroded crater rim the flat-topped peaks crop up like stumpy fingers of an upturned hand. The two mountains are comparable in bulk, but Elgon is lower. It's below the snowline and less precipitous, which is encouraging if the thought of tackling the "loneliest park in Kenya" was putting you off.

Part of the east side of the mountain is enclosed within the confines of **Mount Elgon National Park**. Outside this zone is a forest reserve, with some restrictions on movement due to the presence of poachers, cattle rustlers, and the conflict between a local militia and the Kenyan armed forces (see box, p.301). The park itself, however, is open for business. The easiest way to visit Elgon is by driving in at the main Chorlim Gate, staying just inside the park and visiting the nearby **caves and forest**. There are several relatively easy circular drives and short hikes in this lower part of the park.

On the **moorland** and towards the **peaks**, the smoothing effects of erosion make hiking relatively easy, and there's some bracing walking country. The highest of the peaks, **Wagagai** (4321m; there's also nearby Little Wagagai, at

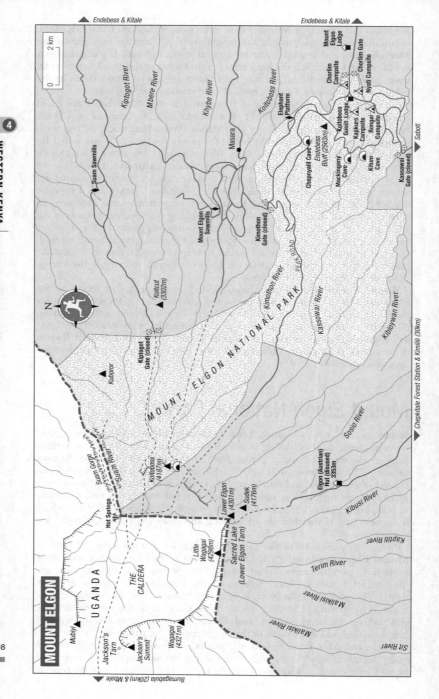

MOUNT ELGON

▲ *Endebess & Kitale*　　　　▲ *Endebess & Kitale*

0　2 km

Kiptogot River

Mbere River

Kimye River

Koitoboss River

Suam Sawmills

Masara

Mount Elgon Lodge

Chorlim Campsite

Chorlim Gate

Nyati Campsite

Elephant Platform

Chepnyalil Cave

Endebess Bluff (2663m)

Koitoboss Guest Lodge

Kapkuro Campsite

Mackingeny Cave

Rongai Campsite

Kitum Cave

Kassawa Gate (closed)

Mount Elgon Sawmills

Kimothon Gate (closed)

▶ *Saboti*

Koitcut (3302m)

N

Kimothon River

PEAK ROAD

Kassowai River

M O U N T   E L G O N   N A T I O N A L   P A R K

Kiboywan River

Kiptogot Gate (closed)

Kubotor

▶ *Chepkitale Forest Station & Kimilili (30km)*

Sosio River

Suam Gorge

Suam River

Koitoboss (4187m)

Koitoboss (4187m)

Elgon (Austrian) Hut (disused) 3353m

Kibusi River

UGANDA

Hot Springs

Lower Elgon (4301m)

Sudek (4176m)

THE CALDERA

Little Wagagai (4298m)

Sacred Lake (Lower Elgon Tarm)

Kaptit River

Terim River

Makisi River

Makisi River

Sit River

Mubiyi

Jackson's Tarn

Jackson's Summit

Wagagai (4321m)

▼ *Bumagabula (20km) & Mbale*

4298m), is across the caldera in Uganda, but the most evocatively shaped peaks (Sudek, 4176m; Lower Elgon, 4301m; Koitoboss, 4187m; and Endebess Bluff, 2563m) belong to Kenya. The mountain has good rock-climbing – the best routes are on the cliffs of Lower Elgon, Sudek and the nearby pinnacles – but you must be properly equipped. You'll also need to clear your plans with the KWS rangers. Up inside the caldera (technically in Uganda), the **warm springs** by the Suam River provide a tempting bath.

Wildlife

The **vegetation** on Mount Elgon is similar to Mount Kenya's, and equally impressive, with bamboo and podocarpus forests (the latter more accessible than Mount Kenya's) giving way to open moorland inhabited by the strange statues of giant groundsel and lobelia. The **wildlife** isn't easily seen until you get onto the moors, but some elephant and a fair few buffalo roam the forest (be extremely wary of both). The best place to see elephants used to be the **Elephant Platform** north of Chorlim Gate, where herds congregated to browse on the acacias, but many were wiped out by poachers in the 1980s, and the remainder became reclusive. It's very rare to see them at the **Elkony caves**, where they regularly used to gouge salt. The Kenya Wildlife Service is confident that poaching is now under control, and estimates the elephant population to be around two hundred. The lions have long gone and, though there are still **leopards** and **servals**, you're not likely to see one. The **primates** are more conspicuous: blue monkeys and black and white colobus crash through the forested areas, troops of olive baboons patrol the scrub, and along the Kimothon River that forms the lower park's northern boundary, there's a scattering of rare de Brazza monkeys.

Practicalities

In most respects, you should treat a trip up Mount Elgon much as you would one to Mount Kenya. However, **altitude** is less of a problem on Elgon and, given several days to climb it, few people will be badly affected by the ascent. The key is to take your time. Access to the national park is easy, with two or three matatus most days from Kitale, and **hiking within the park** is now permitted. If you drive in, you can park and hike on your own, but if you don't have your own vehicle you will need to sign a waiver form at the gate.

It is possible to get to within 4km of Koitoboss peak with a vehicle, but it needs to be an extremely sturdy, high-clearance 4WD, and you will need steely nerves, as it's a steep, rocky and extremely muddy ride up to the road-head where the summit trail starts. Indeed, the route is often completely impassable (Jan & Feb is the best time), and even the area near Chorlim Gate can be extremely treacherous, with slippery tyre-ruts and ample opportunities to bog down or even roll your vehicle.

Timing, guides and equipment

Elgon is best from December to March, rather less good in June and July, and probably not worth visiting when the heaviest rains fall during the April to May and August to September periods. This is a lonely mountain and it's probably best not to go up alone. If you hire a **guide** to accompany you at Chorlim Gate, the official KWS ranger fee is Ksh3000 per day. You're likely to find locals willing to go up for around Ksh1000 per day, but, unlike Mount Kenya, there is no guiding industry here, and finding a good guide is correspondingly harder.

Take a **compass** or GPS and supplies for at least two to three days of self-sufficiency. Suggestions on clothing and equipment can be found in the Mount Kenya section (p.158).You'll need a **tent** if you want to explore beyond the lower park area, and a powerful **torch** if you want to go any distance into the caves. If you are planning more than a short visit, the 1:35,000 KWS map (usually available at Chorlim Gate, but better bought in advance) is better than nothing, and useful for the roads and trails, though it sketchily misses out most of the contours and mixes metric and imperial spot heights. For the high peaks and caldera, it's much more useful to have the topographically accurate *Mount Elgon Map & Guide* published by Andrew Wielochowski (the map of the caldera itself is at a useful 1:50,000; Ⓦwww.ewpnet.com/maps.htm), though the practical details are dated.

Accommodation

Inside the park itself, and on the slopes of the mountain, wild or campsite **camping** ($15) is the most obvious option and is your only choice if you are hiking deep within the park. There are three public campsites near Chorlim Gate – *Chorlim*, *Rongai* and *Kapkuro*. Situated 1km from the gate, in a clearing in the woods, *Kapkuro* also has four good **bandas** ($25 per *banda*, $35 during holidays), each with a bedroom with one double and one single bed, plus bedding, a basic kitchen and a bathroom with hot water delivered when required – but no electricity. If you want something more comfortable, and with electricity, there's the old warden's house, just up from Chorlim Gate, which has been converted into the self-catering *Koitoboss Guest House* ($180 for the whole house), with six double beds, a well-equipped kitchen with a big fridge, two bathrooms (both with a bathtub, one with a shower) and the promise of generator electricity from 7 to 10pm.The garden is full of impala, bushbuck and waterbuck. It's a very nice spot, though perhaps a little pricey for fairly basic comforts.The *bandas* and guesthouse are often available on the day, but to be sure, book in advance with KWS (Ⓣ020/600800, Ⓔreservations@kws.go.ke).

Mount Elgon Lodge (Ⓣ020/2094643 or 0722/875768; BB ❹) is located 1.5km outside the park on the track leading up to Chorlim Gate from Kitale. Although it's an interesting old pile, you can't get away from the fact that the main house is desperately run-down and the ten cottage rooms in the garden only slightly less so. **Camping** in the grounds is an accepted, and very acceptable, alternative to taking a room (Ksh600, including use of bathroom and showers). If you do stay, be sure to order lunch or dinner in advance (Ksh450) and get them to show you round the old house.

Crossing into Uganda

If you want to cross the mountain **into Uganda**, you will need to make arrangements in advance with the senior warden (Ⓣ054/310456, Ⓔmenp @swiftkenya.com), who will coordinate with the Ugandan parks authorities on the west side of the mountain. You'll need to hire a Kenyan ranger to accompany you as far as the warm springs on the border, where you are handed over to the care of a Ugandan ranger (or vice versa if coming the other way), and you will also have to visit Suam to complete border formalities before going through the park.

The **Suam** border post is easily reached by road, and a lot more easy-going than those further south at Malaba and Busia. Suam is accessible by regular matatus from Kitale and Endebess. On the Ugandan side, there are matatus to Kapchorwa and thence to Mbale, where you'll find onward transport to the rest of Uganda.

Routes up Mount Elgon

There are five **principal routes** up the Kenyan side of Elgon, but only **Chorlim Gate** is currently open. The **Kimothon** and **Kiptogot** routes on the north side of the park and the **Kimilili** and **Kassawai** routes up the south side have been closed for years. They may physically be accessible, but using them to enter the park (there are no facilities for registering your details or paying) is not permitted.

Chorlim Gate and the Peak Road

The only entrance currently permitted into the **national park** is **Chorlim Gate**, 22km from Kitale. Matatus usually run three times a day to *Mount Elgon Lodge* and Chorlim Gate from Kitale (leaving around 3–5pm, depending on passenger numbers), and there are frequent services to **Endebess**, from where it's a fairly easy two-hour walk if you don't get a lift. If you're driving, fill up with fuel in Kitale, and head northwest towards Endebess along the tarmac road. After 9km, the road splits, with the tarmac continuing to Endebess and a *murram* road bearing left for Chorlim Gate. About 6km further you reach a crossroads (right to Endebess, left to **Saboti** and the A1, straight ahead to Chorlim Gate).

Once inside the park, install yourself near the gate at one of the campsites or *bandas*, or at the self-catering *Koitoboss Guest House*. These are the obvious bases for visiting the **Elkony Caves** (see overleaf). For **Koitoboss Peak** (4187m), follow the driveable track or "Peak Road" into the moorlands to the road-head on the southern border of the park at 3500m, allowing three to four hours to cover the 30km. You leave your vehicle here, and it's a three-hour hike up the upper Kimothon valley to the pass at the southern base of Koitoboss peak, where there are flat (but cold and windy) places where you can camp. You can then make the one-hour scramble to the top, or take a two- to three-hour diversion to the Suam warm springs in the caldera.

Mayhem on Elgon

Despite the tranquility inside the national park, communities around the southern slopes of Mount Elgon have been embroiled in land disputes with the government since colonial times, and wracked by violent episodes over the past two decades. The most recent began in 2005 with the formation of the **Sabaot Land Defence Force**. Formed to resist a forced resettlement programme, the SLDF rapidly degenerated into a brutal **insurgency** that terrorized unsupportive Sabaot villagers and Okiek tribespeople alike, with murder, mutilations and rape, and is estimated to have displaced 66,000 people and killed more than six hundred. Early in 2008, as the world watched the post-election clashes in Eldoret, Kisumu and Naivasha, the Kenyan military went on a **rampage** in the southern Elgon foothills, arresting every Sabaot man over the age of 15, torturing and raping villagers suspected of involvement with the SLDF, and, according to the local MP, Fred Kapondi, killing more than 150 people. As reported by Human Rights Watch, the Red Cross and the UN Special Rapporteur on Extrajudicial, Summary or Arbitrary Executions, Philip Alston, it seemed that the Kenyan armed forces believed they could get away with murder, and, if anyone noticed, the even worse atrocities committed by the SLDF would cover for them. In May 2008, the army cornered and shot the SLDF's military commander, 25-year old Wycliffe Komon Matakwei, and arrested or killed most senior members of the militia, though questions remain about their funding and political control. For now, the insurgency seems to be over, but as ever, the issues of landlessness, official abuses and legal whitewash remain.

The Elkony Caves

Perhaps Elgon's most captivating attraction is the honeycomb of **caves** on the lower slopes. Some of these were long inhabited by one of the loosely related Kalenjin groups, the **Elkony** (whose name, in corrupted form, was given to the mountain), and used both as living quarters and as livestock pens at night. There is evidence that the caves had a ritual function as well – **Chepnyalil Cave** contains a structure that might have served as an altar or shrine, and its walls are painted with a red-and-white frieze of cattle. The caves are also linked with Luhya circumcision ceremonies, in which boys spent their month-long initiation period covered from head to toe in the white diatomite powder found in the area, before returning home as men. The Elkony were officially evicted from the caves by the colonial government, who insisted that they live in the open "where they could be counted for tax", but several caves were still occupied by extended families within living memory.

The largest and most spectacular cave is **Makingeny Cave**, close to the road and marked by a cascade falling over the entrance. It makes a good hike teamed up with its neighbour, **Kitum Cave**, a twenty-minute hike to the south. Early explorers believed that some of the caves were artificial, one report referring to "thousands of chisel and axe marks on the walls". In fact, generations of elephants were responsible: the well-signposted Kitum Cave was the mineral fix of local elephants, and on rare occasions they still walk into the cave at night to gouge the salt-flavoured rock from the walls with their tusks. If you're exceptionally lucky, a night vigil at Kitum Cave may be repaid by a visit from the elephants; but if not, the thousands of bats and the sounds of the forest are good compensation.

The Uganda road: Webuye and Malaba

Although it's the least interesting part of western Kenya to look at – mostly undulating **grasslands** and Kenya's largest **sugar-cane** fields – the route through Malaba is a good alternative to that via Busia (see p.263) for travellers passing between Kenya and Uganda. Should passenger rail services resume, it will undoubtedly become the main border crossing point, as indeed it once was.

If you're making your way to the south from this district down towards Kakamega and Kisumu, the busy A1 will take you through some fine stands of tropical forest, heralding the **Kakamega Forest** to the southeast.

Webuye Falls and Chetambe's Fort

WEBUYE is the site of the giant Panafrican (or "Pan") Paper Mills, which dominated the countryside around until 2009, when the world recession resulted in their closure. The explanation for the factory's location is the abundant water provided by the Nzoia River, which comes gushing through rock clefts behind the mills, at **Webuye Falls**. There's really no centre to Webuye itself, but there is a Barclays **ATM**.

Also at Webuye, on top of the steep scarp that rears up beyond the town, are the remains of **Chetambe's Fort**. This was the site, in 1895, of a last-ditch stand by the Bukusu group of the Luhya tribe against the motley line-up of a British punitive expedition, which had enrolled Ugandan, Sudanese, Maasai and even other Luhya, troops. A predictable massacre, in this case by Hotchkiss gun, took place, with negligible losses on the attackers' side, and equally few survivors

Elija Masinde's cult of the ancestors

In the 1940s and 1950s, there was a resurgence of **Bukusu resistance** and nationalism in the *Dini ya Msambwa* (Cult of the Ancestors) movement, spearheaded by the charismatic prophet-rebel, **Elija Masinde**. The heart of the movement was in the Elgon foothills between Kimilili and the Ugandan border. It called for the eviction of all *wazungu* and the transfer of their property to Africans. As the *Dini* spread, there were violent confrontations with colonial forces, and a number of deaths. Masinde was sent into internal exile but, by now a folk hero, his followers kept the sparks of resistance alive throughout the more organized uprising of Mau Mau in the Central Highlands, until Independence was finally obtained. The movement collapsed in the early years of *uhuru*, when Masinde was allowed home to Kimilili and his continued denouncements of all authority and claims to divine inspiration began to lose their coherence. Until his death in the 1990s, he could still be seen on the streets of Kimilili, a rather terrifying figure shouting at the wind.

among the defenders. How the British managed to storm the scarp in the first place, however, is a mystery: presumably the Bukusu were all inside their walled fort at the top. Resistance among the Bukusu continued right up until Independence (see box above).

The "**Fort**" itself is quite unimpressive, and in fact not easy to make out: all that remains these days is a circular field covering a couple of hectares, surrounded by a shallow ditch. The spot where the British placed their deadly gun, opposite the fort's main entrance, is just west of the water tower and is now marked by a small concrete memorial, dated 11.5.88 (the day the emplacement was declared a monument). The people who live nearby are glad to show visitors the site, and can tell you stories from their grandparents of finding bones in the compound area, of women coming here to weep in the evenings, and of animal sacrifices to the dead warriors.

It's exactly 8km from the main A104 road to Chetambe's Fort. Approaching Webuye from the east, turn north (right) towards Kitale on the old road (if you're approaching from the west, go past the big junction for the A1 and turn left after 3.2km). Then, after crossing two railway tracks, in just under 1km, turn right again at the sign for St Matthews ACK Secondary School. Go round the back of the school, bearing right, and follow the *murram* track, east, along the base of the ridge, for 2km until you reach the local *hoteli*, *Webuye Falls Resort*. To reach **Webuye Falls**, fork right here, go 500m to cross a railway track and another 600m to cross a stream, then park 150m up the hill. A short flight of steps takes you up to a rocky panoramic viewpoint, with pretty views in every direction.

For Chetambe's Fort, keep straight on at *Webuye Falls Resort* and pass the KBC transmitter towers. Bear left at a couple of small junctions, keeping to the top of the ridge. Exactly 5.1km from *Webuye Falls Resort* you reach a T-junction. Here you turn sharp left and, after 400m (passing the water tower on the left), you reach the end of the track and the site of the fort.

There's a less complicated, but sweatier, way to reach the fort, straight up the steep escarpment on foot. Exactly 1.5km north of the A1 Kitale road's junction with the A104, there's a *murram* turning to the right (east) near a grove of trees and some buildings. Scramble directly up the scrubby hillside for 400m as the crow flies and you'll reach the top of the ridge, about 150m above the plain. Ask the people at the first compound to show you the fort: it's 200m in front of you.

The road to Uganda

The only town of any size between Webuye and the Ugandan border is **BUNGOMA**, a surprisingly animated commercial town, with its Sharriffs Centre **shopping plaza** and bustling, arcaded main street. There's a Barclays **ATM** (the first you'll find if you're coming from Uganda), but no special reasons to stop. West of Bungoma, the tarmac is smooth and the scenery unexciting until you reach the border crossing at **Malaba**.

If you're heading **south from Bungoma** on the C33, the road starts okay, but seriously deteriorates near Mumias.

Malaba: the Ugandan border

MALABA is less used by passenger road traffic than Busia, but it's where most freight, as well as the (presently freight-only) railway line, crosses the border with **Uganda**. While there are usually endless lines of lorries waiting on both sides, pedestrians can cross without difficulty. Official formalities are relatively simple, and moneychangers are on hand both sides of the border. Try to find out the current rates in advance, watch out for scams and count the currency you're buying carefully before handing yours over.

If you're **arriving in Kenya**, you'll find several bus companies doing the run to Nairobi via Eldoret, of which Akamba (℡0774/431510; departures at 11am & 8pm) has the best reputation. Matatus on the Kenyan side serve Bungoma, Kisumu, Kitale and Eldoret; on the Ugandan side, they run to Tororo, Jinja and Kampala. Few people hang around in Malaba, but if you do need to stay, *Jaki Guest House*, on the south side of the main drag about 500m from the border post, is your best bet, with cheap, plain and simple s/c singles and doubles, or pricier and fancier doubles in the main block (℡055/54004; ❶).

Mumias and Butere

MUMIAS was originally *Mumia's*, capital of the Luhya-speaking mini-state of **Wanga**, and well established by the middle of the nineteenth century at the head of an important caravan route to the coast. **King Mumia**, who came to power in 1880, was Wanga's last king and the present-day town stands on the site of his capital. His ten-thousand-strong army, half of them dispossessed Maasai from the Uasin Gishu Plateau, was largely responsible for smashing Bukusu resistance at Chetambe's Fort fifteen years later (see p.302).

Even at the beginning of Mumia's reign, Europeans were beginning to arrive in the wake of Arab and Swahili slave-traders, who in turn had been settling in since the 1850s with the full accord of the Wanga royal family. By 1894 there was a permanent British sub-commissioner or collector of taxes posted here. King Mumia had always welcomed strangers, and he allowed the slavers to continue their work on other Luhya groups (notably the Bukusu), but he was unprepared for the swift usurpation of his authority by the British, whom he'd assumed were also there to trade. He was appointed "Paramount Chief" of a gradually diminishing state and then, as an old man, was retired without his real knowledge. He died in 1949, aged 100, and with him expired Kenya's first, and only, indigenous, upcountry state, almost without notice.

The town's present **mosque** (just by the junction of the Bungoma and Kakamega roads) was built in King Mumia's honour and its Koran school is just one of about 25 around the town. Mumias has long been a centre of Islam, famous for its coastal ways, but today women in *buibuis* – the long, black coverall of the coast – are rarely seen, and Islam is losing ground to Catholicism. The Catholic church (2km down the Kakamega road) is also reasonably impressive, though neither of the two houses of worship is worth going out of your way for. They do, however, supply a good excuse for visiting what is a charming and lively little market town.

Mumias has KCB and Barclays banks with **ATMs**, and a couple of **places to stay**, of which the best is *St Mary's Guest House* (❶), behind St Mary's Hospital on the Kakamega road just outside town. *Wanga Palace Guest House* (❶), by the Mama Watoto supermarket in the Wanga Castle building, on the main street behind the matatu stand, is also adequate.

For **food**, there are two good places opposite Hass petrol station, just across from the matatu stand. *Crossroads Café* ("The finest cuisine in Mumias" with breakfasts, snacks, *nyama choma*, and even chicken tikka and chips) now has competition from a branch of the Kakamega-based *Lawino 2000* just 100m to the north. There are numerous places to get a drink in the evening, but you might want to give *Club Hookers* a miss.

Around Butere

Leaving Mumias, there's a fast new road to Kisumu via **Butere**. **Buses** serve Kisumu, Kakamega and Nairobi, and there's even one a day direct to Mombasa. **Matatus** run to Kisumu, Kakamega, Bungoma and Busia and most other places in the district. In addition, three times a week, there is an alternative (if you first get a taxi or *boda-boda* down to Butere) in the form of the **Butere–Kisumu train** (Tues, Thurs & Sun at 1.30pm) which runs as an extension of the Kisumu–Nairobi service. The branch line to **BUTERE** was intended to reach Mumias, but never did. Though diesel-hauled since 1988, the train is little faster than it was under steam, taking three hours to cover barely 60km, but it's a boon to rural dwellers with more time than money, as a ticket (third-class only) costs only Ksh115.

If you want to stay in the Butere area, the top recommendation is ☘ *Martha's Guest House* in **Mundeku-Khumutimo** (☎0723/712538 or 0723/976299; ❷) which comprises a variety of creatively themed non-self-contained rooms in the main house and chalets in the large gardens. Built by railway employee James Shiraku Inuyundo in 1935, but officially opened as a guesthouse by Princess Margaret in 1956, this is the quirkiest and most enjoyable place to stay between Lake Victoria and Mount Elgon, with charming grounds, attentive service and good food. In addition, there's a fascinating little museum that crams more into a tiny hut than some of the national museums' establishments do in a large building. To reach *Martha's*, heading south from Mumias towards Butere, a signboard on the highway indicates "Martha's Guesthouse 500 meters away". In fact, you turn left 2.6km down this dirt road in the hamlet of Khumutimo, and it's then 400m down the track, behind an anonymous metal gate. Just 200m further along the dirt road, the grove of large trees on the left is **Omulundu**, a sacred grove of the Luhya elders, never to be cut.

Kakamega and Kakamega Forest

KAKAMEGA is the headquarters of the **Luhya**, a loosely defined group of peoples whose only clear common denominator is a **Bantu language**, spoken in more than a score of vernaculars, which distinguishes them from the Luo to the south and the Kalenjin to the east. Numerically, the Luhya (also spelt Abaluhya or Luyia) are Kenya's second largest ethnic group, and most are settled farmers.

▲ Kakamega forest

Kakamega itself was founded as a buying station on the ox trail known as **Sclater's Road**, which reached here from the coast in 1896. Historically, its only fame came in the 1930s, when gold was discovered nearby and more than a thousand prospectors came to the region. However, very few fortunes were made. In the early 1990s, Kakamega became the first town in Kenya to use the bicycle taxis known as *boda-bodas*, now almost a nationwide institution. Today, it's a lively town, but with little to detain casual visitors. If you're passing through in August of an even-numbered year, however, it's worth being aware that some of the Luhya communities in the district are swept up in exuberant boys' **circumcision parties** – though the actual chop is usually done in hospital and the initiates themselves tend not to be the ones doing the partying. A more sedate event, the **Agricultural Society of Kenya annual show**, takes place at the town's showground every November.

The nearby **Kakamega Forest** is one of western Kenya's star attractions and if you have any interest at all in the natural world, it's worth going far out of your way to see. Fortunately, it's fairly easy to get to Kakamega Forest from Kisumu or, if you've been in the Mount Elgon region, from Webuye along a scenically forested stretch of the A1.

Practicalities

Kakamega is fairly small and manageable. If you arrive here late in the day (or after around 2.30pm in a 2WD vehicle, when the rain often starts to fall), you may want to **stay in town** rather than arrive in the forest after dark. There are Barclays and SCB banks with **ATMs**, and several decent lodgings and places to eat.

The **municipal market**, next to the bus station, is very lively, and particularly so on the big market days (Wed & Sat), when the stalls are swelled by produce from the outlying rural areas. Among the local produce on offer you'll find natural remedies and medicines made from forest plants. For **supermarkets**, Mama Watoto on Cannon Awori Street, and Yako Supermarket on Kenyatta

Avenue, should do the job. Vaghela **bookshop**, on Mumias Road, has a reasonable selection of Kenyan and other English-language fiction.

There's **internet** access at several places in front of the *Ambwere Alliance Hotel* and at Kakamega Cyber Café by the SomKen station on Sudi Road. For matters relating to Kakamega Forest visit the Kenya Wildlife Service office (☏056/20425): go past the *Golf Hotel*, right at the roundabout, follow the road past the DC's office (which it's behind) to the next junction, turn left and it's on the left after 50m.

Accommodation

Ambwere Alliance Sudi Rd, nearly opposite the Total station ☏0721/646948. At the lower end of "mid-range" but decent enough, plain, agreeable and cheap (especially if you skip breakfast), with clean rooms, hot water, mosquito nets and safe parking. There's a bar and restaurant downstairs. BB ❷

Franka Mumias Rd ☏0734/929787.
The secure parking, clean, s/c rooms (some with good views), erratic hot water, a good bar, reasonable breakfasts, and *nyama choma* in the evenings make this, all in all, a reasonable choice. ❶

Golf Khasakhala Rd ☏056/30150, ✆www .golfhotelkakamega.com. Well-insulated rooms (nets and TVs, bathtubs and old-style showers, but no fans or a/c) in a comfortable, tourist-quality hotel from the late 1970s, its pretensions comically clipped by the vultures hopping over the lawns. There's a large pool and gift shop, but rates for non-Kenya residents are too high. BB ❺

Jionee Guesthouse Cannon Awori St ☏020/3557023 or 0722/289819. A friendly little place above the *Snack Stop Café*, offering plain but spick-and-span rooms with nets, though some rooms share bathrooms. ❶

Eating and drinking

In addition to the hotel dining rooms, there are some good, cheap **restaurants** in Kakamega, and plenty of places to **drink** and listen to **music**, too. Cannon Awori Street has a few good eating places: there's a long menu of Kenyan standards at the *Western Café*, and a shorter list of plain but decent Kenyan fare at *Snack Stop Café*. An interesting spot is 🏃 *Lawino 2000*, an innovative western Kenyan specialist ("Our mission: to contribute to a healthy and safety nourishment, through indigenous African cuisines"), serving local dishes, such as *alya* (smoked beef), ranging from Ksh50 to Ksh100, and even wine.

For **drinking places** with character, you're spoilt for choice. The bar at the *Franka* is one of the liveliest drinking holes while *Msafiri Bar* is at the mellower end of the spectrum. The town's only **nightclub**, 🏃 *Stardom*, has a good bar with forest-style decor, and opens up its dance floor on Wednesdays, Fridays and Saturdays for a mix of reggae, rumba and R'n'B.

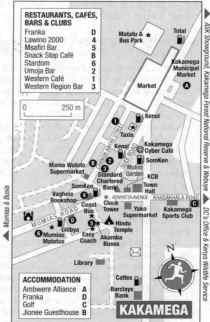

RESTAURANTS, CAFÉS, BARS & CLUBS
Franka — D
Lawino 2000 — 4
Msafiri Bar — 5
Snack Stop Café — B
Stardom — 6
Umoja Bar — 2
Western Café — 1
Western Region Bar — 3

ACCOMMODATION
Ambwere Alliance — A
Franka — D
Golf — C
Jionee Guesthouse — B

KAKAMEGA

Khayega, Shinyalu, Kakamega Forest Reserve ▼ & Kisumu

The Kakamega Forest

Some 400 years ago, **Kakamega Forest** would have been at the eastern end of a broad expanse of forest stretching west, clear across the continent, virtually unbroken as far as the Atlantic. Three hundred years later, after the advent of the human population explosion and widescale cultivation, the forests everywhere had receded, and had reduced Kakamega to an island of some 2400 square kilometres, cut off from the rest of the Guineo-Congolan rainforest. Today, with an area of less than 230 square kilometres, it's a small patch of relict equatorial jungle, famous among zoologists and botanists around the world as an example of how an isolated environment can survive cut off from its larger body.

The Kakamega Forest is a haven of shadowy gloom for more than three hundred species of birds, 45 percent of all the butterfly species ever recorded in Kenya, seven species of primates, as well as snakes, various other reptiles and untold varieties of insects. Many of these creatures are found nowhere else in East Africa because similar habitats no longer exist. The fear among environmentalists now is that even this tiny surviving track of rainforest, unique in Kenya, is in grave danger of being eliminated.

Despite a laudable scheme to educate the local population about the forest (see box overleaf), the lack of any coherent backing or action from the authorities means that its long-term future isn't bright. Pressure from local people, who need grazing for their livestock, land to cultivate, and firewood, amounts to a significant threat. The present area is less than a tenth of what it was in 1900, and its closed canopy cover (which indicates the forest's health and maturity) has dropped from ninety to fifty percent of the total area. This has led to the degradation of the natural habitat, and inevitably, to some species being threatened, some, like the leopard, last seen in 1992, becoming extinct in the forest.

Moving on from Kakamega

The obvious **routes** out of the area lie along the A1, north to Kitale or south to Kisumu. The road down to Kisumu is a real roller coaster, with a final eight-kilometre descent over the picturesque, boulder-strewn Nyando Escarpment, which brings Lake Victoria into view. In clear weather, it allows fantastic panoramas across the sugar fields of the Kano plains towards the massif of the Mau and the Kisii hills. Look out for the florid church on the left, the headquarters of a local denomination that models itself on the Coptic church, founded in Egypt in the early years of Christianity.

If you're heading back to the Rift Valley or Nairobi from Kakamega, it's not necessary to use the busy A1. You can go straight through the Kakamega forest via Shinyalu and out to Kapsabet, where you join an excellent tarmac highway, the C36, to Nabkoi and rejoin the A104.

If you have time and inclination for a diversion somewhat off the beaten track, you could visit the small town of Mumias (see p.304), the sugar belt's biggest processing centre and one of western Kenya's Muslim strongholds. The road from Kakamega is paved and there's regular transport.

Among the **bus routes** available, Akamba (☎020/2365823) runs two daily services to Nairobi, via Kisumu and via Kapsabet, both at 8.30am (Ksh950) and one to Mumias daily at 4pm (Ksh100); Coast Buses (☎020/3577108 or 0722/206453) runs direct, daily services to Mombasa at 4.30pm (Ksh1650): and the comfortable Easy Coach (☎056/30837 or 0738/200313) departs for Nairobi at 8am and 8pm (8hr, Ksh1150). Most **matatus** leave from the main stand on Sudi Road, but those for Mumias have their own stand on the Mumias Road.

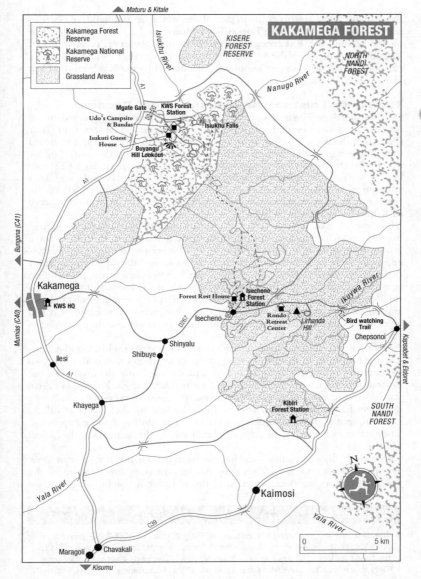

The forest is fragmented, interspersed with open fields of grassland, and the larger, central area has cultivated stream margins, small settlements and even tea plantations (which give the locals an alternative to plundering the forest as a source of income). Two main areas can be visited. The first, which has been accessible for many years, is the central **Kakamega Forest Reserve**, lying east of Kakamega town, somewhat off the beaten track, and managed by the Forest

Department. Most visitors come to part of one of the densest stands of forest in this area, and often stay at the **Forest Rest House** in the glade at its edge. The second section, the **Kakamega Forest National Reserve**, is northeast of Kakamega town, just off the A1 highway, and very easy to get to. This is a strictly controlled zone of 44 square kilometres, maintained by the KWS more or less like a national park.

The central district: Kakamega Forest Reserve

On arrival at the *Forest Rest House* (see opposite), you'll be greeted by an official guide (a member of Kakamega Biodiversity Conservation Tour Operators, KaBiCoTOa for short), whose name should be on the board outside the hut on the path up to the house. You will be given a brief introduction to the region and the conservation work being done by KEEP (see box below) – all guides should have a KEEP identity card, which is attempting to educate villagers and schoolchildren on the outskirts of the forest on the importance of preserving it. There's a daily "recreation" charge of Ksh600 (Ksh150 for children).

It's best to take up the offer of a **guide**, especially if you're a woman on your own (there are several female guides here). Exceptionally, for a profession that usually attracts hustlers, this lot are professional and knowledgeable; their walks are tremendously enjoyable, and they're happy to tailor them to your particular interests. The fee is Ksh300 per person, plus any tip you care to add (about Ksh300–500 for three hours is about right). Expect a wander along the labyrinthine jungle paths, with birds, monkeys, chameleons and other animals pointed out to you, most of which you would miss if you went on your own. A pair of **binoculars** is more or less indispensable if you're out to watch birds.

Among the commoner **birds** are the noisy and gregarious black-and-white-casqued hornbill and the very striking, deep violet, Ross's turaco. You may also see familiar-looking African grey parrots and, circling above the canopy on the lookout for unwary monkeys, the huge crowned hawk eagle. Kakamega's avian stars, however, are the **great blue turacos**, glossy, turkey-sized birds like dowagers in evening gowns. They're easily located by their raucous calls: a favourite spot at dusk is the grove of very tall trees down by the pump house. They arrive each evening to crash and lurch among the branches as they select roosting sites.

The forest draws mammal-watchers as well, particularly for its **monkeys**. Troops are often seen at dusk, foraging through the trees directly opposite the *Forest Rest House* veranda. Apart from the ubiquitous colobus, you can see

---

"Keep our forest"

The Kakamega Environmental Education Programme, or **KEEP** (Ⓦ www.tinyurl .com/mt3ond) was set up by the guides at *Forest Rest House* to combine visits to the forest for local primary and secondary schoolchildren with their school lessons. They hope that by convincing the children of the importance of protecting the forest, the message will spread into the community. A tree nursery has been started to demonstrate basic tree-planting techniques, alongside giving information on waste recycling and more efficient use of firewood. In addition, a butterfly farm has also been set up, with the aim of breeding local butterflies to frame and sell as souvenirs, generating income for the local community from the forest itself. Other sustainable projects in the pipeline include bee keeping and snake farming (for anti-venom production).

Sykes' monkeys and the much slimmer black-cheeked white-nosed monkey (most easily recognized by its red tail). They're often seen milling around with the hornbills. You may also see pairs of giant forest squirrels capering in the treetops – the deep booming call you sometimes hear in the morning is theirs.

At **night**, armed with a powerful torch, you might catch a glimpse of bushbabies, palm civets, genets or even a potto, a slow-moving, lemur-like animal whose name aptly conveys its appearance and demeanour. The forest is also home to several species of fruit bat, of which the hammer-headed fruit bat (*Hypsignathus monstrosus*) is the largest in Africa, with a wingspan of a metre and an enormous head. Other nocturnal Kakamega specialities are the otter shrew, which lives in some of the forest streams, the tree pangolin (a kind of arboreal scaly anteater) and the flying squirrel.

The forest's **reptile life** is legendary, but few people actually see any **snakes**, and you're much more likely to come across **chameleons**. Reptiles spend a good deal of time motionless, especially when frightened, and to see snakes in the dense foliage you have to be experienced. Visible or not, however, snakes are abundant and you certainly shouldn't walk in the forest in bare feet or sandals: the sluggish gaboon viper, growing to a metre or more in length, and fatter than your arm, is a dangerous denizen of the forest floor, though not an animal that seeks confrontation. To avoid a serpentine encounter, simply walk heavily: snakes are highly sensitive to vibration and will flee at your seismic approach.

If you have time for more than one daylight walk, you could ask a guide to show you the way to **Lirhanda Hill**, via a trail that's rich in medicinal plants. You will be shown the leaves, berries and saps that forest dwellers chew, swallow or anoint themselves with to treat various ailments. Lirhanda Hill itself is a lookout point, offering fine views over the whole expanse of forest, with the sombre bulk of Mount Elgon glowering in the distance. Cutting into the hillside near the top is a gold-mining shaft, long disused and now home to a large colony of bats. With a powerful torch and a steely nerve you can grope your way along the tunnel to meet them at close quarters.

Arrival and practicalities

There are several ways of **getting to** the *Forest Rest House*. If you're **driving** from Kakamega, the easiest road is from **Khayega**, 7km south of Kakamega on the A1. The junction is marked by signposts for the Arap Moi Girls' School and the Office of the President. From here, an earth road leads 6km to **Shinyalu**. Keep right at Shinyalu and continue for another 5.3km to **Isecheno**, turning left just after the barrier and a signposted arrow. From the barrier, it's less than a kilometre up the trail to the *Forest Rest House*.

If you're driving from Eldoret via Kapsabet, the road into the forest starts at **Chepsonoi**, on the C39 where you take the right turning (west), signposted "Kisieni 12km D267". Whichever approach you're taking, the surfaces get treacherously slippery in wet weather (especially for low-clearance 2WDs). Given the predictable afternoon rains, this limits you to getting there between 10am and 2pm, when the road is at its driest. Even so, 4WD is advisable.

If you're using **public transport** from Kakamega, the cheapest way is to catch a matatu to Shinyalu. There are occasional matatus from Khayega too, or you could take a *boda-boda* from there. A private **taxi** from Kakamega to Shinyalu (or the *Forest Rest House* if you're lucky) will cost around Ksh1000.

From Shinyalu, it's a lovely hour-long walk to Isecheno. **Shinyalu** itself often has a cattle auction and a major market on Saturdays, when it's worth pausing an hour to soak up the atmosphere of cowboys in the jungle. **From Eldoret**, any bus or matatu heading towards Kisumu via Kapsabet, Chavakali and Maragoli will pass the turning for Isecheno at **Chepsonoi**. From this junction, if you don't get a lift, it takes about three hours to walk through the magnificent forest scenery to the Central District headquarters at Iescheno.

If you stay in one of the Isecheno places (the *Forest Rest House* or *Isecheno Bandas*), you'll find the closest reliable **supplies** are at the *dukas* about 3km away on the road to Shinyalu; so it's best to bring your own food. For candles and simple staples – bananas, *chai*, mineral water, biscuits, sodas and sometimes beer – there's a small *duka* on the way to the pump house, which is open daily. They cook inexpensive meals to order, given a few hours' notice.

Accommodation

Camiha Café At the start of the Isecheno road in Shinyalu ☎0724/142645. If you want to stay somewhere with beer and music, this might fit the bill. It's really just a café and bar, with four basic rooms, bucket showers (hot water on request), food available, and music till late. ❶

Forest Rest House Central District HQ area, reservations in advance through The Forester, PO Box 1233 Kakamega, Western Province, no phone. If you're not too fussy about comforts this wooden chalet is a delight – a kind of budget *Treetops* without the crowds. There are four, three-bedded, s/c rooms up on the first floor, with a long veranda facing onto the wall of forest. There's basic bedding, but you might bring a blanket or sleeping bag, as it can get decidedly chilly early in the morning. You can also camp (Ksh650). There's no electricity and erratic water supplies (when the pump is on, each room has a functioning bathroom and toilet; otherwise you have to fetch water from the pump house). ❶

Isecheno Bandas Central District HQ area next to the *Forest Rest House* ☎0722/619150 ⊛ .tinyurl.com/mt3ond. KEEP's own *bandas* are located right next to the *Forest Rest House* and cost the same, but the money is used locally for KEEP's ongoing community conservation projects. There are five non-s/c *bandas*, with beds, blankets, sheets and pillows, and a separate shower (hot water on request) and toilet block

(with European-style long-drops). As at the *Forest Rest House*, you can either bring food and firewood to self-cater, or make arrangements locally to have meals provided. Ksh500 per person.

Isecheno Blue-Shouldered Guest House 500m south of the Central District HQ area ☎0722/886833. Quirky little homestay named after the blue-shouldered robin-chat, one of Kakamega's unusual birds. Sleeping five in three rooms, the house has a veranda, from where you can watch monkeys in the trees opposite. Meals to order (or bring food and cook your own in the spotless kitchen), and forest walks available (the owner is a Kakamega guide). ❶

Rondo Retreat Centre 2.5km east of the Isecheno junction ☎056/30268 or 0735/894474, ⊛ www.rondoretreat.com. If you want a high level of comfort, this is the upmarket option in the forest, situated in a fine old sawmiller's house built in 1948. This "Christian sanctuary for nature lovers" – owned by a group called the Trinity Fellowship – has wonderful, bright, four-poster bedrooms in cottages set among cool lawns. It's fresh and elegant, with just enough clutter and lack of uniformity to make it feel homely. There's great birdwatching, butterfly-spotting and flower-enjoying, but they don't serve alcohol (though there's no objection if you want to bring your own). HB ❻

Kakamega Forest National Reserve

Driving south down the A1 road to Kakamega from its junction with the A104 at Maturu, you enter the thick forest of the Kakamega forest region after about 14km. Although parts are cleared and there's no lack of people about, it's a very different environment from just about anywhere else in Kenya. Some 22km south of Maturu you reach a cluster of shops and *hotelis* set back from the road. This is the junction for the *murram* road into the

Kakamega Forest National Reserve (Ⓦwww.kws.go.ke/kakamega.html; $20), the part of Kakamega Forest managed by the Kenya Wildlife Service.

If you've got your own vehicle, it's easier to get around this part of Kakamega Forest than the central zone. The forest proper is, in fact, a fair walk from the KWS-run ⚑ *Udo's Bandas and Campsite* ($10 per person), named after the ornithologist Udo Savalli, which is barely 300m from the northern reserve boundary and less than 2km from Mgate Gate. Here there are seven simple thatched *rondavels* (six twins and one with four beds), with bedding, nets and padlocks on the doors, a few pieces of cane furniture, but no other comforts, plus basic cold showers and long-drop toilets nearby. *Banda* prices are likely to go up to reflect the fact that KWS charges $15 for camping. *Udo's* is basic, but the forest environment touches it with a little magic, especially at night. Just before *Udo's* as you come into the reserve, *Isukuti Guest House* ($50 for the whole house) is 1.2km from the main gate. It has four beds in two rooms, a bathroom and kitchen, and is a good deal more spacious and comfortable than *Udo's*, but lacks atmosphere. Both places should be booked in advance with KWS (☎020/600800, Ⓔreservations @kws.go.ke).

A number of driveable and walkable tracks through the coolness of the forest begin just beyond *Udo's*. You have free run of the national reserve on foot. The main trail is well signposted and there are numerous branches and "exit" trails that allow for a relatively quick return when you've had enough of the deep forest. It's not a place you're likely to get lost in, despite its remoteness.

The significant difference between the national reserve here and the forest reserve further south, around Isecheno, is the age of the growth. Many of the **trees** are colossal (indeed some have plaques inviting you to guess the girth – answers round the back). The climate is generally drier and there's a greater diversity of habitat, including ancient forest, young forest and areas of scrub. It's an impressive area and, as in the southern forest, there's a huge variety of bird and plant life, and many monkeys.

An easy excursion from the forest station is to the **Isiukhu Falls**, a rather feeble waterfall 1.5km away along a rocky path. **Buyangu Hill viewpoint**, a four-kilometre drive or walk from the forest station, is much more worthwhile – a precipice with a spectacular vista east across the forest to the Nandi Escarpment. When you get up to the coniferous trees, don't stop. Walk through them another 100m or so, and you'll see the viewpoint tower, up a steep rise (an easy scramble).

The **Kisere Forest Reserve** is a separate area, a 4-square-kilometre, outlying part of the main reserve, home to de Brazza monkeys among other species, and with some superb examples of the prized timber tree, the Elgon olive. Ask the rangers to give you directions: it's 5km from Mgate Gate.

Travel details

Kisumu is the west's transport centre. Buses and matatus run from there to most major centres in this chapter within half a day.

Trains

Kisumu to/from: Butere (3 weekly; 3hr); Nairobi (3 weekly; 13hr).

Buses

Eldoret to/from: Kabarnet (1 daily; 1hr 30min); Kericho (4 daily; 3hr); Kisumu (13 daily; 3hr); Kitale (hourly; 1hr 30min); Malaba (2 daily; 3hr 30min); Nairobi (hourly; 6hr 30min); Nakuru (hourly; 4hr).
Kakamega to/from: Kisumu (frequent; 1hr 30min); Mombasa (1 daily; 14hr); Nairobi (10 daily; 8hr).
Kericho to/from: Kisii (frequent; 2hr); Kisumu (frequent; 2hr); Nairobi (frequent; 5hr); Nakuru (frequent; 2hr).
Kisii to: Homa Bay (4 daily; 2hr); Kisumu (3 daily; 2hr); Migori (5 daily; 1hr 30min); Mombasa (2 daily; 14hr); Nairobi (frequent; 8hr).
Kisumu to/from: Kitale (4 daily; 3hr); Mombasa (5 daily; 14hr); Nairobi (frequent; 8hr); Nakuru (frequent; 5hr).
Kitale to/from: Lodwar (3 daily; 12hr); Nairobi (several services daily and overnight; 8hr).

Matatus

With nearly half the population of Kenya living in this region, matatus are widespread and most minor roads have services. Many also run on bus routes at approximately the same fare, but to less predictable schedules.

Eldoret to/from: Cherangani (1hr); Iten (30min); Kabarnet (1hr 30min); Kakamega (2hr); Kaptagat (30min); Kericho (2hr 30min); Kisumu (2hr); Kitale (1hr); Malaba (2hr 30min); Mumias (2hr 30min); Nairobi (6hr); Nakuru (3hr).
Homa Bay to/from: Kendu Bay (1hr); Kisii (1hr 30min); Kisumu (3hr); Mbita (1hr 30min); Migori (1hr 30min).
Kakamega to/from : Kericho (2hr 30min); Kisumu (1hr); Kitale (3hr); Mumias (40min); Webuye (1hr).
Kisii to: Eldoret (3hr 30min); Homa Bay (1hr 30min); Kericho (2hr); Kisumu (2hr); Migori (1hr 30min); Nairobi (5hr); Naivasha (3hr); Rongo (30min).
Kisumu to/from: Busia (2hr 30min); Kendu Bay (2hr); Kericho (1hr 30min); Kitale (3hr); Luanda Kotieno (2hr 30min); Mbita (4hr 30min); Nairobi (7hr); Nakuru (4hr).
Kitale to/from: Busia (3hr); Cherangani (30min); Endebess (30min); Makutano for Kapenguria (1hr); Malaba (2hr 30min); Nairobi (7hr); Kipsain (30min).

Ferries

Mbita to/from: Luanda Kotieno (4 daily; 45min); Sena (matatu-boat service; 2–5 daily; 1hr) via Takawiri (45min).

Flights

Eldoret to/from: Nairobi (2 daily; 1hr).
Kisumu to/from: Eldoret (1 daily; 20min); Nairobi (several; 1hr).
Kitale to/from: Nairobi (2 daily; 1hr).

The Mombasa road and major game parks

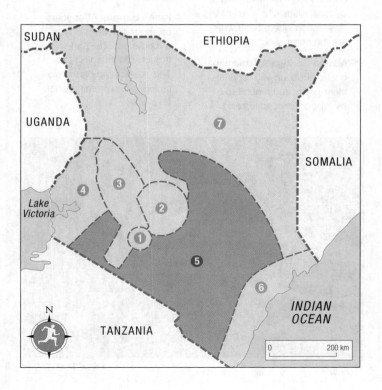

CHAPTER 5

Highlights

* **The Taita Hills** Steep and densely cultivated, the untouristy Taita Hills are like an outcrop of highland Kenya, peaking from the dry plains. Visit the skull caves, where the heads of Taita ancestors are interred. See p.332

* **Selenkay Conservancy** In a remote area north of Amboseli National Park, this community conservation initiative, staffed by local Maasai, is a rewarding destination where bush walks are the norm. See p.343

* **Mzima Springs** A remarkable oasis, bubbling with crystal-clear water and inhabited by hippos, crocodiles and a variety of other species. Check out the walkways and underwater viewing chamber. See p.349

* **The Migration** At any time of the year, the Maasai Mara National Reserve yields an extraordinary diversity of wildlife, but a visit during the annual wildebeest migration can be truly awe-inspiring. See p.374

* **Kinna Bandas** After years off the map, Meru is now a model national park, though still little visited. This welcoming *banda* site includes a swimming pool. See p.381

▲ Hippo, Mzima Springs

5

The Mombasa road and major game parks

T his chapter covers the well-travelled route from **Nairobi to Mombasa** and a number of detours off it, along with the country's most visited **game parks**: Maasai Mara, Amboseli, Meru, Tsavo East and West, and a trio of reserves in the north – Samburu, Buffalo Springs and Shaba.

The **Mombasa Highway** is Kenya's most important thoroughfare, the subject for much of the last decade of a massive resurfacing project, which was more or less completed in 2009. With scenic interest marginal for much of the journey, the temptation is to head straight for the coast, stopping only at the **Amboseli** or **Tsavo national parks**. But there are some rewarding diversions off the highway, which are not greatly explored: east into **Kamba country** and the towns of **Machakos, Kitui and Mwingi**, or south towards the base of **Kilimanjaro** and the **Taita Hills**.

Together with the coast, the **game parks** in this chapter are the most visited parts of Kenya, and the country's archetypal image. This is not to take anything away from their appeal, for visiting any of them is an exceptional experience. In the 24,000 square kilometres covered by the six parks, animals hold sway. Their seasonal cycles and movements, most spectacularly in the Maasai Mara's **wildebeest migration**, are the dominant plots in the natural drama going on all around. Seeing the wildlife isn't difficult, but it does require some patience and an element of luck that makes it exciting and addictive.

It's likely that you will either already be booked on a safari, or you'll book one once in Kenya, either from the coast or from Nairobi. Popular alternatives are to **rent a vehicle**, with or without a driver, or, if you're alone or there are just two of you, and especially if you're on a limited budget, to take a no-frills camping safari. There are details on the ins and outs of booking safaris in Basics, from p.65, and plenty of operators listed in Nairobi (see p.128) and Mombasa (see p.406).

From Nairobi to the coast

Although the **A109 Nairobi–Mombasa route** can seem devoid of interest, any detour into the less well-known parts of **Kamba territory** or down towards the foothills of **Kilimanjaro** can be a really worthwhile antidote to the much hyped attractions of safari-land. There are several stops and sidetracks worth making, though it's much easier to do so with your own vehicle.

There's also a practical reason why you might not simply follow the highway: an excellent but rarely used alternative to the first third of the route, **via Machakos and Makindu**, that avoids what has long been the highway's worst section, in terms of road surface, gradients and traffic. Although the recent improvements on the highway will last for a year or two, there's every likelihood that before this edition's time is out, drivers will be clutching their steering

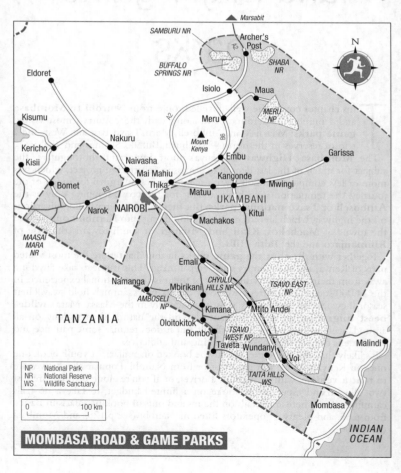

MOMBASA ROAD & GAME PARKS

wheels in despair once again. So the following is a **good tip**. South of Nairobi, taking the Machakos turning, you drive into Machakos and out of the town, southwards, towards the rural centre of Wote (Makueni), eventually rejoining the main highway at Makindu. This route starts off very unpromisingly from Machakos, with 5km of rough tarmac, but it soon becomes an excellent, wide, smooth road, swooping through farmland and hills all the way to Makindu. Machakos to Makindu is 140km, and **Wote**, like a mini-Machakos, with a useful Barclays ATM, is halfway along. Note, if you're doing this detour in the opposite direction, you turn right, in the middle of Makindu, just before the Sikh Temple (see p.326) and drive a straight 5km to the northeast, before the road does a ninety-degree left turn and starts heading reassuringly to the northwest.

Ukambani

One very good way to start a trip heading towards the coast, if you're in no particular hurry, is to take an excursion right into the heart of **Ukambani**, the land of the Kamba people. From **Machakos**, frequent buses and matatus continue to **Kitui**, from where you can get transport further east to Mwingi, north up to Embu, or south down to Kibwezi, back on the Mombasa road.

If you're coming to live or work in Ukambani, you'll be pleased to know that security in the eastern parts of the district, particularly along the once notorious **Garissa highway**, has hugely improved. It's no longer considered any more unsafe than any other Kenya highway, and possibly less so, as the surface is good and traffic generally light. If you're driving to **Matuu**, **Mwingi** or **Garissa**, it's enough to travel by day, stay awake and watch out for camels.

Machakos

The Imperial British East African Company's first upcountry post, established in 1889, **MACHAKOS** is ten years older than Nairobi, and therefore the first capital of Kenya according to some Kamba people. "Machakos", now the capital of Ukambani, is really a corruption of *Masaku's*, after the headquarters of a Kamba chief of the time. It's a name still seen all over town. The **old fort site** is located near the road in the administrative district, though there is nothing left to see.

Distinctly friendly, and overwhelmingly Kamba, Machakos has a backdrop of green hills and a tree-shaded, relaxed atmosphere to its old buildings that is quickly endearing. The weaving of **sisal baskets** (*vyondo*) is a visible industry and a major occupation for many women, either full-time, or behind the vegetable stand in the market. Machakos effervesces and it's a great place to stay for a day or two, especially on Monday and Friday, market days. Look for (though you can scarcely miss) the truly splendid and quite venerable **mosque** and the fine, upstanding **Catholic cathedral**, Our Lady of Lourdes.

Practicalities

The Barclays and Standard Chartered **banks** have ATMs. Apart from the many produce markets scattered about town, there are several **supermarkets**, including Kutata in the town centre and the big **Susu shopping centre** on the way into town from Nairobi. You can get online at Solanq and several other cybercafés. For **buses and matatus** to Nairobi and Mombasa, head for the main stage in the centre of town. For services to Kitui (with connections

5

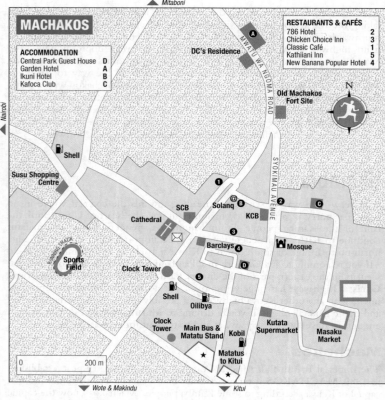

there for Embu and Mwingi), the stage is just up on the Embu road, beside the noisy *jua kali* metalworkers' area.

Accommodation and eating

Machakos has the usual range of **eating places**: *Chicken Choice Inn* is always busy; the *786* is an appealing snack bar and restaurant; *Kathiiani Inn* dishes up good curries and chapatis; the friendly *New Banana Popular Hotel* serves a range of Kenyan dishes; and *Classic Café* is a cheap little corner *hoteli*.

Central Park Guest House Town centre ☎044/21866 or 0722/230932. Clean, well-furnished s/c rooms with nets, TV and instant showers. The first-floor *Central Pub & Restaurant* is a popular local pub with flat-screen TV and big meals (plate of bhajias Ksh120, beer Ksh95). Rates include a solid English-style breakfast. ②
Garden 1km north of the town centre ☎044/20037 or 0722/585637. With views of the Iveti Hills, this is the most upmarket place in town – a muzak-piped, "international-class" hotel with a health club, sauna and steam bath. The carpeted rooms have nets and TV. ④

Ikuuni Town centre ☎044/21166 or 0733/456775. Large and busy watering hole and restaurant, with a warren of uninspiring, s/c rooms tacked on. Discos Wed, Fri & Sat nights, and comedians and other entertainment on Sun afternoons. Ask for a mosquito net. ②
Kafoca Club Town centre ☎0733/960818 or 0720/796124. The Kenya Armed Forces Old Comrades Association is a well-run and fairly wholesome businessmen's hangout, with a bar, TV lounge and a good restaurant with plenty of meat and fish dishes. The clean rooms have nets but old-style showers. Safe parking. ②

The largely dry stretch of central Kenya from Nairobi to Tsavo and north as far as Embu has been the traditional homeland of the Kamba people for at least the last five centuries. They moved here from the regions to the south in a series of vague migrations, in search, according to legend, of the life-saving **baobab** tree, whose fruit can stave off the worst famines, and whose trunks hold vast quantities of water.

With a diverse economy in better years, including mixed farming and herding as well as hunting and gathering, the Kamba slowly coalesced into a distinct tribe with one (Bantu) language. As they settled in the hilly parts, the population increased. But drier areas at lower altitudes couldn't sustain the expansion, so **trade** for food with the Kikuyu peoples in the fatter highlands region became a solution to the vagaries of their generally implacable environment.

In return for farm produce, the Kamba **bartered** their own manufactured goods: medicinal charms, extra-strong beer, honey, iron tools, arrowheads and a lethal and much-sought-after hunting poison. In the eighteenth and nineteenth centuries, as the Swahili on the coast strengthened their ties inland, **ivory** became the most important commodity in the trade network. With it, the Kamba obtained goods from overseas to exchange for food stocks with the highlands tribes.

Long the **intermediaries** between coast and upcountry, the Kamba acted as guides to Swahili and Arab caravans, and led their own expeditions. Settling in small numbers in many parts of what is now Kenya, they were naturally enlisted by the early European arrivals in East Africa. Their broad cultural base and lack of provincialism made them confident travellers and employees, and willing porters and soldiers. Serving alongside British troops during **World War I** gave them insights into the ways of the Europeans who now ruled them. Together with the Luo and Kikuyu, they suffered tens of thousands of casualties in white men's wars. Even today, the Kenyan army has a disproportionately high Kamba contingent, while many others work in the police force and as private security guards.

In the early years of **colonialism**, the Kamba were involved in occasional bloody incidents, but these were usually the result of misunderstandings rather than any concerted rebellion. Although there was a major ruckus after an ignorant official at Machakos cut down a sacred *ithembo* tree to use as a flagpole, on the whole their trade networks and diplomatic skills helped to ease their relations with the British. As early as 1911, however, a Kamba movement rejecting European ways had emerged. Led by a widow named **Siotune wa Kathake**, it channelled opposition to colonialism into frenetic dancing, during which teenage girls became "possessed" by an anti-European spirit and preached radical messages of non-compliance with the government. Later, in the 1930s, the Ukamba Members Association (one of whose leaders was **Muindi Mbingu**) was formed in order to pre-empt efforts to settle Europeans in Ukambani and reduce Kamba cattle herds by compulsory purchase. Five thousand Kamba marched in peaceful protest to Kariokor market in Nairobi – a show of collective political will that succeeded in getting their cattle returned – and the settlers never came to Ukambani in any numbers.

Wamunyu, midway between Machakos and Kitui, was the birthplace of the modern Kamba **woodcarving industry**. Kamba men who served in World War I were introduced to the techniques of wood sculpture by the Makonde ebony carvers of the Tanganyikan coast. Today, the vast majority of woodcarvings in Kenya are still produced by Kamba artists, often in workshops far from Ukambani.

Kitui

Like Machakos, **KITUI**, 100km further east, lies in an impoverished area and, is often badly hit by drought. Despite its proximity to Nairobi, this district is one of Kenya's least developed. The town is small, but there's a sizeable Swahili

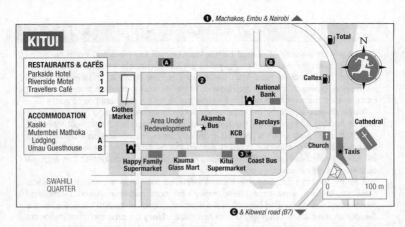

population, descendants of the traders and travellers who criss-crossed Ukambani in the nineteenth century. The town's mango trees were planted then, and are a reminder of the trading tradition. Kitui was the home village of **Kivoi**, the most celebrated Kamba trader, who commanded a large following that included slaves. It was Kivoi who met the German missionary **Ludwig Krapf** in Mombasa, and who guided him to Kitui in 1849, from where he became the first European to set eyes on Mount Kenya. Although it has no sights, Kitui is a busy trading centre, its streets lined with arcaded shops. Look out for **Kauma Glass Mart**, *the* place for drums and plastic religious icons.

Practicalities

There's nowhere to **stay** in Kitui above the budget category, but ⚑ *Mutembei Mathoka Lodging*, Aropu Building, (☎020/2338839 or 0725/879890; **1**) is head-and-shoulders above the others; it's a decent, airy place, with great-value self-contained rooms with nets, instant showers and TVs. Also in the town centre, *Umau* (**1**) is rudimentary, but is friendly and reasonably clean, with nets and a good chance of a tepid shower. On the south side of town on the Kibwezi road, 500m from the end of the tarmac, *Kasiki* (☎0713/966355; **1**) is a peacefully located, basic little guesthouse with a limited bar and restaurant. Hot water is still often supplied in buckets, however. As for food, the Happy Family supermarket is well stocked and busy, and there's a row of cheap **eating** places backing onto the Swahili quarter. Other places to try include the *Parkside Hotel*, the *Travellers Café*, which has good snacks, and the *Riverside Motel*, 1500m out of town on the Machakos road in Kalundu Market, which serves quite good chicken and fish. All three banks have **ATM**s.

Akamba **buses** (☎044/22052) have daily departures to Nairobi (8.30am) and Mombasa (7pm), both via Machakos. The Kitui–Kibwezi road is a tough slog of three hours-plus, much of it rough and dusty, or muddy. Some 20 to 30km at each end is reasonably graded, but the rest is mostly in very poor condition, save for the odd bridge where the road builders have been at work. The road heading north to Embu is tarred and in good condition to Kangonde. There are some morning matatus through to Embu.

Matuu

A thriving trading centre along the Thika-Garissa road, with a KCB bank (ATM), but no Barclays, **MATUU** is busiest at the top of the hill, near the easternmost of the town's two communications masts, where you'll find the main **lodgings**. *Holiday Guest House* (☎067/4355263 or 0734/8137894, Ⓔholidaymatuu@yahoo.com; ❶) offers presentable rooms for two, with DSTV, nets and instant showers; breakfast is a further Ksh200 each. Stepping up a little, *Ndallas Hotel* (☎067/4355425, Ⓔmatuundallashotel@gmail.com; ❹), on the road out towards Thika, is the biggest and classiest establishment in Matuu with rooms of varying quality – none have fans or a/c, but they all have nets, DSTV and hot water (6pm–6am). The pleasant terraces, bar and restaurant are prettified by lots of original paintings.

Mwingi

MWINGI's surprisingly attractive site is an area of rocky hillocks and woodland, 150km east of Thika. Coming from that direction, you first see the town more than 10km before you arrive, spread out across the boulder-dotted hills. Mwingi offers little in the way of sights or entertainment, and only a KCB ATM, but plenty of small **places to eat** and an array of **lodgings**. The best of these by far is *Garden Cottage Hotel* (☎044/822448 or 0710/625599; ❷–❸), exactly 2km north up the C93 Katse road. Popular with local NGOs, this offers pleasant, if slightly unkempt gardens, a small, shadeless pool (Ksh200), and a bar–restaurant and shaded terrace, which improve the value of the rooms and variously equipped cottages. If you'd rather stay somewhere cheaper, give the *Flamingo Executive Guest House* a try (it's on the way up the hill into town from Thika, on the right; ❶). Or check out the popular *Tawfiq*, in the bustling pink and green Salubi House at the Garissa end of town, on the south side of the road (❶).

Garissa

Some 340km east of Thika, on the route to Somalia, **GARISSA** is the capital of North Eastern Province. On the eastern fringes of Ukambani, it's the furthest east you can safely go towards Somalia without an armed escort. With its tarred streets, offices and NGO presence, it feels like the little offspring of Nairobi and Mombasa. While it's reckoned to be Kenya's hottest town (during the day, the thermometer rarely leaves the 32–37°C range), and there are few attractions (the huge Wednesday livestock market is one), the hotels and other services here make it a likely stopover if you're travelling in the region. There are no chain **supermarkets**, but Al-Fatah, on the ground floor of the *Hidig Hotel*, is reasonable, while the KCB and Barclays banks have **ATMs**.

The town spreads out, inelegantly, east of the bridge across the Tana. The three main hotels are: *Nomad Palace*, on Kisimayu Road (☎046/2103242 or

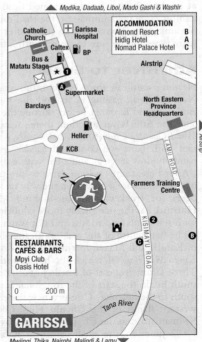

GARISSA

Modika, Dadaab, Liboi, Mado Gashi & Washir

ACCOMMODATION
Almond Resort — B
Hidig Hotel — A
Nomad Palace Hotel — C

RESTAURANTS, CAFÉS & BARS
Mpyi Club — 2
Oasis Hotel — 1

0   200 m

Mwiingi, Thika, Nairobi, Malindi & Lamu

0724/294300, Ⓦnomadpalacehotel.com; BB ❸), a mid-range place frequented by government officials and NGOs, with a small bar opposite; *Almond Resort* on Lamu Road (Ⓣ020/2325721 or 0711/829899, Ⓦwww.almond-resort.com; BB ❸), which has a gym and pool but doesn't serve alcohol; and the simple *Hidig* (BB ❷), opposite the Post Office. Although many establishments in Garissa are dry, finding tasty *pillau* or pasta is easy enough: *Oasis* is a recommended *hoteli* near the bus stage.

Public **transport** between Garissa and Nairobi is mostly reliable, with at least four buses a day in each direction. Transport south along the Tana is more sporadic (and occasionally there are security problems on this route), although there are vehicles every day.

The Mombasa Highway

However you travel south down the Mombasa Highway it's worth knowing that the right side of the vehicle is the best place for scenic views. From this vantage you may, in exceptionally clear conditions, see **Kilimanjaro** (best in the early morning or late afternoon), either on the stretch between the small settlements of Sultan Hamud and Kiboko, or to the west of the Tsavo River.

Although **fuel** and general **supplies** are increasingly available along the road, the only SCB or Barclays **ATMs** are in Voi town, just off the highway, two-thirds of the way to Mombasa (there are KCB ATMs in Mtito Andei and Kibwezi). Driving yourself, in a reasonably fast vehicle, you should reach Voi in less than four hours, while Mombasa is roughly a six-hour journey, though remember, if you've rented, that all PSV vehicles are limited to 80kph. **Driving at night** is best avoided, as dipped headlights and cautious driving are not in fashion, large wild animals on the road can be hard to see, and car hijackings are not unknown. If you have to travel after dark, avoid driving alone, check your spare tyres and be sure to set off with a full tank of fuel.

Athi River to Emali

Heading southeast from Nairobi, the road runs along the east side of Nairobi National Park, passing at its end the junction for the A104 to **Athi River**, Amboseli and Tanzania, before skirting the Kapiti Plains on your right. some 5km after the Athi River junction, there's reasonable **accommodation** at the *Small World Country Club* (Ⓣ045/20486, Ⓦwww.klubhouse.co.ke; ❸), a motel-restaurant with basic self-contained *bandas*, secure parking, unexciting snacks (and painfully slow service), and a bar with a disco at weekends.

After here, there's a long drive to the truckers' stopover of **Salama**, the first of many one-horse towns on the way to Mombasa, providing lodging, food and beers for truckers and lost-looking Maasai. The next settlement, **Sultan Hamud**, has the marginally more salubrious *Park Guesthouse* (Ⓣ044/52209; ❷), with self-contained rooms and hot water.

The first centre of any real significance is **EMALI**, which lies on the boundary of Kamba and Maasai territory. There's reasonable accommodation here at the *Kindu Mall Bar* (❷), which also has an unthreatening 24-hour bar and restaurant. Three kilometres east of Emali, just after the railway flyover, a sharp turn to the south marks the start of the rough *murram* C102 "pipeline road". This heads off south to the Selenkay Conservancy; the east side of Amboseli National Park; the western flanks of the Chyulu Hills; Oloitokitok on the northern slopes of Kilimanjaro; and the Chyulu Gate of Tsavo West National Park. Just beyond the C102 junction, the small centre of **Kibiki** is the regular Friday venue for a major **cattle market**, attracting hundreds of Maasai herders, as well as Kamba people and Kenya Meat Commission buyers. It's an animated scene and worth a pause if your timing is right.

A north turn from Emali leads up into the Machakos Hills with the dramatic rock-mountain peak of **Nzaui** (1830m above sea level, 800m above the plain). If you don't have your own transport, get a matatu from the Emali crossroads to **Matiliku**, some 15km from the main road; Nzaui rears up ahead. With luck, you'll find some schoolchildren to guide you up – it's a popular local trip. From the top of the 500-metre precipices on the south face there are sweeping views across the Kamba and Maasai plains to Mount Kilimanjaro. If you have a vehicle, there's also a lazy way up Nzaui from the north, approached from the village of **Nziu**, further along the same road.

Kiboko

At the petrol-station oasis of **KIBOKO**, 160km from Nairobi, there's **accommodation** in the shape of *Hunter's Lodge* (☎0722/926685; ❹), named after the J.A. Hunter of rhino-potting notoriety (see p.354). The lodge boasts an acacia-backed garden full of vervet monkeys on the banks of the dammed Kiboko ("Hippo") River, with a tranquil birdlife haven over on the other side. Admittedly, service can be sluggish and the food isn't great; on the other hand, the "new rooms" have verandas overlooking the small reservoir and if you're travelling on a low budget, the lodge is a good place to hitch lifts. They also have a campsite by the reservoir (Ksh500). The village of Kiboko itself has a handful of rudimentary lodgings, among which *Wamu Bar*, with nets (☎0721/465841; ❶), is decent enough.

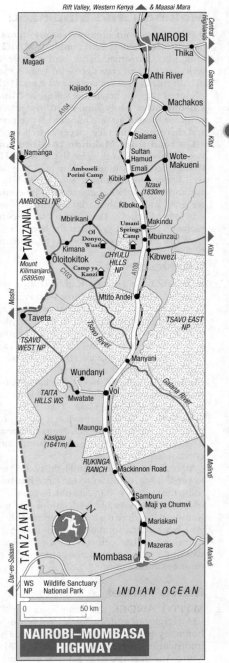

Rift Valley, Western Kenya ▲ & Maasai Mara

NAIROBI–MOMBASA HIGHWAY

WS Wildlife Sanctuary
NP National Park

0   50 km

INDIAN OCEAN

Makindu and Mbuinzau

Back on the main highway, twenty minutes southeast of *Hunter's Lodge*, you pass the ostentatious Sikh temple at **MAKINDU**, sometimes strung with what look like Christmas lights, and prettily unmistakeable. They give a warm welcome here to travellers who want to stay, or have a meal (leave a donation). Alternatively, there are several basic B&Ls.

Some 13km further, in the village of **Mbuinzau**, the **Makindu Handicrafts Co-operative** (daily 7am–6pm) has grown from small beginnings to provide work for more than one hundred active members. You can watch them at work, and there are some nice pieces as well various quirky rejects.

The **road from Makindu to Mtito Andei** is unusually scenic, with grand, sweeping views south over the Chyulu Hills and glimpses of lava flows and strange rock outcrops just to the north. The Kibwezi district is well-known for its **honey**, which you'll be offered – along with **basket ware** and the usual stacks of **charcoal** – by countless sellers along the road. You may see grass and brick huts, distinguishable from human dwellings by their lack of windows. Each contains up to ten **beehives**, owned and tended by local women's cooperatives. When the honey is good, it's delicious, but if there's a dry spell you may be treated instead to something approximating coloured syrup.

Kibwezi

KIBWEZI is a growing Kamba trading town off the highway at the B7 Kitui junction. There's a KCB bank with ATM and a small **market** where you can occasionally buy spiky green **soursops**. One of those fruits you either love or loathe, the soursop is related to the custard apple, but larger and tarter. There are only two places to consider staying in Kibwezi. The water cooler in the lounge and a smoke-where-you-like policy at *Guenter's Guesthouse* (T044/3500247 or 0721/225481; ❷) characterize this German-run bush B&L, where the small, dark, self-contained rooms, with instant showers, are kept immaculately clean. Meals are available (Ksh400), but bring your own beer – there's no bar. *Guenter's* is signposted – go to the very end of his long access lane and round the corner to the left. *Kambua Guest House* (T020/2153201 or 0720/260250; ❷) is completely different, but what it lacks in character and owner's anecdotes, it makes up for in bright self-contained rooms with nets and air-conditioning. They also do meals. Again, it's signposted, off the dirt road that circles around the north side of town.

After Kibwezi, the altitude drops below 900m above sea level and, at this lower altitude, you start to see large **baobabs** along the highway. Some are said to be more than 1000 years old. In the past, they were credited with all manner of spiritual powers and associations (see p.448), and oral history has it that the Kamba were drawn to this area by the sponge-like centres of their trunks, which are a vital source of liquid during droughts. In the low sunlight of early morning or late afternoon, the baobab landscape, with Kamba women working tiny plots of maize between the huge trunks, is one of the highway's most beautiful sights.

Mtito Andei

MTITO ANDEI, the name meaning "Vulture Forest", is a big sprawl of service stations and snackeries, rising out of the dry country by the northern boundary of Tsavo West National Park. There is a smartcard-issuing office and information centre here (see p.61), at Mtito Andei Gate. Fill up on **fuel** in Mtito Andei, as the next petrol station is at Voi, 97km further south.

If you want to stay the night without entering the park, you should find the old way station of *Tsavo Inn* (☎0720/379939; ❺), by the Caltex garage, a pleasant enough retreat, with a tempting pool (Ksh200) and more than fifty, rather tired but clean and secure rooms (nets, but no fans or a/c). The 1963 Michelin map of East Africa, by the lobby, is fascinating. In theory, you can get lunch or dinner (Ksh900), but be prepared to wait if you haven't called ahead. If it's beyond your budget, there are several much cheaper lodgings (❶).

The Tsavo River and Manyani

From Mtito Andei to Voi, the road runs through remote national park country. When you cross the **Tsavo River**, 49km south of Mtito Andei, you're in the spot where two **man-eating lions** played havoc with the building of the railway in 1898, while engineers grappled with the river crossing. The lions seem to have been preternaturally lucky, since they eluded Colonel Patterson's various weapons for nearly a year and killed 28 Indian labourers in that time, as well as the unfortunate Superintendent C.H. Ryall, whom they dragged off a train carriage during the hunt. The Field Museum in Chicago has the two stuffed man-eaters on display.

You're unlikely to see lions at the roadside these days, but between the Tsavo River and Manyani you may well come across **elephants**, always a brick-red colour, thanks to the soil. The Tsavo bridge marks the northern side of a ten-kilometre-wide animal migration corridor linking Tsavo East and Tsavo West, and thus also effectively connecting the northern Kenya ecosystem with that of southern Kenya.

Note that **Tsavo**, although marked as a town or village on some maps, is neither; it's just a bridge and a virtually disused rural railway station. If you want to stay nearby, or just stop for lunch (Ksh750) and a swim in the excellent pool, *Man Eaters Lodge* (☎020/2072392 or 0710/467273, ⓦwww.voiwildlifelodge.com; ❺) consists of 31 tents along the Tsavo River in a private concession just inside the park (no park fees payable). The tent-style rooms have good nets and verandas, decent bathrooms with instant showers, and generator electricity. The lodge, 1km south of the Tsavo river bridge on the east side, is accessed by crossing the railway tracks by the old station. Another possible place to stay nearby, *Patterson's Safari Camp* (☎020/2021674, ⓦwww.pattersonsafaricamp.com; ❼), whose turning is just 500m north of the Tsavo bridge, is located 9km from the highway, on the west bank of the Athi River. With eco-friendly architecture, white sand underfoot and decent tents, there's an intimate, tropical-island feel here. It's not a wildlife-rich area, but you'll see hippos, crocs and elephants, and lots of birdlife.

Some 13km south of the Tsavo bridge, and 2km south of Tsavo East National Park's Manyani Gate (see p.352), the nondescript highway centre of **Manyani** marks the southern side of the animal migration corridor. This has a number of *dukas* and basic *hotelis* refuelling weary travellers. **Manyani prison**, on the west side of the road, was an infamous British Mau Mau detention centre (see p.554).

Voi and around

The only sizeable town between Nairobi and Mombasa is **VOI**. It's a short way off the highway to the east, connected by two access roads, one from the north, and one 6km further south. You drive through the town centre to reach the Voi

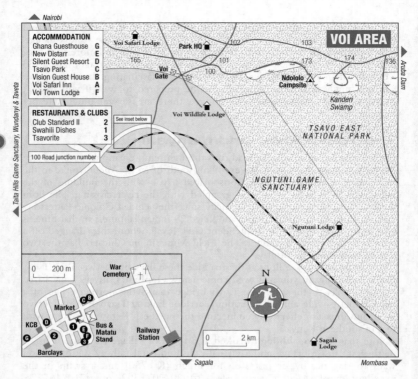

Gate of Tsavo East National Park, 5km to the northeast of Voi. There are plenty of petrol stations, a couple of supermarkets, Barclays and KCB banks with ATMs, and lots of cheap *hotelis*.

Practicalities

The **train** to Mombasa (first class Ksh600, second class Ksh400) departs at 4.30am on Tuesdays, Thursdays and Saturdays, while the Nairobi-bound train (Ksh1300 and Ksh700) passes through town at 11pm on Tuesdays, Thursdays and Sundays. The station (☎043/30098) is ten minutes' walk from the town centre. **Buses** come in all day en route between Nairobi and Mombasa, with some continuing on to Malindi. Buses from Mombasa to Taveta also stop here, and there are matatus to Mombasa and Taveta, as well as Wundanyi in the Taita Hills (last departure around 5pm).

Voi has some good **places to eat**. If you're on a tight budget, make for *Eagle's Hotel* at *Voi Town Lodge* – a popular fry-up place for chicken, curries, birianis, chips masala (Ksh80) and *ugali na sukuma wiki* (Ksh30). The *New Distarr Hotel* is the place for curries, with tasty chicken jeera and fresh passion juice. *Silent Guest Resort* is slightly pricier, with more Western-style dishes, such as pepper steak and chips. *Swahili Dishes* does excellent, coastal-style rice and beans (Ksh80), bhajias and the like. For **beer and music**, the *Tsavorite*, on the same street as the post office, is a decent local nightspot, and *Club Standard II* wakes up at weekends with occasional live music (Ksh150–200 or free with a couple of drinks).

Accommodation

Voi is a safari and tour-drivers' hub, so there's a bit of hustle around the edges of some of the town **lodgings**. For safari lodges and tented camps inside the park see p.352. If you want something outside the park but more park-like, *Ngutuni Lodge* or *Sagala Lodge* (see overleaf) should fit the bill.

Ghana Guest House On the north-side road into town, 500m from the centre ℡043/30291. Clean, s/c rooms with nets, TVs, and instant showers. Corner rooms are nice, and some have balconies. **❶**

New Distarr Town centre ℡043/30277 or 0715/160678. A busy, well-managed warren of a place, with clean, good-sized, s/c rooms, with nets but no fans, and a lively restaurant with good service, doing tasty food. **❶**

Silent Guest Resort Town centre ℡043/30112 or 0720/200078. A well-run hotel but its practically window-less rooms with DSTV, fans and nets (and old-style showers) are overpriced. BB **❸**

Tsavo Park Opposite the bus and matatu stage ℡0721/328567. Decent rooms, with nets and fans, hot water and little balconies. There's a small breakfast room, but they no longer serve lunch or dinner. BB **❷**

Vision Guest House Town centre ℡0722/660113. Very basic but equally cheap s/c rooms with nets, plug sockets and terrifying-looking instant showers. Ask for an upstairs room. **❶**

Voi Safari Inn On the Mombasa highway, 2km south of the north exit for Voi ℡020/8030588 or 0722/484494. Block of dark rooms under a big *makuti* roof, which look more suitable for conducting a brief business relationship than passing a peaceful night. Their motto, "Get received professionally", seems inadvertently to sum it up, yet the spacious public areas are full of safari promise, and the rooms aren't bad, with nets and instant showers. BB **❸**

The Sagala Hills

An unusual day-trip from Voi – with some lovely walking country largely unvisited by tourists – is the **Sagala Hills**, which rise just south of Voi. Regular matatus run the 20km from town to the village of **Sagala**, a small rural centre with a shop, a *hoteli* serving nice *chai* and chicken, and a bar opposite the football field. The **Wray Memorial Museum** (Ksh200), occupies Kenya's second oldest church building, established in 1883 by Reverend Joseph Wray (for the oldest, see p.423), with nineteenth-century photos and other documents. You can stay in Sagala at *Gethsemane Cottages*, with kitchen and verandah (℡043-30705, ✉gethsagal@yahoo.com; BB **❸**). From Sagala, you'll need a local to guide you around – older children will be happy to oblige. A 45-minute walk takes you past a small bridge to the even smaller settlement of **Talio**, which has wonderful views of the Taita Hills, Mount Kasigau and the savanna below. From Talio, small paths lead off through the fields to the base of the hills where there are other little villages (allow an hour or two to get there, depending on the path). Visitors are rare, so be tactful, especially with your camera, and generous with your time. In Talio itself, you can either **stay** locally (someone will happily take Ksh500 to put you up) or pitch a tent somewhere – ask at the school.

Ngutuni Game Sanctuary

Just southeast of Voi, and tucked into the space between the boundary of Tsavo East National Park and the road, lies the **Ngutuni Game Sanctuary** (free). Covering thirty square kilometres, this former ranch has a good network of driveable trails criss-crossing the thorn bush. There's plenty of game here, too, including elephants, lions and large numbers of buffalo. If you're in your own vehicle, you can usually take a ranger for a game drive: alternatively, ask the lodge management for a copy of their map of the sanctuary. While the sanctuary doesn't match Tsavo East or West for spectacle or a sense of wilderness, it makes for a good stopover between Nairobi and Mombasa, or an affordable base for exploring the area. They also do great value **night game drives** (Ksh500 per person, minimum four clients).

There's very good **accommodation** in Ngutuni in the form of ⚑ *Ngutuni Lodge* (☎043/30747, ⊛www.rexresorts.com; ❻), which is popular with mid-market tour groups. Rooms are a decent size and very comfortable (they could possibly do with air-conditioning at this altitude, but the fans work well enough), with good bathrooms, and each has a balcony facing the waterhole, which is floodlit at night. The lodge prides itself on good cooking, and staff are friendly and helpful. The game sanctuary entrance is 13km south of the north exit for Voi and 7km south of the south exit. Once at the gate, it's 5km to the lodge.

Sagala Game Sanctuary

An even more affordable option than *Ngutuni Lodge* lies 3km further south, on the other (west) side of the road. **Sagala Game Sanctuary** is a Swiss-owned ranch covering five thousand acres (20 square kilometres) of savanna and woodland, largely unfenced. The central core includes the attractively low-key and very inexpensive *Sagala Lodge* (☎020/2138102 or 0726/815591, ⊛www.blueskycorporate.com/Sagala_Lodge.html; ❺), set in a shady patch of acacia woodland. The simple rooms, each an individual *banda*, with a terrace, have nets, but no fans, and the generator is on from 6.30pm to 10pm. There's a good swimming pool (if you just want to break your journey, lunch and use of the pool costs Ksh700) and you can also camp here (Ksh400). It's an all-round good place, and there's even a simple game-watching platform, where you can kick back on a sofa with a pair of binoculars and scan the bush in the sanctuary across the fence for the local buffalo and oryx, or for some of the area's two hundred-odd species of birds.

Maungu and the Maungu Hills

After Voi, the road veers across the relentless **Maungu Plains**, also known as the **Taru Desert**, a plateau of "wait-a-bit" thorn and occasional baobabs which forms another, though less significant, migratory corridor for wildlife passing between Tsavo East and the southern plains of Tsavo West. Scenically dreary for much of the year, the plains come alive with colour after heavy rains, and during May and June can be carpeted in convolvulus flowers.

The small town of **MAUNGU**, roughly 25km from Voi, has a couple of B&Ls and, 10km from Maungu down a rough signposted track to the southwest, up in the **Maungu Hills**, is *Rock Side Camp* (☎020/2041443 or 0770/316231, ⊛www.westermannssafari.com; ❻), popular with German visitors. In the shadow of the imposing **"Kale 1" Rock** (which you can climb – it takes about an hour), it offers good food and a pool and is hosted by the owners who live on site. It's worth paying a little extra here for one of the newer, bigger chalets.

Rukinga Ranch

Between Maungu and Mackinnon Road, tucked beyond the rocky hills of the Maungu Range, some 680 square kilometres on the south side of the highway comprise **Rukinga Ranch** and its neighbour adjoining it to the south, **Taita Ranch**. Both are part of a privately run venture to protect wildlife by giving local residents a stake in conservation projects. The combined area is strategically placed on the migration route of plains game, elephant and lion, from the Galana River in Tsavo East to the southern parts of Tsavo West. Despite the thickness of the bush, spotting elephants is usually easy (there are generally around 300 here, and the top count in recent years was 1640), and Rukinga is full of other game, including buffalo, gazelle, and cheetahs.

There's an unusual and very good value natural history base at Rukinga in the shape of **Camp Tsavo** (☎020/8030575 or 0722/530024, ⊛tinyurl.com /yzbzjky), the former "Taita Discovery Centre", now open to independent visitors, where you can stay in *bandas* (FB ❹), or take one or more rooms in the well-equipped and comfortable *Ndovu House* (FB ❺). Affable staff and guides, together with a great deal of wildlife in and around the camp, including a delightful family of genets in *Ndovu House*, make the whole place a charmingly offbeat base. You can opt to participate in a variety of well-thought-out ecological and cultural activities lasting from an hour to several days, and ranging from game drives and night game drives with infra-red, to mountain biking, bush survival skills and village visits – or even have a go at making paper from elephant dung.

Ranch entry fees are included in the accommodation charges. You can find out more from Camp Kenya (see p.32), who include Camp Tsavo in their programmes, and with whom you need to pre-book. Only 4WD vehicles are allowed to enter Rukinga Ranch, and you have to stay at least one night. To reach Camp Tsavo, turn right (southwest) at the brown, earthen "Wildlife Works" sign on the south side of Maungu, 800m south of the Tanzila Jamia Mosque, just over the speed bumps. From the boom gate, just up the track from here, it's 16km to Camp Tsavo, where you'll find all the visitor facilities, *bandas* and *Ndovu House*.

From Mackinnon Road to the coast

Some 11km south of Buchuma Gate, the first place you might stop for refreshments is the long sprawl of **Mackinnon Road**, distinguished by its huge and beautiful **mosque** and the neighbouring burial place of Sayyed Baghali Shah Pir Padree – a holy man who worked on the railway – right alongside the railway track.

East of the small settlement of **Samburu** (no connection with the reserve of the same name), the land is peopled mostly by members of the large **Mijikenda** ethnic group, their distinctive, droopy, thatched cottages often replaced nowadays by more formal square ones, increasingly also whitewashed and tin-roofed in the coastal manner. The **Duruma** Mijikenda of this district herd cattle, make charcoal and grow some sisal – there's little else they can do in such a dry region. The tiny centre of **Maji ya Chumvi** ("salt water") and the growing Mombasa satellite and truckers' town of **Mariakani** ("place of the *mariaka*", the Kamba arrows used in nineteenth-century wars against the Maasai), with its huge steel-rolling mill, bring you closer to the coastal domain. The coast mood really takes over at **Mazeras**, a largely Duruma town from which point on the landscape has a quite different cast, with its mango trees, bananas and cassava, and – encouraging for weary travellers – the sublime sight of thousands of **coconut palms**. For details of Mazeras and the route along the ridge to the north, see p.422. The main road plunges on, down the steep scarp to the Indian Ocean and Mombasa.

If you're driving to the northern coast (for example to Kilifi, Watamu or Malindi), there is an alternative to going into Mombasa and out again through the crowded coastal suburbs, though it's only suitable for high-clearance vehicles. This short cut, along the C107, leads out of the centre of **Mariakani**, heading more or less due east for 19km through the rolling Mijikenda back country to **Kaloleni**, and then for a further 35km northeast through pretty forest and farmland to rejoin the coastal highway a few kilometres south of Kilifi creek. Allow two hours from Mariakani to Kilifi creek.

The Taita Hills

Heading west **from Voi to Taveta** on the badly potholed A23 takes you into a very accessible but largely unvisited region, and in clear weather the magnificent mass of Kilimanjaro looms ahead on the horizon. To get a glimpse of the culture of this region, head up into the **Taita Hills**. From the junction at **Mwatate**, the C104 road twists up 14km into precipitous and beautiful hills, striped with cliffs, waterfalls and dense cultivation, and patches of thick forest. There's a high population density, reasonable prosperity and a strong sense of community up here. Most of the welcoming **Taita people** speak the Taita language, a member of the coastal Bantu family related to Swahili and Mijikenda.

Wundanyi

Regular matatus from Voi pitch through the fertile chasms on the switchback road to the attractive little district capital of **WUNDANYI**. The conifer trees and a babbling brook running past Wundanyi's football field reinforce the feeling of departure from the thorn bush and scrub below. This sense of suspended reality is accentuated by the **cave of skulls**, 1500m outside town, one of many ancestor shrines in the hills (there's one for each clan). The cave in question is on the Mbale road, 400m beyond *Hebron Guest House* (see below), and 700m before you reach *Mwasungia Scenery Guest House* (see below), hidden in a banana grove just below the road. In the niche rest the skulls of nineteen Taita ancestors, exhumed from their graves. Rather than looking for it yourself, ask one of the guesthouses to provide a guide. Traditionally, the shrine was an advice centre where life's perplexities were resolved by consultation with the dead, and where sacrifices were made in times of drought. Christianity has eroded some of the reverence that the Taita once had for these shrines (and traditional dances and rituals have almost disappeared), but they are left undisturbed nonetheless.

Practicalities

There's not much to Wundanyi – just one main street and one side street. Entering the town, you turn right at the T-junction just before the bridge, and, after passing the Shell station, the **KCB** (ATM) and the **post office**, take the first left around the back of the large football field. This leads to **Barclays** (ATM), the *Paradise Hotel*, the helpful Jumwa Solutions Cybercafé, and the *Lavender Garden Hotel*. If you don't turn left, continuing up the hill brings you to the **market** and **matatu stand** on the next left. And that's Wundanyi.

The best **rooms** are at the fairly new *Lavender Garden* (☎020/2437287 or 0733/253084; ❹), overlooking the football field. This new, mid-range hotel has bright, self-contained rooms, equipped with nets, clean bathrooms with instant showers, and low-energy light bulbs. With no competition, prices here are a little steep, so try to get a room at the front for sunset views from the balcony across the valley to the local landmarks of Wesu Rock and the crags of Shomoto Hill, the old Taita execution spot.

On the road to Mbale just out of town (go back to the bridge, turn right and cross the stream and take the right fork after 600m, the very nice ⭐ *Hebron Guest House* (100m from the fork; ☎0723/058078; ❶), is clean and well run, in a peaceful location, and offers dorm beds as well as single and double rooms. About 1.1km further down the Mbale road, and recommended for its helpful owner and lovely location rather than for its slightly ramshackle facilities, is the *Mwasungia Scenery Guest House* (☎0729/554522 or 0734/403225; ❶). This is the best place to settle into if you're interested in finding out more about the Taita people: the owner is knowledgeable, and can take you on walks around the hills to see waterfalls, skull caves and the notorious Shomoto Hill, from which villains were once hurled to their deaths. Rooms are basic, and the house shared with the family, but you can also camp in the orchard (negotiable rates).

There aren't many **places to eat** in Wundanyi. *Paradise Hotel* is recommended for tasty meals and a lively atmosphere – especially emanating from the bar – and the nearby *Lavender Garden* has a busy bar and restaurant. You'll find street food on Wundanyi's big **market days**, Tuesday and Friday. **Moving on** from the town, matatus go direct to Voi and Mombasa, most of them leaving early in the morning. For Taveta, you'll have to change vehicles, down on the A23 at Mwatate.

Taita Hills Wildlife Sanctuary

One place attracting major tourist traffic in this district, particularly visitors on fleeting air safaris from the coast, is the 113-square kilometre **Taita Hills Wildlife Sanctuary** ($30), which isn't in the Taita Hills at all, but in the hillocky lowlands 15km west of Mwatate on the Taveta road. Set up in 1973 by the Hilton hotel chain, the sanctuary is now owned and managed by Sarova Hotels, who successfully balance wildlife and human needs in an environment that, while not being fully natural, seems to work well for both.

For most of the year, the sanctuary is full of wildlife. There are more than fifty species of **large mammals** and three hundred species of birds here, and its small size means the rangers always have a good idea of where the key animals can be seen. It's not uncommon to spot two dozen species in a morning game drive, among them lions, cheetahs, large herds of elephant and buffalo, and all the other southern plains grazers. During the drier times of the year, when the animals are not dispersed, the water sources beneath *Salt Lick Lodge*, on the southern side of the sanctuary, provide waterhole game-viewing, including a very good ground-level hide, far better than you could hope to experience at *Treetops* or *The Ark*. In addition, **night game drives** (9.30pm, two hours-plus; $20), with a guide and driver, are a regular feature and not available in KWS-managed national parks.

Accommodation

Sarova Taita Hills Lodge 500m from the road, just before the sanctuary gate, ☎043/31271 or 0722/410294, ⓦwww.sarovahotels.com. A comfortable bush hotel, with attractive rooms, with nets and fans. Ordinary but copious meals are complemented by a very good pool, and poolside animal-watching over the fence into the sanctuary. FB $480.

Sarova Salt Lick Lodge Inside the sanctuary ☎043/31271 or 0722/410294, ⓦwww.sarovahotels.com. Built on stilts over a chain of waterholes, this looks from a distance like a clump of mushrooms sprouting from the bush. The semi-circular rooms occupy turret-like, conical-roofed houses, linked by aerial walkways, their walls finished in mock-sandbag style, all in keeping with the area's WWI battle history. Architecture aside, remarkable animal-viewing is the hallmark of *Salt Lick*. As you sip your beer over the heads of elephants drinking from the waterhole below, you're literally within touching distance of dozens of trunks. Granted, you're rarely sitting here alone (there's usually a good crowd of locals and tourists), but few lodges in Kenya offer this kind of access. Pachyphile heaven. FB $540.

Taveta, Lake Chala and Lake Jipe

West of the turning for the Taita Hills at **Mwatate**, the A23 road to Taveta runs out of potholed tarmac and you follow the railway line along a corridor through the southern arm of Tsavo West National Park (no fees to pay), mostly in a cloud of orange dust. You're very likely to see some game, especially in the rainy season, but there's nowhere worth stopping on the road itself until you reach Taveta.

Connected to the rest of Kenya by a couple of rough roads and a railway that has had no trains for years, **TAVETA** is situated right on the Tanzanian border and has a mixed population of Taveta, Taita, Maasai, Kamba, Kikuyu and Luo, and even some Makonde, who originally came from Mozambique and were brought to work the sisal estates in the 1930s. For a few moments' reflection, visit the **World War I cemetery** at the entrance to town.

The only paved street in Taveta crosses the railway line and heads straight for the border post, passing Barclays bank (ATM) and Safaricom (internet access Ksh2 per min) on its way. But the town's real main street runs north from the paved road immediately west of the railway crossing. The best **rooms** up here are at the excellent-value ⅌ *Lake Challa Hotel* (☎043/5352240 or 0735/849170; ❶), 400m past the market, which has good self-contained rooms around an internal courtyard, with nets, DSTV, fans and instant showers (and some cheaper "non-renovated" self-contained rooms). They serve good food, and have a relaxed TV bar. One of several competitors, on the paved road to the border, is *Tripple J Paradise* (☎0725/095220; ❶), but it's much inferior to the *Challa*. *Kuwako Bar* (❶), 50m further up the main street from *Lake Challa Hotel*, has magnificent, gaudy murals in its popular bar-restaurant, and dingy, rock-bottom rooms at matching prices.

The best place to **eat** in town is the *Lake Challa*, but otherwise try the *Sarara Hotel*, next door, or the recommended *New Golden Fish* on the street leading to the border post. The local *matoke* stew is popular, though you might baulk at eating eight green bananas in one sitting, even if they are smothered with gravy. The *Gate Way Pub*, just before the railway crossing, is a good place to sink a cold beer and chew on some *nyama choma*.

There are plenty of **matatus** from Taveta to Voi, and **buses** daily to Mombasa. Matatus are most frequent on market days: Wednesday and Saturday in Taveta; Tuesday and Friday in Chumvini/Njukini north of Lake Chala; and Tuesday and Saturday in Oloitokitok, far to the north, near the eastern end of Amboseli National Park.

The **Tanzanian border** post is 5km away, reached by *boda-boda* or *piki-piki*. On the other side, there are regular matatus to Moshi, and thence to Arusha. Moneychangers in Taveta's market sell Tanzanian shillings for Kenyan but, as ever, beware of scams and rip-offs.

Lake Chala

A four-square-kilometre crater lake north of Taveta, **Lake Chala** has one shore in Kenya and the other in Tanzania. Very deep and remarkably blue, it is still paddled over by a few friendly fishermen in their dugouts and is spiritually significant, with lake monster stories part of local folklore. The lake is bilharzia-free and was also believed to be free of crocodiles. However, the death while swimming of a young British traveller in 2002, and the discovery of her body, missing an arm, points to the presence of crocodiles, and you are strongly advised not to swim here. While locals swear the crocodile responsible was killed a few years later, there's no reason to think the reptiles won't colonize the lake again. They are resourceful survivors, and have been known to trek overland for long distances.

Lake Chala is just to the west of the road north to Amboseli. Exactly 7.4km north of the junction outside Taveta (the junction is 3.3km east of the railway crossing), you'll find a stone cairn in a triangle of stones by the road. This is the start of the 1.3km motor track that scrapes over bare rock up the side of the crater to the rim. From the top, it's 800m along the south rim to the ruins of the *Lake Challa Safari Lodge*. You could camp up here but there are no facilities of any kind (the village of **CHALA**, 4km north of the cairn, has the closest basic supplies) and, despite the beauty of the landscape, the uncomfortable dereliction of the place suggests more a short visit than an overnight stay. If you want to find out in advance if the lodge is being restored, contact the *Lake Challa Hotel* in Taveta, which has the same owner.

If you're **driving to Oloitokitok**, 67km north of Lake Chala, note that the road can be very rough going, and is often impassable in the rains, even in 4WD.

Lake Jipe and Grogan's Castle

Another local lake, equally interesting, and totally different, is **Lake Jipe**, 35km south of Taveta. At its northern end, it's fed by Kilimanjaro's snowmelt, passing via Lake Chala's underground outlet, as well as by streams flowing to the south from the Pare Mountains, across the border in Tanzania. Like Lake Chala, Lake Jipe straddles the Tanzanian border. The Kenyan shore is flat and thickly carpeted in reed beds. Several villages along the northern shore make a living from fishing, while the southeastern shore lies inside the almost unvisited southern section of Tsavo West National Park.

There is virtually no public transport to the lake, so unless you want a long day's walk, you'll need to have your own vehicle, or find a car and driver in Taveta to rent for the day – Ksh5000 should cover it. You head east from Taveta along the Voi road, turning right 6.3km from Taveta railway crossing. Look south here and you'll spot the unmistakeable white, hilltop pile that is Grogan's Castle: the 27km road down to Lake Jipe runs straight past it. The flat land between the Voi road and the lake is heavily planted under sisal, in various states of cultivation and abandonment (squatters have moved into the former estate here), as well as cotton and even coconuts.

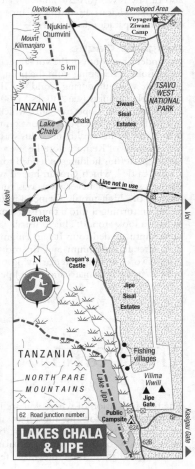

The lakeshore

At **Mukwajoni**, the fishing village 2km before the park gate, you'll find only fish and the most basic provisions, so bring supplies from Taveta. There's nowhere to stay, though someone may be happy to put you up for a small fee. *Lake Jipe Safari Lodge*, (the former *Bobby's Camp*) for which you may see signposts, has been closed for years. When exploring the bush around the lakeshore, you should keep a sharp eye out for **hippos**, especially between the park gate and the village. A feasible target for a couple of hours' walk is the pair of hills, **Vilima Viwili** ("Two Hills"), just outside the park boundary, about 2km east of the track.

Once at the lake, the track becomes confusing as it heads south towards Tsavo West National Park's **Jipe Gate** (see p.346 for park fees and information). Keep as close to the lake as you can, as the gate is directly on the shore. The rangers here are friendly and have little to do; they also have a **boat** (negotiable rates) for a spot of crocodile and hippo-spotting. There's a KWS public **campsite** just inside the gate, with toilets and showers, and three simple twin *bandas* with nets, also run by KWS (℡020/600800, ℮reservations@kws.go.ke; $50). Despite the sometimes vicious attentions of mosquitoes, this is a peaceful and rewarding spot, and a paradise for birders.

Grogan's Castle

Just under 7km south of the Voi–Taveta road, **Grogan's Castle**, a white mansion on an isolated hill rising from the plain, deserves a little detour. This extraordinary residence was built during World War II by Ewart Grogan, one of the most influential early colonists (see "Books", p.604). His mixed reputation was founded on a walk from the Cape to Cairo, which he undertook in 1898, on a notorious public flogging that he carried out on three of his servants (nearly killing one of them), and on his wealth: his status was such that he was able to dictate terms to the governor of Kenya before he even arrived in the colony, and at the peak of his prosperity his holdings extended to more than 2500 square kilometres.

The "castle", which Grogan hoped would become a government agricultural training school (it never was), was run-down for many years, but the current owners, the high-profile former Taveta MP, Basil Criticos, and his wife, seem intent on turning it into a tourism venue of some sort and visitors are welcome to have a look around. There's usually a member of staff on hand to conduct an impromptu guided tour. It's an enigmatic building, much of it stuck together with aircraft aluminium and tin roofs, but refurbishment is gradually taking place. Two enormous circular living rooms give spectacular 360-degree views out towards Kilimanjaro and Lake Jipe.

The parks

The first realization of where you are in Kenya's **big national parks** – among uncaptured, and for the most part unfenced, wild animals – can be truly arresting. It may take you a day or two to adjust, as your normal, "human-centric" view of the world is re-balanced towards a natural environment in which big creatures hunt, die, mate, feed and enjoy themselves all around you in a wilderness landscape not much changed in centuries. Which parks you choose to visit can seem at first like a pin-in-the-map decision: any of them can provide a store of amazing sight and sound impressions.

Amboseli, **Tsavo West** and **Tsavo East** are the three most accessible parks, with ever-busy game lodges, well-worn trails, large numbers of tourists, and large herds of elephant. Amboseli, with its picture-postcard backdrop of Mount Kilimanjaro and guaranteed elephants, is an instant draw, but the flat landscape and lack of tree cover means you may be sharing the stunning vistas with dozens of other safari vehicles. Tsavo East, in contrast, is so huge you can usually escape company completely, although its sheer size makes the same easy for the animals, too. Tsavo West is also huge, but better watered, allowing higher concentrations of wildlife in a varied landscape that includes hills, woodland springs and lava flows in the scenery changes. The little visited, but highly recommended **Chyulu Hills National Park**, to the northeast of Amboseli, has spectacular walking country and two magnificent luxury lodges.

Maasai Mara has the most fabled reputation of Kenya's parks, with horizons of wildlife on every side in a rich, rolling landscape of grasslands and wooded streams. Although it is somewhat isolated in the southwest, coming here is well worth the effort and cost, especially if you can arrange your visit during the yearly **wildebeest migration**. This takes place over eight to ten weeks between early July and early November and is usually at its most spectacular at the end of August. To the northeast of Mount Kenya, on the fringes of Kenya's northern desert region, the adjoining national reserves of **Samburu** and **Buffalo Springs**, and, just to the east, **Shaba National Reserve**, share the bounty of the Ewaso Nyiro River system that flows through them. These reserves have a number of animal varieties not found in the southern parks, including northern races and species of giraffe, zebra, various antelope and ostrich. Each of the reserves is small, even compared with Amboseli, which lends an impression of great concentrations of animals and birds, especially in the dry season when water sources are magnets for the wildlife.

Over to the east of Mount Kenya, verdant **Meru National Park** is one of the country's most beautiful parks, and still very little visited, despite being the platform for showcasing the best work of the Kenya Wildlife Service, and having, among its few places to stay, some of the very best luxury and budget options in the country. KWS's rescue and relaunch of Meru, which in the 1990s had fallen into the hands of bandits and poachers, has been an impressive piece of work.

Read through the advice about safaris, and particularly **guides** (see p.67), before signing up for a safari. If you're **driving**, the numbered junctions ("#17", "#158" and so on) and clearly defined *murram* roads and tracks make most parts of the parks relatively easy to get around, so long as you have a map (though the painted numbers on some cairns are illegible and many maps are out of date). Don't ignore the **distances** involved, especially in the large parks: at 40kph, the speed limit in all the parks and reserves, it can take a long time to make a few centimetres of progress on the map. If you set off somewhere, be sure you have time to get back to base by nightfall, as all the parks close their gates at 7pm, and it's illegal to drive around after that time. If you are changing camp, be sure to inform the management at your destination of your movements. Except at the designated nature trails, or where there's an obvious parking area, stay in your vehicle all the time, even if you break down, in which case rangers will eventually find you.

Amboseli National Park

Amboseli (ⓦ www.kws.go.ke/amboseli; $60; smartcard; see p.61), the Maasai's "Place of Dust", is a small and very touristy park. Scenically, however, it is totally redeemed by the stunning spectacle of **Kilimanjaro** towering over it and, as in those clichéd but irresistible photos taken with telephoto lenses, appearing almost to fill the sky. In the right light, the snowy massif, washed coral and orange, is devastatingly beautiful. Sunrise and sunset are the most likely times to see the mountain, especially during the rainy season when the air is much clearer, but for the most part it remains tantalizingly shrouded in a thick shawl of cloud.

On the animal side, Amboseli, like Tsavo, is **elephant** country par excellence. You will see large herds, some with big tusks. Predators, apart from hyenas and jackals, are relatively scarce (lions are almost absent, thanks to the revenge wrought by the Maasai upon the expulsion of them and their herds from the park), but good numbers of herbivores are present. In the dry season, most of the animals crowd into the impenetrable marshy areas and patches of acacia woodland where food plants are available. But during and shortly after the rains the picture is different, the animals more dispersed and the landscape greener.

Access

The **A104** road from Nairobi is in theory tarmac to Namanga, from where a mercilessly corrugated 76km gravel road leads to the park's centre, at Ol Tukai. The drive takes about four hours from Nairobi. The Namanga–Ol Tukai road is comfortable only at more than 60kph, and very wearing once you're inside the park, where the well-enforced speed limit is 40kph. From **Meshanani Gate**, the alternative route, which cuts right across Lake Amboseli (a seasonal lake that rarely fills deeper than a few inches), is often impassable, and even in dry weather you risk getting bogged down in mud or sand. If you use it, only

▲ Elephants in Amboseli National Park

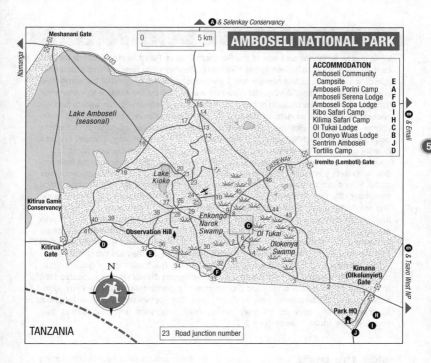

AMBOSELI NATIONAL PARK

0   5 km

ACCOMMODATION

Amboseli Community Campsite	E
Amboseli Porini Camp	A
Amboseli Serena Lodge	F
Amboseli Sopa Lodge	G
Kibo Safari Camp	I
Kilima Safari Camp	H
Ol Tukai Lodge	C
Ol Donyo Wuas Lodge	B
Sentrim Amboseli	J
Tortilis Camp	D

Meshanani Gate

Lake Amboseli (seasonal)

Lake Kioko

Kitirua Game Conservancy

Enkongo Narok Swamp

Observation Hill

Kitirua Gate

Ol Tukai

Olokenya Swamp

Iremito (Lemboti) Gate

CAUSEWAY

Kimana (Olkelunyiet) Gate

Park HQ

N

TANZANIA

23 Road junction number

do so with a guarantee from someone who knows that it's safe, and follow the tracks of previous vehicles.

If you're using public transport, buses and matatus will only take you as far as Namanga, from where you'll have to chance your luck with passing vehicles. Routes on the **east side of the park** are covered on pp.343–344. There are daily Airkenya and Safarilink **flights** from Nairobi's Wilson Airport (around $100 each way) and flights on Mombasa Air Safari from Mombasa and Diani Beach (around $360 return) to the park's only airstrip.

Accommodation

The only budget accommodation is the *Amboseli Community Campsite* (☎0711/674435 or 0722/867394; Ksh500 per person) just outside the park boundary at junction #37. It's a fine, wooded site, though apart from warm sodas, a couple of toilets are the only facilities, and even water supplies can be unreliable. There are also eighteen *bandas* (actually two-person ridge tents, with floor mattresses and thatched roofs; Ksh1000 per person); these have no lighting, but there are bucket showers and European-style long-drop toilets and a kitchen/cooking area, with water provided in buckets. It pays to have a look around before choosing a *banda*, as they are scattered across a wide area.

There are two reliable lodges and a luxury tented camp effectively inside the park, but a clutch of camps and lodges with much less certain credentials has sprung up just outside the park, near Kimana Gate in the southeast. If you're booking a safari that includes a stay in that area, bear in mind that the park's $60 daily entry fee may restrict the number of game drives you do inside Amboseli itself, whose swamp and woodland habitats are worth paying for.

Amboseli's history

What is now Amboseli was part of the Southern Maasai Reserve at the turn of the last century. Then tourism arrived in the 1940s and the Amboseli Reserve was created as a wildlife sanctuary. Unlike Nairobi and Tsavo national parks, created at the same time and sparsely inhabited, Amboseli's swamps were used by the Maasai to water their herds and they saw no reason not to continue sharing the area with the wildlife and – if necessary – with the tourists. In 1961, the Maasai District Council at Kajiado was given control of the area. But the combined destructive capacities of cattle and tourists began to tell in the 1960s and a rising water table in the following decade brought poisonous alkali to the surface and decimated huge tracts of acacia woodland.

Kenyatta declared the 400-square-kilometre zone around the swamps (the present-day Amboseli) a **national park**, a status that formally excluded the Maasai and their cattle. Infuriated, they all but exterminated the park's magnificent long-horned black rhinos over the next few years, seizing on Amboseli's tourist emblem with a vengeance (the surviving rhinos were translocated). The Maasai also obliterated a good part of the lion population, which has still not recovered. Not until a piped water supply was set up for the cattle did the Maasai finally give up the land. Compromise now appears to be the order of the day: in the dry season, you'll see numerous herds of cattle and their herders encroaching well into the park unhindered, as they always did.

The **erosion** of Amboseli's grasslands by circling minibuses did a great deal of damage in the 1980s, turning it into a vehicle-clogged dustbowl that appealed little to animals or tourists. A concerted programme of environmental conservation, road-building and ditch-making was initiated, and this, combined with the toughest approach of any park to off-road driving (including fines and expulsions), has improved the situation enormously.

Inside the park

Amboseli Serena Lodge Southern park area, near the Enkongo Narok swamp ☎045/622622 or 0736/224173, ⓦ www.serenahotels.com. Always busy, but graciously managed, *Serena's* adobe-style architecture is well hidden behind a jungle of tropical plants and creepers. The 92 modestly sized rooms, adorned with animal murals, have built-in nets, ceiling fans, 24-hour electricity and functional bathrooms with constant hot water. There's a large and inviting pool, good wildlife-viewing from the terraces and fairly priced petrol and diesel for sale on site. FB ❽

Ol Tukai Lodge Ol Tukai area ☎045/622275 or 0735/350005, ⓦ www.oltukailodge.com. Set among tall trees and lawns, *Ol Tukai Lodge* has stylish, rustic architecture, beautiful communal areas, and wooden cottages housing the fairly simple rooms, which have nets, and floor fans on request. Half the rooms look out beyond the low-key electric fence towards the Amboseli plains (rooms 1–48, "Elephant View"), and the rest look out towards Kilimanjaro (49–80, "Mountain View"). There's a pleasant pool, and Maasai dances most evenings. FB ❽

Tortilis Camp Just outside the southern park boundary, accessible only via the park ☎045/622195 or 0734/622195, ⓦ www.tortilis-camp.com. Set around a low hill, and named after the *Acacia tortilis* trees of the area, with stunning views of Kilimanjaro, this camp, surrounded by a sensitively low electric fence, is one of Cheli & Peacock's oldest. While not quite offering the same boutique feel as most of the others – it's a little larger and less informal – the seventeen tent-*banda* combinations are stylish enough. Perks include good meals on the terrace (they grow their own veg), a lovely pool, superb birdlife and waterhole game-viewing, plus drives into the neighbouring private game concession. Package $970.

Selenkay Conservancy

Amboseli Porini Camp Selenkay Conservancy ☎020/7123129 or 0722/509200, ⓦ www.porini.com. Deep in the bush, shaded by acacias, this is an intimate and highly enjoyable experience, with nine, very comfortable and spacious en-suite tents, each with a double and single bed, solar lighting, and full bathrooms with hot "safari showers" to order. Few guests drive in themselves and package prices include road travel from Nairobi and all national park and conservancy fees. Closed mid-April–May; no children under 8. Package $1010.

Outside Kimana Gate

Amboseli Sopa Lodge 5km east of Kimana Gate ☎045/622200, ⓦ www.sopalodges.com. The former *Kilimanjaro Buffalo Lodge* has 83 spacious and comfortably furnished rooms, with no nets, fans or a/c, but in a very pleasant garden setting, with good views of Kilimanjaro and a pool. The lodge has no vehicles of its own, and acts as a base for safaris from the coast. FB ❽

Kibo Safari Camp 2km south of Kimana Gate ☎0722/310231, ⊛www.kibosafaricamp.com. The 60-odd diminutive ridge tents here are getting old. It's not luxurious, but has a rough sort of charm, at least compared with neighbouring *Sentrim*, and the pool is a plus. FB ❼

Kilima Safari Camp 500m east of Kimana Gate ☎020 603595, ⊛www.madahotels.com. Owned by the operators of *Fig Tree Camp* in the Mara, this very different beast – a huge investment incorporating lofty public areas, a splendid pool and flamboyant "tent" and chalet designs – was opened in 2009. Too much furniture, uncomfortable beds and not enough shade on site may, hopefully, change with time – it has the potential to be a nice place. FB ❽

Sentrim Amboseli 3.5km south of Kimana Gate ☎0733/852083 or 0722/207361, ⊛www .sentrim-hotels.com. Concrete, even green concrete, is still concrete. And this charmless, shadeless property has lots of it. Sixty identical tents with plywood furniture, fans, electric sockets, room safes and hotel-style bathroom – plus a pool. FB ❼

The route from Nairobi

The A104 through the Kapiti plains is, unfortunately, pretty dull, broken only by the **Maasai Ostrich Farm** (☎045/22505), signposted 7km off on the right 15km south of Athi River. Primarily a commercial farm producing ostrich meat, they also have guided tours, a swimming pool, snacks and large picnic grounds – plus, usually on Sundays, ostrich races.

Further south, in the gentle hills where Maasai country really begins, is the district capital **KAJIADO**. Set among sisal spikes and acacia, it's a friendly market town, an ideal stopover after the hassle of Nairobi. Maasai in all their gear mix with other Kenyans, and the daily **market** is fascinating. The *Kaputiei B&L* (❷) has the best cheap **rooms** in town. For **food**, try *Sizzlers* just down from the *Kaputiei*. The scenic interest picks up after Kajiado, as the road snakes into the hills, giving views of the conical Mount Meru in Tanzania (4565m), and, if the sky's clear, your first glimpses of Kilimanjaro.

Namanga

The hot frontier town of **NAMANGA** sits on the Kenya–Tanzania border, nestled in a wooded valley between steep hills, 130km north of Arusha. It's a big **Maasai** trading centre, and Maasai women hawk armloads of beaded jewellery and other crafts around the town centre. The miniature **glass beads** used in the beadwork are actually manufactured in the Czech Republic, which exports them to Peru and the Native American reservations as well as East Africa. If you want to put a little money into the local economy (the ladies can be very persistent and their big necklaces start at high prices), then buy some copper bangles, which go for around Ksh50 each, with discounts for bulk purchases.

Namanga River Hotel (☎0734/591444, ✉info@namangariverhotel.com; ❹) offers the only mainstream tourist **accommodation**. A colonial-era oddity, composed of wooden cabins set amid pretty gardens, it was the halfway house on the old safari trail between Nairobi and Arusha. The place has a likeable, slightly cranky atmosphere, but is overpriced for what it offers (nets but no fans or a/c, and decent bathrooms, but uncertain hot water). The restaurant is reasonable (lunch Ksh750) and meals are served in the garden. You can also camp in the grounds (Ksh300), using the provided shower and toilet block. A more affordable option is its budget neighbour, *Namanga Safari Lodge* (☎0735/249543; ❷), which has clean, tidy rooms, which are just as good as the hotel's, with instant showers, nets and TV. If you're counting every penny, then *Bongo Salama Guest House* (☎045/523274 ❶) is the one to go for. It's 400m from the town centre (turn left at the junction in the Amboseli direction, then right, then left again). The tiny, strictly no-frills, non-self-contained rooms have nets and clean sheets, while the shared instant showers and squat toilets are decent enough.

The park

In the dry season, Amboseli can seem a parched, unattractive place, with Kilimanjaro disappointingly hazed into oblivion. Heading straight for the park's centre at Ol Tukai, with its lodges, workers, filling station, fences and barriers, doesn't improve first impressions. During the rains, however, it all looks far more impressive, with the shallow and seasonal **Lake Amboseli** partially filled, and a number of other seasonal lakes and ponds – the temporary home of small flocks of flamingos, pelicans, and other migratory species – scattered across the landscape. Balloon flights are usually available.

Ol Tukai is a central oasis of trees and vegetation, a kind of "human reserve", fenced off from the rest of the park, with lodges and other support services, that was formerly the focus of most of the park's human activity. Today *Ol Tukai Lodge* itself is the saving grace at Ol Tukai, for if the derelict appearance of the now-closed *Amboseli Lodge* wasn't enough, the extraordinary elephant destruction of the trees in what was once a pleasant patch of woodland has to be seen to be believed. The Ol Tukai perimeter fence has been breached by the elephants in several places, and a whole avenue of acacias has been taken out by them.

Game drives

Small enough to explore easily in two or three game drives over a couple of days, Amboseli is mostly open country with good visibility. A good first stop is **Observation Hill**. Early in the morning, with Kilimanjaro a pervasive sky-filler to the south, the swamps of **Enkongo Narok**, replenished underground from the mountain top, are looped out in a brilliant emerald sash beneath. You can get out and walk around up here, and chat with the rangers posted on-site.

There's always a concentration of animals around the swamps and along the driveable tracks which follow their fringes. These marshes are permanent enough to keep **hippos** in Amboseli all year, and the park is also home to hundreds of **elephant** and **buffalo** and a raucous profusion of **birdlife**. **Lake Kioko**, between Lake Amboseli and Ol Tukai – most easily seen along the track between junctions #21 and #26, is a particularly worthwhile oasis, and similarly **Olokenya swamp**, with its seasonal lakes north and east of Ol Tukai, is always worth slow exploration.

Lions are quite rare in Amboseli, but **cheetahs** are seen fairly frequently in the woods a little further south, and there must be hundreds of **giraffe** among the acacias. Look out, too, for the beautifully formed, rapier-horned **fringe-eared oryx** antelope, and for **gerenuk**, stretching their long necks up to forage in the trees.

The open plains are scoured by **zebra** and haphazard, solitary **wildebeest**. The two species are often seen together – a good deal from the zebras' point of view because in a surprise attack the predator usually ends up with the less fleet-footed wildebeest. There are tail-flicking **gazelle** out here, too, of both species: the open country provides good protection against cheetah ambushes.

Opinions are divided about the **Maasai cultural bomas** which are set up just outside the park west of *Amboseli Serena Lodge* (between junctions #33 and #34). After paying a fee (from Ksh500 to $30 per person, varying with your perceived ability to pay), you get the right to take as many pictures as you want, and may be treated to a display of traditional dancing, while the Maasai get the right to pitch their curios at you with practised persistence. Try to ensure, at least, that your payment is going to the Maasai, and not to your driver (see box, p.369).

Selenkay Conservancy

North of the park proper, but only easily accessed from it, with a driver-guide who knows the way, the 60-square-kilometre **Selenkay Conservancy** is one of Kenya's pioneering community conservation success stories. Here, Gamewatchers Safaris, one of the country's most environmentally sound safari operators, co-manages *Amboseli Porini Camp* (see p.340) with the local Maasai community. With a maximum of eighteen visitors, there are no time-serving, long-distance staff here: you're looked after by local warriors, generating direct income for their families. Although the area is bushy, with few stretches of open savanna, and wildlife is much less habituated to vehicles than in the park, the game-viewing can still be good, with predators frequently seen, as well as elephants, several species of antelope, and less often observed mammals – there's a porcupine den close to the camp, for example. And the beauty of being here is the chance to go on game walks, rather than game drives, with your Maasai hosts, as often as you like. Down in a sandy area near the seasonal Merueshi River, they have sundowners and bush dinners, while their tree platform, near a waterhole, is a regular bush breakfast and sundowner spot, a favourite especially with younger visitors; it's about 4.5km from camp – a two-hour walk.

Between Amboseli and Tsavo West

There are two routes **east out of Amboseli** (see map, p.325). One heads through **Iremito Gate** to meet the *murram* C102 road at **MBIRIKANI**, a small, Maasai trading centre, where you can turn north to the Mombasa highway at Emali (see p.325). There's no problem driving on the C102 in dry weather, but take care in the wet, when it's definitely 4WD only. The C102 has infrequent public transport. The road from Iremito Gate continues beyond Mbirikani to *Ol Donyo Wuas*, across the Chyulu Hills National Park and down to Kibwezi on the Mombasa highway (see p.325).

The second road is the **C103** to Tsavo West, which leaves the east side of Amboseli at **Kimana Gate** (also known as Olkelunyiet Gate), meeting the C102 23km east of the gate, and 5km south of the trading centre of **KIMANA**. If you need a cheap overnight stay in Kimana, try the *Romunja* or *Paradise* lodgings; both of which offer basic rooms (●). As a result of concerns about **security**, you have to travel to Tsavo West in convoy with an official vehicle, or escorted by an armed guard, although there have been no incidents of banditry since the early 1990s. There are usually 8.30am and 2.30pm departures from both Ol Tukai in Amboseli and Tsavo West's Chyulu Gate, and the journey takes from two to four hours. At other times you can pick up an armed guard from Ol Tukai or the gate, but you'll need to pay him around Ksh500. If you're driving between Amboseli and towns along the C102 (Emali, Kimana, Oloitokitok or Taveta) you don't need security. The concern is with the 66km stretch of the C103 from its junction with the C102 to Tsavo West's Chyulu Gate: there's a roadblock at the start of this stretch where the police will check your security arrangements.

From Kimana junction, it's 3.5km to the C103 junction for Chyulu Gate, and a further 6.5km south to Oloitokitok.

Oloitokitok

With Kilimanjaro towering in front of you, the C102 climbs up to the Maasai country town of **OLOITOKITOK** at an altitude of 1700m, high above the plains. Although it's ignored by 99 percent of tourist traffic, this town is in a stunning location, closer to Kilimanjaro than anywhere else in Kenya. It's a relaxed place to settle into if you're interested in finding out more about the Maasai, as this is their easternmost major centre. Markets happen on Tuesdays and Saturdays. There's a customs post on the north side of town (you'll be waved through unless you're going to Tanzania), but the actual border is 8km further south at Illasit, on the road to Taveta.

Kilimanjaro's **Kibo Peak** is 25km as the crow flies from Oloitokitok; you can arrange climbing tours in town at *Kibo Slopes Cottages*, but don't get caught in Kilimanjaro National Park without having paid the park fee. And obviously you'll need to have your papers in order (Tanzanian visa and yellow fever certificate).

Practicalities

Oloitokitok has fuel, a post office and KCB and Equity **banks** that both change money (but no ATM). Apart from the post office itself, there are several **internet** cafés that are a little pricier than usual. The *Kilimanjaro* bar and *hoteli* is a good spot for a drink or a bite to eat, with a restaurant and a little roof terrace. It's down the hill from the Oilibya petrol station. Of the various **B&Ls**, the Christian-run *Safaris Guest House* (☎045/622088; ❶), with nets, electric sockets, instant showers and squat toilets is well run. *Ntawuouh Guest House* (☎045/622248 or 0723/088589; ❶) offers similar services (and European toilets), but get a room at the end with an outside window. Superior to everywhere else in town is ⚑ *Kibo Slopes Cottages* (☎045/622091, ⓦwww.kibos-lopescottages.com; ❹), 700m down a track to the east of the customs post (left if you're coming from the north), with very clean and tidy self-contained rooms, some with good views, and four-bed cottages for the same price. There's a bar and restaurant and pretty gardens, and it's a well-established base for climbing Kilimanjaro (around $1075 per person, plus entry fees of $50 per person).

On market days there's a fair amount of **matatu** traffic between here and Emali, as well as a service south to Taveta (some leave the day before the market to get to Oloitokitok). At other times, you will have to take pot luck with transport – start early.

From Oloitokitok to Taveta

Unexpected tarmac sweeps invitingly south out of Oloitokitok to the Tanzanian border crossing and market town of **Illasit**, where the tarmac veers off to the right towards Moshi in Tanzania. The road that continues to Taveta starts well, with graded grey gravel skirting the flanks of Tanzania, at least as far as the dispersed centre of **Njukini-Chumvini**. From here to **Lake Chala**, however, it's in a poor state and impassable to most vehicles after heavy rain. From Chala to **Taveta** (see p.334) it's much better.

Much of the scenery along this route is beautiful, the landscape changing from scrubby cattle pasture to plots of sisal and maize – marking the end of Maasai territory – and patches of acacia woodland, cut by streams and dotted with swamp. There are only a few settlements, acting as market centres for Maasai and Taveta farmers, but **Rombo** is notable for its very fine mosque with its soaring minaret.

Chyulu Hills National Park

The **Chyulu Hills National Park** (ⓦ www.kws.go.ke/chyulu.html; $50; see p.62), which follows the spine of the geologically recent Chyulu Hills lava ridge – only formed around 500 years ago – is one of Kenya's least visited and least developed national parks. Aside from the wildlife and the glorious scenery (the hills stood in for the less impressive Ngong Hills for the filming of *Out of Africa*), the main attraction is **Leviathan Cave**, the world's second-longest lava tube. At present, you need to be a dedicated and well-equipped caver to explore Leviathan, but there are plans to make at least part of the cave more easily accessible. **Wildlife** is present in great numbers, though what you'll see varies constantly: the plains between the C102 from Emali to Kimana, known as the "pipeline road", and the hills are often speckled with game, including giraffe, buffalo, eland, zebra and wildebeest, while in the glades of the forested hills themselves you can see elephant and giant forest hog and even, in the park's northwestern corner, towards the Makedo Gate, around fifteen **black rhinos** living on the lava flow and under constant KWS surveillance. The crest of the Chyulus is wreathed in mossy cloud forest, constantly watered by the clouds that make the landscapes here so ravishingly beautiful.

Access

The park's Makedo Gate can be reached from Makutano on the C102 Emali–Oloitokitok road, while the Kibwezi Gate is reached from a junction 1.5km south of Kibwezi on the Nairobi–Mombasa road. You can also get into the park from either of the lodges, *Ol Donyo Wuas* or *Campi ya Kanzi*. Whichever way you go, you'll need to be in a sturdy 4WD and preferably have a guide: the terrain inside the park is steep and hard going.

Accommodation

Accommodation in the park itself is limited to a single **campsite** ($25) by the park HQ, 1200m inside Kibwezi Gate, but there's an affordable tented camp and two outstanding **luxury places to stay** outside the park limits, any one of which would make a good base.

Campi ya Kanzi At the southern end of the Chyulus, 20km north of the C103 Amboseli–Tsavo West road on the Kuku group ranch ⓣ045/622516 or satellite +88/2165/1103557, ⓦwww.maasai.com. Passionately conceived, award-winning, Maasai-Italian eco-collaboration of eight, tented cottages and a stone and thatch central building, constructed without tree-felling. Package $1100, plus $100 per person daily community levy.

Ol Donyo Wuas On the western flank of the Chyulus, 29km east of Mbirikani on the C102 ⓣ0726/772047 or 0725/571025, ⓦwww.oldonyowuas.com. Astonishingly chic bush lodge, consisting of ten extremely stylish and spacious suites in six separate lodges, each with their own plunge pools, roof terraces, outdoor showers and private views. Guests gather for meals and eat at one vast table, with the owners, legendary safari pilot Richard Bonham and family. The superb riding stable has twenty horses, including tough *boerperds* from South Africa (the only ones in East Africa). Highly recommended: one of Kenya's very best lodges. Package $1060 plus $80 per person daily community levy.

Umani Springs Camp On the northeast side of the park, 7km from the Mombasa road south of Kibwezi along the same dirt road as Kibwezi Gate ⓣ0721/317762. Modest tented camp set deep in the forest, closed for refurbishment at the time of writing. The owner is a keen caver and, with advance notice, the camp may be able to help organize a caving trip to Leviathan Cave. FB ❻

Tsavo West National Park

The combined area of **Tsavo West and Tsavo East national parks** makes this by far the biggest wildlife reserve in Kenya, and one of the largest in the world, sprawling across 19,000 square kilometres of dry bush country, an area almost the size of Wales and more than twice the size the size of Yellowstone National Park in the USA.

Of the two Tsavos, **Tsavo West** (ⓦwww.kws.go.ke/tsavo-west.html; $50; smartcard, see p.61), encircled by roads and encroaching human populations, is the most visited and the most developed. Yet within its vast 7000 square kilometre extent, the popular part that receives nearly all visitors is a "mere" 1000 square kilometres, known as the **developed area**, located between the Tsavo River and the Mombasa highway. Here, a combination of magnificent landscapes and good access and facilities (*Kilaguni* and *Severin* both welcome casual visitors, and *Kilaguni* has fuel supplies), attracts visitors in large numbers, while the well-watered, volcanic soils support wooded grasslands and a great quantity and diversity of animal life – though it's not always easily observed.

Access

As with all the parks, there's no public transport into Tsavo by road, so if you're not on an organized safari, you need to drive or fly. Nairobi's Wilson Airport has daily **flights** on Safarilink or you can fly from Mombasa and Diani Beach with Mombasa Air Safari.

If you're coming by road, the small service town of **Mtito Andei** (see p.326) is mid-way between Mombasa and Nairobi and is itself easily reached by bus or matatu. If you are hoping for a lift into the park, however, you could be in for a very long wait: while **Mtito Andei Gate West** is relatively busy, you won't see a stream of vehicles passing through. From the gate, it's around an hour's drive to any of the four main lodge/camp focuses (see "Accommodation" below). The information centre at the gate has interesting background about Tsavo West, as well as a small shop selling cold drinks.

Once you're in the park, if you're driving yourself, you'll soon come to appreciate your dependency on the accuracy of the marker cairns at the numbered junctions: unfortunately, at the time of writing, the signage in the park is woefully inadequate, with many numbers illegible and distances underestimated. A handheld GPS is very useful.

Accommodation

A lack of modestly priced **accommodation** is less of an obstacle in Tsavo West than in most of the other main parks. For a start there are two **campsites** (both $25) in the developed area. The first is *Chyulu Campsite* just outside Chyulu Gate, 600m north of junction #26, with basic European-style toilets, running water for the showers and shacks for camping under (assuming a smallish dome tent). The second, and sometimes the busiest, is *Kamboyo Campsite*, just north of junction #3, near the park HQ not far from Mtito Andei Gate, which is nice enough, with plenty of easy pitches under shady trees, and a promising-looking shower and squat toilet block. But unfortunately it has no water, so you'd need to bring your own. There are also several KWS-designated "special campsites" along the north bank of the Tsavo River.

If you're not equipped to camp, there are **mid-priced, self-catering** options in the shape of the *bandas* at *Rhino Valley Lodge* and *Kitani Safari Lodge* and the house rental at *Kamboyo House*, near the park HQ.

Finch Hatton's Tented Lodge 9km south of junction #29, 65km from Mtito Andei Gate ☎020/8030936 or 0720/444419, ⓦwww.finchhattons.com. With 31 tents (1 to 7 are best) planted around springs and lakes full of hippos and crocs, this is named after the aristocrat who introduced royalty to the bush. Owner-managed, with flair, you're served multi-course dinners, on good china and linen by befezzed waiters, as Mozart tinkles above the evening frog chorus. But it's not everybody's porcelain cup of tea – too big and fancy to call boutique, and not comfy enough, with no nets. The dated snob appeal, and food that veers wildly from sublime to second rate, are solidly offset by large and well-built tents, and the site's truly remarkable natural environment, similar to Mzima Springs. There's free wi-fi around the bar and a good pool. Their own airstrip is 3km away. FB $540.

Kamboyo Guest House 2km northeast of junction #3, by the park HQ and research centre ☎020/600800, ⓔreservations@kws.go.ke. Well located, above a small waterhole, with views to the south from the large upstairs balcony and ground-floor veranda, this spacious, clean and decently furnished house has seven beds, firewood on demand, gas and electricity. The generator is usually on from 8.30–11.30am, 2.30–5.30pm and 6.30–10.30pm. Whole house, depending on season, Ksh8000–10,000.

Kilaguni Serena Safari Lodge Off junction 8, about 30km from Mtito Andei Gate ☎020/8030800 or 0734/699865, ⓦwww.serenahotels.com. Dating from 1962, the oldest park lodge in Kenya is a perennial favourite with many repeat visitors, as much as anything for its prime site and terrific wildlife ambience, with a spectacular panoramic overlook of two, floodlit waterholes. There's a busy atmosphere and it's very often full but standards are high. The rooms, in thatched cottages (most facing the wildlife action, with views towards the Chyulu Hills and Kili from the balconies) aren't big, but are well laid out, with nets, fans and power points. There's a modest pool, and a petrol station open 7am–4pm & 6–7pm, with prices about 10 percent above the pump price in Mtito Andei. FB ❽

Kitani Safari Lodge Next to *Severin Safari Camp*, ☎0722/650819, ⓦwww.severin-kenya.com. The former *Kitani Bandas*, now competently managed by Severin, comprises eight, very comfortable, twin or double *bandas*, with nets, free firewood, bathrooms, good kitchens with gas cookers, and electric sockets. *Banda* #3 has the best views but all share the intimate connection with the Tsavo environment. Guests can go to the main camp to

eat or swim (you'll need to drive or call them to arrange transport). *Banda* only, $85, extra bed $20.

Ngulia Safari Lodge 48km west of Tsavo Gate, 6.5km south of junction #18 ☎043/30140 or 0722/139393, ⓦwww.safari-hotels.com. Somewhat isolated in the more hilly, eastern side of the park, this dated, 1970s-apartment-block-style hotel offers small rooms, with nets and floor fans but no other frills, but tremendous views over the plains far below. The two small waterholes by the terrace attract buffalo, but the immediate area has less wildlife appeal than the other lodges, for which compensation comes in the form of controversial, nightly leopard-baiting. Usually busy with minibus tours from Mombasa, it's well-maintained, with a small pool, and casual visitors are welcome. They also do night game drives (from $65, for up to three guests). FB ❼

Rhino Valley Lodge 3.5km from junction #18 ☎0725/517832, reservations ☎0721/328567, ⓦwww.tsavocampsandlodges.com. The location, nestled on the steep north slopes of Ngulia Hill, offers sweeping vistas from the terrace bar-restaurant and there's a waterhole opposite *bandas* #4, 5 and 6, sometimes visited by translocated black rhinos. But like *Ngulia*, you don't get the concentrations of wildlife you find around *Kilaguni* or *Severin*. There are six *bandas* and a family room with fully equipped kitchens and eighteen more basic *bandas* with no kitchen. Electricity, powering sockets and fridges, is supplied from 6–11am and 5–8.30pm. The ❻ rate for FB is negotiable. Self-catering per *banda* (extra bed $30) $100.

🏃 **Severin Safari Camp** Off junction #36, 8km from Mzima Springs ☎0722/650819, ⓦwww.severin-kenya.com. Enthusiastic, hands-on, German management is responsible for the distinctive flavour of this very cool, thoughtfully conceived camp of tents and luxury *bandas*, sprawled on a flat, bushy plain, teeming with wildlife. Casual visitors are welcome for meals that are well out of the ordinary (try the cook-your-own hot stone grill with dipping sauces), the superb pool and the rejuvenating massage spa, all witnessed by a ceaseless parade of giraffe, antelope, warthogs and birdlife attracted by the camp's five waterholes. Free wi-fi throughout. Tent 16 and *banda* 3 have the best views. FB ❼

Voyager Ziwani Camp Just outside Ziwani Gate, about 40km south of the developed area, but most easily reached from the Taveta–Voi road ☎043/30506, ⓦwww.heritage-eastafrica.com. On a glorious site on the Sainte stream, dammed to create a hippo and crocodile pool, *Ziwani* has 25 fairly basic tents on plinths under thatched roofs. Long overdue a complete refurb, it was undergoing one at the time of writing, so should be much improved. Although a good hour's drive south of the park's main attractions (from which it is sometimes cut off when river floods wash away the crossing points over the Tsavo River), the local bonuses such as early-morning walks and night game drives – both possible because it's outside the park boundaries – more than compensate. FB $405.

The developed area

The **developed area** is hilly, and there's an unending succession of fantastic views across the plains, dotted with volcanic cones and streaked with forest at the water margins. When the animals are abundant, every turn in the track seems to bring you face to face with zebra, giraffe, huge herds of buffalo, casual prides of lions, or methodical, strolling elephants, almost orange from the dust. An unusual species to look for is the beautiful and shy **lesser kudu** antelope – always, it seems, running away.

One large mammal you're less likely to see is the black rhino. In the 1960s, Tsavo had as many as nine thousand **black rhinos** – the biggest population in Africa. By 1981, they had been poached to barely one hundred individuals across Tsavo West and East (see box, p.354). The situation today has improved, and about 65 of Tsavo West's eighty rhinos are now in the safety of the **Ngulia Rhino Sanctuary** (daily 4–6pm; free) where you're almost bound to see one if you drive around for a while. You can always visit the holding pen in the middle of the sanctuary to inspect the latest arrivals. In addition, another fifteen rhinos live free in the park itself, under constant surveillance.

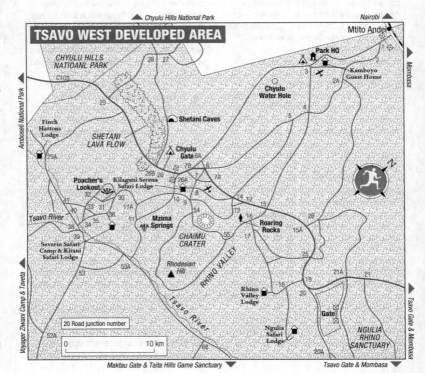

▲ Chyulu Hills National Park   Nairobi ▲

TSAVO WEST DEVELOPED AREA

Mtito Andei

CHYULU HILLS NATIOANL PARK

C103

28 27

Park HQ

2

3

2A

Kamboyo Guest House

Mombasa

29

Chyulu Water Hole

4

Finch Hattons Lodge

29A

SHETANI LAVA FLOW

▲ Shetani Caves

5

Amboseli National Park

Chyulu Gate 6A

26B 26

6

Poacher's Lookout

Kilaguni Serena Safari Lodge

26A

7A

7

32

41

33 31

30

11A

8

Tsavo River

34 35 36

11

Mzima Springs

10 9

54

14 12

15

28

38

39

Severin Safari Camp & Kitani Safari Lodge

CHAIMU CRATER

13 16

55

17

Roaring Rocks

15A

25

53

54A

Rhodesian Hill ▲

RHINO VALLEY

Rhino Valley Lodge

18

19

20

21A 21

Voyager Ziwani Camp & Taveta

Tsavo River

Gate

NGULIA RHINO SANCTUARY

52A

20 Road junction number

0   10 km

66

Ngulia Safari Lodge

20A

Tsavo Gate & Mombasa

▼ Maktau Gate & Taita Hills Game Sanctuary   Tsavo Gate & Mombasa ▼

The little circuit that takes you around the foot of **Rhodesian Hill** is recommended too, and **Poacher's Lookout**, near *Severin*, is a very promising place for a quiet scan with binoculars. There's a thatched shelter on this prominent hilltop, where you can sit in the breeze. Note that the summit is 4.5km from junction #32, not 2km as marked.

Mzima Springs

The biggest attraction in Tsavo West is **Mzima Springs**, 500m south of junction #11, 48km from Mtito Andei and close to both *Kilaguni Lodge* and *Severin Safari Camp*. This stream of crystal-clear water was made famous by Alan Root's 1983 film *Mzima: Portrait of a Spring*, which followed crocodiles and hippos in their underwater lives. It's a delightful, and popular, spot, so you're advised to arrive very early to avoid a possible tour-bus atmosphere. With luck, some of the night's animal visitors may still be around, while the luxuriant growth around the water reverberates noisily with birds and monkeys. You can walk around freely, as elephants and predators rarely visit, but there are KWS rangers posted by the car park to look after you, just in case.

There are two large pools, connected by a rush of rapids and shaded by stands of date and raffia palms. The upper (or long) pool is the favoured **hippo** wallow, while the **crocodiles** tend to retreat to the broader expanse of water lower down. It's worth walking around this lower pool to the right where, if you're stealthy, you have a good chance of seeing a croc – just make sure there's not one on the bank behind you. This word of caution applies equally to hippos, but they seem settled in their routine, content to snort and flounder en masse. At the side of the top pool, a circular underwater **viewing chamber** has been built at the end of a short pier. With luck (and it doesn't happen on every visit), you'll see the unforgettably comic tip-toeing of an underwater hippo, or the sinuous, streamlined stealth of a crocodile in motion, as well as the blue swirl of large fish.

Mzima Springs' water is filtered to aquarium transparency by the lava of the **Chyulu range**, just to the north of here: the porous rock absorbs the water like a sponge and gravity squeezes it out into the springs. A direct pipeline from Mzima to Mombasa, completed in 1966, is the source of most of the city's **drinking water**. Engineers, summoned by the National Park's trustees, devised a way of taking water from beneath the lava, but above the spring, preserving the area's integrity. There are one or two signs of the pipeline, but most are unobtrusive.

You don't have to be a botanist to enjoy Mzima's two **tree trails**, with examples of various trees labelled with their common uses and their English, local and botanical names. It's easy to spend a couple of hours in the area: try to sit for a while completely alone on the bank and you'll begin to piece together the ecological miracle of the place, as the mammals, birds and other creatures forget about your presence. And look out for **sycamore figs**, the spectacular tree that features in the extraordinary nature documentary *The Queen of Trees* (Mark Deeble & Victoria Stone, 2006; widely available on DVD) about the symbiotic relationship between the sycamore fig and the tiny fig wasp.

Game-viewing at Kilaguni and Severin lodges

You may not be staying in the relative luxury of *Kilaguni* or *Severin*, but a visit to either can be highly rewarding, for the pleasure of sitting on the terrace with a cold beer, or having lunch (allow \$25), watching the enthralling natural circus going on a few yards away. At *Severin*, guests and wildlife are on exactly the same level, making the experience very intimate, while the **waterholes** at *Kilaguni*, spread beneath the panorama of the Chyulu Hills, are a well-known magnet for human as well as animal visitors.

At *Kilaguni*, dazzling **birds** hop everywhere, **agama lizards** skim along the walls (the miniature orange and blue dragons are the males in mating drag), **hyraxes** have been known to scamper between the tables and **dwarf mongooses** are regular visitors. Out by the waterholes, scuffling **baboon troops**, several species of **antelope** and **gazelle**, **buffalo**, **zebra**, **giraffe** and **elephant** all provide constant spectacle, with the possibility of the occasional kill adding tension. At dusk, **bats** swoop, while **genets**, **jackals** and **hyenas** lurk near the floodlights, drawn by the smell of dinner – though, thankfully, the lodge has stopped the practice of baiting them with meat scraps.

While *Kilaguni* is a dead cert for full-on animal action, the odds are against it keeping its absolute pre-eminence indefinitely, as the much newer *Severin* begins to make a mark. The camp at *Severin*, far from dominating the landscape, seems to be absorbed by its environment, and there's nothing to stop the animals treating the whole camp as their own. Signs warn visitors not to stray off the paths, but you'll need little reminding, as families of **warthogs** trot past the terrace, **impala** and **giraffe** nibble audibly, and **lion kills** take place close to reception. Unlike *Kilaguni*, guests at *Severin* have to be escorted to and from their tents after dark.

Ngulia Safari Lodge

Ngulia Safari Lodge is a stopover on the annual southern migration of hundreds of thousands of European **birds**, but the reasons for its attraction for the birds – apart from its isolated lights – aren't really known. Kenyan and overseas ornithologists and amateur birders gather at the end of November for a fortnight to identify and ring the birds that are trapped in mist nets (20,000 in 2008) to build up a picture of their migration routes. If you'd like to participate, contact the lodge or your national bird-watching organization for information.

Lava flows and caves

The lava that purifies Mzima's water can be seen in black outcrops all around this part of Tsavo. The main park road from Amboseli to Chyulu Gate runs right across the spectacular **Shetani lava flow** (it starts about 10km east of junction #29 and continues east for more than a kilometre). Only 200 years old, the eruption that spewed it out was evidently a cataclysmic event for local people, and is still the focus of stories about fire and evil spirits (*shetani* means "devil" in Swahili). People are said to have been buried under the hot lava, and legend has it that their plaintive cries can be heard on certain nights. The local people appease the ghosts with offerings of food which, of course, are gone by daybreak.

At several places you're allowed out of your vehicle to explore the lava, which is brittle, honeycombed and unstable. After only two centuries, very few plants have yet taken hold. It is also possible to climb up to the volcano's **crater rim**, but this can be surprisingly hard work on the scree and shouldn't be attempted in the heat of the day. Less strenuously, there are some small **caves** that are worthy of investigation, though you'll need a powerful torch to get very far. They are 5.5km up the high-clearance-only track that climbs the flank of the volcano, north of junction #26B. After 5km, start looking out on the right side of the track for a uselessly unmarked cairn, an oil drum, and a fig tree that covers the entrance.

Tsavo East National Park

Northeast of the highway, the railway, and the apparent natural divide that separates Kenya's northern and southern environments, lies **Tsavo East National Park** (Ⓦ www.kws.go.ke/tsavo-east.html; $50; smartcard, see p.61). Although it is the larger part of the combined Tsavo parks, the sector north of the Galana River has few tracks and is much less visited. South of the river, the great triangle of flat wilderness, with **Aruba Dam** in the middle, has become popular with safaris operated from the coast, since it offers a pretty sure chance of seeing plenty of animals, in a very open environment.

Apart from some tumbled **crags and scarps** near Voi, and the rocky cleft of the **Galana River** (fed by the Tsavo and the Athi), Tsavo East is an uninterrupted **plain of bush**, dotted with the crazed shapes of baobab trees. It's a forbiddingly enormous reserve and at times over the last three decades has seemed an odd folly, especially since its northern area was closed to the public for many years due to the long war against elephant and rhino **poachers** (see box, p.354). Since the 1990s, this campaign has been largely won and the elephants are once again on the increase, their numbers swelled by a major KWS translocation operation that moved three hundred elephants from Shimba Hills (see p.425). Rhinos are still very rare in Tsavo East and numbers exceedingly hard to estimate but it's believed there may be about fifty individuals, mostly in the north. With the northern sector secure and rangers in place, the whole of Tsavo East was opened for tourism in 2006, though infrastructure north of the Galana is still basic.

Access

There are no scheduled **flights** to Tsavo East at the time of writing, but access via the gates along the Mombasa highway is relatively straightforward. From north to south, these are: **Mtito Andei Gate East**, which gives access to the northern sector; **Voi Gate**, the park's smartcard point of issue, 7km from Voi (see p.328); **Manyani Gate**, near Mudanda Rock; and **Buchuma Gate** at the southern tip, little more than an hour's drive from Mombasa.

On the east side of the park, **Sala Gate** offers access from Malindi. It's 105km due west of the coastal resort, and there is a small cluster of camps and lodges just outside the park boundary. If you're driving from Malindi, you'll find the first 40km over coral rock quite jarring, but the views across the Sabaki plain are good. The remaining 65km over red *murram* and gravel are mostly fairly smooth, though heavy rain can cause delays. Allow three hours to reach the gate, and be prepared to make a fixed 7am start from the police barrier outside Malindi. You have to travel in convoy – although as with the convoy between Amboseli and Tsavo West (see p.343), there no longer appears to be any security threat. If you try this route by public transport, you'll find few matatus venture west of **Kakoneni**, 30km from Malindi.

Accommodation

Tsavo East's **accommodation** options are more numerous and varied than you might expect. The following listings include most of those inside the park itself, but outside the park you'll find cheaper options, as well as one or two good lodges and tented camps. Those outside the park, around Voi and off the Mombasa Highway, are covered on pp.328–330, while just outside Sala Gate, on the road between the park and Malindi, is a small cluster of fairly basic camps where you might find yourself booked on a safari, or need to call in for lunch or a last-minute overnight

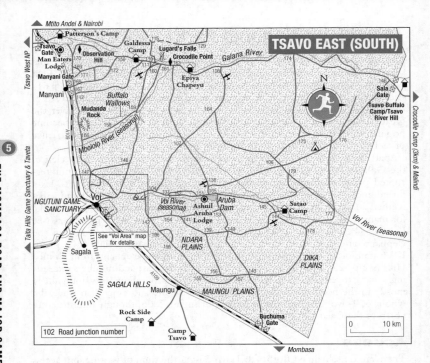

▲ Mtito Andei & Nairobi

TSAVO EAST (SOUTH)

102 Road junction number

0   10 km

▼ Mombasa

stay. Just 200m east of Sala Gate, *Tsavo Buffalo Camp* and *Tsavo River Hill* (both
℡0711/844544 or 0722/576542, Ⓦwww.coralkeymalindi.com) are two sides of
the same Italian-run operation, where you can get lunch for Ksh750. *River Hill* is
the slightly more upmarket choice, with fake gold taps and ornate furnishings in
large rondavels (FB ❼) while *Buffalo* has basic, small cottages with nets (FB ❺).
Some 3km further east is *Crocodile Camp* (℡0733/295349,Ⓦwww
.africansafariclub.com; no children under 8; FB ❻) which offers small, air-
conditioned tents, and much preferable cottages, also air-conditioned but without
nets, all set along the river. Casual visitors are welcome for lunch (Ksh750). It's in
a good spot and you enter reception across a small pond, whose bridge is festooned
with fat monitor lizards.

There's only one public **campsite** in the park, *Ndololo*, run by KWS ($25),
which is 7km from Voi gate, at the western edge of Kanderi Swamp and off
junction #173. This has showers, toilets and free firewood, but no other
facilities.

🏃 **Epiya Chapeyu** 5km east of junction #163,
on the south bank of the Galana River
℡020/3749796, Ⓦ www.epiya-chapeyu-camp.
com. Unstuffy, Italian-run camp in a lovely location.
The fourteen tents are closely spaced, the better
ones in the front row facing the river, but they don't
have nets or front decks. You are, however, down
close to the river. Not fancy, but very good value,
and casual visitors are welcome for lunch
(Ksh1000). FB ❻

🏃 **Galdessa Camp** 4km north of junction #111
on the south bank of the Galana
℡020/523156, Ⓦwww.galdessa.com. This
spectacular, Italian-owned luxury camp is stunningly
conceived and located above the river. With
wonderful staff and ambience, lavish and comfortably furnished *banda*-tents, superb, hearty, Italian
cooking and extraordinary attention to detail, it's by
far Tsavo East's best camp. It's situated in one of the
few areas of Tsavo East where you have a chance of

spotting black rhino and elephants are nearly always seen crossing here. Closed May. FB $420.

🏃 **Satao Camp** Off junction #144 ☎ 043/30204 or 020/2038669, ⓦ www.sataocamp.com. Engagingly managed by its experienced safari host, *Satao* has a fine, low-key ambience, with its thatch-covered, slightly old-fashioned tents, ranged beneath big trees. The atmosphere suits visitors who want to relax in the bush and enjoy the wildlife – elephants, occasional lions and plains game attracted to the waterhole. As well as the ordinary tents, there are larger "suite" tents, for a thirty percent surcharge, with fridges and large beds. Solar-heated hot water is only available in the evenings. FB ❼

Voi Safari Lodge 3km north of Voi Gate on a rocky crag ☎ 043/30019, ⓦ www.safari-hotels.com. Not to be confused with the brashly oversized *Voi Wildlife Lodge* (just outside the park on the east side of town). Inside the park but on the south side of town, this fifty-room lodge is quite busy enough, and similar in many respects to its sister establishment, *Ngulia Safari Lodge* in Tsavo West. Admittedly, the rooms aren't huge, but despite the shortcomings of its style (it's actually a rather fun 1970s glam-kitsch: look out for the photo of Miss World 1972), this is a perennial favourite for its near-guaranteed game-viewing from the terrace, and the magnificent panorama plunging to the horizon. FB ❼

Around the park

With minibus safaris increasingly taking in Tsavo East, the emptiness of the park is no longer as overwhelming as it was, but the park's vastness means that for much of the time, you will still have the pleasure of exploring the wilderness completely alone. It's easy to get away off the two or three beaten tracks, and you may find something special – a **serval** perhaps, or a **striped hyena**. You're also very likely to see some of Tsavo's **elephants**.

Tsavo East's elephant orphans

Until a few years ago, the scarcity of mature bull and matriarch **elephants** was still noticeable after so many had been killed by poachers (see box overleaf). These days, good-sized herds and large tuskers are increasingly common. As well as the KWS relocation of elephants from the coast, much of the hard work in re-establishing elephants in Tsavo East has been done by the **David Sheldrick Wildlife Trust** based in Nairobi (see p.138). If you "adopt" an orphan (minimum $50; ⓦ www.sheldrickwildlifetrust.org), you can make arrangements to visit the release facilities, either at the stockade near Voi Gate or the one near the Ithumba park headquarters in the far north. The trust has an exclusive-use self-catering camp at **Ithumba** ($450; book through the trust), with three twin tents under thatched roofs, a communal area, and three staff, though it's expensive for a DIY place. These visits are only available to sponsors by pre-arrangement.

Game drives

Most **game drives** from the camps near the Galana River use the main dirt road along the south bank of the river, and then strike south along the roads following tributary *luggas*, up into the higher bush country between the Galana and Voi rivers. Lions, and occasionally cheetahs, can be seen along these water courses. The **Galana River** itself, with its fringing cordon of branching **doum palms**, creates a captivating backdrop, the sandy river bed often dotted with wildlife in the dry season.

West of junction #110, above the confluence of the Tsavo and Athi Rivers and the start of the Galana, is **Observation Hill**, while downstream, east of junction #160, are the gently spectacular **Lugard's Falls**, where you're allowed to park and clamber around the bizarrely eroded rocks. Even in relatively dry conditions, the falls, progressing from foaming rapids to narrow cascades gouged deep into the rock, are quite impressive.

In Tsavo, as throughout the country, the question of how to manage the **elephants** is still the paramount one. While several other countries permit trophy hunting, it has been illegal in Kenya since the 1970s and the policy here is to hunt the poachers and allow the elephants to reach their own natural balance within the defined park territory. Zoologists are divided about whether there is an optimal elephant population for a park like Tsavo, especially as natural weather patterns and now climate change are so significant. The destruction by elephants of Tsavo East's fragile woodlands and ongoing human-elephant conflict in the farmlands around the perimeter are perennial concerns.

Such questions have been submerged for many years by the overbearing problem of **poaching**, which at one time looked like it would wipe out the elephants completely. In 1967, the combined Tsavo parks' elephant population was more than 30,000. It went down to 5300 in 1988, and today stands at around 12,000. Elephants are long-lived and intelligent animals with complex kinship patterns, and the social structure of the herds in many districts was badly distorted in the 1980s, with many older animals killed and too many inexperienced younger elephants unable to fend for themselves or to act as role models for infants. The poachers had changed too; they were no longer marginalized Kamba farmers killing an occasional elephant with an old gun or poisoned arrows, but a new breed of well-connected gangster, equipped with automatic weapons, wiping out whole family groups in a single attack.

The international **ivory trade moratoriums**, in place from 1989, stopped the ivory trade in its tracks, and had an immediate effect on the numbers of new elephant corpses being logged in Tsavo East. Equally dramatic was the unprecedented aggression with which the Kenyan parks authorities started carrying out their duties under the bluntly pragmatic new Director of the Kenya Wildlife Service, **Richard Leakey**, with poachers liable to be shot on sight.

The pressure from some countries to reopen the ivory trade has been strongly resisted by Kenya and although there was a rise in poaching during the 2009 drought, the security of Tsavo's elephants is currently as good as it has been for decades. The price of tusks in the Far East, however, is running as high as $1500 per kilo and the turmoil in neighbouring **Somalia** is potentially a huge threat.

Tsavo East's **black rhinos** are much further down the path to annihilation. Their number in Kenya is estimated at around 570 (compared to 330 in 1989, at the height of the poaching), a figure that is perhaps twenty percent of the total population of the species. More than 95 percent of Kenya's rhinos, most of them in Tsavo, were killed in the 1970s. This escalation was largely due to a major expansion of the market for rhino horn in China (where powdered horn is used in traditional medicine), and in **Yemen** where oil money put the rhino-horn dagger-handle, traditionally the prerogative of the rich, within reach of thousands of Yemeni men. Many tons of horns were smuggled out of Mombasa by dhow before the authorities made any effort to halt the trade.

Yet the savage groundwork in rhino extermination had been done long before. After World War II, the Makueni area southeast of Machakos was designated as a Kamba resettlement area, and the colonial Kenya Game Department sent in one J.A. Hunter to clear it of unwelcoming rhinos. He lived up to his name, shooting 1088 black rhinos.

Today there are maybe fifty black rhinos in Tsavo East, and there are breeding populations in a number of ranches and sanctuaries around the country, while the concept of **saving the rhino** has become a national cause. Nevertheless, as long as there's a market for the horn, currently valued at up to $5000 per kilo, rhinos will remain under threat.

A kilometre east of the falls, another short diversion takes you to **Crocodile Point**, something of a let-down as the crocs are extraordinarily hard to see unless you get up close, which you're no longer allowed to do. Hippos are easier to spot from the vantage point.

Heading south from the Galana, any of the park roads from junctions #150, #111, #110, #161, #163, #108 or #174 can yield good results. **Buffalo Wallows Lugga** (junction #110, then #159), is often rewarding, with the chance of seeing a leopard, and plenty of birdlife. Some 20km further southwest, just north of junction #158, **Mudanda Rock** is particularly recommended. It resembles a scaled-down version of Australia's Uluru, and towers above a natural dam which, during the dry season, draws elephants in their hundreds.

Starting out from the relatively busy Voi area, the wooden margins of the **Voi River** often hide a profusion of wildlife, and this area is one of the most promising in the park. Try the **Ndololo Campsite** at junction #173 and the pretty **Kanderi Swamp loop** at #174. Keep your windows up when driving through the tall grass and undergrowth, not only for security against large animals, but as a defence against the tsetse flies that may mistake your vehicle for a large animal.

Until 2007, the most obvious focus in Tsavo East was the formerly beautiful **Aruba Dam** on the Voi River, the marshy fringes of which were an excellent spot for bird- and animal-watching, and where decrepit *Aruba Lodge* nestled in the trees on the north shore. Sadly, a large tour operator has ruined the area with an obtrusive new mass-market lodge constructed inside a large fenced compound, and it will be years, if ever, before the area recovers. As of 2009, the lake was dry.

The park's **northern sector** is most easily accessed from Mtito Andei Gate East, but in the dry season it's also possible to cross into the northern sector over the Galana river bed at junction #160, the only crossing point. Beware of mistaking mud for the smooth rock bed: unwitting drivers sometimes get stuck. On the western side of the northern sector lies a huge, ancient lava flow, in the shape of the **Yatta plateau**, stretching from Mtito Andei towards the Galana River, above the east bank of the Athi River.

Maasai Mara National Reserve

For a long list of reasons, **Maasai Mara** (no single website, but see Ⓦwww.maratriangle.org; $60; see p.62) is the best animal reserve in Kenya. Set at nearly 2000m above sea level, the reserve is a great wedge of undulating **grassland** in the remote, sparsely inhabited southwest part of the country, snuggled up against the Tanzanian border and, indeed, an extension of the even bigger **Serengeti plains** in Tanzania. This is a land of short grass and croton bushes (Mara means "spotted" because of the yellow crotons dotted on the plains), where the wind plays with the thick, green mantle after the rains and, nine months later, whips up dust devils from the baked surface. Maasai Mara's climate is relatively predictable, with ample rain, and the new grass supports an annual **wildebeest migration** of up to one and a half million animals from the dry plains of Tanzania.

At any time of year, the Mara has abundant wildlife. Whether you're watching the migration, or a pride of lions hunting, a herd of elephants grazing in the marsh, or hyenas squabbling with vultures over the carcass of a buffalo, you are conscious all the time of being in a realm apart. To travel through the reserve in

▲ Maasai, Maasai Mara

August or September, while the wildebeest are in possession, feels like being caught up in the momentum of a historic event. There are few places on earth where animals hold such dazzling sway.

With its plentiful vegetation and wildlife, the reserve's **eco-system** might at first appear resilient to the effect of huge numbers of tourists. However, the Mara is the most visited wildlife area in Kenya, and the balance between increasing tourist numbers and wildlife can't be maintained indefinitely. Off-road driving kills the protective cover of vegetation and can create dust bowls that spread like sores through the effects of natural wind and water erosion and become muddy quagmires in the rains.

The vast majority of visitors come on pre-booked air or road safari packages, which can work out cheaper than making independent arrangements. If you're travelling on a budget, you'll have to accept that the reserve is not a cheap option and even organized budget-camping safaris can seem expensive (see p.129). While it is possible to access the area by public transport, and then camp or stay in budget establishments, the experience is likely to leave you just wishing you'd saved a little more before coming here. If you can afford it, there's nothing to stop you renting a vehicle, ideally with an experienced driver-guide (see p.67), and visiting entirely independently, while staying at camps or lodges you've booked directly.

When deciding **where to stay** in the Mara region, don't be unduly swayed by whether a lodge or camp is inside the **reserve proper**: all the **conservancies** and **group ranches** outside the reserve have excellent wildlife viewing and their own special features, and can be less crowded than the busiest parts of the reserve (accommodation listings for these areas start on p.364). If you're visiting for the migration, at some point you're going to want to head towards the Mara River to try to witness one of the famous **wildebeest crossing points**. For this, accommodation on the western side of the reserve might be a good idea, and it tends to be at a premium at that time. There's a lot to be said, however, for camps that are far from others, such as *Offbeat*, *Mara Porini* or *Cottar's*, that give you those moments early in the morning when it's just you, the animals and the sun coming up over the plain.

Access, orientation and fees

Access is most straightforward, and most expensive, by the scheduled daily **air services** from Nairobi's Wilson or JKIA airports that set down at one or more of the eight airstrips in the reserve and adjoining group ranches and conservancies (duration and order of landing depends on passengers requirements: it's quite informal). The price is around $120 each way. You can also fly to the Mara from Lewa Downs, Nanyuki, Samburu, Diani Beach and Mombasa. The turbo-prop flights are thoroughly enjoyable, with animals clearly visible below as you approach each airstrip.

If you **drive to the Mara**, you should use a 4WD vehicle. Although hard-surfaced roads are making gradual advances into the region, the final approaches still have a gravel or mud surface and that's the condition of all the routes inside the reserve and in the adjoining conservancies to the north and east. If you decide to drive, give yourself plenty of time. Check that you know the precise location and final directions for your destination, especially if it is in some remote *lugga* on one of the group ranches (getting to lodges or camps inside the reserve is usually relatively straightforward as the dirt roads are easy to follow and establishments usually signposted). Various routes and options are covered over the next couple of pages. In the reserve area, **fuel** is usually available at *Fig Tree*, *Keekorok*, *Sarova*, *Serena* and *Simba* lodges, but as usual you should carry a full, spare jerrican.

Without your own transport, even if you manage to get to the Mara, you'll need a vehicle if you want to do game drives, as there are no public tours. You may find a vehicle by asking around the villages at Talek, Sekenani or Ololaimutiek gates or in the neighbouring budget campsites – expect to spend $100 to $150 per day

The history of the Maasai Mara

When the reserve was created, today's familiar scene of plentiful wildlife looked very different. Traditionally, the **Maasai** lived in some harmony with the wildlife, hunting only lion as a ritual exercise and, in times of famine, the beasts they called "wild cattle", the eland and buffalo. When the first European **hunting safaris** made the Mara world-famous in the early years of the last century, the white hunters were ransacking a region recently deserted by the Maasai. Smallpox had ravaged the Maasai communities and rinderpest had torn through their cattle herds. By 1961, the white hunters had succeeded in bringing the Mara's lion population down to nine, and the Maasai Mara (sometimes spelled Masai Mara) was created as a game sanctuary to be administered by the Maasai District Council at Narok. In 2001, management of the **Mara Triangle**, the section of the reserve west of the Mara River, administered by the Trans-Mara County Council based at Kilgoris, was handed over to a body called the **Mara Conservancy**, a non-profit management company. Over the last decade, management of this area has been considerably better than in the rest of the reserve, with greater transparency of gate receipts, better success against poachers, and improved road maintenance. Outside the reserve proper to the north, most of the Maasai **group ranches** east of the Mara river have in recent years converted from pasturelands to wildlife conservancies, and all of them now have their own entry fees, usually levied by the camps and lodges where guests stay. Safari operators and local community leaders have recently transformed much of the largest group ranch, Koiyaki, into the **Mara North Conservancy**.

to rent some kind of serviceable van, pick-up or 4WD, with a driver. As well as the usual $50–70 game drives available at most lodges and the larger tented camps, you can often find $20–30 game drives (depending on group size) at the budget camps near the eastern gates. You'll need to pay reserve, group ranch or conservancy fees pretty much wherever you go.

Roads and sectors

Fast **roads**, with improved, hard-core surfaces and theoretically uncrossable banks and ditches alongside them (to deter off-road driving), have been laid in various parts of the reserve, especially in the east, and there is now a good all-weather route from Talek Gate to Sekenani Gate, inside the reserve. During the rains, however, and for some weeks after, the western parts of the reserve can be very wet and treacherous.

The only permanent route across the Mara River is the long haul between *Keekork* and *Mara Serena* via Mara New Bridge on the southern boundary. Heading north from *Mara Serena* to Oloololo Gate, however, the main road skirts the western edge of Olpunyata Swamp, which is completely impassable in wet weather. Similarly dreadful is the shorter but ill-defined jumble of tracks known as the New Mara Serena Road, on the eastern edge of the swamp, for which you'd definitely need a guide in wet weather, and plenty of time even in the dry season. Likewise, the crossings over the tributaries of the Talek are often impassable.

In terms of structuring your visit, think of the reserve proper in three parts. In the far west you have the **Mara Conservancy**, also known as the **Mara Triangle**, between the Mara River and the Oloololo Escarpment. This lush, green area is only accessible from Oloololo Gate in the north, or by crossing the Mara New Bridge in the far south. Then you have the **Musiara sector** in the north, which is bounded by the Mara and Talek rivers, and is the location of *Governor's Camp* and *Intrepids*. Some of the most photogenic wildebeest river-crossings can be seen here. And finally you have the **Sekenani sector**, the largest part of the reserve, bordered by the Talek, Mara and Sand rivers, with *Keekorok*, the oldest lodge in the reserve, in its centre.

Outside the reserve, nearly a dozen **conservancies**, **group ranches** and **private game ranches**, usually run in partnership with the local Maasai communities, offer wildlife-viewing that is often the equal of what you'll see in the reserve proper – increasingly reflected in their management practices, conservation work and prices. From 2011, the most important of these, the **Mara North Conservancy**, will become a zone exclusively for the use of the camps and lodges that are its members, with the aim of limiting visitor numbers and excluding outside minibus tours.

Reserve, group ranch and conservancy fees

Reserve, group ranch and conservancy fees are best handled by your safari operator or lodge/camp. They will add the cost to your bill (you may never see the tickets, but if you have any concerns, check that hologrammed tickets for your stay have been issued and stamped). Mara Conservancy tickets, covering the Mara Triangle, are transferable to the Musiara-Sekenani side of the reserve, and vice versa. The rangers at gates and airstrips invariably accept cash only. Group ranch and conservancy tickets, which should also have a silver hologram set across the central tear, usually cost the same, or a little more than reserve tickets, and are, unfortunately, not usually valid for the reserve itself (although some group ranches have swung deals with the reserve authorities to include a certain duration inside the reserve for each visitor). Like reserve tickets, group ranch tickets work on a 24-hour basis. This means in practice that most visitors staying in the reserve don't venture north into the group ranches, while visitors staying on group-ranch based properties usually make just one, full-day trip into the reserve proper, especially during the migration, when some camps cover this cost themselves.

Access from Narok

Driving to the Mara **from Nairobi**, you take the lower road to Naivasha, down the escarpment, turning left at the unpleasantly burgeoning truck stop of **Mai Mahiu** (allow one to two hours to get here from Nairobi depending on traffic). The newly surfaced 92-kilometre road from Mai Mahiu to **Narok** (not much more than an hour's drive) is mostly in excellent condition and you sweep across stupendous vistas of range lands. Cattle are the economic mainstay here, but extensive wheat fields are pushing south. Once through Narok, if you branch left onto the **C12 highway** after 3km, the road makes its way south towards **Sekenani Gate** and the eastern section of the reserve, where *Keekorok Lodge* and the eastern reserve headquarters are the main human focuses. This route has a good surface for around half its length, and the remaining gravel section to the gate is also in decent condition. Allow two hours from Narok to the gate.

Access to the western end of the reserve from Nairobi is much faster since completion of the **B3 highway** linking Narok with Sotik. West of the C12 turn-off outside Narok, there are three main turnings south off the B3. The first is at **Olulungu**, 32km west of Narok, signposted to *Mara Safari Club*. This route goes via the small centres of **Ngorengore** and **Lemek** and becomes the notorious **C13**. The second turning off the highway, 51km from Narok, is signposted to Ngorengore and eventually joins up with the C13. Even with a 4WD, the C13 is for dry weather only, and even then has very difficult patches of deep mud along the way. If it's been raining, the wet clay can make escaping from ruts impossible. The third turning south off the B3 is at **Mulot**, 53km from Narok, where a private road (toll Ksh500) takes you south, a few kilometres away from the west bank of the Mara river towards *Mara Safari Club* and others outside the reserve, and ultimately joins the C13 a few kilometres short of the **Musiara Gate**.

Narok

NAROK is the funnel through which the majority of road transport enters the Mara. It's a bumpy, hustly mess, but is the last guarantee of fuel, a cold drink or almost anything for more than 80km before you enter the reserve. If you arrive here after 5pm, you may well end up having to stay the night, as you won't have time to get into the reserve itself by nightfall (the gates close at 7pm).

Despite its touts and garish tourist bazaars full of carvings and beads, Narok is lively and interesting, always full of Maasai on shopping expeditions or doing business at the market (on the higher north side of the town centre, to the right as you go through town towards the Mara). The small but perfectly formed **Narok Maa Cultural Museum** (daily 9am–6pm; Ksh200), after the Kobil station, on the right as you come into town, is an excellent introduction to the Maasai way of life. The walls have a fascinating collection of photographs taken by Maasai women.

Practicalities

The main **matatu** stage is across from Kenol on the west side of town. Matatus from Narok run through the group ranches along the C13 via Mara Rianta to Lolgorien (and occasionally as far as Migori). You're likely to see lots of plains game along the way – so long as you can see out of the window – so you could, at a pinch, get a flavour of the Mara district eco-system without entering the reserve proper or paying any fees (public transport using this route is exempt). Local matatus also run to Sekenani Gate at least twice each day. Again, if your budget doesn't stretch to any kind or organized safari, this is better than nothing. See overleaf for information about where to stay on a budget.

Barclays, on the north side of the main road, opposite the **post office**, halfway down the hill, and the KCB, also on the left, 300m west of Kobil, further down the hill, both have **ATMs**. There's **internet** access at Sky Apple Enterprises on the left, 100m past Barclays.

The best place for a **drink or a bite to eat** is *Kenol Restaurant* (daily 6.45am–10.30pm), part of the Kenol petrol station and supermarket, under the trees on the left side of the main road heading out of town on the west side. They do good **food** and fresh juices. *Hillside Club*, on the south side of the main road on the way into town, with a terrace overlooking the street, does good chicken and *kienyeji*, and at night features a bizarre mix of traditionally garbed Maasai and westernized Kenyans drinking and listening to reggae.

Accommodation

Almis Guest House Around the corner from the Hass petrol station (turn right at Hass, and right again) ☎0722/7931212. Large rooms, with instant showers and nets, though some bathrooms are only separated by shower curtains from the rest of the room. Good security and space for one or two cars to park safely in the courtyard. ❶

Aminstar Further up the hill past the *Almis* ☎0723/234744. Busy, Somali-run place with 27 rooms and a welcome "no prostitution" policy. Third-floor rooms have double beds, nets, instant showers and TVs (but few outside windows), while rooms on the second floor are twins with no nets (but with TVs and instant showers). The decent restaurant serves tasty pillaus and other dishes. ❶

Chambai Up on the north side of town behind the mosque ☎050/22591 or 0722/957609. This, the tallest building in town, has Narok's best rooms. Clean and spacious, they have nets, instant showers and TVs. Overall, a very decent place, with a bar and restaurant and a big, safe car park. ❷

Access from Bomet and the west

Approaching the Maasai Mara from Kisumu, Kericho or Kisii, all routes converge on **BOMET**, an overblown village of just three streets running round the back of the petrol station, and containing a small market, a few meagre *hotelis* and *dukas*, a KCB (with ATM), a post office, and some very basic lodgings. Past Bomet, the surfaced **B3** heads southeast for Narok, crossing the Amala/Mara River. The easiest route into the reserve is via the toll road from the Mulot junction, mentioned on p.359. A difficult alternative is the unpaved **C14** for Sigor and Kaboson, but though shorter than going via Mulot, this is very rough and difficult to navigate; stop regularly along the way to check with local people that you're on the right track. The first important (and unmarked) turning is about 5km south of Bomet. At **Kaboson** the C14 continues northwest, back towards Kilgoris and Kisii; turn off left in order to cross the Mara River and join the **C13**.

Access from Tanzania

Entry is not permitted directly from Tanzania's Serengeti National Park into the Maasai Mara at the Maasai Mara reserve's Sand River Gate, and there are no other gates or routes between the two. Most people coming from Tanzania, cross the border at Sirari-Isebania and head north 20km to Suna-Migori, before turning east on the unsurfaced C13 road towards the Mara. See p.275 for the start of this route. Once you reach **Lolgorien**, 46km from Suna, the road is mostly good *murram* all the way through to the Mara, with turnings to the long-closed *Olkurruk Mara Lodge* after 65km and *Kensington Mara West Camp* after 66km. After 70km you reach the junction for the road down to **Oloololo Gate**. Keep going northeast and you cross the Mara River, climb up to the straggling settlement of **Mara Rianta** and then reach the turning down to the **Musiara Gate**.

Accommodation

The region's hundred-odd **lodges and camps** are scattered across the national reserve and the adjoining group ranches and conservancies. Although competition between them keeps standards fairly high in every price range, it's worth choosing where to stay very carefully, as they vary greatly in style and atmosphere: one person's sumptuous luxury will be another's garish opulence, while a place that seems delightfully informal and in keeping with the environment to one visitor may just come across as a bit plain and unpolished to another. Regardless of how long you stay, all the lodges and camps, with the exception of the budget places outside the reserve, operate on at least full board (FB) basis, and their rates include all meals. They expect guests to arrive for lunch and leave after breakfast. Some are set up to provide a "package", which includes all meals and drinks, including alcohol, and two or more game drives per day. **Booking ahead** is essential, especially at popular times (Christmas/New Year and the July–September migration season).

The mid-range to luxury **lodges** and **tented camps** vary greatly in price, and offer vastly different levels of service. There's nothing intrinsically cheaper about sleeping under canvas. Quite the opposite, in fact: the cheaper places are pack-'em-in lodges, while the most expensive establishments are boutique tented camps, with rosters of bronze and silver guides among the staff. Except where noted, all the mainstream lodges and camps have vehicles and driver-guides on site. Neither FB nor package prices usually include reserve or conservancy fees: allow another $60 to $90 per person per day.

Camps and lodges on the **conservancies and group ranches** outside the reserve are able to offer guided walks and night drives. Not all do so, and night drives are being discouraged in some areas, but walking (strictly a daytime activity) is highly recommended if you get the chance: you will need to sign a disclaimer, and will be accompanied by an armed guard. These are also the areas where horseriding safaris, and occasional escorted cycling safaris, operate.

Camping

Simple **campsites** are found at several of the gates and generally charge around Ksh500 per person per night. Most have only the most basic facilities, though drinking water is usually available. You can expect some good-natured pestering by rangers and others, who will try to extract money by guiding you on game drives in your vehicle. Note that the Oloololo and Musiara gates have no nearby settlements (the village of Mara Rianta is a few kilometres to the north), while outside the Talek, Sekenani and Ololaimutiek gates, ramshackle "villages" of *mabati* houses, shops and bars have sprung up. The most remote of the reserve gates, Sand River Gate, has no settlement and very limited facilities.

The Triangle has eight "**private campsites**" in excellent locations, but with no facilities whatsoever. These are for exclusive use, and there's a Ksh7500 per week booking fee in addition to the $25 per person daily fee (enquiries via Ⓦ www.maratriangle.org/campsite-bookings).

If you're travelling independently on a low budget, or you're on one of the budget camping safaris (probably sleeping in little dome tents or the basic *bandas* available near some of the gates), be particularly careful about general security and theft, and beware of **baboons**. These sometimes intimidating monkeys are prone to grab anything that looks inviting, whether edible or not, and dash off with it to examine it later. You would be asking for trouble if you left your tent unguarded. If you can't be sure that the whole site is completely safe and supervised, then you'll need to leave an *askari* behind on an agreed fee to guard your tent while you're out on game drives. Or else pack up completely each morning.

Remember, even as a basic, DIY camper, you're expected to pay **reserve or conservancy fees**, depending on which bit of grass your tent is pitched on.

Mara Conservancy Headquarters The *Iseiya* and *Elaui* campsites are near the Triangle's Iseiya headquarters and *Mara Serena Safari Lodge*. Despite being close to human activity, their facilities are very limited. $25.

Oloololo Gate Welcoming campsite run by the Mara Conservancy, with showers and toilets and wonderful views of the escarpment. You can drive to nearby Mara Rianta village for basic supplies. $25.

Sand River Gate Best of the gate campsites, with toilets, water and firewood available and nicely located in a spot where animals come to drink at night. This site acquired notoriety after the murder here of Julie Ward in 1988, but there's no reason to let that deter you. No nearby supplies. $15.

Sekenani Gate The campsite at the gate itself is pretty basic, but 2km down the track to the east, the public campsite at *Olperr Elongo Camp* (ⓦ www.biketreks.co.ke) has toilets, showers and good security. $10.

Talek Gate There are quite a few campsites along the north bank of the Talek River, east of the gate. Several are the permanent bases of camping safari operators, including Best Camping and Gametrackers. *Riverside Campsite*, five minutes' walk west of the bridge and Talek Gate, is a well-established, Maasai-owned, public site with a shared kitchen, hot showers and flush toilets. Ksh400.

Budget tented camps and banda sites

The following places are outside the Sekenani and Ololaimutiek gates and offer simple tents, with beds and bedding, and usually basic *bandas*.

Acacia Camp Ololaimutiek Gate ⓣ0736/255224 or 0728/415572. A well-run place, owned by the African Travel Company and mostly catering for overland tours. Meals, on request ($10). Camping (Ksh500) or 2-bedded ridge tents, with shared showers and toilets (but bedding $10 extra). ❸

Amicabre Camp Ololaimutiek Gate ⓦwww .amicabretravel.com. Pleasant site, with small tents with separate shower and toilet blocks. Limited bar and catering possibilities. ❶

Big Time Camp Ololaimutiek Gate ⓣ020/2218841 or 0722/570722, ⓦwww.bigtimeholidays.com. Busy and well looked after, with shady groves for the tents, and an on-site bar-restaurant. BB ❸

Enchoro Wildlife Camp Ololaimutiek Gate ⓣ0710/322787, ⓦtinyurl.com/yh53rc3. A cut above the very cheapest places near this gate, on a shady site, with decent-sized, s/c ridge tents under

shelters and a bar-restaurant. Dorm beds also available ($10). FB ❺

Mara Sidai Camp Ololaimutiek Gate ⓣ0723/147289. The best of the bunch near this gate, on a shady site, with neat little ridge tents under shelters, and a small bar-restaurant. BB ❸

Mara Springs Camp Sekenani Gate ⓣ020/242133 ⓦtinyurl.com/m7xwww. Large site, with a number of options, including basic, ridge tents, and permanent tents with built-in WC and shower, supplied with generator electricity. The ablutions blocks are basic, but quite clean. BB ❸

Riverside Camp Talek Gate ⓣ0720/218319 or 0733/994181, ⓦwww .riversidecampmara.com. For the Mara, this offers excellent value, with neat s/c *bandas* (though no fans or nets), some with good river views, plus a dining room and bar. BB ❹

Lodges and camps in the National Reserve

The **accommodation** inside the reserve includes affordable mainstream lodges (*Mara Simba*) and one of the most expensive camps in the region (*Governors' Il Moran*). Inevitably, key routes, river crossings and animal viewing spots can become crowded in the reserve, especially over Christmas and during the migration.

The Mara Conservancy (Mara Triangle)

Little Governors' Camp On the west bank of the Mara, in the Mara Triangle just upstream from *Governor's Il Moran* (Musiara Airstrip) ☎ 020/2734000, ⓦ www.governorscamp.com. Accessed from the Musiara sector by a rope-pulled boat across the Mara, and hidden in the trees, with wonderful birdwatching, this has seventeen tents, all facing an oxbow marsh of the Mara. There's no fence and plenty of animal action, with elephants, buffaloes and hippos keeping the *askaris* very busy. But the tents' style (or lack of) is very similar to that of the other camps in the *Governors'* group. Package $972.

Mara Serena Safari Lodge On a hilltop in the Mara Triangle, above the Mara River (Serena Airstrip) ☎ 050/22253 or 0733/222500, ⓦ www.serenahotels.com. Located in the heart of the Triangle, close to the migration crossings, this lodge is intriguingly designed, based on a recreation of two Maasai *enkangs*, with smallish but appealingly cellular, cave-like rooms, with nets. Most have good views. Pool. FB $430.

Musiara sector

Governors' Main Camp On the east bank of the Mara, near Musiara Gate (Musiara Airstrip) ☎ 020/2734000, ⓦ www.governorscamp.com. Close to the fantastic game-viewing of the Musiara marsh, this large, busy, highly regarded operation has 37 tents – 28 facing the river and 9 facing the plain. Unfortunately, with heavily framed tents, basic furniture and utilitarian bathrooms, their standards are slipping relative to other camps. The three *Governors'* camps have two bronze guides between them. Package $990.

Governors' Il Moran Camp On the east bank of the Mara, just upstream from the main *Governors'* (Musiara Airstrip) ☎ 020/2734000, ⓦ www.governorscamp.com. The ten huge, steel-framed tents, which all face the river (though unfortunately the camp footpath runs in front of tents 1–5) are old-fashioned and mounted on ugly concrete plinths, but more spacious and better furnished than the main camp. When you're paying this much, however, you'd at least expect some comfy seating on your terrace. With the blandly featureless bar and mess area, this is massively overpriced. Package $1288.

Mara Bush Camp Close to Ol Kiombo Airstrip, on the banks of the Olare Orok ⓦ www.marabushcamp.com. Operated by the excellent Sunworld Safaris

(see p.130) and open only for the wildebeest migration, this is a highly recommended, ten-tent camp, offering tremendous value for money. Battery-charging in the lounge tent while the generator is on from 6.30–11pm. Closed Nov–June. FB ❽

Mara Explorer On the north bank of the Talek River, just upstream from sister camp *Mara Intrepids* (Ol Kiombo Airstrip) ☎ 050/23054 or 0722/105333, ⓦ www.heritage-eastafrica.com. Upmarket sister of *Mara Intrepids*, this boutique camp is very peaceful, with seven double and three twin open-plan tents, all with decks facing the river, and open-air baths. As it's unfenced, guests use radios to summon the *askaris* after dark. Generator until midnight (sockets in tents). Guests can use *Intrepids'* pool, with free transfers. *Explorer* and *Intrepids* share three bronze guides & one gold. Closed mid-April to mid-June. Package $1185.

Mara Intrepids On the north bank of the Talek, just downstream from sister camp *Mara Explorer* (Ol Kiombo Airstrip) ☎ 050/23054 or 0722/105333, ⓦ www.heritage-eastafrica.com. This shady camp of thirty tents (all with four-poster beds and nets) on a bluff overlooking the river is a perennial family favourite – the *huge* family tents have a double, a twin and a large living area (room for up to six). Popular activities clubs for children and teens, watchtower (very good for migration photos), and pool. Three bronze guides & one gold. Package $940.

Rekero Camp On the north bank of the Talek, close to its confluence with the Mara (Ol Kiombo Airstrip) ⓦ www.rekero.com. Seasonal tented camp, in dense woods in the middle of the reserve, and excitingly in the thick of the migration from July to October. You rely on solar power (central battery-charging), kerosene lamps, and bucket showers and enjoy convivial evenings with fellow guests, guides and hosts (many bronze guides and one silver), surrounded by the noises of the night. Closed April & May. Package $1220.

Sekenani sector

Keekorok Lodge In the heart of the reserve's Sekenani sector (Keekorok Airstrip) ☎ 050/22680 or 0733/999916, ⓦ www.wildernesslodges.co.ke. This 101-room lodge is the oldest in the reserve, dating from 1963. Although the smallish rooms and furnishings are showing their age, the Keekorok eco-system adjusted long ago to the lodge's presence, and there's good game-viewing in the vicinity. The hippo bar and elephant deck, out on the boardwalk in the papyrus swamp, are a bonus.

▲ Ballon safari

Good pool, and the best shop in the Mara. One bronze & one silver guide. FB $440.

Mara Simba Lodge On the south bank of the Talek River, 6km northwest of Sekenani Gate (Keekorok Airstrip) ☎050/222590, ⓦwww.marasimba.com. Opened in 2005, this has 84 identical hotel-style rooms in blocks of four, with fans, all overlooking the river, and seventeen cabin-style "tents". Public areas are on decks ranged out over the Talek. Usually the busiest lodge in the Mara, with an international mix of guests, and the cheapest in the reserve itself by some margin. Pool. FB ❼

Sarova Mara Camp Off the main C12 entrance road, 2km inside Sekenani Gate (Keekorok Airstrip) ☎050/22386 or 0736/187002, ⓦwww.sarovahotels.com. The most accessible of the reserve's camps and lodges is well managed and always busy and welcoming, with plenty of nice touches, such as vegetarian options at every meal. The large pool and jungly gardens are fun, and it's worth seeking out James Saruni Ole Tira, the charming on-site elder and naturalist. FB $503.

Kimintet Group Ranch and Oloololo Game Ranch

Carved out of the **Kimintet Group Ranch**, on the west bank of the Mara, the ten square-kilometre private **Oloolo Game Ranch** adjoins the main reserve, with access to the Mara Triangle, via the Oloololo Gate, just minutes away. Oloololo is the subject of an ongoing dispute between its foreign owners and their Maasai partners and the rest of the Kimintet community. Ranch fees are included in overnight stays.

Bateleur Camp Adjoining *Kichwa Tembo* on Oloololo Game Ranch (Kichwa Tembo Airstrip) ☎050/22464, ⓦtinyurl.com/ld3odj. More exclusive than its co-owned neighbour, this has eighteen, very comfort-able, cabin-style "tents" with huge bathrooms, tucked in two wings among the trees on either side of a small lap pool, each with a four-poster bed and an armchair-furnished deck overlooking the plains. Both camps are discreetly fenced, lie on the fringe of a belt of African greenheart forest, and have superb birdlife. Package $1000.

Kichwa Tembo Camp Adjoining *Bataleur*, on Oloololo Game Ranch ☎050/22465, ⓦtinyurl .com/ackln2. Emerging from the trees at the foot of the Oloololo Escarpment, this long-established favourite has excellent food and, unusually, two female driver-guides. The modestly furnished, old-fashioned tents are basic for the price, and have no electric sockets (battery-charging and wi-fi are available in the central area). It's great for children, however, with a lovely decked pool and large lawns facing the plains. Package $1000.

Balloon flights

At around $450 per person for the ninety-minute flight plus a breakfast with sparkling wine, **"balloon safaris"** are the ultimate safari treat. Just watching the inflation and lift-off at dawn is a spectacular sight. In order to avoid frightening the animals unduly, however, there is a minimum height below which the balloons are not permitted to fly. It's a memorable experience, but photographic opportunities can be limited, depending on the light (don't bank on every shot being a winner: the animals are mostly far below). If you're not staying at a lodge or camp with a launch site, the operators will come and pick you up. After breakfast, you do a game drive on your way back to your lodge. Depending on your budget, you may want to leave your booking until the last minute, as two-for-one deals are sometimes available. Operators include:

Adventures Aloft Ⓦwww.madahotels.com. Flights from *Fig Tree* and *Siana Springs* camps.

Balloon Safaris Ⓦtinyurl.com/yh72bwu. Flights from *Keekorok*.

Governors' Balloon Safaris Ltd Ⓦtinyurl.com/lyyhqr. Flights from *Little Governors' Camp*.

Transworld Kenya Ⓦwww.transworldsafaris.com. Flights from *Sarova*, *Serena* and *Mara Safari Club*.

Olonana On the west bank of the Mara on Kimintet GR (Kichwa Tembo Airstrip) ☎020/6950002 or 020/6950244, Ⓦwww.sanctuarylodges.com. Lavishly appointed eco-camp, with comfortable public areas and huge tented rooms, which have spectacular views over the river. *Olonana* is unusual for the personal attention it pays to guests and the welcome extended to children. Pool and spa. FB, including drinks, $1060.

Mara North Conservancy

A large part of Koiyaki Group Ranch is now the 320-square kilometre **Mara North Conservancy** (Ⓦwww.masaimaranorthconservancy.com; daily fee $60), though some of the camps that are members of the conservancy are not geographically on Koiyaki land. The MNC is classic savanna bush country, the land broken into ridges by bush-choked *luggas*, and with high densities of game. The wildlife includes several, much-studied lion prides, such as the Acacia pride and the Gorge pride, named after the iconic **Leopard Gorge**, 5km northeast of Musiara Gate.

Elephant Pepper Camp Off the C13 in the MNC (Shikar Airstrip) ☎020/603054, Ⓦwww.elephantpeppercamp.com. In a dense grove, with eight lovely tents pitched in two wings each side of the stylish central area, this is owned by boutique safari operator Cheli & Peacock, on a private lease of four square kilometres. The camp uses a non-permanent construction (no cement), for minimal impact and is entirely solar-powered; they have five bronze guides. Closed 1 April–15 June. Package $1090.

Karen Blixen Camp On the east bank of the Mara, in the MNC (Shikar Airstrip) ☎0737/499707 or 020/883898, Ⓦwww.karenblixencamp.com. Danish-owned, this innovative, unfenced camp has 22 tents along the river (home to forty hippos) or on raised platforms.

Although the environment is still adjusting, the naturalistic grounds (all trees and bushes planted come from within a 5km radius), grey-water recycling and gas water-heaters for each tent, are all promising signs. Tents have cooler-boxes and 24hr solar-powered sockets. Small pool. FB $610.

Kicheche Camp On Lemek Group Ranch, but a member of the MNC (Ngerende Airstrip) ☎020/890541 or 0733/607786, Ⓦwww.kicheche.com. Located in a thickly wooded, animal-rich *lugga*, this is personally hosted and great value, with a maximum of 22 guests in big, comfy, new tents, with bucket showers to order and views across the plains. A favourite with photographers, Kicheche has near-resident cheetahs and leopards, as well as excellent meals and 24hr electricity. Ten bronze and five silver

5

guides. The adjoining *Kicheche Private Camp*, with seven smaller tents and its own kitchen and mess, is cheaper and ideal for a group. Closed April & May. Package $730.

Offbeat Mara In the MNC (Musiara Airstrip) ☎0722/433268 or 0735/667421, ⓦwww .offbeatsafaris.com. A hidden jewel in the Mara, this exceptional, boutique tented camp is unusually informal, unpretentious and enjoyable. The six reasonably sized tents are surrounded by untrammelled bush – no clipped lawns or electric fences here, nor any other vehicles around, just fantastic wildlife right in front of you. Charming hosts, really outstanding staff and silver guides, and excellent, generous meals and wine. Package $800.

Royal Mara Safari Lodge On the east bank of the Mara, in the MNC (Shikar Airstrip) ☎020/7123356, ⓦwww.royalmara.com. New camp, with eight vast, ostentatious tented cabins that appear to have cost half the Mara's forests in their construction. With beds and chairs hewn from tree trunks and every varnished surface covered in carvings and fussy details, it won't suit everyone, but the care taken with guests, and the cuisine, service and game drives here have all been commended. Motorized bicycles available, and tame eland orphans in camp. Competitively priced. Package $800.

Saruni Far to the north, in the MNC (Ngerende Airstrip) ☎0734/764616, ⓦwww.sarunicamp.com. One of Cheli & Peacock's very stylish properties, with just six, roomy, breezy cottages overlooking a bird- and game-filled valley far to the north of the Mara plains, which you can see through a cleft in the hills. With very good food, free wi-fi, awesome showers and the wonderful Masai Wellbeing Space (free massage with each booking), this is a highly recommended base, especially if you're as happy doing local game walks as game drives. One bronze & two silver guides. Package $1190.

Serian Spanning the Mara, 6km north of the C13 road, in the MNC ☎0735/922222 or 0735/427077, ⓦwww.serian.net. Owned by rugby fan and former hunter Alex Walker, this is one of the region's most attractive and individual-istic camps, with seven tents on the east bank and four more (called *Ngare Serian*) across the river via a splendid suspension bridge. The super-comfort-able tents are dubbed "marquees" and bathrooms are daringly "adjoining" rather than en-suite. A private driver-guide for each tent is part of the package. With generator electricity only in public areas, and solar and kerosene in tents for lighting, this is a stylish lesson in how to create a beautiful and eco-friendly camp. Package $1150.

Olare Orok Conservancy

The 230-square-kilometre **Olare Orok Conservancy** (ⓦwww.oocmara.com; daily fee $80, allows access to the reserve), on the reserve boundary north of the Musiara sector, is unusual for its highly focused conservation work and the success of its community integration. Funds are channelled from visitors to the Maasai landowners, who also have access to the conservancy's grasslands during times of drought. Tusk Trust and the International Fund for Animal Welfare are both donors, and the wildlife-viewing is exceptional, with all the predators present.

Mara Plains Camp On the Ntiakatek River and also a member of Mara North Conserv-ancy (Ol Kiombo Airstrip) ☎0732/242389, ⓦwww .maraplains.com. Tucked into woodland, surrounded by open savanna, the former *Films Safaris Camp* has eight, elegant, hexagonal tents on decks (two facing the plains, six the river). Superb views from the front of the camp go clear across the migration grazing grounds. Run by film and photography pros who share their expert knowledge. 24hr generator and tent sockets. One gold guide. Package $1220.

Porini Lion Camp Near the seasonal Ntiakatek River (Ol Kiombo Airstrip) ☎020/7123129,

ⓦwww.porini.com. Silver eco-rated camp managed in collaboration with the local Maasai community, in a brilliant game-viewing area particularly renowned for big cats – far from other camps, but close enough to the reserve if you want. The ten, very spacious and airy tents are run as responsibly as possible, with full recycling, and the staff, all from the local community, are paid significantly higher wages than the norm. Guests eat together. Bronze & silver guides. Closed mid-April to end May. Package, including all fees, $1280.

Ol Choro Oirowua Conservancy

A private conservancy bounded by the Mara River, the 70-square-kilometre **Ol Choro Oirouwa** (ⓦolchorro.blogspot.com; daily fee $40) is a largely pristine area. It's away from the routes of most visitors, and while it's also off the wildebeest migration route, the relative absence of other tourist vehicles makes game drives very rewarding. There's a highly regarded rhino sanctuary here (see p.373).

Fairmont Mara Safari Club On the east bank of the Mara, off the C14 (Ngerende Airstrip) ℡020/2216840, ⓦwww.fairmont.com. Modish, rather formal tented camp, with fifty riverside tents, in shady grounds linked by concrete paths. It's a peaceful base, with a beautiful public deck area and heated pool, and very large, tile-floored tents (though a little closer together than you might want at these prices), with four-poster mosquito net beds and city-hotel amenities. Wi-fi available. FB $618.

Richard's Camp In Ol Choro Oirouwa Conservancy (Ngerende Airstrip) ℡0733/700015, ⓦwww.richardscamp.com. A very enjoyable, high-end bush camp, run by an energetic, fun-loving team, with eight tents, solar lighting, hot water by the big bucketful and battery-charging in the office. The owner Richard Roberts is a pilot, and his Cessna 180 or little yellow biplane are available for scenic flights over the Mara (or wherever you can afford). Three bronze guides & one silver. Closed May. Package $1190.

Olderikesi Group Ranch

The remote **Olderikesi group ranch** (ⓦtinyurl.com/yfaox6s; daily fee $90), southeast of the main reserve, has only one, spectacular, **camp** – *Cottar's*. The district is teeming with wildlife (including some huge lions), especially since the camp negotiated an agreement with the Maasai stakeholders in the area to create a "no cattle" zone around the camp in exchange for the community charges levied from visitors.

Cottar's 1920s Camp On Olderikesi GR, close to the Tanzanian border (Keekorok airstrip) ℡0733/479752 or satellite +86/7253/04417254, ⓦwww.cottars.com. The finely tuned retro atmosphere, organic gardens and ten huge, sumptuous tents are just the icing on the cake, for this is one of the best wildlife camps in Kenya, in a game-rich area, with a low human population density. Exceptionally good vehicles, and the bronze guide and two silver guides are outstanding. Pool. Package $1560.

Ol Kinyei Conservancy

A new conservancy, with just one camp from which the local group ranch members benefit substantially, **Ol Kinyei** (fees included in overnight stays) covers 35 square-kilometres of bush and plain. Happily bypassed by the lines of vehicles driving between Narok and Sekenani gate, this is an area in which guided walks and a good degree of cultural immersion are the norm. *Ol Seki Camp* is just outside Ol Kinyei, on a private concession on Koiyaki Group Ranch.

Mara Porini Camp 5km west of the C12 road (Siana Airstrip) ℡020/7123129, ⓦwww.porini.com. Like other *Porini* camps, in the Amboseli area and further west in the Mara (see *Porini Lion*, opposite), this eco-camp is run in partnership with the local community. The unfenced camp has just six very nice tents and a communal mess. Game walks are a popular feature and guests eat together – the intimate atmosphere is a million miles from the Mara's mainstream lodges. Bronze & silver guides. Closed mid-April & May. Package, including all fees, $1210.

Ol Seki Camp On the Koiyaki Group Ranch, 10km west of the C12 road (Siana Airstrip) ℡020/2425060 or 0733/822870, ⓦwww.olseki .com. On a bluff at the end of a ridge, with a 270-degree panorama, *Ol Seki* (*ol seki* is the sandpaper tree, which conveys peace and harmony) has just six, wonderful twelve-sided tents on platforms, with mind-blowing views and amazing sunsets. Eco-friendly char-dust briquettes provide 24hr hot water; most of the staff are local; and $30 per bed night goes to the local community. Closed April & May. Package, including all fees, $1380.

Oloirien Group Ranch

Most of the land of this huge group ranch (no fees), lies west of the Oloolo Escarpment, far from the main areas of the reserve, and as a consequence the district is relatively little visited. To the south of the one, spectacularly sited lodge, *Kensington Mara West*, lies the abandoned *Olkkurruk Mara Lodge*, built to house Sidney Pollack and his actors Robert Redford and Meryl Streep, during the filming of *Out of Africa* in 1985.

Kensington Mara West On the crest of the Oloololo Escarpment, overlooking the Mara Triangle (Kichwa Tembo Airstrip) ☏0734/849293, ⊛www.marawest.com. Perched to enjoy some of the best views over the Mara, this unusual, small and very good value tented camp is twenty to thirty minutes' from the Mara Triangle. Accommodation is in economy tents with shared bathrooms (FB ⑥) or very comfortable en-suite "tented chalets". FB ⑧

Siana Group Ranch and Conservancy

Siana Group Ranch (⊛tinyurl.com/yz4zv39; daily fee $40) covers a vast area, stretching from Sekenani Gate to Ololaimutiek Gate. It includes numerous budget camps and *banda* sites, especially near the gates, but the full involvement of the local Purko Maasai community has only recently started. The core **Conservancy** area being promoted by *Siana Springs* and *Sekenani Camp* will be a 100-square-kilometre, minibus-free, wildllife sanctuary.

Mara Hippo Safari Lodge outside Ololaimutiek Gate ☏0725/355549, ⊛www.marahippo.co.ke. Recently opened, in a pretty, thickly wooded valley, with 62 tents, cottages and rooms and mostly German, Dutch and Danish guests. Modest, but well managed, if somewhat overpriced for what it offers. FB ⑦

Mara Sopa Lodge outside Ololaimutiek Gate (Siana Airstrip) ☏050/22195 or 0722/567858, ⊛www.sopalodges.com. Equalling *Keekorok* (see p.363) in size, this has a hundred rooms, all quite spacious and with pull-around nets. The public areas are impressive and there's a good pool overlooking the wooded valley but it's more of a resort than a game lodge. There's little wildlife to see from the lodge, even with binoculars, and it's a fair drive to the central parts of the reserve. FB ⑦

Sekenani Camp on the reserve boundary 6km southeast of Sekenani Gate (Keekorok Airstrip) ☏050/22454 or 0722/147810, ⊛www.sekenani-camp.com. Unusual and affordable camp, with a good atmosphere, on a ridge in the forest. Tents are all on raised platforms, accessed through tunnels cut through the trees, with bathrooms nicely illuminated by plastic sheeting in the *mabati* roofs above the tents. The area sees elephants, buffaloes and lots of birdlife. Well worth considering if you've been to the Mara before and want somewhere a little different. FB ⑧

Siana Springs Intrepids on Siana Group Ranch, 7km east of the C12 road (Siana Airstrip) ☏050/22553 or 0722/761993, ⊛www.heritage-eastafrica.com. Although somewhat remotely sited, the mature forest here, with ponds and lawns on a 45-acre plot, and colobus monkeys, warthogs and other wildlife in camp, makes this worth considering, especially for families – and there's a nice pool. The old-style tents are tidy and decent, but nothing to write home about. Two bronze guides. FB $825.

Talek area of Koiyaki Group Ranch

The mostly mainstream camps and lodges along the north bank of the Talek are often thought of as being inside the reserve. In fact they are all in the southern-most part of Koiyaki Group Ranch (daily fee $40), which means that game walks and night drives are possible. Although the area's human population is steadily increasing, access into the reserve itself is easy via Talek gate and the Talek bridge, with the plains of the Sekenani sector and the confluence of the Talek and Mara rivers equally close.

Basecamp On the north bank of the Talek, close to Talek Gate (Ol Kiombo Airstrip) ☏020/3877490, ⊛www.basecampexplorer.com. This award-winning camp, one of the Mara's most eco-friendly places to stay, runs on solar energy, uses composting toilets and recycles all waste. The twelve comfy tents with verandas, Kilgoris-grass-thatched roofs and open-air showers, seem to grow out of the environment. Two bronze guides & one silver. FB ⑧

Fig Tree Camp On the north bank of the Talek, close to Talek Gate (Ol Kiombo Airstrip) ☏050/22163, ⊛www.madahotels.com. Lovely location on an oxbow peninsula, but in a busy area.

The chalets in fragrant gardens, or comfortable tents overlooking the river, are all quite closely spaced. Small pool and treetop bar. Game walks ($25) and night game drives ($40) are also available. One silver guide. FB ❽

Ilkeliani Camp On the north bank of the Talek looking out onto the Mara plains (Ol Kiombo Airstrip) ☎0733/258120 or 0723/475684, ⓦwww.ilkeliani.com. Spacious and eco-friendly establishment with seventeen well-spaced tents along the river in a fifty-acre compound, with

nature walks possible. Old-style tents (with sockets for battery-charging) are powered by solar panels and a rarely needed generator. FB $450.

Tipilikwani Camp On the north bank of the Talek, 4km southeast of Talek Gate (Ol Kiombo Airstrip) ☎020/4450035, ⓦwww.atua-enkop.com. Don't be put off by the bafflingly uninviting entrance of security fences and scrub; this opened in 2007, and has excellent, light public areas, a fabulous deck and twenty alluring tents draped around a loop of the Talek. FB $780.

Game drives

The Maasai Mara is the one part of Kenya where the **concentrations of game** that existed in the nineteenth century can still be seen. The panorama sometimes resembles one of those wild-animal wall charts, where groups of unlikely looking animal companions are forced into the artist's frame. You can see a dozen different species in one gaze: gazelle, zebra, giraffe, buffalo, topi, kongoni, wildebeest, eland, elephant, hyena, jackal, ostrich, and a pride of lions waiting for a chance. The most interesting areas, scenically and zoologically, tend to be westwards, signalled by the long ridge of the Oloololo Escarpment. If you only have a day or two, and you're inside the reserve, you could do worse than spend most of your time here, near the **Mara River**.

It sometimes seems, however, that wherever there are animals there are **people** – in minibuses, in Land Cruisers, in rented Suzukis, often parked in ravenous, zoom–lens–touting packs around understandably irritable lions, leopards and cheetahs (the official limit is five vehicles around an animal at any one time). This popularity is highly seasonal, and can be overbearing around Christmas and during the migration, but it need not spoil your visit. If you aren't driving yourself, encourage your driver to explore new areas (obviously not off-road) and perhaps stress you'd rather experience the reserve in its totality than tick off animal species.

Visiting Maasai villages

One diversion you're likely to be offered, especially if travelling on an organized safari, is a visit to a **Maasai** *enkang*, usually incorrectly called a *manyatta* (an *enkang* is an ordinary homestead, a *manyatta* a ceremonial bush camp). Forget about the authenticity of tribal life: this is the real world. Children and old people are sick, young men have moved to the towns, and everyone wants your money. Unprepared and uncomfortable, most visitors find the experience either depressing or a bit of a rip-off, or both. You'll pay around $20 per person if organized by your lodge, camp or safari driver, or around Ksh500 per person if you arrange it yourself, for the right to have a look around, peer inside some dwellings, and be on the receiving end of a determined sales pitch to get you to buy souvenirs. Because of the supposed sales opportunity, safari drivers have for decades paid a tiny fee to the headman of their chosen village and kept the bulk of the cash as a huge commission. A number of initiatives are now changing this, however, and the best operators and camps have worked hard to make the experience less mercantile and more worthwhile for both parties. If you can forget any TV-documentary illusions, and actually sit down and talk to the Maasai (there will always be people who speak a little English), the experience can be transformed and full of interest and laughter.

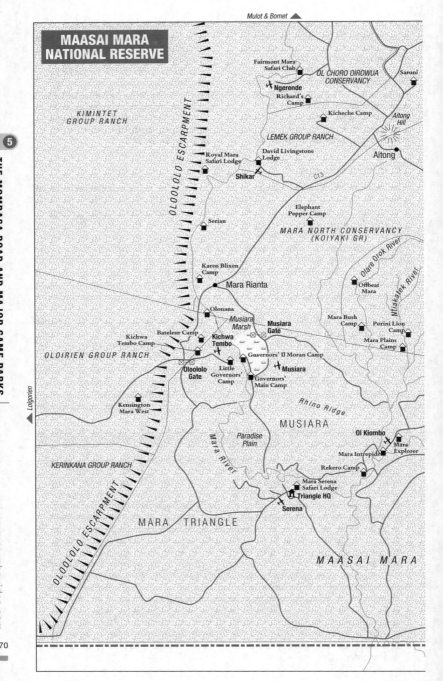

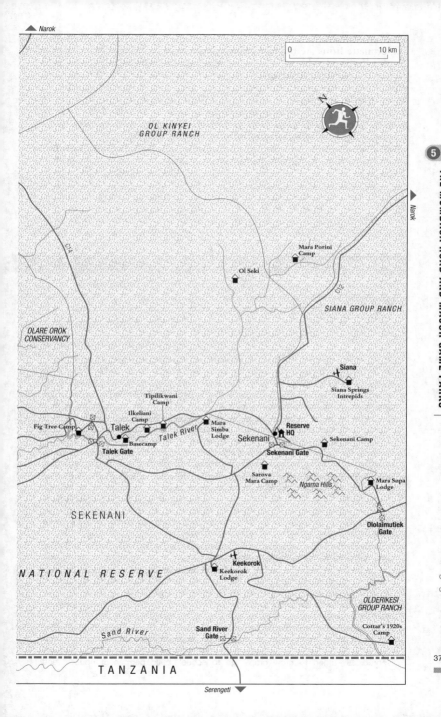

The animals

Big brunette **lions** are the best-known denizens of the Maasai Mara. Between five hundred and a thousand lions live here, and there are usually several prides around the **Musiara Swamps**, which are dry much of the year. It is sometimes possible to watch them hunt, as they take very little notice of vehicles. The **Mara Predator Project**, run by Living With Lions, is creating an online ID database of the North Mara prides. Lodge guides use the lions' facial whisker spots to identify individuals and visitors are encouraged to get involved by reporting sightings at ⓦ marapredatorproject.blogspot.com.

While lions seem to be lounging under every other bush, finding a **cheetah** is much harder (they can quite often be seen on the *murram* mounds alongside the Talek–Sekenani road). These are solitary cats – slender, unobtrusive and somewhat shy – and vulnerable to harassment. Their natural hunting times are dawn and dusk, but there is evidence that they are turning to hunting during the middle of the day, when the humans are shaded in the lodges. This is not a good time of day for the cheetah, which expends terrific energy in each chase and may have to give up if it goes on for more then thirty or forty seconds. When they move, cheetahs

The Maasai

After deep reflection on my people and culture, I have painfully come to accept that the Maasai must change to protect themselves, if not their culture. They must adapt to the realities of the modern world for the sake of their own survival. It is better to meet an enemy out in the open and to be prepared for him than for him to come upon you at home unawares.

Tepilit Ole Saitoti, writing in *Maasai* (Elm Tree Books/Abrams)

Of all Kenya's peoples, the **Maasai** have received the most attention. Often strikingly tall and slender, dressed in brilliant red cloth, with beads, metal jewellery, and – for young men – long, ochred hairstyles, they have a reputation for ferocity, pampered by an arch superiority complex. Traditionally, they lived off milk and blood (extracted, by a close shot with a stumpy arrow, from the jugular veins of their live cattle), and they loved their herds more than anything else, rarely slaughtering a beast. They maintained rotating armies of spartan warriors – the **morani** – who killed lions as a test of manhood. And they opposed all interference and invasion with swift, implacable violence. Their scorn of foreigners was absolute: they called the Europeans, who came swaddled in clothing, *iloridaa enjekat* or "those who confine their farts". They also derided African peoples who cultivated by digging the earth – the Maasai even left their dead unburied – while those who kept cattle were given grudging respect so long as they conceded that all the world's cattle were a gift from God to the Maasai, whose incessant cattle-raiding was thus righteous reclamation of stolen property. **Cattle** are still at the heart of Maasai society. There are dozens of names for different colours and patterns, and each animal among their three million is individually cherished.

Some of this noble savagery was undoubtedly exaggerated by Swahili and Arab slave and ivory traders, anxious to protect their routes from the Europeans. At the same time, something close to a **cult of the Maasai** has been around ever since Thomson walked *Through Maasailand* (see p.603) in 1883. In the early years of the colony, Governor Delamere's obsession with the people and all things Maasai spawned a new term, "Maasai-itis", and with it a motley crop of romantic notions about their ancestors, alluding to ancient Egypt and Rome, and even to the lost tribes of Israel.

The Maasai have been assailed on all sides: by uplands farmers expanding from the north; by eviction from the tourist/conservation areas within the Maasai Mara boundaries; and by a climate of opposition to their traditional lifestyle from all around. Sporadically urged to grow crops, go to school, build permanent houses, and exhibit marvellous speed and agility and, if you're lucky enough to witness a kill, it's likely to take place in a cloud of dust a kilometre from where the chase began.

Leopards are more rarely seen, though there are plenty of them. You can give yourself a serious case of risen hair when you come across their footprints down on the sandbanks at the edge of the Mara River outside the reserve boundary, where guided walks are permitted. They are largely nocturnal and prefer to remain well out of sight. Their deep, grating roar at night – a grunt, repeated – is a sound which, once heard, you carry around with you.

Rangers are certain to know the current news about the **black rhinos** – every calf born is a victory – though finding them is often difficult. Check out the thickets of desert date trees (*Balanites*) near *Little Governors'* marsh, or Rhino Ridge, where one or two of the reserve's surviving *faru* are sometimes obligingly positioned. There are also some **white rhinos** in the area, brought in from South Africa and living in the Ol Choro Oirouwa Rhino Sanctuary in the conservancy of the same name, close to *Mara Safari Club*. The sanctuary (Ⓦolchorro.blogspot.com; $5 entry) is upstream along the Mara River, well to the north of the reserve.

generally settle down and stop being a nuisance, the Maasai face an additional dilemma in squaring these edicts with the fickle demands of the **tourist industry** for traditional authenticity. Maasai dancing is *the* entertainment, while necklaces, gourds, spears, shields, *rungus* (clubs), busts (carved by Kamba carvers) and even life-sized wooden *morani*, to be shipped home in a packing case, are the stock-in-trade of the souvenir shops. For the Maasai themselves, the rewards are fairly scant. Few make much of a living selling souvenirs, but enterprising *morani* can do well by just posing for photos, and even better if they hawk themselves in Nairobi or down on the coast.

Many men persevere with the status of **warriorhood**, though modern Kenya makes few concessions to it. The *morani*, arrested for hunting lions and prevented from building *manyattas* for the *eunoto* transition in which they pass into elderhood, have kept most of the superficial marks of the warrior without being able to live the life fully. The ensemble of a cloth tied over one shoulder, together with spear, sword, club and braided hair, is still widely seen, and after circumcision, in their early days as warriors, young men can still be encountered out in the bush, hunting for birds to add to their elaborate, taxidermic headdresses. But there is considerable local frustration and, when the pasture is poor, the *morani* have little compunction about driving their herds into the reserve to compete with the wildlife.

With improved medical and veterinary facilities having eased the hardships of the traditional way of life, the Maasai have been expanding again, with **land** the biggest issue. The Maasai have still not fully come to terms with the idea of individual ownership of it, although the recent introduction of wildlife conservancies run by Maasai Group Ranches seems at last to be providing a steady source of income from tourism.

The **lifestyle** is changing: education, MPs and elections, new laws and new projects, jobs and cash, all impinge on Maasai communities – with mixed results. The traditional Maasai staple diet of curdled milk and cow's blood is rapidly being replaced by *ugali*. Many Maasai have taken work in the lodges and tented camps, while others end up as security guards in Nairobi. For the majority, who continue to live semi-nomadic lives among a welter of constraints, the future would seem to hold little promise. But that stubborn cultural pride – the kind of hauteur that keeps a cattle-owner thoroughly impoverished in cash terms, while he counts his 220 beasts – may yet insulate the Maasai against the social upheavals that seem certain to rock the lives of many Kenyans in the twenty-first century.

Maasai Mara's other heavyweights are about in abundance. The Mara River surges with **hippo**, while big families of **elephant** traipse along the forested river and stream margins and spread out across the plains when there's plenty of vegetation to browse. The park is home to an estimated thousand or so elephants, with another five hundred living in the districts beyond its boundaries.

Buffalo are seen all over and can be menacing when they surround a vehicle on its own. It is the solitary old bulls that you need to watch out for – their reputation is not exaggerated. Tourists' vehicles get stoved in quite often, so always back off.

Among all these outstanding characters, the herds of humble grazers can quickly fade into the background. It's easy to become blasé when one of the much-hyped "big five" (elephant, rhino, buffalo, lion, leopard) isn't eyeballing you at arm's length – but those are the hunter's trophies. **Warthog** families like rows of dismantled Russian dolls, **zebra** and **gazelle**, odd-looking **hartebeest** and slick, purple-flanked **topi** are all scattered with abandon across the scene. The topi are peculiarly characteristic of Maasai Mara, and there are always one or two in every herd standing sentry on a grass tussock or an old termite mound. Topi and **giraffe** – whose dream-like, slow-motion canter is one of the reserve's most beautiful and underrated sights – are often good pointers for predators in the vicinity: look closely at what they're watching. The reserve also has rare herds of **roan antelope** – swaggering, horse-sized animals with sweeping, curved horns, that you'll see elsewhere only in Ruma National Park near Lake Victoria.

The wildebeest migration

It is the annual **wildebeest migration**, however, that has planted Maasai Mara so firmly in the popular imagination. With a lemming-like instinct, the herds gather in their hundreds of thousands in May and June on the withering plains of Serengeti to begin the long, streaming journey northwards, following the scent of moisture and green grass in the Mara. They arrive in July and August, pouring over the Sand River and into the Sekenani side of the reserve, gradually munching their way westwards towards the escarpment in a milling, unsettled mass, and turning south again, back to the Serengeti, in October. Never the most graceful of animals, wildebeest seem to play up to their appearance with unpredictable behaviour; bucking like wild horses, springing like jack-in-the-boxes, or suddenly sprinting off through the herd for no apparent reason.

The **Mara River** is the biggest obstacle they come up against. Heavy rains falling up on the Mau Range where the river rises can produce a brown flood that claims thousands of animals as they try to cross. Like huge sheep (they are, in fact, most closely related to goats), the brainless masses swarm desperately to the banks and plunge in. Many are fatally injured on rocks and fallen branches; others are skewered by flailing legs and horns. With every surge, more bodies bob to the surface and float downstream. Heaps of bloated carcasses line the banks; injured and dying animals struggle in the mud; while vultures and marabou storks squat in glazed, post-prandial stupor.

The migration's full, cacophonous impact is awesomely melodramatic – both on the plains and at the deadly river crossings. This superabundance of meat accounts for the Mara's big lion population. Through it all, the **spotted hyenas** scamper and loiter like psychopathic sheep dogs. Half a million wildebeest **calves** are born in January and February before the migration, of which two out of three perish without returning to the Serengeti.

Each year the timing, duration and scale of the migration is different: if you want to know how things are looking in the run-up to your visit, check out ⓦ wildebeestmigration.blogspot.com.

Samburu–Buffalo Springs

Up in the north of the country, in the hot, arid lowlands beneath Mount Kenya, **Samburu National Reserve** ($40; see p.63) was set up in the late 1960s, a tract of country around the richest stretch of the Ewaso Ngiro (or Uaso Ngiro) River. In this region, the combination of near-permanent water (the river usually stops flowing for a month or two around January) and forest shade on the banks draws plentiful wildlife in the dry season and maintains many of the less migratory species all year round. While the wildlife spectacle doesn't always match that of the southern parks, the peace and scenic beauty of Samburu is unquestionable and, in the kind of mood swing which only an equatorial region can produce, the contrast with the fertile farming country of the Highlands just a few dozen kilometres to the south couldn't be more striking. In the background, the sharp hill of **Koitogor** rises in the middle of Samburu Reserve, making a useful reference point. And on the horizon, 30km to the north, looms the gaunt red block of **Ol Olokwe** mountain. **Buffalo Springs National Reserve** ($40), the continuation of Samburu on the south side of the river, and **Shaba National Reserve**, further upstream, are often treated as if they were just part of "Samburu". But they remain distinct reserves, with their own entrance fees.

Isolated incidents of **banditry** still occur around Archer's Post and on the roads into the reserves. Security is generally good, but if you're driving yourself, it's always worth having a chat with the police at the checkpoint just north of Isiolo.

Access

If you're circling Mount Kenya, Samburu Reserve is close at hand, a couple of hours north of Nanyuki. Buses and matatus run down onto the hazy plain as far as **Isiolo** (p.530) at the end of the tarmac. If you don't have a car, waiting at the Isiolo police barrier will usually get you a lift into the reserve itself in a few hours, although there are one or two matatus which venture up to Archer's Post.

▲ Close encounters with cheetas

If you're **driving**, you may be required to wait at the police checkpoint for a convoy to form for the short continuation to the Ngare Mara Gate; you won't wait long, as safari vans cover the stretch every day. Remember to fill up with fuel before leaving Isiolo, though *Samburu Game Lodge* usually has supplies, sold at a twenty percent mark-up. Both Airkenya and Safarilink have **flights** from Nairobi to the Samburu lodges. Note that the 24-hour **fees** chargeable in each reserve apply even if you're only in transit from one to the other: if you enter, you pay.

Accommodation

There's an increasing range of **lodges and tented camps** in Samburu-Buffalo Springs, though in recent years they've often seemed too many for the number of visitors. If you're **camping on a budget**, the obvious place to base yourself is the campsite next to *Samburu Game Lodge* (Ksh500). It's not wonderful, but you can use the lodge's pool, bars and restaurant and if you don't have a vehicle you may even manage to get a lift around the reserve. If not, you always have the option of booking yourself onto a morning or evening game drive on a lodge Land Cruiser ($70). Note that the **baboons** at the campsite here are beyond being an amusement; leave your tent and its contents under guard. The fact that baboons sometimes fall victim to crocs at the water's edge seems less distressing after you've been in the area a day or two.

Samburu has three other campsites on the north bank of the Ewaso Ngiro River, a few kilometres to the west of the bridge and park HQ. There are no facilities except at the furthest of these – *Buffalo Special Campsite* ($15), which has toilets and showers.

There are four public campsites in the Champagne Ridge area of **Buffalo Springs Reserve**, not far from the main gate, Ngare Mara. The camping area is a pretty one, among the acacias, and abounds with giraffe and other animals.

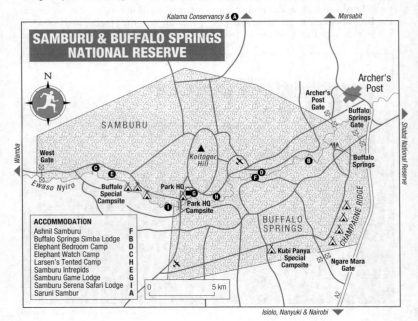

There's also one so-called special campsite in Buffalo Springs – *Kubi Panya*, on the Maji ya Chumvi stream.

Lodges and tented camps

Ashnil Samburu On the south bank, in Buffalo Springs reserve 12km from Ngare Mara Gate Ⓦwww.ashnilhotels.com. Twenty-four rather small, low tented chalets, with hot, single-layer canvas roofs, mini-safes and floor-standing fans, but no nets. Generator electricity. Pool. FB $400.

Buffalo Springs Simba Lodge Ⓦwww .marasimba.com. Under construction in 2009 on the site of the old *Buffalo Springs Tented Camp*, this lodge looks like a Californian residential development and will offer seventy cool, high-ceilinged rooms, ranged along a flood meander of the Ewaso Nyiro, most with good views. Two pools. FB $360

Elephant Bedroom Camp On the north bank, in Samburu reserve ☏0724/614281, Ⓦwww .atua-enkop.com. Well-designed, beautifully furnished, light, airy tents (two doubles and ten twins). Very appealing, designer bush living. FB $600.

Elephant Watch Camp On the river, west of the reserves ☏020/891112 or 0722/524751, Ⓦwww.elephantwatchsafaris.com. Elephant specialist Oria Douglas-Hamilton's camp on the sandy riverbank, with six superb, individually fitted-out and variously shaped tents, with massive nets, and rambling, open-air bathroom-shower-toilets (bucket showers). Three bronze guides. Closed April & Nov. Package $1230.

Larsen's Tented Camp On the north bank, in Samburu reserve Ⓦwww.wildernesslodges.co.ke. Twenty tents, on a fenced plot, all facing the river. Tents have concrete floors, with fans but no nets, and sockets, minibars, tea-making and safes. Electricity, supplied by a generator, is turned off at midnight. There's a nice, open-air massage suite, looking across to Koitogor rather than the river, and ther's a pool. It's all very comfortable and well-appointed but it's slightly stuffy, and lacks soul. Package $750.

Samburu Intrepids On the north bank, in Samburu reserve ☏064/30811 or 0722/795569, Ⓦwww.heritage-eastafrica.com. Built on stilt platforms (for when the river floods), in a dense, riverside thicket, the pleasant, modestly sized tents here have good bathrooms and wooden floors. Double-sized family tents are also available. All tents are river-facing, and one is disabled-friendly. The fine, expansive, public deck areas reach over the river bank and are shot through with indigenous trees. Bronze guide, and children's and teen's activities clubs. Good pool. FB $530.

Samburu Game Lodge On the north bank, on a heavily wooded broad bend of the river near the reserve HQ ☏0720/626366, Ⓦwww .wildernesslodges.co.ke. The oldest lodge in Samburu, this is very well sited, with great tree cover, rooms in blocks and thatched chalets, with nets and fans, close to the river, excellent views and no fence (the bank provides an adequate boundary along most of the river frontage). Still popular, but very tired, and in need of an overhaul. Nice pool with shaded surrounds. Leopards are still baited and crocs fed daily. FB ❽

Samburu Serena Safari Lodge On the south bank, just outside Buffalo Springs reserve ☏064/30800, Ⓦwww.serenahotels.com. This 62-room lodge is big, and feels it. The twins and doubles in sloping-roofed chalets are pretty, but quite small, with nets and fans, and bright, fresh shower rooms. There are eight larger rooms in a block. The river regularly floods, hence the dyke at the front, and there's a pool above the river, near the croc feeding point. Wi-fi available. FB ❽

Saruni Samburu In the Kalama Conservancy, 8km north of Archer's Post, then through a gate of the Kalama Conservancy on the highway, and 11km west ☏0734/764616 or 0725/540572, Ⓦwww.sarunisamburu.com. Unlike anywhere else in the Samburu district, this sensuous rock and steel vision of an architect and designer, (another Cheli & Peacock property), clinging to a bare, rocky col north of Samburu, is completely beguiling: sit and gaze at Mount Kenya far to the south, swim in the pool, and recharge your spiritual batteries. Package $1190.

Exploring Samburu-Buffalo Springs

Except during and immediately after the rains, scrubby bush country takes up most of the reserve district, but there are some large acacia thickets, especially in the eastern part of **Buffalo Springs**. The **springs** themselves are a welcome target; two pools of clear if weedy water, the smaller of which has been sanitized with concrete for the benefit of swimmers and, most of the time, the exclusion of crocodiles (be sure to check before jumping in). The

Leopards at Samburu

Samburu's **leopards** used to be a regular sight – at least from the terraces at the *Serena* and *Samburu Game* lodges, both of which baited the trees on the opposite bank with haunches of meat every evening. Between drinks and dinner, guests got a floodlit view of the stealthy predator reduced to giant pussycat. The stampede for cameras never encouraged the leopards to stay long, so efforts were made to attach the meat firmly to the trees. It was all pathetically contrived (and forget worthwhile pictures or videos at that distance), and eventually opinion, and the reserve authorities, turned against the practice, especially when leopards took to patrolling the lodge paths in search of scraps, posing a serious danger to the hotels' natural inhabitants. These days, *Serena* still baits regularly, with *Samburu Game Lodge* a less certain leopard-benefactor. The jury is still out on how bad the practice is (a habituated leopard may lose the skills and motivation to hunt) but if you don't see leopards like this, it's only with luck or dogged persistence that you will see one in the wild.

larger one is the water supply for Archer's Post. While looking out for crocs, you should also beware of lions, which sometimes rest under the bushes by the neighbouring natural waterhole.

The dry country ecosystems are prone to large variations in animal populations as they move in search of water and grazing, which means that Samburu's **wildlife** can occasionally be disappointing. Some visitors, however, have tremendous luck and Samburu-Buffalo Springs can provide consistently excellent animal-watching. The best areas are often along the south side of the river in Buffalo Springs Reserve, close to *Samburu Lodge*. Poaching wiped out the rhinos from here years ago, but **lions** are often seen.

Meanwhile, the locally burgeoning **elephant herds** have ruined some sections of the riverine forest. Various rare or more localized races and species compensate, though, and are often seen here in large numbers. Among these, the **reticulated giraffe** with its beautiful jigsaw marking, **Grevy's zebra**, the large, finely striped species that has a bushy mane and outsized ears, the **Somali ostrich**, which has blue rather than pink legs, and the **gerenuk**, the antelope that stands on its hind legs to reach foliage, are all common and conspicuous. Samburu's **birdlife** is diverse and prolific and includes the marshal eagle, pygmy falcon, Egyptian goose and several species of hornbill.

Shaba National Reserve

Across the rutted surface of the Isiolo–Marsabit road lies the **Shaba National Reserve** ($60; see p.63), where Joy Adamson experimented with the release of hand-reared leopards. Highly recommended, Shaba is much less visited than Samburu or Buffalo Springs. If you're driving, you're likely to enter the reserve at **Natorbe Gate** (6km from the A2 highway junction a couple of kilometres south of Archer's Post) on a road that rolls up and down through a **lava field**. The landscapes of Shaba are a lot more varied than you might expect, with the dramatic bulk of **Bodich** mountain rising behind the river to the north, and steep hills, culminating in **Shaba** peak, pressing in on the south.

If you're not driving to Shaba, you'll arrive on one of Safarilink's twice-daily **flights** to the airstrips at *Sarova Shaba Game Lodge* and Chaffa, close to *Joy's Camp*.

For animals, **Shaba** is quite the equal of its two neighbours, with lots of elephants, jackals, lions and plains game, including beautifully marked Grevy's zebra, reticulated giraffe and the gerenuk, which rarely if ever drinks, extracting water from morning dew on leaves. Scattered waterholes are the usual targets of visitors, who sometimes spend long periods just watching and waiting from their vehicles. Unusually, you are permitted to walk in various places in Shaba. The rangers at the gate can point out where. If you need fuel, you can usually get it at *Sarova Shaba*.

You might consider venturing out of the reserve to the east to visit **Chanler's Falls**, 30km beyond Chanler's Falls (Gafarsa) Gate on the Ewaso Ngiro River, but double-check the security situation first with the rangers – there's no one here except Samburu herders.

Accommodation

There are two simple **campsites** in Shaba ($10); the better one is on the banks of the Ewaso Ngiro some 9km from Natorbe Gate. Neither has any facilities. Otherwise, the only accommodation in the reserve is at the following two, completely different, establishments.

Joy's Camp ⓣ020/3513563 or 0725/957321, ⓦwww.joyscamp.com. Whatever you might feel about the late Ms Adamson, who made her home here, never has a camp been so aptly named. The palatial, Bedouin-style tents, gleaming with soft fabric and glass details, and perfectly spaced along a 1km stretch of buffalo-grazed marsh, seem to breathe relaxation. The birdlife is fantastic and the swimming pool, meals and generally chic ambience, sublime. When you're ready to go game-watching, there are excellent bronze and silver guides. The perfect honeymoon camp. Package $1190.

Sarova Shaba Game Lodge On the south bank of the river at the western end of the reserve ⓣ064/30638 or 0736/900038, ⓦwww.sarovahotels.com. Very attractively landscaped, with a superb swimming pool and streams running through public areas, but the fact that local herders were prevented from using the crystal-clear spring which feeds them (a well was dug for them instead) jars a little. The eighty standard rooms have fans, but rotten old nets that don't really work (and you need them with all that water running around). Crocodile-feeding and viewing, daily at 7.30pm. FB ⑧

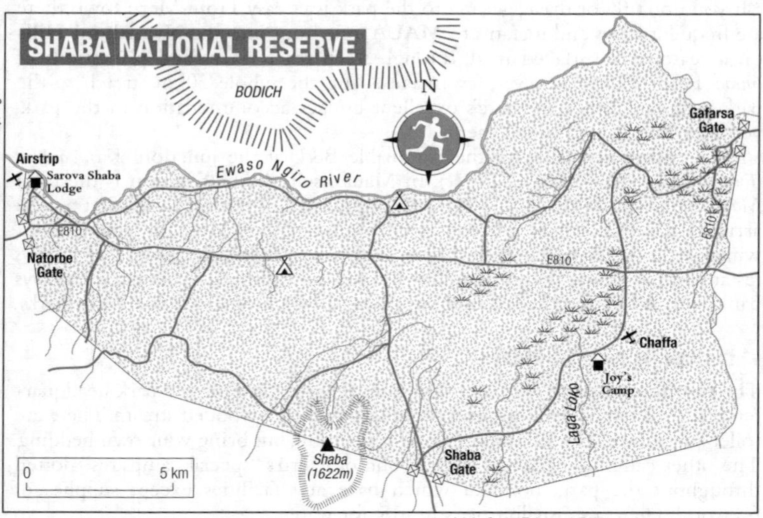

Meru National Park

You don't see **Meru National Park** (Ⓦwww.kws.go.ke/meru.html; $50; see p.63) on many safari itineraries. Of the main parks covered in this chapter, it is the least visited, most unspoiled and pristine. Abundantly traversed by **streams** flowing into the Tana River on its southern boundary, and luxuriantly rained upon, the rolling **jungle** of tall grass, riverine forest and swamp is lent a hypnotic, other-worldly quality by wonderful stands of prehistoric-looking **doum palms**.

True, the **animals** aren't always as much in evidence here as they can be in some other Kenyan parks, but the even more noticeable absence of minibuses and Land Cruisers more than compensates. After visiting some of the less bushy parks, where the animals can be spotted from miles away, Meru's intimate, unusual landscape is quickly entrancing.

Meru is the area where the Adamsons released their most famous lioness **Elsa** back into the wild, and where their later series of experiments with orphaned cheetahs was cut short by the murder of Joy Adamson. The adjoining **Kora National Park** was the home of George Adamson, murdered by poachers in August 1989 when he drove through their barricade. Kora, and the three national reserves south and east of Meru – **Bisanadi**, **Mwingi** and **Rahole** – are all in the Land Rover expedition category, a total of 4500 square kilometres of scrub and semi-desert, and dense forest where they fringe the Tana River. Because of the history of poor security in the area, you need to check out the situation very carefully with KWS if you're considering entering the Kora area.

Access

Most visitors to Meru National Park arrive on the daily **flight** on Airkenya from Nairobi's Wilson Airport. If you're **driving**, the route from Meru town (see p.170) to Murera Gate is straightforward. Gradually, as you descend, the highlands scene gives way to the lank grass, termite cathedrals and the scattered trees and streams that characterize the park's savanna.

If you don't fly or drive, getting to the park isn't easy. From Meru town there are frequent buses and matatus to **MAUA**, one hour into the **Nyambeni Hills** on a reasonably surfaced road, through steep tea terraces and plantations of *miraa*. From Maua, however, few matatus run the whole 30km stretch to the park gate, and although there's excellent budget accommodation in the park, you may find it hard to get there.

For a **room** in Maua, try the reasonable B&L at the junction, *Kiringo Hill Tourist Lodge* (Ⓣ0722/852517; ❶). In Maua itself, the best option is the calm *Maua Basin Hotel* (Ⓣ0720/175415; ❹), signposted 300m off to the left as you arrive, with a choice of self-contained rooms in the "Museum" and "Basin" wings – the latter is the best choice, with more light. The hotel's *Hotsprings* restaurant has a long menu (Ksh200–400 for most dishes). Maua has a Barclays bank with **ATM** and the last **fuel supplies** (there's no fuel for sale in the park).

Accommodation

The **public campsite** ($25) is 18km from the gate near the old park headquarters, on a stretch of open ground running down to a wooded stream. There are toilet and shower blocks, and firewood is plentiful, but bring your own bedding. The other camping option is to pick one of Meru's "special campsites" dotted throughout the park, none of which have any facilities except supplies of firewood. There are usually rivers nearby for water.

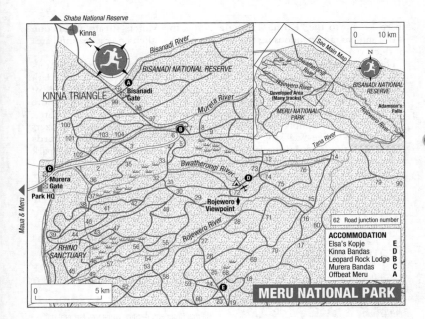

MERU NATIONAL PARK

Map labels (from image):
Shaba National Reserve
Kinna
Bisanadi River
BISANADI NATIONAL RESERVE
KINNA TRIANGLE
Bisanadi Gate **A**
Murera River
Murera Gate **C**
Park HQ
Maua & Meru
Bwatherongi River
Rojewero Viewpoint
Rojewero River
RHINO SANCTUARY
D
E
0   5 km

See Main Map
Bwatherongi River
Rojewero River
Developed Area (Many tracks)
MERU NATIONAL PARK
BISANADI NATIONAL RESERVE
Adamson's Falls
Rojewero River
Tana River
0   10 km

62 Road junction number

ACCOMMODATION
Elsa's Kopje   E
Kinna Bandas   D
Leopard Rock Lodge B
Murera Bandas   C
Offbeat Meru   A

Elsa's Kopje On Mughwango hill 020/3513564 or 0722/509387, www.elsaskopje.com. Arguably Kenya's best lodge, and among the world's top places to stay, the magnificence of *Elsa's* is partly down to its stunning rocky hilltop location, with a 360° panorama that simply drives away cares. But the details are all spot-on, too – an infinity pool cleaved from the rock; birds, comical hyraxes and lizards everywhere; outrageously good food and wine; and completely delightful cottages, each open-fronted to let in the sky, with its own private deck among the shrubs and crags. Three silver guides for bush walks and day and night game drives. Package $1190.

Kinna Bandas Near the old park HQ 020/600800, reservations@kws.go.ke. On a shady site, the former *Bwatherongi Bandas* offers three s/c twin and one family *banda*, with very large rooms, nets and bathrooms, but no cooking facilities. On the plus side, the caretaker's tame giraffe, Duse, which accompanies him everywhere, is a hit with every visitor. Possibly even more appealing is the excellent swimming pool in the middle of the site, complete with recliners and cleaning robot. Ksh3500 per *banda*.

Leopard Rock Lodge Along the Murera river 020/600031 or 0733/333100, www.leopardmico.com. French-owned, this strangely out-of-place and overpriced lodge has fifteen huge rooms, converted from two-room *bandas*, now each occupying an entire *banda*. Pool. FB $680.

Murera Bandas By Murera Gate 020/600800 reservations@kws.go.ke. Three *bandas*, each with two bedrooms – one double, one single – and a shared barbecue area. Large groups can be accommodated in a nearby dormitory which has bunk beds and a central kitchen. $50 per *banda*.

Offbeat Meru 1.3km east of junction #99 0722/433268 or 0735/667421, www.offbeatsafaris.com. Real bush camp in a lovely, remote setting, with wonderful forest birdsong in the early morning. Proper, large tents with good mosquito screens (no nets inside) and bucket showers to order. Very good meals in the laid-back mess tent, shared with the hosts and other guests. Bronze & silver guides. Pool Package $670.

Exploring the park

Meru's many tracks are all good gravel and most **junctions** have signposts and numbered cairns. There are still plenty of enticing areas to investigate without going too far. Driving in through Murera Gate, for example, turn immediately sharp left up to the "**Kinna Triangle**", cross the Murera stream at junction #102 and pass a stupendous fig tree on your left. You then enter a beautiful area of thick vegetation, tall trees and high grass.

The **Rojewero River**, the park's largest stream, is an interesting water-course: densely overgrown banks flash with birds and monkeys and dark waters ripple with hippos, crocs and turtles. Large and very visible herds of **elephant**, **buffalo** and **reticulated giraffe** are common, as are, in the more open areas, **gerenuk**, **Grevy's zebra** and **ostrich**. Predators seem scarce, though they may simply be hidden in the long grass – the smaller grazers must have a nerve-wracking time of it here. Large numbers of **leopards** captured in the stock-raising lands of Laikipia have been released in the park in recent years, but as usual you have little chance of seeing them.

The park's **Rhino Sanctuary** (4WD only) is on the right when you enter the park at Murera Gate. The couple of dozen white rhinos are doing well, the similar number of black rhinos suffering somewhat from tsetse flies. They're monitored around the clock.

Travel details

Road details for the main Nairobi–Mombasa route are given in Chapters 1 and 6.

Trains

Voi to/from: Mombasa (3 weekly; 4hr); Nairobi (3 weekly; 9hr).

Buses

Kitui to/from: Machakos (4 daily; 1hr); Mombasa (daily; 7hr); Nairobi (3 daily; 4hr).
Garissa to/from Mombasa (daily; 8hr); Nairobi (4 daily; 6hr).
Machakos to/from: Mombasa (daily; 8hr); Nairobi (frequent; 1hr); Voi (daily; 4hr).
Maua to/from: Meru (3 daily; 1hr); Nairobi (3 daily; 6hr).
Namanga to/from: Nairobi (daily; 4hr).
Narok to/from: Nairobi (several daily; 4hr).
Taveta to/from: Arusha (1 daily; 4hr); Mombasa (4 daily; 5hr); Nairobi (2 weekly; 8hr); Voi (4 daily; 3hr).
Voi to/from: Mombasa (frequent; 2–3hr); Nairobi (frequent; 4–5hr).

Matatus

Kitui to/from: Embu (daily; 3hr); Kibwezi (daily; 4hr); Machakos (frequent; 1hr).
Namanga to/from: Nairobi (frequent; 4hr).
Narok to/from: Nairobi (frequent; 4hr).
Oloitokitok to/from: Emali (2–3 daily; 3hr); Taveta (market days; 2hr).
Taveta to/from: Voi (frequent; 3hr).

Voi to/from: Mombasa (constant; 2–3hr); Nairobi (frequent; 4–5hr); Wundanyi (several daily; 1hr 30min).

Flights

Flight times are approximate, depending on routing and airstrips visited in each park/reserve.
Amboseli to/from: Diani Beach & Mombasa (Mombasa Air Safari; daily; 1hr); Maasai Mara (Mombasa Air Safari; daily; 1hr 30min); Nairobi (Airkenya and Safarilink; 2 daily; 40min–1hr 15min); Tsavo West (Mombasa Air Safari; daily 15–30min).
Chyulu Hills (Ol Donyo Wuas) to/from Nairobi (Safarilink; daily; 1hr).
Maasai Mara to/from: Diani Beach & Mombasa (Mombasa Air Safari; daily; 2hr 30min); *Lewa (Safarilink; daily; 2hr); *Loisaba (Safarilink; daily; 1hr 10min); Nairobi (Airkenya and Safarilink; 5 daily; 45min–1hr 15min); *Naivasha (Safarilink; daily; 40min); *Nanyuki (Airkenya and Safarilink; 2 daily; 1hr 30min); Tsavo West (Mombasa Air Safari; daily; 1hr 45min).
Meru to/from: Nairobi (Airkenya; daily; 1hr 10min–1hr 40min).
Samburu/Buffalo Springs/Shaba to/from: Nairobi (Airkenya and Safarilink; 2 daily; 1hr 20min–1hr 40min).
Tsavo West to/from: Nairobi (Safarilink; daily; 1hr).

* flights only operate southbound to Maasai Mara.

The Coast

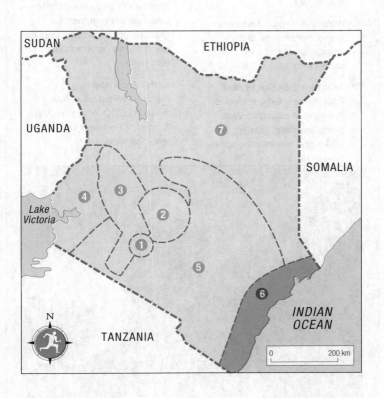

SUDAN

ETHIOPIA

UGANDA

Lake Victoria

SOMALIA

7

4   3

2

1

5

6

TANZANIA

INDIAN OCEAN

N

0   200 km

CHAPTER 6 # Highlights

* **Fort Jesus** Seven centuries of coastal history are on show in Mombasa's fascinating castle-museum. See p.396

* **Tiwi Beach** The reef is close to the shore here, and there are some excellent, low-key cottage developments. See p.429

* **Wasini** A tiny, undeveloped island community, with wonderful diving and snorkelling. See p.445

* **Arabuko-Sokoke Forest** East Africa's largest tract of indigenous coastal forest offers excellent guided walks and the chance to see monkeys and lots of birds and butterflies. See p.452

* **Gedi** Try to visit this lost city first thing in the morning or as the sun goes down, when the ruins are at their most atmospheric. See p.455

* **Watamu** The stunning bays, islets and casuarina-shaded beaches are matched by glorious coral gardens and good diving opportunities. See p.457

* **Lamu** A compelling, history-soaked city-state and UNESCO World Heritage Site, with no roads or vehicles. See p.476

▲ Fort Jesus, Mombasa

The Coast

The coast is a world apart from "upcountry" Kenya and in many ways it feels like a different country. For a start, **Mombasa**, Kenya's second city, is a much easier place to enjoy than Nairobi. With its sun-scorched, colonnaded streets, this is the quintessential tropical port – steamy and unbelievably dilapidated, but not lacking in atmosphere – and it's fun to shop here, stroll the old city's alleys, or visit Fort Jesus. To the north and south of Mombasa there are superb **beaches** and a number of tourist resort areas, but nothing, as yet, highly developed in the Florida or Spanish *costa* sense. You can certainly enjoy yourself having a lazy time at a beach resort, but there's a lot more to the coast than recliners, swimming pools and buffet meals.

Most obviously, the beaches are the launch pad for one of the most beautiful **coral reefs** in the world. With equipment, you can do some spectacular dives, but even with a simple snorkel and mask, which are easily obtained, you can explore beneath the surface, to discover what really is another world. The two most spectacular areas are enclosed in **marine national parks**, around Watamu and Malindi, and at the island of Wasini.

The string of **islands** that runs up the coast – Wasini, Funzi, Chale, Lamu, Manda, Pate and Kiwaiyu – are all very much worth visiting. Apart from their beach and ocean attractions, most of them have some archeological interest, which is also a constant theme on the mainland: the whole coast is littered with the **ruins** of forts, mosques, tombs and even one or two whole towns. Some of these – including **Fort Jesus**, the old town of **Lamu** and the ruined city of **Gedi** – are already on the tourist circuit, but there are dozens that have hardly been cleared and make for quite compelling excursions.

Islam has long been a major influence on the coast, and the traditional, annual fast is widely observed during the month of **Ramadan**, when no food or drinks are consumed during the hours of daylight. Visiting the coast at this time might leave a slightly strange impression of a region where everyone is on night shift, but in practical terms it usually makes little difference. The end of Ramadan is marked by major **festivities**, as are several other Muslim holidays throughout the year. See p.56 for dates.

Resort areas and where to go

Plenty of visitors – perhaps the majority, in fact – treat the coast as their main destination in Kenya, combined with a short safari inland. There are four main, popular **resort areas**. First and foremost is the suburban district north of Mombasa island, often known as "**North Coast**", around half an hour to an hour from the airport; further north comes **Watamu**, about two hours from Mombasa; and lastly **Malindi**, another twenty minutes beyond Watamu. South

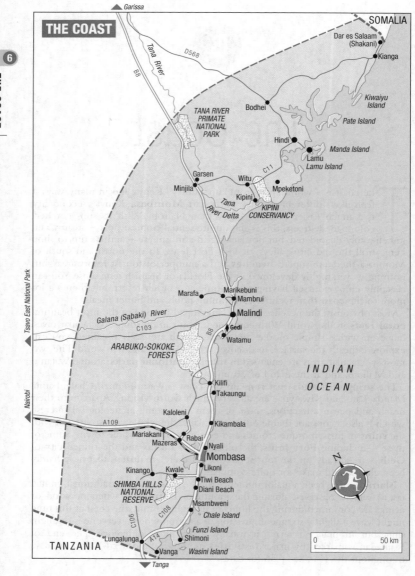

of Mombasa, the main focus of the "**South Coast**" is Diani Beach, about an hour-and-a-half's drive from the airport on a good day (the ferry can delay you). Apart from the odd small development, the rest of the coast is virtually untouched by tourism.

In many areas along the length of Kenya's coast, the sea is very shallow at low tide and in some places it's impossible to swim except at high tide. If you're concerned about the state of the tides, consult the **tide tables** in the online edition of *Coast Week* (Ⓦwww.coastweek.com/tides.htm). The lagoon inside the reef is reasonably safe for swimming all year round. Beyond the reef, however, conditions can be radically different. If you're planning to go beyond the reef – to dive or go fishing, for example – always check that your boat has a useable life jacket for each passenger.

If you're on a budget, a word of warning: tempting as it can be, **sleeping out** on the beaches is nearly always unwise because of the danger of robbery. Although there are one or two very remote areas where you might get away with it, you'll usually have to find a room or pitch your tent at one of the few campsites.

Seasons

This part of Kenya, with its monsoon climate, is the region most affected by the **seasons**. The somewhat unpredictable "long rains" between April and June are a much cheaper and quieter season than the rest of the year. While the beaches tend to be damp and the weather overcast during this low season, you can make big savings on pre-booked holidays or, if you're travelling independently, reduce your hotel or rental costs by fifty percent or more – and if you're diving, the **water clarity** is still good. It's worth noting, however, that smaller hotels, especially the more upmarket establishments, often close during the low season. While the sea is warm all year (averaging 25–30°C), underwater visibility varies greatly, from as little as five metres from June to September, to as much as thirty metres in December. October, November and March are usually the best overall months for weather and water visibility, though it can be very hot in February and March in the build-up to the "long rains". As for the Indian Ocean's **monsoon winds**, they always blow onshore: the dry, moderate *kaskazi* wind blows from the northeast from November to April; then the moister and stronger *kusi* blows from the southeast from May to October (the changeover period is often very gusty), and in this season large quantities of **seaweed** often sweep up onto the beach. In July, August and September there is generally quite a strong breeze, with choppy seas. From December to February, on the other hand, it's hot and dry, and much calmer.

Environment and wildlife

The hundreds of kilometres of sandy **beach** that fringe the low-lying coastal strip are backed by **dunes** and coconut palms, traversed by scores of streams and rivers. Flowing off the plateaus through tumbling jungle, these waterways meander across a narrow, fertile plain to the sea. In sheltered creeks, forests of **mangrove** trees cover vast areas and create a distinctive ecological zone of tidal mud flats.

Wildlife on the coast is in keeping with the region's lush, intimate feel. The big game of upcountry Kenya is more or less absent (though Shimba Hills National Park near Mombasa is an exception), but smaller creatures are abundant. **Monkeys** are especially common, with troops of baboons seen by the road, and vervet and Sykes' monkeys frequently at home in hotel gardens. **Birdlife** is prolific – if you have even a mild interest you should bring binoculars. On the **reptile** front, snakes, those brilliant disguise artists, are rarely seen, but lizards skitter everywhere, including upside down on the ceiling at night, and bug-eyed chameleons waver across the road, sometimes making it to the other side. So do **giant millipedes**, up to 30cm long: this harmless scavenger is known as the "Mombasa Express", after the famously slow train. **Insects** are here in full force although efforts to eradicate mosquitoes are paying off (thankfully) and most, including the glorious **butterflies** of the Jadini and Arabuko-Sokoke forests, are attractive participants in the coast's gaudy show.

Travel

For details on arrival at Moi International Airport in Mombasa, see p.392. If you **fly** to Diani Beach, Mombasa, Malindi, Lamu or Kiwaiyu you'll save a day's travel, or more. Note that it's only the flights to Mombasa and Diani Beach, with occasional views of Kilimanjaro, that are interesting in themselves. On the other hand, flying up to Lamu from Mombasa or Malindi offers stunning views over jungle and reef (see relevant city listings and chapter "Travel details" on p.500).

The overnight **train journey** between Nairobi and Mombasa used to be a Kenyan travel highlight. While its unreliability makes it difficult to recommend unreservedly (elephants on the line and more mundane problems mean it's often hours late), it's a trip worth doing at least once. For more details see p.44.

The constant stream of **buses from Nairobi to Mombasa** provides the cheapest transport, and you can stop anywhere en route if you want to explore. It's best to travel by day to reduce the chance of accidents and the very rare incidents of banditry.

If you're **driving**, or you're in a rented vehicle with a driver, you'll be pleased to know that, as of 2009, the highway is in good condition for its whole length, for the first time in decades (see p.317).

Mombasa and around

Arriving in **Mombasa** by plane or train in the morning, there's ample time, if you don't find the heat too much, to head straight out to the beaches (Mombasa island has no proper beaches of its own: the nearest is Nyali Beach – see p.411). But you should consider spending a day or two in Mombasa itself, acclimatizing to the coast, catching the cadences of *Kiswahili safi* (pure Swahili) and looking around Kenya's most historic city. If you have time, there's a recommended trip you can make inland, well off the beaten path to the northwest, to the **Mijikenda country** between Mazeras and Kaloleni. If you would rather take this latter detour before reaching the coast proper – and it's a pleasant introduction to the coastal region – buses from Nairobi can drop you at **Mazeras** (see p.331), a short bus ride from Mombasa.

Mombasa

There's a sense of community and depth of history in **MOMBASA** that Nairobi lacks. Sleazy, hot and physically tropical in a way that could hardly be more different from the capital, Mombasa is the slightly indolent hub of the coast. Faded, flaking and occasionally charming, the city centre – neatly isolated by sea from its suburbs – feels like a small town that was once great.

Mombasa is an **island**, linked to the mainland by two causeways to the west, by a bridge to the north, and by a ferry to the south. At the city's heart is the **Old Town**, a lattice of lanes, mosques and cramped houses sloping gently down to the once-busy dhow harbour. **Fort Jesus**, an impressive

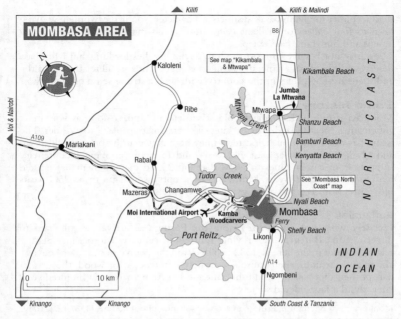

MOMBASA AREA

Kilifi

Kilifi & Malindi

B8

Kaloleni

See map "Kikambala & Mtwapa"

Kikambala Beach

Jumba La Mtwana

Ribe

Mtwapa Creek

Mtwapa

Shanzu Beach

Voi & Nairobi

A109

Mariakani

Bamburi Beach

Kenyatta Beach

Rabai

Tudor   Creek

See "Mombasa North Coast" map

NORTH COAST

Mazeras

Changamwe

Nyali Beach

Moi International Airport

Kamba Woodcarvers

Mombasa

Ferry

Shelly Beach

Port Reitz

Likoni

INDIAN OCEAN

A14

0   10 km

Ngombeni

Kinango

Kinango

South Coast & Tanzania

reminder of Mombasa's complicated, bloody past, still overlooks the Old Town from where it once guarded the harbour entrance. It's now a national monument and museum.

From the Old Town, clustered all around you, and mostly within easy walking distance, lies the whole expanse of downtown, modern Mombasa, with its wide streets and relative lack of high-rise buildings. While you won't doubt it's a chaotic city, the atmosphere, even in the commercial centre of what is one of Africa's busiest ports, is invariably relaxed and congenial. Rush hours, urgency and paranoia seem to be Nairobi's problems (as everyone here will tell you), not Mombasa's. And the gaping, marginal slums of many African cities hardly exist in Mombasa. It's true that **Miritini** and **Chomvu** and especially **Likoni** and **Changamwe** are burgeoning mainland suburbs that the municipality has more or less abandoned, but the brutalizing conditions of Nairobi's Kibera are absent.

Despite the palm trees, the sunshine and the happy languor, all is not bliss and perfection. **Street crime**, though it hardly approaches Nairobi's level, is still a problem, and you should be wary of displaying your valuables or accepting invitations to walk down dark alleys. But, as a general rule, Mombasa is a far less neurotic city than Nairobi and, in stark contrast to the capital, there's nowhere in the centre that could be considered a no-go area, even at night. The climate partly explains it, but, at an hour when central Nairobi is empty except for taxis and *askaris*, Mombasans can be seen taking a stroll in the warm night, old men converse on the benches in Digo Road, and many shops stay open late.

Ethnically, Mombasa is perhaps even more diverse than Nairobi. The Asian and Arab influence is particularly pervasive, with fifty mosques and dozens of Hindu and Sikh temples lending a strongly Oriental flavour. Still, the largest contingent speaks Swahili as a first language and it is the **Swahili civilization**

that accounts for Mombasa's distinctive character. You'll see women wearing head-to-foot *buibuis* or brilliant *kanga* outfits, and men decked out in *kanzu* gowns and hip-slung *kikoi* wraps.

You may not be able to resist the lure of the beaches for long, but Mombasa deserves a little of your time; the small-town freedoms are still relatively healthy and there are few places in the country with such a strong sense of identity.

Some history

Mombasa is one of East Africa's oldest settlements and, so long as you aren't anticipating spectacular historical sites, it's a fascinating place to wander. The island has had a town on it, located somewhere between the present Old Town and Nyali Bridge, for at least 700 years, and there are enough documentary snippets from earlier times to guess that some kind of settlement has existed here for at least 2000 years. Mombasa's own optimistic claim to be 2500 years old comes from Roman and Egyptian adventure stories.

Early tales

Precisely what was going on before the Portuguese arrived is still hard to discern. **Ibn Battuta**, the roving fourteenth-century Moroccan, spent a relatively quiet night here in 1332 and declared the people of the town "devout, chaste and virtuous, their mosques strongly constructed of wood, the greater part of their diet bananas and fish". But another Arab writer of a hundred years later found a less ordered society:

Monkeys have become the rulers of Mombasa since about 800 AH [1397 AD]. They even come and take the food from the dishes, attack men in their own homes and take away what they can find. When the monkeys enter a house and find a woman they hold congress with her. The people have much to put up with.

Early Portuguese visitors

Mombasa had considerably worse depredations to put up with after **Vasco da Gama's** expedition, full of mercenary zeal, dropped anchor on Easter Saturday 1498. After courtesy gifts had been exchanged, relations suddenly soured and the fleet was prevented from entering the port. A few days later, richer by only one sheep and "large quantities of oranges, lemons and sugar cane", da Gama went off to try his crude diplomacy at Malindi, and found his first and lasting ally on the coast.

Mombasa was visited again in 1505 by a fourteen-strong Portuguese fleet. This time, the king of Mombasa had enlisted 1500 archers from the mainland and people stored arsenals of stone missiles on the rooftops in preparation for the expected **invasion** through the town's narrow alleys. The attack, pitching firearms against spears and poisoned arrows, was brutal and overwhelming. The town was squeezed on all sides and the king's palace (of which no trace remains) was seized. The king and most of the survivors slipped out of town into the palm groves which then covered most of Mombasa island, but 1513 Mombasans had been killed – as against five Portuguese.

The king attempted to save Mombasa by offering to become a vassal of Portugal, but the request was turned down, the Portuguese being unwilling to lose the chance to loot the town. The victors picked over the bodies in the courtyards and broke down the strongroom doors until the ships at anchor were almost overladen. Then, as a parting shot, they fired the town. The narrow streets and cattle stalls between the thatched houses produced a conflagration that razed Mombasa to the ground.

Portuguese occupation

In 1528, the Portuguese returned once again to wreck and plunder the new city that had been built on the ashes of the old. In the 1580s, it happened twice more. On the last occasion, in 1589, there was a frenzied **massacre** at the hands of the Portuguese on one side and – coincidentally – a marauding tribe of cannibal nomads from the interior called the Zimba on the other. The Zimba's unholy alliance with the Europeans came to a treacherous end at Malindi shortly afterwards, when the Portuguese, together with the townsfolk and three thousand Segeju archers, wiped them out.

Remarkably, only two years after this last catastrophe, Mombasa launched a major land expedition of its own against its old enemy, Malindi. The party was ambushed on the way by Malindi's Segeju allies, who themselves stormed and took Mombasa, later handing over the town to the Portuguese at Malindi. The Malindi corps transferred to Mombasa, the Malindi sheikh was grandly installed as sultan of the whole region, and the Portuguese set to work on **Fort Jesus**, dedicated in 1593.

Once completed, the fort became the focus of everything that mattered in Mombasa, changing hands a total of nine times between the early seventeenth century and 1875. The first takeover happened in 1631, in a **popular revolt** that resulted in the killing of every last Portuguese. But the Sultan, lacking support from any of the other towns under Portuguese domination, eventually had to desert the fort and the Portuguese, waiting in Zanzibar, reoccupied it. They held it for the rest of the seventeenth century while consolidating their control of the Indian Ocean trade.

Omani rule

Meanwhile, the **Omani Arabs** were becoming increasingly powerful. As Dutch, English and French ships started to appear on the horizon, time was running out for the Portuguese trading monopoly. Efforts to bring settlers to their East African possessions failed, and they retreated more and more behind the massive walls of Fort Jesus. In 1696–98 Fort Jesus itself was besieged into submission by the Omanis who, with support from Pate and Lamu, had already taken the rest of the town. After 33 months almost all the defenders – the Portuguese corps and some 1500 Swahili loyalists – had died of starvation or plague.

Rapid disenchantment with the new Arab rulers spilled over in 1728 into a mutiny among the fort's African soldiers. The Portuguese were invited back – for a year. Then the fort was again besieged, and this time the Portuguese gave up quickly. They were allowed their freedom, and a number were said to have married and stayed in the town. But Portuguese power on the coast was shattered for ever.

The new Omani rulers were the **Mazrui** family, who soon declared themselves independent of Oman, outlawing slave-trading in Mombasa, and directly challenging the **Busaidi** family who had just seized power in the Arabian homeland.

British takeover

Intrigue in the Lamu Archipelago led to the Battle of Shela (see p.478) and Lamu's unwittingly disastrous invitation to the **Sultan of Oman**, Seyyid Said, to occupy its own fort. From here, and by now with **British** backing, the Busaidis went on to attack Mazrui Mombasa repeatedly in the 1820s.

There was a hiccup in 1824 when a British officer, **Captain Owen**, fired with enthusiasm for defeating the slave trade, extended British protection to

Mombasa on his own account, despite official British support for the slave-trading Busaidis. Owen's "Protectorate" was a diplomatic embarrassment and – not surprisingly – did not last long. The Busaidi government was only installed when the Swahili "twelve tribes" of Mombasa fell into a dispute over the Mazrui succession and called in Seyyid Said, the Busaidi leader. In 1840, he moved his capital from Oman to Zanzibar and, with Mombasa firmly garrisoned, most of the coast was soon in his domain. Surviving members of the Mazrui family went to Takaungu near Kilifi and Gazi, south of Mombasa.

British influence was sharpened after their guns quelled the mutiny in 1875 of al-Akida, "an ambitious, unbalanced and not over-clever" commandant of Fort Jesus. Once British hegemony was established, they leased the **coastal strip** from the Sultan of Zanzibar and Fort Jesus became Mombasa's prison, which it remained until 1958. It was opened as a museum in 1962.

Arrival and orientation

If you've never been to Africa before, flying into Mombasa and merely getting the transfer bus or taxi to your hotel throws you into the place more quickly than arriving in Nairobi's cosmopolitan embrace. You may even experience some level of **culture shock** from the poverty, the heat, the noise and the general upfront nature of everything.

Once on Mombasa island, for orientation purposes, think of **Digo Road**, with the main market and GPO, as the city's spine: head up it to the north and you cross the **Nyali Bridge** to the main Mombasa beach resorts; go down it to the south and you come to the **Likoni ferry** to the south coast mainland. East of Digo Road is the **Old Town** and some sedate streets of government offices. West of Digo Road you have (from north to south): **Jomo Kenyatta Avenue**, leading to the airport and the Nairobi highway; **Haile Selassie Road**, leading to the railway station; and **Moi Avenue**, Mombasa's main tourist strip, with its famous tusk arch, known simply as "the Tusks".

By air

Moi International Airport is situated some 10km from the city centre on the mainland. If you haven't got a **visa**, they are usually issued on the spot without delay – payment in cash only. There are **bank booths** for exchanging money just outside the customs area, and ATMs.

There is no airline or public bus service from the airport into town, and the nearest **matatu** service is a kilometre away. To get there, walk 1km to the first row of small shops at the road junction for Magongo, where you can pick up a matatu to the GPO.

Several **taxi** companies which service the airport, including Kenatco, Prime and Sacco, have fixed rates that are posted up near where their representatives wait, or which they'll show you on request. The price to the centre of Mombasa is Ksh900–1200, depending on the street you want. Fares are also fixed for the beach resorts, depending on your hotel: Nyali Ksh1300; Bamburi Ksh1800, Tiwi Ksh3100, Diani Ksh3700–4700, Malindi Ksh10,500.

You can also arrange to have your pre-booked **car rental** vehicle meet you. Avis and Budget have desks at the airport, and most rental companies will oblige, though you'll usually need to visit their office in town to complete the paperwork and pay the deposit.

There's never any problem with **airport parking** in the car park just outside the terminal building (Ksh40/hr or safe, long-term parking at Ksh300/day).

By train

Though the service now runs only three times a week, the night **train** from Nairobi is still a good way of arriving in Mombasa (full details on p.44). When you walk out of the station into the glare of the morning sun, **Haile Selassie Road** is directly ahead, leading in one straight kilometre to the city's main north–south thoroughfare, **Digo Road**. If you pick a taxi out of the swarm awaiting the train's arrival, Ksh200–300 should be the going rate to be taken to any town-centre hotel – unlikely to be more than a five to ten-minute ride.

By road

Arriving by **road from Nairobi**, first impressions can be dismal. You come over the Makupa Causeway alongside the railway, then diverge from it on the island to head 4km straight down **Jomo Kenyatta Avenue**. Although there have been various clean-up efforts over the years, "shabby" is still the adjective that comes to mind as you bump down this erstwhile showcase avenue, a scene of broken windows, crumbling facades and out-of-date hoardings smothering the street from its inception, via the triumphalist Independence Roundabout to its final disintegration in the diesel-laden environment of the Mwembe Tayari bus parks. If you get out of a bus or matatu at Mwembe Tayari and walk on down Kenyatta to Digo Road your mood should lift a little.

If you're driving into the city, there's rarely any problem **parking**. Uniformed parking wardens patrol the streets, and will sell you a Ksh50 ticket, entitling you to park as many times as you like over the course of the following 24 hours. Beware of faded yellow "no parking" road markings on some kerbs: there are one or two nimble and corrupt wheel-clamping teams on the loose, ready to take advantage of unwary visitors.

City transport and information

With no bus services, **city transport** comes down to taxis and more informal services. Kenatco (℡041/2227503, Ⓦwww.kenatco.co.ke), based out of Ambalal House, Nkrumah Road runs a reliable 24-hour **taxi** service with fixed

---

Mombasa's ferries

Driving or taking public transport to Mombasa from the south, the road runs into the sea at the swarming suburb of Likoni, where you take the **Likoni ferry** across Kilindini Creek to Mombasa island (10min; 4am–1am every 15min; 1am–4am hourly; pedestrians and cyclists free, cars Ksh90). T-shirted security guards now look out for pickpockets and security has greatly improved, but it's still wise to keep valuables tucked away and your car windows up. While main bus services use the ferry, if you're travelling by matatu, you change vehicles and cross on foot. The other ferry across Kilindini Creek, the **Mtongwe ferry**, is a free commuter service, but only for foot passengers, operating daily from 5–10am and 3–9pm.

prices. Otherwise, choose between **matatus**, which run from the GPO to Nyali Bridge, Tudor Docks and the Likoni ferry; **taxis** (Ksh200–400 to go anywhere on the island, but firmly agree the price first); **tuk-tuks** (Ksh100–250); **piki-pikis** (Ksh100–200); and **boda-bodas** (Ksh50–100). Alternatively, getting around the city centre is easy enough, and sometimes faster, on **foot**.

The city's **tourist office**, operated by the Mombasa and Coast Tourist Association, is on Moi Avenue, between the Tusks and the Shell station (Mon–Fri 8am–4.30pm, Sat 8am–12.30pm; ☎041/2225428). Although offering little in material terms, the staff are helpful, and can advise you on transport and accommodation.

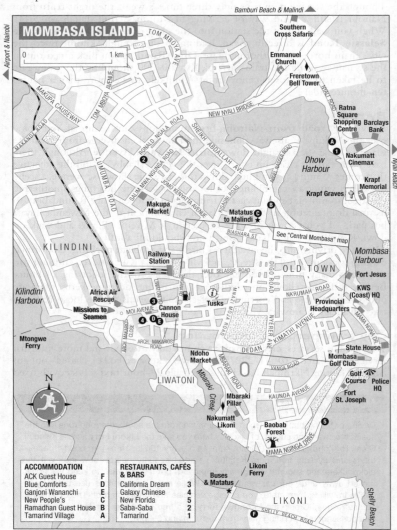

Bamburi Beach & Malindi ▲

MOMBASA ISLAND

0   1 km

Airport & Nairobi ◀

Southern Cross Safaris

Emmanuel Church

Freretown Bell Tower

Ratna Square Shopping Centre   Barclays Bank

Dhow Harbour

Nakumatt Cinemax

Krapf Memorial

Krapf Graves ✝

TOM MBOYA AVE

NEW NYALI BRIDGE

Nyali Beach ▶

Makupa Market

Matatus to Malindi ★

Railway Station

See "Central Mombasa" map

Mombasa Harbour

KILINDINI

OLD TOWN

Fort Jesus

HAILE SELASSIE ROAD

Tusks

Provincial Headquarters

KWS (Coast) HQ

Kilindini Harbour

Africa Air Rescue

Missions to Seamen

MOI AVENUE

Cannon House

State House

Mombasa Golf Club

Mtongwe Ferry

ARCH. MAKARIOS ROAD

DEDAN

Golf Course

Police HQ

Ndoho Market

Fort St. Joseph

LIWATONI

Mbaraki Pillar

Nakumatt Likoni

Baobab Forest

Likoni Ferry

Buses & Matatus ★

LIKONI

SHELLY BEACH ROAD

Shelly Beach ▶

N

ACCOMMODATION	
ACK Guest House	F
Blue Comforts	D E
Ganjoni Wananchi	
New People's	C
Ramadhan Guest House	B
Tamarind Village	A

RESTAURANTS, CAFÉS & BARS	
California Dream	3
Galaxy Chinese	4
New Florida	5
Saba-Saba	2
Tamarind	1

Tiwi Beach, Diani Beach, Shimba Hills NP & Shimoni ▼

Accommodation

None of Mombasa's main resort hotels is located on the island, and barely any of the city's hotels are of international standard. Note that **water supplies** in Mombasa are unreliable, and many cheap places feature the telltale buckets and plastic basins which indicate that water sometimes has to be carried up. Even when the pipes are working, hot water is rare in the cheap places (and the instant, electric showers are rare), but in this climate you're unlikely to miss it.

Cheap lodgings

Berachah Lodge Haile Selassie Rd, at the corner of Digo Rd ℡0725/006228 or 0722/673798. The s/c rooms here, with nets, fans and TV, aren't bad value, and have decent bathrooms. There's also a nice, very cheap first-floor *hoteli*. BB ②

Blue Comforts Archbishop Makarios Rd ℡041/2351111. Good-value standby. The rooms have nets and fans, but upgrading to one with a/c and TV isn't worth the doubling in price. BB ②

Excellent Haile Selassie Rd ℡041/2227683, Ⓔblueedgehotels@hotmail.com. Good-sized, clean s/c rooms with nets and fans (and 2 with a/c for a small supplement) but noisy on Sundays when the Jesus Joy Centre holds services on the roof. Busy *hoteli* at street level. BB ②

Josleejim Duruma Rd ℡0722/975799. Sizeable, very friendly place, with reasonable facilities, including safe parking. The s/c rooms have no nets but fans and clean sheets make it overall decent value for money. BB ②

New Daba City Guest House Mwembe Tayari Rd, next to Coast Bus ℡0727/603227. Clean and respectable cheapie with s/c rooms, nets and hot water. Excellent value. ①

New People's Abdel Nasser Rd, right by the main bus and matatu offices ℡0727/103426. Big, noisy, long-established and very male-dominated block, with some s/c rooms. Handy if you're taking a morning bus up to Malindi or Lamu. ①

Ramadhan Guest House Abdel Nasser Rd ℡0720/336979. A good-value cheapie with airy, reasonably clean non s/c rooms with fans and nets. ①

Up Country Guest House Raha Leo St ℡020/8017626. Reasonably looked after and clean, if a bit shabby, with fans, nets and sockets in s/c rooms. Cheaper, non s/c rooms are also available. ①

YWCA Corner of Kaunda Ave and Kiambu Ave ℡0727/806979, Ⓔywcamsa@gmail.com. Pleasant ambience with good security and a cafeteria (6am–8.30pm), open to men (upstairs) as well as women (downstairs), and couples can share rooms, none of which are s/c. Best value for long stays, but book ahead. No curfew, but no guests in rooms. BB ②

Hotels

ACK Guest House Shelly Beach Rd, Likoni, 500m from the ferry dock (turn first left coming from Mombasa) ℡041/2151521 or 0723/712588, Ⓦwww.ackguesthouses.or.ke. The Anglican Church of Kenya's coastal retreat might seem an odd choice, but the 26 clean, spacious rooms, with fans, TVs and large bathrooms (but no nets) are well looked after, and the pool is clean and a good size. BB ③

Castle Royal Moi Ave ℡041/2220373 or 0720/843072, Ⓦwww.sentrim-hotels.com. Mombasa's most venerable hotel, formerly the *Palace*, dating from 1909. Period on the outside, modern on the inside, with a/c rooms (all with DSTV and, in theory, wi-fi), and corridors open at both ends to allow a through breeze. All it lacks is a pool. BB ⑤

Ganjoni Wananchi Archbishop Makarios Rd ℡020/2332053, Ⓦganjoniwananchihotel.com. Popular, upcountry-style hotel, with busy bar and restaurant and competitively priced rooms with TV and fans (or a/c for a Ksh500 supplement). BB ③

🏃 **Lotus** Corner of Mvita and Cathedral roads ℡041/2313207, Ⓦwww.lotushotelkenya .com. Located on a quiet corner not far from Fort Jesus, with a vaguely Oriental feel, and overflowing with greenery, it's not surprising the plain but very neat, clean rooms with a/c and TV are often full. BB ④

Manson Mohdar Mohamed Habib Rd ℡041/2222419–21, Ⓦwww.mansonhotel.com. Large, clean rooms of variable size in a 7-floor block, some with balconies, some with fans, others a/c. TV lounge and bar-restaurant on the ground floor. Secure, and reasonable value overall. BB ③

🏃 **New Palm Tree** Nkrumah Rd ℡020/8025682 or 0732/334200. Once quite a grand place that still has bags of charm, despite the frayed edges. Alcohol is prohibited, however. Rooms are spacious and clean, with fans and a/c but no nets. There's also a sunny first-floor courtyard. A good deal, and worth reserving. BB ④

Royal Court Haile Selassie Rd ℡041/2220932 or 0722/412867, Ⓦwww.royalcourtmombasa.co.ke. Modern business-class hotel, close to the station, with good-sized rooms with spotless bathrooms, facing out over town. Rooftop bar-restaurant, plunge pool and gym. BB ⑤

 Tamarind Village Cement Rd, Mkomani (north across the Nyali Bridge, and turn right) ☎041/474600 or 0725/959552, ⓦwww .tamarind.co.ke. Spacious, very comfortable, serviced apartments, all with wonderful views across to the Old Town. ⑥

The City

Mombasa doesn't have a huge number of sights, but most visitors will want to check out its main one, **Fort Jesus**, in the shadow of which lies Mombasa's **Old Town**, still an atmospheric hive of narrow lanes, mosques and carved Swahili doorways. In the modern town centre, the **tusks** that feature on so many postcards are not wildly exciting, though fans of 1930s architecture might appreciate one or two of the buildings from that era on Digo Road. Further afield, there's a **baobab forest** and a seventeenth-century **pillar tomb** which are worth a visit.

Fort Jesus

For all its turbulent past (see p.391), **Fort Jesus** (daily 8am–6pm; Ksh800, children Ksh400; ☎041/2312839), a classic European fortress of its age, is today a quiet museum-monument. Surprisingly spacious and tree-shaded inside its giant walls, it retains a lot of its original character, despite having been much repaired over the centuries. The curious angular construction was the design of an Italian architect and ensured that assailants trying to scale the walls would always be under crossfire from one of the bastions.

The best time to visit is probably first thing in the morning. Look out for the restored **Omani House**, in the far right corner as you enter the fort. Avoiding head contact with the lintel, climb up to the flat roof for a wonderful view over Mombasa. Interesting in their own way, too, are the uncomfortable-looking, wall-mounted **latrines**, overhanging the ditch just south of the Omani House, which would presumably have been closed in with mats. It is immediately obvious that Fort Jesus was not so much a building as a small, fortified town in its own right. The ruins of a church, storerooms, and possibly even shops are up at this end and, to judge by some accounts, the main courtyard was at times a warren of little dwellings. Captain Owen described it in 1824 as being: "a mass of indiscriminate ruins, huts and hovels, many of them built wherever space could be found but generally formed from parts of the ruins, matted over for roofs."

Most of the archeological interest is at the seaward end of the fort, where you'll find the **Hall of the Mazrui** with its beautiful stone benches and eighteenth-century inscription. A nearby room has been dedicated entirely to the display of a huge plaster panel of **wall paintings**, made with carbon and ochre by bored Portuguese sentries. Their subjects are fascinating: ships, figures in armour (including the captain of the fort wielding his baton), fish, and what seems to be a chameleon. Illiteracy precluded much writing but, oddly enough, there's nothing obscene either. The small **café** above the room with the wall paintings serves first-class lime juice, and the museum **restaurant**, behind the ticket office, has a lunch dish each day and various snacks.

Fort Jesus Museum

The **museum**, on the eastern side of the fort where the main soldiers' barracks block used to be, is small, but still manages to convey a good idea of the age and breadth of Swahili civilization, and also has a decent display of Mijikenda ethnography (see p.423). Most of the displays are of pottery, indigenous or imported, some from as far afield as China and some of it over a thousand years old. A number of private collections have contributed pieces and there's probably still a wealth of material in private hands. Look out for the big carved door taken from the Mazrui house in Gazi (p.441) and also the extraordinary whale vertebra used as a stool. The museum has a good exhibit on the long-term project to recover as much as possible from the wreck of the *Santo Antonio de Tanna*, which sank in 1697 while trying to break the prolonged siege of the fort. Some seven thousand objects have already been brought to the surface, but the bulk of the ship itself remains nine fathoms deep in the harbour.

The Old Town

From Fort Jesus, the **Old Town** is an easy objective. First impressions, though – of a quarter entirely devoted to gift and **curio shops** – are none too encouraging. This turns out to be purely the result of Fort Jesus' adjacent car park and tourist appeal, and the shops don't extend far into the Old Town. Further west, away from the fort, the stores are smaller, and correspondingly cheaper and less pretentious, with a couple of genuine antique shops along Kibokoni Road and the famous Noor Ala Noor cloth emporium on the corner of Kibokoni and Old Kilindini roads. For more about buying crafts, see *Crafts and shopping* colour section.

Mosques and other architecture

The Old Town is not, in fact, that old. Most buildings date from the nineteenth century, and though there may be foundations and even walls that go back many centuries, you'll get a clearer guide to the age of the town from its twenty or so **mosques**.

The **Mandhry Mosque** on Bachawy Road, founded in 1570, is officially the oldest, and has a striking minaret, but it's rarely open to visitors. The **Basheikh Mosque** on Old Kilindini Road, painted in green and white, is also acknowledged to be very old – "about 1300", they'll tell you, though this may be exaggerated. Entering the mosques – as long as they aren't locked – is usually all right for men if you're properly dressed (no shorts) and take your shoes off. Sometimes you may be expected to wash hands and feet. Women, however modestly dressed, will usually be politely refused.

Much of the other **architecture** in the Old Town is profoundly influenced by the Indian-style Zanzibari tastes of the Busaidi occupiers of the nineteenth century. This is particularly noticeable in the elegant fretwork balconies and shutters still maintained on a few houses, notably on **Ndia Kuu**. For older relics, you'll have to look further – there are a number of quite ancient tombs along the seafront, especially towards the northern end of the Old Town, some of which have pillars; this is the part of Mombasa considered to pre-date the Portuguese.

Returning south along the twisting **seafront road**, you come to the gigantic **Burhani Masjid** – the mosque of the Bohra community, renowned traders of Indian origin. In the unassuming setting of the Old Town, it is an imposingly massive edifice.

The Jain temple

Heading up towards Digo Road, you might enjoy stopping by at the **Jain temple** (daily 10am–12.30pm; free; remove shoes and anything made of leather), whose entrance is in Langoni Road. This sublime creation – intricate icing sugar outside, scrupulously clean and scented within and decorated in dozens of pastel shades – was only built in 1963. Jainism is an Indian religion, pre-dating but related to Buddhism, and commonest in Gujarat (original home of the majority of Kenyan Asians), which holds all life to be sacred. The temple interior is ornamentally magnificent: the painted figurines of deities in their

▲ Airport & Nairobi

Nyali Bridge & North Coast ▲

ABDEL NASSER ROAD

MUYAKA ROAD

FAZA ROAD

SHAFI ROAD

JOMO KENYATTA AVENUE

BIBI WA

BARINGO ROAD

BIASHARA STREET

JOE KADENGE STREET

MACKAWI ROAD

GEORGE MORUBA STREET

BUNGOMA STREET

BIASHARA STREET

Akamba Bus Services

Modern Coast

Total

Tahmeed ★

Falcon Buses

Sikh Temple Complex ④

Kaloleni Buses & ★ Matatus

Kobil

Coast Bus Ⓐ

Old KBS Station

War Monument ③

JOMO KENYATTA AVENUE

Barclays Bank ⑥

MWEMBE TAYARI ROAD

Ⓒ

DURUMA ROAD

BAJUNI ROAD

Raha Leo STREET

KWA SHIBU ROAD

Ⓑ

Zilizopendwa Music Store

Public Health Dept

ASANIFU KOMBO STREET

HOSPITAL STREET

TURKANA STREET

KONZI RD

⑧
⑨
⑩

Railway Station ◄

Swaminarayan Temple

HAILE SELASSIE ROAD

Ⓕ

Total Ⓓ

⑫ ⑬

Omar Hussein Cycloduka

Oilibya

KCB

MAUNGANO ROAD

MSANIFU KOMBO STREET

Library

TURKANA STREET

TAITA ST.

STREET

GUSII

Southern House

Tusky's Bandari

AGA KHAN ROAD

SHIMONI STREET

WHITE FATHERS ROAD

⑮

⑯

⑰

MAUNGANO RD

CHEMBE ROAD

MERU ROAD

⑲

⑳

TANGANA ROAD

MACHAKOS ROAD

Mombasa Uni Plaza

LIONS CLUB MOMBASA PWANI ROAD

MERU RD

Kant Stationers

Farway Travel Centre ㉑

Reinsurance Plaza

BUNIU ROAD

Uhuru Gardens

Tusks

Harria's Gift Shop

Freed Building

Barclays Bank

Ketty Tours

MOI AVENUE

Ⓗ

Commercial Bank of Africa

Jubilee Insurance Building

Shell

ⓘ

㉔

Wimpy

WAKATWA ROAD

Gapco

Safaricom ㉓

Diamond Trust Building

NGONYO ROAD

CUSTOM HOUSE ROAD

MOI AVENUE

㉕

Regal Chambers

MOHTAR QUAMED HABIB ROAD

KAMUNDE LANE

SAUTI YA KENYA ROAD

Web Corner @

Hare Krisna Temple

Mombasa Sports Club

MNAZI MMOJA ROAD

㉖

MPYA ROAD

CHIEF ALI BIN NAAMAN ROAD

GIBSON NGOME RD.

GIBSON NGOME RD.

Ⓙ

Playing Fields

Shree Visha Oshwal Varik Community Swimming Pool

MAKARIOS ROAD

N

△

Commonwealth War Cemetery

DEDAN KIMATHI AVENUE

Little Theatre Club

ACCOMMODATION
Berachah Lodge E
Castle Royal H
Excellent D
Josleejim C
Lotus I
Manson J
New Daba City A
New Palm Tree G
Royal Court F
Up Country B
YWCA K

Kilindini Docks ◄

▼ Likoni Ferry & South Coast

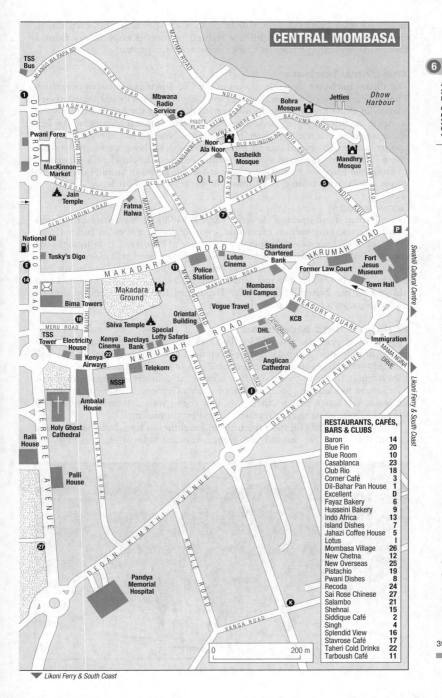

Dhow Harbour

TSS Bus

DIGO ROAD

Pwani Forex

MacKinnon Market

National Oil

Tusky's Digo

Bima Towers

TSS Tower

Kenya Airways

NSSF

Ambalal House

Holy Ghost Cathedral

Ralli House

Palli House

NYERERE AVENUE

MLANGO WA PAPA RD

KUZE ROAD

MZIZIMA ROAD

BIASHARA STREET

NEHRU ROAD

KERICHO STREET

LANGONI ROAD

Jain Temple

Fatma Halwa

OLD KILINDINI ROAD

MARIAKANI LANE

SAMBURU

WACHANGAMWE ST

KIBOKONI STREET

NYERI ROAD

Mbwana Radio Service

PIGOTT PLACE

KITUI ROAD

Noor Ala Noor

Basheikh Mosque

OLD KILINDINI RD

NDIA KUU

MWEA TABERE ST

Bohra Mosque

Jetties

BACHUMA ROAD

OLD TOWN

Mandhry Mosque

NDIA KUU

BACHAWI ROAD

MAKADARA ROAD

Lotus Cinema

Police Station

MWAGOGU ROAD

Makadara Ground

Shiva Temple

Special Lofty Safaris

Oriental Building

Kenya Cinema

Barclays Bank

NKRUMAH ROAD

Telekom

MERU ROAD

BALUCHI STREET

Electricity House

Standard Chartered Bank

MAKUTUBU ROAD

Mombasa Uni Campus

Vogue Travel

KCB

DHL

Anglican Cathedral

CATHEDRAL CLOSE

CATHEDRAL ROAD

NGOMENI LANE

KAUNDA AVENUE

TREASURY SQUARE

Former Law Court

Fort Jesus Museum

Town Hall

NKRUMAH ROAD

P

Immigration

MAMA NGINA DRIVE

MVITA ROAD

DEDAN KIMATHI AVENUE

MTIKINDANI ROAD

MKINDANI ROAD

KWALE ROAD

Pandya Memorial Hospital

VANGA ROAD

K

Swahili Cultural Centre

Likoni Ferry & South Coast

0   200 m

Likoni Ferry & South Coast

RESTAURANTS, CAFÉS, BARS & CLUBS

Baron	14
Blue Fin	20
Blue Room	10
Casablanca	23
Club Rio	18
Corner Café	3
Dil-Bahar Pan House	1
Excellent	D
Fayaz Bakery	6
Husseini Bakery	9
Indo Africa	13
Island Dishes	7
Jahazi Coffee House	5
Lotus	I
Mombasa Village	26
New Chetna	12
New Overseas	25
Pistachio	19
Pwani Dishes	8
Recoda	24
Sai Rose Chinese	27
Salambo	21
Shehnai	15
Siddique Café	2
Singh	4
Splendid View	16
Stavrose Café	17
Taheri Cold Drinks	22
Tarboush Café	11

niches are each provided with a drain so they can be easily showered down, while around the ceiling, exquisitely stylized pictures portray scenes from a human life, including a familiar snake temptation in a garden.

The dhow harbour

The **dhow harbour**, along the shores of the Old Town, is somewhat overrated. There are usually one or two boats in port but you can no longer expect to see dozens, let alone hundreds, of dhows, even at the end of the northeast monsoon in April, traditionally the peak time for arrivals: seasonal variations are less important now that the big *jahazis* have engines. Nor are you likely to have the opportunity to go aboard one of these exotic vessels, though a number of big dhows have been converted as dinner-cruise vessels (see below). Still, the area is an enjoyable place for a stroll, especially at weekends, when families dress up to go for a walk and children leap around in the sea below Fort Jesus.

Dhow cruises

The German tour operator Severin (☎041/5485001, Ⓦwww.severin-kenya .com) offers, among various excursions, evening dhow cruises on Tudor Creek ($99), followed by a son-et-lumière performance at Fort Jesus, and dinner in the courtyard of the fort. Any Mombasa or North Coast hotel will make a reservation for you. Dining cruises are also offered by the *Tamarind* restaurant (see p.403; ☎041/471747, Ⓦwww.tamarind.co.ke; $75), who have outfitted two old *jahazis*, the Nawalilkher and the Babulkher, for Swahili seafood dinners under sail, with a band in accompaniment.

Walks around Mombasa

For the most part, the rest of Mombasa's pleasures are simple. Strolling, with plenty of cold-drink stops, is a time-honoured Mombasan diversion. You will probably want to see that immortal double pair of **elephant tusks** arching over Moi Avenue. To get to them, you have to run the gauntlet of curio booths that have almost hidden the cool hideaway of Uhuru Gardens, with its Africa-shaped fountain. And when you get there, you may regret your determination to view the tusks close up, as they're revealed as grubby aluminium.

More rewarding, if you have the time and inclination for a **long walk**, is the circuit that takes off around the breezy, seaward side of the island down

▲ Camels on beach

Mama Ngina Drive: a fine morning's or evening's walk, when it seems to become the meeting place for half of Mombasa's Indian population. You can get back to town on a matatu from the Likoni ferry dock. There are lots of places to sit and watch the waves pounding the coral cliffs through the break in the reef. On the clifftop, protruding from the far side of the **golf course**, are the stumpy, insignificant remains of Fort St Joseph, built in 1826 to defend Mazrui Mombasa against the attacks of the Busaidi Omanis. Come down this clifftop promenade at weekends or late afternoon and you'll find plenty of other people doing the same – there are even food stalls and streets entertainers. At the end of Mama Ngina Drive is an extensive stand of enormous **baobab trees**, frequently associated with ancient settlements on the coast.

Finally, to the west of the Likoni ferry roundabout is a huge pillar tomb, the **Mbaraki Pillar**. Supposedly the burial place of a seventeenth-century mainland sheikh, the chief of one of the "twelve tribes", its eight-metre height is impressive enough, but it is these days dwarfed by nearby warehouses. To get to it from Likoni, turn left immediately before Ndoho Market, then follow the road round to the left about 200m, before branching right down a broad, dirt road between warehouses for a further 200m, behind Nakumatt Likoni. The pillar is on the right, near the cliffside, with a small mosque alongside.

Eating

The city is full of places to eat, and **street food and drinks** are much better and more widely available than in Nairobi. During the day, you can get green coconuts (drink the coconut water, then scoop out and eat the jelly-like flesh); sugar-cane juice, freshly pressed from the cane; and cuplets of *kahawa thungu* (thick bitter coffee, usually flavoured with ginger or cardamom). After dark, you'll find what are effectively full meals for Ksh100 or so, including *nyama choma*, chapattis, spicy little chicken kebabs and freshly fried potato and cassava crisps, by the bus stalls up Abdel Nasser Road and along Jomo Kenyatta Avenue and Mwembe Tayari Road, as well as on other busy corners.

Snacks and juice bars

Dil-Bahar Pan House Digo Rd, at the corner of Bungoma Street. Indian snacks, *pan* (see box, p.402), excellent *chai* and good juices including melon, watermelon, and occasionally even custard apple. A calm refuge, or a place to read the paper.

Fayaz Bakery Jomo Kenyatta Ave. A good range of cakes and biscuits, with a fair stab at cheesecake and doughnuts as well as local specialities such as passion cake.

Husseni Bakery Turkana St. Nice selection of cakes and snacks. Mon–Sat 9am–12.30pm & 2.30–7.30pm, closed Sun.

Jahazi Coffee House Ndia Kuu, Old Town. Beautifully decorated, joint Canadian-Kenyan venture in an eighteenth-century house near Fort Jesus, serving delicious coffee with cardamom , cinnamon and cloves, *mahamri* and other snacks. As well as the café it serves as a cross–cultural meeting place and book exchange.

Pistachio Chembe Rd. Hard to beat for quality ice cream and various kinds of coffee, but not cheap.

Siddique Café just off Pigott Place, Old Town, next to Mbwana Radio Service music shop. Friendly little snack bar with cold drinks and fresh *maji ya miwa* (sugar-cane juice).

Taheri Cold Drinks House Nkrumah Rd (closed weekends). Juices, samosas, sausages, meat pies and kebabs. Good for a weekday snack.

Restaurants

Mombasa is well supplied with good, **cheap restaurants**. Especially if you're newly arrived from upcountry, they are one of the city's chief delights, as a discernible cuisine involving coconut, fish, chicken, rice and beans, and incorporating

Asian flavours, begins to make an impression on your palate. Phone numbers are given in the reviews whenever it's a good idea to book. The places covered below appear on the Central Mombasa map except where noted.

Swahili food

Island Dishes Kibokoni St. Wonderful Swahili dishes, including vegetables and fish with coconut, *mkate wa kima* ("Swahili pizza" also known as *mkate mayai*), and various fruit juices, with mango and chilli sauce on the table to spice it up if you like it hot, and sometimes tamarind if you prefer it sweet and sour.

Recoda Moi Ave, near the Tusks, ☎041/2223629. One of the oldest and most famous Swahili restaurants in Mombasa, relocated from the Old Town, and sadly stripped of most of its character. The food is good and cheap, but tends to be generic diner fare, much the same as you can find anywhere else in town – pilaus, birianis, chicken tikka, and a few special Swahili dishes if you're lucky. Daily 8.30am–midnight.

Tarboush Café Makadara Rd. Open-air eating and a great spot for grills, with *shawarmas*, shish kebab, "chicken tikka" and curries plus good naan bread and gorgeous juices. An excellent place to check out the Afro-Indo-Arabian combination that makes up the local cuisine. Daily 7am–late.

Fast food & hotelis

Baron Digo Rd. Really more of a beer hall than a restaurant, but there's decent food at moderate prices, with pizzas, grills and fish dishes (around Ksh400–500 a meal).

Blue Fin Meru Rd (closed Sun). Fish or chicken and chips, and other reasonably priced fry-ups, plus juices and daily specials.

Blue Room Haile Selassie Rd. Self-service place with tiled tables, fans, a cool courtyard and a menu dominated by burgers and pizzas, plus a few vegetarian choices. Their internet access is a bonus.

Corner Café Corner of Jomo Kenyatta Ave and George Morura St. Popular and lively place, with tables outside (as well as in) the tiny premises, offering a range of filling dishes and snacks, including kebabs.

Pwani Dishes Turkana St. Cheap and cheerful diner, with lots of stews and basic Kenyan dishes in large servings at low prices. Daily 7am–10pm.

Mombasa Village Mji Mpya Rd. Very popular open-air beer and *nyama choma* spot, with live music and grilled meat (minimum order 500g), including beef, lamb, pork chops and goat ribs. Be prepared to wait a while for them to cook it.

Indian cooking

Indo Africa Haile Selassie Rd, ☎041/2317529 or 0721/743556. North Indian mutton and fish dishes, Jeera chicken and vegetarian options. Decor notable for being absent, though the food is reliably good (and less fiercely spicy than at the adjacent *New Chetna*). Try the prawn or fish masala, or *muttar paneer* (home-made cheese, cooked with peas) for vegetarians. Around Ksh1000 for two, including a drink. Daily (except Tues evening) noon–2.30pm & 7–10.30pm.

Lotus Hotel Corner of Mvita and Cathedral rds. Clean and efficient, with steaks, grills and curries. Expect to pay around Ksh600 for a meal.

New Chetna Haile Selassie Rd. A long-time favourite for snacks and sweets on the left, and tasty South Indian vegetarian dishes at low prices on the right. The all-you-can-eat *dhal* is superb, but the food can be very hot, so treat with caution. Full dinners around Ksh300, most dishes around Ksh100. Daily 8am–9pm.

Pan shops

Highly characteristic of Mombasa are the Indian **pan shops**, often doubling as tobacconists and corner shops. Worth trying at least once, *pan* is a natural digestive and stimulant that encourages salivation. Its main ingredient is a chopped or shredded "betel nut", actually the areca palm nut, which is flavoured with your choice of sweet spices, chopped nuts and vegetable matter, syrup, and white lime, from a display of dishes, all wrapped in a hot-sweet, dark-green leaf from the betel vine, known as *pan* in Urdu and Hindi. Adding tobacco is another option, but best avoided by novices. Pop the triangular parcel in your mouth and munch – it tastes as exotic and unlikely as it sounds – spitting out the copious juice as you go. Two of the best *pan* counters in town are at the *Dil-Bahar* café (see p.401) and the *New Chetna* restaurant (see above).

Shehnai Fatemi House, Maungano Rd
℡041/2312492. Mughlai specialities with a good reputation, in a spacious and light interior with somewhat regal furniture. You're spoilt for choice: try *achar gosht* (mutton cooked in spices and flavoured with pickles), or *machi tandoorwalli* (oven-baked marinated rock cod). Vegetarian meals around Ksh500, non-veg Ksh750. Tues–Sun noon–2pm & 7–10.30pm.

Singh Mwembe Tayari Rd ℡041/493283. A bit of a walk from the centre of town, but worth it for the very tasty Punjabi curries. Tues–Sun noon–2.30pm & 7–10.30pm.

Splendid View Maungano Rd. Fish and prawn dishes with butter or garlic are the speciality here, and very tasty they are too, at around Ksh300 a throw. Mon–Sat 11am–2pm & 4.30–10.30pm, Sun 5–10.30pm.

Stavrose Café Sheikh Jundani Rd/Maungano Rd. A small place that's been serving Indian snacks, tikka dishes and kebabs for years. Lunches around Ksh300. Mon–Fri 9am–7.30pm, Sat 9am–3pm.

Foreign cuisines

Galaxy Chinese Archbishop Makarios Rd (see "Mombasa Island" map, p.394) ℡020/2138611.

Variable Chinese food, and relatively pricey – if you want to be extravagant, try the pan-fried lobster with ginger and garlic, otherwise expect to pay around Ksh2500 for two, including drinks. Daily 11am–2.30pm & 6–11pm.

New Overseas Chinese Korean Moi Ave, 200m west of the Tusks ℡041/2230729–30. Good-value Cantonese and Korean cooking, focusing on seafood, with more expensive specialities including steamed crab, tuna fish *sashimi*, and *kimchi* (spicy pickled cabbage) soup, all at around Ksh500–800. Daily 11am–3pm & 5.30–11pm.

Sai Rose Chinese Nyerere Ave ℡0721/497973 or 0714/219693. A better restaurant than hotel, with crispy duck Ksh1250 and most dishes Ksh450 or Ksh500. Daily 11am–3pm & 6pm–midnight.

Tamarind Cement Rd, Mkomani (north across the Nyali Bridge, and turn right) ℡041/474600, ⓦwww.tamarind.co.ke. With a sublime location above Tudor Creek, this is unequivocally the best restaurant in Mombasa and the only one specializing in seafood. Tempting dishes and a pricey wine list mean you're unlikely to come away from dinner with change from Ksh4000 a head.

Drinking and nightlife

Despite the city's overwhelmingly Muslim population, you won't go thirsty. There are several **nightclubs** too, but the busiest clubs and discos tend to be in the resort area north of Mombasa (see "Nightlife" sections on p.415 & p.418). Most clubs are free, but on popular nights (Wed, Fri & Sat), men are charged up to Ksh300 entry, while women are admitted half-price or free.

Long before the clubs open, a stroll around the generally safe Old Town will uncover one or two **coffee-sellers** serving black *kahawa* from traditional high-spouted jugs. A perfect accompaniment to the coffee is perfumed almond *halwa*. This is a local speciality, not the sesame sweet of the Middle East, but more like Turkish delight. One of the best places to buy it is *Fatma Halwa Shop* (℡0722/269573; Mon–Sat mid-morning until 1am) at the corner of Langoni and Old Kilindini roads.

There are few straightforward bars in Mombasa: try the bar by the *Excellent Hotel* – a large and restful old-timers' place, mercifully free of prostitutes; or visit the *Lotus Hotel*, which is one of the nicest places in town for a civilized beer.

Clubs and live music

Unless you want to be repeatedly accosted by prostitutes (or, if you're a woman, by gentlemen who all believe they're the man you're looking for) it's best to visit most of the following clubs with at least a companion, if not in a group. The following are marked on the Central Mombasa map (p.398), unless otherwise noted.

California Dream Hotel Moi Ave 400m west of the Tusks, at the corner with Liwatoni Rd (see "Mombasa Island" map, p.394). The former, alluringly named *Jam Rescue Hotel* has

traditional Kikuyu and Swahili music on Wed, Fri and Sat nights.

Casablanca Mnazi Moja Rd, just off Moi Ave ⓦcasablancamombasa.com. On the site of the old

Sunshine Club, this draws a big mixed crowd to a lively terrace, and the prostitutes gather here in force, especially upstairs. They can be a pain – or a laugh – depending on your mood. Relatively expensive drinks and food.

New Florida Nightclub & Casino Mama Ngina Drive, overlooking the ocean, 2km from the city centre (see "Mombasa Island" map, p.394). Attempts to create a slick impression, with floor shows and glitter, but similar in most respects to its Nairobi namesake. It does benefit from the terrace by the ocean, a pleasant little gaming room (opens 6pm, free entry until 7.30pm) and keg beer.

Saba-Saba Corner of Jomo Kenyatta Ave and Ronald Ngala Rd, through an unmarked entrance distinguished by the plants on the first-floor terrace (see Mombasa Island map, p.394). The bar at the front isn't very inspiring, but head out to the open terrace at the back, where the action is. There's often live music, even in the day, and always a sweaty, local atmosphere.

Salambo Moi Ave. By day a dozy bar with limited snacks, this comes to life at night as the city centre's only really local disco. Mon–Sat there's a mix of Congolese sounds, soul and reggae, with midnight shows, acrobats, dancing and beauty contests. Open 24/7.

Club Rio Baluchi St, behind the post office. Formerly *Toyz*, this is central Mombasa's only DJ club. Wed, Fri and Sat nights are packed, and drinks tend to become more expensive as the night wears on, but other nights can be deserted. Generally hassle-free, and gay-friendly.

Arts and culture

Cultural and artistic life in Mombasa is a bit limited. The **British Council** (First-floor, Jubilee Insurance Building, Moi Ave ☎041/2223076, ⓦwww .britishcouncil.org) and **Alliance Française** (Freed Building, corner of Moi Ave and Kwa Shibu Rd ☎041/2225048, ⓦwww.ambafrance-ke.org) occasionally sponsor events, but you can't guarantee anything. There's no equivalent of Nairobi's relatively flourishing arts and gallery scene.

Cinemas The Kenya, on Nkrumah Rd, is the most promising. Otherwise, try the Lotus on Makadara Rd. Both survive on a diet of Bollywood, with a few American films thrown in. For a modern cinema experience, the closest and best cinema on the coast is the Nyali Cinemax at Nyali Plaza, with four screens.

Libraries Kenya National Library, Msanifu Kombo St (Mon–Thurs 8am–6.30pm, Fri 8am–4pm, Sat 8am–5pm); Fort Jesus Museum (archeology; Mon–Fri 8am–12.30pm & 2–4.30pm). The small a/c library at the the British Council (details above; Mon–Thurs 7.45am–4.30pm, Fri 7.45am–1pm) has recent UK newspapers: temporary membership is available for Ksh200 per day (bring your passport).

Theatre The Little Theatre Club, Mnazi Moja Rd (☎041/2229258), used mainly to be an outlet for amateur dramatics in the expat/settler community, but of late it has been hosting productions by drama groups from all over the coastal region, as well as music performances. Seats usually cost around Ksh200.

Shopping

Mombasa is a good city for **shopping**, with a generally wide choice, and fewer hassles as you window-shop than in Nairobi. Once you know where to go for crafts, the business of buying souvenirs improves markedly.

The main tourist street is the stretch of Moi Avenue **between the Tusks and Digo Road** and the pavement is periodically lined with souvenir stalls (though their abundance fluctuates with the fortunes of the tourist industry). Sisal baskets, soapstone, beadwork and fake ebony carvings make up most of what's on offer. Those at the Digo Road end of Moi Avenue tend to be the most aggressive at touting their wares, and getting past without stopping is not easy, while if you do halt, making cool decisions can be difficult. The line of stalls on **Chembe Road** seems to be in something of a backwater, and they're more fun to deal with.

If you're **buying crafts** in Mombasa, first go and have a look at ⵌ Harria's Gift Shop (Mon–Sat 9am–6pm; credit cards accepted) in Regal Chambers, Moi

Mombasa Carnival

Every November, Mombasa holds a **"Cultural Carnival"**, with parades of floats, representing everything from churches to community self-help groups and business associations. They converge on Moi Avenue and stream under the Tusks. Although this isn't a traditional festival, having been invented a few years ago by the Kenya Tourist Board, it incorporates elements of Mombasa tradition, such as the competitive **drumming and marching teams** known as *beni* or *ngoma* (see p.586), that you're bound to see (and hear) if you're in the crowd. You'll find lots of street food, crafts hawkers and an increase in pickpockets – beware.

Avenue, near the Tusks. It consistently offers good deals and you may even be able to get things here more cheaply than on the street.

The usual rules apply when **bargaining** – don't start the ball rolling if you're not in the mood and never offer a price you're not prepared to pay. If you want quite a few items, it's worth browsing for a well-stocked stall and then, as you reach one near-agreement after another with the stallholder, add a new item to your collection. This way you should be able to buy well-finished *vyondo* (sisal baskets) in the range of Ksh600–1000, small soapstone items for Ksh150–500, and simple bracelets and necklaces for around Ksh100, or even less.

It's much harder to estimate what you should pay for **carvings** as the price depends as much on the workmanship as on the size of the piece. Again, take a look in Harria's for an idea. If you want to buy carvings, consider making a special trip to the enormous **Kamba Woodcarvers Village**, near the airport (ⓦ www.akambahandicraftcoop.com; coming from the airport, it's on the left about 300m before you reach Magongo Road, the main road leading into the city). While it may appear that the art of woodcarving has been reduced here to not much more than a human conveyor belt, the village is in fact a cooperative, with willing members who are only too pleased to see visitors.

Markets

For a completely different retail experience, visit **Mackinnon Market**, the city centre's main one, which has a splendid abundance of tropical fruit, including such exotics as jackfruit and soursops (like a bigger, tarter version of a custard apple). Behind the market, there are several good sweet shops and a row of stores devoted to spices, coffee and tea.

Apart from the Mackinnon and the big street market off Mwembe Tayari, there's **Makupa market** in the heart of Majengo, the island's low-income housing district. A colourful, multipurpose market with a busy, rural atmosphere, it's well worth a visit. Go 1.5km northwest along Jomo Kenyatta Avenue, then turn left at Salim Mwa Ngunga Road.

Cloth and domestic items

Mombasa is also a cheap place to buy the coast's famous **fabrics**. For genuine Indian **sarongs**, have a rummage through the Old Town. Noor Ala Noor, on the corner of Kibokoni and Old Kilindini roads, is an enjoyable shop. For the latest *kanga* designs check out the shops in **Biashara Street** (especially the section between George Morura Street and Digo Road), where new designs are sold before they become available anywhere else in Kenya. It's worth checking prices in several shops before buying, and perhaps going in company so you can bargain for several lots at once (they are always sold in pairs and you should be looking to get a pair for around Ksh400 or less). It's actually quite difficult, however, to knock prices down more than a token Ksh50 for the sake of politeness, as business is just too good.

Beyond Mackawi Road, Biashara Street shifts from textiles to a less gaudy section of **household goods** – winnowing trays, coconut graters, palm bags, mats, spoons, furniture and the like – more mundane, but just as interesting to browse.

Music

If you have even a passing interest in African **music**, Mombasa is as good a place as any to stock up on a few CDs. Prices are low: expect to pay between Ksh300 and Ksh1000 for a CD, depending on how legitimate the copy is. The best place for finding traditional Mijikenda music and Mombasa *taarab,* as well as traditional songs from the Wa-Bajuni people of Lamu district, is Mbwana Radio Service (☏041/2221550), just off Pigott Place in the Old Town. Kikuyu and other Kenyan sounds, as well as the ubiquitous gospel pop, are available from the more permanent shops: try Zilizo Pendwa Music Store, a hole-in-the-wall shop up an alley just off Raha Leo Street.

Safaris from Mombasa

Mombasa is important as a **safari hub**, with ninety percent of safaris starting from the coast visiting Tsavo East or Tsavo West. With a number of daily flights further afield, however, even the Maasai Mara is accessible for a short safari, though less than two nights isn't recommended.

Expect to pay $180 for a one-day safari to Tsavo East, including lunch, or from $270 staying overnight, depending on the lodge and your group size. Air safaris to the Maasai Mara start at around $1000 for two nights, including the flight. Safaris should always include all transport and transfers, meals, park fees for the full duration of your stay, and at least two three-hour game drives each day.

Safari operators

African Quest Safaris Mezzanine floor, Palli House, Nyerere Ave, ☏041/2227052 or 0722/410362, ⊛www.africanquest.co.ke. Large operator offering competitively priced lodge safaris. Two bronze guides.

🏃 **Farways Safaricentre** Msanifu Kombo St, ☏0733/773434 or 0734/855261, ✆farways@africaonline.co.ke.
Good value and very personal service from a small, long-established agent with an excellent network of operator contacts, including car rental, Zanzibar trips, accommodation bookings and safaris.

Glorious Safaris ☏041/476518 or 0733/239412, ⊛www.glorioussafaris.com. Busy operator with strong British ties, offering competitively priced local excursions and safaris to Tsavo East and West.

Kedev Off Links Rd, Nyali, ☏041/5487356 or 0733/410566, ⊛www.kedev.de. Tailor-made safaris to Tsavo and beyond, with a personal touch. Customers can also stay in Kedev's own guesthouse in Nyali.

Ketty Tours Ketty Plaza, Moi Ave, ☏041 2229572 or 041/2312204, ⊛www.kettytours .co.ke. Solid operator with good experience and a large rental fleet.

Pollman's Tours and Safaris Pollman's House, Malindi Rd, Bamburi ☏041/2014980 or 0721/786553, ⊛www.arpsafaris.com. One of the biggest operators (you'll see their vehicles everywhere) with reliable, mainstream safaris. One bronze guide.

🏃 **Southern Cross Safaris** Southern Cross Centre, off Nyali Bridge (northbound, mainland side, immediate first exit on the left) ☏020/2434600, ⊛www.southerncrosssafaris.com. Highly respected operators and agents, with four bronze and four silver guides and their own *Satao* camps.

Special Lofty Safaris First-floor, Hassanali Building, Nkrumah Rd ☏041/2220241, ⊛www .lofty-tours.de. Conscientious German-Kenyan operator running its own safaris. The main draw is experience and Land Cruisers, a more personal way of travelling than minibus.

Car and bike rental

Renting a car for an independent safari, prices tend to be a little cheaper in Mombasa than in Nairobi, especially if you deal with a local company. Most of the safari operators (see opposite) also rent vehicles with or without a driver. Expect to pay from around Ksh4000 per day or Ksh25,000 per week for a Nissan Sunny saloon. Mombasa has no bike rental, but Omar Husein Cycloduka, Haile Selassie Road near Maungano Road (Mon–Sat 8.30am–1pm & 2–6pm; ☎041/2225899), has a good selection for sale, and you can re-sell. Heavyweight roadsters with racks start from Ksh4500, while mountain bikes range between Ksh5000 and Ksh8000.

Avis Mombasa Southern House, Moi Ave, Nkrumah Rd ☎041/2220465 or 0720/741625, or at Moi International Airport ☎020/2386421, ⓦwww.avismombasa.com.

Bike the Coast 0722/873738, Go Kart Track, Bamburi ⓦbikethecoast.com. Small, Swiss-owned operator specializing in half-day bicycle tours – an unusual and highly recommended option, although the tours that go inland require a bit of leg work.

Budget Associated Motors, Jomo Kenyatta Ave ☎041/2221281 or at Moi International Airport ☎041/2434759, ⓦwww.budget.com.

Distance Tours & Car Hire Wimpy Building, Moi Ave (near the Tusks) ☎041/2222869 or 0721/200496, ⓦwww.distancetours.com. Centrally located fleet-owner with a good reputation.

Pedo Bikes Kongoni Rd, near Mamba Village roundabout on the mainland north of Nyali Bridge ☎041/471193. Motorbike rental.

Unik Car Hire & Safaris Ground floor, Fatemi House, Maungano Rd, off Haile Selassie Rd ☎041/2226310, ⓦunikcarhire.com.

Listings

Banks There are one or more branches of each of the three main banks in the city centre, all with ATMs, Pwani Forex on Digo Rd (Mon–Fri 8.30am–5pm, Sat 8.30am–1pm) offers good exchange rates.

Bookshops Kant Stationers, on Moi Ave, and Citizen's Bookshop, at the corner of Jomo Kenyatta Ave and Joe Kadenge St, are the best, but both easily eclipsed by the Nakumatt supermarkets (see "Supermarkets", below).

Consulates Canada c/o Noorudin Tejpar, Farways Safaricentre, Msanifu Kombo St ☎041/2223307, ⓔfarways@africaonline.co.ke (Mon–Fri 8am–6pm, Sat 9am–1pm); Netherlands, c/o Maersk Kenya Ltd, Maritime Centre, Achbishop Makarios Close ☎041/2314190 or 0727/272645, ⓦtinyurl.com /kpcckq (Mon–Fri, 9am–2pm); Tanzania 12th floor, TSS Tower, Nkrumah Rd ☎041/2228595, ⓔtancon@africaonline.co.ke (Mon–Fri 8am–3pm, visas $50 and two passport photos); UK c/o James Knight, Seaforth Shipping, 2nd floor, Cotts House, Moi Ave ☎041/2220023 or 0722/410901, ⓔJames.Knight-HonCon@fconet.fco.gov.uk (Mon–Fri 9am–2pm).

Golf Mombasa Golf Club ☎041/2228531. Nine holes: Ksh1500. For Nyali Golf and Country Club, see p.412.

Hospitals & Emergencies Pandya Memorial Hospital, Dedan Kimathi Ave (☎041/2313577 or 0722/206424, ⓦwww.pandyahospital.org), is hygienic and efficient, and has an ambulance service, as does St John's Ambulance Service (☎041/2490625). Africa Air Rescue (AAR) Health Centre, Manyara Building, Mogadishu Rd, off the western end of Moi Ave (opposite Missions to Seamen), is open 24/7 (emergencies ☎041/312405).

Immigration You can get visitor's pass extensions at the immigration office near Provincial Headquarters on Mama Ngina Drive (☎041/2311745), but leave enough time, as you always have to wait.

Internet access Web Corner on Mohdar Mohamed Habib Rd near the Tusks (Mon–Sat 8am–8.30pm, Sun 10am–7pm), among several others.

Kenya Wildlife Service Mama Ngina Drive, ☎020/2405089 (daily 6am–6pm). Point of issue and point of sale for National Park smartcards.

Mobile phones Safaricom's main customer centre on Moi Ave (Mon–Fri 8am–5.30pm, Sat 8.30am–2pm) is efficient.

Pharmacies The staff at Diamond Arcade Pharmacy, Diamond Trust Building, Moi Ave (Mon–Fri 8am–6pm, Sat 9am–2pm; ☎041/2316351), are pleasant and helpful. Island Chemist, by *Josleejim Hotel* in Duruma Rd, is open late (Mon–Sat 8.30am–8.30pm, Sun 9am–8.30pm).

Supermarkets Nakumatt Likoni, Mbaraki Rd, near the Likoni ferry (open long hours) and Nakumatt Cinemax, Nyali (open 24/7); Tusky's Bandari, Haile

Selassie Rd and Tusky's Digo, Digo Rd (both Mon–Sat 7.30am–8.30pm, Sun 8am–7.30pm).
Swimming pools The Shree Visha Oshwal Varik Community swimming pool complex (daily 5.30am–7.30pm; Ksh300) is the best place to swim, with a good-sized lap pool, spring board and paddling pool.

Vaccinations For yellow fever, you first have to go to the Town Hall, Treasury Square, and pay (Ksh600), and then to the Public Health Department in Msanifu Kombo St, opposite the end of Hospital Rd (Mon–Fri 8am–4.30pm, closed lunchtime).

Moving on from Mombasa

Matatus to most destinations north of Mombasa, including Bamburi, Shanzu and Mtwapa, can be caught anywhere along Digo Road. Matatus to Malindi congregate at the south end of Abdel Nasser Road, near the junction with Mackawi Road, by the mosque. For Kaloleni and Voi, they leave from the Kobil station at the junction of Mwembe Tayari Road and Jomo Kenyatta Avenue.

Buses

Bus company booking offices are spread along Abdel Nasser Road (for the north coast as far as Lamu) and Jomo Kenyatta Avenue and Mwembe Tayari Rd (for Nairobi, the south coast and Tanzania). You can buy through-tickets to central and western Kenya on Akamba, Coast and Mash, but all services go via Nairobi, usually requiring a change of buses. Competition on all routes is fierce, and some operators are more reputable than others. The safest is reckoned to be Akamba, but Mash has a good reputation for comfort, while there's little to choose between the bus companies running up and down the coast. For reasons of safety and comfort, the overnight journey to Nairobi isn't recommended.

Akamba Jomo Kenyatta Ave, ☎041/2490269 or 020/3500964, Ⓦwww.akambabus.com: Nairobi (Ksh1000) dep 9am, 2pm, 9pm; Kampala (overnight; Ksh2600) dep 2pm.
Coast (Coast Air, Coastline, Coast Pekee) Mwembe Tayari Rd ☎041/3433166: Nairobi (Ksh1100–1800) dep morning and evening.
Falcon Jomo Kenyatta Ave, opposite Kobil ☎041/4900776: Malindi (Ksh200), Lamu (Ksh700), both daily.
Mash Mwembe Tayari Rd, ☎041/2491955 or 041/3432471; Nairobi (Ksh1100–1800).

Modern Coast Jomo Kenyatta Ave, ☎041/2495812 or 020/2023776 (8am–8pm): Nairobi (Ksh1200–1400) dep 8.30am & 5pm.
Tahmeed Jomo Kenyatta Ave, ☎0729/356561: Lamu (Ksh600; every morning); Dar es Salaam (Ksh1200; dep 6.30am).
Tawakal (Pwani Tawakal) Abdel Nasser Rd, ☎0722/550111 Ⓦwww.pwanitawakal.com: Malindi (Ksh200), Lamu (Ksh700), dep morning.
TSS Abdel Nasser Rd, ☎041/2221839: Malindi (Ksh200), Lamu (Ksh600), dep morning.

Trains

The overnight **train** (see p.44) for Nairobi leaves Mombasa on Tuesday, Thursday & Sunday at 7pm, and arrives, in theory, around 9am the next morning. However, don't count on making any further transport connections until the afternoon. You can also disembark in Voi (around midnight). It's best to buy tickets in person from the station, ideally on a Tuesday, Thursday or Saturday morning when the train arrives and the station is open, from 8am onwards.

Flights

If you're coming from the South Coast be prepared for **delays at the Likoni ferry**. A taxi from Mombasa island to Moi International Airport currently costs Ksh1000 with Sacco Airport Taxis (☎041/433211), and roughly the same with Kenatco (☎041/2227503) There are no buses or matatus to the airport, but a matatu from Jomo Kenyatta Avenue to Magongo will drop you less than a kilometre short. Domestic departure tax is always included in the price of your ticket, as is (normally) the international departure tax of $20.

You can fly domestically from Mombasa to Nairobi (one-way $60), Malindi (one-way $35) and Lamu (one-way $85), and Mombasa Air Safari runs a daily service from Mombasa to Maasai Mara ($290; return $400), via Ukunda (Diani Beach), Tsavo West and Amboseli. They also fly daily between Mombasa and Diani Beach/Ukunda ($20).

Airlines

Airkenya Moi International Airport ℡041/3430217 or 0720/050940, ⓦwww.airkenya.com.
Fly540 Ground Floor, Mombasa Trade Centre ℡041/2319078 or 0710/540540, ⓦwww.fly540.com.

Kenya Airways Electricity House, Nkrumah Rd ℡041/2227613 or 0734/105201, ⓦwww.kenya-airways.com.
Mombasa Air Safari Moi International Airport ℡0734/400400 or 0734/500500, ⓦwww.mombasaairsafari.com.

North of Mombasa

While the **north coast** is busier, brasher, and much less pastoral than the **south coast**, the resorts are closer to Mombasa and the airport, and there are more targets for day-trips, though it's not as appealing if you simply want to stretch out on the beach. The resorts start with Nyali, just ten minutes' drive from the city centre. If you're driving, watch out for the dangerously high, unmarked **speed bumps** that are a feature of the coast road.

Nyali and Nyali Beach

Nyali, the comfortable resort suburb of Mombasa on the north side of Tudor Creek, has a few minor items of interest – apart from some of the North Coast's main hotels. It was the site of **Johan Ludwig Krapf**'s first missionary toehold on the east coast. Four years before Livingstone arrived in Africa, in May 1844, Krapf landed at Nyali with his wife and baby daughter. His wife died of malaria on July 13, their baby the next day. The pathetic graves – now rather overgrown – can be found at the end of the road leading past the *Tamarind Restaurant* (see p.403) and a couple of cement silos. Opposite, on a small knoll, is the stone **Krapf Memorial**.

There's another reminder of Mombasa's history in the site of the **Freretown Bell**, at the Nyali Road junction. The bell was erected by the Society of Freed Slaves in the 1880s to warn the people of Freretown (named after Sir Bartle Frere, who founded the freed slave community here) of any impending attack by Arab slavers. The bell hung silently under its small stone arch until the 1920s when it was removed for safekeeping to the nearby Emmanuel Church (Freretown's parish church, erected in 1889), where it is still in use. The bell you see at the Nyali Road junction is a plastic replica.

Accommodation

Whether you're staying in one of the big hotels or not, all of them will arrange dhow trips and scuba and snorkelling excursions. In the evenings they put on bands, acrobat shows and other entertainments. Independent **restaurants**, **bars** and **clubs** are thin on the ground in Nyali: people tend to check out the other hotels, go into Mombasa, or explore further north (see p.415).

Bahari Beach Mount Kenya Rd ℡041/472822, ⓦwww.baharibeach.net. Built in 1971 and refurbished in 1997, this doesn't have much character and can feel stuffy. In common with most Nyali hotels, the rooms – which are reasonably spacious and have balconies – lack sea views. HB ❼

Foreign ideas have long shaped the society, language, literature and architecture of the coast. Immigrants and traders from **Arabia**, **Persia** and **India** have been a subtle and gradual influence here. They would arrive each year in March or April on the northeast monsoon, stay for a few months, and return in September on the southerly monsoon.

Some, either by choice or mishap, would be left behind. Through intermarriage from the earliest times, a distinct ancient civilization called **Swahili** emerged. Swahili, a name which is thought to derive from the same Arabic root as *sahel*, meaning edge or coast, is also a language, known to its speakers as **Kiswahili** (or even more correctly kiSwahili). Like all old languages used by trading peoples, Swahili contains strong clues about who its speakers mixed with, and is full of Arabic-derived words and peppered with others of Indian, Portuguese and English origin.

The Swahili are not a "tribe" in any definable sense – they are the result of a mixed heritage: families who can trace their roots to foreign shores in the distant past tend to claim superior social status. And, while Swahili culture is essentially **Muslim**, people's interpretation of their religion varies according to circumstance.

The towns

Like the Swahili language, it used to be thought that the **towns** of the coast began as Arab or even Persian trading forts. It is now known that Mombasa, Malindi, Lamu and a host of lesser-known settlements are essentially ancient African towns that have always tolerated and even encouraged peaceful immigration from overseas. With the odd exception, however, efforts to compromise their independence were met with violent resistance. The **Portuguese** were the least successful. When they arrived at the end of the fifteenth century, cultural memories of the Moorish occupation of their own country were still fresh. Accommodation to Islam was not on their agenda and, despite a long acquaintance with the coast, they never established an enduring colonial presence. They fared better in Goa on the Indian coast, further along the same monsoon trading route.

The slave inheritance

Historically, **slavery** on the coast was less a black-and-white moral issue than is normally assumed. Although refugee and convict slaves were not uncommon, pawn-slavery was a more structured version of the institution. For example, the **Mijikenda** peoples (see p.423), who lived in the coastal hinterland, maintained close links with the coastal towns, trading their produce and providing armed forces when the towns were under threat, and receiving, in exchange, goods from overseas, especially cotton cloth and tools. As traders, the Swahili periodically accumulated surpluses of grain on the coast at times of severe drought inland. In exchange for famine relief, Mijikenda children or marginalized adults would then be taken to the towns by their relatives and fostered with Swahili families with whom they had links – to become pawns, or in effect domestic or farm slaves. Later, they married into their adoptive families, or paid off the debt and returned inland. But sometimes circumstances altered and, for various reasons, a small number of these indentured labourers were sold overseas, though the trade was always fairly insignificant.

When, in the late eighteenth century, the **slave trade** itself became a major aspect of commerce, and the available foreign goods (firearms, liquor and cloth) became irresistible, then any trace of trust in the old arrangements vanished. The weak and defenceless were captured and sold to slavers from the coast, often to end up on Dutch or French plantations in the Indian Ocean, or in Arabian households. And, with the domination of the Sultan of Oman on the coast in the early nineteenth century, and the large-scale migration of Arab families to East Africa, slaves from the far interior were increasingly set to work on their colonial coastal farms and plantations. When the British formally freed the slaves in 1907, they became a new social class in Swahili society.

Kigotho's Links Rd ☎041/472855 or 0734/517026, ✉kigothohotel@yahoo.com. Although it doesn't seem to fit, and it's not on the beach, this is quite a nice place to stay, and very inexpensive for the area. The bright, quite spacious rooms, have fans (but no nets or a/c), plus a kitchenette with fridge and cooking facilities. There's a cheap bar and *nyama choma* joint, and a small pool. BB ❹

Mombasa Beach Mount Kenya Rd ☎041/471861, ⓦwww.safari-hotels.com. Despite the clumsy 1970s architecture, there's a good atmosphere here – largely the result of its shady, clifftop location and the fact that it attracts many more African guests than its competitors. Good staff and two pools (one huge, the other down near the beach) compensate for the rooms, which are in urgent need of a complete refit. HB ❼

Nyali Beach Bungalows Rd ☎041/471567 ⓦwww.nyalibeach.co.ke. Pleasant, bustling, generally well maintained, but under receivership in 2009, this is one of the coast's oldest hotels, dating from 1946, with two good pools, five restaurants, and extensive gardens. The standard Garden Wing rooms are okay, but only the marginally more expensive Palm Wing rooms have sea views, and all of them need a refurb. HB ❼

Nyali Beach Holiday Resort Bungalows Rd ☎041/472325 or 0725/849111, ⓦnyalibeachresort.com. Mediterranean-style development right by the beach, with two pools. Most of the sixteen large, clean rooms, with a/c, nets and TVs, face both the pool and the beach, as do the self-catering apartments or "cottages". Restaurant, games room and safe parking. HB ❻

Reef Mwamba Drive ☎041/471771 ✉reef @africaonline.co.ke. Once one of Nyali's best, this large and still friendly 1972 resort (last renovated in 2004) is looking tired and unloved, and its peak season prices are excessive for the standard – though off-season, if you're not too fussy, it's still good value. Wide mix of clients and fairly basic food. HB ❼

Voyager Beach Resort Barracks Rd ☎041/475114, ⓦwww.heritage-eastafrica.com. Impressive communal areas, all meshwork *makuti* ceilings and marble-look floors, and maintained to a generally high standard (all rooms have nets, a/c, tea-making, TVs and safes) make this easily the best hotel in Nyali. *But* it's worth knowing this is also a very big hotel (232 rooms), with a fun-loving, largely British clientele enjoying three restaurants, four bars, nightly shows and 24-hour snacks. If you want a quiet time on the beach, look elsewhere. Facilities include tennis, a PADI diving school (the very good ⓦwww.buccaneerdiving.com) and all the water sports you'd expect. AI ❼

Nyali Beach

Nyali Beach is good, but crowded at weekends and holidays, and the reef here is quite far out while the beach is fairly narrow, especially at the northern end, and high tide can largely cover it. There are several points of access, but the easiest is by the entrance to *Nyali Beach Hotel*.

One curiosity at the southern end of Nyali Beach is the so-called **Shiva Cave**, containing several *lingams* (phallic representations of the Hindu god Shiva) in the form of stalagmites, and a rock formation resembling the elephant-headed Hindu god Ganesh. The site was discovered by an Indian doctor, who treated a local farmer who had been attacked by a swarm of bees in the cave, after the farmer had found his cow rubbing her udders on the stalagmite – a set of circumstances rich with Hindu symbolism. The area, which includes a pleasant ledge overlooking the ocean, is maintained as a temple by the local Hindu Union, but visitors are welcome – remove your shoes.

Mamba Village, Nyali Golf Club & Wild Waters

Behind Nyali Beach and the hotels, you can't miss **Mamba Village** (daily 8am–6.30pm; Ksh650, children Ksh350) on Links Road. Nothing to do with poisonous snakes, this is the biggest crocodile (*mamba*) farm in Kenya. Pools in

Dhow trips and diving

For details of **dhow**-trip operators, see the box on p.441. Information on **scuba diving** is in the box on p.436.

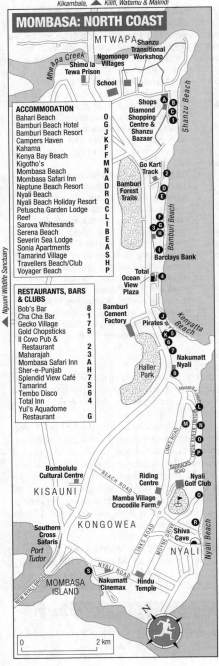

MOMBASA: NORTH COAST

Kikambala, Kilifi, Watamu & Malindi

MTWAPA

Mtwapa Creek

Shimo la Tewa Prison

Nguuni Wildlife Sanctuary

Ngomongo Villages

Shanzu Transitional Workshop

School

Shanzu Beach

Shops

Diamond Shopping Centre & Shanzu Bazaar

Go Kart Track

Bamburi Forest Trails

Bamburi Beach

Barclays Bank

Total Ocean View Plaza

Bamburi Cement Factory

Pirates

Kenyatta Beach

Nakumatt Nyali

Haller Park

Bombolulu Cultural Centre

KISAUNI

BEACH ROAD

Riding Centre

MOUNT KENYA ROAD

LINKS ROAD

BARRACKS ROAD

Nyali Golf Club

Mamba Village Crocodile Farm

KONGOWEA

Southern Cross Safaris

Port Tudor

Shiva Cave

Nyali Beach

MOINE DRIVE

LINKS ROAD

NYALI

NEW NYALI BRIDGE

NYALI ROAD

MOMBASA ISLAND

Nakumatt Cinemax

Hindu Temple

ACCOMMODATION

Bahari Beach	O
Bamburi Beach Hotel	G
Bamburi Beach Resort	J
Campers Haven	K
Kahama	F
Kenya Bay Beach	F
Kigotho's	M
Mombasa Beach	N
Mombasa Safari Inn	A
Neptune Beach Resort	D
Nyali Beach	R
Nyali Beach Holiday Resort	Q
Petuscha Garden Lodge	C
Reef	L
Sarova Whitesands	I
Serena Beach	B
Severin Sea Lodge	E
Sonia Apartments	A
Tamarind Village	S
Travellers Beach/Club	H
Voyager Beach	P

RESTAURANTS, BARS & CLUBS

Bob's Bar	8
Cha Cha Bar	1
Gecko Village	7
Gold Chopsticks	5
Il Covo Pub & Restaurant	2
Maharajah	3
Mombasa Safari Inn	A
Sher-e-Punjab	H
Splendid View Café	7
Tamarind	S
Tembo Disco	6
Total Inn	4
Yul's Aquadome Restaurant	G

0   2 km

---

a former quarry house thousands of crocodiles at all stages of growth, alongside a freaks sideshow of congenitally deformed croc-lets. The overall effect – croco-burgers in the snack bar, 5pm Pavlovian bell-ring feedings, and unlimited saurian souvenirs – is tacky, and the crocodile trail sits unhappily with the skin-farming half of the "village", which is not on show. Also part of the empire is the adjacent **Botanical Garden and Aquarium** (same hours and ticket) and the *Mamba International Nightclub*. Further down Links Road, the same organization also offers **horseriding** (☏041/3415778; beach rides Ksh950 per hr).

Next door, the slides at Wild Waters **waterpark** (Tues–Fri 10am–6pm, Sat & Sun 11am–6pm, closed Mon; Ksh850; ☏0726/337000, ⓦwww.wildwaterskenya.com) are a hit with children and energetic adults and its bar and café and various amusements are open until 10pm.

Across the road from Mamba Village is the 18-hole course at **Nyali Golf and Country Club** (☏041/471589 or 0722/414477, ⓦwww.nyaligolf.co.ke). It's an enjoyable course and, despite stuffy indications to the contrary on the website, is open to visitors. In addition to the golf, there's a pool, squash and tennis, and a bar-restaurant.

From Nyali Bridge to Kenyatta Beach

Beyond the Freretown Bell and the junction for Nyali – always jostling with people trying to get transport to their shifts at the hotels – the main coast road, **Malindi Road**, ploughs through

an area of burgeoning suburban growth. This is the Kenya
appear in the brochures: ignored by the resort developers beca.
from the sea, the primitive living conditions and milling activity he ι
as a shock if you're fresh off the plane. Matatus from Mombasa GPO ι
Nasser Road come along this way, usually going as far as Mtwapa town o ι..
other side of Mtwapa Creek before returning to the city. There are two ver $\jmath$
worthwhile visits in this area – **Bombolulu** and **Haller Park** – both of them
recommended outings whether you're travelling independently or exploring
from your beach hotel.

Bombolulu Workshops and Cultural Centre

Just off Malindi Road, 3km north of Nyali Bridge, **Bombolulu** is a crafts
training school and manufacturing centre, employing more than 150 disabled
people, mostly polio victims, in its five handicraft workshops (workshops
Mon–Fri 8am–12.45pm & 2–5pm; showroom Mon–Sat 8am–6pm; Cultural
Centre Mon–Sat 8am–5pm; Ⓦwww.bombolulu.org; free). The **jewellery
workshop** is the programme's biggest money-spinner, with hundreds of
original designs in metal and local materials, including old coins and seeds,
exported to the USA and Europe, where you'll come across them in charity
gift catalogues. The shop is an excellent place to buy crafts, with somewhat
lower prices than you'll find in the souvenir shops. There's also a **cultural
centre** (Ksh650, including transport from nearby hotels), incorporating
recreations of six tribal homesteads around a central restaurant and dance
floor, where traditional crafts, cooking and farming skills are demonstrated.

Haller Park, the Forest Trails & Nguuni Sanctuary

Some 5km north of Bombolulu, **Haller Park** (also called Baobab Adventure and
Bamburi Nature Park; daily 8am–5pm; Ksh600, children Ksh300; Ⓣ041/2101000
or 0722/410064, Ⓦwww.bamburicement.com/baobabadventures) is the outcome
of an unusual attempt to rehabilitate a quarry. The Bamburi Cement Factory,
whose giant kilns are visible from miles around, and whose familiar brown sacks
are seen all over Kenya, has been scouring the land here for limestone since 1954.
In 1971, it began a concentrated programme of tree-planting in an effort to rescue
the disfigured landscape, putting a small-is-beautiful principle into conservation
practice, making a modest, but terrifically successful, contribution in a land of huge
wildlife parks. Later, as the project gained momentum, fish breeding was established, and large numbers of mammals and birds introduced, including several
hippos. One of the hippos, **Owen**, is an orphan of the 2004 Indian Ocean
tsunami, washed out to sea from his Sabaki River home, and later famously
befriended here by **Mzee**, an elderly giant tortoise. Feeding time is 11am and 3pm
for the giraffes, 4.30pm for the crocodiles, and 4.45pm for the hippos.

  The footpaths twist through dense groves of casuarina, a tree known for its ability
to withstand a harsh environment, across ground which is mostly below sea level,
permanently moist with salty water percolating through the coral limestone rock.
The fish-farming side of the operation experiments with different types of **tilapia**,
a freshwater fish highly tolerant of brackish conditions, many tons of which now
reach shops and restaurants every year, including the park's own *Whistling Pine
Restaurant* (daily 12.30–3pm & 7.30–10pm; Ⓣ041/5487464) where they serve
ranched game meat from Nguuni Wildlife Sanctuary (see below).

  On a similar theme and also managed by Bamburi Cement, are the newer
Bamburi Forest Trails (daily 8am–6pm; Ksh300, children Ksh150). The
entrance is 4km further north, opposite the turning for *Bamburi Beach Hotel*.
Intended mainly for joggers and cyclists, there are four looping tracks, and

r use on the trails (Ksh300 per hour). There's also a

...uni Wildlife Sanctuary (☏041/5485901; pre-booked ...nburi Forest Trails) is the third of Bamburi Cement's ...ting, and well-known for its herds of farmed **eland** and ... ostrich farm.

...d Bamburi beaches

...ring stretches of beach, together with Shanzu just to the ..., are the heart of the "North Coast". If you're out for the day, there s... n most cases, be little difficulty in visiting a hotel and using its facilities. The exceptions are the all-inclusive places, which naturally charge admission (usually around Ksh3000 for the day or evening, including lunch or dinner and all drinks). The beach itself is entirely public; it's the access to it which has been progressively restricted by the hotel developers. Either way, *Whitesands* and *Serena Beach* are the nicest hotels along this stretch.

Kenyatta Municipal Beach is almost the only beach in the country where you'll see droves of ordinary Kenyans by the seaside. There's a great family atmosphere here – and consequently little or no hassle. The beach goes far out at low tide, exposing plenty of coral pools and vast stretches of sand for undisturbed walks. There are sailing boats for rent and trips offered (check they have life jackets), and at the fringes under the low coconut trees pedlars sell ice creams and sodas, snacks and drinking coconuts, while others rent out inflated car inner tubes. For many, though, the main attraction is *Pirates* (daily, pools 9am–5pm, restaurant and bar 9am–midnight; ☏041/5487119 or 0722/750277, ⊛www.cemkenya.com/pirates), a combination of waterslides, restaurant and breezy bar. The two slides are a required outing for kids: they're as good as you'll find anywhere, and consist of a long, steep, fast slide, with a big jump, and a curling, gentle alternative for the little ones. They cost Ksh300 per day, or Ksh100 for just the children's pools. The restaurant serves good, if not amazingly cheap, Mediterranean food and the beach bar is the venue for popular nightly discos, with a mixed crowd and a variety of music.

For something different, try the Swiss-run **go-kart track** at the northern end of Bamburi, just off the main road (Tues–Sun 4–10pm; Ksh1100 for 10min; ☏0721/485247, ⊛www.mombasa-gokart.com).

Practicalities

There are three shopping centres along the main road from Nyali to Shanzu. The biggest is the Nova Centre, which includes a large Nakumatt **supermarket**, a good bookshop, Books First (with an internet café), various food and drink outlets and Barclays and KCB ATMs. Should you need a **doctor**, Dr Buran (☏041/5485238) has a surgery here. Further north, Ocean View Shopping Plaza, next to the *Sai Rock* (former *Ocean View*) hotel, has a branch of the efficient Commercial Bank of Africa with an ATM, and Shaban Mini-Mart where you can change cash at good rates. And the Bamburi shops just north of *Whitesands* include a small **post office** and another Barclays, again with an ATM.

Accommodation

Nearly thirty **beach hotels** throng the six-kilometre shoreline that makes up Bamburi beach.

Bamburi Beach Bamburi Beach, ☏041/5485611, ⊛www.bamburibeachkenya .com. Unexceptional mid-sized resort hotel with a nice pool, but slow service. On the plus side, most rooms have sea views. Facilities include a PADI diving school, glass-bottomed boats, snorkelling, squash courts and a gym. Most guests are on AI. HB **7**

Bamburi Beach Resort Malindi Rd, Bamburi Beach ☏020/2048275 or 0733/474482, ⓦwww.bamburiresort.com. Budget beach hotel just above the sands, with a cheap bar, a deck and pool. The airy, s/c rooms have a/c and nets and you can also self-cater if you want. Discounts for longer stays. **4**

Campers Haven Kenyatta Beach, on the site of *Jamboree* club/restaurant, south of *Pirates* ⓔcampers_haven@yahoo.com. Seasonal campsite (Ksh500) and overlanders' rendezvous that varies from dead to thronged. Some decent s/c rooms. **4**

🏃 **Kahama** Malindi Rd, Bamburi Beach ☏041/5485395 or 0729/487446 ⓦwww.kahamahotel.co.ke The former *Octopus Hotel*, just back from the beach, is pretty good all round for the price, with 32, decent, spacious rooms with nets and TVs and a good pool. The *Pitcher and Butch* sports pub is located here, with regular music nights and live bands. The price is very fair, though they bump it up increases about 300 percent at Christmas. BB **4**–**6**

🏃 **Kenya Bay Beach** Bamburi Beach ☏041/5487600, ⓦwww.kenyabay.com. One of the old generation, from the 1970s, but much better maintained than many others. Although it's simpler and feels smaller than most Bamburi hotels, it still has 106 rooms (a/c, nets, TV, safe), very good staff and a good mix of nationalities. There's a water-sports centre and free wi-fi in the lobby. BB **5**

Neptune Beach Resort Off Malindi Rd, Bamburi Beach North ☏041/5485701 ⓦwww.neptunehotels.com. Slightly downmarket, but

refreshingly lacking in pretension, this is a fun package destination with excellent food, good staff, lots of activities and watersports, and a cheerful atmosphere. BB **6**

Sarova Whitesands Malindi Road, Bamburi Beach ☏041/5485926 or 041/5485652 ⓦwww.sarovahotels.com. One of the biggest hotels in Kenya, with the longest seafront on the North Coast and not a *makuti* roof in sight. The grounds include extensive, interconnecting pools and busy restaurants, and the rooms all have nets, a/c, DSTV and large safes. You can do all the activities you'd expect, and there's wi-fi throughout, but the personal touch is missing. HB **8**

Severin Sea Lodge Off Malindi Rd, Bamburi Beach ☏041/5485001, ⓦwww.severin-kenya.com. Large, well-run resort hotel, with excellent sports and watersports and incredibly motivated staff. Rooms have the lot – a/c, TV, nets, safes and balconies. The *Imani Dhow* restaurant is a converted, beached Zanzibari *jahazi*. Great value for fifty weeks of the year: prices more than double over Christmas/New Year. HB **6**–**8**

Travellers Beach/Travellers Club Malindi Rd, Bamburi Beach ☏041/5485121, ⓦwww.travellersbeach.com. Big, package-tour set-up that crams a lot of rooms into the half-board *Beach* on one side and the all-inclusive *Club* on the other. You can swim into the lobby then slide out again, but you can't go on the beach at high tide, when it's submerged: four pools, and lots of activities compensate. Dull gardens, and somewhat tenement-like room blocks, though the rooms are spacious and well-appointed. They have a very good Indian restaurant. HB **8**

Eating, drinking and nightlife

Apart from the hotel restaurants there are plenty of other **eating and drinking places**, most of which line the unpretty Mombasa–Malindi road. Most places offer free transport from nearby hotels.

Bob's Bar Birgis Complex, near Nova Centre ☏020/2021775 or 041/471000 (open 24/7). Also known as *Murphy's Irish Pub*, this is a convivial place for a drink, with a mix of tourists and locals, flat screens for sports and good live music, usually on Thurs & Sun.

Gecko Village 200m north of Nova Centre, Malindi Rd, Bamburi Beach ☏0724/333209. A 24hr bar and eatery with live music Wed and Sun from 6pm. There's an eclectic mix of food on offer, from *nyama choma* to mulligatawny soup and guinea fowl in red wine sauce (mains around Ksh500– 800). Drinks include a legit bottled version of palm wine – not quite the real thing, but close.

Gold Chopsticks At *Baobab Holiday Resort*, Malindi Rd, Bamburi Beach ☏041/5485496. Bamburi branch of Mombasa's supposedly upmarket Chinese restaurant *Galaxy*, specializing in seafood dishes such as pan-fried lobster with garlic and ginger. If the à la carte crustaceans are beyond your budget, opt for the Sat night or Sun lunchtime buffet, which include vegetarian options (Ksh1000). Plan on at least Ksh1500 per head.

Il Covo Pub & Restaurant Off Malindi Rd, Bamburi Beach North (north of *Neptune Beach Resort*) ☏020/2071020 or 0735/4526867, ⓦwww.ilcovo.net. Upmarket Italian and Japanese restaurant and beach bar. Sushi, pizzas and Italian

Turtles

Several parts of Shanzu Beach, notably at *Serena Beach Hotel* are popular egg-laying sites for **sea turtles**. There are educational talks about these endangered marine reptiles at the hotel (Mondays, 7pm), where motorized watersports are banned.

dishes done with more authenticity than you'd expect. A bit pricey – pastas Ksh800-plus and carpaccio starters about the same – but recommended.

Maharajah Outside the *Indiana Beach Hotel*, Malindi Rd, Bamburi ☎041/5485895. North Indian tandoori with a seafood twist – dishes on offer include fish tikka or tandoori lobster, but there are plenty of chicken options too. Curries and tandoori dishes around Ksh600, seafood Ksh1150. Daily 2–10.30pm.

Sher-e-Punjab *Travellers Beach Hotel* ☎041/5485121. Unusual among the hotel restaurants for having a reputation for style and quality. Vegetarian (paneer tikka, vegetable kebabs), chicken (jalfrezi, korma), and Mughlai (rogan josh, Mughlai birianis) dishes, and a very good-value Sun lunchtime buffet, including vegetarian options. Count on Ksh1200–1500 per head. Daily 12.30–2.30pm & 7.30–10.30pm.

Splendid View Café Next to *Gecko Village* (see above) ☎041/5487270 (Tues–Sun midday–2pm & 7–10pm, closed Mon). This Indian Mughlai doesn't have any kind of view, unless you gaze on the splendidly tacky fantasy paintings. The food is

good, though, with unusual specials like Baluchi mutton *sajji* (whole roast leg of lamb), chicken, seafood, and a daily tandoori BBQ. Shaded outdoor area. Under Ksh800 per head.

Tembo Disco 300m north of the *Splendid View*, ☎020/2024330 or 0722/411873, ⓦwww.tembodisco.de. Huge garden bar-restaurant and underground disco playing a mixture of music (Congolese, Kenyan, hip hop, soul, reggae), with occasional shows and predictable low-key hustle. Women Ksh100, men Ksh150. Daily; bar 24/7, restaurant 6pm–6am, disco 9pm–5am.

Total Inn By the Total garage, Ocean View Shopping Plaza, Malindi Rd. If you wondered where hotel staff can afford to eat, the answer is in places like this: basic African dishes and not a lobster in sight. Good conversations, and most items are less than Ksh100.

Yul's Aquadome Restaurant Next to *Bamburi Beach Hotel*. Very reliable spot on the beach, based at Yul's watersports centre, with one of the longest (and most consistently available) menus on the coast, and now more than twenty years old. Great pizzas and steaks, excellent boneless chicken and naan bread, and very good ice cream. Gets busy at weekends. Daily 9am–11pm.

Shanzu

At the northern end of the stretch of coast between Mombasa island and Mtwapa Creek, **Shanzu Beach** is dominated by exclusive (if not particularly upmarket) holiday clubs, although it does have a couple of other attractions that may appeal to some. The most unusual of these, 1km east of the Mombasa–Malindi road and copiously signposted, is **Ngomongo Villages** (daily 9am–5pm; Ksh700; ☎041/5487063; ⓦwww.ngomongo.com). Like Bamburi Nature Park, this is a reclamation project, but of a landfill site, rather than a quarry, and with a twist: as well as trees, it's been furnished with a collection of regional homesteads, complete with inhabitants in traditional dress, representing eight of Kenya's tribes. Don't expect authenticity, but you should be able to look forward to an enjoyable couple of hours in this ethnic theme park – though they're very dependent on regular visitors to stay open (as the occasional pestering for tips as you walk round makes clear). There are musicians and herbalists to watch and talk to and hands-on activities like archery, Luo-style hook fishing, grain pounding and tree planting. The *Trekkers Bar & Restaurant* onsite specializes in African dishes.

Also worth a visit is the **Shanzu Transitional Workshop for Disabled Young Women** (Mon–Sat 9am–6pm; ☎041/2223078), 350m east of Ngomongo, run by the Mombasa Girl Guides. Here, a group of women get on-the-job training in practical crafts skills, turning out a small selection of well-made clothes (including great Bermuda shorts), jewellery and leatherwork, all of which is for sale.

Next to *Sonia Apartments*, in Shanzu, you'll find a large cluster of **shops**, including a cybercafé and the very good Kelele Record Shop, which sells local CDs.

Accommodation

Most of the hotels at Shanzu are run by African Safari Club, and not open to walk-in guests. Unfortunately, it's also a magnet for North Coast prostitutes, so cheaper places tend to be sleazy.

Mombasa Safari Inn Shanzu Tourist Rd, Shanzu ℡0733/430996. One of the few cheapies in Shanzu, in the little "town centre" itself – friendly, and with modern s/c rooms. It has a popular outdoor bar and restaurant (see below). ❷

Petuscha Garden Lodge Shanzu Beach ℡041/5485860, ℮petuschahotel@yahoo.com. Kenyan-German run, with spotless, comfortable rooms with a/c, fans and room safes, fronting onto a small pool and gardens. Use of split-level sitting room with plenty of books. BB ❺

Serena Beach Shanzu Beach ℡041/5485721 ⓦwww.serenahotels.com. Beautifully put together in a mélange of Moorish and Swahili designs, and very stylishly maintained, this is the standout proposition on this stretch of coast, and indeed anywhere between Mombasa and Mtwapa. As in all Serena hotels, the standard rooms (a/c, DSTV, safes) are on the small side and drinks are pricey. There are lots of activities, most of them free to guests, including floodlit tennis and a/c squash courts, snorkelling, canoeing, and sailing, and they take good care of children. PADI diving school. HB ❽

Sonia Apartments Shanzu Tourist Rd, Shanzu, ℡041/5480426 or 0711/909161. Spacious two-room apartments, with cooking facilities and a/c, arranged around a courtyard restaurant and sometimes noisy 24hr bar. ❹

Responsible snorkelling, diving and fishing

Coral reefs are the world's most fragile ecosystems. A reef is a living entity: every cluster of coral consists of thousands of individual organisms called polyps, constantly growing outwards as the older ones die and calcify and become covered in new growth. Solid though it seems, coral is extremely sensitive to sea temperature increases, and of course very vulnerable to physical damage by tourists or fishermen. When snorkelling, diving or fishing, it's worth bearing the following points in mind:

When mooring a boat, ensure you use established buoys, or drop anchor well away from the coral.

Dive and swim carefully, and never touch the coral. Even gentle abrasions can kill some polyps and coral suffocates if covered with silt or sand thrown up by a careless swipe of fins. If you wear fins, use them only in open water and use your hands to swim when near coral.

Don't feed the fish, as it may cause stress and encourages dependency. It also destabilizes the food chain and can cause some species to become aggressive (just like monkeys).

Don't collect souvenirs. Collecting shells, dead coral and starfish disrupts the ecosystem and is illegal in most countries, including Kenya – as is all trade in sea-turtle products. Getting caught when you arrive home can land you in serious trouble. Equally, buying marine souvenirs, rather than collecting them yourself, is no excuse, although they are widely for sale. Although not enforced, selling shells is illegal.

Big-game fishing (the season runs Sept–March) reduces the population of natural predators, increasing the populations of their prey, in turn increasing pressure on organisms further down the food chain. Among the sports fishing fraternity, falling catch rates have spurred talk of introducing quotas. Happily, most boat charterers now operate a tag-and-release policy.

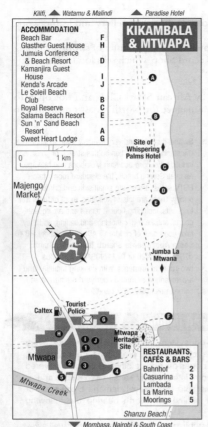

Kilifi, ▲ Watamu & Malindi   ▲ Paradise Hotel

KIKAMBALA & MTWAPA

ACCOMMODATION	
Beach Bar	F
Glasther Guest House	H
Jumuia Conference & Beach Resort	D
Kamanjira Guest House	I
Kenda's Arcade	J
Le Soleil Beach Club	B
Royal Reserve	C
Salama Beach Resort	E
Sun 'n' Sand Beach Resort	A
Sweet Heart Lodge	G

0   1 km

Majengo Market

Site of Whispering Palms Hotel

Jumba La Mtwana

Caltex

Tourist Police

Mtwapa Heritage Site

Mtwapa

Mtwapa Creek

RESTAURANTS, CAFÉS & BARS	
Bahnhof	2
Casuarina	3
Lambada	1
La Marina	4
Moorings	5

Shanzu Beach

▼ Mombasa, Nairobi & South Coast

Eating, drinking and nightlife

Shanzu is pretty tacky when it comes to eating places and watering holes, with most places catering purely for a captive market of package tourists. Don't expect to find any ordinary Kenyan eateries. The *Mombasa Safari Inn* is a cheery bar and restaurant with good grills, (main courses around Ksh600). The bar attracts prostitutes, but the outdoor atmosphere is mellow, and it's open daily from 8am until the last customer leaves. Another place worth trying is the *Cha Cha Bar*, next to the *Petuscha*, a pleasant and laid-back outdoor bar-restaurant under an octagonal *makuti* roof, where you'll pay around Ksh700 for a main course or Ksh1500 for seafood (food daily until 11pm, bar open later). The working women here are less of a hassle than at other Shanzu venues, and there's occasional live music in the evenings.

Mtwapa

Mtwapa Creek marks the edge of Greater Mombasa, where tropical suburbia, with its villas, super-markets, clubs, restaurants – and poverty – is more or less left behind. From here on, the road heads with fewer distractions up to Kilifi, Watamu and Malindi.

The town of **MTWAPA** itself is in many ways the most pleasant of the main-road settlements, with a more established feel than Nyali-Bamburi-Shanzu, and a more ordinary Kenyan atmosphere – including a rash of unpleasant speed bumps. The obvious reasons to pause here are **boats** and **big fish** – the beautiful **creek** is a focus for yacht owners and game fishermen – but there are also some low-key places to stay and a few good spots for eating, drinking and nightlife. There's also a Barclays with **ATM**. If you have a few hours to spare, don't overlook the fascinating **ruins of Jumba la Mtwana** and **Mtwapa Heritage site** just north of the creek mouth.

Accommodation

Beach Bar Maweni Beach, on the corner of the creek mouth and the ocean (signposted from Kenol station: 20min walk or take a *piki-piki*) ☎0720/852327 or 0720/852327, ℮thebeachafrica @gmail.com. German-owned campsite (Ksh500) with some fairly basic bandas, with nets and paraffin lamps. It's a seasonally popular hangout spot, with food and cold drinks available. **❷**

Glasther Guest House Down a turning on the west side of the main road, directly opposite the one that leads to the *Sweet Heart*. Down-at-heel, but you'll find it okay if you're counting every penny. **❶**

Kamanjira Guest House On the east side of the main road about 600m north of the bridge ☎0733/824633. Clean, well-kept s/c rooms, but can get very hot and stuffy. **❷**

Kenda's Arcade (aka *New Kenda's*) Behind the *Casuarina* ☎041/5480148 or 0725/580256 ⓦwww.kendashotels.com. Clean, modern rooms, with nets and fans, though it gets noisy late at night from their bar. ❷

Sweet Heart Lodge East of the main road, just north of the market ☎041/495598. Clean, properly managed and reasonably comfortable, this is the best B&L in Mtwapa. BB ❷

Jumba la Mtwana

Well worth stopping for, and worth an excursion in its own right, are the ruins of **Jumba la Mtwana** (daily 8am–6pm; Ksh500). This national monument, one of three between Mombasa and Malindi, is the remains of a wealthy fourteenth- or fifteenth-century Swahili community. The sign for the three-kilometre access road is 2km north of Mtwapa Creek bridge. If you're travelling by public transport and are dropped off at the junction, you have a good chance of getting a lift down here.

The phrase *jumba la mtwana* means "mansion of the slave", but the settlement has been deserted for some 500 years and probably had a different name in the past. It's a small site in an enchanting setting among baobabs and lawns, just above the beach. This seems a strange place for a town, right on an open shore with no harbour, and it's possible the inhabitants were pushed here by raiding parties from inland groups, and relied on Mtwapa Creek as a safe anchorage for the overseas traders who would have visited yearly. Jumba is fortunate in having good water, but why it was deserted, and by whom, remains a mystery.

Compared with Gedi, further north (see p.455), Jumba's layout is simple. Though it lacks the eerie splendour of that much larger town, it must once have been a sizeable settlement; there were three mosques within the site and a fourth just outside. Most of the population would have lived in mud-and-thatch houses, which have long since disintegrated. In Swahili culture, building in stone (in fact, coral "rag" of different densities) has traditionally been used for mosques, and was the preserve of certain privileged people, principally the long-settled inhabitants of a town. Newcomers would almost always build in less durable materials appropriate to their shorter-term stake in the community.

The best of Jumba's mosques is the **Mosque by the Sea**, which shows evidence of a separate room for women, something which is only nowadays becoming acceptable again in modern mosques. The cistern where worshippers washed is still intact, with coral foot-scrapers set nearby and a jumble of tombs behind the north wall, facing Mecca. One of these has a Koranic inscription carved in coral on a panel facing the sea and must have been the grave of an important individual:

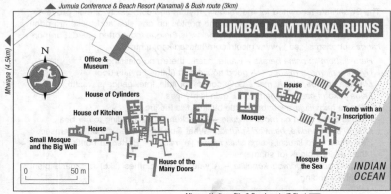

▲ Jumuia Conference & Beach Resort (Kanamai) & Bush route (3km)

JUMBA LA MTWANA RUINS

N

Office & Museum

House of Cylinders

House of Kitchen

House

Small Mosque and the Big Well

House of the Many Doors

Mosque

House

Tomb with an Inscription

Mosque by the Sea

INDIAN OCEAN

◄ Mtwapa (4.5km)

0   50 m

▼ Mtwapa Heritage Site & Beach route (2.5km)

Every soul shall taste death. You will simply be paid your wages in full on the Day of Resurrection. He who is removed from the fire and made to enter heaven, it is he who has won the victory. The earthly life is only delusion.

The **people of Jumba** seem to have been very religious and hygienic – virtues that are closely associated in Islam. Cisterns and water jars, or at least the remains of them, are found everywhere among the ruined houses, and in most cases there are coral blocks nearby which would have been used to squat on while washing. The latrines are all stone-lined with long-drops. Of course, it is possible that the poorer people of Jumba lived in squalor in their mud huts, yet even the **House of Many Doors**, which seems to have been a fifteenth-century lodging house, provided guests with private washing and toilet facilities.

Jumba Beach is a good place to while away an afternoon – in fact, late afternoon, when the atmosphere hangs among the ruins like cobwebs, is probably the best time to come. Strange but attractive **screw pines** grow in the sand, aerial-rooted like mangroves. It's a good spot for a swim and a picnic: there are toilets and showers by the ticket office.

Old Mtwapa

If Jumba stoked your interest, you may be intrigued to visit the virtually unexcavated ruins at **Mtwapa Heritage Site** in the five hectares of thick forest behind Mtwapa's tiny beach, just to the north of the creek mouth. They're easily reached on foot from Mtwapa town (take the track to the right by the huge baobab tree on the way down to the beach). Old Mtwapa dates from the twelfth century and scattered here are the remains of more than sixty houses, a mosque and a tomb. Although it's a gazetted monument, there's no actual protection of the site, and its security looks uncertain: for more background go to Ⓦtinyurl.com/kjb2up. Meanwhile, enjoy the strange jungle ruins while you can: if you come down here soon after dawn, you'll also see plenty of monkeys, hornbills, monitor lizards and even dik-diks.

Restaurants, bars & clubs

Bahnhof Opposite *Casuarina*. Formerly German, now British-owned sports bar, with big screens, pool tables, DJs and plenty of cold beer. It's usually heaving to the point of overflowing on a Saturday night, but always a good place to catch the local vibe.

Swahili proverbs and sayings

The Swahili are renowned for the imagery, rhythm and complexity of their **proverbs**. *Kangas* always have some kind of adage printed on one side and these are often traditionally Swahili. The first one listed below is the one most often heard. For more *kanga* aphorisms, see Ⓦwww.glcom.com/hassan/kanga.html.

Haraka, haraka: haina baraka – Haste, haste: there's no blessing in it.
Nyumba njema si mlango – A good house isn't (judged by) its door.
Mahaba ni haba, akili ni mali – Love counts for little, intelligence is wealth.
Faida yako ni hasara yangu – Your gain is my loss.
Haba na haba kujaza kibaba – Little by little fills the jug.
Kuku anakula sawa na mdomo wake – A chicken eats according to her beak.
Mungu alihlolandika, haliwezi kufutika – What God has written cannot be erased.
Heri shuka isiyo kitushi, kama shali njema ya mauwa – Better an honest loincloth than a fancy cloak (of shame).
Mke ni nguo, mgomba kupalilia – A wife means clothes (like) a banana plant means weeding.

Casuarina 300m north of the bridge on the east side of the road. Although often full of prostitutes, the pleasant, *makuti*-roofed *Casuarina* is a perennial favourite among locals and more adventurous tourists and expats, with a good atmosphere, discos from 6pm–6am, occasionally traditional dancers at weekends, and good, char-grilled meat and seafood at all hours. Open 24/7.

🏃 La Marina on the north shore of the creek, east of the bridge: turn right at the signboard 550m north of the bridge, and head along the dirt track for 1.5km ☎020/2434726 or 0723/223737, ⓦwww.lamarina-restaurant.com. Mtwapa's top restaurant, comparable with the *Tamarind*, but much more affordable, the former *Aquamarine* serves conventional meals on the creek shore – a very atmospheric spot for dinner (expect to spend around Ksh2000/head) and also offers "champagne dhow cruises", with a barbecue lunch or dinner and music and other entertainments.

Lambada on the east side of the road through Mtwapa, north of *Casuarina* ☎0722/726630. Going for a less atmospheric, more Euro-disco feel than its neighbours in Mtwapa, *Lambada* has a big dance floor, a sports bar, a small, "splash disco" pool and sometimes live acts at weekends.

Moorings on the north side of the creek, west of the bridge: turn left 300m north of the bridge ☎041/5485045 or 0723/032536, ⓦwww.themoorings.co.ke. This floating restaurant, in a fine, breezy location is a good place for talk and tales – and to hook up with others, either in person or via the notice board. They have reasonably priced drinks and snacks, and a mainly seafood menu that vies with *La Marina* for quality – though it tends to be inconsistent. Main courses Ksh600–1200. Tues–Sun 10am–midnight.

Kikambala

If you're staying in Mombasa or one of the North Coast resorts, the low-key resort area around **KIKAMBALA**, a few kilometres north of Mtwapa, is about as far as you'd want to come for a day-trip. Parts of the coastal strip here are still thickly forested and the beach itself is a glorious white expanse, though it's two to three kilometres from the highway. With the countryside here being very flat, the sea goes out for nearly a kilometre, and the lagoon isn't deep enough to swim in except at high tide (see tide tables, p.387). The Israeli-owned *Paradise Hotel* at Kikambala was the location of an al-Qaeda **suicide bombing** in 2002 in which sixteen people died, including two Israeli children and five members of a Giriama dance troupe. The tragic episode achieved notoriety when the hotel was rebuilt, but the dancers' families received scant compensation.

Accommodation

The Kikambala **hotels** are virtually the last on the coast north of Mombasa until you reach Kilifi. Vehicles normally approach the beach properties from the northern access road, 7.4km north of Mtwapa Bridge (signposted for the *Sun'n'Sand Hotel*). Coming from the south, you can also cut down to the beach from the turning in **Majengo**, 5.3km north of Mtwapa Bridge, a sandy road that heads straight to the *Jumuia Conference and Beach Resort*. There are few independent restaurants or bars at Kikambala, and most people stick to their hotels.

Jumuia Conference & Beach Resort Beachfront road, Kikambala (5.3km north of Mtwapa Bridge, then 3km along *murram*) ☎020/3548318 or 0710/288043, ⓦwww.resortjumuia.com. Formerly known as *Kanamai*, this sprawling, pretty place under the coconuts, run by the National Christian Council of Kenya, has been comprehensively updated in recent years. The rooms, while not cutting-edge-elegant, are spacious and well furnished, with good fans and nets. Large pool. BB ❺

Le Soleil Beach Club Beachfront road, Kikambala (3.2km along northern access road) ☎041/32195, ⓦwww.lesoleilkenya.com. More like tropical office blocks than a hotel, and always in need of a good spring clean, this is as tacky as it is popular, with a cosmopolitan variety of budget package tourists on all-inclusive deals. AI ❻

Royal Reserve Beachfront road, Kikambala, just north of *Jumuia* ☎20/2057155 or 0722/205220, ⓦwww.royalreserve.us. Good-value, homely,

US-style, a/c apartments, sleeping four to six, with nets, DSTV and kitchenettes, in a beachfront complex with pool and restaurant. There's a good feel here, and plenty of activities, but it's as divorced from the real Kenya as it's possible to be. ⑥
Salama Beach Resort Beachfront road, Kikambala (just south of *Jumuia*) ☏0733/736979 or 0723/527145, ⓦwww.salama-beach-resort .com. Cool, attractive, German-owned bungalow-style hotel, right by the beach, with an infinity pool, opened in 2007. Rooms have terraces and a/c (small supplement) and their *Maridadi* restaurant has a good rep. BB ⑥

Sun'n'Sand Beach Resort Beachfront road, Kikambala, 2.1km down the northern access road ☏020/2057950 or 0722/204799, ⓦwww .sunnsand.info. One of the oldest hotels on the Kenya coast, originally built in 1932 and most recently revamped in 2004 – it's one of Kenya's biggest, with three hundred bright, functional rooms, furnished in some style. Four pools, with diving boards, an extended "river" and slides. Lots of activities, including a kids' club. There are several small shops and *dukas* near the gate if the club atmosphere begins to get claustrophobic. AI ⑧

Note: if you're **continuing north** past Kikambala, see p.447.

Inland from Mombasa

MAZERAS is just a short hop up the hill from Mombasa. If you're coming from Nairobi, this small town marks the end of the long vistas of scrub; it's perched right on the edge of the steep scarp, amid bananas and coconuts. If you're travelling by road, it isn't a bad idea to break your journey here and savour the new atmosphere. The *hotelis* serve good, flavourful, coastal *chai* and Mazeras has a slightly unkempt **botanical garden** (daily 6am–6pm; free) on the Mombasa side of town, which makes a good break for the travel-weary en route from Nairobi. Across the road and up the hill a little way is a **mission** and its century-old church, signs of an evangelical presence in the hills behind Mombasa that goes back, remarkably, over 150 years.

For historians of Methodism and the Church Missionary Society or, possibly more likely, connoisseurs of palm wine, the **road to Kaloleni**, 22km north of Mazeras, is a required sidetrack (see the Mombasa Area map on p.389). It's a wonderfully scenic drive in its own right, looping through lush vales, with a wide panorama down to the coast to the east. Masses of **coconut trees** sway all around and, invariably, there are groups of flamboyantly dressed Mijikenda women walking along the roadside: leaving the highway you're instantly back in rural Kenya.

There are frequent buses and matatus from Mombasa to Kaloleni via Rabai (from the Jomo Kenyatta/Mwembe Tayari junction) which makes this an easy day-trip away from the coast. If you arrive in Kaloleni before mid-afternoon, you'll be able to catch a matatu further north to Kilifi, and from there back to Mombasa or onwards to Malindi. If you're driving, note there's no petrol station in Mazeras, and only irregular fuel in Kaloleni, so fill up in Mombasa or Mariakani.

Rabai

RABAI, capital of the **Wa-Rabai Mijikenda** and site of the first Christian mission to be established in East Africa, is the first village you come to, 4.5km from Mazeras. It's also one of only two Mijikenda villages still occupying its original *kaya* (for more on *kayas*, see p.437). A German pastor, the Reverend **Johan Ludwig Krapf**, came here in 1846 after losing his family at Nyali (see p.409), and left his mark on the community when, 41 years later, the imposing **St Paul's church** was erected. The centre of the village, marked by a cluster

The Mijikenda peoples

The principal people of the coastal hinterland region are the **Mijikenda** ("Nine Tribes"), a loose grouping whose Bantu languages are to a large extent mutually intelligible, and closely related to Swahili. They are believed to have arrived in their present homelands in the sixteenth or seventeenth century from a quasi-historical state called Shungwaya, which had undergone a period of intense civil chaos. This centre was probably located somewhere in the Lamu hinterland or in the southwest corner of present-day Somalia. According to oral tradition, the people who left it were the Giriama, the Digo, the Rabai, the Ribe, the Duruma, the Chonyi, the Jibana, the Kauma and the Kambe (not to be confused with the Kamba of the interior).

All these tribes now live in the coastal hinterland, the **Giriama** and the **Digo** being the largest and best-known. Like so many other Kenyan peoples, the Mijikenda had age-set systems that helped cut across the divisive groupings of clan and subclan to bind communities together. And these involved some fierce traditions: the installation of a new ruling elders' age-set, for example, required the killing and castration of a stranger. This, like most of the milder practices of tribal tradition, was abandoned in the early twentieth century.

The Mijikenda have always had a diverse **economy**. They were cultivators, long-distance traders, makers of palm wine (a Digo speciality now diffused all over Mijikenda-land), hunters, fishermen and herders – the Duruma especially and, at one time, the Giriama, were almost as fond of cows as the Maasai. They still maintain local market cycles. These are four-day weeks in the case of the Giriama: days one and two for labour, day three for preparation, and day four, called *Chipalata*, for the market.

Despite acquiring all the trappings of modern life along with most Kenyan peoples, the Mijikenda have been unusually successful at maintaining their cultural identity. They warred with the British in 1914 over the imposition of taxes and the demand for porters for World War I. And they have preserved a vigorous conservative tradition of adherence to their old beliefs in spirits and the power of their ancestors. While this is very apparent from the resurgence of interest in preserving their traditional sacred groves, or *kayas* (see p.437), it's also notable in the relative ease with which you can pick up CDs of **traditional music**, especially in Mombasa: wonderful rhythms and some very delicate *chivoti* flute melodies.

If you're a little off the beaten track, are really interested and have time to spare, even casual enquiries will elicit invitations to **weddings** or **funerals**, where the old traditions – and music – are still very much the centrepieces, despite a veneer of Christianity or Islam. Many Mijikenda have found conversion to **Islam** helpful in their dealings with coastal merchants and businessmen. The conversion seems to be the latest development in the growth of Swahili society, and that change is probably the biggest threat to Mijikenda cultural integrity.

of school rooms and sports fields, lies 500m off the main road on the right as you come into Rabai from Mazeras. For the church and museum, fork left after 200m.

Opposite the entrance to St Paul's, the first church to have been built (1846–48) now houses the modest **Rabai National Monument** (daily 8am–6pm; Ksh500). Not the most exciting place in Kenya, it contains a few well-presented photographs but little else. The ticket, however, includes a guided tour and explanation, with visits to a full-scale replica of the *kaya* (tourists are not allowed to wander through the real one), and the village's nearby viewpoint over the countryside. Adjacent to the museum is the house where Krapf used to live, and the nearby cottage of Johann Rebmann, Krapf's proselytizing partner, is used as a school room. Between them, the two missionaries managed to explore a great deal of what is now Kenya without the demonstrations of firepower so many of their successors thought necessary. Krapf worked out the grammar of the Swahili language and produced a translation of the Bible.

Ribe

RIBE (the main village of the Wa-Ribe Mijikenda) is more substantial than Rabai, but harder to get to. Some 7km from Rabai, a road snakes up to the right from the deep valley floor: Rabai village – a few small shops and a basic bar-restaurant – is 1.5km along here.

Fifteen minutes' walk from Ribe centre, through the *shambas* and dense undergrowth, is a tiny **cemetery**, regularly cleared of weeds and creepers, near the site of Ribe's Methodist mission, itself crumbled to its foundations and now completely overgrown. It isn't hard to find, and it's worth visiting if only to take a look at the pathetic graves of those few **missionaries** who struggled all the way here before succumbing in what must have been nearly impossible conditions. They were often very young: the Reverend Butterworth, whose carpentry skills ensured him a welcome arrival, died aged 23, just two months after getting there; they used his new tools to make the coffin. It isn't surprising that the cemetery faces out to sea: towards Mombasa, supplies, the mail and new settlers.

Kaloleni

The paved road comes to its end at **KALOLENI**. On the way, you pass through dense coconut groves where many of the trees have been initialled to avoid ownership disputes. The tapping of **palm wine** (*mnazi*), banned by the government, is still widely practised here, with the **Giriama** section of the Mijikenda leading the field. They call palm wine "the mother of the coconut", since tapping the trees for juice hinders formation of the nuts.

Tapping is done by cutting off the flower stem, binding it tightly and allowing the sap that would have produced new coconuts to collect in a container – usually a baobab pod – tied to the end. Here it ferments rapidly and has to be regularly collected. Variations in the local demand for *mnazi*, which is most often drunk at community gatherings like weddings and funerals, and in the coastal market for *copra* (the dried coconut flesh used in soap and oil manufacture), tend to influence the owners of trees in their decision whether to tap or to grow *copra*. You will see trees incised with step-notches (enabling the tapper to reach the top), that end several metres below the crown, indicating that a tree has been left for several years to develop coconuts.

Although, strictly speaking, illegal, **palm wine** is locally available up and down the coast. In Kaloleni, it usually comes in plastic mineral-water bottles, and costs about Ksh100 a litre. You drink it (discreetly) through a reed straw with a coconut-fibre filter.

The only places to **stay** in Kaloleni are two basic guesthouses, the tin-roofed *Bububu Guesthouse* (℡0734/794039; ➊) near the bus and matatu stand, which at least tries, with rooms available by the hour, day or night, and the cheaper but even more basic *makuti*-roofed *Kaloleni Guesthouse* (➊), 700m up the old Kilifi road behind the post office and near St Luke's hospital. Neither has electricity or running water, and washing is done with buckets.

Moving on, there are frequent buses and matatus back to Mombasa via Rabai and Mazeras, or to Mariakani, for Nairobi, and less frequent matatus north to Kilifi, 40km away (catch these at the bottom of the hill by the Kilifi junction). The road to Kilifi is particularly memorable for its scenes of local life in the coconut groves and forests – it's a great route to drive (see p.331) or cycle along, though sometimes difficult after heavy rain.

The South Coast

South of Mombasa, a continuous strip of beach runs between Likoni and Msambweni, backed by palms and broken once or twice by small rivers. Along the whole coast south from Mombasa to the Tanzanian border, there's just one highly developed resort area, **Diani Beach**. South of Diani, the coast is little known and, in most tour operators' minds at least, nobody stops again until they reach **Shimoni**. This is great news if you have the time to go searching out untrodden beaches. With your own vehicle, or on an organized trip, you can also visit the **Shimba Hills National Park** and the neighbouring **Mwaluganje Elephant Sanctuary**, either overnight or on an easy day-trip excursion.

The fact that you have to take the **Likoni ferry** (see p.393) emphasizes the south coast's separation from Mombasa, and the queues and usual delays have tended to deter hotel developers a little. **LIKONI** itself is a busy suburb of Mombasa, straggling down the southbound road for nearly 5km. A coast road, served by infrequent matatus, runs around the creek mouth to the east (see "Mombasa Island" map, p.394), to **Shelly Beach**, facing the ocean. Named for its shells and once a popular local resort area, the beach is narrow and the sea here only feasible for swimming at high tide. With the closure of the big *Shelly Beach Hotel*, all the local alternatives have also closed.

Shimba Hills National Park

Kenya's most underrated wildlife refuge, **Shimba Hills National Park** (Ⓦ www.kws.go.ke/shimba.html; $20) is less than an hour's drive from Mombasa, even less from Likoni and, at 400m above sea level, wonderfully refreshing after the humidity on the coast down below (take some warm clothes). The hilly park of scattered jungle and grassland is comparatively little visited, which is all to the good. It has a wonderful game-viewing lodge and one of the best-situated camping and *banda* sites anywhere.

The most straightforward option for visiting Shimba is on a **safari from Mombasa** or from the coast. Trips from most coast hotels and travel agents cost about $100 for a day-trip or $250 for a trip including an overnight at *Shimba Lodge* on a full-board basis.

The Digo

Most of the people who live along the southern coastal here are **Digo**, and their neat rectangular houses, made of dried mud and coral on a framework of wood, are a distinctive part of the lush roadside scene. Digo women tend to dress very colourfully in multiple kangas. Although they belong to the Mijikenda group of peoples, the Digo are unusual in traditionally having **matrilineal inheritance**: in other words they traced descent through the female line, so that a man would, on his death, pass his property on to his sister's sons rather than his own. It is an unusual system with interesting implications for the state of the family and the position of women. However, the joint assault of Islamic and European values over the last century has shifted the emphasis back towards the male line, and in many ways, women in modern Digo society have less freedom and autonomy than they had a hundred years ago.

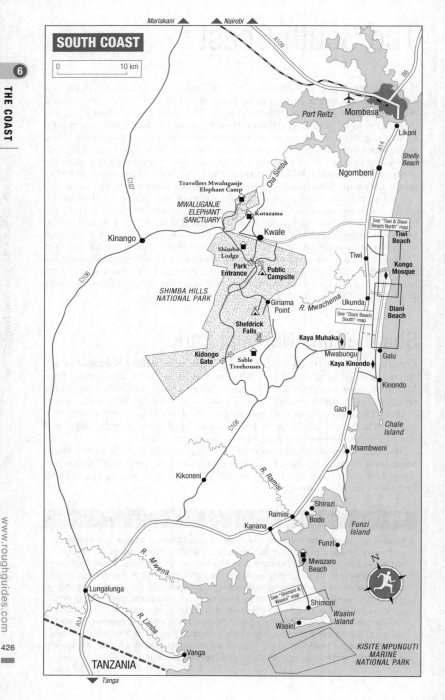

Mariakani ▲   ▲ *Nairobi* ▲

A109

B8

Port Reitz

Mombasa

Likoni

Ngombeni

Shelly Beach

A14

C107

Travellers Mwaluganje
Elephant Camp

Cha Simba

MWALUGANJE
ELEPHANT
SANCTUARY

Kutazama

Kwale

See "Tiwi & Diani
Beach North" map

Tiwi
Beach

Kinango

Shimba
Lodge

Tiwi

Kongo
Mosque

Park
Entrance

Public
Campsite

C106

SHIMBA HILLS
NATIONAL PARK

Giriama
Point

R. Mwachema

Ukunda

See "Diani Beach
South" map

Diani
Beach

Sheldrick
Falls

Kaya Muhaka

Kidongo
Gate

Sable
Treehouses

Mwabungu

Kaya Kinondo

Galu

Kinondo

C108

Gazi

Chale
Island

Msambweni

R. Ramisi

Kikoneni

Shirazi

Ramisi

Bodo

Funzi
Island

Kanana

Funzi

R. Mwena

Mwazaro
Beach

Lungalunga

R. Limba

See "Shimoni &
Wasini" map

Shimoni

N

A14

Wasini

Wasini
Island

TANZANIA

KISITE MPUNGUTI
MARINE
NATIONAL PARK

Vanga

▼ *Tanga*

Kwale and the park gate

There are fairly frequent **matatus** to Kwale from the Likoni ferry dock, but no obvious way of visiting the park from there unless you're lucky with a lift. The park's **main gate** is 3km beyond Kwale, along the elephant-dunged *murram* road to Kigango. If you're **driving**, it's best to have a high-clearance 4WD to enter the park itself. You should get away with an ordinary car in dry weather, but some park roads may be too rough for it: the rangers at the gate will tell you.

The small district capital of **KWALE** doesn't have a lot to offer, but there are two **lodgings**, of which *Golden Guesthouse* (℡0722/605646; ❷) is the best, offering fairly clean, self-contained rooms, with nets.

Around the park

Although the park is famous for its thick **forest**, one of the easiest places to experience the forest is at *Shimba Lodge* itself, rather than on a game drive. You can see most of the **primates** from the lodge, too – colobus, Sykes' and vervet monkeys, as well as bushbabies and greater galagos – and **leopards** range in the same area. Other predators are rare in Shimba Hills: the lions have gone, but you might see a **serval**.

You are likely to see **elephants**, especially from the vantage of Elephant Hill or at the nearby **Sheldrick Falls**, particularly if you go early in the day. There are armed guards at Elephant Hill who will escort you to the falls. It's a very pretty walk down a steep hillside, and then partly wooded to the falls themselves, but quite a long hike back up again. Take drinking water, and swimming gear if you want to splash in the pool. Allow about three hours for the excursion. There were around six hundred elephants in Shimba until the translocation of half of them to Tsavo East in 2005. The remaining three hundred are still arguably more than Shimba can support: fortunately, the creation of the Mwaluganje Elephant Sanctuary (see overleaf) has been a great success.

Buffalo are fairly common, as are **bushbuck** and several species of **duiker**. Look out also for the park's small herd of **Maasai giraffe**, the product of a tentative experiment. Although Shimba had never had giraffe naturally, a few individuals were introduced in the 1990s, though the jury is still out on whether they can thrive here. **Ostriches** have also been introduced.

Shimba is best known for its indigenous herds of **sable antelope**, magnificent animals as big as horses, with great, sweeping horns. The park is their only habitat in Kenya. You may well see groups of chestnut-coloured females but the territorial, jet-black males, for which the species is named, are more solitary and harder to find. If you have a guide he'll know where to look, but they're most commonly seen in the area overlooking the ocean, between the public campsite and Giriama Point.

Accommodation

One of the best things about the Shimba Hills is ⚑ **Shimba Lodge** (℡0722/200952, ⓦwww.aberdaresafarihotels.com; no children under 7; FB ❼). Like *Treetops* (see p.187), it's a "tree-hotel", though superior in all respects to the original. Check-in is normally from 3pm, but if you're driving up yourself and give advance notice, you can arrive for lunch. Although the standard rooms, with nets, and shared showers and toilets, are very basic for a lodge, when there are bushbabies on the branch outside, a fish eagle in the trees opposite, and monitor lizards hunting by the lake below, you don't spare too much thought for luxuries. The best feature is the tree-level **walkway**, which runs for 100m to a platform high above a small clearing where elephants often visit. After dark, spotlights illuminate bushbabies, hundreds of bats and a whirling hailstorm of jungle insects. It's a memorable evening – and the food is always good.

You can also **camp** at two sites in the park ($15 per person). The main public campsite is located at one of the best vantage points in the park, about 3km from the main gate. The four, twin-bedded *bandas* here, *Sable Bandas* (℡020/600800, ✉reservations@kws.go.ke; $35 per person), are adequate, though the bedding, lamps, shower and nearby toilet are unreliable, and you need to treat the water. The setting, however, is sublime: a thickly forested bluff hundreds of metres above the coconut-crowded coastal plain. It's well worth spending the night up here just for the sunrise.

Mwaluganje Elephant Sanctuary

To the northwest of Shimba Hills National Park lies the **Mwaluganje Elephant Sanctuary** (℡0722/343050; $30, children $10). Situated on the slopes of the privately owned Goloni Escarpment, it's a remarkable success story of community ecotourism, created in 1995 to defuse conflict between the local Duruma farmers and the district's elephants, which had made a habit of trashing crops and killing farmers. After consultation between the local people, KWS and the Eden Wildlife Trust, 240 square kilometres were set aside for the sanctuary, separated along a third of its boundary from farmland with electric fencing, but with a corridor left open to Shimba Hills to keep the elephants' migration route open.

The low-lying areas around the Manolo River are dominated by baobab, while thick brachystegia forest covers the escarpment's flanks, and harbours one of the densest concentrations of elephants in Africa. You're guaranteed to see elephants and, in time, it's hoped that threatened species can be relocated here from other parts of Kenya. Other mammals are thin on the ground, but there's prolific birdlife.

The main gate is beyond the Shimba Hills park entrance, 14km west of Kwale, then 2km along a signposted track to the right. The only **accommodation** in the sanctuary is *Travellers Mwaluganje Elephant Camp* (reservations through *Travellers Beach Hotel* in Bamburi: ℡041/5485121, Ⓦwww.travellersbeach.com; FB ❼). Set along the shoulder of a low hill, facing a well-established elephant trail and waterhole, there are twenty twin-bedded tents under thatched roofs, each with bathrooms and electricity. It's not fancy, but the experience is fun.

Outside the sanctuary, on the Goloni ridge north of Kwale, there's a stunning place to stay in the shape of ⚜ *Kutazama* on the Goloni ridge north of Kwale (℡020/2040651 or 0722/410468, Ⓦwww.kutazama.com; package $940). It's a beautifully designed house, blending with the landscape, and full of tribal artefacts. It has just two, very luxurious and secluded, but quite different, guest suites, each with a deck and spa pool. Stunning views, walks in the area and an infinity pool overlooking a great loop of the Cha Shimba River make this a perfect honeymoon hideaway. A more affordable but still highly attractive place to stay in the Shimba Hills is *Sable Vally Treehouses* on the southeastern slopes below the park (℡0724/558642 and 0733/602588; Ⓦwww.destination-adventures.com; AI $410). For what you get – a very private, elevated room (one of just two among the trees), with your own staff, in a superb location – this is great value.

Tiwi Beach

On the coast south of Mombasa, the first real magnet is **Tiwi Beach**, which lies a couple of kilometres to the east of the main road. Popular among budget travellers having a bit of a splurge, Tiwi rates as genuine tropical paradise material and attracts lots of Anglo-Kenyan families down from Nairobi. The reef lies just offshore, and there are good snorkelling opportunities at high tide, especially at the northern end. With the exception of the large *Tiwi Beach Resort* at its southern end, Tiwi is still cottage territory, with a handful of plots vying for business. The main drawbacks (though you might think they're advantages) are the relative isolation of the beach from Mombasa and Diani, and the lack of restaurants and bars outside the cottages and guesthouses. The clear advantages are fewer tourists and fewer beach boys. In the dry season, you can walk to the end of Tiwi Beach and wade across the Mwachema River to Diani Beach and the strange Kongo Mosque, right next to the *Indian Ocean Beach Resort*.

There are two **access roads** down to Tiwi Beach from the main South Coast highway. The northern road (signposted for *Sand Island*, *Capricho* and *Maweni*) is a narrow sandy track some 17km from the Likoni ferry; the second, about 1.5km further south, has a bigger clump of signboards and is much wider. Using either road, you're strongly advised not to walk, especially if you have luggage with you: these roads through the cashew woods have seen a number of robberies over the years. Waiting for a ride won't be a huge problem, certainly on the southern access road, where there's a fairly frequent taxi service (Ksh400–500), and most of the beach properties will happily pick you up for free from the main road if you contact them in advance. Taxis to Tiwi Beach from Mombasa airport cost about Ksh3000.

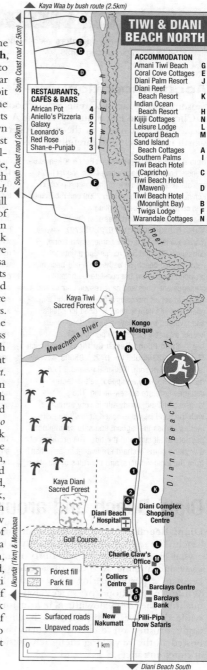

Kaya Waa by bush route (2.5km)

TIWI & DIANI BEACH NORTH

ACCOMMODATION

Amani Tiwi Beach	G
Coral Cove Cottages	E J
Diani Palm Resort	J
Diani Reef	
Beach Resort	K
Indian Ocean	
Beach Resort	H N
Kijiji Cottages	L
Leisure Lodge	N
Leopard Beach	L M
Sand Island	
Beach Cottages	A I
Southern Palms	
Tiwi Beach Hotel	
(Capricho)	C
Tiwi Beach Hotel	
(Maweni)	D
Tiwi Beach Hotel	
(Moonlight Bay)	B F
Twiga Lodge	
Warandale Cottages	F N

RESTAURANTS, CAFÉS & BARS

African Pot	4
Aniello's Pizzeria	6
Galaxy	2
Leonardo's	5
Red Rose	1
Shan-e-Punjab	3

South Coast road (2.5km)

South Coast road (2km)

Tiwi Beach

Reef

Kaya Tiwi Sacred Forest

Kongo Mosque

Mwachema River

Diani Beach

Kaya Diani Sacred Forest

Diani Complex Shopping Centre

Diani Beach Hospital

Golf Course

Forest fill

Park fill

Charlie Claw's Office

Colliers Centre

Barclays Centre

Barclays Bank

Ukunda (1km) & Mombasa

Surfaced roads

Unpaved roads

New Nakumatt

Pilli-Pipa Dhow Safaris

0   1 km

Diani Beach South

For details of **dhow-trip operators**, read the box on p.441. Information on scuba-diving can be found in the box on p.436.

Accommodation

Seasons on Tiwi tend to reflect the school holidays of their regular clients, and at Christmas and Easter, and in July and August, advance booking is a very good idea. There isn't much in the real budget range, but the extra expense is well worth it if you choose carefully.

Amani Tiwi Beach Resort Tiwi Beach ⓦ kenyaluxuryhotel.com. The beach's only large, tourist hotel, an establishment with one of the longest pools in Kenya. It burned down early in 2009 and rebuilding was continuing at time of writing.

🏃 **Coral Cove Cottages** Tiwi Beach ☎ 040/3300010 or 0722/732797, ⓦ www.coralcove.tiwibeach.com. Large, stand-alone cottages with good bathrooms and an attractive, palm-shaded beach, all bathed in a laid-back mood provided by low-key but consistently helpful management. Dogs and cats, rescue parrots and a troupe of vervet monkeys are all part of the atmosphere.The sea here is shallow, good for children, and favoured by egg-laying turtles. Cook/housekeeper available for Ksh700 per day. ❹

🏃 **Sand Island Beach Cottages** Tiwi Beach ☎ 0733/660554 or 0722/395005, ⓦ www.sandislandtiwi.com. Well-maintained if fairly rustic, the six fully equipped, self-catering cottages here are all sea-facing. The long-established, shady site is very attractive, with the sand island exposed at low tide just metres across the lagoon, and safe swimming possible at all states of the tide. The products of a working citrus orchard are available, as is fish from the local vendors, and the ruins of old slave quarters stand in the grounds. ❹

Tiwi Beach Hotel Tiwi Beach ☎ 040/3300012 or 0722/328365, ⓦ www.mawenibeach.com. The former *Maweni Beach*, *Capricho* and *Moonlight Bay* properties, amalgamated under a single management, includes self-catering cottages and hotel rooms. *Maweni* has a variety of cottages with stunning sea views in beautiful gardens roamed by dik-diks; *Capricho* is slightly pricier, with well-designed vault-roofed cottages and plenty of cool space; and *Moonlight Bay* has four cottages and a restaurant. You can hire the services of a cook for Ksh500 per day. There's also a restaurant at *Moonlight Bay* and a pool bar at *Maweni*. ❺

Twiga Lodge Tiwi Beach ☎ 040/3205126 or 0721/577614. Lively, secure and good value, this hostel and campsite trades on a reputation established in the 1970s, and is perennially popular with budget travellers and overlanders with their own vehicles. The cheap rooms are simple but good-value (some have verandas), and the superior rooms, which cost twice as much, are big, bright and airy. You can also camp (Ksh300 per person). There's an adequately stocked shop and the bar-restaurant is lively and does decent food (meals 8am–9pm; bar open as late as the last drinker). ❸

Diani Beach and around

Diani Beach ought to fulfill most dreams about the archetypal palm-fringed beach. The sand is soft and brilliantly white; the sea is turquoise and usually crystal-clear; the reef is a safe thirty-minute swim or a ten-minute boat ride away; and, arching overhead, the coconut palms create pools of cool shade and keep up a perpetual slow sway as the breeze rustles through their fronds. While competition for space always threatens to mar Diani's paradisal qualities, the 2008 downturn in tourism knocked out some of the hotels, while the droves of hustlers, or "beach boys", dwindled to a few relatively easily brushed-off diehards. Security has been tightened up, with *askaris* posted all the way along the beach outside every property, and tight security at hotel entrances.

If you're coming to Diani by **public transport** from Mombasa, first take the Likoni ferry and then catch a matatu for "Diani" or "Beach". If there are no direct matatus, get one to Ukunda (see p.440), and then make a connection down to the beach road. Taxis from Mombasa cost around Ksh3700 to Ksh4700, depending on your final destination. If you're flying to Diani Beach airstrip you'll find you arrive right in the middle of things, less than ten minutes' drive from most hotels along the beach.

Running three hundred metres behind the beach and separated from it by bush, the **Diani Beach road** feels like Kenya's number-one strip in the high season. Fortunately, forest and scrubby bush separate the road from the shore, though more of the **Jadini Forest** disappears every year as one new plot after another is cleared. Apart from too many would-be **estate agents** and **travel agents**, there are one or two genuinely good **tour operators and safari agents** along the strip, together with an increasingly heavy scattering of **shops** – though thankfully no shopping malls as yet – a Barclays with an **ATM**, a **post office** and several **cybercafés**, not to mention an ever-changing list of **restaurants and bars**, happily including some that have been pleasing visitors for years.

Accommodation

Although there are one or two good **hotels** north of the Ukunda junction, the much longer beachfront to the south retains some flicker of the pre-hotel era, and this is where most of the remaining forest is. To the north, the scene is brasher and more despoiled. Many of the thirty-odd hotels offer all-inclusive deals, as well as full- or half-board or bed and breakfast, and most provide some sort of nightly

▲ Harvesting coconuts for juice

entertainment, including cheesy bands and troupes of dynamic acrobats. Most all-inclusives are open to casual visitors: you'll pay from Ksh1500 to Ksh2000 for a daytime wrist band, including lunch and all drinks and normal activities, and around Ksh1800 to Ksh3000 for the evening equivalent.

Budget accommodation along the beach is sparse, although there are one or two places to camp. If you're with your family or in a group, renting a cottage is invariably better-value than taking hotel rooms, and gives you the chance to cook local food – or have it cooked for you. Most self-catering places are regularly visited by fruit and fish vendors.

The distances in the following listings are from the Ukunda junction on the Diani Beach road, next to Barclays Bank. For locations, depending on whether places are north or south of the Ukunda, junction, see either the "Tiwi & Diani Beach North" map on p.429 or the "Diani Beach South" map, on p.431.

Camping, budget rooms and self-catering cottages

Diani Beachalets 6.9km south ☎020/2170209 or 0734/408324, ⓦwww .dianibeachalets.com. Great-value, welcoming and homely, this peaceful refuge is right on the beach and has a variety of accommodation, from simple, non s/c two-bed *bandas* with shared showers and cooking area, to roomy s/c cottages with kitchen and veranda. The site is visited by duiker antelopes, bushbabies, colobus and Sykes' monkeys, and baboons. *Banda* ❶, cottage ❷

Diani Campsite 1.4km south ☎0722/683900. Once something of an institution when it was *Dan Trench's* (Trench was the elderly character who opened up Diani Beach in the 1960s), this site fell

on hard times, but its new incarnation is a popular standby, with small, well-maintained s/c, self-catering cottages, slightly overpriced, but all with kitchens and nets, plus camping (Ksh300; cooking facilities available), safe parking, and the busy *Winds* bar-restaurant. ❹

Diani Marine Village 3km south ☎040/3202367 or 040/3203451, ⓦwww.dianimarine.com. A great-value dive base, and whether you're diving or not, the decent, *banda*-style accommodation, with fans and nets (no a/c) make it well worth considering. BB ❻

Kijiji Cottages 600m north ☎0724/255473 or 0722/326151, ⓦwww .kijijicottages.com. The best cottages on Diani Beach, innovatively designed and extremely well kept, with a choice of different shapes and sizes, all spacious, comfortable, secluded and well-furnished. Sea-facing cottages cost more (the three-storey *Bonde* is the finest of the lot, with a superb terrace). There's a pool, and regular visits by monkeys and bushbabies. A daily cook/cleaner is included with each cottage. **5**

Stilts 3km south, opposite *Ali Barbour's Cave* restaurant ☎ 0722/523278, ⓦ www .dianibeachkenya.com. Just over the road from the beach, but right in the bush, with non s/c *bandas* on stilts, well-shaded pitches for camping (Ksh300), a good bar-restaurant (mains around Ksh500, pasta Ksh400, chips Ksh150, salad Ksh200, and plenty of wildlife. Solar lighting in rooms and no electric sockets – charge your batteries at the bar. **3**

Tandoori Guesthouse 3.5km south, on the west side of the road, behind *Tandoori Bay Restaurant* ☎ 040/3202020. The cheapest rooms in Diani, and very reasonable for the price: clean, some of them pretty large, all with nets – three s/c, three non-s/c. **2**

Vindigo Cottages 700m south ☎ 040/3202192 or 0733 579702, ⓦ www.vindigocottages.com. Seven self-catering cottages in woodland, with a pleasing rustic feel. The kitchens are fully equipped and the rooms are very private, if a little basic, with electricity and decent bathrooms. Some have lovely views over the beach through the trees. A cook can be hired for Ksh500 per day. **4**

Warandale Cottages 600m north ☎ 040/3202186, ⓦ www.warandale.com. On the same plot as *Kijiji*, and sharing the pool, these six cottages are smaller and simpler, but still extremely pleasant, fresh and spacious. Three are sea-facing, others (cheaper) are set back among the trees, with the advantage of more likely bushbay and monkey sightings. A daily cook/cleaner is included with each cottage. Good discounts May–June & Sept–Nov. **4**

Wayside Beach Apartments 1.4km south, between the main road and the defunct *Trade Winds* hotel ☎ 040/32031196 or 0722/820913, ⓦ www.kenyaurlaub.com. Urban-style, German-owned two- to six-bed self-catering apartments in a building around a good pool and spa, but not right on the beach. **4**

Hotels north of the junction

Diani Reef Beach Resort 1.5km ☎ 040/3202723 or 0722/205679, ⓦ www.dianireef.com. Built in the 1970s and revamped in 2005, complete with under-lobby aquarium, this is one of the largest hotels on the coast, on a steep stretch of beach, with three restaurants, five bars, and 143 rooms, all cool and comfortable, but with little to distinguish them but the size of their balconies.

The pool feels too small for the number of guests, but facilities are good, including all the watersports, a diving school, the *Ace* casino, *Dunes Nightspot* (9pm–late) and *Maya* spa. HB **7**

Diani Palm Resort 2.4km north ☎ 040/3202423, ⓦ www.dianipalmhotel.com. Although on the landward side of the road, the beach is just 400m away, and this part-Swiss-managed hotel offers all the essentials, with less fuss and at far less expense than most of its neighbours. The 22 s/c rooms are fresh and clean (if a little basic), with nets, TV and fridge. There's a reasonably priced bar-restaurant and a good-sized pool. BB **4**

Indian Ocean Beach Resort 3.4km ☎ 040/3203730, ☎ 020/4445818, ⓦ www .jacarandahotels.com. The northernmost property on Diani Beach (it shares its boundary with Kongo Mosque) opened in 1992, with – at the time – state-of-the-art, Lamu-style rooms. It still manages to feel a little special, and is popular for weddings and honeymoons. The one hundred rooms have cute, alcove bathrooms, fridges, safes and tea-making kit, and upstairs rooms incorporate very pleasant balconies looking out across the baobab-studded gardens. The oceanfront rooms are worth the small supplement. On the down side, the pool is too shallow and rather exposed. BB **7**

Leisure Lodge 1km ☎ 040/3203624 or 040/3202620, ⓦ www.leisurelodgeresort.com. One of the earlier Diani hotels (1971) but slickly revamped, and in a striking location on low cliffs hollowed by bat-filled caves, above a fine, tree-shaded beach. Five pools soak up the guests from 170 rooms and there's a casino (9pm–3am), and an 18-hole, par 72, 6084-metre golf course. Standard rooms lack sea views, but come with a/c, nets and DSTV. PADI diving school, windsurfing school and tennis. HB **7**

Leopard Beach 700m ☎ 040/3202721 or 040/3202110, ⓦ www.leopardbeachresort.com. Once stylish, now slightly formal hotel set in lush gardens with ponds and waterfalls, friendly if inconsistent staff, a good atmosphere and generally decent food. Superior rooms and cottages have sea views, but overall the 158 rooms vary from very good to verging on unacceptable for this standard. It's a big place, and overpriced at peak season, especially with its one, modest pool. Steps lead down to the beach. PADI diving school. HB **7**

Southern Palms Beach Resort 2.7km ☎ 040/3203721 or 0733/333366, ⓦ www .southernpalmskenya.com. Bright, welcoming package hotel, with a spring in its step. The average-sized rooms, with screened windows (no nets), TV, fridge and safe are perhaps a bit blandly cosmopolitan (and top-floor rooms are a bit of climb), but the overall, fun approach, with two enormous, 80-metre, freeform pools, four restaurants, five bars and a kids' club, make it ideal for families. PADI diving school ("Diving the Crab"), windsurfing, floodlit tennis courts, squash, gym. HB ❼

Hotels south of the junction

🏃 **Asha Cottages** 2km, ☎0723/644945 or 0727/624626, ⊛www.ashacottages.com. Cool, light, airy, family-run, boutique hotel, right by the beach, with just five rooms, and water heated by solar panels. Pool, and excellent seafood meals (Ksh2000). They capture rainwater, separate and recycle all waste, and donate a percentage of income to community projects. BB ❻–❼

Baobab Beach Resort 5.9km ☎040/3202623 or 040/3202526, ⊛www.baobab-beach-resort.com. The 1970s *Robinson Club Baobab* is now an elegant and well-kept all-inclusive, part of the big TUI group, located at the southern end of Diani Beach on a coral rock promontory. With 239 rooms, including the 2008 *Maridadi* wing (much bigger rooms) and the separate *Kole Kole Resort* (south of the promontory) it's a busy place, on a sizeable plot – though they have cleared much of the indigenous forest – with a reputation for good food. Clients can use all three parts of the resort. "Diving the Crab" PADI diving school. AI ❼

Diani Sea Lodge 3.3km ☎040/3203438, ⊛www.dianisea.com. Large, German-owned, slightly downmarket, Mediterranean-style version of the jointly owned *Diani Sea Resort*. The rooms are a let-down: despite the good-sized double beds, a/c and frame-fitted nets, most are small, in bungalows set back in the gardens. Pool and children's pool, gym, tennis court, crazy golf, windsurfing and PADI diving school. Mainly German clientele. AI ❼

Diani Sea Resort 1.9km ☎040/3203438, ⊛www.dianisea.com. Built in 1991 and much more cheerful than its sister hotel, with good service, nice staff and plenty of things to do. Again, most guests are German, many on long stays. Great pool, gym, tennis and squash courts, crazy golf, windsurfing and PADI diving school. AI ❽

🏃 **Flamboyant** 2.8km ☎040 3202033 or 0714/456130, ⊛www.dianibeachkenya.com. Large family house, adapted as a modest but comfortable hotel, sleeping twenty guests in a variety of a/c rooms with fans and nets. There's a good pool, tennis and squash. Separate cottages – *Baobab* and *Desert Rose* – are also available (from Ksh20,000 sleeping up to 8). BB ❼

🏃 **Kinondo Kwetu** 12km, on Kinondo beach ☎040/3300031or 0710/251565, ⊛www.kinondo-kwetu.com. Far south of Diani Beach proper, *Kinondo Kwetu* ("Our Home at Kinondo") mixes Scandinavian cool and Kenyan warmth in a beguiling combination, with lots of African art, sumptuous fabrics and dark wood, catering for a maximum of 38 guests. The breeze-cooled rooms, none of which lock (or need to) have stylish, bright interiors; there's excellent cuisine; charming Swedish hosts; and almost nobody on the beach (though note the beach is narrow, the reef far out and the lagoon shallow at low tide). Free airport transfers, sauna, sports and non-motorized watersports, plus a PADI diving school and riding stables. AI $970.

LTI-Kaskazi Beach 300m, ☎040/3203725 or 040/3300114, ⊛www.kaskazibeachhotel.com. Well run and competitively priced, successfully balancing package-tour prices with a friendly atmosphere. While the rooms are ready for a refurb, the public areas are still stylish enough, decorated with Arabic motifs, white-tiled floors and tinkling fountains. There's also the sad little ruined seventeenth-century "Diani mosque" in the garden, which is basically just an old wall. AI ❼–❽

Neptune Paradise Village 8.5km, on Galu Beach ☎040/3202350 or 040/3300046, ⊛tinyurl.com/n3jny2. Decent rooms ("Paradise" are superior to "Village") in tightly packed rows of two-storey *bandas* (few with sea views), on a plot that requires lengthy, shadeless walks and has been extended seawards to the point where there is no beach left at high tide. Reasonable facilities include two pools and a diving school. The co-owned *Neptune Palm Beach*, 200m to the south, is more luxurious. Renovation to the "Paradise" rooms in 2009 should see improvements. AI ❼

Papillon Lagoon Reef 5.5km ☎020/2331338 or 0725/204777, ⊛www.rexresorts.com. Middle-market, mid-sized mostly all-inclusive hotel, with 119 rooms and a good reputation for value-for-money stays, but inconsistent service and mediocre food. Rooms, of which eighteen have sea views, are better than adequate: spacious, comfortable, with a/c and fans, useful room safes (extra payment) and balconies. Free windsurfing and snorkelling for AI guests, and free diving demos available in the pleasant pool. AI ❼

🏃 **Pinewood Village** 10.8km, on Galu Beach ☎020/2080981 or 0723/957080, ⊛www.pinewood-village.com. Well managed, Mediterranean-style resort hotel on a quiet stretch of beach south of the main Diani strip, all set in pretty gardens. Take an ordinary room and eat in the restaurant, or a suite and get the services of your own chef thrown in. 58 rooms in cottages of two doubles upstairs and one suite downstairs, with great a/c, nets and safes. There's a good gym and the popular Aqualand watersports centre down on the beach. HB ❼–❽

Shaanti Holistic Health Retreat 6.4km
☏040/3202064 or 0721/363343, ⓦwww
.shaantihhr.com. With just eight rooms, the most
unusual establishment on Diani bills itself as a yoga
and meditation health retreat and is just about far
enough south of the busiest part of the beach to do
so convincingly. The food is vegetarian and rates
include yoga and meditation sessions, but therapies
and massage treatments are extra. FB $500.

🏃 The Sands at Nomad 4.8km
☏0724/262426, ⓦwww.thesandsatnomad
.com. The most appealing hotel on Diani Beach is
this boutique beach lodge of cool, well-designed
rooms and cottages (though standards and prices
vary greatly) tucked among baobabs close to the

shore, with 37 rooms and suites, and very personal
service. There's a good beach bar and restaurant,
the HQ of the "Diving the Crab" PADI diving school,
5m-deep pool (good for dive training), and a
kitesurfing school. BB ❼–❽

🏃 Water Lovers Ocean View 2.2km
☏0735/790535 or 0727/008840.
ⓦwww.waterlovers.it. Both friendly and trying to
be eco-friendly, with six cottages and a villa,
largely powered by solar panels, this small,
recently built hotel lies in a coconut grove more
or less on the beach. The centrepiece is a small
infinity pool above the sands. The Italian-slanted
restaurant goes in for local produce and home
cooking. BB ❼

Along Diani Beach

As on other beaches in Kenya, all of Diani Beach is open to the public, and
there are **access paths**, some signposted, between many of the hotels: if you
can't find one, you can always access the beach by visiting one of the hotels. If
you're doing something that depends on having enough beach (football or
volleyball) or sufficient sea depth (wind- or kitesurfing, or snorkelling in the
lagoon), it's worth checking the **tides** (see p.387), as the lagoon often drops to
ankle depth at low tide, while all but a thin strip of the beach is generally under
water at high tide.

Enjoying yourself on Diani isn't difficult. The sheltered lagoon behind the reef
is ideal for **windsurfing** (Ksh1000/hr or often free to all-inclusive guests) and
kitesurfing (one-day courses from $70). Most hotels also offer snorkelling gear
(again, free to all-inclusive guests, or you can rent it for about Ksh500), and you
can then float out across the lagoon towards the **reef**. You need to be a reasonably confident swimmer: there are no strong currents nor any real danger, but
the reef is 600 to 1000m away and swimming back on the ebb tide can be
tiring. Alternatively, a trip to the reef on one of the outrigger **canoes** is highly
recommended. The crews know all the good spots for snorkelling and it should
cost you Ksh1000 to 2000 for up to three hours of pottering about with a
captain and one crew. One of the best areas is directly opposite *Baobab Beach
Resort*, about 300m out towards the reef, where there is a cluster of coral heads.

Beach boys

Spending some peaceful time on the beach can sometimes seem virtually impossible
because of the **hustlers** plying their wares, their camel rides, their boat trips, or just
themselves. Fortunately, the problem has abated in recent years, but a few
beach-boy pesterers, in theory all licensed in some way, still hang on. People have
different ways of dealing with them. Ignoring their greetings is considered rude, and
may well not deter them. One solution is to strike up a friendship of sorts with one
beach boy, to buy at least something, or to go on a boat trip. Once you have a friend,
and have done some business, you should find you can then use the beach with
fewer hassles from the others. It's not so easy for single women, but the principle for
most situations still applies – don't fight it. There is no need, incidentally, to feel
physically threatened on the beach. Every hotel has its *askaris* (security guards)
posted along the boundary between the hotel plot and the beach, and they usually
stay alert to the slightest sign of trouble – which is rare indeed.

Diving on the South Coast

Many hotels have **dive centres**, where you can do everything from a basic beginner lesson plus assisted dive (around $140) to a full course giving you an internationally recognized PADI qualification ($700 for the Open Water Diver). Before choosing a centre, take time to compare their equipment, and ask them about their environmental policy, safety procedures and general experience. They should at the very least have up-to-date PADI accreditation, and ideally be affiliated to Scuba Schools International (SSI). One of the oldest and best-established outfits, with an excellent reputation and good equipment, is **"Diving the Crab"** (☎0723/108108, ⓦwww .divingthecrab.com) who have several dive bases on Diani Beach. **Diani Marine**, who run the Diani Marine Village, also have an excellent reputation.

If you already have scuba certification, single dives cost around $100. If you're a complete novice, you can often take a free dip in the pool wearing diving equipment, to test your affinity – most people find breathing underwater curiously addictive. If you're qualified, but haven't dived for a while, you should take a pool check at one of the hotels' PADI schools, which is usually free of charge, before going out to sea.

When you tire of the beach and the sea, or of just lying under the palm trees, you could **rent a bicycle** and go off exploring – from about Ksh500 per half-day. There's also *Leisure Lodge's* **golf course** (see p.433). For details of **dhow-trip** operators, see the box on p.441. Various other possibilities are mentioned in the listings on p.439.

If you're on Diani Beach in early June, look out for the local community fund-raiser, **Diani Rules** (ⓦwww.dianirules.com), which you're liable to get roped into. From goat races to dhow races, Frisbee tournaments and volleyball, it's all grist to the mill and part of a three-day party that usually swirls around one or other of the hotels, usually raising money for Kwale District Eye Centre.

Kongo Mosque

For a short cultural excursion, visit the **Kongo Mosque** at the far north end of the beach, at the mouth of the Mwachema River. It's most easily reached through the grounds of the *Indian Ocean Beach Resort*. Beyond the boundary fence and inevitable *askari*, the Kongo Mosque is surrounded by venerable baobabs. Also known as Diani Persian Mosque, the building is enigmatic and disconcerting, the barrel-vaulted mosque with its five heavy wooden doors brooding like a huge tomb under the trees. Named after the former forest of the area, the mosque is thought to be either fourteenth- or fifteenth-century and the one remaining building – maybe the only stone one – of a Wa-shirazi settlement here (see p.443) that grew up around the first safe anchorage south of Mombasa. If you want to take a close look, take photos, or even have a chance of going inside if you're suitably dressed, you should first introduce yourself to one of the elders who are usually sitting nearby. A small "donation for the upkeep of the mosque" is expected.

Jadini Forest wildlife

For a walk, or a jog, head south along the Diani Beach road, which has more shade than the northern stretch. Towards the end of the tarmac surface are some wonderful patches of jungle, comprising the dwindling **Jadini Forest** ("Jadini", disappointingly, turns out to be an embellished acronym made from the initials of members of a white settler family who once owned most of the land around here). There's the almost obligatory snake park, but if you'd like to search for some animals in the wild rather than support this venture, then several of the tracks leading off inland will take you straight into magnificent areas of hardwood forest, alive with birds and butterflies, and rocking with vervet and colobus monkeys – try the tracks between *Jadini Beach Hotel* and *Shaanti Retreat*. The most impressive stands of forest are the isolated *kayas*, or **sacred groves**, of which there are at least three along the Diani Beach road: **Kaya Diani**, on the north side of the Leisure Lodge golf course; **Kaya Ukunda**, west of the entrance to *Diani Sea Lodge*; and **Kaya Kinondo**, south of *Pinewood Village*. Kinondo is the first *kaya* to be officially opened to visitors (see "The Mijikenda Kayas", p.437).

The **Angolan colobus monkeys**, whose population is estimated at around 1500, have come in for special attention since the early 1990s, as concern has mounted over land encroachment and deaths from speeding cars. The resultant campaign, spearheaded by the Wakuluzu Colobus Trust, has put up warning signs, speed bumps and the ingenious wire, rope and wood "colobobridges" at known danger spots over the road, which the monkeys quickly learned to use. You can pick up more information at **Colobus Cottage** (6.8km south; Mon–Sat 8am–5pm; ☎0711/479453, ⓦwww.colobustrust.org) and learn about the trust's active campaigns to halt illegal tree-felling by local hotel owners. If you have time and flexibility, they welcome volunteers here. Of the other monkeys, **baboons** are most common, and can be quite aggressive. Their diet of hotel leftovers means they've multiplied greatly, and are not afraid of humans, so keep your distance. Overly tame **Sykes' monkeys** are also becoming a nuisance: don't leave things on your hotel balcony.

The Mijikenda Kayas

Each Mijikenda tribe (see box, p.423) has a traditional **kaya** central settlement, a fortified village in the forest of between five hectares and three square kilometres, usually built on raised ground some distance from the coast, but sometimes right by the shore. Some Mijikenda peoples built only one *kaya* while others built secondary *kayas* or even whole clusters. The *kayas* are considered to be the dwelling place of ancestral spirits, although they are now sacred glades rather than fortified villages.

In theory, each *kaya* contains a *fingo* – a charm said to derive from the Mijikenda's ancestral home of Shungwaya. Most *fingo* have been lost or, like the **grave posts** called *kigango* (*vigango* in the plural) that also used to be a feature of every *kaya*, stolen for private collections of "primitive art" or loft-converters' ideas of interesting *objets d'art*.

Today, many *kayas* are neglected, but they are still remembered and visited by tribal elders. Along with the belief in their sacred qualities comes a local conservation tradition: undisturbed and uncultivated, they represent a unique biological storehouse on the East African coast. A WWF-backed botanical research programme, the Coastal Forest Conservation Unit, run by the National Museums of Kenya, is slowly mapping out the *kaya* ecosystems. In 2008 the *kayas* were collectively inscribed as a **UNESCO World Heritage Site** (ⓦwhc.unesco.org/en/list/1231). More than twenty have so far been given legal status and paper protection, and elders are being encouraged to reassert their authority over them before property developers move in. There may be more than fifty altogether, though some could be so small that they will disappear under the bulldozer before anyone remembers them.

The first *kaya* to open to visitors is **Kaya Kinondo** (daily, 8am–5pm, except on Chipalata, the fourth day of the Digo week; ☎0722/446916, ⓦwww.kaya-kinondo-kenya.com), at the southern end of Diani Beach. You visit with a Digo guide (payment is still informal rather than by ticket), wrapped in a *kaniki* (indigo-dyed calico sarong) which you will be loaned, and while photography is encouraged (except at grave sites), you are expected to show deep respect for the impressive forest environment.

If you're a **bird-watcher**, Diani's hotel gardens offer spectacular entertainment, though the status of the Jadini forest's threatened species is uncertain. Look out for southern banded snake-eagle, spotted ground-thrush, plain-backed sunbird and Fischer's turaco, all of which have been seen here, though the spotted ground-thrush not since the 1980s.

You're unlikely to come across **snakes**. Whether harmless green tree snakes, egg-eaters or pythons, or more rarely poisonous mambas, those that get anywhere near the hotels tend to be bludgeoned to death by enthusiastic *askaris* who also use their sling shots to keep their local monkeys on the run. The forest used to be the haunt of **leopards**, but they haven't been seen in this part of the coast for decades now. Venture into the forest at night, however, preferably with a guide, and you will see eyes in the dark – usually those of **bushbabies**.

Eating, drinking and nightlife

The following listings, with distances given from the Ukunda junction, include some of the best, and some of the best-value, places to eat and drink. Finding food for **self-catering** is straightforward enough, with stalls along the beach road, fish and fruit vendors doing the rounds of the various cottage and *banda* sites, and several supermarkets, including a new Nakumatt (see "Listings", opposite).

Restaurants, bars and cafés

African Pot 300m north. By *Coral Beach Cottages*, a pleasant bar serving cold beer and the usual Kenyan fare (tilapia, stew, *pilau*) at reasonable prices (around Ksh300), for Diani.

Ali Barbour's Cave 2.8km south ☎040/3202033 or 0714/456130, ⊛www .dianibeachkenya.com. Bizarrely built inside a 150,000-year old coral cave, you enter the restaurant at ground level and descend a staircase. The lavish French and seafood menu (lobster bisque and chilli crab among the highlights) is well presented and a meal runs to around Ksh5000 for two without wine. Daily from 6pm.

Al Manara "Sails" Beach Bar and Restaurant 7.8km south ☎0716/135225. Changing lunch menu of seafood or meat dishes, with starters around Ksh500, mains Ksh800–1100. Dinner is a huge, set menu, generally priced at Ksh1800–3000 depending on what's on it (call ahead). Daily until late.

Aniello's Pizzeria Just south of Colliers Centre. A reliable standby for wood-fired oven pizzas (Ksh450–500), pastas around Ksh500 mark, meat and fish (Ksh600–700). There's another branch of *Aniello's* – a snack bar with a shady terrace – at Bahirini plaza. Daily 10am–11pm.

Bull Steak House 600m south, behind Petro filling station. Not recommended for vegetarians, *Bull* serves very large slices of high-grade Angus, with T-bones at Ksh1500, or rib-eyes for just over half that. In the sausage department, it also serves one-metre bratwursts.

Forty Thieves Beach Bar & Restaurant 2.8km south. This famous local watering hole is a good place for a daytime drink and perfect in the evening when its beachfront is floodlit. Discos on Wed, Fri & Sat; live band and curry buffet on Sun; English premiership football and other sport on TV; quiz nights.

Galaxy Diani Complex Shopping Centre, 1.5km north ☎0720/418563. Good Chinese restaurant with main dishes at around Ksh500–800. Free pick-up from hotels. Daily 11.30am–2.30pm & 6–10.30pm.

Leonardo's Colliers Centre ☎0750/501707. Notable for the pair of ostentatious "Range Rovers" built from wood and leather and usually parked outside, this fancy Italian joint is all wood with a fabric roof. Pasta and pizza Ksh500–800, other mains around Ksh100. Daily 10.30am–11.30pm, last food orders 10.15pm.

Mr T Roof Garden Bar & Restaurant 9.2km south. Although a little overpriced for the standard menu of tourist seafood and African dishes (main courses Ksh500–800), the breeze through the trees and convivial company keeps people coming back.

Ngiri Bar and Restaurant Diani Beach Shopping Centre, 1km south ☎0727/970787 or 0772/970787, ⊛www.ngiribar.com. Friendly, English-run sports bar and pub-style restaurant serving tasty dishes at fair prices (Ksh1000 per head, including a drink). The English food, with locally sourced produce, includes great breakfasts and a range of daily specials. *Ngiri* is also a conveniently located networking and info exchange – the owners seem to know everyone on the beach. Daily until late.

Nomad Beach Bar/Red Pepper 4.8km south ☎0724/262426 or 0735/373888.

Popular beach bar (wildly so at times), with snacks, pizzas, seafood and its famous Sun lunch curry buffet (Ksh1000) a real family affair, with regular live jazz or a one-man band. The *Red Pepper* part of the restaurant is devoted to excellent Japanese and Thai food – they do a fantastic buffet for which you should allow around Ksh2500 per head. Daily 6.30am–midnight.

Red Rose Pub and Restaurant North of the junction, past Diani Complex Shopping Centre, ☎0722/571613. European beach food – pepper steaks, spaghetti Bolognese – good prices. Open daily.

Shan-e-Punjab Diani Complex Shopping Centre, 1.4km north ☎040/320116. Punjabi restaurant and snack bar with an open-air garden, serving

vegetarian and non-vegetarian dishes. Most dishes around Ksh400–500 for a meal. Free transfers from anywhere in Diani. Daily 1–11pm.

Sundowner 7km south. A cheap and unpretentious restaurant and bar, serving brilliant African food, seafood (crab, octopus or tuna and rice) plus some German dishes, even fish fingers and chips, all freshly prepared, in a laid-back atmosphere.

Tandoori Bay Opposite *Diani Sea Lodge*, 3.5km south. Popular all-day TV bar, with down-to-earth Kenyan food at moderate prices – though no tandoori dishes.

Winds *Diani Campsite*, 1.5km south. Popular diner and TV bar at *Diani Campsite*. Fry-ups and sandwiches around the Ksh250 mark, as well as grills (Ksh400) and salads (Ksh300).

Nightlife

To get around Diani Beach at night without your own vehicle, you'll have to rely mostly on taxis. Any restaurant or hotel will call one for you: they never take more than a few minutes, but always agree the price firmly before getting in. While everyone will warn you about walking on the beach at night, under a full moon it's a pleasure that's hard to resist. With no valuables, especially in a group, you're very unlikely to have any problems.

Giriama dancing is the big entertainment that is often touted. It's perhaps not something to go out of your way to find, but is fun if you happen upon it. A couple of professional troupes work the hotels, performing acrobatically to the accompaniment of superb drumming. You're also likely to happen across **Maasai dancers**, invariably the real thing, though they come from various locales. The guttural polyphonic singing is fascinating, though the performances usually end with a "Maasai market" where they sell overpriced and not necessarily authentically Maasai trinkets. Rarest of all are the **Taarab bands** (see p.599), who sometimes play in hotel dining rooms on special occasions or public holidays. Such entertainment is very seasonal and you won't find much going on when it's quiet.

Apart from the usually cheesy hotel discos, there are several independent **night clubs** along the road, each with its own idiosyncrasies, all with at least a trace of sleaze (couples who visit will usually be ignored, but single men can expect lots of business-like propositions, and women without male partners will be constantly chatted up). None of the discos start to warm up before 11pm. The best night spot is ✻ *Shakatak*, opposite Diani Sea Lodge (3.5km south of the junction; Ⓦwww .shakatak-kenya.com; daily 9pm–late; Ksh150), with a wooden dance floor and air conditioning. It's a bit of a dive, but it does play the best music mix on the strip. Lower-key places include the small dance floor at *Tandoori Bay*, just north of *Shakatak*, and *Mambo Jambo* at the *Bull Steak House*, 600m south of the junction.

Listings

ATMs, banks & forex bureaux Barclays by the Ukunda junction has an ATM that's operational day and night; KCB has an ATM at Diani Beach Shopping Centre; as does Fidelity Bank at the Baharini Plaza. Maritime Forex by the Petro filling station is open office hours.

Bicycle, motorbike and quad-bike rental Bicycle rental outlets come and go: ask at your

hotel. Diani Bikes, based at Bazaar Shopping Centre, rent out their yellow bicycles at negotiable rates. Motorbikes are available from Glory Car Hire, Diani Beach Shopping Centre (Ⓦwww.glorysafaris .com). Quad Bikes are available from Excursion Quads (1.3km south of the junction; ☎0721/459258 or 0733/434475) starting at €60 for two hours, including hotel transfers.

Car rental Saloon cars start from around $50/day. Try Glory Car Hire, Diani Beach Shopping Centre (Ⓦ www.glorysafaris.com); or Ketty Tours, Petro filling station (Ⓦ www.kettytours.co.ke).

Flights from Diani You can fly from Ukunda airstrip (just west of the beach road, 1.5km south of the junction) to Nairobi with Safarilink (Ⓦ www .safarilink-kenya.com) and Airkenya (Ⓦ www .airkenya.com) for $125, and to Tsavo West, Amboseli and Maasai Mara with Mombasa Air Safari (Ⓦ www .mombasaairsafari.com; $270 regardless of destination); MAS also offers connections to Mombasa for its service to Malindi ($55) and Lamu ($120).

Internet access Relatively expensive compared to Mombasa, but available at several places, of which the best is the cool, new cybercafé on the upper tier of the rebuilt Diani Beach Shopping Centre. Others include Top Africa, on the north side of Colliers Centre, Forty Thieves Beach Bar, and Hot Gossip just north of the post office.

Medical services Dr Rekhi and Dr Raj (☎ 040/3202435), at the small, modern Diani Beach Hospital, next to Diani Complex Shopping Centre, are recommended.

Notice boards There are notice boards at most of the shopping centres, usually outside the supermarkets, or try Ngiri Bar & Restaurant at Diani Beach Shopping Centre.

Pharmacy South End Pharmacy, at Diani Beach Shopping Centre, is good.

Post office 500m south of Diani Beach Shopping Centre.

Supermarkets Muthaiga Mini Market, at Diani Beach Shopping Centre is a little expensive; Onjiko's, behind the Petro filling station is cheaper and has a deli counter. A new Nakumatt was due to open on the south side of the road to Ukunda, early in 2010.

Taxis Most hotels have taxis in their forecourts, and there's a stand opposite Barclays Bank, or try Diani Beach Shopping Centre, where the chairman of the taxi drivers' association is based.

Travel agents & tour operators There are various safari agents by the Petro garage and in the shopping centres along the strip: shop around. DM Tours & Safaris at Diani Beach Shopping Centre (☎ 0722 470382, Ⓦ www.dmtours.net) and Julius Safaris (☎ 040/3300299 or 0721/769771 Ⓦ www.julius-safaris.com) both have good names; Bush2Beach, Golf Villas, behind Diani Hospital (☎ 040/3202575 or 0722/411566, Ⓦ www.beach2bushkenya.com) is more expensive but highly regarded.

Ukunda

Until a few years ago just a village on the highway, **UKUNDA** is now a scruffily burgeoning town and the main service centre for the resort hotels, strung out along the Likoni–Lungalunga road, with a post office, a KCB bank with ATM, several petrol stations, a number of places with internet access, and hundreds of *dukas*. Only marginally touched by tourism, except insofar as many of its residents work in the hotels, Ukunda has a life of its own. If your holiday isn't otherwise adventurous, it's worth a visit to see something of Kenya a little more authentic than the strip. There are several cheap **B&Ls**, the best of which is *Corner Guesthouse* (☎ 0724/173484; ❶), just north of the junction for the beach road. For **nightlife**, almost anything here comes as a shock after Diani's more urbane delights. All the bars can seem (and sometimes are) pretty rough places, so go with a Kenyan friend if you can.

South to Shimoni

South of *Pinewood Village* (see p.434), the Diani Beach road returns to gravel, although it continues in a driveable condition, past one or two secluded properties around Kinondo, and past Kaya Kinondo itself. There's little transport down here, so you're likely to be driving or walking. You get to a hard right-hand bend, then 100m later a sharp left turning for Chale Point. An exclusive little beach lodge, *The Cove Retreat* (☎ 0724/558642 or 0733/602588, Ⓦ www.destination-adventures .com; no under-17s; AI $480), is just down on the beach at this junction.

Chale island is 4km further south, and 300m offshore. The island, once an uninhabited beauty spot, was acquired in the early 1990s by a property developer,

Dhow and snorkelling trips

Several **excursion operators** are based at Diani Beach. All will pick you up from your hotel either for free or for a nominal extra charge. For the most part, the dhows are not under sail but are powered by on-board or outboard motors. All can be booked direct, or though your hotel. Always ensure there's a usable life jacket for each passenger.

Charlie Claw's office at *Leopard Beach Hotel*; ☎040/3203154 or 0722/205154, Ⓦwww.wasini.com. Day-long dhow, snorkelling and dolphin-searching trips at Kisite Mpunguti Marine National Park, with a seafood lunch at their own restaurant at the northwest end of Wasini island, which also has a large, landscaped swimming pool. $100–130 including park fees, drinks, lunch, community visits and all equipment, with pick-up from North or South coast, or direct from Shimoni. Scuba-diving, if you're qualified or want to try, costs an additional $50 for one dive, or $80 for two.

"Diving the Crab" at *The Sands at Nomad*; ☎0723/108108, Ⓦwww.divingthecrab .com. Bird-watching, dolphin-watching and snorkelling trips by motorboat to mangrove channels near Chale island. Around $100 for a full day, including lunch and drinks.

East African Whale Shark Trust at Aqualand, next to *Pinewood Village* ☎0720/293156, Ⓦwww.giantsharks.org. EAWST organize in-water, whale shark encounters, especially during the peak, Feb–March whale shark season. Prices vary depending on group size and duration, but expect around $150/person.

Paradise Divers Barclays Centre ☎0722/806170, Ⓦwww.salamamarine.com. Run trips to Kisite-Mpunguti Marine National Park, in cooperation with the people of the village of Mkwiro, on the less developed and less visited eastern end of Wasini island. Prices negotiable.

Pilli-Pipa Dhow Safaris Colliers Centre; ☎040/3203559 or 0722/244694, Ⓦwww.pillipipa.com. Small-group dhow day-trips to Kisite Marine Park for outstanding snorkelling (field guides, masks, snorkels and fins provided), with a late lunch of crab claws, good wine and Swahili food at a private house on Wasini island. Departures most days at 8.30am from Shimoni jetty. $100–120, including marine park fees, all equipment and transfers.

---

with the help of two local MPs, despite being public land and a gazetted Mijikenda *kaya*. The resulting resort, the largely Italian-patronized *Sands at Chale* (☎040/3300269 or 0733/610455, Ⓦwww.thesandsatchaleisland.com; FB $490–565), owned by *The Sands at Nomad* in Diani, angered local people and wiped out acres of natural vegetation. The owners claim the development has been sensitive, that only a third of the island has been built upon and that the other part is a nature reserve. Even if you're comfortable with that, there's a package feel to the resort which you wouldn't expect in the location, and the food is nowhere near as good as at the other *Sands*. You reach it by boat, or by tractor at low tide. But not without a reservation – the island has been well and truly privatized.

If, instead of driving down to Chale Point you keep straight ahead, you emerge, after exactly 3km of slightly rough-and-ready coral rag road, onto the main highway down to Tanzania, at a point 13km south of Ukunda.

Gazi

Down the main coastal highway south of Ukunda, **GAZI** is next, a sleepy little village just off the road. It was once headquarters of the Mazrui leader **Sheikh Mbaruk ("Baruku") bin Rashid**, who acquired a reputation for torturing prisoners after half-suffocating them in the fumes of burning chillis. The story was perhaps intended to discredit him as he was the principal figure behind the

Mazrui Rebellion of 1895, an uprising against British authority that saw Mbaruk flying a German flag at his house and supplying his men with arms donated by the Germans. The British had to send for troops from India and fighting continued for nine months before an Omani puppet regime was re-established and the rebels crushed. Mbaruk died in exile in German Tanganyika. Baruku's mansion is now a primary school, which you can look around out of school hours. More than 150 years old, it was obviously a very grand place – the heavy ceiling timbers show that it once had an upper storey – but it is now sadly neglected.

There are two turnings to Gazi, which lies between the road and the shore. The first is 3.1km from the Chale island/Diani South turning. The village itself lies back from a deep, mangrove-filled bay and has no beach to speak of. Gazi Beach, about 2km south of the village, is more promising, and this is the location of a new beachside tented camp, *Gazi Retreat* ⊕0724/558642 and 0733/602588, ⊛www.destination-adventures.com; no under-17s; AI ❼). Local women in Gazi manage the **Gazi Women's' Mangrove Boardwalk**, a quarter-kilometre trail through the mangroves, which is worth visiting, especially for bird-watchers, as the modest donations support the community.

Msambweni and Funzi island

Continuing down the highway from Gazi, **MSAMBWENI** is a sizeable village with a famous leprosarium. The road to the beach goes through the village, following the coast for several kilometres before turning back to the highway. The beach is lovely – low cliffs and less uniformity than Diani – and there are no beach hassles down here, but the tide goes out for miles, with lots of rock pools, so it's not ideal for snorkelling or for most watersports.

There's limited **accommodation** at Msambweni, but what's here is exceptionally good. You ideally need your own transport, though you could manage with taxis. Several of the places are self-catering houses, with staff, including the beautiful *Samawati House* and *Chingwede House* (both ⊕040/52060, ⊛www.samawati.co.ke; $180–280/night), which share a large plot on the palm-studded shore southeast of the village. Further south, ⚒ *Msambweni House* (⊕020/3577093 or 0723/697346, ⊛www.msambweni-house.com; closed May; AI $610–1010) is a fabulous boutique hotel, the pride of its Belgian owner-designer, rising from the edge of the highest cliffs on the Kenyan coast above a remote beach complete with caves and a private dining area. *Msambweni*'s huge and inviting infinity pool is only matched by the opulence of the coolly palatial rooms and really superb food.

If, instead of returning north to the main road from Msambweni, you follow the coastline, you eventually reach **Funzi island**, separated from the mainland by a narrow channel that you can walk across at low tide. Unlike exclusive Chale, you can easily camp on the island if equipped for a fair amount of self-sufficiency, and Diani operators run bird- and crocodile-watching day-trips here. The village of **Funzi** is at the southern end, about 6km from the mainland, and there are beaches and sections of reef scattered close to the forested shore on both sides of the island. The stone and thatched cottages of the attentively managed *Funzi Keys* (⊕040/3202044, ⊛www.thefunzikeys.com; closed May & June; FB $640–840), surrounded by mangrove creeks, and accessed only by boat at high tide, are a big hit with most visitors, though it seems overpriced when compared with other, similar hideaways, and there's no beach on site.

Ramisi and Shirazi

The coast highway passes through verdant regions of parkland, with borassus, doum and coconut palms (borassus palms are the ones with a bulge in the trunk, like pythons that have swallowed a goat) interspersed with swampy dells. Further south, the landscape becomes one of rolling fields of sugar cane, culminating in **Ramisi**, which was the coast's main sugar-producing area, until the closure of its factory.

On the shore, just before you reach Ramisi, is the tiny and very old settlement of **SHIRAZI**, also known as Kifunzi (which means "little Funzi"). Any of the tracks through the sugar fields on the left of the road will take you to the hamlet – a scattering of houses in the jungle and a small harbour among mangroves. The people of Shirazi call themselves **Wa-shirazi** and are the descendants of a once-important group of the Swahili-speaking people. During the fifteenth and sixteenth centuries, they ruled the coast from Tiwi to Tanga from their eight settlements on the shore, one of which is believed to have been this village. Around 1620, these towns were captured by the Wa-vumba, another Swahili group. The Wa-shirazi, now scattered in pockets along the coast, speak a distinctive dialect of Swahili. Historians used to think that they originally emigrated from Shiraz, in Persia, but it now seems likely that very few of them have Persian ancestry and that the name was adopted for political reasons. Like many villages on the coast, Shirazi is a backwater in every sense. The people cut a small quantity of *boriti* (mangrove poles), though much less than they used to; they fish; and they also grow produce in their garden plots, which are continually being raided by monkeys. But the setting is memorably exotic and worth the two-kilometre detour from the main road. They may not have cold sodas at Shirazi, but they do have coconuts and tranquillity.

Just a couple of hundred metres south of Shirazi rests the enigmatic hulk of a Friday mosque, its *mihrab* still standing. Elders in Shirazi, who describe how earlier inhabitants were routed by the Maasai and fled to the Comoros Islands, remember when the mosque was still intact, though by the beginning of the twentieth century it had already been abandoned. The mosque is now surrounded by a modest tourist development, *Paradise Lost*, which principally acts as a bar-restaurant base for clients who come down here on crocodile-watching trips on the Ramisi River. A pleasant swimming pool is overlooked by limited **accommodation** in *Amani House* (☎040/3203513, ⓦ www.paradiselostkenya .com; FB ❼), which has two double, self-contained rooms with nets and fans, a shared living area, a balcony and kitchenette (but no cooking facilities) and a pleasant roof terrace, set somewhat improbably with a spa pool.

Shimoni

In the 1980s, the US had its eye on **Wasini** – the rocky sliver of an island just offshore from the village of **Shimoni** – as a potential naval base. Fortunately the idea was shelved, and Shimoni, 14km down a picturesque sand and mud road from the highway, remains relatively untouched and fascinating.

If you're driving down to Shimoni yourself it's worth calling at *Mwazaro Beach* (see p.445), which has to be one of the country's most eco-friendly establishments and welcomes casual visitors for meals or drinks. *Mwazaro*, which means "prayer place", is on a beautiful, lonely beach, opposite the delta of the Ramisi River, with forests of **mangroves** all around (eight of the nine species native to Africa can be found here and the owners of Mwazaro have replanted some ten square kilometres), excellent **snorkelling** at the nearby reef, and creek- and sea- trips available.

Most visitors only pass through little **Shimoni** itself when coming here for dhow trips to Wasini and the Kisite-Mpunguti Marine National Park, but it's worth an hour or two of your time. The "**slave caves**" (daily guided tours

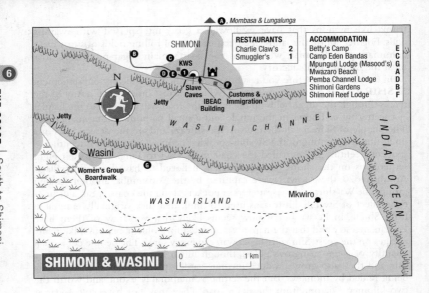

8.30–10.30am & 1.30–6pm; Ksh200) after which Shimoni was named (*shimo* means cave in Swahili) have achieved fame locally, if not much further afield, through the melodramatic warblings of Kenyan-born singer Roger Whittaker's song *Shimoni*, which was recorded in the caves. Based on the evidence of iron rings in the rocks, it's believed that they were used to store slaves prior to shipment to Zanzibar. Historians from the National Museums of Kenya are looking for further evidence, and with 5km of silted-up caverns to excavate they may have some way to go. These are caves into which you descend from ground level. Once you're down, shafts of sunlight pierce through holes in the forest floor to illuminate the stalactites and dangling lianas quite beautifully.

The ruined two-storey building opposite the caves ticket office was formerly the headquarters of the **Imperial British East African Company**, dating from 1885. The nearby **fish auction house** by the jetty is also interesting – there's an auction every morning – though exciting captures like marlin and shark are rarely on the slab.

Practicalities

There are direct **matatus** from Likoni to Shimoni, but they can be infrequent, and tend to run mostly early in the morning. Vehicles for Lungalunga will drop you at the junction where you shouldn't have much trouble getting a lift.

There are fairly frequent **cargo dhows** motoring from Shimoni to Pemba (3hr; Ksh2000) and sometimes straight to Zanzibar (6hr; Ksh3000); if you've lined up a passage, you should report to the customs and immigration offices in Shimoni.

Although Shimoni is small, the demand for **accommodation** by big-spending game-fishermen has spawned several places to stay. The Pemba Channel (the Tanzanian island of Pemba lies 50km offshore) is considered one of the world's very best stretches of sea for hunting big fish: **marlin** weighing a quarter of a tonne (550 pounds) and **tiger sharks** close on half a tonne race through these waters, marlin at recorded speeds of more than 100kph (60mph).

If you're looking for **lunch** or **dinner**, aside from visiting a couple of basic *hotelis*, or popping across for lunch at *Mpunguti Lodge* or *Charlie Claw's* on Wasini (see

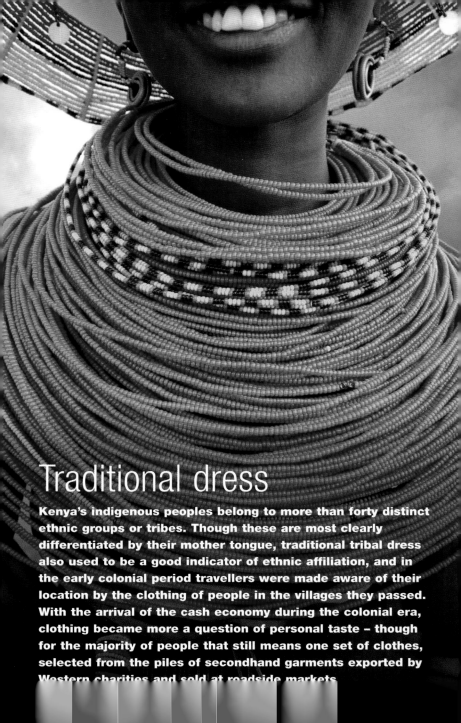

Traditional dress

Kenya's indigenous peoples belong to more than forty distinct ethnic groups or tribes. Though these are most clearly differentiated by their mother tongue, traditional tribal dress also used to be a good indicator of ethnic affiliation, and in the early colonial period travellers were made aware of their location by the clothing of people in the villages they passed. With the arrival of the cash economy during the colonial era, clothing became more a question of personal taste – though for the majority of people that still means one set of clothes, selected from the piles of secondhand garments exported by Western charities and sold at roadside markets.

Swahili woman in *buibui* ▲

Maasai warrior ▼

Swahili

The Swahili (see p.410) are almost exclusively Muslim and have adopted several variations of traditional Islamic dress from the Middle East. The basic garment for men is the **kikoi**, a colourfully woven sarong that reaches from waist to shins, often in brilliantly contrasting colours. They are not to be confused with the less expensive *kangas*, wraps of printed cotton worn exclusively by women and usually featuring Swahili proverbs and epithets. For men, formal wear consists of topping a shirt and *kikoi* with a long cotton **kanzu** – a gown, usually white and usually worn with a neatly embroidered skull cap or **kofia**. For high-status Swahili women, formal attire is the **buibui**, a black cloak and shawl that completely conceals the woman's identity, leaving only a tiny gap, or a gauze veil, to see through.

Maasai and Samburu

Of all Kenya's peoples, the **Maasai** (see p.372), particularly their men, decked in brilliant red cloth, with beads, jewellery and – for young men – long, ochred hair, have received perhaps the most attention from outsiders. Although the wearing of red cloth is as close to a "national costume" as any in Kenya, it does not long predate the colonial period: throughout most of their history in Kenya, the Maasai wore skins and had no use for cotton cloth. Today, the warrior ensemble of a cloth tied over one shoulder, together with weapons and braided hair, is still widely seen, while young men can be encountered out in the bush, hunting for birds to add to their elaborate, taxidermic headdresses.

The **Samburu** (see p.520), who split from their Maasai-speaking cousins around the seventeenth century, wear

similar attire – though men often go bare-chested. Like other pastoralists, they tend to appear in shirts and trousers only for rare visits to town. Maasai and Samburu women invariably wear **kangas** these days, and most women cover their breasts, an innovation of the late twentieth century. Long earrings and stacks of bead necklaces are, however, still the norm.

Kikuyu

Among the mixed farming and trading people of the Mount Kenya region, traditional costume was in many respects similar to that of the Maasai. The **Kikuyu** (see p.147) dressed exclusively in animal skins, tanned, softened and sewn together. Goatskin was the preferred material, but sheepskins were also used. The Kikuyu have a long history of smelting and iron-working, so volumes of heavy metal jeweller were also worn, especially by women. By the middle of the twentieth century, most Kikuyu men had adopted European clothes and blankets, but women tended to be more traditional. Today, however, Kikuyu fashions for both sexes are cosmopolitan. "Traditional" costume, worn for dances or cultural events, includes goatskins, worn over cloth wraps, and plenty of ornamentation, as well as white face and body paint, or *karia andus*, made of lime.

Turkana

You'll still see older **Turkana** (see p.508) people in more remote parts wearing very few clothes or, in some cases, animal skins. Stacks of heavy jewellery, ostrich egg necklaces and beadwork are also very common, and men usually sport lethal wrist-knives known as *aberait* – bracelet-like blades sheathed with strips of leather.

▲ Traditionally dressed Kikuyu

▼ Turkana Lady

Giriama

Living along the coast between Kilifi and Malindi, but traditionally not in the towns or along the shore, the **Giriama** (see p.450) are part of the Mijikenda ("nine tribes") ethnic group. They trace their ancestry back to a semi-mythical state or cultural heartland called Shungwaya, in present-day southern Somalia. The most distinctive Giriama dress form, the **rinda**, is a kind of kilt worn by women. In pre-colonial times it was made of grass or leaves but, as high-status, imported cotton cloth became available, women started making their *rindas* out of pleated *kanga* material, emulating the grass skirt, and stuffing a bustle of coconut fibre under the waistband at the back to accentuate the buttocks as the old-style *rinda* had done. By the turn of the century, many Giriama women had adopted Swahili-style *kanga* dresses, but on the backcountry roads you will still see old ladies with the traditional padded backside.

Giriama dance performance ▲

Luo elder ▼

Luo

For the cattle-herding-turned-fishing **Luo** (see p.252), traditional dress consisted of very little and, until World War I, many people typically went naked or wore scanty loincloths of skin or sisal. Today, the Luo, who live around Kisumu and on the shores of Lake Victoria, are one of the most Westernized of all Kenya's tribes, and you'll find Luos working in the civil service, the tourist industry or in business, throughout the country.

Traditional dress is history, and you'll only see it for special ceremonies, when senior elders may don huge plumes of feathers, embellished with tusks and metal ornamentation.

overleaf), your best bet is *Smuggler's*, an up-country-style bar-restaurant just west of the slave caves, where you can usually get chicken, beef or goat, either stewed or roasted, accompanied by rice, ugali or chapatti. They also do good breakfasts.

Accommodation

Betty's Camp 500m west of the village centre ℡0722/434709, ⓦwww.bettys-camp.com. Aiming at the budget game-fishing market ($450 per day, maximum four people), this has a choice of small, stuffy, non-s/c ridge tents, with fans, or modest rooms with ceiling fans (2 small and non-s/c, 1 large and s/c) in a large, quaint rondavel, with a shared, breezy, top-floor lounge area. There's a pleasant pool (Ksh750 for non-guests), but it's well-overpriced for the facilities and standards. BB ❻

Camp Eden Bandas 300m west of the village centre ℡020/3549520 reservations ℡020/600800 ⓔreservations@kws.go.ke. Managed by the local Kenya Wildlife Service rangers, and wonderful for naturalists on a budget, *Camp Eden* is a group of seven, airy and clean, if fairly rudimentary, *makuti*-roofed *bandas* in the forest; three of them s/c, four non-s/c (the latter have basins outside, but share squat loos and showers). There's mains electricity, but it's best to bring your own drinking water. You can also camp ($8). ❷

🏃 **Mwazaro Beach** 1km off the Shimoni road, 7.5km from the highway ℡0722/711476, ⓦwww.keniabeach.com. "Where God makes holidays" is how the German owners describe this eco-resort at a Digo *kaya* where approval was sought and granted for the low-key, sustainable development of 10 *makuti* cottages and 4, more

comfortable, coral rag rooms, all with fitted nets, and powered exclusively by wind and solar energy. Excellent, Zanzibari set meals. Camping also possible (Ksh500). FB ❻

Pemba Channel Lodge 800m west of the village centre ℡0722/205020, ⓦwww.pembachannel.com. The speciality at this small lodge (six simple, but comfortable cottages, catering for a maximum of twenty guests) is big-game fishing ($550 per day, maximum four people). It's a pleasant enough place, and has a pool, but you only stay here if you're fishing or diving (four-day dive trips aboard their 18-metre, live-aboard, motor yacht *Kisiwani* start at $1750 per person for a minimum of six). FB ❼

Shimoni Gardens 2km west of the village centre ℡0722/710050, ⓔkigless@swiftmombasa.com. Small, breezy rooms made of cane, reed and *makuti*, or sturdier stone-built cottages, not actually on the shore, but not too far away, with a bar and restaurant, plus a separate beach bar, and its own boats for snorkelling and fishing expeditions. ❹

Shimoni Reef Lodge 300m east of the village centre ℡0722/400476 ⓦwww .shimonireeflodge.com. Aimed less at sport fishermen than at divers. Pleasant enough accommodation in ten, whitewashed split-level cottages with separate bedroom and lounge areas, floor fans and nets, but rather average food. Salt water pool. HB ❻

Wasini island and offshore

WASINI isn't far offshore, but there's no standard, cheap and simple way for tourists to reach the island. The snorkelling-cruise operators speed pre-booked lunchers across the channel in their boats (see box, p.441), but if you're not one of these, you'll have to hire a motor boat on the spot, at a price of Ksh1500 to Ksh3000 depending on your bargaining skills. Meanwhile, you'll see local people using *jahazi*, the sailing boat "matatus" that are really the same kind of vessel, and which, despite resentment from the tourist-boat captains, you should be able to use, too (Ksh100).

Only 5km long and 1km across, Wasini has about a thousand inhabitants, and is totally adrift from the mainstream of coastal life. There are no cars, nor any need for them: you can walk all the way around the island in a couple of hours on the narrow footpaths through the bush. With something of Lamu's cast about it, the island is completely undeveloped, and people tend to be conservative in dress – something you should be sensitive to while visiting (don't wander around in a swimming costume). The village of **Wasini**, an old Wa-vumba settlement, is built in and around its own ruins. It's a fascinating place to wander and there's even a small pillar tomb which still has its complement of inset Chinese porcelain. The **beach** in front of the village (and in fact the shores all round the island) – littered with shells, pottery shards, pieces of glass and scrap metal – are a beachcomber's paradise that you could explore for hours (though be wary of pocketing sea shells or any artefacts).

Behind the village is a bizarre area of long-dead **coral gardens**, raised out of the sea by changing sea levels, but still flooded by twice-monthly spring tides. Walking along the **boardwalk** (daily 9am–5pm; Ksh100), built by a local women's group, with funds going towards education and healthcare in the village, through the coral grottoes, with birds and butterflies in the air, gives you the surreal impression that you're snorkelling on dry land. The ground is covered by a short swathe of sea grass – the tasty *mboga pwani* (sea vegetable) – and patrolled by fleets of small crabs with enormous right claws. Beyond the coral garden, the boardwalk continues into the mangroves, giving an excellent chance to visit an environment not usually easy to access.

Accommodation in Wasini is very limited (as much by the island's total reliance on rainwater as by anything else), but you can stay at *Mpunguti Lodge* (T0722/566623; camping Ksh300, dorm beds Ksh500, FB ❹), commonly known as *Masood's*, a simple, rustic affair without electricity, though flush toilets and showers have been installed, some rooms are self-contained, and rainwater tanks provide sufficient water for most of the year. The owner has a collection of Wasini's old pottery and ceramics.

The village of **MKWIRO**, at the eastern end of Wasini, is still largely a fishing village. The inhabitants have traditionally had little contact with Wasini village, but the arrival of Paradise Divers (see p.441) means they are now also engaging with the tourist economy.

Kisite-Mpunguti Marine National Park

Wasini has ideal conditions for **snorkelling**, with limpid water all around, and the waters offshore are the most likely area on Kenya's coast for seeing dolphins. Several operators (see p.441) run full-day trips in large dhows to the reefs around Kisite island, part of **Kisite–Mpunguti Marine National Park** (W www.kws .org/marine.html; park fee $20), which is actually made up of Kisite National Park, which covers 11 square kilometres, and Mpunguti National Reserve, which has less protection and which covers 28 square kilometres. The area is renowned for having some of the best snorkelling in Kenya. Similar trips, on a more ad hoc basis, can be arranged with boat captains at the dock in Shimoni: depending on the number in your party, demand on the day and the kind of vessel provided, the price for a three-hour trip could range from Ksh3000 to Ksh10,000, excluding park fees. You'll get the most out of the day by getting down here as early as possible, adding lunch to the deal, and making a whole day of it. Always check that there are enough life jackets, and that they're useable.

The boats normally go out of the Wasini channel to the east, then turn south to pass the islets of **Mpunguti ya Chini** and **Mpunguti ya Juu** ("little" and "great" Mpunguti) on the port side. Some 5km further southwest, **Kisite islet**, a coral-encircled rock about 100m long, is the usual destination and anchoring point. The best parts of the Kisite anchoring area are towards the outer edge of the main "coral garden". There are fish and sea creatures in abundance here, including angel fish, moray eels, octopuses, rock cod or grouper and some spectacularly large sea cucumbers up to 60cm (2ft) long. At certain times of the year, however, the water is less clear, and repeated anchorings have destroyed much of the coral in at least one small area. Ask the crew if you'd like to try to find a better area: the **Mako Koke Reef**, the other main part of Kisite marine park, is about 4km further west. The KWS headquarters, by *Eden Bandas*, where you buy **park tickets**, has a good display of information about local marine wildlife.

Vanga

Kenya's southernmost settlement, **VANGA** is the largest coastal town to have been left alone by the tourist industry. There are odd matatus from Likoni and Ukunda, but no lodgings and no formal *hotelis*, so take supplies.

To get here you travel down one of the country's most beautiful roads, the quiet highway that swoops across green plains and baobab-dotted hillsides from the Shimoni junction to the border town of **Lungalunga**. Here, you'll need to stop to explain your movements to officials. Midway between the customs check and the immigration barrier you turn left to start the 17km *murram* road to Vanga. The track skims the Tanzanian border through *shambas* and tunnels through tall forest. Vanga itself is in the **mangroves**, approached along a causeway that regularly floods on the spring tide, despite the sea wall.

The big old house on the seafront is a nineteenth-century **British customs house**, in the care of the National Museums of Kenya. Many of the other houses in the village were constructed during **World War I** by General Paul von Lettow-Vorbeck, to billet troops he had recruited in German East Africa to fight the British. It is said that the cache of gold from which he paid them is buried under a baobab tree, but that it is cursed: several people are said to have defied the curse and not survived.

Assuming you haven't come in search of buried treasure, **dugout canoes** can be rented very cheaply for wobbly punting trips through the mangroves. You should be able to find someone in the village who'll organize **accommodation** for you: you might even try to round up some palm wine and a goat and make a party of your visit.

Onwards to Tanzania

If you want to get to Dar es Salaam on the same day, you'll need to be at the border by 9am. After completing formalities on the Kenyan side, take a matatu or taxi or walk the 6km to **Horohoro** on the Tanzanian side. The journey to Tanga by *dala dala* (matatu) takes two-and-a-half hours from there, and it's a further five hours to Dar.

There are **moneychangers** at both border posts, but ascertain the current rate before starting negotiations, and always check the notes carefully before handing yours over. If you're buying Tanzanian shillings with Kenyan, you usually get the best rate on the Tanzanian side, and in fact you'll get them at a better rate here than you will in Tanga or Dar.

From Kilifi to Malindi

Between Mtwapa Creek and **Malindi**, the landscape is a diverse collage, from rolling baobab country and sisal plantations as you near **Kilifi** to groves of cashew trees further north. Thick, jungly forest and mangrove swamp characterizes **Mida Creek**, and there's a more compact, populated zone of *shambas* and thicket as you approach Malindi. **Kilifi creek** and **Takaungu creek** are both stunning, the clash of blue water and green cliffs almost

Baobab stories

The **baobab**'s strange appearance has a number of explanations in Kenyan mythology. The most common one relates how the first baobab planted by God was an ordinary-looking tree, but it refused to stay in one place and wandered round the countryside. As a punishment, God planted it back again – upside down – and immobilized it.

Baobabs may live well over 2000 years, putting them among the longest-lived organisms that have ever existed. During a severe drought, their large green pods can be cracked open and the nuts made into a kind of flour. The resulting "hungry bread" is part of the common culture of the region. Even in normal times, they have their uses: the tangy white pith of the fruit is boiled with sugar to make a popular bright red sweet that you will see on sale at street stalls.

unnatural. There is lots of scope for **beach hunting** along this part of the coast. Malindi and, to some extent, Watamu have been developed, but Kilifi functions largely as a Giriama market-centre and district capital, while Takaungu seems virtually unknown, a throwback to pre-colonial days. There's also superb snorkelling at the **marine national parks** at Watamu and Malindi. And the ruined town of **Gedi**, deep in the forest near Watamu, is one of the most impressive archeological sites in East Africa.

Kilifi and around

Between Kikambala and Kilifi lies a major **sisal–growing** area, focused around the small town of **Vipingo** (one or two *dukas* and *hotelis*, but not much else). As far as the eye can see, arrow-straight rows of fleshy-leafed, cactus-like sisal plants stretch in every direction, the remaining **baobab trees** standing out bizarrely. Towards Kilifi, the road bucks through a hilly area and the baobabs grow more profusely amid the scrub.

Takaungu

Ten kilometres south of Kilifi, there's a turn-off to the right to **TAKAUNGU**. Although there are a couple of matatus most days from Mombasa direct to Takaungu, the chances of a lift are relatively slim if you happen to get dropped off at the turning, but the walk (5km) is not too long. Takaungu is enchanting – a quiet, composed village of whitewashed Swahili houses on a high bluff above **Takaungu Creek**, with a perfect, ocean-facing **beach**, situated 1km east of the village. There are three mosques and one or two small shops and *hotelis*, but no lodgings. If you want to stay in the village and you speak a little Swahili, people will put you up for a very reasonable price. Food supplies are variable: women will prepare food if you ask, and especially if you supply the ingredients. There's no produce market, but a small fish market by the creek – be there when the catch arrives to get the tasty ones. If you're at the other end of the budget spectrum, *Fig House* (☎0722/415447, ⊛www.fighousekenya.com; sleeps 8–11; Ksh40,000), on the north side of the creek, is a beautiful self-catering hideaway with staff, pool and private tunnel to the creek shore – it's accessible by road from the Kilifi side.

Takaungu Creek is startlingly beautiful, the colour of blue çuraçao, and absolutely transparent; the small swimming beach on the stream is covered at high tide, but you can still dive from the rocks. Upstream, the creek disappears between flanks of dense jungle. When you're ready to move on, the tiny, council-operated rowing boat provides a slow, very cheap service across the

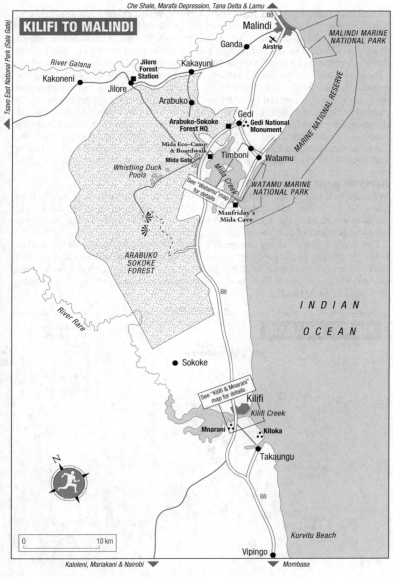

narrow creek to the Kilifi side; from there, it's a five-kilometre (90-minute) walk through the sisal fields to Kilifi bridge.

Kilifi, Mnarani and the creek

Kenya's coastline was submerged in the recent geological past, resulting in the creation of the islands and drowned river valleys – the creeks – of today. **KILIFI**, a small but animated place, is on such a creek. When the Portuguese knew it, Kilifi's centre was on the south side of the creek and called **Mnarani** (still the name of the village on that side). Together with Kitoka on the north side of Takaungu Creek, and a settlement on the site of the present town of Kilifi, these three constituted the mini-state of Kilifi.

In recent decades, as the **Giriama** tribe of the Mijikenda (see p.423) has expanded, Kilifi has become one of their most important towns. Giriama women used to be quickly noticed by everyone for their unusual dress, incorporating a padded backside, although this is now only seen in rural areas. Older women still occasionally go topless but younger women invariably cover up, at least in town (see the "Traditional Dress" colour section). The Mijikenda peoples, and the Giriama especially, are known as great sorcerers and practitioners of witchcraft, and Kilifi is still the frequent scene of accusations that sometimes reach the press.

Arrival and information

With the building of the **bridge** in the 1980s, Kilifi's economy was dealt a hard blow. All the creek-side trade made possible by the ferry's endless delays and breakdowns ceased (the ferry itself is now a half-submerged wreck), and many bars and *hotelis*, and half the town's lodgings, closed.

The town is draped along the north side of the creek to the east of the bridge. If you're driving you'll probably pass it by. Even most bus and matatu travellers only see it from the inside of the vehicle while more fares are being picked up. But staying the night in Kilifi is a perfectly good plan and certainly better than arriving late in Malindi.

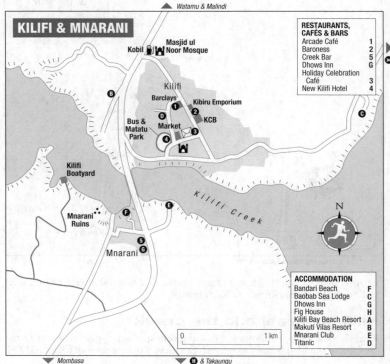

There are Barclays and KCB banks in town, both with **ATMs**; the **post office** is near the market; and there are several **internet cafés**, of which the one beneath the *Titanic Hotel* is the best bet (Mon–Sat 8am–5pm). Kilifi's **Oloitipitip Market** is always bursting with fresh fruit and vegetables, but good **supermarkets** are in short supply. Kibiru Emporium (daily) has a good range of wines and spirits, plus cold drinks.

There's no shortage of **transport** to Mombasa and Malindi. Northbound, most buses to Lamu and Garissa pass through around 8am.

Accommodation

Accommodation in Kilifi ranges from basic town lodgings to one or two pleasant resort hotels, including the very popular and secluded *Mnarani Club*.

Kilifi Town

Bandari Beach Mnarani, on the south shore of the creek, 300m off the road between *Dhows Inn* and the Mnarani ruins. Small guesthouse that used to host parties of game fishermen from Germany, now run as a family home/lodging house. Adequate if you're on a low budget, with half-decent s/c rooms with fans. BB ❷

Dhows Inn Mnarani, at the south side of the bridge ☎041/522028. Popular boozer and restaurant with big, clean, good-value s/c rooms in the garden, each with two large beds, fan, nets, and electric sockets. Good meals include stews and fried fish around the Ksh200–300 mark. BB ❷

Makuti Vilas Resort North side of the bridge, west of the highway ☎041/7522371 or 0734/873704, ⊛www.makutivillas.com. Budget tourist-class establishment, with 36 good-sized s/c rooms with nets and ceiling fans and good bathrooms, but a murky pool and an uncertain welcome. More positively, their pizzas are usually very good. BB ❸

Mnarani Club South side of the creek, entrance near the bridge ☎041/522318, ⊛www.mnarani .co.za. Comfortable package resort, overlooking Kilifi creek from expansive gardens, with a good international mix of clients, decent food and good service and animation. There are two categories of rooms and it's worth paying a bit extra for the more spacious and breezy Creek rooms, with stable doors, windows on two sides, a/c and fridge. The views over the creek from the hotel's pool are glorious, and there's a private beach. BB ❻

Titanic Town centre, reception at the back of the hotel at street level ☎041/522370 or 0726/363437, ⊛www.hoteltitanickenya.com. This big central lodging house offers a seemingly unlimited variety of rooms. Go for a room on the top floor if you want a window with any kind of view, though rooms tend to be small up here. All have fans, TVs and good nets, and the better rooms are very spacious. Non-residents' rates are overpriced, but negotiable. BB ❹

Kilifi Beach

Distances for the following are given from the main Mombasa–Malindi road.
Baobab Sea Lodge 3.2km ☎041/522570, ⊛www.madahotels.com. Attractively sited amid densely planted gardens and baobabs, in a pleasant position on a bluff above the shore, just north of the creek mouth at the south end of the beach. Tennis courts and a good pool with lots of shade, but no sea-swimming at low tide. The rooms, while simple, are spacious and attractively furnished, with a/c, good nets, fans, fridges and safes, but they lack sea views. FB ❻–❼

Kilifi Bay Beach Resort 6.5km ☎041/522264, ⊛www.madahotels.com. The best of Kilifi's hotels, with a stunning location right down on the beach (the best rooms have stupendous sea views; all have balconies), mature tropical gardens with coconut palms, a freedom pool for when the tide is out, great four-poster beds, spacious *makuti*-roofed communal areas, good service and decent breakfasts. Diving and watersports can be arranged. FB ❼–❽

Mnarani and the beaches

There's little of **sightseeing interest** in Kilifi itself. Its two main **mosques** – one a stumpy shed in the town centre, the other a newer and attractively minareted blue, green and white temple, the Masjid ul Noor, at the north junction – more or less sum it up, but across the creek are the more interesting **Mnarani ruins** (7am–6pm; Ksh500). The ruins sit under the trees high above the water near the old ferry landing and then up a rather steep flight of steps.

The small site is archeologically famous mainly for the large number of inscriptions found on its masonry, all in a difficult form of monumental Arabic. They can be seen in several places, in particular in the well-preserved *mihrab* of the main mosque. Just behind this is a very tall octagonal white pillar tomb, which dominates the remains. In front of the mosque, a precipitous well plummets right down to creek level. A little way removed from the main mosque (signposted in front of the office), a smaller mosque is hidden away among the baobabs. As a whole, the site is pretty and quite photogenic, though if you're not a specialist its most memorable aspect is its superlative position.

The real **beaches** around Kilifi are mostly accessible only through private property, and the best are up on the open coast to the northeast of the town. Along this ten-kilometre tarred road, however, there are several fairly recent developments.

Kilifi Creek

Kilifi's seaside-settler and sailing community tends to hover around the informal bar-restaurant at **Kilifi Boatyard** (☎041/525067, ⓦwww.kilifiboatyard.com), which is *the* place for making contacts if you have any ideas of Indian Ocean crewing in mind, and also a possible place to make contacts for sea-fishing excursions. There's no public transport here: if you don't have your own vehicle you'll have to walk, unless you can get a lift. It's a little further up the south side of the creek from the old ferry landing, accessible via a dirt road from the old main road, 1km inland, then 2km down a steep gravel road to the waterfront. Easier access on foot is along the shore of the creek, but this is only possible at low tide. *Kilifi Boatyard* is a friendly place, with fine views of the creek and the dramatic bridge. They turn out fresh and simple seafood dishes, including fish and chips, or crab samosas (dishes Ksh200–750), and there's a notice board for exchanging news and trading kit.

Eating

The *New Kilifi Hotel* is a busy local joint near the bus station, serving good cheap meals and snacks. *Arcade Café* (Mon–Sat, 7am–8pm; around Ksh100–200) does tasty meals in fresh, clean surroundings in the small shopping arcade it shares with Postbank. The same people offer the exact same menu at their *Holiday Celebration Café* on the ground-floor terrace of the *Watergate Hotel*. If you want something more upmarket, try the popular ⚲ *Baroness* (daily 7am–midnight; mains Ksh400–700) by the KCB bank, where local dishes are joined by the likes of pork fillet in pineapple sauce. **Nightlife** is concentrated on the main junction in Mnarani, south of the creek, where the *makuti*-thatched *Creek Bar* concentrates on *bango*, while the bar of the nearby *Dhows Inn* plays Western tunes.

Arabuko Sokoke National Park

The cashew trees lining both sides of the road north of Kilifi soon give way to tracts of jungle where monkeys scatter across the road and hornbills plunge into the cover of the trees. This is the **Arabuko Sokoke Forest** (ⓦwww.kws.go.ke /arabuko.html; $20), the largest patch of indigenous coastal forest in East Africa. At one time it would have covered most of the coastal hinterland behind the shoreline settlements, part of an ancient forest belt stretching from Mozambique to Somalia. There are some 400 square kilometres to explore, though you'll need a vehicle, or a few days for some walking. A tiny part of the area (six square kilometres in the far north) was declared a national park in 1991.

The bans on cutting timber and clearing bush for agriculture aren't popular with **local residents**, many of whom see the forest as a useless waste of land. To combat this ill feeling, the Kenya Wildlife Service, National Museums of Kenya and a forest support group, the Friends of Arabuko Sokoke (Ⓦwww .watamu.net/foasf.html), have pioneered a number of projects to make conservation worthwhile for the community, including butterfly farming (see p.457), a bee-keeping scheme in which villagers are given low-cost beehives to produce honey from forest flowers (it's sold at the Forest Visitor Centre), and the harvesting of medicinal plants under licence.

Practicalities

Whether driving or walking, head first for the **Forest Visitor Centre**, 1.5km south of the Watamu junction on the Malindi–Mombasa road. They have **guides** available to escort you (see below) and you can camp at the main site beside the Visitor Centre ($15) or, if you book ahead, stay in the Tree House ($15), a large platform in the branches, with enough space for a two-person dome tent. **Walking** in the forest is best in the morning or late afternoon, and although this isn't the Amazon, a degree of preparation is a good idea if you plan on venturing far down any of the tracks leading off the main road. The Visitor Centre maps are adequate for the main trails but a GPS unit would be helpful if you're venturing off the main trails (though the signal can be weak under the trees). Official **ASF guides**, all professional and well versed in forest ecology, are available at the Visitor Centre (or booked in advance on Ⓣ0734/994931). You can also book them for fantastic **night walks**, which would be impossible on your own. A regular early-morning **bird walk** (Ksh100) usually leaves the Visitor Centre on the first Saturday of every month at 6.30am.

Wildlife

Beside **elephants** (usually evidenced by their dung), **Sykes' monkeys** and **yellow baboons**, the forest also shelters two rare species of mammal. The 35cm-high (14-inch) **Aders' duiker** is a shy miniature antelope that usually lives in pairs, while the extraordinary **golden–rumped elephant shrew**, which has been adopted as the symbol of the forest, is a bizarre insectivore, about the size of a small cat, that resembles a giant mouse with an elongated nose, running on stilts. In one of those mystifyingly evolved animal relationships, it consorts with a small bird, the **red–capped robin chat**, which warns it of danger and in turn picks up insects disturbed by the shrew's snufflings. Your best chance of seeing a shrew is to look for its fluttering companion among the tangle of branches: the shrew will be close by. Elephant shrews can usually be seen (but not for long – they're very speedy) on the walk along the Nature Trail close to the Visitor Centre, or along the sandy tracks further inside the forest. You may also spot one darting across forest trails ahead of you. The exceedingly rare **Sokoke bush–tailed mongoose** is unlikely to put in an appearance – there have been no sightings since the mid-1980s. The forest is also home to six globally threatened **bird species**, including the small **Sokoke scops owl**, which is found only in the red-soiled *Cynometra* section of the forest, and the **Sokoke pipit** – both very hard to spot, although guides can help locate them. The other endangered birds are the **Amani sunbird**, **Clarke's weaver**, the **East Coast akalat** and the **spotted ground thrush**, a migrant from South Africa. As well as its wealth of mammals and birds, the forest is, in Africa, second only to the Okavango Delta in Botswana for the diversity of its **frog** population, a fact very much in evidence after heavy rain.

Exploring the park

A **nature trail** takes you from the Visitor Centre around the first part of the forest. After rain, this area is spectacularly adorned with the nests of foam-nest tree frogs. It takes most of a morning, but it's an easy walk and makes an excellent introduction to the forest and its medicinal uses. Take water and insect repellent with you. Another easy walk is to the **tree house**, a viewing platform high up a tree by a former sand quarry, from which you get superb vistas over the forest.

If you're short of time, there are several **driving routes**, ideally with 4WD, which are also suitable for bikes. The main route starts at the Mida entrance, 2km south of the Visitor Centre on the main Mombasa–Malindi road, and goes up to the viewpoint through Brachystegia forest – look out for the rare Amani sunbird on the way. From the viewpoint, which looks east over the forest to Mida Creek and the Indian Ocean, a walking track continues a further 2km to a second viewpoint that looks west onto *Cynometra* forest and a large, exposed escarpment. There are other paths along the western edge of **Whistling Duck Pools**, at the junction between the Brachystegia and *Cynometra* forest on the main driving track between the Mida entrance and the viewpoints. These ponds are a favourite haunt for white-faced whistling ducks, little grebe and open-billed storks, as well as the odd elephant.

Mida Creek

Although not part of Arabuko Sokoke Forest, Mida Creek, which extends inland from the coast to main road, is an interesting and unusually accessible area of tidal mud, grassland and mangrove forest, and popular with naturalists. The main target here is **Mida Creek Mangrove Board Walk & Bird Hide**, 3km south of the Arabuko Sokoke visitor centre, and signposted about 1km off the main road. You park at the little information hut, then pay your fees (Ksh150, plus Ksh200 per hour for your guide for up to four visitors) and are escorted out through the mangroves to commune with the tidal ecosystem for as long as you like. If you're a keen birder, you might want to check the tides before your visit (see p.387). The best time to see waders is as the tide comes in.

For **accommodation** in the area, the board walk's neighbour, the charming and welcoming ⚶ *Mida Eco-Camp* (☎0729/213042, ⓦwww.midaecocamp .com; BB ❷), is a gem of place, a Giriama community project with private UK input. The handful of quirky rooms in various experimental formats (nets, shared toilets and showers, solar power, but no room sockets) is complemented by a blissfully relaxing, open-air tree-platform lounge area where everyone tends to congregate for a cold beer, while watching the sun go down. The community's Giriama dance troupe often performs in the evening. You can also camp very cheaply (Ksh200). Meals are highly recommended (around Ksh700) and the staff, who all benefit directly from every guest, will go out of their way to look after you. They particularly welcome children.

If you want Robinson-Crusoe-esque remoteness, without sacrificing your comforts, *Manfriday's Mida Cove* – four individually serviced villas around a pool above the beach at the mouth of Mida Creek – will fit the bill, which tends to be fairly high (☎020/2335387 or 0721/388401, ⓦwww .manfridays.com; FB ❽). To reach it yourself, turn east at Matsangoni, 29km north of Kilifi Bridge (or 17km south of the Watamu junction at Gedi) and ask for "Papu's Hotel".

Gedi ruins

Dense forest in the area may help to explain the enigma of **GEDI**. This large, thirteenth- to seventeenth-century Swahili town was apparently unknown to the Portuguese, despite the fact that they had a strong presence only 15km away in Malindi for nearly a hundred years, during a time when Gedi is judged to have been at the peak of its prosperity. Baffingly, Gedi, sometimes spelled Gede, is not mentioned in any old Portuguese, Arabic or Swahili writings and it has to be assumed that as it was set back from the sea and deep in the forest its scale and significance were never noticed.

Any Mombasa- or Malindi-bound bus or matatu can drop you off at the Kobil station at Gedi junction, where the Malindi–Mombasa road meets the turn-off for Watamu. The junction is a ten-minute walk from the site, which is clearly signposted.

The **ruins** (daily 7am–6pm; Ksh500) are confusing, eerie and hauntingly beautiful, especially in the late afternoon. Even if you're not that interested in visiting historical sites, don't miss this one. Forest has invaded the town over the three centuries since it was deserted, and baobabs and magnificent buttress-rooted trees tower over the dimly lit walls and arches.

Gedi has a sinister reputation and local people have always been uneasy about it. Since 1948, when it was opened to the public, it has collected its share of ghost stories and tales of inexplicable happenings. Some of this cultural baggage may derive from the supposed occupation of the ruins in the eighteenth century by the **Oromo** (probably ancestors of the Orma, who live along the Tana River). At the time, the violent and unsettled lifestyle of the Oromo was a major threat to the coastal communities. Even today, Gedi tingles spines easily, and particularly if you are on your own. James Kirkman, the archeologist who first worked at the site, remembers: "when I first started to work at Gedi I had the feeling that something or somebody was looking

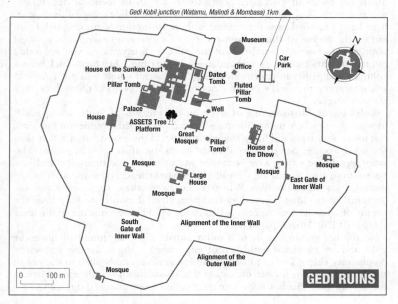

Gedi Kobil junction (Watamu, Malindi & Mombasa) 1km

Museum
Office
Car Park
House of the Sunken Court
Dated Tomb
Pillar Tomb
Fluted Pillar Tomb
Palace
Well
House
ASSETS Tree Platform
Great Mosque
Pillar Tomb
Mosque
House of the Dhow
Mosque
Large House
Mosque
East Gate of Inner Wall
Mosque
South Gate of Inner Wall
Alignment of the Inner Wall
Alignment of the Outer Wall
Mosque
0   100 m
GEDI RUINS

out from behind the walls, neither hostile nor friendly but waiting for what he knew was going to happen."

The more time you spend at Gedi, the further you seem from an answer to its anomalies. The display of pottery shards from all over the world in the small **museum** shows that the town must have been actively trading with overseas merchants, yet it is 5km from the sea and 2km from Mida Creek; and the coastline has probably moved inland over the centuries, so it might previously have been even further away. At the time, with the supposed Oromo threat hanging over the district, sailing into Mida Creek would have been like entering a lobster pot. The reasons for Gedi's location remain thoroughly obscure and its absence from historical records grows more inexplicable the more you think about it.

The site

The town is typical of medieval Swahili settlements. It was walled, and originally covered just under a quarter of a square kilometre – some 45 acres. The majority of its estimated 2500 inhabitants probably lived in mud-and-thatch huts, on the southern, poorer side of town, away from Mecca. These have long been overwhelmed and dissolved by the jungle. The palace and the stone town were in the northern part of the settlement. When the site was reoccupied at the end of the sixteenth century – archeologists have established that there was a hiatus of about fifty years – a new inner wall was built, enclosing just this prestigious zone.

The **Palace**, with its striking entrance porch, sunken courts and honeycomb of little rooms, is the most impressive single building. The concentration of **houses** outside its east wall is where most of Gedi's interesting finds were made and they are named accordingly: house of the scissors, house of the ivory box, house of the dhow (with a picture of a dhow on the wall). If you have been to Lamu, the tight layout of buildings and streets will be familiar, although in Gedi all the houses were single storey. As usual, sanitary arrangements are much in evidence: Gedi's toilets are all of identical design, and superior to the long-drops you find in Kenya today. While many of the houses have been modified over the centuries, these bathrooms seem original. Look out for the **house of the sunken court**, one of the most elaborate dwellings, with its self-conscious emulation of the palace's courtyards. As you go, watch out for the **ants** that have colonized many of the ruins. They form thick brown columns and gather in enormous clumps. Be careful where you put your feet when stepping over walls. And try not to stand on the walls themselves: they are very fragile.

Gedi's **Great Mosque**, one of seven on the site, was its Friday mosque, the mosque of the whole town. Compared with other ruined mosques on the coast, this one is very large and had a *minbar*, or pulpit, of three stone steps, rather than the usual wooden construction. Perhaps an inkling of the kind of people who worshipped here – they were both men and women – and their form of Islam, comes from the carving of a broad-bladed **spearhead** above the arch of the mosque's northeast doorway. Whoever they were, they were clearly not the "colonial Arabs" long believed by European classical scholars to have been the people of Gedi: it's hard to believe that Arabs would have made use of the spear symbol of East African pastoralists.

Nearby is a good example of a **pillar tomb**. These are found all along the coast and are associated with men of importance – chiefs, sheikhs and senior community elders. The fact that this kind of grave is utterly alien to the rest of the Islamic world is further indication that coastal Islam was distinctly African for a long time. Such tombs aren't constructed any more, though there's a nineteenth-century one in Malindi. It looks as if the more recent waves of Arab immigration to the coast have tended to discourage what must have seemed to them an eccentric, even barbaric, style.

The **dated tomb** close to the ticket office gives an idea of Gedi's age. Its epitaph reads 802 AH – or AD 1400. Also by the office, the **museum** exhibits various finds from the site, including imported artefacts such as Chinese Ming vases and even Spanish scissors.

It's easy to spend hours at Gedi, and rewarding to walk down some of the well-swept paths through the thick jungle away from the main ruins. In the undergrowth, you catch spooky glimpses of other buildings still unexcavated. ASSETS, the Arabuko Sokoke Schools & Ecotourism Scheme (Ⓦ www .assets-kenya.org), has built a nature trail and an observation platform (Ksh100), high in a baobab overlooking the palace. With patience you may see a **golden-rumped elephant shrew** (see p.577). Gedi also has monkeys, bushbabies, tiny duiker antelope and, according to local belief, a huge, mournful, sheep-like animal that follows you like a shadow down the paths.

Kipepeo Butterfly House

By the entrance to Gedi ruins is **Kipepeo Butterfly House & Farmers' Training Centre** (daily 8am–5pm; Ksh100). This butterfly farm (*kipepeo* means "butterfly" in Swahili) helps local residents benefit from the proximity of the forest by exploiting the overseas market for exotic butterflies as preserved specimens and subjects in walk-through butterfly houses. Local people net the adult butterflies in the forest, and the eggs laid by the females are harvested. When hatched, the caterpillars are maintained on their food plants until they pupate, at which point the pupae (chrysalises) are brought to Kipepeo to be shipped to foreign customers, and the breeders are paid. Visitors to the centre can see the insects at various stages of their life cycle and the centre also provides information on the Arabuko Sokoke Forest (see p.452), and sells local handicrafts and honey. Morning is the best time to visit, when the butterflies are most active and you have a chance of seeing them emerging, and their wings expanding.

Watamu

After Gedi, **WATAMU** can seem a bit superficial, consisting simply of a small agglomeration of hotels, a strip of beachfront private homes, a compact village shaded by coconut trees, and the beach. One or two big hotels cater to all-inclusive holidaymakers, but there are good reasons to come here if you're travelling independently or on a budget, including the superb marine park, some interesting wildlife initiatives, youthful nightlife (sporadically) and the beautiful beach itself. Watamu is comfortable with tourists, and despite tourism's high profile, there's an easier-going atmosphere here than at Diani, Malindi or Mombasa's north coast. As most of the beach is within the marine park, KWS regulations tend to be more strictly enforced to keep hawkers away.

This is an exceptional shoreline, with three stunning bays – **Watamu Bay**, the **Blue Lagoon** and **Turtle Bay** – separated by raised coral cliffs and dotted with tiny, sculpted coral islets. Watamu is good for **diving** – and a good place to get qualified, with several diving schools – and out in the **Watamu Marine National Park**, when the visibility is good, the submerged crags of living coral gardens and their swirls of brilliant fish can still seem magically vivid,

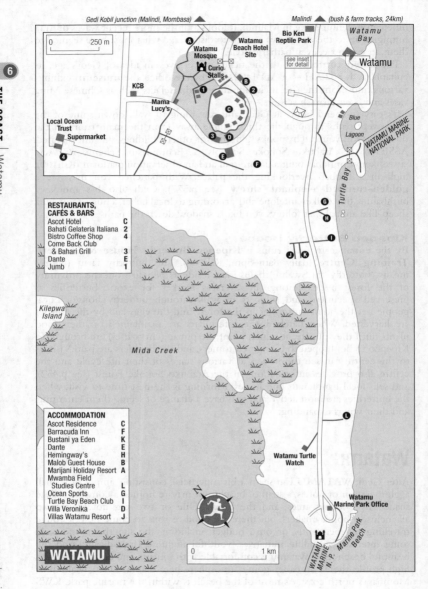

Gedi Kobil junction (Malindi, Mombasa) ▲   Malindi ▲ (bush & farm tracks, 24km)

0   250 m

Watamu
Mosque

Watamu
Beach Hotel
Site

Bio Ken
Reptile Park

*Watamu
Bay*

see inset
for detail

Watamu

Curio
Stalls

KCB

Mama
Lucy's

Local Ocean
Trust

Supermarket

Blue
Lagoon

WATAMU MARINE
NATIONAL PARK

Turtle Bay

**RESTAURANTS,
CAFÉS & BARS**
Ascot Hotel   C
Bahati Gelateria Italiana   2
Bistro Coffee Shop   4
Come Back Club
  & Bahari Grill   3 E
Dante   1
Jumb

*Kilepwa
Island*

Mida Creek

ACCOMMODATION
Ascot Residence   C
Barracuda Inn   F
Bustani ya Eden   K
Dante   E
Hemingway's   H
Malob Guest House   B
Marijani Holiday Resort   A
Mwamba Field
  Studies Centre   L
Ocean Sports   G
Turtle Bay Beach Club   I
Villa Veronika   D
Villas Watamu Resort   J

Watamu Turtle
Watch

Watamu
Marine Park
Office

WATAMU MARINE N. P.   Marine Park Beach

N

WATAMU

0   1 km

although like elsewhere they are suffering from contact damage and the rise in
sea temperature.

Watamu village is a weird mixture of unhurried fishing community and
Europhile souvenir centre. The traditional rubs elbows with the pseudo-hip;
Samburu and Maasai *morani* in full ochred splendour stand around waiting for
photographers; and the Jamia Mosque has a notice that reads "All Muslims are
Well Come for Prayers. No Trespass. By Management."

Arrival and information

Getting to Watamu is easy, with frequent matatus making the run from Malindi. Buses and matatus travelling the coast highway will drop you at the Gedi junction, leaving you to walk, hitch a lift, wait for a local matatu, or take a cab for the last, dead-straight, 6km. Coming into Watamu itself, you pass the **post office** before reaching the beach road T-junction, along which matatus scud up and down all the time. Just north of the junction, if you continue up the beach road a little way past the turning for the supermarket, a road off to the right takes you into the village (the KCB bank, with **ATM**, is on the left).

Bicycle rental is offered by a number of outlets, especially in high season when it gets quite competitive (Ksh500–1000 per day, depending on season and number of days). Bikes are a great way of getting to know Watamu, with the Gedi ruins and anywhere on the beach road easily reachable in thirty minutes or so.

Accommodation

There's a wide variety of **accommodation** in the village itself – everything from humble and uninviting B&Ls to a pleasant holiday hotel. The very central places risk being loud at night, thanks to nearby nightclubs.

Watamu's beach hotels and lodgings are a mixed bag. Several focus on water sports, with diving and game fishing the main activities. The big fishing competition in the first or second week of March can make accommodation scarce, but May and June usually see excellent low-season rates. Matatus usually only go as far south as *Turtle Bay*, where *piki-pikis* or *boda-bodas* can be hired to take you further south.

It's possible to camp at *Ocean Sports*.

Village accommodation

Ascot Residence Village centre ☎042/32326 or 0721/267761, ⓦwww.ascotresidence.com. Good-value, two-room studios (sleeping four), with nets and fans but no a/c, and a large, dolphin-shaped pool. The pleasant, breezy public areas get fairly lively in high season. Most guests are Italian. BB ❹

Dante On the way down the hill into the village ☎042/32243. Small, but homely s/c rooms with fan, but not much else. Rates are negotiable. ❶

Malob Guest House On the way down the hill into the village ☎042/32260 or 0727/293077. Friendly, but a bit dark and dingy and the eight s/c rooms, with nets and fans, aren't very clean. ❷

🏄 **Marijani Holiday Resort** North of the village ☎0735/258263, ⓦwww.marjani-holiday-resort.com. Friendly, informal German-run place, with fifteen, comfortable and very good-value rooms (four-poster beds, nets, fans, fridges, spotless bathrooms) in two stylish houses. All rooms have fridges, some have kitchens. BB ❸

🏄 **Villa Veronika** On the way down the hill into the village ☎0729/785306 or 0726/642007. Stylish B&L, with local women and children always milling around, with very acceptable, fresh, bright rooms, some s/c, with nets and

fans, around a courtyard. Very clean, with a shady, intimate, almost Mediterranean feel. BB ❷

Beach hotels and other accommodation

The following listings are arranged from north to south. Unless otherwise noted, they are all on the beach.

Barracuda Inn ☎042/32223 or 042/32522, ⓦenglang.barracuda-inn.com. Unusual hotel with impressive *makuti*-vaulted reception, well worth considering for its location on the shore of the Blue Lagoon, and great views. Ground-floor rooms are more spacious – all have a/c – and there are tennis courts and pool. BB ❻

🏄 **Ocean Sports** ☎042/32008 or 0724/389732, ⓦwww.oceansports.net. Slightly macho place, whose reputation ("Open Shorts") has sailed before it for years. During holiday times it swarms with young Anglo-Kenyans doing their own thing, but the staff are great, as is the food, and it's right on the beach. All 44 rooms have nets, fans, a/c and safes and pleasantly rustic bathrooms, but foam mattresses on the beds is disappointing. Tennis, squash, two pools, PADI diving school. Adjoining campsite ($20). HB ❻

Hemingway's ☎042/32624, ⊛www.hemingways.co.ke. From Oct–April, landing big fish is high on the agenda here, but this is a really good, mainstream hotel where the atmosphere tends towards the formal and there's nothing much for children – or non-fishing adults. Superior rooms in the new wing are very nice, large with huge beds, a/c and sea views, but no TVs. Two pools. HB ❽

🏃 **Turtle Bay Beach Club** ☎042/2332003 or 0721/830604, ⊛www.turtlebay.co.ke. Expertly run, all-inclusive holiday club, full of happy holidaymakers, mainly from the UK. Lots to do, lots to eat, and plenty of cheap booze. The gardens are cramped, but facilities include two pools, tennis and PADI diving and windsurfing schools and free bicycles and watersports. Staff and management actively participate in local community and environmental initiatives – they have a silver rating from Ecotourism Kenya. AI ❼

Bustani ya Eden West of the road, not on the beach ☎0712/122101. Plain, tidy, comfortable, s/c, chalet-style rooms, with fans and nets, attached to a locally renowned bar-restaurant, with reasonably priced seafood and African dishes. BB ❷

Villas Watamu Resort 400m west of the road ☎042/32487 or 0722/66357, ⊛www.villas-watamu.com. A Mediterranean-style self-catering villa complex with a dramatic line in verandas and a huge pool, as well as a restaurant. The beach is a 15-min walk, but security is good (half the villas are occupied by the local tourist police) and the rates, for spacious a/c accommodation with fully equipped kitchens, are very reasonable. BB ❹

🏃 **Mwamba Field Studies Centre** ☎020/2335865 or 0720/100680, ⊛www.arocha.org. Formerly *Mrs Simpson's*, this guesthouse is now run by the Christian conservation group A Rocha, though it is open to all and is only evangelical about the environment. They have 14 beds in various clean, simple s/c rooms with nets, and camping pitches (Ksh1000/person). Snorkelling gear, bird walks and turtle-watching are all available and it's close to the nearly deserted beach. Staying is on a FB basis only, including for campers, and is very good value. FB ❹

Watamu Marine National Park

The **Watamu Marine National Park** (⊛www.kws.org/marine.html; $15) stretches along the coast from the Blue Lagoon to Mida Creek. Its **total exclusion zone** for fishermen has not been greeted with rhapsody all round. On the other hand, tourists come in larger numbers every year and Watamu hasn't gone far wrong in identifying their needs. This is a highly rated **snorkelling** and **diving** territory, where the reef is reasonably close to shore, still mostly in good condition and the water crystal clear in the right season. Harmless **whale sharks** visit the area regularly, a highlight for any diver.

If you've never taken a swim before in a shoal of coral fish, the spectacle can be breathtaking: every conceivable combination of colour and shape – and a few inconceivable ones – is represented. The ostentatious dazzle of some of them, especially the absurd parrot fish, can be simply hilarious. The most common destination is the "**coral gardens**", a kilometre or two offshore, where the boat drifts, suspended in 5 to 6m of scintillatingly clear water. Here, over a group of giant coral heads, where fish naturally congregate, you enter the unusual park. If you dive to the sea floor, you'll get an intense experience of sharing the undersea world with the fish and the coral. Watch out for the small, harmless octopuses that stay motionless until disturbed and then jet themselves across the sea bed – they're brilliant masters of disguise, altering their form and colour to match their surroundings. If such adventures aren't your forte, the glass bottoms of the boats provide an alternative view – but it's often a rather obscure and narrow one.

For **visits to the park**, *Ocean Sports* and *Hemingway's* both run glass-bottom boat snorkelling trips. Otherwise, you'll have to haggle with the boatmen along the beach, or outside the park headquarters and ticket office down at the south end of the Watamu road at Temple Point. Expect to pay around Ksh1000 per person (not including park fees) for a three-hour trip in a glass-bottomed boat combining the coral gardens with, at high tide, a trip along Mida Creek. Masks, snorkels and sometimes fins are provided, but remember to take plenty of sun cream and a T-shirt.

Other activities and excursions

Watamu's **beach** is beautiful, with its coral outcrop islands within swimming distance of the hotel gardens. Although they mostly started as **fishing** and **diving** centres, many of the hotels are getting involved with **community and environmental projects** that channel tourist excursion money into the local economy.

Diving

From October to March, when the water is clearest, the **diving** possibilities are extensive. **Turtle Reef**, a few hundred metres offshore, offers big shoals of surgeon and parrot fish around high coral heads. Further out, a popular site is **Moray Reef**, where at least one, very large moray eel has become used to visiting divers. Further north, a good spot for beginners is the shallow **Drummers Reef** site, where you can see blue-spotted rays, napoleon wrasse and scorpion fish, and, fairly often on the landward side, **turtles**. There are three dive centres at Watamu, the best plan is probably to visit all of them and make your own assessment of their competence and suitability. Remember that marine park fees are extra ($15 per day, payable at the KWS Marin Park office at the end of the beach road, or to your operator).

If you're a qualified diver, each dive will cost around €30 to 40 including equipment, less with your own equipment. There are reductions if you book a series of dives, and small supplements for night- and wreck-dives. If you haven't dived for a while, you should be asked to do a check-out dive (usually free) or a one-day refresher. If you're a beginner, you can do either a one-day, one-dive course (around €100), or opt for a PADI course of four dives over five days – leading to Open Water certification – for around €400.

Dive operators

Aqua Ventures Based at *Ocean Sports*
☎042/32420, ⓦwww.diveinkenya.com. Long-establised leading operator, with PADI Open Water certification €450. BSAC Premier Centre (the only one in Kenya), used by the British army for dive training. Underwater digital camera hire at €30 per dive.
Blue Fin Diving Next to *Blue Bay Village*
☎0722/261242, ⓦwww.bluefindiving.com. Based

in Watamu from Nov–April and Malindi from July–Nov, but offering diving year-round (from intro dives to PADI Open Water certification – €340) from many of Watamu's hotels.
Turtle Bay Beach Club ☎042/32003 or 0733/295487 ⓦwww.turtlebay.co.ke /dive_centre.html, www.turtledive.com. Single dives for qualified divers: €33; PADI Open Water certificate: €460.

Fishing

The **game-fishing** season runs from July to mid-April (there is no legal season as such, but few boats go out in the rough seas between May and July), with the main season for **billfish** – those with spikes on their snouts, including sailfish and black, striped and blue marlin – roughly November to mid-March. Other species commonly hooked include wahoo, kingfish, dorado, bonito, giant trevally and various sharks, including some big tiger sharks and bull sharks. If you're fishing between July and October, before the wind swings round, it's good to be aware that conditions can be rough – it's not for the fainthearted. While some fish are caught for eating and invariably killed and sold by the crew (yellow fin tuna particularly), all captains have a policy of tag-and-release for sharks and billfish. The fish are tagged for migration research, and a $5 bounty paid for delivery of tags from recaptured fish.

The biggest sea-fishing centre in Watamu is *Hemingway's* (☎042/32624, ⓦwww.hemingways.co.ke); with trips around £500 for up to four people for a day. Alternatively, the following, highly recommended, Watamu-based **independent boat owners** offer a day's fishing from around £400 to 450, usually for a group of four or five, with lunch and drinks included. They're normally prepared to be a little more flexible than *Hemingway's* on the question of what time you have to be back on shore.

Alleycat Fishing ☏ 020/2335871 or 0722/734788, ⓦ www.alleycatfishing.com.

Tarka ☏ 0722/282573, ⓔ tarka@swiftmalindi.com. **Unreal** ⓔ unreelfishing@gmail.com.

Groupers, dolphins and whale sharks

At the entrance to Mida Creek is a famous group of caves. Known as the "**Big Three Caves**", these are the meeting place of a school of **giant groupers**, or rock cod, that once numbered only three but are now many more. Up to two metres long and weighing more than 300kg (660 pounds), these are placid, stationary monsters – thankfully enough, for anyone intrepid enough to dive down a few metres for a closer look. The site is a good kilometre offshore and there are some moderate currents, so boat trips normally only take place at the turn of neap high tides, when visibility, depth and currents give the optimum conditions. You need a permit from the park warden to visit the Big Three Caves, which is usually given freely. Less predictable sea excursions are also arranged in quest of **dolphins and whale sharks**. These are fairly frequently seen offshore, but it's become accepted practice to pay only a nominal charge for the trip if you're unsuccessful. Check it out before signing up (with any of the diver operators listed on p.461).

Bio-Ken reptile park

About 1.3km north of the Gedi junction is a superb little **reptile park**, Bio-Ken (daily 10am–noon & 2–5pm; ☏ 042/32303, ⓦ www.bio-ken.com; Ksh700), which breeds green and black mambas for anti-venom, and houses a large collection of snakes, plus a few tortoises and a token crocodile. It's an interesting visit, and you'll be guided round by someone who actually knows a bit about reptiles – one of the staff is a silver-level safari guide.

Watamu Turtle Watch

Among environmental initiatives, one in which many hotels participate, and which individual tourists can contribute to, is **Watamu Turtle Watch** (ⓦ www .watamuturtles.com; Mon–Sat 9.30am–12.30pm, 2–4.30pm), a project to protect the eggs of threatened marine turtles from poaching by paying local people to guard nests. The same group also pays fishermen to hand in turtles that have got ensnared in fishing nets for treatment of their injuries and release back into the sea – anything from eight hundred to a thousand turtles every year. The office and information centre has some shady quarantine pools where you can usually "meet" recovering turtles.

August brings lots of sea grass to Watamu, and turtles mate and lay in the same month. The **eggs**, which are buried en masse on the beach in pits dug by the females with their flippers, and then covered in sand, take 60 to 75 days to incubate, so October and November are commonly the months when nests usually hatch. Watamu's turtles are mostly the green and hawksbill species. Despite extensive research and observation, it is still not known survives where the babies go after hatching. What is clear is that only one in a thousand survives to maturity.

Visitors can sponsor a turtle for release or a nest for guarding (you can see the nest sites if you walk down the Watamu peninsula towards Temple Point). Turtle Watch is informed when nests that are being guarded start to hatch, so, if you contact them, you may be able to go and see the baby turtles scuttling down the sand like tiny clockwork toys. Mwamba Field Studies Centre (see p.460) is be a good place to be based if you don't want to miss anything.

Eating and drinking

There are one or two places to **eat, drink or get a snack** on the way into the village. By the supermarket, the *Bistro Coffee Shop* (Mon–Sat 8am–5pm) does very nice, fresh-ground coffee, cakes, quiches, shakes and juices. *Bahati Gelateria Italiana* (☎0724/079856; daily 5am–8pm) is a popular, Italian-run ice cream parlour and snack bar. *Ascot Residence* caters mainly to Italians, and has a wood-fired pizza oven (authentic pizzas), and wine at moderate prices.

For **bars and nightlife**, the *Dante* is usually enjoyable, and has cheap beer, but it no longer bothers with meals, and the *Come Back Club & Bahari Grill* is popular and open late for drinks and simple meals. *Jumbo* is a lively bar with mostly inexpensive, local, food.

Malindi and around

When Vasco da Gama's fleet arrived at **MALINDI** in 1498, it met an unexpectedly warm welcome. The king of Malindi had presumably heard of Mombasa's attempts to sabotage the fleet a few days earlier and, no friend of Mombasa himself, he was swift to ally himself with the powerful and dangerous Portuguese. Until they finally subdued Mombasa nearly one hundred years later, Malindi was the Portuguese centre of operations on the East African coast. Once Fort Jesus was built, Malindi's ruling family was invited to transfer their power base there, which they did, and for many years Malindi was virtually a ghost town as its aristocrats lived it up in Mombasa under Portuguese protection.

Malindi's reputation for **hospitality** to strangers has stuck, and so has the suggestion of sell-out. It has an amazingly salacious reputation, and although there was a slump in German tourism after the first AIDS-awareness crisis in the 1980s, a quick glance in some of the bars suggests that the sex safari is back in full swing, now dominated by Italians. As a growing zone for the cultivation of Euros, Malindi is slipping towards cultural anonymity: it can't seem to make up its mind whether it wants to be a Mombasa or a Lamu. While its old centre clings on to some Swahili character, it lacks Lamu's self-contained tranquillity. And although it makes a good base for visits to Gedi and the Arabuko Sokoke Forest, and for a trip to Lamu, it remains unashamedly geared towards beach tourism.

Consequently, whether you enjoy Malindi or not depends a little on how highly you rate the unsophisticated parts of Kenya, and whether you appreciate a fully fledged resort town for its facilities or loathe it for its tackiness. It also depends on when you're here. During December and January, the town can sometimes be a bit nightmarish, with everything African seeming to recede behind the swarms of window-shopping tourists and Suzuki jeeps.

Fortunately, Malindi has some important saving graces. Number one is the **coral reef** south of the town centre. The combined Malindi/Watamu Marine National Park and Reserve encloses some of the best stretches on the coast, and the Malindi fish have become so used to humans that they swarm in front of your mask like a kaleidoscopic snowstorm. Malindi is also a **game-fishing** centre with regular competitions, and it's also something of a surfing, windsurfing and kitesurfing resort, too. Good-sized rollers steam into the bay through the long break in the reef, opposite the town, between June and late September, whipped up by the southerly monsoon (*kusi*) wind. The surfing isn't world class, but it's fun, and good enough for boogie boards.

Despite the heavy reliance on tourism, Malindi still has some interest as a Kenyan town with an ancient history, and a few places of interest other than its beach and

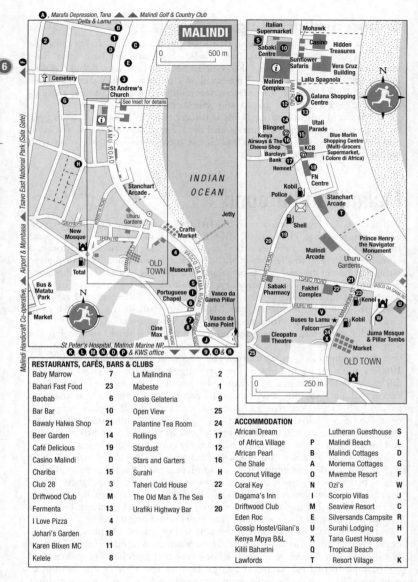

MALINDI

0   500 m

INDIAN OCEAN

OLD TOWN

RESTAURANTS, CAFÉS, BARS & CLUBS

Baby Marrow	7	La Malindina	2
Bahari Fast Food	23	Mabeste	1
Baobab	6	Oasis Gelateria	9
Bar Bar	10	Open View	25
Bawaly Halwa Shop	21	Palantine Tea Room	24
Beer Garden	14	Rollings	17
Café Delicious	19	Stardust	12
Casino Malindi	D	Stars and Garters	16
Chariba	15	Surahi	H
Club 28	3	Taheri Cold House	22
Driftwood Club	M	The Old Man & The Sea	5
Fermenta	13	Urafiki Highway Bar	20
I Love Pizza	4		
Johari's Garden	18		
Karen Blixen MC	11		
Kelele	8		

ACCOMMODATION

African Dream		Lutheran Guesthouse	S
of Africa Village	P	Malindi Beach	L
African Pearl	B	Malindi Cottages	D
Che Shale	A	Moriema Cottages	G
Coconut Village	O	Mwembe Resort	F
Coral Key	N	Ozi's	W
Dagama's Inn	I	Scorpio Villas	J
Driftwood Club	M	Seaview Resort	C
Eden Roc	E	Silversands Campsite	R
Gossip Hostel/Gilani's	U	Surahi Lodging	H
Kenya Mpya B&L	X	Tana Guest House	V
Kilili Baharini	Q	Tropical Beach	
Lawfords	T	Resort Village	K

0   250 m

OLD TOWN

reef. An interesting old Swahili quarter, one or two "ruins", a busy market, shops, *hotelis* and plenty of lodgings all balance out the tourist boutiques, beauty salons and real estate agencies. There's a broad range of places to stay, eat, drink and be entertained. As for the **Italian influence**, the new resident expats have brought the town riches that nowhere else in Kenya can boast – some of the best pizzas, pasta and ice cream in the whole of Africa – even if the suspiciously dormant state of some Italian businesses makes you wonder how legitimate they all are.

Note that the shore can get very windy around September, and during June, July and November the beach becomes covered in **seaweed** – many hotels clear their beachfronts daily, though the seaweed is clean and perfectly harmless, and in fact prevents erosion of the beach (clearing it is prohibited within the limits of the marine park). It's also worth knowing that the headland of **Vasco da Gama Point** marks a locally important division. To the north, the sea water is often reddish-brown and cloudy – full of the soil erosion brought down by the Sabaki River, especially after rain – and, to the south, the Marine Park encloses a zone of often aquarium-clear water.

Arrival, orientation and information

If you're arriving from the south, you'll end up at the main **bus station** and matatu area, about ten minutes' walk south of town along the Mombasa road; a taxi or *tuk-tuk* to the centre shouldn't cost more than Ksh200, or Ks500 to the furthest beach hotels. Coming from Lamu or Garissa, you'll be dropped by the bus companies' booking offices in the town centre between the market and the messy, noisy high street where the cheapest of the B&Ls are found. The main focus of town is from here up to the misleadingly named Uhuru Gardens (a dusty patch of shade) and then north along the commercial Lamu Road.

Note that **Lamu Road**, increasingly built up with little malls and new developments, but happily still shaded by big trees, is set far back from the **seafront** (you can't usually see the sea from the town centre). The beach in this part of town, when you do get out to it, is windswept and less appealing than you might imagine. For more of a seaside atmosphere, the seafront **Vasco da Gama Road** is pleasant, especially in the late afternoon. For the real McCoy, beach-wise, you need to go south of town to the aptly named **Silversands Beach**, complete with reef-fringed lagoon, palm trees and the inevitable beach boys.

Malindi **airport** is barely 3km south of the town centre and you can walk into Malindi in half an hour. Matatus heading to the main stage (which is about halfway between the airport and the town centre) will pick you up on the main road just outside the airport; otherwise, taxis charge around Ksh800 to beach hotels, or Ksh500 into town.

If you need to park at the airport, you can do so safely under the trees outside the small terminal building (Ksh40 per hour, Ksh200 per day). The airport has a shady little snack and drinks bar you'll get to know well if your flight is delayed.

The **tourist office** (Mon–Fri 8am–12.30pm & 2–4.30pm; ☏042/20747) is on Lamu Road, at the very back of the Malindi Complex building, on the first floor. Staff don't have much in the way of information, but are the people to contact if you have a serious complaint about a hotel, safari operator or restaurant.

Accommodation

There's plenty of **accommodation** on offer, though over Christmas room availability can be tight. The cheap town lodgings also fill up in high season, during Maulidi and at the end of Ramadan. Tourist establishments usually vary their prices seasonally by up to fifty percent. You can **camp** just south of town at *Silversands*, or near the marine park office (☏042/2120845 or ☏020/600800, ✉reservations@kws.go.ke; $15), which also has a clutch of nine, twin-bedded, non-s/c, self-catering *bandas* ($25 per banda, $35 during peak periods – good value and worth considering if you want to do a lot of snorkelling in the marine park. You'll need to be fairly self-sufficient to stay there – much easier if you have a vehicle.

Budget rooms and camping

Dagama's Inn Vasco da Gama Rd, on the seafront ☎042/2131942. A variety of rooms, some s/c, simple but clean, with nets. Best are the two front rooms overlooking the beach, with fans and a balcony. **①**

Gossip Hostel/Gilani's Vasco da Gama Rd, on the seafront ☎042/2120307. Above the restaurant, and overpriced. The four big and breezy upstairs rooms at the front with balconies are the best reasons to stay here. BB **②**

Kenya Mpya B&L Mama Ngina St ☎042/2130461. Big enough rooms in a four-storey block, not all s/c or with fans, with cleanish sheets. **①**

Lutheran Guesthouse Lamu Rd, town centre ☎042/30098. Set in a large garden, with double rooms only (clean and mosquito-netted with fans, two s/c), plus two self-catering bungalows, each for four people (Ksh2000/day). There's a no-alcohol policy. BB **②**

Malindi Cottages Lamu Rd ☎042/2121071. Pretty little set-up that has, sadly, fallen on hard times. The one-bedroom cottages are really just s/c double rooms, though reasonable enough for the price. The two-bedroom ones are better value (Ksh4000), with kitchens, small verandas and large sitting rooms, all set in gardens with a pool in dire need of maintenance. No bar or restaurant. **②**

Moriema Cottages off Lamu Rd ☎0726/416981. Each of the plain and simple cottages here has gas rings, a sink and fridge (as well as fans and nets), so you can self-cater if you want to, but there's

also a reasonable restaurant, and breakfast is included. BB **③**

Ozi's Vasco da Gama Rd, on the seafront ☎0721/104099 or 0736/888879, ⓔozi@swiftmalindi.com. Very secure, friendly, and popular with travellers, *Ozi's* is arranged around a central courtyard. None of the rooms are s/c, though all have ceiling fans and the shared showers and toilets are clean. It's next to the Juma mosque, so you may be woken by the early prayer call. Free laundry. BB **②**

Silversands Public Campsite Casuarina Rd, 1.8km south of the Total roundabout ☎042/2120218 or 0710/287386. Owned by *Ozi's* (see above). Hard ground, and not much shade, but if you want to camp, this is it, and at least it's secure and close to the beach. There are three, clean, unisex shower/ toilets, a small communal terrace and food preparation area, and a basic provisions kiosk. Ksh300.

Surahi Lodging off Lamu Rd ☎042/30452. Above the Indian restaurant of the same name are these nine reasonable s/c rooms with fan, net and one big bed in each. Secure, comfortable and quiet. Negotiable rates. **③**

Tana Guest House Uhuru Rd ☎042/30940. While basic, the *Tana* is clean and well kept, with nets and fans, and is very handy for buses to Lamu. Rooms in the main block can be stuffy and hot, but there are slightly dearer s/c rooms around a quiet courtyard at the back. Good, busy *hoteli* downstairs with plenty of choice. **①**

Hotels in the town centre and north

All the upmarket hotels have pools, but the beach is some 500m east of Lamu Road and relatively little used. Watersports are very limited at most of these hotels – with no reef offshore, there's no snorkelling, and the current makes windsurfing only feasible if you're experienced. One exception is the excellent *Che Shale*, a 30-minute drive from Malindi, north of Mambrui.

African Pearl Lamu Rd ☎0725/131956, ⓦwww.africanpearl.com. Personably managed hotel with cool, spacious rooms, plus four self-catering cottages with kitchens, and a fully equipped gym. The best rooms are characterful and comfortable and have large verandas (some are a/c too), and they're located in a charming old house with a nice veranda, a good pool, and a bar-restaurant (with *nyama choma*) at the front near the road. Good value if you choose one of the best rooms. BB **④**

Che Shale 24km north of Malindi, and 6km off the main road (transfer Ksh2500 from town) ☎0722/230931, ⓦwww.cheshale.com. Literally on the beach – and what a beach – this is

one of Kenya's best mid-budget beach bases, opened in 1978, but now re-envisioned as a kitesurfing centre. With just five s/c, wood and palm-mat *bandas*, sand underfoot and cool hosts, staff and fellow guests, this is *The Beach* incarnate, without the horrors. The separate *Kajama bandas* (BB **⑤**), 200m north, are the non-s/c, non-electric, budget option. Closed May & June. HB **⑦**

Eden Roc Lamu Rd ☎042/2120480, ⓦwww .edenrockenya.com. Large old package-tour place, with huge and largely untended gardens stretching several hundred metres down to the dunes and beach. Friendly if somewhat disorganized management and mostly German guests. Rooms with a/c, or smaller rooms with fans. BB **④**

Lawfords Lamu Rd ⓣ042/2121265. Owned by the Italian *Coral Key*, this completely renovated Malindi institution, set in spacious palm-filled gardens, has been transformed. All the rooms are suites, done out in a confident, European design, with powerful a/c, safes, TV, cool bathrooms and designer beds. Two pools, and very well-equipped pampering from Lawford's Spa. BB ❼–❽

Mwembe Resort off Lamu Rd ⓣ042/2130573, ⓦwww.mwemberesort.com. Shady, green hideaway on an extensive plot at the back of town, with spacious Mediterranean-style suites (a/c, safe, fridge, DSTV) and self-catering villas (Ksh22,000 for up to 4 people), scattered around a large pool. Facilities include tennis and *Lorenzo's* restaurant on site, and the private Rosada beach at Silversands. BB ❻–❼

Seaview Resort Lamu Rd ⓣ042/2130427 or 0735/432371, ⓦwww.seaviewresortmalindi.com. Low-key development in a pleasant, wooded setting. The big rooms, with a/c, fans and TV are quite nicely done, and there's a good pool. Self-catering cottages are also available (Ksh4200 sleeping up to 4). Good value overall. BB ❹

Hotels south of the town

Protected by reefs, this is where the greatest development has taken place in the last few years, with one **resort hotel** after another reaching almost down to Casuarina Point. Most are Italian-owned or managed, and Italian visitors comprise the majority of guests. Taxis shouldn't cost more than Ksh1000 from town to Casuarina Point, or Ksh400 to the *Driftwood*, and less by *tuk-tuk* or *boda-boda*. Distances are south of Uhuru Gardens in town.

Coral Key 2km south, on Silversands Rd ⓣ042/30717 or 042/2130715, ⓦwww.coral keymalindi.com. Lively and sporty Italian-run resort, with rooms in 38 two-storey brick buildings, but not all a/c. Five pools, children's pools, and a good Italian restaurant and pizzeria. Activities include tennis, a climbing wall and a disco every Friday. BB ❻–❼

🏃 **Driftwood Club** 2.7km south, on Silversands Rd ⓣ042/2120155, ⓦwww .driftwoodclub.com. With good food and a deserved reputation among the local Anglo–Kenyan community, the *Driftwood* is highly recommended – friendly and excellent value (especially for families, as under 12s pay a fraction of adult rates). As well as rooms in the gardens (a/c, nets), there are two luxury a/c cottages sharing a private pool and three, a/c, self-catering villas. Membership (Ksh5000 joining, Ksh3500 annually) entitles you to fifteen percent off. Facilities include squash, a modest pool and wi-fi (Ksh600/day). BB ❻

Kilili Baharini 4km south, on Casuarina Rd ⓣ042/2120169 or 042/2121264, ⓦwww .kililibaharini.com. Rather a classy set-up, with rooms organized in small enclaves, each group clustered around its own pool. There's also a bigger main pool. The a/c rooms are fresh, with tasteful Swahili-style furniture. Big on massage treatments and very popular with Italian visitors. BB ❼

Planhotel: Coconut Village/Malindi Beach/ Tropical Village/Dream of Africa 3km south, on Casuarina Rd ⓣ042/2120444 or 042/2131673 or 042/2131728, ⓦwww.planhotel .com. Stretched along 500m of shoreline, this is an all-inclusive Italian-slanted holiday resort, encompassing four different plots, each with a different hotel, ranging from the cheap(ish) and cheerful *Coconut* (AI ❼–$410) to pricey *Dream* (AI $492–620). *Tropical Village* has more than a hundred rooms; the others one hundred between them. Guests can use the extensive facilities across the four hotels. AI ❼

Scorpio Villas 1km south, on Vasco da Gama Rd, not directly on the beach ⓣ042/2120194, ⓦwww .scorpio-villas.com. Small-scale, Italian-owned "village", in a plot dense with tropical vegetation, rebuilt since a fire in 2007. The a/c rooms with nets, DSTV, fridges and safes are characterful, with Swahili-style four-poster beds. Three pools. Good value, with lunch and dinner supplements only Ksh600 each. BB ❺

The Town

Other than the beach and the sea, strolling in town is the main pastime and not without its idiosyncratic rewards. The old part of Malindi is a half-hour diversion: interesting enough, even though there's nothing specific to see and few of the buildings date from before the second half of the nineteenth century. But the juxtaposition of the earnest and down-to-earth business of the old town with the *mzungu*-mania only a couple of minutes' walk away on Lamu Road produces a schizophrenic atmosphere that epitomizes Malindi. Archeologically, Malindi's offerings are scant. The two **pillar tombs** in front of the Juma (Friday) Mosque on the waterfront are fine upstanding examples of the genre, though the shorter one is only nineteenth century. This being Malindi, its appearance is sometimes described as "circumcised", though Islamic scholars on the coast do not of course accept the phallic label applied by foreigners.

Malindi's other monuments are Portuguese. The **Vasco da Gama Pillar** (1499), down on the point of the same name, makes a good target for a stroll. Unfortunately, the cross, made of Lisbon limestone, stands on a rapidly eroding rocky outcrop and looks close to toppling into the sea. The **Portuguese Chapel** is a tiny whitewashed cube of a church now covered with *makuti*, whose foundations were laid in the sixteenth century on the site of a Portuguese burial. The most recent Portuguese bequest is the ugly 1959 **Monument to Prince Henry the Navigator** on the seaward side of Uhuru Gardens. A nineteenth-century trader's shop on the waterfront has been made into a town **museum** (daily 9am–6pm; Ksh500), with a coelacanth fish downstairs, and some photographs of archeological sites on the coast upstairs, plus temporary exhibitions, but not quite enough to justify the rather steep entry fee.

Snorkelling and watersports

Board-based watersports – **surfing**, **windsurfing** and **kitesurfing** – and **diving** and **snorkelling** are Malindi's touristic *raison d'être*. Unfortunately, diving is somewhat marred by the Galana (Sabaki) River's outpouring of thousands of tons of prime red topsoil from the upcountry plateaus. The cloudy water prevents any coral growing north of Vasco da Gama Point and the sea in this north part of Malindi is muddy-brown from November to January. The good diving and snorkelling season, in the area starting from Vasco da Gama Point southwards, lasts only from July to October. During the April to June long rains, it's low season and not great for clarity, while between November and March, silt makes the water too murky and the larger hotels usually organize daily excursions for their guests to dive or snorkel in Watamu.

Seasonal variations aside, with your own gear you can **snorkel** in the lagoon, or snorkel out to the inside edge of the reef anywhere north of the marine park. At the park boundary at Casuarina Point the reef hugs the shore, and it runs north to its conclusion off Vasco da Gama Point, where it's more than 900m from the beach.

Malindi Bay is the main **surfing** beach (June to the end of September, when the swell is on) and surfboards are available from some of the tourist hotels in town. The beach here is a good five to ten minutes' walk from the road. There are several public access points (see map, p.464), and some hotels will allow use of their beach access for a small fee, which means you can use their pool and leave your things on their guarded premises.

Malindi is one of the world's **kitesurfing** hotspots. Learning at *Che Shale*, (see p.466), the beach lodge which is partly responsible for the development of the sport, costs €260 for a five-to seven-day residential course, on top of your accommodation. The best seasons for this are January to April and July to mid-October.

Malindi Marine National Park

Trips out to the **marine park** (daily 6am–6pm; Ⓦ www.kws.org/marine.html; $15) can be arranged with the boat-trip salesmen who make their rounds of the beaches and hotels most mornings. Alternatively, make your own way down to the park office and very pretty beach at **Casuarina Point**, 5km from town, where you can choose your boat and captain. Be sure to check out the condition of masks and snorkels, and insist on a set for each member of the party. Fins, assuming they have any that fit you, are not likely to be up to much. You should find a little room for discussion but won't be able to knock down prices much below the current going rate of Ksh3000 (excluding park fees) for two hours, especially at peak seasons; in fact your outing may be somewhat curtailed if you bargain too ruthlessly.

The six square kilometres of the national park take in the loveliest areas of coral garden, between 1km and 4km offshore, and the trip is worth every shilling you finally agree on. Unless you have a mortal fear of snorkelling, don't bother with the **glass-bottomed boats** (about Ksh3000–5000 for two hours), which generally have small, not very clear windows. The **snorkelling** itself is sublime and, especially if you've never done it before, an unforgettable experience.

Dive centres and diving schools

There are two main dive centres in Malindi, and you should probably visit them both before deciding which one to use. Remember marine park fees are extra ($15 per day). For general advice and information, see the Watamu account (p.460) and the boxes on p.417 and p.436.

Blue-Fin Based at *Tropical Beach Resort* ☏0722/261242, ⓦwww.bluefindiving.com. Based in Malindi from July–Nov and in Watamu from Nov–April, but offering diving year-round (from intro dives to PADI Open Water certification – €340) from many of Malindi's hotels.

Upinde Based at *Mariposa Restaurant* south along the beach from *Scorpio Villas* ☏0723/962123 or 0735/418570, ⓦupindediving.com. One-day introduction courses and five-day PADI Open Water qualification courses.

The Marafa Depression

Northwest of Malindi, the **Marafa Depression** is the remains of a large sandstone ridge, now reduced by wind, rain and floodwater to a series of gorges, where steep gullies and narrow arêtes alternately eat into or jut from the main ridge wall. The colours of the exposed sandstone range from off-white through pale pink and orange to deep crimson, all capped by the rich tawny topsoil. It's particularly dramatic at sunset.

"Hell's Kitchen" is the common nickname for this impressive landscape, though the locals call it Nyari – "the place broken by itself" – and tell numerous moralizing stories about its dark origins. The main one sets the word of a monotheistic, all-powerful deity against traditional wisdom, and tells how the people of a village that once stood here were warned by God about a forthcoming miraculous event. They were commanded to move out and all did so, except one old woman, who refused to believe such nonsense. The village and the old lady disappeared a short while later, leaving Nyari.

To get to Marafa, take the road out of Malindi heading north, turn left on the other side of the Galana (Sabaki) bridge and from there go via **Marikebuni** and **Magarini**. You're looking at a round trip of about 80km. Alternatively, a handful of matatus run to Marafa village every day, or you could hire a cab and negotiate the price – between Ksh5000 and Ksh10,000. To get to the gorge itself, fork right at the end of **Marafa** village, and the canyon is about 500m along on the left, hidden until you're right at its edge. At the lip of the gorge (Ksh250 community fee), it's easy to descend the steep path to the bottom, where you can count on spending an hour or two exploring the natural architecture of what looks like an early *Star Trek* set. It's good to do so with a guide from the village, especially if you come in a group, but be sure to settle the price before setting off.

Eating, drinking and nightlife

There are two basic options for **eating** in Malindi. The first is ordinary *hoteli* fare plus a scattering of Indian-style juice and samosa bars dotted about the **market** and Lamu bus company area. The second is a much higher-price bracket that includes the big hotels and a small number of more lavish restaurants catering mainly for tourists. It's worth remembering that the main package market here is Italian, and some of the Italian-run places do very fine Italian food.

Malindi Market is celebrated for fruit and vegetables – second, on the coast, only to Mombasa's. Malindi's speciality is smoked sailfish, absolutely delicious and often available as a starter. Cheese is available from The Cheese Shop in Utalii Parade on Lamu Road (Mon–Sat 8am–9pm), from the Italian supermarket at the Sabaki Centre, and from Pappa i Chakula (Mon–Sat 8.30am–12.30pm & 2–6pm), a little Italian deli at the back of the Blue Marlin shopping centre, which also has fresh pasta, olives and salami. See also "Supermarkets" in Listings, p.473.

Hotelis and cheap restaurants

Bahari Fast Food In the town centre near Juma Mosque. Good, tasty, cheap food but, despite the name, often rather slow.

Bawaly and Sons Halwa Shop In the town centre near Uhuru Gardens. Long-established spot, famous for its fragrant version of the gooey jelly sweet. The minimum order is 250g, but you can eat a small amount on the spot and have the rest wrapped up to take away. Tiny cups of spiced *kahawa* come free. Daily 8.30am–12.15pm & 3–5.45pm.

Café Delicious Kenyatta Rd. A small diner serving breakfasts, snacks and basic cheap meals.

Chariba Lamu Rd. Good value fry-ups and African dishes. Sukuma Ksh30, *chai* Ksh20. Daily 6am–10pm.

Johari's Garden In the garden of the FN Centre Building. Excellent-value, large portions of well prepared, fresh Kikuyu dishes – you can eat well for Ksh100. Lovely fresh passion juice Ksh 40. Daily 6am–9pm.

Oasis Gelateria Silversands Rd, 1.8km from Uhuru Gardens. This big snack bar is very good – as much for its delicious omelettes and espresso as for the forty flavours of ice cream. Daily 8am–midnight in high season, otherwise 3–11pm.

Open View By the big Total roundabout. Good Kikuyu food including meat stews and *githeri,* and plenty of cold beer.

Palantine Tea Room Mama Ngina St, next to *Kenya Mpya B&L.* Large and busy local place, serving *ugali* or chips with everything. Cheap, and open round the clock.

Stars and Garters Lamu Rd, next to Barclays Bank. Brash and busy *makuti*-roofed complex, especially popular for the flat screen TVs showing English football. Good range of snacks, and fuller meals too, including pasta, seafood and grills, and there's a disco most evenings.

Taheri Cold House Fakhri Complex, Tsavo Rd. A good spot for juices, snacks and cheap meals. Try the "Zanzibari mix" – vegetable-based snacks in your choice of sauce. Tues–Thurs 7.30am–8.30pm, Fri–Sun 7.30am–11pm.

Upmarket restaurants

Baby Marrow Vasco da Gama Rd, near the Portuguese Chapel ☎0727/581682. One of Malindi's best dining houses, *Baby Marrow* aims for Italian bush elegance. Starters include smoked sailfish, and mains feature lots of crab and lobster dishes (Ksh1000–2000), and meat dishes for around Ksh1000. Expect to pay around Ksh2000 per head, not including drinks. Daily 11am–2pm & 6–11pm.

Baobab Vasco da Gama Rd, on the seafront next to the Portuguese Chapel. Moderately priced curries, Italian and African dishes (Ksh350–600), and pricey seafood (from Ksh1000). Popular as much for its food as for the cheap, cold beer and sweeping views over the beach and fishing boats. Daily 8am–11pm.

Bar Bar Sabaki Centre, Lamu Rd. A little piece of Italy in Kenya, with authentic and tasty pizzas and pasta (Ksh400–750), and pricier meat and seafood dishes, rounded off with excellent espresso.

Driftwood Club Silversands beach ☎042/2130569. Always a good place to eat, but the Sunday curry buffet is worth planning your day around, and prices in general are reasonable. Starters include smoked sailfish and seafood bisque, and the salads and chocolate cake are good, too. Members (see "Accommodation") get twenty percent off à la carte meals.

I Love Pizza Vasco da Gama Rd, on the seafront ☎042/2120672. The pizzas and pasta dishes here (Ksh300–750) are really not bad, though they push their more expensive seafood, which is also good. Modestly upmarket and ever-popular. Daily noon–3pm & 7–10pm.

Karen Blixen MC Galana Shopping Centre, Lamu Rd. A bit of a tourist trap, Italian-style, with pleasant tables under the shade outside. Attractions include some rather pricey pizzas (Ksh800), pasta and light lunches, even including *prosciutto* with melon.

La Malindina Off Lamu Rd, at the back of town ☎042/2131449 or 042/2120045.

Specializing in, and only serving, seafood, a typical set meal (Ksh4000) at this food-lover's restaurant starts with seafood salad with fish carpaccio, followed by spaghetti *fruits de mer*, then a choice of crab, lobster or prawns, desert and coffee. Non-seafood tastes can be catered for, with notice. Wines (Italian and South African) range from Ksh1800–3000. One service daily, at 8.45 for 9pm.

 The Old Man & The Sea Vasco da Gama Rd, on the seafront ☎042/2131106. Rather quirky, Moorish-style restaurant with an international menu, specializing in seafood and steaks, with some vegetarian dishes, and seemingly benefitting from its location right by the seafront to deliver a strong Indian Ocean twist to its dishes. Not outrageously expensive, with mains mostly in the Ksh350–650 range. Daily noon–2.30pm & 7–11pm.

Surahi Off Lamu Rd, at the back of town ☎042/2130452. A good North Indian restaurant, with a few moderately priced dishes and an uncluttered, cool dining room. Dishes include rogan josh and mutton chilli masala, and fish and vegetarian options, mostly featuring *paneer* cheese. Daily except Wed 11am–3pm & 6–10pm.

Bars and Clubs

After dark, especially in high season, Malindi's clubs and bars throb with action and, regardless of your gender, status or, increasingly, even your age, you're unlikely to avoid being propositioned, and not necessarily by a commercial sex worker. Entry charges are rare unless entertainment has been laid on. International African musicians sometimes perform at *Market Village*, inside the Malindi Showground off the Mombasa road.

Beer Garden Lamu Rd, next to *Stars and Garters*. Come for a beer and bratwurst to start the evening. Burgers and steaks available too. Daily 9am till late.

Casino Malindi Lamu Rd. With free entry to anyone gambling. It's almost worth playing a few hands just to watch the grim-looking Italian bosses tending their novice Kenyan croupiers. Daily 9am–5am.

Club 28 Lamu Rd, adjacent to *Eden Roc Hotel*. This small nightclub has its ups and downs, but it's good when it hits the mood. Daily from 10pm. Ksh300.

Fermenta Galana Shopping Centre. Expensive Italian joint that plays Euro-trash when not inflicting karaoke. Daily from 8pm.

Kelele Next to *Baby Marrow* restaurant, Vasco da Gama Rd. *Kelele* ("Noise") is a pleasant, open-air, beer-garden and club hangout, nicely done, and run by local Kenyans.

Mabeste International Klub Lamu Rd. Pool bar and restaurant with a good variety of snacks, fried food and curries.

Rollings Lamu Rd. A bar popular both with local residents and tourists, with *nyama choma* daily, and live music at weekends.

Stardust Lamu Rd, opposite Galana Shopping Centre. The busiest club, especially in peak season, when half of Malindi – Italians and Kenyans alike – seem to be here waggling their backsides in time to 1980s cheese.

Urafiki Highway Bar Kenyatta Rd. Cheerful and unpretentious bar with tables inside and out.

Crafts and shopping

There are two main outdoor areas to head for when you're in the buying mood. Most obvious is the **crafts market** on the seashore below the old town. Naturally, if you stray down here you'll be pounced upon, and leaving without buying anything isn't easy. On the other hand, you can also leave with all sorts of little free gifts if you strike the right bargain. The other area is the **Malindi Handicraft Co-operative** (daily 8am–6.30pm), 2.5km west of the new market and matatu stage, where you can see and freely photograph the woodcarvers at work. There's no bargaining at the shop, but you can discuss prices direct with the carvers and place specific orders.

Alternatively, for more expensive crafts and the possibility of browsing unhurriedly, try one of the **upmarket shops** along Lamu Road, just to the north of Uhuru Gardens. Prices tend to be high, but visits are useful for checking comparative values and gauging prices.

Shops

Hidden Treasure Lamu Rd, opposite the Sabaki building. A shop whose wares are ranged around a garden, with lots of decor and furnishings, mostly reproduction Chinese lacquered chests and the like.
I Colore di Africa Blue Marlin Shopping Centre, Lamu Rd. Large, Italian gifts-and-interiors shop with a great variety of attractive items from East Africa, Europe and the Far East.
Lalla Spagnola Lamu Rd, just north of the Galana shopping centre. High-end interior design and furnishings, including lots of owner-made

and owner-commissioned stuff from Lamu and the Far East.
Malindi Arcade Lamu Rd, near Uhuru Gardens. Lots of top-quality crafts and *objets d'art*, including old Lamu silver and jewellery as well as more familiar items available on the street.
Mohawk Lamu Rd, opposite the Sabaki building. Two shops: on the left, nice beaded designer sandals, bags, cushions, ladies' clothes, accessories and jewellery; on the right, tableware, furnishings, wall hangings, mirrors and knick-knacks.

Listings

Airlines Kenya Airways, Utalii Parade (☎042/2120237) cancelled its daily flights to JKIA Nairobi in 2009 and it's not clear if they will resume. Airkenya, North Coast Building; opposite the FN Centre, Lamu Rd (☎042/2120411); Fly540 (agent is North Coast Travel ☎042/2130312 or 042/2120370); Mombasa Air Safari, based at the airport (☎0734/400400 or 0722/500500, ⊛www .mombasaairsafari.com).
Banks Barclays, KCB and Standard Chartered banks all have 24-hr ATMs.
Car rental There are no full-service car rental firms in Malindi. Sunflower Safaris, opposite the Italian Supermarket (☎0722/716539 or 0733/822282), rents out Land Cruisers with a driver, seating up to eight passengers, for around Ksh9000 per day. Otherwise, private taxi and 4WD owners will meet your requirements: ask your hotel front desk. Prices for saloons start from Ksh5000 per day around town.
Cinemas Cleopatra Theatre, by the big Total round about, screens English premiership football matches.

Golf Malindi Golf and Country Club ☎042/2120404, features an unusual eleven-hole (fifteen-tee) course behind the dunes on the north side of town.
Honorary Consuls The Italian honorary consul (the only diplomatic representative in Malindi; Mon–Fri 9am–noon ☎0722/825392 or emergencies ☎0722/224750) has an office in the Sabaki Centre, behind *Bar Bar*.
Hospitals The Italian-run St Peter's Hospital on Casuarina Road (☎042/2120086 or 0735/601304) is well run and has an ambulance service.
Immigration On the second floor of a decrepit-looking building on the waterfront road by the Juma Mosque (☎042/2120149).
Internet access The going rate in Malindi is Ksh2 per min: try Blingnet, opposite Barclays or Hemnet (with webcams) in the Blue Marlin shopping centre.
Kenya Wildlife Service Casuarina Point (daily 6am–6pm). Point of issue and point of sale for National Park smartcards.

Moving on from Malindi

From the main **bus and matatu park**, there are frequent services to Gedi, Watamu, Kilifi and Mombasa, and infrequent local matatus and buses for points inland. In addition, some matatus for Watamu leave from the town centre by the market in Mama Ngina Road.

Flying to **Lamu** is an experience not to be missed (see p.488 for airlines), but **buses** are much cheaper. Services start off from Mombasa, and pass by their Malindi booking offices in the centre of town by the market at around 8.30am each day. The companies serving Lamu are Falcon (☎042/2130850), Tahmeed (☎0729/356561), Tawakal (☎042/2131832), and TSS (no office – pay on bus) and tickets cost Ksh500–600. It's advisable to buy your ticket for Lamu the day before – otherwise you may have an exceedingly uncomfortable standing-up experience to look forward to. Whether travelling by bus or **driving** your own vehicle to Lamu, you'll have to change onto a **boat** at Mokowe.

In terms of **flights from Malindi**: Airkenya flies daily to Nairobi's Wilson airport; Mombasa Air Safari operates seasonally to Mombasa (dep 6.40pm; $35) and Lamu (dep 5pm; $50) and Fly540 flies daily to Lamu and JKIA Nairobi.

Pharmacy Sabaki Pharmacy (daily 8am–9pm), Kenyatta Rd, at the corner of Tsavo Rd.

Supermarkets There are several small places in the shopping arcades up Lamu Rd in the town centre, the best – with the widest range – being Multi Grocers in the Blue Marlin shopping centre.

Taxis Baobab Taxis (☎042/2130499) has fixed rates posted opposite the Portuguese Chapel on the baobab tree that serves as its HQ. *Tuk-tuks* are cheaper, *boda-bodas* cheaper still.

Travel agents A good scattering along Lamu Rd and the seafront all offer similar services, including safaris to Tsavo East. Try *Ozi's Guest House*, whose owner runs African Concept (Ⓦwww.africanconcept.co.ke) or Sunflower Safaris (see "Car Rental", opposite).

The Tana Delta

North out of Malindi, the **road to Lamu** sets off as a tarmac highway, crosses the Sabaki (Galana) River and passes one or two resort developments and the anachronistic little seaside town of **MAMBRUI**, with its pretty mosque, semi-ruined pillar tomb and the unusual spectacle of cows on the beach. The idyllic kitesurfing base of *Che Shale* (see p.466) is further up the coast on the south side of the **Ras Ngomeni peninsula**. About 60km north of Malindi, you leave the *shambas* and scattered homesteads behind and enter the bush of the **Tana Delta**, with the road arrowing straight across the flat, gentle landscape, brown and arid, or grey–green and swampy, depending on the season.

The former ferry-crossing town of **Garsen** has been sidelined by the tarmac **New Garsen Causeway**, which sweeps over the Tana River 7km to the south of the flyblown town before petering out into a dirt track for the rest of route to Lamu. If you want to break your journey, Garsen has a KCB bank with an **ATM** and, in season, some of the best and cheapest **mangoes** in Kenya.

Between the river and the end of the trip, the scenery can pall, but if you're on the bus, the journey is always enlivened by the other passengers and by stops at various small Tana delta towns and villages. Occasional flashes of colour – the sky-blue cloaks of **Orma** herders or the red, black and white of shawled **Somali** women – break up the journey, along with wonderful **birdlife** and some **big game**, too: especially giraffe and antelope (notably waterbuck), and even the odd elephant if you look hard enough. The road passes right through the recently created **Kipini sanctuary** (see p.475).

Tana River National Primate Reserve

Some 40km north of Garsen, straddling the Tana River, lies the **Tana River National Primate Reserve** (Ⓦwww.kws.go.ke/tana-river.html; $20), the 170-square kilometre refuge for two of Kenya's rarest and most beautiful monkeys, the **Tana River red colobus** and the **Tana River mangabey**. This is a remote area, with little in the way of supplies, so you'll need to bring provisions with you.

If you're **driving** here, the Baomo or Mchelelo tracks to the river are the ones to use, though the latter doesn't seem to be signposted from the road. If you want to try to visit the reserve using **public transport**, you simply need to allow time for unforeseen delays and a fair amount of walking or canoe-poling. Buses heading for Garissa occasionally stop in **Mnazini** village, just outside the southern end of the reserve. Otherwise, buses will drop you on the Garissa road, 6km to the west. If the district is flooded, a canoe ride from the road, following the Mnazini track to the village itself, will take about an hour – local **Pokomo boatmen** will happily pole you for a small fee.

Mnazini is a fine, coastal-style village beneath mango trees. There are no lodgings, but *hotelis* will take you in for the night once you've cleared your stay with the sub-chief and the headman. The shops have basic provisions, but north

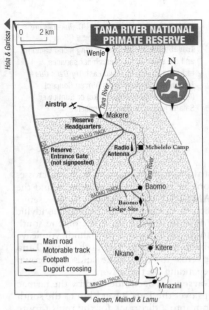

TANA RIVER NATIONAL
PRIMATE RESERVE

0   2 km

Wenje

N

Tana River

Airstrip

Makere

Reserve
Headquarters

MCHELELO TRACK

Reserve
Entrance Gate
(not signposted)

Radio
Antenna

Mchelelo Camp

Tana River

BAOMO TRACK

Baomo

Baomo
Lodge Site

Main road
Motorable track
Footpath
Dugout crossing

Nkano

Kitere

MNAZINI TRACK

Mnazini

Garsen, Malindi & Lamu

of Mnazini there's nothing in the way of food apart from a little fruit and garden vegetables.

Nobody in the area knows the Tana River National Primate Reserve by that name. Locals all refer to **Mchelelo**, the site of the primate research headquarters. The 12km walk to get there from Mnazini involves two river crossings, and a guide is essential to lead you through the bush and gallery forest. You enter the forest just after **Kitere** and reach the site of the former *Baomo Lodge* after 7km. At Mchelelo, there are two very basic **self-service tents** available to rent from KWS (price to be discussed) but essentially no other facilities.

Wildlife

Although little is laid on for the few visitors who come, you may well be given a detail of armed rangers on the anti-poaching force to accompany you as you walk the trails looking for **red colobus** and **crested mangabey monkeys**. Continued human encroachment on the forest, which is increasingly split into small intact zones, threatens both species, and the colobus very rarely leave the trees, limiting them to whichever patch they find themselves in.

Your chances of seeing both kinds of monkey are good, and the other highlights of the reserve are mostly avian: the superb birdlife includes goliath heron, Pel's fishing owl, southern banded snake eagle and the exceedingly rare Tana River cisticola, not to mention vast numbers of Palaearctic migrants in season. **Mammals** in the reserve, apart from the rare primates, include blue monkeys, baboons, Grevy's and Burchell's zebra, oryx, lesser kudu, and even lions, giraffe and buffalo. On the east side of the park you can see elephants, and there's also a small seasonal population of the endangered Hunter's hartebeest, or hirola. If you're interested in making a boat trip on the sluggish river, dodging the large numbers of hippos and crocodiles, you're likely to find local boatmen willing to take you.

Kipini and around

If you have a 4WD vehicle and a fair amount of patience, the trip to Lamu can be stretched over several days, with time to explore the fascinating region around the **Tana Delta**. This area includes the dune-shrouded coast and the small town of **Kipini**, with the Swahili ruins of **Ungwana**, **Shaka** and **Mwana** along the shore to the east, within a few kilometres. If you're interested in exploring down here, try to see the warden of the museum at Fort Jesus for further information. These sites were partially excavated in the 1970s and 1980s, but have since largely returned to bush and jungle. Ungwana is the most impressive, with an unusual mosque with two *mihrabs* and strange tombs with cruciform markings.

As yet almost wholly untouched by tourism, a visit to the district around the fishing village of **Kipini** at the mouth of the Tana and the larger market centre of **Witu**, 21km inland, repays the slight effort of getting here and finding somewhere to stay. **Kipini** was once the headquarters of Tana River District, before that title was shifted to Hola at the time of Independence. Nowadays, its former importance is evident only in a mixed population of Orma, Pokomo, Bajun, Somali and Swahili, who get by on fishing, small-scale farming and some herding.

To get to Kipini by public transport, leave the Lamu bus at Witu, where there's a connecting matatu to the village (most **buses** heading for Lamu or Malindi pass through Witu during the morning). Kipini has no formal **lodgings**, but you should be able to stay with a local family for few hundred shillings. Village *hotelis* serve delicious *dalasini* cinnamon tea. Alternatively, you could stay in **Witu** itself (again, no formal lodgings), and rent a **bicycle** locally for getting around.

Kipini Wildlife and Botanical Conservancy

The Kipini Wildlife and Botanical Conservancy (Ⓦ www.kipiniconservancy .org; no fees; contact the conservancy in advance), northeast of Kipini is a former ranch – the Nairobi Cattle Ranch – that failed, largely because of tsetse fly, and has now been reborn as a wildlife sanctuary. The people of the area, traditional hunter-gatherers, the **Boni**, are now mostly subsistence farmers. The conservancy is still in its infancy, but the intention is to create a viable natural resource, modelled on the former ranches of Laikipia. As you'll see if you stop off here, the area is full of **wildlife**, including elephants, giraffe, buffalo, lesser kudu, hirola, lions, the odd dugong in the creeks and, they claim, hunting dogs.

Delta Dunes and the Lower Tana Delta Trust

It's possible to stay near the delta mouth at the highly appealing, castaway-style *Delta Dunes* (Ⓣ 0721/322745 or 0723/538930, Ⓦ www.tanadelta.org; closed 1 June–15 July; package $1000 plus $50 per person conservation fee), up on the bush-covered sand dunes near the ocean, with six *bandas* made from driftwood, mangrove poles and *makuti*. Stays include all meals and drinks, boat trips, fishing, game and bird walks and village visits.

Delta Dunes works with thirteen thousand local people – Orma herders and Pokomo farmers – through the community's **Lower Tana Delta Trust**, and a proportion of income from guests goes direct to community bank accounts. But despite progress at the micro level, the threats to the delta region seem to be accumulating: after the failure of a highly damaging irrigation and rice-growing project in the 1990s, the latest disastrous idea is a gigantic biofuel project, carpeting more than 200 square kilometres of bush and flood land with **sugar-cane plantations** for cheap ethanol. While the project would create employment, its social and environmental costs have been deliberately underestimated by vested interests, and if it goes ahead it may have devastating consequences for the entire region (for more information, see Ⓦ www.tanariverdelta.org). The community is hopeful that the delta can be put under international protection as a **Ramsar Site** – a wetlands area of global importance.

The Lamu Archipelago

A cluster of hot, low-lying desert islands tucked into the coast near the Somalian border, **Lamu** and its neighbours have a special appeal that many visitors find irresistible. While every town and village has its distinct character, together they epitomize a separate spectrum of Swahili culture, a world apart from the coconut beaches of Mombasa and Malindi.

To a great extent the islands are anachronisms: there are still almost no motor vehicles, and life moves at the pace of a **donkey** or a **dhow**. Yet there have been considerable changes over the centuries and Lamu itself is now changing faster than ever. Because of its special status in the Islamic world as a much-respected centre of **religious teaching**, Saudi aid has poured into the island: the hospital, schools and religious centres are all supported by it. At the same time, Lamu's tourist economy has opened up far beyond the budget travellers of the 1970s. Foreign investors are eagerly sought and new **guesthouses** and **boutique hotels** go up every year, especially in Shela, which has more room than Lamu town. Islanders are ambivalent about the future. A string of all-inclusive resorts along the beach, a bridge to the mainland and a **US naval base** all seem possible, and a new **port** is virtually certain. Undoubtedly, all would contribute to the destruction of Lamu's historic character.

But the damage that would be done goes further than spoiling the tranquillity. The Lamu archipelago is one of the most important sources for knowledge about pre-colonial Africa. **Archeological sites** indicate that towns have existed on these islands for at least 1200 years. The dunes behind Lamu beach, for example, are said to conceal the remains of long-deserted settlements. And somewhere close by on the mainland, perhaps just over the border in Somalia, archeologists expect one day to uncover the ruins of Shungwaya, the town that the nine tribes that comprise the Mijikenda people claim as their ancestral home. The whole region is an academic's delight, a source of endless confusion and debate, and a place where there is still real continuity between history and modern life.

Lamu island itself, most people's single destination, still has plenty to recommend it, despite the inevitable sprouting of satellite dishes, cybercafés and souvenir shops. It has the archipelago's best beach and its two main towns, Lamu and Shela. **Manda island**, directly opposite, is little visited except as Lamu's gateway to the outside world (the airstrip) though its own beach is beautiful and there are several delightful places to stay. **Pate island**, accessible by dhow or motorboat, but completely off the tourism radar, makes a fascinating excursion if you have a week or more in the area. **Kiwaiyu island**, not quite within the archipelago, but exotic and alluring enough to be worth the effort, is a wisp of dunes and beach 9km long and less than 1km across, lying to the northeast of the other islands, with just two, superb, beach camps.

Lamu

Perhaps best left until the end of your stay in Kenya, **LAMU** may otherwise precipitate a change in your plans as you're lulled into a slow rhythm in which days and weeks pass by unheeded and objectives get forgotten. The deliciously lazy atmosphere is, for many people, the best worst-kept secret on the coast. All the senses get a full work-out here, so that actually *doing* anything is sometimes a problem. You can spend hours on a roof or veranda just watching the town go by, feeling its mood swing effortlessly through its well-worn cycles – from prayer call to prayer call, from tide to tide, and from dawn to dusk.

If this doesn't hit the right note for you, you might actually rather hate Lamu: hot, dirty and boring are adjectives that have been applied by sane and pleasant people. You can certainly improve your chances of liking Lamu by not coming here at the tail end of the dry season, when the town's gutters are blocked with refuse, the courtyard gardens wilt under the sun and the heat is sapping.

Lamu is something of a **myth** factory. Conventionally labelled an "Arab trading town", it is actually one of the last viable remnants of the **Swahili civilization** that was the dominant cultural force along the coast until the arrival of the British. In the 1960s, Lamu's unique blend of beaches, gentle Islamic ambience, funky old town and a host population well used to strangers, was a recipe which took over where Marrakesh left off, and it acquired a reputation as Kenya's Kathmandu; the end of the African hippie trail and a stopover on the way to India. Shaggy foreigners were only allowed to visit on condition they stayed in lodgings and didn't camp on the beach.

Not many people want to camp out these days. The proliferation of guesthouses in the heart of **Lamu town** encourages an ethos that is more interactive than hippie-escapist. Happily, visitors and locals cross paths enough to avoid any tedium – though for women travelling without men, this can itself become tedious (see p.492). Having said that, there can hardly be another town in the world as utterly unthreatening as Lamu. Leave your room at midnight for a breath of air and you can stroll up a hushed Harambee Avenue, or tread up the darkest of alleys, and fear absolutely nothing. It's an exhilarating experience.

If you want to spend all your time on the **beach**, then staying in **Shela** is the obvious solution, and there's an ever-growing range of quite stylish possibilities there, though hardly anywhere really inexpensive.

Some history

The undeniably **Arab** flavour of Lamu is not nearly as old as the town itself. It derives from the later nineteenth century when the **Omanis**, and to some extent the **Hadhramis** from what is now Yemen, held political and cultural sway in the town. The first British representatives in Lamu found themselves among pale-skinned, slave-owning Arab rulers and the cultural and racial stereotypes that were subsequently propagated have never completely disappeared.

Lamu was established on its present site by the fourteenth century, but

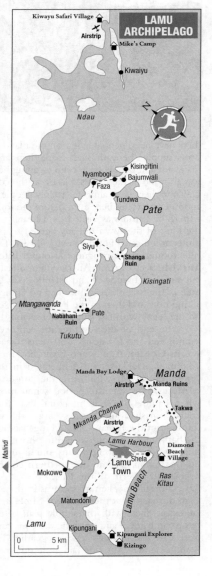

LAMU ARCHIPELAGO

Kiwayu Safari Village
Airstrip
Mike's Camp
Kiwaiyu
Ndau
Kisingitini
Nyambogi · Bajumwali
Faza
Tundwa
Pate
Siyu
Shanga Ruin
Kisingati
Mtangawanda
Nabahani Ruin
Pate
Tukutu
Manda Bay Lodge
Manda
Airstrip
Manda Ruins
Takwa
Mkanda Channel
Airstrip
Lamu Harbour
Diamond Beach Village
Malindi
Lamu Town
Shela
Mokowe
Ras Kitau
Matondoni
Lamu Beach
Lamu
Kipungani
Kipungani Explorer
Kizingo

0   5 km

▲ Lamu waterfront

there have been people living on the island for much longer than that. The fresh-water supplies beneath Shela made the island very attractive to refugees from the mainland and people have been escaping here for two thousand years or more. It was also one of the earliest places on the coast to attract settlers from the Persian Gulf and there were almost certainly people from Arabia and southwest Asia living and intermarrying here even before the foundation of Islam.

In 1505, Lamu was visited by a heavily armed **Portuguese** man-of-war and the king of the town quickly agreed to pay the first of many cash tributes as protection money. For the next 180 years Lamu was nominally under Portuguese rule, though the Portuguese favoured Pate as a place to live. In the 1580s, the **Turkish** fleet of Amir Ali Bey temporarily threatened Portuguese dominance, but superior firepower and relentless savagery kept them out, and Lamu, with little in the way of an arsenal, had no choice but to bend with the wind – losing a king now and then to the Portuguese executioners – until the Omanis arrived on the scene with fast ships and a serious bid for lasting control.

By the end of the seventeenth century, Lamu's Portuguese predators were vanquished and for nearly 150 years it had a revitalizing breathing space. This was its **Golden Age**, when Lamu became a republic, ruled over by the *Yumbe*, a council of elders who deliberated in the palace (now a ruined plot in the centre of town), with only the loosest control imposed by their Omani overlords. This was the period when most of the big houses were built and when Lamu's classic architectural style found its greatest expression. Arts and crafts flourished and business along the waterfront made the town a magnet throughout the Indian Ocean. Huge ocean-going dhows rested half the year in the harbour, taking on ivory, rhino horn, mangrove poles and cereals. There was time to compose long poems and argue about language, the Koran and local politics. Lamu became the northern coast's **literary and scholastic focus**, a distinction inherited from Pate.

For a brief time, Lamu's star was in the ascendant in all fields. There was even a famous victory at the **Battle of Shela** in 1812. A combined Pate-Mazrui force landed at Shela with the simple plan of capturing Lamu – not known for its resolve in battle – and finishing the construction of the fort which the Nabahanis from Pate had begun a few years earlier. To everyone's surprise, particularly the Lamu defenders, the tide had gone out and the invaders were massacred as they tried to push their boats off the beach. Appalled at the overkill and expecting a swift response from the Mazruis in Mombasa, Lamu sent to Oman itself for Busaidi protection and threw away independence forever. Had the eventual outcome of this panicky request been foreseen, the Lamu *Yumbe* might have reconsidered. Seyyid Said, Sultan of Oman, was more than happy to send a garrison to complete and occupy Lamu's fort – and from this toehold in Africa, he went on to smash the Mazrui rebels in Mombasa (see p.391), taking the entire coast and moving his own sultanate to Zanzibar.

Lamu gradually sank into economic collapse towards the end of the nineteenth century as Zanzibar and Mombasa grew in importance. In a sense, it has been stagnating ever since. The building of the Uganda railway from Mombasa and the banning of slavery did nothing to improve matters for Lamu in economic terms, and its decline has kept up with the shrinking population. However, the **resettlement programme** on the nearby mainland and – in recent years – a much safer road from Malindi, has led to a revived upcountry commercialism taking root around the market square.

Lamu Town

Perhaps surprisingly for so laid-back a corner of Kenya, there's no shortage of things to do in **LAMU TOWN**. An UNESCO World Heritage site, it's unendingly fascinating to stroll through, with few monuments but hundreds of ancient houses, arresting street scenes and cool corners to sit and rest. And the **museum** outshines all others in Kenya bar the National Museum in Nairobi.

Maulidi, a week-long celebration of Muhammad's birth (see p.56 for dates), sees the entire town involved in processions and dances, and draws in pilgrims from all over East Africa and the Indian Ocean. For faithful participants, the Lamu Maulidi is so laden with *baraka* (blessings) that some say two trips to Lamu are worth one to Mecca in the eyes of God. If you can possibly arrange it, this is the occasion to be in Lamu, but unless you make bookings, you'll need to arrive at least a week in advance to have any hope of getting a room. The other principal festival of the year is the **Lamu Cultural Festival** held in November to promote Swahili culture and heritage. With donkey and dhow racing, swimming, dancing and traditional craft displays, including carving, dhow-building, embroidery and henna decoration – all of it fairly competitive – the festival engages the town for the best part of a week.

Arrival

The bus trip or drive ends at **Mokowe** dock, on the mainland, where a chugging *mtaboti* (motorboat taxi, Ksh100) takes you around the creek for the thirty-minute ride to the town. The *mtabotis* are timed to coincide with the buses, though there are other less frequent services throughout the day. Grab your luggage, ignore the touts pulling you every which way, and jump on the boat which seems fullest – they all go to Lamu. Don't be misled by anyone trying to sell you a *mtaboti* charter; just wait for the next public *mtaboti* with everyone else. If you drove up, remove all your valuables and leave your vehicle in the car park where it should be safe (tipping the *askari* beforehand may improve security further).

Planes land on Manda island, across the harbour directly opposite the town. If you're staying a few days only and then flying out, it's a very good idea to go straight to the appropriate airline office on arrival to **reconfirm** your return seat. The short boat trip from the airstrip (Ksh100 to Lamu Town on boats run by the airlines) gives you a wonderful introductory panorama of Lamu's nineteenth-century waterfront.

Once you're at the harbour, you'll inevitably be met by a bevy of **beach boy hustlers** offering to take your baggage and guide you to a hotel. Some work for hotels or guesthouses and are just trying to fill rooms; some think they may get lucky with a quick tip for helping you; others genuinely want to be your guide for the duration of your stay. It's difficult to avoid these characters and they certainly won't allow you to stand around on the quayside looking at your map, so it's best to know in advance how to get to your preferred destination from the jetty. As usual, firmness, smiles and robust clarity are the best course. If you don't want a guide, be quite clear about that, and if they follow you anyway, explain what has happened to the hotel receptionist. The whole palaver is usually over very quickly as they turn their attentions to the next boatload of arrivals. If you need a guide in Lamu – and they can be useful and informative – your best bet is to ask other travellers to recommend one, or visit the **Tourist Office** and be sure your guide has a proper ID card. You'll need to tell any guide you engage which places you would like to visit and agree a fee: Ksh500 per day is about right.

Orientation and information

Initially confusing, Lamu town is not the random clutter of houses and alleys it appears. The town is divided into two main parts – **Mkomani** is the northern end and **Langoni** the southern. When discovering Lamu for yourself, you shouldn't get lost too easily if you remember that **Harambee Avenue** – also known as the Usita wa Mui ("Town Street") or Njia Kuu ("Main Road") – runs parallel to and fifty metres behind the waterfront, and that streets leading into town all run slightly uphill.

Lamu's **Tourist Information Office** (☎042/633132) is at the north end of town on the waterfront, next to *Lamu House*.

Accommodation

The better **lodgings** are generally those on the waterfront or those with a height advantage; places on Harambee Avenue tend to be suffocatingly hot. There's also a growing number of relatively pricey lodgings and private houses in **Shela** (see p.491) – which has become an alternative, upmarket base to Lamu town. In December, January, July and August, and particularly during Maulidi, room avail-ability can be tight, so **book ahead** if you can. Between April and June, you may find some places closed. **Room prices** depend on the season as well as your bargaining skills – haggling is possible at most lodgings, even those places charging eye-watering sums. The size of your group, how long you intend to stay and when you will actually pay are all useful bargaining chips. Unless the town is heaving with visitors, you shouldn't have any problem getting a discount. If you like the place, aim to agree a rate for the duration of your stay and then pay daily.

As well as hotels and guesthouses, it's often possible to rent **private houses** by the week or month. Some of these are occupied part of the year by their owners (often Nairobi-based Lamu-philes) and rented out the rest of the year in part or in whole, while others are second homes belonging to local families. The quantity and standard of furnishing varies, but there's always a kitchen and usually a cook and cleaner – often the same man (you'll pay an extra negotiated rate for his services). Put the word out that you're interested in finding a house, and they'll find you.

Budget and mid-range

Amu House ☎042/4633420. Extremely \attractive and welcoming, this is a restored, American-owned stone house with newer rooms added on top, built in the same style and offering really good value. The doubles and triples are airy, with large bathrooms. Dinner available upon request. BB ❹

Bahari ☎042/4633172. Basic but spacious s/c rooms on several floors, around a cool, plant-filled courtyard. Features include amusingly tokenistic "four-poster" beds, nets and fans, and most rooms have a fridge. Laundry Ksh30 per item. The excellent rooftop terrace is a good place to meet travellers. Haggle hard. BB **2**

Bush Guest House ☎0729/234102. Rooms in a tall building accessed from an alley between Harambee Ave and the sea. Only two rooms are s/c, but all are secure, with nets and fans, and not too small. There's also a rudimentary kitchen and communal lounge, and a rooftop. **1**

Café Bustani ☎0722/859594, ✉lamuchonji @yahoo.com. One very nice, s/c, top-floor room, with good ventilation, Swahili four-posters with nets and fan and a large bathroom. Terraces close to the room, and they do good coffee. BB **2**

Casuarina Rest House ☎042/4633123. A warren of rooms on the seafront, with nets and fans, in a nice position, but very basic. Okay if you're prepared to put up with rudimentary comforts and security. Two rooms are s/c. **2**

Hapa Hapa Guest House ☎042/4633145. Behind the popular eating place of the same name, this has two big double rooms at the front, both with fans but rather poor ventilation (the lower one has a TV, but go for the upper one). BB **3**

House of Mwana Kupona ☎0735/980848. Owned by Nairobi-based expats, the home of the famous nineteenth-century female poet Mwana Kupona is rented as a whole house, with a shared kitchen, two large, secure rooms, plus several other, pleasant, more flexible rooms with double beds. BB Ksh8000 per day to sleep up to seven.

Jannat House ☎042/4633414 or 0726/288817, ✇www.jannathouse.com. Atmospheric, Swedish-owned boutique hotel with fifteen, s/c and non-s/c rooms (nets and fans), a very nice, small pool, a bar-restaurant and a dhow, *Jannat*. Arranged around a heavily planted courtyard with much of its original decoration (*zidaka* stuccowork niches and furniture) still intact, plenty of terraces with comfy chairs and lovely views over the town. BB **5**

🏃 **Kilimanjaro** ☎0721/141924, ✉info@kilam_ lamu.com. Managed by a personable local DJ, this is a very good choice, with a nice chill-out scene on the rooftop and a popular Sunday jazz breakfast. The kitchen is available if you want to self-cater. The penthouse with the big double bed is best, and the same price as the six other rooms. BB **3**

Lamu Archipelago Villa ☎042/4633247. The s/c rooms here aren't that great – just a bit too small, and rather plain – but the position, right on the waterfront, is a plus. The rooms at the front are much the better ones. BB **2**

Lamu Guest House ☎042/4633338. A well-maintained old house right in the heart of things, which has been owned by the same Indian family for seven generations. It's inevitably somewhat hot

and stuffy given its location, but the ceilings are high and there are nets and fans; a few of the rooms are s/c. Good-value. **1**

New Mahrus ☎042/4633001 or 0720/574446. Although not on the waterfront, this rambling old place with its own creaking, run-down charm, has a great location by the square, looking across to the fort. It's one of the cheapest places in town, with single, non-s/c rooms for just Ksh300, but rooms could be cleaner and security is rather uncertain. The upper rooms, facing the square are best. BB **2**

🏃 **Nyuma Gereza** ☎020/8023732 or 0722/721232, ✇www.nyumagerezahotel .blogspot.com. Located behind the fort, and personably run by its devoutly Muslim owner (no alcohol or beach boys in rooms), this excellent new conversion has ten s/c rooms with fans and nets, and guests have use of a kitchen. **2**

Pole Pole Guest House ☎042/4633344. Getting a bit run-down, but still pleasant, and very good value, especially if you're used to B&Ls. It has a fantastic roof terrace with a bird's-eye view from the roof, one of the highest in town. Nets and fans in most rooms. **2**

🏃 **Sultan Palace** ☎0728/991280, ✇www .sultanpalacelamu.com. Dramatic, tall house, next to and (surprisingly) owned by *Petley's*, with four large rooms, each with two or three large beds. Steep stairs lead up to a splendid, top-floor lounge area under the *makuti* eves. BB **4**

Sunsail ☎042/4632065 or 0722/666303. Situated in the old stone "Mackenzie" trader's house on the waterfront, the rooms here have high ceilings and smart tiled bathrooms, but this doesn't compensate for their small size – and only the two at the front have sea views. Unfortunately the roof terrace is enclosed. Still, reasonable value for money. BB **3**

Sunshine Guest House ☎042/4633087 or 0711/183469. Pleasant, if slightly mouldering place tucked in a corner in the heart of Mkomani, with a good terrace. Rooms are s/c, with fans and nets, and while bathrooms are a bit decrepit, it remains very good value, especially if you haggle, and the use of the kitchen (with cooker and fridge) is a bonus. **1**

🏃 **Wildebeest** ☎042/4632261 or 0723/687408. Fascinating, old, gallery-cum-apartments, with a hair-raising multiplicity of steep, Escher-like staircases, owned by a Nairobi-based American artist, managed by a Lamu artist-caretaker, and stuffed with artwork and bric-a-brac. Breakfast and other meals available. Exceptional value. **2**

Yumbe House ☎042/633101 or 0725/352117. A cut above the average lodging, this has ten, mostly quite spacious, s/c rooms, including some good-value singles, all with fans, nets and fridge (a nice touch), above a well-planted courtyard. The top room is easily the best. Check when booking as you may be put up at *Yumbe Villa*, their annexe, a few minutes' walk away, which is not as nice. BB ❸

Expensive

🏃 **Baytulkher** ☎0725/617996, ✉baytulkher@talktalk.net. Decorated in funky, bright colours, with naïve paintings, this is a beautiful, well-lit, airy house, with spacious s/c rooms, bathrooms you can enjoy (rather than want to leave quickly) and lots of quiet corners for rest and contemplation. The huge top floor "suite" opens on all sides, and has great views. BB ❻

🏃 **Lamu House** ☎042/4633491, ⓦwww .lamuhouse.com. A stunning conversion, based on two traditional houses, Salama and Azania, each with five s/c suites with private terrace, really comfortable beds and superb bathrooms. Rooms downstairs can be a little dark: ideally get one upstairs at the front. There are also two cool, white courtyards with plunge pools, and a decent swimming pool as well. Rates include a

daily transfer to the beach and back. Excellent on-site restaurant. BB ❼

New Lamu Palace ☎042/4633272, ⓦlamuparadiseholidays.com. Three-storey hotel, co-owned with *Petley's* (see below), with a restaurant and bar. Only four of the 22 cramped, s/c, a/c rooms face the sea, and the sea-view ones are not worth the hefty supplement for one small window. The seamless, tourist-class style must appeal to many (and many guests are on Lamu packages), but look elsewhere and you'll get a better deal for half the price. BB ❻

Petley's Inn ☎042/4633272, ⓦlamuparadise holidays.com. Under the same ownership as *New Lamu Palace* (see above), for which it serves as an annexe, *Petley's* is Lamu's oldest hotel but sadly devoid of historic interest after multiple owners and a fire. The small, high-ceilinged rooms have fans and nets (the best two face the sea); some have a/c; but none are rooms you could spend time in. There's a small roof-level pool and a lively rooftop bar. Breakfast is served in the *New Lamu Palace*. BB ❻

The Town

Very few towns in sub-Saharan Africa have kept their original **town plan** so intact (Timbuktu in West Africa is another), and Lamu's history is sufficiently documented, and its architecture well enough preserved, to give you a good idea of how the town developed. The main division is between the **waterfront** buildings and the town behind, separated by **Usita wa Mui**, now Harambee Avenue (actually a narrow alley for the most part). Until around 1830, this was the waterfront, but the pile of accumulated rubbish in the harbour had become large enough by the time the fort was finished to consider reclaiming it, and, gradually, those who could afford to, built on it. The **fort** lost its pre-eminent position and Lamu, from the sea, took on a different aspect, which included Indian styles such as arches, verandas and shuttered windows.

Behind the waterfront, the **old town** retained a second division between **Mkomani** district, to the north of the fort, and **Langoni** to the south. These locations are important as they distinguish long-established Mkomani from still-expanding Langoni. This north–south division is found in most Swahili towns and reflects the importance of Mecca, which is due north of Lamu.

The town is divided further into forty *mitaa* or **wards**, roughly corresponding to the idea of blocks in a modern city. The names of these suggest a great deal about how the town once looked. **Kinooni** ("whetstone corner") boasts to this day a heavy block of stone on the corner for sharpening swords, reputedly imported from Oman, and Utakuni ("main market") ward still has a row of shops, even though most of the buildings on this north side of town are now purely residential.

It is difficult to construct a guided tour of Lamu – serendipity comes to everyone here, and in any event, you're better off exploring whenever you have a spare hour or two – but the following ideas are well worth pursuing whenever you lack the energy for the beach. Note that while the National Museums of Kenya has tried to impose a charge of Ksh3000 to visit Lamu's four main sites (the museum, the fort, the house museum and the German post office museum), there's not a great deal of take-up at that price and most visitors pay separately.

It's another good reason to take out temporary membership of the Kenya Museum Society (see p.111) if you're in Nairobi.

Stone architecture

Lamu's **stone houses** are perfect examples of architecture appropriate to its setting. The basic design is an open box shape enclosing a large courtyard, around the inner walls of which are set inward-facing rooms on two or three floors, the top floor forming an open roof terrace with a *makuti* roof. The rooms are thus long and narrow, their ceilings supported by close-set timbers or mangrove poles (*boriti*). Most had exquisite carved doors at one time, though in all but a few dozen homes these have been sold off to pay for upkeep. Many also had *zidaka*, plaster-work niches in the walls to give an illusion of extended space, which are now just as rare. Bathroom arrangements are ingenious, with fish kept in the large water storage cisterns to eat mosquito larvae. In parts of Lamu these old houses are built so close together you could step over the street from one roof to another.

The private space inside Lamu's houses is barely distinguishable from the public space outside. The noises of the town percolate into the interiors, encouraged by the constant flow of air created by the narrow coolness of the dark streets and the heat which accumulates on upper surfaces exposed to the sun.

Lamu Museum

The one place you should definitely count on devoting an hour or so to is **Lamu Museum** (daily 8am–6pm; Ksh500; ⓦ www.museums.or.ke). The house, built in 1891 on the waterfront, once served as a British colonial government residence. Of Kenya's regional museums, this is the one that best lives up to its name. There's no need to fill spare rooms here with game trophies and trivia; the region's history provides more than enough material.

As you enter, there's a large aerial photo of the town for a fascinating bird's-eye insight. Elsewhere, exhibitions of **Swahili culture** – architecture, boats and boat-building, and domestic life – are displayed. There are also rooms devoted to the non-Swahili peoples of the mainland: farmers like the **Pokomo**, **Orma** cattle herders and **Boni** hunters. Two magnificent ceremonial **siwa horns**, one

---

Tradition and morality in Lamu

A number of **old photographs** on display in the museum belie pronouncements about "unchanging Lamu". The women's cover-all black **buibui**, for example, turns out to be a fashion innovation introduced comparatively recently from southern Arabia. It wasn't worn in Lamu much before the 1930s when, ironically, a degree of emancipation encouraged women of all classes to adopt the high-status styles of purdah. In earlier times, high-born women would appear in public entirely hidden inside a tent-like canopy called a **shiraa**, which had to be supported by slaves; the abolition of slavery at the beginning of the twentieth century marked the demise of this odd fashion.

Outsiders have tended to get the wrong end of the stick about Swahili seclusion. While women are undoubtedly heavily restricted in their public lives, in private they have considerable freedom. The notion of **romantic love** runs deep in Swahili culture. Love affairs, divorces and remarriage are the norm, and the *buibui* is perhaps as useful to women in disguising their liaisons as it is to their husbands in preventing them.

All this comes into focus a little when wandering through the alleys. You may even bump into some of Lamu's **transvestite** community – cross-dressing men whose lifestyle, which derives from Oman, is accepted and long established. In fact, the more you explore, the more you realize that the town's conventional image is like the walls of its houses – a severe facade concealing an unrestrained interior.

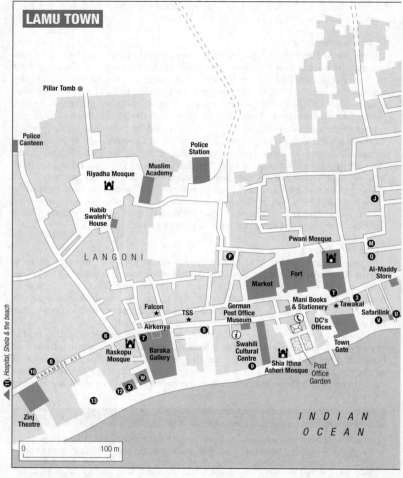

LAMU TOWN

▲ Kipungani   ▲ Matondoni

Pillar Tomb ●

Police
Canteen

Riyadha Mosque

Muslim
Academy

Police
Station

Habib
Swaleh's
House

L A N G O N I

Pwani Mosque

P

Fort

Market

Al-Maddy
Store

Falcon ★   TSS ★   German
Post Office
Museum

Mani Books
& Stationery   ★ Tawakal   3

Safarilink

Airkenya   5

ⓘ

DC's
Offices

V   U

6   7

Raskopu
Mosque

Baraka
Gallery

Swahili
Cultural
Centre
9

Shia Ithna
Asheri Mosque

Town
Gate

8

10   HARAMBEE AVE

Post
Office
Garden

12 X W

13

Zinj
Theatre

I N D I A N

O C E A N

0   100 m

◀ Hospital, Shela & the beach

J

M

O

T

in ivory from Pate, the other from Lamu itself, and made of brass, are the prize
exhibits – probably the oldest surviving musical instruments in sub-Saharan
Africa. The Pate *siwa*, slightly more ancient, dates from 1690. Wooden imitations
are on sale all around town.

The museum can arrange guided tours to archeological and historical sites on
Manda and Pate islands: contact the curator in person, or email via the Nairobi
headquarters.

Lamu Fort Museum

The **fort**, which was begun in 1809 and completed in 1821, seems oddly
stranded in its modern-day position, deprived of its role as defender of the
waterfront. It served as a prison until 1984, but it's now a national monument
and open as the **Lamu Fort Museum** (same times and prices as Lamu

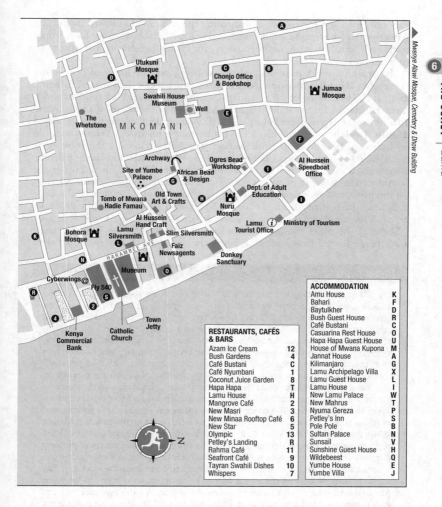

RESTAURANTS, CAFÉS
& BARS

Azam Ice Cream	12
Bush Gardens	4
Café Bustani	C
Café Nyumbani	1
Coconut Juice Garden	8
Hapa Hapa	T
Lamu House	H
Mangrove Café	2
New Masri	3
New Minaa Rooftop Café	6
New Star	5
Olympic	13
Petley's Landing	R
Rahma Café	11
Seafront Café	9
Tayran Swahili Dishes	10
Whispers	7

ACCOMMODATION

Amu House	K
Bahari	F
Baytulkher	D
Bush Guest House	R
Café Bustani	C
Casuarina Rest House	O
Hapa Hapa Guest House	U
House of Mwana Kupona	M
Jannat House	A
Kilimanjaro	G
Lamu Archipelago Villa	X
Lamu Guest House	L
Lamu House	I
New Lamu Palace	W
New Mahrus	T
Nyuma Gereza	P
Petley's Inn	S
Pole Pole	B
Sultan Palace	N
Sunsail	V
Sunshine Guest House	H
Wildebeest	Q
Yumbe House	E
Yumbe Villa	J

Museum), as well as housing the town's **library** and acting as a gallery space. It's always fun to walk round the ramparts, getting bird's-eye views of the town, and there's usually an interesting art show or a **temporary exhibition** of photos or local archaeological finds on display.

Mosques

When you start checking out some of Lamu's 23 **mosques**, you'll find that any tone of rigid conformity you might expect is lacking. Most are simple, spacious buildings, as much local men's clubs as places of prayer. There's no special reason to enter them; their doors are always open and there's little to see. Male visitors, suitably dressed, are normally allowed inside; female visitors are generally excluded. The oldest-known mosque is the **Pwani Mosque**, by the fort, parts of which date back to the fourteenth century. Lamu's current Friday mosque is the **Jumaa**, the big one in Pangahari ("sword-sharpening place") ward. Unfortunately, the **Mwenye Alawi Mosque**, at the north end of town, which was once Lamu's only exclusively female mosque, has been taken over by the men, leaving the women to pray at home.

The star of Lamu's mosques, as well as being one of the youngest, is the sumptuous **Riyadha Mosque** located well to the back of the town, in Langoni. Built at the beginning of the twentieth century, the mosque has brought about a radical shift in Lamu's style of Islam, and indeed in the status of Lamu in the Islamic world. It was founded by a sharif, a descendant of the prophet, called **Habib Swaleh**, who came from the Hadramaut (present-day Yemen) to settle in Lamu in the mid-nineteenth century. His house, close by the mosque, is acknowledged with a plaque, but is basically a simple wattle-and-daub structure, containing a caretaker's bed and a few old papers. Habib Swaleh and his group introduced a new freedom to the five-times-daily prayers, with singing, tambourines and spontaneous readings from the Koran. They attracted a large following, particularly from the slave and ex-slave community, but gradually from all social spheres, even the aristocratic families with long Lamu pedigrees.

Some of the other mosques later adopted the style, but the Riyadha, apart from being Lamu's largest mosque, is still the one most closely associated with

Dhow trips

Where the hotel hustlers left off after you settled in, the dhow-ride men take up the challenge. You'll be persistently hassled until you agree to go on a trip and then, as if the word's gone out, you'll be left alone. The fact is your face quickly becomes familiar to anyone whose livelihood depends upon tourists. Dhow trips are usually a lot of fun and, all things considered, very good value. The simplicity of Swahili sailing is delightful, using a single lateen sail that can be set in virtually any position and never seems to obstruct the view. Sloping past the mangroves, with their primeval-looking tangle of roots at eye level, hearing any number of squeaks and splashes from the small animals and birds that live among them, is quite a serene pleasure.

There are limitless possibilities for dhow trips, though only a short menu of possibilities is usually offered. The cheapest trip is a slow sail across Lamu harbour and up Takwa "river", fishing as you go, followed by a barbecue on the beach at **Manda island**, then back to town. This might commence with some squelching around in the mud under the mangroves, digging for huge bait-worms. If the trip is timed properly with the tides, you can include a visit to **Takwa ruins** or, for rather more money, you can stay the night on the beach behind the ruins and come back the next day. This is usually done around full moon. Takwa has to be approached from the landward side up the creek, and this can only be done at high tide. A further variation has you sailing south through Lamu harbour, past the headland at Shela and out towards the ocean for some **snorkelling** over the reefs on the southwest corner of Manda around **Kinyika rock**. Snorkel and mask are normally provided, but bringing your own is obviously much better. Although all dhows should carry enough useable life jackets, this is particularly essentially if you're venturing beyond the reef, where the seas can be very rough and accidents happen all too often.

The **price** you pay will depend on how many are in your party, where you want to go, for how long, and how much work it's going to be for the crew. Agree on the price beforehand (a full day with lunch starts from around Ksh1000 per person) and pay up afterwards, although some captains may ask you for a small deposit to buy food. Be clear on who is supplying food and drink, apart from any fish you might catch.

Cameras are easily damaged on dhow trips, so wrap them up well in a plastic bag. And take the clothes and drinks you'd need for a 24-hour spell in the Sahara – you'll burn up and dry out otherwise.

this kind of inspirational worship. Non-Muslim men who visit while worship is in session are likely to be invited in and encouraged to sit cross-legged with the rest of the assembly. Any sense of stale ritual is far removed: the atmosphere is light, the music infectious. The Riyadha is also famous as the spiritual home of Lamu's annual **Maulidi** celebration (see p.479).

Next to the Riyadha is the big, square **Muslim Academy – a major teaching establishment**, and like the Riyadha itself, and so much else in Lamu, heavily under Saudi patronage. Both men and women are allowed to have a look around, but there's very little to see. More interesting are some of the students, who come from all over the Islamic world.

Other sights

After the fort, the only other national monument in Lamu (though you may not believe it when you see it) is the fluted **pillar tomb** behind Riyadha Mosque. This may date from as far back as the fourteenth century, and the occasional visit by a tourist might persuade the families in the neighbourhood that it's worth preserving; it can only be a matter of time before it leans too far and collapses on a passing child. In the middle of town, by a betel vine plot, is another tomb, that of **Mwana Hadie Famau**, a local woman of the fifteenth or sixteenth century. This has been walled up and has lost the porcelain-embedded pillars that would once have stood at each corner.

The **Swahili House Museum** (daily 7.30am–5.45pm; Ksh500, children Ksh250) in Mkomani is an eighteenth-century house that's been restored to an approximation of its original appearance. Unfortunately, the guided tour (included in the entrance fee) is brief and the house is very small, consisting only of a small courtyard, two sleeping galleries, two toilets and an upstairs kitchen and roof. The best Lamu houses are still in private hands.

On the waterfront is the **Donkey Sanctuary**, funded by a UK-based animal charity (Ⓦ drupal.thedonkeysanctuary.org.uk). They'll show you round in the morning and are always happy to receive donations, which they use for free veterinary care of animals that are otherwise sometimes literally worked to death. More than animal-lovers, they have had a significant impact economically, too, with their twice-yearly donkey de-worming programme in the Lamu archipelago.

Heading north out of town, through the wards of Tundani ("fruit-picking place") and Weyoni ("donkey racetrack"), you reach the **cemetery**. This is the goal of many religious processions and strolling up there makes an interesting short walk. You then come out by the slaughterhouse and rubbish dumps, populated by marabou storks. In the inlet behind them, several large **dhows** and smaller boats are moored. Many are rotting, but one or two are quite new, even unfitted. If you have dreams of owning a dhow (they make great houseboats), you're looking at around $7000 for a 12-metre hull. The price depends largely on the time required to build it – two years isn't unusual.

Eating and drinking

There are enough **restaurants** and passable *hotelis* in Lamu to enable you to eat out twice a day for a week without going back to your first port of call. A fine balance has been achieved between what is demanded and what can be supplied: yoghurt, fruit salad, pancakes, milkshakes and puréed fruit juices have become Lamu specialities. Superb lobster and crab dishes, oysters, snapper and delicious steaks of swordfish, barracuda and shark are also on many menus – it's a nice change to find a fishing town where you can actually eat seafood relatively affordably. Upcountry staples – beans, curries, pilau, steak, chicken, chips, eggs, even *ugali* – are available from a number of ordinary **hotelis** crowded along Harambee Avenue, particularly in Langoni. Also along Harambee Avenue, you'll find tiny mutton kebabs and cakes on sale at night; they cost next to nothing and are usually delicious. **Prices** are fairly standard, Ksh40 to Ksh100 for shakes and juices, depending on size, and Ksh400 to Ksh500 for full meals. Cheaper places, that don't go out of their way to attract tourists, serve meals for Ksh 100 to Ksh200.

If you spend any time in Lamu, you'll probably run into someone offering you a "genuine" Swahili **dinner at home**. At its best, this is a great way of seeing how the majority of Lamu's inhabitants live, and the food can be delicious. On the other hand, the price demanded at the end (which, like everything in Lamu, depends mainly on how hard you haggle and your perceived ability to pay) might not necessarily be any cheaper than eating in a decent restaurant. As in a restaurant, you should pay after your meal, not before.

If you enjoy doing your own **cooking** (several lodgings have kitchens you can use), a whole new world starts to open up. The **produce market** in front of the fort – run for the most part by upcountry women – has everything you'll need, with separate sections for meat, fish, and fruit and vegetables. For **fish and shellfish**, get there very early: by 9am all the interesting stock has been sold. Lamu has wonderful fruit and is famous for its enormous, aromatic **mangoes**, but you should also try the unusually sweet, juicy **grapefruit**. While you're here, you might also find one of Lamu's traditional exports, **betel**, the green vine you

Moving on from Lamu

The **bus companies** running daily to Mombasa via Malindi are Falcon, Tahmeed, Tawakal and TSS. Departures from Mokowe jetty on the mainland start at 7am and the first *mtaboti* ferries leave Lamu Town at 6–6.30am to connect. Buy tickets (about Ksh600 to Mombasa) the day before or earlier to be sure of a seat (booking offices hours generally daily 8.30am–12.30pm, 2.30–4.30pm & 7–8.30pm). Tawakal is the fastest, costs a little more then the others and sells out more quickly. It also runs more service, until late morning or early afternoon (usually 7am, 11am and 1pm).

There are currently four **airlines** connecting Lamu with Kiwaiyu, Malindi, Mombasa and Nairobi – unfortunately, **Kenya Airways**, under *Casuarina Guesthouse* (⏀042/4632040–1) has cancelled its Lamu service.

Safarilink, next to the *Sunsail Hotel* (042/4632211; daily 8am–5pm, early closing on Sun) has daily flights to Wilson airport, Nairobi (4pm; $162) and Kiwaiyu airstrip (3.30pm; $48), but no service April–June and only four days a week 1 Nov–15 Dec

AirKenya on Harambee Avenue in Langoni (⏀042/4633445 or 042/4633063; daily 8am–5pm), has a daily flight to Nairobi Wilson (5pm; $175 or $335 return)

Fly540 (⏀042/632054; Mon–Fri 8–noon & 2–5pm, Sat 8–noon) flies daily direct to Nairobi JKIA (5.55pm; Ksh12,000), and via Malindi (Mon–Sat 11.55am, Sun 3pm; Ksh3,770)

Mombasa Air Safari (bookings care of Safarilink) flies in high season to Mombasa (Ksh7000) via Malindi (Ksh3500), dep. 6pm.

Getting a ride on a **cargo dhow** from Lamu to Mombasa can be relatively straight forward, assuming it's the right time of year (roughly once a week from December–March). There are no fixed prices and you should accept that your well-being and security are your own responsibility. Having found an agreeable captain, you'll need to visit the District Commissioner's secretary's office for a form absolving the captain and the government of all responsibility in the case of mishap. Take one copy to the captain, which he'll present when he files his crew and passenger manifest. They'll tell you it's a 36-hour trip to Mombasa, but count on up to three or even four days. Bring fruit and anything else you anticipate needing to break the monotony of unvarying fish and *ugali* meals. You should get a passage for around Ksh2000 or less.

see trailing out of all the empty plots in town. The sweet hot-tasting leaves are
wrapped around other ingredients, including white lime and betel nut, which
stains the teeth red, to make *pan* which you chew (see p.402). For something
sweeter, try the *halwa* shop on Harambee Avenue in Langoni, and there's a good
bakery facing the right side of the fort. **Supermarkets** are listed overleaf.

The only stand-alone bar in town is *Petley's Landing* on the waterfront, below
the hotel of the same name. It's a horrible, noisy music bar, and has nothing to
do with its namesake.

Snack bars and local hotelis

Azam Ice Cream On the waterfront in Langoni.
Lamu's only ice cream parlour, with a half-decent
selection of flavours. Daily 9.30am–1.30pm &
4–10pm.

Coconut Juice Garden Harambee Ave. Good
juices and shakes, blended as you wish –
combinations include passion and pawpaw, and a
sublime coconut and banana. Mon–Sat.

New Masri Harambee Ave, across from the *New
Mahrus*. Swahili curries and fish dishes served to
an assortment of locals and tourists.

Rahma Café Harambee Ave. Popular local teashop
and *hoteli*.

Tayran Swahili Dishes Harambee Ave, Langoni.
Locals squeeze together at shared tables in this
tiny chop house to eat fried fish, beans, samosas
and *mandaazi*.

Restaurants and travellers' cafés

Bush Gardens On the waterfront,
Mkomani. Competing for the same business
as *Hapa Hapa* (see below) but more upmarket, this
seafood and kebab place has a popular following
and a charming proprietor. The food varies from
average to first-rate (the grilled garlic fish is
magnificent) and prices are reasonable – shakes
Ksh50–100, fish around Ksh450. Daily 7am–10pm.

Café Nyumbani Harambee Ave, opposite *Lamu
House* ☎0721/151304. Popular first-floor restaurant for breakfasts, lunches and dinners, with a
wide variety of prices and dishes (mains Ksh250–
1000). The speciality is barbecued seafood in garlic
and tamarind sauce. You have to call or text several
hours in advance (or the day before) to order food,
but it's well worth it.

Hapa Hapa on the waterfront, Mkomani. Popular,
central seafront rendezvous – the food is inexpensive, generally good and occasionally excellent.
And then there are the famous pint jugs of freshly

pressed juices, shakes and smoothies. A good
place to people-watch, or just daydream.

Mangrove Café Next to *Petley's*. Popular
travellers' café serving up freshly squeezed
juices and snacks.

Lamu House On the waterfront, Mkomani
☎042/4633491, 🖰www.lamuhouse.com. With its
terrace cleverly tucked away behind a low wall,
eating here is more relaxing than in some of the
more exposed restaurants. Although not cheap, it's
not as expensive as you might imagine (Ksh1500
for three courses, without drinks), and the seafood
dishes are invariably fragrant and well-prepared.

New Minaa Rooftop Café Just off Harambee Ave,
Langoni. A pleasant roof-terrace restaurant that's
also a good place to mingle with the locals. Serves
good fried fish, beans in coconut and chapattis.

New Star Harambee Ave, Langoni. Under a
dilapidated roof, this Lamu institution (30
years and still going strong) is one of the few
restaurants catering equally to travellers and locals,
and one of the cheapest in town, with tasty stew
and rice for Ksh120. Especially good for breakfast
before an early-morning walk to the beach. Daily
5.30am–10.30pm.

Olympic On the waterfront, Langoni. Popular, long-
established beachfront place for fresh juices,
snacks and rice and fish-based meals.

Seafront Café On the waterfront, Langoni. This
travellers' restaurant offers coconut fish or beans,
rice, pilau and *karanga*, though standards are
variable. Daily until midnight.

Whispers Harambee Ave, Langoni
☎042/4632024 or 0721/527647. It may be
slightly pretentious, but the real espresso and
wonderful cakes, pizzas, pastas and salads are
hard to resist. Unless, that is, you're really counting
the pennies – it's expensive when a snack and a
coffee can cost Ksh500. Has a deli section and
does take-outs, though portions tend to be on the
small side. Daily 9am–9pm or later, usually closed
May & June.

Shopping

Woodcarving shops are mostly found in Mkomani, along the waterfront and in
Harambee Avenue. Model dhows, chests, furniture and *siwa* horns are all

attractive but bulky. Beautifully hand-carved safari chairs are also a hassle to carry, but the prices make them worth acquiring. Wooden trays are an opportunity to have something lighter and useful that also shows off Lamu craftsmanship. If you have something in mind, and a day or two in hand, you can always order a particular piece or design. Some of the shops selling **jewellery** and trinkets have genuinely old and interesting pieces: look out especially for tiny lime caskets in silver, earlobe plugs in buffalo horn or silver, and old coins.

A number of **tailors** along Harambee Avenue will run up shirts, trousers, shorts and skirts very cheaply in a day or so. The easiest way to end up with something that fits is to provide a model garment for them to copy. Langoni is the place to hunt out pairs of printed ladies' *kangas* and men's woven *kikoi* wraps.

Shops

African Bead and Leather Design Near the arch in Mkomani. Sourced from a community workshop near the *Tamarind* in Mombasa, they have leather bags, beadwork and beaded sandals, and handmade fashion.

Baraka Gallery Harambee Ave, Langoni. Even if it's expensive, the wares here are so diverse and attractive – from silver and glass jewellery to intricate basketware, leather goods and paper crafts – that it's a must-visit for souvenir hunters. Daily 9am–1pm & 3.30pm–7.30pm.

Lamu Silversmith On Harambee Ave just up from the *Lamu Guest House*. Long-established and recommended craftsmen who will design to order.

Ogres Bead Workshop Just off Harambee Ave, Mkomani. Run by two brothers from Nairobi, this workshop sells wonderful handmade jewellery. Custom pieces made to order.

Old Town Art and Crafts Mkomani. Big shop of carvings, paintings and jewellery – the sort of stuff you don't easily find elsewhere in Lamu. Like an upcountry souvenir emporium, but in a relaxed atmosphere.

Listings

Bank KCB, on the waterfront, is the only bank in Lamu (Mon–Fri 9am–3pm, Sat 9–11am), and has an ATM.

Books and newspapers Mani Books & Stationers, near the fort, sells newspapers and magazines. For a selection of books, visit the offices of Lamu Chonjo magazine, at *Café Bustani* in Mkomani, near the Swahili House Museum.

Cinemas The Zinj Theatre on Harambee Ave in Langoni screens international and Bollywood films. It also occasionally screens live English Premiership or European Champions League football matches.

Discos There's usually a disco, sometimes with a Ksh50 or Ksh100 entrance, on Fri & Sat at the *Civil Servants' Club*, about 1km south of the GPO (entrance on the waterfront).

Henna painting A number of women around town offer henna designs for hands and feet, for which you can expect to pay around Ksh500 for both hands or both feet. The best women have portfolios of designs to choose from – you'll see them in one or two shop fronts and private doorways. If done properly, your hands or feet will be bound in cloth for twelve hours and the design should stay for up to six months, or a year on nails.

Hospital The Saudi-funded hospital, out in the direction of Shela (☎042/4633012), attracts patients from a huge part of northeastern Kenya. There are also several private clinics – ask around.

Internet access Cyberwings, next to *Petley's*, has webcams (daily 9am–9pm, sometimes closed around 1–2pm; Ksh1.50 per min); *New Mahrus Hotel*, first floor (Ksh2 per min, Ksh100 per hr).

Library The town library (Mon–Fri 8am–12.30pm & 2–5.30pm, Sat 10am–noon; ☎042/4633201) is on the top floor of the fort. It has a surprisingly good collection, with lots on Lamu, as well as a sixteenth-century Koranic manuscript.

Speedboat charter Not exactly in keeping with the spirit of Lamu's lifestyle, it certainly gets you from A to B effectively, but drinks diesel fuel and is thus expensive. You can hire a boat from Al-Hussein, which comfortably seats four, plus captain and "small captain"; their office is on Harambee Ave in Mkomani (☎042/4633509), and they can also be contacted through Al-Hussein Hand Craft, 200m further south. Rates are around Ksh8000 to Pate, Ksh10,000 to Faza and Ksh15,000 to Kiwaiyu. In Shela, *Peponi* offers a similar service at similar prices.

Supermarkets/general stores There are no big shops in Lamu. If you can't get it at Al Maddy Store, Harambee Ave (daily 9am–12.30pm & 5–10pm in theory, but often shuts earlier) or Bagdam Store, Harambee Ave (Mon–Sat 8.15am–12.30pm & 4–10pm, Sun 8.15am–12.30pm), you probably can't get it.

Swahili lessons Being suffused in Swahili culture, Lamu is a good place to learn the language – the

Tourist Information Centre (see p.480) can put you in touch with a teacher. Alternatively, ask at the Department of Adult Education on Harambee Ave or at Lamu Museum.

Tide tables Check out *Coast Week* or, if you can get online, ⓦ www.coastweek.com/tides.htm.
Visa extensions Immigration office in the District Commissioner's (DC's) offices on the waterfront.

Around the island

The one place everyone goes on Lamu is, of course, the **beach**, on the oceanfront, past Shela village, and it more than repays the slight effort of getting there (see map, p.477). The walk is enlivened by the village of **Shela**, on the headland 3km south of Lamu town at the mouth of the creek. It's also possible to catch a **boat** from Lamu to Shela for Ksh150 per person, sailing or motoring in a local boat with others (30–40min), or around Ksh600 if you charter a faster boat working as a water taxi (10mins).

Fewer people see the **interior** of Lamu island itself, which is a pity, as it's a pretty, if rather inhospitable, reminder of how remarkable it is that a town exists here at all. Much of it is patched into *shambas* with the herds of cattle, coconut palms, mango and citrus trees that still provide the bulk of Lamu's wealth. The two villages you might head for here are **Matondoni**, on the north shore of the island, by the creek, and **Kipungani**, on the western side.

Shela

SHELA was once a thriving, self-contained community: Shela's people trace their ancestry back to Manda island and speak a dialect of Swahili quite distinct from that of Lamu town. After the demise of slavery, however, and the coming of the Europeans, it was in limbo for decades; then, post-Independence, it found itself midway between rural decline and upmarket tourist boom. Since the turn of the century that balance has definitively altered: the tourists have won. Most of the fine old houses have been bought by foreigners and converted into ravishing holiday homes, decked in bougainvillea. But there's a surge in new building, too, sending multi-floored hotels up above the palms. In global terms, the boom is still small-scale, but intense enough to have already overshadowed Shela's only historical sight; the strange and much-photographed **Friday Mosque**, built in 1829, which stands out for its unusual, rocket-shaped minaret and once stood out high above every other building. Not any more. If you're suitably dressed, you can ask to visit and may even be able to go to the top.

Accommodation

While Shela can be a hedonistic place to pass a few days, it doesn't offer the thrill of staying among the mosques and street life of Lamu town itself. In addition, the price of **rooms** here can be up to twice what they would be in town, and there are few **restaurants** aside from those in the hotels. In addition to hotels and guesthouse rooms, though, there are now more than twenty self-catering **houses** to rent, with prices start at around $200/night. For more information, contact Lamu Retreats (☏020/600482, ⓦ www.lamuretreats.com) or Lamu Homes & Safaris (☏020/4446384, ⓦ www.lamuhomes.com).

Shella Bahari Guest House on the waterfront 100m north of *Peponi* ☏042/4632046, ⓦ www.shellabahari.co.ke. You pay a premium for the location here, right next to the water. The five rooms, all s/c and different rates, are simple but nicely done and there's an excellent restaurant downstairs. BB ❸

Jannataan in the centre of Shela ☏0711/972590 or 0722/729219. Big, new place with a good, deep pool, though unshaded. However, it's essentially just a modern hotel, even with the fake *zidaka*-style ceilings. Seventeen rooms on five floors, so there are good views from the top – just no atmosphere. BB ❺

Island in the centre of Shela ⊤042/4633290 or 0712/670961. An older-style place, with spacious, attractively furnished rooms, all with nets on frames and instant showers, and a restful atmosphere. Rooms 16 and 17 are especially appealing – almost open-air, like sleeping on the roof but in privacy and comfort. The *Barracuda* rooftop restaurant is good and reasonably priced, but doesn't have an alcohol licence. Sometimes closes May to mid-June. BB ❹

🏃 **Kijani House** on the waterfront north of Shela ⊤042/4633235 or 0725/545264, ⓦwww .kijani-lamu.com. Comfortable and pretty, environ-mentally conscious, Swiss-owned hotel, with eleven beautifully done rooms (with solar-heated showers, fans, frame nets and safes) around tropical gardens, and their own fruit farm close by. There are also two small pools, a restaurant serving Italian-style set menus, and a bar with a nice range of Italian and South African wines. Closed May & June. BB ❼

Peponi ⊤042/4633421 or 0734/203082, ⓦwww .peponi-lamu.com. Shela's main beachfront focus, where everyone stops in for a cold drink (or a good single malt), *Peponi* is fabulously situated, and offers superb food (some would say the best on Lamu). But if you're staying – and it's quite expensive for what you get – pay the extra for rooms in the main house, as the standard rooms in chalets across the lawn are not that special. Good pool. Closed May & June. BB ❼

🏃 **Pwani Guest House** overlooking *Peponi* ⊤042/4633540. Stylish, roomy house, co-owned with the *Shella Bahari*. The three doubles and two singles (all s/c) offer various options, but all are a good deal, by Shela standards, with their old furniture, antique stucco work and soft light. Breakfast and dinner are served on the rooftop terrace, which has beautiful sea views. BB ❹

Shella Rest House up past *Island Hotel*, turn first right and then left ⊤042/4633091 or 0734/771372. Co-owned with the much pricier *Shella Royal House*, this old place has nine, rather uncared-for, non-s/c rooms, all very different, including a funny one on a converted balcony with only curtains for privacy (and security). Even without haggling, these are the cheapest rooms in Shela. ❸

Shella Royal House ⊤042/4633091 or 0722/698059, ⓦwww.shellaroyalhouse.com. A bright and breezy place, with yellow floors and stairs. The rooms, all with mahogany four-posters, are of varying standards. There's a great swing bed on the roof terrace, perfect for lounging, with a 360-degree view, and a fabulous "honeymoon room" on the top floor. BB ❻

Shela White House at the top of the alley leading past *Pwani Guest House* ⊤042/4633091 or 0711/972590. Three s/c rooms in a stand-alone, three-storey house, of which two are sea-facing and s/c. They can cook food to order, or you can use the kitchen. Roof terrace. BB ❻

Stopover on the waterfront, south of *Kijani House* ⊤042/4633370 or 0738/710514, ⓦwww .stopoverrestaurant.com. Five simple, but nicely done, s/c rooms directly on the seafront near the dhow harbour, all opening out onto balconies with sea views. There's a ground-floor restaurant overlooking the sea, serving great fish curries. The three first-floor rooms can be rented out as a self-catering apartment with kitchen facilities. BB ❻

Shela beach

A usually deserted twelve-kilometre sickle of white sand, backed by empty **sand dunes**, Lamu's **beach** is the real thing; you half-expect Robinson Crusoe to come striding out of the heat haze. Unprotected by a reef, the sea here has some motion to it, and it is one of the few places on the coast where, at certain times of the year, you can body-surf (August is probably best). Unfortunately, women may find that wanderers along the beach can be a nuisance, muggings are not unheard of, and there were two rapes a few years ago, so stay within shouting distance of other sunbathers and preferably go to the beach in company.

All that said, the **sun** is a more likely assailant. There's absolutely no cover and you'll often find that the wind is too strong for erecting a sunshade. Ordinary sunscreen cream is available in town. Coconut oil, also sold in town, is used by some people to avoid drying out, but you need a deep tan to begin with, otherwise your skin fries.

Matondoni and Kipungani

MATONDONI is the most talked-about destination on Lamu apart from Shela and the beach, but in truth, it's not wildly exciting and its fame as the district's principal dhow-building centre seems misplaced. However, the walk there is a fine one if you start early (the soft sand track isn't fun in blazing sunshine). A sane, enjoyable alternative is to go by **donkey**: fix up a beast through your guesthouse reception, or you can take one of the sand dhows on its trip from Lamu jetty to Matondoni, get some lunch and walk back, following the telephone wires.

If you really want to look around the whole island, proceed from Matondoni to **KIPUNGANI**, one hour's walk from the end of the beach (4hr from Shela village). This is the halfway mark on the round-the-island walk; the whole trip takes eight or nine hours at least. It is useful to know the state of the tides for the stretch from Matondoni to Kipungani, as you can take a direct route through the mangroves at low tide (but don't get caught out). Kipungani has an upmarket **hotel**, 1500m before the village, in the shape of *Kipungani Explorer* (ⓦwww.heritage-eastafrica.com; closed Easter–June; FB $525–590), a delightful "desert island" complex of fourteen simple mat-and-*makuti* thatch *bandas* up on the beach, with a bar and restaurant decorated with driftwood and the products of beachcombings. The food is superb, the views over the sands and channel are exceptional, and the welcome, service and sense of blissful isolation are everything you could ask for. Excursions, windsurfing and snorkelling trips are all on offer, and there's a pool, too. If you don't want to walk or ride, you can get there direct from Lamu town by speedboat (30min), or more slowly by dhow.

On the southwest tip of the island lies 🍴 *Kizingo* (ⓣ0733/954770 or 0722/901544, ⓦwww.kizingo.com; closed May & June; FB ❽), a secluded eco-lodge, created in partnership with nearby Kipungani village. There are six thatched *bandas* nestled among the sand dunes, each with perfect sea views, and the food served up at the restaurant is wonderfully fresh. From November to April you can swim with wild bottlenose dolphins and between November and June turtles lay eggs on the beach; the owners will take guests to watch the newborn turtles make their way into the ocean. If you want to rent a house in this remote part of Lamu, there are now several lavish, new beachfront properties on a 24-acre private stretch between *Kizingo* and *Kipungani Explorer*. Check out ⓦkizingonibeach.com for more details.

Manda Island

Practically within shouting distance of Lamu town, **Manda** – with next to no fresh water – is almost uninhabited and, apart from being the site of the main airstrip on the islands, and the location of the old ruined town of **Takwa** (favourite destination of the dhow-trip operators) is not much visited either. Significant archeologically for the ruins of Takwa and Manda, the north side of the island is also the location of the fabulous *Manda Bay Lodge* (ⓣ0722/203329 or 0722/203109, ⓦwww.mandabay.com; package $1210). This exclusive beach camp of palm mat, wood and *makuti* bandas in an extravagantly beautiful setting is a perfect honeymoon retreat. When you're not participating in every conceivable water sport, or taking a sundowner trip on the lodge's own enormous dhow, you can swing in your hammock and be entertained by a huge variety of birds (there are bird baths outside every *banda*).

You can also walk from the lodge to the nearby **Manda ruins**, just fifteen minutes away. The population of this town is estimated to have been around three thousand. It's a fascinating, barely excavated site, with baobabs poking through the old walls. The remnants include the *mihrab*, and most of the walls, of a sizeable mosque. Watch out for **snakes** – the island has a diverse variety.

Much more affordable is the delightful 🍴 *Diamond Beach Village* (ⓣ0720/915001, ⓦwww.diamondbeachvillage.com; closed 15 April–30 June; BB ❺) on the southern arm of Manda, facing Shela. Simple self-contained bandas (and a rather wacky treehouse in a baobab), sound environmental principles, and a superb beachfront location add up to a very fine place to stay. They have evening electricity and pride themselves on great food.

The island is criss-crossed with paths through the jungle, should you be taken by the urge to spend a day there. Using a local boat, the price to Manda beach from Lamu jetty is Ksh150. Rumours have been flying around the archipelago that an American naval facility, a new seaport for northeast Kenya, or a gas terminal for the finds around Garissa, is going to be built on Manda. It looks increasingly like it will eventually be all three, though perhaps not until the strife in Somalia has been resolved. The hoteliers and farmers were given notice to leave a few years back and the dredgers started clearing the channels. For the moment, though, it's all quietened down again.

Takwa ruins

Whether you make a flying visit to **Takwa** (daily 8am–6pm; Ksh500), a thirty-minute boat ride from Lamu, or sleep out on the beach behind it, the site is well worth seeing. A flourishing town in the sixteenth and seventeenth centuries, it was deserted (as usual, no one knows why), and is in many respects reminiscent of Gedi (see p.455). As at other sites, toilets and bathrooms figure prominently in the architecture. In Islam, cleanliness is so close to godliness as to almost signify it – the Takwans must have been a devout community. The doors of all the houses face north towards Mecca, as does the main street with the **mosque** at the end of it. The mosque is interesting for the pillar at one end, which suggests it was built on a tomb site (that of a founder of the town perhaps), and for the simple lines of its *mihrab*, so different from the ornate curlicues of later designs. Another impressive **pillar tomb** stands alone, just outside the town walls, its date translating to about 1683, and it still occasionally attracts pilgrims from Shela (some of whom claim their ancestry lies in Takwa), who come here to pray for rain.

Takwa has been thoroughly cleared but, in order to preserve it for the future, hardly excavated at all. What has been found, however, suggests an industrious and healthy community, living in an easily defensible position with a wall all around the town, the ocean on one side behind the dunes, and mangroves on the other. Despite this, they appear to have left in a panic and, as usual, there's ample room for conjecture about why. Part of the great appeal of Kenya's ruined towns lies in the open debate that still continues about who, precisely, their builders and citizens were, and why they so often left in such evident haste. And there's always the fascinating possibility that old Swahili manuscripts will turn up to explain it all.

There's a simple dormitory-style *banda* available at the ruins, where you can **stay** for Ksh2000 for the whole place. Facilities are minimal (take food and water), but the setting is magnificent.

Pate Island

Only two hours by ferry from Lamu, totally unaffected by tourism and rarely visited, **Pate island** has some of the most impressive ruins anywhere on the coast and a clutch of old Swahili settlements which, at different times, have been as important as Lamu or more so. There are few places on the coast as memorable.

Pate is mostly low-lying and almost surrounded by mangrove swamps; no two maps of it ever agree (ours on p.477 shows only the permanent dry land, not the ever-changing mangrove forests that surround it in the shallow sea), so getting on and off the island requires deft awareness of the tides. Its remoteness, coupled with a lack of information and no transport on the island, deters travellers. In truth, though, Pate is not a difficult destination, and is an easier island to walk around than Lamu, with none of that island's exhausting soft sand.

Some history

According to its own **history**, the *Pate Chronicle*, Pate was founded in the early years of Islam with the arrival of Arabian immigrants. This mini-state is supposed to have lasted until the thirteenth century, when another group of dispossessed Arab rulers – the **Nabahani** – arrived. The story may have been embellished by time but archeological evidence does support the existence of a flourishing port on the present site of Pate as early as the ninth century. Probably by the fifteenth century the town exerted a considerable influence on most of the quasi-autonomous settlements along the coast, including Lamu.

The first **Portuguese** visitors were friendly, trading with the Pateans for the multicoloured silk cloth for which the town had become famous, and they also introduced gunpowder, which enabled wells to be easily excavated, a fact which must have played a part in Pate's rising fortunes. During the sixteenth century, a number of Portuguese merchants settled and married in the town, but as Portugal tightened its grip and imposed taxes, relations quickly deteriorated. There were repeated uprisings and reprisals until, by the middle of the seventeenth century, the Portuguese had withdrawn to the security of Fort Jesus in Mombasa. Even today, though, several families in Pate are said to be Wa-reno (from the Portuguese *reino*, "kingdom"), meaning of Portuguese descent.

During the late seventeenth and eighteenth centuries, having thrown out the old rulers and avoided domination by new invaders like the Omani Arabs, Pate underwent a **cultural rebirth** and experienced a flood of creative activity similar to Lamu's. The two towns had a lively relationship, and were frequently in a state of war. At some time during the Portuguese period, Pate's harbour had started to silt up and the town began to use Lamu's, which must have caused great difficulties. In addition, Pate was ruled by a Nabahani king who considered Lamu part of his realm. The disastrous Battle of Shela of 1812 (see p.478) marked the end of Lamu's political allegiance to Pate and the end of Pate as a city-state.

Practicalities

A *mtaboti* **water taxi**, one of three plying the route, leaves every day except Friday for Pate island's main dock at **Mtangawanda** (a quiet spot on the island's southwest tip), which takes two to three hours, then **Faza** (another hour) and finally **Kisingitini** (another half hour). The boats usually leave from the municipal jetty in Lamu about an hour before high tide. Since the dredging of the **Mkanda channel**, between Manda and the mainland, they can reach Mtangawanda at any state of the tide, but getting close enough to Faza and Kisingitini still requires careful timing. Pate town lies in the southeast corner of the island at the head of a creek so shallow that it's difficult to get up there even in a flat-bottomed boat at high tide.

Rather than taking the *mtaboti* water taxi, you could choose to take a dhow to Pate. Alternatively, if you have less time but can afford to spend a lot more, you might look into taking a speedboat (see "Listings", p.490) which would enable you to reach Pate town direct, at high tide, in less than half an hour. But timing is critical, only small boats can make it at all, and you have to wait until the next high tide to get out of Pate creek again – unless the speedboat captain goes round to Mtangawanda or Siyu, leaving you to walk.

The obvious plan, having walked from Mtangawanda dock to Pate town (allow at least an hour), is then to walk through **Siyu** to Faza, returning to Lamu by ferry from there. The walk from Pate town to Faza can be done in a day if the tides force an early start, but you may well find yourself wanting to stay longer and breaking for at least a night in Siyu.

Accommodation is rarely a problem (normally, you'll be invited to stay by someone almost as soon as you arrive in a village), but as there are no proper lodgings, an insect-proof **tent** is a useful back-up. If you plan on spending several days on Pate, and especially if you're interested in the archeology of the region, you should ask at Lamu Museum and Lamu Fort for **advice**.

It's wise to take **water** with you (five litres if possible) as Pate's supplies are unpredictable and often very briny. Most islanders live on home-produced **food** and staples brought from Lamu and, although there are a few small shops on the island, it's a good idea to have some emergency provisions (which also make useful gifts if required). **Mosquitoes** and flies are a serious menace on Pate, especially during the long rains. The shops sell mosquito coils but it's also worth carrying some repellent for use during the day.

Pate town

From the dock at Mtangawanda there's more than one route to Pate town. The old path, a narrow **footpath** through thick bush, the *ndia ya Pate*, or "path to Pate", is the one old people will show you, and, once on the trail it's easy to follow. You cross a broad, tidal "desert", pockmarked with fiddler crab holes, then climb a slight rise to drop through thicker bush, and arrive after an hour on the edge of town. However, since the dredging of the Mkanda channel, Patean labourers have been working at enlarging the dock at Mtangawanda and a tractor and trailer, carrying a barrel of fresh water for concrete-mixing, follows a new **motorable road** back and forth throughout the day, and will usually give you a lift.

Despite its small size, **PATE** could hardly be described as a village. Yet, reduced to the status of sub-location, its only link with government an assistant chief, its sole provision a primary school, the town is today a mere shadow of its former self. But at least its inhabitants are said to remain the richest on the island, thanks to their cash crop, **tobacco**, possibly introduced by the Portuguese and certainly grown here longer than anywhere else on the coast.

After Lamu, Pate comes as a series of surprises. There's no electricity, no alcohol and, apart from the tractor and a few motorbikes, no vehicles. The town plan is pretty much the same – a maze of narrow streets and high-walled houses – but here the streets are made of earth, and the houses are built of coral and dried mud, unplastered and somehow forbidding. The overall layout is confusing, with little slope, as in Lamu, to help your orientation. Pateans do, in fact, refer to the "upper" and "lower" parts of town – Kitokwe and Mitaaguu respectively. The lower part is down near the town dock, which is only briefly underwater at high tide. If you arrive from Mtangawanda in the "upper" part of town – reputedly poorer and less friendly – you're likely to be struck immediately by the *Wapate* – the **people**, and notably the women. Brilliant, determined ladies, with short, bushy hair and rows of gold earrings, stare out directly, unhidden by *buibuis*. If you speak any Swahili, you're likely to find the dialect here unrecognizable. *Wazungu* are rare and, after Lamu's characteristic studied repose (well, beach boys aside), Pate is arrestingly upfront in its dealings with foreigners.

The Nabahani ruins

More layers are peeled off Pate's enigmatic exterior when you start to explore the ruins of the **Nabahani** town just outside the modern one. The walls, roofless buildings, tombs, mosques and unidentifiable structures, stretched across several acres, are fascinating, the more so perhaps because this isn't an "archeological site" in the commonly expected mould. Farmers cultivate tobacco and other crops in the stony fields between the walls.

Boys will guide you around the ruins for a small payment, but don't expect anyone to take you at night; although it's very beautiful in a full moon, you'll have to go alone because the locals are afraid of the *djinn* and ghosts living there. Most impressive are the **Mosque with Two Mihrabs**, a nearby house that still has a facing of beautiful *zidaka* (niches) on one wall, and the remains of a sizeable mansion. This last building, you'll be told, is a **Portuguese house**. Certainly, the worn-down stumps of bottle glass projecting from the top of one of its walls do lend it a curiously European flavour, and in the plaster on another wall are scratched two very obvious galleons. Its ceiling slots are square for timbers rather than round for *boriti*, as elsewhere in the ruins.

Shards of pottery and household objects lie in the rubble everywhere, but many of the interiors of the buildings are so clogged with tangled roots and vegetation that getting in is almost impossible. It is worth persevering, however: the sense of personal discovery is exciting.

Many of the walls and buildings have already been demolished to obtain lime for tobacco cultivation. Without weighty financial backing, it's hard to see how the National Museums of Kenya could preserve the remains of old Pate as well as compensate the farmers. Gradually, tragically, it is all returning to the soil.

Siyu

The walk from Pate to Siyu is a slightly tricky eight kilometres. Having set off in the correct direction, you will find the first half-hour fairly straightforward; if in doubt, bear right. You come to a crossroads (easily missed unless you look backwards) and turn right. This narrow red dirt path soon broadens into a track known as the *barabara ya gari* (the "motor highway" – there was once a car there); it takes you to a normally dry tidal inlet where you veer left a little before continuing straight on through thick bush for another hour to reach Siyu. Wherever the bush on either side is high enough you may come across gigantic spiders' webs strung across the path. The spiders are brightly coloured, non-hairy, and merely waiting for insects, but they are nevertheless intimidating. Fortunately, they have the sense to build their webs high up and well out of the way.

Siyu is even less well documented than Pate. Still less accessible by sea, the town was a flourishing and unsuspected centre of Islamic scholarship from the |seventeenth to the nineteenth century and apparently something of a **sanctuary** for Muslim intellectuals and craftsmen. While Lamu, Pate and other trading towns were engaged in political rivalry and physical skirmishing, Siyu never had its heart in commerce or maritime activities, and never attracted much Portuguese attention. Instead, there was enormous devotion to **Koran-copying**, **book-making**, **text illumination**, and cottage industries like the **woodcarving** and **leatherwork** for which it's still famous locally. Siyu **sandals** are said to be absolutely the best (though plastic flip-flops have forced almost all the makers out of business), and Siyu **carved doors** are among the most beautiful of all Swahili doors, with distinctive guilloche patterns and inlays of ground shell.

The sources of wealth and stability for Siyu's flowering are a little mysterious, but the town's agricultural base obviously supported it well and it was probably the largest settlement on the island in the early nineteenth century, with up to thirty thousand inhabitants. In 1873, the British vice-consul in Zanzibar could still describe Siyu as "the pulse of the whole district".

These days you wouldn't know it. Less than four thousand people live here, and signs of the old brilliance are hard to find. Siyu lost its independence and presumably much of its artistic flair when the Sultan of Zanzibar's Omani troops first occupied the fort in 1847 – though it was twenty years before the Omanis were able to hold it for more than a brief spell.

The Town

Built in the early nineteenth century (no one knows for sure by whom), **Siyu Fort** is the town's most striking building and indeed, in purely monumental terms, the most imposing building anywhere in the Lamu archipelago. Substantially renovated, it is one of the few surviving traces of the glory days. It's freely accessible, though watch out for dangers like the well and the unstable walls. Around the outskirts of Siyu on the south side are a number of quite impressive **tombs**. The big domed tomb with porcelain niches dates from 1853.

Most of Siyu's houses today conform to the "open-box" plan typical of the Kenyan coast: yellowish mud with a ridged *makuti* roof, open at each end. These houses stand, each on its own, with no real streets to connect them so, that although it's larger than Pate, Siyu feels far more like a village. The cultural isolation of these communities from each other, a separateness which continues to this day, is easily appreciated after arriving in Siyu from Pate. There are still few *buibuis* here, but there's much less jewellery in evidence and the atmosphere is altogether less severe.

Shanga ruins

You'll need the help of a good guide if you hope to visit the ruins of **SHANGA**, a large Swahili town at least 1000 years old, which would be almost impossible to find unaided. Expect to pay around Ksh1000 for a guide. Shanga is on the south coast of the island, about an hour's walk from Siyu. You literally have to hack your way through the undergrowth when you arrive at the ruins. The most impressive sight is the white pillar tomb, eminently phallic, which you come to first. The very large Friday mosque nearby and a second mosque nearer the sea are only the most obvious of innumerable other remains in every direction.

Excavations at Shanga have revealed a walled site of five hectares with five access gates and a cemetery outside the walls containing 340 stone tombs. There was even a sea wall. Inside the town, 130 houses were surveyed, together with what looks to have been a palace similar in some respects to the one at Gedi. Shanga is believed to have been occupied from the ninth to the fourteenth centuries and, in a pattern that may sound familiar, no very convincing reasons have been found for its abandonment, nor for why it was never mentioned by travellers and traders of the time.

A limited amount of work has been done to restore some of the plaster in a set of *zidaka* wall niches and on the fluted pillar tomb, but on the whole the excavations only seem to have encouraged the jungle. Getting from one ruin to the next isn't easy. Dangerously camouflaged **wells**, and **snakes**, both of which are common, enliven the Shanga experience. If you walk on down to the sea – and assuming you have a certain capacity for hardship in paradise – there's a beautiful **beach** and some ideal camping spots. Perhaps needless to say, you would need to be completely self-reliant, and preferably in a group.

Faza

From **Siyu to Faza** the walk is shorter than from Pate to Siyu and more interesting, through waist-high grass, fertile *shambas* and sections of bush. It takes about two hours, but you'll need guidance, at least as far as the airstrip which was inherited from a 1980s oil-prospecting venture. From there it's straightforward. An hour or so out of Siyu, you reach the first *shambas*.

Faza itself is almost an island, surrounded by tidal flats and mangroves. A secondary school, health centre, police station (with nothing to do) and even a post office have made Faza the most important settlement on Pate island. There's even a Land Rover ambulance donated by Saudi Arabia. Fishing is the commonest occupation, with much of the catch going to a cold room at Kisingitini, from where it's shipped to Mombasa.

As a contemporary Kenyan rural centre, Faza makes an interesting place to walk around and you're almost certain to have plenty of time to fill before the boat leaves. A fine evening stroll takes you across the mud on the concrete causeway to the thickets on the "mainland", where the island's expanding secondary school is located. The other villages on the island, all fairly modern and bunched together, lie within a forty-minute walk of Faza: **Kisingitini**, **Bajumwali**, **Tundwa**, and the closest, **Nyambogi**.

Faza's ruins

Archeologically, **Faza** has less to offer than its neighbours. It was one of the most defiant Swahili towns over any attempts to usurp its independence, and was razed by the Pate army after a dispute over water rights in the fifteenth century, and again by the Portuguese in 1586 after collaborating with the Turkish fleet of Amir Ali Bey. On this occasion, the entire population was massacred and the head of Faza's king was taken to Goa in a barrel of salt to be paraded triumphantly in the streets. Faza's unfortunate history may partly account for its relative lack of ruins, but one success is commemorated in the **tomb** of Seyyid Hamed bin Ahmed al-Busaidy, commander-in-chief of the Sultan of Zanzibar's forces, who met his death in 1844 under a hail of arrows. His grave or *kaburi*, with a long epitaph, lies just outside the town.

There are several ruined mosques around Faza, including the very crumbled **Kunjanja** mosque. The ruins of the eighteenth-century **Mbwarashally**, or **Shala Fatani** mosque, merit a visit, however. Now theoretically protected by the National Museums of Kenya, most of the mosque is a pile of rubble. Its *mihrab*, however, turns out to incorporate exquisite and unusual heart motifs, including the Islamic creed, or *shahada*, inscribed within an inverted heart shape.

Kiwaiyu

From Faza you're within striking distance of the desert island retreat of **Kiwaiyu** (also spelt Kiwayu), about an hour by *mtaboti*, if you can find one. A group **dhow charter** in Lamu is probably more realistic: you can charter a small dhow for four or five days for Ksh5000 to Ksh8000 a day. That should include breakfast and dinner for a small group, snorkelling and fishing gear, and plenty of fresh water. You can expect to spend at least 24 hours on the journey in each direction, depending on wind, tides and the skill of the crew. The experience of sailing, the nights under the stars, and the company of the Swahili crew are altogether highly recommended. Kiwaiyu also has Airkenya **flights** from Nairobi and Safarilink flights from Nairobi via Lamu.

The island is a long strip of sand dunes, held in place with low scrub and the odd tree and fronted on the ocean side by a superb beach. The village of **Kiwaiyu**, near the southern end of the island, has limited provisions at a couple of shops. Twenty-minutes' walk to the south, you reach a private fishing lodge on the high southern tip of the island. From here, the empty, ocean-facing beach, with the reef close offshore, is just a scramble down the sandy hillside. There are one or two first-class **snorkelling** spots off this southern tip of the island, with huge coral heads and a multitude of fish. Ask for precise directions as it's possible to spend hours looking and still miss them.

Luxury lodges

There are two **luxury lodges** at Kiwaiyu. ⚓ *Mike's Camp* (☎0733/963813 or 0733/583627; Ⓦwww.mikescampkiwayu.com; closed May & June; FB $580), about 2km north of Kiwaiyu village, is a group of seven spacious, comfortably furnished *bandas* of palm mats and wood, planted on the crest of the island to catch the breeze. The camp, run by the completely laid-back and affable Mike Kennedy, is only accessible up the inside channel between Kiwaiyu and the mainland at high tide. Their little shop sells articles made by local people from recycled odds and ends, and they also have possibly the coldest beers in Kenya and brand-new diving equipment: there's fantastic coral right off the beach down on the ocean side. Rather wonderfully, *Mike's* is run entirely on wind power.

Much more luxurious and slightly bigger – more of a hotel in feel, perhaps – but absolutely stunning as a place to stay, is ⚓ *Kiwayu Safari Village* (☎0735/598858, Ⓦwww.kiwayu.com; closed 1 May–23 July; package $1330) nestled on a pristine, palm-shaded beach across the channel from the northern end of Kiwaiyu, on a spectacular, deep bay, within the Kiunga Marine National Marine Reserve. The combination of extremely spacious, palm- and grass-thatch cottages (the fans are inside the enormous nets), snorkelling and watersports, and superb food (dinner is served right on the beach most evenings) makes for an extraordinary place to get away from it all.

Travel details

Trains

Mombasa to/from: Nairobi (3 weekly; 14hr).

Buses

Mombasa to/from: Busia (2 daily; 15hr); Dar es Salaam (3 daily; 14–16hr), via Tanga (7hr); Garissa (2 daily; 8–10hr); Kisumu (5 daily; 14hr); Lamu via Kilifi and Malindi (6 daily; 7–8hr); Malaba (1 daily; 15hr); Malindi via Kilifi (approximately hourly; 1hr 30min); Nairobi (frequent, but especially around 7am and 7pm; 7–9hr).

Matatus

Likoni to/from: Diani Beach (occasional; 45min); Kwale (40min); Lungalunga (2hr); Msambweni (1hr); Shimoni (1hr 30min); Ukunda (30min).
Mombasa to/from: Bamburi (15min); Kaloleni (1hr 30min); Mazeras (30min); Malindi (1hr 30min); Mtwapa (30min)

Flights

Kiwaiyu to/from: Lamu (1–2 daily; 30min); Nairobi Wilson (1–2 daily; Airkenya and Safarilink; 2hr).
Lamu to/from: Malindi (Kenya Airways and Mombasa Air Safari; 1–2 daily; 30min); Nairobi (1–2 daily; Airkenya, Fly540, Safarilink; 1hr 30min).
Malindi to/from: Nairobi JKIA (Kenya Airways; 2 daily; 1hr 15min); Nairobi Wilson (Airkenya; 3–6 weekly; 1hr 30min).
Mombasa to/from: Nairobi (Kenya Airways 6–7 daily; 1hr); Ukunda-Daini Beach (Mombasa air safari; daily; 10min).
Ukunda (Diani Beach) to/from: Amboseli, Maasai Mara, Nairobi, Tsavo West. Safarilink and Mombasa Air Safari (daily in season).

7

The North

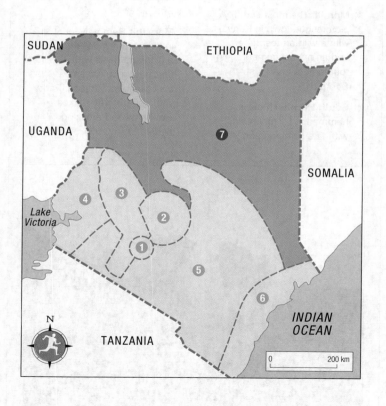

CHAPTER 7 # Highlights

* **Central Island National Park** Totally untouched volcanic sanctuary in the middle of Lake Turkana, where Nile crocodiles breed. A memorable boat trip from the lake's western shore. **See p.511**

* **Maralal** The most scruffily picturesque town in Kenya, with a wild atmosphere and an annual camel-racing tournament in August. **See p.514**

* **South Horr** Lush oasis hemmed in by mountains, with fine camping and great opportunities to meet Samburu people. **See p.521**

* **Loiyangalani** End-of-the-world kind of place on the eastern shore of shimmering Lake Turkana, home of the fishing and croc- and hippo-hunting Elmolo people. **See p.523**

* **Marsabit** Remotely located in the northern deserts, a highland oasis with a fascinating cultural mix. Visit Marsabit National Park with superb crater lakes, elephants and amazing birdlife. **See p.534**

▲ Samburu warrior leading baggage camels

The North

There is one half of Kenya about which the other half knows nothing and seems to care even less.

Negley Farson, *Last Chance in Africa*

You rarely think of deserts in Kenya, but **the north** – more than half the country – is an arid zone, cinder-dry for more than ten months of the year. The old "Northern Frontier District" remains one of the most exciting and adventurous parts of Africa: a vast tract of territory, criss-crossed by ancient migration routes, and still tramped by nomadic Samburu, Boran, Rendille, Gabbra, Turkana and Somali herders. Unfortunately, it also has a dangerous reputation, with livestock-rustling and tribal feuding widespread. Banditry, and the spillover from Somalia's civil conflict, makes it too risky to visit the whole area east of the Isiolo–Marsabit–Moyale road (see the box on p.529 for further advice and precautions). By contrast, the huge area of northwest Kenya, if not exactly trouble-free, is certainly not too risky to visit, and incidents involving tourists are virtually unknown.

The target for most travellers is the wonderful jade splash of **Lake Turkana** – very remote and highly unpredictable in nature (when British sailors first ventured out on it, they reckoned it could turn "rougher than the North Sea"). To get there, you have two main options: going on an organized camping safari, or taking the matatus and lorries that ferry goods and people from the hub of highlands Kenya. Comparatively few visitors drive themselves, though it's becoming more popular with expat and Kenyan 4WD fans. NGOs, and most people on business, tend to fly to the north.

Because of the layout of the **roads** and **tracks** that radiate north from the Central Highlands, you'll need to make a decision about which "spokes" to cover. It's hard to get from east to west, or vice versa, without going back south, so don't be over-ambitious. Bus and matatu services are patchy at best, whilst lorries and hitching lifts can work out, but are exhausting. If you're driving, having enough water, fuel and mechanical know-how should be your priorities since you'll need to be almost self-sufficient. In practical terms, the current situation limits you to the two main routes up to Lake Turkana (one from Kitale, one from Maralal), the Mathews Range north of Samburu and, with caution, the route to Marsabit, which then doubles back to Turkana via North Horr.

Although the landscape is parched for most of the year, when the **rains** do come (usually around May) they can have dramatic effect, bringing torrents of water along the ravines and *luggas* (watercourses) and tearing away bridges and concrete fords with a violence that has to be seen to be believed. Flood waters often sweep over the plains to leave an ooze of mud and, within twenty-four

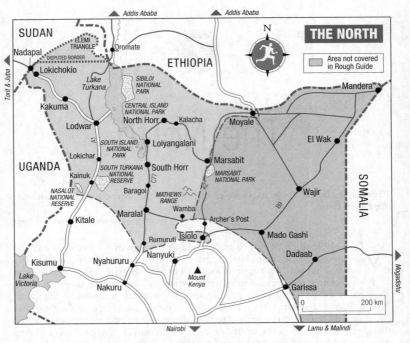

hours, new shoots. In these conditions, you can easily be stranded – even along the now notoriously broken-up paved road to Lodwar. However, if your plans are flexible, being up north during the rains is an exciting time to explore. Needless to say, driving any vehicle yourself in the rainy season, unless it's a sturdy 4WD, is not recommended.

Turkana

Straddling the Ethiopian border at its northern end, **Lake Turkana** stretches south for 250km, bisecting Kenya's rocky deserts like a turquoise sickle. It's hemmed in by sandy wastes and black-and-brown volcanic ranges, and the lake scene changes constantly. The water, a glassy, milky blue one minute, can become slate-grey and choppy or a glaring emerald green the next.

The lake was discovered for the rest of the world only in 1888 by the Hungarian explorer **Count Samuel Teleki de Szék** and his Austrian co-expeditionary **Ludwig von Höhnel**. They named it Lake Rudolf after their patron, the Crown Prince of Austria. Later, it became eulogized as the "Jade Sea" in travel writer John Hillaby's book about his camel trek. The name "Turkana" only came into being during the wholesale Kenyanization of place names in the 1970s. By then, it had also been dubbed the "Cradle of Mankind", the site of revelatory fossil discoveries in the field of **human evolution**. It was also becoming a great excuse for a week of rough travel in a safari lorry or a get-away-from-it-all weekend in one of the handful of lakeshore lodges. There are fewer lodges now than there were in 1980, and apart from those that remain, and one or two windy campsites, the tourist infrastructure is nil. And there's still only one paved road, from Kitale to Lodwar (in dire condition) and on to Lokichokio.

Ecology and climate

Lake Turkana is the biggest permanent desert lake in the world, with a shoreline longer than the whole of Kenya's sea coast. Yet 10,000 years ago its surface was 150m higher than today. It spread south as far as the now desolate Suguta Valley and fed the headwaters of the Nile. Today it has been reduced to a mere sliver of its former expanse. A gigantic natural sump, with rivers flowing in but no outlets, it loses a staggering three metres of water through **evaporation** from its surface each year (nearly a centimetre every day). As a result, the lake water is quite alkaline – although you can just about drink it, and it's not hostile to all aquatic life.

The prehistoric connection with the Nile accounts for the presence of enormous **Nile perch** (some weighing more than 100kg) and Africa's biggest population of **Nile crocodiles** – some 10,000 to 22,000 of them. Turkana is one of the few places where you can still see great stacks of crocs basking on sand banks. There is a profusion of **birdlife**, too, including European migrants seen most spectacularly on their way home between March and May. **Hippos**, widely hunted and starved from many of their former lakeshore haunts through lack of lake grazing, manage to hang on in fairly large numbers, though you won't see many unless you go out of your way.

Climatically, Turkana is extremely hot and dry for ten months of the year, and very humid during the rains. It is notorious for its strong easterly **winds** that puff and gust energetically most of the time and occasionally become demonic. The squalls whipped up by the wind are the cause of most accidental deaths of local people on the lake, rather than hippos or crocodiles.

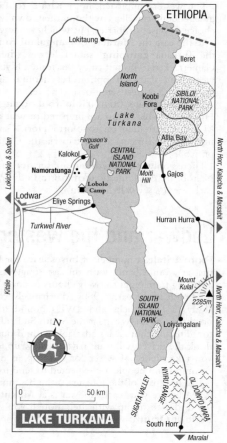

LAKE TURKANA

The **people** most likely to be encountered are **Turkana** (p.508) on the western and southern shores, as far round as Loiyangalani, **Samburu** (p.520) south of Loiyangalani, **Elmolo** (p.526) to the north of Loiyangalani, and **Gabbra** (p.534) further east. The Turkana and Samburu are pastoralists, who hold their cattle in great reverence; the Gabbra herd camels; while the Elmolo are traditionally property-less hunters and fishers.

Turkana's **water level** is subject to wild fluctuations. From the mid-1980s to 1997, the level receded steadily, leaving parts of the former shoreline more than 8km from the lake. But heavy El Niño rains in 1998 led to a six-metre rise in the lake level in less than a year. Fish stocks recovered and former fishing communities rediscovered their vocation. Since then, however, the level has fallen again, the lakeshore receding by as much as a kilometre in some places.

Getting there

There are **three road routes** to Turkana: one to the western shore that starts in Kitale, and two to the eastern shore from Maralal and Marsabit (the latter very remote). There is no route connecting the east and west shores, the volcanic **Suguta Valley** forming a blazing hot barrier.

The western approach, from **Kitale to Lodwar**, is the one used by most independent travellers without their own vehicles. For **transport**, there's a choice of buses or lorries, but whichever way you do it the road is diabolical.

To the east, the **Maralal–Loiyangalani route** is the one traditionally used by the Turkana **camping safari** lorries (the main operators these days are Gametrackers, who return by this route). If you can afford around $1000 for the week-long trip, this option has definite advantages, including magnificent scenery and a great sense of adventure.

The third route, from **Isiolo to Loiyangalani** via **Marsabit** and **North Horr**, is feasible if you are prepared to wait longer for lifts, first from Isiolo to Marsabit, and then on to North Horr. Gametrackers uses this route on its northbound Turkana Truck trip via the Chalbi Desert (route details are given on p.538).

There's only one **scheduled air service** to Turkana, Fly540's daily flight from Nairobi JKIA's domestic terminal to Lodwar, via Kitale. Fares are around $120 each way (Ⓦ www.fly540.com).

Lodwar and the western lakeshore

From Kitale, a number of **buses** leave for Lodwar in the early morning (the first at around 6am), with the last stragglers leaving just after midday, taking anything from eight to twelve hours to cover the 285km of what remains of the road built in the early 1980s. Alternatively, you might try **hitching** – there are always a few trucks and 4WDs bound for the aid centre at Lokichokio, northwest of Lodwar near the South Sudan border, and finding a vehicle is not too difficult, though it's advisable to find out the going rate in advance if you think the driver will want paying (allow up to Ksh1000 to Lodwar). Make sure you take plenty of water for this trip, as delays and breakdowns are all too common and people are expected to fend for themselves.

The best part of the journey is the beginning, covered in Chapter 4. The last ATM before you reach Lodwar is at **Makutano** (see p.296), where it is also a good idea to fill up with fuel, though you should be able to find that further north at **Ortum**.

After the Marich Pass, you come out of the Cherangani Hills and onto the plain, passing from Pokot into Turkana territory when you cross the Turkwel River just before **Kainuk** – an occasional flashpoint for inter-communal violence. The change of scenery is dramatic, but from the thorny wilderness of the **Turkana Plains** beyond, it's hard to extract much of scenic interest, although if you're travelling by bus or lorry, the regular stops to pick up increasingly wild-looking passengers maintain gently heightening expectations as you head north.

Nasalot and South Turkana National Reserves

At Kainuk, there is a possible detour to the **Nasalot National Reserve** ($15), which bounds the northern slopes of the mountains and the southern fringes of the south Turkana plains. From the gate, 6km off the Lodwar road (signposted on the left), the winding paved route drops several hundred metres into the heat, with plunging precipices and spectacular views all round, to the **Turkwel Gorge** and **hydroelectric dam**.

As the reserve is mostly covered with thick bush, **spotting animals** isn't all that easy: the elephants here, though larger than their southern cousins, hide themselves pretty well, and your best chance of seeing them is on the paved road at dawn or dusk. You'd be unusually fortunate to see any of the reserve's lions and leopards. Camping is not allowed, but there are some good value **bandas** by the dam.

Beyond Nasalot back on the main A1 Lodwar road, another detour to the right takes you to the **South Turkana National Reserve** ($15), which lacks Nasalot's scenic grandeur, but is where the elephants migrate to between March and July.

Lodwar

For most Kenyans, mention of **LODWAR** conjures up remote and outlandish images of the badlands, an aberrant place where anything could befall you. And the Turkana District capital is, to put it mildly, a wild town, and somewhat unformed and incongruous in this searing wilderness. During the 1980s it became Kenya's desert boomtown, the lake's fishing, the possibility of oil discoveries and the new road from Kitale all encouraging inward migration. While **Turkana people** have always predominated, **Luo** and **Luhya** also arrived in search of opportunities. With the exhaustion of farming country in the south, Lodwar and the area around it became increasingly attractive to pioneers and cowboys of all sorts. But this expansion has now fizzled out and Lodwar has returned to being a sleepy frontier town.

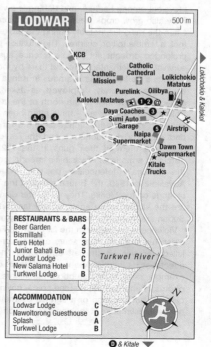

LODWAR

0 — 500 m

KCB
Catholic Mission
Catholic Cathedral
Loikichokio Matatus
Purelink
Oilibya
Kalokol Matatus
Daya Coaches
Sumi Auto Garage
Airstrip
Naipa Supermarket
Dawn Town Supermarket
Kitale Trucks

Lokichokio & Kalokol

Turkwel River

RESTAURANTS & BARS	
Beer Garden	4
Bismillahi	2
Euro Hotel	3
Junior Bahati Bar	5
Lodwar Lodge	C
New Salama Hotel	1
Turkwel Lodge	B

ACCOMMODATION	
Lodwar Lodge	C
Nawoitorong Guesthouse	D
Splash	A
Turkwel Lodge	B

D & Kitale

Until a few decades ago, the **Turkana**, the main people of the western shore of the lake, had very little contact with the outside world, or even with the Republic of Kenya. Turkana people did not traditionally wear much in the way of clothing, though the women wear several tiers of beads around their necks and, if married, a metal band too. Turkana men are rarely seen without their *akichalong*, a small wooden headrest, like a stool, which they recline on at any opportunity. Many still wear a wide bracelet on their wrists called an *aberait*, which is in fact a weapon. Although it's usually covered with a leather guard, the edge of the *aberait* is razor-sharp, and can be wielded in a fight like a slashing knife, while leaving the hands free.

Linguistically, the Turkana are related to the Maa-speaking Samburu and Maasai. Indeed, along the northwest shore of the lake, the people are probably an old mixture of Turkana and Samburu, although, like the Luo (also distantly related by language), the Turkana did not traditionally practise circumcision. They moved east from their old homeland around the present-day borders of Sudan and Uganda in the seventeenth century. The desolate region between the lake and the Ugandan border that they now occupy is barely habitable land, and their daily struggle for existence has profoundly influenced the shape of their society and, inevitably, helped create the funnel into modern Kenya that Lodwar, with its road, has become.

The Turkana are more individualistic than most Kenyan peoples and they show a disregard for the ties of clan and family that must have emerged through repeated famines and wars. Some anthropologists have suggested that loyalty to particular **cattle brands** is a more important indicator of identity than blood ties or lineage. Although essentially **pastoralists**, always on the move to the next spot of grazing, the Turkana, with characteristic pragmatism, have scorned the taboo against fish so prevalent among herders, and **fishing** is a viable option that is increasingly popular. They also grow crops when they can get seeds and when there's adequate rainfall. Often the rains fail, notably during the prolonged drought of the early 1980s, which took a terrible toll on children. The situation had eased up until 2007, when, again, a prolonged drought set in. Life is once again very much a matter of day-to-day survival, supplemented here and there by food aid.

Turkana **bellicosity** is infamous in Kenya (Turkana migrants to the towns of the south are frequently **employed** as *askaris*). Relations with their neighbours – especially the Merille to the north of the lake, the Samburu to the south, and the Pokot to the southwest – have often been openly aggressive. British forces were engaged in the gradual conquest of the Turkana – the usual killings, livestock raids and property destruction – and they succeeded, at some cost, in eventually disarming them of their guns in the 1920s. But the Merille, meanwhile, were obtaining arms from Abyssinia's imperial government, and they took advantage of the Turkana's defenceless position. When war was declared by Italian-held Abyssinia in 1940, the British rearmed the Turkana, who swiftly exacted a savage revenge on the Merille. They were later disarmed again. Now, it is the Turkana who are the victims once again: in the far north, heavily armed Toposa raiders from Sudan are thought to have killed as many as ten thousand Turkana in recent years.

Violence is no **longer** in the air down at **Ferguson's Gulf** – though you might see older Turkana men with scars on their arms and chests to indicate who they've killed: females on the left upper arm and chest, males on the right. Turkana directness is unmistakeable in all their dealings with *wazungu*. They are, for example, resolute and stubborn bargainers, while offers of relatively large sums for photos often leave them stone cold – not necessarily from any mystical fear of the camera, but because of a shrewd estimation of what the market will stand, and hence, presumably, of their own reputation.

Apart from just hanging around and taking in the scene, there's not a lot to do. If you have the time and energy, you can **hike** up one of the hills behind the town (the guides from *Nawoitorong Guesthouse* are best, see below). Lodwar's canopy of acacias makes it surprisingly invisible below, but the view stretches for miles. For **handicrafts**, you'll find good woven baskets on sale at the *Nawoitorong Guesthouse*. If you plan any walking, you might want to pick up a pair of **5000-mile shoes** (flip-flops, or thongs, made from old truck tyres), which are comfortable and virtually unbreakable, and can be found in the streets behind *New Salama Hotel*.

Practicalities

Lodwar is an incredibly hot, dusty town most of the year, but for a short stay you may find the rough, frontier atmosphere exhilarating. There's a KCB **bank** with an ATM, a **post office** and a number of places to stay. If you need to get **online**, Purelink, in the town centre, can handle that, but if you need real speed and reliability, you'll have to present yourself to the Catholic Mission on the north side of town (when their school computer lab is free, they charge Ksh2 per min for a decent connection). If your **vehicle** needs looking at after braving the road from Kitale, Sumi Auto Garage comes highly recommended, and is one of the few used by NGOs. Mt Elgon Tyre Repair are also trustworthy.

   Buses to Kitale gather in the main street around *New Salama Hotel*, and almost always leave in the evening, around 7 to 8pm, travelling by night. The one daily bus to Nairobi, run by Daya Coaches, leaves from its office next to the *Euro Hotel* (which is owned by the same proprietor). If you want to travel to Kitale by day, head down in the morning to the roundabout at the eastern end of the main street, where you can flag down a **lorry** heading south. Local lads may also offer to help you find a vehicle for a small tip. **Matatus** for Kalokol, and an occasional one to Kitale, leave from the main stage in the centre of town, near the buses, but vehicles for Lokichokio have their own stage on the east side of town, opposite the Oilibya filling station.

Accommodation

None of the following has hot water as such, and the supply is invariably tepid rather than cold, especially by evening time.

Lodwar Lodge ℡0721/339094. Formerly *Nature Lodge*, and owned by the MP for Turkana North, this place burned down, but has now risen phoenix-like, and revamped, with a restaurant, outdoor bar and *bandas*. ❷

   Nawoitorong Guesthouse 1km south over the Turkwel bridge, then 1.5km east ℡054/21208, ℮edfrhp@imul.com. Part of the Turkana Women's Conference Centre, a cooperative set up in 1984 by four women who began baking bread together, *Nawoitorong* is made of local materials, is partly solar-powered, and uses profits to help Turkana women's education. It still bakes its own bread, and serves, occasionally excellent, food. There are good showers, the non-s/c rooms in the main compound are spotless and have great mosquito nets, but lack privacy and can be noisy; the three s/c cottages (Ksh1400) are better but more expensive. By far the best place to stay in Lodwar but some way out of town. BB ❶

Splash Clean, friendly and relatively secure, with s/c rooms, with fans and nets, named for African countries and regions, rather than numbered. *Splash* can be a bit of party place as it's so popular and is consequently often noisy at night. Good breakfasts (Ksh100) and other food available (order in advance), and cold beer. Secure parking in a gated compound at the back. ❶

Turkwel Lodge ℡054/21099. The most present-able of the town-centre lodgings, clean s/c rooms with nets and ceiling fans, plus a good bar and restaurant out front. The rooms are reasonably quiet, and there's secure parking. ❷

Eating and drinking

For **food** supplies the two main supermarket/grocery stores, Naipa and Dawn Town, will fulfil most of your needs.

Beer Garden Lodwar's only disco, operating Fri & Sat nights, with a mix of Kenyan music and reggae.

Bismillahi Clean and cheap, with attentive service. *Nyama choma*, pilau, *mboga*, chapattis, and cold sodas.

Euro Hotel Opposite Oilibya, near the Loki stage. Open round the clock for tea, chapattis, *mandaazi* and all the usual staples.

Junior Bahati Bar Near the Loki stage. Has a pool table inside, and drinking *bandas* outside.

Lodwar Lodge Convivial outdoor bar.

New Salama Hotel By the main transport stage. Serves tasty meat and fish stews.

Turkwel Lodge Cooks up good, solid meals, usually chicken, and has outdoor seating for drinkers.

Kalokol

Though Ferguson's Gulf is the only easily accessible place to head for on the lakeshore, the village you want initially is called **KALOKOL**. Several matatus make the 60km trip every day from Lodwar. Kalokol has a surprising amount of hassle for such a small place, and only one basic **lodging**, *Kalokol Tours Lodge & Hotel* (℡0735/467251; ❶), which is cheap and run-down, with stuffy shacks for rooms and an erratic water supply. While **food** supplies have improved a little with the opening of a few *dukas*, it's not a bad idea to bring at least some fruit with you from Lodwar. The lodging should be able to rustle up a basic meal for you, or try the Somali-run *Loima Hotel*, but don't expect gourmet cuisine.

Kalokol's main appeal (and the reason for the hassle), is that it is especially good for buying **Turkana crafts**: wonderful (and far too big) baskets, rich-smelling, oiled head stools (*akichalong*), ostrich shell necklaces, and an array of snuff and tobacco horns made of cow horn (traditionally) or pieces of plastic piping. When you've had enough, take a matatus back to Lodwar, but don't leave it till too late in the afternoon. Otherwise, you can try your luck hitching – far from guaranteed, though occasionally trucks go all the way through to Kitale.

The dancing stones of Namoratunga

During the journey between Lodwar and Kalokol, look out for the **standing stones of Namoratunga**, 15km west of Kalokol some 50m off on the south side of the road. Although they're easy to miss, being only a small cluster of metre-high cylindrical stones, the Turkana have the habit of balancing small rocks on top of them, so you'll know them when you see them. Like a miniature Stonehenge, the pillars are a spiritual focus and the scene of a major annual gathering of Turkana clans, usually in December. The stones pre-date the arrival of the Turkana, but little is known about them, even by the people themselves (the name "namoratunga" is used by Turkana to describe any standing stone site). One theory is that the stones were aligned with the positions of important stars in Eastern Cushitic astronomy and were used to determine the dates of ritual ceremonies. Some people call them "dancing stones", following a legend that told of a tribe dancing on the site, who were turned to stone by the ridicule of a group of new arrivals, the Turkana. More plausible reasons for their existence might be the concentration of haematite and copper ore around the site, the smelting of which (for making weapons) has historically had ritual significance. Uphill from the stones you'll find several raised rock cairns covering ancient graves, some perfectly delineated with larger regular stones. It's fascinating site, and all rather mysterious.

Ferguson's Gulf

Kalokol is about 3km from the shallow waters of **Ferguson's Gulf**: just follow the river course as it drains east. *Lake Turkana Fishing Lodge*, or what remains of it, stands at the tip of the sand spit on the other side of the gulf. Depending on the water depth, you'll need to be either rowed or poled across, or you can wade or walk.

Hanging out by the lake here is fascinating, with the constantly mutating background of the western shore across the bay, as well as the closer prospect of Turkana fishermen, hundreds of species of birds, and the occasional glimpse of crocodile or hippo on the water surface. From a distance, the activity at the water's edge seems silent since the wind whips all sound away, lending the whole scene a slightly dream-like quality.

Down on the shore you can talk with the children who follow you every-where, and who often speak good English. If you make friends, you can be taken looking for snakes (be careful), to see *tembo* brewing (always by women) or, if you're lucky, to a dance. Teenagers' and children's dances happen several times a week, but they're best when there's a full moon: the boys tie cans of stones to their ankles and pretend to ignore the girls' flirting.

When you're tired of wandering around, being mobbed by toddlers, watching the fishermen paddling out on their waterlogged rafts, and the pied kingfishers hovering and plunging over the shallows, you might consider having a **swim**. The water is quite clear and always pleasantly warm, but you should be extremely wary of crocodiles. People may tell you it's safe, but going in is always a risk.

Central Island National Park

A trip to the five-square-kilometre **Central Island National Park** (Ⓦ www .kws.go.ke/central-island.html; $20) is highly recommended. This is one of two island national parks in the lake (the other is the less accessible South Island), which, together with Sibiloi National Park on the northeast shore of the lake, are a UNESCO World Heritage Site. Central Island is a unique triple volcano poking gauntly out of the water. The island covers just five square kilometres, most of which is taken up by two crater lakes (a third has dried up) hidden behind its rocky shores. One of the lakes is the only known habitat of an ancient species of tilapia, a reminder of the time when Lake Turkana was connected to the Nile. The island is the nesting ground for big colonies of water birds but, like some African Galapagos, it really belongs to the reptiles. Crocodiles breed here in the largest concentration in Africa, and at the right time of year (usually April and May) you can witness the newly hatched baby crocs breaking out of the nests and sprinting with loud squeaks down to the crater lake where they'll pass their first season. The vegetation is scant, but some of the sheltered lees are overgrown with thick grass and bushes for a short period each year, and the nests are dug beneath this foliage.

Boat trips are expensive: expect to pay Ksh7000 to 10,000 for the round trip in a motorboat, depending on your bargaining skills. The park warden or one of his rangers normally accompanies you on each visit. Do be sure, however, that the boat is thoroughly lake-worthy, equipped with life jackets, and that the crew know what they are doing. Vicious squalls can blow up fast and it's more than 9km to the island.

Eliye Springs

Eliye Springs, 66km south of Lodwar, used to be *the* place for travellers on the lakeshore and it still attracts the occasional overland truck and self-sufficient 4WD weekenders. Getting there and back is the main problem, as there's no public transport. You can **rent a vehicle** with a driver for the day, at around Ksh7000 (4WD advisable as the trail gets very sandy towards the end). Alternatively, it's possible to take the lakeshore **walk** from Ferguson's Gulf – hire a guide (Ksh3000), load up with water and follow the lake south for 45km. A night walk by moonlight is best, but watch out for crocodiles.

Eliye Springs readily compensates for the hassles of the journey – a paradisal place with rustling doum palms watered by hot springs, gorgeous views, and nothing to do except lounge about and swat flies. *Eliye Springs Bandas* (T0734/995719, Wwww.eliyespringsresort.com; camping Ksh500; ❶) is once again operating, with tents and *bandas*, showers and toilets, cold drinks and meals of chicken or fish, and even a swimming pool. About 25km south of Kalokol, on the shore, the high-end *Lobolo Camp* (T020-3541811, Ejadesea @africaonline.co.ke; FB ❽), in another lakeshore oasis, should reopen during the course of this edition.

Kakuma, Lokichokio and Southern Sudan

A good paved road allows fast travel from Lodwar up to Lokichokio, passing the huge refugee camp at **Kakuma**, 144km northwest of Lodwar. Set up for refugees fleeing the civil war in southern Sudan, this sprawl of huts and shacks follows the banks of the Tarach *lugga* for nearly 10km. It is now being used for the overspill of Somali refugees from Dadaab camp in eastern Kenya. Kakuma has food and basic lodgings (and usually fuel), but nothing to warrant a stopover.

The border town of **Lokichokio** (also spelled Lokichoggio and often just called Loki) is an unremittingly dry and rocky place, and even more of a cowboy town than Lodwar, with an eclectic mix of international fixers, tribal Turkana, haggard relief workers, businessmen, doctors, pilots, nurses and missionaries. During the civil war in southern Sudan, it was the main UN aid centre, and, although much scaled down since the 1990s, remains a major supply base for NGOs in Sudan, with a tarmac airstrip and bars for NGOs.

The **post office** is at the north end of town, off the Juba road and opposite immigration. There's a KCB bank with an **ATM** in the UN compound off the Lopiding road, and a forex bureau, together with the ALS airline offices, at *KATE Camp*.

The cheapest **lodgings** in Loki are mostly on the Juba road. Try the decent self-contained rooms at *Wananchi Hotel* (❷), on the way to the post office, next to Eureka Chemist. Not quite so clean and tidy are the rooms at *Makuti Guesthouse* (❷), opposite the *Sunbird* (T0735/199217; ❷), which has clean, decent-sized, non-self-contained rooms with nets and fans. If you want your meals included, try *Breeze Camp*, at the NPA compound on the Lopoding Road, which offers simple quarters with shared facilities and all meals for just Ksh2350 a day per person. For something with real comfort, however, you're looking at a fair bit more: *Afex Ensuite*, *Aircon Suite*, *748 Camp* (T0720/772335) or *KATE Camp* (T0723/502576) offer a selection of self-contained tents, hard accommodation units, or traditional *tukuls* (round huts) with three meals – and sometimes laundry – included, for around $50 to $70 per person per day.

If you want to get down to Nairobi quickly, then ALS's reliable flights will do the job (T0723 502 576; Mon, Wed, Fri, Sun; dep 4.15pm; 1hr 30min; from $175 one-way). They fly up to Rumbek in South Sudan on the same days (dep 10.15am; 1hr 30min; from $250). East African Safari Express also does the Loki–Nairobi run, three times a week ($190). They use a jet, so the journey is just one hour and you fly into Nairobi JKIA.

If you're planning to head overland to **Southern Sudan**, you can get a visa for $50 at the GoSS (Government of Southern Sudan) border post at **NadaPal**, where you'll also need to show your yellow fever certificate. Before leaving Kenya, you must first formally exit the country by getting stamped out at the immigration office in Loki: it's near the barracks on the Juba road just across the *lugga* on the north side of town (daily 6am–6.30pm). If you're entering Kenya here, you get a Kenyan visa.

Maralal, the Mathews and East Turkana

From Nairobi, the journey up to **Loiyangalani** en route to Turkana is a good deal shorter in distance than to the west shore, but even full tilt on the rough roads it's a long, two-day **drive**. The roads are incredibly rough for most of the way and to be sure of arriving you'll need 4WD and spare fuel. Even then, if you go during the rainy season, you could be held up for 24 hours or more at several points waiting for floodwaters to subside.

The obvious solution is to sign up with one of the few operators offering **Turkana camping safaris**. Most people thoroughly enjoy these trips, coming back loaded with amazing souvenirs and photographs, and stories of weird and wonderful encounters. One drawback is the brevity of the trips and the fact that they run to an itinerary. The best company, Gametrackers, uses converted trucks (or Land Cruisers for small groups). Its weekly round trips (departing Fridays) via the Chalbi Desert are unique and highly recommended.

If your budget is tight, but you have time and a flexible attitude and don't want a spoon-fed adventure, you'll get the maximum exposure to Turkana and the north from travelling completely independently and without your own vehicle. This may require patience: there's little **public transport**, and you may effectively have to hitch rides north of **Maralal**.

Routes to Maralal

The easiest route to Maralal, the **C77**, rolls up from Nyahururu via Rumuruti: tarmac to Rumuruti, and then poor-quality *murram* to Maralal (it's feasible without 4WD, but not if you value the health of your car). **Rumuruti** (onomatopoeic Maa for "mosquito") is hardly noticeable any more and merely marks the end of the paved road, but this former Maasai stronghold of western **Laikipia** (see p.182) was settled by British soldiers after World War I and many of their ranches still exist. However, there's some very good game country in the vicinity, so you might want to stay nearby. In Rumuruti itself, the *Jojas Hotel* and the *Laikipia Club* both have low-priced self-contained rooms (❶), while there are good, cheap eats at the *Buffalo Village Inn*. North and east of Rumuruti, several **ranch-stays** – including *Bobong Campsite*, *Sosian*, *Mutamaiyu*, *Loisaba*, *Sabuk* and *Ol Malo* – are reviewed in the Laikipia section of Chapter 2 (see p.183). At **Suguta Marmar** (the boundary between Central Province and the Rift Valley), 15km north of the Baringo junction, and 20km south of Kisima, there's little more than a livestock auction yard, and a basic checkpoint, plus a few cheap *hotelis*. **KISIMA** is a flyblown little place, but significant as a junction: on the south side of town, the road heading off to the east is the C78 – it's 86km to Wamba and 176km to Isiolo.

An alternative route to Maralal is the lonely but well-constructed *murram* road from **Lake Baringo**, which in its earlier stages has breathtaking views back over the lake and some fascinating Pokot villages on the way.

The third route to Maralal is the maddeningly corrugated **A2** from **Isiolo** past Archer's Post (p.533), which then heads west as the **C79** past the turn for **Wamba**, where it becomes the **C78**. Despite a continuation of the A2's washboard surface, scenically the C79/78 has everything to recommend it, including some magnificent desert buttes and sweeping views over the valley of the Ewaso Nyiro River, which flows east through Samburu Reserve. The garishly decorated Babie Coach operates the Isiolo to Maralal route, every other day in each direction, usually packed full of Samburu warriors (5–6hr; Ksh700). Matatus run daily in both directions.

Maralal

Some of the Laikipia settlers who ended up around Rumuruti would have dearly liked to set themselves up around the cool, conifer-draped highlands of **MARALAL**. But even before British administrators made this the district capital, Maralal had been a spiritual focus for the **Samburu people** and, despite some dithering, the colonial administrators didn't accede to the settlers' demands.

Maralal is a peculiar town, spread with abandon around a depression in the hills. Samburu people trudge its dusty streets, with a brilliant collage of skins, blankets, beads, brass, and iron, and a special smell, too – of sour milk, fat, and cattle. You'll see warriors in full rig on bicycles; warriors with braided hair and bracelets, but wearing jeans and singlets; women decked with flanges of necklaces; old men with sticks; and young men carrying old rifles. The main town centre watering hole is the *Buffalo Hotel*: the place sets itself up for Wild West comparisons and the climate is appropriate – unbelievably dusty, almost always windy and, at 2220m, sharp enough at night for log fires. All it needs is wolves – and even there hyenas fill the role with their nocturnal whooping.

The regular arrival of safari lorries means that Maralal has plenty of persistent souvenir salesmen. Yet despite this, it's a good place to get to know the Samburu and especially worthwhile during Christian holidays. Many Samburu around the town have become Catholics and the colourful procession on Palm Sunday – mostly thousands of women, waving branches and leaves – is riveting.

A notable resident of Maralal until 1994 was the travel writer and Arabist **Wilfred Thesiger**, who had made the town his home and had adopted a number of orphaned boys. Thesiger made his name with his accounts of the Shia Arabs of southern Iraq and the Bedu of the Arabian peninsula, and followed up these achievements with several books on Kenya, notably *My Kenya Days*. Among the Samburu he found equally congenial companions for his old age.

If you neglect to visit the liberally signposted **Kenyatta House** (free), don't fret. The fact that Kenyatta was detained here in 1961 before his final release doesn't really improve the interest of this unexceptional and almost empty bungalow. In a way it seems a pity that it's a slightly unloved national monument and not some family's home.

Maralal International Camel Derby

The Maralal International **Camel Derby** makes for a strange weekend during the second week of August. Anyone can enter, or just be a spectator, as dozens of competitors from East Africa, Europe, China, Australia and South Africa battle it out over 12-kilometre amateur and 42-kilometre semi-professional stages. There is also a tie-in with the Kenya Amateur Cycling Association, which organizes mountain-bike and amateur cycling races. The events are based at the *Yare Club & Camp* (see p.516), where you can get more details.

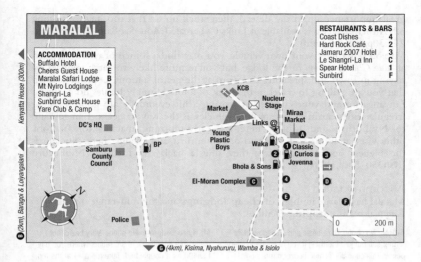

MARALAL

ACCOMMODATION
Buffalo Hotel	A
Cheers Guest House	E
Maralal Safari Lodge	B
Mt Nyiro Lodgings	D
Shangri-La	C
Sunbird Guest House	F
Yare Club & Camp	G

RESTAURANTS & BARS
Coast Dishes	4
Hard Rock Café	2
Jamaru 2007 Hotel	3
Le Shangri-La Inn	C
Spear Hotel	1
Sunbird	F

Kenyatta House (300m)

(2km), Baragoi & Loiyangalani

KCB

Nucleur Stage

Market

Miraa Market

Links @

DC's HQ

Young Plastic Boys

Waka

Classic Curios

Samburu County Council

BP

Bhola & Sons

Jovenna

El-Moran Complex

Police

0   200 m

(4km), Kisima, Nyahururu, Wamba & Isiolo

Guides and crafts

On arriving in Maralal, you'll invariably attract a flock of annoying "guides" offering evening excursions to see **traditional dancing** in nearby *manyattas*, or else visits to local **Samburu witch doctors** and **blacksmiths** and **Turkana villages**. Use your judgement before accepting, making it absolutely clear how much you are prepared to pay.

An attempt to tame the guides by organizing them into disciplined groups is the **Young Plastic Boys' Co-operative Self-Help Group**, so named after the street children who used to make dolls and trinkets using plastic bags and cartons. They have now progressed, under the guidance of the Kenya Wildlife Service and various NGOs, to carving and selling woodcrafts, spears and other touristy items. Their shop is in the market, and sells a decent range of Pokot, Turkana, Rendille and Samburu crafts, and they should also be able to sort you out with a guide, should you need one. If you want to look further for crafts, seek out a Plastic Boys offshoot, Classic Curios, a little crafts shop opposite the *Jamaru Restaurant*.

Maralal National Sanctuary

Although it's not particularly worthwhile to do a game drive around the **Maralal National Sanctuary**, your patronage of *Maralal Safari Lodge* (see p.516) is very welcome, and you can sit on the terrace, by the bar and restaurant, and watch a succession of wildlife from the surrounding sanctuary and Yamo Forest, including zebra, baboon, impala, eland, warthog, buffalo and hyena, file up the hill to the concrete waterhole a few metres away. The lodge is just a short way out of town to the southwest. If you want to swim in their occasionally sparkling pool, there's a charge of Ksh250 for non-guests.

Practicalities

If you're **continuing north**, note that Maralal is the last place where you can rely on supplies of **petrol** (25 percent more expensive here than in the Central Highlands), and **change money** – at the KCB (with ATM), at *Yare Club & Camp* or at *Maralal Safari Lodge*. If **beer** is important to you (and it can assume great importance up in the desert), then stock up on that too before heading off. **Internet** access is available at Links Cybercafé (Mon–Sat 8am–7.30pm, Sun 2–7.30pm; Ksh2/min)

If you don't have your own vehicle, you may find a source of **rides onward** at *Yare Club & Camp* or the lodge, but you're more likely to catch vehicles by staying in town and spreading the word at the petrol stations. Let it be known that you are willing to travel in the back of a lorry. Supply lorries do go up to Loiyangalani and your chances of scoring a lift eventually are good. Finding irregular rides, again with transport vehicles, is the way to get to Baragoi, and to Nyahururu and Isiolo. There are early-morning matatus for Nairobi, otherwise catch one to Rumuruti or Nyahururu, and change there. Nucleur is the biggest operator in town: they shuttle back and forth to Nyahururu (Ksh350–500) all day.

Accommodation

Maralal has a large number of **cheap lodgings** and the mid-range *Yare Club & Camp* also has **camping** facilities.

Buffalo No phone. Ultra-basic and a shadow of its former self but just the thing if you're counting every penny. This centrally located boozer offers single-bedded rooms, around a small courtyard. The rooms (all non-s/c) cost Ksh200 – possibly the cheapest in Kenya and definitely the cheapest in this book. ❶

🏃 **Cheers Guest House** ☎065/62204 or 0722/655877. twenty-five bright, clean rooms (with decent bathrooms, TV, nets, and all-day hot water – in theory), a cheap laundry service and a busy, upcountry-style restaurant on the ground floor. All told, it's a modest gem. ❶
Maralal Safari Lodge 2km southwest of the town centre ☎0720/924523 or 0724/906327. Although it's seen better days, it's hard not to like this old place, with its weather-beaten cabins like an old-style ski lodge, high, pitched roofs and the interiors fitted out in solid wood. While comfy enough, with pretty gardens and genial staff, it's extremely tired and in need of a complete refit. Bathtubs only, no showers, but plenty of hot water. Meals are very pricey and the small pool a little too green and cold to be tempting. Optional log fires in rooms. HB ❼

Mt Nyiro Lodgings No phone. Very basic, but clean, in a little block of s/c rooms where you pay Ksh400 for a double bed. Take room #1 at the top, which gets the best breeze. Safe parking. Hot water mornings only. ❶
Shangri-La ☎0726/527699 or 0726/912525. Very good value, clean and tidy rooms, with instant showers, TV and nets. ❶

🏃 **Sunbird Guest House** ☎065/62015 or 0722/622947. Fantastically clean, fresh rooms, with electricity, all charmingly and reassuringly well managed, with a wholesome *hoteli* attached for the wholesome clients they prefer to welcome. Great value. ❶

🏃 **Yare Club & Camp** 4km down the Isiolo road ☎065/62295, ⓦwww.yaresafaris .co.ke. Maralal's main tourist centre, with some pleasant thatched *bandas*, a decent campsite (Ksh400), a well-stocked bar and a hard-working kitchen (order well in advance). Slightly ramshackle, but cosy and well looked after, and the little cabins have electricity and hot water. Activities include camel rides ($3 per hour) and guided walks in the district ($25/day). BB ❸

Eating and drinking

Maralal has several **decent places to eat**, as well as the usual run of cheap and filling *hotelis*. A night spent in the town's numerous **bars** can be exhilarating, infuriating, silly and occasionally dangerous – though you may not notice. *Buffalo Hotel* used to be the best of the lot, but most of the colourful expats and other characters in the area have faded away, and you are now more likely to encounter wheedling con merchants and a host of bizarre local nutcases. So, until the *Buffalo* is sold and reinvented as a theme pub, the best bars around town are *Yare*, which is always heaving with Samburu drinkers and pool players, and the little frequented *Maralal Safari Lodge*.

Coast Dishes Delightfully friendly local restaurant ("The neighbourhood will never be the same again" they proclaim in large letters on their facade) selling rice-based dishes, *mchele*, pillau, chapattis and *mahamri*. Fill up for Ksh200.

Hard Rock Café Excellent little place with cheap snacks and friendly owners, who are generous with advice on travel in the region.

Jamaru 2007 Hotel Big *hoteli* with a good variety of food, including chapattis and samosas, and meat-and-carb dishes such as pillau and *karanga* for around Ksh250.

Le Shangri-La Inn El-Moran complex. Would-be upmarket restaurant at Maralal's first "mall", with its neighbours a Safaricom centre and the *Ice cream and Yoghurt Palace*.

Spear Hotel Reliable and popular *hoteli*, with a great atmosphere, widescreen TV, breakfasts, curries and samosas.

Sunbird Smart *hoteli* with an outdoor garden area. Order ahead for meals, which are good value and well prepared, most friedly dishes, with some greens and salads (around Ksh200 per plate). Beer can be served only with food.

The Mathews Range and Wamba

In terms of the vastness of the north, the **Mathews Range** is virtually on Maralal's doorstep. The range, most of which is a forest reserve, is impressively wild hill country, with Mathew Peak (Ol Doinyo Lenkiyo) rising to 2375m. Lower down, the mountains are heavily cloaked in forest and thick bush; unusual vegetation includes "living fossil" cycad plants, giant cedars and podocarpus. Among the animal life, you can look out for (but shouldn't expect to meet) small numbers of black rhinos – every one of them known and tracked, for its own safety, by forest guards and their Samburu staff – and really outstanding butterflies. This is first-rate walking and exploring country for hardy travellers, but you need to be fully self-sufficient, and that includes carrying all your food requirements.

First target if you're visiting the Mathews is **WAMBA**, a one-street town 5km off the C78/79 highway, roughly midway between Maralal and Isiolo. You can get the odd matatu here from Maralal, or use the Babie Coach, which passes by the Wamba turning just after midday (heading out from Maralal one day, coming back from Isiolo the next). The big mountain you can see outside town (9km to the peak as the crow flies) is a southern outlier of the Mathews, **Warges** (2688m). Guides from Wamba will take you up there, though they'll stress how full of wild animals it is and how much their lives (not yours of course) are at risk. Wamba's main focus is its large, modern Catholic **hospital** outside town, the best in northern Kenya. One of the few **B&Ls** in town is *Saudia Lodge* (❷), with clean and pleasant rooms. There are a few *dukas*, though they offer little in the way of fresh food beyond basic fruit and vegetables. You could also try *Imani Bar & Restaurant*, which serves the usual limited range of stews and a reasonable *githeri*.

Southeast of Wamba, between Warges and Ol Olokwe (the impressive mesa by the A2 highway from Isiolo to Ethiopia) the community-managed **Namunyak Wildlife Conservation Trust** manages 750 square kilometres of rugged bush and forest. Here, with Warges rearing behind, is one of the north's best tented camps, *Sarara* (ⓦ www.sararacamp.com; closed April, May & 15 Oct–15 Dec; package $1220; conservation fee $60). From here, you can do game walks, go fly camping with camels, or do all the game drives you like. There are rich pickings for birders with frequent sightings of Gambaga flycatcher, shining sunbird, tiny cisticola, stone partridge, and Kenya's largest nesting colony of Ruppell's vultures. You might also see klipspringer, Chandler's mountain reedbuck, and (very rarely) leopard and elephant. Back at the camp, there's an infinity pool hewn out of the rock, and a waterhole offering very close-up viewing.

Camel safaris in the north

Desert Rose Camels ☏020/3864831 or 0721 322745, ⓦdesertrosekenya.com. Expertly guided and flexible camel or horseback expeditions in and around the Mathews, Ndoto and Nyiru mountain ranges, from $200/day. Base is the delightful *Desert Rose Lodge* (package $1000), between Baragoi and South Horr. This is perfect for children and teens, with its swimming pool, home-grown fruit and veg, exciting local walks and nearby natural waterslide.

Karisia Camel Safaris ☏020/891065 or 0721/836792, ⓦkarisia.com. Camel-assisted walking safaris in the Karisia Hills and Mathews Range, from $185/day. Base is Tumaren Ranch, near the village of Kimanjo, 80km southeast of Maralal.

Ol Maisor Camels ☏062/32718, 0735/243075 or 0722/936177 (SMS only), ⓔolmaisor@africaonline.co.ke. Camel-assisted walking safaris as far north as Lake Turkana. Base is the family-friendly *Bobong Campsite*, north of Rumuruti (see p.183).

Wild Frontiers ☏+88216 43334103 (satellite), ⓦwildfrontierskenya.com. Camel-assisted walking safaris, with one or two riding camels always available.

Kitich Camp and campsite

The main route from Wamba is towards the bush-luxury *Kitich Camp* and the nearby KWS station campsite. If you're driving with a 4WD, you basically set off towards Barsaloi (Parsaloi) along a rough road that commences just half a kilometre along the Wamba access road. From here you drive 15km, then turn right and do a further 17km to **Ngelai** (follow the yellow stones), which is the location of the local airstrip. Some 6km further, you fork left to ford the **Ngeng River**. With the mountains looming all around, this is the way into the heart of the Mathews; the KWS campsite is a couple of kilometres up the track on the other side, and *Kitich Camp* some 4km further north. Note that there's no fuel along the way and normally none for sale at *Kitich*.

If you're on foot, find a guide in Wamba and set off cross-country, direct to Ngelai, crossing several *luggas*. You'll see almost nobody on the way. The distance is about 30km and it's an exhausting day's walk. Check with the KWS guys in Wamba that the site is still open. Ngelai has a Lutheran mission (2km out of the centre to the north) and a single shop, which may put you up for the night if you can't make the final 8km to the campsite before nightfall.

Once you reach the **KWS campsite** you'll find it pleasant and shady, with showers and toilet, and water available from the nearby pools. Note that there is no food available at the campsite and, while you can fish in the river, there's a limit to how much catfish a person can stand.

Kitich Camp (ⓦwww.kitichcamp.com; closed April–June & Nov; package $960; $40 per day conservation fee) itself, nestled unobtrusively on the river bank beneath towering giant figs and recently reopened for visitors after years on the back burner, is one of Kenya's most legendary locations, with just four, generously sized, dark canvas tents, huge open-air, stone showers, and unusual touches like sand floors in the public areas. Their very personally hosted style, with walking in the forested hills the main activity, leaves a lasting impression of a remote and beautiful wilderness. There are some fine **excursions**, including short walks up the valley to wonderful, deep, rock pools where you can swim. Wherever you go around here, you'll need a guide to escort you through this very game-rich area. There are elephants everywhere, buffaloes, hyenas, leopards and plenty of more innocuous creatures. You really have to watch yourself, especially if you go down near the river. It's a lot of fun, but take care.

North from Maralal: into Samburu-land

The first stretch of the road **north from Maralal** climbs higher into the *Podocarpus* **forests** of the Maralal national sanctuary, before dropping down across the Lopet Plateau to the Elbarta Plains, 15km east of the scorching Suguta Valley. The northern boundary of the sanctuary has been scarred by climatic changes and the wholesale burning of much of its valley sides, presumably to make way for cattle pasture.

Some 20km from Maralal, a detour to the left takes you through the village of **Poror**, past a large wheat-farming project and, after 6km, to the dramatic scimitar edge of the **Losiolo Escarpment**. There is a charge of Ksh100 per person to enter the area and Ksh200 to Ksh500, depending on your bargaining skills, to camp. The Rift Valley is, by its nature, bordered from end to end by vertiginous escarpments and each one seems more impressive than the last. But Losiolo is not just an escarpment; it's a colossal amphitheatre dropping down to the Suguta Valley, 2000m below. Try to get here very early in the morning while the air is still clear. From Poror, the road north is increasingly rough and hot as it drops down through the Samburu Hills on to the Lopet plateau. Settlements from here on are few but evenly scattered. The first two – **Morijo** and, 20km north, **Marti** – each have basic *chai* kiosks, one or two Somali-run *dukas*, a mission and a police station.

Baragoi

Sitting 37km north of Marti is **BARAGOI**, in the heart of the barren Elbarta Plains, watered only occasionally by run-off from the Samburu Hills and Ndoto Mountains. The *lugga* that skirts the town is dry for much of the year, and in times of drought local women dig pits into it for water, up to 6m deep. It's a blistering, dusty and unforgiving land, dotted here and there with sun-bleached bones and populated only by red-robed semi-nomadic herders armed with spears or bows and arrows to protect their cattle, goats and camels against the endemic rustlers (*ngorokos*).

First settled in the 1930s, Baragoi retains its original function as the region's major livestock market, attracting both Samburu and Turkana for whom the town also marks the invisible boundary between their respective grazing lands. For a while, during the late 1990s, things changed quite fast, as former soldiers from Kenya's UN peacekeeping battalion in Bosnia (many of whom were Samburu from this area) returned to Baragoi with dreams of setting up businesses with their earnings. The remains of the mini-construction boom can still be seen in the town centre, but no fortunes were made.

The livestock market and courtship dances

Down off Bosnia Street to the northwest of town is the **livestock market**. It's a gentle, unhurried affair where old men with gnarled hands and ostrich plumes in their hair play *ngiles* (or *mbau*) with stones and seeds on "boards" carved out of the bone-dry earth as they wait for business to arrive. Here, Samburu deal with Rendille and Turkana, some of whom spend up to seven days walking their livestock south from the lake. In turn the Samburu, and sometimes Turkana, trek southeastward for five or six days to reach Isiolo where, with luck, they resell their animals at a profit.

If the herder is of **courting** age (a warrior, in Samburu a *moran*; or in Turkana a *lmoli*), Isiolo is also where he buys the beads, necklaces and bangles with which to woo his bride. Once back home, he will not only present her with these gifts,

The Samburu

The **Samburu** are historically close to the Maasai. Their languages are nearly the same (both Maa) and culturally they are virtually indistinguishable to an outsider. Both came from the region around present-day northwest Turkana in the seventeenth century. The Samburu turned east, establishing themselves in the mountain pastures and spreading across to the plains; the Maasai continued south.

Improvements in health and veterinary care over the last century have swelled the Samburu population and the size of their herds. Many in the driest areas of their range in the northeast have turned to camel herding as a better insurance against drought than cattle. Since livestock is the basis of relations between in-laws (through the giving of "bride wealth" from the husband to his wife's family), having camel herds has disrupted patterns of marriage and initiation into new generations because camel herds increase more slowly than cattle herds. Memories, recording every transaction over successive generations, are phenomenal (the Samburu have only just begun to acquire writing in the last couple of decades).

The Samburu age-set system, like many others in Africa, is a complicated arrangement to which a number of anthropologists have devoted lifetimes of investigation. Essentially it's a gerontocracy (rule by old men) and the elders are assured, by the system they manipulate, of having the first choice of young women to marry. The promiscuous and jingoistic – but, by Samburu reckoning, still juvenile – warriors are forced to wait, usually until their thirties, before initiation into elderhood and subsequent marriage and fatherhood bring them a measure of real respect. In turn, they perpetuate the system on their own sons, who have everything to gain by falling in line and much to lose if they withdraw their stake in the tradition, perhaps by going to Nairobi or the coast to look for work.

For women the situation is very different. They are married at 15 or 16, immediately after their (still widely performed) clitoridectomy and before they have much chance to rebel. But they may continue affairs with their *morani* boyfriends, the unmarried juniors of their new, much older husbands. This polygamy in itself seems to be an important motivating force for the whole generation system. For the warriors and their girlfriends, there's a special young people's language – a vocabulary of conspiratorial songs and idioms – which has to be modified with the initiation of every age-set, so that it's kept secret from the elders.

This highly intricate system is now beginning to collapse in many areas, with a widespread disruption of pre-colonial ways; even the circumcision initiation of boys to warriorhood is less of a mass ceremony. While herds are still the principal criterion of wealth, people in some areas are turning to agriculture. There are enormous problems for such initiatives, especially when there's no aid or government support, but they do show that the standard stereotypes don't always fit. As for the *morani* warriors, opportunities for cattle-raiding and lion-killing have diminished with more efficient policing of their territories, although there are still frequent clashes with the Turkana on their northern borders. For some, tourist hunting has taken over: *morani* in full rig, striding past the beach hotels, are no longer an unusual sight.

but also mime and sing the attributes of the animals that will provide him and his family with their means of survival. For these semi-nomads, animals are the source of all wealth, and the young herder must represent them favourably to attract the attention and confidence of a bride. To this end, he selects a single castrated bull, camel or goat, which he then mimics, indicating with his hands and gestures its size, colour, the shape of its horns, even its temperament. There's a comical side to all this, too, for even the poorest herder, whose beast may only be a goat with lopsided horns, must dance to attract a spouse and does this by raising a few smiles with a self-deprecating parody of his goat. Dances are held almost nightly in the *manyattas* on the outskirts of town (ask around at the market or else try one of the *manyattas* behind the primary school). These are wild and hugely enjoyable events, where you'll certainly be made welcome – though cameras are generally not acceptable.

Practicalities

There's no ATM or forex bureau, nor any internet access in town, but there is a **post office** (Mon–Fri 8am–5pm) and a decent **vehicle mechanic** (Dalfer Welders, opposite the post office). Emergency **fuel** can usually be had, at a price, from Mount Ngiro Supplies. When you're ready to move on, you'll usually have to line up a lift with a supply truck or a mission 4WD – ask at the lodgings and *hotelis*. The police station on the north side of town is helpful in finding likely drivers, but be prepared to wait all day. The basic but clean *New Highbury Pub and Lodging* (❶) is the best place to **stay**, with a decent bar. There's better food, though, at the *Ramada Hotel*.

South Horr

Baragoi marks the end of the forbidding Elbarta plains, as the road now climbs into ravine and mountain country, fantastically green if there's been rain. Some 30km north of Baragoi, a track to the left towards Nyiru, signed by a red gas cylinder, leads to Desert Rose Camel Safaris, who organize camel treks based out of their *Desert Rose Lodge* (see p.518).

There's a positive jungle all year round at the oasis village of **SOUTH HORR** (*horr* means "flowing water"), wedged tightly between the Nyiru and Ol Doinyo Mara mountains. With its pleasantly somnolent atmosphere, ample shade and relaxed herders lounging under the trees, this is a great place to bunk down for a night or three, and making friends is easy despite the language barrier. There are a few cheap *hotelis* and cold drinks at *Arsenal Inn*, but only rarely beer. There's a choice of half a dozen basic **B&Ls** (all ❶) and good, dirt-cheap **camping** at

▲ Women in traditional dress

the *Forest Department Campsite*, located up a rough trail to the west of the road a kilometre south of South Horr. Facilities consist of long-drops, an *askari*, and a river that provides drinking water (once you've purified it), bathing spots and a means to wash the dust out of your clothes. This site, a short walk from South Horr village where most vehicles stop, is a good base for meeting up with supply or mission vehicles.

The **mountain forest** around South Horr hides lots of wildlife and bursts with birds and butterflies, though unfortunately, many of the elephants and buffaloes have been poached. You can be guided by Samburu *morani* up the lower slopes of Nyiru and Ol Doinyo Mara, or, more ambitiously, on the stiff hike up to **Nyiru peak**, with its stunning views over Lake Turkana. If you're thinking of doing any more daring expeditions in the region, **camel hire** should cost in the region of Ksh1000 per beast per day, plus the negotiable fee for your guide and any other guards or companions. Be careful if you're embarking on anything way off the beaten track. Many local men who like to sell themselves as **guides** have led surprisingly sheltered lives and they don't know the desert like the backs of their hands any more than you do. Real knowledge and experience are sought after, and more expensive.

Well worth a visit in the village itself is **SALTLICK** (Semi-Arid Lands Training and Livestock Improvement Centres Kenya), which concerns itself with supporting the local pastoralist communities through honey-production projects and cash-crop experiments involving the acacia gum tree. They're a mine of information on Samburu culture. For a more intimate experience, you might try asking about the **camel market**, held on occasions a few kilometres south of the village at a roadside well.

Samburu dance performances

Around South Horr, you are likely to have the mixed pleasure of **Samburu dancing**, especially if you're on an organized safari. For about Ksh500, you are allowed to take as many pictures of the dancers as you want. Scepticism is briefly swamped by the hour-long jamboree that follows. A troupe of *morani* goes through an informal dance programme, flirtatiously threatening the audience with whoops and pounces. Young women and girls join in – sometimes with the evident disapproval of older Samburu onlookers – to be mock-propositioned with whisks of the men's ochred hair-dos. Meanwhile, there's the constant offering of necklaces, trinkets, spears, tobacco pouches and more photo poses, to be negotiated individually with those who are too old or too young to dance. It's best not to worry about the fleeting illusion of "authenticity" on these occasions, but to accept them for what they are: vivid, funny, dynamic entertainment.

From South Horr to the lake

After South Horr, the track winds down between the Nyiru Range to your left and the Ol Doinyo Mara mountains to the right, before opening onto featureless plains of black lava with the gaunt massif of **Kulal** dominating the northern horizon. The lava is hard and jagged – a vicious test for tyres – and the track itself, pummelled to a fine dust, can become a quagmire after a rainstorm. This is Turkana territory. The numerous **stone circles** and **cairns** around here are the remains of settlements and burial sites, which, with a keen eye, you'll learn to recognize all over the region. Most distinctive are the low semicircular constructions, which you'll see in use as you approach the lake: these serve as shelters against the viciously hot wind that blows almost incessantly off the flanks of Kulal. The burial cairns are by no means as ancient as they appear, as traditionally neither the Turkana nor Samburu (who migrated from this area a few hundred years ago) buried their dead, but instead simply left the bodies out in the open for wild animals to eat. The more important members of the community, such as blacksmiths and respected elders, were sometimes buried under cairns, or were left in a hut whose door would be walled up. The site would be abandoned and thereafter never again be used for human habitation. Since Independence and the rise in the power of Christian missions, however, both Turkana and Samburu are now obliged to bury their dead.

Just when you were beginning to wonder, **Lake Turkana** appears as the road drops away in front: usually a stunning vista of shot blues and greens, with the black, castellate silhouette of South Island hanging as if suspended between lake and sky. Descending a little further along a viciously rocky stretch of road (known to drivers as The Staircase), you come down to several bays. People have swum here in the past but this is really inadvisable because of crocodiles. You pass a few frail and temporary fishing settlements and, an hour or so later, reach Loiyangalani.

Loiyangalani and around

LOIYANGALANI – "the place of the trees" – is a small community far from metropolitan Kenya, a vague agglomeration of grass huts, mud huts, tin shacks, a police station, a school, a few campsites, and a luxury lodge. The land around is mostly barren and stony, scattered with the carcasses of livestock, with palm trees and acacias clustered around the settlement's life source, a **hot spring** of fresh water. This empties into two small pools near the police station, one visited by men, the other by women.

The village came into being in the early 1960s with the *Oasis Lodge* and its airstrip, and the Italian mission to the **Elmolo** people, a small group who live by hunting and fishing on the southeastern lakeshore. Somali raiders ransacked both establishments in 1965, but since then the two institutions have been left alone. The mission is now starting to thrive and its net of influence has reached most of Loiyangalani's more permanent inhabitants, especially the children who attend the school.

For all its apparent drabness, the village isn't dull. When you've had enough of haggling for artefacts and fantastic quartz, onyx, amethyst and other semi-precious stones – as well as the odd fossil – collected from Kulal, you can wander over to the springs and the school. You'll inevitably pick up a cluster of teenagers – Turkana, Elmolo, Samburu, Rendille – eager to practise their English. Swahili has never made much impact up here and English is the usual teaching medium. Education is perhaps the most positive of the major influences, including tourism, state interference and Christianity, that pressurize local customs and traditions.

Loiyangalani's Italian-funded **Desert Museum** (daily 9.30am–6pm; Ksh500) is a purpose-built exhibition space overlooking the lake, a couple of kilometres north of town. Although it displays photos about the eight different tribes of the north, and deserves support, what's on offer – an information centre, essentially – is a bit too limited for the entry price.

Loiyangalani's "beach" is a grubby strip a couple of kilometres down the road. Many of the loose stones on the shore shelter scorpions (their stings are not serious) and carpet vipers (whose bite is very serious). In the evenings, **dances** often take place around Loiyangalani – informal, energetic, pogo-ing perform-ances for fun, that are always worth checking out. Track them down by the

God's work

The **Loiyangalani mission**, while changing the structure of traditional society through conversions to Catholicism (particularly sweeping among the Elmolo), is at the same time helping to make local people sufficiently independent to resist unwanted change and to make choices about their future, by helping to set up income-generating schemes such as shops, boats and the service station. Some of the Italian missionaries are extremely open and informative and the chance to talk to them may well arise if you're around for a few days. For non-Christians, however, the whole concept of missionaries and their work can be difficult to swallow. For all their schools and clinics, it's difficult to escape the feeling that the local people – for so long "untouched" by the outside world – managed very well with their original beliefs and traditions, which underpinned their society, cosmology and relationships. With Christianity now ascendant, the old structures are breaking down fast and some risk being lost completely. And by preferring to convert children, rather than their more obstinate parents, the deeper morality of the well-meaning missionaries is questionable at best.

booming sound of collective larynxes. It's the girls who ask the boys to dance, and you're welcome to join in (no cameras allowed unless permission is expressly given and paid for, usually Ksh500 per person).

If you're in Loiyangalani in late May or early June, you're likely to find the **Turkana Cultural Festival** taking place (2008 and 2009 were its first two years). It's organized by the German embassy and the Goethe-Institut with some EU funding and coordination by the National Museums of Kenya (W www.museums.or.ke; contact E mibrahim@museums.or.ke). Samburu, Turkana, Rendille and Gabbra gather in their thousands, in finest traditional garb, to dance and sing. And of course, to sell crafts.

Practicalities

There are few shops in Loiyangalani, and apart from fresh fish, only a limited variety of **food**: it's a good idea to bring at least some of your own. The centrally located *Cold Drink Hotel* claims to give "best service, no matter how long it takes" but is nothing special, and has a tendency to charge tourist rates even though their fridge is always out of action. The *New Salaama*, just off the main drag, serves good, spicy Somali food, while *Mpasso Bar* is a pleasant thatched-roof, open-air compound with snacks, cold beers, and a games area with darts and a pool table.

Accommodation

Wherever you stay in Loiyangalani, be prepared for wind and dust: it just never stops. Campers, in particular, tend to struggle a bit, because pegs get yanked out and everything blows away.

Gametrackers Camp 7km south of Loiyangalani on the lakeshore. Probably Lake Turkana's most perfect site, operated by Gametrackers for their Turkana safaris, with thatched *bandas* facing out over the lake. There's little shade, and the *bandas* are small and cramped, but the views are unparalleled. Gametrackers use it for only two or three times a week. You should be able to deal with the caretaker. Camping Ksh400. ❶

Mama Changa's Loiyangalani centre. Down-to-earth B&L run by a lady who, apart from supplying much of the Turkana's beadwork necklaces and bracelets, has eighteen cleanish and adequate rooms at the back of the misnamed *Cold Drink Hotel*, each with a kerosene lamp and free drinking water. The place to meet up with non-camping, low-budget travellers (and drivers, should there be any). ❶
Mosaretu Camp Adjacent to *Oasis Lodge*. Run by the local branch of the women's Maendeleo ya

Wanawake movement. Apart from camping (Ksh200 per tent), there are five traditional *bandas* under the palm trees, with mosquito nets and mattresses. Facilities include toilets, showers, a curio shop and a shared kitchen. The same people also own *Rhino Camp* on the other side of town. ➊ **Oasis Lodge** On the northern edge of the village. ☏0722/829423 or 0729/954672. Well-guarded, German-run lodge of fairly basic chalet-style rooms, that tries to be exclusive, and certainly charges as if it were (buoyed by its role in Fernando Meirelles' film *The Constant Gardener*). There's a Ksh500 daily entrance fee to casual visitors, which entitles you to swim in the two pools and soak up the great views from the bar-restaurant. Fishing trips can be organized for Nile perch, tiger fish and tilapia. Their vehicle rental with driver – useful for visiting Sibiloi National Park – is expensive at around $180 per day for their battered Land Rovers. Bargain hard for all services, and double-check the price before signing up to anything. Closed mid-May to mid-June. FB ➐

Palm Shade Camp Behind the *Cold Drink Hotel*. A clean site with a handful of cool *bandas* with nets, plus filtered water, good toilets and showers from the hot springs, and a communal kitchen. They'll cook good meals for you if you provide money for food and a few hundred shillings for the cook's fee. Generator till late evening. Camping Ksh450.

South Island National Park

If you want to visit **South Island National Park** (Ⓦwww.kws.go.ke; $20), you should first ask about a trip at *Oasis Lodge*, but spread the word and you may find a much cheaper means of getting there. It's a thirty-kilometre round trip, so the weather needs to be fair. Although the warden doesn't always grant permission to camp there for the night, if you get the chance, it's one of the weirdest places to stay: its volcanic vents, rising some 300m above lake level, give out a ghostly luminous glow that has long put off local fishermen from venturing there.

Mount Kulal

With perhaps more guarantee of success, you could make a stab at climbing **Mount Kulal** (2285m). There are two summits, joined by a narrow and dicey ridge. The climb itself, once you're on the right track, is straightforward enough, but talk to some gem-hunters who should be guide you up for a negotiable fee. Note that, although Kulal seems to tower over Loiyangalani (its summit is more than 1900m above the lake), two days is barely enough to walk to the base and back, and the summit is 25km east of Loiyangalani as the crow flies. Factor in wind, dust and heat and you can see why you'd be well advised to get transport as far up the mountain as possible before you start climbing (expect to bargain hard, and end up paying Ksh10,000–12,000 for the vehicle hire, with driver). The views from the top are fabulous, with the lake on one side and the searing Chalbi Desert on the other, and bird-watchers have the added incentive of a rare species of **white-eye** peculiar to the mountain. Bring all the **water** you will need, as there are no supplies on the mountain.

Elmolo Bay

The last viable community of **Elmolo people** lives at **Elmolo Bay**, 8km north of Loiyangalani. To visit them, you pay a fixed fee per person (Ksh1000) to the headman, for freedom to roam the village, including the right to take photos and a trip to the island opposite the bay to look for crocodiles. During the week, many children are at school in Loiyangalani; they come home at the weekend, which is the best time to visit. Impromptu dances start and little hands are slipped engagingly into yours for a walk around the low, grass huts. If you have a digital camera you'll be extremely popular with the village children, eager to look at their image on screen. You will also be shown the "market", a

The Elmolo

The people of Loiyangalani with the best claim to being the original inhabitants are the **Elmolo**. The Elmolo call themselves *el-Des*, but their usual name comes from the Samburu *loo molo onsikirri*, "the people who eat fish". They once inhabited South Island, but now occupy a couple of islands in Elmolo Bay, and a few clusters of grass huts on the torrid shores 8km north of Loiyangalani. Most of the six hundred-strong community lives here, partly by **fishing** and the occasional heroic crocodile or hippo hunt (officially banned), and partly by **cash receipts** from tourist visitors.

The Elmolo are enigmatic. At the time of Teleki's discovery of the lake, they spoke a **Cushitic** language, the family of languages to which Somali and Rendille belong. Recent linguistic research on historical migrations points to their having arrived on the shores of Lake Turkana at a very early time – perhaps more than 2000 years ago. They seem to have no tradition of livestock herding, which might have been kept up if they had turned, like the Turkana, to fishing as a supplement. Today they speak the Samburu dialect of Maa (the last Elmolo-speaker died in March 1998) and have started to inter-marry with the Samburu. This, as well as the mission's influence, has been quite significant in raising their numbers (from less than 200 fifty-odd years ago) and also in diluting their cultural identity. Once strictly monogamous, polygamy isn't uncommon now, and they also send many children to the school in Loiyangalani as weekly boarders. On the slope, right behind the village, looms the fairly recent Catholic Church.

All this signals the final curtain for a culture and history that has been largely ignored or denied. The conventional wisdom about hunter-gatherers in Kenya is that they are often the descendants of pastoralists who lost their herds. But if the Elmolo are, as some say, pastoral Rendille who took to fishing in order to survive, then it's strange that they have never tried to replace their herds. For without herds, they could never hope to pay bride wealth for wives from their non-fishing neighbours in the traditional way. A better explanation, and one favoured by the Elmolo themselves, is that their people have always been fishermen and hunters and, until very recently, pressures from other tribes, particularly the Turkana, had pushed them almost to the point of annihilation.

By the end of the twentieth century, the Elmolo fishing culture was rubbing off on other ethnic groups and even the Samburu had started to eat fish. As long ago as 1972, Peter Matthiessen wrote in *The Tree Where Man was Born*:

> The Samburu and Turkana may linger for weeks at a time as guests of the Llo-molo, who have plenty of fish and cannot bear to eat with all these strangers hanging around looking so hungry. Other tribes, the Llo-molo say, know how to eat fish better than they know how to catch them . . . "We have to feed them," one Llo-molo says, "so that they will feel strong enough to go away."

The Elmolo are a charming and hospitable people, and how they survive in their chosen environment is hard to imagine. Outwardly similar in dress and appearance to the other people of the area, they are slightly smaller, but the bowed legs that are supposed to be the characteristic result of their diet seem to be confined to the older people – you might have thought all that fish would give them strong bones.

Incidentally, don't get worried when a mother hands you her child, then asks for money; she's not selling her offspring, but simply wants you to sponsor the child's education with a large wad of cash.

circular stall in the centre of the village with beadwork, belts, fertility dolls and gourds. It's a novel, disturbing experience that contrives to be stage-managed and voyeuristic at the same time. Because of their friendliness, their small number and the increased interest shown in them, the Elmolo risk being taken

▲ Ceremonial dancing, Turkana tribe

advantage of by tourists. However, the usual rules apply: ask before you take pictures and be generous with your time and your wallet.

Over on the island – which, because of the drop in the level of the lake, you can now reach by a causeway – you should see **crocodiles** if you walk softly and approach the far shore cautiously. On the island's stern, rocky beaches, the remains of Elmolo fish picnics and old camps, even the occasionally virtually fossilized hippo tusk, can be found everywhere.

Sibiloi National Park

Sibiloi National Park (ⓦ kws.go.ke/sibiloi.html; $20), with its relatively abundant **wildlife** and famous **fossil sites**, provides a powerful incentive to go further north. Access is a problem, however, unless you have your own 4WD, as vehicles heading there from Loiyangalani are extremely rare and you could easily wait a week or more. You need a high clearance 4WD, particularly for the first section along the northern flanks of Mount Kulal, and then a full day's drive should get you to the park headquarters at Alia Bay. Be sure to get clear directions from as many people as you can in Loiyangalani, as most maps are useless. Driving along the Loiyangalani-to-North Horr road, turn north after some 45km, when the road begins to drop down from Mount Kulal's rocky shoulder. From here, a completely desolate track heads more or less due north for 40km to the settlement of **Hurran Hurra**, where a left turn should bring you to the camel watering-point and settlement of **Gajos**, another 40km northwest. Another left here (heading west, then northwest) begins the descent down towards the lake and the national park itself. **Camp Turkana**, near the shore just south of Alia Bay, marks the park's southern boundary where you'll find the park headquarters. The National Museums of Kenya base at **Koobi Fora** (ⓦ www.kfrp.com) is another 30km further north.

The Koobi Fora field schools

Possibly the best way of visiting the fossil sites is by timing your trip to coincide with a **field school** organized by the National Museums of Kenya in tandem with Rutgers University in the USA (ⓦwww.koobifora.rutgers.edu). Approximate dates are mid-June to the end of July.

Apart from **flying in** (around $1000 return from Nairobi's Wilson Airport – you'll need to find an amenable pilot who has a plane available and a spare day), an alternative way of getting here is by boat from Ferguson's Gulf on the lake's western shore, near Kalokol (p.510). There's an infrequent National Museums supply boat from here.

Discoveries in human prehistory

Sibiloi was created to protect the sites of numerous remarkable **hominid fossil** finds that have been made since 1968 by Richard Leakey's, and latterly Kamoya Kimeu's, teams from the University of Nairobi. The park, more than 1600 square kilometres of rock desert and arid bush, is an exceptional source because many of the fossils are found on the surface, blown clean by the never-ending wind. The finds set back the dates of intelligent, cooperative, tool-making behaviour among hominids further and further all the time, but most of the species concerned are assumed to have died out. The crucial discoveries that will link humankind to our prehuman ancestors have yet to be made. One striking find made at Sibiloi in 1972 was the skull labelled "1470", first thought to be of a *Homo habilis* ("Handy man") and then renamed *Homo rudolfensis* ("Rudolf man"), which is about 1.9 million years old. Although quite different from other species of early human-like primates, with its large brain and big, flat face, Rudolf man may yet be shown to be a direct ancestor of modern *Homo sapiens*.

As more and more hominid discoveries are made at Sibiloi (more than two hundred so far), as well as in Ethiopia, Tanzania, and on the other side of Lake Turkana (where excavations have yielded the earliest *australopithecine* yet discovered, *Australopithecus anamensis*, dated to between 4.2 and 3.9 million years), the evolutionary theories continue to flesh out.

The so-called **museum** at the "expedition" headquarters in Alia Bay, where some of the fossils (including part of a one-and-a-half-million-year-old elephant) are supposedly displayed *in situ*, isn't easily traced; all that was found on a last attempt were empty ranger buildings and unhelpful staff. You can **camp** there, though ($15), and there are supposedly **bandas** available, too (❷).

Animal life

At times, Sibiloi National Park has a surprising wealth of **wildlife**. Indeed, until the 1930s, there were large numbers of elephant living here. Rainless years, ivory hunters, and especially the increase in the herds of livestock, contributed to their demise. But lion, cheetah, hyena, both kinds of zebra (the ordinary Grant's and the finer-striped, taller Grevy's), giraffe, ostrich, Grant's gazelle, topi, kudu and gerenuk all occur here, though there's no guarantee you'll see much. Because of the protection from hunters, hippos and crocodiles are numerous. The tree cover is minimal: the only trees you might see are in the petrified forest of stone trunks, at the Sibiloi Fossil Forest, a few kilometres east of the park HQ – reminders of the lush vegetation of the lakeshore in prehistoric times.

The northeast

Travel in northeastern Kenya has a special quality. The normal stimuli – passing scenery, animals, people and fleetingly witnessed events – are replaced with a massive open sky, shimmering greenish-brown earth, and, just occasionally, a speck of movement. It might be some camels, a pair of ostriches, or perhaps a family moving somewhere with their donkeys. It's a sparse, absorbingly simple landscape, and not the least of its attractions is the restful absence of hassle and shove, and a solitude hardly found anywhere else.

Northeastern Kenya has a single and limited travel circuit: north through **Isiolo** to **Marsabit National Park**. Most people who make it as far as the border town of **Moyale** are going on to Ethiopia and up to Addis Ababa on the tarmac highway that starts as soon as you cross the border. East of the Isiolo–Marsabit–Moyale road, the administrative outposts of **Mandera** and **Wajir** are considered too dangerous to visit (or rather the long journeys across the desert to reach them are viewed as being at risk of bandit attack). Although in practice most travellers, even in the northeast corner, survive the truck journeys quite

Travel in the northeast – a warning

Northeastern Kenya has long had a reputation for lawlessness, but what was sometimes dismissed as the exaggerations and ignorance of "down-country" Kenyans acquired a more brutal reality in the 1990s, which continues to this day.

Since the flight of Somalia's dictator Siad Barre in 1991, and that country's anarchic disintegration into warring fiefdoms, northeastern Kenya has borne the full brunt of Somalia's desperate refugee crisis, with increasingly violent bandits targeting commercial vehicles, foreign aid workers and refugee camps.

The northeast is also home to pastoralist tribes who frequently engage in livestock rustling and clash over grazing and water rights. All this has been made more volatile by the prolonged drought in the region. And whatever the complicated situation on the ground, you can be sure of one thing: there are more people than before with guns, ammunition and little else.

The military presence in the northeast is pervasive: roadblocks, vehicle searches and armed escorts are part of everyday life, yet for all this the military presence is also almost entirely ineffective. Very seldom do reported incidents result in arrests. Indeed, some accuse the police of being complicit in the crimes.

We've endeavoured to note the current security situation for all parts of this chapter, but you're strongly advised to seek advice on the ground before travelling anywhere covered in the following pages, as the situation can change quickly. For example, the area between Isiolo and Archer's Post, including Samburu and Buffalo Springs National Reserves, suffered a number of attacks on villages and tourists in the late 1990s. Although the situation in the parks is now controlled by the KWS, two relatively low-key attacks near Archer's Post at the height of the drought in September 2009 led several tour operators to temporarily withdraw their safaris.

The main no-go area at the time of writing is the entire region east of the A2 Isiolo–Marsabit–Moyale road and north of the A3 Thika–Garissa road (but not including Shaba National Reserve or Meru National Park, both of which are safe). If you're driving in the northeast, always use your judgement, ask advice everywhere you go, and always stop at police checkpoints. You will quite often be asked to travel in convoy, or, if you have space, to take an armed policeman as an escort to your next stop. Driving at night, incidentally, is not only the height of folly, but also illegal.

unscathed, unless you have a visceral desire to reach the most far-flung corners of Kenya, you're not missing out hugely by not going to them.

Isiolo

ISIOLO is the northeast's most important town and the hub for travel to Marsabit and Moyale. Southernmost of the "Northern Frontier" towns, Isiolo is on the border between two different worlds – the green highlands and the desert. A measure of the untamed badlands beyond is indicated by the three military training schools based here: Infantry, Combat Engineering and Artillery, as well as a tank regiment. Isiolo is a frontier in every respect. The **Somali influence** here is something noticeable everywhere in the northeast, and Isiolo is one of their most important towns in Kenya. It was here that many veteran Somali soldiers from World War I were settled: recruited in Aden and Kismayu, they gave up their nomadic lifestyle to become livestock dealers and retail traders.

The town is lively and welcoming, relatively safe and generally hassle-free. It's also a cultural kaleidoscope, with Boran, Meru, Samburu and some Turkana inhabitants as well as the Somalis. To someone newly arrived from Nanyuki or Meru, the upland towns seem ordinary in comparison. Women from the irrigated *shambas* around Isiolo sell cabbages, tomatoes and carrots in the busy market; cattle owners, nomadic camel traders and merchants exchange greetings and the latest news from Nairobi and Moyale; in the livestock market, goats scamper through the alleys; while hawkers stroll along the road raising their

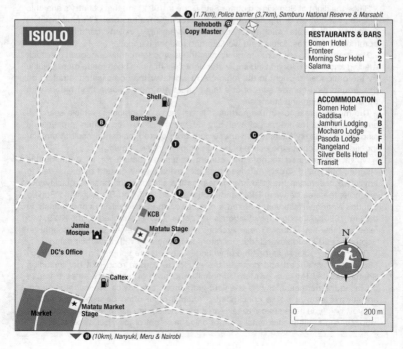

ISIOLO

▲ Ⓐ (1.7km), Police barrier (3.7km), Samburu National Reserve & Marsabit

Rehoboth @
Copy Master

Shell

Barclays

Ⓑ

Ⓒ

❶

Ⓓ

❷

Ⓕ

Ⓔ

❸

KCB

Jamia
Mosque

Matatu Stage

Ⓖ

DC's Office

Caltex

Market

★ Matatu Market
Stage

N

0   200 m

▼ Ⓗ (10km), Nanyuki, Meru & Nairobi

RESTAURANTS & BARS

Bomen Hotel	C
Fronteer	3
Morning Star Hotel	2
Salama	1

ACCOMMODATION

Bomen Hotel	C
Gaddisa	A
Jamhuri Lodging	B
Mocharo Lodge	E
Pasoda Lodge	F
Rangeland	H
Silver Bells Hotel	D
Transit	G

Somali swords and strings of bangles to the minibuses heading up to Samburu National Reserve. And, in the shade, energetic *miraa*-chewing and hanging around are the major occupations. *Miraa* has a long history in Somali culture, and the Nyambeni Hills, where most of the Kenyan crop is grown, are just 30km away (p.172).

Practicalities

If you get a late **bus** from Nairobi you'll arrive in the middle of the night, and the town can be seen glittering out on the plain far below for an hour or more before you get there. During Ramadan, lanterns glow along the pavements for the *miraa* sellers and most of the shops are still open. There are branches of KCB and Barclays banks here, and both have **ATMs**. **Internet** access is available at Rehoboth Copy Master (Mon–Fri 8am–6pm, Sat 8.30am–6pm; Ksh1.50/min).

Accommodation

Isiolo has one reasonable, mid-range **hotel**. Of the more humble **lodgings**, all are cheap – some of the cheapest in Kenya – and several surprisingly good value. You can **camp** at the *Gaddisa*, out of town. There's also a good place 10km south of town in the form of the shaded *Rangeland Hotel*.

Bomen Hotel ☎064/52272 or 0733/712275. The best and most expensive in town: clean, polite and serving good lunchtime buffets in its restaurant. Rooms lack fans, but are s/c and have nets, TVs, instant showers, and hot water mornings and evenings. The breezy top-floor suites are relatively good value for Ksh1500 extra. BB ❸

Gaddisa Out of town, 2km up the Garba Tula road (turn right at the police barrier) ☎0724/201115 or 0735/646370, ⓦwww.gaddisa.com. Semi-abandoned trophy development, still kept up by the staff. The seven rooms, facing onto the garden, are decent and clean, but very ordinary. The insanely huge, deep pool was never fit for purpose, and is being converted, somehow, into half-pool, half underground bar/night club – which seems even more dangerous. Camping Ksh450. BB ❻

Jamhuri Lodging ☎064/2065 or 0722/384544. Newly renovated, clean, courteous and mellow (no alcohol or prostitutes allowed), and incredibly cheap, although rooms are non-s/c. Hot water mornings only. The nets are a bit perfunctory, and/or badly hung, but the instant showers look safer than usual. Secure parking in the compound. ❶

Mocharo Lodge ☎064/2385. With its top-floor "suites", with TV and nets, and a good dining room downstairs (breakfast Ksh200), this is probably the best value for money in town. Safe parking in courtyard. ❶

Pasoda Lodge ☎0726/416602. Basic, courtyard-style B&L – all rooms are s/c with clean sheets and nets, and water from plastic basins. Inexpensive meals available, and safe parking. They also have a bar with a pool table. Very cheap. ❶

Silver Bells Hotel Between the *Bomen* and *Pasoda* ☎064/2251. Clean, quiet and mid-priced, with a bar, this has seventeen rooms, all inward-facing around the courtyard, with nets and hot water mornings only. The restaurant does plates of inexpensive staples. ❶

Transit ☎064/52083 or 0726/846378. Simple, clean rooms with nets, fans and instant showers, on a par with *Mocharo*, or even better. Forty-eight rooms, and a good place all round, but as usual, not many rooms have outward-facing windows. Breakfast Ksh250. ❶

Rangeland 10km south of Isiolo ☎0720/060038 or 0721/434353. Set in pleasant grounds, around which hyraxes scamper, the s/c rooms in the garden cottages are decent value, with nets but no other extras. A little above the average B&L, this is a popular out-of-town drinking spot, and tends to be noisy in the evenings. BB ❷

Eating and drinking

Most of the Somali *hotelis* provide excellent **food**, day and night. Now that you're in the northeast, you'll see pasta (usually spaghetti) appearing quite prominently on menus – one of the better Italian bequests to the Somalis.

Bomen Hotel Ground-floor bar and restaurant, doing grills, with most dishes Ksh300–400, and beer for Ksh100. Popular outdoor *nyama choma* grill.

Fronteer Garish and popular disco/bar in outlandish contrast with the rest of the town. The *Frontier Café* part of the establishment has long

been popular for the good spiced *chai* for next to nothing a glass.

Morning Star Hotel Pretty good, down-to-earth *hoteli* – especially noted for its samosas.

Salama Friendly and popular place, recommended for an early breakfast or the very good spaghetti with gravy.

Shopping and guides

Isiolo is one of the best places to buy copper, brass and aluminium **bracelets**. Prices are generally around Ksh50 for the simple ones, and from Ksh200 for the heavier, more complicated designs, if you can bargain effectively (starting prices are much higher). Short "Somali swords" in red leather scabbards are also much in evidence. The "sharp boys" who mob you near the markets will invariably offer to guide you to one of the few blacksmiths in town to watch the fascinating process of twisting the wires for the bangles. Profits come from buying rough bangles, then polishing and selling them. If you go, you're generally expected to make a purchase and tip a few shillings to the boys. While the bangle and knife salesmen throng as soon as you sit down for a *chai*, their approach is rarely aggressive. Women offer small wooden dolls with woven hair, which in the past were given to young girls as both toys and fertility charms.

Some of the former "sharp boys" have recently teamed up to start the **Utamaduni Self-Help Group**, based just north of the police barrier, which aims to organize and rehabilitate homeless and orphaned youth in community-based projects (for example, by building small bridges over sewage ditches). Though some of their members are still a little rough around the edges, it's a laudable venture, and the best place to get a **guide** for visiting local *manyattas* (they must have an ID card; you should pay no more than Ksh1000 for a full day). For trips further afield, test the guide first on a one-day trip in the environs of Isiolo before trusting him on a longer journey.

Moving on from Isiolo

When heading north, waiting in Isiolo is a predictable part of the trip. The only public transport onwards from Isiolo is to Wamba (see p.517) and Maralal via Archer's Post, details for which are given opposite. Otherwise, there are no buses and only limited matatu services north or east from Isiolo, so your only options for travel to Marsabit and Moyale are either **self-drive** or **hitching a ride** with a truck in the convoy. If you're lucky, you might get a lift with one of the mission or aid vehicles. Note if you're driving that Isiolo is the last guaranteed **fuel** stop until Maralal or Marsabit. The police/KWS barrier is very much in operation on the north side of Isiolo. You'll need to tell them where you're going, and, depending on the recent situation on the road, possibly join a convoy for your onward journey.

To Nairobi via the Central Highlands

There are several daily **bus** services to Nairobi via Nanyuki, leaving between 6.30 and 7.30am and taking five to six hours (Ksh400–500). For matatus it's best to be at the market stage before sunrise – last departures at 6am are not unheard of. The fare for the hop to Nanyuki (1hr 30min) is Ksh200.

North to Marsabit and Moyale

Matatus go as far as Archer's Post, which is only helpful if you're visiting Samburu or Shaba national reserves (see p.375 & p.378). There's often a direct bus to Marsabit and Moyale from Nairobi two or three times a week, though schedules vary through the year depending on demand. Otherwise, try for trucks at the **police roadblock** 3km north of Isiolo, where drivers sign their vehicles out of town. There are usually a few heading up to Moyale daily, and most take passengers (Ksh500 to Marsabit and Ksh1000 to Moyale). Unless you pay extra, you'll have to stand on top of the load along with the other, usually male, passengers, although given the state of the roads, this can be more comfortable than sitting down. Alternatively, Gametrackers' Turkana Bus passes through Archer's Post early in the morning most Saturdays, which – if the driver's amenable – can take you as far as Marsabit, probably for a fee. The 262km to Marsabit takes seven to ten hours, with the next leg to Moyale (245km) anything from ten hours to two days, depending on the state of the road and the frequency of hold-ups – natural, mechanical or human.

West to Maralal

The **Isiolo–Archer's Post–Maralal** run is served by Babie Coach, an exotically named converted truck with no other special features, that makes the journey between Isiolo and Maralal (or vice versa) on alternate days, leaving one town at around 9am to reach the other five to six hours later (Ksh700). On the days that Babie Coach is on its homebound run to Isiolo, you may find the odd matatu going to Maralal. If you're **driving** the route yourself, bring enough fuel for the whole journey – there are usually no supplies at Wamba.

To Marsabit and North Horr

No matter what speed you go, this is a fantastically uncomfortable trip, with rocks, ruts and corrugations that shake smaller vehicles to breaking point.

Passing over the occasionally dry Ewaso Nyiro River and a police barrier, you hit the agglomeration of shiny-roofed shacks and rows of *dukas* that is **ARCHER'S POST**. This is as far north as you'll get by matatu, although lifts into Samburu and Shaba national reserves (see p.375 & p.378) may be forthcoming from Kenya Wildlife Service personnel, who frequent a number of particularly good bars. There are some **rooms** here, too, should you fail: try *Acacia Shade Inns* (❶), which also has a **campsite** (with no guarantee of security). Note that there's no **fuel** at Archer's.

North of Archer's Post, the road veers northwest and for thirty minutes the great mesa of **Ol Olokwe Mountain** (or Ol Doinyo Sabache) spreads massively across the horizon in front of you. If you're travelling independently with your own vehicle, you'll be in a position to climb it: take the Wamba road and stop at the first village, **Lerata**; find the General Store and start asking for the Namunyak Conservancy manager. You can climb Ol Olokwe in a day from Lerata with a crack-of-dawn start. Fees include a $20 conservation fee and whatever you negotiate for your guide – around Ksh1000 for the day is about right, or more if you're in a group.

For several hours north of Ol Olokwe you roar across the flat **Kaisut Desert**. **Laisamis** isn't much of a break – a windblown cluster of low, tin-roofed huts, offering sodas and toothbrush sticks to passers-by – and the **Losai National Reserve** isn't any different from the rest of the scenery. The **approach to Marsabit**, though, is unmistakeable. The road begins to climb and suddenly you're on a hilly island in the desert, a region of volcanic craters, lush meadows and forest. The branches of the trees on the steep slopes are disguised by swathes of Spanish moss, looking at first glance like algae-covered rocks in shades of grey and green.

Identities in the northeast can be confusing to foreigners. The largest group are the **Boran**, part of the **Oromo peoples** (formerly called Galla, an Amhara term of abuse), whose homeland was near the Bale Mountains in Ethiopia, from where they suddenly exploded out, in all directions, in the sixteenth century. The pastoral Boran developed and flourished in what is now southern Ethiopia, but Menelik's conquest of the area and the oppressive Amhara regime caused some of them to move down to the lowlands of northern Kenya, a much less suitable region for their cattle. The first Boran arrived in Marsabit only in 1921.

Similarly, recent Ethiopian immigrants to the region between Marsabit and Moyale are the **Burji**, an agricultural people who were called down by colonial administrators in the 1930s who wanted crops grown. The Burji took quickly to Western education and trade, and as a result dominated Marsabit politically in the first decade after Independence. There's traditionally little love lost between the nomadic Boran and the settled Burji.

At around the time of the Oromo expansion, another group of people – the forefathers of the Gabbra – arrived in northern Kenya, causing havoc in the region, only to be themselves pressured by the ensuing expansion of **Muslim Somalis** from the east. The ancestors of the **Gabbra** became "Boranized" to the extent that they changed their language and adopted Boran customs. Although most Boran and Gabbra, especially those who adopted a more sedentary life, have adopted Somali styles in dress and culture, they eschew Islam, preferring their own religions.

The **Rendille**, to the northwest of Marsabit, look and act like Samburu, with whom they are frequently allied; they speak a language close to Somali but have non-Muslim religious beliefs. They normally herd camels rather than cattle and, to a great extent, continue to roam the deserts, facing the prospect of settling down without any enthusiasm at all and visiting Marsabit only for vital needs or a brief holiday.

In Marsabit itself, distinctions other than superficial ones were becoming increasingly hard to apply by the 1990s, as people intermarried, sent more children to school, and absorbed new ideas from Nairobi – and Christian missionaries. Still, language and religious beliefs remain significant in deciding who does what and with whom, and, outside the town, individual tribal identities are as strong – and potentially bloody – as ever. Since the Turbi massacre in 2005 (Turbi is a remote village 150km north of Marsabit), when Boran warriors attacked Gabbra villagers during a flare-up of customary inter-tribal cattle rustling, and killed sixty people, Marsabit has seen a deep chill in relations between the different peoples. Nearly ten thousand Gabbra refugees crowded into the town, and at present Gabbra and Boran barely speak to one another, let alone inter-marry.

Marsabit town

MARSABIT is a surprise. It's hard to prepare yourself, after the flat dust lands, for this fascinating hill oasis, in the desert but not of it. Rising a thousand metres above the surrounding plains, *Saku*, as the mountain is known by locals, is permanently green, well watered by the clouds that form and disperse over it in a daily cycle. The high forest is usually mist-covered until late morning, the trees a characteristic tangle of foliage and lianas.

The town is the capital of the largest administrative district in the country, as well as a major meat- and livestock-trading centre. Small and intimate in feel, the lively cultural mix in the main market area is the biggest buzz: transient **Gabbra** herdsmen and **Boran** with their prized short-horn cattle, women in the printed shawls and chiffon wraps of **Somali** costume rubbing elbows with ochred **Rendille** wearing skins, high stacks of beads and wire, and fantastic braided hairstyles. There are government workers here, too, from other parts of Kenya, and a scattering of **Ethiopian immigrants** (mainly Burji) and refugees. For some Marsabit background, try Mude Dae Mude's novel *The Hills are Falling* (1979), now out of print but you might still find a copy in Nairobi. If you're interested in **traditional music**, ask for George's Music Store.

Walks out of town

There are a number of trips you can make on foot from Marsabit in a few hours or less. The easiest, with rewarding views, is the short walk up to the big wind-powered **generator** on a hill just west of the town. Turn left just before the police barrier and simply follow the path.

A longer excursion takes you up to the **VOK transmitter** behind the town, an excellent morning or afternoon hike through lush forest with magnificent panoramas of the whole district from the top. There are wells up here, too (see below). During the rainy season, everything is tremendously green and you walk over flowering meadows through clouds of butterflies.

From there, you should be able to see the closest sizeable crater, **Gof Redo**, about 5km north of the town in the fork of the roads to Moyale and North Horr. Follow the North Horr road until you see tracks branching off right after about 500m, and heading for a low col about 1.5km ahead: the gentler west side of the crater wall rises up here. There are some *manyattas* on the southwest rim, and you should be able to hire a guide quite easily if you want to go down inside for an hour or two. The crater is quite a favoured hideout for greater kudu, and there's a population of cheetah around here too.

Even easier is a walk to the "**singing wells**" near Ulanula. These are less exotic than they sound, but they're still a good excuse to explore. Ulanula is a conical peak to the west of the Isiolo road, about 6km from town. Leaving Marsabit, you cross two bridges, then turn left and climb 200–300m up a narrow, tangled ravine. A concrete holding-tank, visible from the road, gives the place away. Behind it are two natural wells, the first with a wooden trough in front, the second longer and apparently deeper, containing a fluctuating depth of brown, frog-filled water. A silent pump house stands by.

The **singing** is done not by the wells but by the Boran herders who use them. When the water is low, human chains are formed to get it out with luxuriantly leaking leather buckets and singing helps the work. At the driest times of the year you may be lucky and witness this, but try to get here early. Animals are usually driven to the wells after dawn, and it's a brisk 75-minute

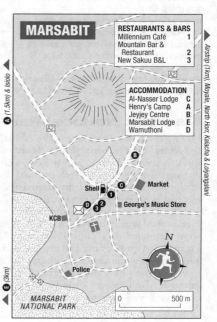

MARSABIT

Airstrip (1km), Moyale, North Horr, Kalacha & Loiyangalani

RESTAURANTS & BARS
Millennium Café — 1
Mountain Bar & Restaurant — 2
New Sakuu B&L — 3

ACCOMMODATION
Al-Nasser Lodge — C
Henry's Camp — A
Jeyjey Centre — B
Marsabit Lodge — E
Wamuthoni — D

Shell

Market

George's Music Store

KCB

Police

N

MARSABIT NATIONAL PARK

0   500 m

www.roughguides.com

535

walk from town. Go out there in the late afternoon, though, and you should get a lift back with one of the day's vehicles up from Isiolo.

Practicalities

If you're **moving on** from Marsabit by any available transport, you'll find that one or two trucks do occasionally spend the night in Marsabit, en route from Moyale or Isiolo. The best place to wait is at the **police checkpoint** on the Isiolo road. Ask around the petrol stations if you're trying to hitch a lift to Loiyangalani.

There's a KCB with an **ATM**, a **post office** and several reasonable places to **eat and drink** in town. The *Millennium Café* serves good chips and samosas, and there's very cheap food in a lively atmosphere at any time of day from the *hotelis*: hefty pancakes, *githeri*, *mandaazi* and *nyama choma*. The *hotelis* double as butchers so you can select your own slab for roasting from the carcasses hanging up. There's also a well-stocked shop and grocery stall opposite the Shell station. If you're thirsty, try the *Mountain Bar & Restaurant* which is the die-hards' drinking den, or try *New Sakuu B&L* next door.

Accommodation

There's a fair spread of cheap accommodation in town. Whichever place you choose, ask about **hot water** before moving in, as nights can get chilly (by some accounts, *Marsabit* means "place of cold") and lukewarm showers are no fun. In recent years, Marsabit has experienced terrible problems with **water supplies**, however, let alone worrying about hot showers, and some lodgings truck water in for their guests. To **camp**, most people head for Henry's Camp, but you can also camp at the national park's main gate.

Al-Nasser Lodge Town centre, by the market. Very cheap. ❶

Henry's Camp In a builder's yard in a shallow valley west of the town centre. Excellent, Swiss-run campsite with clean showers and toilets and extra touches like cold beer and home-made bread. Camping Ksh300.

Jeyjey Centre Town centre, by the Isiolo–Moyale road ☏069/2296. Camping Ksh200. Owned by former Saku MP Jarso Falana, who brings water in from miles away to supply guests. Formerly *the* place to stay, but increasingly rowdy and noisy in recent years, and very much a second best after Henry's ❶

Wamuthoni Town centre, near the post office. A basic hotel with clean rooms and shared hot showers. ❶

Marsabit National Park

Having made the long journey to Marsabit, you'll certainly want to get into the **Marsabit National Park** (Ⓦ www.kws.go.ke/marsabit.html; $20). The forest is wild and dense and the two crater lakes idyllically beautiful. Except during the long rains (March to June), there's a good chance you'll see some of the long-tusked Marsabit **elephants**, relatives of the famous Ahmed – a big tusker to whom Kenyatta gave "presidential protection", with elephant guards tracking him day and night (now replicated in fibreglass in the National Museum in Nairobi). His replacement, Mohammed, whose tusks were estimated at a cool 45kg each side, has also gone to the elephant's graveyard. As well as big tuskers, the park is renowned for its **greater kudu**, and there's a wide range of other wildlife. Between the nearly impenetrable forests of the peaks and the stony scrub desert at the base of the mountain, however, you'll need a little luck for sightings. This is a rewarding park, but one where you have to look hard.

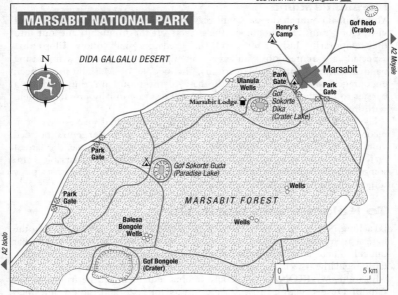

Practicalities

The park's **main gate** is at the edge of town, past the bank and the District Commissioner's office. It's not often visited and you may be in for a long wait if you want a lift around its forest tracks, but government officers and soldiers garrisoned in town do drive up to the **lodge** fairly frequently. This short trip, with the view over the first lake – Gof Sokorte Dika – and its forested rim, is a lot better than nothing. You might also be able to convince an armed ranger to escort you on foot as far as the first lake (a Ksh500 payment should be enough). This is a wonderful walk through the forest, with clouds of butterflies and the occasional mouth-drying encounter with buffalo or elephant.

Don't attempt to **drive in the park** without 4WD, as many of the roads are steep and tend to be ridiculously muddy.

There's a **campsite** near the main gate, 100m down the hairpin to the left of the ranger's house ($15). It's a wonderfully shaded place, somewhat overrun with baboons. There are several other places to camp in the park. Gof Sokorte Guda (Lake Paradise), a stunning, dark pool a kilometre across for much of the year, has wonderful sites on its crater rim, where a night could be thrillingly spent – lion, leopard and the rare and shaggy striped hyena are all seen and heard from time to time. This *Lake Paradise Special Campsite* ($15), requires an obligatory accompanying ranger.

Marsabit Lodge (℡0733/809919; FB ❻) sits on the shore of Gof Sokorte Dika, its outstanding views and the exquisite beauty of its location compensating for the shabby rooms and spooky emptiness – the place has been semi-closed for years. Elephants are no longer common visitors, since the salt that lured them is no longer laid out, but you can see buffalo and other wildlife converging at the lake below.

Marsabit's fauna

Your animal count in the park will very much depend on the season of your visit. Good rains can encourage the grazers off the mountain and out into the temporarily lush desert, and the predators will follow. **Elephants** especially are tremendous wanderers, sometimes strolling into town, causing pandemonium. More problematically, the people of Marsabit have been encouraged to cultivate around the base of the mountain, thus creating a barrier to the elephants' free movement and unintentionally providing them with free lunches.

The **birdlife** in the park is amazing: almost four hundred species have been recorded, including 52 different birds of prey. Very rare **lammergeiers** (bearded vultures) are thought to nest on the sheer cliffs of Gof Bongole, the largest crater, which has a driveable track around its ten-kilometre rim. Marsabit is also something of a **snake** sanctuary, with some very large cobras – this isn't a place to go barefoot or in sandals.

To Kalacha and North Horr

Reaching North Horr from Marsabit is getting easier, though continuing the logical next step down to Lake Turkana and Loiyangalani is still somewhat difficult. There is a more or less regular passenger truck that leaves Marsabit fairly regularly, as well as various mission, NGO and GK vehicles.

En route, **MAIKONA** is a friendly Gabbra settlement on the fringes of the **Chalbi Desert**, with a thriving daily market for goats and cattle (the camels which become ubiquitous from here on tend to be traded at Isiolo). As with all the villages up here, keep your camera out of sight, and ask permission if you want to take **photographs**: belief in the camera's evil eye is prevalent. *Mazingira Tourist Lodge* (❶) has a couple of rooms.

The Maikona springs are the last fresh water for 35km until you reach **Kalacha Goda** – the equally important springs near the small town of **KALACHA**. Kalacha has a few basic *dukas* and bars; a good mission-run **campsite** (Ksh300), with decent showers and a rather inventive swimming pool/water tank; and good *bandas* and camping at *Chalbi Safari Resort* (☎0722/267695, ❸; camping Ksh400), owned by the twin brother of the local MP, with meals available, and also with a small pool. The best accommodation in the area is ⚡ *Kalacha Camp* (☎0722/207300 or 0711/311479, Ⓦkalacha.org; FB including alcoholic drinks ❽, or self-catering $110 per person; huge discounts for residents), which has comfortable, self-contained twin-bedded *bandas* and, once again, the joy of a small **swimming pool**, partly shaded by the communal mess area. While you're in Kalacha, the **Catholic Church**, with its interior beautifully adorned with Ethiopian paintings, is well worth a look.

From Kalacha to North Horr, the track streaks out over blinding white salt pans and shifting soft sands, ducks behind straggly oasis clusters of half-dead palm trees, and finally loses itself in a vast orange expanse rimmed only by the hulks of very distant mountains. The exact path of the road varies annually, and in April it's often impassable when the rains come. **NORTH HORR**, when you finally reach it, is a welcome haven, with a handful of *dukas*, the Somali *Mandeleo Hotel*, opposite the mosque, for traditional food, rooms at the *Mandera Tourist Hotel* (❶), and a bright yellow phone box. From here on down to Loiyangalani, the terrain becomes even tougher as the road painfully climbs the northern foothills of Mount Kulal, but the view when you crest the ridge, looking down over the lake far away, can be spellbinding.

To Moyale and Ethiopia

From Marsabit, the **journey to Moyale**, which straddles the Ethiopian border, takes upwards of ten hours, depending on the vehicle. For the first three of these you descend from the mountain's greenery past spectacular craters – **Gof Choba** is the whopper on the left – to the forbidding black moonscape of the **Dida Galgalu Desert**. Dida Galgalu means "plains of darkness", according to one Boran story. Another account derives it from Galgalu, a woman buried here after she died of thirst trying to cross it. The road arrows north for endless miles, then cuts east across watercourses and through bushier country beneath high crags on the Ethiopian frontier. En route, you pass the turning to the small village of **Sololo** on the Ethiopian border, arrestingly sited between soaring peaks that can be climbed for stunning views over the northern plains and Ethiopian highlands. Sololo has a mission, which may let you camp in their grounds, and a single lodging, the *Treetop*.

There are some magnificent, towering **termite mounds** along the northern part of the route. They're a sight that seems quintessentially African, yet one that can quickly be taken for granted, like leafless trees in a northern winter. As the distances roll away, the 250km from Marsabit to Moyale is resolved in just a few bends, a couple of minor scenery changes. Over distances that would take days to cover on foot you can see where you have been and where you are going – the pastoralists' conservatism echoed in the landscape.

The road doubles north again and winds up through the settlements of Burji farmers – an agricultural people who emigrated from Ethiopia early in the twentieth century (see box, p.534) – past their beautifully sculpted houses and sparse fields, to Moyale.

Moyale

Straddling the Ethiopian border, **MOYALE** makes Marsabit look like a metropolis. Though the town is growing rapidly, the centre is small enough to walk around in fifteen minutes. You'll find several sandy streets, a pretty mosque, a few *dukas*, a bar, a camel-tethering ground, two petrol stations (one of which occasionally belies its defunct appearance), a big police station, a fairly large market area, a KCB with ATM, and an incredibly slow post office. Moyale is not much to write home about in fact, and there's not a lot to do except wander around, perhaps try some camel milk (very rich and creamy) and pass the time of day with everyone else, with or without the aid of *miraa*, universally popular in the northeast (see p.172).

The most interesting aspect of Moyale is its **architecture** – at least, the good number of traditionally built houses that are still standing. The Boran build in several styles, including circular mud-and-thatch huts, but in town the houses are rectangular, made of mud and dung on a wood frame, with a flat or slightly tilted roof projecting 1 to 2m to form a porch, supported by sturdy posts and tree trunks. The roof is up to 50cm thick, a fantastic accretion of dried mud, sticks, scrap, and vegetation. Chickens and goats get up there, improving the roof's fertility, and every time it rains another layer of insulating herbage springs up. As a result, the houses are cool while the outside temperature hovers above 30°C for most of the year.

Accommodation, eating and drinking

Accommodation is very limited and all firmly in the budget category – and the local *hotelis* and bars are equally basic when it comes to **meals and drinks**. The water in Moyale can be briny at times and it's worth bringing a few litres of drinking water with you. Even if you're not travelling on to Addis (see below), you're likely to want to visit Ethiopia for a much better range of food and drink. On the Kenyan side of the border, you'll find several fairly unsavoury **lodgings**, of which the *Sherif* (❶) is marginally the best, but there's really little to choose between them. If you have a tent, your best bet is to **camp** at the KWS (Kenya Wildlife Service) campsite (Ksh400), a simple plot often used by overland vehicles, with showers and decent toilets but no other facilities. The **Catholic mission** has also extended a warm welcome and a safe camping spot to overlanders in the past (donations welcome), although they don't offer any facilities at all, so you need to be fully equipped.

Into Ethiopia

Even if you're not intending to travel in **Ethiopia** (and if you haven't got a visa already, you won't be able to do so), the most interesting prospect in Moyale is to cross the valley into Kenya's neighbouring state and spend a few hours there. For Kenyans and Ethiopians, the border is an open one. For foreigners wanting to have a short look around, which is permitted even without a visa, there are just a few formalities on the Kenyan side, none on the Ethiopian, and crossing is easy.

    Ethiopian Moyale is larger than its Kenyan counterpart and noticeably more prosperous, with piped water, and a long-established electricity supply. There are several bars, and several decent hotels, of which the best is the *Koket Borana* (☎046/ 4441161 or 0911/451023; BB ❷), with clean, self-contained rooms and excellent meals in the restaurant. In town, there are lots of simple stores, and plenty of eating places. You can pay for everything in Kenyan shillings. The market buzzes colourfully with camels and goats, piles of spices, flour and vegetables. Otherwise, life here seems much the same as over the border, but easier. As a back-door view of Ethiopia, however, it is no more representative than the other side of town is of Kenya.

Travel details

On the main axes – Kitale–Lodwar, Nyahururu–Baragoi and Isiolo–Moyale – you will rarely be stuck for a ride too long. Least frequented is the route up to Loiyangalani and this, together with Isiolo–Moyale, has no reliable bus service.

Buses

Isiolo to/from: Maralal (every 2 days; 6–8hr); Nairobi (several daily; 5–6hr).
Lodwar to/from: Kitale (6 daily; 12hr); Lokichokio (1 daily; 3hr); Nairobi (1 daily; 18hr).
Maralal to/from: Nairobi (2 daily; 7hr); Nyahururu (2 daily; 3–4hr).

Matatus

Isiolo to/from: Maralal (daily; 6hr); Meru (several daily; 1hr); Nairobi (2–3 daily; 5hr); Nanyuki (several daily; 2hr).

Lodwar to/from: Lokichokio (3hr by Nissan, 2hr 30min by Peugeot); Kalokol (1hr).
Maralal to/from: Nairobi (several daily; 6hr); Nyahururu (several daily; 3hr).

Flights

Lodwar to/from: Nairobi JKIA (Fly540; daily; 1hr 30min).
Lokichokio to/from: Nairobi Wilson (ALS; 4 weekly; 1hr 45min).

Contexts

Contexts

History

Kenya's pre-colonial past is still the subject of endless conjecture, and it can be difficult for the traveller to make much sense of it – especially since the physical record in ancient architecture is virtually nonexistent upcountry. On the coast, settlement ruins, old documents and the Islamic tradition help to convey the past. What follows, up to the colonial period, is a much condensed overview, intended to pull together the historical accounts of individual peoples that are given throughout the Guide. More emphasis is given here to the history of the last hundred years or so.

The cradle of humankind

Kenya is quite likely to be the place where human beings first evolved. Some of the oldest remains of **ancestral hominids** have been found in the Tugen Hills, and the remains of what are thought to be our later ancestors have been found on the shores of Lake Turkana. Even so, concrete evidence of the origins of humanity remains scant, and new finds could easily turn the latest theories upside down.

The East African **Rift Valley** is ideal territory for the search for human origins: volcanic eruptions have repeatedly showered thick layers of ash and cinders over fossil beds, building up strata that can be reliably used to compare ages. The **Leakey** family has been instrumental in much of the work that has been done. Olduvai Gorge in Tanzania was the first major site to disclose evidence of human prehistory, and Louis Leakey and his wife, Mary, worked there from the 1930s. Their son, Richard, went on to explore the Turkana region and found even older fossils, putting Kenya under the spotlight of scientific attention. A suggestion in support of the "cradle of humankind" idea is that the Rift Valley's very formation – a major event on the earth's crust, which began some twenty million years ago – could have been the environmental spark that was the catalyst for human evolution.

In 2000, the Tugen Hills yielded finds from around six million years ago, of a hitherto unknown species named *Orrorin tugenensis*. It was possibly the **first hominid** – that is to say, the first known specimen of a creature on our side of the evolutionary divide between humans and the modern-day great apes – although *Sahelanthropus tchadensis*, discovered in Chad in 2002, is another possible contender. The *O. tugenensis* remains were of a creature that was still an ape, but one that walked upright on two legs. Specimens have also been found in Kenya of the hominids known as **australopithecines**, which seem to have appeared around 4.2 million years ago. Samples of *Australopithecus anamensis*, the earliest known australopithecine, were unearthed on the east side of Lake Turkana in 1965. Examples of later australopithecines have also been found in Kenya, but it is no longer thought that these were our direct ancestors. Evidence that they were not comes in the form of **fossil skull 1470** (its catalogue number), discovered by Bernard Ngeneo in 1972 and now in the National Museum in Nairobi (see p.113). Dated at 1.9 million years old, it was first believed to be an example of *Homo habilis* ("Handy man") and later renamed *Homo rudolfensis*. It proved that the earliest members of our genus, *Homo*, had co-existed with the later australopithecines.

Almost as important, was the discovery in 1984 of the nearly complete 1.6-million-year-old skeleton of 12-year-old "**Turkana Boy**", a member of the later species *Homo erectus* ("Upright man"), the immediate ancestor of the human species, found at Nariokotome on the western shore of Lake Turkana. It was probably *Homo erectus* who developed **speech** and discovered how to make **fire**, while improving enormously on the **tool-making** efforts of *Homo habilis*. **Olorgesailie** and **Kariandusi** are two "hand axe" sites, probably belonging to *Homo erectus*, which have been used within the last five hundred thousand years. And it was *Homo erectus* who, if the "cradle" theory is right, spread the humanoid gene pool to Asia, Europe and the rest of Africa, where, over the next few hundred thousand years, *Homo sapiens* emerged on the scene.

Early inhabitants: up to 1600

Real history begins with *Homo sapiens*, living as **hunter-gatherers**. Numbering probably fewer than a hundred thousand, living in small units of several families, and either staying in one place for generations or moving through the country according to the dictates of the seasons, these earliest human inhabitants of Kenya may have been related to the ancestors of present-day Pygmy and Khoisan (Bushmen) peoples, and probably spoke "click" languages similar to those of today's Khoisan peoples of southern Africa and Tanzania. Remnant hunter-gatherer groups still live in remote parts of Kenya – the **Boni** on the mainland near Lamu, the **Sanye** along the Tana River and the **Okiek** and **Dorobo** in parts of the Highlands – but the languages they now speak have mostly been adopted from neighbouring peoples. The hunting and gathering way of life has persisted in the cultural memories of most Kenyan peoples, and some of the groups who still practise it may have been offshoots from farming or herding communities that broke up during droughts.

The earliest distinct migration to Kenya was of **Cushitic**-speaking people from the Ethiopian Highlands. Occasional hunters and gatherers themselves, they were also livestock herders and farmers. Over the centuries, they filled the areas that were too dry for a purely subsistence way of life. They also absorbed many of the previous inhabitants through inter-marriage. Having herds and cultivating land brought up questions of ownership, inheritance and water rights, and an elaboration of social institutions and customs to deal with them. The Cushites had a strong material culture, using stone, particularly obsidian, to produce beautiful arrowheads, knives and axes, and they made a whole range of pottery utensils. They left evidence of their settlements in burial cairns and living sites at places like Hyrax Hill, near Nakuru. The same people may have built the irrigation works still used today along the Elgeyo Escarpment, west of Lake Baringo. For the most part, the earliest Cushites were absorbed by peoples who came later and they adopted new languages and customs. The changes were not all one-sided, however: **circumcision** and **clitoridectomy** (so-called female circumcision), practised by the early Cushites, became important cultural rituals for many of the peoples who succeeded and absorbed them.

The **Somali** and **Rendille** of the northeast are the main groups still speaking Cushitic languages, although their arrival in Kenya was more recent. Today, only the Boni speak a language related to the Southern Cushitic of the first farmers and herders, although the Boni themselves are hunter-gatherers.

For present-day Kenya, the most important arrivals began to reach the country in the first few centuries AD. From the northwest and the headwaters of the Nile came the **Nilotic**-speaking ancestors of the so-called **Kalenjin** peoples; from the west and south came speakers of **Bantu** languages, forebears of today's **Kikuyu**, **Gusii**, **Akamba** and **Mijikenda**, among others. (Bantu, a word coined by twentieth-century linguists, derives from the common stem for "person" – *ntu* – and the plural prefix *ba*. The word is not found in any of the six hundred contemporary Bantu languages spread across the continent, but it may have been the one used for "people" in the proto-language before it diversified.)

Along with their languages, the new arrivals brought new technologies, including iron working. **Iron** had enabled the Bantu to spread from the Nigeria/Cameroon area across central Africa, clearing the virgin forests and hoeing the ground for their crops. Eastwards, they encountered new Asian food crops – bananas, yams and rice – some of which arrived in East Africa by way of the Indonesian colonization of Madagascar. This new diversity of foods helped people to settle permanently in chosen regions. The Kalenjin peoples consolidated in the western highlands. The Bantu were particularly successful and, as their broad economic base took hold across the southern half of Kenya, their languages quickly spread. Herding, hunting, fishing and gathering were important supplements to the agricultural mainstay, while trade conducted with their exclusively pastoral or hunter-gatherer neighbours, especially in iron tools, carried their influence further. By about 1000 AD, Kenya's Stone Age technology had been largely replaced by an Iron Age one and, as human domination of the country increased, the beginnings of real specialization in agriculture and herding set in among the different tribes.

Down on the **coast**, Bantu immigrants mixed, over several hundred years, with the Cushitic-speaking inhabitants and with a continuous trickle of settlers from Arabia and the Persian Gulf. With the advent of Islam, this mélange gradually gave rise to a distinct culture and civilization – **Swahili** – speaking a Bantu language laced with foreign vocabulary. The Swahili were Kenya's link with the rest of the world, trading animal skins, ivory, agricultural produce and slaves, for cloth, metals, ceramics, grain, ghee and sugar, with ships from the Middle East, India and even China. The Swahili were the first Kenyans to acquire firearms. They were also the first to write their language (in the Arabic script) and the first to develop complex, stratified communities based on town and countryside. Swahili history is covered in more depth in Chapter 6.

Later arrivals: 1600–1885

New **American crops** – corn, cassava and tobacco – spread through Kenya after the Portuguese arrived on the coast in the early sixteenth century. They hugely increased the country's population capacity, while enabling a greater degree of permanent settlement and providing new trade goods.

At about this time, a pastoral **Nilotic**-speaking people, distantly related to the earlier Kalenjin arrivals, began a migration from the northwest. These were the first **Luo**-speakers who, some generations earlier, had left their homeland (around Wau in southern Sudan) for economic reasons: in the alternately flooded and parched flatlands around the Nile, unusual conditions could be catastrophic and forced communities to flee. The Luo ancestors were always on the move, herding, planting, hunting or fishing. Politically, they had a fairly complex organization, as, for months on end, while the Nile flooded, communities would be stranded in concentration along the low ridges. Several good years might be followed by drought, and population pressure then forced less dominant groups to go off in search of water and pasture. The overall trend was southwards. Groups of migrants picked up other, non-Luo-speakers on the way, gradually assimilating them through intermarriage and language change, always drawing attention with the impressive regalia and social standing of their *ruoth* – the Luo kings.

On the shores of Lake Victoria, where the Luo finally settled, sleeping sickness is thought to have wiped out many of their herds. But they were pragmatic, resourceful people, whose background of mixed farming and herding during the era of migration supported them. They turned to agriculture and, increasingly, to fishing.

Another Nilotic, pastoral people, the **Turkana**, appeared in Kenya later in the seventeenth century. Linguistically closer to the Maasai Nilotes, they seem to have shared the Luo resilience to economic hardship and they, too, have more recently turned to fishing. Also like the Luo, and almost unique among Kenyan peoples, they have never practised circumcision.

The Maa-speakers – **Maasai** and **Samburu** – were the last major group to arrive in Kenya, and their rise and fall had far-reaching effects on neighbouring peoples. Moving southwards from the upper Nile valley, from the beginning of the seventeenth century, they expanded swiftly thanks to their nomadic pastoral lifestyle, and in a few generations they were transformed from an obscure group into a dominant force in the region. Culturally, they borrowed extensively from their neighbours, especially the **Kalenjin** peoples, who spoke **Nandi**. Nandi words and Kalenjin cultural values were adopted, including circumcision, the age-set system and some ancient (originally probably Cushitic) taboos against eating fish and certain wild animals. It's likely that much of the "traditional" Maasai appearance also owes something to these contacts. The Maasai migration was no slow spread. Their cattle were periodically herded south and other peoples were raided en route to enlarge the herds; by 1800, they were widely established in the Rift Valley and on the plains, everywhere between Lake Turkana and Kilimanjaro. In response to Maasai dominance, many of the Bantu peoples adopted their styles and customs. Initiation by genital mutilation, probably already practised by most Bantu-speakers, was imbued with a new significance – especially for the Kikuyu – by intermarriage and close, if not always peaceable, relations with the Maasai.

Severe **droughts** in the nineteenth century pushed the Maasai further and further afield in search of new pastures, bringing them into conflict, and trade, with other peoples. Drought, disease and rinderpest epidemics (which killed off their cattle) were also responsible for a series of **Maasai civil wars** in the second half of the nineteenth century that disrupted the **trading networks** that had been set up between the coast and the interior. These were mainly controlled by Swahili, Mijikenda, Kamba and Kikuyu traders. Dutch, English and French goods were finding their way upcountry, and American interests were already being served during this period, as white calico cloth (still called *amerikani* today) became a major item of profit. In the last throes of the slave trade's existence, **slaves** were being exported from western Kenya and Uganda.

Largely in response to slavery and widespread fighting, the first **missionaries** installed themselves upcountry (the earliest went inland from Mombasa in 1846). Throughout this period, the Maasai disrupted movements in their territories, attacking Swahili slavers, Bantu traders and explorer-missionaries alike. The Maasai *morani* were specifically trained for raiding – a kind of guerrilla warfare – but, while their reputation lived on, they were bitterly divided among themselves and not organized on anything like a tribal scale.

By the time Europe had partitioned the map of Africa, the Maasai, who could have been the imperialists' most intractable enemies, were unable to retaliate effectively. The **Nandi** of the western highlands, the main people of the Kalenjin group, had begun to take the Maasai's place as Kenya's most feared adversaries, and put up the stiffest resistance. They were organized to the extent of having a single spiritual leader, the *orkoiyot*, who ruled what was in effect a theocracy. Their war of attrition against the British delayed advances for a number of years. But the Nandi did not have the territorial advantage that would have helped the Maasai, and the assassination of their *orkoiyot*, **Koitalel**, by the British, destroyed their military organization.

On the coast, the **Sultanate of Oman**, which had ousted the Portuguese from Mombasa in 1698, ruled the whole region between Lamu and Mozambique, and made Zanzibar its capital in 1840. Oman was already under British influence, and officially a British protectorate, when the country split in 1856; Zanzibar, including what is now the coast of Kenya, became a sultanate in its own right. (Coastal history is covered in more detail on p.390.)

The scramble for Africa

All Kenya's peoples resisted colonial domination to some degree. In the first twenty years of British attempts to rule the region, tens of thousands were killed in ugly massacres and manhunts, and many more were made homeless. Administrators – whose memoirs (see "Books", p.604) are the most revealing background for that period – all differed in their ideas of the ultimate purpose of their work and the best means of imposing British authority.

British interests in East Africa at the close of the nineteenth century had sprung from the European power struggle and the "scramble for Africa". The 1885 Berlin Conference chopped the continent into arbitrary spheres of influence. Germany was awarded what was to become Tanganyika; Britain got Kenya and Uganda. In 1886, formal agreements were drawn up and Kilimanjaro was ceded to Victoria's grandson, the Kaiser, giving each monarch a snowcapped, equatorial mountain.

Uganda was the focus of British interest, since Kenya – decimated by drought, locusts, rinderpest and civil war – seemed largely a deserted wasteland. And Uganda was strategically important for **control of the Nile** – which had long been a British preoccupation. But rivalry wasn't far beneath the seemingly amicable surface and Germany clearly had Uganda earmarked too. Britain's claim was in danger of lapsing if Uganda could not be properly garrisoned and supplied, and Kenya was the necessary base from which to do that.

In 1888, the British government granted permission for commercial operations in Uganda to the **Imperial British East Africa Company** (IBEAC), which, for sea access, leased a wide swath of southern Kenya from the Sultan of Zanzibar. The British also authorized the IBEAC to administer Uganda and that section of Kenya on their behalf. The company officers – mostly young and totally inexperienced English clerks – established a series of trading forts at fifty-mile intervals in a line connected by a rough ox-track leading from Mombasa into Uganda. Machakos, Murang'a and Mumias all began as IBEAC stations.

The IBEAC eventually went bankrupt, having failed to establish any kind of administration. The British government stepped into the breach in 1895, declaring a **protectorate** over Uganda and Kenya. Having thus acquired the region, the British decided to build a **railway**. This classic, valedictory piece of Victorian engineering took six years to complete and cost the lives of hundreds

Whether called peoples, ethnic groups or **tribes** (the term "tribe" has no pejorative connotation in Kenya), Kenyans have a multiplicity of racial and cultural origins. Tribes have never been closed units and families often include members of different tribes, though tradition and a degree of negotiation determine identity, usually through either the father's line, or through the mother's brother's line. In some respects ethnic identities are breaking down as class, political and national ones emerge. Nevertheless, politics still tends to have a strong ethnic dimension, and inter-tribal prejudice is still commonplace and occasionally becomes violent, as in the 2007–2008 clashes.

The most enduring ethnic distinction is **language**. A person's "mother tongue" is still important as an index of social identity, and a tribe is best defined as people sharing a common first language. Many people speak three languages (their own, Swahili and English) or even four if they have mixed parentage. English is a first language for a small but growing minority and English and Swahili (or Kiswahili as it's correctly known) are the country's dual official languages.

Indigenous tribes make up about 99 percent of the population. The largest tribe is the Kikuyu, based in the central region, who make up about 20 percent, followed by the Kalenjin from the Rift Valley (15 percent), the Luhya of western Kenya (14 percent), the Luo from the Nyanza region around Kisumu (12 percent), and the Kamba from the region east of Nairobi (11 percent). Many visitors are surprised that little more than two percent of the population are Maasai or Samburu.

Kenya also has a considerable and diverse **Asian** population (perhaps more than 100,000 people), predominantly Punjabi-and Gujarati-speakers from northwest India and Pakistan. Most of them live in the main cities. Descendants in part of the labourers who came to build the railway, they also include many whose ancestors came in its wake, to trade and set up businesses. Some of these families, notably on the coast, have lived in Kenya for centuries. There's a dispersed, Christian Goan community, too, identified by their Portuguese surnames, who tend to have less formalized relations with other Kenyans. A diminishing Arab-speaking community remains on the coast.

Lastly, there are still an estimated 34,000 **European** residents – a surprisingly motley crew from British ex-servicemen to Italian aristocrats scattered through the highlands and the rest of the country, some four thousand of whom hold Kenyan citizenship. Some of Kenya's white tribe maintain a scaled-down version of the old planter's life, and a few still hold senior civil service positions. Increasingly, however, the community is turning to the tourist industry for a more secure future.

Main language groups
There's a wide range of spellings in use, and names also vary depending on whether the name refers to the language or the people.

Bantu-speaking
Western Bantu: Luhya, Gusii, Kuria
Central Bantu: Kamba, Kikuyu, Embu, Meru, Mbere, Tharaka
Coastal Bantu: Swahili, Mijikenda, Segeju, Pokomo, Taita, Taveta

Cushitic-speaking
Southern Cushitic: Boni
Eastern Cushitic: Rendille, Orma, Boran, Gabbra ("Oromo" is often used collectively for all four languages), Somali.

Nilotic-speaking
Lake-River Nilotic: Luo
Plains Nilotic: Maasai and Samburu (Maa-speakers), Turkana, Teso, Njemps, Elmolo
Highland Nilotic: Kalenjin (Nandi and its dialects), Marakwet, Pokot, Tugen, Kipsigis, Elkony

of Indian labourers. Financially, it was a commitment that grew out of all proportion to the likely returns and continued to grow long after the last rail was laid. But its completion transformed the future of East Africa. From now on, the supply lines were secure and the interior only a month's journey from Europe by ship and rail. Suddenly, the prospects for developing the cool, fertile Kenya highlands looked much more attractive than the distant unknowns of Uganda and its powerful kingdoms.

More immediately, the railway physically divided the **Maasai** at a time when they were not united, and moreover were moving into alliances with the British. Their grazing lands, together with the regions of the **Kalenjin** peoples and the **Kikuyu** on the lower slopes of the highlands, were to become the heartland of the white settler colony.

The Kenya colony

Many people in Edwardian Britain saw Kenya as a land of opportunity: a new New Zealand, or even a Jewish homeland (a party of Zionists was actually escorted around Kenya but declined the offer). It was Sir Charles Eliot, the Protectorate's second governor, who was the main mover behind the **settlement scheme**. While some colonialists urged consideration for the "rights of natives", the growing clamour of voices claiming the support of British taxpayers – who had met the bill for the railway – outweighed any altruism. Eliot's extravagant reports on the potential of British East Africa were published, and government policy was thereafter directed towards getting the settlers in and making the railway pay. And so a trickle of landless aristocrats, middle-class adventurers, big-game hunters, ex-servicemen and Afrikaners (the farming land was also advertised in South Africa) began travelling up the line. Using ox-wagons to get to the tracts of bush they had leased, they started their farms from scratch. Lord Delamere, governor himself for a time, was their biggest champion. In the years leading up to World War I, the trickle of settlers became a flood, and by 1916 the area "alienated" to **European settlers** had risen to 15,000 square kilometres of the best land. Imported livestock was hybridized with hardy, local breeds; coffee, tea, sisal and pineapples were introduced and thrived; European crops flourished and cereals soon covered vast areas.

Nearly half the land worth farming was now in the hands of settlers, but it had become clear that it was far from empty of local inhabitants. Colonial invasion had occurred at a low point in the fortunes of Kenya's peoples and, unprepared for the scale of the incursion, they had been swiftly pushed aside into "native reserves" or became squatters without rights. As populations recovered, serious land shortages set in. The British appointment of "chiefs" – whose main task was to collect a tax on every hut – had the effect of diverting grievances against colonial policy onto these early collaborators and laying the foundations of a class structure in Kenyan society. Without a money economy, employment was the only means available to pay taxes and, effectively, a system of forced labour had been created. The whole apparatus quickly became entrenched in a series of **land and labour laws**. A poll tax was added to the hut tax; all African men were compelled to register to facilitate labour recruitment; squatters on alienated land were required to pay rent, through labour; and cash cropping on African plots was discouraged or banned (coffee licences, for example, were restricted to white farmers). The highlands were strictly reserved for white settlement, while land not owned by Europeans became Crown Land, its African occupants "tenants at will" of the Crown and liable to summary eviction.

Asians, too, were excluded from the highlands. While the leader of Kenya's Indians, **A.M. Jeevanjee**, had called for the transformation of Kenya into the "America of the Hindu", the proposal never came near consideration by the British. Barred from farming on any scale – except in the far west, where they developed sugar cane as an important crop – Indians concentrated on the middle ground, setting up general stores (*dukas*) across the country, investing in small industries and handling services.

World War I

World War I had a number of profound effects, although there were comparatively few battles in Kenya itself. Some 200,000 African porters and soldiers were conscripted and sent to Tanganyika (German East Africa), where 50,000 of them died. **General von Lettow Vorbeck**, the German commander, waged a dogged campaign against British forces despite the fact that his own were vastly outnumbered. After the Armistice, Kenyan troops who returned were deeply influenced by the experience. They had seen European tribes at war with each other; they had experienced European fallibility, and witnessed the kind of organization used to overcome it.

Sir Edward Northey, governor of Kenya at the time of armistice, pushed his **Soldier Settlement Scheme** through without difficulty. Its aim, to increase revenue by doubling the settler population in Kenya to nine thousand, seemed promising enough to a government sapped by war. But the Soldier Settlement Scheme was bitterly resented by Africans, particularly those who had fought alongside the soldiers and were now excluded from their gains.

Early nationalism and reaction

Political associations sprang up among ex-servicemen and those with a mission-school education: the Kikuyu Association, the Young Kikuyu Association and the Young Kavirondo Association. **Harry Thuku,** secretary of the Young Kikuyus, realized its potential and re-formed it as the East Africa Association in order to recruit on a nationwide basis. The hated registration law by which every African was obliged to carry a pass – the *kipande* – was a prime grievance, but tax reduction, introduction of land title deeds and wage increases were demanded as well. Alliances were built up with associations of embittered Indians and 1921 saw a year of protests and rallies. These culminated in Thuku's detention and the shooting by police of 25 demonstrators at a mass rally calling for his release. He remained in detention for eleven years.

The Indian constituency eventually secured two nominated seats (not elected) on the Legislative Council. Africans, meanwhile, remained voiceless, landless, disenfranchised and segregated by the **colour bar**.

As the settlers became established, they began to contribute appreciably to the income of the colony (which Kenya had officially become in 1920). Most of them seem to have believed that they were the founders of what would be a long and glorious era of white dominion. Indeed, settler self-government, along Canadian or South African lines, was a declared aim. African demands were hardly heeded by the authorities, but the Colonial Office was in a difficult position over the **Indians**, who were already British subjects and whose demands for equal rights they had trouble in refuting. Tentative proposals to give them voting rights, allow unrestricted immigration from India and abolish segregation caused indignation among the settlers. Their **Convention of Associations**, already arguing the case for white home rule, formed a "Vigilance Committee", which worked out detailed military plans for rebellion, including the kidnapping of the governor and the deportation of the Indians. Sensing a crisis, the Colonial Office drew up a white paper and a grudging settlement was reached that allowed five Indians and one Arab to be elected to the Legislative Council (the colony's local government), alongside eleven Europeans.

The primacy of African "interests", admirably reiterated yet again in the Devonshire Declaration of 1923, was still denied any real expression. A system of **de facto apartheid** was being practised. It was in this climate in the 1920s and 1930s that, floating above their economic troubles, the settlers had their heyday – the **Happy Valley life** so appallingly and fascinatingly depicted in *White Mischief* (see p.608) and other books.

Education, Kenyatta and the Kikuyu

The opportunities available to Africans came almost entirely through **mission schools** at first. Again, there was conflict between government and settlers on the question of **education**. The Colonial Office was committed, on paper at least, to the general development of the country for all its inhabitants, while the white farmers were on the whole adamant that raising educational standards could only lead to trouble. A crude form of Swahili had become the language of communication between Africans and Europeans. But the teaching of English was a controversial issue that hardliners foresaw eventually rebounding on government and settlers alike. In frustration, the Kikuyu set up self-help **independent schools** in the 1930s, primarily in order to teach their own children English.

Whether barring access to English education would ultimately have made any difference is debatable, but by the late 1930s there were already enough educated Africans to pose the beginnings of a serious challenge to white supremacy. One of these was **Jomo Kenyatta**. Born some time between 1889 and 1895 near Kiambu, just north of Nairobi, and educated at the Scottish Mission Centre in nearby Thogoto, Kenyatta adopted his name from the traditional beaded belt (*kenyatta*) he always wore.

After Thuku's imprisonment and the bloodshed at Nairobi in 1921, the East African Association was dissolved and was succeeded by the **Kikuyu Central Association** (**KCA**), which Kenyatta joined in 1928. The KCA was the spearhead of nationalism and lobbied hard for tax reductions, a return of alienated land, and the election of African representatives on the Legislative Council. It also protested against missionary efforts to outlaw **female circumcision**, on the grounds that the church was attempting to undermine Kikuyu culture. This last conflict led to a leadership crisis in the KCA and for a number of years threatened to swamp other issues.

Kenya survived the 1929 stock market crash and the resulting global **depression** as the colonial government became increasingly committed to the struggling settlers it was now bailing out. Exports fell catastrophically; coffee planting by non-whites was still prohibited and the tax burden continued to be placed squarely on Africans. Faced with this crisis, even some of the settlers began to accept that large-scale changes were in order. Just as awareness was growing that the economy could not survive indefinitely unless Africans were given more of a chance to participate, Kenya was thrown into World War II.

World War II

Perhaps not surprisingly, soldiers were easily recruited into the **King's African Rifles** when Italian-held Ethiopia (then Abyssinia) declared war on Kenya in 1940. Volunteers wanted money, education and a chance to see the world; conscripts, filling the quotas assigned to their chiefs, faced a life at home or on the native reserve that was no better than enlisting. Propaganda immediately succeeded in casting Hitler's image as the embodiment of all racist evil. Some Africans thought the war, once won, would improve their position in Kenya. They were partly right. Military campaigns in Ethiopia and Burma owed much of their success to African troops, and during the war their efforts were glowingly praised by Allied commanders.

On the soldiers' return, a new awareness, more profound than that felt by those returning from World War I, came upon them. The white tribes of Europe had fought the war on the issue of self-determination; the message wasn't lost on Africans. Yet still, in almost every other sphere of life, they were demeaned and humiliated. The KCA had been banned at the outbreak of war, allegedly for supporting the Italian fascists, and African political life was subdued. Real change, for 99 percent of the population, was still a dream.

Kenya's food-exporting economy had done well out of the war and it was clear the colony could make a major contribution to Britain's recovery. The postwar Labour government encouraged economic expansion without going far enough to include Africans among the beneficiaries. Industrialization gathered momentum and there was a rapid growth of towns. There was also further promotion of **white immigration** – a new influx of European settlers arrived soon after the war – and greater power was given to the settlers on the Legislative and Executive Councils. Population growth and intense **pressure on land** in the rural areas were leading to severe disruptions of traditional community life as people were shunted into the reserves or else left their villages to search for work in the towns. On the political front, militant **trade unionism**, dominated by ex-servicemen, gradually usurped the positions of those African leaders who had been prepared to work with the government.

Postwar African politics

A single African member, Eliud Mathu, was appointed to the Legislative Council in 1944. More significant, however, was the formation of the **Kenya African Union** (**KAU**), a consultative group of leaders and spokesmen, whose first president was Harry Thuku, set up with the governor's approval to liaise with Mathu.

Kenyatta had spent most of the period between 1931 and 1946 in Britain, campaigning for the KCA, studying anthropology under Bronisław Malinowski at the London School of Economics and writing his homage to the Kikuyu people, *Facing Mount Kenya*. His **return** in 1946, to an unexpectedly tumultuous welcome, signalled a real departure for African political rights and the birth of a new current of nationalism. The KAU was transformed into an active political party – and ran straight into conflict with itself. The **radicals** within the party wanted sweeping changes in land ownership, equal voting rights and abolition of the **pass law**, under which all black Kenyans were restricted in their movements and forced to carry an internal passport. The **moderates** were for negotiation, educational improvement, multiracial progress and a gradual shift of power. They were not convinced that their best interests lay in confronting the British head-on; they had all achieved considerable ambitions within the settler economy. Kenyatta, elected KAU president in 1947, was ambitious himself, but the Europeans mistrusted his intentions and rumour-mongered about his personal life and his communist connections (he had visited Russia during his time abroad).

Despite Kenyatta's efforts to steer a middle course, the KAU became increasingly radical and Kikuyu-dominated. While Kenyatta angled to give the party a multitribal profile to appease the settlers, he also managed to sacrifice some moderates in the leadership for the sake of party unity. There were defections as well: several radicals joined an underground movement and took oaths of allegiance against the British. Oath-taking groups emerged secretly all around the Central Highlands and, by 1951, a Central Committee was organized to coordinate insurgent activities.

The Mau Mau Rebellion

The Central Committee began murdering its opponents and attacking white-owned property in what became known as the **Mau Mau Rebellion**. The origin of the name is obscure; it may derive from *muma*, a traditional Kikuyu oath; but the insurgents never used it, calling themselves the **Land and Freedom Army** (**LFA**). The British accused the KAU leadership of involvement, but this seems unlikely, although the insurgents used Kenyatta's name in their propaganda. The LFA consisted largely of young men from the rural periphery of towns like Nyeri, Fort Hall (Murang'a) and Nairobi, and membership was overwhelmingly Kikuyu. One of the main factors prompting them into violent action was that land seizure by the settlers meant they no longer had enough land to feed themselves. Many insurgents had taken part in strikes during the late 1940s, and others were ex-soldiers who had fought for the British and learned guerrilla warfare in Burma and other campaigns.

In August 1952, following arson attacks on the homes of people who had refused to take the Mau Mau oath, the government imposed a curfew on three districts of Nairobi. But in October, **Chief Waruhiu wa Kungu**, the government's most senior African official, was murdered in Nairobi after making a speech condemning the Mau Mau. The British reacted by declaring a **State of Emergency**, and arresting any suspected insurgents. Within ten days, they had detained nearly four thousand people.

Kenyatta had played a delicate political game, condemning strikes and even oath taking, but ready to seize on any chance to exploit the situation. Now he and other KAU leaders were arrested and interned for their supposed part in the uprising. Thousands of **British troops** were sent to Kenya, and a **Kikuyu Home Guard** was formed to combat the Mau Mau, but the hardcore guerrillas fled from their villages and lived off the jungle for months on end, launching surprise attacks at night. They relied on considerable support from Kikuyu homesteads for supplies, intelligence reports and stolen weapons.

By early 1953, the rebels were becoming more daring. In January they murdered a settler family, the Rucks, including their 6-year-old son, and in March, a party of 83 insurgents raided **Naivasha police station**, releasing 173 detainees and seizing a large quantity of weaponry. Almost simultaneously, a force of some one thousand insurgents attacked the village of **Lari**, northwest of Nairobi, whose residents were largely Kikuyus loyal to the colonial regime, many of them Home Guard members. The insurgents burned down their homes and hacked to death more than eighty people. The following day, Home Guard reprisal killings of Mau Mau sympathizers in the district topped one hundred, killed in a series of mass shootings.

The British now declared "**Special Areas**" in which anyone who failed to stop when challenged would be shot, and "**Prohibited Areas**" – including the Aberdare range and Mount Kenya – in which all Africans would be shot on sight. In April 1954 they put Nairobi under military control, rounding up all the city's Kikuyu residents and detaining seventeen thousand of them, before extending the operation to other Kikuyu areas. By the end of the year, there were 77,000 prisoners, held in more than fifty British **concentration camps** throughout the country, where they were subject to arbitrary acts of brutality and murder at the hands of British troops. At one point, a third of the entire male adult Kikuyu population was being held in detention.

Under emergency powers, a policy of "**villagization**" was also enforced: by the end of 1955, more than a million people – almost the entire Kikuyu population – had been forcibly resettled in villages policed by guards and fenced with barbed wire. It was during this period that the cluster of closely related small tribes known today as the **Kalenjin**, acquired their name, which means "I tell you" in their common language, Nandi. Forging together the Nandi, Pokot, Elgeyo, Marakwet, Tugen and others under a single umbrella, it was largely the creation of the colonial authorities, seeking to recruit and reinforce support against the Kikuyu-dominated Mau Mau.

British atrocities

At its height, in 1953–54, the insurgency consisted of some fifteen thousand guerrillas, but little by little the British hunted them down. By September 1956, only around five thousand remained. The **end of the revolt** came in October 1956 with the capture and execution of **Dedan Kimathi**, the LFA's commander-in-chief. The State of Emergency nonetheless continued until 1960, when it was abandoned after news escaped into the press that British troops had bludgeoned detainees at **Hola** detention camp, killing eleven and injuring sixty, causing outrage in Britain.

During the uprising, insurgents had murdered 32 white settlers and around two thousand African civilians. Fifty British troops lost their lives. The British had hanged 1090 rebels – more than in any other colonial uprising – and claimed to have killed around eleven thousand guerrillas, destroying much of the documentation about the detention camps before Independence. New evidence, however (see "Books", p.609), suggests that British forces killed more than fifty thousand people, and perhaps as many as one hundred thousand. Many of these, uncommitted to Mau Mau, yet living in key locations as far as the British were concerned, were caught, sometimes literally, in the crossfire. The evidence, also shows that torture was a widespread tool of interrogation: thousands of detainees and villagers were subjected to gross **human rights abuses** while being screened and questioned, ranging from mutilation to rape, many of which resulted in death.

No British officials, nor any of the settlers who were also involved, have yet been prosecuted for atrocities committed during the Emergency. Nor has Britain yet paid any compensation or made any formal apology.

Independence: uhuru

With the Emergency over, the KAU leaders still at liberty set about exploiting the European fear of a repeat episode. Anything that now delayed the fulfilment of African nationalist aspirations could be seen as fuel for another revolt. There was no longer any question of a South African-style, white-dominated independence. Settlers, mindful of the preparations for independence taking place in other African countries, began rallying to the cry of multiracialism in a vain attempt to secure what looked like a very shaky future.

At the 1960 Lancaster House Conference in London, called to discuss Kenya's future, African representatives won a convincing victory by pushing through measures to give them majorities in the Legislative Council and the Council of Ministers. The members of these bodies, all nominated by the colonial authorities, included **Tom Mboya**, the prominent and charismatic Luo trade unionist, and the radical politician **Oginga Odinga** (another Luo), as well as **Daniel Arap Moi** and the Mijikenda leader **Ronald Ngala**. A new constitution was drawn up and eventual access to the "White Highlands" was accepted. The declaration promised that "Kenya was to be an African country": the path to independence was guaranteed; British Prime Minister Harold Macmillan said as much in his "**Wind of Change**" speech to the South African parliament at the time the Lancaster House Conference was meeting. The settlers perceived a "calamitous betrayal", with universal franchise and African-dominated independence expected within a few years.

Minority tribal associations, meanwhile, foresaw troubles ahead if the Kikuyu/Luo elite achieved independence for Kenya at the cost of the smaller constituencies. In 1960, the Kenya African National Union (**KANU**) was formed, dominated by the Kikuyu and Luo politicians who had campaigned most prominently against British colonial rule. Soon after, a second, more moderate party, the Kenya African Democratic Union (**KADU**), was created, with Britain's help, to federate the minority, largely rural-based, political associations in a broad defensive alliance against Kikuyu/Luo domination. One of KADU's leading members was **Daniel Arap Moi**.

Elections were held in 1961, KANU emerging with nineteen seats against KADU's eleven. But KANU refused to form a government until Kenyatta was released. A temporary coalition government was formed, composed of KADU, European and Asian members. Kenyatta was duly released and, six months later, a member resigned his seat, making room for him on the Legislative Council. In 1962, Kenyatta became Minister for Constitutional Affairs and Economic Planning – a wide portfolio – in a new coalition government formed out of the KADU alliance and KANU. Despite a second London conference to try to reach an agreement about the federal constitution demanded by KADU, the question was left in the air. Independence elections the following year seemed to answer the constitutional question: KANU emerged with an even greater lead and a mandate for a non-federal structure. On June 1 – **Madaraka Day** – Kenyatta became Kenya's first prime minister. And on December 12, 1963, control of foreign affairs was handed over and Kenya became formally **independent**.

The Kenyatta years: harambee

It was barely sixty years since the pioneer settlers had arrived. Many of them had panicked, sold up and left before Independence, but others decided to stay under an **African government**. Despite his years in detention, Kenyatta turned out to have more consideration for their interests than could have been foreseen. He held successful meetings with settlers in his home village; his bearded, genial image and conciliatory speeches assuring them of their rights and security quickly earned him wide international support and the respected title Mzee (Elder). Many Europeans retained important positions in the administration and judiciary.

Milton Obote and Julius Nyerere, leaders of newly independent Uganda and Tanzania, held talks with Kenyatta on setting up an **East African Community** to share railways, aviation, telecommunications and customs. The union was formally inaugurated in 1967. There was a mood of optimism: it looked very much as if Kenya had succeeded against all the odds.

But there were urgent issues to contend with, among which **land reform** and the rehabilitation of freedom fighters and detainees were the most pressing. Large tracts of European land were bought up and a programme to provide small plots to landless peasants was rapidly instigated. Political questions loomed large as well. On December 12, 1964, Kenya became a republic, its head of state no longer the Queen, but rather President Kenyatta. KADU was dissolved "in the interests of national unity", its leaders absorbed into the ruling KANU party, making Kenya a de facto one-party state. For the sake of "national security", British troops were kept on, initially to quell a revolt of ethnic Somalis in the northeast and an army mutiny in Nairobi. A defence treaty has kept a British force at Nanyuki ever since.

There was heavy emphasis on **harambee** (pulling together), endorsed by Kenyatta at all his public appearances. *Harambee* meetings became a unique national institution: fund-raising events at which – in a not untraditional way – donations were made by local notables and politicians towards self-help education and health programmes. During the 1960s and 1970s, hundreds of *harambee* schools were built and equipped in this way. But the ostentatious gifts, and particularly the guaranteed press coverage the next day with donors listed in order of value, sometimes reduced the *harambee* vision of community development to an exercise in patronage and competitive status seeking.

On the **economic front**, the first decade of independence saw remarkable changes and rapid growth. The settlers' fairly broad-based crop-exporting economy was a powerful springboard for development, and not difficult to transfer to African control. While many large landholdings were sold *en bloc* to African investors, smaller farmers began to contribute significantly to export earnings through coffee, tea, pyrethrum and fruit. Industrialization proceeded at a slower pace: Kenya's mineral resources are limited and the country relies heavily on oil imports. **Foreign investment** wasn't especially beneficial, as investors were given wide freedoms to import equipment and technical skills and to re-export much of the profit.

The resettlement programme was abandoned in 1966, its objectives "largely attained". But many peasants, having been squatters on European farms, were now "illegal squatters" on private African land. Thousands migrated to the towns where unemployment was already a serious problem. Kenya was becoming a class-divided society. **Growth**, rather than a radical redistribution of wealth, was the government's main concern. Although by 1970 more than two-thirds of the European mixed farming lands were occupied by some fifty thousand Africans, and the overall standard of living had improved considerably, income disparities were greater than ever. **Kikuyu domination** was strongly resented by other groups, although it was perhaps inevitable that the people who had lost most and suffered most under British rule should expect to receive the most benefits from independence.

Political opposition

It was in this climate that KANU's leadership split. **Oginga Odinga**, the party vice president, resigned in 1966 to form the socialist **Kenya People's Union** (**KPU**) and 29 MPs joined him. The ex-guerrilla Bildad Kaggia became deputy head of the KPU and a vocal agitator for poorer Kikuyu. Kenyatta and Mboya closed ranks in KANU and prepared for political conflict. KPU was anti-capitalist and pro-non-alignment, while KANU – led in this respect by Tom Mboya – stressed the need for close ties with the West, and for economic conditions that would attract foreign investment. The KPU's stand was denounced as divisive, and the party was barely tolerated for three years, its members harassed and detained by the security forces, its activities obstructed by new legislation and constitutional amendments.

In KANU, Odinga's post of vice president was taken, briefly, by Joseph Murumbi and then, with behind-the-scenes encouragement from the British (keen to avoid a radical in the job), by Daniel Arap Moi. Odinga had strong, grassroots support in the Luo and Gusii districts of western Kenya. But **Tom Mboya**'s supporters came from an even broader base, including many poor Kikuyu. By the end of the 1960s, speculation was mounting about whether he would be able to take over the presidency on Kenyatta's death. As the Mzee's right-hand man he was widely tipped to succeed – a possibility that alarmed Kenyatta's Kikuyu supporters. In July 1969, Mboya was gunned down by a Kikuyu assassin in central Nairobi. No high-level complicity in the murder was ever brought to light, but Mboya's death was a devastating blow to Kenya's fragile stability, setting off shock waves along both class and tribal divisions. There was widespread fighting and rioting between Kikuyu and Luo, fuelled by years of rivalry and growing feelings of Luo exclusion from government. During a visit by Kenyatta to Kisumu – where he attended a public meeting at which Odinga and his supporters were present – hostility against his entourage was so great that police opened fire, killing at least ten demonstrators.

The KPU was immediately banned and Odinga detained without trial. Although the constitution continued to guarantee the right to form opposition parties, non-KANU nominations to parliament were, in practice, forbidden. There was a resurgence of oath taking among Kikuyu, Meru and Embu, pledging to maintain the Kikuyu hold on power. The Kikuyu contingent in the army was strengthened and a new force of shock troops, the **General Service Unit** (**GSU**), was recruited under Kikuyu officers; independent of police and army, it was to act as an internal security force. In the early 1970s, Kikuyu control – of the government, the administration, business interests and land – gripped tighter and tighter.

Internationally, however, Kenya was seen as one of the safest **African investments** – a model of stability only too happy to allow the multinational corporations access to its resources and markets. The development of the tourist industry helped give the country a positive profile, and, in comparison with most other African countries, some still fighting for independence and others beset by civil war or paralyzed by drought, Kenya's future looked healthy enough. But in achieving record economic growth, foreign interests often seemed to crush indigenous ones. An elite of profiteers – nicknamed the **wabenzi** after the Mercedes Benzes they favoured – extracted enormous bribes out of transactions with foreign companies. Nepotism was blatant and Kenyatta himself was rumoured to be one of the richest men in the world. For the majority of Kenyan people, life was hardly any better than before Independence. Students poured out of the secondary schools with few prospects of using their qualifications; population increase was the highest in the world; and, most damaging of all, land distribution was still grossly unfair in a society where land to grow subsistence crops was the basic means of survival.

In 1975, in the first ever explicit public attack on the Kikuyu monopoly of power, the radical populist MP **J.M. Kariuki** warned that Kenya could become a country of "ten millionaires and ten million beggars". He was arrested for his pains then released and, some weeks later, found murdered in the Ngong Hills. A massive turnout at his funeral was followed by angry **student demonstrations**. "Kariuki's death", wrote the then outspoken *Weekly Review*, "instils in the minds of the public the fear of dissidence, the fear to criticize, the fear to stand out and take an unconventional public stance." In the following years, a number of other MPs were detained, and the issue of landlessness ceased to be one that many people were prepared to shout about.

Kenyatta retreated into dictatorial seclusion, propped up by close Kikuyu cronies. As parliament, and even the cabinet, took an increasingly passive role in decision-making, the pronouncements from the Mzee's "court" began to be accompanied by vague suggestions of threats to his government from unspeci- fied foreign powers. By 1977, the **East African Community** had ceased to function. Delayed elections, hostility towards socialist Tanzania, further deten- tions and growing allegations of corruption formed the sullen backdrop to **Kenyatta's death**, in bed, on August 28, 1978.

Kenya under Moi: nyayo

The passing of the Mzee took Kenya by surprise. There was a nationwide outpouring of grief and shock, but for many, also a sense of relief, and anticipation that the future might better reflect the ideals of twenty years earlier. Vice president **Daniel Arap Moi** smoothly assumed power and quickly gathered popular support with moves against corruption in the civil service (where the mass of Kenyans felt it most), his stand against tribal nepotism (he himself was from the minority Kalenjin), and the release of all Kenyatta's political prisoners.

But the honeymoon was short. In the first year or two of his presidency, Moi's **nyayo** (footsteps) philosophy of "peace, love and unity" in the wake of Kenyatta found wide appeal, and his apparent honesty and outspoken attacks against tribalism impressed many, making him friends abroad. But economic management was weak, and the failure to make any adjustments in economic policy in favour of the rural and urban poor caused growing resentment at home. Oginga Odinga and other ex-KPU MPs were prevented from standing in the 1979 elections. Student protests began again and the closing of the university became an annual event. On the international scene, the whole Indian Ocean region became strategically important with the fall of the Shah of Iran and the Soviet invasion of Afghanistan. Kenya developed closer ties with the USA, extending military facilities to American vessels in exchange for gifts of grain after a failure of the harvest in 1983.

On Sunday August 1, 1982 – three months after constitutional amendments were pushed through to make Kenya officially a one-party state (to prevent Oginga Odinga registering the new Kenya Socialist Alliance party) – sections of the Kenya Air Force attempted a **military coup**. Without support in the other armed forces however, the coup was easily put down by the army and the GSU, who killed scores of perceived coup supporters. The coup attempt heralded a new clampdown on students (the university was dissolved) and dissident voices, such as that of Oginga Odinga, who was placed under house arrest.

Despite Moi's efforts to throttle all dissent, the groundswell of resentment continued to grow. An opposition group, **Mwakenya** (a Swahili acronym for Union of Nationalists to Liberate Kenya), attracted attention through its pamphlets calling for the replacement of the Moi government, new democratic freedoms and an end to corruption and Western influence. Hundreds of people were arrested, and some of their defence lawyers were in turn arrested themselves. In 1987, an **Amnesty International** report condemned Kenya's human rights record, as detainees died in custody and prisoners were routinely tortured and kept in waterlogged cells beneath Nyayo House in Nairobi. Public meetings of more than five people were banned, and all dissent, even within KANU, was crushed.

The path to multiparty democracy

In February 1990 **Robert Ouko**, the Luo foreign minister favoured by the West and widely viewed as a potential successor to the presidency, was murdered, sparking off a week of nationwide **rioting**, most violent in Ouko's home town of Kisumu. July of that year saw Central Highlands towns in violent tumult as public opposition to the government mounted, and a Nairobi pro-democracy rally on July 7 (**Saba Saba** – Swahili for 7/7, as the event came to be known) degenerated into a riot, leading to dozens of deaths in street battles with armed police.

Moi blamed "hooligans and drug addicts" for the Saba Saba riots, and the government came down hard on journalists, stifling local newspapers and accusing the foreign press, and particularly the BBC, of mischief-making. Relations with the international community plummeted. Against the prevailing, post-Cold War trend in Africa, Moi's stubborn resistance to the adoption of a multiparty system riled his overseas backers. He seemed barely aware of the new global consensus and the hard reassessment of aid distribution taking place among the rich countries.

In 1991, the steady build-up of an opposition lobby became so powerful it could no longer be dismantled. Oginga Odinga – effectively Kenya's elder statesman – set up the **Forum for the Restoration of Democracy (FORD)** in association with his son **Raila Odinga** and the influential Law Society chairman, **Paul Muite**. FORD quickly attracted government opponents from all quarters. Moi called them "rats" that would be "crushed", but by the end of 1991, Kenya's immediate future was increasingly out of the president's control. **John Troon**, the ex-Scotland Yard policeman hired by Moi to investigate Ouko's murder, revealed that the greatest suspicion fell on the president's closest advisor Nicholas Biwott, and his internal security chief, Hezekiah Oyugi, both of whom were sacked, arrested and later released "for lack of evidence", but not reinstated.

Although now internationally renowned as a wildlife conservationist, Richard Leakey rose to prominence as a palaeontologist from the shadows of his eminent parents Mary and Louis Leakey. He published several books and eventually became head of the National Museums of Kenya in Nairobi.

In 1989, facing an international outcry over the poaching of elephants and the serious impact that was having on the tourist industry, President Moi hired Leakey to take charge of the newly formed **Kenya Wildlife Service** (KWS). Leakey's first move was a characteristically bold one: he invited the world's press to watch Moi ignite Kenya's US$3 million stockpile of confiscated **ivory** – producing the most memorable photo opportunity of the Moi presidency. He went on, with Moi's support, to create anti-poaching units and briefed them to shoot to kill any poachers in the parks. The World Bank and other donors were so impressed that they gave more than US$140 million in grants. The poaching stopped, elephants and rhinos were saved from the brink of extinction, and Kenya's international image was partially restored.

But Leakey's success went too far for some local politicians, particularly in Maasailand. His confrontational approach to the balance of human and animal needs in the parks – all humans out – infuriated many. And he seemed incorruptible: the KWS had dried up completely as a source of patronage.

In June 1993, on a routine flight at the controls of his Cessna plane, Leakey crashed, losing both legs in the accident. Foul play was suspected, but not proven. Within months he was walking on artificial limbs, anxious to get back to work. But there had been a mood change in his employers. Noah Ngala, tourism minister at the time, announced that evidence of corruption and mismanagement had been unearthed at the KWS. No more bitter irony could be imagined. In January 1994, Leakey resigned from the KWS and was replaced by the less trenchant David Western, an advocate of human-animal coexistence.

In the wake of this, the major donor nations suspended balance-of-payment support to Kenya for six months, pending economic and political reforms. Moi got the message. Within days he announced there would be multiparty elections for the next parliament and a free vote for the presidency at the end of 1992.

The 1992 elections

FORD found the transformation from opposition lobby group to **political party** very hard to manage. As a party it was promiscuous in the welcome it extended to every ex-KANU minister who made the leap, and with elections approaching, it promptly split into three factions, each with its own presidential candidate. The split revealed the **ethnic divisions** of multiparty politics, and it became impossible to enter the political arena without constant reference to the tribal affiliations of the politicians and their supporters. Dozens were killed and thousands made homeless in tribal violence in the Rift Valley, mainly between indigenous Kalenjin people who supported Moi, and migrant farmers and traders from central Kenya.

Using a combination of fraud, ballot-stuffing, manipulation of electoral rules, physical prevention of opposition candidates from presenting nomination papers, printing money to buy off the voters, and changing the polling date at the last minute, Moi made sure that he and his party won the **1992 election**. But for the first time in years, there was also an elected multiparty opposition, including the three FORD factions, and the Democratic Party (DP) under former Vice President Mwai Kibaki, who came third in the presidential poll behind Moi and Odinga. KANU had almost no MPs from Kikuyu or Luo areas.

Despite dubious practices in the elections, the international community was unimpressed with the fractious opposition, and the **IMF** and **World Bank** decided that there had, in the end, been wide support for the incumbents. After a row in which Moi called their economic demands "suicidal and dictatorial", donor nations agreed to pick up the aid programme, two years after it had ceased, although this did little to refill the coffers pilfered since the end of the 1980s. The aid was contingent on a dramatic raft of privatizations – including post and telecoms, the railways and the national produce and cereals board – intended to stimulate the economy and reduce the opportunities for embezzlement.

The 1997 elections

Several years of economic slowdown followed, with strikes by teachers and nurses, mass demonstrations for constitutional reform and the breakdown of relations with the IMF. Senior figures in the main opposition parties (FORD-K, FORD-A and the DP) agreed to work together, with a single presidential candidate for the **1997 elections**, the economist and career politician Mwai Kibaki. **Richard Leakey** (see box opposite) coordinated the alliance and raised funds. By June 1997, the opposition, and particularly students, were howling for reforms in advance of the elections. Police stormed Nairobi University to stop a rally commemorating the 1990 Saba Saba demonstrations, and left more than a dozen dead while brutally putting down protests that had broken out around the country.

Religion in Kenya

Varieties of **Catholicism** and **Protestantism** are dominant in the Highlands and westwards, and are increasingly pervasive elsewhere. In the Rift Valley and the far west, especially towards Lake Victoria, there are many minor Christian sects and churches – more than a thousand denominations in all – often based around the teachings of local prophets and preachers.

Broad-based, non-fundamentalist **Sunni Islam** dominates the coast and the northeast, and is the fastest growing religion in the country. Many towns have several mosques, but one usually serves as the focal Friday mosque for the whole community. The Aga Khan's Ismaili sect is an influential Asian constituency with powerful business interests. Politically, Kenyan Muslims tend towards moderation, but there is a certain cultish and invariably contradictory admiration for **Osama Bin Laden** among disaffected youth on the coast. An irrational fear of Islam was spread by some missionary groups in the run-up to the 2007 elections, and persisted in a mistrust of US president Barack Obama's background and his presumed (and unsubstantiated) support for the the ODM.

Hindu and **Sikh** temples are found in most large towns, and there are adherents of **Jainism** and the **Bahai** faith, too.

Indigenous religion (mostly based around the idea of a supreme god and intercession between the living and the spirit worlds by deceased ancestors) survives as an inclusive belief system only in the remotest areas of northern Kenya, among the remaining Okiek (or Ndorobo) hunter-gatherers in a very few forests, and among pastoralists like the Maasai. While it is continually under threat from Christian missionaries, its influence over the lives of many nominally Christian or Muslim Kenyans remains powerful.

For the rest of the year, repression alternated with promises of reform, punctuated by a series of national strikes until, in November 1997, parliament removed some of the legislation restricting freedom of movement and speech. Despite this, Mombasa erupted in violence in August 1997, when two police stations were attacked, six policemen killed, weapons stolen and dozens of upcountry people later killed and thousands more expelled by armed gangs who terrorized the district of **Likoni**. Notices circulated "reclaiming" the coast for its indigenous inhabitants, and demanding the largely Kikuyu newcomers return to their home districts.

Elections were held in December, and the vote, predictably, split along ethnic lines. The Kalenjin constituencies of the Rift Valley, along with the Maasai and Samburu, the Somali, Turkana, coastal and many Luhya and Kisii constituencies, largely voted for Moi and KANU. Mwai Kibaki's DP did well in the Kikuyu areas, in whose heartland, not even Jomo Kenyatta's son, **Uhuru Kenyatta**, could win a seat for KANU. Raila Odinga, with his National Development Party (NDP), was well supported, but only locally in Luo-land. Moi won the presidential election with 2.4 million votes; Kibaki came second with 1.9 million.

Moi's final term

The aftermath of the elections saw discussion on constitutional reform getting under way, with Moi bringing opposition figures on side. Raila Odinga was made chair of the constitutional reform committee and Richard Leakey was appointed as cabinet secretary with special responsibility for combating corruption. In June 2001, KANU and Odinga's NDP joined together in a formal coalition, Odinga joining the cabinet as energy minister.

With elections approaching in 2002, Odinga dissolved the NDP, which merged into KANU, a move that Moi hoped would bring Luo voters over to the party. The opposition also did some merging, when twelve groups, including FORD-K and the DP, joined to form the National Alliance Party of Kenya (**NAK**). Meanwhile Moi decided to back Uhuru Kenyatta as KANU's presidential candidate. Kenyatta was widely seen as a figurehead who would front a new regime on Moi's behalf, and Moi's backing of him particularly annoyed Raila Odinga, who had hoped to be the party's candidate. He and a number of other KANU grandees resigned their ministerial posts and set up a "Rainbow

Al-Qaeda in Kenya

On the morning of August 7, 1998, a van containing 800kg of TNT exploded in the parking lot behind the US embassy in Nairobi. In the embassy itself – the terrorists' intended target – some forty people, twelve of them Americans, perished; but the brunt of the blast was borne by the adjacent four-storey Ufundi Cooperative House. The resulting carnage led to 263 deaths and more than five thousand people injured, nearly all of them Kenyans, and property damage estimated at around $500 million. It is widely suspected that local al-Qaeda operatives were responsible for the attack, as well as the bombing of the US Embassy in Dar es Salaam, just a few minutes later.

Before the December 2002 elections, Kenya's tourist industry was shaken by an al-Qaeda suicide bomb attack on the Israeli-owned *Paradise Hotel* at Kikambala that killed sixteen people, simultaneous with a failed attempt to shoot down an Israeli-bound charter flight leaving Mombasa.

In September 2009, a US helicopter raid over Somalia killed Saleh Ali Saleh Nabhan, the Kenyan-born al-Qaeda suspect who is believed to have organized both attacks.

Alliance" within the party, opposed to Kenyatta's candidacy. In October they left KANU and formed the Liberal Democratic Party (LDP), which joined with the NAK to form the **National Rainbow Coalition** (**NARC**), with a single presidential candidate, Mwai Kibaki. NARC won a landslide victory in the December **2002 elections**, and KANU was turfed out of government for the first time since Independence.

All in all, **Moi's legacy** was not great: under his 24-year rule, living standards had fallen; respect for human rights had decreased; and ethnic strife had worsened, in part due directly to his divide-and-rule politics. With Moi and KANU out, Kenyans as well as the country's financial backers were now hoping for better.

Kenya under Kibaki

Kibaki took up the presidency with a promise of **constitutional reform** within one hundred days. More than 2500 days later, Kenya was still waiting. The biggest wrangle involved the proposed post of prime minister, which Odinga saw as his, apparently following a secret deal (the Memorandum of Understanding, or "**MoU**", with Kibaki). Part of the problem was that NARC was a loose alliance of politicians and ethnic blocs, and it soon began to fragment without Moi as a common opponent to unite it. A constitutional convention was set up at the **Bomas of Kenya** conference centre in April 2003, but in a **draft constitution** passed in June 2005, the Bomas proposals were shot through with amendments tabled in parliament, most notable among them the provision that the post of prime minister be in the president's gift. However, the amendments also included a radical shake-up of Kenya's **land laws**, including proposals that women should have the right to inherit land, that foreigners should not be able to own land and that foreign 1000-year leases be reduced to 99 years. Odinga and several other cabinet ministers opposed the proposed constitution, which went to the country in a **referendum** in November 2005. The ballot-paper symbol for a "yes" vote was a banana, for the "no" vote an orange, and politicians who favoured the original Bomas proposals joined forces with those who wanted no change at all in an Orange Team, to campaign for a "no" vote, headed by Odinga.

The referendum was peaceful and transparent and resulted in a two-to-one rejection of the proposed constitution. His plans thwarted, Kibaki dismissed his entire cabinet, and then re-appointed them all, with the exception of Odinga and the Orange Team, who moved over to join KANU in opposition, marking the death of the NARC coalition. Constitutional reform was left in the air.

In other fields, Kibaki's reform ideas fared better. In 2003, his administration introduced **free primary education** for all, bringing schooling to 1.5 million more children, although the move has been beset by logistical problems, teacher shortages, and a fall in schools' performance, with private schools dominating exam league tables. Post-Moi, the **press** was largely freer, although in an infamous raid in 2006, masked policemen stormed the offices of the Standard media group (which includes KTN TV, owned by the Moi family), burning papers, smashing equipment and seizing tapes. The Kibaki faction, and in particular the president's outspoken wife, had been infuriated by negative press and stories they alleged were fabricated, but neither Kibaki nor Moi had anything to say about the raid.

For years, any reference to **multiparty politics** by KANU leaders was accompanied by dire warnings of the bloody consequences for tribal harmony of such a system. Once the government was forced into a corner on the issue by foreign aid donors, the prophecy was quickly realized. Ethnic allegiances swamped the new political order before it had even consolidated, so that the opposition parties were unable to formulate policies and election strategies that were free of ethnic considerations.

For decades, the Rift Valley and other normally unproductive areas had been the destination for **migrants** from the Kikuyu, Luo and Luhya tribes, who bought up marginal farmlands, and tried to apply their farming techniques among the local Kalenjin and Maa-speakers while benefiting from local aid and subsistence initiatives. Victims of the early attacks in Rift Valley Province described organized gangs of youths terrorizing non-Kalenjin homesteads and villages, while local police arrived too late to do anything or just stood by.

In electioneering terms, the violence usually proved counterproductive, as the government lost more votes from disgust with their inaction than it gained from forcing opposition voters out of marginal KANU constituencies. Probably the aim was simply to demonstrate to the world at large that multipartyism in Africa leads to tribal violence. In this – to the Moi government's lasting shame – it succeeded.

The violence consisted of the looting of property, the theft of livestock, the burning of houses, and the beating up or killing of anyone who got in the way of the perpetrators. Their message was, "Get off our land", and thousands of victims moved to refugee camps outside Eldoret, Nanyuki and other towns. During the 1990s, at least three thousand people were killed in violence between different language groups in the Rift Valley, western Kenya and on the coast, and at least three hundred thousand displaced in **ethnic cleansing**. The violence would build up in the run-up to the elections and, in late 1992 and 1997 (and to a lesser extent in 2002), tensions ran high in traditional flashpoints.

As the results came in after the **2007 presidential elections**, both Raila Odinga and Mwai Kibaki declared victory, but it was Kibaki's swearing in on December 30 that sparked an instant, violent reaction across the country. Gangs of non-Kikuyu, Odinga supporters rampaged in the Rift Valley, in Kisumu and on the coast, attacking Kikuyu homes and businesses, killing men, women and children and, in an attack that received wide media coverage, burning a church in Eldoret sheltering fleeing Kikuyus, killing 35 people. There were running battles in Nairobi's slums between club- and machete-wielding youths of different tribes. By the end of January 2008, when talks brokered by former UN secretary-general Kofi Annan were finally under way, more than 1300 people had been killed and more than half a million displaced. The majority of the victims were Kikuyu, but other tribes were the targets of Kikuyu reprisal attacks and the police shot dead more than 100 demonstrators and looters. Unlike previous bouts of politically inspired ethnic violence, most of which had taken place in rural areas, the **2007–2008 clashes** were intense, and took place largely in towns, where foreign media were able to relay the unfolding carnage as it happened.

The IMF and the World Bank resumed lending to Kenya in 2003 after the new government set up a five-year **Economic Recovery Strategy**, with a commitment to **fighting corruption** while opening up to **privatization**. The anti-corruption campaigner **John Githongo** was appointed Permanent Secretary for Government and Ethics, reporting directly to Kibaki. But high-level **corruption** continued virtually unabated. In 2005, the then British High Commissioner Sir Edward Clay memorably accused "gluttonous" officials of "vomiting on the shoes of donors" in a "looting spree" that had cost Kenya hundreds of millions of dollars. The scandal, which largely focused on the security industry, came to be known as **Anglo-Leasing** (the name of one of the companies involved) – a web of scams in which government money was paid to non-existent companies or for bogus or massively inflated contracts. Githongo took his job seriously and uncovered so much sleaze that when he presented his findings to the president, they were met with indignation rather than approval. He received death threats and had to flee into exile in the UK.

Public support for Kibaki's new Party of National Unity (**PNU**) government was wearing very thin as the country prepared for the 2007 elections, in which Kibaki was the PNU's candidate and Odinga, representing the Orange Democratic Movement, his rival. Kibaki's distant, hands-off, technocratic style was never going to endear him to voters outside his political heartland. Throughout the Rift Valley, the west and on the coast there was outright hostility to what was perceived to be a "Mount Kenya Mafia" running the country. The violent response to the elections, rigged by a government bent on staying in power, almost led to the break-up of Kenya itself in the **tribal clashes** of 2007 to 2008 (see box opposite).

The Grand Coalition: 2008–

The **Grand Coalition** that eventually emerged from the electoral and societal wreckage of the clashes was led by **Mwai Kibaki**, who retained the presidency, and his ODM opponent, **Raila Odinga**, who became prime minister. Their bloated government, consisting of twenty highly paid ministers from each party grouping, attempted to buy off every interest group by giving all senior politicians a cabinet job. And Kibaki continued to wield huge powers inherent in the still unreformed constitution.

The **police** and their paramilitary wing, the General Service Unit (**GSU**), continued to behave as if answerable to no one. While the eyes of the world saw unarmed youths gunned down by police officers during the clashes, far more dangerous targets were also being disposed of. In Nairobi's Mathare district and other slum areas in the Highlands, hundreds of alleged "Mungiki thugs" have been shot since 2007 (see p.147) and on Mount Elgon in the far west, in a local war that saw little coverage outside Kenya (see p.301), hundreds of people from the Sabaot sub-tribe of the Kalenjin were killed, tortured or raped. In an embarrassingly public humiliation in 2009, the administration was lambasted by the UN Special Rapporteur on Extrajudicial, Summary or Arbitrary Executions, **Philip Alston**, for its poor human rights record. Two weeks after Alston's speech, two human rights activists were shot dead in a traffic jam in Nairobi in broad daylight. Student demonstrations in response to the killings resulted in more casualties, from police bullets. The chief of police and most senior officers were sacked and replaced in August 2009, but this may have had more to do with potential legal cases against senior politicians implicated in the post-electoral clashes than from any genuine effort to clean up the police force, whose moral bankruptcy has driven generations of Kenyans to despair.

The prospect that politicians and others accused of inciting violence during the 2007–2008 clashes might face prosecution at the International Criminal Court in **The Hague**, if they are not brought to justice in Kenya, raised the stakes for the Kibaki-Odinga alliance in 2009. There is a widespread belief in Kenya that the clashes were not spontaneous but orchestrated by senior figures on both sides of the political divide. In a theatrical gesture, in July 2009, Kofi Annan took an envelope containing the names of fifteen key suspects to the Hague.

Kenya's prospects at the end of the first decade of the twenty-first century would look doubtful even if it had a healthy environment and a strong

Women's rights and FGM

Women's groups flourish across the country, but tend to be concerned more with improvement of incomes, education, health and nutrition than social or political emancipation. The government-sponsored Maendeleo ya Wanawake Organization (MYWO) started to help women at a very basic level in the 1950s. It now encourages economic independence and, with a nominal annual membership fee, almost every woman in Kenya can belong. The umbrella group teaches basic literacy, family planning and nutrition and is also working hard to abolish the practice of ritual **female genital mutilation** (FGM). This is carried out as a rite of passage on a significant proportion of Kenyan girls, and is more prevalent in some ethnic groups (the Gusii and the Maasai, for example, where it may still affect up to fifty percent) than others. Unsurprisingly, it is more common in rural areas and among uneducated people than in cities and among those with schooling. Kenya is a signatory to the UN's Human Rights Convention, which proscribes genital mutilation, and the government promised in 1990 to ban the practice, but a motion calling for its prohibition was heavily defeated in parliament in 1996, and it remains legal. Women's' groups are meanwhile trying to persuade rural communities to accept a mutilation-free "alternative rite of passage", with some success.

Kenya is still used as something of a contraceptive testing ground, with less stringent rules on over-the-counter drugs than many countries. Depo-Provera, high-level oestrogen pills and the Dalkon Shield have all been foisted on Kenyan women. For information and contacts, visit the website of the National Council of Women of Kenya ⓦ www.ncwk.or.ke.

economy (despite rapid economic growth as it recovers from Moi's decades of mismanagement, living standards have not improved visibly or widely). But the crippling **2009 drought**, after the successive years of failure of the rains to provide enough water for cultivation and pasture saw ten million Kenyans needing food aid. Although tourism had to some extent bounced back after the clashes, the 2009/10 safari season saw tourists driving through scenes of devastation, with the carcasses of cattle and wild animals scattered in the worst affected parks and desperate pastoral communities breaking apart and moving to the cities. Heavy rains at the end of 2009 brought some relief, as well as flooding.

Climate change is the most likely cause of the extreme weather, and Kenya has a very public focus for the destruction wrought by increased atmospheric carbon dioxide – the **farmers**, sold questionable rights under the Moi and Kibaki governments in the 2700-square-kilometre **Mau forest**, on the western side of the Rift Valley, who have cut a large percentage of the tree cover on what is Kenya's biggest water catchment area. With the Mara River in 2009 running at the lowest levels ever seen, and some rivers flowing north to the Rift Valley completely dry, there was strong public support for evicting the settlers and replanting the forest, as prime minister Odinga demanded. Unfortunately, there were no clear plans for resettling the twenty thousand families or compensating them for their purchases – even if their title deeds proved to be genuine.

Kenya's **future** seems more uncertain than ever; the combination of human and natural disasters almost overwhelming; the old spectres of corruption and tribalism remaining to be vanquished; and the problems of landlessness, unemployment and poverty looming larger than ever. It's not a bright outlook, and Kenyans are nervously anticipating the **next presidential election**, scheduled for December 2012.

Wildlife and the environment

D
espite huge losses since the early twentieth century, and continued environmental damage (see p.584), Kenya still teems with **wildlife**. While visiting some of the country's forty-odd parks and reserves can almost guarantee sightings, even outside the parks, if you travel fairly widely, you're almost certain to see various gazelles and antelopes, zebra and giraffe – and even hippo, buffalo, crocodile and elephant. Monkeys and baboons can be seen almost anywhere and are a regular menace.

If this impression of abundant wild animals seems alarming, rest assured that the danger is minimal. Visitors rarely see big cats outside the parks, and enraged elephants are no more a realistic cause for concern than the few remaining rhinos, which live entirely within the parks; while buffaloes, though plentiful, are only really dangerous when solitary. The two animals you should perhaps be a little wary of are **hippos** (especially on land) and, in any lake or river below about 1000m, **crocodiles**.

The country's **birdlife** is even more noticeable than its mammals, and astonishingly diverse, attracting ornithologists from all over the world and converting many others as well. There are more than a thousand species in all, ranging from the thumb-sized **red-cheeked cordon bleu** to the **ostrich**.

Kenya's natural habitats

Kenya's location astride the equator, with a great range of altitude and in a climate zone affected by monsoon winds, give it a remarkably diverse range of ecosystems for a country its size. These local environments, from lowland rainforest to savanna grassland, high-altitude moorland to desert, and coral reef to mangrove swamp, provide equally varied habitats for its extraordinary fauna and flora.

Highland forests

The characteristic natural landscape in the **highlands** is patches of evergreen trees separated by vast meadows of grasses – often wire grass and Kikuyu grass. The true highland forest, typically found only above 1500m, contains different species of trees from lowland forest, and does not normally grow as tall or dense. Typical species include **camphor**, *Juniperus procera* (the East African "cedar") and *Podocarpus*. The better-developed forests are found on the wetter, western slopes of the highlands. Above the forest line, at altitudes of 2500m and higher, you get stands of giant bamboo, while along the lower, drier edges of the highlands, the stands of trees tend to be interspersed with fields of tall grass, where you commonly also find various species of olive.

The main **highland forests** are on mounts Kenya, Elgon and Marsabit, plus the Aberdare range and the Mau Escarpment. **Mount Kenya** displays a high altitude plant community known as **Afro-Alpine**, which is very similar to that found in the Great Lakes region of Uganda, Rwanda and Congo. The highest part of the montane forest belt, above 2900m, is characterized by a giant form of St John's

Wort, while above this, you find giant heather and Proteus trees and, at even higher altitudes, marshy moorland with tussock grasses, giant groundsel and giant lobelia.

Lowland forest and woodlands

West of the Rift Valley, the 240 square kilometres of the **Kakamega Forest**, and a few adjacent outliers, are examples of the Guineo-Congolan **equatorial forest**, which is more typically a feature of central Africa and is now very restricted within Kenya. Many bird and plant species not encountered elsewhere in Kenya are found here.

In the lowlands, Kenya has few areas of woodland and rainforest left; they're mainly restricted to the coastal strip, and the banks of the lower **Tana River**. **Lowland woodlands** are found inland of the coastal forest strip and away from the rivers. Forming more open forest areas, where the ground flora is dominated by grasses and the forest canopy covers as little as twenty percent of the area, the trees in such woodlands can be quite stunted, and may average only four to five metres high. The soils of these forests quickly lose their fertility when cleared for agriculture, and many of the remaining areas are degraded.

The rain forests, all threatened by human incursion, include **Witu Forest** near Lamu, the **Mida-Gedi forest**, the **Sabaki River Forest** near Malindi, several forest fragments in the **Shimba Hills** and the **Ramisi River Forest** on the southern coast. Several of the *kaya* sacred areas, such as Kaya Diani and Kaya Kinondo, are similar, although they're too small to have a rainforest microclimate.

The most important area of natural forest is the **Arabuko–Sokoke Forest**, south of Malindi. Arabuko-Sokoke is unique in that it comprises a largely unbroken block of 420 square kilometres of coastal forest, consisting of *Brachystegia* woodland (containing a huge variety of birdlife), dense *Cynometra* forest, and zones of mixed lowland rainforest that are very rich in plants, mammals and insects.

Large areas of the coastal plain itself are covered in relatively moist, tree-scattered grasslands. On the beach itself, tall **coconut palms** and the rather weedy-looking **casuarina** (known as whistling pine) dominate the high-tide line.

Grasslands

Grassland with scattered trees – the wooded savanna that is the archetypal image of East Africa – covers vast areas of Kenya, both in the **Lake Victoria basin** (which includes the Maasai Mara ecosystem), and **south and east of Mount Kenya** at elevations of 1000m to 1800m. This type of ecosystem prevails because of regular fires. Many of the trees that persist are broad-leaved and deciduous, protected from fire damage by their corky bark. In areas with a similar altitude, but with more erratic rainfall, a thin scattering of tall, flat-topped acacia trees, along with shorter acacias, occurs amongst the grassland.

Desert and semi-desert

Typical desert and semi-desert flora comprises **thorn bush and thicket**. Thirty kilometres inland from the Indian Ocean, beyond the fringes of the Arabuko-Sokoke Forest, is the eastern edge of the **Nyika wilderness**, which stretches west to the edge of the highlands. Nyika is characterized by an often impenetrably thick growth of stunted, thorny trees, which are grey for most of the year, but become green during the rainy season. Scaly-barked species such as acacia and euphorbia occur in this plant community.

Desert grass–bush and the drier **desert scrub** communities cover nearly seventy percent of the land area of Kenya, mainly in the east and north. These areas are below 600m and have unreliable rainfall, suffering long droughts, a lack of regular flowing water and strong winds. Vegetation is sparse and scrubby, with bushes and occasional, widely scattered tall trees, mainly baobab and acacia (*mwangi* and *mgunga*). Where the ground is free of bushes it may be covered by dispersed bunches of grass and other low shrubs. However, much of the soil surface here is bare.

The true desert habitat is drier still and plant life is very limited in some areas. Many of those trees and bushes that are present are dwarf. Large areas are bare, stony desert with a thin, patchy growth of desert grasses and perhaps a few bushes along dry river margins or dry watercourses.

Wetland habitats

There are very few permanent **riverine habitats** in Kenya, because the country is so dry, but those river systems that exist are extremely attractive to birds and mammals. The best examples are the **Tana** and the **Athi–Galana-Sabaki** systems.

The savanna of the **Great Rift Valley** is dotted with bird-rich lakes, ranging from the two freshwater lakes – Naivasha and Baringo – to intensely saline ones like Magadi and Bogoria. The Rift Valley acts as a magnet to wintering migrants from Europe and northern Asia.

The vast expanse of **Lake Victoria** is an example of an oligotrophic lake – one fed mainly by rainwater rather than inflowing rivers. As a result, it has a relatively low nutrient concentration. A feature of the lake is its papyrus beds and marshlands, harbouring birds found nowhere elsewhere in Kenya.

Two major habitat types, sandy beach and mangrove forest, dominate Kenya's **coast**. The coral reefs and one or two offshore rocky islands provide refuge for birds, but there are no breeding sites of pelagic seabirds (birds of the open ocean).

Mangrove (*mkoko*) swamps are found in many parts of the coast. The largest tracts are in the Lamu Archipelago, and this is the area from which most mangrove poles (*boriti*) are cut for construction, but all the coastal creeks have a natural bordering of mangroves. There are also areas of saline grassland on the landward side of some of the mangrove thickets. Although interesting to visit by boat, mangrove forests are not noted for their faunal diversity. One unusual animal you're bound to see is the **mudskipper**, a fish on the evolutionary road to becoming an amphibian.

Mammals

Kenya has more than a hundred species of large, native mammals. The majority are grazers, browsers and foragers at the lower end of the food chain – animals such as monkeys and antelopes. The plains are still home, however, to the last surviving community of **megafauna** in the world – the giant species, including elephant, rhino, lion and giraffe – that would have been out-numbered by dozens of other, equally enormous species in prehistoric times. The so-called "Big Five" (elephant, black rhino, buffalo, lion and leopard) were the hunter's trophies of the early twentieth century, but are still a fixation in the minds of many driver-guides and their clients, and invariably the topic of conversation around the campfire. But don't ignore the less glamorous animals: there can be just as much satisfaction in spotting a serval cat or an uncommon antelope, or in noting rarely observed behaviour, as in ticking off one of the more obvious status symbols.

Primates

There are twelve species of primates in Kenya, excluding *Homo sapiens*. They range from the pint-sized, slow-motion, lemur-like potto, found in Kakamega Forest, to the baboon. Kenya no longer has any great apes (the family to which the gorilla and the chimpanzee belong), although they probably only became extinct in the western forests, of which Kakamega is a relic, in the last five hundred years, during which time the region was widely settled by humans. Today, the primate you are certain to see almost anywhere in Kenya, given a few trees, is the **vervet monkey** (p.15), a small, lightweight monkey that has no difficulty adjusting to the presence of humans and their food. The vervet is one of the guenons – typical African monkeys, with distinctive facial markings and hairstyles, all wonderfully adapted to a life on the prowl for fruits, leaves, insects and just about anything else small and tasty. Almost as common in certain areas, notably on the coast, is **Sykes' monkey**, also known as the blue monkey (p.15). At Diani Beach, a number of Sykes' troops have become notoriously accustomed to stealing food from hotel dining tables, and large males will even raid bedrooms. Upcountry populations of Sykes' monkey appear to be more timid.

It's upcountry where you are most likely to see the beautiful, leaf-eating **black-and-white colobus monkeys** (p.14) although they can also be spotted in the Diani forest. They are usually found high in the tree canopy; look out for the pure white young. The related **Tana River red colobus** is only found in the remote Tana River National Primate Reserve, which also shelters a small population of **Tana River crested mangabey**, a partly ground-dwelling monkey with a characteristic Mohican-style crest of hair. Other rare or more localized monkeys include: the **red-tailed guenon** (or black-cheeked white-nosed monkey) of the far west; the stocky but distinguished looking **De Brazza monkey**, with its white goatee, found almost exclusively in Saiwa Swamp National Park; and the **Patas monkey** (p.15), a moustachioed plains runner of the dry northwest and Laikipia.

In a safari lodge, you are quite likely to see **bushbabies** at night (see p.15), as they frequently visit dining rooms and verandas. There's a large, cat-sized species (the greater galago) and a small bushbaby not much bigger than a kitten (the lesser galago). Both are engaging animals, with sensitive, inquisitive fingers and large eyes and ears to aid them in their hunt for insects and other small animals.

On safari you'll have plenty of opportunities to watch **baboon troops** up close (p.14). Large males can be somewhat intimidating – disconcertingly so towards women, whom they easily identify as less physically threatening than men. Troops, averaging forty to fifty individuals, spend their lives, like all monkeys, in clear, but mutable social relationships. Rank and precedence, physical strength and kin ties all determine an individual's position in this mini-society led by a dominant male. The days revolve around the need to forage and hunt for food (baboons will consume almost anything, from a fig tree's entire crop to a baby antelope found in the grass). Grooming is a fundamental part of the social glue during times of relaxation. When baboons and other monkeys perform this massage-like activity on each other, the specks they pop into their mouths are sometimes parasites – notably ticks – and sometimes flakes of skin.

Rodents and hyraxes

Rodents aren't likely to make a strong impression on safari, unless you do a night game drive. In that case you may see the bristling back end of a **crested porcupine** (p.16) or the frenzied leaps of a **spring hare**, dazzled by headlights or a torch. In rural areas off the beaten track you may occasionally see hunters taking home **giant rats** or **cane rats** – shy, vegetarian animals, which make good eating. Kenya has several species of **squirrel**, the most spectacular of which is the giant forest squirrel, with its splendid bush of a tail, and the nocturnal flying squirrel – which actually glides, rather than flies, from tree to tree, on membranes between its outstretched limbs. Both are most likely to be seen in Kakamega Forest. Very widespread, however, are the two species of **ground squirrel** – striped and unstriped – which are often seen, dashing along the track in front of the vehicle.

Rock hyraxes (p.20), which you are certain to see at Hell's Gate National Park and on Mount Kenya, look like they should be rodents. In fact the rock hyrax and closely related tree hyrax are technically ungulates (hoofed mammals) and form a classificatory level entirely their own. Their closest living relatives are elephants, with which they share distant common ancestry. Present-day hyraxes are pygmies compared with some of their prehistoric ancestors, which in some cases were as big as a bear. Rock hyraxes live in busy, vocal colonies of twenty or thirty females and young, plus a male. In a few places they are extremely tame and wait to be fed by passing hikers. Usually, however, they are timid in the extreme – not surprising in view of the wide range of predators that will eat them.

Carnivores

Kenya's carnivores are some of the most exciting and easily recognizable animals you'll see. Although often portrayed as fearsome hunters, pulling down plains game after a chase, many species do a fair bit of scavenging and all are content to eat smaller fry when conditions dictate or the opportunity arises.

Of the large cats, **lions** (p.19) are the easiest species to find. Lazy, gregarious and physically large – up to 1.8m in length, not counting the tail, and up to a metre high at the shoulder – they rarely make much effort to hide or to move away, except on occasions when a lot of vehicles intrude. They can be seen in nearly all the parks and reserves, and their presence is generally the main consideration in determining whether you're allowed out of your vehicle or not. Popular parks where lions are normally absent are Hell's Gate and Lake Bogoria (you can hike in both). Parks inhabited by lions, but in which you can generally hike, include Aberdare and Mount Kenya. "Man-eating" lions appear from time to time but seem to be one-off feline misfits. Normally, lions hunt cooperatively, preferring to kill very young, old or sick animals, and making a kill roughly once in every two attacks. When they don't kill their own prey, they will happily steal the kills of cheetahs or hyenas.

Leopards (p.19) may be the most feared animals in Kenya. Intensely secretive, alert and wary, they live all across the country except in the most treeless zones. Their unmistakeable call, which sounds something like a big saw being pulled back and forth, is unforgettable. Although often diurnal in the parks, they are strictly nocturnal wherever there is human pressure: they sometimes survive on the outskirts of villages, carefully preying on different herds of domestic animals to avoid a routine. They tolerate nearby human habitation and rarely kill people unprovoked. For the most part, leopards live off any small animals that come their way, pouncing from an ambush and dragging the prey up into a tree where it is wedged and may be consumed over several days – the so-called "leopard's larder". Melanistic (black) leopards are known as panthers or black panthers, and seem to be more common in some areas (Mount Kenya and the Aberdare range for example) than others.

In the flesh, the **cheetah** (p.19) is so different from the leopard, it's hard to see how there could ever be any confusion. Cheetahs are lightly built, finely spotted, with small heads and very long legs. Unlike leopards, which are highly arboreal, cheetahs never climb trees. They live alone, or sometimes briefly form a pair during mating, and hunting too is normally a solitary activity, dependent on eyesight and an incredible burst of speed that can take the animal up to 100kph (70mph) for a few seconds. Cheetahs can be seen in any of the large, upcountry parks.

Other large Kenyan cats include the beautiful part-spotted, part-striped **serval** (p.19), found in most of the parks, though somewhat uncommon; and the aggressive, tuft-eared **caracal** (p.18), a kind of lynx, which is seen even less often than the serval, favouring drier zones like Tsavo East and Samburu.

The biggest carnivore after the lion is the **spotted hyena** (p.18); it is also, apart from the lion, the meat-eater you will most often see. Although considered a scavenger par excellence, the spotted hyena is a formidable hunter, most often found where antelopes and zebras are present. Exceptionally efficient consumers, with immensely strong teeth and jaws, spotted hyenas eat virtually every part of their prey, including bones and hide. Where habituated to humans, they sometimes steal leather shoes, unwashed pans and trash from tents and villages. Although they can be seen by day, they are most often active at night – when they issue their unnerving, whooping cries. Clans of twenty or so animals are dominated by females, which are larger than the males and compete with each other for rank. Curiously, female hyenas' genitalia are hard to distinguish from males', leading to a popular misconception that they are hermaphroditic. Not surprisingly, in view of all their attributes, the hyena is a key figure in local mythology and folklore. The slighter and much rarer **striped hyena**, a usually solitary animal, is occasionally glimpsed very early in the morning.

The commonest members of the dog family in Kenya are the **jackals**. The black-backed or silver-backed jackal (p.17) and the similar side-striped jackal can be seen just about anywhere, both species usually in pairs. The golden jackal is most likely to be seen in the Mara. **Bat-eared foxes** (p.16) are also not uncommon, and unmistakeable in appearance. However, the unusual and rather magnificent **hunting dog** (p.17) is now extremely rare in Kenya, having been present in reasonable numbers fifty years ago. Canine distemper has played a big role in its decline, as have human predation and habitat disruption. There are a number of packs in the country, and if the opportunity exists to see them – in Laikipia, for example, and now in the greater Mara area, too – you will hear about it.

Among smaller predators, the unusual **honey badger** or **ratel** (p.17) is related to the European badger and has a reputation for defending itself extremely fiercely. Primarily an omnivorous forager, it will tear open bees' nests (to which it is led by a small bird, the honey guide), its thick, loose hide rendering it impervious to their stings.

The largely arboreal **genet** (p.18) is reminiscent of a slender, elongated domestic cat (in fact they were once domesticated around the Mediterranean, but cats proved better mouse-hunters). In fact they are viverrids, related to mongooses, and are frequently seen after dark around national park lodges, even scampering around the roof beams.

Most species of **mongoose** (p.18) are also tolerant of humans and, even when disturbed out in the bush, can usually be observed for some time before disappearing. Their snake-fighting reputation is greatly overplayed: in practice they are mostly social foragers, fanning out through the bush like beaters on a shoot, rooting for anything edible – mostly invertebrates, eggs, lizards and frogs.

The **civet** (p.17) is a stocky animal, resembling a large, terrestrial genet. They're not often seen, but they are predictable creatures that wend their way along the same paths at the same time, night after night, so if there's one in the neighbourhood, you'll see it.

Elephants

Elephants (p.20) are found throughout Kenya – almost all the big plains and mountain parks have their populations. These are the most engaging of animals to watch, perhaps because their interactions, behaviour patterns and personality have so many human parallels. Like people, they lead complex, interdependent social lives, growing from helpless infancy, through self-conscious adolescence, to adulthood. Babies are born with other cows in close attendance, after a 22-month gestation. The calves suckle for two to three years, from the mother's two breasts between her front legs.

Elephants' basic **family units** are composed of a group of related females, tightly protecting their babies and young and led by a venerable matriarch. It's the matriarch that's most likely to bluff a charge – though occasionally she may get carried away and actually tusk a vehicle or person. Bush mythology has it that elephants become embarrassed and ashamed after killing a human, covering the body with sticks and grass. They certainly pay much attention to the disposal of their own dead relatives, often dispersing the bones and spending time near the remains. Old animals die in their seventies or eighties, when their last set of teeth wears out and they can no longer feed.

Seen in the flesh, elephants seem even bigger than you would imagine – you'll need little persuasion from those flapping, warning ears to back off if you're too close – but they are at the same time surprisingly graceful, silent animals on their padded, carefully placed feet. In a matter of moments, a large herd can merge into the trees and disappear, their presence betrayed only by the noisy cracking of branches as they strip trees and uproot saplings.

Managing the elephant population (see box, p.354) leads to arcane ecological puzzles in which new factors keep emerging; current wisdom suggests that elephants are in a way "architects" of their environment. Overpopulation is usually the result of old migration routes being cut off, forcing the animals into unnatural reserves – like the Mara – where their massive appetites can appear to be destructive. Adults may consume up to 170kg of plant material daily – more than three thousand tons of foliage through the Mara's collective elephant gut each month. However, this foliage destruction by crowded herds also puts new life into the soil. Acacia seeds sprout more readily after being eaten and dunged by elephants than if they simply fall to the ground: dung beetles tackle the football-sized elephant droppings, break them into pellets and pull them into their burrows where the seeds germinate. Elephants also dig up dried-out water-holes with their tusks (they're either right- or left-tusked, in the same way that humans favour one hand or the other), providing moisture for other animals.

Rhinos

There are two species of **rhinoceros** (p.20) in Africa – the hook-lipped or black rhino, and the much heavier wide-lipped or white rhino. Both are on the brink of extinction in the wild. The shape of their lips is far more significant than any alleged colour difference, as it indicates their respective diets (browsing for the black rhino, grazing for the white) and favoured habitats (thick bush and open grassland respectively).

Rhinos give birth to a single calf, after a gestation period of fifteen to eighteen months, and then the baby is not weaned until it is at least a year or sometimes two years old. Their population growth rate is slow compared with most animals – another factor contributing to their predicament.

Native white rhinos have been extinct for several hundred years in Kenya, but reintroduced animals (principally from South Africa) have always done well and can be seen in several parks and reserves, as well as in private and community wildlife sanctuaries.

The slightly smaller black rhinos were, until the mid-1970s, a fairly common sight in most of the parks. In the 1960s, Amboseli, for example, had hundreds of magnificent black rhinos, some with graceful, long upper horns more than a metre in length. The facts behind their rapid and depressing decimation are given in some detail on p.354. Today, there are around six hundred black rhinos in Kenya. You can see them in the Maasai Mara reserve and at Lake Nakuru, Nairobi, Aberdare, Meru and Tsavo West national parks, and increasingly in conservancies in Laikipia, northwest of Mount Kenya.

Hippos

Hippopotamuses (p.22) are highly adaptable, and found throughout Kenya wherever rivers or freshwater lakes are deep enough for them to submerge and have a surrounding of suitable grazing grass. By day they need to spend most of their time in water to protect their thin, hairless skin from dehydration. After dark, hippos leave the water to spend the whole night grazing, often walking up to 10km in one session. In the Maasai Mara, they wander across the savanna; at Lake Naivasha they plod through farms and gardens; and everywhere they are rightly feared.

Hippos can be found everywhere from the humid estuary of the Tana River to the chilly mountain district of Nyahururu, including the briny Lake Nakuru in the central Rift Valley and Lake Turkana in the semi-desert of the northwest.

Hippos are reckoned to be responsible for more human deaths in Africa than any other animal. These occur mostly on the water, when boats accidentally steer into hippo pods, but they can be aggressive on dry land, too, charging and slashing with their fearsomely long incisors. They can run at 30kph if necessary and have a small turning circle. Although uncertain on land (hence their aggression when cornered), they are supremely adapted to long periods in water. Their nostrils, eyes and ears are in exactly the right places and their clumsy feet become supple paddles – as can be seen, if you're lucky, from the underwater observatory at Mzima Springs in Tsavo West National Park.

Zebras

Zebras (p.21) are closely related to horses and, together with wild asses, form the equid family. Of the three species of zebra, two live in Kenya. Burchell's has thick stripes and small ears and is found in suitable habitats in most parts of the country, while Grevy's is a large animal with very fine stripes and big, saucer-like ears, restricted to Tsavo East and the northern parks and reserves.

Burchell's zebras found in Kenya are mostly the *granti* subspecies and often called Grant's zebras. In the far north, they tend to have a very short mane, or even none at all. In Tsavo West and other parts of southern Kenya, they tend to exhibit the "shadow striping" typical of the species in southern Africa (fawn stripes between the black ones). In Amboseli and the Mara, Burchell's zebras gather in migrating herds up to several thousand strong, along with wildebeest and other grazers. In contrast, Grevy's zebras live in small territorial herds.

Pigs

The commonest wild pig in Kenya is the **warthog** (p.21), regularly sighted throughout Kenya up to altitudes of over 2000m. Flighty and nervous, warthogs are notoriously hard to photograph as they're generally on the run through the bush, tails erect, often with their young in single file. They shelter in holes in the ground, usually old aardvark burrows, and live in family groups, usually a mother and her litter of two to four piglets, or occasionally two or three females and their young. Boars join the group only to mate, and are distinguishable from sows by their prominent face warts, which are thought to be defensive pads protecting their heads during often violent fights. Although a favourite prey animal of large cats, the warthog's survival doesn't appear to be threatened, although its rooting and wallowing behaviour often brings it into conflict with farmers.

Two other, much rarer pigs, both nocturnal, live in Kenya: the huge, dark-coloured **giant forest hog**, a bristly, big-tusked pig which lives in the highlands and is most likely to be seen from a tree hotel on Mount Kenya or the Aberdare range; and the **red river hog** or **bush pig**, which is very rarely seen, though not uncommon in dense forest, close to agriculture and river margins.

Giraffes

The tallest mammals on earth, **giraffes** (p.22) are common and unmistakeable. Non-territorial, they gather in loose, leaderless herds and spend the day browsing on the leaves of trees too high for other species (acacias and combretums are favourites), while at night they lie down and ruminate. Bulls test their strength while in bachelor herds. When a female is in heat, which can happen at any time of year, the dominant male mates with her. She will give birth after a gestation of approximately fourteen months. More than half of all young, however, fall prey to lions or hyenas in their early years.

Kenya has three types of giraffe, differentiated from each other by their pattern and the configuration of their short horns. Most often seen is the **Maasai giraffe**, with two horns and a very broken pattern of dark blotches on a buff or fawn background. This is the giraffe you'll see in the Maasai Mara, Amboseli and Tsavo West. Roughly north of the Nairobi–Mombasa road (coincidentally a natural dividing line) lives the dramatically patterned **reticulated giraffe**, which normally has three or five horns and boldly defined chestnut patches on a very pale background. The more solidly built **Rothschild's giraffe**, which has a pattern more like crazy paving (also with well-defined blotches) and usually two horns, is found only in parts of western Kenya (and over the border in Uganda). There's disagreement among zoologists over whether any of the giraffe's subspecies should be accorded the status of separate species – particularly concerning the reticulated giraffe – but they all interbreed.

Hollow-horned ruminants

This category of mammals includes the buffalo and all the antelopes. The **buffalo** itself (p.22) is a very common and much-photographed safari animal, closely related to the domestic cow. Buffaloes live in herds of one hundred to three hundred and rarely make much effort to move when vehicles approach. Indeed, they aren't troubled by close contact with humans, and you don't have to read the papers in Kenya long before finding an example of buffaloes trampling crops or goring a farmer.

The rather ungainly **hartebeest** family (p.23) includes one of the rarest antelopes in Kenya, the hirola or Hunter's hartebeest of the lower Tana River. The Coke's hartebeest or kongoni, however, is found widely in southern Kenya, and **topi** (p.23) are practically emblematic of the Maasai Mara, their main habitat, where herd sentries are commonly spotted standing on old termite mounds. The **wildebeest** (p.23) is also particularly associated with the Mara.

Of the **gazelles**, the most obvious are **Thomson's** and **Grant's** (p.24), seen at the roadside in many parts of southern Kenya. The range of Grant's gazelle extends further north to encompass the northern parks (Samburu and Meru) where "Thommies" are absent. The **gerenuk** (p.23) is an unusual browsing gazelle able to nibble from bushes standing on its hind legs (its name is Somali for "giraffe-necked"). Although considered an arid land specialist, its range encompasses most of Kenya east of the Rift Valley. The **impala** (p.24), although not a gazelle, is closely related and very common throughout much of Kenya.

The **reedbuck** (p.24) and **waterbuck** (p.25) are related: both spend much time in or near water. The common or Bohor reedbuck has a patchy distribution in southern Kenya, whereas the waterbuck is common in many central and southern areas.

Some of the smallest antelopes in the world are quite easily seen in Kenya. Found all over the country, **Kirk's dik–dik** (p.25) is a common miniature antelope, measuring no more than 40cm in height, which usually pairs for life. The **suni**, which is uncommon, but can be encountered almost anywhere in forest cover, is even smaller, at just 32cm. Other small Kenyan antelopes – all fairly widespread but nowhere common – include the surprisingly aggressive **steenbok** (p.28) which, despite a height of only 50cm, defends itself furiously against attackers; the **oribi** (p.28), with its charming foreplay (when the female is in heat, the male pushes his head under her hindquarters and pushes her along on her forelegs like a wheelbarrow); and the **klipspringer** (p.28), which has hooves wonderfully adapted for scaling near-vertical cliffs.

The duikers (from the Dutch for "diver", referring to their plunging into the bush) are larger – the **common duiker** (p.28) is around 60cm high – though they appear smaller because of their hunched posture. The common duiker is found throughout the country in many habitats, but most species are choosier and prefer plenty of dense cover and thicket. These include the tiny Zanzibar duiker (whose range in Kenya is restricted to the Arabuko-Sokoke Forest), the widespread red duiker and blue duiker, and the more localized black-fronted duiker (Mount Kenya and Mount Elgon) and yellow-backed duiker (Mau forest).

Kenya's big antelopes are the *Tragelaphinae* – twisted-horn bushbuck types – and the *Hippotraginae* – horse-like antelopes. The **bushbuck** itself (p.26) is notoriously shy – a loud crashing through the undergrowth and a flash of a chestnut rump are all you are likely to encounter. The **bongo** is a particularly impressive member of this group, now confined to the highlands of Mount Kenya, the Aberdare range and possibly the Cheranganis and Mau Escarpment. The **sitatunga** (p.26) is a smaller, semi-aquatic relative, found only in one or two remote corners of western Kenya (including at the very accessible Saiwa Swamp National Park, where they are easy to see), and at Lewa Conservancy in Laikipia. Also easily spotted, almost anywhere in the country, is the huge, cow-like **eland** (p.26), with its distinctive dewlap. The two species of kudu are not uncommon where they exist at all, but they are very localized. Both are browsers. You're most likely to see **greater kudu** (p.26) at Lake Bogoria or Marsabit and **lesser kudu** (p.27) in Tsavo West or East.

The horse-like antelopes include the fine-looking **fringe-eared oryx** (p.27), that is found almost everywhere except the Mara; the massive **roan antelope** (p.27), restricted to the Mara and Ruma National Park in western Kenya; and the handsome **sable antelope** (p.27) which lives only in Shimba Hills National Park.

Other mammals

Of Kenya's other mammals, you're not likely to see more than a glimpse. Rarest of all is the **dugong**, the marine mermaid-prototype, of which there are believed to be a handful of individuals remaining, drifting in the shallows around the Lamu Archipelago.

The insectivorous **elephant shrews** are worth looking out for, simply because they are so weird. Your best chance of a sighting is of the golden-rumped elephant shrew, at Gedi on the coast.

The **aardvark** (p.16) is one of Africa's – indeed the world's – strangest mammals; a solitary termite-eater weighing up to 70kg. Its name, Afrikaans for "earth pig", is an apt description, as it holes up during the day in large burrows – excavated with remarkable speed and energy – and emerges at night to visit termite mounds within a radius of up to 5km, to dig for its main diet. It is most likely to be seen in bush country, well scattered with tall termite spires.

Pangolins are equally unusual – nocturnal, scale-covered mammals, resembling armadillos and feeding on ants and termites. Under attack, they roll themselves into a ball. The ground pangolin, the only species found in Kenya (most pangolins are arboreal), lives mainly in savanna districts.

Kenya's many **bats** will usually be a mere flicker over a waterhole at twilight, or sometimes a flash across your headlights. The only bats you can normally observe in any meaningful way are fruit bats hanging from their daytime roosting sites. The hammer-headed fruit bat, sometimes seen in Kakamega Forest, has a huge head and a wingspan of more than a metre.

Birds

Kenya boasts the second-highest bird list in Africa (after Congo), at more than 1070 species (this compares with no more than three hundred for Britain and around six hundred for North America). Nearly eighty percent of Kenya's birds are thought to breed in the country, with the remainder breeding during the northern summer in the Palaearctic region (Europe, north Africa and northern Asia) but wintering in tropical Africa. Many of these are familiar British summer visitors, such as swallows, nightingales and whitethroats. In winter, the migrant terns and waders can sometimes dominate Kenya's shorelines, and the Palaearctic swallows and warblers may comprise a large proportion of the birds in bush land habitats.

If you're a novice **birder**, Kenya is an excellent place to start. No amount of wildlife documentaries can do justice to the thrill of glimpsing your first colourful bee-eaters (twelve species have been recorded in Kenya, three or four of which you might expect to encounter), watching rollers and shrikes swoop from perches to hunt insects, or seeing groups of vultures wheeling and dipping as they prepare to arrive at a kill. The wide variety and accessibility of habitats makes bird-watching in Kenya highly rewarding. The keenest independent bird-watchers might expect to encounter more than six hundred species in a four-week period, whereas some of the organized birding tour groups, living and breathing birds for a three-week period, might record more than seven hundred species in that time; one tour group holds the African record of 797 species in 25 days. However, even for those just dipping into the hobby or with limited time and choice of itineraries, Kenya offers some wonderful surprises. The following brief round-ups cover some of the more noticeable species.

Distribution

Only a few species of birds are found throughout Kenya. Three that will become familiar to sharp-eyed visitors are the **laughing dove**, the **African drongo** (an all-black crow-like bird with a forked tail) and the **grey-headed sparrow**. Most other species have well-defined distributions dependent on habitat type, itself a reflection of altitude and rainfall patterns.

Part of Kenya's bird diversity can be explained by the large numbers of species reaching the edge of their known ranges inside its borders. These include birds originating in the Horn of Africa but having their western or southwestern limits in Kenya (for example, the Somali bee-eater), species widespread in southern Africa which reach their northern limits here (such as the rufous-bellied heron), coastal species that are confined to the east (for example, the mangrove kingfisher), species from west African equatorial forests whose ranges just overlap the forest patches in west Kenya (for example, the grey parrot), and species occurring along the southern edge of the Sahel that reach the extreme southeast of their range in Kenya (for example, the Abyssinian roller).

Many Kenyan birds display two more or less separate populations, one on the coast, and the other in the highlands. This is determined by habitat: the coastal areas tend to have less rain than the highlands, and are much hotter, with a more severe dry season. In some species, such as the widespread speckled mousebird, two distinct races are evolving.

Endemic and near-endemic species

Of more than a thousand species of bird found in Kenya, there are only six **endemic species**. Although these species are unlikely to be encountered by the novice and can be difficult to identify, their existence serves to emphasize Kenya's remarkable birdlife. They comprise two species of cisticola (small, skulking species, found in dense vegetation), a species of lark found only in the Marsabit and Isiolo areas, Sharpe's pipit (found in high grasslands in western and central Kenya), Clarke's weaver (found only in and around the Arabuko-Sokoke Forest), and Hinde's pied babbler (found in the vicinity of Kianyaga near Embu).

Many bird-watchers are attracted to Kenya by the large number of **near-endemic species**, confined to northeast Africa, for which Kenya offers a reasonably accessible chance of a sighting. These include Heuglin's bustard, the Somali bee-eater (a very pale, open-country bee-eater found in the north and often noted at Samburu), Hartlaub's turaco (a green species of turaco, only found in highland forests in East Africa), and the small Sokoke Scops owl found most easily around the Arabuko-Sokoke Forest.

Large walking birds

Several species of large, terrestrial or partly terrestrial birds are regularly seen on safari. Their size and common form of locomotion (though the secretary bird and marabou stork can both fly perfectly well, and the ground hornbill is not flightless) makes them the species most frequently spotted by non-ornithologists.

The locally common, distinctive **ostrich** is found in dry, open plains and semi-desert. The world's biggest bird, at up to 2.5m high, it is virtually absent from the coastal strip, but can readily be seen in Nairobi National Park and most other parks.

The **secretary bird** is a large, long-tailed, long-legged bird, grey-white in colour with a scraggy crest (the quills of which gave it its name), black on the wings and with black "stockings". A bird of dry, open bush and wooded country, often seen in pairs, it is most commonly noticed stalking prey items that it has disturbed. Prey includes beetles, grasshoppers, reptiles and rodents, sometimes up to the size of a hare. Secretary birds are scarce in western Kenya and on the coast, but can be seen easily in Nairobi National Park.

The **marabou** is a large, ugly stork, up to 1.2m in height, with a bald head and a dangling, pink throat pouch. Most specimens look as if they're in an advanced state of decomposition. The marabou flies with its head and neck retracted (unlike other storks) and is often seen in dry areas, including towns, where it feeds on small animals, carrion and refuse. A large population of marabous is usually considered a sign that waste management is a problem in the area.

Another reasonably common walking bird is the **ground hornbill**. This impressive bird lives in open country and is the largest hornbill by far. Black, with red face and wattles, it bears a distinct resemblance to a turkey. It's not uncommon to come across pairs, or sometimes groups, of ground hornbills, especially in the Mara, trailing through the scrub on the lookout for small animals. They nest among rocks or in tree stumps.

Flamingos and ibises

Many visitors to Kenya are astounded by their first encounter with **flamingos** – a sea of pink on a soda-encrusted lake, accompanied by the salt-rich smell of the lake and the stench of the birds' guano. Two species are found in Kenya, the greater flamingo and the lesser flamingo. Both are birds of the Rift Valley lakes and adjacent areas, and are colonial nesters.

Much the commoner of the two is the **lesser flamingo**, which is smaller, pinker and has a darker bill. The Rift Valley population of lesser flamingos, with more than a million birds gathering at one time at lakes Bogoria and Nakuru, is one of only three main populations in Africa. This species is nomadic, moving in relation to fluctuating food supplies, water levels and alkalinity, and flocks can leave or arrive at an area in a very short period of time – an estimated 400,000 birds have been recorded leaving Lake Bogoria over a seven-day period. Lesser flamingos feed by filtering suspended aquatic food, mainly blue-green algae that occurs in huge concentrations on the shallow soda lakes of the Rift.

Greater flamingos can occur in their thousands but are considerably fewer in number than the lesser species. They are bottom feeders, filtering small invertebrates as well as algae. Although greater flamingos tend to be less frequently nomadic than their relatives, they are more likely to move away from the Rift Valley lakes to smaller water bodies and even the coast.

The most widely distributed **ibis** species (stork-like birds with down-curved bills) is the **sacred ibis**, found near water and human settlements. It has a white body with black head and neck, and black tips to the wings. Also frequently encountered is the **Hadada ibis**, a brown bird with a green-bronze sheen to the wings and noisy call in flight, found in southern Kenya near wooded streams and cultivated areas.

Water birds

Most large water bodies, apart from the extremely saline lakes, support several species of **ducks and geese**, many of which breed in Europe, but overwinter in Africa.

Several species of **herons, storks and egrets** occur in areas with water, or can be observed overflying on migration. The commonest large heron is the black-headed heron, which can sometimes be found far from water. Mainly grey with a black head and legs, the black heron can be seen "umbrella-fishing" along coastal creeks and marsh shores: it cloaks its head with its wings whilst fishing, which is thought to cut down surface reflection from the water, allowing the bird to see its prey more easily.

The **hammerkop** is a brown, heron-like bird with a sturdy bill and mane of brown feathers, which gives it a top-heavy, slightly prehistoric appearance in flight, like a miniature pterodactyl. Hammerkops are widespread near water, and build large, conspicuous nests that are often taken over by other animals, including owls, monitor lizards and snakes.

Guineafowl

Four species of these large, grey game birds are found in Kenya. The **vulturine guineafowl** is a bird of very arid areas, recognized by the long tapered feathers hanging from the base of the neck over a royal-blue chest. The well-known **helmeted guineafowl**, a bird of moister areas, has a bony yellow skull protrusion (hence its name). The crested and the Kenya crested guineafowl are both birds of thickets.

Birds of prey

Kenya abounds with birds of prey – kites, vultures, eagles, harriers, hawks and falcons. Altogether, more than 75 species have been recorded in the country, several of which are difficult to miss.

Six species of **vulture** range over the plains and bush and are often seen soaring in search of a carcass. All the species can occur together, and birds may travel vast distances to feed. The main differences are in feeding behaviour: the lappet-faced vulture, for example, pulls carcasses apart; the African white-backed vulture feeds mainly on internal organs; the hooded vulture mainly picks from bones.

Two other birds of prey that are firmly associated with East Africa are the **bateleur**, an eagle that is readily identified by its silver wings, black, stumpy body shape and chestnut-red, wedge-shaped tail; and the **fish eagle**, generally found in pairs near water, often along lake shores.

Cranes and bustards

Uganda's national bird, the **crowned crane**, is found in southern and western Kenya. It is a distinctive, elegant bird, the head crowned with an array of golden plumes. Crowned cranes are often seen feeding on cultivated fields or in marshy areas, invariably in identical pairs.

Some nine species of **bustard** occur in the plains and grasslands of Kenya. These large, open-country species are long-legged and long-necked and are very well camouflaged among the browns and yellows of their habitat. The heaviest flying bird in the world, the Kori bustard, is commonest in the Rift Valley highlands. Bustards are affected by intensive, small-scale agricultural and human presence, and several species have undergone a decline in Kenya.

Parrots and lovebirds

Eight species of *Psittacidae* have been recorded in Kenya, three of which are introduced. The parrot species that you're most likely to see is the **brown parrot**, which occurs in wooded areas in the west of the country. Lovebirds are small, green, hole-nesting parrot-relatives and are readily seen in the acacias around Lake Naivasha, where a feral breeding population of **yellow-collared lovebirds** has become established. This species has been introduced to Kenya from Tanzania, and hybridizes with the introduced and very similar **Fischer's lovebird**.

Go-away birds and turacos

These distinctive, related families are found only in Africa. Medium-sized and with long tails, most **turacos** and **go-away birds** (named after their call) have short rounded wings. They are not excellent fliers, but are very agile in their movements along branches and through vegetation. Many species are colourful and display a crest. The largest, the magnificent **great blue turaco** (blue above, and green and brown below) is found only in the western forests in Kenya – notably at Kakamega, where it is one of the largest birds in the forest. Other turacos are generally green or violet in colour, and all are confined to thickly wooded areas. Open-country species, such as the widely distributed and common **white-bellied go-away bird**, are white or grey in colour.

Mousebirds

Three species of **mousebird** are found in Kenya. Their name derives from their rapid scampering through thick tangles of branches using unusually well adapted claws. They can be identified by their slight crests and their long, tapering tails. Generally grey or brown in colour, they're noisy and feed actively in quite open vegetation. The **speckled mousebird** is a very common species throughout southern Kenya, often found in small groups at forest margins and in suburban gardens.

Rollers, shrikes and kingfishers

A family of colourful birds of the African bush, **rollers** perch on exposed bushes and telephone wires and chase flying insects. They take their name from their impressive courtship flights – a fast dive with a rolling and rocking motion, accompanied by raucous calls. Many have a sky-blue underbody and sandy-coloured back, and long tail streamers are a distinctive feature of several Kenyan species. The **lilac-breasted roller** is a common and conspicuous species.

Shrikes are found throughout Kenya. Fierce hunters with sharply hooked bills, they habitually sit on prominent perches, and eat insects, reptiles and small birds.

Kingfishers are some of Kenya's most noticeable birds, with eleven species found here. They range from the tiny **pygmy kingfisher**, which feeds on insects and is generally found near water, to the **giant kingfisher**, a shy fish-eating species of wooded streams in western Kenya. Several species, which eat insects rather than fish, can often be seen perched high in trees or on open posts in the bush where they wait to pounce on passing prey. A common and widespread insectivorous species is the **chestnut-bellied kingfisher**.

Hornbills

Named for their long, heavy bills, surmounted by a casque or bony helmet, hornbills generally have black and white plumage and several species are common open-country birds. Their flight consists of a series of alternate flaps and glides. When in flight, hornbills may be heard before they are seen, the beaten wings making a "whooshing" noise as air rushes through the flight feathers. Many species have bare areas of skin on the head, with the bill and casque often in bright colours that change with the age of the bird. Twelve species have been recorded in Kenya, including the **silvery-cheeked hornbill**, sometimes seen in Nairobi. Hornbills have interesting breeding habits: the male generally incarcerates the female in a hollow tree, leaving a hole through which he feeds her while she incubates the eggs and rears the young.

Sunbirds

Sunbirds are bright, active birds, feeding on nectar from flowering plants, and distributed throughout Kenya, wherever there are flowers or flowering trees and bushes. More than 35 species have been recorded in the country, with many confined to niche habitats. Common species in the Nairobi area are **variable** and **scarlet-chested sunbirds**. Males are brightly coloured and usually identifiable, but many of the drabber females require very careful observation to identify them.

Starlings

The glorious orange and blue starlings that are a common feature of bush land habitats and are usually seen feeding on the ground, belong to one of three species. The **superb starling** is the most widespread of these, found everywhere from remote national parks to gardens in Nairobi. It can be identified by the white band above its orange breast. Similar starlings are the larger **golden-breasted starling**, often seen in Tsavo National Park, and **Hildebrand's starling** (also orange-breasted), which is commonest around Machakos but can be encountered all over southern Kenya.

Weavers and whydahs

These small birds are some of the commonest and most widespread of all Kenyan birds. Most male **weavers** have some yellow in the plumage, whereas the females are rather dull and sparrow-like. In fact, many species appear superficially very similar; distinctions are based on their range and preferred type of habitat. Weavers nest in colonies and weave their nests into elongated shapes, which can be used to help in the identification of the species. Many nests are situated close to water or human habitation and sometimes hang suspended. The **golden palm weaver** is the species you'll commonly see on the coast, often in hotel gardens where they form chattering colonies in palm trees.

Whydahs are also known as widow birds. The **paradise whydah** has extremely ornate tail feathers, with the central pair of tail feathers flattened and twisted into an unmistakeable crest-like tail. Male paradise whydahs are mainly black, and perform a strange bouncing display flight to attract the females.

Reptiles and amphibians

There is only one species of crocodile in Kenya – the big **Nile crocodile**, which, left to grow, can reach 6m or more in length and is considered a cunning and dangerous animal. You'll see them in the Mara River, in the Tana, at Mzima Springs in Tsavo West, in great numbers in Lake Turkana and, if you take the trouble to look, in many other rivers and large bodies of water.

Kenya has many species of **snake**, some of them quite common, but your chances of seeing a wild specimen here are more remote than in Australia or the USA, or even certain parts of Europe. In Kenya, as all over Africa, snakes are both revered and reviled and, while they frequently have symbolic significance for local people, that is quite often forgotten in the rush to hack them to bits with a panga as soon as they're discovered. All in all, snakes have a very hard time surviving in Kenya.

Common **non-poisonous species** of snake include the rock python (a constrictor that can grow up to five metres or more in length), the egg-eating snake and the sand boa. Common **poisonous species** include the green and black mambas (fast, agile, arboreal snakes), the boomslang, the spitting cobra and the dangerous puff adder, which is probably responsible for more bites than any other, on account of its sluggish disposition – most snakes flee on detecting the vibrations of human footsteps.

Tortoises are quite frequently encountered on park roads in the morning or late afternoon. Some, like the leopard tortoise, can be quite large, up to 50cm in length, while the hinged tortoise (which not only retreats inside its shell but shuts the door, too) is much smaller – up to 30cm. In rocky areas, look out for the rare and unusual pancake tortoise, a flexible-shelled species that can put on quite a turn of speed but, when cornered in its fissure in the rocks, will inflate to wedge itself inextricably. Several species of terrapins, or freshwater turtles are commonly found in ponds and slow-flowing streams. On the coast, sea turtles breed and it's not unusual to see them from boats during snorkelling trips.

Lizards are harmless, often colourful and common everywhere. The commonest are **rock agamas**, the males often seen in courting "plumage", with brilliant orange heads and blue bodies, ducking and bobbing at each other. They live in loose colonies often near human habitation; one hotel may have hundreds, its neighbour none. The biggest lizards, **Nile monitors**, grow to nearly 2m in length and are often seen near water. From a distance, as they race off, they look like speeding baby crocodiles. The other common monitor, the smaller savanna monitor, is less handsomely marked: you can often see them basking on top of termite mounds.

A large, docile lizard you may come across is the **plated lizard**. Growing to 40cm, this mild-mannered reptile is often found around coastal hotels, looking for scraps from the kitchen or pool terrace. Also mainly on the coast, at night, the translucent little aliens on the ceiling are **house geckos**, catching moths and other insects, and worth encouraging. By day, their minuscule relatives, the **day geckos** (velvet grey and yellow), patrol coastal walls.

In the highlands you may come across prehistoric-looking three-horned **Jackson's chameleons** creeping through the foliage. There are several other species of chameleon, living in most parts of the country, which, owing to their excessive slowness, you are most likely to see squashed flat on the road.

In the **amphibian** world, you tend to hear examples long before you see them. You may come across the odd toad, sitting under a footpath light, waiting for insects to drop to the ground. There are, however, dozens of species of frogs and tree frogs, ranging from the common squeaker to the red and black rubber frog.

Environmental stewardship

The growth of tourism in Kenya has been spectacular, from just a few thousand visitors each year at the time of Independence to more than a million today. It has been a boon for the economy, but **environmental degradation** as a direct consequence of tourists is evident in parks and reserves from the Maasai Mara to Amboseli, Aberdare and Samburu, as well as on the beaches. You should do all you can to mitigate your impact. Even if you're visiting Kenya on an organized tour, you can ensure your driver sticks to the park rules about off-road driving – by far the most damaging side effect of high visitor numbers – by requesting that you are not taken closer to the wildlife than the legal limits.

Leaving aside the safari industry, the rate of **clearance** of Kenya's remaining areas of indigenous forest is alarming, worsening the problem of soil erosion, and consequently the silting-up of lakes, rivers and estuaries. Illegal "land grabbing" has been making headlines since the mid-1990s and there have been countless legal moves, demonstrations and protests against the expropriation of public land for private gain. The government responded with the 1999 Environment Conservation Management Act, which protects forest areas that are officially gazetted, and allows members of the public to oppose de-gazetting. This did not stop the government from announcing, in 2001, the excision of 6700 square kilometres from gazetted forests for development, resulting in widespread protests by environmentalists, and attempts in the High Court to halt the move. Some of the land was eventually re-gazetted. The area most affected is the **Mau Forest** on the Mau Escarpment in the western Rift Valley, damage to which has led to disastrous climatic and environmental changes in the surrounding watersheds. Other areas still threatened by land grabbing and illegal logging include most of the Kakamega Forest and parts of the Mount Kenya Forest, the coastal mangroves, and the Arabuko-Sokoke Forest.

If you're at all concerned about the impact of tourism or environmental matters, or want to further your knowledge, get in touch with the organizations listed below.

Contacts

African Wildlife Foundation ⓦwww.awf.org. AFW runs an African Heartlands programme in eight key conservation areas including Kenya's Samburu, involving species conservation (particularly elephants and rhinos) and wildlife management.

African Bird Club ⓦ www.africanbirdclub.org. Enthusiasts' association, producing an excellent regular bulletin and occasional well-produced monographs and itineraries.

East African Wildlife Society ⓦ www.eawildlife.org. Influential Kenya-based group, centrally involved in the movement to ban the ivory trade (achieved in 1989), and remaining active in other areas, recently raising awareness about marine and wetlands protection. Publishes an excellent magazine, *Swara*.

Ecotourism Society of Kenya ⓦ www.ecotourismkenya.org. A local organization promoting sustainable tourism. They award bronze, silver and gold ratings to hotels, lodges, tented camps and tour operators.

Friends of Nairobi National Park ⓦ fonnap.wordpress.com & nairobinationalpark.wildlifedirect.org. Works to keep the migration route to the park from the south open, and to raise awareness among Nairobians about the remarkable environment on their doorstep.

Green Belt Movement ⓦ www.greenbeltmovement.org. Grassroots conservation and women's movement founded by the Nobel Peace Prize winner Wangari Maathai.

Kenya Forests Working Group ⓦ www.kenyaforests.org. Concerned with conserving and managing Kenya's forests.

Kenya Tourism Concern ☏ 020/535850, c/o ⓦ www.tourismconcern.org.uk. Kenyan sister organization to the UK's Tourism Concern, a campaigning organization working for more fairly traded forms of tourism.

Nature Kenya ⓦ www.naturekenya.org. Natural history enthusiasts' and conservationists' website with several strands of interest and a good, online newsletter.

Wildlife Direct ⓦ wildlifedirect.org. Conservation fund-raising meets conservationists' network, including more than fifty blogs from the field in Kenya. Chaired by Richard Leakey, this is a superb resource and focus.

Music

Although Kenya's music is less well known abroad than the sounds of many other African countries, home-grown genres are widespread and full of vitality. Nairobi's audiences and recording facilities have long been a draw for musicians from all over east and central Africa, bringing a pan-African musical flavour to the city.

Some of Kenya's purely **traditional musical cultures** have survived more intact than others, however, as gospel music has all but obliterated traditional folk music in many areas. Among the Kikuyu and Kalenjin, for example, traditional music is almost extinct, while elsewhere you often need time and local people's trust before being able to witness the sacred events at which traditional styles are usually performed. Kenyan **gospel** itself is sadly not like the uplifting version of African American churches in the United States, but tinny and synthesized.

As for what you could broadly call Kenyan **pop music**, there is no single identifiable genre, but a number of styles that cross-fertilize and borrow freely from one another. In the case of the extremely widespread **benga** style, many musicians perform most of their songs in one of the local indigenous languages. Other musicians, especially those playing rumba styles, aim at a broad national audience and invariably perform in **Swahili**. Others offer a local variant of the **Congolese** sound, with lyrics in **Lingala** (an important Congolese language, understood by almost no one in Kenya).

Traditional music

Music has traditionally been used to accompany ceremonies, events and **rites of passage**, from celebrations at a baby's birth to songs of adolescence and warrior-hood, and from marriage, harvests and solar and lunar cycles to festivities, religious events and death. The oldest of Kenya's musical traditions is **ngoma**, a term which, in most Bantu languages of Kenya, refers to a specific kind of drum and a related dance; *ngoma* is nowadays used generally to describe all the facets of a musical performance, including the groups and their accompanying dances.

Although an inter-ethnic *ngoma* called *beni* ("band") emerged on the coast at the beginning of the twentieth century and spread inland to many tribes (you can still witness this anachronistic, marching-band form on special occasions in Lamu), *ngoma* music today is usually specific to a language group or tribe and uses the respective vernacular and local dance rhythms. Whether in the town or the country, *ngoma* also provides most of the music used during the life-cycle festivities of birth, initiation/circumcision, marriage and death, Look out for recordings by Luhya *sukuti* groups, the *sukuti* being the central drum of these ensembles.

The following is a brief tribe-by-tribe run-down of more easily encountered traditional music and instruments.

Kamba and Chuka

The **Kamba** are best known for their skill at drumming, but this tradition has sadly now all but disappeared. To find any musicians, you'll have to go well off the beaten track in the Ukambani region east of Nairobi. Like that of the Kamba, **Chuka** music from the east side of Mount Kenya is drumming genius, and is likewise almost extinct. Your only hope is to catch one of the very few remaining bands who sometimes pop up at tourist hotels.

Bajuni

The **Bajuni** are a small ethnic group living in the Lamu Archipelago and on the nearby mainland, and are known musically for a recording of an epic women's work song called *Mashindano ni Matezo* ("Competition is a Game"). One of very few easily available recordings of women singing traditionally in Kenya, it features counterpoint vocals that gradually become hypnotic, punctuated by metallic rattles and supported by subdued drumming. You can find it in Lamu, Kilifi and Mombasa.

Boran

The **Boran**, who live between Marsabit and the Ethiopian border, have a rich musical tradition. The Arab influence is readily discernible, as are more typically Saharan rhythms, and most distinctive is their use of the *chamonge*, a large cooking pot loosely strung with metal wires. Recordings are difficult to obtain, but you can try asking in Isiolo or Marsabit.

Gusii

Gusii music is perhaps Kenya's oddest. The favoured instrument is the *obokano*, an enormous version of the Luo *nyatiti* (a lyre) which is pitched at least an octave below the human voice, and which can sound like roaring thunder. They also use the ground bow, essentially a large hole dug in the ground over which an animal skin is tightly pegged. The skin has a small hole cut in the centre, into which a single-stringed bow is placed and plucked: the sound defies description. Ask around in Kisii and you should be able to pick up recordings easily enough.

Luhya

Luhya music has a clear Bantu flavour, easily discernible in the pre-eminence of drums. Of these, the *sukuti* is best known, sometimes played in ensembles, and still used in rites of passage such as circumcisions. Recordings are easily available in Kakamega and Kitale, and in some shops in the River Road neighbourhood in Nairobi.

Luo

The **Luo** are best known as the originators of *benga* (see p.590). Their most distinctive musical instrument is the *nyatiti*, a double-necked, eight-string lyre with a skin resonator, which is also struck on one neck with a metal ring tied to the toe. It produces a tight, resonant sound, and is used to generate sometimes remarkably complex, hypnotic rhythms. The instrument was used in the fields to relieve workers' tiredness, the music typically beginning at a moderate pace and quickening progressively, while the musician sang over the sound. The lyrics cover everything from politics and social changes since the Europeans arrived, to moral fables and age-old legends. Look out also for recordings of the *onand* (an accordion) and the *orutu* (a single-stringed fiddle).

Maasai

The nomadic lifestyle of the **Maasai** tends to preclude the carrying of large instruments, and as a result their music is one of the most distinctive in

Kenya, characterized by a total lack of instruments and by some astonishing polyphonous, multi-part singing. This can be call-and-response, and sometimes women are included in the chorus, but the most famous form is warrior songs, where each man sings part of a rhythm, more often than not from his throat (rather like a grunt), which woven together with the calls of his companions creates a pattern of rhythms. The songs are usually competitive (expressed through the singers alternately leaping as high as they can) or bragging – about how the singer killed a lion, or rustled cattle from a neighbouring community. The Maasai have retained much of their traditional culture, so singing is still very much used in traditional ceremonies, most spectacularly in the *eunoto* circumcision ceremony in which boys are initiated into manhood to begin their ten- to fifteen-year stint as *morani*, or warriors.

If you're staying in one of the big coastal hotels or in a safari lodge in Amboseli or the Maasai Mara, you're likely to have a chance to sample Maasai music in the form of groups of *morani* entertaining guests.

Mijikenda

The **Mijikenda** of the coast have a prolific musical tradition which has survived Christian and Islamic conversion and Swahili cultural absorption, and is widely available on CD throughout the coastal region. Performances can occasionally be seen in the larger hotels. Most of the music available is from the Giriama section of the Mijikenda, whose roots are inland of Kilifi and Malindi. Like the Kamba, the Mijikenda are superb drummers and athletic dancers. The music is generally light, overlaid with complex rhythms, and impossible not to dance to. Listen out also for the *kiringongo* music of the Chonyi Mijikenda, which features the xylophone (an instrument otherwise unknown in Kenya).

Samburu

The only recordings of **Samburu** music are tracks on occasional compilations. Like their Maasai cousins, whose singing it closely resembles, Samburu musicians make a point of not playing instruments – at least in theory. In practice, they do play small pipes, and also a kind of guitar with a box resonator and loose metal strings – which seems to be related to the *chamonge* of the Borana. But these are played purely for pleasure, or to soothe a crying baby, and are not deemed proper "music" by Samburu traditionalists. Listen out also for the sinuously erotic rain songs sung by women in times of drought. For recordings, ask around in Maralal, or among the staff at lodges and tented camps in the Samburu, Buffalo Springs and Shaba reserves.

Turkana

The Turkana are one of Kenya's remotest tribes, and in large part are still untouched by Christian missionaries. Their traditional music is based loosely on a call-and-response pattern. The main instrument is a kudu antelope horn with or without finger holes, but most of their music is entirely vocal. A rarity to listen out for are the women's rain songs, sung to the god Akuj during times of drought. As traditional music is still played on ceremonial occasions (and being nomadic, the Turkana rarely have access to electricity), finding CDs or old cassettes is difficult, but try asking around in Loiyangalani. You're usually welcome to join performances in Loiyangalani for a small fee.

Popular music

Until the mid-1990s, the defining elements of Kenyan popular music had always been the interplay of guitars, with prominent solos, and the **cavacha** rhythm – a kind of clavé beat, popularized in the mid-1970s by Congolese groups such as Zaiko Langa Langa and Orchestra Shama Shama. While rapid-fire percussion, usually on the snare or high hat, continues to underlie a great sweep of Kenyan music, it's worth noting that the scene is very

Taarab music

Taarab (or *tarab/tarabu*), the main popular music of the coastal Swahili people, has a special place in coastal society. It has a long tradition in the festive life of the Swahili, especially at weddings, and is also the traditional music of entertainment in all the coastal communities. Many of the lead singers and bandleaders of *taarab* groups are women, almost unique in Kenyan traditional music. Furthermore, the music has strong Arabic/Islamic overtones in instrumentation, especially in the haunting vocals. Earlier *taarab* groups used the full Arabic orchestra, including violins and the lute-like *oud*. Today, the main instruments are mandolin or guitar and either an Indian harmonium or a small electronic organ or piano, plus a variety of local, Arabic or Indian drums. Hindi movies, with their strong musical component, are very popular among the coastal people and this has led to many features of Indian music being absorbed into *taarab*.

On Lamu island, the old centre of Swahili culture, most weddings today are served by a few amateur *taarab* groups, with professional groups bussed up from Mombasa only for well-to-do marriages. **Zein Musical Party**, the most famous of these groups, and now based in Mombasa, is the heir of Lamu's *taarab* tradition. Zein l'Abdin was born in Lamu in 1939 and hails from a family in which the Swahili arts were highly valued. Together with the Swahili poet Sheikh Nabhany, Zein has unearthed a number of poems, dating back to the nineteenth century, which he has included in his repertoire. But Zein isn't just a fabulous singer and composer; he also ranks as the finest *oud* player in East Africa and is well known throughout the Islamic world.

Maulidi Musical Party, **Zuhura & Party** and **Malika** have, for the past three decades, been Mombasa's main wedding favourites. Singer Maulidi Juma and his group are at ease both with traditional Swahili wedding songs and the Hindi-style songs so characteristic of Mombasa *taarab*, with Swahili words set to tunes from the latest Bollywood movie. Some of their rhythms are rooted in local *ngoma* traditions, and bandmaster Mohamed Shigoo's keyboard work is especially original, with a strong flavour of harmonium (which he used to play earlier in his career) and *nzumari* (a local double-reed horn). Shigoo and the Maulidi Musical Party used to back Malika (Asha Abdo Suleiman) when she was visiting from Somalia, where she lived for a while in the 1970s and 1980s. After the outbreak of the civil war, she was based in Mombasa, where she was much in demand – few can rival her stage aura – and she now lives in the US and continues to perform at Somali and Swahili weddings. Mombasa's other female star is the enchanting **Zuhura Swaleh**, whose energetic songs have a firm base in the local *chakacha* rhythms and lyrics. The *taishokoto* is a prominent sound in her group.

With Malika off the scene, and Maulidi and Zuhura now well into their 60s, the audience is looking for new stars. Sitara, second voice in Maulidi Musical Party for some years, emerged with her own group Diamond Star, taking half of Maulidi's band with her. She was popular with the young wedding audience for her Swahili covers of some of the latest Western and Indian pop songs, but sadly died in 2000. A more recent appearance on the scene is Yusuf Mohamed "Tenge", following in the steps of Maulidi and Juma Bhalo, who used to be the hero of Indian-style taarab.

different to that of fifteen or twenty years ago: the ranks of the elder generation of pop musicians have thinned all too quickly in recent years, with a
startling number of experienced younger musicians having also died. HIV/
AIDS may be a factor in many of these cases but that is rarely confirmed.
Whatever the causes, the effects have been devastating, not only in the loss
of creative talent, but also because with the passing of these musicians goes
the living memory of the evolution of Kenyan music. Partly as a result of
this changing of the guard, a new generation of musicians and producers
with quite different backgrounds, training and experience is beginning to
make its mark.

The arrival of the guitar

From the early 1950s on, with the coming of recording and broadcasting, the
introduction of new instruments and the more widespread use of the **guitar**,
an acoustic guitar-based music developed as accompaniment to songs sung in
Swahili. A basis for Swahili-language popular music had already been laid by
the *beni* groups flourishing in East African towns during the first half of the
twentieth century. *Beni* songs, as well as the new guitar songs, featured the
robust social commentary so beloved of Kenyans. The songs were usually in
the form of a short story and often commented on actual events or issues, or
recounted personal experiences of the musician. Romantic lyrics were almost
non-existent, even in songs dealing with men and women.

The guitar styles themselves developed out of different instrumental
techniques and musical perceptions, but they were influenced by the records
available at the time, mainly from other parts of Africa. Kenyan musicians of the
period cite the finger-picking style of **Jean Bosco Mwenda** and **Losta Abelo**,
both from Katanga (Shaba Province in Democratic Republic of the Congo),
and **George Sibanda**, from Bulawayo in Zimbabwe, as important inspirations.
From this period, the notables of Kenya's acoustic guitar styles were **John
Mwale**, **George Mukabi** (directly out of the Luhya *sukuti* tradition) and **Isaya
Mwinamo**.

The 1960s saw the introduction of **electric guitars** as well as larger groups
(of three to four guitars). Finger-picking guitarists from western Kenya and the
smoother, driving, electric-guitar sound of groups like **Equator Sound Band**
(Equator was a leading record label of the time), featuring the songs of **Daudi
Kabaka**, **Fadhili William**, **Nashil Pichen** and **Peter Tsotsi**, dominated the
airwaves and the record stores. Daudi Kabaka reigned as the "King of Twist",
the twist being essentially a fast version of the South African rhythm found in
songs such as "The Lion Sleeps Tonight". Into the 1970s, while Kabaka's
African Eagles and others continued to play their brands of Swahili music,
many top Kenyan groups, such as the Ashantis, Air Fiesta and the Hodi Boys,
were playing Congolese covers and international pop, especially soul music, in
the Nairobi clubs.

Benga and other modern styles

In the 1970s, a number of musicians began to define the direction of an
emerging form, **benga**, which more than any other Kenyan music became
Kenya's most characteristic pop sound. Although it originated with the Luo
people of western Kenya, practically all the Kenyan guitar bands play variants
of it, and today most of the regional or ethnic pop groups refer generally to
their music as *benga*.

As a pop style, *benga* actually dates back to the 1950s, when musicians began adapting traditional dance rhythms and the sounds of the *nyatiti* and *orutu* to the acoustic guitar and later to electric instruments. During its heyday in the 1970s and early 1980s, *benga* music dominated Kenya's recording industry and was very popular even in west and southern Africa.

By any measure, the most famous *benga* musician is **D.O. Misiani** – guitarist, vocalist, and leader of **Shirati Jazz** until his tragic death in a road accident in 2006. Born in Shirati, Tanzania, just south of the Kenyan border, Misiani is regarded as one of the founders of *benga*. His style is characterized by soft, flowing, melodic two-part vocal harmonies, a very active, pulsating bass line that derives at least in part from traditional *nyatiti* and drum rhythms, and stacks of invigorating guitar work, the lead alternating with the vocal.

Three other important *benga* artists (all departed) are the pioneering **Collela Mazee** and **Ochieng Nelly** – either together or separately in various incarnations of **Victoria Jazz** and the **Victoria Kings** – and **George Ramogi** with his Continental Luo Sweet Band. The 1990s saw the emergence of **Okatch Biggy** (Elly Otieno Okatch) with **Heka Heka** and **Prince Jully** (Julius Okumu) with the **Jolly Boys Band**. Today Heka Heka (and the band's various offshoots) and the Jolly Boys are still flourishing. After Prince Jully's death in 1997, Jully's wife, Lillian Auma, began fronting the Jolly Boys as Princess Jully, and she continues to draw enthusiastic crowds.

One Luo name which doesn't fit neatly under the *benga* banner is **Ochieng Kabaselleh** with his Luna Kidi Band. His songs were mostly in Luo, but sometimes with a liberal seasoning of Swahili and English. Likewise, his melodies and harmonies were from the *benga* realm but the rhythm, guitar work, and horns suggested influences from the Congolese/Swahili-dominated sound. Kabaselleh, who languished in prison for several years for "subversion" in the 1980s under the Moi regime, returned to the music world with a flood of new releases in the 1990s. He died in 1998.

A related group started by Kabaselleh with several of his brothers in the late 1970s continues today as **Bana Kadori**. Originally brought together as recording artists, they are still active performers.

Luhya

Many of Kenya's famous guitarists and vocalists come from the Luhya highlands just to the north of Lake Victoria and Luo-land. This was the ancestral home of early finger-picking guitarists like **John Mwale** and **George Mukabi**, as well as **Daudi Kabaka** and another twist proponent still active in the music business, **John Nzenze**. While these musicians achieved broad popularity through Swahili lyrics, other Luhya musicians stayed closer to their home areas both musically and linguistically. In *benga* style, **Sukuma bin Ongaro** is famous for his humorous social commentaries. Even if you can't understand the language, his music is great to dance to and, of course, has some superb guitar licks.

Shem Tube is a Luhya vocalist/guitarist whose music straddles both past and present – though it is his past that has given him a following in Europe, thanks to a vintage compilation in the *omutibo* style featuring his group **Abana ba Nasery** (the Nursery Boys). Coming together as a trio in the early 1960s, Abana ba Nasery used traditional Luhya rhythms and melody lines, but their two-guitar line-up and three-part vocal harmonies, with rhythms scraped from the neck ridges of an old Fanta bottle, presaged elements of modern Kenyan pop. Although they've never earned enough money to buy their own electric guitars and amps, Abana ba Nasery have had a string of local hits as an electric band under the stage names Mwilonje Jazz and Super Bunyore Band.

Kikuyu

As Kenya's largest ethnic group, the Kikuyu of Central Province and Nairobi are a major market force in Kenya's music industry. Perhaps because of this large "built-in" audience, few Kikuyu musicians have tried to cross over into the national Swahili or English-language markets.

Kikuyu pop has a traditional melodic structure, quite distinct from those of the Luo and Luhya of western Kenya. Most often the songs incorporate elements of *benga* and *cavacha*, but it's not unusual for there to be a dose of country and western, reggae or Congolese soukous. From the 1970s into the 1990s, the king of Kikuyu pop was indisputably **Joseph Kamaru**, who over the course of his career carved out something of his own musical empire, including a large performing band and dancers, two music stores and a recording studio. Still going strong in 1993, Kamaru shocked his fans by announcing that he had been "born again" and retired from music performance to devote his efforts to evangelism and gospel music promotion.

At least a part of the void left by Kamaru was filled by Jane Nyambura, one of very few female headliners in Kikuyu pop. Known simply as **Queen Jane**, she's a staunch advocate of the inclusion of traditional folk forms and local languages within contemporary pop, an approach that has limited her radio exposure, but hasn't prevented her and four of her brothers and sisters from make their living from the band. Competing with Queen Jane for top honours among the Kikuyu audience are **J.B. Maina** and **Mike Rua**.

Kamba

Kamba pop music is firmly entrenched in the *benga/cavacha* camp, though it has distinctive features of its own. One is the delicate, flowing rhythm guitar, the flow often reminiscent of the old carousel calliope, which underlies many arrangements. While the primary guitar plays chords in the lower range, the second guitar, often in a high register, plays a fast pattern of fills. This is discernible in many of the recordings of the three most famous Kamba groups: the **Kalambya Boys** and **Kalambya Sisters**; **Peter Mwambi and his Kyanganga Boy**; and **Les Kilimambogo Brothers Band**. With socially relevant lyrics, intricate guitar weaves and a solid dance-beat backing, Les Kilimambogo Brothers began recording in Swahili and achieved widespread popularity in Kenya, though their career was brought to an end by the death of leader **Kakai Kilonzo** in 1987. These days, a new generation of musicians is drawing the limelight away from the old guard, with **Ken wa Maria** (Kennedy Wambua) and his **Yatta International** dominating the Kamba market.

Congolese

Congolese musicians have been making musical waves in Kenya since the late 1950s, but it wasn't until the mid-1970s, after the passing of the American soul craze, that music from Congo began to dominate the urban nightclubs. One of the first Congolese musicians to settle in Kenya during this period was **Baba Gaston**, who had already been in the business for twenty years when he arrived in Nairobi with his group Baba National in 1975. A prolific musician, he stole the scene until his retirement as a performer and recording artist in 1989. Following Gaston, groups such as **Super Mazembe**, **Les Mangelepa** (some of Gaston's own musicians), as well as **Samba Mapangala** and an early version of Mapanagala's **Orchestra Virunga** took hold in the city. This period is still regarded as the golden age of Lingala music in Kenya and it flourishes locally with plenty of CD reissues available in the shops.

Congolese music remains popular in a number of clubs in Nairobi and the larger Kenyan towns. In fact, some of the musicians of this golden period can be found performing today in various Mazembe and Mangelepa successor bands. The veteran Congolese star **Lessa Lassan** continues with his group **Popolipo**, and there are plenty of aspiring young Congolese émigrés waiting in the wings for their turn to shine.

In both Congolese and Swahili popular music, **rumba** has always been a major ingredient. Songs typically open with a slow-to-medium rumba that ambles through the verses, backed by a light percussion of gentle congas, snare and high hat. Then, three or four minutes into the song there's a transition – or more often a hiatus. It's goodbye to verses and rolling rumba as a much faster rhythm, known at the *seben*, highlighting the instrumental parts, especially solo guitar and brass, takes over with a vengeance. Swahili music over the last thirty years has been largely faithful to this two-part structure, although today, both Swahili and Congolese musicians often dispense with the slow portion altogether and crack straight into the *seben*.

Swahili bands: the Tanzanian influence

Kenya's own brand of **Swahili pop** music has its origin in the Tanzanian pop styles of the 1970s, though the Kenyan variety has followed a separate evolutionary path from the Tanzanian mainstream. In addition to the stylistic features it shares with the Congolese sound (light, high-hat-and-conga percussion and a delicate two/three-guitar interweave), the Kenyan Swahili sound is instrumentally sparse, allowing the bass to fill in gaps, often in syncopated rhythms. While the Congolese musicians are famous for their vocals and their intricate harmonies, Swahili groups are renowned for their demon guitarists and crisp, clear guitar interplay. Trumpets and saxes are common in recorded arrangements but usually omitted in club performances because of the extra expense.

One of the first Tanzanian groups to migrate to Kenya was **Arusha Jazz**, the predecessor of what is now the legendary **Simba Wanyika Original** (*Simba Wanyika*: "Lion of the Savanna"). Founded by Wilson Peter Kinyonga and his brothers George and William, the group began performing in Mombasa in 1971. In 1975, with Tanzanian recruit Omar Shabani on rhythm and Kenyan Tom Malanga on bass, the brothers shifted to Nairobi where, over a twenty-year period, they were favourites of the city's club scene and made scores of recordings. They broke up in the 1990s after the deaths of George and Wilson.

The **Wanyika** name is also famous in East Africa for several bands that emerged from Simba Wanyika Original. The group's first big split occurred in 1978 when the core of supporting musicians around the Kinyonga brothers left to form **Les Wanyika**. Under the leadership of Tanzanian lead guitarist John Ngereza, they remained one of Nairobi's top bands right up until his death in 2000. Their rumba music was distinguished by imaginative compositions and arrangements, a typically lean, clean sound and the delicious blend of Professor Omari's rhythm guitar mastery with John Ngereza's lead guitar and Tom Malanga's bass. The vocals, too, were wonderful, handled by Ngereza, whose inclusion as a guest artist on Orchestra Virunga's 1997 US tour finally brought him some international exposure. Sadly, 1998 saw the death of Professor Omari, who had composed many of the group's early hits, and following the death of John Ngereza, the Les Wanyika name lasted only a few months before the group broke up.

Another important figure in the Wanyika story is Tanzania-born **Issa Juma**, who quickly established a name for himself in Kenya as a premier vocalist in the early days of Les Wanyika. Issa formed Super Wanyika in 1981 and over the next

Swahili pop lyrics

These are two songs you're almost certain to hear, sooner of later, regardless of where you stay or how you travel.

Jambo Bwana
by Teddy Kalanda Harrison

Jambo, jambo Bwana	Greetings, greetings Bwana
Habari gani?	How are you doing?
Nzuri sana	Very well
Wageni, mwakaribishwa	Visitors, you are all welcomed
Kenya yetu	In our Kenya
Hakuna matata	There are no problems
Kenya ni nchi nzuri	Kenya's a beautiful country
Hakuna matata	There are no problems
Nchi ya kupendeza	A pleasing country
Hakuna matata	There are no problems
Nchi ya maajabu	A country of wonders
Hakuna matata	There are no problems
Nchi yenye amani	A country of peace
Hakuna matata	There are no problems

Malaika
Authorship disputed, first popularized by Fadhili William (translated by Farouk Abdillah)

Malaika, nakupenda malaika	Angel, I love you angel
Malaika, nakupenda malaika	Angel, I love you angel
Nami nifanyeje, kijana mwenzio?	And me, what shall I, your boyfriend, do?
Nashindwa na mali sina wee	If I weren't struggling for money
Ningekuoa malaika	I would marry you angel
Nashindwa na mali sina wee	If I weren't struggling for money
Ningekuoa malaika	I would marry you angel
Pesa zasumbuwa roho yangu	Money is the source of my heartache
Pesa zasumbuwa roho yangu	Money is the source of my heartache
Nami nifanyeje, kijana mwenzio?	And me, what shall I, your boyfriend, do?
Nashindwa na mali sina wee	If I weren't struggling for money
Ningekuoa malaika	I would marry you angel
Nashindwa na mali sina wee	If I weren't struggling for money
Ningekuoa malaika	I would marry you angel
Kidege, hukuwaza kidege	Little bird, I'm always dreaming of you, little bird
Kidege, hukuwaza kidege	Little bird, I'm always dreaming of you, little bird
Nami nifanyeje, kijana mwenzio?	And me, what shall I, your boyfriend, do?
Nashindwa na mali sina wee	If I weren't struggling for money
Ningekuoa malaika	I would marry you angel
Nashindwa na mali sina wee	If I weren't struggling for money
Ningekuoa malaika	I would marry you angel

few years had a series of hits featuring half a dozen other variations on the Wanyika names. One of the most prolific artists of the 1980s, he was perhaps the most versatile and creative of the Swahili artists in his willingness to take his music in different directions. His recorded output features many numbers that were a kind of fusion of Swahili rumba and *benga*.

Foremost among other Tanzanians and Kenyans performing in the Swahili style are the **Maroon Commandos**. Members of the Kenyan Army, the Commandos are one of the oldest groups in the country. They first came together in 1970 and were initially mainly a covers band playing Congolese hits, but by 1977 they had become a strong force in the Swahili style with the huge Taita-language hit "Charonyi ni Wasi." The Commandos have proved to be quite experimental at times, mingling Swahili and *benga* styles and occasionally adding a keyboard and innovative guitar effects. Currently, the only other serious proponents of the Swahili rumba sound are **Abdul Muyonga and Everest Kings**.

Tourist and international pop

Where Kenyan pop meets the tourist industry, at the coastal resorts around Mombasa, bands can make a living just playing hotel gigs. These bands typically feature highly competent musicians, relatively good equipment and a fairly polished sound. The best of them are worth catching: they typically play an eclectic selection of old Congolese rumba tunes as warm-ups, popular international covers, a few Congolese favourites of the day, greatest hits from Kenya's past, and some original material that leans heavily towards American and European pop, but with lyrics relating to local topics.

The most successful Kenyan group in this field has been the oddly named **Them Mushrooms** (also called **Uyoga**, Swahili for mushroom). The band managed to graduate from the coastal hotel circuit when they moved to Nairobi in 1987, but their music lives on at the coast, in particular their crowning achievement, the tourist anthem "Jambo Bwana" (see box opposite). While the Mushrooms are proud to take credit for this insidiously infectious bit of fluff, they have shown over their long career that they have serious musical intentions, having been involved in a series of highly successful and diverse collaborations, including one with one of Kenya's earliest guitar pioneers, **Fundi Konde**, and other projects with *taarab* star Malika and the Kikuyu singer Queen Jane. Since 1993, the band have returned to their reggae roots.

Them Mushrooms' long-time counterpart in the hotel circuit, **Safari Sound**, have the distinction of having made Kenya's best selling album ever in *The Best of African Songs*, a veritable greatest hits of hotel classics with songs such as "Malaika", a beautiful composition about ill-starred love (see box opposite).

The evolving scene

In the early 1990s, the Kenyan music business was at a low point. Piracy and diminishing sales meant that, as a business, recorded music was hardly worth the effort – and the music that was being produced at the time hardly seemed worth buying anyway. By the mid-1990s, however, a number of factors had set the stage for a radical departure from the styles of previous generations. For one thing, Kenya experienced the rise of commercial **FM radio**, which helped acquaint Kenyans with reggae, ragga, house, dancehall, hip-hop and R&B from abroad. Also around this time, **new technology** made recording much more affordable, and a new breed of independent Kenyan producer began to emerge. New groups were formed, performing in styles inspired largely by music from abroad, but adding local elements in language, subject matter and sometimes melody and instrumentation. **Tedd Josiah**, **Bruce Odhiambo** and **Suzanne and Gido Kibukosya** were among the producers who were instrumental in shepherding along these new artists, often with quite different musical intentions, from hip-hop covers of African pop classics to gospel balladry.

Eric Wainaina, who brought together an innovative mix of Kenyan pop sounds with American soft-rock influences, was one of the stars of this new generation of Kenyan musicians, especially in the turbulent early years of multi-party democracy, when his lyrics about corruption and poverty resonated across the country. Some of the best material of the time was showcased on two CDs put together by Josiah – *Kenyan: The First Chapter* and *Kenyan: The Second Chapter*. Notable from the first of these is **Kalamashaka**'s "Tafsiri Hii", the trio's trendsetting Swahili hip-hop song addressing the reality of street life. *The Second Chapter* introduced the duo **Gidigidi Majimaji**, perhaps the most innovative and successful of Kenya's new breed of music stars, blending clever lyrics, African rhythms and instruments and contemporary hip-hop. In much the same way that Josiah's *Chapters* CDs introduced a host of new artists to radio and the public, the production house known as **Ogopa Deejays** have released three compilations featuring acts who have become fixtures of the Kenyan pop charts: **Redsan**, **Kleptomaniaks**, **Wahu**, **Big Pin**, **Mr Lenny** and the late **E-Sir** are just a few of many successful Ogopa artists. Much of the Ogopa sound is encompassed by the style known as **kapuka**, built on a mixture of Kenyan hip-hop, ragga and house. Kapuka gets plenty of airplay and *kapuka* artists are often featured at corporate-sponsored events and festivals.

Kenyan **hip-hop** artists draw a distinction between their music and *kapuka*, criticizing the latter for its shallowness and lack of meaningful social content. They point out that a great many *kapuka* practitioners have never experienced the hardships of the poor in the urban slums; instead, their love songs and party music represent the African middle class. And indeed, one of the biggest of today's stars is the wealthy rapper **CMB Prezzo**, who brags about his fortunate circumstances in his music. Always the showman, Prezzo makes it a point to be seen arriving at his concerts with a well-dressed entourage in the flashy cars. He even hired a helicopter to airdrop him into a music awards ceremony, scoring points for brazen style, but no awards. Similar in sound to *kapuka* but lyrically deeper, the **genge** genre promoted by rival production house Calif Records, aims to be music for the masses. Calif artistes **Jua Cali** and **Nonini** have scored some massive hits in recent years.

While hip-hop and dancehall sounds underlie much of Kenya's music today and are especially popular among teens and young adults, contemporary Kenyan music has gone off in many directions and with numerous fusions. Traditional instruments have returned in several pop forms. Drawing on Luo traditions, the group **Kenge Kenge** combines *orutu* fiddle, flute, horn, vocal harmonies and lively percussion on traditional Luo drums. Their high-energy music guarantees a packed house any night of the week. Taking these Luo musical elements in a different direction, *ohangla* musicians such as **Tony Nyadundo** and **Osogo Winyo** combine traditional percussion with keyboard, harmonica, and drum kit for an updated version of the music formerly reserved for funerals, country beer parties, and celebrations such as for the birth of twins. This is must-see entertainment when performed live but less compelling for non-Luo speakers when listening on CD.

Another segment of Kenya's new music scene includes musicians looking to their traditions for elements they can use to reshape contemporary pop. **Yunasi**, **Kayamba Afrika** and US-based **Jabali Afrika** emphasize rich vocal harmonies blended with traditional African percussion and stringed instruments, along with guitar, bass and keyboards. **Nairobi City Ensemble** takes a slightly different approach in their album *Kalapapla*. The group begins with what they term "authentic melodies" from traditional roots but makes the sound completely contemporary with modern instruments, guest rappers, and the thoughtful use of traditional stringed instruments like the Luo *nyatiti* and *orutu*. Finally, singer-songwriter and guitarist **Suzzana Owiyo** deserves special mention for her innovative approach to bringing the melodies and instruments of her traditional Luo culture into modern pop. All these efforts attract great critical interest and, despite being largely ignored by Kenyan radio and most under-30s, have resulted in financial support from cultural exchange organizations like the Alliance Française and the Goethe-Institut, and invitations to the artists to perform in music festivals across Africa and overseas.

Discography

Music shops throughout Kenya will have CDs by many of the following artists. Online MP3 stores also carry an increasing range of tracks. You can usually find a few CDs of **traditional music** locally, though you may have to persevere a little to find someone who sells them. **Kentunes** is the first dedicated Kenyan music online store (Ⓦkentunes.com).

Abana Ba Nasery *Classic Acoustic Recordings from Western Kenya* (GlobeStyle, UK). A charming collection of finger-picking acoustic guitar music. The central position of the solo guitar in Kenya's electric groups is anticipated here in Shem Tube's solos.

Abana Ba Nasery *!Nursery Boys Go Ahead! The Guitar and Bottle Kings of Kenya* (GlobeStyle, UK/Xenophile, US). This CD captures the crisp ABN sound in recordings made on their 1991 UK tour. It also involves the trio in some interesting collaborations with European artists.

H.N. Ochieng Kabaselleh & the Lunna Kidi Band *Sanduku ya Mapendo and Achi Maria* (Equator Heritage Sounds, US). From the area around Lake Victoria, Kabaselleh was one Kenyan bandleader whose music always stood apart – an interesting mix of Luo *benga*, Swahili rumba and Congolese influences, exemplified by these two collections of Kabaselleh's double-A-sided singles from the 1980s.

🏃 **Kakai Kilonzo** *Best of Kakai Vols 1 & 2* (Shava Musik, Germany). From the mid-1970s until his death in 1987, Kakai was at the top of the Kamba music scene in

Kenya, and with catchy Swahili lyrics and a tight *benga* sound, he had fans from across the country. This is a fine compilation of vinyl singles from the 1980s which usually featured a song split between the A- and B-sides, but which here have been neatly stitched back together.

Fundi Konde *Fundi Konde Retrospective Vol 1 (1947–56)* (RetroAfric, UK). Full of enticing, vintage Kenyan pop: imagine a vocal line like a mellow, two-part "Chattanooga Choo Choo", add a smooth, jazzy electric guitar, bass and clarinet, and you have the ingredients for the typical Konde track. Konde's heyday was the 1950s, but he was rediscovered in the 1990s through his collaboration with Them Mushrooms.

🏃 **Gidigidi Majimaji** *Ismarwa* (A'mish, US). The duo of Joseph Ogidi and Julius Owino burst onto the scene with their song "Ting' Badi Malo" (found on the *Rough Guide to Kenyan Music*). *Ismarwa* was a brilliant debut album, beautifully combining a strong rhythmic component with tantalizingly fresh acoustic sounds. The alternative take on *Ting Badi Malo* found here, with its foghorn bass (mimicking a traditional horn), light acoustic guitar, and tight Luo rap, is much rootsier than the version on the Rough Guide CD.

Golden Sounds Band *Swahili Rumba* (Naxos World, US). Led by the brilliant saxophonist/arranger Twahir Mohamed, Golden Sounds played rumba music in the tradition of the Wanyika bands and Maroon Commandos. Repeated listens are required before you really begin to appreciate all that this album offers, in the evolutionary development of musical motifs over tracks lasting around eight minutes apiece.

Les Wanyika *Paulina: The Best of Professor Omari Shabani and John Ngereza* (Tamasha, Kenya). Les Wanyika were the last of the great Swahili rumba bands in the "Wanyika" lineage, dating back to the early 1970s, and this album is a gem, bringing together some of their finest material. The eloquent interplay of the guitars of John Ngereza and Professor Omari is stunning.

Samba Mapangala & Virunga *African Classics* (Sheer Sound). From the mid-1970s to the early 1990s, Virunga were one of Kenya's most exciting groups. Mapangala has since relocated to the USA but is still a favourite in East Africa. Each song is like a ten-minute story, exploring different combinations of rhythm, melody and harmony right to the finish. This collection pulls together some of the best tracks of Samba's 25-plus years under the Virunga name, with classics such as Malako, Yembele, and Sungura, plus three songs never before released outside Kenya.

Maroon Commandos *Shika Kamba* (Sound Africa, Kenya). Tilting a little more towards Congolese rumba in this release, the Maroon Commandos are still a great sound as Kenya's longest running rumba group.

Collela Mazee and Victoria B Kings Band *Jessica* (Equator Heritage Sounds). Classic Luo *benga* music of the late 1970s and early 1980s: a pounding beat, pulsing bass, and brilliant guitars, each track ending with a luscious guitar solo.

D.O. Misiani & Shirati Band *Benga Blast!* (Earthworks/Stern's, UK) and *Piny Ose Mer/The World Upside Down* (GlobeStyle, UK). Daniel Owino Misiani was one of the founding fathers of *benga* music: these are both fine collections of his work, the former in glorious mono, being the rough, unpolished sound of the old Pioneer House studios.

John Amutabi Nzenze & Friends *Angelike Twist* (Equator Heritage Sounds). John Nzenze is a pioneering figure in Kenyan music who started his recording career as a teen back in the 1950s. This compilation beautifully highlights his contribution to the acoustic finger-picking guitar styles of the 1950s and the electric "twist" style that followed in the 1960s.

Ayub Ogada *En Mana Kuoyo* (Real World, UK). Based in the UK, Ayub Ogada is a Luo who has been exploring and bridging cultural boundaries over the last two decades. This enthralling, low-key, largely acoustic album, has beautiful melodies and captivating rhythms, and features elements of the Luo tradition.

Orchestra Super Mazembe *Giants of East Africa* (Earthworks/Stern's, UK). Congolese group Super Mazembe played the dance halls and bars of Kenya for nearly thirty years before their demise. In songs such as "Kasongo" and "Shauri Yako", they exemplified the definitive sound of Congolese rumba in East Africa. Mazembe's early 1980s LP, *Kaivaska*, kindled much of the early enthusiasm for African music in the UK and Europe. This collection includes five of the best songs off *Kaivaska*, including "Kasongo", plus "Shauri Yako".

Suzzana Owiyo *Mama Africa* (ARC Music, UK). This debut from a talented singer-songwriter is a delightful mix of traditional instruments, Owiyo's acoustic guitar and electric sounds with a few rough edges. *Yamo Kudho* (Blu Zebra, Kenya) picks up where *Mama Africa* left off, in a more polished, tighter package, delivering sublime melodies with a bright acoustic sound and mixing in traditional Luo *orutu*, *oporo* (horn), and percussion.

Simba Wanyika Original *Pepea* (Stern's, UK). Their one and only European CD release, superbly produced, allowing the band to shine on fresh recordings of some of their biggest hits of the previous twenty years.

Eric Wainaina *Sawa Sawa* (Wainaina/Kaufmann Prod, USA/ Kenya). Originally part of the Five Alive singing group of the mid-1990s, Wainaina went off to the USA to study at the Berkley College of Music. Spanning a broad range of styles, from up-tempo African dance rhythms to ballads and smooth jazz, this album found Kenyans readily connecting with the song "Nchi ya Kitu Kidogo" (Nation of Kickbacks), decrying, albeit with great humour, the way bribery has permeated Kenyan society. For Swahili speakers, there are comic interludes from the Kenyan stand-up troupe Redykyulass. He followed up with a meticulously produced modern pop album, *Twende Twende* (Enkare, Kenya).

Compilations

Kenya Dance Mania (Earthworks/Stern's, UK). An excellent introduction to Kenya's various styles. *Dance Mania* includes some classics of the 1970s and 1980s, such as Les Wanyika's "Sina Makosa" and Maroon Commandos' evergreen hit "Charonyi Ni Wasi".

Kilio cha Haki (UpToYouToo, Netherlands). Its title translating as "A cry for justice", this album was the outcome of a month-long recording project initiated by a Dutch foundation, bringing together 38 talents from Nairobi's slums, to create innovative hip-hop. The excellent notes transcribe and translate the poignant Swahili lyrics. Proceeds go towards local development.

The Nairobi Beat: Kenyan Pop Music Today (Rounder, USA). A cross-section of mid-1980s Kenyan pop put together by the author of

this article. It showcases some of the best examples of regional *benga* styles: Luo, Kikuyu, Kamba and Luhya, plus a couple of Swahili and Congolese dance tunes for good measure.

The Rough Guide to the Music of Kenya (World Music Network, UK). A sampling of the many styles of Kenyan popular music, including the guitar-centric *benga* and Swahili rumba styles, *taarab* from the coastal region, current day "traditional" sounds, and the shifting sounds of the younger generation (including Gidigidi Majimaji's "Ting Badi Malo").

Zanzibara 2: 1965–1975 (Buda Musique, France). A delightful collection of *taarab* music recorded by Mombasa's Mzuri Records. Features songs by the likes of Zuhura Swaleh, Zein l'Abdin and Maulidi Juma.

Written and researched by **Doug Paterson** (Ⓦeastafricanmusic.com), with contributions from Jens Finke on traditional music (Ⓦwww.bluegecko.org) and Werner Graebner on *taarab*.

www.roughguides.com

Books

There is no shortage of reading matter on Kenya. For pre-departure reading, the growing body of **Kenyan literature** provides a good foretaste. Usual high street and online retailers, or used book suppliers, will have most of the titles in this section (or can order them), although a few may be more easily available in Kenya. In the UK, the Africa Book Centre is an excellent source (www.africabookcentre.com).

Literacy has massively improved in Kenya in recent decades and more than ninety percent of the population can now read, a high figure in Africa. Bookstores in Nairobi, Mombasa and in the tourist hotels have imported paperback selections. Locally printed books are sometimes very cheap, and provide insights into Kenyan life you wouldn't otherwise find. Although a number of Kenyan authors have written in the country's indigenous languages, English still predominates. The excellent *Kwani?* website (www.kwani.org), run by Caine-prize winning writer Binyavanga Wainaina, is an excellent resource. Titles marked 🏃 are particularly recommended.

Climbing and diving guides

Iain Allan *The Mountain Club of Kenya Guide to Mount Kenya and Kilimanjaro*. For fully equipped alpinism, this is indispensable.

Anton Koornhof *The Dive Sites of Kenya and Tanzania*. Highly recommended, with detailed text on every major site, beautifully illustrated and with thoughtful sections on environmental matters.

Andrew Wielochowski *Mount Kenya 1:50,000 Map and Guide*. Covers just the mountain itself, and includes a detailed rundown on the huts and technical information for those scaling Nelion and Batian.

Helmut Debelius *Indian Ocean Reef Guide*. Field guide to all the main species of fish and invertebrates, with excellent identification photos.

Wildlife guides

Michael Blundell *Field Guide to the Wild Flowers of East Africa*. Botanical companion in the Collins series.

🏃 **Jonathan Kingdon** *The Kingdon Pocket Guide to African Mammals*. The definitive handbook, abridged to this still detailed, soft-cover, game-viewing format, with identification illustrations and distribution maps for each species.

Dave Richards *A Photographic Guide to the Birds of East Africa*. More than three hundred photos, this is ideal if you're a holiday birder.

Chris Stuart and Tilde Stuart *Field Guide to the Larger Mammals of Africa*. Beautifully illustrated and well edited field guide published in 2006.

Nigel Wheatley *Where to Watch Birds in Africa*. Tight structure and plenty of useful detail make this a must-have for serious bird-watchers. Twenty-five pages on Kenya.

Zimmerman, Turner and Pearson *Birds of Kenya & Northern Tanzania*. Weighty and comprehensive coverage for the serious birder, also available in a more portable paperback edition.

Coffee-table books

Mohamed Amin *Cradle of Mankind* and *Portrait of Kenya*. Stunning photographs of the Lake Turkana region, by the award-winning maverick photo-journalist Amin, killed in the Comoros plane hijack in 1997.

Yann Arthus–Bertrand *Kenya from the Air*. Superb images of the country from the eagle's viewpoint.

Paul Goldstein and Roger Hooper *Dotted Plains, Spotted Game*. Captured entirely in the Mara, an impressive collection of images, concentrating on the big cats.

Mitsuaki Iwago *Serengeti: Natural Order on the African Plain*. Simply the best volume of wildlife photography ever assembled, this makes most glossies look feeble. If you're trying to persuade someone to visit East Africa – or if any aesthetic argument were needed to preserve the parks and animals – this is the book to use.

David Keith Jones *Shepherds of the Desert*. Brilliant photos, many in black and white, with a text more lucid and less superficial than most glossies; this book

concerns itself only with northern Kenya.

Nigel Pavitt *Kenya: A Country in the Making 1880–1940*. A much-admired production in Kenya itself, where many people – particularly Euro-Kenyan settler families – feel a connection to one or more of the 720 digitally restored photos in this sumptuous tome.

Brian Jackman and Jonathan Scott *The Marsh Lions*. Beautifully produced and painstakingly researched study of the big cats and other animals around the Musiara Marsh in the Maasai Mara Reserve.

Jonathan Scott and Angela Scott *Stars of Big Cat Diary*. Valedictory volume for fans of the series.

Tepilit Ole Saitoti and Carol Beckwith *Maasai*. The Maasai coffee-table book, with some photos too much to take at reading distance. Exquisite, but largely staged, portraits of Maasai culture (and even Beckwith's camera can't disguise the tourist souvenirs in the background). Variably interesting, chauvinistic text, which plays the cult value of the Maasai for all it's worth.

Arts

Jane Barbour and Simiyu Wandibba *Kenyan Pots and Potters*. This comprehensive description of pot-making communities includes techniques, training, marketing and sociological perspectives.

Susan Denyer *African Traditional Architecture*. Useful and interesting, with hundreds of photos (most of

them old) and detailed line drawings.

Frank Willett *African Art*. An accessible volume; good value, with a generous illustrations–text ratio.

Geoffrey Williams *African Designs from Traditional Sources*. A designer's and enthusiast's sourcebook.

Travel and general accounts

David Bennum *Tick Bite Fever.* Memoir about growing up in an expat household in the 1970s from a British newspaper journalist. Full of acid wit, this is an amusingly dry alternative to more cloying accounts.

Bill Bryson *Bill Bryson's Africa Diary.* A brief but typically engaging book, recounting Bryson's travels around Kenya learning about the work of Care International. All profits go to the charity.

Bartle Bull *Safari: A Chronicle of Adventure.* A great, macho slab of a book, jammed with photos. It's grotesque but utterly compelling – even if the cruelty and foolish waste of the hunting era is a bit emotionally wearing.

Negley Farson *Behind God's Back.* An American journalist's account of his overland journey across Africa on the eve of World War II. A lively book if you can stomach the alarming shifts between criticism of the colonial world and participation in its worst prejudices.

John Hillaby *Journey to the Jade Sea.* An obvious one to read before a trip to Lake Turkana. Hillaby's account of his walk in the early 1960s was an adventure, as he writes, "for the hell of it", with sprinklings of tall stories and descriptions of loony incompetence.

Corinne Hoffmann *The White Masai.* Equally ridiculed and revered, an extraordinary account, effectively a journal, of a Swiss woman's extended love affair with a Samburu man, and her life in Barsaloi in the early 1990s.

J. Ludwig Krapf *Travel, Researches and Missionary Labours during an Eighteen Years Residence in Eastern Africa.* The account of the first missionary at Mombasa, and the first European to set eyes on Mount Kenya.

Peter Matthiessen *The Tree Where Man Was Born.* Wanderings and musings of the Zen-thinking polymath in Kenya and northern Tanzania, first published in 1972. Enthralling for its detail on nature, society, culture and prehistory, and beautifully written, this is a gentle, appetizing introduction to the land and its people.

George Monbiot *No Man's Land.* A journey through Kenya and Tanzania, providing a shocking exposé of Maasai dispossession and trenchant criticism of the wildlife conservation movement.

Cynthia Moss *Elephant Memories: Thirteen Years in the Life of an Elephant Family.* Moss is one of the world's leading authorities on the social life of the African elephant – a fascinating, moving account of her work in Amboseli.

Dervla Murphy *The Ukimwi Road.* Murphy's bike ride from Kenya to Zimbabwe becomes – for her – a trip through lands lost to AIDS and neo-colonialism.

Shiva Naipaul *North of South.* A classic account of the late Naipaul's life and travels in East Africa in the 1970s. Caustic but always readable and sometimes hilarious, the insights make up for occasionally angst-ridden social commentary and some passages that widely miss the mark.

Barack Obama *Dreams from My Father: A Story of Race and Inheritance.* In which, in 1988, the forty-fourth president-to-be of the USA spends five weeks and 140 pages visiting his father's side of the family in Kenya.

This part of the book is a gentle, thoughtful conclusion as Obama hangs out in Nairobi, goes to the Mara, and visits his father's grave in Kogelo.

Craig Packer *Into Africa*. A professor of ecology, evolution and behaviour, Packer puts it all to good use in day-by-day reflections during an eight-week field trip.

Joyce Poole *Coming of Age with Elephants*. Deeply sympathetic account of studying the social and sexual behaviour of elephants in Amboseli alongside Cynthia Moss.

Keith B. Richburg *Out of America; a Black Man Confronts Africa*. Nairobi bureau chief for the Washington Times from 1991–94, Richburg discovered that he was American, not African, and preferred it that way. A rather depressing read and unfortunately likely to stoke the flames of moral relativism.

Rick Ridgeway *The Shadow of Kilimanjaro*. The American adventurer and film-maker took a walk in 1997 through the bush from Kilimanjaro to Mombasa – mostly through Tsavo West and East, along the Tsavo-Galana River. Robust, readable and full of passionate enthusiasm for the wild country and the wildlife.

Wilfred Thesiger *My Kenya Days*. The account of thirty-odd years in northern Kenya by a very strange man indeed – an old Etonian noble savage with no interest in modern Africa, wedded to his own ego and a reactionary, glamour-laden view of his tribal companions.

Joseph Thomson *Through Masai Land: A Journey Of Exploration Among The Snow-Clad Volcanic Mountains And Strange Tribes Of Eastern Equatorial Africa*. First published in 1885, these two volumes detail Thomson's African journeys of exploration.

Daisy Waugh *A Small Town in Africa*. A year in the life of Isiolo – good gap year preparation.

Evelyn Waugh *A Tourist in Africa*. First published in 1960, Waugh's diary of a short trip to Kenya, Tanganyika and Rhodesia is determinedly arrogant and uninformed, but funny, too – and brief enough to consume at a single sitting.

Essays

Wahome Mutahi *How to be a Kenyan*. A satirical view of Kenyan life by one of the country's most popular newspaper columnists. Painfully funny, and close to the bone.

Renato Kizito Sesana *Father Kizito's Notebook*. Kenyan life from the Catholic perspective of Father Kizito's weekly columns in the *Sunday Nation*. Full of insights into the struggle to survive that Kenyans call life, infused with humour and compassion.

Colonial writers and biographies

Isak Dinesen (Karen Blixen) *Out of Africa*. This has become something of a cult book, particularly in the wake of the movie. First published in 1937, it describes Blixen's life (Dinesen was a nom de plume) on her Ngong Hills coffee farm between the wars. Read today, it seems to hover uncertainly between contemporary literature and historical document. It's an intense read – lyrical, introspective, sometimes obnoxiously and intricately racist, but worth pursuing and never superficial, unlike Sydney Pollack's film. Karen Blixen's own *Letters from Africa 1914–1931*, translated by Anne Born, gives posthumous insights.

Elspeth Huxley *The Flame Trees of Thika: Memories of an African Childhood* and *The Mottled Lizard*. Based on her own childhood, from a prolific author who also wrote numerous works on colonial history and society, including *White Man's Country*, a biography of the settlers' doyen, Lord Delamere, and *Out in the Midday Sun: My Kenya* – both as readable, and, to be fair, as predictable, as any. Her last book, *Nine Faces of Kenya* is a somewhat dewy-eyed anthology of colonial East African ephemera. More interesting is the collection of her mother's letters, *Nellie: Letters from Africa*, which includes compelling coverage of the Mau Mau years from the pen of a likeably eccentric settler.

Beryl Markham *West with the Night*. Markham made the first east–west solo flight across the Atlantic. This is her only book about her life in the interwar Kenya colony, drawing together adventures, landscapes and contemporary figures.

Richard Meinertzhagen *Kenya Diary 1902–1906*. The haunting day-to-day narrative of a young British officer in the protectorate.

Meinertzhagen's brutal descriptions of "punitive expeditions" are chillingly matter-of-fact and make the endless tally of his wildlife slaughter pale inoffensively in comparison. As a reminder of the savagery that accompanied the British intrusion (Meinertzhagen is notorious as the murderer of the Nandi chief, Koitalel, during a meeting), and a stark insight into the complex mind of one of its perpetrators, this is disturbing, highly recommended reading. Good photos, too.

Edward Paice *Lost Lion of Empire: The Life of Ewart Grogan DSO, 1876–1976*. Fascinating biography of one of the Kenya colony's most rumbustious movers and shakers.

Judith Thurman *Isak Dinesen: The Life of a Storyteller*. A revisionist biography that was much used as a source for Sydney Pollack's *Out of Africa* film.

Errol Trzebinski *The Lives of Beryl Markham*. In which, among much else, it is suggested that Markham did not, and could not, have written *West with the Night*.

Sarah Wheeler *Too Close to the Sun: The Audacious Life and Times of Denys Finch Hatton*. Stylishly written biography of the colony's coolest dude, the enigmatic lover of Karen Blixen, who died at the controls of his plane in 1931, aged 44.

Kenyan fiction in English

Chinua Achebe and C.L. Innes (eds) *African Short Stories*. A collection that treats its material geographically, including Kenyan stories from Jomo Kenyatta, Grace Ogot, Ngugi and a spooky offering (*The Spider's Web*) from Leonard Kibera.

Thomas Akare *The Slums*. A bleaker read than Meja Mwangi (see p.606), but also more humane. Without quotation marks, the dialogue melds

seamlessly into the narrative; there are no doubts about the authentic rhythms of Kenyan English here. But much is assumed to be understood and there's much that won't be, unless perhaps you're sitting under a 25-watt light bulb in a River Road B&L.

Charlotte H. Bruner (ed) *Unwinding Threads: Writing by Women in Africa*. East Africa features Kenyan writers Charity

Ngugi wa Thiong'o

Ngugi wa Thiong'o, the dominant figure of modern Kenyan literature, currently lives in the USA: although his books in English are not banned in Kenya, his political sympathies are unwelcome.

Ngugi's work is art serving the revolution – didactic, brusque, graphic and unsentimental. He writes in Kikuyu, then translates his work into English. His novels, especially the later ones, are unforgiving: the touch of humour that would leaven the polemic rarely comes to the rescue. Powerful themes – exploitation, betrayal, cultural oppression, the imposition of Christianity, loss of and search for identity – drive the stories along urgently.

Ngugi's style is heady, idealistic and undaunted, never teasing or capricious. Disillusioned with English, his first work in Kikuyu, in collaboration with Ngugi wa Mirii, was the play *Ngahiika Ndeenda* (*I Will Marry When I Want*), and its public performance by illiterate peasants at the Kamiriithu Cultural Centre in Limuru got him detained for a year. *Detained – A Writer's Prison Diary* is a retrospective of Kenya's history up to 1978, woven into the daily routine of political detention during Kenyatta's last year.

All of Ngugi's writings in English are in print. Try *Secret Lives* for short stories, *Weep Not, Child* for a brief but glowing early novel, or, for the mature Ngugi, *Petals of Blood* – a richly satisfying detective story that is at the same time a saga of wretchedness and struggle. Others include *The River Between*, on the old Kikuyu society and the coming of the Europeans; *A Grain of Wheat*, about the eve of independence; *Devil on the Cross* (originally written in detention on scraps of toilet paper); and *Matigari* ("The Patriots"). *Matigari*, first published in Kikuyu in 1986, had a remarkable effect in the Central Highlands. Rumours circulated that a man was spreading militant propaganda against the government of Daniel Arap Moi. The police even tried to track him down, before realizing their mistake and confiscating all copies of the book.

His epic, satirical novel, *The Wizard of the Crow*, was his last work of fiction, published in 2006 to huge acclaim, before he started to write autobiographically about his childhood: *Dreams in a Time of War* is published in 2010. Apart from *I Will Marry When I Want*, Ngugi has written two other plays, *The Black Hermit* and *The Trial of Dedan Kimathi* (with Micere Mugo). His contribution to Kenyan literature is enormous, and delving in is rewarding, if not always easy.

Waciuma and the excellent Grace Ogot, whose *The Rain Came* is a bewitching mystery myth, combining traditional Luo tales with her own fiction in a perplexingly Western form.

John Kiriamiti *My Life in Crime.* This racy autobiographical account, penned in prison by a professional robber, was so successful that the author went on to write two novels (*Son of Fate* and *The Sinister Trophy*) plus an account of his time as a villain told from his fiancée's point of view (*My Life with a Criminal: Millie's Story*).

J. Roger Kurtz *Urban Obsessions, Urban Fears: the Postcolonial Kenyan novel.* Explores the relationship between Kenyan fiction in English and the city of Nairobi, and includes a comprehensive bibliography of all the Kenyan novels in English since Ngugi's *Weep Not, Child* was published in 1964.

Charles Mangua *Son of Woman.* Mangua tells the tale of a son of a prostitute and his misadventures: hard-bitten and cynical, but engaging nonetheless. In a very different style, his second novel, *A Tail in the Mouth*, looks at the Mau Mau rebellion through the eyes of a young man caught up in it and swept along by events.

Ali Mazrui *The Trial of Christopher Okigbo.* A clever "novel of ideas" from the US-based political scientist, who always succeeds in infuriating both critics of Kenya and its supporters.

🏃 **Meja Mwangi** *Going Down River Road*; *Carcass for Hounds*; *Kill Me Quick*. Popular author Meja Mwangi is lighter and more accessible than Ngugi, his fiction infused with the absurdities of urban Nairobi slum life. *Going Down River Road* is his best-known work – perfect for reading *in situ*, with convincing scenes, chaotic action and sharp dialogue. Mwangi was shortlisted for the Commonwealth Writers' Prize with *Striving for the Wind* (1992), which is set in a rural rather than urban location.

🏃 **Ngugi wa Thiong'o** *Decolonising the Mind: The Politics of Language in African Literature*. Ngugi, who writes fiction in Kikuyu, has long been closely associated with attempts to move Kenyan literature

and African literature in general towards expression in the readers' mother tongues (see box p.548).

M.G. Vassanji *The In-between World of Vikram Lall*. Remarkable epic – winner of the 2003 Giller Prize for Canadian fiction – of multiple alienations and the power of corruption in a world of competing moralities. Lall is the chief protagonist, a Ugandan Asian exiled to Canada having been named Kenya's most corrupt man.

🏃 **Binyavanga Wainaina** *Discovering Home*. A collection of short stories, including the final shortlist for the 2002 Caine Prize for African Writing. Wainaina takes Kenyan humour, tragedy, and especially the meaning of home for diaspora Kenyans, and mounts them in a beautiful frame.

Kenyan poetry

The oldest form of written poetry in Kenya is from the coast. **Swahili poetry** reads beautifully even if you don't understand the words. Written for at least 300 years, and sung for a good deal longer, it's one of Kenya's most enduring art forms. An *Anthology of Swahili Poetry* has been compiled and rather woodenly translated by **Ali A Jahadmy**, but some of Swahili's best-known classical compositions from the Lamu Archipelago are included, with pertinent background. There's a more enjoyable anthology of romantic and erotic verse, *A Choice of Flowers*, with **Jan Knappert**'s idiosyncratic translations and interpretations, and the same linguist's *Four Centuries of Swahili Verse*, which expounds and creatively interprets at much greater length.

Upcountry poetry in the sense of written verse is a recent form (though oral folk literature was often relayed in the context of music, rhythm and dance). *The Penguin Book of Modern African Poetry*, edited by Ullie Beier and Gerald Moore, is a hefty and catholic selection, with a good selection of Kenyan contributions.

Kenya in foreign fiction

Justin Cartwright *Masai Dreaming*. A compelling novel by a Booker- and Whitbread-nominated writer, juxtaposing a film-maker's vision of Maasai-land with the barbarities of the Holocaust, linked by the tapes of a Jewish anthropologist.

Adam Foulds *The Broken Word*. Moving, gripping and beautifully crafted novella-length prose poem about a young recruit swept up in the hunt for Mau Mau guerrillas.

Jeremy Gavron *Moon*. Vivid short novel about a white boy growing up on a farm during the Mau Mau uprising.

Martha Gellhorn *The Weather in Africa*. Three absorbing novellas, each dealing with aspects of the Europe-Africa relationship, set on the slopes of Kilimanjaro, in the "White Highlands" of Kenya and on the tourist coast north of Mombasa.

David Lambkin *The Hanging Tree*. A human-nature-through-the-ages saga which makes a good yarn – in fact, several yarns.

John Le Carré *The Constant Gardener*. The spymaster turns his hand to a whodunnit, in which a campaigner against the misdeeds of Big Pharma is raped and murdered. Her husband, a British diplomat, starts his own investigation. A brilliantly crafted story (although not always convincing in its portrayal of expat society) and now a multi-Oscar-winning movie by Fernando Meirelles.

Barbara Wood *Green City in the Sun*. A sprawling saga, in which, among a slew of fizzing plot lines, a settler family come into conflict with a Kikuyu medicine woman. One of the few credible novels about the realities of colonial Kenya by a *mzungu* writer.

History and peoples

Kenya in African history

Guy Arnold *Africa: a Modern History*. A huge reference history of the continent from 1960 up until 2000, that places Kenya in context and succinctly ticks all the boxes linking present conditions with past causes.

Richard Dowden *Africa: Altered States, Ordinary Miracles*. Respected journalist and director of the Royal African Society, Dowden's wealth of experience and inimitably human engagement are

expressed through a collection of extended essays, including a brilliant encapsulation of Kenya's downward spiral of greed and corruption.

Christopher Hibbert *Africa Explored: Europeans in the Dark Continent 1769–1889*. Entertaining read, devoted in large part to the "discovery" of East and Central Africa.

Alan Moorehead *The White Nile*. A riveting account of the search for the source and European rivalries for control in the region.

Roland Oliver and J.D. Fage *A Short History of Africa*. Dated, but still the standard paperback introduction.

Thomas Pakenham *The Scramble for Africa*. The story of how the European powers rushed to exploit Africa in the name of commerce, Christianity and civilization, in the last two decades of the nineteenth century.

Kenya in general

Jeffrey A. Fadiman *When We Began There Were Witchmen*. Recounts the story of the Meru people from their mythical origins in Shungwaya in northeastern Kenya to the decimation of Meru culture by a tiny handful of missionaries and colonial administrators.

Terry Hirst *The Struggle for Nairobi*. Sort of large-format "Nairobi for Beginners" that manages to make town planning (or the lack of it) fascinating, bringing together a mass of otherwise hard-to-get information about the city's growth.

Jomo Kenyatta *Facing Mount Kenya*. A traditional, functionalist, anthropological monograph, but written by a member of the society in question – in this case, the Kikuyu – under the

supervision of Bronislaw Malinowski at the LSE, shortly before World War II. One of the few scholarly works ever written on traditional Kikuyu culture, this is as interesting for the insights it offers on its author as for its quite readable content. Good Kikuyu glossary.

Maxon and Ofcansky *Historical Dictionary of Kenya*. From a reliable series that covers nearly every African country, this is an A to Z of Kenya's history and includes an extensive bibliography.

Thomas Spear and Richard Waller (eds) *Being Maasai*. Articles about Maasai identity – a subtle and interesting field, and vital reading for anyone concerned with the ethnic politics of modern Kenya.

Coastal history

G.S.P. Freeman-Grenville *The East African Coast*. Fascinating, vivid and often extraordinary – a series of accounts from the first century to the nineteenth.

Sarah Mirza and Margaret Strobel *Three Swahili Women*. Three histories of ritual, three women's lives. Born between 1890 and 1920 into different social backgrounds,

these biographies document enormous changes from the most important of neglected viewpoints.

James de Vere Allen *Swahili Origins: Swahili Culture and the Shungwaya Phenomenon*. The life work of a challenging and readable scholar, bound to raise a fascinating field of study to new prominence.

Protectorate and colonial Kenya

James Fox *White Mischief*. Investigative romp through the events surrounding the notorious unsolved murder of Lord Errol, one of Kenya's most aristocratic settlers, at Karen in 1941. Well told and highly

revealing of British Kenyan society of the time. Michael Radford's 1987 film version is equally enjoyable, and a good deal more stimulating than the *Out of Africa* movie.

Charles Miller *The Lunatic Express.* The story of *that* railway. Miller narrates the drama of one of the great feats of Victorian engineering – as bizarre and as madly magnificent as any Wild West epic – adding weight with a broad historical background of East Africa from the year dot. The same author's very readable *The Battle for the Bundu* follows a little-known corner of World War I, as fought out on the plains of Tsavo between British Kenya and German Tanganyika.

The Mau Mau rebellion

David Anderson *Histories of the Hanged: Testimonies from the Mau Mau Rebellion in Kenya.* Previously published as *Britain's Dirty War in Kenya*, this deeply researched study concludes that the British response to Mau Mau was unnecessarily harsh and of doubtful legality, and that many Mau Mau trials were flawed.

Caroline Elkins *Britain's Gulag: The Brutal End of Empire in Kenya.* Pulitzer prize-winning study of Britain's network of Mau Mau detention camps. Less dispassionate, and more one-sided than *Histories of the Hanged* (Elkins spends little time discussing Mau Mau atrocities), Elkins has been accused of exaggeration. But this book is nevertheless a shocking indictment of the army's methods, and the reports of torture and abuses committed on and witnessed by survivors provide strong support for the legal cases that some have lodged.

Tabitha Kanogo *Squatters and the Roots of Mau Mau 1905–63.* Delves into the early years of the "White Highlands" to show how resistance, and the conditions for revolt, were built into the relations between the settler land-grabbers and the peasant farmers and herders ("squatters") they usurped. Strong on the role of women in the Mau Mau movement.

J.M. Kariuki *Mau Mau Detainee: The Account by a Kenya African of His Experience in Detention Camps.* A remarkably forbearing account of life and death in the detention camps. Kariuki's vision for the future of Kenya and his loyalty to Kenyatta have a special irony after his assassination in 1975.

David Throup *Economic and Social Origins of Mau Mau.* An examination of the story from the end of World War II, covering the colonial mentality and differences in efficiency between peasant cash-cropping and more wasteful plantation agriculture.

Post Independence

Jean Davison *Voices from Mutira: Change in the Lives of Rural Gikuyu Women 1910–1995.* Unselfconsciously moving and particularly interesting for the attitudes it documents on bride price and genital mutilation.

Anthony Howarth *Kenyatta: A Photographic Biography.* A roughly hewn biography composed of an amalgam of black-and-white photographs, news clippings and quotations. It doesn't pretend to be exhaustive, but manages to capture the spirit of the leader and the struggle for independence.

Joseph Karimi and Philip Ochieng *The Kenyatta Succession.* Worth tracking down – a good read about how the clique surrounding Kenyatta planned to seize power when he died, murdering Moi in the process. By good fortune, Kenyatta died in the wrong place: his cronies would have been far worse than Moi.

Kenneth King *Jua Kali Kenya*. First serious study of Kenya's important informal sector – the self-employed fixers and manufacturers who work under the "hot sun" (*jua kali*). Great photos.

Tom Mboya *The Challenge of Nationhood*. The vision of Kenya's best-loved statesman – and a Luo – assassinated in 1969 for looking like a popular successor to Kenyatta.

Andrew Morton *Moi: the Making of an African Statesman*. Strange subject for the author of *Diana: Her True Story* and a strangely compelling book is the result. While it would be impossible to deny this is a sycophantic biography – Morton's reported conversations with Moi usually dry up just as the reader formulates the critical question – simply getting access to the notoriously defensive president was remarkable in itself. The research is here; there are insights, but also too many factual inaccuracies and

lacunae not to cast suspicion over the whole account. It is, after all, an authorized biography.

Bethuel Ogot and William Ochieng (eds) *Decolonization and Independence in Africa 1940–93*. The standard work on these years, asking how much the difficulties of Kenya and other countries are linked to the colonial past and the process of growing away from it.

Michaela Wrong *It's Our Turn to Eat: The Story of a Kenyan Whistle Blower*. "To eat" is a Kenyan euphemism for helping yourself to what doesn't belong to you – what those in power have been doing since Independence. A book that few retailers are comfortable selling in Kenya, British journalist Michaela Wrong's jaw-dropping account narrates the story of what happened when anti-corruption czar John Githongo tried to do his job. Essential reading.

Language

Language

Swahili

Surprisingly, perhaps, **Swahili** is one of the easiest languages to learn. It's pronounced exactly as it's written, with the stress nearly always on the penultimate syllable. And it's satisfyingly regular, so even with limited knowledge you can make yourself understood and construct simple sentences.

In Kenya, you'd rarely be stuck without Swahili, but it makes a huge difference to your perceptions if you try to speak it. People are delighted if you make the effort (though they'll also tend to assume you understand more than you do) and for travels further afield in East Africa, and especially in Tanzania, some knowledge of Swahili is a very useful backup. Don't forget that for many Kenyans Swahili is another foreign language they get by in, like English.

The language has spread widely from its coastal origins to become the lingua franca of East Africa and it has tended to lose its richness and complexity as a result. Upcountry, it is often spoken as a second language with a minimum of grammar. On the coast, you'll hear it spoken with tremendous panache: oratorial skills and punning (to which it lends itself with great facility) are much appreciated. Swahili is a Bantu language, and in fact one of the more mainstream of the family, but it has incorporated thousands of foreign words, the majority of them Arabic, but including Portuguese and English. Far more of this Arabic inheritance and borrowing is preserved on the coast. The "standard" dialect is derived from Zanzibar Swahili, the dialect the early missionaries learned and first transcribed into the Roman alphabet. **Written Swahili** is still not completely uniform, and you'll come across slight variations in spelling, particularly on menus.

Swahili language books and courses

There are several published language **courses** around. *Teach Yourself Swahili* by Joan Russell is an excellent book and CD, with practical Swahili that you can use from the beginning. *Kiswahili kwa Kitendo* ("Swahili by Action", by Sharifa Zawawi) is the best bet if you find ordinary grammars indigestible. The free online resource Mwana Simba (Ⓦmwanasimba.online.fr/E_TABLE.htm) includes grammar as well as an extensive dictionary. As for **phrasebooks**, try the pocket-sized *Rough Guide Swahili Dictionary Phrasebook*, which includes links to MP3 files to practice your pronunciation at Ⓦtinyurl.com/yhwqwyn.

Swahili pronunciation

Once you get the hang of voicing every syllable and remember that each vowel is a syllable and that nothing is silent, **pronunciation** is easy. However, odd-looking combinations of consonants are often pronounced as one, double-length syllable. **Mzee**, for example, is pronounced "mz-ay-ay" (rhyming with "hey") and **shauri** (troubles, problem) is pronounced "sha-oo-ri" while **mgonjwa** (ill) has just two syllables "mgo-njwa".

You'll often come across an "**m**" where it looks out of place: this letter can precede any other. That is because it's a noun prefix (usually replaced in the plural with "wa-" or "mi-"), as in **mtoto** (child; plural **watoto**) or **mti** (tree; plural **miti**). Just add a bit of an "m" sound at the beginning; "mm-toto". If you say "um-toto" or "ma-toto" you'll be misunderstood. "Ng" followed by an apostrophe makes a sound like the "ng" in banger, not Bangor (try saying "banger" without the "ba", and then use it in a word like **ng'ombe** – cow or beef). Without the apostrophe, the ng is like two separate letters as in "finger" (as in **nguo** – garment, clothes).

For memorizing, it often helps to ignore the first letter or syllable. Thousands of nouns, for example, start with "ki" (singular) and "vi" (plural), and they're all in the same noun class.

A as in Arthur

B as in bed

C doesn't exist on its own

CH as in church, but often sounds like a "t", a "dj", or a "ky"

D as in donkey

DJ like the "j" in pyjamas

DH like a cross between dhow and thou

E between the "e" in Edward and "ai" in ailing

F as in fan

G as in good

GH at the back of the throat, like a gargle or a French "r"

H as in harmless

I like the "e" in evil

J as in jug

K as in kiosk, sometimes like soft "t" or "ch"

KH like the "ch" in loch

L as in lullaby, but often pronounced like an "r"

M as in Martian

N as in nonsense

NG as in finger or hunger, with a clear "g" sound

NG' as in wrong or banger, with no "g" sound

O as in orange, never as in "open" or "do"

P as in penguin

Q doesn't exist (except in early Romanized texts; now "k")

R as in rapid

S as in Samson

T as in tiny

TH as in thanks, never as in "them"

U as in lute

V as in victory

W as in wobble

X doesn't exist

Y as in you

Z as in zero

Swahili words and phrases

The words and phrases listed here are all in common usage, but Swahili (like English) is far from being a homogeneous language, so don't be surprised if you sometimes get some funny looks. And, for lack of space for explanation, there are a number of apparent inconsistencies; just ignore them unless you intend to learn the language seriously. These phrases should at least make you understood.

Greetings and terms of address

Tourists are greeted with **Jambo?** or more correctly **Hujambo?** (a multipurpose greeting, meaning "Things?" or "Problems?"). If you don't speak any Swahili, replying **Jambo** is fine, but if you want to make an effort, say **Sijambo** ("No problems") and continue with one of the following:

News? Habari?

Your news? Habari yako?

What news? Habari gani?

Good, thanks	Nzuri	Very (a common emphasis)	Sana
How goes?	Mambo?	Mister	Bwana (pl. mabwana)
Well, thanks	Nzuri	Addressing an adult woman	Mama
What's up?	Vipi?		
Cool, sweet	Safi		
Cool, excellent	Fiti	Addressing an old lady	Bibi
Hello? Anyone in?	Hodi!		
Come in! Welcome! (also said on offering something)	Karibu	Addressing an old man	Babu
		Youth, teenager	Kijana (pl. vijana)
Goodbye to one/many	Kwaheri/ni	Child	Mtoto (pl. watoto)
Thank you to one /many	Asante/ni	What's your name?	Jina lako nani?
		White, European	-zungu (eg mzungu white person; wazungu, white people)

LANGUAGE | Swahili words and phrases

Basics

My name is/ I am called	Jina langu/Nina itwa	when?	lini?
Where are you from?	Unatoka wapi?	now	sasa
Where are you staying?	Unakaa wapi?	soon	sasa hivi
		why?	kwa nini?
I am from ...	Ninatoka	because	kwa sababu
I am staying (at/in)	Ninakaa	but	lakini
See you!	Tutaonana!	who?	nani?
Yes, that's right	ndiyo	what?	nini?
No	hapana; siyo; la (Arabic heard mostly on the coast)	which?	gani?
		true	kweli
		and/with	na
I don't understand	Sifahamu/Sielewi	or	au
I don't speak Swahili, but	Sisemi kiswahili, lakini	isn't it?	siyo?
		I'm English (or British)/Scottish/ Welsh/Irish/ American/ Canadian/ Australian/ a New Zealander/ Kenyan:	Mimi ni mwingereza/ mskochi/mwelsh/ muairish /mwamerika/ mkanada/ mwaustralia/ mnyuziland/ mkenya
How do you say ... in Swahili	Unasemaje kwa kiswahili ...?		
Could you repeat that?	Sema tena		
Speak slowly	Sema pole pole		
I don't know	Sijui		
where (is)?	wapi?		
here	hapa		

The plurals for nationalities begin with "Wa-" instead of "M-".

Signs and common phrases

Danger	Hatari!	And two phrases you're more likely to hear than to ever say	
Warning	Angalia!/Onyo!		
Fierce dog!	Mbwa mkali!	Take a picture of me!	Piga picha mimi!
No entry!	Hakuna njia	Help the poor!	Saidia maskini!

www.roughguides.com

615

Adjectives and idioms

good (with a prefix at the front)	-zuri	problems, hassles	wasiwasi, matata
bad (ditto)	-baya	friend	rafiki
big	-kubwa	sorry, pardon	samahani
small	-dogo	It's nothing	Si kitu
a lot of	-ingi	Excuse me, let me through	Hebu
other/another	-ingine	What's up?	Namna gani?
not bad	si mbaya	If God wills it (heard often on the coast)	Inshallah
OK, right, fine	sawa		
fine, cool	safi		
completely	kabisa	please	tafadhali (rare upcountry and not heard much on the coast either)
thing(s)	kitu (vitu)		
No problem	Hakuna wasiwasi/ Hakuna matata		

Daily needs

Where can I sleep?	Naweza kulala wapi?	Give me/Bring me (can I have?)	Nipe/Niletee
Can I stay here?	Naweza kulala hapa?	again/more	tena
room(s)	chumba (vyumba)	enough	tosha/basi
bed(s)	kitanda (vitanda)	expensive	ghali sana
chair(s)	kiti (viti)	cheap (also "easy")	rahisi
table(s)	meza	fifty cents	sumni
toilet, bathroom	choo, bafu	Reduce the price, come down a little!	Punguza kidogo!
men, women	wanaume, wanawakea		
washing water	maji ya kuosha	shop	duka
hot/cold water	maji moto/baridi	bank	benki
I'm hungry	Nina njaa	post office	posta
I'm thirsty	Nina kiu	café, restaurant	hoteli
Is there any ...?	Iko ...? or Kuna ...?	telephone	simu
Yes there is ...	Iko ... or Kuna ...	cigarettes	sigara
No there isn't any	Haiko ... or Hakuna ...	I'm ill	Mimi mgonjwa
How much?	Ngapi?	doctor	daktari
money	pesa	hospital	hospitali
What price ...?	Bei gani ...?	polisi	police
How much is ...?	Pesa ngapi ...?	tip, bribe	chai
I want...	Nataka ...		
I don't want ...	Sitaki ...		

Travel and directions

travel	kusafiri	taxi	teksi
journey	safari	bicycle	baiskeli
bus(es)	bas, basi/mabasi	train	treni
car(s), vehicle/s	gari (magari)	plane	ndege

boat/ship	chombo/meli	This road, it goes to ...?	Barabara hii, ni njia ya ...?
petrol	petroli	I'm going to...	Nenda ...
road, path	njia/ndia	Move along, squeeze up a little	Songa!/Songa kidogo
highway	barabara		
on foot/walking	kwa miguu	Let's go, carry on	Twende, endelea
When does it leave?	Inaondoka lini?	straight ahead	moja kwa moja
When will we arrive?	Tutafika lini?	right	kulia
slowly	pole pole	left	kushoto
fast, quickly	haraka	up	juu
Wait!/Hang on a moment!	Ngoja!/Ngoja kidogo!	down	chini
Stop!	Simama!	I want to get off here	Nataka kushuka hapa
Where are you going?	Unaenda wapi?	The car has broken down	Gari imevunjika
To where?	Mpaka wapi?		
From where?	Kutoka wapi?		
How many kilometres?	Kilometa ngapi?		

Time, calendar and numbers

What time is it?	Saa ngapi?	Sunday	jumapili
four o'clock	saa nne (ie 4hr past dawn or dusk, in other words 10am or 10pm)	1	moja
		2	mbili
		3	tatu
		4	nne
quarter past	na robo	5	tano
half past	na nusu	6	sita
quarter to	kasa robo	7	saba
minutes	dakika	8	nane
daytime	mchana	9	tisa
night-time	usiku	10	kumi
dawn	alfajiri	11	kumi na moja
morning	asubuhi	12	kumi na mbili
early	mapema	20	ishirini
yesterday	jana	21	ishirini na moja
today	leo	30	thelathini
tomorrow	kesho	40	arobaini
last week/this week/next week	wiki iliopita/wiki hii/ wiki ijayo	50	hamsini
		60	sitini
this year	mwaka huu	70	sabini
this month	mwezi huu	80	themanini
Monday	jumatatu	90	tisini
Tuesday	jumanne	100	mia moja
Wednesday	jumatano	121	mia moja na ishirini na moja
Thursday	alhamisi		
Friday	ijumaa	1000	elfu
Saturday	jumamosi		

Menu and food terms

The lists below should be adequate for translating most Swahili menus and explaining what you want, though bear in mind that spelling may vary.

Basics

chakula	food	maziwa	milk
maji	water, juice	yai (mayai)	egg(s)
barafu	ice	samaki	fish
meza	table	nyama	meat
sahani	plate	mboga	vegetables
kijiko	spoon	mchuzi	sauce
kisu	knife	matunda	fruit
uma	fork	ingine	more, another
chupa	bottle	nusu	half
hesabu	bill	choma	roast
chumvi	salt	chemka	boiled
piripiri	pepper	kaanga	fried
mkate	bread	moto	hot
siagi	butter, margarine	baridi	cold
sukari	sugar		

Snacks

chapatti	unleavened, flat wheat bread, baked on a hot plate or in an oven (tandoor)	maziwalala	yoghurt (literally "milk asleep")
		mkate mayai	"egg-bread"; soft thin dough wrapped around fried egg and minced meat
halwa	gelatinous sweetmeat, like Turkish delight		
keki	cake	samosa	deep-fried triangular case of chopped meat and vegetables
kitumbuo	deep-fried rice bread		
mandaazi	deep-fried sweet dough, sometimes flavoured with spices, known as mahamri on the coast	tosti/slice	slice of bread

Dishes

frigisi	chicken giblets	matoke	green banana, usually boiled and mashed
githeri	Kikuyu dish of beans and corn, sometimes with meat	mboga	vegetables usually potatoes, carrots and onions in meaty gravy
irio/kienyeji	potato, cabbage and beans mashed together	mchele	plain white rice
kima	mince	michicha	spinach cooked with onions and tomatoes

pilau	rice with spices and meat
sukuma wiki	boiled green leaves, usually a kind of spinach
ugali/sima	cornmeal boiled to a solid porridge with water, occasionally milk; yellow ugali is considered inferior to white but is more nutritious

| uji | porridge or gruel made of millet; good for chilly mornings |
| wali | rice with added fat and spices (almost pilau) |

Meat

kondo	lamb	ng'ombe	beef
kuku	chicken	nguruwe	pork
mbuzi	goat	nyama choma	roast meat
mushkaki	kebab; small pieces of grilled, marinated meat on or off the skewer	steki	steak, grilled meat

Fruit

limau	lime	nazi	coconuts
machungwa	oranges	ndimu	lemon
madafu	green coconuts	ndizi	bananas
maembe	mangos	papai	papaya/pawpaw
mastafeli	soursops	parachichi	avocado
matopetope	custard apples	pera	guava
nanasi	pineapple	sandara	mandarins

Vegetables

maharagwe	red kidney beans, often cooked with coconut	ndizi	bananas or plantains
		nyanya	tomatoes (also means grandmother)
mahindi	corn	sukuma wiki	greens, usually kale or collard greens
mbaazi	pigeon peas, small beans	viazi	potatoes
mtama	millet	vitunguu	onions
muhogo	cassava		

Drinks

busaa	maize beer	changa'a	hootch, illegal spirits
chai, chai kavu, chai strungi	tea, black tea, strongly spiced tea	mnazi	coconut palm wine
		muratina	porridgey Kikuyu honey and millet beer

mabziwalala	fermented milk/almost yoghurt	bia, tembo	beer
kahawa	coffee	pombe	booze

Swahili animal names

Animal is **mnyama** (plural **wanyama**) but the names of most species are the same in singular and plural.

Aardvark	Muhanga	Kudu	Tandala
Baboon	Nyani	Leopard	Chui
Bat-eared fox	Bweha masigio	Lion	Simba
Bird (also means plane)	Ndege	Lizard	Mjusi
		Mongoose	Nguchiro
Buffalo	Nyati	Monkey (usually Sykes' monkey)	Kima
Bushbaby	Komba		
Cane rat	Ndeze	Oribi	Taya
Caracal	Simbamangu	Oryx	Choroa
Cat	Paka	Ostrich	Mbuni
Cheetah	Duma	Otter	Fisi maji
Chimpanzee	Soko	Pangolin	Kakukuona
Civet	Fungo	Pig, hog	Nguruwe
Colobus monkey	Mbega	Porcupine	Nungu
Crocodile	Mamba	Ratel	Nyegere
De Brazza's monkey	Kalasinga	Reedbuck	Tohe
Dog	Mbwa	Rhinoceros	Faru
Duiker	Nsya	Roan antelope	Korongo
Eland	Pofu	Rock hyrax	Pimbi
Elephant	Ndovu	Sable antelope	Pala hala
Elephant shrew	Sange	Serval	Mondo
Genet	Kanu	Shark	Papa
Gerenuk	Swala twiga	Snake	Nyoka
Giraffe	Twiga	Springhare	Kamandegere
Grant's gazelle	Swala granti	Steinbok, grysbok	Dondoo
Ground squirrel	Kindi	Suni antelope	Paa
Hare, rabbit	Sunguru	Thomson's gazelle	Swala tomi
Hartebeest	Kongoni	Topi	Nyamera
Hedgehog	Kalunguyeye	Tortoise	Kobe
Hippopotamus	Kiboko	Tree hyrax	Pembere
Horse, ass	Punda	Vervet monkey	Tumbili
Hunting dog	Mbwa mwitu	Warthog	Ngiri
Hyena	Fisi	Waterbuck	Kuru
Impala	Swala pala	Wild cat	Paka pori
Insect, bug	Mdudu	Wildebeest	Nyumbu
Jackal	Bweha	Zebra	Punda milia
Klipspringer	Mbuzi mawe		

Regional languages

The following brief lists are intended only for introductions and as a springboard for communication. If you'll be spending time in a particular linguistic region, you may be surprised at how difficult it is to track down useable primers and phrasebooks for these languages.

Kalenjin (Rift Valley)

Hi, hello	Chamgei	1	Akenge
Sleep well	Rui komie	2	Aena
Goodbye	Sai sere	3	Somok
Thank you	Kongoe	4	Angwan
Good	Kararan	5	Mut
Yes	Uoi	6	Lo
No	Adja	7	Tisap
How are you?	I amu ne?	8	Sisit
Fine	Misi	9	Sokol
I am hungry	Ama rubet!	10	Taman

Kamba (Ukambani, east of Nairobi)

How are you (sing.)?	Wimuseo?	Goodbye/go well (staying, pl.)	Endai noseo
Fine (sing.)	Nikuseo		
How are you (pl.)?	Mwiaseo?	1	Imwe
Fine (pl.)	Twiaseo	2	Ile
How are things?	Maundu mailye ata?	3	Itatu
Things are well	Maundu ni maseo	4	Inya
No problem /nothing wrong	Aiyie	5	Itano
		6	Thanthatu
Goodbye (leaving, sing.)	Tiwa noseo	7	Muonza
		8	Nyanya
Goodbye (leaving, pl.)	Tiwai na useo	9	Kenda
Goodbye/go well (staying, sing.)	Enda noseo	10	Ikumi

Kikuyu (Central Highlands)

How are things?	Kweruo atia?	1	Imwe
Fine!	Ni kuega!	2	Igiri
Are you well? (pl.)	Wi mwega/Muri ega?	3	Ithatu
Response ("Nothing wrong")	Asha, ndi mwega	4	Inya
		5	Ithano
Goodbye (when you're leaving)	Tigwo na wega	6	Ithathatu
		7	Mugwanja
Goodbye (when you're staying)	Thii na wega	8	Inyanya
		9	Kenda
		10	Ikumi

Luhya (Kakamega & western Kenya)

Good morning	Vushele (boo-sher-ae)	1	Indala
Hello, Good afternoon	Mulembe (moo-rem-bae)	2	Zivili
		3	Vizaka
Good evening	Vwakhila (wah-hee-ra)	4	Zinee
Responses	Vushele muno,	5	Ziranu
	Mulembe muno,	6	Zisasava
	Vwakhila muno	7	Saba
How are you?	Karina?	8	Munane
Well, very well	Malahi (ma-lay-ee),	9	Tisa
	Malahi sana	10	Likhomi
Thank you	Urio muno (or-e-om-ono)		
Goodbye	Vulahi (vu-lay-ee)		

Luo (Lake Victoria)

How do you do?	Iriyo nade?	5	Abich
Response	Ariyo maber!	6	Auchiely
Thank you	Erokamano	7	Abiriyo
1	Achiel	8	Aboro
2	Ariyo	9	Ochiko
3	Adek	10	Apar
4	Angwen		

Maa (Maasai)

Greetings to a man	Lo murrani! Supa!	1	Obo
Response	Ipa!	2	Aare
Greetings to a woman	Na kitok! Takuenya!	3	Okuni
		4	Oonguan
Response	Iko!	5	Imiet
Thank you (very much!)	Ashe (naleng!)	6	Ile
		7	Oopishana
Goodbye!	Sere!	8	Isiet
		9	Ooudo
		10	Tomon

Glossary

These words are all in common usage. Remember, however, that plural forms often have different beginnings.

AFCO Armed Forces Catering Ordnance

Age-set/age grade Generation who have passed through rites of passage together, often including people of widely differing chronological ages

ASK Agricultural Society of Kenya

Askari Policeman, security guard, soldier

Banda Any kind of hut, usually round and thatched

Bangi, Bhang Marijuana

Baobab Species of tree whose trunk retains water

Barabara Main road

Bau Traditional calculation game of pebbles and holes

Boarding & Lodging (B&L) Cheap guesthouse

Boda-boda Bicycle taxi

Boma A fort or defensive stockade, often used to mean a small village or cluster of huts

Boriti Mangrove poles, used on the coast for building and exported to the Gulf states for the same purpose

Buibui The black cover-all cloak and scarf of Swahili women

Bwana Mister, a polite form of address

Chai Not just tea, but also the common term for a tip, or more often a small bribe or persuasion

Choo Toilet (pronounced "cho")

Day & Night Club Drinking bar

Duka Shop, store

Duka la dawa Chemist

Enkang Maasai village

FORD Forum for the Restoration of Democracy, opposition political party

Fundi Mechanic, craftsman, expert

Gari Car

Gema The ethnic grouping of Gikuyu (Kikuyu), Embu and Meru

GK Government of Kenya

Group ranch Community-owned grazing area with title deeds, rather than traditional rights

Harambee "Pull together" – the ideology of peaceable community development espoused by Jomo Kenyatta. Harambee meetings are local fund-raising gatherings for schools, clinics, etc.

Hoteli Small restaurant, tea shop or café

Jamhuri Republic

Jiko Kitchen or cooker

Jua kali "Hot sun" – open-air car repairer's yard or small workshop

Kanga Printed cotton sheet used as a wrap, often incorporating a motto

Kanisa Church

KANU Kenya African National Union, Kenya's ruling political party

KBC Kenya Broadcasting Corporation

KWS Kenya Wildlife Service

Kikoi Brightly coloured woven cloth

Laibon Maasai spiritual leader, with the status of regional headman

Lugga/Laga Dry river valley (usually in the north)

Mabati Corrugated-iron roofing sheets

Maendeleo Progress, development

Madaraka Independence

Magendo Corruption, bribery, abuse of power

Majimboism The creation of federal blocks in formerly heterogeneous regions – these days associated with ethnic cleansing

Makonde Beautifully worked Tanzanian woodcarving, typically in ebony and representing entwined spirit families

Makutano Junction

Makuti Palm-leaf roof common on the coast

Malaika Angel

Malaya Prostitute

Mama Common term of address for married women

Manamba Matatu tout, "turnboy"

Manyatta Temporary cattle camp, often loosely used for a village (Maasai)

Maskini The poor, beggars (**Saidia maskini!** "Help the poor!")

Matatu Shared minibus

Mbenzi Member of the rich elite (presumed to have a Mercedes; plural **wabenzi**)

Mgeni Guest, tourist (pl. **wageni**)

Miraa Qat, a natural stimulant

Mkenya Kenyan (pl. **wakenya**)

Moran Man in the warrior age group of Maasai or Samburu (pl. **morani**)

Msikiti Mosque

Mtalii Tourist (pl. **watalii**)

Mtoto Child (pl. **watoto**)

Mungiki Anti-establishment Kikuyu youth cult that violently rejects Western values

Mungu God

Murram Red or black clay soil, usually referring to a road

Mwananchi Person, peasant, worker (pl. **wananchi**)

Mzee Old man – "the Mzee" is Kenyatta

Mzungu White person (pl. **wazungu**)

NCCK National Christian Council of Kenya

NDP National Development Party, mainly Luo

Ngai Supreme god of the Kikuyu and other groups

NGO Non-governmental organization

Nyama Animal, game, meat

Ngoma Dancing, drumming, party, celebration

Njia Road, path

Nyayo "Footsteps" – the follow-in-his-footsteps philosophy of post-Kenyatta Kenya propounded by President Moi

Panga Multi-purpose short machete carried everywhere in the countryside

Pesa Money, cash

Pombe Booze

Rondavel Round hut or small house (see **banda**)

Safari Journey of any kind

Shamba Small farm, plot

Sista Informal term of address to young woman

Slum Any area of poor housing (no pejorative connotation)

Soda Fizzy drink, but also a euphemism for a tip

Soja Soldier, watchman, guard

Stage Matatu stand

Uhuru Freedom, independence

Ukimwi AIDS

Ulaya Europe

Wageni See **mgeni**

Wananchi See **mwananchi**

Watu Literally "people", but often used slightly disparagingly by expats and Anglo-Kenyans, especially when referring to their staff

Wazungu See **mzungu**

Travel store

...Unforgettable

Located next to Kenya's internationally acclaimed
Watamu National Marine Park Turtle Bay presents
an acknowledged, award winning eco-resort.

Crystal clear waters rich in corals, white sandy shores,
unspoilt coast and forest all provide unforgettable reasons
as to why so many visitors return to this tropical paradise.

Kenya's responsible resort

DRIVE YOUR MOUSE WILD!

LETS GO TRAVEL

UNIGLOBE ®
beyond expectation **Travel**

Head Office, Nairobi.
Tel: (254-20) 4447151/4441030.
E-mail:info@letsgosafari.com
www.letsgosafari.com

With 400 lodges, hotels, community
lodges and 200 safaris to choose from,
click your mouse onto www.letsgosafari.com
and you can find yourself on a comprehensive
journey in East Africa. Let our experienced travel
advisors help you find that special place in Kenya.

"Setting the standard for a high quality eco-friendly safari experience in Kenya."

KICHECHE
camps

SOUTHERN CROSS SAFARIS
Connoisseur Safaris
www.southerncrosssafaris.com
www.southerncrossscuba.com
www.sataocamp.com
www.sataoelerai.com

EXCELLENCE THROUGH EXPERIENCE

Established in 1957, Southern Cross Safaris is one of Kenya's most experienced and respected tour operators. Our philosophy is simple: we want to create the perfect safari package - having recently won 5 awards for excellence, including the 'Best Tour Operator in Kenya 2005, 2006, 2007 and 2008' Travel News & lifestyle Award,we believe we can fulfil our promise and deliver an unforgettable African Experience.

Southern Cross Safaris' extensive operation in East Africa ensure the best safari on offer whether it be in Kenya,Tanzania, Uganda or Rwanda; We also own 2 of our own exclusive camps including Satao Camp in Tsavo East & Satao Elerai at the foot of Mt.Kilimanjaro, bordering Amboseli National Park. Our expertise also spreads to the marine world, with Southern Cross Scuba operating 5 watersports bases located at Pinewood Village, Indian Ocean Beach Club, Leopard Beach Resort & Spa, Leisure Lodge Resort and Diani Reef Beach Resort & SPA.

We operate using the most modern four wheel drive vehicles; experienced drivers; qualified, multilingual specialised guides; our own private aircraft; and offer accommodation in a choice of lodges, camps and hotels. Our service is highly personalised and safaris are tailored to suit individual requirements. Our knowledge and experience of Africa is unsurpassed - we will ensure that your dream safari becomes a reality

Southern Cross Centre
Email: sales@southerncrosssafaris.com
Tel: +254 (0) 20 2434600/1/2/3

Driftwood
Malindi - Kenya

A tropical paradise...

Books change lives

Book Aid International
www.bookaid.org

Poverty and illiteracy go hand in hand. But in sub-Saharan Africa, books are a luxury few can afford. Many children leave school functionally illiterate, and adults often fall back into illiteracy in adulthood due to a lack of available reading material.

Book Aid International knows that books change lives.

Every year we send over half a million books to partners in 12 countries in sub-Saharan Africa, to stock libraries in schools, refugee camps, prisons, universities and communities. Literally millions of readers have access to books and information that could teach them new skills – from keeping chickens to getting a degree in Business Studies or learning how to protect against HIV/AIDS.

What can you do?

Join our Reverse Book Club and with your donation of only £6 a month, we can send 36 books every year to some of the poorest countries in the world. For every two pounds extra you can give, we can send another book!

Support Book Aid International today!

 Online. Go to our website at **www.bookaid.org**, and click on 'donate'

 By telephone. Start a Direct Debit or give a donation on your card by calling us on 020 7733 3577

Book Aid International is a charity and a limited company registered in England and Wales.
Charity No. 313869 Company No. 880754   39-41 Coldharbour Lane, Camberwell, London SE5 9NR
T +44 (0)20 7733 3577   F +44 (0)20 7978 8006   E info@bookaid.org   www.bookaid.org

So now we've told you about the things not to miss, the best places to stay, the top restaurants, the liveliest bars and the most spectacular sights, it only seems fair to tell you about the best travel insurance around

WorldNomads.com
keep travelling safely

Recommended by Rough Guides

Travel

Andorra The Pyrenees, Pyrenees & Andorra Map, Spain
Antigua The Caribbean
Argentina Argentina, Argentina Map, Buenos Aires, South America on a Budget
Aruba The Caribbean
Australia Australia, Australia Map, East Coast Australia, Melbourne, Sydney, Tasmania
Austria Austria, Europe on a Budget, Vienna
Bahamas The Bahamas, The Caribbean
Barbados Barbados DIR, The Caribbean
Belgium Belgium & Luxembourg, Bruges DIR, Brussels, Brussels Map, Europe on a Budget
Belize Belize, Central America on a Budget, Guatemala & Belize Map
Benin West Africa
Bolivia Bolivia, South America on a Budget
Brazil Brazil, Rio, South America on a Budget
British Virgin Islands The Caribbean
Brunei Malaysia, Singapore & Brunei [1 title], Southeast Asia on a Budget
Bulgaria Bulgaria, Europe on a Budget
Burkina Faso West Africa
Cambodia Cambodia, Southeast Asia on a Budget, Vietnam, Laos & Cambodia Map [1 Map]
Cameroon West Africa
Canada Canada, Pacific Northwest, Toronto, Toronto Map, Vancouver
Cape Verde West Africa
Cayman Islands The Caribbean
Chile Chile, Chile Map, South America on a Budget
China Beijing, China, Hong Kong & Macau, Hong Kong & Macau DIR, Shanghai
Colombia South America on a Budget
Costa Rica Central America on a Budget, Costa Rica, Costa Rica & Panama Map
Croatia Croatia, Croatia Map, Europe on a Budget
Cuba Cuba, Cuba Map, The Caribbean, Havana
Cyprus Cyprus, Cyprus Map
Czech Republic The Czech Republic, Czech & Slovak Republics, Europe on a Budget, Prague, Prague DIR, Prague Map
Denmark Copenhagen, Denmark, Europe on a Budget, Scandinavia
Dominica The Caribbean
Dominican Republic Dominican Republic, The Caribbean
Ecuador Ecuador, South America on a Budget
Egypt Egypt, Egypt Map
El Salvador Central America on a Budget
England Britain, Camping in Britain, Devon & Cornwall, Dorset, Hampshire and The Isle of Wight [1 title], England, Europe on a Budget, The Lake District, London, London DIR, London Map, London Mini Guide, Walks In London & Southeast England
Estonia The Baltic States, Europe on a Budget
Fiji Fiji
Finland Europe on a Budget, Finland, Scandinavia
France Brittany & Normandy, Corsica, Corsica Map, The Dordogne & the Lot, Europe on a Budget, France, France Map, Languedoc & Roussillon, The Loire, Paris, Paris DIR, Paris Map, Paris Mini Guide, Provence & the Côte d'Azur, The Pyrenees, Pyrenees & Andorra Map
French Guiana South America on a Budget
Gambia The Gambia, West Africa
Germany Berlin, Berlin Map, Europe on a Budget, Germany, Germany Map
Ghana West Africa
Gibraltar Spain
Greece Athens Map, Crete, Crete Map, Europe on a Budget, Greece, Greece Map, Greek Islands, Ionian Islands
Guadeloupe The Caribbean
Guatemala Central America on a Budget, Guatemala, Guatemala & Belize Map
Guinea West Africa
Guinea-Bissau West Africa
Guyana South America on a Budget
Holland see The Netherlands
Honduras Central America on a Budget
Hungary Budapest, Europe on a Budget, Hungary
Iceland Iceland, Iceland Map
India Goa, India, India Map, Kerala, Rajasthan, Delhi & Agra [1 title], South India, South India Map
Indonesia Bali & Lombok, Southeast Asia on a Budget
Ireland Dublin DIR, Dublin Map, Europe on a Budget, Ireland, Ireland Map
Israel Jerusalem
Italy Europe on a Budget, Florence DIR, Florence & Siena Map, Florence & the best of Tuscany, Italy, The Italian Lakes, Naples & the Amalfi Coast, Rome, Rome DIR, Rome Map, Sardinia, Sicily, Sicily Map, Tuscany & Umbria, Tuscany Map, Venice, Venice DIR, Venice Map
Jamaica Jamaica, The Caribbean
Japan Japan, Tokyo
Jordan Jordan
Kenya Kenya, Kenya Map
Korea Korea
Laos Laos, Southeast Asia on a Budget, Vietnam, Laos & Cambodia Map [1 Map]
Latvia The Baltic States, Europe on a Budget
Lithuania The Baltic States, Europe on a Budget
Luxembourg Belgium & Luxembourg, Europe on a Budget
Malaysia Malaysia Map, Malaysia, Singapore & Brunei [1 title], Southeast Asia on a Budget
Mali West Africa
Malta Malta & Gozo DIR
Martinique The Caribbean
Mauritania West Africa
Mexico Baja California, Baja California, Cancún & Cozumel DIR, Mexico, Mexico Map, Yucatán, Yucatán Peninsula Map
Monaco France, Provence & the Côte d'Azur
Montenegro Montenegro
Morocco Europe on a Budget, Marrakesh DIR, Marrakesh Map, Morocco, Morocco Map,
Nepal Nepal
Netherlands Amsterdam, Amsterdam DIR, Amsterdam Map, Europe on a Budget, The Netherlands
Netherlands Antilles The Caribbean
New Zealand New Zealand, New Zealand Map

DIR: Rough Guide **DIRECTIONS** for short breaks

Available from all good bookstores

ROUGH GUIDES
Don't Just Travel

For more information go to www.roughguides.com

NOTES

NOTES

NOTES

Small print and

Index

A Rough Guide to Rough Guides

Published in 1982, the first Rough Guide – to Greece – was a student scheme that became a publishing phenomenon. Mark Ellingham, a recent graduate in English from Bristol University, had been travelling in Greece the previous summer and couldn't find the right guidebook. With a small group of friends he wrote his own guide, combining a highly contemporary, journalistic style with a thoroughly practical approach to travellers' needs.

The immediate success of the book spawned a series that rapidly covered dozens of destinations. And, in addition to impecunious backpackers, Rough Guides soon acquired a much broader and older readership that relished the guides' wit and inquisitiveness as much as their enthusiastic, critical approach and value-for-money ethos.

These days, Rough Guides include recommendations from shoestring to luxury and cover more than 200 destinations around the globe, including almost every country in the Americas and Europe, more than half of Africa and most of Asia and Australasia. Our ever-growing team of authors and photographers is spread all over the world, particularly in Europe, the US and Australia.

In the early 1990s, Rough Guides branched out of travel, with the publication of Rough Guides to World Music, Classical Music and the Internet. All three have become benchmark titles in their fields, spearheading the publication of a wide range of books under the Rough Guide name.

Including the travel series, Rough Guides now number more than 350 titles, covering: phrasebooks, waterproof maps, music guides from Opera to Heavy Metal, reference works as diverse as Conspiracy Theories and Shakespeare, and popular culture books from iPods to Poker. Rough Guides also produce a series of more than 120 World Music CDs in partnership with World Music Network.

Visit www.roughguides.com to see our latest publications.

Rough Guide travel images are available for commercial licensing at www.roughguidespictures.com

Rough Guide credits

Text editor: Emma Gibbs
Layout: Ankur Guha
Cartography: Jasbir Sandhu, Deshpal Dabas
Picture editor: Emily Taylor
Production: Rebecca Short
Proofreader: Susanne Hillen
Cover design: Daniel May and Chloë Roberts
Photographer: Suzanne Porter
Editorial: Ruth Blackmore, Andy Turner, Keith
Drew, Edward Aves, Alice Park, Lucy White,
Jo Kirby, James Smart, Natasha Foges, Róisín
Cameron, James Rice, Lara Kavanagh, Emma
Traynor, Kathryn Lane, Monica Woods, Mani
Ramaswamy, Harry Wilson, Lucy Cowie, Alison
Roberts, Joe Staines, Peter Buckley, Matthew
Milton, Tracy Hopkins, Ruth Tidball; **Delhi**
Madhavi Singh, Karen D'Souza, Lubna Shaheen
Design & Pictures: **London** Scott Stickland,
Diana Jarvis, Mark Thomas, Nicole Newman,
Sarah Cummins; **Delhi** Umesh Aggarwal, Ajay
Verma, Jessica Subramanian, Pradeep Thapliyal,
Sachin Tanwar, Anita Singh, Nikhil Agarwal,
Sachin Gupta.

Production: Liz Cherry
Cartography: **London** Ed Wright, Katie Lloyd-
Jones; **Delhi** Rajesh Chhibber, Ashutosh Bharti,
Rajesh Mishra, Animesh Pathak, Karobi Gogoi,
Alakananda Roy, Swati Handoo
Online: **London** Faye Hellon, Jeanette Angell,
Fergus Day, Justine Bright, Clare Bryson, Aine
Fearon, Adrian Low, Ezgi Celebi; **Delhi** Amit
Verma, Rahul Kumar, Narender Kumar, Ravi
Yadav, Debojit Borah, Rakesh Kumar, Ganesh
Sharma, Shisir Basumatari
Marketing & Publicity: **London** Liz Statham,
Louise Maher, Jess Carter, Vanessa Godden,
Vivienne Watton, Anna Paynton, Rachel
Sprackett, Laura Vipond; **New York** Katy Ball,
Judi Powers; **Delhi** Ragini Govind
Reference Director: Andrew Lockett
Operations Assistant: Becky Doyle
Operations Manager: Helen Atkinson
Publishing Director (Travel): Clare Currie
Commercial Manager: Gino Magnotta
Managing Director: John Duhigg

Publishing information

This ninth edition published May 2010 by
Rough Guides Ltd,
80 Strand, London WC2R 0RL
14 Local Shopping Centre, Panchsheel Park,
New Delhi 110017, India
Distributed by the Penguin Group
Penguin Books Ltd,
80 Strand, London WC2R 0RL
Penguin Group (USA)
375 Hudson Street, NY 10014, USA
Penguin Group (Australia)
250 Camberwell Road, Camberwell,
Victoria 3124, Australia
Penguin Group (Canada)
195 Harry Walker Parkway N, Newmarket, ON,
L3Y 7B3 Canada
Penguin Group (NZ)
67 Apollo Drive, Mairangi Bay, Auckland 1310,
New Zealand
Cover concept by Peter Dyer.

Typeset in Bembo and Helvetica to an original
design by Henry Iles.
Printed in Singapore
© Richard Trillo, 2010
Maps © Rough Guides

668pp includes index
A catalogue record for this book is available from
the British Library
ISBN: 978-1-84836-137-9

1   3   5   7   9   8   6   4   2

Help us update

We've gone to a lot of effort to ensure that the
ninth edition of **The Rough Guide to Kenya** is
accurate and up-to-date. However, things change
– places get "discovered", opening hours are
notoriously fickle, restaurants and rooms raise
prices or lower standards. If you feel we've got it
wrong or left something out, we'd like to know,
and if you can remember the address, the price,
the hours, the phone number, so much the better.

Please send your comments with the subject
line "**Rough Guide Kenya Update**" to ©mail
@roughguides.com. We'll credit all contributions
and send a copy of the next edition (or any other
Rough Guide if you prefer) for the very best
emails.

Have your questions answered and tell others
about your trip at ® www.roughguides.com

Acknowledgements

For generous assistance on the first edition, my continuing indebtedness to Jeremy Torr for the wonderful English Cycles mountain bike that got my round Kenya, and to Rosie Mercer, Jackie Switzer and the Khans in Kisii. To Rough Guide authors who have updated several recent editions – Emma Gregg, Daniel Jacobs, Jens Finke, Nana Luckham and Okigbo Ojukwu – and to Tony Stones for the wildlife piece and Doug Paterson and Werner Graebner for music, my grateful thanks. On this edition, many thanks to everyone in Rough Guides' editorial and cartography departments, especially my editor Emma Gibbs for her skill and patience and to proofreader Susanne Hillen and page designer Ankur Guha.

On this edition, hugely appreciated assistance and support came from: Marisa Marsden at Hills Balfour Synergy; the ever-calm and resourceful Ndolo Kaleli, who drove me the extra mile many times to get the job done, and even hacked through fallen trees in the Kinangop; and Margaret Gordon and family for generous hospitality. Warm thanks and boundless gratitude go to my co-researchers and travelling companions Matt Brown, Robert Gordon and Alex Trillo, and to Teresa, David and Phoebe who came along for some of the ride in Kenya (the good bit) and put up with the long hours back at home (the not-so-good bit).

For help on the ground in Kenya, grateful thanks to: Petra Allmendiger (Sandai), Simon Ball (Kensington Camps), Jane, Julia & Dick Barnley (Sirikwa Safaris), Sissa and Richard & Tara Bonham (Ol Donyo Wuas), Florence Bouchou (Lamu House), Mohanjeet Brar & Jake Grieves-Cook (Gamewatchers), John Buckley (Safarilink), Steve & Annabelle Carey (Sosian), Philippe Cauviere, Eva Njeru & Sean Walwyn (Fairmont), Stefano Cheli, Sue Heath & Charlotte Bourke (Cheli & Peacock), Susan and Tony Church (Longonot Ranch House), John Cleave (Mombasa Air Safari), Melba Correia & Ian Taplin (Rex Resorts), Calvin Cottar, Björn Forslind & Isaac Rotich (Cottar's), Lara Cowen & Jamie Hendriksen (Joy's Camp), Damian Davies (Turtle Bay), Deepa Darbar (Exclusive African Treasures), Alan Dixson (Let's Go Travel), Cornelia & Peter Frank (Finch Hattons), Fuzz & Bimbi Dyer and Caragh Roberts (Manda Bay), Paul Goldstein, Greg Monson and Andy & Sonja (Kicheche), Anne Kanini (Kenya Tourism), Mohez Karmali (Concorde Cars), Edith Kabiru & Fabrizio Molinaro (Galdessa), Jenny Larby (Driftwood), George Moorhead (Kiwayu), Larry Mvoi & Andrew Muir (Severin), Bella and Michael Nicholson (Cruising Cruisers), Gabriele Nowak (Sunworld), Joan Nthiga (Sarova), Joseph Ouma Oluoko (Erokamano Destinations), Riccardo Orizio, Gio Risso & Neil Unsworth (Saruni), Juergen Pietz & Manja Seifert (Severin), Claire Roadley (Ethos Marketing/Serena), Caro Roberts & Ross Withey (Samatian), Torben Rune (Southern Cross), Raj Shah (Naiberi), Race Tavasi Masumba (KWS), Ida & Filip Trygg-Andersson (Kinondo Kwetu), Clare & John Upton (Tortilis), Frederik Vanderhoeven (Msambweni House), Cindy Voorspuy (Deloraine), Verity Williams (Sabuk), Piers Winkworth (Offbeat), Louise Wood (Safari & Conservation Co.)

For extra-generous help with information and introductions: Aden Abdi for the Garissa account, Alnavaz Amlani (El Paraiso), Justin Aniere (Che Shale), Richard Argiriou, Margaret Asiko, Jonathan Bending (Colobus Cottages), Phillipa Bengough (Laikipia Wildlife Forum), Phil and Jill Benn, Sara Blackburn (LivingWithLions.org), Richard Bradley (Lion TV), Leah Buckman, Tamsin Corcoran-Brennan, Nick Demille, Rob Dodson (Wildlife Works), Michael Dyer (Borana), Simon Englefield (Camp Kenya), Rachael Feiler (Diamond Beach), Felicity Fowkes (Mida Eco-Camp), Anthony Friscia & Erin Kane, Rosalie Faithfull (Mwamba FSC), Linda Gaymer (Crescent Island), Darren & Emma Geary (Ngiri Bar), Kerry Glen & James Christian (Karisia), Rolf Gloor (PoViLo), Andrew Gordon, Paul Harrison, William Kimosop (Lake Bogoria NR), Will Knocker (Silole), Melia van Laar (Castle Forest Lodge), Kerin Larby (Bush & Beyond), Ann Lipson, Kathryn Maitland, Carolyn McIntyre (GirlSoloInArabia.com), Iregi Mwenja, Steve Mullens & Sally Cox (Charlie Claw's), Frankline Nyakundi (Serena), Catherine Nyako (Kenya Museum Society), Helmut Opitz, Bruce Pike, Susanne Porter (SuzannePorter.com), Jessica Rawley, Paul Roden (Marich Pass FSC), George Sphikas (Royal Mara), John Round-Turner (Oserian), Donatella Sala, Elodie Sampere (Lewa), Melissa Shales, Graham Stirling and Justin Tilley.

Readers' letters

Thanks to all the readers who have taken the time to write in with comments and suggestions (and apologies if we've inadvertently omitted or misspelt anyone's name):

Ina Blanke, Steve Bull, Mike Butler, Stroma Cole, Mark Fairweather, Mary Furnivall, Tim Gonyou, Andy Graham, Robert Hack, Zen Geb, Cindy Heazlit, Vicky Hill, Daniel Hofer, Terry John Hummerston, Romena Huq, Jill Jolliff, Alex Keto, Stefan Kleineisen, Julia Laube, Chuck Ludlam, Colin Macbeth, Njeru Mbogo, Bruce Methven, Joe Mitchell, Ron and Viv Moon, Stephen Mustoe, Rachel L Myers, Caroline Njeri, Pippa Oakeshott, Helga Pfeiffer, Jim Puckett, Franziska Rebscher, George Ritchie, Nicolas Van Rossem, Gerhard Rötzer, Kelly Rust, Juergen Schulz, Adam Smith, Morgan Smith, Bea Staley, Dave Tucker, Torsten Volker, David Weatherby, Felicia Webb, Irmtraud Welter.

Photo credits

All photos © Rough Guides except the following:

Introduction
Flamingos over Lake Magadi © Steve Bloom Images/Alamy
Detail of necklaces of a Maasai woman © Ripani Massimo/SIME/4Corners
Hippopotamus submerged in natural pool © Paul Sounders/Corbis
Maasai warriors © Hugh Sitton/Corbis
Mosque at Lamu © John Frumm / Hemis/Axiom
Aerial view of Nairobi © Canali Pietro/SIME/4Corners

Things not to miss
01 Wildebeest crossing Mara River © Steve Bloom/Photolibrary
02 Lake Turkana © Courtesy of Kenyan Tourist Board
03 Groundsel plants on Mount Kenya © Julius Lando/Photolibrary
04 Nyama Choma © Richard Trillo
07 A diver moves in close to a reef in the Indian Ocean off Kenya © Stephen Frink/Corbis
08 Tiwi Beach © Julia Bayne/Robert Harding
12 Birdwatching © Richard Trillo

Wildlife
Zebras and buffalo © Steve J. Benbow/Axiom
Yellow Baboon © David Garry/iStock Pictures
Black & white Colobus Monkey © Craig Dingle/iStock Pictures
Patas Monkey © http://www.flickr.com/photos/35603785@N04/3384088318
Sykes Monkey © Lee Dalton/NHPA
Bush Baby © Stephen Dalton/NHPA
Aardvark © Nigel Dennis/NHPA
Pangolin © Heinrich van den Berg/iStock Pictures
Bat-eared Fox © wrangle/iStock Pictures
Wild Dogs © Liz Leyden/iStock Pictures
Honey Badger © Anthony Bannister/NHPA
African Civet © Nigel Dennis/NHPA
Genet © Nigel Dennis/NHPA
Banded Mongoose © Rich Kirchner/NHPA
Caracal © Duncan Noakes/iStock Pictures
Cheetah © Nigel Dennis/NHPA
Leopard © Peter Malsbury/iStock Pictures
Lion © Sean Randall/iStock Pictures
Serval © Martin Harvey/NHPA
Rock Hyrax © Hansjoerg Richter/iStock Pictures
Black Rhino © Andy Rouse/NHPA
Zebra © Maurizio Ascione/iStock Pictures
Grevy Zebra © Christian Musat/istock Pictures
Bush Pig © vario images GmbH & Co.KG/Alamy
Rothschild Giraffe © Klaas Lingbeek- van Kranen/iStock Pictures
Reticulated Giraffe © David Keith Jones/Images of Africa Photobank/Alamy
Red Hartebeest © Nico Smit/iStock Pictures
Topi © Bernd Zoller/imagebroker/Alamy
Blue Wildebeest © Irving N Saperstein/iStock Pictures
Gerenuk © Mark Wilson/iStock Pictures
Grants Gazelle © Icarus Images /iStock Pictures
Thompsons Gazelle © Peter Malsbury/iStock Pictures

Reedbuck © AfriPics.com/Alamy
Kirk's Dik-dik © The Africa Image Library/Alamy
Common Duiker © Tim Davies/Alamy
Suni © David Keith Jones/Images of Africa/Alamy
Sitatunga © Clive Druett/Papilio/Alamy
Bushbuck © Cobus Olivier/iStock Pictures
Eland © Adrian Assalve/iStock Pictures
Lesser Kudu © http://www.flickr.com/photos/txzeiss/2772236533
Fringe Eared Oryx © http://www.flickr.com/photos/7326810@N08/3327584804
Sable © Nico Smit/iStock Pictures
Roan Antelope © Nigel Dennis/NHPA
Steenbok © James Warwick /NHPA
Grysbok © Nigel Dennis/NHPA
Oribi © Joe McDonald/NHPA
Klipspringer © http://www.flickr.com/photos/brianscott/3398492439

Traditional dress colour section
Masai woman wearing beaded necklace © Jim Zuckerman/Corbis
Kikuyu dancers wearing traditional costumes sitting under tree © Frantisek Staud/Alamy
Old Turkana lady © Courtesy of Kenyan Tourist Board
Giriama tribal dancing, Mombasa, Kenya © World Pictures\Photoshot
Luo elder with headdress of ostrich feathers and hippo tusks, Kisumu © Images of Africa Photobank /Alamy

Crafts and shopping colour section
Making traditional basket, Kibwezi © Liba Taylor/Robert Harding
Pair of sandals made from old car tyre © Mark Boulton/Alamy
Muslim man playing a SIWA, Lamu island © Images of Africa Photobank/Alamy
Nairobi city market craft stall © Thomas Cockrem/Alamy

Black and whites
p.103 The *Norfolk Hotel* © Fairmont The Norfolk
p.122 Live music in Nairobi © Getty Images
p.158 Mount Kenya © David W Breed/Photo library
p.196 Hells Gate National Park. Early morning ground mist surrounds Fischers Tower © Nigel Pavitt/Photolibrary
p.306 Kakamega Forest © Steffen Foerster/iStock Pictures
p.338 Amboseli National Park © Konstantin Kalishko/iStock Pictures
p.375 Safari © Kenyan Tourist Board
p.400 Camels on beach © PNS/Tips Images
p.502 At sunrise, a Samburu warrior leads baggage camels down the Milgis lugga © Nigel Pavitt/PhotoLibrary
p.521 Women in traditional dress © http://www.flickr.com/photos/ferdinandreus/3614763420/
p.527 Turkana tribe, ceremonial dancing © Steve Turner/Photolibrary

SMALL PRINT

Index

Map entries are in colour.

www.roughguides.com

J

K

N

Map symbols

maps are listed in the full index using coloured text

Regional Maps

Motorway	✈ Airport
Minor roads (mostly unpaved)	✗ Airstrip
Main roads (mostly paved)	Park/reserve
Footpath	Forest
Railway	Beach
Ferry route	Glacier
River	
International border	
Chapter division boundary	**Town Maps**
Mountain range	Roads
▲ Mountain peak	Unpaved roads
Escarpment	∴ Ruin
Cliff	◉ Accommodation
Hill	▣ Restaurant
Viewpoint	★ Bus stop
Crater	Petrol station
Cave	⊞ Hospital
Waterfall	@ Internet access
Marshland	ⓘ Information office
Spring	© Telephone
General point of interest	✉ Post office
Lighthouse	Ⓟ Parking
Picnic area	Monastery
Golf course	✿ Synagogue
Gate	Mosque
Lodge	▲ Temple
Park HQ	Church
⚠ Campsite	Building
⊙ Monument	Stadium
Cemetery	Cemetery

www.roughguides.

The last word ...

The vast majority of visitors to Kenya arrange and book their whole trip in advance. The best lodges and guesthouses are heavily over-demanded for much of the year. Turning up on the doorstep is simply not an option, you need to book well ahead of time. Transport too needs to be pre-planned, with overland safari companies running short of decent vehicles and internal airlines often operating at maximum capacity. Add to that the complexity of linking all these components together and you start to understand exactly why even the most hardened independent travellers suddenly find themselves booking through a travel agent.

The good news is that the safari world, Kenya included, is serviced by some exceptional specialist travel companies, staffed by people with genuine enthusiasm, in depth knowledge and real first hand experience of travelling and working in Africa. These guys should be able to take the hard labour out of trip planning, get you deeper under the skin of the place and even deliver the whole thing at a lower price than if you had booked all the elements individually.

One of the leading companies involved in putting together tailormade safaris to Kenya is Africa Travel Resource, which specialises in innovative and off the beaten track trips to suit a broad range of budgets. Whether or not you ultimately end up arranging your trip with them, it may well be worth taking a good look at their website www.africatravelresource.com, which has for some time been widely regarded as the leading internet resource for travel to East Africa.

leading internet resource for travel to kenya

www.africatravelresource.com

306 880770   usa/canada +1 888 487 5418